Madeleine Sophie Barat
1779–1865

Scene

Two women: Elizabeth, whose marriage has broken up. The shock has disturbed her and she has not slept for twenty-four hours. Her friend, Elise, has come to tell her that one of the villagers was found drowned that morning.

ELIZABETH: I've been sitting here since yesterday, seeing it all, over all the world. Everything we trust in lets us down . . .

ELISE: Who are you that you should not be let down, as you call it, by the chances and accidents of life? Who are you that you should not be let down by your feelings and your blood and your nerves and your reasoning, like any other human being? The marvel is not that we are fallible and foolish, but that we have the wit to see it and to go on in spite of it. We are burdened with error and prejudice, like a rich field covered with stones, and the marvel is not that we stub our toes against the stones, but that we have sense enough to clear them away – even if we only clear the little patch that is ourselves. And even then, I have realised, we clear it not only for ourselves, but for the toes of other people who come after us . . . I don't know whether there is a God or not, but I do know that there is humanity, that there is a rich field, and that there are tons of stones to be cleared away . . .

extract from Willa Muir, *Imagined Corners* (Edinburgh, 1996), pp. 276–7.

MADELEINE SOPHIE BARAT
1779–1865

A LIFE

Phil Kilroy

Paulist Press
New York / Mahwah, N.J.

ISBN: 0-8091-0526-8

Published by arrangement with Cork University Press.
Published by Paulist Press
997 Macarthur Boulevard
Mahwah, New Jersey 07430 USA

www.paulistpress.com

Printed and bound in England by MPG Books Ltd., Cornwall

CONTENTS

ILLUSTRATIONS

The publishers gratefully acknowledge the following copyright holders for permission to use the illustrations herein: General Archives of the Society of the Sacred Heart Rome; Society of the Sacred Heart National Archives USA; Bibliothèque Nationale de France; Archives Départmentales de l'Yonne; Archives Communales, Ville de Joigny; Ville de Joigny, Archives Municipales; Archives Historiques, Archevêché de Paris; Archives Historiques, Archevêché de Besançon. Special thanks is extended to Studio Foto Bresson di Fabrizio Ferraro, Rome.

ACKNOWLEDGEMENTS

T
here are many colleagues and friends to thank for their help and encouragement over several years. I owe a special debt of gratitude to Helen McLaughlin, who commissioned this biography of Sophie Barat to mark the bicentenary of the Society of the Sacred Heart in 2000. The two major collections of the archives of the Society of the Sacred Heart are held in Rome (Italy) and in Poitiers (France) and I would like to thank the archivists there in a particular way: Anne Leonard in Rome and Marie-Thérèse Carré in Poitiers. I also appreciate the help of Mary C. Wheeler and Ann McManus, former archivists in Rome. My thanks to Elizabeth Farley and Margaret Phelan, Society of the Sacred Heart National Archives, USA, St Louis, Missouri; to Mary Coke, Provincial Archives, London; to Maire O'Sullivan and Eileen Brady, Provincial Archives, Dublin. Their expert, unfailing help, either while I was working in the archives or by fax, phone and email, has been essential in the preparation of this biography.

I would like to thank the librarians and archivists of the following institutions for their courteous help: in France: Archives Nationales, Paris; Archives Départementales de l'Yonne (Auxerre); Archives Communales de la Mairie de Joigny; Bibliothèque Municipale, Joigny; Archives du Ministère des Affaires Etrangères; Bibliothèque Nationale; Bibliothèque Historique de la Ville de Paris; Ecole Nationale des Chartes; Archives du Séminaire de Saint-Sulpice; Bibliothèque Marguerite Durand; Archives de l'Archevêché de Paris, Archevêché de Besançon, Archevêché de Chambéry, Archevêché de Toulouse, Evêché de Poitiers, Evêché d'Amiens; Archives de la Compagnie de Jésus, Vanves; Archives de la Congrégation de la Mission, Paris; Archives des Carmelites, Clamart; Archives Privées de la Maison de Gramont d'Aster, by kind permission of the duc de Guiche. In Rome: Archivio della Provincia d'Italia, Villa Lante, Sainte Rufine; Archives de la Trinité des Monts; Vatican Archives; Congregation for Institutes of Consecrated Life and Societies of Apostolic Life; Congregation for Saints; Archivium Historicum Societatis Iesu; Archives de l'Ambassade de France près le Saint-Siège; Archives of the Society of the Holy Child Jesus. In the USA, Archdiocesan Archives, New Orleans.

I am indebted to Françoise Mayeur, Claude Langlois, Jacques Gadille, Michelle Perrot, Leigh Whaley and Jim Livesey, Thomas Morrissey, Guy Avanzini, Marie-France Carreel, Monique Luirard, J.B. Lyons, Gilbert Humbert, Laura Bowman, M.D. Nobecourt, Marie-Joseph Vie and the late Pierette Chevrant for their help and generosity, especially in the early stages of my research. They gave graciously of their time and expertise. I owe a special debt of gratitude to Jeanne de Charry, a most generous colleague whose scholarship and published work were essential in the preparation of this biography. At the time of going to press the final volume of the letters of Sophie Barat and Philippine Duchesne, edited by Jeanne de Charry, had not been published. I acknowledge with gratitude the gracious gift of a copy of these letters. I am grateful also to Claire Dykmans who co-ordinated transcriptions of the 14,000 letters of Sophie Barat. Without this aid the biography could not have been produced in time to celebrate the bicentenary of the Society of the Sacred Heart in the year 2000.[1]

I am grateful to the following for the transcription of some, almost illegible documents and letters, and for translations of French and Italian documents: Ghislaine de Menditte, Concepión Santamaria, Hélène Carré, Maria Aluffi Pentini, and in particular Gerard Oates. I thank Joan Stephenson, who translated much of the correspondence of Sophie Barat and Eugénie de Gramont, and who recognised the classical, especially Latin, allusions in these letters. For several years I have been deeply indebted to François Vincent for his skill as a French tutor in Armagh. All this support has been essential in the realisation of this project. Furthermore, I am grateful to those who read chapters of the manuscript and offered criticism and encouragement: Mary d'Apice, Patricia Byrne, Dolores Dooley; Anne O'Keeffe, Marie McCarthy and Marie Louise Martinez. I am especially grateful to Patty Dougherty, who read sections of the book, and who has been source of insight and knowledge shared over many meetings in Paris. In the final months of writing Rebecca Rogers and Margaret MacCurtain read the entire manuscript. They made essential comments and suggestions which I have tried to integrate into the presentation of the biography. To them both I express my deep gratitude.

Many friends and colleagues have given me help and inspiration over the years, in Ireland (Armagh and Dublin), France, Italy, Australia and the United States. Particular thanks are due to the communities in France where I have worked, especially in Lowendal, Paris; and to the community at the Villa Lante, Rome. Their hospitality and their interest in the biography facilitated research and writing.

Finally, I would like to thank the staff of Cork University Press, for their encouragement and interest in the project and who have ensured the publication of this biography in three languages.

Phil Kilroy

---

[1]   The sixty-eight volumes of transcriptions are not definitive, critical editions of the letters of Sophie Barat. All the letters cited in this biography have been checked with the originals, held in the General Archives of the Society of the Sacred Heart, Rome.

INTRODUCTION:
SOPHIE BARAT, 1779–1865

This biography tells the life of a nineteenth-century Frenchwoman, Madeleine Sophie Louise Barat. The story begins in 1779 in the little Burgundian town of Joigny and then moves to Paris, where Sophie sets out on a long, adventurous journey. She could never have imagined then that she would found the Society of the Sacred Heart and that by the time of her death in 1865 she would preside over an international community of 3,359 women, who were inspired by a spiritual ideal and offered a service of education in Europe, north Africa, north and south America. Yet this happened and in the process Sophie Barat herself was shaped and enriched by the interaction of her personal, inner journey, her network of relationships and the spiritual ideals which motivated her and her friends. These three elements informed, modified and transformed Sophie Barat over the course of a long life. She emerged from this crucible of formation as a pioneer who, in the company of many gifted companions, had forged her own style of leadership. When she died at eighty-five years of age, sixty-three of them had been spent in leadership.

When Sophie was a child in Joigny the spirit of the Enlightenment was gradually permeating the consciousness of European society, insisting that human beings, endowed with rational capacities, could succeed in making sense of their lives, indeed transform them into a work of art. Part of this consciousness was a critique of the institutions of society, especially the church. The anti-clerical stance among the French *philosophes* in particular came at a time when the Catholic church itself had undergone radical change. Although it had reformed itself successfully in accordance with the decrees of the Council of Trent, in the wake of the Reformation it had become a church closed in upon itself and showed distrust of life and of the world. The church focused on the authority of the bishops and clergy, and on the reform of clerical training and care of parishes. It had gradually become élitist and frowned upon local, popular expressions of Catholicism, discouraging many of the practices of popular religion. This Tridentine church in France was marked by Jansenism, a reform movement rooted in the theology of predestination. By the late eighteenth century Catholics in France were weighed down, first by an image of God which was severe, threatening and demanding, and then by the conviction that human nature was profoundly sinful, that human beings were incapable of doing any good act. It was considered almost impossible to make a good confession and communion, such was the sinfulness of the human being, and the mediation of the clergy was seen as the only hope of bridging the gap between God and the sinner. The impact of this view of human nature was that the practice of approaching God in sacrament had diminished, especially among the male members of the population.[1] As a child and young adult in Joigny Sophie imbibed these varying strands of religious experience. The region of the Yonne was considered to be among the most Jansenistic in France and it affected Sophie profoundly.

Sophie Barat's childhood experiences were bound up with France on the eve of the Revolution. Her adolescence was marked by the unrest and turbulence of 1789, of the fall of the monarchy and Reign of Terror, and the memory of these events stayed with Sophie throughout her life. She lived through the momentous times of the Revolution, the Empire of Napoleon, the restoration of the Bourbons, the July Revolution and the 1848 revolutions. Indeed the impact of the French Revolution reverberated throughout the nineteenth century and Sophie's own journey weaves its way in the midst of further unrest, further revolution and further change. Yet she was not revolutionary in the political sense, rather she was counter-revolutionary, since her experience of the Revolution, especially of the Terror in Joigny and Paris, made her fearful of the extremes of revolutionary energy. Her abiding instinct, expressed in her relationships and in her understanding of institutions, was to conserve, to restore, to repair, to renew.

Sophie was living in Paris when the Revolutionary period gave way to the rise of Napoleon and the establishment of the Empire. At this time many women all over France, in a bid to restore the primacy of religion and the place of the church, initiated small communities focused on social work, mostly in education and health.[2] These projects began in towns, villages and cities, and gradually mushroomed throughout France and Europe into the wider world. Sophie Barat was part of that impulse and energy. Between 1800 and 1820 thirty-five new communities of women, including the Society of the Sacred Heart, were founded in France; and each year between 1820 and 1880 six new communities were founded. The founders of these communities came from all sections of French society, and included fifty-three from the lower bourgeoisie, among them Sophie Barat herself.[3]

Sophie Barat and the other numerous women who established new congregations of women in France in the early nineteenth century were welcomed and valued by the clerics within the church because they were desperately needed. Long before the Revolution the church had become progressively the place where more women than men worshipped and took an active part in the life of the parishes. So while the value of women in themselves was not recognised in the Declaration of the Rights of Man (1789), in the church women were seen as the way to bring men back to the practice of the faith. In that respect and for that purpose, women were necessary. That need opened a space for initiatives for women like Sophie Barat. The market for education and health care was immense and between them these women carved out certain areas to work in, and displayed great entrepreneurial skills in maintaining and extending their communities within their chosen area. Sophie Barat's chosen area was the education of young women of the aristocracy and upper middle classes and the education of the poor. To this purpose, she established boarding schools and poor schools, usually on the same property.

Like other founders of similar communities, Sophie struggled within herself and within the church, and indeed within society in general, to find her voice, her mode of action and manner of governing. She discovered her personal style of leadership slowly and learnt gradually how to articulate it. She used a rhetoric, in conversation and letter-writing, which enabled her to overcome obstacles and pursue her goals in a world where the leadership of women was greeted with suspicion and often with outright hostility.[4] With the benefit of our consciousness today we can grasp what Sophie Barat was straining after in her day. But she lacked the words, the social constructs and the general acknowledgement of the issue of women in society which have come to the fore in our time. Without such social confirmation and assurance, Sophie Barat forged a path with her colleagues in the Society of the Sacred Heart, with church and with government bodies, in Paris, in Rome and throughout the areas where the Society was present during her lifetime.

This was a formidable achievement because, like all women of her time, Sophie was affected by the low image women had in society generally. In her home town, Joigny, one of its most notable citizens, Edme Davier, the founder of the school where Sophie's brother, Louis Barat, was educated, published his portrayal of women:

> A woman is a spoilt creature who changes appearance and character just as she wishes. She is dishonest in her thoughts, scheming in her emotions, calculating in her views, flighty in her conversations, coquettish in her manners. She has affected airs, is deceitful about her virtues, self-interested in her generosity, and hypocritical about her economies. She is always crafty, always ambiguous and always telling lies. Now that, more or less, is what women are like.[5]

The view of women as secondary and inferior to men was deeply embedded in the consciousness of that time. In the realm of religion it was couched in theological language and internalised in the life of prayer and the practice of faith. The *philosophes* of the Enlightenment, who critiqued the institutions of church and state, did not promote the equality or the rights of women, or indeed the equality and rights of the servant and non-propertied classes. Rather they presumed that men (white, wealthy and educated) were the norm and women were measured against this assumption.[6] The radical thinkers and activists of the Revolution, with the notable exception of Condorcet, concurred with this judgement. Women who had hoped for inclusion in the Revolutionary spirit found they had been useful only for a time, a common experience of women in any revolutionary period.[7] Negative views towards women were further reinforced by Napoleon whose Civil Code defined the limited rights and extensive duties of women for the nineteenth century. The code imposed rigid legal subordination on women in the family and in the state.[8]

It is all the more remarkable then that in her leadership of the Society of the Sacred Heart, and more by her actions than her rhetoric, Sophie Barat did not operate from a negative view of women. She was enabled to do this because she offered a service which was needed in the church and in society. She was also well served by her realism, her sense of truth and her capacity to learn from experience. But, most of all, she made an inner, spiritual journey in the course of which she continually strove to transform her image of a severe, harsh Jansenist God into one of warmth and love and vulnerability. Though her outer success was the focus of her fame in the nineteenth century and beyond, her inner achievement had greater, long-term consequences for the image of the divine, of the holy, in our time.

Sophie Barat was endowed with a remarkable capacity for human relationships and she used that gift to good effect in her leadership of the Society of the Sacred Heart. However, it took continual efforts throughout her life to face into her own self-image, her image of God, her shadow self and the shadow self of her colleagues. On the one hand, the image of God could be cold, empty, harsh, critical and emotionally frozen. On the other hand it could be warm, full of energy, gentle, generous-minded and vulnerable. It demanded all her courage to trust enough to let go of old certainties, old burdens. In her testament to the Society of the Sacred Heart, read after her death, she admitted she had only realised a part of what she had searched for all her life and that her journey was not over, nor was that of the Society of the Sacred Heart.

A deeply religious woman, Sophie Barat's life was lived within the basic belief in the existence of God, revealed in Jesus Christ. For her the Catholic church was the church of Christ and she was faithful to its teaching, nourished by the sacraments and attentive to the requirements it made of her as superior general of the Society of the Sacred Heart. She loved and practised many devotions which stemmed from either medieval France or the ultramontane[9] movement of the nineteenth century. While she did not question any of the fundamental aspects of her faith-world, Sophie's needs and her own experience of life led her to question, to challenge and change what had been given to her as immutable. So while Sophie retained the rhetoric of conformity she moved as she needed to meet the requirements of the moment. In a world where women's powers and skills were not readily recognised and valued by either men or women, Sophie

Barat found her way within constrictions and achieved her goals. In that sense she was the supreme diplomat, forced to use a type of language to make herself understood. She had no script to follow, few models to learn from and she was often compelled to work on her own. She prepared the way for a new space and place for women far beyond her own time. Gerda Lerner notes, when explaining why she had chosen certain women for her study on the creation of feminist consciousness:

> I have included many women who would not have defined themselves as feminist in their own time, even allowing for the fact that the word itself did not appear until late in the nineteenth century. Such women would have denied that they were concerned with problems of women as such and several of them were explicitly opposed to women's rights movements. I have included some of them, such as female mystics or early proponents of women's education, because their work and thought directly contributed to the development of feminist consciousness, whether they so intended or not.[10]

When people met Sophie Barat they saw a woman just 150 cm (4 feet 11 inches) in height, with a mobile face and lively manner, a brisk walk and impetuous movements, and some may have asked themselves: How could someone so in touch with her world, who handled enormous finances with facility and skill, who negotiated agreements with church and state, be a woman of God? Could she be called loyal to the church when she was often critical of the clergy and indeed of bishops? How could someone who was so direct and blunt with her own colleagues, and so devastating in her remarks about others, be truly holy? Many spoke of Sophie Barat's natural charm and popularity, but were these the grounds of sanctity? Many recorded her brusque and impatient manner, her impetuous and curt attitude; some criticised her for her chauvinism. Others accused her of Gallicanism[11], others still of ultramontanism. All such remarks about this rich, complex personality were true in part. But they only looked in from the outside, they judged the appearance of the woman rather than the woman herself. Sophie Barat defied the nineteenth-century image of the holy person, of the holy woman, of the woman of obedience. To get her measure it is necessary to examine the full extent of her integrity, her fidelity to a vision and her lack of an inflated self-centred ego.

In any event, Sophie herself never made claims to personal perfection. She recognised some of her limitations and was blind to others. She was a product of her time and culture and she was affected by circumstances which impelled her to shape the Society of the Sacred Heart. She had her own consciousness and her own personal journey to make in life, with personal hurdles and challenges. It was a life lived constantly in the public eye, in the presence of her colleagues and wider circle of friends, family and business contacts. This often proved stressful for Sophie. Yet she functioned best in her role and found her relationships through her leadership of the Society of the Sacred Heart. Few glimpsed the private, reticent Sophie Barat behind the role and there, in that private space, she struggled and came to terms with herself and made sense of her life.

This biography tells the story of how Sophie Barat gradually assumed and consolidated her leadership in the Society of the Sacred Heart, a lengthy process which extended from 1800 to 1851. It is not a history of the Society of the Sacred Heart as such, nor is it a history of the Society of the Sacred Heart's contribution to education, though there are elements of both in the book. The archival material for this study of Sophie Barat is immense and accessible and it allows her personality to emerge as she speaks her way through the text.[12] Many biographies of Sophie Barat have already been written in several languages. While most of them are based on edited, published material from the archives of the Society, all have relied on two sources: the life by Adèle Cahier written immediately after the death of Sophie Barat but not published until 1884,[13] and the life written by Louis Baunard and published in 1876 specifically in view of the beatification/canonisation process which was initiated in 1872.[14] By far the more reliable of the two is that by Adèle Cahier, who gathered and organised all the archival material on Sophie Barat.

This biography is based on the primary material on Sophie Barat and Society of the Sacred Heart, contained in extensive archives held within and without the Society of the Sacred Heart. During her life Sophie Barat was always called Sophie by her family and friends. After her death she was known as Madeleine Sophie Barat. In this biography the name Sophie has been retained. Biography is an exercise in memory, a way of retrieving the life-story of the person, of telling their story, again. It can also disclose incomplete or disrupted narratives and can jog personal and collective memories, long hidden and forgotten. Biography is never final, definitive, finished. When the narrative is repeated, when the story is retold, hidden possibilities are released around the person and their time and new light thrown on their significance. By trying to tell some of the truth about a person and their time in history, a biography rescues both from a stereotyping which threatens to falsify the true person in their time and setting. Sophie Barat would appreciate such an approach. She once remarked: 'A historian should tell the truth'.

— 1 —

JOIGNY AND PARIS, 1779–1800

During the evening of 12 December 1779 a fire broke out in medieval Joigny. Starting in the rue Neuve it quickly spread to the rue du Puits Chardon and then forked right, along the ruelle des Chartreux, threatening to engulf the houses on the rue du Puits Chardon from both sides. It stopped just three houses from where Madame Barat was expecting her third child. She heard the cries and tumult in the streets a few short yards away and was filled with fear. All Jacques Barat and his son Louis could do was to move her to a room at the back of the house where there was less noise. Although she was only seven months pregnant fear and terror propelled her into labour. For some hours mother and child struggled for life. Finally, at eleven o'clock that night, Madeleine Sophie Barat was born two months prematurely and was considered so fragile that early the following morning she was baptised in the parish church of St Thibault, a few yards from the family home.[1]

Sophie's baptism was rushed and though godparents had been arranged in advance, there was no time to call them to the church. And so at 5 a.m. on 13 December a local woman, Louise-Sophie Cédor, on her way to the early Mass, and Sophie's brother, Louis Barat, stood in as her godparents. She was named Madeleine Sophie. Though Louise-Sophie Cédor disappeared from Sophie's life, her elder brother, Louis, took his duties as godfather seriously and he was to play an important role in her life.

People in Joigny remembered the fire, how two houses in the rue Neuve were consumed like a box of matches. They were built of wood and the cellars of both houses, where wine was stored, contained dried vine shoots and fodder which

7

fuelled the flames. They remembered it too because of the child who had been born in panic, and those who saw her grow up among them called her 'the miracle child'. Later when Sophie Barat herself told the story of her birth, she told how when neighbours asked 'how did you come into the world?' she knew the answer they wanted to hear was: 'by fire!'[2] The tale was passed on and many years later it would be recreated in the form of a miracle story: Sophie Barat was saved from the fire for she had a task in life, a destiny which marked her out from birth.[3] The Barat family had visible reminders of what could have happened, for the first floor of each of the first three houses on their street, the rue du Puits Chardon, had to be rebuilt. Certainly the dramatic circumstances of her birth marked Sophie profoundly, especially since she was to experience the fire and fury of revolution again and again throughout the course of her life.

Sophie Barat was born into a family whose ancestors had lived in Joigny for generations and were proud of their roots in the Bourgogne. The town of Joigny had been founded in the year 996; it had known a long and varied history, first under the dominion of the dukes of Burgundy, and later as part of the kingdom of France. By the eighteenth century, administrative, fiscal and judicial and religious rights had become so exceedingly complex and oppressive that sometimes families did not know under whose jurisdiction they lived. While Joigny belonged to the region (généralité) of Paris and was governed by an Intendant of the King, it was also in the diocese of Sens, and belonged to the chief bailiwick of Sens. In January 1790, when Sophie was nine years old, the Constituent Committee of the National Assembly divided France into eighty-nine *départements*. The *département* of the Yonne was carved out of the dioceses of Auxerre, Sens, Langes and Autun and subdivided into seven municipalités/districts of which Joigny was one. The actual town of Joigny was divided into ten sections and the Barat family lived in the second of these, the area of Calvary and the town of Joigny.[4] This section contained the Hôtel de Ville and the parish church of St Thibault and was therefore central to the life of the town.

The climate in Joigny was healthy, with no extremes of heat or cold. The geographical situation of the town, which was built along the river Yonne and surrounded with woods, favoured both the people and the land. The air was pure and bracing, the food wholesome; the water of the area was reputed to possess healing qualities, while the wine was good and gentle on the system. Even recovery from illness was quick and complete. In 1783 the local doctor, Edme-Joachim de la Mothe, noted the good health of the people, some of whom lived very long; indeed one woman was said to have lived to 183 years of age.[5] In 1790 the population of Joigny was estimated at 4,923, divided into active citizens, (those who paid the high taxes and had a vote), and non-active citizens (those who did not vote).[6] The economy of the town was based essentially on wine-making and the sale of wood or furniture, with cultivation of land for crops and the raising of animals as subsidiary. Three market days were held each week, on Wednesday, Friday and Saturday. Fair days were held on 2 January, 10 August, 14 September and 1 October.

Sophie Barat described herself as the daughter 'of an artisan, a barrel maker; he was called a vine grower . . . my father made the barrels and sold them'.[7] Jacques Barat (1742–1809) was born in Joigny, on the rue des Menuisiers (now rue Jean Chéreau). Being a wine-grower and a cooper was considered a noble trade with centuries of culture and spirituality behind it. The wine-grower's life was rooted in the earth and followed its seasons. Two cycles succeeded each other in the year, one after the feast of St Martin in November when harvest was over and the vineyards were resting in winter, the other after the feast of St Vincent in January when the vines were tended and first pruned, to prepare for the new harvest. The grape harvest was the high point in the year and every member of the family was involved in gathering the fruit in the vineyards and bringing it in for pressing. In the late eighteenth century the vineyards in Joigny stretched from Saint-Aubin to Paradis, to the Côtes St Jacques and finally to Verger Martin. Jacques Barat owned or rented vineyards in Saint-Aubin, Paradis and Verger Martin.[8] In addition to this he made barrels during the winter and he sold them and his wine at the market in Joigny, in Paris and at least as far as Lorraine and Flanders.[9] Thus he spent much of his life out in the vineyards or in the cellars of his house, making his barrels and watching the wine ferment during the winter months. Here he welcomed his friends and heard about all that was going on in Joigny. The cellars were in reality underground villages where a great deal of business was carried out and social contacts maintained.

Jacques Barat married Madeleine Fouffé (1740–1822) in 1767. She came from a wealthier background than her husband and unlike him she had a basic education. She was a sensitive woman, who enjoyed reading and was affected by the spirit of the Enlightenment. She had great ambitions for herself and her future family, having the experience of mixing with legal and merchant families in Joigny.[10] Her parents approved of the marriage and they gave the couple a present of their own home on 6 rue du Puits Chardon. The census taken in Joigny in 1754 indicated that the Fouffé family were living there at the time and that Madeleine Fouffé had been born there. It was a sturdy house, built after the great fire of 1530 when half of Joigny had been destroyed, and it had the distinction of having a fine staircase indoors. It was a generous marriage gift and Madeleine Fouffé's parents moved to a smaller house next door.[11] The newly-weds now possessed a ground floor with a kitchen and two rooms for fermenting wine; a first floor with two bedrooms and a second floor consisting of a loft, an attic room with a chimney and alcove. There were two cellars in the house where the wine was stored.[12] Jacques talked to his neighbours in the roomy cellar downstairs, while Madeleine invited her guests to join her in the kitchen, to read and discuss the new ideas of the day.

The marriage began with great hope and by the standards of the day the Barats were comfortably off.[13] This is confirmed in the Declaration of Goods which all citizens in Joigny were required to make in 1791, in view of taxation. Jacques Barat listed his properties in the area and it is clear that he owned most of his vineyards and rented no more than three from local landowners. In total he worked four arpents and seventy perches (approximately five acres) of land in the area of Joigny and Saint-Aubin. In the context of the time, when landowners in the area were considered quite wealthy if they worked twenty arpents of land, Jacques Barat belonged to the artisan and lower bourgeois class, and had an adequate income through his vines and his skill as a cooper.[14] The land he owned or rented, on which the vines were planted, were long, thin strips, 'parcelles en lanière', and were scattered over Saint-Aubin, Paradis and Verger Martin. Jacques Barat also declared his domestic property, no. 6 rue du Puits Chardon, as a house which included space for fermenting wine ('vinée'). Again it is clear, in comparison with what other owners declared and paid in tax, that the Barat family had ample means of existence and within their own peer group would have been considered quite comfortable.[15] With his vineyards and his skill as a cooper, and with the security which Madeleine Fouffé brought to the marriage in the form of the house, the Barat household was established on a sturdy financial footing.

Their first child, Louis, was born on 30 March 1768. Two years later Marie Louise was born on 25 August 1770 and nine years later Sophie was born, during the night of the fire, 12–13 December 1779. Why there was such a gap between the birth of the two sisters remains unknown; medical records do not exist for this period nor are there any indications within the family archives regarding miscarriages or ill health. Certainly Sophie was welcomed with joy and relief and she was a vivacious child, full of feeling and fun. Perhaps due to the dramatic circumstances connected with her birth and her delicate and fragile state of health, this child, their youngest, drew the warm affection and protective love of her parents. Indeed these early years at home established in her a basic sense of her own goodness which did not totally desert her even when faced with destructive experiences in adolescence and later in adult life. Moreover, the climate of Joigny served to strengthen her constitution and she grew into a confident young person. She became aware of her own self at an early age, possibly because of the premature nature of her birth which may have awakened her consciousness abruptly. She told her nephew Stanislas in 1832 that though she was getting old, 'Nevertheless I feel it is only yesterday that I began to think, for I was only seventeen months old when I became conscious that I existed. So it is fifty-one years since I began to think . . .'[16]

Although the physical and emotional conditions of her life were nurtured in the early stages of her development, the spiritual atmosphere within which Sophie grew up was different. In 1856, she spoke about her family background and explained how Jansenistic it was and how much this marked her own life. 'It is good that you know I was born into a Jansenist family . . . very attached to this sect which has always been the declared enemy of the devotion to the Sacred Heart.'[17] Jansenism marked Sophie's spirituality profoundly. The deep rift within Counter-Reformation Catholicism had been given extreme expression in the work of Cornelius Jansen, a Dutch theologian who taught at Louvain and died as bishop of Ypres in 1638. He taught that only the predestined would be saved, that Christ had not died for all, and that human beings were not free to resist God's grace. Any form of compromise with the world was condemned. The emphasis in Jansenism was on the innate evil within the human being. God was portrayed and presented as a severe judge whom it was almost impossible to please or appease. The role of the priest as confessor and spiritual director became dominant within this context. Before receiving communion, detailed confession of sin to a priest was required and priests were taught to give absolution cautiously. Sometimes only after several confessions over several months, when at last the priest thought the penitent worthy of receiving communion, was absolution granted. It was a dark, heavy religion, and it gave the clergy great power over the inner lives of men and women. The negative view of God and of human nature was very influential in France from the early seventeenth century, and just as the Jesuit theologians of the sixteenth century had clashed with the Calvinist theology of predestination, so they also challenged the severity of Jansenist teaching on salvation in the seventeenth and eighteenth centuries. It was a struggle between Christian optimism on the one hand and a tragic vision of the human situation on the other.

While Jansenism had begun as a theological movement, it became politicised in France in the wake of papal condemnations of its teaching. Several popes condemned Jansenism and required that at ordination priests take an oath rejecting its tenets. At the request of Louis XIV, Pope Clement XI comprehensively condemned Jansenism in 1713, in the Bull Unigenitus. From that period papal rejection of Jansenism became identified with the monarchy, and Jansenism became aligned with the French *parlement*, the body which protected legal rights and ratified the acts of the monarch. The French bishops and members of the clergy were divided on their acceptance of the Bull Unigenitus, and those who differed from the pope and from the king had recourse to the protection of *parlement*. Through theological differences and open debates, through prohibitions from receiving the sacraments and through restrictions on the clergy in their administration, Jansenism gradually spread from the textbook to the pulpit out into French society, causing inner divisions and often public turmoil in towns and villages. Jansenism captured the minds and spirits of many of the clergy and laity in France and became a catalyst for debate in a way the originators could not have anticipated. When the Gallican tradition of the French Church became allied with the doctrine of Jansenism, a powerful combination was forged, which threatened both royal and papal authority in late eighteenth century France. The region of Yonne was especially influenced by Jansenism.[18] It was into this atmosphere that Sophie Barat was born in Joigny.

The Fouffé family in particular was marked by the spiritual teaching of Jansenism and Madeleine Fouffé brought this into her marriage. As a child she had grown up with the tensions in the town caused by the two opposing camps, the followers of the teaching of Jansen and those who rejected that and adhered to Rome. Matters in Joigny came to a head in 1730 when the bishop of Soissons, Jean-Joseph Languet de Gergy, was appointed archbishop of Sens (1730–53) and openly opposed the acknowledged leader of Jansenism, the archbishop of Auxerre (1704–54), Charles de Thubières de Caylus.[19] A confrontation was inevitable; it had been growing ever since the papal declaration Unigenitus in 1713. In this context, the appointment of Archbishop Languet de Gergy to Sens was an effort on the part of Louis XV to stay the power of Jansenism in both Sens and Auxerre. After his installation in 1731, Languet de Gergy moved actively against it. He totally reorganised the seminary at Sens which was steeped in Jansenism; he replaced the large and small catechisms, also deeply Jansenistic and he engaged a Capuchin priest to preach against Jansenism. This offensive was further signalled by his advocacy of the cult of the Sacred Heart.

Yet the cult of the Sacred Heart need not have polarised the communities in the diocese of Sens. Some aspects of the devotion had an appeal for Jansenists, especially the accent on the nothingness of the human being overwhelmed by the divinity and glory of the Heart of Jesus. However, the more devout form of devotion to the Sacred Heart, with a greater accent on the humanity and vulnerability of Christ incarnate, was the aspect of the devotion espoused by Languet de Gergy.[20] Because of the scandal of this warm image of the divine, Jansenists were bitterly opposed to this form of devotion to the Sacred Heart, a devotion which would become highly politicised during the French Revolution.

The newly appointed archbishop visited Joigny twice, in 1731 and in 1732, and there met strong resistance. Rather than immediately confronting the community, Languet de Gergy chose a slower approach, gradually filling the three parishes in Joigny, St André, St Jean and St Thibault with anti-Jansenist priests. He was less tolerant of the nursing sisters at the Hôtel-Dieu in Joigny since they had direct contact with the people in the town. That community was dispersed and replaced by new members, nominees of the archbishop. The parish priest of St Thibault, who until now had remained silent on controversial issues, formally denounced the Jansenist, anti-Rome, influences in the parish in 1732. His successor did the same in 1736. In practical terms this meant that members of the parish had to accept the papal teaching of the Bull Unigenitus or be refused the sacraments. From this period on, those who adhered to Jansenism in Joigny went to Auxerre to fulfil their Easter duty of confession and communion, and there were cases of men and women being refused the last sacraments unless they conformed. Women in Joigny particularly opposed the archbishop and for several years there was an ongoing battle between the parish priest at St Thibault and some women in the parish. The issue of administration of the sacraments actually became a lawsuit, for the women successfully appealed to *parlement* and had the parish priest removed for nine years.

Jansenism in Joigny was quite complex: for some it was about discipline and penance in life, especially in the area of confession and communion; others saw Jansenism as a stance within which to establish freedom from the church of Rome and from certain members of the clergy; others again saw it as a corrective of royal power and privilege. Jansenism was certainly used in Joigny during this period in power struggles and lawsuits between families and the church.[21] As children and young adults both Jacques Barat and Madeleine Fouffé would have been aware of this controversy in their parish of St Thibault, and this was the atmosphere within which Sophie Barat herself grew up. It was the background and foundation of spiritual life in the family and Sophie encountered it in her mother, father and in her elder brother Louis, and of course she internalised it herself. She recalled this atmosphere in which she grew up: 'People spoke in front of the child of a [religious] community divided as a result of Jansenist ideas ... Sophie said to herself "I want to be a religious but I will only join a community where all live in harmony, not in rebellion" '.[22]

Sophie's brother, Louis Barat, was a serious boy and from an early age he showed great interest in studies. This was encouraged by his parents, especially his mother, and they employed a tutor for him at home. His tutor prepared him for entry to the Collège St Jacques in Joigny and he was ready to go there at nine years of age, certainly earlier than was usual. He was a successful student and won several prizes each year. One day he came home from school and told his mother he wanted to become a priest. She was very pleased and welcomed his decision. It would be a mark of distinction and a cause for family pride. His love of study had already shown that Louis would take a path different from his father and the news of his decision came as no surprise. Though comfortably off financially the Barat family could not aspire to becoming socially equal with the nobility. Priesthood in the family, however, meant access to the second estate in the land and Louis's decision redounded on the Barat and the Fouffé families. Opinion in the town held that Louis Barat was unsociable and quite odd. While a student at St Jacques Louis would frequently preach to his schoolfellows. Not surprisingly, he made few friends and spent breaks between classes alone in a garden. He chose to spend his First Communion day in seclusion. There is no evidence that Louis tried to teach his father, nor indeed that they had a bond as deep as that between mother and son. Neither did his father attempt to block him in his studies, his vocation, or in his increasingly dominant position in the house.[23] Shy of women, Louis was at ease only in the company of his mother and sisters and he tried to preach to and teach them. He had no challenge from his mother who adored him and sadly there are no records for this period regarding Marie-Louise. She may have gone to school locally, and unlike Louis she probably did not have a tutor coming to the house. Until her marriage in 1793, the history of the second child of the family remains unrecorded. In the entries of the marriage banns Marie-Louise is described as a linen worker, 'ouvrière en linge', the first reference to her activity at home before marriage.[24]

In 1784, when he was sixteen, Louis Barat left the Collège St Jacques in Joigny and began his studies for the priesthood at the seminary at Sens which from 1675 was in the hands of the Lazaristes. It had been influenced by Jansenism in the seventeenth century while Henri de Gondrin was archbishop (1646–74). His successor, Jean de Montpezat de Carbon (1674–85) had reacted against this and in 1675 had invited the Lazaristes to take over the seminary, thus moving away from the strongly Jansenist influence which had existed there.

This policy was continued in the eighteenth century by Archbishop Languet de Gergy and by the time Louis Barat arrived at the seminary Jansenism no longer held any official sway. Training for priesthood generally lasted three or four years. The seminarians followed a monastic form of life from 5 a.m. to 10 p.m., and every moment of their day was accounted for in detail. The method of teaching was in the form of commentaries on selected texts of approved authors and the content of the classes was focused on the Bible, scholastic and moral theology, cases of conscience, the catechism, dogma, and preaching.[25] It was a basic, rudimentary training of clerics destined to work in parishes, teach the commandments of God and of the church, say Mass, administer the sacraments and officiate at church ceremonies. It was typical of the formation given in the seminaries of the Lazaristes in France.[26]

Although ordained deacon, Louis was too young for ordination as a priest and he had to return home to Joigny and wait until he was twenty-one. He needed to work and he was well qualified to teach in his old college. Louis was appointed to the staff there on 15 January 1787 as teacher of the fifth and sixth classes with a salary of 600 livres. In their report on the Collège in January 1792, the authorities in the Department of the Yonne commented on the unusual gifts of learning possessed by the rector Saulnier and by the deacon Barat. Commenting further on Louis Barat they noted his youth and his known austere way of life.[27] While he was teaching Louis continued the ascetic form of life which he had already developed there as a boy. He also continued his own studies concentrating on foreign languages and on mathematics. However, this did not satisfy his intellectual needs, and so he went to Paris to follow courses in the College of the Four Nations.[28] This puzzled his mother who thought that her son was destined to be ordained a priest for ministry in one of the parishes. But Louis had plans to leave Joigny and become either a Trappist monk or a missionary. He would have preferred to become a Jesuit but the order had been suppressed in France in December 1764, by command of Louis XV, and dissolved in the church in July 1773 by Pope Clement XIV.

Sophie was nearly eight years old when Louis returned from Sens and began living at home again. He was eighteen, a teacher and he had decided to take on the education of his little sister. This was not questioned, for the characteristics Louis had displayed as a studious, serious, withdrawn boy had been confirmed and developed in Sens and the fact that he was ordained deacon and destined for priesthood gave him authority and power within the family.[29] On his return home Louis met his little sister, now a lively child, full of talk and charm, doted on by her parents and older sister, clearly very intelligent. Sophie herself admitted that until she was about seven she was thoroughly spoilt at home, but that after 1786, Louis 'took immediate responsibility for my education and became not only my Master but took over the place of Papa and Mama'.[30] His original responsibility as godfather was now expanded into parenting and the little child of eight fell completely under his power. In her history of the early life of Sophie, Geneviève Deshayes sums up this influence wryly:

She was confided to the care of her brother, who was more concerned about the spiritual development of his sister than experienced in the physical care such a fragile and delicate child needed . . . He dreamed of making her a saint and for this reason did not neglect her education . . . He made her work without the breaks necessary for her age and suited to her physical strength. She was truly imprisoned; maybe if she had been less held she would have gained less too; but her body suffered always from the effect of this handling in childhood.[31]

That Sophie became the focus for Louis's sense of responsibility was more than likely due to the circumstances of her birth. When his mother had given birth prematurely to little Sophie during the night of the fire, it was Louis who at the age of eleven had rushed to the church at 5 a.m. with the baby in his arms to have her baptised. If Sophie had died without baptism the teaching of the church then declared she was lost forever, would be cast into oblivion and never have the vision of God. She had been in danger then of a double death, and Louis had rescued her from both. He saw this as a trust given him not just for that moment but for life. No child could have forgotten that night and the sense of urgency and drama surrounding the birth of Sophie. The relief and triumph of the task accomplished stayed with Louis Barat all his life and despite his outward severity he genuinely felt great tenderness for his little sister. His manner of showing it, however, was seriously damaging to Sophie.[32]

Sophie was a great contrast to her ascetic brother and it is possible that Louis was jealous at how Sophie was treated by her parents; he may also have resented her charm and intelligence which were remarkable in such a young child. One of the neighbours in rue du Puits Chardon, who was a tax lawyer, enjoyed talking to Sophie. He was impressed by her questions and by her own assessment of what he told her, even though she was only six at the time.[33] The child was precocious and perhaps Louis, a young man of eighteen, felt that he should intervene, take her education in hand, and direct her energies in the way he thought best for the sake of her soul. Certainly it felt like this to Sophie. She felt this heavy hand and remembered well that once, when she was arguing with her mother, Louis told his mother that Sophie needed to be slapped for her rudeness, something her mother would never do.[34] Nor did Louis, then.

It was clear that Sophie was gifted and that she was ready for a teacher. There seems to have been no question that she would go to school either to the Benedictines in the parish of St André or to the sisters at the Hôtel de Dieu in the town.[35] In the first years Louis taught her to read and write, to learn some scripture, Latin and mathematics, providing her with a strong, basic education. When she had absorbed this he began teaching her the same content that he had taught the boys in St Jacques and expected her to do all the work he had set them. Just as Louis had had a tutor, now Sophie was getting the benefit of Louis's education. It was an unusual education for a young girl and probably unique in Joigny at this time. During these years Sophie made her First Communion, at the age of eleven.[36] She was prepared for this by the local priest and she went to St Thibault's regularly for catechism class. She was so tiny and her voice was so low that she was asked to stand on a stool when answering her questions. Indeed she was so small that the date of her first communion was in doubt until the curate persuaded the parish priest to examine her for himself and see that she was quite ready. On her communion day her mother presented her with her own prayer book which she had bought in 1754. It was a Christian handbook, containing the liturgy of the Mass, the New Testament and Psalms and the Imitation of Christ. Sophie used it for the rest of her life.[37]

Later in life, Sophie admitted that though she loved her brother and knew that he loved her, she had always been afraid of him and often had trembled before class with him. Homework was constant and she had little time to play. From time to time Louis went to Paris to study in the College of the Four Nations, probably during 1790–91 when access was more possible. Then Sophie, with the collusion of her mother, raced up the vineyards to play. Such release was short-lived, for Louis usually came back unannounced and Sophie was dragged back to the books. Louis could not allow Sophie the childhood he never had himself, nor had he the insight to let her develop differently. Life at home was solemn and serious in these years, from 1787 until 1791, when Louis's hold over Sophie was strong. There was little respite for her and no insight into her own needs at a very critical time when she was approaching puberty. Sophie often referred to this experience in later life, remarking wryly that she had learnt early that life had no pleasures without pain and disappointment. This affected her judgement profoundly, to the extent of distrusting the good in life and of dreading what could happen, especially in the wake of success.[38] Once Sophie had made her communion Louis expected her to attend the 7 a.m. Mass daily at St Thibault's with the boys. The students from the College had their designated place in the church for Mass. So too had Sophie Barat. She first had a seat in the Place du Rosaire, no. 8.

> I had to be ready to go to the schoolboys' Mass which was at 7 a.m. One morning, when I really wanted to sleep, my brother came and asked: 'Where is Sophie?' I heard him and in fear I buried myself in my bedclothes. 'Do you think that she is so lazy?', said my mother. Taking this as a reply my brother said nothing further. But I cried out: 'I'm here'. So Louis said: 'get up immediately and be at Mass at the same time as I am'. I was so afraid that I took just five minutes to dress.[39]

Louis showed his ill-judgement when he decided to take Sophie to an exorcism. Sophie was eleven at the time and Louis exposed her to a traumatic and bizarre experience which most adults would find daunting. In 1790 a young dressmaker in Joigny became possessed by thirteen devils. She belonged to the parish of St André and the reason for the possession was said to be a bad communion. In a town where the spirit of Jansenism was strong a bad communion could signal the presence of the devil and the path to hell. The priest in St André knew the girl's family well because her mother cooked for him in her home and he was therefore a daily visitor to the house. He asked the three teachers from the Collège St Jacques, Saulnier, Fromentot and Barat for advice. They examined the girl for some time and in the end they decided that the vicar of St André and Louis Barat would perform an exorcism on her. This took many sessions and Louis took Sophie with him on several occasions.[40] Later in life she spoke of this experience which had frightened her and increased her awe of her brother. In the account of the exorcism it was recorded that Louis Barat 'who was a very learned young man' spoke to the devil in Greek, Latin and Italian. The entire process was a demonstration of clerical learning, power and dominance over the young dressmaker, but the real source of her disturbance was never discovered.

Demonic disturbances in Joigny were symptomatic of the growing, explosive unrest in late eighteenth-century France and soon this would intrude upon Sophie's life. The meeting of the Estates General in Paris in May 1789 impacted quickly upon Joigny and in September of the same year plans were initiated by twenty-three citizens in the town to change radically the municipal structures. By January 1790, 251 active citizens were called upon to vote and the new authority was put in place.[41] From her bedroom window which looked out on to the Hôtel de Ville Sophie could see and hear much of the political activity of the town; she would also have heard her parents talking about such meetings. By April 1791 a Patriotic Association (Société des Amis de la Constitution) had been formed in Joigny[42] and by 1793 the Terror was being felt there and in the neighbouring towns and villages. In Joigny several citizens were in close touch with the most radical clubs in Paris and made no secret of their total commitment to revolutionary politics.[43] The implications of the Revolution began to dawn on the Barat family when Louis became caught up in the debate surrounding the Civil Constitution of the Clergy, passed in July 1790. The main provisions of the constitution were a new ecclesiastical organisation for the church in France, a new system of appointment of bishops and priests, a new system of ecclesiastical government and the payment of bishops and clergy by the state. It was to be a French church established without papal endorsement. Clerics were required to take the oath to abide by the Civil Constitution of the Clergy by January 1791 and the archbishop of Sens, Cardinal Loménie de Brienne, and almost all the clergy of the Yonne, conformed to this directive. And so with the priests of Joigny, including his friend Saulnier, Louis Barat took the oath in St Thibault's on 16 January 1791. Some months later Louis learnt that the pope had condemned the Civil Constitution of the Clergy and consequently the taking of the oath. Louis made his decision and, with Saulnier, the former rector of St Jacques, he formally retracted his oath on 2 May 1792.

The retraction had an immediate effect and while at first Louis Barat tried to hide in the attic at home, the danger became too great both for himself and the family so he fled to Paris. There he was denounced by a former student of the Collège St Jacques, was arrested on 23 May 1793 and imprisoned for two and a half years. He only escaped the guillotine through the courage of a friend.[44] Even then, when he was released in 1795 there was no place for him in Joigny and he returned to Paris to seek ordination and exercise his ministry there, in secret. Louis's retraction of the oath put the Barat family in danger. For a year their goods were sequestrated and the house was put under surveillance. Madame

Barat made a formal request to the town authorities on Louis's behalf, pleading that since he was not ordained he could not be considered a non-constitutional priest.[45] A year later the sequestration of the family goods and the surveillance on the house were removed. This decision was taken, not because Louis Barat had not been ordained, for in the eyes of the authorities he was a cleric in minor orders. Rather the grounds for the removal of the constraints on the Barat household were due to the fact that Louis Barat was not a member of the nobility. It took some time to prove this to the authorities, since it was presumed that most of the clergy were members of the nobility. Sophie remembered that for a time in Joigny people pointed her out as an aristocrat, perhaps as a way of taunting the family in their distress.[46]

From 1790, the Revolution gained momentum in the daily lives of the people of Joigny. The new calendar was introduced. One of the churches, St Jean, was renamed the Temple of the Goddess of Reason. Citizens were invited to process to the 'temple', hear speeches and sing patriotic songs and in this way celebrate the advent of the Revolution. St Thibault's had been used regularly from 1790 for town meetings and was closed to Christian worship for a year, from 1794 to 1795.[47] There was great unrest generally in the Yonne region, expressed in food riots stemming from the danger of famine following the severe winter of 1788–89 and the consequent rise in food prices. In September 1790 and in the spring of 1793 there was famine in Joigny which inflamed revolutionary spirit and anger.[48] In February 1792, vineyard workers rioted in Joigny. Joigny was alive with the Revolution; clubs and masonic groups were well informed with regard to events in Paris, especially during the period of the Terror when anti-clerical feeling was rife and liable to erupt into violence.[49] Most of the priests in the district of Joigny had either renounced their ministry or been deported; others were in hiding or in prison. When Louis Barat was arrested in August 1793 in Paris, the Barat family was truly frightened, for prison in Paris was considered the antechamber to death.[50] This was indeed a traumatic time for all the family, certainly for the young Sophie. As a much older woman she still had not forgotten the effect of the singing of the 'Marseillaise'. In 1840 when there was unrest in Paris, the 'Marseillaise' was sung in the streets and when the singing woke her up she felt she was back in Joigny, a young girl of twelve or thirteen.[51]

Over a period of months the entire context of Sophie's life had altered. Her studies stopped and she had more time to devote to sewing and to helping her father in the vineyards. In 1792, when she was thirteen, Sophie Barat was described as a linen dressmaker when she acted as godmother to Louise-Sophie Guillot. In 1795 when she acted as godmother to Pierre Barat, Sophie was described as a vine-grower.[52] The family did not know whether Louis Barat would ever come back. He could die in prison or be guillotined. Sophie had to go forward and make her own life. With her needle she could earn money and work from home. She was now the only child at home with her mother and father: just before Louis was arrested in Paris Marie-Louise married Etienne Dusaussoy on 12 March 1793. Etienne Dusaussoy belonged to a legal family. His grandfather was a lawyer and his father was a solicitor in Joigny. Etienne was a tailor and owned two haberdashery shops on the Grande Rue. On account of his wealth he was deemed an active citizen, with voting rights.[53] This then was a good marriage for Marie-Louise and for the Barat family, one to which Madame Barat readily consented. This was her milieu and she hoped that in time Sophie too would marry well and remain close to her in Joigny. Indeed, during these years Sophie was essential company for her mother, especially after Marie-Louise's marriage and Louis's imprisonment in Paris.

Louis's absence from home allowed Sophie much greater intellectual freedom. She read *Don Quixote* and enjoyed the tale enormously; she was absorbed by the huge tomes of *Clarissa* by Samuel Richardson, a highly moral tale then popular in France; she read Virgil in Latin and confessed later that she was afraid that on the Day of Judgement she would hear Christ say of her: 'with regard to the pleasure she took reading Virgil: This is not a Christian, but a "Virgilienne"'.[54] Her need for fun found expression as she played and walked freely with her friends in the vineyards. Her mother encouraged this vivacity and often invited neighbours to the house in the evenings. With great pride she would ask Sophie to read to her guests. The tales of Marmontel were in vogue at this time and Sophie read them aloud to the company. These tales were popular in the fashionable salons of Paris and somewhat risqué and Sophie found some of them embarrassing to read aloud. Her mother did not seem to notice. One evening she was rescued from her embarrassment by a perceptive young man who often came to the house in the evening. He pointed out to Madame Barat that Sophie did not enjoy the *contes* and that she should not be compelled to read them aloud.[55]

Once Madame Barat heard in August 1793 that Louis had been arrested and put into prison even Jacques Barat could not console his wife. She was deeply upset and she began to lose interest in food and cried all day long. Events in Paris, at the height of the Terror, were frightening and certainly Louis was in danger daily from the guillotine. Louis XVI had been executed in January 1793 followed by Marie-Antoinette in October of that year, and Madame Barat felt anything could happen. Her anxiety was all the greater for lack of information and endless rumours. Gradually Madame Barat stopped eating and nothing could persuade her to sit down at table with Sophie and her father. Sophie made her mother's favourite dishes but these held no attraction for her. One day she prepared peas in a certain way her mother liked. When these were refused, Sophie, exasperated, decided to not to eat either. Her mother was taken aback at this and questioned Sophie who answered curtly that she had no intention of eating anything at all unless her mother did too. The ruse worked and Madame Barat began to take some food. But she had been pushed too far emotionally and physically and for a time she lost her mental balance. One day when Jacques Barat was out in the vineyard and Sophie was alone with her mother, Madame Barat had a seizure and began to fall about the house. This was frightening for Sophie and though she knew she should have gone for her sister, Marie-Louise, she did not want to tell her. Instead she looked after her mother quietly and brought her back to health, 'by dint of care and loving caresses she became herself again'.[56] Sophie became increasingly more responsible for her mother and helped her in family business affairs, for since the beginning of their marriage Jacques Barat had left all this work to his wife. Sophie accompanied her mother in the town for all business matters and she showed herself astute and deft in business affairs. On one occasion a solicitor asked to talk to her mother about conditions regarding the buying and selling of some land. Madame Barat had given some contradictory information but Sophie was able to clarify the situation quickly for the solicitor who admired her grasp of the financial and legal affairs of the family.[57]

From the time Louis retracted the oath in May 1792 until his imprisonment in Paris, Madame Barat gradually underwent a profound spiritual change. The deterioration in her health broke down some of her prejudices and inner resistance to the image of a warm, compassionate God. Sophie recalled the impact of this change on her mother and how it came about. Just before Louis was arrested in August 1793 he sent his mother a present of two pictures of the Sacred Heart of Jesus and of Mary:

> In a print shop Louis found two very fine engravings, one representing the Sacred Heart of Jesus and the other the holy Heart of Mary. He bought them and sent them to Madame Barat, and forgetting her former prejudices, she welcomed her beloved son's gift with joy. And despite the remarks of her family, for one of her sisters was particularly trapped in the error [of Jansenism] she had the two images framed and they remained there [in the kitchen] throughout the Terror, without ever being insulted, or even remarked upon in the frequent visits made to the house during these times.[58]

Anything Louis sent was precious and Madame Barat placed the pictures in full prominence as a sign of her love. Political Jansenism (as well as some streams of spiritual Jansenism) had always been critical of devotion to the Sacred Heart. However, the Barat family probably did not know how dangerous it was to display the pictures, for devotion to the Sacred Heart was directly linked to the Bourbons. In 1688 Margaret Mary Alacoque had urged Louis XIV to add the emblem of the Sacred Heart to the arms of the Bourbon dynasty. In 1729, Archbishop Languet de Gergy of Sens had dedicated his biography of Margaret Mary Alacoque to the queen. The symbol of the Sacred Heart was closely linked also with counter-revolutionary movements in France.[59] But all this mattered not at all to Madame Barat. She displayed the pictures because Louis had sent them. Certainly the pictures impressed Sophie and introduced her to a new image of God, of Christ, of Mary, and later on she recognised that Louis's gift was significant for herself as well as for her mother.

Having spent two years in prison, first in St Pelagie, then in Bicêtre and finally in the Luxembourg, Louis Barat was released following the fall of Robespierre in 1795. He had been through horrendous experiences and seen dreadful events. He had also met some extraordinary people in prison, especially many priests, some of whom went to the guillotine and some who like him managed to survive.[60] On his release Louis went home to Joigny, relieved and exhausted after his harrowing experiences. He saw that Sophie was growing up quickly, and while she had no plans other than staying in Joigny and settling down eventually to marry and have a family, Louis certainly had plans for her. Perhaps with a clearer vision of what life was about, resulting from his raw experience in several prisons in Paris, close to death for two and a half years, Louis Barat saw possibilities for his sister slipping away from her while she remained in Joigny. He knew how much his parents loved and spoilt Sophie, the only child at home; how Sophie herself enjoyed her life, her work, her fun, and in particular how dependent Madame Barat had become on her, especially after Marie-Louise's marriage. Seeing this after two years in jail gave Louis another perspective on life. He could not stay in Joigny as the political situation was too volatile to ensure his safety and that of his family. He had to return to Paris and he was determined to take Sophie with him to complete her education.

At first Madame Barat would not hear of this. Over many years she had hoped to keep Louis in Joigny, but from the beginning Louis's horizons were wider and he never intended staying there. Once Madame Barat realised that Louis would go, her hopes had rested on Sophie. Now she too was about to leave home, her youngest and most delicate child, whom she hoped would be with her in her old age. It was a huge disappointment, especially since Sophie had never expressed a desire to go to Paris. Louis consulted Jacques Barat on his own and explained why he wanted to take Sophie away to Paris. It is hard to know what Louis said that convinced his father but by dividing his parents he managed to detach Sophie from her mother and from Joigny.[61] Perhaps he pointed out that Sophie could be commissioned, as had other girls in the town, to work in the barracks making uniforms for the army. In 1793 the girl who had been possessed was ordered to go there and had died from the persecution she suffered at the hands of tormentors who knew her past. Louis would have heard this news and would have wanted to remove Sophie from even the possibility of being called up for this service. A persuasive argument indeed.[62] Moreover, Louis had long since assumed dominance over his father and easily won him round to this point of view. With this understanding he returned to Paris and from there he wrote to Sophie, encouraging her to join him.[63]

Sophie herself was torn but she finally decided to go to Paris in 1795. Why did she go to Paris with Louis? It is possible that Sophie herself had no motivation other than the pressure of her brother. At just sixteen years of age she was still afraid of him, was in awe of him, especially of his certainties and she was trapped by thinking that what he said was what God wanted. Even Geneviève Deshayes, who knew Sophie from 1801, indicates in her own personal memoirs that she did not know whether or not Sophie had decided then on some form of religious life.[64] Nor was it clear if even Louis thought Sophie was destined for this. In 1795 there were no communities able to receive candidates since all religious congregations with solemn vows had been suppressed in February 1790.[65] Many years later Sophie recalled the reasons for her leaving home at such a critical time during the Revolution and she remembered how neighbours at home had been critical of her parents:

> My poor parents, guided by a more elevated spirit than their [neighbours], had to endure their accusations, criticisms and mockery of my priest brother who when released from prison at the fall of Robespierre, began teaching me Latin, history and literature: 'What madness', they said in the neighbourhood, 'to make such a delicate girl study subjects beyond her station in life ... When my brother saw how my parents were being attacked he suggested that he take me to Paris with him, now under the Directory, which in comparison to the dreaded Constituent Assembly appeared to offer some security ... My mother refused point blank. But on a second journey to Joigny my brother considered that I was wasting my time, as he wanted me to finish my studies, he persuaded my father to let me go. My mother gave in, for she saw with natural complacency that this would be a kind of victory in the modest social circles of Joigny. God used this motherly pride, [and] the apparent ambitions of my brother to make his little sister an educated woman.[66]

Louis came to fetch Sophie after the grape harvest in 1795. He had been ordained to the priesthood secretly that year on 19 September, by Bishop Jean Baptiste de la Tour Landry. Whatever hesitations his mother may have had about Sophie would have been swept away by the added authority of Louis's ordination.[67] They left for Paris after the harvest and took rooms in a house belonging to Madame Duval, no. 4, rue de Touraine, in the heart of the Marais district of Paris, not far from the Bastille. This was a safe house where the identity of Louis Barat as priest would be kept secret and here he exercised a clandestine ministry. There were three other women with Sophie: Octavie Bailly, Marie-Françoise Loquet and a woman named Marguerite, Madame Duval's maid. They all followed the order of day laid down by Louis Barat. It was a life of silence, hours of prayer, meagre food, fasting, study and little sleep. The day began with prayer, Mass and then breakfast on dry, rough bread. In the mornings they had no hot drink for breakfast and if they had not finished a piece of study the previous day, that had to be done before they broke their fast on dry bread and cold water. Classes consisted of study of the Fathers of the Church, mathematics, Latin and the Scriptures.

Louis paid particular attention to Sophie's intellectual development. She was quick at her work, and to hold her back and allow the others to catch up, Louis gave her other tasks, such as learning long psalms in Latin by heart, especially Psalm 50, and then translating them into French. Nothing escaped his eye and if he saw that she was enjoying a particular piece of work, he would immediately change to something different. All works of literature which had fed her imagination were forbidden. All spontaneity was curtailed. For example he noticed that she was making something for him and was getting great pleasure and joy from that; he made sure she could never finish it. Another time she did manage to finish something for herself and he threw it in the fire. The same happened to a gift she made for his birthday. He left her nothing to enjoy. According to his perspective his purpose was 'to destroy her nature and replace it with grace'. But her companions found it very difficult to watch and they criticised her brother for such harsh treatment of his sister. Sophie herself felt singled out from the others and treated much more severely. He regulated her life in every detail, and even refused to allow her food her mother sent from home.[68] Many years after the death of Sophie, one of her colleagues testified how Sophie's health suffered from the treatment of her brother, first in Joigny but especially in Paris, noting in particular that her digestive system had been ruined.[69] Louis Barat lived the life of a Trappist monk and expected his younger sister to do so too, without any of the exceptions required by her age and health.

Sophie was pushed very hard indeed, to breaking point. In the end, by her own account, she began to laugh. What kind of laughter was it? Was it an echo of her own bitter disappointment in the vineyards at home when she was called in to face Louis on his sudden returns from Paris? Or was it that life could never be trusted to promise anything other than pain and disillusion? A laugh of despair, of never getting it right? A laugh that receded into a permanent smile of surrender and capitulation? A laugh, finally, that falsified her judgement and told her that life was death? When one of her companions asked her why she seemed not to be distressed by such treatment, Sophie replied that others had more to put up with than she had and she would offer her pain to God. In other words she took refuge by spiritualising the pain and in this way she was able to cope. Perhaps it kept her sanity in a world that had become bleak and hard. She told them: 'I understand nothing; I think nothing; if I'm told to do something, I obey'. It was a form of trauma, whereby she conformed outwardly in order to survive.[70] Not only was the outer frame of her life monitored by her brother but her spirit too was imprisoned when Louis Barat became her confessor. On her arrival in Paris she first had a young priest, Philibert de Bruillard, as her confessor and she had found him very helpful.[71] Yet Sophie decided to change and she asked her brother to be her confessor, perhaps under pressure from Louis. It is clear that she felt obliged to take this step and that it was not a free choice on her part. Louis Barat had neither the preparation nor the experience to guide his sister spiritually, but he thought he had at the time. Using St Jerome as his model, Louis corrected every failing in Sophie; he exaggerated her faults and painted them in the most lurid colours. He required her to go to confession every day and to confess the least fault in detail; his inexperience and rigidity led to misunderstandings in the area of confessing faults and this compounded her sense of guilt. He gave her penances and trials on a daily basis. His method was to humiliate her to the depths and to require absolute obedience to him. Soon she lost her own sense of worthiness and often refused to go to communion. When this occurred Louis would call to her from the altar and insist that she receive the host, thus compounding her scruples. Once she took sugar before Mass deliberately so that having broken her fast she could not receive communion; in this way the weight of worry was removed. Louis called to her from the altar and she had to reply in public and receive a public scolding at the end of Mass. This experience of having her soul seared daily by examination of conscience remained with her for life. Yet while she was in deep inner pain, her spirit was not quite crushed. Later on she was asked how she survived such an experience and she admitted that 'I did not always receive what was happening to me with gratitude. I cried a great deal.'[72]

Life in Paris was a form of prison for Sophie. Louis refused to let her leave the house unless he considered it was really necessary. Once her mother came to Paris to visit both of them. Madame Barat and Sophie went out for a walk and they met a cousin of the family in the street. The cousins were so delighted to meet that they hugged each other warmly. Afterwards, even though she knew there was nothing in it other than sheer joy at seeing a friend, Sophie, now well programmed by Louis Barat, had scruples and felt she had to confess her action. She was very frightened and thought the best time to tell Louis was just before Mass, as that was probably the time he would be the most understanding. She plucked up her courage to tell him. He was furious and in his anger he slapped her across the face. Then he turned away and proceeded to say Mass. Sophie cried all during that Mass and afterwards she had to go to confession to Louis during which the episode was re-examined in detail. Such pressure deepened the self-doubt and guilt which had begun to root in Sophie and which dogged her all her life.

Sometime while she was in Paris Sophie had arrived at a decision about her life. She told her brother she had decided to join a Carmelite community, though there was no question of being able to join any contemplative community at the time since these had been abolished in February 1790. How Sophie had reached this choice is hard to know, for her inner life was in turmoil and her judgement uncertain. Perhaps it was a wish, an aspiration, and as such it gave her a direction. At eighteen she needed that security. It certainly pleased her brother and this may have motivated her also and provided her with the approval he so often withheld. However, the intense time in Paris was coming to an end. Political events in the city threatened a return to the temperature of the Terror and Louis was forced to flee to the Ile de Rhé (or perhaps Cayenne) and Sophie was able to return home once again. Madame Barat hoped that this time she would stay at home in Joigny for good.

Men were attracted to Sophie. Her confessor in Joigny told her she should get married and settle down like her older sister, Marie-Louise, raise a family and find her happiness in that way. Indeed Madame Barat hoped and even planned that Sophie would marry someone in or around Joigny. There was every reason to believe that Madame Barat's hopes would be realised. Sophie had had friendships with boys as she was growing up and she resumed them when she returned to Joigny in 1797. But she had changed and gradually this became apparent. Once Sophie visited friends of her mother out in the country, a family which was well thought of in the area. The mother was fond of Sophie and had openly declared that if she had a daughter like Sophie she would be a happy woman. During this time, there was a party for the sons in this family and Sophie was invited. At the party a young man, attracted to Sophie, came and offered her a bouquet of flowers. Overwhelmed and over-sensitive from her rigorous experience in Paris, Sophie found this attention too much for her. She reacted strongly, threw the flowers on the ground and in no uncertain terms made it clear she would not accept such presents. Her reaction was out of proportion to the simple act of offering flowers and there was panic in her outburst.[73] Louis Barat cast long shadows in Sophie's life even when he was miles away.

However, Sophie was able to enter into the family life of her sister Marie-Louise who by 1798 had had three children: Louis Etienne (1794–1873), Stanislas (1797–1879) and Célestine (1798–1823). Louis remembered his young aunt taking him for walks along the river or in the vineyards, and although these memories may have been romanticised in the light of Sophie's later achievements, they show her at ease and enjoying her time with the children. She settled back into life in Joigny profoundly marked by the experience in Paris. Indeed she needed respite from the impact of Louis on her life, for her health had been permanently damaged. Some years later the results of his action were pointed out to Louis, but it is likely that he never grasped the extent of the damage Sophie suffered at his hands.

Yet it was Louis who had recognised the gifts of his younger sister and felt that she would have wasted her time and talents had she remained in Joigny. In teaching her what he could, firstly at home and later in Paris, Louis opened and prepared her mind for a different life and a different way of being, which she then called becoming a Carmelite. Few young women of the time would have had the educational advantages offered her and Sophie was gifted enough to avail of all she received. Basically Louis passed on to Sophie what he had received in the Collège St Jacques and later on in Sens and Paris. Before going to Paris in 1795 Sophie had begun to explore literature and poetry, through the books her mother was providing and the evening meetings in the house and Sophie never forgot what she had read at home in Joigny, even when Louis firmly steered her in another direction, that of theology, scripture and religious history. It was the classics in particular which had kept the windows of her imagination open, especially reading Virgil and Ovid, whose works she cited in her letters later on in life. Nor did she forget La Fontaine, quoting from the tales frequently in her letters and conversations. At the age of eighteen she had more learning and skill than most of her generation, anywhere.

Sophie's time of respite at home was not destined to last. In 1799 it was safe to return to Paris and when Louis resumed his ministry there Sophie joined him. The routine of classes and study recommenced. This rhythm was interrupted only when Sophie returned home to help her father and mother at the grape harvests, a time of hard work but of release too from the constraints of Paris. In the course of the autumn in 1800, while Sophie was in Joigny, Louis made the acquaintance of a priest called Joseph Varin in Paris. This meeting was to change the lives of both Louis and Sophie Barat forever, in ways neither could have imagined or foreseen.

– 2 –

PARIS AND AMIENS, 1800–1806

The period from autumn 1799 to autumn 1802 was a watershed in the life of Sophie Barat. During these months she became intimately bound up with several influences and movements current within France, the Austrian Empire and Italy, and she was introduced to several people who would affect her profoundly. This transition period in Sophie's life began when she went home to Joigny for some months in the summer of 1800, planning to return to Paris after the grape harvest in the autumn. Louis Barat had remained in Paris and while she was away he had met Joseph Varin. As Joseph Varin talked Louis Barat saw his own future taking shape. While Louis's life had been lived within the confines of France, Joseph Varin had moved all over Europe in his quest for religious life. Joseph-Désiré Varin d'Ainville had been born into a legal family in Besançon on 7 February 1769. He had a brother and a sister, and had been particularly close to his mother who was widowed when Varin was a boy. He decided early on in life to become a priest and at the age of fifteen went to the seminary of St Sulpice in Paris where he came under the influence of Jacques-André Emery, the rector of the seminary.[1] He also formed close friendships with two of his colleagues, Léonor de Tournély and Charles de Broglie. However, Varin was a restless man, impetuous and keen for action, and he grew bored with study and impatient with life in the seminary. When he was twenty he left St Sulpice to become a soldier. He joined the counter-revolutionary army led by the Prince de Bourbon-Condé and fought to restore the Bourbons to the throne of France.

The violent campaigns of 1792 and 1793 exposed him to the brutality of war and the deaths of many friends on the field of battle. Unable to take more, he sought out his former colleagues of St Sulpice and found them at Venloo in Holland. He discovered that de Tournély had initiated an association of priests called the Society of the Sacred Heart which worked actively for the restoration of the Jesuits in France. Varin decided to join this Society formally on 20 July 1794. He learnt some days later that his mother had been guillotined in Paris on 19 July along with 1,300 other victims of revolutionary violence. This double experience of the futility of violence confirmed Varin in his choice and he took an active part in the development of the new association.[2] For some months de Tournély led this small group of men over warring Europe and finally settled in Hagenbrunn near Vienna. There the little group lived a very austere life, rather more in keeping with the life of Trappist monks than Jesuits in waiting. Indeed at this time they saw themselves essentially as contemplatives, and left their solitude only to minister in surrounding parishes.[3]

In January 1796 de Tournély decided to found an association of women, also called the Society of the Sacred Heart. Like the male association, their inspiration would be drawn from the Jesuit rule[4] but lived out differently, adapted to women and to their non-clerical status.[5] He saw these women as contemplatives, involved in education and in nursing, but firmly cloistered in accordance with the customs of religious life prior to the Revolution. He hoped the Princess Louise-Adélaïde de Bourbon-Condé, abbess of the noble chapter of Remiront in France, though at this period an émigrée in Austria, would support this venture.[6] She did respond initially to de Tournély's invitation, but the style of life to which de Tournély was calling her did not match her own desires for a life of greater solitude, and after a short time the project of a women's association fell through. Despite the setback, de Tournély assured Joseph Varin that his ideal would be fulfilled, one day, and that a women's association called the Society of the Sacred Heart would exist. De Tournély died in July 1797 and never saw his hopes realised. Yet de Tournély's initial impulse was not lost, and though it was muted for a time it re-emerged some years later, in France.

Joseph Varin was elected to replace de Tournély as leader of the Fathers of the Sacred Heart. The possibility of the women's association was kept alive by Archduchess Marie-Anne of Austria (1770–1809), sister of the emperor, Francis II. She was attracted to religious life and was nominated abbess to the Chapter of St George at Prague. Her two ladies-in-waiting, both sisters, Louise (1770–1845) and Léopoldine (1773–1834) Naudet, followed her there and they adopted the Jesuit rule for their way of life. They maintained contact with Louise-Adélaïde de Bourbon-Condé but, as with de Tournély, she showed no desire to join with them. However since Joseph Varin had established a noviciate in Prague for the Fathers of the Sacred Heart, he had regular contacts with Marie-Anne and the Naudet sisters in Prague. Not knowing quite what to do he asked a former Jesuit, Nicholas de Diessbach, to accept responsibility for the formation of the little group, but de Diessbach died in 1798 and no one else was available to take his place.[7]

At this point new developments in Italy determined the future of this little group of women and indeed of the Fathers of the Sacred Heart themselves.

Nicholas Paccanari (1771–1811), a native of Trent in the north of Italy, and then a layman, sought to establish a religious association of men. His ultimate goal at the beginning was to work for the restoration of the Jesuits and he used his considerable persuasive gifts of eloquence to establish his association, which he called the Fathers of the Faith. This group was largely composed of former Jesuits and of new members who worked for their restoration. Paccanari had the ear of Pope Pius VI and this directly affected the little group founded by Léonor de Tournély.[8] For when the Fathers of the Sacred Heart wrote to the pope for approval of their association, Pius VI asked them to merge with the Fathers of the Faith founded in Italy by Paccanari. In order to proceed with the merger of the two associations of men, Paccanari travelled to Prague to meet Joseph Varin and his companions. From his first meeting with him, Joseph Varin was completely won over by Paccanari and he enthusiastically urged his colleagues to agree to the proposed merger.

Varin told Paccanari of the small group of women in Prague who were searching for some form of life inspired by the Jesuit rule. Paccanari explained that in addition to founding the group for men, he had written a rule of life for an association of women, to be called the Diletti di Gesù, the Beloved of Jesus, and that he was searching for a group of women who would adopt this way of life. The association had two aims: one active, the other contemplative. The active aim was the education of youth, of boarders and day pupils; the making and washing of church linen and ornaments and the accommodation of wealthy lay women in the monastery while making their spiritual exercises. The contemplative aim was the sanctification of the members through spiritual exercises within the monastery, prayer, spiritual reading, examination of conscience and regular confession. In other words, a full active life in the field of education and a full contemplative life within the cloistered world of nuns. Paccanari's vision held firmly to the old understanding that the only model of religious life was the monastic form, and that all formal recognition of the work of women in the church could only come within those parameters. Paccanari's ideas were not unusual. They were held by other religious men and women all over Europe and remained almost unchanged throughout the nineteenth century and well into the twentieth century.[9] Paccanari proposed to Joseph Varin that the group in Prague follow the rule he had written and to Varin it seemed an admirable and tidy solution to their need for some structure and form of life. After some deliberation together, during which Paccanari replied to all the questions and doubts on the part of both men and women, the Fathers of the Sacred Heart joined the Fathers of the Faith and accepted Paccanari as their leader; and the three women agreed to follow the rule of the Diletti di Gesù.[10] Thus the original ideals of Léonor de Tournély were recast and reshaped by these new developments. Certainly Paccanari had persuasive powers; he overcame and prevailed over the doubts and hesitations of both the men and the women in Prague. Besides, he had the backing of the pope and this appeared to guarantee stability and security. The use of the title 'Sacred Heart' was central to Varin and his colleagues as well as to Marie-Anne of Austria, but Paccanari argued that it would be politically impossible to use this title in public for the present. They agreed not to use the name 'Sacred Heart', at least for the time being, and through this decision something of de Tournély's vision was lost.[11] The merger of the men's association took place in April 1799 and the beginning of the Diletti di Gesù in June 1799. Later on in the summer of 1799 Paccanari presented his rule of life for the Diletti to the pope and received verbal approval for it. The little community of three moved first from Prague to Padua and then finally to Rome at the invitation of the pope. There they began their new form of life as the Diletti di Gesù.[12]

When Joseph Varin met Louis Barat in Paris in June 1800 the Fathers of the Faith and the Diletti di Gesù were ready for expansion into France and Joseph Varin was charged with the task of heading that movement.[13] Louis Barat was interested in all Joseph Varin told him and felt that it resonated with his own desire to join a group inspired by the Jesuit rule, that worked towards the restoration of the Jesuits in France. In the course of their conversation, Joseph Varin asked Louis Barat about his family in Joigny. Louis Barat mentioned that he had a sister of eighteen years of age who knew Latin and could translate the classics with ease and was a good rhetorician. Not long afterwards, Sophie returned to Paris and Joseph Varin went to see her, hopeful that she would be interested in joining the Diletti. In later years he often recalled this meeting, and especially the anticipation he had beforehand:

> [I met] a small person, very simple, very plainly dressed and almost completely in peasant clothes. I can still see her arriving from her village by coach to rejoin her brother in Paris. He wanted to devote his life to our little society of the Fathers of the Faith and had only one problem, that of finding out what to do with his sister for whom he was responsible . . .[14]

The Carmelite communities in France were still unable to regroup and accept new members so there was no immediate possibility of Sophie joining one. Joseph Varin spoke enthusiastically to Sophie of the aims of the new congregation and asked her to consider joining the community about to start in Paris. It is clear that he did not in any way see her as the leader of the group in France, either then or for quite some time. For her part Sophie had come to Paris in order to enter the Carmelites there, as soon as it was possible for the community to resume receiving members. She told this to Joseph Varin and he countered her wishes with his enthusiasm, presenting the huge needs in France after the Revolution. He argued that the education her brother had given her at home and in Paris could not be buried in a time of crisis, hidden in a Carmelite monastery. He told Sophie the story of de Tournély, of his desire to see a community of women devoted to the spirituality of the Sacred Heart and involved in the education of young women. Sophie simply said she would think about it. Joseph Varin retorted that the time for thinking was over and that she should follow her destiny. This conviction overwhelmed Sophie and led her to accept the proposal that she join the Diletti and let go of her plan to become a Carmelite.[15]

But the implications of what she had done haunted her and later in life, especially in times of crisis, Sophie questioned the way she had let herself be orien-
tated by others who said it was God's will for her. Her formation to passivity by
her brother, Louis, weakened her own initiative, made her doubt her own judgement and believe in the convictions of others before her own. It was a form of
blind obedience, highly valued in spiritual teaching and practice at the time, as
well as the perceived role for women in society generally. It seemed the right
thing to do and she responded to the pressure. But it took her a long time to own
what she had done, accept what it made her and recognise it as her destiny. At
the time, little was clear, except that this group called the Diletti was beginning
in France and that she could join it as a member. By meeting and working with
the challenges placed before her in 1800, at the age of twenty-one, and somehow intuiting that this could be her way, Sophie went forward and with three
other women committed herself to the Diletti di Gesù.

The three other women were Sophie's companions in the rue de Touraine:
Marguerite (Madame Duval's maid, whose family name is not recorded), Octavie
Bailly and Marie-Françoise Loquet. Sophie and Octavie still lived as paying
guests of Madame Duval's. Marguerite had expressed the hope of joining a religious association, and Octavie, like Sophie, had decided to enter the Carmelites
when political circumstances allowed.[16] Marie-Françoise Loquet did not live in
the house at the rue de Touraine, though she was a frequent visitor there. She
ran a small school for young workers in her own house and she was trained as a
catechist. She was the author of several spiritual novels and was quite well
known in Paris at the time, at least in church circles. Joseph Varin considered
her to the be the leader of the little group in the process of being affiliated to
the Diletti di Gesù.[17] They took some days of retreat to prepare for their commitment and celebrated their affiliation to the Diletti on 21 November 1800,
with a religious ceremony followed by a festive meal.[18] Soon afterwards, Louis
Barat left Paris to make his noviciate in the Fathers of the Faith and took all his
belongings with him, except a picture of the Virgin Mary which he wanted
Sophie to have, and which she kept all her life. It was the end of an era for brother and sister, both setting out on new journeys. 'He heard my confession before
he left and after that he told me to sing at Mass. I had to do it . . . he left without saying goodbye to me.'[19]

Sophie was twenty when she began this new phase in her life, and from the
beginning she took the commitment seriously. Her letters home told the family
what was happening and how her life as a member of the Diletti was unfolding.
She appeared confident and assured in her correspondence, as if she had found
a way of life that suited her. She retained regular contact with her sister, Marie-
Louise, whose marriage was stressful, though the causes of this are not fully
known. Certainly the births of her children left Marie-Louise in need of support
and encouragement. Sophie tried to encourage her and pull her out of long bouts
of depression and weariness. Sophie realised that bringing up a family was difficult for Marie-Louise and she promised in time to try and help her with the

education of the children. Marie-Louise was the only sibling left in Joigny and Sophie wanted to assure her that she would not desert her, though she delivered quite a sermon in the process:

> I hope that your illness will not have any consequences . . . you will suffer less if you gain some strength and do not weigh yourself down with depressing thoughts. You need to be aware that the [marriage] state you are in, by God's Providence, of necessity brings with it these thoughts and afflictions. Do not waste them, make use of your suffering to bring you merit by living a truly Christian life and by patiently putting up with all the sufferings you endure. You see, my dear sister, I will not give you any human consolation, for that is both insufficient and empty. I can only offer you the comforts of religion . . . soon you will realise that with a bit of effort everything comes to an end, even the most difficult things. Believe me I have had this happy experience. And even though my position is not like yours, I had to suffer something and I assure you that I have always taken great consolation from the little efforts that I made . . . good sister, open your heart to me. Ah! If you only knew how I feel your plight and how, if it was possible, I would love to take half of your burden away. That moment will come. In the meantime Providence wishes that you carry on alone for a little longer. . . . When you have a minute write and tell me of your sufferings and your hopes, indeed everything that concerns you. Despite the little time I have I will try to respond. . . . Above all tell me about your children. . . . Greet tenderly all your little family for me, and be assured that I remain always with the same love your sister and your friend . . . greet father and mother for me. [20]

For some months life continued much as it had been before, though now Joseph Varin was confessor in the little community. While the women had made a formal commitment they had yet to find and adopt a definite work of education. At this period the Fathers of the Faith were active as missionaries in France, keen to try and establish their communities and schools. With this purpose in mind Joseph Varin visited Amiens in April 1801. This was a key visit, not just for the Fathers of the Faith but also for the little group in Paris. Louis Sellier (1772–1854)[21] had run a school in Amiens since 1799 and when he decided to enter the Fathers of the Faith in 1801 he offered his school to the association. During his visit Joseph Varin met several women who were engaged in good works in the town, among them were Geneviève Deshayes, Hyacinthe Devaux, a former Benedictine nun, and her niece, Henriette Grosier.[22] In her record of these times Deshayes tells how she had been searching for some spiritual path after the trauma of the Revolution, while Hyacinthe Devaux was trying to recover some form of religious life. With the help of her niece, Henriette Grosier, she ran a small boarding school in the rue Martin-Bleu-Dieu in Amiens but both were finding it difficult to sustain the work alone. Having received news about a new women's congregation, described in a brochure and in the newspapers in France, they were attracted to it, even hoping that the school could be the focus of the new congregation in Amiens. The brochure on the Diletti presented their work as that of 'learned women who would work in the spirit of St Francis de Sales and Fénelon and educate young women'. Joseph Varin explained the genesis of the Diletti, and as with Sophie and the others in Paris, he stressed the original impulse and idea of Léonor de Tournély, as well as the importance of the name Society of the Sacred Heart.[23]

Deshayes and Grosier decided to join the Diletti, but Hyacinthe Devaux was less sure, though she agreed to consider the possibility. Joseph Varin thought that the little group in Paris could merge with that in Amiens and establish the school as their common project. He considered Marie-Françoise Loquet the obvious leader though he had no real knowledge of her at all. He chose her because she was a writer and she appeared to have more experience than the others. Loquet arrived in Amiens on 9 September 1801 and began immediately to organise the venture. She arranged that Deshayes would join Henriette Grosier and her aunt at rue Martin-Bleu-Dieu to work with them in running the school. This negotiation took longer than expected since Hyacinthe Devaux could not reach a decision to hand over the school, but eventually the deeds were surrendered to Loquet on 15 October 1801, though Madame Devaux decided not to join the new community. A month later Sophie Barat and Octavie Bailly joined Loquet, Grosier and Deshayes in Amiens and the community was complete. Now the Diletti had both members and an educational project in France. At their first meeting Geneviève Deshayes studied both Sophie and Octavie, these two close friends. Their arrival was greeted with enthusiasm, in particular that of Sophie:

> Even to see . . . Sophie did our hearts good. Her reputation for piety, virtue and talent had gone before her and everyone loved her before they had met her. But her gentleness, her angelic, unassuming air, something which only she had, won all our hearts. . . . Octavie, though really good and very virtuous, nevertheless did not have the same charm, the same affability.[24]

In any event Octavie had little time to make an impression in Amiens as she was sent to Rome immediately to be trained as mistress of novices; she would return in the winter of 1803.

Sophie and Henriette took responsibility for teaching in the school; Geneviève took weaker pupils who needed individual attention and she looked after the infirmary in the house. Originally there were twenty boarders in the school and soon after the new opening this rose to forty. In January 1802 the community announced that they would give free classes to the poor of the town and the response was immediate. Sixty-five pupils turned up on the first day, which presented the small group with an enormous task, for they were few in number and had limited experience in the field of education. They wrote to Joseph Varin asking him to try and find more teachers to cope with the number in both schools and he promised to do so. Léopoldine Naudet in Rome, superior general of the Diletti, also promised to send personnel. In the meantime they devised a method for teaching so many by dividing the day pupils into groups of fifteen, and putting an older pupil in charge of each group. The teachers taught the group leaders, and each group leader passed on what she had learnt to her group.[25] The boarding school needs were much more demanding and the teachers themselves needed help in preparing their classes. By this time the Fathers of the Faith had taken over the school established in Amiens by Sellier and one of the teachers there, Nicholas Loriquet,[26] promised to help. However this did not begin until the following year, 1803.

The educational work was daunting and Marie-Françoise Loquet's ineptness as a leader, and her unsuitability for her task in Amiens, compounded the problems of the little group. Because she was a writer of some repute, Joseph Varin had expected her to be effective in this educational project. In fact this was an unhappy, negative experience for her and for her companions in Amiens. Her inconsistencies were marked. She spoilt the pupils and imposed no discipline in the school, least of all on her own niece who had come to the school with her aunt. She had fits of temper and tantrums, which lasted a long time; she withdrew from all teaching herself and from the life of the little group. She imposed an austere order of day which she herself did not observe. She allowed the cook, formerly employed by Hyacinthe Devaux, to run the house and was unaware that very often the little community had inadequate food. Her cats had total freedom in the house day and night. All finances were held in her hands and funds became very tight. She insisted that the little group wear the costume of peasant women but her choice of head dress and of clothing was odd and drew ridicule from the townspeople. Lacking all experience of religious life and thrown together to live out some ideal of which they knew little, the group had no means or indeed time to address the situation. But Geneviève Deshayes reacted strongly for she was aware of how sick in the mind Loquet was, and she tried to deal with the problem with little immediate success. Since all were so inexperienced and had no yardstick by which to measure their experience, they did not trust their own judgement. They hesitated to speak their minds or were too absorbed in surviving to question openly the abnormality of the situation.[27]

For some time no one outside saw what was going on. Once the group was established Joseph Varin left Amiens to resume his journeys, preparing the way for the Fathers of the Faith in France. He was confident that Loquet was capable of leading the group and quite unaware of the difficulties he left behind. He asked his colleague, Nicholas Jennesseaux, rector of the college at Amiens, to be the confessor of the community and probably thought that was enough. During his short visits to the community Joseph Varin perceived nothing amiss and most of the members certainly did not complain at the time. It was only years later that they reminisced with wry amusement on their silence and collusion in a situation that became increasingly bizarre. Deshayes's memories were very clear and she knew well that the type of education given under the leadership of Loquet had little to do either with Francis de Sales or Fénelon.[28]

These were difficult months. The running of the school was left to Henriette, Geneviève and Sophie. They were supposed to learn how to teach and look after children, and at the same time learn about religious life but there was no one present who had experience in either of these areas. The pupils liked Sophie but she could not hold them in class or at recreation or indeed when they were out on walks in the town. She was often sick and had to be cared for by the others. She lived very much in her own world and dreamed of going on the missions to Canada, an attractive idea in a situation where the immediate challenges were overwhelming and her self-confidence tested.[29] Certainly on two occasions she was so absorbed in her own world that she actually did not attend to or perceive what was going on around her. One was Sophie's unawareness of the misbehaviour of Loquet's niece in the refectory; the other happened on the morning of her vows. On both occasions Sophie seems to have lost consciousness of where she was and had to be brought back to reality. It is evident from her correspondence with Joseph Varin that she felt lost, somewhat disconnected and unsure of herself. He tried to assure her and give her a way of moving out of such inner pain, especially the scourge of scruples which he noted as the particular effect of Louis Barat's formation. Out of touch with the situation in Amiens, Joseph Varin urged Sophie to speak openly about her concerns to Loquet, convinced that Sophie would receive good advice and help.[30] In a way this time in Amiens, from November 1801 to December 1802, was a continuation of her lifestyle in Paris with Louis Barat. As in Paris so in Amiens Sophie had a rigorous life of prayer and work, a leader who demanded full obedience, and a regime of poor food and inadequate sleep. This austere way of life was mitigated by the friendship of Grosier and Deshayes and the camaraderie that developed in the course of sharing so much in such close quarters.

By the early spring of 1802 Joseph Varin had found three more women ready to join the little community in Amiens: Adèle Jugon, Anne Baudemont and her friend, Mlle Capy. All three had been in contact with Joseph Varin and they had heard about the new congregation through friends or through accounts in newspapers. Adèle Jugon worked very effectively as a catechist in the parish d'Etoilles in Paris; Anne Baudemont and Mlle Capy had both been religious in the Clarissan order in Rheims. Anne Baudemont had tried unsuccessfully to restore her community after the Terror and Joseph Varin had invited her to try the new congregation.[31] All three were a welcome addition to the house and were greeted with some relief. Indeed, later on in the year the school moved to another part of Amiens (to the rue Neuve), to facilitate the growing number of boarders though the number of day pupils had to be reduced.[32] Despite the chaotic government of Marie-Françoise Loquet, the numbers in the boarding school were actually growing, though the state of the community had reached breaking point.

Sophie continued to write home at this time and did not mention any of the difficulties she was having in Amiens. She admitted that she had not written home much, but neither had she heard from either her parents or Marie-Louise. Indeed it was Louis who had written to Sophie, given her news of the family and told her that Marie-Louise was overburdened. It is not clear whether this was due to marriage difficulties or financial problems, though some prolonged family stress is hinted at in the correspondence over the years between Sophie and her sister. Indeed Marie-Louise had given birth to two more children, Marie

Thérèse in 1801 and Hubert Xavier in 1802. Neither of the children lived for more than two years and they were a source of continual concern and anxiety during these months. Sophie desperately wanted to have details:

First of all give me news of your health and that of your little family. I do not know if it has increased or decreased, to the extent that if I were in the desert I would not be more ignorant in your regard. If I do know anything about you it is indirectly and from strangers. Do you believe that I am no longer interested in what touches you, have I become so detached from you that nothing about your house and family can draw me for a moment [?] Oh! No, my dear sister, it is not like that, the friendship I have for you has not changed at all. Even if I do not express it anymore by emotion and tears, it is no less in my heart and only more solid and purified.[33]

Sophie hoped that her parents had become used to the fact that she would not be coming home that autumn, breaking another pattern of her life. She also realised that the family were very disappointed at Louis's short visit home.[34] Sophie reminded her sister that Louis had never expressed any desire to settle at home and Sophie did not expect that he would ever return home permanently. But both she and Louis were very aware of their parents and of their sister and had discussed the education of the nieces and nephews. Sophie told Marie-Louise to make sure that Célestine got a good start in education so that when she was old enough she could join the school in Amiens. Above all she asked her sister not to repeat what their mother had done, becoming too possessive and so finding separations from her children so difficult that she became quite ill. She asked Marie-Louise to look after their parents. She was worried about her father, and asked Marie-Louise to try to get him to work less hard. Sophie reminded her sister how Jacques Barat loved his eldest daughter and she was sure she could persuade him: 'to understand that you would prefer to have less and keep him for a few years more. Tell him to give more time to the practice of religion and talk to him often on this beneficial topic'.[35]

The critical situation in Amiens was addressed in December 1802 when Louise Naudet, a delegate of the superior general of the Diletti, visited the community and very quickly saw what was happening within it. She stayed in Amiens for several months to assess the situation and she concluded that Loquet had to be removed. It took some time to persuade Loquet that religious life was not for her but she left Amiens in December 1802, when it was clear that Louise Naudet was not going to change her mind. The next task was to appoint her successor. While Sophie was young, shy and unable to express herself, Adèle Jugon considered that Sophie was the only person among them capable of leadership. On the other hand, Anne Baudemont spoke at length to Louise Naudet and suggested that, with her own gifts and especially her experience of religious life prior to the Revolution, she herself was the most suitable for leadership in the community. Louise Naudet took the advice of Jugon and to the surprise of all decided to appoint Sophie. Certainly Joseph Varin had not thought of Sophie as the leader and it was only when Louise Naudet held firmly to her choice that he was persuaded to concur. Sophie accepted the role reluctantly, with surprise, even dismay. In some way she sensed that life would never be the same again.[36] Many years later, when the Society of the Sacred Heart was well known, Louise Naudet would remember with evident pleasure and satisfaction that she had appointed Sophie leader in Amiens.[37] For her part Sophie always retained great affection for Louise Naudet and appreciated her mark of trust and confidence at a critical time in her life.

There was a great sense of relief at the departure of Loquet for all in Amiens: they had been living a type of captivity which had created enormous tensions, both in the community and in the school. This situation was inherited by Sophie when she began her role as leader of this community on 21 December 1802. Her scope for leadership was limited however since Joseph Varin remained in charge of the community. As well as by his visits to the house, he guided Sophie through letters and insisted that she present all decisions to him for approval before they were executed. She was also accountable to Léopoldine Naudet and to Nicholas Paccanari in Rome. Moreover, Joseph Varin appointed two priests in Amiens, Fr Bruson and Fr Sambucy de Saint-Estève, as advisers to Sophie and as confessors to the school and the community.[38] In the spring of 1803 Nicholas Loriquet started to work on a plan of studies for the school as well as giving classes to the teachers. Within the community Anne Baudemont was named assistant to Sophie and Geneviève Deshayes was charged with the studies in the school, despite the fact that Deshayes herself recognised that she was in no way gifted for this.

Sophie found her new role burdensome. She began losing sleep and her appetite as she felt the task to be beyond her capacities. Despite her protests Joseph Varin continued to insist that she was the person for the task. He urged her to trust God and her friends who had confirmed the choice. But the community were concerned and Mlle Capy tried to nurse Sophie, who was by all accounts difficult to look after as she was so reticent about her body. By July 1803 she was in such poor health that Joseph Varin promised that if it became necessary he would name Mlle Capy to replace her.[39] But Mlle Capy herself had a mental breakdown in October 1803 and despite their best efforts the community could not take care of her. Adèle Jugon, who had recently left the community, came from Paris to take Mlle Capy to the Salpêtrière hospital there, which had a special section for the mentally ill. This breakdown weighed heavily on Sophie and her colleagues and they had to endure the criticisms of the local people in Amiens, and later of the Capy family and the priests of her home town, Rheims, who were taken aback that Capy had been sent away to the asylum in Paris.[40] In September 1803 Louis, in a new awareness of Sophie's physical needs, expressed concern for her health. He told Marie-Louise that Sophie needed a long rest at home in Joigny but that until the community was more solidly established she was indispensable at Amiens. He admitted however that she was bearing up much better than he had hoped.[41]

Sophie did not get that holiday. Indeed all focus on Sophie's health was diverted for a time on to Capy's illness, but by the spring of 1804 it was clear that Sophie had become very ill indeed and was in danger of death: 'Threatened for some time with a form of cancer this generous soul offered it to God to suffer secretly . . . all that was painful and distasteful in it for human nature . . .'[42]

After a time Sophie could no longer fight the illness secretly. One of the community saw what was happening, probably Geneviève Deshayes, and she warned Joseph Varin that Sophie was seriously ill. It is clear that she was embarrassed by her illness, and did not want to see a doctor. She tried to force her body to get better, and had a certain contempt and impatience for it. Besides, 'her extreme delicacy of conscience on the question of modesty was added to her other repugnance'. Her illness was probably gynaecological and Sophie's natural diffidence was compounded by the attitudes to the body she had received in the formation she received from Louis Barat. Joseph Varin insisted that she be cared for by a nurse and that she go to the Sisters of Charity in Paris who were well-known experts in the treatment Sophie needed so urgently. He was annoyed when she ignored him. She preferred to hope for some kind of a healing miracle. He insisted that she follow the advice of the infirmarian, Deshayes, and the chaplain, Bruson.[43] It is clear that all the priests around knew about her illness and that Joseph Varin used the pressure of their criticism to force her finally to do something about it. Sophie did go to Paris for treatment which lasted several weeks and while her condition was alleviated she was not fully cured. Nevertheless the treatment prevented further deterioration of her health and Sophie was able to remain in office as superior. But she needed care and she admitted that she only felt really well again in August 1806.[44]

Meanwhile the community grew in number. In the autumn of 1803 Catherine de Charbonnel (1774–1857) and Marie du Terrail (1771–1813) joined the community. Both were highly educated women, deeply affected by the Revolution.[45] Nicholas Loriquet was impressed at the knowledge possessed by de Charbonnel and by her capacity to communicate it and he recognised that she had the ability to teach her own colleagues. Her very presence in the house helped to establish the reputation of the school and numbers there began to grow. The school confessor, Saint-Estève, gradually took over the direction of the school and it was only a matter of time before he gradually assumed full authority in both school and community.[46] However, in the more immediate future, events happening elsewhere overtook the little community in Amiens and forced it to separate from the congregation of the Diletti in Rome. Since 1802 the Fathers of the Faith had become progressively uneasy with the leadership of Nicholas Paccanari, gradually realising that he had no intention of ever joining the Jesuits should they be restored. This was difficult for Joseph Varin to accept, because at their first meeting in Prague he had been won over by this strong personality. The situation then became more problematic when suspicions were raised regarding Paccanari's personal life. The leader of the Fathers of the Faith in London, Jean Rozaven, went to Rome and investigated the rumours.[47] Within months Paccanari was accused of sexual misconduct and was brought to trial before the Holy Office in Rome. He was found guilty of the sin of sodomy and he was jailed. The public image and reputation of the Fathers of the Faith and the Diletti were discredited in Rome, and Paccanari's behaviour forced all the members to reconsider their position.[48]

In addition, in France the Fathers of the Faith were under heavy suspicion from the government of Napoleon. They were suspected of plotting to subvert the power of the state since they looked beyond France for their ultimate authority and, worst of all, were suspected of being disguised Jesuits. This and the condemnation of Paccanari led the Fathers of the Faith to break links with Italy and to restrict their own activities to France from 21 June 1804. Without any prior consultation of the little community in Amiens, Joseph Varin wrote to Rome and informed Marie-Anne of Austria and Léopoldine Naudet that the Diletti in Amiens were no longer under their authority. During a visit to Amiens he told the older members of the community some of the details. The key decision was that the community was under his sole authority and responsible to him for all decisions now that the link with Rome was broken. Such high-handedness on the part of Joseph Varin can be explained partly by his embarrassment over the case of Paccanari. However, it also underlines his assumption that he had the authority to regulate the life of the community at Amiens. It was an abrupt end to a slowly growing relationship with the Naudet sisters and was confusing to all in Amiens, especially when they considered the enthusiasm with which Joseph Varin had introduced the Diletti to each of them.[49]

The break with Louise Naudet was a great loss of support for Sophie. Louise had been the first to recognise her potential gifts and had affirmed and assured her when she felt unable to fulfil her task in her community. When Sophie went to Rome in 1833 and 1837 she made sure to visit Louise who had chosen to live alone there. Léopoldine had moved to Verona and founded her own congregation, the Holy Family of Verona. This separation directly impacted on the Amiens community – Octavie Bailly had returned from Rome in October 1803, disillusioned at what had happened to the Diletti there, she told Sophie that she had decided to return to her first choice and join the Carmelites in Paris, although she had been trained to oversee the novices at Amiens. Her departure from Amiens in August 1804 was a personal loss for Sophie; they had been friends in Paris and had planned to enter Carmel together.[50] In September the community moved again to another more suitable location in Amiens and the schools continued to grow. The name of Diletti di Gesù was replaced by the Association des Dames de l'Instruction Chrétienne, a title which explained their work and contribution in society and did not link them in any formal way with the Fathers of the Faith, thus avoiding the suspicions of the government.

Much had been achieved in a short time. Gifted and unusual women had gathered together for a common project. They were beginning to work out their teaching philosophy and reach further into the deeper motivations for their life together. Now that the influence of Paccanari and the Diletti was receding, the search for a spiritual goal became urgent and there were several influences at work in Amiens which would prove difficult to integrate. Strong characters were at work, struggling for power and control. The next eleven years would clarify several strands of religious life which at this stage were embryonic and tentative. On the one hand there was the influence of Joseph Varin, bearing the impulse of Léonor de Tournély and later Nicholas Paccanari until his fall. However, Joseph Varin had never lost sight of what de Tournély had dreamed for the future and he wanted to hold that ideal central. On the other hand, Anne Baudemont came to Amiens at the invitation of Joseph Varin, and she sought to make her mark in this new venture, convinced that she had by far the longest experience of religious life. Others, like Geneviève Deshayes, Henriette Grosier and Catherine de Charbonnel, marked by the horrors of the Revolution, had initiated good works and were searching for some form of community life. Sophie Barat and Octavie Bailly had decided to enter the Carmelites but had been deflected by the enthusiasm of Joseph Varin and Louis Barat into joining the Diletti.

This was the beginning of Sophie Barat's long and painful journey towards expressing her own vision. She was able to talk about it only much later when she explained the origin of her own idea of religious life. It began during the Revolution, when she was in Paris and witnessed or heard about the desecration of churches and the persecution of religion. The king and queen had been executed; priests and nuns were being persecuted, exiled or guillotined. The young Napoleon had twice humiliated the city of Rome and the office of the pope. The place of religion in society and the sense of God were being eroded or at least held in contempt. In the midst of such upheavals Sophie and her friends searched for some way to create a counterbalance, to restore what had been profaned. They sought to restore religious values and to atone for such attacks on the sense of the sacred.[51] Many years later Sophie spoke about these early years. She outlined the original impulse, rooted in her experience of the Revolution:

The first idea of the Society that we had . . . was to gather as many as possible of the true adorers of the Heart of Jesus in the Eucharist. . . . At the end of the Terror and of the abominations of the Revolution against religion and the Blessed Sacrament . . . all hearts vibrated together in unison: Make reparation to Jesus Christ in the Blessed Sacrament . . . was the rallying cry . . . No two pious people meeting together would talk without trying to find some means of bringing Jesus Christ back into family life. . . .

My original idea of our little Society of the Sacred Heart was to gather young girls together and establish *a little community which night and day would adore the Heart of Jesus, whose love had been desecrated in the Eucharist.* But I said to myself, when we are twenty-four religious, able to replace one another on a prie-dieu for perpetual adoration, that will be something, and yet little enough for such a noble goal. . . . If we had *young pupils* whom we formed in the spirit of adoration and reparation, now that would be different! and I saw hundreds, thousands of adorers before a *perfect, universal monstrance,*[52] *raised above the Church.*

'That is it' I said to myself, as I was praying before a lonely tabernacle: 'we must dedicate ourselves to the education of youth, renew in souls the solid foundations of a living faith in the . . . Blessed Sacrament; [and] there fight the traces of

Jansenism which had led to [such] impiety. With the revelations of Jesus Christ to Blessed Margaret Mary concerning the devotion of reparation . . . to the Heart of Jesus in the Blessed Sacrament, we will raise up a multitude of adorers from all the nations, to the very ends of the earth.[53]

This was a visionary insight, in direct response to the Revolution. It was a response founded on Sophie's belief in God, in Christ and in the church. All that was sacred to her world was being torn apart and devalued. With her companions Sophie felt the need to renew a society which had become brutalised and violent, both in its sense of God and in its respect for human life. Over the years this intuition matured and developed and expanded into seeing education as the means and the way to renew society in its depths. She always returned to that initial hope and desire to heal and renew society in France after the ravages of the Revolution.

The demise of the Diletti in Rome created a hiatus in the community in Amiens, one which the chaplain at Amiens, Sambucy de Saint-Estève, was ready to fill with his projects. He had an able ally in Anne Baudemont and when Joseph Varin's enthusiasm for a new foundation in Grenoble required Sophie's absence from Amiens in November 1804, Joseph Varin named Anne Baudemont as Sophie's replacement as superior while she was away. Saint-Estève was confirmed as confessor to the community, to the school and special adviser to Anne Baudemont. It was to prove a powerful combination. Leaving Amiens was momentous for Sophie: she was setting forth on her first of many journeys of foundation. Indeed, the image of travelling described her life, for she was in continual movement and until the period after 1852 Sophie was rarely in one place for longer than a few months. She set off for Grenoble to meet a woman of remarkable courage and determination. Philippine Duchesne had persisted in her desire for religious life throughout the Revolution and had come through daunting obstacles to realise her goal. By the time Sophie arrived in Grenoble in December 1804, Philippine Duchesne had procured a building and had begun a school with a small group of women who shared her ideals. This achievement was the fruit of a long, uncertain and painful process.

Philippine Duchesne, born in Grenoble on the 29 August 1769, was the daughter of Pierre François Duchesne (1743–1814) and Rose-Euphrosine Périer (1748–1797) and she was baptised Rose-Philippine. Her father was a skilled lawyer and politician, a formidable product of the Enlightenment, radical and anti-clerical in his thinking. Her mother came from a wealthy merchant family, was well educated and devoted to the care of her five children in the home. The Duchesne and Périer families shared a large house in the centre of the town where strong, lifelong bonds of friendship were forged at this time between Philippine Duchesne and her cousins, especially Josephine Périer. Until she was twelve Philippine and her cousin Josephine shared a governess at home and were taught reading, writing and arithmetic, as well as some household skills. Their brothers had a tutor, the Fr Raillanne. However, it was customary for young girls to be sent to boarding school to prepare for their First Communion and so in 1781 Philippine and Josephine were sent to the Visitation Convent in Grenoble, Ste Marie d'En Haut. They made their First Communion in the following year and they remained there as boarders for four years. Not only did Philippine enjoy her education there but she showed every sign of entering the community and becoming a Visitation nun. On learning this her parents removed her quickly from the school in 1784 and hoped that in time she would forget about it. But the desire persisted and when Josephine married Fortunat de Savoye-Rollin in 1788, Philippine asked her parents for permission to enter Ste Marie d'En Haut. On their refusal she simply went to the convent and refused to return home; at this her parents relented and allowed her to enter the community on the condition that she would not make her vows until she was twenty-five.[54]

Soon Philippine's life became caught up in political events. By 1792 the Revolution was in full spate, all convents and monasteries were suppressed and Philippine was forced to leave Ste Marie d'En Haut and return home once more. Her parents were relieved but Philippine was bitterly disappointed and tried to continue to live a form of religious life at home. She spent some of that time in the family home some miles outside Grenoble at Grâne and later nearby with her maternal grandmother at Romans. She returned to Grenoble and worked with the poor and destitute of the town, often at great risk to her own safety. During these years nothing was clear, the whole of France was in turmoil and Philippine could find no light, no future, no worthwhile reason to look forward and plan. In her search for some path, she made a pilgrimage to Louvesc, the shrine of St Francis Regis, to pray for guidance. There she met an elderly Jesuit who confirmed her vocation to religious life. This moment in her life remained with Philippine into old age and was a source of courage for her in times of great difficulty. After 1795, the persecution of the church became less intense and there was a hint of change in the air which gave Philippine grounds to hope that religious life would be restored. She visited her aunt in the Visitation convent in Romans and saw that the community there was beginning to regroup. Encouraged by this she decided to return to Grenoble and contact the former Visitation community in the hope of resuming her former life in Ste Marie d'En Haut.[55]

Her first task was to gain legal access to the convent, sequestered during the Revolution, and she succeeded with the help of her cousins in Grenoble. From December 1801 to December 1804 Philippine tried in vain to reinstate religious life in Ste Marie d'En Haut, but the former community members were either too old or too dispirited to resume their life in the monastery. Some indeed tried but it was not possible to reinvent the past there, even though other Visitation monasteries in France were in process of being restored. Philippine's enthusiasm brought both criticism and downright antagonism on her head, from the former community as well as the general public. It proved to be an incredibly difficult task and she was often advised by family and friends to give up her plans. Only the local clergy supported her efforts and defended her motives. Her courage and the conviction that she was destined to restore religious life in Ste Marie d'En Haut gave Philippine the energy to persist.

With bitter disappointment, she gradually recognised that she could not re-constitute religious life with her former companions. Nevertheless, she perse-vered in her ideal and began to search for some group either to join or at least be affiliated to for support and encouragement. She had heard about the Diletti di Gesù in Italy and as early as 1802 had thought of joining them, ready even to go to Rome if necessary. While waiting for some contact to be made with this new congregation, and to give her some form of credibility in the town, Philippine asked one of the clergy to write a rule of life for her and present it to the bish-op. This was approved in March 1803 under the name 'Daughters of the Propagation of the Faith'.[56] During 1803 one of the local clergy, Pierre Rivet, went to make his retreat in Belley, a town north of Grenoble, where the Fathers of the Faith were established. Philippine asked Rivet to talk to Joseph Varin about the possibility of becoming affiliated to the Diletti in Amiens. Joseph Varin was not there but his colleague, Pierre Roger[57] showed great interest in what Rivet had to tell him about the small group of women in Grenoble and gave him the rule of the Diletti to copy out and bring back to Philippine Duchesne. Soon after, Roger paid a visit to Ste Marie d'En Haut and reported all to Joseph Varin. The possibility of a merger between Amiens and Grenoble became strengthened when both Joseph Varin and Roger paid a visit to Ste Marie d'En Haut in July 1804 and began to plan the fusion of the two communities. At the end of the visit Joseph Varin told Philippine that Sophie, 'our invalid', would visit them soon and effect the fusion.[58] By this time all links with the Diletti in Rome had been severed and it is not clear if Joseph Varin told Philippine then about the crisis in Rome concerning Paccanari or indeed about the original vision of Léonor de Tournély. But he did tell Sophie and the community in Amiens that it was worth going not just to Grenoble but to the ends of the earth to meet someone of the calibre of Philippine Duchesne.[59]

On the way to Grenoble Sophie managed to spend a week at home with her family, and see the new baby, Sophie Dusaussoy, who had been born the previ-ous March. The break gave her a chance to tell her parents what was happening in her life. Sophie could see how they were ageing and relying more and more on Marie-Louise. It was a short visit and Sophie left home in early December. She arrived in Ste Marie d'En Haut on 13 December 1804, accompanied by two of the community members from Amiens, Rosalie Debrosse and Catherine Maillard, and two priests, Pierre Roger and Fr Coidy.[60] Sophie retained a vivid memory of her arrival, on foot, up the steep path to the convent, the enthusias-tic welcome of Philippine Duchesne and the sense of being overwhelmed by the expectation laid upon her.[61] While Philippine and her four companions, Marie Rivet, Emilie Giraud, Marie Balastron and Adélaïde Second,[62] greeted Sophie with relief and joy, it took time for them all to get used to the new situ-ation. Some avoided Sophie for a time through either fear or shyness. Yet there was a sense of adventure and an awareness that new paths were opening up for these women which must have made them both excited and apprehensive. Sophie herself was under some strain. She had been very ill and was still quite fragile in health. She came to Grenoble in the role of leader, though she had no specific terms of reference at all since all links with the Diletti were broken. She admitted later on in life that she had little idea then of what she should do or initiate. No wonder she was perceived as serious and withdrawn, a distant figure, hard to approach and easier to avoid. It was an impression that she would often make throughout her life, at least in new situations.[63]

Sophie decided to start the training of these women after Christmas and to precede it by a time of prayer together. Pierre Roger offered to give a retreat to launch the group. This proved to be extraordinarily helpful because his inexperience and poor judgement provided daily amusement for everyone and created real bonds of friendship. Roger himself said it was a retreat that he would never forget. His daily exhortations and testing of the women were so bizarre that Philippine was afraid that they would all leave the house in dismay. To allay her anxiety she whispered assurances to them during the sermons which only added to the laughter. Roger's aim was to create conditions for a new start in life and he tried to preach so persuasively that he would make them weep for their past sins and weaknesses. To this purpose he adopted a dramatic, theatrical style, such as might have been used on parish missions. But since the group was very small this soon turned into burlesque. Finally, on the last day of the retreat the entire group, including Roger, fell about laughing in the little prayer room. Such an experience helped more than anything else to break down barriers of shyness and reserve between the women, and to bond them together. It certainly made their beginnings memorable.[64]

The noviciate began in earnest in early January 1805 and for the next eleven months Sophie was responsible for the formation of these women in Grenoble. This task was difficult, for since the rupture with the Diletti Sophie had no official rule of life as a source of reference. No record exists of the content of her formation plan during these months. However, an insight into her views on religious life can be gleaned from the two changes she proposed to make in the house. The first was the abolition of the monastic grilles which the Visitation order had prior to the Revolution. The grilles symbolised the separation of the religious from the wider community, the cloister required by the Church for all women religious who took the solemn vows of religion. To request that the grilles be abolished represented a huge break with the past and Philippine struggled for a long time against their removal. Sophie tried to explain to her why the grilles had to go but Philippine accepted the change reluctantly, without ever really understanding why such forms could not be part of this new experience of religious life.[65]

Sophie also asked the little group to drop the recitation of Office in choir in favour of prolonged silent prayer. She, following the Diletti, saw this as a more suitable form of prayer for women who needed to rest their voices after teaching all day. Again Philippine Duchesne resisted this and, despite the support of

Fr Roger, this time Sophie did not succeed. Indeed during the retreat Roger asked the community not to say Office and immediately the local people in Grenoble criticised them for not praying as the former members of the Visitation monastery. Sophie too was criticised. The people thought that she was far too young to be in charge. They resented her insistence on having fewer visitors to the house, the fact that there were only young women accepted into the community and of course her removal of the grilles from the building. Such efforts to replace some monastic forms of religious life, as well as the task of trying to blend the old and the new, were formidable.[66]

From the beginning Sophie introduced a disciplined order of day in Grenoble, based on the pattern in Amiens. While it did not occur to Sophie to write a rule of life herself at this period, she asked Joseph Varin several times for some written guidelines. The women could make no formal commitment without some legal structure which local authorities in Grenoble could recognise. Finally, in early November 1805, Joseph Varin and Roger travelled to Grenoble and set to work to adapt the rule of the Diletti for the community at Grenoble.[67] They submitted their work to the local bishop, Claude Simon, who accepted it as a provisional rule of life for the little group in Ste Marie d'En Haut. On 21 November 1805 five novices made their first vows thus completing the first stage of the foundation. By this time Sophie had been absent from Amiens for over a year and it was time to return and establish the leadership of the congregation on a firmer footing. Not only had the community in Grenoble been established but in the autumn of 1805 Joseph Varin had asked Henriette Grosier to leave Amiens and begin a community in Belley, near Lyon, where the Fathers of the Faith had a college.[68] Having three communities required a leadership election to decide who would have the overall responsibility for the congregation.

The fact that Joseph Varin ensured that someone was named to replace Sophie while she was in Grenoble indicated that the model the Association would adopt would be that of several communities, in different geographical areas, and governed by a superior general elected for life. The monastic model of single, autonomous communities, each governed separately and independently, was not the one Joseph Varin had in mind. This led to a struggle for leadership in this little association which had been brewing for several months and came to a head when Joseph Varin announced an election for superior general was to be held in Amiens in January 1806. Such a struggle was inevitable. Much had happened to the community and school in Amiens since Sophie had left. Political circumstances forced the houses to have little communication with one another. Indeed Joseph Varin wanted all contacts between Amiens and Grenoble to be restricted and filtered through him. There is no doubt that the government was very suspicious of all religious groups and that any indication that communities were linked would be treated severely, especially if they were associated with the Fathers of the Faith. In quite specific directives to Anne Baudemont in March 1805 Joseph Varin urged her to try to solve all difficulties in Amiens within the community and if necessary with the help of Saint-Estève. Only in cases of real impasse was she to write and consult Joseph Varin himself. She was to act alone, in concert with her own advisers within the community, and there was no mention of any role at all for Sophie. In the minds of both Joseph Varin and Anne Baudemont, Sophie had left to form another community and there was no further immediate need for her in Amiens. The only reference to Sophie in his words of advice was to urge Baudemont to form her community in the way that Sophie was in process of doing in Grenoble.[69]

Independent communities would have seemed quite normal to Anne Baudemont, since her former community in Rheims had been completely autonomous. The Fathers of the Faith and the Diletti had developed a different vision, of communities linked together structurally for purposes of government and exchange of personnel, after the model of the Jesuits. Now there was a conflict of models, and the attitude of the government to the Fathers of the Faith, and towards any communities of women who had contact with them, favoured the model of independent, autonomous communities, familiar to Anne Baudemont. This left Sophie in an ambiguous position. While she had been formally replaced in Amiens by Anne Baudemont during her absence, almost immediately after her departure several important changes were made there over which she had not been consulted.

In a short space of time the two women with whom she had started off in Amiens, Geneviève Deshayes and Henriette Grosier, had left the community. Deshayes had been appointed headmistress of the school but after a few weeks had resigned and left Amiens for Grenoble. In her own accounts Deshayes derides her own intellectual capacities but it is hard not to suspect that she was forced out of the position by Anne Baudemont. Joseph Varin was in thrall to Anne Baudemont and to Saint-Estève and accepted their assessment of the situation in Amiens. Their views and their pressure made Geneviève Deshayes ill and she was forced to leave the house in that state. Joseph Varin told Sophie that everyone, including Saint-Estève and Loriquet, breathed a sigh of relief when Deshayes left Amiens. Joseph Varin appointed Grosier to succeed Deshayes in the school from February 1805, while keeping her responsibility for the novices. Yet she too was removed from Amiens by Joseph Varin, in June 1805, for the proposed foundation of a new house of the congregation in Belley. Again it was a sudden move and even Grosier herself was not told where she was going until Joseph Varin wrote to her at Grenoble and informed her of what was happening. Thus in the space of a few months, Sophie, Henriette and Geneviève found themselves together again, this time in Grenoble. The gaps in Amiens were filled by Anne Baudemont and Saint-Estève, and both proceeded to put their stamp on the community and school, drawing up a prospectus for the school and constitutions for the community.

Sophie complained to Joseph Varin about the decisions taken at Amiens, as well as the manner in which such decisions were communicated to her. She voiced her suspicions of the influence of both Anne Baudemont and Saint-Estève. Although young and inexperienced, Sophie did not accept without protest this high-handedness on the part of Joseph Varin, Saint-Estève and Baudemont. Her views, however, were interpreted by Joseph Varin as evidence of a stubborn and independent spirit. He urged her to trust him and Anne Baudemont and Saint-Estève and not be so suspicious. Yet Joseph Varin often opened letters addressed to her and decided which of them she should receive. It was particularly distressing when he withheld a long letter from Louise Naudet, written to Sophie and explaining what had happened in Rome to Paccanari and to the Diletti.[70] Joseph Varin exercised both authoritarianism and censorship under the guise of prudence, barely disguising a desire to maintain control of both Amiens and Grenoble. Through his manner of acting Sophie was doubly cut off from Amiens: on the one hand he gave Anne Baudemont and Saint-Estève all the support and authority needed in Amiens; on the other hand, he chided Sophie when she wanted to be consulted and involved in decisions over Amiens. He concurred with her understanding of her role, however, and ensured that all legal acts of the congregation were signed by Sophie herself or at least were signed in her name.[71]

Anne Baudemont was a woman of strong character, of immense energy and dispatch, thorough and hard-working, competent in what she undertook and well tried during the Revolution. Although she had decided to join the newly established Diletti, and even formally rescinded her vows as a Clarissan, she retained her love and devotion to all the monastic practices of her earlier religious life. This must have been strengthened when the community of the Diletti collapsed through its implication in the Paccanari affair, leaving a vacuum in the community at Amiens regarding rules and constitutions. In leading the community and indeed the school at Amiens, she insisted on monastic observance of rules and all infringements were punished. Her spirituality expressed itself in strange practices. For example, during the school retreat she decorated a room with skulls, darkened the windows and then read stories of demonic possession to the girls. Perhaps even more bizarre were her mood swings. She would break into uncontrollable laughter, in which everyone was expected to share, until she suddenly reverted to the role of stern leader, 'whose eyebrows made all tremble'. Her very unpredictability gave her enormous power.[72]

Saint-Estève was much younger than Anne Baudemont and came from a very different background. Jean-Baptiste-Louis Sambucy-St-Estève was born in Millau en Rouergue in 1771 and went to Paris to train for the priesthood. He studied at first in the Collège de Juilly and later in 1787 at St Sulpice. The seminary was closed during the Revolution and Saint-Estève went to Versailles and tutored the three sons of the comte de Quelen, one of whom (Hyacinthe de Quelen) later became the archbishop of Paris. He taught the boys humanities, philosophy, rhetoric and scripture, a basic foundation for their future education. Saint-Estève was ordained in 1795 and remained in Versailles until he joined the Fathers of the Faith in Amiens in 1801. In his capacity as chaplain to the school he exercised great influence there, with the full approval of Baudemont and without opposition from the reticent head of studies, Catherine de Charbonnel.

He was inspired by Fénelon, by the royal school of St Cyr and by the convent of the infant Jésus, its Parisian counterpart. He introduced the music of St Cyr to Amiens and designed elaborate celebrations for the public oral examinations and distribution of prizes.[73] Though Joseph Varin was critical of the extravagant exhibitions at the school and said so to Sophie in 1805, he continued to give Saint-Estève his full support and approval.[74] Anne Baudemont and Saint-Estève worked well together. It was a powerful combination and the pressure in the house to go along with them was almost irresistible. Those who did not accept were eased out of the picture, and Joseph Varin facilitated their exodus. When the community at Amiens broke with the Diletti, Saint-Estève was well placed to work on new constitutions for the community and Joseph Varin approved and allowed him all the scope he wanted in this regard.

Sophie returned to Amiens on the morning after her birthday, 13 December 1805. It was quite clear that the community had changed in her absence and that no one was quite sure how to deal with her arrival in the house. Those who knew her best were in Grenoble. Perhaps in a move to isolate her, Baudemont placed Sophie in a room at the far end of the house, access to which was across a court-yard opposite Baudemont's window. Thus all Sophie's movements and her visi-tors could be observed easily, an uncomfortable position to be in while waiting until 18 January for the election of the superior general. Joseph Varin and Pierre Roger came at Christmas and preparations began for election and for a review of the progress of the little congregation.[75]

They had two decisions to make, one concerning the superior general and the other concerning the name of the group. With regard to the name, there was a definite return to the original impulse of de Tournély. The title of the congre-gation would be Daughters of the Sacred Heart of Jesus and the Jesuit rule would be the source of the future constitutions of the community. They then proceeded to the election of the superior general in the presence of Joseph Varin, Roger and Saint-Estève. The two candidates were Anne Baudemont and Sophie Barat. The community at Grenoble sent written votes: Catherine Deshayes, Philippine Duchesne, Henriette Grosier and Catherine Maillard; the members from Amiens who had a vote were Catherine de Charbonnel, Félicité Desmarquest, Henriette Ducis, Adèle Bardot, Anne Baudemont and Sophie Barat. Sophie was elected leader for life by a majority of just one vote, evidence of a deep split between Amiens and Grenoble. It was clear that there was no place for Sophie in Amiens, that the election was a disappointment in the house and that she lacked the support of the community there. Even Joseph Varin tended to communicate directly with Baudemont and send messages to Sophie via Baudemont or indeed via the priests in Amiens. Clearly he still thought she did not possess the capacity to lead and that her election was an error. After some awkward weeks in Amiens, Sophie decided to return to Grenoble.[76]

On the way there she stopped to see her parents in Joigny, remaining at home for several weeks, a time of respite for her and joy in the family. By then Marie-Louise's next child, Zoé had been born in 1805 and Sophie found herself able

to relax with her nieces and nephews after the tensions in Amiens. Indeed Louis
Barat, then teaching in the seminary, L'Argentière, a foundation of the Fathers
of the Faith at Lyon, was concerned about Sophie's health and asked Joseph
Varin to let her stay at home until she was really rested. Varin objected since he
was unwell and due to take the waters at Vichy. He needed to see Sophie urgently on several items of business. In view of this, he asked her to be in Lyon by
early May, cutting short her holiday. In Lyon they discussed the constitutions of
the congregation which Saint-Estève and Baudemont were working on and the
possibility of a new foundation. Two of the Fathers of the Faith, Louis Enfantin
and Louis Lambert, had met several women in Bordeaux who were anxious to
live in a religious community. Joseph Varin hoped that they could travel together to Bordeaux sometime later on in the summer and see if the group was interested in joining their communities.[77] Their business arranged, Sophie continued
her journey back to Grenoble and Joseph Varin left for Vichy.

— 3 —

JOURNEY INTO NEW PLACES, 1806-1811

W hen Sophie returned to Grenoble she was still in poor health and needed care. The doctor in Amiens had given her a strict diet 'for my Purgatory' as she wryly remarked to Philippine Duchesne. She continued to find it difficult to accept this and asked Philippine not to draw attention to her personal, physical needs.[1] She was warmly welcomed back to Grenoble especially by Philippine and Geneviève Deshayes, and she was at home in a house where she was both wanted and respected. But she had barely settled back when she received a letter from Joseph Varin urging her to travel immediately to Poitiers. There two women lived in the former monastery of Les Feuillants and had the nucleus of a school. It was too difficult a project to realise on their own and they were on the point of handing both school and monastery over to the diocese of Poitiers. Joseph Varin thought they would change their minds if Sophie could speak to them, especially if she could suggest the possibility that some of the group in Bordeaux would go to Poitiers and form the basis of a new community. He also informed Sophie of a projected foundation in Ghent (which formed part of northern France at this period). Although she was superior general, there was no question of consulting her about this and the negotiation was entirely in the hands of Saint-Estève. Thus while the community in Amiens, under the leadership of Saint-Estève, was establishing a new house in Ghent, Joseph Varin proposed that Sophie initiate a foundation in Poitiers.

Sophie set out immediately and the journey proved to be one of the most important in her life. She took Henriette Girard[2] with her, a member of the community in Grenoble since 1805, a woman much older than Sophie and capable of looking after her en route. They set out on 10 July and went first to Lyon and then by Moulins, Limoges, and Bellac to Poitiers. Details of the journey are graphic and recorded in several documents, clearly the source of many conversations over the years.[3] In the first place Sophie remembered that on that journey she was cured of the illness which had dogged her since 1803. Writing to Philippine Duchesne in August 1806, when she had reached Poitiers, Sophie told her what had happened in the course of the journey. She admitted that at the beginning she felt very ill, indeed quite miserable and wondered whether she could survive the journey at all. But strangely, once she had left Lyon and was on the way to Moulins she grasped that something was happening to her body. Despite the July heat, the actual travel itself and the stops on the way, Sophie realised that in the course of one night her illness had reached a crisis point and had then disappeared. She felt genuinely well:

> You know what state I was in when I left you. When I arrived in Lyon the heat of the journey had increased my illness and I was worse than last year. Far away from my dear Samaritan I thought that no one else could heal me for I felt she was as necessary for the care of my body as she thought I was for her soul. I made this complaint quietly to Our Lord and I told him how disagreeable this would be for me on the journey, close to people who could recognise my ailment. Alone and without wanting to confide in anyone I remained peaceful after this complaint . . . I had not left Lyon when all had disappeared and yet I had done nothing to heal the illness. On the contrary, on the way it had been extremely hot then, I had had very little sleep, as well as bad food and dirty inns. At the time I am talking about everything added to my ailment and yet all disappeared in a night. I am completely healed.[4]

However it happened, Sophie was completely relieved of the illness which had dogged her from the winter of 1803. This gave her a real sense of liberation and she began to enjoy the journey to Poitiers, despite all its hazards and uncertainties. The quality of lodging was varied and sometimes less than basic; they had to deal with curious travelling companions and the task of finding carriage drivers for each part of the route. For example, at Limoges, a carriage driver, Cadence, offered to take the travellers to Poitiers for a very reasonable price. Sophie took him at his word and found that the carriage was really an open cart, full of merchandise and drawn by cattle. Henriette Girard was angry at this arrangement but Sophie held to it and they mounted the cart outside the town, to avoid being watched by the people. They covered very little ground that day and by ten o'clock in the evening it was time to stop at an inn for the night:

> This room corresponded well enough with that which Gresset depicts in his Chartreuse. The university of rats came there for their meetings in the middle of the night, and since we stayed in an isolated house we would have been really frightened had we not placed all our trust in God.[5]

The next day they got up early and set out again and while Cadence had promised that they would get to the next village, Bellac, in time for Sunday Mass it soon became clear that they would not reach the church in time. However, by chance they came upon a little village where Mass was about to begin. There:

> The high Mass was sung in such a ludicrous pitch that in any other circumstances it would have led to laughter . . . the parish priest announced the feast of St Madeleine and . . . to entice [the congregation] to come and hear Mass that day, he promised them a high Mass for the dead![6]

The travellers progressed slowly towards Poitiers and as they approached the outskirts of the town, on 23 July, it began to rain heavily. They had little protection and so were soon soaked. Sophie had decided that they would leave the cart before entering the town but the weather forced her to change her plans. She remembered ruefully the stir they caused as they entered Poitiers, wet, dishevelled and travelling in a cart drawn by cattle. They had tried to hide themselves by creating a type of curtain around them, but people looking out from the first floor of their houses could see in. Besides the cart made a terrible noise in the street and people stared at this strange sight on a damp July evening. Cadence dropped them far from their destination and Sophie asked a man passing by to take them to the monastery of Les Feuillants. He agreed to help them but soon handed them over to his wife while Sophie and Henriette took shelter in a doorway as he explained where the two travellers wished to go. This woman brought Sophie and Henriette to their destination. They arrived bedraggled and travel-weary at the monastery of Les Feuillants:

> So here I was with someone to introduce me, and dressed in such a way that left nothing to vanity, I arrived humbly at Les Feuillants, the home of Mlle Chobelet.[7]

The monastery originally belonged to the congregation of Notre Dame, a branch of the Cistercian order. The community had dwindled to five prior to the Revolution and, with all the other monastic communities in France, was dissolved in 1790. In 1802 two women, Lydie Chobelet and Josephine Bigeu, still lived in the vast building and had tried in vain to establish a school for girls in the former monastery. Like Philippine Duchesne in Grenoble, and Geneviève Deshayes and Henriette Grosier in Amiens, the women had been active during the height of the Revolution, doing whatever they could to help stabilise society, especially trying to provide education for young women. Lydie Chobelet was born in 1765 in Soullans, in the Vendée. During the Revolution she and her two sisters were forced to flee for safety as the Vendée was a centre of resistance to the Revolution. They moved to Poitiers where they lived together with several other women and opened a school for children. They also housed a priest and for this they were imprisoned for a time. When they were released Lydie Chobelet decided to establish a religious community in Poitiers and asked her friends to consider this proposal. Her younger sister, Pulcherie, decided to go to Tours and found a school of her own there. Shortly after that their eldest sister died. All the other members of the group joined religious communities in the town and only Josephine Bigeu remained. She was born in Poitiers in 1779 and had joined the Chobelet sisters in 1798. While her parents were not wealthy, they ensured that she had some formal education. This gave her confidence to stay with Lydie Chobelet and try to keep the school in operation. However, after a time both had come to the conclusion that they could no longer carry on.

They had decided to cede the building to the diocese and at this point Lambert intervened and asked them to wait until Sophie Barat came to Poitiers. Thus, the arrival of Sophie in their midst on the 23 July was their last hope.[8]

After a meal and some introductions, Lambert arrived and all four had a long discussion. Sophie explained the goals of the Association she represented and how the communities lived and worked. Lambert went to see the clergy[9] and showed them the rule of the Association.[10] Both the women and the clergy seemed satisfied with what they heard and were ready to accept that the monastery and school become part of the Association des Dames de l'Instruction Chrétienne. However, Sophie had some difficulty explaining her role in the Association, the anomaly of being a superior general who travelled around without a fixed abode. This puzzled the priests and they asked her which of the houses was the centre of the Association. Sophie realised that they wanted Poitiers to be the centre and so she made no mention of Amiens. Indeed a similar, potential difficulty had arisen in Grenoble, and when she was leaving there in early July Joseph Varin had advised her to tell the bishop of Grenoble that her absence in Poitiers would be very brief. Now in Poitiers Sophie settled the affair for the moment when she told the priests that she would try to live for as much of her time as possible in Poitiers, especially since it was going to be the noviciate of the Association.

However, it was more than just a question of where the centre of the Association was to be located. The clergy also wanted her to indicate clearly that she was under the authority of a bishop – in the nineteenth century it was inconceivable that a woman could be free from control of either husband, brother or guardian, in other words free from the supervision of a male figure. In view of this, Sophie's mobility raised questions. A young woman travelling around France at this period was unusual especially during the upheavals of the Napoleonic era. At this time however the expansion of the Association to Grenoble and Poitiers provided Sophie with a freedom and mobility unusual for women in her time. Sophie allowed that freedom to both form and shape her, especially in the period after 1806 when Joseph Varin was no longer so present and when Louis Barat's influence was lessening. In a short time Sophie convinced Lydie Chobelet and Josephine Bigeu, and the local clergy, that the Association could further the work of education in Poitiers.

The possibility of women from Bordeaux coming to help build up the school was a key factor in their decision and Sophie decided to go there immediately. All she knew at this stage was that there were women in Bordeaux who had declared an interest in religious life, but had not succeeded in finding a community to accept them. There were six in particular, led by Thérèse Maillucheau, who, greatly fired by a retreat given in Bordeaux by Enfantin and Lambert, had decided that if they could not find a community to receive them they would form one themselves. They met and decided to act:

Let us make use of the fact of the mission taking place, let us be generous and leave our families without telling them. Everyone agreed with this plan. One of the young women, called Angélique, whose parents were dead, owned a vineyard in the area where there was a kind of small hut. That was the place they chose as the place of retreat.[11]

After the evening instruction, given by one of the missioners, the young women waited until their families had left the church and then they made their way to the vineyard. Despite the pleas of their parents the little group refused to return home and stayed in the vineyard for three months, creating their own form of community life. During this period they were a source of curiosity for the local people, mocked by many on the way to and from church and mourned by their families and friends. This was more than a passing phase and both Enfantin and Lambert realised they had to take some responsibility for this situation, if only to ease the criticism and concern expressed by the families. They contacted Joseph Varin to ask him to send Sophie Barat immediately to Bordeaux in the hope that the group could be accepted into the Association. In the meantime Enfantin arranged better accommodation for them in Bordeaux within a convent run by Madame Vincent, and he gave them a rule of life to follow until Sophie could come herself and take the situation in hand.[12]

Sophie Barat arrived in Bordeaux on 12 August 1806 with the intention of meeting those women and seeing if they were ready to set out with her and begin religious life in Poitiers. However, Enfantin had presumed that Sophie would establish the Association in Bordeaux and indeed had promised the parents of the young women that this would happen. Knowing the commitment of the Association to Poitiers, both Sophie and Lambert thought this was not feasible. Moreover, the wing in the convent where the six women lived was owned by Madame Vincent, who herself was in the process of negotiating a fusion of her community with that of Julie Billiart in Amiens. In the light of the needs of Poitiers and the proposed fusion with Julie Billiart, it was inappropriate for Sophie to initiate anything at this time in Bordeaux. However, she promised that one day she would return and establish a community in the city. Her task during this visit was to choose which of the women she thought could join the Association in Poitiers.

News of Sophie's arrival spread quickly and over a period of several days Sophie met and examined, not just the six women living in the convent, but many others who were searching for some form of religious commitment. She interviewed at least thirty women and chose eight whom she thought capable of life in the Association. What criteria she used in her choice is not known, though she did say that she could not take certain women on account of the opposition of their families. Once the parents of those she had chosen had agreed to allow their daughters to leave Bordeaux, Sophie thought it best that they travel in three groups, to avoid drawing attention to such an exodus. Sophie sent two groups ahead of her and decided that she and Thérèse Maillucheau would travel together and visit the Maillucheau family at Saint-André de Cubzac, not far from Bordeaux. The family had opposed Sophie for a time and she needed to assure them, for not only Thérèse, who was the leader of the original group of six, but also four other women from the village had asked to join the Association. When she had spoken to the families about the Association they were more confident in trusting her though Thérèse's father could not reconcile himself to his daughter's decision.[13]

Sophie set out for Poitiers and while there were no hitches on the way:

> Nevertheless, I had a little accident. I got out of bed during the night and walked on a stone and turned my ankle badly. The nerves were torn . . . my foot grew swollen and by the time I arrived in Poitiers I could not walk. I would not have known how to get back to our house, which is very far from the carriage office where the coaches stop, except that Mme de la Charpagne, our good friend, who lives nearby, had been on the lookout for me for several days to collect me on her way, as she had done for those of my companions who had preceded me.[14]

Although she had only arrived in Poitiers in late July, Sophie had already made a good friend in Madame de la Charpagne who lived near the set-down place for travellers. She made a meal for the travellers and then bound Sophie's foot so that she could walk back to Les Feuillants, as there was no transport available to take her there.

Sophie had been away the best part of a month and through her negotiations in Bordeaux had brought hope and new life to the situation in Poitiers. For with the arrival of the eight women from Bordeaux the future of the school and community of Les Feuillants was assured. Now the household consisted of Sophie Barat, Henriette Giraud and ten novices. There were nine boarders in the school, Marie the cook, Madeleine the shepherdess, and a gardener. It was time to begin both the initiation of these women into the Association and the development of the boarding school started by Lydie Chobelet and Josephine Bigeu.[15] There was a great sense of setting out on a new journey. Sophie asked the women to live the experience with generosity, courage and joy. They had all invested their idealism in the project, had come on long journeys and this was not the time to falter. The programme of formation was Sophie's own responsibility, though she had some help from the local clergy and from the Fathers of the Faith giving missions occasionally in the area. On 9 September 1806, the morning after the opening of the noviciate, Sophie called the group together and outlined the daily programme which all would be expected to follow. The day was a blend of prayer, manual work, study and recreation. Sophie gave a conference twice a week, on Wednesdays and Sundays, on various aspects of religious life and on the feast days of the liturgical year. She insisted on spiritual reading and explained its value in deepening reflective powers; for the same reason she insisted on two reflections a day, one at midday and one in the evening. She continually encouraged such reflection, to help each one build up inner spiritual resources and the capacity for insight into their own lives. Even though Sophie herself was either the same age as these women, or in some cases younger, she had a great deal of personal experience to draw upon when guiding them. This stemmed from her formation and experience at home in Joigny, then in Paris, Amiens and Grenoble.

She consulted Lydie Chobelet and Josephine Bigeu with regard to the running of the house and the sharing out of responsibilities among the members. There was a great deal of cleaning, repairs and furnishing to be done in the old monastery. As in Grenoble in 1804, so in Poitiers the people were curious to know what exactly these women were doing in such a big building and soon they began to criticise them for reaching beyond their station in life, by studying and preparing for a teaching profession. In fact as Sophie herself noted they were cooking, sewing, cleaning, learning the basics of grammar and of Latin, nothing more, and yet the townspeople were suspicious of them and indeed of her. Old moulds were being broken and such innovation evoked resentment. Certainly a group of independent women, living alone, and intent on a common project, was an innovation as well as a source of curiosity.[16]

This was also a time for Sophie to explore her own ideas regarding religious life and carve out her style of leadership. Throughout her life Sophie stressed the importance of personal relationships in dealing with people, and here at the beginning this quality underlined her way of treating the members of the community. While she detailed structures for those being trained, she also gradually learnt to read individuals and their particular needs. Over a period of time this blend of structure and a capacity to recognise individual needs became characteristic of her government. At this stage in her life, however, it was experimental and tentative and Sophie had to find her way as she went along. During these two years neither Joseph Varin nor Louis Barat visited Poitiers and this gave her space and scope to work out her ideas on her own. On the other hand she was in regular correspondence with Joseph Varin (though these letters no longer exist) and in this way she took part in the ongoing project of writing the constitutions of the Association. However, it became progressively clearer to Sophie that the task of writing the constitutions had been taken over by Saint-Estève and the circle around him in Amiens. Even Joseph Varin took little if any part in it, other than to report progress to Sophie in Poitiers and even that became rare when he moved to Besançon.

At her own initiative and according to circumstances as they arose, Sophie continued to accept new members into the noviciate and to consider the possibility of new foundations. Her major concern, however, was the noviciate and she had to come to terms with several issues which threatened to have serious repercussions. Her inexperience in dealing with young enthusiastic women made her unaware of the stresses and strains that they were carrying. Some of these arose from their own life-stories, some from their temperaments, and some from their imagination of how religious life should be lived. Sophie too had her own ideal of religious life. In her leadership role she felt bound to epitomise the perfect religious woman – she stressed the monastic practice of public penance and long periods of prayer in the chapel, hard work and a certain cult of fasting and of cutting down on food. The issue of fasting was central to Sophie and she held to the model initiated by her brother in Paris. It reached an unhealthy level when during a retreat most of the food presented by the cook was returned to the kitchen uneaten. Thérèse Maillucheau remembered years later that Sophie's example of eating little food took away their appetites.[17] Sophie led the group in trying to model what she was asking them to do and to be. It was far too much, and only when the health of some in the group actually collapsed did Sophie begin to reflect on what she was doing and she realised that health had to be safeguarded if the prayer and work were to be sustained. But at this time she herself had not found a balance and there was an unhealthy exaggeration in her behaviour and in the example she gave to others. She admitted later that she had made some mistakes, and prepared those in formation more as Carmelites than as prayerful women involved in the work of education.[18]

Most of her life Sophie found it difficult to accept her ill health and yet she talked about it and struggled with it intensely, always expecting more of herself than she was able to give. By the same token she was unable to accept laziness, either in herself or in others. She assumed that she would work hard in life and expected others to do the same. It is clear that while she presented herself as the model for the life she was preparing these women to lead, she herself was unable to live it. In effect she was unable to fast, to spend long hours especially at night in the chapel or to work without respite. But she tried to do so and regularly her health failed and she was forced to take rest. When any in the community became ill or were genuinely in need of her then all her tenderness poured out in care for them, but it took her some years to grasp that prevention was better than destroyed health.

In her manner of governing, Sophie was both distant and close, at different times and for different reasons. She had a short fuse and punished faults in all sorts of ways, either by imposing extra penances or demanding difficult work or a type of work individuals felt incapable of doing. Sometimes she ignored those at fault, for days at a time, or refused to speak to them when they approached her. Even at times of recreation she could appear at one time severe and distant and at another time lively and warm. She was as needy and mysterious as any of the others and yet she was their leader. In a sense she was a different person with different people; added to that was the complexity of her own moods and temperament, not to say the state of her health and her effort to present herself as a model for the community. She was finding her way as a leader and this was an added stress. She had a need for quiet and order and withdrew from the group every two weeks saying she was going into retreat on her own. It is more likely that she was taking time to rest and recover from the strain and stress of the life she was leading. Indeed this tendency to either become ill or go into retreat became a coping mechanism for Sophie Barat throughout her life. She probably did not recognise it and may have unconsciously used ill health to attain the solitude she so desperately needed. Certainly she insisted on silence in the house except at times of recreation and would correct the least infringement of it. It was necessary to instil an atmosphere of quietness in the community so that individuals could think about their future and find a rhythm to their own life of prayer and reflection. There was a practical point to this also. Sophie suggested that silence in the corridors be strictly observed, even during the day, so that those who needed to rest, those who were ill or tired could rest in peace. She also asked that when they met to relax each should learn to listen to one another and not interrupt incessantly, appealing to basic courtesy in this regard.

Yet, however much Sophie insisted on the order of day, on hard work, fasting, prayer and spiritual reading, she instinctively treated each member of the community differently. Her own moods and difficulties gave her insight into the needs of others, so that she did not hold to the outer form of life if the inner struggle needed something different. This approach became the hallmark of her government and it ensured a basic flexibility even years later, when the expansion of the communities demanded some structural uniformity. Later on in life she spoke about this period of her life in Poitiers, with its beginnings and its intensities and reminisced with affection about the different characters in the community. She told three stories from this period and they give as much insight into Sophie herself as into the people in question.

These stories are recounted in some detail.[19] The first concerns the arrival of a new member, Madeleine du Chasteigner, a native of Poitiers, who had asked to enter the new community before Sophie went to Bordeaux. She had been active during the Revolution, visiting the sick in the town, going to the prisons, teaching catechism to the children. She had already tried living in a religious community in Poitiers and that had not worked out. While she wanted to live the new form of life in Les Feuillants she was shocked at the penitential practices in the community and the long periods of silence required during the day. The contrast with her former life was stark and it took her a long time, and many long conversations with Sophie, to settle into the inner rhythm of the community. She desperately wanted to be part of it but it cost her imaginative character dearly. She wrote out an imaginary conversation she had with the devil, and through this she worked out her difficulties; she shared the piece with Sophie who read it and then suggested that she burn it in front of her. Burning the paper was a way of moving on, letting go, but in later years Sophie regretted this action. The piece of writing was both graphic and amusing and well worth recording. At the time, however, it represented a source of great suffering to du Chasteigner. What had she expected in Les Feuillants? Did Sophie ever question the shock this woman received? The contrast between life at home and life in the monastery was very real. Perhaps that was part of its attraction and the source of its challenge.

The second story showed how Sophie dealt with Thérèse Maillucheau, a different person with different needs. Thérèse Maillucheau had a strong attraction for prayer and the contemplative life and showed great determination in achieving a break with her family in order to pursue her desire. She wanted to withdraw from common life and spend long hours in prayer, something which Sophie only allowed her to do in the evening and at night time. During the day she gave

Thérèse basic jobs, such as feeding the cattle and house cleaning – in other words work that was real and constant and needed to be done daily. Again, Sophie had a life long affection for Thérèse Maillucheau and from this time both shared a great love of the mystics. She valued and admired the desire for prayer and mystical experience and yearned herself for time and space to pray. Yet she was concerned about the need to ground this desire in the reality of life, especially in hard, daily work that was vital to the life of the community.

The final story was about Henriette Girard. She had travelled with Sophie from Grenoble in July 1806, and was as much a novice as anyone else though longer in the Association. She was extremely scrupulous. She struggled with feelings of inadequacy and could not cope alone with her worries and anxieties. She began going to Sophie daily to unburden herself and normally this eased her mind for a time. On one occasion Sophie refused to see her, as she was too tired, too busy or too aware that a real dependency had developed in Henriette. Later on in the day, unable to cope with the uncertainty, Henriette left Sophie a written message asking for an appointment, to no avail. At the end of the day, having still not spoken to Sophie, Henriette had to take part in the evening relaxation of the community. She showed nothing of her inner turmoil and panic. Finally, just before going to bed, Sophie visited her in her room and they had a good talk on how to manage worries and scruples and yet not to expect an instant cure. She also explained how the tyranny of trying to be perfect drags down the human spirit and dissipates energy, and Sophie urged her to use her reflective powers to counterbalance her feelings. Such guidance must have eased the inner pain of Henriette and given her courage to face into herself. It was wise advice and one Sophie had to discover herself in the turmoil of Louis's treatment of her, especially in Paris from 1795 to 1797.

In these stories of three members of the community, facets of Sophie's own life were being played out in front of her and in dealing with them she was looking at her own life. She was also giving them the benefit of her own experience. For example, du Chasteigner, like Sophie, had lived through the horrors of the Revolution and was now trying to adapt to a very different life. She was a vital, enthusiastic and imaginative woman, full of fire and spirit. Now she was embracing a way of life that seemed to dampen that spirit. She wondered if she could actually take on the challenge and what it would mean for her, indeed what it would do to her. Thérèse Maillucheau was attracted to a contemplative life and had thought of religious life in these terms. She was courageous and determined and had taken steps in Bordeaux to try and realise her dream. Her time in Poitiers forced her in another direction and only her trust in the Providence which led her to Sophie allowed her to stay with and commit herself to the new community. All her life she struggled to keep her feet on the ground, while maintaining her attraction for the contemplative form of life she desired. Henriette Girard was a deeply emotional and loving woman and tried to reach the very demanding standards which Sophie set. She struggled with scruples and the desperate need to talk about them with someone who understood. Thus she was dependent on Sophie for support and approval and to be acknowledged in public. Once she had assured herself that she was on good terms with Sophie she could function and do what was required. Throughout her life Sophie was caught between dependency and the desire to be free and autonomous. For many years she looked to others for support and approval, and grieved when it was missing or withheld. Only as a much older woman, in her late fifties, was she to face her life, her work and her leadership on her own, alone.

Bonding within the community was deepened when, drawing upon her experience in Amiens, Sophie suggested that each member of the community tell her life story during evening recreation. This must have been exciting since so many had dramatic experiences during the Revolution. Sophie devised a way of assuring that each story could be heard without interruption. She stuck a pin in a candle at the beginning of recreation and so each one knew how long she had that day to tell her story.[20] Through such sharing, bonds of friendship were developed and all were drawn to Sophie in particular as the leader and teacher of the group. Inevitably, emotional dependencies were formed. This too came to be a mark of Sophie's leadership for she used her capacity to draw people to great effect throughout her life. Sometimes the actual dependency concerned her and she tried to deal with it, either talking to the group about being too attached to her or trying to distance herself from the needs of individuals. She had encouraged the community members to go to her in need and did not mind if it was once or even twice a day. However, such a rhythm could not be sustained and she tried to put limits on such access. Each time she went away she spent a great deal of time preparing the group for her absence and this may have increased the dependencies. In addition to her stress on structure and on personal relationships within the community, Sophie was also learning of the power and influence of her own personality.[21]

By the late spring of 1807, the monastery buildings had been made ready for a school, but the boarding school pupils did not increase in numbers that year. Nevertheless the community held a prize-giving in September 1807. This formal ceremony was organised by Marie d'Olivier who had come from Amiens to Poitiers in April 1807 because of ill health. She modelled the prize-giving on how Saint-Estève and Baudemont had produced it the previous year in Amiens.[22] However, it did not have the desired effect of drawing new pupils and it was necessary to try and find more boarders and extend the type of education the community was prepared to offer. New possibilities had opened up when Henriette Bernard had joined the community in November 1806.[23] She had been running a poor school some miles away in Niort and had sixty pupils whom she did not wish to abandon. Thus before entering the community at Poitiers, Bernard arranged that her school would be taken over by a local religious in Niort and she hoped that in due time the new community in Poitiers might take responsibility for her poor school. Certainly in the course of 1807 Sophie investigated the possibility of a foundation in Niort, and though she could not respond immediately she promised that she would consider seriously a community there at a later date. But it gave her the idea to open a poor school in Poitiers. She knew from her own experience in Amiens that a poor school was a sure way of drawing pupils generally. Thus Sophie decided to buy a small house adjoining the monastery and to open a poor school before the end of 1807.[24] She wrote to the local priests and asked them to send the poor children of the parish to the new school where they would be taught the catechism as well as reading, counting and manual skills. This was an immediate success and by June 1808 the school was working so well that Sophie was able to consider the other poor school in Niort. She visited the town, not just about the poor school founded by Henriette Bernard but also to see about a property for a boarding school.

In October 1807 an unusual woman asked if she could enter the new community in Poitiers. Suzanne Geoffroy was a native of Poitiers and had tried on several occasions to initiate some form of religious life. As was the practice in the community each told her life story during recreation and Suzanne Geoffroy's probably took several evenings to recount.[25] When Sophie heard the story of her life she was both moved and heartened, though perhaps not all of it was told in public. Suzanne Geoffroy was born on 6 December 1761, in the village of Tellié, in the diocese of Poitiers. She was the eldest of nine children and when she was six or seven an aunt and uncle, who had no children of their own, asked to be allowed to bring her up. She was a vivacious child and found it hard to concentrate at studies, despite the fact that she had a tutor at home. As a young woman she was attracted to the Carmelites in Poitiers and in 1787 asked to join the community there. However, the prioress felt that Suzanne was not called to live their life and advised her to speak to her Jesuit confessor in the town. Although the Jesuits were suppressed in France many of them served quietly in parishes. Suzanne spoke to Fr Drouard and he told her to wait for some time. When she pressed him to be more explicit he told her that she was destined to enter an order which would be founded in Germany and later brought into France by a little girl who in 1787 was still playing with her dolls. He explained that he received this prophecy from another Jesuit, Fr Nectoux, who was his teacher in Poitiers before the suppression of the Jesuits. Fr Nectoux had foretold the horrors of the French Revolution, the growth of the counter-revolution movement and the triumph of religion (by the return of the Bourbons), all in highly apocalyptic terms. He described the future Association of women in some detail, saying it would be devoted to the Sacred Heart, modelled on the Jesuits, and characterised by gentleness and humility. However, Suzanne Geoffroy did not meet Sophie Barat until 1807 when she asked to join the newly formed Association, then called the Dames de l'Instruction Chrétienne. Her arrival and the stories she told affected Sophie deeply.

When Sophie met Joseph Varin for the first time she knew nothing of course about these predictions of the Society of the Sacred Heart and of her role in it. In 1800 she understood that she was entering an order already established in Italy, the Diletti di Gesù. At this period there was no question of Sophie initiating a group of women for a particular work; rather she became part of a project already begun several years earlier, originally inspired by Léonor de Tournély. Now from Suzanne Geoffroy she heard another story, another myth, in which she herself was a central figure. She was described in the prophecy of Fr Nectoux as the founder of the Association in France. Sophie never commented on what this meant to her and indeed in her Journal of Poitiers she omitted the actual phrase: 'she who is destined to be the founder of this congregation in France is still playing with her dolls'.[26] It was obviously too direct and personal to record such a direct reference to herself but she saw the connection between the stories of de Tournély and Nectoux. Indeed some years later Suzanne Geoffroy was asked to speak about the prophecies of Fr Nectoux at the general council of 1820. This was at the time when the Association had emerged from a prolonged crisis over its origins, purpose and leadership, and needed to record its founding myth and history.[27] In 1807 it was encouraging for Sophie to hear Suzanne Geoffroy's story. An imaginative picture of her role and destiny was a source of energy and courage for Sophie as she found her way forward in Poitiers. It was also a help to her as she looked back over the events in her life since she left Joigny in 1800. She had joined the new association of the Diletti di Gesù; she had taken part in the foundation of the community and school in Amiens, and was appointed the leader there in December 1802. This was a difficult role for her: there were many strains in the community and school, and she herself was in poor health. In June 1804 the personal scandal surrounding Paccanari forced the Fathers of the Faith to sever all contacts with Italy, and Joseph Varin took it on himself to break all links with the Diletti di Gesù. This left Sophie as the leader of a community which suddenly found itself on its own. In the autumn of 1804, again at the initiative of Joseph Varin, Sophie had travelled to Grenoble to meet Philippine Duchesne and plan the union of the little community in Grenoble with that of Amiens. From then on Sophie's role as superior general was ambiguous and she complained that events were being negotiated over her head. By her own admission Sophie found this mode of procedure difficult to accept, despite the opinions of both Louis Barat and Joseph Varin.[28]

Indeed in Amiens the community had come more and more under the influence of the confessor, Saint-Estève. He exercised complete control over Anne Baudemont, whom Joseph Varin had appointed superior when Sophie went to Grenoble in 1804. It was clear even by 1806, when Sophie returned to Amiens for the election of the superior general, that the community and school in Amiens had begun to establish its own identity. This was a necessary development since the break with the Diletti forced the community to build their future from within their own resources and not in reference to Paccanari and the Diletti di Gesù in Rome. Moreover with the virtual absence of Joseph Varin from Amiens and the gradual marginalising of the Fathers of the Faith by the French government at this time, the community at Amiens came more and more under the influence of Saint-Estève. This was even more pronounced when he decided to leave the Fathers of the Faith at this time in order to avoid harassment from the government.

In 1805 school examinations at Amiens were held in public followed by distribution of prizes and both events were celebrated with pomp and ceremony. This was to gain approval from the town authorities and to attract new pupils to the school. However Joseph Varin thought the event too extravagant and ostentatious.[29] In a report of the Département de la Somme for 1806 the school at Amiens was listed as belonging to the 'School of the Ladies of the Institution of Amiens', run by Anne Baudemont. In 1807, due in great part to the efforts of Saint-Estève, the houses of the Dames de l'Instruction Chrétienne were approved by Napoleon. The petition to be presented to Napoleon was drawn up by Saint-Estève in December 1806. This petition, which was submitted to the minister of religion (Portalis), by the bishop of Metz, André Jauffret, stated that the community was composed of some former religious of several orders and some lay women who were in process of forming a new association. In the petition the Dames de l'Instruction Chrétienne stated that they were no longer connected with the Fathers of the Faith (suspected by Napoleon and soon to be suppressed). They indicated a plan to adopt either the rule of the Ursulines or that of the Association of Notre Dame, both acceptable to the government of France. They claimed that they fulfilled a useful service to the state in the field of education, not only in Amiens but also in Grenoble, Belley, Poitiers and Ghent. On these grounds the community asked for formal approval from the emperor.[30] In March 1807 Napoleon signed a decree which gave provisional recognition of the community and its work in Amiens, in France and in the future, in the colonies. This was a necessary step on the road towards formal, full recognition by the state. However, the Secretary of State's minutes, taken at the Imperial camp at Osterode, made no mention of any community other than Amiens, though Article V provided for expansion of the Association precisely through the provisional recognition of Napoleon.

Nowhere in the documentation presented to Napoleon was Sophie Barat mentioned as superior general of the Association. Indeed, while the office of superior general was noted in the articles presented it was not stated who held that office nor that it was for life. While this was the understanding at Sophie's election in Amiens in January 1806, it went unacknowledged in the subsequent documentation. This may have been a prudent decision on the part of Saint-Estève since the role of superior general for life could have raised Napoleon's suspicions. Such roles implied a number of communities united under one head and it had echoes of the Jesuit form of government. In any event, the actual process of seeking authorisation from Napoleon was carried on apart from Sophie though she certainly knew that it was being discussed and prepared by Saint-Estève. Nevertheless, she noted in her journal that it was Joseph Varin who informed her at the beginning of Lent in 1807 that the petition had actually been presented. Since no letters between Joseph Varin and Sophie have survived for the period 1806 to 1814 it is hard to know how much both knew of what was happening in Amiens. At this time Saint-Estève enjoyed the total confidence of Joseph Varin, who in any event was pleased to have no part in the presentation of the petition to Napoleon. He was already suspect in the eyes of the government.

For her part, Sophie had reservations about the procedure and thought it premature.[31] She thought it best that the Association retain a low profile and wait until much later in its development before requesting approval. She was quite satisfied to use the rule being worked upon since 1806 and saw it as provisional in the sense that she thought that over a long period of time the text would be refined and defined.[32] Though she may not have seen the actual decree of provisional approval from Napoleon in March 1807, Sophie sensed that her place in the documentation had been sidelined. No wonder she doubted the wisdom of the process initiated by Saint-Estève and the community in Amiens. Clearly the community there saw no place for her, except as a local superior in one of the foundations, either Grenoble or Poitiers. Nevertheless, however real Sophie's reservations were, some form of legal recognition was necessary if the Association was not to risk dissolution by the government. In the Decree of Messidor, 22 June 1804, Napoleon had declared that no religious associations of either men or women could be constituted without formal legal authorisation from the government. While Grenoble had struggled, with the help of Joseph Varin and Philippine Duchesne's family, to gain legal recognition for Ste Marie d'En Haut, some form of government recognition would be necessary to show to local authorities in the areas where the community wished to establish schools.

In this context it was politically astute to seek recognition. Indeed the image of a successful and expanding religious Association was further underlined when the community petitioned the Prefect of the Department of the Somme for permission to move to bigger premises in Amiens in 1807. The Amiens community presented itself as the birthplace of the Dames de l'Instruction Chrétienne, with several other foundations within France. They explained that their educational vision came from three sources: St Cyr, near Versailles, the Enfant Jésus in Paris and Lambesech in Provence. Fénelon's *Education of Young Girls* was taken as their basic source of inspiration. As well as members of the religious community teaching in the school, lay teachers were hired also to teach writing, drawing, music (the harp, piano and singing), deportment and dance. There was a poor school too, with 160 pupils, and classes there were free. Both schools were quite separate although the boarding school pupils were expected to clothe the poor students and in particular to provide First Communion dress. All such details show the context and background within which Saint-Estève, with the co-operation of community, worked. Without doubt, it was useful and necessary work.[33]

As stated in the petition to Napoleon, the community stressed again that their schools in Amiens were so valued that requests had come from Lyon, Grenoble and Poitiers and the community sent members to the three cities to found schools there. The community and the schools in Amiens were both expanding and a move was needed urgently to a bigger property. They needed the space, not just for the boarding school and poor school, but also for a noviciate to train young women and the possibility of offering hospitality to women who wanted to live in the community as paying guests. While several dioceses within France had offered them large buildings and sums of money, they preferred to stay in Amiens if they could get larger premises and they hoped the Prefect could meet their needs by allowing them to move to the larger premises of the seminary. Clearly this community was prosperous and planning its future carefully.[34] This had come about through the determination of Saint-Estève and Anne Baudemont as well as the active collaboration of the women who formed the community. Legally Sophie Barat was the superior general and despite the independence of the Amiens community, documents had to be sent to Sophie for signature. But she had no effective role in the development of Amiens. Sooner or later Sophie would have to confront the situation and she decided to take the matter in hand and visit Amiens in the summer of 1808.

The task that lay ahead of Sophie in Amiens was daunting and Joseph Varin had not helped to prepare her for this. On the one hand he encouraged her personally in a warm persuasive way and was particularly concerned about her state of health. He found her independent spirit difficult to accept, and was wary of her criticism. He tended to dismiss her reservations and hesitations regarding Saint-Estève and Baudemont, and urged a passive response, suggesting that she confine herself to her own immediate responsibilities. In 1805, when Sophie was in Grenoble, she expressed her concern regarding developments in Amiens. Joseph Varin was taken aback at what he read as criticism of his administration:

> You know me and you know how I dislike pretence and disguise, and so I ask you to have full confidence in all that I will say to you on different occasions about the state of your [religious] family. It is very important for your peace of mind and for your happiness that you really know the truth and bring your judgement to bear upon it. As for the rest, I know that with you I have no need for preambles to gain your credence.[35]

Joseph Varin undoubtedly respected Sophie but he did not perceive her capacity for leadership for quite some time, certainly not before 1814. He was easily influenced by outward displays of enthusiasm and competence and less impressed by another, more reticent style, such as Sophie's. From the beginning he had given Saint-Estève his full support and every freedom to do what he thought best in Amiens. Even after her election as superior general, and while she was still in Amiens, Joseph Varin wrote to Anne Baudemont rather than Sophie. This was a source of difficulty in a house where Sophie knew her presence was resented and her authority not accepted. When Sophie indicated the difficulty Joseph Varin appealed to flattery, indicating how little he understood her position in Amiens:

> Even though I did not write to you I did not leave you in the dark about what concerned me. Mr B[lanc] on the one hand, and Madame Baudemont on the other have given you news of my journey which was very good indeed. When I am

pressed for time with several people whom I ought to write to, you among them, I see where it is appropriate to begin. I leave you to the end, unquestionable proof of a firm friendship.[36]

Joseph Varin often excluded Sophie from consultation and told her only about decisions after they had been made. Sometimes he read letters addressed to Sophie and decided whether or not she should receive them. At the time of the crisis over Paccanari in Rome, Louise Naudet had written to Sophie but Joseph Varin had chosen to destroy the letter:

I forgot to tell you there was a letter for you from M[ada]me Louise. The community at Amiens sent it to me and I burnt it. It was largely about her two friends Marie-A[nne] and Julie, and most imprudent besides.[37]

Again when Joseph Varin, at the request of Saint-Estève and Baudemont, removed Geneviève Deshayes from the school in Amiens, Sophie was only informed of the decision in retrospect:

Do not have any worries over Mde Desh[ayes]'s change of work. I can assure you that this change has given me great satisfaction. I sense a real joy in it. She has been given other responsibilities more in keeping with her health and which give her more pleasure. She sent me a letter for you but it was so difficult to read that I burnt it, to spare your eyesight. Do not tell her that. I took a glance at it and it contained nothing very important.[38]

Despite several observations made by Sophie critical of Saint-Estève's actions in Amiens Joseph Varin upheld his colleague and told Sophie that she was too suspicious and independent minded. She had expressed concern about Saint-Estève's spiritual guidance of some of the community in Amiens, indeed even Anne Baudemont was concerned about this. But Joseph Varin defended Saint-Estève and invoked the rights of confessors:

You need to place a little more trust in the wisdom of those who know and guide the conscience. Whatever goes on in the depths and in secret between the soul and God, through the advice of an enlightened director, needs no other sanction, as long as the rights of others are not damaged.[39]

However to ease her concerns Joseph Varin agreed to talk to Saint-Estève. But in reality Joseph Varin had complete confidence in Saint-Estève and supported him fully. He invited Sophie to do the same. When the question of seeking approval from Napoleon arose, Joseph Varin suggested that they leave the negotiation to Saint-Estève:

Let us not distrust the wisdom of dear M. de S[ambuc]y, but leave this concern to loving Providence which seems to have chosen him as its instrument. I have already written to him in this sense about the matter.[40]

Sophie did not share Joseph Varin's enthusiastic praise of Saint-Estève and indeed thought he was unsuitable to formulate the petition for the Emperor. Joseph Varin brusquely cast her view aside:

Dear M. de S[ambuc]y writes to me by every post and is always pushing ahead for the important business which concerns you. You thought I was going to put a stop to his gallop. But, truly, no. I thought about it deeply in prayer before the good God and I felt within myself a great sense of trust in letting Providence act. So I have encouraged him [Sambucy].[41]

Repeatedly, Joseph Varin overrode Sophie. He urged her constantly to obey and conform to what he considered was best for the Association. He frequently accused Sophie of too much independence of spirit and urged her to submit her judgement to his:

Oh yes! strip yourself entirely of your own will and do not keep even a shred of it under pretext of devotion and a higher perfection. The highest perfection I want you to have is the complete suppression of your intense inner struggles, which I can see in you when your own will is crossed, either in the role you exercise, or on the question of penances . . . and in the end, accept everything with good grace and in liberty of spirit.[42]

The language of spirituality was weighty and prevented Sophie being able to insist on her point of view at this time. In time her intuitions would be justified but until 1814 Joseph Varin perceived little amiss in Amiens and found Sophie's views on Saint-Estève groundless. Moreover Saint-Estève had left the Fathers of the Faith when they were suppressed in 1807 and so Joseph Varin had even less contact than ever with him. In the light of this stance Sophie had a real task in convincing Joseph Varin that Saint-Estève was becoming progressively more powerful in the Association and assuming the role and task of founder. This was a painful discovery for Joseph Varin, and one that he recognised very slowly. By temperament Joseph Varin was impetuous and impulsive, and attracted to colourful personalities, either men or women. He was easily taken in by extravagant claims and gave them undue weight and value, as in the case of Paccanari. He consulted erratically, changed his mind a great deal and was quite unpredictable in his attitudes and actions. On the other hand, Sophie's qualities were much more low key and less effusive and were hidden behind her presumed inexperience. He did not value and respect what she had to offer and so her warnings escaped him, as he later ruefully accepted.

Apart from these serious blocks in communication, Joseph Varin's own position in France was precarious and he wished to become less involved and less associated with the women's communities. Napoleon was in process of ensuring that the Catholic church was subservient to the state and to the emperor. In this context the government suppressed the Fathers of the Faith in France in November 1807, as they were suspected of being underground Jesuits. The members of the Fathers of the Faith were ordered to return to their dioceses of origin. Joseph Varin went to Besançon and remained there until 1814 when the reign of Napoleon was drawing to a close.[43] He occasionally made visits to Paris but his contacts with Amiens and the growth of that community seems to have been almost completely severed during these years. No letters between Joseph Varin and Sophie Barat exist from June 1806 to October 1814. During this period when all former members of the Fathers of the Faith were resident in their diocese of origin, Sophie was left alone to deal with the developments within the little Association. She had three houses to care for: Poitiers, Grenoble and Niort. In her capacity as superior general, she was also responsible for Amiens, and by 1808 Amiens had founded communities in Ghent and Cuignières which were also, at least in theory, the responsibility of Sophie Barat.

The new foundation in Cuignières was a practical decision taken in view of the uncertainty regarding religious life in France at this time, especially after the suppression of the Fathers of the Faith in November 1807. In view of this, Baudemont bought a house in Cuignières, three miles from Clermont in the diocese of Beauvais. In the event of the community having to vacate Amiens, Cuignières would serve as an asylum. The decision to actually send a community there was taken in Amiens on 2 March 1808 and three members of the Amiens community went there. The beginnings were miserable, with regard to housing and relations with the local priests and people. The community recovered from such an unpromising start and gradually wove their way into the life of the village, first by nursing the sick in their homes, then setting up a poor school, followed by a boarding school.[44]

The foundation in Ghent, then in French territory, had been undertaken by Saint-Estève and negotiated with the bishop of Ghent, Maurice de Broglie. In 1806, the bishop had invited the community in Amiens to establish a school in his diocese and offered the former Cistercian abbey of Doorseele for their accommodation. The actual foundation began in May 1808 when eight members from the Amiens community inaugurated the community and school in Doorseele. They were led by Marie-Antoinette de Peñaranda (1779–1830), a Belgian of Spanish origin, who had just completed her initial training in the noviciate at Amiens. A boarding and a poor school opened in October 1808 and soon Belgian women began to ask for admission to the community. In January 1809 the prefect of the *département* granted the community legal status, in view of the decree of approbation granted by Napoleon in March 1807. All seemed to augur well, the communities and schools were prospering at Amiens, Ghent and Cuignières.[45]

In July 1808 Sophie decided to travel to Amiens for a formal visit to the community, fully aware that this would be a difficult stay for her. She knew that she needed some preparation for a task which would demand a great deal of energy and insight. She decided to take Thérèse Maillucheau with her, first to Paris and then to Amiens. In Paris they stayed with Madame de Gramont d'Aster, who had lodgings in the convent of the Sisters of St Thomas de Villeneuve in Paris.[46] Sophie had met Madame de Gramont d'Aster on previous visits to Paris, especially during her prolonged stay in 1804 with Madame Bergeron. The two women, one from the nobility and the other from the petit bourgeois class, became good friends, and a relationship of mutual ease and respect developed. Charlotte-Eugénie de Boisgelin (1766–1836) was the widow of the duc de Gramont d'Aster and former lady-in-waiting to Marie-Antoinette. During the

Revolution the family fled France, setting up house in London. There, with her sister, Madame de Chabannes, Madame de Gramont tried to establish a school in Hyde Park. The duc de Gramont died in London in March 1795 and a year later Madame de Gramont d'Aster and her children returned to France. They lived for some years in Amiens and then moved to Paris.⁴⁷ By the time Sophie met Madame de Gramont her two daughters were at school in Amiens and one of them, Eugénie de Gramont, had entered the noviciate there in 1806, just before the election of Sophie as superior general. Sophie and Eugénie de Gramont were to become close friends, over many years.⁴⁸

Thérèse Maillucheau recorded Sophie's stay in Paris as well as her subse-quent visit to Amiens in August 1808.⁴⁹ During her time in Paris Sophie met with Jean Montaigne, rector of St Sulpice.⁵⁰ She knew him through the contacts which Madame de Gramont had with the church of St Sulpice, for Eugénie and Antoinette had attended the catechism classes there when they recommenced in 1804.⁵¹ Jean Montaigne (1759–1821) was a Sulpician and a friend of the Fathers of the Faith. He was known and well-regarded in Paris for his gifts as a spiritual director and became Sophie's counsellor at this time. Sophie outlined the origins of the Association and the critical situation as she saw it. After some reflection, Montaigne warned Sophie, several times: 'there is a seed of destruc-tion in your midst; but someone very powerful and close to God is praying for you and for your order'.⁵² It helped Sophie to hear her intuitions confirmed and her stay in Paris with Madame de Gramont and her visits with Jean Montaigne gave her time to build up her inner resources and prepare her for her visit to Amiens. Strengthened and assured, she and Thérèse Maillucheau set off for Amiens in August 1808. When they reached Amiens, they found that Saint-Estève was now considered the founder of the Association. There were thirty-two members in the community, fifty-two boarders and 140 in the poor school. It was evidently prosperous and successful.

At the head of this community was Anne Baudemont, powerful and influen-tial. Her assistant and director of the school was Catherine de Charbonnel, (1774–1857), a highly intelligent and educated woman, though somewhat over-awed by Baudemont. Teresa Copina, Italian in origin and formerly a Dilette, was the director of novices. Henriette Ducis (1774–1844), born in Versailles, was guided by Saint-Estève into the community at Amiens. Félicité de Sambucy, eldest sister of Saint-Estève, who had been an Ursuline religious in the monastery of Clermont-Ferrand, joined the community in Amiens and without any initial training was accepted immediately as a full member of the commu-nity. This was the core group which greeted Sophie in August 1808. Few knew her personally, for Félicité Desmarquest had left Amiens to start the foundation in Cuignières in May 1808 and soon, in 1810, Catherine de Charbonnel would move to Poitiers to take charge of the studies in the school there.

Sophie's arrival was greeted with great outward show of affection and the changes in the house presented to her for approval, but it was clear that there was no question of her either ratifying them or indeed vetoing them in any way.

She was expected to agree to all she saw and allow the life in the house and community to continue. Sophie was impressed by the evident success in Amiens and she accepted the educative work of the community as well as its plan of studies for the school. Clearly the community was engaged in a task which answered their own desires and aspirations and fulfilled a need in French society. In ways, Sophie Barat was irrelevant: her role as superior general did not affect them except in the legal sphere. Sophie recognised this and initially tried to adapt herself to their form of life. The perspectives and expectations of the community belonged to the world of the Ancien Régime. Most of them had lived as religious before the Revolution and were for the most part from the nobility, though some were quite penniless. On the other hand Sophie had neither wealth nor social status, nor had she any experience of religious life prior to joining the Diletti.

In view of such circumstances Sophie had no option but to accept what she found in Amiens and try to work with what had developed there during her absence. She found that there was no place for her role since Anne Baudemont was the leader in the house, completely under the influence of Saint-Estève and considered by the local authorities as the superior general of the Association. Clearly Sophie was superfluous. She was in fact ostracised and she relived the experience of 1806, when on arrival in Amiens for the election of superior general, she had been basically ignored. Acutely aware of her position, Sophie for the next six years stayed only intermittently in Amiens: August–September 1808; November 1808–May 1809; June–July 1811. Sophie's only option was to continue exercising her role as superior general in the other houses. Her letters offered spiritual direction to the members in the other houses and her advice was warm and loving and gave no hint of the problems she was encountering in Amiens.[53] She was more open with Philippine Duchesne and told her how much Philippine's letters were a support to her, and she admitted that when Thérèse Maillucheau went to Grenoble she really missed her company in Amiens. Sophie made constant references to the cross in her letters, a way of saying that she was suffering, and she asked Philippine to pray that she would not be frightened by any demand God would make of her.[54] It was dark time, full of enigma, with little light for the path ahead.

— 4 —

A SEED OF DESTRUCTION, 1811–1815

Since Sophie had left home in 1800 she had remained in regular contact with her parents and sister in Joigny and took great interest in all that was happening at home. Her contact with Louis was more sporadic. When he and Sophie parted in the autumn of 1800 he went to Lyon and with Pierre Roger organised a college for boys there. This lasted barely a year as the government suppressed the college in 1802, but the Fathers of the Faith decided to resite the college in St Galmier and Louis was sent to run it. That site was closed by the government the following year and the college was once more transferred, this time to Belley. Louis taught there and in 1803 he became a finally professed member of the Fathers of the Faith. For the next two years Belley was his base and there he taught the boys and gave missions in the surrounding parishes. He travelled to Paris in December 1804 when Pope Pius VII was present at the coronation of Napoleon in Notre Dame. Though Louis stayed for some weeks in Paris he had returned to Belley by the time Sophie arrived in the city, in March 1805. In the autumn of that year Louis was transferred to the junior seminary at l'Argentière which Cardinal Fesch had asked the Fathers of the Faith to run. While he was there Louis visited Grenoble several times between 1805 and 1808. Sometimes Sophie was there and she found his visits a source of pain. She remained fearful of Louis and found herself deeply troubled when he was present in the house. She spoke to Joseph Varin about the effect her brother had on her. Joseph Varin had already noted this fear. In 1801 he had written:

> I do not know what your dear brother, and mine, could possibly have ordered you
> to do which was capable of bringing such trouble and anxiety to your soul. But I

70

cross out and erase every line, to the very last word, which is not an expression of joy, happiness and encouragement.[1]

The fear was still there in 1805 when Louis visited her in Grenoble. Joseph Varin was surprised at how tenacious this fear was and while he could understand that some problems in the Association had caused Sophie suffering:

> what really astonishes me is that your other form of suffering is only increased rather than dispelled when you meet your brother. What! Have you not yet found out who is behind this, no one less than the dark spirit! And if you have discovered this, then you are still taken in by it! Oh! Please, I beg you, may all such useless worries be dispelled by the time I arrive. Do you need an angel from heaven to reassure you? And if you refuse to believe in Jesus Christ in the person of his minister, will you have more faith in an angel? Courage, trust and blessed audacity.[2]

Sophie could not easily break the hold Louis had over her personal life. Louis himself noticed Sophie's reaction to his presence and spoke to Joseph Varin about it. But neither understood the source of Sophie's stress. When writing to his sister Marie-Louise in 1803 Louis had expressed concern over Sophie and his admiration at what she was doing.[3] But he was unable to express the care and concern he felt to Sophie personally. On the other hand Philippine Duchesne felt no fear of Louis and between 1806 and 1808 a lifelong friendship was formed between them. Louis shared Philippine Duchesne's longing for the missions, and her austerity of life won his full approval. However, these contacts came to abrupt end. In November 1807 Napoleon ordered all the Fathers of the Faith to reside in their home dioceses,[4] and early in 1808 Louis made plans to return to Joigny.

Louis's contacts with the community at Grenoble marked the beginning of his guidance of several members of the Association. Yet while Sophie herself approved of and often encouraged this she was quick to point out if Louis overstepped his limits. In this respect Sophie, in her role as superior general, was able to act independently of Louis. Once one of the community in Niort received conflicting advice from Louis Barat and asked Sophie what to do:

> I am not in the least surprised that my brother prefers prolonged periods of prayer to your embroidery, and that he laments the time you give to it. Long ago he tore up all that I made, saying that it was time lost. You know how useful embroidery is to us and I want you to learn how to *nuance* this. It is not the quantity of work that I ask . . . nor do I insist on the time you give to it. Take the time you can for embroidery but make sure always that your spiritual exercises, grammar and the other subjects come first.[5]

By the end of 1808 Louis was back in Joigny. He taught for a short time in his old school, Collège St Jacques in Joigny, and then was appointed to the parish of St-Fargeau where he ministered for almost three years.[6] Having Louis back in the vicinity of Joigny was a comfort to Madame Barat. Although only sixty-seven, Jacques Barat was ailing and by late May 1809 he had become seriously ill. Sophie went to see her father in early June and planned to stay at home for some time.

However, she was called away urgently to Poitiers and while she was there Jacques Barat died on 25 June. Sophie rarely spoke of her father and when Philippine sympathised with her on his death, Sophie's reply was very restrained:

> Thank you for your kind sympathy on our recent loss. It was indeed truly painful; but the sorrow was eased by hope and by the prayers which you offered for this admirable father.[7]

She was much more forthcoming about her mother. When Emilie Giraud made presents of a blouse and slippers for Madame Barat, Sophie wrote to her:

> If only you knew how much my mother loved me! Being deprived of me was the martyrdom which heaven reserved for her. Pray for her and for all the family.[8]

Louis's time in St-Fargeau came to an end in 1811 when he was invited to teach in the seminary in Troyes. Almost immediately he ran into conflict with the government for he refused to subscribe to the Four Articles of 1682. These Gallican articles were added to the Concordat drawn up by Napoleon in 1802[9] and the clergy were obliged to subscribe to them. Louis Barat refused. An anonymous letter was sent to the emperor which complained as much about the content of Louis's theology as his ultramontanism:

> Indeed Mr Barat is far from knowing how to guide and bring up young men destined in our time to become ministers of religion! I know better than anyone else the spiritual situation at the seminary at Troyes and the extent of the damage which the bizarre ideas of this visionary have produced . . . This mania for strange devotions, revelations and small miracles. Alas! What would happen to a seminary so directed[?][10]

Napoleon passed the letter on to the minister of police and the matter was dealt with quickly. Louis Barat was ordered to leave not only the seminary but also the region of the Yonne. He was given the choice of where he wished to go and he chose Bordeaux since he knew some of the clergy there. He was allowed a few days to leave, to call in Joigny and Migennes and then he was given a passport to travel to Bordeaux. From this time he was a watched man even though the authorities recognised that while Louis Barat rejected the conditions of the Concordat with Rome, he was no revolutionary.[11]

Both Louis and Sophie were concerned about the education of their nieces and nephews. They now numbered eight, since the birth of Elisa in 1807 and of Dosithée in 1809, in all, two boys and six girls. The eldest boy, Louis, was already at school at St Acheul's, Amiens, and in 1803 Louis arranged with Marie-Louise that Stanislas should go there also.[12] The state of Etienne Dusaussoy and Marie-Louise's marriage is hard to gauge. Indeed Sophie rarely mentions her brother-in-law in her letters and then only in the usual courtesies. Sophie told Marie-Louise that when the girls were ready she would find places for them in the schools.

By 1810, Julie Dusaussoy (1800–1842) had been sent to Grenoble and was later joined by her sister, Elisa (1807–1839). Thérèse (1798–1823) went to

Poitiers, and Sophie (1804–1886) to Ghent, then to Amiens and finally finished school in Paris. The education of the girls was complete when Zoé (1805–1894) and Dosithée (1809–1823) went to school in Amiens.

Sophie followed the progress of her nieces with interest. She asked Philippine Duchesne to be firm with Julie in the beginning as the child had a strong will and could be difficult. A year later Sophie was still concerned about Julie's progress and behaviour and asked that she change class, in the hope that her behaviour would change. A change of school might have helped but she had more nieces to educate in other schools and places were limited.[13] Elisa Dusaussoy arrived in Grenoble in 1812, just five years old, and when Sophie visited the house in February 1813 she could see that both nieces were doing well in the school. Julie had grown up to the extent that she was able to look after Elisa, and Elisa even then could read, was beginning to write and could sew well for her age. By the following year, however, the little girl was showing signs of stress. She was too young to mix with the older boarders and Sophie asked Marie Balastron to look after the child who had become so anxious to please that she had begun telling lies:

> What you tell me about Elisa really upsets me. Could you not find a way of stopping her from lying and pretending so much? I mean, win her trust, treat her gently and convince her that she will be loved and treated well when she tells the truth. I noticed that this child is very self-centred and has such a strong need to please that even the hint of being scolded or disapproved of will easily bring about her deviations. There is no way she should be praised for behaving badly, but maybe by winning her back gently and by giving her a bit of freedom when she is with you, she will be less demanding on you. For the rest, since I am so far away and unable to follow her up, and I am told hardly anything about her, I cannot give any other advice . . . this is the age to correct faults that develop, later it will be more difficult . . . Will you allow her have some short outings from time to time in the hills?[14]

Sophie Dusaussoy was sent to the school in Ghent in 1810/1811 and her aunt was able to followed her education more closely. She praised her progress and chided her failures. Apparently Sophie's behaviour in the school was not always up to standard and letters from her aunt urged her to do better. Life was not easy for Sophie Dusaussoy. She was lonely, she wanted to see her parents and wondered why they did not visit her in Ghent. Aunt Sophie comforted her in her letters, gave her news of her parents and urged her to write home often. She told her how her brothers and sisters were progressing and sometimes made comparisons between Sophie's progress and that of her sisters in the hope that Sophie would be shamed into behaving better.[15] Thérèse Dusaussoy went to school in Poitiers in 1809/1810 and when Sophie visited the community there in March 1812 she was pleased with her niece's progress.[16] However that did not last and in 1814 Sophie wrote to Marie-Louise in Joigny exasperated with her nieces and in particular with Thérèse. She was forthright in her criticisms:

> In general all your children are very difficult to bring up: moodiness, stubbornness and pride rule them. Thérèse has become impossible, she treats her companions

and her teachers as her inferiors and in the most rude manner. Think of my embarrassment! She had to be publicly humiliated. I had to rebuke her severely myself.
She is a bit better but according to what Madame Grosier wrote to me she is not
convinced even a little that this means work. It is really wrong to bring children up
beyond their station when they are not alive to their situation! I was almost tempt-
ed to send her home to Joigny to let her see with her own eyes what awaits her in
life: work and suffering. . . . Sometimes I think that you have a lot to thank God for
in giving you the opportunity of having your children brought up far from you . . .
especially with your incorrect way of treating them, giving them all they want at
one moment and scolding them later for everything.[17]

Yet despite Sophie's evident irritation with her nieces and her criticism of her
sister's parenting, she suggested in 1815 that Zoé go to Poitiers and Dosithée, the
youngest, go to Cuignières. She also kept an eye on her nephews, Louis and
Stanislas. While Louis Barat had arranged their education and watched over their
studies in Amiens and Bordeaux, Sophie followed them up too, especially when
they left school. When Louis Dusaussoy began his studies for the priesthood in
Paris he continually pressed his aunt for money for clothes and lodging, something which Sophie found hard to refuse. She knew that ready cash was not easy
to find for all the children's needs, since the Dusaussoy family had suffered financial losses during the later years of Napoleon's reign. Etienne and Marie-Louise
Dusaussoy paid fees for their children by sending wine to the houses where the
children were at school. Sophie also had the use of the Dusaussoy home if she or
her friends were travelling. She asked if a room could be set aside for such occasions. Joseph Varin stayed there with a friend, and Sophie arranged that Josephine
Bigeu, then in Grenoble, could have a short holiday in Joigny en route to Paris in
1814. With Julie and Elisa at school in Grenoble, Josephine Bigeu's visit was a
chance for the parents to have firsthand news of their children.

Taking care of nieces and nephews was relatively easy in comparison to dealing with the situation of the Association in Amiens. Sophie recognised that
Saint-Estève had invested great personal ambition and energy in the Amiens
community. As subsequent events would show, Saint-Estève was pursuing his
own agenda and used his considerable charm to convince the community in
Amiens that he had both the vision of life they were seeking and the capacity to
realise it. There was no secret about his motives in assuming the role as founder
of the Association des Dames de l'Instruction Chrétienne. Both Saint-Estève
and his brother Gaston de Sambucy (who was master of ceremonies in the imperial chapel of Napoleon) wanted to provide secure accommodation for life for
their sister, Félicité de Sambucy.[18] They were in the process of family empire
building and the community colluded with it since it answered their own needs
and aspirations, at least to a degree. Anne Baudemont was convinced that she
was destined to lead the community and the monastic model suited both her
experience and her temperament. Saint-Estève thus could not contemplate having a superior general for life in his scheme of things, nor could he conceive of
a Jesuit model of government, whereby houses of the Association could

exchange personnel and have interaction between the houses built into their way of life. He had already clashed in Amiens on these points with Julie Billiart, founder of the Sisters of Notre Dame de Namur. He had convinced both Joseph Varin and the local bishop that she was incapable of governing her community and should be removed. In reality her crime was to have withstood the pressure that Saint-Estève placed upon her. Nevertheless, he won his case and Billiart was ordered by the bishop to leave Amiens. She took her community to Namur, in Belgium, where it prospered.[19]

Secure in the approval granted by Napoleon in March 1807, Saint-Estève worked on a rule of life for the community at Amiens. While it was one thing to have a provisional approval from Napoleon it was another to draw up a rule in view of approval from the pope. Between 1807 and 1811 a rule of life had been worked upon by several Fathers of the Faith, and certainly Sophie used that work in progress in Poitiers between 1806 and 1808. By 1811 Saint-Estève had finalised the text and no further contributions were made by the Fathers of the Faith since they had been suppressed in 1807. This text was presented to the community at Amiens in 1811. The rule was consistent with the aims of Saint-Estève: to welcome former religious into the Association and to have teachers for their work of education. The actual rule was an amalgam of several rules of associations already founded, but basically taken from that of the Sisters of Notre Dame of Jeanne de Lestonnac of Bordeaux. The influence of the Ursulines was also quite strong and indeed the community in Amiens celebrated the feast of St Ursula rather than that of the Sacred Heart. Two key elements were missing from Saint-Estève's rules of life for the community. Firstly, the term of office of superior general was no longer for life, but for ten years. This reflected communities modelled on the monastic pattern of federations rather than on the Jesuit model of all communities united, symbolised in the Association by the role of superior general for life. Furthermore the role of superior general was curtailed by the powers given to the local community to receive new members and later accept them for integration into the Association. Secondly, the inspiration of de Tournély was lost: the spirituality of the Sacred Heart of Jesus was not presented as the focus of the Association, nor the need to bring this spirituality to bear on the formation of the members of the Association, or on the manner in which they carried out their work. Clearly Saint-Estève and the community in Amiens, in so far as they were involved in the actual writing of the rules, were reconstituting religious life as they knew it before the Revolution.[20]

Sophie had left Grenoble in November 1810 and spent some weeks visiting Lyon, Joigny, Paris and Cuignières. She arrived in Amiens in mid-January 1811 to take part in the final discussions on Saint-Estève's proposed rules. Only Sophie, Anne Baudemont and her council were at the final voting sessions on 2 February 1811. They voted to adopt the rules and to present them to the community at Amiens and to the other houses of the Association for approval. On the evening of 2 February 1811 the rules were presented to the professed members of the Amiens community and they were accepted on a trial basis. The next stage was to present them to the communities of Ghent, Grenoble, Poitiers and Niort. Curiously, Saint-Estève did not travel round the communities himself but left it to Sophie to present the new rules.

Sophie spent from February to May in Ghent and tried to explain the new rule to the community. After time to reflect, the community rejected the new rule on the grounds that that the loss of the role of superior general for life threatened the vision they had adopted, which was based on the Jesuit rule. This was a key point. The Amiens community understood that new foundations were to be independent and linked only by bonds of affection. The Ghent community saw communities in close union with one another, expanding globally, and maintaining a corporate sense of unity which was actualised and symbolised by the office of superior general for life. On that basis they expressed grave doubts and it was clear to Sophie that the community at Ghent would not accept the rules proposed by Saint-Estève. With that knowledge she left Ghent and journeyed to Poitiers, Niort and Grenoble to assess the response there to the new rules. Here, there were equally negative reactions, though for different reasons. In these three other houses, the lack of devotion to the Sacred Heart as well as the lessening of Eucharistic devotion provoked a strong response. In particular, the two original members of the Amiens communities, Geneviève Deshayes and Henriette Grosier, were clear that they could not accept the new rule. Polarisation set in and Sophie knew she would have to take the initiative in order to retain unity and find a way to the future.[21]

Through the reactions of the communities outside of Amiens she had become clearer in her own mind of her role in the Association. She knew also that her election as superior general in 1806 was valid and she had no intention of resigning. Increasingly, a power struggle between two models of religious life, and between two leaders, Saint-Estève and Sophie Barat was emerging. Through this process Sophie herself became the focus for both unity and for division, a role she would experience several times in the course of her life. Sophie also kept in touch with Joseph Varin, meeting him at Vichy in June, then in Paris in July 1810.[22] Despite what she told him he continued to support Saint-Estève. Nor would he accept the criticism which Louis Barat had made of Saint-Estève, in particular regarding his move away from the Jesuit model of religious life and from the spirituality of the Sacred Heart, both key elements in the original vision of de Tournély. Through his visits to Grenoble, his conversations with Philippine Duchesne and Geneviève Deshayes as well as his contacts with other members of the Association in Poitiers and Niort, Louis had become aware of the shift created by Saint-Estève. However, this difference of opinion between Joseph Varin and Louis had potential to damage Sophie. In October 1811 Sophie warned Geneviève Deshayes not to let the Amiens community know of the difference of opinion between her brother and Joseph Varin. But Louis made his views clear to his sister and told her he would prefer to withdraw from contact with her and the Association rather than risk dividing the members further. Sophie was relieved at his decision as Louis's involvement would only compound an already difficult position.[23]

Room for change was created when Saint-Estève was arrested on 6 June 1812 and jailed in Paris, ostensibly for political activity in Amiens and for interfering with the affairs of the local diocese. He was imprisoned at St Pélagie first and then transferred to a mental home in St Jacques.[24] His absence from Amiens gave Sophie an opportunity to plan her return there in her role as superior general. She initiated this process in October 1812 when she decided to travel to Besançon and discuss the future with Joseph Varin; the following year she and Geneviève Deshayes both met Joseph Varin again and they agreed that Sophie would have to discuss some key revisions to the rules with Saint-Estève and insist on her rightful place in Amiens. Varin thought Saint-Estève would accept the changes Sophie wanted but that Geneviève Deshayes should not accompany her to Amiens. Geneviève Deshayes was opposed to the rule of Saint-Estève and the stance of the community at Amiens and she would certainly not have remained quietly on the sidelines.[25]

Sophie went to Paris in November 1813 to discuss affairs with Jean Montaigne and to prepare for her meeting with Saint-Estève, who was still under house arrest in Paris. It is not clear who, or if anyone, accompanied Sophie to the meetings with Saint-Estève, though possibly Jean Montaigne was present in his capacity as her adviser. Certainly Henriette Ducis travelled from Amiens in December 1813 and acted as secretary for the meetings. While these minutes have not survived, two key concessions were won when Saint-Estève agreed firstly that Sophie herself was superior general for life, though it was understood that those who succeeded her would be appointed for ten years. He also agreed that Sophie was also local superior in Amiens, thus effectively deposing Anne Baudemont. She had achieved what she thought was necessary to maintain the basic unity of the several communities in France, but Saint-Estève knew that he had a hold on the women in Amiens, especially his own sister, Félicité de Sambucy, as well as Teresa Copina, Henriette Ducis and Eugénie de Gramont.[26]

As soon as the meetings in Paris were completed, Sophie set off for Amiens, to implement what had been agreed. Her arrival there in January 1814 generated tension and resentment. The new situation was untenable from the start – in Amiens Sophie was surrounded by women whose first loyalties were to Saint-Estève and Baudemont. The original composition of the community council had only changed by the addition of one member, Eugénie de Gramont. Assistant general to Anne Baudemont, she hardly knew Sophie Barat and was loyal both to Saint-Estève and Anne Baudemont. Eugénie de Gramont became assistant general to Sophie and Anne Baudemont became treasurer general; Félicité de Sambucy continued as assistant to the local superior, now Sophie Barat herself. Teresa Copina was director of novices; and Henriette Ducis remained secretary general. Thus Sophie was isolated among the followers of Saint-Estève. Such a situation was untenable and tension mounted in the house.

Tension was also mounting in France. The empire of Napoleon was falling apart and the area around Amiens was overrun by armies on manoeuvres. On 4 April 1814 Napoleon abdicated and the path was open for the restoration of the

Bourbons. There was great hope that Pius VII would restore the Jesuits and when they were formally reinstated in the church in August 1814, the Fathers of the Faith sought admission to the Jesuit noviciate in France. Saint-Estève was released from prison on 5 April and, aware that his presence was unwelcome in the diocese of Amiens, he found himself an appointment as secretary to Mgr Cortois de Pressigny, bishop of St Malo, the newly appointed ambassador to the Holy See. The opportunities for peace as well as the imminent departure of Saint-Estève for Rome prompted Sophie Barat to go to Paris and arrange a meeting with him in May 1814. Joseph Varin was free to travel again and went to Paris to attend the meeting with Sophie, Jean Montaigne, and Saint-Estève. This was the first time that Joseph Varin had met Saint-Estève in several years and he had yet to recognise the personal ambition of Saint-Estève with regard to the Association. There was a certain pressure at the meeting in that Saint-Estève's departure was imminent and any decisions regarding the constitutions would have to be made quickly. During the meeting Saint-Estève proposed that he try to get the rule of the Association approved in Rome and that he even try to open a house of the Association in Rome. After some deliberation together, the group decided to accept Saint-Estève's proposals that he present the rule in Rome for approval. But they insisted that Saint-Estève agree to some modifications to the rule he had drawn up in 1811. These modifications would be sent to him in Rome. Sophie Barat consented to Saint-Estève's role in Rome on the understanding that she would present the rule of 1811 and the modifications to it to the general council of the Association which she hoped to convene shortly. Only when that council had completed its work should Saint-Estève proceed to seek approval in Rome.[27]

Some weeks later, towards the middle of July 1814 Sophie returned to Paris to deliberate with Joseph Varin on the modifications to the rule. This coincided with the time when many of the Fathers of the Faith entered the Jesuit noviciate in Paris, under the leadership of Pierre de Clorivière. As Joseph Varin and Sophie worked together on the modifications they wished to make to the rule of Saint-Estève it slowly dawned on Joseph Varin that the rule of Saint-Estève was far from the inspiration of de Tournély. It was a key moment of recognition and one that required a radical decision. Both Sophie and Joseph Varin agreed that entirely new constitutions would have to be written, that those of Saint-Estève were foreign to the initial inspiration of de Tournély.[28] They asked another colleague, Julien Druilhet, to work with them in drawing up another rule of life. This would retrieve the intuition of Léonor de Tournély and be centred on the Heart of Christ. Sophie Barat had tried to voice her misgivings many times and had never been heard. While this decision was heartening, it was only the prelude to a deepening crisis for Sophie and the Association.

The eighteen months between the departure of Saint-Estève for Rome and the opening of the general council in Paris in November 1815 mark the final stage in Sophie Barat's assumption of authority in the Association. This period both formed and revealed her personality and stamped the nature and style of her authority within the Association. After a long period in which she had been deliberately sidelined by Saint-Estève, Sophie began to steer her way through a labyrinth of intrigue in ways that might have seemed weak, haphazard and inept. Yet, despite appearances, what is remarkable at this time is the clarity with which Sophie read events as they unfolded and how she found her own style of leadership in response to those events. The contrast between her style of leadership and Saint-Estève's was very marked. Saint-Estève's was that of a powerful and dominant influence in Amiens where practically all the community fully approved his proposed constitutions. His colourful and overbearing personality had rendered Sophie powerless in Amiens. His grandiose projects and plans for the future of the Association were assuring for the membership there and in a time of uncertainty this was attractive. Sophie Barat could offer nothing like that and she had neither the temperament nor the inclination to enter into competition with him. It was her nature and style to wait and to watch the future unfold and then judge when and how to act. Whereas Saint-Estève sought to make the future happen, Sophie Barat chose the moment to respond to events and situations. For several years Sophie's tendency to hold back suited Saint-Estève, but by 1814 she had read the situation within the Association carefully and realised that the time had come to act. Over the years Sophie had been led by the conviction that Providence would point the way and her task was to wait until a path opened up and showed her how to proceed. That path had begun to open in 1808 and led slowly to the negotiations in Paris in June 1814. The final confrontation between Sophie Barat and Saint-Estève was yet to come and it would prove far more demanding than Sophie could have imagined. With his departure to Rome, Saint-Estève took the conflict into a new and wider context. Sophie would have to contend with the daunting prospect of Saint-Estève trying to force a resolution of the issue in his favour, with the support of the church authorities in Rome.

At the conclusion of the negotiations in Paris in June 1814, Sophie understood that the outcome of their discussion would be debated by a general council of the Association first and that this body would or would not formally authorise Saint-Estève to proceed in Rome. Saint-Estève's interpretation was different. He claimed that he had been authorised to begin the process of seeking approval for the constitutions in Rome. Thus when he arrived in Rome as secretary to the newly appointed French ambassador, Saint-Estève set about seeking approval for the rule he had written immediately, building his own future as the superior general of the Association. To further this aim his letters to Joseph Varin alluded to the easy access he had to the pope, to the cardinals and to the bishops, as well as to the newly re-established Jesuits in Rome. In this way he created the illusion of a strong base from which he could negotiate the future of the Association. When Joseph Varin intimated in a letter that he had undertaken further modifications of the constitutions Saint-Estève presumed that these would be minor and easily incorporated into his own 1811 constitutions. Indeed, he urged Joseph Varin to send on the 'corrections', as he called them, as quickly as possible. He hinted that the Association could not be named 'Dames du Sacré Coeur de Jésus', suggesting that the pope had expressed his wishes in this regard. He also added casually that he was in the process of getting a house in Rome for the Association.[29] Saint-Estève had taken the initiative into his own hands and was busily carving out a niche for himself in Rome.

Following his pattern of former years, Saint-Estève did not communicate directly with Sophie Barat and it was through Joseph Varin that she learnt what Saint-Estève was doing in Rome to further his hold over the Association. She promptly wrote to Saint-Estève and in the most polite, diplomatic terms complained of his silence in her regard. While recognising that it had been agreed that he would in time negotiate approval for the Association in Rome, she firmly reprimanded him for going too fast.

> Allow me to make an observation in this regard. You have already submitted our rules for examination; perhaps, following on this, now you will seek formal approbation. Before proceeding any further would it not be prudent to wait until the final draft has been completed and accepted by a general council of the Society. Indeed, to respond to the general desire of all the houses, with the exception of Amiens, which is less demanding on this point, *all* would prefer to have the rule of the Jesuit Institute adapted as far as possible for women, particularly since France has regained its freedom.
>
> As soon as this final draft is completed and accepted by the Society we will send it to you and then you may submit it for examination and approval.... There is yet another point with which you must comply, concerning the name which we will adopt for the Society. You are aware that the [name] *Sacred Heart* has been agreed on by all with, it could be said, a kind of enthusiasm. It would be quite difficult to gain acceptance of another ... so you will readily understand that just as it is for the Society to submit its constitutions to the Pope, it is also its responsibility to choose its name. ... This question of the name will be the concern of the general council as well as everything regarding the constitutions. The outcome of this council will be sent on to you, as we agreed verbally before you left [Paris]. ... This is the only way that we can possibly take to restore and create *one body* in the Society.[30]

This was a new Sophie Barat and one that took Saint-Estève by surprise, even though her actions since December 1813 had made it clear to all that she had taken up a new position and that she would not tolerate the situation he had created. Her letter also conveyed to Saint-Estève that it was no longer a question of modifications to his rule, agreed on in Paris in 1813 and 1814. Rather she told Saint-Estève that since his departure for Rome she and Joseph Varin had decided not to present the text of 1811 to the general council. Even with the modifications agreed on in June 1814, it would never be accepted by the vast majority of the membership. To his dismay, Saint-Estève realised that an entirely new text was in the process of being drawn up and this work, not his, would be the material for deliberation at the general council of the Association. All his grandiose plans in Rome were in jeopardy. During October and November 1814 Saint-Estève wrote to Sophie Barat, Joseph Varin and Pierre de Clorivière, in a bid to retain his dominance over them and the Association. He tried to play off

Joseph Varin and de Clorivière against Sophie, implying that only she was the source of opposition to his plans in Rome. He hinted that Joseph Varin must force Sophie to take what he called 'an open attitude, devoid of prejudice, full of trust and independent of the views of some of her companions'; otherwise all in Rome would assume that the Association had either 'a really defective superior or a poor council'.[31] Clearly he had been taken aback by her letter of September 1814 and could not believe it was the same person he had sidelined and rendered ineffective for so long in her role as superior general of the Association. Yet Saint-Estève had every reason to suspect that the Fathers of the Faith, most of whom had decided to join the Jesuits in Paris, were now his greatest critics and Sophie Barat's greatest supporters.

Something of the intrigue and confusion Saint-Estève tried to create at this time was expressed in a long letter he wrote to Clorivière in November 1814. He told Clorivière that he was acting with the approval of the pope, cardinals and Jesuits of Rome. In that context he alluded to the permission which Clorivière had given Joseph Varin, though a Jesuit novice, to write new constitutions of the Association des Dames de l'Education Chrétienne. Saint-Estève warned Clorivière that the pope, following his predecessors, refused to allow women adopt the Jesuit rule, nor would he approve of a Jesuit being closely involved with a women's congregation. Besides, Saint-Estève continued, between 1800 and 1814 Joseph Varin had not written a rule for the Association; even since the summer, despite promises to send his modifications to Saint-Estève in Rome, nothing at all had arrived from Paris. He rejected Sophie's role as superior general and declared she was incapable of governing the Association, and he insisted that he had been recognised as the sole superior of the Association. He was convinced that Joseph Varin should order the communities of the Association either to conform to Saint-Estève's leadership or to withdraw from the project of seeking approval from Rome.[32] There was a certain rationale to this point of view. It was true that Joseph Varin had withdrawn from all direct contact with the Association since 1808 and had indeed made no effort to contribute to a rule of life for the Association. Sophie herself at no time sought to write a rule of her own. There was then a lacuna which Saint-Estève had filled when he wrote the rule in 1811.

Certainly by this time Saint-Estève's anger was roused and his reply to Sophie barely disguised his fury. He had been taken aback at the tone and content of her letter. He was convinced that she was a mouthpiece for others, that she could not be speaking in her own right. He put himself in the role of an old friend betrayed and he accused her of insincerity, prejudice and contradiction. He could not understand, especially since their last meeting in Paris, how she could not see the influence of the Jesuit rule in the work he had written in 1811 and indeed modified at her request in 1813 and 1814. It was certainly adequate for Rome and already the Jesuits there, as well as other clerics, had given it their approval. Besides, and this was the core of the problem, it was his work, not hers. He hinted that there were some members of the Association in France ready to come to Rome and join other women there, ready to live according to his rule of life. Indeed already several properties in Rome had been offered him for the use of a community.

He countered her objections to his activities in Rome and repeated that he had the ear of the pope, cardinals and Jesuits there. In particular he recounted a conversation he had had with Pius VII, in August 1814, over the question of women adopting the Jesuit rule. Just as Urban VIII in the seventeenth century had rejected the efforts of Mary Ward to adopt the Jesuit rule, so the present pope would not allow any Association of women to adopt the Jesuit rule, nor would he allow the Jesuits to become involved in the guidance of such Associations. He claimed the pope had said:

> My predecessors destroyed the Jesuitesses. I do want them either and even less so the Ladies of the Faith. I will never permit Jesuits to become involved with women religious; it is contrary to the rules of their founder.[33]

Saint-Estève hinted that the Jesuits in Rome were critical of Clorivière, of his involvement with groups of religious women in Paris, including the Association.[34] Thus by innuendo and veiled threats Saint-Estève tried to silence the views of Sophie Barat. However, by this time the Jesuits in Paris, especially the former Fathers of the Faith, had seen through Saint-Estève and realised how serious the situation in the Association had become. Saint-Estève realised this and wrote to Joseph Varin in November 1814, defending his actions with regard to the Association. He hinted that the Jesuits in Rome were critical of both Joseph Varin and Sophie Barat and that they fully approved of Saint-Estève's constitutions. Indeed he claimed that all in Rome were amazed at the news that Joseph Varin, Sophie Barat and others were in the process of critiquing the work of Saint-Estève with a view to make the constitutions reflect the Jesuit rule more closely.[35]

These were forceful opinions and neither Sophie nor Joseph Varin had any possibility of weighing their accuracy. Yet once they had taken the decision in Paris to write another rule of life for the Association, both Sophie and Joseph Varin had anticipated a strong reaction from Saint-Estève. Indeed Joseph Varin wrote to Sophie almost with a sense of relief: 'so the storm which I have watched gathering round your head for some time, and indeed round mine too, has finally erupted'.[36] It was ironic, for Sophie had seen this storm coming for several years and had tried to convince Joseph Varin of the impending crisis. Then Joseph Varin could not accept her views. Even in 1814 he still saw her more as a member rather than as truly the leader and it took him a long time to acknowledge Sophie Barat's key role in establishing the Society of the Sacred Heart. He never fully recognised that she, and indeed Louis Barat, had held firm to the original impulse of Léonor de Tournély at a time when both he and Saint-Estève, in different ways, had let it drop. Thus, when Saint-Estève's reply to Sophie, of 23 October 1814, arrived with letters to Varin and de Clorivière, Joseph Varin opened Sophie's letter and read it himself. He may have had Sophie's permission to read letters, since the post was uncertain and both had anticipated a strong reaction from Saint-Estève. He certainly was curious to read anything from Rome and would have found it difficult to wait. In any event, Joseph Varin had censored her correspondence mail for many years and this old habit died hard.

Saint-Estève's letters convinced Joseph Varin and de Clorivière that some concerted reply would have to be made, to counter his accusations and prevent Saint-Estève playing one off against the other. In November 1814 Sophie was in Amiens and Joseph Varin wrote to tell her of their plan. Pierre Roger, in Paris at this time as he had entered the Jesuit noviciate, agreed to draft a letter for Sophie to sign. Varin suggested that Sophie should send the letter to the provincial of the Jesuits in Italy, Louis Panizzoni,[37] and a copy to Saint-Estève as well. At the same time both Joseph Varin and Clorivière would write separate letters to Panizzoni, supporting Sophie's views and they would ask a member of secular clergy, Fr Perreau (1766–1837)[38] who was well known in Rome, to write a letter of support also. The letter prepared by Roger described how Sophie Barat, Joseph Varin and Pierre de Clorivière viewed the affairs of the Association in the autumn of 1814. Panizzoni needed some background information for he had no knowledge of the Association des Dames de l'Instruction Chrétienne, except that it had had links with the disgraced Paccanari. The purpose of Sophie's letter[39] was to give Panizzoni an explanation of the origins of the Association and the role played by Sophie Barat and Joseph Varin in its evolution. The role of the Fathers of the Faith in the Association was played down. On account of the scandal surrounding Paccanari in Rome, they wanted to avoid drawing attention to the close connection of the Association with the Fathers of the Faith. In any event, this had been less marked after 1807 when the restrictions placed on the Fathers of the Faith during the reign of Napoleon had curtailed their contacts with the communities. Sophie told Panizzoni that the promise of peace in France had led her to hope that the time had come to establish the Association on a firmer footing. She explained that Saint-Estève, who had directed the house at Amiens for ten years, had written a rule but the membership in general, with the exception of some in Amiens, did not accept the text. She had given it every chance, had even tried to persuade the communities to adopt the work of Saint-Estève, but to no avail. The general body of the Association did not recognise it as expressive of their spirit.

Sophie explained that, in view of this failure to win consensus, she had proposed that the best way forward was to write a new text of constitutions and rules and have them accepted by the members of the Association. Then, after a period of trial of some years, these could be presented to the authorities in Rome for approval. In this context she had been taken aback to learn that Saint-Estève had gone ahead and presented his own work to the pope, the cardinals and the Jesuits, and that he was in the process of acquiring properties in Rome.

> Allow me, on my own behalf and on behalf of my companions in four of the houses of the Society, as well as a large number of those in the fifth house (which has

been under the guidance of M. de Sambucy) to beg you to persuade M. de Sambucy to suspend his proceedings. Ask him to wait until all minds and hearts are united by the common rules which the Society itself will ratify. Without this step, and knowing the views of my companions, I have every reason to fear that the authority and the rules drawn up by M. de Sambucy would only be accepted by a few. It seems to me that our Society, having been founded for France and composed of French women, requires this delay in order to test what appears to be most suitable for it, in accordance with its goal, for the glory of God and the desire to bear the name of the Society of the Sacred Heart and be entirely devoted to this Sacred Heart.[40]

This was clearly a reclaiming of the original vision of Léonor de Tournély and a return to the sources, to the founding myth of the Society of the Sacred Heart. This was confirmed some days later when Joseph Varin wrote a strong letter to Saint-Estève.[41] Replying to Saint-Estève's accusation that Association members wanted to be 'Jesuitesses' Joseph Varin reminded Saint-Estève:

Your former friend, Mr l'abbé de Tournély, [who] should be regarded as the original founder of this Society since he originally initiated the project and the plan in Germany; its realisation in France is truly only the consequence of that [impulse]. Mr de Tournély . . . never planned to have Jesuitesses, but only an association of women consecrated to the Sacred Heart and entirely devoted to education. They were to take from the rule of St Ignatius what would help them fulfil their goal. Thus they are Dames du Sacré Coeur and not Jesuitesses.[42]

He also replied to Saint-Estève's four major criticisms: that the Association had made little progress over fourteen years; that Joseph Varin could have healed the divisions in the Association if he so wished; that since he had decided to become a Jesuit Joseph Varin had no right to be involved in the Association; that Saint-Estève alone was responsible for the Association. Joseph Varin declared that it was a kind of miracle that the Association had actually survived and expanded, despite the chaos of the Revolution and Empire. Now the aim was to continue quietly for some years in France, consolidate the Association and not rush into the process for seeking formal approval in Rome. However, the Association had been precipitated into a process of seeking approval in Rome by Saint-Estève, who was indeed 'a seed of destruction'. Joseph Varin saw his own role as laying the foundation for the new Association 'following the insights of M de Tournély' and in this context he rejected Saint-Estève's claim to leadership as both untrue and divisive. No one had given Saint-Estève the right to try and force the Association to adopt what he sought to impose. Let the work of Saint-Estève prosper and even develop in Rome. For their part the communities of the Association in France wanted to carry on quietly and wait much longer before seeking formal approval. As Sophie had done in September, now Joseph Varin let Saint-Estève know clearly that the understanding reached in Paris in June 1814 no longer obtained. The work and activities of Saint-Estève were firmly rejected.[43] Varin sent Sophie a copy of this letter and assured her that the others were writing to Rome in support of her and the Association. Joseph Varin had finally grasped something of the destructiveness of Saint-Estève's activity not only in Rome but over many years in Amiens.[44] Furious at the way that not only Sophie Barat but now Joseph Varin were thwarting his plans, Saint-Estève's replies contained ominous threats about what could happen both to Joseph Varin and to the Association if they continued to resist him.[45]

Sophie entered a bleak time. In November 1814 while letters were going to Rome confronting Saint-Estève, the members of the community in Ghent decided not only to reject the rule of Saint-Estève but also to separate from the Association des Dames de l'Instruction Chrétienne in Amiens, and so from Sophie Barat. It was the end of a struggle which had gone on since February 1811, when the community initially refused to accept the rule drawn up by Saint-Estève. Sophie herself had visited Ghent from February to May 1811 and had been unable to persuade the community, especially the superior, Marie-Antoinette de Peñaranda, even to try the rule. In 1812 Saint-Estève and Anne Baudemont had sent Henriette Ducis to see if she could win over the members of the community, but she too had no success. In the summer of 1814, when he was beginning to travel more, Joseph Varin went to Ghent to see what he could do, but he also failed to convince them at least to remain with the Association.[46] Sophie herself had not visited since the modifications to the rule of Saint-Estève were agreed upon in Paris in 1813 and 1814. However, it was not just resistance to the rule of Saint-Estève which led the community at Ghent to seek separation. They were concerned that Sophie Barat and her advisers had Gallican sympathies, but this may have been just an excuse to justify separating from Amiens. The bishop of Ghent, Maurice de Broglie, encouraged the community to separate from Amiens. He had received Julie Billiart in 1809 when Saint-Estève succeeded in driving her out of Amiens and tried to destroy her work.[47] Besides, by the winter of 1814 the political alignment of Belgium had changed and it no longer belonged to France but to the Netherlands. The diocese no longer formed part of France and the separation of the community mirrored the political reality.

By early December each member of the community at Ghent had to choose either to stay in Ghent or return to Amiens. All the French members of the community and at least one Belgian returned to Amiens. Little Sophie Dusaussoy had to leave the boarding school also and she travelled with those returning to Amiens and joined the boarding school there. By late December the break was effected and Ghent separated from the body of the Association. This loss had a profound effect on Sophie. It was the culmination of a long period of stress and weariness. She became so seriously ill with 'the warning signs of a complicated sinus infection' that she asked to receive the last sacraments. Her death was expected and even Louis Barat was prepared for it. He wrote from Bordeaux: 'if my sister dies just send me a sheet of white paper with a black seal. I will understand'.[48] The crisis lasted for three weeks and left Sophie very weak throughout the early spring of 1815.

This was precisely the time when she needed energy and strength to deal with the new situation in Amiens, created by the arrival of the members from

Ghent and the general unrest in the community. Her old friend Louis Sellier, in St Acheul's, Amiens, urged her to confront the community with the fact that Saint-Estève was in no way the founder or the superior of the Association and announce that those who could not accept that were free to leave and join him in Rome. But Sophie had neither the energy nor the inclination to exert her leadership like that. Varin agreed with Sellier but 'Madame Sophie is so weakened by suffering and so deprived of all help, that she is in no fit state to act with the firmness that this situation requires'. His only hope was that with his letter to Saint-Estève, supported by others, Sophie would be able to act more frankly.[49] While aware of her physical weakness he still urged her to try to establish some ascendancy over the growing unrest and unease in the house. He advised her to convene her own council in the house: Eugénie de Gramont, Félicité de Sambucy, Teresa Copina and Henriette Ducis, all of whom were negotiating directly with Saint-Estève. It was an impossible situation, yet Joseph Varin urged Sophie to try:

> I think that you would do well to convene your council and to propose firmly and calmly that the time has come to restore union among the members of the Society and in consequence of this to restore a sole authority, a spirit of obedience and the observation of the rules. Tell them clearly that M. de Sambucy neither is nor ever has been the superior [general], that the Society has never recognised him as such, neither has any competent authority conferred that role upon him. You need to say that those in Amiens can no longer continue to call him their superior, unless they want to break with the Society. Moreover in a few months time you will convoke a general council of the Society and a common path will be adopted. [Say also] that the response made to M. de Sambucy and even more the experience of his damaging influence . . . forces you to present yourself and act as superior [general].[50]

Joseph Varin urged Sophie to forbid the meetings of small groups within the community. Some in the house were writing to and receiving letters from Saint-Estève, either through his sister, de Sambucy or through contacts in the town and Joseph Varin urged Sophie to censor all letters coming in and going out of the house. He also suggested that she talk individually to those who were supporting Saint-Estève and persuade them that they had no future in the Association if they persisted in following him. This advice was well intended but did not make Sophie's path any easier in Amiens. Besides, Joseph Varin was far away in Paris, embarking upon his noviciate as a Jesuit and could only help from afar. For Sophie the relief was that at last there was common perception among the former Fathers of the Faith, now Jesuit novices in Paris, concerning Saint-Estève and his intrigue within the Association. Indeed the extent of Saint-Estève's activity in the Association had only dawned on Joseph Varin the previous year. Only then did he begin to grasp something of the burden Sophie carried and which certainly was central to her illnesses and exhaustion. For their part both Montaigne and de Clorivière sent messages of support from Paris, aware of the complexity of the situation Sophie was enduring virtually on her own.[51] In Amiens, however, she had the firm friendship of Madame de Gramont d'Aster, (mother of Eugénie and Antoinette de Gramont) and this had been a real support over many years. Madame de Gramont had entered the community in 1813 and saw at first hand what was happening in the house, especially to her eldest daughter, Eugénie.[52]

In Rome, Saint-Estève's opposition to Sophie Barat continued and he worked hard to create the conditions which could attract his followers in Amiens to join him there. He continued to search for a property where a community could be housed and he wrote about this to the inner circle at Amiens. Madame de Gramont d'Aster was aware that Saint-Estève had written to her daughter, Eugénie in November 1814, inviting her to go to Rome and found the new community in the Trinité des Monts. For her part, Madame de Gramont d'Aster was acutely aware that both her daughters were influenced by Saint-Estève. She wrote to the French ambassador to the Holy See, Mgr Cortois de Pressigny:

> We have been told, Monsignor, that certain people have spoken to the pope about our little Society and that he has deigned to offer us the monastery of the Holy Trinity on the Piazza di Spagna. Moreover, my elder daughter, Madame de Gramont had been proposed to initiate this foundation. Enthusiasm for a large enterprise can arouse a moment of fantasy in a young religious but her selection is not valid for it has not been made by our superior general. I beg your excellency to present our deepest apologies to the pope for being unable to take responsibility for this establishment. Please explain to him the needs of our Society, still in its infancy, and aware of the need to consolidate its growth before expanding. Would it not be very imprudent, at least for a few years, to establish this house so far from our superior general and from the centre of the new-born Society itself. It was founded only for France, and since at present it has only a rudimentary rule of life, the Society needs to concentrate on creating authentic constitutions to serve as its firm foundation. This is an important grace which the Society can only hope to receive from God, by prayer, silence and humility.[53]

In such a critical situation, a letter from Madame de Gramont d'Aster, a member of the court nobility, was far more effective and influential than any representation Sophie Barat could have made at this time and it would reach the places in Rome where Saint-Estève could be countered. Besides, Sophie was ill in December 1814 and Madame de Gramont d'Aster realised the gravity of the situation. She knew that it would be a great triumph for Saint-Estève if Eugénie de Gramont was persuaded to join him in Rome, for she was assistant to Sophie Barat and sub-mistress of novices at Amiens. Eugénie de Gramont decided to ask advice from her old teacher, Gaston de Sambucy de Saint-Estève, (brother of Saint-Estève). He suggested that she defer her decision for the time being, until she was clearer in her mind.[54] Meanwhile the intrigue continued and spread. A contemporary account of the period 1812–15 in Amiens, written by Marie de la Croix (1792–1879) records how the inner circle had strengthened its hold within the community and continued to plan its future with Saint-Estève. Marie de la Croix had entered at Amiens in April 1812[55] and gradually came to realise that she had joined a very divided community. By then, not only was Saint-Estève considered by many to be the founder of the Association but he also enjoyed the reputation of a saint among some in the community, which had increased to the status of martyr when he was imprisoned.

For the inner circle in Amiens (Eugénie de Gramont, Félicité de Saint-Estève, Teresa Copina and Henriette Ducis), their greatest hope for the future lay in the women who had recently joined, like Marie de la Croix. Because of that, the fourteen women in the noviciate were completely isolated from the rest of the community, and in particular from Sophie herself:

> We were forbidden to have any communication with the professed members of the community. Under the pretext that her illness required total rest, Sophie Barat was closeted away in the little house where she lived, and with the exception of those who looked after her, none of the members of the community dared visit her.[56]

Sophie's increasing self-confidence and resolute refusal to accept Saint-Estève's views and activities were difficult to explain to the new members. While Saint-Estève was presented to the novices as one ready to work closely and harmoniously with the pope and church authorities in Rome, insinuations were made that Sophie was Gallican, that she strove to be independent from the authority of Rome and that she would work only with French bishops who held Gallican sympathies. It was, as Marie de la Croix later recognised, a process of character assassination. The mistress of novices, Teresa Copina, described how Saint-Estève had tried to enlighten Sophie and help her see the errors of her ways, but to no avail. Rather he had encountered uncompromising resistance and so decided that he had to go to Rome to get the problem resolved by the pope. Remarks to this effect were made casually and regularly:

> We studied in silence . . . while the sub-mistress of novices was leaving her room and locking it after her. . . .she said to us while walking briskly by us: 'Ah! My little ones! never forget that whoever is not in the barque of Peter is cast into the water!'. She disappeared and left us astonished!
> My mistress of novices took me aside and during quite a long walk . . . she told me that she regretted having to speak but that she was forced by circumstances to share a sad and sorrowful truth: that in France the four articles of the Gallican church existed, a source of error and of disagreement with the Holy See. Many of the bishops were ardent defenders of these articles and by a misfortune which could only be deeply regretted and which daily became more dangerous Sophie Barat herself accepted these four articles. Her boundless trust in those who created this heresy placed us all in imminent danger of being lost![57]

Marie de la Croix admitted that she had no idea at this time of what 'Gallican' meant except that it was surely a negative quality. In her innocence Marie de la Croix suggested that they all go to Sophie and ask her there and then to change in order to save herself and the Association. The reaction was of immediate panic, for Copina thought that Marie de la Croix would go directly to Sophie herself:

> Now you force me to tell you what I would have preferred to hide from you. Sophie Barat is an extremely shrewd woman. Her warmth of manner which enchants you

is merely a front to win us all and make us fall into dire difficulties. See now what charity has prevented me telling you.[58]

Sophie continued to be unwell and her precarious state of health was used in July 1815 as an excuse to have her removed from the house. The doctor in Amiens was asked to prescribe a period of complete rest and convalescence in Cuignières but Sophie refused, knowing well what was going on in the house. Pressure was placed on her when her council asked the vicar general of the diocese and ecclesiastical superior of the house to order her to obey the doctor. Sophie had no choice but to leave Amiens. A charade was played out the night before she left, 21 July 1815. She came to the window of her room and the community and school sang her a farewell concert. Marie de la Croix composed verses, Antoinette de Gramont accompanied her on the guitar and flowers were offered by Eugénie de Gramont with wishes expressed for a speedy return. When Sophie asked to see Marie de la Croix privately after the concert, ostensibly to thank her for her verses, it was clear that Sophie was well aware of the situation in the house and that leaving under such circumstances was painful.[59] Her silence unnerved those who were working against her and they feared Sophie's power. Marie de la Croix herself saw the contradictions inherent in the actions of the women in the community. From this time while Marie de la Croix continued to attend the meetings of the inner circle, she began to question the quality and indeed the purpose of the religious life she experienced in Amiens.

As the months wore on the secret meetings became more intense. These were attended by Eugénie de Gramont, Teresa Copina, Félicité de Sambucy, Henriette Ducis, Antoinette de Gramont and Marie de la Croix. During these meetings either Eugénie de Gramont or Henriette Ducis would read and comment on the rule of Saint-Estève. They shared his letters from Rome, telling them of his plans for them, denigrating Joseph Varin with sarcastic, critical remarks about him and his role in the Association. Concretely, Saint-Estève invited them to join him and form part of the new venture in Italy. They discussed this proposition in detail and two of the little group, Copina and Sambucy, decided that they would definitely join Saint-Estève in Rome. Eugénie de Gramont facilitated their departure, convinced that she too would take the road to Rome in due time, hopefully with her sister, Antoinette de Gramont. Marie de la Croix was taken aback and asked Eugénie de Gramont if she hadever consulted her mother over such an important decision:

> My mother? she said, but her all too human love for Sophie has completely blinded her. I have done everything possible to enlighten her but have not managed to succeed. I am going to say nothing more to her but I want at least to save Antoinette.[60]

Saint-Estève's pressure on Eugénie de Gramont to join him in Rome had clearly created tension between mother and daughter. Furthermore since Madame de Gramont d'Aster had joined the community in Amiens later than Eugénie de Gramont, within the community the daughter was senior in rank to her mother. It was a strange position for both of them. In effect Eugénie de Gramont ignored her mother's opinions at this time and continued to plan her move to Rome. Indeed she proposed to Marie de la Croix that they both talk to individuals in the community and discover which of them would be ready to go to Rome. She rehearsed with Marie de la Croix what to ask and how much information to give to each one. Marie de la Croix began with an older member from Belgium, Madame Gillot,[61] who chuckled at the possibility of Sophie Barat being Gallican and she explained to the young woman what Gallicanism really entailed. She assured Marie de la Croix that Sophie was far too prudent to get involved in the debates around gallicanism and thought that the accusations against Sophie were merely a pretext to break off from the Association. She advised Marie de la Croix to extricate herself from all the intrigue around her and regain her freedom. Indeed from the autumn of 1815 Marie de la Croix was in turmoil over her future and wanted to talk to Louis Sellier, from the seminary of St Acheul nearby. This was refused. She then tried to speak to the bishop of Soissons, who had suggested initially she enter at Amiens; this too was refused. When Sophie asked that Marie de la Croix be sent to Cuignières an excuse was found to keep her in Amiens. Finally a letter came from Saint-Estève suggesting that the women travel in two groups to Rome, one by land and the other by sea. Marie de la Croix was to go by sea, with Henriette Ducis and begin the journey to Rome by first stopping at the home of Ducis's brother at Versailles. At this point Marie de la Croix knew that she would have to leave not just Amiens but the Association; she had decided to become a Carmelite in the hope of reaching peace there.[62]

In the meantime Saint-Estève's grandiose plans in Rome had not been realised. He did not succeed in procuring the Trinité des Monts in Rome but got instead the much smaller convent of St Denys aux Quatre Fontaines. By the summer of 1815 he was frantic for personnel and in desperation decided to write to Sophie Barat under a pseudonym, a last resort and ruse.[63] Calling himself Stephanelli, he urged Sophie not to resist the path God was clearly asking her to take as the leader of the Association. She and her communities in France must join the Association, approved by the pope. Failure to do so would incur excommunication of all the members of the Association in France. He suggested that she must know that many members of the Association were already planning to go Rome and unless she submitted to Saint-Estève there would be a schism. He proposed that since Saint-Estève was accepted in Rome as the lawful superior of the Association, the best way to resolve the difficulties was for Sophie Barat to resign as superior general and leave the future in the hands of Saint-Estève.

Sophie received this ultimatum in early August when she was in Cuignières, exiled there by the community in Amiens but certainly regaining strength. She told Joseph Varin about the strange letter from the unknown Stephanelli. He in turn discussed the letter with Jean Montaigne and both realised even more clearly what Sophie was carrying:

After Our Lord, who is your chief friend, I do not believe that you could find two more devoted friends, ready to do their best to share your burdens and make them easier to carry.[64]

Joseph Varin sent her a draft of a reply which she could use as a working basis for her own letter to Saint-Estève. She wrote to 'Stephanelli' on the 23 September 1815 and challenged the author of the letter to declare his identity. She remarked ironically that it could not possibly be Saint-Estève since even he could not claim so boastfully to be the founder of the Association, the author of 'splendid constitutions' (the words of Stephanelli) approved by the pope and by the congregation of bishops and religious in Rome. She admitted that she had been so taken aback by the letter that she had shared it with some colleagues. They had the same reaction. Then, pretending that she did not think it was Saint-Estève who had written the letter, she commented on Saint-Estève to the fictitious 'Stephanelli', outlining what he had done to destroy the inner unity of the Association at Amiens and her authority as superior general. Indeed, she wrote, Saint-Estève had claimed that he had received approval from the pope for his institution in Rome but had provided no documentation to prove it. In any event the Association had not authorised him to act in their name so it could not be bound by any approval Saint-Estève might have received for his foundation in Rome. If that were binding then the bizarre logic was that every religious congregation in France would be bound by Saint-Estève's institution in Rome. The truth was that the Association was not ready yet to seek approval for its constitutions in Rome. It would do so when they had more experience, had tried out their rule of life and had lived in several dioceses in France.

− 5 −

GENERAL COUNCIL, 1815

Over the months Sophie had recognised that the fundamental weakness in her position was the absence of an alternative rule of life, to counter that of Saint-Estève. Both Joseph Varin and de Clorivière had accepted that new constitutions would have to be written, but the work had not started because Sophie was too ill in the winter and spring of 1814–15. In March 1815 she had been well enough to travel to Paris to begin working on the text of the new constitutions with Joseph Varin and Julien Druilhet. This was cut short abruptly by the dramatic return of Napoleon from exile in Elba. The king, Louis XVIII, fled the city and the political situation in Paris was too volatile to continue work on the constitutions. Sophie was forced to leave Paris with the work which was so desperately needed left undone.

However, Napoleon's return to power proved short-lived. He promised a liberal constitution but failed to convince a nation weary of war. The coalition of European powers which had defeated him in 1813 and 1814 completed his downfall at Waterloo on 18 June 1815. Following his exile to the island of St Helena, the Napoleonic empire was dismantled and the Bourbons were restored to the throne of France. In the hope that political stability was assured, later in the summer of 1815 Sophie wrote to Pierre de Clorivière in Paris. She asked him to allow Joseph Varin, in addition to his commitments as a Jesuit novice, to resume work on the constitutions:

> The abuses and ills which I confided to you have not lessened. Indeed I could say that they have only increased. The most distressing of all is that several members of the Amiens community, having been sent to other houses, have brought with

them this spirit and have imperceptibly won over those who govern. This is a source of bitter pain for the [other] superiors who remain faithful to me. The remedy . . . for this germ of division, which extends to nearly all the houses, is the one that you have recognised yourself. That is: to be in a position to offer the membership constitutions drawn up according to the spirit of St Ignatius. The majority aspire to that. This work, which all constantly urge me to undertake, is the only thing which will stabilise the members, win back hearts and reunite minds. I admit that if I cannot hold on to the hope of seeing an end to our troubles soon, I do not know if I can in conscience continue to govern this association.[1]

Sophie received a prompt reply from de Clorivière and Joseph Varin. Both agreed on the gravity of the situation and invited Sophie to come to Paris as soon as she was able to travel and to bring a companion to look after her as she was still so frail in health. They assured her that her friends in Paris were ready to do all they could to help her.[2] A month later Joseph Varin wrote again and passed on the advice of her friend and counsellor, Jean Montaigne. Montaigne suggested that before going to Paris to finish the work on the constitutions and hold the general council, Sophie should visit the community in Amiens and say clearly in public that each one was free to leave the Association and join that of Saint-Estève. The same choice could be given to the other communities once the council met in Paris. However, he advised her to communicate the situation to the local bishop in each diocese, to ensure his support if there was question of needing an arbiter to decide which group owned the house and property. In other words, he feared that a schism was inevitable, that the Association was in the process of breaking up.

Indeed this view was confirmed in early September when Sophie learnt that two of the community at Amiens had left for Rome. Saint-Estève's sister, Félicité de Sambucy and Teresa Copina left on 8 September, 1815, ostensibly without saying anything to the community at Amiens, though they gave Eugénie de Gramont letters of explanation for Sophie Barat. Teresa Copina also wrote a formal letter to Eugénie de Gramont. The whole affair was a well-rehearsed charade. Eugénie de Gramont had been party to all the preparations and admitted in a letter to Sophie that she had provided both women with Saint-Estève's former servant, Leonard, as travelling companion.[3] Eugénie de Gramont also wrote a letter to Sophie, telling her of the 'surprise' she had when she saw they had left the house. Nevertheless, she told Sophie that she understood why they had gone and she hoped that soon Sophie herself would accept the wishes of the pope and join the community at St Denys in Rome:

I hope that soon we do likewise. I think . . . that this is essential. It would be a real blow if there was a schism; misfortune awaits those who do not accept the views of the pope. Moreover, do not believe that I am thinking of leaving you . . . I repeat, there is only one path ahead and that is for us all to join what you have been unable to prevent happening.[4]

Sophie herself was aware how critical the situation had become. The divisions originally contained within the community at Amiens had now spread to the other houses in France, mainly through letters and changes of personnel. Certainly the superiors and their councils in the houses had become aware of the confrontation between Saint-Estève and Sophie Barat. For a while there were at least thirty-five in Amiens ready to follow Saint-Estève. In Poitiers at least fifteen had sided with him, and from his knowledge of the situation, Joseph Varin thought the other houses would soon follow suit.[5] There had been criticism of Sophie Barat already in Poitiers, and indeed in Niort, among some of the community and among several of the local clergy. This was increased by the arrival of Anne Baudemont in the winter of 1814. She had left Amiens where the situation had become impossible for both herself and for Sophie. In the spring of 1814 Sophie agreed to let Baudemont try to found a new community in Rheims, where she had been a religious before the Revolution. By September 1814 it was clear that the project could not succeed and rather than have her return to Amiens Sophie asked her to go to Poitiers. This did not succeed either and by November 1814 Anne Baudemont asked Sophie to free her from her 'terrible prison' in Poitiers. In the spring of 1815 Sophie allowed her to renew her efforts to found a community in Rheims. This project failed again and Baudemont returned to Poitiers where she continued to be unhappy. After some months in the community she decided to separate from the Association and join Saint-Estève in Rome.[6]

Thus Sophie had every reason to worry over the situation in Poitiers and in the neighbouring community in Niort. While she was unable to visit the houses at this time her friend, Robert Debrosse, went there for her with instructions to find out what was going on in both houses and what the local clergy were thinking.[7] He discovered that two of the clergy in Poitiers were critical of Sophie and one in particular, the vicar-general of the diocese, Soyer, was actively promoting the cause of Saint-Estève. However Debrosse learnt that only a core group in the community had any idea of what was happening, but they were key people: Henriette Grosier, Catherine de Charbonnel, Lydie Chobelet and Marie Prevost. He noted some hesitations on the part of de Charbonnel, regarding her loyalty to Sophie Barat; he also noted that Marie Prevost was in touch with Soyer, though he thought it was a useful contact and probably in the interests of Sophie to encourage it. Soyer wanted to inform the entire community about the situation in the Association and Debrosse knew that this certainly would polarise the members. What none knew at the time was that Saint-Estève had written to Soyer and offered him the position of superior general of the Association in France.[8] Debrosse told Sophie that while Soyer was a powerful adversary he could be won over by flattery and attention. One member of the clergy, Jean de Beauregard, was supportive of Sophie Barat and a positive influence in the community, and he remained a faithful friend then and indeed throughout his life. Sophie's former colleague in the foundation of Poitiers, Louis Lambert, had many questions but he wrote to Sophie Barat herself and was satisfied with the answers he received. Debrosse also visited Niort and found that only four members of the community knew about the conflict with Saint-Estève and that they were loyal to Sophie Barat. Suzanne Geoffroy admitted that since Soyer had been supportive of her during a critical time in her life, she would find it hard to oppose him if a crisis arose.[9] Thus there was a holding situation in both Poitiers and Niort which could be lost if Soyer decided to speak out in public. Instead he chose to write to the pope to seek clarification regarding the position of Saint-Estève and await a reply before taking further action.[10]

At this time too Saint-Estève attempted to draw Philippine Duchesne to his side and thus influence the community of Grenoble. Soon after writing the 'Stephanelli' letter to Sophie Barat in August 1815 Saint-Estève wrote to Philippine, also under the pseudonym of 'Stephanelli' and invited her to join him Rome. He told her that Sophie Barat's refusal to join the Association founded in Rome had led to her dismissal and to the appointment of a new superior general from within the communities. He asked her to tell the community what had happened though he requested all to observe secrecy, a ploy to prevent communication with Sophie Barat. He also assured Philippine that her vocation for the missions would be easily facilitated, once she had arrived in Rome.[11] Some weeks later he wrote a second letter to Philippine Duchesne, critical of Sophie Barat and angry at her resistance to the wishes of the pope expressed in her reply to his letter of 5 August 1815. He accused her of contradictions and bad faith. He was also critical of Joseph Varin, describing him as 'the colleague of Paccanari', a term of contempt.[12] Thus, throughout the autumn of 1815 there was growing unrest in all the communities in France but most of all in Amiens. This was the outcome of nearly twelve years of continual unrest and intrigue there which reached a pitch in the period 1812–15, spreading throughout the Association and threatening to destroy it.

By mid-September Sophie had recovered her energy sufficiently to allow her to travel to Paris and to work for some weeks with Joseph Varin, Pierre de Clorivière and Julien Druilhet, preparing the new constitutions. She chose not to go to Amiens on the way to Paris, unwilling to precipitate a confrontation in the community. She decided instead to call both Eugénie de Gramont and Marie de la Croix to Paris and so remove her key opposers from the house.[13] By November 1815 the text of the new constitutions was ready to be presented to the general council of the Association and Sophie sent letters of convocation to the members chosen asking them to travel to Paris in time for the opening of the council on 1 November 1815. She convened the general council in one of the apartments in the convent of St Thomas de Villeneuve, which Madame de Gramont d'Aster had retained after her entry into the community at Amiens. The task that lay before them was to seek union and agreement. If that could be achieved in Paris then there was every hope that the divisions within the communities could be healed. The actual composition of the general council was crucial and Sophie structured that carefully.

This council was composed of two representatives of each house of the Association: the superior, in virtue of her role, and a professed member of the community, in theory the oldest, named by Sophie Barat. Grenoble was represented by Josephine Bigeu and Philippine Duchesne; Poitiers by Henriette Grosier and Catherine de Charbonnel; Niort by Suzanne Geoffroy and Emilie Giraud; Amiens by Henriette Girard and Eugénie de Gramont; Cuignières by Félicité Desmarquest and Geneviève Deshayes. These represented the oldest members of the Association, with two exceptions: in Poitiers Anne Baudemont was passed over in favour of Catherine de Charbonnel, while Eugénie de Gramont, by no means the oldest in Amiens, had to be included since Sophie knew that no union could be effected without her being present.

For over a month the members of the general council discussed the draft of the new constitutions written by Sophie Barat, Joseph Varin, Julien Druilhet and Pierre de Clorivière. The constitutions presented in Paris were influenced not just by the Jesuits but also by rules of several congregations, and certainly by the great educational orders and traditions in France, notably that of St Thomas de Villeneuve, the Ursulines and the royal school of St Cyr. While Sophie recognised that the Heart of Christ was the central focus of the Association, she readily adopted or borrowed from the educative traditions of her time.[14] Most of all the council members heard once again the story of the original impulse to found the Society of the Sacred Heart: Léonor de Tournély's dream, the evolution of the Diletti in Italy and France, the suppression of Paccanari and consequently the separation of both Amiens and Grenoble from the Diletti, followed by the efforts to find identity and unity in France.

On 17 December 1815, when elections to offices had been completed, the general council formally accepted the constitutions as their way of life. This act of acceptance by the members of the general council established the new name of the Association. It was to be called Society of the Sacred Heart of Jesus. Josephine Bigeu, Catherine de Charbonnel, and Henriette Grosier were elected assistant general to Sophie Barat; Félicité Desmarquest, Suzanne Geoffroy and Eugénie de Gramont were elected members of the general council; Philippine Duchesne was elected secretary general.[15] These were the women with whom Sophie Barat would implement the consensus they had achieved in Paris, at least on paper. Sophie Barat was confirmed as superior general for life and this necessitated the appointment of an ecclesiastical superior, to satisfy church law. This appointment was useful as it would give Sophie some independence from diocesan bishops, especially in allowing her to travel freely within dioceses and facilitate exchange of personnel between the houses. It would also help in legal negotiations with the government. The general council asked the grand aumônier of France, Mgr de Talleyrand-Périgord, to accept this office in the Society of the Sacred Heart. He agreed and delegated his secretary, Fr Perreau, to act in his name. This was a happy choice since Perreau was a good friend of Joseph Varin and had already written to Rome denouncing Saint-Estève. Talleyrand-Périgord had strong Gallican sympathies and was closely aligned to the restored Bourbons.

During the general council the issue of Saint-Estève was thoroughly debated. Indeed he had sent material for consideration.[16] Clearly, it was more the personality and the ambition and perhaps the vanity of Saint-Estève which had driven a wedge between Sophie Barat and his followers in the Association. But by the end of the council in Paris the members rejected his interventions and affirmed Sophie Barat's leadership. Sophie then sought to communicate the outcome of the council in a letter to the membership. This was the first time she had written to all the houses in her capacity as superior general and it marked the beginning of her formal assumption of authority. In this letter she outlined the purpose and the outcome of the council in Paris, and how through their deliberations the Association now had a rule of life and a new name 'Society of the Sacred Heart'. At no point in her letter did Sophie mention Saint-Estève by name.

> The task was to overcome this seed of disunity which had been growing among us for several years and which could have had disastrous consequences. All of us had to bond together and follow the same rule of life, in accordance with God's design revealed in the foundation of this little Society. The Society at its origin was essentially founded on devotion to the Heart of Jesus and must be so dedicated and consecrated to the glory of this Divine Heart that all the works and functions it undertakes are related to that chief purpose . . . such is the glorious and attractive aim of our little Society: we become holy ourselves by taking the divine Heart of Jesus as our model, trying as far as we are able to unite ourselves to his feelings and innermost dispositions; and at the same time we dedicate ourselves to extending and promoting the knowledge and love of this divine Heart by working for the sanctification of souls. . . . I repeat, this is the destiny of the Society of the Sacred Heart which God graciously revealed at our origins. And if the turbulent times during which the Society began in France did not permit us to publicly declare our consecration to the Sacred Heart of Jesus, now we believe we would be totally failing God's plan if we did not refer to the origins of the Society in order to take our true spirit and fulfil our destiny. . . . On seeing the constitutions and rules . . . you will have no difficulty in recognising that they are modelled as far as possible on those of St Ignatius, and that we have taken from them all that would suit our way of life.[17]

Sophie's letter was a clear statement of the purpose of the Society of the Sacred Heart, told officially for the first time. The story began with Léonor de Tournély, then moved to the origins of the Diletti in France until its dissolution and the consequent beginning of the Association des Dames de l'Instruction Chrétienne; the evolution continued and eventually led to the confrontation with Saint-Estève and the general council of 1815. This was the story which would be told and retold, and handed on as the origin and source of the Society of the Sacred Heart, the record of its founding myth, the initiation of a spiritual movement. Sophie signed her first letter 'Barat'. With the exception of times of political unrest when caution was needed Sophie Barat always signed her letters thus, even to very close friends. This letter of December 1815 signalled the end of a long journey for Sophie and the triumph of her hopes. Yet she was very aware that she still had to face a legacy of the years of Saint-Estève's ascendancy in Amiens, one which would not be easily modified or effaced.

During the general council in Paris Sophie wrote a letter to her old colleague in Poitiers, Louis Lambert, since he had asked her to explain why she so resolutely opposed Saint-Estève.[18] In the context of the events which happened during the Council, and aware that Saint-Estève had been exposed as a mischief maker, Sophie was free to be explicit and forthright in her letter. She summarised the problem with Saint-Estève as twofold: he wanted to change the original purpose of the Association; his manner and mode of government was unacceptable. In a long exposé Sophie showed how over a period of several years Saint-Estève had sought to change the original purpose and name of the Association and replace it with those of his own design. He had taken leadership of the community at Amiens in ways quite beyond his role as chaplain to the community and school.

Sophie admitted to Lambert that she was well aware that by her silence over many years she could be accused of having tacitly given her approval to Saint-Estève. However, in her letter to Lambert, and indeed to others at this time, she rejected this judgement of her. She argued that she had been forced to tolerate what she could not control and she did so in order to maintain peace, hoping that in time the divisions could be healed. From at least 1807 she had sensed that the situation was not healthy. Her basic instincts were correct but at that time she had no way of proving her suspicions. Indeed she told Lambert that she realised by 1813 that something concrete would have to be done to curtail the action of Saint-Estève. She had won concessions from him in 1813 and in 1814 which she had hoped would help the communities find some common ground for their future together. Yet her method of procedure did not prevent the community in Ghent severing their links with the Association in the winter of 1814. Despite this, Sophie refused to accept that her attempt to win approval for Saint-Estève's rule in the Association could be interpreted as weakness. Rather it was her role as a peacemaker and a focus for union which pushed her into such a contradictory position:

> My silence on these innovations cannot be regarded as a sign of approval. My authority over the house at Amiens was rendered ineffective because Mr de S[ambucy] took everything into his own hands there. For the sake of peace I decided to tolerate what I could not prevent, hoping that time would reconcile minds and hearts. Two years ago I believed that the moment for this had come. . . . Then, in the desire for peace, I urged all the houses to accept Mr. de S[ambucy]'s constitutions. That is why there are objections now to the opposition I have taken, as if I am contradicting myself, but my actions then [in 1813] should be seen as a painful sacrifice endured for the sake of peace.[19]

She then indicated to Lambert how the manner of Saint-Estève's government was destructive and divisive, but rather than speak of her own pain in this regard she told the story of Julie Billiart. She outlined how Saint-Estève had destroyed the work of Julie Billiart in Amiens and influenced the bishop to force her to leave the diocese. Sophie had worked closely with Julie, though they had their own tensions and difficulties, and initially Sophie did not grasp what Saint-

Estève was doing to Julie.[20] She was taken aback when Saint-Estève then insisted that the Association take over the work of Julie Billiart in Amiens, thus forcing her to collude with Saint-Estève. With hindsight, and especially with the exposure of Saint-Estève in 1815, Sophie could see clearly that what happened to Julie Billiart had been happening in slow motion to her also. She saw that from 1807 Saint-Estève had tried to take over the Association, change its nature and purpose, and that he wanted rid of her, in the same way that he had got rid of Julie Billiart and indeed of anyone who opposed him. And he had succeeded to a great degree, since he disempowered Sophie by turning most of the community in Amiens against her. As she told Lambert:

> Unfortunately there is great similarity between Saint-Estève's treatment of Julie [Billiart] and her Society and the way he has treated ours over several years. In fact he was only the confessor at Amiens. Very soon, by changing the spirit and the rule of life, he wanted to make himself the superior and the new founder of the entire Society. I did not attribute this claim to him. You will see in the letter he addressed to me under the name of Stephanelli that he claims to be the only one who can be named superior and founder of our Society. . . .what means has he used to achieve his goal? You ask for facts and these are known: he created a faction in the house at Amiens which did not recognise the authority of the superior general, and for a long time she lived in that house like a stranger.[21]

Sophie's letter to Lambert showed that by Christmas 1815 she had come through years of stress and uncertainty; she had survived a strategy of isolation and alienation, and she had achieved a clarification and definition around the Association which allowed it to name itself anew and definitely as the Society of the Sacred Heart. Though Saint-Estève's power was rejected by the general council he did not surrender his claim to be the founder of the Society. Until at least 1818 he continued to cause mischief and unrest, and he retained communication with Eugénie de Gramont for many years afterwards. He created mischief in Paris for the Society of the Sacred Heart, by accusing the Jesuits there of interfering in the life of the Society. He tried to prevent the Society of the Sacred Heart from making a foundation in Chambéry, maintaining that he was the founder and that Sophie Barat was a usurper. In 1817 de Clorivière wrote to the general of the Jesuits, outlining in detail the steps Saint-Estève had taken from 1802 to control the Dames du Sacré Coeur and destroy the power of the superior general, Sophie Barat.[22] By then, however, the authorities in Rome had recognised the ploys of Saint-Estève and in the end the pope ordered him to leave the city in the summer of 1825.[23]

In the years 1808–15 Sophie was seriously ill several times. It is not clear what those illnesses were, but the stress, strain and exhaustion of those years certainly created conditions for illnesses. In her letters at this time Sophie complained of fevers and general weariness. In 1811, a year when she suffered continually from sore eyes, Sophie went to Poitiers for the month of August, by order of the doctor, to rest and have goat's milk.[24] This seemed to help for early in 1812 she told Philippine Duchesne that she was in very good health and this was maintained throughout that year.[25] By 1813 she was ill again in Grenoble throughout the month of February. She was well looked after by Philippine Duchesne and Marie Balastron and they insisted she follow the directions of the doctor. This proved to be quite an achievement for Sophie who was very stubborn when ill and wanted to resume normal life too soon.[26]

Sophie Barat idealised the importance of fasting and found it difficult to let go of that and accept her state of health. She wanted to live common life and could not manage to do so. Joseph Varin asked her to accept that reality and to eat properly for the sake of the task she had been given. In particular Sophie found it difficult to accept that she could not fast during Lent. In Ghent in 1811, during Lent, she told the community how Joseph Varin had challenged her in public over her unwillingness to accept reality about food and fasting. Visiting a community, during Lent, she had asked to eat on her own to avoid the community seeing that she was not fasting. Joseph Varin turned up unexpectedly in the house and was shown into her room. She hid her meal under the bed but Joseph Varin saw it:

> What do I see there? But, Father. . . . I was very embarrassed . . . and I admitted as much to him . . . Father, I am not fasting. He said, how can you have such small ideas about your companions, you are afraid that they will think less of you. Come on now, call the community here. Everyone was brought to my room, even those who were with the children. . . . I certainly was very embarrassed.[27]

However embarrassing the incident was at the time, it helped Sophie to accept her limitations and it created a bridge between her private and public image which enabled her to stop concealing her frailty. Nevertheless, she had a great deal to contend with and her constant illnesses during these years point to real pressure of work and of worry. Fundamental to her illness was the effect of the regime imposed by Louis Barat in Paris which permanently damaged her digestive system. Throughout her life Sophie struggled to come to terms with that and had to accept that she would never be a physically strong leader. Her body simply collapsed under stress, especially the stress of perceiving what was wrong and yet being unable to do anything about it immediately. During long periods either in bed or confined to her room, Sophie had time to reflect, to read and to consider her next step. The illnesses, which were real, actually gave her contemplative space to work at another level and achieve insight and courage for the path ahead. At critical moments in her life Sophie Barat intuitively knew how to withdraw into her own world, even if she never consciously recognised what she was doing at the time.

Moreover, Sophie had a rich inner world to take refuge in, one which she cultivated by prayer and reading. From her letters at this time it is clear that she read the Bible regularly, especially the Canticle of Canticles from the Old Testament and the gospels and letters from the New Testament. She shared this reading with some members of the Association and in her letters alluded constantly to phrases from the Canticle. She read the mystics, St Gertrude, St

Catherine of Genoa, St Catherine of Siena, St Bernard, St Teresa of Avila and St John of the Cross. In conversations she cited St Augustine, St Francis de Sales, St Francis de Paul and St Madeleine de Pazzi. At this time of upheaval and change the Book of Revelation was central to the thinking of Pierre de Clorivière, and Sophie too was influenced by this apocalyptic literature. Clorivière lent her some of his writings and commentaries on the Book of Revelation and all her life Sophie retained an interest in apocalyptic literature.[28] In her own personal life of prayer she had a deep trust in Providence and a sense that she had a task in life given her.[29]

In addition to strengthening her own resources Sophie had forged strong relationships within the Association. Through letter-writing and visits Sophie kept in touch with individual members in a warm, personal way and gradually she created a network of friendships. As she visited the houses she had ongoing discussions with Philippine Duchesne, Thérèse Maillucheau, Henriette Grosier, Geneviève Deshayes and Suzanne Geoffroy. These conversations were continued through the medium of letters and Sophie commented on all the concerns of the Association. She wrote to Emilie Giraud and Adrienne Michel about the issues in Ghent and in Amiens, and she assured Madeleine du Chasteigner in Poitiers that the Association would certainly not take a monastic form, despite the efforts of the community at Amiens.[30] Yet at this stage in her life no one person in particular stands out as her closest friend and confidante. Indeed Teresa Copina had described Sophie as a shrewd woman, who kept her counsel and played her cards carefully, rarely expressing her thoughts: 'she is a profoundly astute woman; she never says what she thinks and pretends to have feelings she does not possess!'[31] Sophie's reticent power coupled with her natural charm and attractive manner were a powerful combination and one which few could resist. She had both distance and closeness in her presence and she could speak without self-disclosure.

By the close of 1815 Sophie Barat possessed the means to draw the members of the Society of the Sacred Heart together in unity. The original insight of Léonor de Tournély, that of a group of women devoted to the Heart of Christ and working in the field of education, had been retrieved. New constitutions had been written, voted and accepted by the representatives of the congregation. Sophie's own authority had been confirmed and she had a governing body, voted and accepted, whose task was to work with her in governing the congregation. In reality it was a new phase in the evolution of a group of women whose lives had touched over fifteen years, whose stories affected one another and whose memories held the record of the years. Each brought to the newly named and newly defined congregation their own history of why they had joined in the first place as well as the motivation for staying within it now.

By 1815 there were 108 women in the Sociey of the Sacred Heart and the average age was thirty-nine.[32] Such growth testified to steady development over fifteen years, no mean achievement in the turbulent times of the French Revolution and subsequent rise and demise of Napoleon. There were sixty-two

professed members, forty-four were teaching sisters and eighteen were domes-
tic/coadjutrix sisters; forty-six had completed initial training and were awaiting
final profession, while seventeen novices and seven postulants were in formation. The geographical and social background of these women was varied: they
originated from all parts of France, from the rural areas and classes; from artisan
and petit bourgeois families, from middle-class families of town and country,
from the court nobility and from the landed nobility. The marked class distinctions which obtained later in the communities had not fully emerged yet and
there was a certain fluidity in the designation to teaching or domestic work.

In the early days in Poitiers there was little distinction of function within the
community:

> Lay sisters were not very numerous in the early days. Their work had to be done
> as well as the other tasks which each member of the community was named to do
> in the house.[33]

By 1814 roles and functions within the communities were being defined more
quickly and those who entered were being placed according to their natural gifts,
either to work within the community and school as domestic servants, or to work
within the school as teachers. In 1814 Sophie wrote to Emilie Giraud at Niort:

> You ask for three class teachers immediately, saying that you have only lay sisters
> which adds to your overwork. Three teachers all at once. That's a tall order! You
> know . . . class teachers are not trained in dozens! I hope that Madame Grosier will
> be able to send you one and later we will prepare another for you. . . . You have only
> lay sisters in your house. That is true and it is a great abuse which you will experi-
> ence even more later on. From now on you see how wrong it is to accept more lay
> sisters than you need; this must be avoided. I see very clearly from your work list
> that you are all overworked.[34]

The women who wished to enter the Association sought a life of prayer and
service within the community. They discovered the Association in a variety of
ways. Sometimes they had heard about it from friends and often Joseph Varin himself, Saint-Estève or some of the Fathers of the Faith advised women to join one
of the communities. As the work of the Association developed and schools grew
in number, so did the need for teachers and for domestic help to see to the running of the kitchen, the laundry, the infirmary in each house. Gradually a division
between intellectual work and manual work was created and, since the members
of the community mirrored society in general, manual work became devalued. In
the Association this became even more emphasised as it became increasingly identified with aristocratic and wealthy bourgeois families in France and beyond.

When the Jesuits were restored in France Pierre de Clorivière wrote to the
general of the Jesuits indicating that he had accepted a good number of Jesuit
brothers into the order. He explained that brothers were needed in the schools
to do the domestic work, to give good example. Besides it was dangerous to
employ secular help at this time. The restoration of the Jesuits was momentous
enough and the less people knew about their lives then the more secure they

were. Yet de Clorivière received a sharp rebuke from the general who told him not to use the Jesuit brothers in the schools as domestic servants. He insisted that that the number of brothers in each community should be few and that they should be quite distinct from the domestic servants in the house. The goal was to have a few brothers in every community and as many domestic helpers as needed. De Clorivière was disappointed at this directive and complained that it was extremely difficult to get domestic help in France at that time, 'given the general demoralisation of that class in society'. It was expensive to hire them, hard to train and then keep them, and those who stayed often asked to enter with the Jesuits.[35] Sophie Barat did not have the resources and experience of the Jesuits at this time; nor did she have the finances to employ women as domestic servants in the communities and schools. However, she was aware even at this early stage that the balance in the numbers between coadjutrix sisters and teaching sisters was important.

The years 1800–15 saw the gradual emergence of a clash of consciousness between monastic models of religious life and other, more mobile, forms. This newer consciousness was influenced by the Jesuit rule which represented a different form of religious life for men, established in the sixteenth century by Ignatius of Loyola. Women were attracted to this as an alternative form of religious life which offered greater mobility and ease of contact with society. It represented new possibilities which Sophie Barat readily recognised. In her letter to Lambert in December 1815, Sophie complained that one of the problems with Saint-Estève was the number of former religious he accepted. She saw this as damaging the new initiatives she wished to take:

> All former members of religious congregations are accepted in his house. Yet he knows quite well that in the Society we believe that, while not excluding [such religious] . . . we need to exercise great caution in admitting them. You will readily understand . . . that a house open to receive religious from all the orders could not preserve its own spirit for long.[36]

Yet the Society of the Sacred Heart had been forged in this struggle between old and new forces, and most of those affected quite profoundly by Saint-Estève remained in the Society after 1815. Sophie Barat had to deal with this throughout her life, either consciously or unconsciously. In the end the Society of the Sacred Heart was a blend of the old and new, and over the next fifty years Sophie placed her stamp on the congregation. The number of disputes and divisions she dealt with during her years in office attest to the fundamental differences which existed at the heart of the congregation from the beginning. In the Society of the Sacred Heart Sophie herself would be the focus for unity but also the butt of criticism. Her leadership role and style kept the Society together, and while there were times when it almost fell apart and disintegrated, yet it survived. As she picked up the threads after the general council of 1815 Sophie Barat began her long term of office which formed and shaped her personally and facilitated an extraordinary flowering of women's communities in France and beyond.

While the general council had managed to distance itself from Saint-Estève and reach consensus on new constitutions, the minds and hearts of many in Paris and in the communities had yet to be won over. A vision for the future had been articulated by four people, Sophie Barat, Joseph Varin, Julien Druilhet and Pierre de Clorivière. It was Sophie's task to ensure that this vision was communicated to members of the Society of the Sacred Heart in such a way that each could recognise the inspiration for her own life and commitment within the group. By Christmas 1815 Sophie had initiated this process by her letter to all the communities and in time she would visit each of the houses. However, even before the opening of the general council in November 1815, Sophie had anticipated that the work of winning hearts and minds would be difficult everywhere but especially so in Amiens. She knew that if she was to create the conditions for unity and peace there she had to establish her ascendancy over Eugénie de Gramont and Marie de la Croix. Both were influential, although Eugénie de Gramont had a more public profile in view of her seniority in the community. Before convening the general council in Paris in 1815 Sophie had recognised that it was crucial to have Eugénie de Gramont publicly on her side. To ensure this she asked Eugénie join her in Paris some days before the opening of the council and suggested she bring Marie de la Croix as her travelling companion. On the journey to Paris Eugénie de Gramont warned Marie de la Croix to watch her words carefully and to give no hint to Sophie that they were planning to join Saint-Estève in Rome. For her part, Marie de la Croix had already decided to tell neither Sophie Barat nor Eugénie de Gramont that she was planning to leave the Association altogether.

Going to Paris was a watershed for Marie de la Croix. Her old friend and counsellor, Pierre Ronsin,[37] had written to her in Amiens. He had prepared Marie de la Croix as a young adult for baptism and later he suggested she enter the community at Amiens and he knew that serious problems had arisen there. He had heard about the stance Marie de la Croix had taken in the community and he wanted to know why she had chosen to follow Saint-Estève rather than Sophie Barat. Recognising that this letter presented a possible escape for her, Marie de la Croix replied and asked Ronsin to explain to Sophie that she needed a quiet place in Paris to make a retreat and think out her future. Sophie accepted this request and arranged for her to stay with the Visitation community on the rue des Postes, while the general council of the Association was in session. Marie de la Croix had barely arrived at the Visitation convent when Pierre Ronsin called to see her. She found herself unable to speak to him openly, other than that she had decided to become a Carmelite. Realising that he could not help her then, Ronsin asked her to see Joseph Varin. She agreed although she did not know Joseph Varin at all and anything she had heard about him in Amiens was negative.

Yet from Joseph Varin Marie de la Croix heard the story of the origins of the Association, a story which been silenced in Amiens. Varin went back to the beginning and told her the story of Léonor de Tournély, of his vision of a congregation of men and women devoted to the Heart of Christ. He explained

Sophie Barat's place in the story as well as her task in governing the Society. He exposed the reality behind the projects Saint-Estève was devising in Rome. Joseph Varin left Marie de la Croix with plenty to think about and after some days' reflection she realised that she wanted to remain with Sophie Barat. But she had one final query regarding Sophie personally. This was a delicate issue (at least for Marie de la Croix), and one we still do not have information on. Whatever it was it had to be resolved before she could in good conscience commit herself fully to the Society of the Sacred Heart. Again she found it hard to talk to Ronsin about this and asked to go to confession to Joseph Varin. Her worry concerned Sophie Barat herself. In reply to her query Joseph Varin commented:

> Sophie [your mother] has made the vow of Saint Teresa. Since she has the obligation to follow the way of perfection, how could she have meant what you understood her to have said[?][38]

This is a mysterious phrase and it is has not been possible yet to discover what Marie de la Croix was worried about. Sophie had taken the vow of St Teresa of Avila, to do the most perfect thing in all circumstances. Perhaps Sophie Barat had behaved or spoken in a way that shocked Marie de la Croix to such a degree that she felt she could not accept her leadership. In another account of the same incident, Marie de la Croix noted that Joseph Varin resolved her questions concerning Sophie Barat and that out of respect and love for Sophie she had resolved never to speak of it again.[39] Her difficulties about Sophie resolved, Marie de la Croix, in a moment of fervour and without consulting anyone, made a vow of perfection. When Pierre Ronsin discovered this, he reprimanded her sharply for acting so impetuously. But the damage had been done and somehow Saint-Estève heard about it. He used this as an excuse to complain about Ronsin to the general of the Jesuits. Pierre de Clorivière wrote to Brzozowski, in defence of Pierre Ronsin's direction of Marie de la Croix. He explained Ronsin's role in her life, from her conversion and baptism until her entry into the community at Amiens:

> Impetuously, in a moment of unusual fervour, she made a number of rash vows to God, striving for what she imagined to be the most perfect state. She was reprimanded for this by Fr Ronsin who undertook to confer with the vicars general and other well known, distinguished clerics. Following these consultations, the letter which Fr Ronsin wrote to MM [Marie de la Croix] contained nothing unusual, despite what Mr de Sambucy claims.[40]

Marie de la Croix remained at the Visitation convent for two weeks after which period Eugénie de Gramont went to see her on her own, to discover the outcome of her reflection. When she learnt that Marie de la Croix had decided to stay with Sophie, Eugénie de Gramont told her that she too had resolved not to follow Saint-Estève to Rome. She had come to this decision after a long talk with Gaston de Sambucy Saint-Estève, the brother of Saint-Estève.[41] Gaston de Sambucy had prepared Eugénie de Gramont for her first communion and he was in an excellent position to speak frankly to her about his brother and warn her against leaving for Rome. He convinced Eugénie de Gramont that she should not go to Rome either then or ever.

Both women, for different reasons, had decided not to proceed with their plans to join Saint-Estève. While Eugénie de Gramont said nothing at all either to Sophie or to her colleagues in Paris, Marie de la Croix told Sophie of her decision immediately and asked to make her vows. Pierre Ronsin was aware of the damage the inner circle of women had done in Amiens and he thought that before her vows Marie de la Croix needed to acknowledge her part in damaging the reputation and character of Sophie. He insisted that she write to those in Amiens who had been aware of her activity and try to undo some of the harm. In response to his demand, Marie de la Croix wrote a detailed account of her actions in Amiens. In a burst of remorse she fell into the trap of taking full responsibility upon herself for everything that had taken place in the community and named no one else. Then something happened which scarred Marie de la Croix for life. She showed her letter of self-accusation to Ronsin who decided to read it out to Sophie when, accompanied by Eugénie de Gramont, she arrived at the Visitation convent to bring Marie de la Croix back to St Thomas de Villeneuve. In the course of this dramatic reading Marie de la Croix was profoundly upset and broke down in tears. Sophie responding to her evident stress, reached out and let her know that she forgave her. What disturbed Marie de la Croix most of all then was that Eugénie de Gramont remained totally silent throughout that meeting:

> This was one of the worst moments of my life. I am sure that even Fr Ronsin himself regretted putting us both through such torture. And Madame de Gramont, who was present, must have suffered greatly herself, knowing well the role she had in it, and she must have feared being compromised at any moment. I said nothing about her. At that moment nature was stronger than grace. She had not got the courage to utter even the slightest word to ease my predicament and I drank the cup of suffering alone, to the dregs.[42]

Sophie was quite aware of the role and influence played by Eugénie de Gramont in Amiens. Yet she did not speak out that day either. Perhaps she did not yet know of the extent of Eugénie de Gramont's collusion with Saint-Estève. Maybe she did know about it and decided not to humiliate her in the presence of Marie de la Croix. She may also have sensed the journey Eugénie de Gramont would have to make, not just with her but with the community at Amiens, would in the long run entail a bigger loss of face perhaps than that of Marie de la Croix. The general council was at a critical stage and during one of its final sessions Eugénie de Gramont had been elected as one of the three general councillors to Sophie Barat. Even then Eugénie had not spoken publicly of her decision to uphold Sophie Barat and accept the new constitutions proposed in Paris. Josephine Bigeu wrote to Madame de Gramont d'Aster on 20 December 1815 that 'Madame Eugénie has not yet spoken frankly to our Mother'. Thus, even at the end of the general council in Paris Sophie was not sure where Eugénie de

Gramont really stood with regard to the Society of the Sacred Heart. Apparently Fr Soyer had written to Eugénie de Gramont and told her about the letters he had received from authorities in Rome, unmasking Saint-Estève. Yet she still held back and Sophie remarked in a letter to Soyer 'Madame de Gramont, enlightened by your recent letters seems to be ready to join us'.[43] So there was a cloud of uncertainty around her which Sophie may not have known how to dispel just then. In this context Sophie could not confront Eugénie de Gramont with the truth of her own actions.

Marie de la Croix's confusion was compounded some days later when in the course of a ceremony all the religious present publicly accepted the new constitutions and rules. This included a public act of acceptance of Sophie Barat as the superior general. Marie de la Croix was stunned to see Eugénie de Gramont take part in the ceremony and accept her own election to a position of trust: 'I was surprised to see Madame de Gramont accept this, for I considered her to be much more responsible than I was in the whole affair [at Amiens].'[44] The effect of Eugénie de Gramont's betrayal and dishonesty, both in private and then in public, remained with Marie de la Croix for life. Out of loyalty to Sophie she never spoke of it in public and wrote her pain down in 1872/3 when Sophie was dead and even then only in response to a formal request for memoirs of Sophie Barat. Marie de la Croix had to watch the friendship of Sophie Barat and Eugénie de Gramont grow over many years. She witnessed the very public and generally successful profile of Eugénie de Gramont in Paris, and yet she had knowledge she could not share with anyone. Her only and essential link with sanity was her relationship with Sophie and when this was gone, after Sophie's death in 1865, there were no bonds left within which she could hold secrets. In the final years of her life the old pain emerged. No one could understand the wanderings of her mind. Adèle Lehon, the superior general at the time, recorded that Marie de la Croix spoke of the pain of being used and how she kept repeating that she had been the victim of superiors. Her friend and confessor in Bordeaux took her accounts seriously and after her death published them in four volumes, without the knowledge of the Society of the Sacred Heart. These volumes were considered to be so damaging to the Society of the Sacred Heart and to the reputation of Sophie Barat that they were ordered to be destroyed.[45] The central government of the Society feared that if the books became public the beatification process for Sophie Barat would be interrupted, if not terminated. Marie de la Croix had too many secrets to hold. In 1815 she had gone to Paris, to make a retreat and find her own integrity and she had left there to begin a double life. To be betrayed at twenty-one in a such a public way, by a key member of the Society of the Sacred Heart, was profoundly disturbing and ultimately it led to the disintegration of Marie de la Croix.

However, at twenty-one her life lay before her. She went back with Sophie and Eugénie to the convent of St Thomas de Villeneuve where the general council was completing its work.[46] Sometime over that Christmas in Paris Eugénie de Gramont finally did speak frankly to Sophie telling her that she had decided not to join Saint-Estève in Rome and that she would form part of the newly named Society of the Sacred Heart. She also wrote a letter to the community in Amiens and told them that Saint-Estève had not received approval for his association in Rome and that she fully accepted the work of the general council. This was a courageous act and made Sophie's return to Amiens easier, for with Eugénie de Gramont publicly on her side she could begin the work of reconciliation there. Eugénie de Gramont also had the courage to precede Sophie's arrival in Amiens and prepare the way for her return. While Madame de Gramont d'Aster was delighted with her daughter's decision, Eugénie's sister, Antoinette de Gramont, was furious and accused Eugénie of capitulation. For a time she refused to make her final commitment to the Society of the Sacred Heart.[47] Some in the community accepted that they had been mistaken in their views of Saint-Estève and indeed of Sophie Barat; others were so angry with Eugénie de Gramont that they refused to listen to her and studiously avoided her in the house; two of the community wrote to Rome asking for written proof that Saint-Estève's association had not been authorised and that the newly named Society of the Sacred Heart had approval from Rome.[48]

Sophie and Marie de la Croix arrived in Amiens on 23 January 1816 and Sophie certainly was under no illusion about the difficulty of the task ahead. Marie de la Croix thought that there would be few members left in the house, for she was convinced that many had left for Rome. In fact no one had left, indicating that it was the sense of drama and secrecy which had created the impression, even the illusion of numerous, imminent departures. This made Sophie's task even more difficult since those who opposed her for years were still there. Her old friend Madame de Gramont d'Aster was her greatest ally; she welcomed her back warmly and recorded the process of reconciliation initiated by Sophie on her return. She was systematic: for the first few days she held no community meetings, but chose to speak privately to individuals. In reality there was little she could say in public to a community so divided. Some were relieved that the crisis was over, and were happy to talk to Sophie; others wanted to talk to her but could not bring themselves to do it; and some deliberately avoided her.[49]

After five days of working with individuals, Sophie decided to have a community meeting and during it she pointed out how far the members of the community were from living the kind of life they had chosen with such idealism. It was a firm, if gently delivered rebuke to all. She asked for no public discussion, but rather an inner recognition on the part of each one as to where she stood in her spiritual commitment. She gave an account of the work completed in Paris by the general council: the acceptance of the constitutions, the elections to offices in the Society and the choice of the name, Society of the Sacred Heart. She proposed a process for the community: that they all make a novena in honour of the Heart of Jesus and Mary and in the course of the nine days consider the new constitutions. On the second day the confessor, Fr Dubas, came to the house for the weekly confessions of the community. By this time individuals were so challenged and disturbed that individual confessions lasted more than an hour and all were completed only after three days. Throughout this time Sophie continued with the reading and commentary on the new constitutions and by the end of the novena the entire community had spoken to her in private and acknowledged her as the lawful superior general.

However the next step – when formal acceptance of the new constitutions would be made by each member in public – was more delicate. Sophie Barat's authority in the Society of the Sacred Heart had to be publicly accepted by the members individually. Prior to proceeding to this stage Sophie paid a visit to the bishop of Amiens, Jean-François Demandolx (1804–1819). No friend of Saint-Estève's, the bishop was relieved that the divisive situation in Amiens had been resolved. He formally approved the constitutions and accepted Sophie Barat as the legal superior general of the Society of the Sacred Heart. Once this had been confirmed Sophie then suggested that the community make a retreat in preparation for the commitment each would take to live by the new constitutions. She gave a conference each evening during the retreat while Fr Dubas gave two talks during the day. One evening, as Sophie stood up to leave the conference room, one of the community publicly asked her pardon for the manner in which she had been treated in Amiens over the years. The tension was broken at last that evening and the rest of the community also asked forgiveness. Sophie was so taken aback that she had to sit down again and it became clear to all present that she was deeply moved. Only then did the community glimpse some of the pain inflicted by the coldness and antipathy shown her over the years. She responded finally by saying that she did forgive and accept them, and that it was time old wounds were healed. They embraced one another and a sense of joy and release pervaded the house. A great burden had been lifted from everyone. By carefully planning the process of reconciliation, Sophie herself had broken through into the hearts of the community and created warmth and life and a sense of hope for the future.

Sophie Barat had resolved the profound divisions in Amiens by presenting the community with a vision of life that resonated with each one's idealism and transcended all their real differences. Again and again she presented the story of the origins of the Society of the Sacred Heart, speaking of the spirituality of the Heart of Christ as the centre and focus for unity. She did it in an attractive, convincing and inspiring way, communicating the spiritual end and purpose of their lives as central to the work of education. She had the gift and the capacity to win hearts and minds and this time in Amiens she had the authority to transform the situation. More at peace and ease with themselves and with one another, the members of the community were ready after this process of reconciliation to commit themselves to the Society of the Sacred Heart and to accept Sophie Barat as leader. For some more days Sophie continued to instruct the community each day on the new constitutions and to consolidate the inner life of the community. The formal ceremony of commitment was carried out on 29 February 1816, signalling the end of the crisis in Amiens, the resolution of years of division.[50]

Sophie was careful to involve Eugénie de Gramont in all the tasks she undertook in Amiens at this time, giving public proof of her trust and confidence.
There was a certain symbolism throughout this period in that Sophie Barat gathered the hearts and minds of individuals and Eugénie de Gramont taught the
community to sing office and perform religious ceremonies, tending to the outward, public presentation of the Society of the Sacred Heart. Sophie's manner
of reconciling minds and hearts in Amiens provides an insight into her style of
leadership. She set about her task quite methodically and with great deliberation. There was no doubt in her own mind of the goal she wished to achieve and
she reached it slowly. Her approach was based on personal relationships, on
speaking the truth directly to another, and then trusting the integrity of the
person, their own inner light and honesty. Once she had done that she respected each one's personal, spiritual journey. It was effective, especially in Amiens
in 1816. It could look weak and hesitant, especially to those who looked to
another, more aggressive model of leadership. As Teresa Copina had remarked
to Marie de la Croix, Sophie Barat was a shrewd woman and she grasped the
measure of what she could or could not do in a given situation. Essentially, it was
the art of the possible, down to earth, pragmatic and effective, rooted in common
sense and her own deep religious commitment.

It was this quality of leadership which won acceptance in Amiens. Many in
the community came from the court or landed nobility, or from wealthy bourgeois families. Sophie Barat was from a different milieu, a sturdy, respectable
and comfortable background, but nevertheless definitely petit bourgeois. For
Sophie to return to Amiens and implement a radical reform in the community
required courage and insight on her part, but it also required recognition on the
part of the community that Sophie held the spiritual authority to do it. At any
other level many in the community in Amiens could not have accepted Sophie's
role in the Society. Her style of leadership freed them to continue on their own
inner journey. But it was more than that. At the level of her own inner world of
prayer, the style she assumed reflected the warmth of heart she drew from her
understanding of the Heart of Christ, as well as a strong reliance on the best intuition and integrity of each person.

Whereas in Amiens Sophie had no difficulty in having the constitutions of
1815 accepted by the bishop, the response in the diocese of Poitiers was different. On her return from the general council in Paris, Henriette Grosier had given
Fr Soyer a copy of the constitutions and had asked him and the other vicars general of the diocese to accept them as the authentic voice of the newly named
Society of the Sacred Heart. In response, the vicars general of Poitiers drew up
a statement on 16 January 1816 which criticised the 1815 constitutions on several points. Most of them concerned the authority of the local bishop over religious communities, but it was clear that Soyer in particular resented the
independent stance the Society had taken.[51] Whereas by the winter of 1815
Soyer had realised that Saint-Estève had had no right to offer him the role of
superior general of the then Association des Dames de l'Instruction Chrétienne,

he did consider that he had authority over the houses in Poitiers and Niort. This had been confirmed in a letter from the French ambassador to the Holy See, in December 1815.[52] That letter had been accompanied by one from Saint-Estève warning Soyer that the general council in Paris would try to remain exempt from the authority of the local bishop over their communities.[53] Perhaps Soyer remembered a conversation he had with Sophie Barat in 1806 when she arrived to establish the community in Poitiers. The vicars general of that time, Soyer, Pradel and Beauregard, asked Sophie to clarify where the centre of the Association (the mother house) was to be situated. She led them then to believe that Poitiers would be her preferred option, though she warned that she would have to travel a great deal. It was a diplomatic answer to a potential conflict of power and control. She had already hinted to the bishop of Grenoble that his diocese was her preferred option, for he had asked the same question. Whereas in 1806 this question was very theoretical for Sophie, by 1815 there were five houses of the Society and more were being planned.

In addition to these difficulties, the idea of a community of women having a superior general for life challenged the customary hold that local bishops and priests had over communities of women in their dioceses and parishes. Moreover, a woman who exercised the role of superior general for life could be viewed as potentially far too independent in comparison to the role women generally exercised in society. A superior general could visit communities all over the country, make personnel changes between the houses of the congregation, effect changes in policy, without the express authority of the local bishop. She had, at least potentially, the power of a medieval abbess, not just over one community, but over clusters of communities, in different dioceses. Even abbesses did not effect changes of personnel between houses, nor did they regularly visit communities. Thus in Poitiers in 1816 the traditional clerical power and control over women's religious communities was at stake. This was enshrined in church law and indeed by the general laws of society whereby all women had of necessity to have a male figure in control of them: father, brother, husband, guardian. The vicars general sensed that the new constitutions of the Society of the Sacred Heart represented a system which would take power from them. That the decisions of a general council, held in another diocese (in this case, Paris), could be binding in Poitiers was a new concept for these clergy and one they resisted. The ordinance of January 1816 contained their objections and Henriette Grosier sent it to Fr Perreau asking for advice on how to deal with it.

When Sophie arrived for a short stay in Paris she and Perreau discussed how best to reply to the vicars general of Poitiers. They agreed that they had to take a strong stand in this situation, for if every bishop or diocesan authority wanted to adapt the 1815 constitutions then the unity of the Society of the Sacred Heart would easily be fragmented. Besides, the ordinance from the vicars general could be used to divide the community at Poitiers. In his capacity as ecclesiastical superior general of the Society, Perreau replied to Grosier's request for advice, clearly supporting the 1815 constitutions in their entirety. He noted that if the local clergy disapproved of some parts of the constitutions they were free to do so, but they could not block the work of a general council. They could allow the constitutions to be lived in their diocese without having to approve of every article. However if they chose to forbid a community to live the constitutions, or part of them, then the community would leave and go where they could live by the 1815 constitutions. By the same token, if members of the community at Poitiers were not at ease with the 1815 constitutions they too were free to leave and find their future elsewhere. It was a strong, clear letter of support for the Society. Besides, Perreau was aware that there were links between Soyer and Saint-Estève, though he may not have known then that Saint-Estève had offered the role of ecclesiastical superior general to Soyer, a role that was given to Perreau at the general council in Paris.[54] And indeed there were divisive elements in the community at Poitiers and until the summer of 1816 Anne Baudemont was still a member of the community. By stating the freedom either to accept or reject the 1815 constitutions, on the part of the local clergy or the community, Perreau effectively cut off the possibility of collusion between the two parties.

In her capacity as superior of Poitiers, Henriette Grosier was the focus of Soyer's criticism and she left him in no doubt about the position of the Society of the Sacred Heart. The issue of the 1815 constitutions was complicated by a personality clash between them which made communications difficult. Henriette Grosier wrote to Soyer on 23 February 1816, conveying the contents of Perreau's letter. Soyer was furious and countered by threatening to withdraw personally from all involvement with the community at Poitiers. This was potentially serious, for Soyer's role vis à vis the community had legal implications in so far as he acted in the name of the bishop and his co-operation was needed to fulfil the local, legal requirements of government and church authorities. No community could ignore that reality.[55] Thus Soyer's threat was a ploy to provoke a reaction, not just from Henriette Grosier but also from Sophie Barat. Some weeks later Sophie wrote to pacify Soyer and persuade him not to withdraw his support from the community and indeed from the Society of the Sacred Heart. She knew very well that tensions existed between Henriette Grosier and Soyer; she also knew that he had no such difficulties in Niort where his old friendship with Suzanne Geoffroy ensured that some mutual understanding could be reached. Indeed, Soyer had visited Niort and accepted the same constitutions without difficulty. However Sophie expressed the hope that the differences between Grosier and Soyer could be resolved:

> I do not doubt that the frank and clear discussions which Madame Grosier has had with you will have dispersed the clouds which threatened the union and harmony. Harmony should characterise your relations since both of you have such noble aims to do good.[56]

She asked him to reconsider his threat to withdraw from the community, if only out of consideration of the old friendship they had had from the early days in Poitiers. She outlined some of her plans for the future, asked his opinion on them and indicated that she would visit Poitiers soon and all could be smoothed out then. She picked her words carefully: having emerged from one prolonged crisis with Saint-Estève she could not afford to begin another with Soyer. She also knew that Soyer was in touch with church authorities in Rome. Anything adverse in Poitiers could be reported to Saint-Estève who would try anything to regain his position of power. Nevertheless she in no way compromised Henriette Grosier and when Soyer implied further criticism of her in his reply to Sophie, she defended Grosier and deflected the criticism on to herself. However, it was clear that the strain was telling on Henriette Grosier and Sophie decided that Grosier should leave Poitiers, for a short time, to relieve the situation.

During a visit to Poitiers in May 1816 Sophie met Soyer and in a frank exchange she managed to smooth out any remaining problems. The situation was further eased by the departure of Anne Baudemont, who had finally decided to join Saint-Estève in Rome. Using the fact that she needed a superior for Amiens, Sophie appointed Henriette Grosier to this office and replaced her in Poitiers with Catherine de Charbonnel.[57] Soon after Sophie's visit to Poitiers, Soyer received a letter from the pope confirming that Saint-Estève had received no authorisation either to found the house in Rome, St Denys aux Quatre Fontaines or to govern the Association in France.[58] Tension finally eased in Poitiers when Soyer was named bishop of Luçon in 1817 and so moved to the neighbouring diocese, an altogether easier situation for the Society of the Sacred Heart. To his credit Soyer remained a faithful supporter of the Society and of Sophie Barat. In 1818 he defended Sophie in a difficult situation in Chambéry, engineered by Saint-Estève and Anne Baudemont, their last effort to regain control over Sophie Barat and the former members of the Association des Dames de l'Instruction Chrétienne.

If her handling of the community at Amiens showed how Sophie Barat could deal with internal problems within communities, the manner in which she resolved the potentially damaging situation with the clergy in Poitiers displayed her skill in dealing with authorities outside the Society of the Sacred Heart. She had taken advice from Fr Perreau on how to act and was able to adapt it as it suited her. The style was her own and she managed to blend the capacity to compromise (what she called 'for the sake of peace'), with maintaining her long-term goal and vision. Thus she genuinely did consult Soyer on some issues of no great importance within the Society, clearly more to smooth ruffled feathers than allow him power within the congregation. His later boast to his friends that Sophie Barat consulted him on matters pertaining to the congregation indicated that she had achieved what she wanted. Again and again in the course of life, and in her leadership of the Society of the Sacred Heart, Sophie Barat exercised the art of compromise and in this way she negotiated her way around intractable situations or intransigent people. She rarely confronted directly and when she did it rarely worked for her. She learnt that she had a gift for persuasion, a way of winning people, of creating bonds of affection and friendship, and she had discovered that she could use that gift to further her own aims for the Society and avoid making enemies.

The first six months of 1816 were an intense and busy time for a woman who had been so ill the year before. She collapsed with exhaustion after her visit to Poitiers where she had spent so much time and energy sorting out the problems there:.

> Everywhere there is work to do and everywhere I suffer from my little illnesses. At Poitiers, Niort and Bordeaux I was almost continually in pain. When I arrived in Paris, after a difficult night journey by coach, shivering and thirsty from fever, I went straight to bed. I could do no work for a week. That is how my life is, almost all the time.[59]

But these months after the general council of 1815 were also energising for Sophie Barat. Letters and news from Rome continued to confirm the church's rejection of Saint-Estève's claims over the Society of the Sacred Heart,[60] and this served to consolidate Sophie's authority both within and without the Society. For his part Fr Perreau exercised his role of ecclesiastical superior general clearly and positively. He advised Sophie, either through letters or meetings, while recognising the latitude she needed to deal with the reality on the ground. She had gained a new relationship with Joseph Varin, who in the course of 1815 had seen Sophie really for the first time in her own light and strength. In February 1816 he ended a letter to her:

> You know what I mean to you, because to me you are mother, sister and daughter. My feelings tell me this and they are summed up in this single word: Your very devoted in our Lord Jesus Christ, Joseph.[61]

Once the major difficulties had been resolved in Amiens and Poitiers, Sophie had other tasks to address during these months. Her role as superior general had to be further strengthened. To that purpose Fr Perreau advised her to remove Eugénie de Gramont as superior in Amiens. Madame de Gramont d'Aster agreed with this, more from the point of view of her daughter's health, never very robust and under strain for some months. Linked with this proposal, in Sophie's mind, was the presence of Marie de la Croix in Amiens. When the community, originally established in Cuignières in 1808, was transferred to Beauvais, early in 1816, Sophie sent Marie de la Croix there, to prepare for the official opening of the house and to work in the school.[62] The removal of Eugénie de Gramont was more delicate, for she was in charge of the novices and the school, and if Sophie was absent she replaced her as superior of the house. Sophie had not changed any of Eugénie's roles in the house after the general council. While this was an act of trust on Sophie's part it was also a gamble. Yet just then Sophie could do little else, at least until the situation in the house had become calmer. Besides, Sophie was getting to know Eugénie de Gramont in some depth and she was learning to trust her, and to appreciate her qualities of leadership. She told Thérèse Maillucheau in April 1816 how much she admired Eugénie de Gramont's fine spirit.[63] For her part, Eugénie de Gramont appeared to have changed and to regret her previous actions. While Perreau recognised that Eugénie de Gramont and her sister, Antoinette (with some reluctance), had accepted the 1815 constitutions and the leadership of Sophie Barat, he was still much more wary of both of them than Sophie. His point was that the superior in Amiens should be someone who had always remained loyal to Sophie Barat, and he suggested that Eugénie de Gramont be replaced by Josephine Bigeu.[64] In that way Sophie could leave Amiens with a free mind and concentrate on her task of governing the Society.

Indeed Sophie had come to a decision regarding her own future residence. She had come to the conclusion that while Amiens was the cradle of the Society it could not be its centre in the future. Too many painful things had happened there and both she and the Society needed a change of focus to symbolise a new direction. Early in 1816, even while engaged in the task of establishing peace in Amiens and in Poitiers, Sophie began looking for suitable accommodation in Paris, for a noviciate and for a school. She had decided that the capital would be the centre of the Society of the Sacred Heart, giving her and indeed all the membership a fresh start. Yet it was much more than that. This was a dramatic period in the history of France, with all eyes focused on the capital. Paris in 1816 belonged to Counter-Revolutionaries. In their view there was much to do in the field of education, in the task of restoring what had been lost, destroyed and devalued in the course of the Revolution and the Napoleonic Empire. Thus, by choosing to go to Paris at this time, Sophie was identifying the Society of the Sacred Heart very closely with the politics of the day. Her friend, Fr de Lamarche, the former chaplain to the Carmelites of Compiègne who were guillotined during the Terror, identified the role of the Society of the Sacred Heart as renewing the values of religion in society:

> This is what I mean: I am your Society's oldest friend. Before its birth I gave all the encouragement possible to such a Society. I have followed all its developments. I have wept for all the tribulations it has endured. . . . [I have been] deeply convinced for the past thirty years that religion in France would owe its renewal to the Sacred Heart (as I have publicly preached). I have always believed in the need for a Society to be *clearly called* the Society of the Sacred Heart, in order that the Lord operate his greatest miracle ever in France.[65]

Perreau also recognised the importance of becoming established in Paris, and made practical suggestions to enable the initiative to be successful:

> What particularly concerns me is the composition of the house in Paris and the disadvantage of having in the same house as your novices one or two individuals who could lead them to the hope of living some day under another rule of life, that of Mr de Sam[bucy] . . . be warned, Madame, that if some of your sisters entertain thoughts of joining the house in Rome, as soon as Mr de Sam[bucy]s rules are approved, you will never attain perfect union and oneness of spirit among your ladies. . . . for this reason I fear the presence in your noviceship of those who have such sympathies; furthermore the house in Paris is the very one where it is essential that there should be no conflict of ideas.[66]

Perreau argued that in Paris only those who were totally committed to the constitutions of 1815 should be members of the formation community. In that way there would have be a complete break with the past. Again, Eugénie de Gramont did not fit this requirement and Perreau made it clear that she should not form part of the initial formation community in Paris. This did not present a problem for Sophie since at this time she envisaged two separate groups in Paris, one involved in formation and the other running a school. She hoped Eugénie de Gramont could take charge of the new school. This appointment would remove her from Amiens and ensure that she had no influence over new members to the Society of the Sacred Heart. In fact, however, the school and the noviciate communities were housed initially in the same buildings in Paris, as a temporary measure, and both lived in close proximity. In a short time the one became identified with the other, with the school maintaining its dominant position of influence in society.

— 6 —

AMIENS TO PARIS, 1816–1820

In the wake of the general council and the reconciliation effected in Amiens, all pointed to Paris as the strategic centre for the Society of the Sacred Heart. Such a move would shift the focus from Amiens and give Sophie the free hand she needed. Throughout February and March 1816 Philippine Duchesne, now secretary general of the Society, was making preparations for the new house. After a long search the only property she could find ready for immediate renting was on the rue des Postes, quite near the Jesuits, and the formalities were cleared for moving in by 15 April 1816.[1] Sophie herself arrived on 29 April, on her way to Poitiers, and saw the amount of work and time needed to get the house ready for a large number of women. She decided to form the nucleus of the noviciate by bringing the novices from Grenoble and Amiens and appointing Josephine Bigeu to be in charge of them. She was replaced in Amiens conveniently by Henriette Grosier, for whom a change from Poitiers was needed, at least for a time. On 16 July six women came from Grenoble: three choir novices, one coadjutrix novice, and two coadjutrix postulants. The following day five women arrived from Amiens: four choir novices and one choir postulant, and they were accompanied by Eugénie de Gramont.

The house was too small for the purposes of both noviciate and school, and so Perreau's warning to Sophie about keeping novices apart from Eugénie de Gramont was impossible to heed. Whereas in the summer of 1816 there were just two students in the proposed school, by October there was quite a large group, all from the aristocratic or wealthy section of society. Alexandrine de Riencourt remembered her arrival in Paris, to join the noviciate, in October 1816:

When I arrived at the rue des Postes on the 16 October the boarding school, though not very big was already thriving . . . The novices were so cramped for space that our dormitory was a very small room and in the evenings we had to crawl our way across an attic to reach it. Even the noviciate work room was turned into a bedroom at night for a senior pupil.[2]

By September 1817 the cramped situation had created health hazards, illnesses hit both the school and the community and two novices and three students died. Eugénie de Gramont became ill herself and had to leave Paris for some weeks for a change of air in Amiens. Sophie suffered from rheumatism but nothing more serious. When one of the girls, Caroline, was at death's door and all hope of saving her life was lost, Sophie told Eugénie de Gramont, then convalescing in Amiens:

Caroline is very ill indeed. I will hide it from you no longer, we have little hope of her living. She is an angel. She received all the sacraments last Sunday in full consciousness. She received communion and today she received the scapular . . . That is our only consolation. I am torn apart at the grief of her father.

The following day she wrote:

Our dear Caroline is dead . . . or rather she has begun to live her true life in the heart of God where she sped yesterday at 10 p.m., after a long and peaceful agony. She has appeared before God rich in innocence and in merit, for she could not have been more pious during her illness. Let us thank God then while we feel his hand upon us, and let us not distress ourselves as do unbelievers who have no hope at all of meeting again.[3]

It was not just the health of the community and school that concerned Sophie at this time. Living closely together, in circumstances so overcrowded that Sophie and Eugénie were obliged to share a room, created personal difficulties for Sophie. Her growing friendship with Eugénie de Gramont had become a source of gossip in the houses outside Paris. Trust was growing between them and when they lived together in Paris, embarked on a new, common project, their intimacy grew. By 1817, Sophie told Thérèse Maillucheau that Eugénie was her support and consolation in countless difficulties. A great deal of her affection was expressed in concern for Eugénie's health and well-being and in the midst of epidemics Sophie was concerned about Eugénie's health most of all. She asked Marie Prevost at Amiens for fruit and warm shoes, while she asked her family in Joigny to send grapes and a special kind of cake, a *toufette*, made only in Joigny. After a short time Sophie recognised that Eugénie de Gramont had become indispensable to her.[4]

There were good reasons for this; Sophie had to depend on Eugénie de Gramont. There was no one else in the rue des Postes on whom Sophie could rely to lead the actual task of education. Two key members of the Society were fully occupied in the house. The noviciate was the responsibility of Josephine Bigeu and even she was absent for a time in 1817, overseeing a new foundation in Quimper. Although Philippine Duchesne was present in Paris, Sophie had accepted that she must be allowed to realise her missionary dream and preparations were afoot for her departure to Louisiana in the spring of 1818. On the other hand Eugénie de Gramont needed Sophie because their friendship gave her a sense of inclusion in the Society of the Sacred Heart, especially following her previous stance in Amiens. Her sense of having been duped by Saint-Estève as well as her need for acceptance in the Society led, for a time, to an overdependence on Sophie Barat. Sophie responded with friendship and warmth and showed her affection publicly, both in the community and in the letters she wrote while absent from Paris. And while it was politically necessary for Sophie to win and retain the affection of Eugénie de Gramont, she grew to love this formidable woman, whose personality was so marked that her congenital deformity was easily forgotten. For a time Eugénie suffered extreme remorse for what she had done and Sophie used that to bond their friendship. They were seen together a great deal and soon became the subject of comment and criticism.

When apart they exchanged letters and expressed their genuine friendship and feelings for one another often through concern for each other's health. On a visit to Beauvais, Sophie became ill and wrote:

> How I miss my Eugénie! here I am prostrate in bed, drenched in perspiration and full of pain. I dared not hope to have you here, for I know that your presence and your gentle care of me would have been a comfort that I ought to sacrifice, thinking that I am worthy of nothing . . . I got your kind, short letter . . . I read it with tender emotion, but nevertheless I would have wished that you were stronger and that there would have been no need for tears to fall.[5]

And on another occasion:

> You get upset too easily, my dear Eugénie, and I find your anxiety about me really difficult, for basically I have very good health which means I can fight all illness and this makes me fear I will live to be eighty years of age. Indeed from the time I started to have bad health, I have got used to it and am putting on weight even while I am ill . . . you see then that you are upsetting yourself in vain by weeping over my suffering, while you need so much to look after yourself, to rebuild your own health which is so impaired . . .[6]

Yet Sophie was deeply concerned about Eugénie de Gramont and expressed this in her letters. She was absorbed in and by their relationship and found ways to talk about this. On leaving Paris for a visit to Beauvais Sophie wrote to Eugénie:

> I think of you almost all time in the presence of the Heart of Jesus. I make great plans for your perfection. Oh! my dear daughter, everything else passes with this world and with us, and God is always God above all things. Tell me your news quickly. The jolting of the carriage has blunted neither my heart nor my imagination . . .[7]

Sophie's concern was expressed in the minute instructions she gave Eugénie when it was time for her to return to Paris, after convalescing in Amiens:

> This is what I forgot. I haven't told you to wrap up well, and, if the weather is wet and cold, you must wear more clothes, especially when you are travelling (leave off

your cotton stockings, put on floss-silk ones, wear two petticoats, and gloves). In short, wrap up sensibly so as to avoid catching cold.[8]

Apart from the fact that Sophie needed Eugénie to be in sufficient health to run the new school in Paris, there is no doubt that their friendship was a source of joy to Sophie at this time. Madame de Gramont d'Aster had been Sophie's staunch friend in the difficult years and now Eugénie not only had turned away from Saint-Estève but she had transferred her loyalty to Sophie Barat. The joy and comfort of their friendship was a support for Sophie who was going through a bleak time personally just then. She admitted to both Eugénie de Gramont and Thérèse Maillucheau that she was struggling with depression. She needed spiritual guidance and could not find anyone to talk to in Paris. Over several years Jean Montaigne had been a good friend to her, she felt he understood her from the inside and she had learnt to trust him. After the general council of 1815 Montaigne had become very ill and was unable to continue spiritual direction. And so Sophie remarked wryly that in the whole of Paris, she could not find anyone to talk to in depth about herself and she could only see a desert opening up before her.[9] Even Eugénie de Gramont could not help her, for whenever she spoke about her inner pain, Eugénie became so upset herself that Sophie decided to say no more to her. The sadness and depression undoubtedly came from exhaustion. Sophie was overworked and over stretched in every direction, not just with the general administration of the Society but with the serious illnesses and the deaths in the community school in Paris, aggravated by the absence of Eugénie for some weeks in the autumn of 1817. She confided some of her burden to Thérèse Maillucheau, telling her of:

> my own particular difficulties regarding how badly I am supported here, for I send the best members away to other houses, . . . My anxieties are caused by those who ought to be helping me and who are presumed to be a great source of help in my work here . . . Others sense the sadness I carry in the depths of my soul. I am no longer gentle or patient enough. This is really wrong. For everyone has their own load to carry and we cannot ask them to take on other's burdens as well. Yet that is what happens when we cannot control our emotions. I have lost all my cheerfulness. I am truly a wet blanket at recreations . . . I can barely speak to anyone about my troubles.[10]

Thus in her personal, spiritual life Sophie was feeling bereft and alone. In her task of leadership she also found herself quite isolated and without support. Even though she had been given three assistants general in 1815, Josephine Bigeu, Catherine de Charbonnel and Henriette Grosier, none of them lived with her in Paris. She could not afford to have them with her as there were few capable of taking leadership of the houses, or of negotiating new foundations. Josephine Bigeu was involved in the foundation of Chambéry at this time; Catherine de Charbonnel was responsible for that of Lyon and Henriette Grosier was in charge of Amiens for a time and then returned to Poitiers. In addition to assistants general, Sophie had also been given four councillors who were equally involved in establishing houses, Félicité Desmarquest in Beauvais, Suzanne Geoffroy and

Emilie Giraud in Niort. Sophie recognised that Geneviève Deshayes was unsuitable for that type of leadership and she counted on being able to entrust other tasks to her in Paris. Thus all those who were elected to help Sophie Barat in the government of the Society were fully occupied and with the exception of Eugénie de Gramont, were unable to help Sophie in the day-to-day running of the Society.

Thus over a period of time, first in Amiens and then in Paris, Sophie Barat and Eugénie de Gramont were thrown together by circumstances and their friendship was mutually supportive. The experience of those who had known the inside story of Amiens was different. They kept their distance from Eugénie de Gramont and found it hard to trust her, knowing the extent of her former commitment to Saint-Estève and the Roman project. Some could only view the growing friendship between Sophie and Eugénie with apprehension, and perhaps with jealousy. Yet Sophie's love for Eugénie was not exclusive and she had other deep friendships in the Society. After a visit to Grenoble Sophie found it hard to leave Thérèse Maillucheau:

> On leaving you I was so upset and my heart felt such anguish that I could say hardly anything on the journey. This was a sad journey for when I was thinking of you, of your problems, of your worries which will tumble down upon you, I found it hard to hold back my tears. My whole being had stayed with you . . . It would be a real pleasure to return to live near you for six months, to go and see you a few times, and you, too, could come and give me your help . . . this is just a hope . . . which lessens quite a lot the bitterness of our separation.[11]

In the early days Sophie and Thérèse had shared a great deal in Poitiers and both felt nostalgia for those days of relative freedom from responsibility. Yet Sophie was realistic and reminded Thérèse that since they had not always got along so easily when they lived together, perhaps they should modify their expressions of loneliness for one another.[12] This was the century of tears and sentimentality, when so much was expressed in exaggerated expressions of feeling. Sophie was of her time and her letters to individuals, like Eugénie de Gramont, need to be read in conjunction with those to other friends and colleagues to the get the measure of her affection and grasp how much was couched in the conventional language of the day.[13]

Sophie was aware of and sensitive to criticisms concerning the relationship between herself and Eugénie de Gramont. She responded furiously to the indiscretions of Marie Balastron who had been in Paris from 1816 to 1818, and had returned to Grenoble in the autumn of 1818. On her return she had gossiped about the lack of discipline in the community in Paris and how Sophie and Eugénie de Gramont were constantly together:

> Instead of remaining discreet and only speaking positively of Paris, you said openly at recreation that Madame de Gramont is always in my company . . . that here we live in a state of continual dissipation . . . you know how much contact I am obliged to have with the headmistress; she helps me with my correspondence and her health requires great attention as well . . . a little fairness would have required silence on your part.[14]

Sophie reminded Balastron how constricted the space was in the rue des Postes, where all were obliged to live closely together, though she remarked dryly that since Balastron's departure there had been much more quiet and peace in the house. The point, however, had been taken and Sophie warned Eugénie not to express her affection so openly. By 1819, while visiting the communities in different parts of France, Sophie warned Eugénie that limits would have to be put on their times together in Paris since she had heard comments regarding their relationship everywhere she went. She also asked her not to write separate letters to her so often, but to slip her letters into the general business post forwarded to Sophie while on visitation. She also advised Eugénie not to announce in community when she received personal letters from her as the other members resented this favouritism. Concerned that her affectionate letters to Eugénie could fall into the hands of other readers, Sophie asked Eugénie to destroy them and Sophie kept few of Eugénie's letters to her.[15]

While she had apparently won over Eugénie de Gramont, Sophie herself was learning how to handle deep affection, both in herself and in the love others showed her. When she showed one of Eugénie's letters to Thérèse Maillucheau in Grenoble, she remarked that she too had felt like that about Sophie.[16] So had Madeleine du Chasteigner and Marie Balastron and indeed Sophie's attractiveness as a leader was noted throughout her life. This influenced the manner in which Sophie Barat governed the Society of the Sacred Heart. She based her authority on personal relationships created with key people and it was through these carefully formed friendships that she shaped and formed the Society. This mode of government fulfilled Sophie's emotional needs and, despite the criticism, Sophie found her friendship with Eugénie de Gramont helped her. It gave her energy and filled emotional spaces in her being, spaces that had been unexplored and most definitely suppressed by Louis Barat. Indeed when one of the community scolded her for writing long letters to Eugénie de Gramont, on the grounds that it would tire her, Sophie replied that, on the contrary, writing to Eugénie gave her energy and joy. She told Eugénie about this in a letter and she ended:

> All yours . . . I am afraid that this phrase, which when used by others is often merely politeness, is only too true in your case.[17]

Her personal contacts with the members of the Society, either through letters or visits to houses, gave her immense pleasure. By temperament she was both choleric and sanguine and so was able to be immediately both curious and interested in all that went on around her, affected by it for a time and then able to let it go for a while, until either the next visit or the next letter. Her mode of government took relationships and individuals into account and this led her to develop the gift of reaching compromise and harmony, often in situations that seemed insoluble.

Those who were wary of the relationship between Sophie and Eugénie de Gramont feared for Sophie herself and acted out of friendship for her.

Undoubtedly some of the criticism of the relationship came from the recent past, when Sophie Barat and Saint-Estève were in open conflict and Eugénie de Gramont herself was deeply involved in undermining Sophie and planning her exit to Rome. The general council of 1815 marked the confirmation of Sophie Barat as leader and the reinstatement of the original impulse of Léonor de Tournély. In that context Perreau's warning about the importance of a new start in Paris, free from the influence of Saint-Estève, was good advice. Members of the Society, first in Paris and later in the other houses, viewed the growing relationship with Eugénie de Gramont with suspicion. The Jesuits in Paris, especially those who had helped Sophie confront Saint-Estève, saw her now hand in glove with the woman who had steadily plotted against her to win over the community to Saint-Estève. Pierre Roger was suspicious of the dependency between the two women and he forbade Eugénie to write so often to Sophie when she was away from Paris. Julien Druilhet let Sophie know that he doubted Eugénie's loyalty to the Society of the Sacred Heart. Pierre Ronsin, who knew a great deal through Marie de la Croix, also expressed his doubts about Eugénie's integrity.[18]

The reservations of Sophie's friends were not mere jealousy and resentment and they continued to voice their criticism. They saw Eugénie de Gramont as a cold, distant woman who lived alongside rather than with the community. Sophie knew that Eugénie acted independently and remained aloof from other members of the community in Paris. She preferred to deal with Sophie alone and this stance deepened misgivings within the community. For her part Sophie urged Eugénie to treat the other women in the community with more respect and to work with them, rather than ignore them.[19] Yet when Thérèse Maillucheau wrote a strong letter criticising Eugénie de Gramont's attitude to the other members of the Society teaching in the school in Paris, Sophie defended Eugénie vigorously and would not accept the criticism at all. Rather she blamed the bad spirit of some in the community and suggested that Eugénie be allowed to prove herself. The past was painful and had affected everyone, but it was over and it was best to face the future positively.[20] Nevertheless, Sophie advised Eugénie to tread carefully with Catherine de Charbonnel and Geneviève Deshayes, as both women were well aware (though in very different ways) of the extent of Eugénie de Gramont's activity in Amiens prior to 1815 and they found it hard to watch her deepening friendship with Sophie.[21]

If Saint-Estève had truly disappeared in 1815, then the relationship between Sophie and Eugénie may have been regarded with less apprehension. But Saint-Estève was still active in 1817 and 1818, seeking to insinuate himself into the Society of the Sacred Heart. When his sister, Félicité de Saint-Estève, died in Rome Saint-Estève claimed restitution of her property in Amiens, and Anne Baudemont also claimed recompense for her goods in Amiens. Sophie asked Eugénie to write to Anne Baudemont, clarifying that in fact the Society of the Sacred Heart owed neither Félicité de Saint-Estève nor Anne Baudemont any money. On the contrary, Sophie knew well that the money the Association had expended on the two women far exceeded the revenues they had offered the community at Amiens. Nevertheless, to keep the semblance of charity and in the hope of finally severing all ties with Saint-Estève and Anne Baudemont, Sophie decided that Anne Baudemont should be given the money she asked for, as well as any of the goods in Amiens that she claimed as her own:

> When will we be free of all dealings with this good man? I look forward to the day when he will have no more cause to write to us. [Anne Baudemont] does not seem to be at all happy where she is . . . What a sad old age she will have! My heart really goes out to her.[22]

The final confrontation between Saint-Estève and Sophie Barat came in the summer of 1818, while Sophie Barat was in the process of establishing a house in Chambéry. Formal negotiations had almost been concluded with the church and town authorities, when Anne Baudemont arrived in Chambéry, accompanied by Saint-Estève's servant Leonard. Sophie had a cordial meeting with Anne Baudemont, during which nothing contentious arose. However, when Anne Baudemont met the archbishop of Chambéry, Mgr de Solle, she told him that the Society of the Sacred Heart was an offshoot from her own foundation in Rome. She also implied that Sophie Barat had rebelled against her authority and that of the pope. The archbishop asked Sophie for an explanation and she had no difficulty in providing extensive and decisive proof of the authenticity of the Society of the Sacred Heart and of her leadership. It was the measure of her own authority and position then that Sophie could request and receive prompt written endorsement of her authority from well-placed clerics. She asked the grand aumônier of France, Cardinal de Talleyrand-Périgord, his secretary and acting superior general of the Society of the Sacred Heart, Fr Perreau, the bishops elect Soyer and Beauregard (formerly vicars general of Poitiers), to clarify the situation with the archbishop. Within a few weeks the matter was resolved in her favour and Sophie was able to proceed with the foundation of the house.[23]

During these weeks of tension in Chambéry, Saint-Estève himself, though still in Rome, continued to create disturbance. He wrote to Eugénie de Gramont and told her that a reconciliation had been effected between Sophie Barat and Anne Baudemont, and that Teresa Copina had written from Rome in the most friendly terms to Sophie.[24] In his letter Saint-Estève reminded Eugénie of her former loyalty to him and renewed his claim to be the founder of both the Society of the Sacred Heart in France and of the Association in Rome.[25] At the same time Leonard, following the instructions of Saint-Estève, had left Chambéry and travelled to Paris and then to Amiens to see Eugénie de Gramont, to try and renew old bonds. Sophie feared Leonard more than Anne Baudemont. Over the years in Amiens Saint-Estève had used Leonard in his negotiations with Sophie Barat and with Julie Billiart and both had found him an oppressive and sinister man.[26] Thus at the very time when Sophie Barat and Eugénie de Gramont were drawing close together, their relationship was being tested by these tensions. However, Eugénie withstood the pressures Saint-

Estève was placing upon her by his letters and through the visit of Leonard. In any event it had become clear to her that there was no future with Saint-Estève. Eugénie wrote to him and stated her position regarding the claims of the Association in Rome and her role in the past in Amiens. She made it clear that she regretted what she had done:

> I lay at the foot of the Cross the grief which these unfortunate matters have caused me and to which I have contributed only too much by my credulity and trust. Advantage was taken of my youth, and I regret having spent it in a manner of little benefit to my salvation.[27]

And so while Eugénie de Gramont was unable to speak frankly in December 1815, when Marie de la Croix admitted her mistakes, by 1818 she was able to disavow and bitterly regret her past actions in Amiens.[28]

The fact that Eugénie had rebuffed the overtures of the Association in Rome encouraged Sophie and justified, at least in her own eyes, the trust she placed in her. But she knew that their friendship was being criticised and she complained: 'Who has loved their friends more than Jesus did when he was on earth?'[29] Sophie valued their friendship, its own goodness and truth, and had no intention of breaking it. However she repeated once again that they had to be careful about their relationship and not spend so much time together:

> Oh! If only you knew how I have suffered since we have been separated, as a result of the complaints and criticisms I have received on this subject! With regard to telling you who it was and how it was said, I really did not want to find out, only that I feel the need to act more prudently with regard to my exterior behaviour and I advise you to do the same . . . for we must admit that women are small-minded![30]

Sophie did not recognise that there was more to the criticism than mere pettiness. She could not see that the relationship between Sophie Barat and Eugénie de Gramont was the subject for public comment among members of the Society precisely because Sophie herself had created great expectations for the house in Paris. She had presented it as pivotal in the growth of the Society of the Sacred Heart. From there the spirituality of the Society would radiate, carried by the women who had been trained at the source and centre. It would form and shape the members and ensure corporate unity and common vision. This was what Sophie had planned, what Perreau had supported and what her old Jesuit friend, Joseph Varin, had heartily endorsed. It was Sophie's basic vision. Those who most criticised her relationship with Eugénie de Gramont feared that her intuition could be compromised. And yet Sophie certainly needed someone like Eugénie de Gramont in Paris to help initiate the school, and she thought her love and her authority could keep Eugénie's actions in check. What Sophie would have to learn again and again was that Eugénie de Gramont always acted independently and rarely consulted her own colleagues. Sophie would also learn that Eugénie could return to ignoring her as she had done in Amiens. Her own continual presence in Paris and firm hand would be always needed. As the Society expanded and Sophie was absent from Paris for prolonged periods of time, her control of Eugénie slipped and progressively became more difficult to regain. So while there was always a genuine, loving relationship between them, Sophie struggled to control Eugénie de Gramont and modify her influence on the Society of the Sacred Heart in Paris.

Throughout this period the Society continued to expand. In a short period of time three new houses had been established in France. One was founded in Quimper where, in March 1817, the Society took over a school already in existence in a former Capuchin monastery, well situated and set in vast gardens. The school had been run by the Visitation nuns but by 1816 they lacked the personnel to continue. Mlle de Saint-Pern, who had endowed the school, asked Bishop Dombidau de Crouseilles to contact Sophie Barat in Paris and ask her to send a community to Quimper. The prospect was attractive to Sophie since the school and buildings were already established and so Josephine Bigeu spent some weeks there early in 1817, arranging the transfer of the schools to the Society of the Sacred Heart. By March all had been completed and in May Madame de Gramont d'Aster arrived to be the superior and Josephine Bigeu returned to Paris with Mlle de Saint-Pern who had decided to enter the Society.[31] Since 1816 a foundation in Villeurbanne, near Lyon, had been projected but came to fruition only in February 1819 when Sophie Barat decided to buy the château of La Ferrandière, in Villeurbanne. There a school was founded in March that year and in July 1820 a poor school was opened.[32] In the same year a new community was founded in Bordeaux, fulfilling a promise Sophie had made in 1806. The occasion for the foundation was an orphanage in need of personnel, for by 1819 Madame de Lalanne, widowed in 1816, could no longer run it alone. She had been attracted to religious life and even before her husband died she had formed a small group of women and they had taken the vows of religion in 1812. In 1819 Madame Lalanne wished to endow the Society of the Sacred Heart with her orphanage and to enter the Society. Sophie accepted the offer of the orphanage in principle but could not act on the decision until 1819. In that year she sent Suzanne Geoffroy from Niort to Bordeaux to oversee the change of ownership. Once this had been done Madame Lalanne was named superior of the community and fully absorbed into the Society of the Sacred Heart in a few short months.[33]

Difficulties abounded in these beginnings and each situation called for a vast amount of planning, prolonged negotiations and searches for personnel. At this time Sophie received many requests for foundations and only regretted that she could not respond to them all. Her courage and vision were best seen in her decision to let one of her oldest friends, Philippine Duchesne, leave for America early in 1818. Since 1815 Sophie had received invitations from several mission areas. Initially Sophie hoped that the first foundation of the Society outside of France could have been in Martinique, since it was a French colony and contacts would have been easier than with Louisiana. In addition, Eugénie de Gramont's brother was governor-general of Martinique and that contact would have been helpful.[34] Yet in spite of that possibility Sophie agreed that

Louisiana was to be the first house of the Society outside of France and helped Philippine prepare for the long journey. Such plans on the part of a congregation which had so recently come through a prolonged crisis were a sign of self-assurance and self-confidence.

From the time she was a boarder in Grenoble, in Ste Marie d'En Haut, Philippine had heard about the missions to the Indians in Louisiana and had dreamed of going there. The Revolution had interrupted her religious life but not her longing to go on the missions. In 1806 Philippine had begun to plan going to China and had spoken of this hope to Sophie Barat. Philippine had also been inspired by Marie de l'Incarnation and her mission to the Indians in Canada.[35] So had Sophie. In Amiens Sophie had spoken to Louise Naudet about her missionary hopes. However, Naudet felt that Sophie was destined to remain in France and this seemed to be confirmed when Sophie was elected superior general for life in 1806.[36] When Philippine was elected secretary general of the Society in December 1815 her hopes of going on the missions seemed to have been set aside indefinitely.[37]

Yet by the spring of 1818 Philippine Duchesne and four companions were on their way to New Orleans. This time Louis Barat was the catalyst for the decision. From his visits to Grenoble Louis Barat had known of Philippine's longing to go to the Indians in Louisiana and he had encouraged her to hold on to her dreams. Indeed he shared her longing for the missions. In 1816 Louis met the newly ordained Bishop of Louisiana, Louis Dubourg (1766–1833) in Bordeaux and told him about Philippine's longing to go on the missions. He wrote to Sophie about his meeting with bishop Dubourg, and he told Philippine that she should be ready to go back to America with the bishop and realise her lifelong desire to live and work with the Indians. Philippine was excited and told Sophie about it. Sophie sensed immediately that the agenda was no longer in her own hands:

> Just imagine, Philippine has kept on dreaming of her house across the sea and my brother has almost paved the way there for her. Despite the dread that this undertaking causes me, perhaps we are going to see it succeed. I tremble at the thought. Pray for this, but say nothing just now for fear some may get excited about it. We live in a century where people move about for little reason and it is not easy to restrain everyone's imagination.[38]

Sophie realised that the arrival of Bishop Dubourg in France was significant though clearly the possibility of Philippine going away was momentous for the little congregation, especially at this juncture. When Dubourg arrived in Paris in January 1817 he went to the rue des Postes, to see Sophie Barat and Philippine Duchesne. Initially Sophie's instinct was to agree that the Society would make a foundation in Louisiana and the bishop left the house presuming that the decision had been made. However, Joseph Varin and Louis Perreau persuaded Sophie to change her mind, for they felt Philippine could not be spared just then in France. Some months later, in May 1817, Bishop Dubourg visited Sophie again and was disappointed to learn that the decision had been changed. At this point Philippine impetuously took the matter into her own hands and begged Sophie in the presence of Dubourg to let her go this time. Sophie could not resist such directness and there and then agreed.

Neither Sophie nor Philippine knew what lay ahead. In the nineteenth century the world of the missions was one of adventure, of heroism, of entering into a new world, crossing frontiers and opening up new horizons. It was a path open to religious women, giving them an autonomy unusual for any women at this time. The church supported such initiatives in view of the purpose of the missions.[39] Although this was a huge personal loss for Sophie, she recognised that her task was to let Philippine fulfil her missionary call within the Society. Philippine was certainly going into frontier territory in every sense of the word. The diocese of Louisiana and the Floridas extended then from the mouth of the Mississippi to the Rocky Mountains. In the eighteenth century this diocese had been governed by the bishop of Quebec and then, after 1762, by the bishop of Havana, (Cuba), reflecting first French and then Spanish political alliances. In 1793 Pope Pius VI established Louisiana and the Floridas as an independent diocese with the bishop's residence centred at New Orleans. For a short time, in 1800, it reverted to France. However in May 1803 the United States negotiated the Louisiana Purchase with Napoleon. For the sum of $15,000,000 a vast tract of land, stretching from the Gulf of Mexico to the Rocky Mountains in the north west, was added to the Union, although the state of Louisiana was only formally admitted to the Union in 1812. When Bishop Dubourg was appointed in 1815 he inherited old tensions and unresolved difficulties, stemming from French and Spanish influences in the church and the severe financial straits in which the clergy found themselves. There had been no bishop in Louisiana since 1802, and Dubourg had to thread his way carefully to assert his authority.[40]

In every sense of the word then Philippine Duchesne was going out into the unknown, into a new world where the United States of America was expanding rapidly, especially since the Louisiana purchase. At forty-eight years of age, she faced into the challenge with energy. Her goal was to reach the Indians in Louisiana and Dubourg had promised her that she would be able to live and work with them. For her part Sophie Barat recognised that the expansion of the Society of the Sacred Heart into Louisiana was historic and she anticipated that Philippine Duchesne would need scope and freedom to act in a wholly new context. To this purpose Sophie drew up a formal document, headed with this statement:

> Considering before the Lord the great distances which separate us from the community at St Louis, as well as the difficulty in granting the necessary permissions according to our Institute, I invest Mother Duchesne, superior of the house which we are opening in Louisiana (Upper) with the authority detailed as follows . . .[41]

Sophie delegated a great deal of her authority to Philippine Duchesne. In the new situation, Philippine could accept new members into the Society and admit them to first vows. Acceptance for final profession remained in the hands of Sophie. Philippine could send away any women she felt would not fit into the

Society; she could adapt the dress if the situation/climate so required; she could use more money than sanctioned in Paris if the needs of the poor were in question; she could buy property and build; she could appoint those in charge; they could leave the confines of the community, cloister, if the educational needs of the children so required or if they needed to go to Mass. All the permissions given were conditional on Philippine keeping Sophie informed and working in harmony with local church authorities. Sophie discussed this document with Philippine the night before she left Paris and they tried to describe the unknown as best they could imagine. For someone whose authority had been so challenged for several years and only confirmed in 1815, Sophie Barat showed real trust and confidence in Philippine. Both women continued to be faithful to one another, now from a distance. Contact was retained by letters, and while in the evolution of the Society in America they had some misunderstandings, their deep affection for one another did not wane.

Philippine and Louis Barat were old friends. Louis admired Philippine's ruggedness and envied her departure for Louisiana. But characteristically he could not say directly to her what he felt. Instead he told her that she would need three generous women to accompany her, 'but they must be great souls, and among women great souls are very rare'. He even assured Philippine that God would make an exception in her own case and 'not require you to be wholly a great soul'.[42] Sophie Barat found three such 'rare souls', and invited them to join Philippine Duchesne. Octavie Berthold (1787–1833), was Swiss, born a Calvinist and later a convert to Catholicism. She entered in Grenoble in 1814 and completed her noviciate in the rue des Postes in Paris in 1816–17. Since she was named to go with Philippine, the time of preparation for her final commitment in the Society of the Sacred Heart was shortened and she made final profession in February 1818. She had no specific call for the missions but felt that she should do something heroic to mark her entry into the Catholic church. Eugénie Audé (1792–1842) was from Savoy and had entered in Grenoble in 1815 and like Octavie Berthold she completed her noviciate in Paris. She had asked to go on the missions with Philippine and Sophie had decided to let her go. Her profession was also anticipated and she actually made her final commitment to the Society the morning of her departure for Louisiana. Catherine Lamarre (1779–1845) had entered in Amiens as a coadjutrix sister and was professed there in 1806. She had helped to found the house at Cuignières, a very difficult task at the time, for the community there experienced great poverty as well as opposition from the local people. She had offered to go on the missions to Martinique but found the challenge of going as far as Louisiana daunting and frightening. This affected her all her life as a missionary:

> she . . . often repeated that she had told Fr Sellier, Madame Prevost and indeed you yourself that she did not feel that she had the courage to go so far away. I responded by saying that I was sure that you would not have chosen her if she had not been willing to go, and even asked you to let her go. At this she repeated that *she had*

indeed asked to go to Martinique because she thought it was near, but she had felt repugnance for Louisiana.[43]

On the morning of 8 February 1818, Philippine and her three companions left Paris, on the first stage of the long journey, first to Bordeaux, then to New Orleans and up the Mississippi river to St Louis. On the way to Bordeaux, the four travellers stopped at Poitiers. There they were joined by a member of the community at Niort, Marguerite Manteau (1771–1841). She had entered the community at Poitiers as a coadjutrix sister and was professed there in 1809. She had been ill in Niort and set out for Bordeaux while still quite unwell. In view of such a long voyage ahead Philippine was concerned and complained to Sophie that no one had warned her of this.[44] But she had time to convalesce in Bordeaux while Philippine and the others, with the help of Louis Barat, arranged the final details for the journey and got the provisions they needed for the journey.[45] They finally left France on 19 March 1818, on the ship, *The Rebecca*. It was a journey into the unknown, undertaken with both joy and apprehension, and Philippine's accounts of the actual sea voyage are graphic and evocative. After seventy days at sea they reached New Orleans on 29 May 1818. They stayed with the community of Ursulines in New Orleans for some weeks until they could arrange the next stage of the journey up the Mississippi, to St Charles rather than to St Louis, and there they set up the first little community and school.[46] From this small beginning they would offer educational opportunities to young women in the territory west of the Mississippi, and establish schools and communities in Louisiana. It would prove to be rugged, pioneer work, tough, arduous and demanding, at times thankless and discouraging. Their life on the missions would expose them to realities their colleagues in Europe would never know: the meeting and clashing of cultures and traditions, stemming from French, Spanish and American influences; discrimination against Creoles, against Indians, against immigrants; slavery as part of the economy of the country. And they would become part of that culture and country as it strove to define itself, struggle with it and place their own stamp on it too.

The loss of Philippine Duchesne as secretary general was an added burden at this time, and she was not replaced until the general council of 1820. Indeed when Philippine Duchesne left for Louisiana in February 1818, Sophie's health collapsed and for most of 1818 she suffered constant illnesses, the root of which was exhaustion. Her attacks of rheumatism were frequent, her fevers recurred; her eyes were affected and for a time prevented some letter-writing.[47] She suffered constantly from insomnia and especially from diarrhoea:

> The doctor here thinks that it is the stomach nerves which are not working and that in time they will wear out. According to this diagnosis there is nothing which can be done to remedy the situation and that I will have to suffer this illness, often acute, for as long as it pleases Our Lord.[48]

As soon as Sophie recovered sufficient health and energy she resumed her work which by now had begun to take on a certain pattern. This was a blend of prolonged stays in Paris, followed by visits either to houses already established or to possible new areas for growth. Thus while she made Paris her base between August 1816 and March 1818, she paid two short visits to Amiens, in August/September 1816 and again in September 1817, taking in Beauvais this time as well. In the late spring of 1818 she went on a long journey, visiting her mother and sister in Joigny, and then proceeding on to Lyon, Grenoble and Chambéry. She returned to Paris in September 1818 and remained there until the following September when she set out for Autun, Lyon, Chambéry and Grenoble, returning to Paris in December 1819. She remained there until August 1822. Wherever she was, Sophie maintained contact with members of the Society through letters, which became her major source of communication, of formation, of decision-making and of continuity in relationships.

Sophie remained in touch with her family too, by letters and by visits. By this time her mother had become unable to live on her own and so the family home had been sold and Madame Barat had moved in with Marie-Louise on the Grande Rue in Joigny. Like so many families in the town, the Dusaussoys had suffered economic hardship in the closing years of the empire. Coupled with loss of income was the series of bad harvests. Sophie told Stanislas, then at school at Bordeaux:

> They are in great difficulty, for the bad weather has robbed them of their corn and wine harvest. Poverty is so great generally that trade is at a standstill, and the little your parents do for you costs them greatly.[49]

The situation was no better in October 1816:

> I got news of your family a few days ago. Poverty is great in Joigny. The quality of bread has never been so bad; there is no hope of a grape harvest, and if the wood does not mature, then income is lost for the second year.[50]

Two years later, on her way to Grenoble, Sophie paid a visit home and found the situation worse. The family was really needy and she realised with dismay that their financial situation had changed dramatically. Sophie's former criticism of her sister and brother-in-law's parenting indicated how little she knew of their plight. She told Eugénie de Gramont:

> When I was at Joigny I saw real poverty and in my own family too. I promised some help for those children born for better things. Without saying who it is for, ask Fr Perreau for his old overcoat, and send it to my sister who will have it collected. If he can add an old pair of trousers etc. that would be a kindness. You see, . . . I really count on your devotion to all that concerns me, since I ask you to see to my private business . . .[51]

A few weeks later, Sophie thanked Eugénie:

> Thank you very much . . . for your kindness in sending clothes to my sister. These are for relatives who once were among very rich and who now have come down in the world, like so many others.[52]

Two years later, Etienne Dusaussoy died at the age of fifty-five.[53] A marriage that had begun so well in 1793 ended in early financial ruin. Years later Sophie told her niece, Sophie Dusaussoy, that when her father died he had left little money either for her mother or for the children.[54] A silence hangs around Etienne Dusaussoy: there are few references to him in any of the letters and documents of the period, and these references are general and vague, so it is difficult to assess the quality of the marriage of Etienne Dusaussoy and Marie-Louise Barat. Certainly Sophie and Louis felt responsible for the education their nieces and nephews. Indeed Sophie was a mother-figure for them, as much at the centre of their affections as their mother and father, if not more. This only increased when Etienne Dusaussoy died.

Knowing how hard-pressed the family was in Joigny Sophie was anxious that Stanislas and his sisters would work hard, if only to be able to earn their living in the future. She took great interest in them all. Both Louis Barat and Sophie found it hard to get Stanislas to work seriously. Sophie urged him to grow up, to leave childhood behind and face the reality that he would need to earn money. Indeed she challenged them all to face the reality of life and not live in illusion.[55] When Julie Dusaussoy decided to enter the Society of the Sacred Heart Stanislas was furious and tried to stop her. Sophie was equally furious with her nephew and told him not to interfere with his sister's life:

> What advantage can you offer your sisters in the world? What dangers will they not be exposed to in the world? Certainly a vocation should not be foisted upon them and for this you can address yourself to us. But if you really loved them, should you not encourage them to practise the virtue and the noble feelings they express? At least they do not follow your example for they make use of the good education they have received . . . *But* your letter . . . was still so badly written, with poor spelling and in a style that is dull and careless. No one would ever think you had been to school! Alas! when real sensitivity is not part of the person's being, then their culture is like something that is sown on stony ground: all it produces is a few wild shoots, without roots, and which dry up or are knocked down at the first storm! . . . I look forward to hearing from you.[56]

Stanislas was also furious at his aunt. Sophie was amused:

> Really . . . The description of your rage at my letter amused me for a moment for I thought this storm at sea was like the tempest that the prophet speaks of: Iracimini et nolite peccare [be angry and sin not]. If it were really true, then that would prove to me that you are truly choleric by temperament.[57]

When the time came for Stanislas to leave Bordeaux, Sophie had tried to find a place for him in Amiens, with the Jesuits, and explored the possibility of his going to Grenoble to study law.[58] This did not materialise for, as Sophie told her nephew, he would need more training to be a lawyer and she felt he did not have the capacity for that. The standard of his handwriting prevented him getting a job as a private secretary so she urged him to make good use of his time in Amiens. He eventually got a post in the ministry of finance in Paris.

Sophie urged her nieces to work hard. She watched over their health and every detail of their studies. In her letters to them individually she told them how everyone was progressing and gave them what family news she had heard.

She saw that they made their first communion and were confirmed. She wondered why little Elisa misbehaved and was intrigued at her precocious charm. She was pleased when Sophie won prizes in Amiens and remarked that she could do better if she were not so lazy. She was anxious that Julie would learn the piano as long as the lessons were free. She also wanted Julie to learn how to embroider and this time Louis Barat actually bought the threads for his niece, something that made Sophie smile to herself. Changed times indeed. Every year Julie sent a present of her embroidery work to her parents and Sophie was pleased with this achievement; she was less so with Julie's basketwork and drawing for these were not essential to earning a living.[59] Yet when Julie declared that she wished to enter, Sophie suggested that she learn to dance. For:

> I am so tired of telling the novices that they must hold themselves properly, that I despair of training those who have bad deportment.[60]

Sophie Dusaussoy was at school for some years in Amiens. Her aunt was taken aback at her bad accent and wanted to change her from the school.[61] She thought first of Grenoble and then Paris, and eventually little Sophie arrived at the rue des Postes.

Paris was not the answer, as Sophie told Thérèse Maillucheau:

> She [Sophie] has a great need of some help to enable her to finish her education, which she could not do at Amiens where the type of life is so common. She has become a real *Picarde* in language and in her manners. We have not got a place for her in Paris, and besides this would be to bring her from one extreme to another. I want to avoid putting her here with girls, who almost without exception are from the nobility. She will become either too elevated or too ashamed, if she has the intelligence to see it![62]

Sophie appreciated the care the communities gave her nieces, though many in the Society had nieces in the schools also and Sophie was vigilant over their welfare too.[63] She hoped that most of her nieces would enter and that she could continue to see to their welfare in this way. They all expected her to write to them, to send them gifts and see them especially when she was in the house. She also wrote to their teachers in the different houses either to get progress reports or to ask them to attend to some trait of character which needed reform. And Sophie did all this at a time when she was occupied with implementing the 1815 Constitutions, dealing with new foundations and maintaining existing ones, as well as dealing with the final efforts of Saint-Estève to retain power over the Society of the Sacred Heart. Sophie worried about their futures and at times was wearied by them all. When one of Catherine de Charbonnel's nieces died in Poitiers Sophie remarked wryly to Thérèse Maillucheau:

> I would have suffered less if I had lost my nieces. Alas! I would have willingly given them for all those who were taken from us. At least I would be happy about their fate. What kind of future do those [my nieces] have who are going to stay in the world.[64]

Sophie and Louis Barat shared their interest in and responsibility for their nieces and nephews and they remained in contact by letter or by visits when Louis came to Paris occasionally. Louis was fond of his nieces, especially Thérèse and Julie. When Stanislas was at Bordeaux Sophie urged him to benefit all he could from his uncle. Louis Barat also retained contact with the Society through his visits to the houses in Bordeaux, Poitiers and Niort. He gave retreats in the houses, to the pupils and to the members of the community, writing letters of a devotional nature to the communities. His preaching and writing were deeply affected by the apocalyptic literature and language which Pierre de Clorivière had employed in the formative years in Paris when the Jesuits were being restored in France after the revolution. Louis also wrote religious poetry and songs which were sent around the houses and used for devotions in the communities. Several volumes of these were compiled over the years, containing the hymns and songs and the names of those to whom they were dedicated. These included individuals, Sophie herself, Philippine and the early members of the Society; they also included communities, especially those in Grenoble and Bordeaux.[65] Louis Barat also corresponded with Philippine Duchesne and supported her in the early years of her difficult mission, one he had longed to go to himself.[66]

By 1820 Sophie realised that two situations in the Society of the Sacred Heart urgently required attention. One was the need for more space for the noviciate, the community and the school in Paris. The other was when to convoke the second general council of the Society. Both were a sign of the vitality of the Society of the Sacred Heart, of its expansion within and beyond France and of the need to accommodate the growing number of women who wished to join. Sophie returned to Paris in January 1819 and set about dealing with these two issues. She had recognised for some time that there was not enough space in the rue des Postes for the community and school. The property had been taken in 1816 as a temporary base in Paris. Unable to find anything bigger and suitable, in 1818 Sophie negotiated renting an adjacent building on the rue d'Arbalète which was connected with the house on the rue des Postes through a shared garden. There the novices could be housed but, though it was an improvement, it did not solve the basic problem of accommodation because both school and noviciate were growing rapidly. It could only be an interim solution and Sophie complained to Thérèse Maillucheau that she was tired of going between two houses and getting wet and muddy. Alexandrine Riencourt hinted in her memoirs that their privacy was often invaded by the workers in the nearby factory who had access to their work through the garden.[67] The real solution was to find a property to house both school and noviciate comfortably, with room for expansion.

— 7 —

PARIS, RUE DE VARENNE, 1820-1825

In 1820, then, Sophie set about choosing another, bigger property in Paris to consolidate the presence of the Society in the capital. It had to be large enough to function as the centre, the mother house, of the congregation, where Sophie could oversee the formation of new members, and also to accommodate a large boarding school in the capital. That year Sophie also began planning the next statutory general council of the Society and she decided to advance it by one year, in view of pressing issues which needed to be addressed. In her formal letter of convocation Sophie pointed out that the general council of 1815 had established the Society of the Sacred Heart on a solid base and ratified rules and constitutions which expressed the goals of the congregation.[1] However there had not been enough time to explore other essential issues, especially that of education, and Sophie wished to take these up in the coming general council:

> As the Society, by the grace of God, has increased its number of foundations, rules which were formulated in the early days were either increased or reduced in each house. This was done according to what was thought necessary for the greatest good of the pupils. Without being aware of it, houses differ from one another on a number of points. One of our most cherished aims is to establish uniformity of practice throughout the Society. So we think it is a matter of urgency, before expanding any further, that we consolidate those houses already in existence, by prescribing all that could contribute to their good, both spiritual and temporal.[2]

This was all the more urgent as the Society was expanding rapidly and Sophie wanted the general council to articulate some clear educational directives common

135

to all the schools, in France and beyond. In particular she wanted the 1810 plan of studies revised. Another function of the general council was to review the life of the Society and in view of this Sophie asked each member to prepare in advance their assessment of the last five years. More concretely she requested an account of the personnel in the houses, especially their gifts and capacities, with some indication regarding which members were available for transfer to other parts of France or indeed to Savoy or to Louisiana. She also asked for a report on the schools, in particular the level of studies and the number of students in each school. Finally, she asked for a report on the income and expenditure of each of the houses, and on the material condition of the buildings. In all, it was an opportunity for her to get an overview of the rapidly expanding Society.

By this time there were ten houses of the Society, governed by Sophie Barat and six councillors general, who had been elected in 1815: Josephine Bigeu (Chambéry), Catherine de Charbonnel (Villeurbanne), Henriette Grosier (Poitiers), Suzanne Geoffroy (Niort), Geneviève Deshayes (Paris) and Eugénie de Gramont (Paris). These formed the governing body but they did not represent all the houses. Acting on the advice of Joseph Varin, Sophie invited not only the six general councillors of the Society but also the superiors of those houses not represented by the general councillors: Marie Elizabeth Prevost (Amiens), Félicité Desmarquest (Beauvais), Gabrielle de Gramont d'Aster (Quimper), Félicité de Lalanne (Bordeaux) and Thérèse Maillucheau (Grenoble). Philippine received her formal invitation as a mark of inclusion in the ongoing affairs of the Society, though of course she could not travel from Louisiana.[3] By any standards these were remarkable women, colleagues of Sophie Barat, all ready to move forward with her. Sophie had a warm relationship with each one and while there were some she could more readily resonate with personally, she knew how to draw the best from each for the sake of the task in hand. At the deepest level they all shared a common vision, sought the divine in their lives, and had a common wish to serve others.

From late July in 1820 members of the general council began to arrive in Paris, in time for the formal opening of the council on 15 August 1820. From the moment of their arrival in the rue des Postes it was clear that space was urgently required in Paris and this was a subject of discussion from the beginning. Despite the added space rented on the rue d'Arbelète, there was not enough room to accommodate the community, the noviciate and the school. The number of women who wished to join the Society was increasing as were the pupils in the school. The first sessions of the council were taken up with this reality which had to be addressed without delay. The question of the need for alternative accommodation in Paris was agreed on easily. The real difficulty was how and where to find a suitable property in Paris. After lengthy discussions the council decided to bid for the Hôtel Biron, a property on the rue de Varenne situated in the Faubourg Saint-Germain.

Sophie had already considered the Hôtel Biron as early as 1817 and had wanted to buy it then. It seemed ideal, in terms of accommodation and spacious gardens. It was also in a much healthier location than the rue des Postes. However, the asking price then of 700,000 francs was far beyond her means and Sophie continued to search elsewhere. Other prospective buyers found it either too big or too costly and the property remained on the market. Three years later when the owner, the duchesse de Charost, heard that Sophie Barat was interested in buying the property, she reduced the price in view of the work of education the Society of the Sacred Heart would carry out there. Her decision made it possible for the general council to make a bid for the Hôtel Biron, even though it was a vast amount of money to spend in one transaction.

The Hôtel Biron, built between 1728 and 1731, was owned by a rich financier and lawyer, Abraham Peyrenc de Moras, from Languedoc. He wanted to build the finest house in Paris and appointed the architect Jean Aubert to draw up plans for such a project. The design of the house and gardens reflected the wealth of its owner. The style was rich, sumptuous and extravagant. In 1736 the Hôtel was bought by the duchesse de Maine who made few changes or additions to the work initiated by Peyrenc within the house. However she built a smaller house on the property, the Petit Hôtel, and this was completed in 1738. On her death in 1753, the house was bought by Antoine de Gontaut, duc de Biron, and his name was retained for the property when he died in 1788. He added little to the decorative work within the Hôtel, concentrating instead on developing the gardens and establishing their reputation for beauty and order. When the duchesse de Biron was guillotined in 1794 the property passed to her nephew the duc de Béthune-Charost, though he did not live there. In 1797 he rented it out to a small group of businessmen and artists who ran public balls and festivals in the Hôtel Biron for a few years. On the death of the duc de Béthune-Charost, the duchesse de Béthune-Charost administered the property and rented the Hôtel to the Papal Nuncio, Cardinal Capara, from 1806–08 and afterwards to the Russian Embassy until 1811. When the Society of the Sacred Heart purchased it in 1820, the Hôtel Biron had been empty for nine years.[4]

The actual location of the Hôtel Biron, on the rue de Varenne, affected the public image of the Society of the Sacred Heart profoundly. The Hôtel was situated on the left bank of the Seine, in the heart of the Faubourg Saint-Germain. This area of Paris comprised five long streets: the rues de Bourbon, de l'Université, de Grenelle, de Varenne and Saint-Dominique. There after the Revolution, even before the Restoration of the Bourbons in 1815, the nobility and aristocracy of the Ancien Régime had returned and gradually picked up mentally where they had left off in 1789. They had become a counter-court to that of Napoleon in the Tuileries.[5] Later, after the long awaited return of the Bourbons to the Tuileries there was only a bridge across the Seine between the king and the Faubourg Saint-Germain. Throughout the course of the year noble families moved between the Court, the Faubourg Saint-Germain, Versailles and the country, in well-planned cycles. A great deal of power and patronage was enclosed within a few streets of the city of Paris. Across the Seine, beside the Tuileries, in the Faubourg Saint-Honoré, lived the nobility and rich middle-class families of more liberal political tendencies, a blend of views influenced by the Revolution and the Empire. In the years immediately after 1815 there was easy flow of contact between the two Faubourgs, on both sides of the river, with the Court as their focal point of unity. In the years after the Restoration, the Faubourg Saint-Germain was known not only for the beauty of its houses and gardens but also as the centre of aristocratic life in Paris, committed to the Bourbon family and to the preservation of old values and traditions, a bastion of noble exclusiveness. In hindsight, it was a backwater, swimming against the tide of change which had erupted in 1789.[6] It was a risk to take root in such an environment in Paris, and Sophie and the members of the general council took advice from the bishops, the Jesuits and some members of the secular clergy.[7] All advised buying the Hôtel Biron and, as far as records show, there were no dissenting voices or hesitations. On the contrary, the bishops in particular welcomed the purchase of the Hôtel Biron. Such a step represented another sign of the restoration of the Catholic church in France, after a long period of persecution. Indeed the process of the rehabilitation of the Catholic church in France was brought about to a great extent by religious communities of women and is one of the hallmarks of nineteenth-century French Catholicism.[8]

Once the decision was taken to buy the Hôtel Biron, Sophie's immediate task was to find the money somehow and close the bid on the property. This she managed to do in a short period of time and by 5 September 1820 the house and gardens of the Hôtel Biron had been sold to Sophie Barat for 365,000 francs. She raised the money by petitioning the king and by borrowing from creditors. The first response from the king to her request for money gives an indication of the politics operating in the Court and in the Faubourg Saint-Germain. When Sophie petitioned the king, Louis XVIII, through one of the novices, the comtesse de Marbeuf, widow of the comte de Marbeuf, the widow's strong links with Napoleon worked against the petition. However, when the duc de Gramont, Eugénie de Gramont's uncle, took the matter in hand he negotiated a donation of 50,000 francs immediately from the king, with a promise of another 50,000 the following year. The gift was conditional upon the king's right to nominate pupils to five free places in the school annually. The rest of the money was borrowed. The marquis de Montmorency and two business men in Amiens, Laurent and Morand, between them lent her 265,000 francs at a reduced interest. She agreed to pay all her debts by 1824.[9] This was a huge transaction and Sophie carried out this major purchase with ease and professionalism. For her it was a pragmatic decision. The Society needed a large property to do its work and fulfil very specific needs. Her consistent plan was to establish a centre for the Society of the Sacred Heart in Paris, and from there govern the rapidly growing number of communities and schools.

While the negotiation to buy the Hôtel Biron was in process, Sophie continued to preside over the work of the general council. During the times of daily prayer and reflection, Joseph Varin recalled the story of the Society of the Sacred Heart, from the initial impulse of Léonor de Tournély all along its strange and difficult journey, to August 1820 in Paris. This was necessary as some had not heard the whole story from the beginning. Others told their story, too. Suzanne Geoffroy told of the prophecies of Fr Nectoux prior to the Revolution. Nectoux told of the little girl in France still playing with dolls, who in time would found a congregation devoted to the Sacred Heart in her own country. This was now accepted to be a reference to Sophie and her role in the Society of the Sacred Heart, and the council decided that the time had come to record the early stories and myths. Twenty years of existence, first as Diletti, then as Dames de l'Instruction Chrétienne and finally as the Society of the Sacred Heart was quite a span of time. Several council members were commissioned to write the history of each of the houses so that these stories could be preserved and passed down through the generations to come.

Those present at the council were formidable women with strong ideas and points of view; as a matter of course differences between them arose during the sessions. Since the 1815 council Saint-Estève had continued to interfere in the affairs of the Society and had tried to force a fusion with the community of St Denys in Rome. Moreover, the Society was still in its infancy and a great deal had yet to be articulated. Any reference to tensions in the general council were suppressed in the minutes, but some mention was made of them in letters and Marie Balastron in Grenoble heard and spoke about them. Sophie wrote to her at the end of the council, clearly angry at the gossip:

> I hasten to . . . reassure you about the imprudent account of our council . . . there was total agreement throughout, and the short discussions needed to clarify matters resulted in the most satisfactory outcome for the good of the Society. Tell this to those who have been distressed, like you, to hear the contrary. It is essential for the good of the Society that false impressions are not given.[10]

The last thing Sophie needed just then was unrest in the houses, created by rumours and gossip. A basic unity had been achieved at the council because the tasks they had in hand were essential and were a focus for unity. The council addressed the subject of education, the major work of the Society. Sophie was aware that more attention was required with regard to the preparation of the teachers and the content of the curriculum. Several key documents which had been drawn up between 1804 and 1815 were reviewed and evaluated in 1820. A prize-giving booklet, published in 1805, outlined in some detail the content of the education given to the girls at Amiens during the early period.[11] It was an ambitious and comprehensive programme and in time the teachers discovered how much of it they could actually deliver to the students. In the early years in Amiens, especially between 1803 and 1805, the community had a good colleague in Nicolas Loriquet, the prefect of studies in the boys school run by the Fathers of the Faith in Amiens. He had helped the community both to prepare for their classes and to draw up texts for use in the school.[12] He had drawn up his own plan of studies for the boys' school and placed that at the disposal of the community, and this had obviously influenced the 1804 plan of studies.[13]

The plan dealt with the timetable, the number and order of classes, the content and the method of teaching. It covered a four-year course with the possibility of one or two more years of further studies for older pupils. The basic course of studies included reading, French grammar and spelling; arithmetic; history, geography and literature.[14] Another plan was drawn up in 1806 quite similar in content but the curriculum was expanded. It included religion, Latin, foreign languages, *arts d'agrément* (music, dancing, drawing), mythology, domestic economy and handwork. A further plan of studies was drawn up in 1810, with some small modifications to the text of 1806. This remained in force until 1820, when Sophie Barat asked the general council to revise the plan of studies and assess what improvements could be made to the standard of teaching.

Sophie asked Nicholas Loriquet, who by then had joined the Jesuits, to come to the general council and advise on the revision of the plan of studies. By this time Loriquet's own plan of studies, drawn up between 1805 and 1807, had been adopted in the Jesuit schools in France, as had his two-volume history of France.[15] The council examined the 1810 plan of studies for three days. Apart from some minor changes they found it adequate to the needs of the schools at this time. They recognised that the real difficulties lay in the lack of properly trained teachers, as well the mixed abilities of the pupils. These were matters Sophie Barat would address again and again in the course of her life. In February 1818 she had written to Thérèse Maillucheau, commenting on the quality of the teachers in the Society and the difficulty of providing adequate training for them:

> We are very short of competent teachers. The greatest difficulty is finding larger premises. We are obliged to send the older novices away to make room for the new ones. How few ask [to enter the Society] who have gifts for teaching![16]

The period of noviciate was two years, normally preceded by six months' postulancy. It was a short time in which to prepare women for commitment to religious life and for the task of teaching, which most were destined for in the Society. In Paris, not only were few entering with some previous formal education but even the time in the noviciate itself had to be shortened owing to lack of space and indeed to the pressure for personnel on the houses. In these circumstances Sophie counted on the superiors or the headmistresses in all the houses to continue the training of the teachers. She gave Eugénie de Gramont the task of training the young teachers as well as the pupils:

> It looks as if your boarding school is going to give you plenty of work. God will help you and soon I will too. Act with moderation and courage. Everywhere in this age children demand hard work. It is essential that you devote time to the teachers, let them talk to you and bring you up to date, and receive from you the guidance they need. In this way all act in harmony and understand each other. All have goodwill but they need to be trained since most have no experience.[17]

A month later she noted with appreciation:

Mother de Charbonnel tells me that you have shown the firmness which was necessary and which has produced the happiest results. To maintain this improvement you must insist on discipline, you must give authority to the teachers and uphold that authority in the school, and you need to meet the teachers regularly so that you act in harmony. Urge them to be constantly vigilant, to correct the pupils, and yet to do so without damaging them, speaking to them gently in the language of reason.[18]

She urged Thérèse Maillucheau to use the weekly community conferences on school affairs as a way of forming the young teachers, as long as the meetings were carefully prepared and properly run.[19] She was glad when there were few pupils in the new house at Villeurbanne in 1819 as this gave the time needed to prepare the core teaching group.[20]

Each school presented different needs and problems, according to the area in which it was established, and Sophie was often torn by the needs of each. Niort concerned her for it needed strong leadership:

One work which causes me sorrow is the little Providence of Niort, because it is failing for lack of leadership. It is an important foundation which deserves sacrifices on our part to support it . . . Will we not answer to God if we allow a house like that to suffer, even perish, for it is more useful than those we support with so many efforts. For in the end the children in the other [boarding] schools are not without resources, their wealth will allow them to have a good education. But for the orphans, it is total loss. Truly, the poor do not touch our lives enough.[21]

The needs in the school in Paris were of another order. There Sophie asked Eugénie de Gramont to retain an essential simplicity in the school, always a struggle for Eugénie after her early years under the influence of Saint-Estève:

I think it is important that you do not allow any acting of plays on feast days in the course of the year. These upset the routine in the school, put the pupils in a state of excitement and take them away from their work. These children, who are so easily distracted by nothing, ought to be guided towards simplicity. If they do play charades, then I think this should be only occasionally and without dressing up. For dressing up creates bedlam and leads to total disarray. Here then are some of my thoughts which I place before you. We need to take every means to find out what helps them best. But such children! They truly belong to their time![22]

Beauvais had different needs. Sophie visited there in April 1818 and was delighted to see that the school had over eighty boarders as well as 400 poor children at the free school, some of whom were being taught craft skills to enable them to earn a living. In addition, every Sunday between four and five hundred women attended classes given by several teachers in the community.[23] There in 1817 the prefect of the department (Oise) asked Sophie to adopt the Lancastrian method of teaching.[24] He suggested it would be especially useful when dealing with the numbers of poor children during the week and the adults on Sundays. However by this time the method had become politicised and it was a source of tension in the struggle for power in the schools. The Catholic church condemned the method as heretical, since it was initiated by English Protestants, but in reality it was a test of strength between the church and government.

Sophie was aware of the opinion of the clergy of Paris and politely informed the prefect that though she recognised the value of the method, she could not implement the Lancastrian method in Beauvais as it would fly in the face of church authority.[25] She warned Thérèse Maillucheau also to avoid the method even though it was being promoted in Grenoble:

> Regarding the new music method which you mentioned, known as the Lancastrian method, you must reject it, despite its advantages. Apparently there would be serious problems, and some have already arisen, were the Dames du Sacré Cœur to adopt this teaching method . . . You need to give this question your full attention. I have refused permission for the Lancastrian method everywhere. Here we use a method . . . by which several pupils learn at the same time. It is certainly not inspired by the Lancastrian method and yet real progress has been made by the pupils.[26]

The question arose in Savoy and in Louisiana whether or not to admit day pupils. Normally fees were requested only from those who were boarders in the schools and these fees were for food, heating and material needs, not for tuition. In order to maintain the school Sophie kept an eye on the fees in each school and recommended that they be increased if necessary.[27] In this context, day pupils presented a problem for while they could pay fees Sophie was not sure if they should be asked to so do. Philippine told her that if they did not take fees from the day pupils they would have no income at all. In Chambéry, the same issue arose and to both Sophie replied that they could take pupils and charge them a fee, but the pupils had to be educated separately.[28] Sophie's beliefs regarding education was inclusive in that she believed that education was the right of all, but, like so many of her generation, she did not see that social classes could be educated together. Referring to the school in Paris, Sophie spoke her mind:

> Our pupils especially cause us much concern. They are full of themselves and like only what pleases them. I put them to shame one day when I informed them that we were really punished by having only the nobility and that henceforth I would prefer [to have] the middle classes . . . One in particular objected strongly to this threat.[29]

By twentieth-century standards, education had a limited function for the women of nineteenth-century France: education for women at this time was seen as a preparation for marriage, motherhood, good housekeeping, letter-writing and the capacity to hold polite conversation, both as hostess in the home and in public. Sophie Barat thought that a basic education would enable the pupils to fulfil the expectations of their families and of society in general. She understood the role of women in society as that of wife and mother; as members of religious communities, either of the Society of the Sacred Heart or other congregations; or as single women, devoted to a life of good works in society. These roles could be lived out in private or in public, but they were tasks that their education in school should prepare them to accomplish. Women were called to revitalise the life of the family, the life of the church and life in the world, according to their calling. Sophie Barat hoped that the education offered by the Society of the Sacred Heart would be solid and thorough enough to help women fulfil their destinies in life.

The general council of 1820 also reviewed the spiritual life of the Society. While no substantial changes were made to the constitutions and rules of 1815, some recommendations were passed which circumscribed the activity of the members of the Society. The most significant of these referred to travel and mobility in the area of work. The council defined more precisely than before those situations when members of the Society could leave the houses, either for travel or business. Members were no longer free to go to spas and take the waters as a health cure. More significantly, whereas before some had left the confines of the house and property to work with the poor in particular, all works of the Society were to take place now within the house. For this reason, the council directed that only those properties which were large enough to accommodate a school and community, and which had extensive gardens attached for farming and for recreation, could be accepted in the future. The number of visitors and the occasions upon which they could enter the parts of the house and gardens reserved for the community and the school was defined, though access to the gardens was less strict.[30] Joseph Varin finally presented his summary of the constitutions and rules, a task he had been asked to do in 1815 and completed hastily in 1820. The council decided this should be read each month in every community, with the letter of St Ignatius of Loyola on the virtue of obedience. Another task was to draw up a text of the rites of religious ceremonies, called a Ceremonial, outlining the procedure for initiation into the Society, and for final commitment. Clearly Sophie and the council were preparing documentation in view of seeking formal approval from the pope, something Sophie Barat saw as essential for the Society, especially after the upheavals with Saint-Estève. Such approval would ratify her own authority, establish a certain independence for the Society of the Sacred Heart in France and make access to other parts of the world easier. At the same time Sophie hoped it would finally lessen if not remove the capacity of Saint-Estève, and those associated with him, to disturb and divide the Society.

The general council concluded its work on 13 October 1820 with the elections to office. Catherine de Charbonnel, Josephine Bigeu and Henriette Grosier were elected assistants general to Sophie Barat; Félicité Desmarquest, Suzanne Geoffroy, Lydie Chobelet, Geneviève Deshayes, Eugénie de Gramont and Marie Prevost, in that order, were elected general councillors to Sophie Barat. Catherine de Charbonnel was elected bursar general, Henriette Grosier admonatrix to Sophie Barat, and Henriette Ducis secretary general of the Society, replacing Philippine Duchesne. It was clear that while Eugénie de Gramont was not a popular vote among the electors she had enough supporters to be elected as fifth general councillor.[31] Undoubtedly she had gifts and skills which were being used to good effect in the rue de Varenne. She had also contributed greatly to the public profile of the Society in Paris and indeed in France. But she was regarded as a cold, distant woman and had few friends in the Society. Her friendship with Sophie was a source of unease among some members of the Society. This was the tension which Marie Balastron had heard about in Grenoble and which Sophie either refused to acknowledge or simply did not see.

For Sophie the general council of 1820 had been a consolidating experience. The council had confirmed the overall vision and goals of the Society of the Sacred Heart. Members were elected to the roles and offices, though since Sophie Barat had been elected for life in 1806 her role was not open for election. Some points in the rules and constitutions had been clarified and in the light of experience modified or changed. The plan of studies had been considered adequate to the needs of the students, but the need for good teachers was underlined. The council had also taken time to reflect on the origins of the Society and appointed several members to write its history. Once the council closed Sophie began planning the move from the rue des Postes to the Hôtel Biron. She went to see the property again and decided which sections would be used by the school and which by the community and noviciate. The actual Hôtel Biron would be used only by the school. The community would live in the stables area, in the buildings formerly used by the servants and horses. Some of the students in the rue des Postes were brought over to see their new school and they were delighted to know they would be in the actual Hôtel Biron, intrigued and impressed as they were by its splendour and flamboyant decoration. However, when they arrived some weeks later to begin life there in the boarding school a great deal of the splendour and decoration in the Hôtel had been removed. While Sophie did not wish to change the outward beauty and style of the Hôtel Biron, she did simplify the inner decorative work, and was especially anxious to remove the painting and ornamentation which she considered too sensuous. Later art critics would condemn her for this, lamenting the loss of eighteenth-century artistic work. Yet, it is important to remember that she belonged to her time and acted in the spirit of the guidelines issued in 1810 by the municipality of Paris. The city authorities established women inspectors for lay schools in Paris and in 1813 these inspectors noted the need to eradicate luxury in boarding schools and in particular to eliminate 'indecent gravings' in the schools which could harm the morals of the pupils. Further legislation in the period following the restoration only confirmed these efforts to avoid frivolity and worldliness in the lay boarding schools for young women in Paris.[32] Sophie Barat would have considered this all the more necessary for a school run by religious, especially in the Faubourg Saint-Germain.

Preparations for moving to the Hôtel Biron were completed quickly and on 10 October 1820 the school and community transferred from the rue des Postes to the rue de Varenne. The duchesse d'Angoulême and the duchesse de Berry visited the school on the 19 November 1820, welcomed officially by Sophie and Eugénie de Gramont. A few days later the duchesse de Berry brought her little daughter to the school and this was seen as a further mark of approval and acceptance. Such visits by royalty were common in Paris at this time and many other schools received such marks of attention, especially in the early years of the Restoration. Yet by receiving such marks of approval and recognition the Society of the Sacred Heart became identified with the Bourbons and ultimately with the forces of reaction.

News of the purchase of the Hôtel Biron reached Louisiana, and Eugénie Audé wrote to Louis Barat about it, expressing her criticism. At a time when the new foundation in Louisiana was poor and struggling to survive in conditions which those in Paris could not even imagine, the expense of the Hôtel Biron appeared enormous. Louis told Sophie about this letter and she wrote to Eugénie Audé, defending the decision:

> I need to say to you in passing that the reflections you made to Father Barat, and I do not know who else, regarding our purchase of the Hôtel Biron, were out of place, to say the least. We are no better off here than elsewhere, thank God, and the stables area where we live is not at all great. I hope we will practise poverty there and I do not think that any of us is more attached to it than to the poorest house. We had to find accommodation, and it was impossible to find it anywhere else. This difficulty led to the decision of the general council to buy the property. Undoubtedly . . . if I had the choice I would not hesitate between your humble abode and ours.[33]

Once the decision was taken by the general council in August 1820 to try and buy the property, a change of tone in the council minutes becomes noticeable. The members in some ways realised the importance of the step they had taken, for they had created a public profile for the Society of the Sacred Heart. They were aware of dangers this new profile of the Hôtel Biron could have for their reputation and so the council members passed recommendations regarding simplicity and poverty of life. When Joseph Varin finally finished the task of writing a summary of the constitutions he included a new accent on the need for simplicity and poverty in the Society. Eugénie Audé's reaction represented some of the impact such a purchase would make on the Society over the years – at the time it seemed an entirely pragmatic decision, providing adequate accommodation in Paris. And although Sophie had no idea then of the long-term effects of buying the new property, many years later she reflected ruefully on the choice she had made in 1820:

> Unfortunately we shall never be able to eliminate the disastrous impression spread throughout France and to other parts of the world, concerning our so-called extravagance at the beginning of the boarding school in Paris. The gilded mansion gave it this reputation and some teachers did not prevent the pupils from spending money needlessly. This unfortunate reputation still goes round the world and each year deprives us of a great number of pupils, to the advantage of other schools . . . So every time these pious people in society either see us or hear of us placing a value on worldly ways, on the nobility, on greatness, or if our conversations are not serious enough, religious, full of zeal for the salvation of all, then we are criticised, judged harshly and often people no longer respect us.[34]

Joseph Varin spoke to the council during its days of prayer before the formal opening, when he knew the Hôtel Biron was on the agenda for discussion. He admitted that Jesuit buildings and schools were very prestigious, indeed no church could be more lavish and extravagant than the Gesù church in Rome. The members struggled to live simply and austerely but it was difficult. In his desire to make money Lavalette had speculated, had destroyed the Jesuits in France and precipitated their suppression.[35] Turning to the Society of the Sacred Heart he warned:

> I can say here that I have met people who believe that the spirit and manners of the Society are still too worldly.
>
> Only six weeks ago someone said to me, referring not only to one of your houses in the provinces: I thought I would enter the Society of the Sacred Heart but I find that it still it has too much of the spirit of the world. So try and steer a middle path, so difficult to find.[36]

Yet long before the Hôtel Biron was purchased in September 1820 the worldly reputation of the Society of the Sacred Heart had already been established. This was no doubt due in part to the school at Amiens, and especially to the influence of Saint-Estève and Anne Baudemont and later Eugénie de Gramont. This reputation existed in the rue des Postes in Paris also. On the occasion of a vows ceremony in Beauvais, in 1816, it was noted by the town authorities that most of the members of the Society came from higher classes of French society.[37] Sophie had acknowledged this in a letter to the archbishop of Bordeaux in April 1819 when there was question of the Society taking over an orphanage:

> ... Mme Lalanne's institution appeals to me in preference to other, more splendid foundations, precisely because of the spirit of poverty, humility and simplicity present there. In my opinion this work will draw us closer to the Heart of our divine Master. Humble and obscure beginnings are more in keeping with His spirit and more appropriate to attract his blessing on our Society ... This work is not at all new to us. It is in keeping with our constitutions to devote ourselves to the education of the poor. It is for that purpose that each of our foundations has a free school and that at Grenoble and Beauvais we have training classes for the daughters of the poor and they are taught trade skills.[38]

The Society of the Sacred wished to develop a form and content of education for girls which was essentially for two groups in society: the aristocracy/upper middle class, and the poor. All innovative actions draw criticisms and as early as 1802, when the Diletti advertised the form and type of education they wished to offer in Amiens, the public mocked their ambition, their audacity in offering a broad wide education for girls:

> an article published in an Italian newspaper was soon copied by the French newspapers. It gave an account of an association recently set up by learned women who, inspired by the spirit of both St Francis de Sales and of Fénelon, devoted themselves to the education of youth, with the title of The Beloved of Jesus ... people speak in several ways about them: some make fun of them especially on account of their description as learned women and because of the predictions they claim,

as if they were announcing a new world and the good that they were called to do in the world. Others, though this was the smallest number, thanked God and praised his mercy when they saw a means which they considered adapted to the needs of the time, destined in the long term to prepare for the renewal of society, which they longed for with all their hearts.[39]

As a woman from a small town in France, from a modest background, Sophie Barat had already done extraordinary things with her life, but who could ever have imagined that she would buy the Hôtel Biron and establish the centre of the Society of the Sacred Heart in the Faubourg Saint-Germain? Of all her decisions, this was the one which was fraught with questions and ambiguities and often threatened to unravel all her work and ideals. At the time it was a pragmatic, indeed courageous, decision but many people had misgivings; Louis Barat was one. He was in no doubt that the city of Paris, never mind the Faubourg Saint-Germain, was a city full of dangers for any who wished to live a Christian life. He was steeped in the Book of Revelations, in the language of the last days, of Antichrist and the falling of the kingdoms of this world, and he used such language until the end of his life. When his nephew, Stanislas Dusaussoy, came to Paris looking for a job, his uncle told him to help Sister Rosalie, a member of the Daughters of Charity, who worked with the poor of Paris:

> This will be a source and channel of blessing for you which will give you the strength to remain in the furnace of Babylon, like the three children, without getting burnt . . . You will require heroic virtue to withstand the attacks of ungodliness and the onslaughts of sensual pleasure. For Paris is the Babylon of Europe . . .[40]

Throughout her life the Hôtel Biron proved to be a constant source of worry and concern for Sophie Barat. In the context of establishing the centre of the Society of the Sacred Heart in Paris, the appointment of Eugénie de Gramont as headmistress of the school was a momentous choice. Eugénie de Gramont remained headmistress in Paris from 1816 until her death in 1846. With her aristocratic background and forceful personality she gradually created the reputation and direction of the Society of the Sacred Heart not only in Paris but also in France and further afield. She was often either considered or treated as the real superior general of the Society. Indeed Eugénie de Gramont's contribution, especially in the years immediately after 1815, blended well with the restoration of the Bourbons and the desire among counter-revolutionaries and indeed the émigrés, to pick up where they had left off in 1789. Thus Sophie's appointment of Eugénie de Gramont allowed Eugénie to reinvent the type and style of school and community in Paris that was very similar to that created by Saint-Estève in Amiens. The irony lay in the fact that the Society of the Sacred Heart needed to be successful in the capital, needed to draw students and novices, needed a public profile. The desire to have a centre and a new start for the Society of the Sacred Heart was of vital importance for Sophie, but there were other forces than hers at work in Paris. She would learn, very painfully, that many of the values of the inner circle of Amiens had been transferred to Paris, as Perreau feared, and she was left to struggle with their influence all her life, hardly admitting to herself, perhaps never really knowing, the hold Eugénie de Gramont had over her and over the Society of the Sacred Heart.

This was far from Sophie's original vision and intention. She envisaged the house in Paris as forming the spiritual centre, the model and inspiration of the Society of the Sacred Heart. All those who joined the Society would receive their initial training there, at the source, and then spread that spirit wherever they went. In Sophie's mind, it was not that Paris was the centre of the Society of the Sacred Heart but that the Society needed a centre which turned out to be Paris. Yet in 1820 she and the general council were caught in the double bind of wanting to live according to the values of the Gospel, while at the same time accepting the help of the powerful in society to actually achieve that goal. In Paris the powerful at this time were the nobility. With Eugénie de Gramont in the community, doors to the king and to patronage were opened. Contemporary pedagogical thinking within the Catholic church valued the education of the aristocracy and wealthy class in society and saw this as the path to restoring a Christian society in France in the wake of the Revolution. Even on the missions Philippine encountered this thinking in Bishop Dubourg and it blocked her way to the Indians. He told Philippine in 1818 that by educating the wealthy, rather than the Indians, she would have greater impact on society. He assured her that the rich would have a good influence on the poor.[41]

In the years following the 1820 general council, except for some weeks away visiting communities in other parts of France, Sophie lived in the rue de Varenne. There, in addition to her work of guiding the Society, she was closely involved in the running of the school. Sophie acted as a bridge between Eugénie de Gramont and the members of the community. Sophie confronted Eugénie over her attitude towards some members of the Society, and she did this either while she was present in the rue de Varenne, or by letter if she was absent for a time from Paris. For example, in 1823, the chaplain in the school asked the students to make a financial contribution to the clerical fund in the diocese. Catherine de Charbonnel, in charge in Sophie's absence, told Eugénie de Gramont and Henriette Ducis, that she thought only the community should contribute money to the clergy. Instead of discussing the issue Eugénie de Gramont completely overrode Catherine de Charbonnel and invited a cleric to speak to the school about the request for money. This direct snub could not be ignored and Catherine de Charbonnel felt it deeply. She was by nature a reserved and painfully shy woman and such a high-handed manner on the part of her colleague both shocked and wounded her. She told Sophie about it and this incident evoked a firm reprimand. Sophie reminded Eugénie that she had a reputation for such rudeness in the Society and that such events only confirmed it:

> You know that these reflections will not stay just there, that they will be passed on to others, and that you will be judged harshly. I tell you again: take care, it is necessary.[42]

By all accounts, the young women at the rue de Varenne were a handful and discipline was difficult to maintain. A contemporary account of the school indicates the level of society from which they came and the level of studies in the school. Marie de Flavigny (1805–1876), later the comtesse d'Agoult and writer under the pseudonym Daniel Stern, began her studies in the rue de Varenne on 28 April 1821. Even at this early stage the reputation of the Hôtel Biron had been established and it had become fashionable to go to school there. Marie de Flavigny had a room of her own, with a piano. She was allowed to have a music teacher come to the school to give her lessons, though always under supervision by one of the community; she could leave the Hôtel Biron any time her relations asked to see her in Paris. The new student was impressed by the grandeur of the house and the opulence of the decoration. These qualities were matched in the religious, who,

> under their black veil, their cross of silver on their breast, and their long rosary at the side, . . . took care not to forget their family background. Most of them were from old families, and some of very noble blood. With rare exceptions, they only accepted pupils from the nobility, either of the court or from the provinces . . . the general tone was in the highest sense aristocratic.[43]

The aristocratic background of the pupils at the rue de Varenne was its distinguishing mark and it created an exclusivity which was impossible to modify.[44] Indeed there was a certain awkwardness when either relations or friends of members of the Society, who did not belong to the nobility, asked to send their daughters to the rue de Varenne. When Félicité Desmarquest wanted her niece to go to the rue de Varenne she asked Sophie to ensure that the girl was not placed in a class with the nobility. The child had to have a special teacher in a special class. The Desmarquest family paid the fees by providing wine for the school and community, a practice of the Dusaussoy family also.[45] Sophie had to insist that Eugénie de Gramont accept Philippine Duchesne's niece, even though the family were wealthy and highly educated. The irony was that many of the aristocracy were penniless and could not afford to pay fees at all. Sophie once remarked drily, they were extremely mean with their money, especially for their daughter's education. Yet when she recognised a genuine need Sophie reduced fees for the nobility, as in the case of the de Choiseul family,[46] because she recognised the needs of this class and was convinced that an educated, Christian élite could transform society. She worried that the scale of fees at the rue de Varenne would prevent pupils being sent there. In 1825, when visiting the houses in the west of France, Sophie heard in Poitiers, Niort and Bordeaux that parents chose to send their daughters to the convent of Les Oiseaux in Paris, rather than to the rue de Varenne, on account of the fees required by the Society of the Sacred Heart.[47]

Marie de Flavigny was critical of many aspects of the education offered and in particular of the leadership of Eugénie de Gramont. While Antoinette de Gramont attracted her and remained for her all her life an image of the 'Eternal Feminine' Eugénie was quite different:

Her sister, Eugénie, a haughty small woman who had a congenital deformity. She had grey, cold eyes, a hoarse voice, long bony fingers and a harsh commanding manner.[48]

While the school saw Eugénie de Gramont daily, Sophie Barat was more distant:

> The superior of the community, Madame Barat, a woman of great authority who did not appear much, sent for me. Speaking in an austere voice she praised me quietly and in a Christian way. She commended my wisdom, my sincere faith.[49]

On one occasion, Marie de Flavigny and her companions decided to give Antoinette de Gramont a bouquet of flowers for her feast. Eugénie de Gramont was furious and refused to allow Antoinette receive the flowers. Marie was called to her office to explain herself and to prepare an apology for the community. At this Marie rebelled, became ill with fever and refused to eat. In the end:

> It was Madame Barat, the superior general, whose unseen and dreaded authority inspired a sort of terror in the boarding school, who had to come to my bedside for I had not slept for a whole week. She rendered full justice to my integrity. She said to me in truly Christian simplicity that they had made a mistake in my case, that they were wrong, that they were sorry, she most of all . . . Without any flattery, or caresses, or promises, by a simple word of truth, Madame Barat calmed and healed me. My hand in hers, reconciled, I listened to the reflections she felt she should make, the warnings she gave me on the disadvantages and the dangers of [having] too strong affections, and the need to moderate even the most legitimate of loves.[50]

The contrasting style of Sophie Barat and Eugénie de Gramont was easily perceived by this young woman. Clearly Sophie Barat was in charge of the school and community and even of the autocratic Eugénie de Gramont. The school needed that care since, because of her congenital physical deformity, Eugénie de Gramont drove herself hard. Yet despite her own experience of frailty, she was unaware of the care needed by young children and by young women in the process of growing up. Eugénie de Gramont accompanied the chronic illness and subsequent death of a pupil with great drama. Such deaths were revered almost to the extent of a cult. Dying at a young age, in extremes of piety and resignation was considered fashionable and a 'grace' for the school. Sophie thought nothing of the sort and she had to reprimand Eugénie de Gramont constantly for not taking care of the pupils at the early stage of their illnesses. She criticised Dr Recamier in Paris and wanted to dismiss him as school doctor:

> in this important matter, my dear Eugénie, you are not without some blame. You certainly look after those who are ill wonderfully. This is acknowledged by everyone, and this applies to Mr Recamier, too. But you make too little of slight illnesses and do not take any preventative measures. Your pupils say this to their parents . . . I have endured much worry and suffering about this, for I know what the complaints are and I know also that you are not sufficiently aware of them. For instance, I myself saw how you treated one of the Moretus [family] for rheumatism in the neck. She needed to be kept warm, to rest in bed and to remain in her room . . .

You constantly sent her to class, and in the end, one day when you saw her more muffled up than usual, you said to her in a sarcastic tone of voice: Soon you will be wearing a mattress. The little girl, really hurt, went to take off the extra clothing; her companions protested and the little girl complained bitterly to one of the community . . . of the way you were treating her . . . Her mother came to the school a few days later.

I am asking you to consider the effect of this and how much harm all such incidents will do to the school. Moreover, they touch our conscience for we are responsible for them body and soul. All these serious problems will disappear if you set aside your own point of view [in this matter], which deep down is kind . . . Everywhere I recommend that we err by more care rather than less . . . Forgive me, my good Eugénie, for speaking so plainly. This matter has been weighing on me for some time . . .[51]

Two weeks later Sophie had to reprimand Eugénie again, for allowing children to sleep in a newly plastered dormitory, endangering their health and creating conditions for an epidemic.[52] Such letters were clear and direct, with no watering down of the truth as Sophie saw it. Eugénie de Gramont was offended by her observations and told Sophie that she felt blamed for the deaths of the pupils in the school. Sophie rejected that interpretation and insisted that Eugénie build on preventative measures for safeguarding the health of the boarders. Sophie often urged Eugénie to make sure the school received proper meals, in good quantity. In hot weather she reminded Eugénie that plenty of liquids were required, that the pupils should have lemon drinks as a precaution; they also needed to be taken into the garden in the evenings and to take exercise by the light of the moon.[53]

When Sophie and Eugénie were together at the rue de Varenne they were a good combination. Sophie was down to earth, practical and shrewd, had a firm hand and a clear overview. Eugénie had social and family connections which established the reputation of the rue de Varenne and of the Society of the Sacred Heart. This created possibilities for the Society's quick growth and expansion. Eugénie had easy access to the sources of power and she cultivated this to a fine art. She found her way about in court circles and knew the nobility of the Faubourg Saint-Germain. She also cultivated the clergy and in particular the archbishop of Paris, Hyacinthe de Quelen. The school was successful. By 1824 there were 106 boarders and, due to lack of accommodation, several pupils came in by day. The numbers gradually increased and just before the Revolution in July 1830 there were 160 boarders. From 1823 Sophie had planned a poor school in the rue de Varenne.[54] This did not materialise but a school for disabled students was opened. Perhaps Eugénie de Gramont, with her own disability, was sensitive to the needs of such children. In any event by 1827 there were twenty-five physically handicapped children in the rue de Varenne and other houses, such as Besançon, Lyon and Turin, were following its example. It was expensive and Sophie was not in favour of this work developing generally in the Society. Despite the growth in numbers in the school, the plan of studies created in 1806 and revised in 1816 and 1820, was superficially implemented in the rue de

Varenne under the leadership of Eugénie de Gramont. The boarders lived a semi-monastic life as the school journals show. Emphasis was placed on religious instruction, religious practices of piety, processions, masses, devotions, confessions. As Eugénie de Gramont was close to the court and to the inner circles of the clergy, visits from royalty and bishops grew more frequent and disrupted the rhythm of the school constantly.

In her memoirs Marie de Flavigny recalled her disappointment at the standard of education given at the rue de Varenne. When she wanted to discuss articles of the faith with Joseph Varin he rejected her intellectual curiosity and avoided her questions. Instead he told her to avoid the influence of the devil and not pry into the mysteries of God. He tried to persuade her to practise devotions of piety but she could not and after a time he desisted. She was surprised to discover that in the senior class of six pupils which she joined in 1823 only two of the six could spell. According to Marie de Flavigny, studies consisted for the most part on the 'arts d'agrément', all in preparation for marriage. She was critical of the books used to teach history and resented the fact that they were the texts written by Nicolas Loriquet. She had read widely before she came to Paris, had met Goethe and Chateaubriand and she moved in circles where art, music and literature were the normal subject of conversation.[55] Thus in many respects Marie de Flavigny was not typical of her contemporaries in the rue de Varenne. Her reading experience before she came to school in Paris was unusual and she certainly found herself starved of intellectual content and satisfaction while she was at the rue de Varenne.[56]

While Marie Flavigny was at school at the rue de Varenne, Marie d'Olivier, a member of the Society in Lyon, presented Sophie with some ideas regarding the quality of education given in the Society, and she suggested how the standard could be raised.[57] She argued that since the Revolution there had been a profound ignorance in society regarding religion and the moral life, and that women would bring about a renewal of society and especially of family life. In view of this, Marie d'Olivier criticised the accent in the curriculum on pious practices of religion, learning by rote and too great an emphasis on the 'arts d'agrément'. More solid instruction was needed as well as training the capacity to think independently. Many of the young women in the school were destined to spend a good deal of their lives in society, in the salons of Paris and other cities of Europe. There they would hear opinions, views and ideas from all quarters of society; church, state, the army, the arts:

> The age we live in is marked by a spirit of reasoning and daring . . . Faith is almost entirely banished from our world . . . Will our pupils keep their integrity if they do not have values which are well thought out . . . if they do not have serious dispositions . . . if, in the end, they do not have in fact what is the true purpose of a wise education, if they have not learnt how to think? How will they protect themselves from the arguments they hear not only in public, but also from their brothers, their husbands, their cousins and even their fathers. That is, from a society which they cannot and should not avoid.[58]

In view of these goals Marie d'Olivier urged the production of three basic texts for the schools, in history, literature and natural history. The teachers in the school should be properly prepared for teaching these texts. The task of preparation of lessons and the actual teaching should be seen as integral to the commitment to religious life. She argued that such discipline and study were an aid to a deeper inner life, especially of prayer. If every school had a nucleus of good teachers then the Society of the Sacred Heart would enhance its reputation for serious studies. Since the Society of the Sacred Heart wished to model itself on the Jesuits there was no need to invent a programme. Rather the Jesuit model of education could be adopted, with the help of the Jesuits.

The following year, Marie d'Olivier wrote another paper for Sophie and for Josephine Bigeu in which she presented her idea of having a periodical not only for past pupils of the Society's schools but for all interested women, from all classes of society.[59] This document was the result of thoughts she had shared with Sophie in the course of conversations. Sophie had asked her to write down her thoughts and present them to her in the form of proposals. Marie d'Olivier argued in the document that her ideal form of education responded exactly to the aim and purpose of the Society of the Sacred Heart: to glorify the Heart of Christ by forming those who would learn to worship God in spirit and in truth. This worship of God had to come from an informed understanding of the Christian life and the Society of the Sacred Heart was founded to educate in this way. The work done in the schools could be reinforced by a journal to which all would be invited to subscribe. Through articles and commentaries as well as the exchange of letters in the journal, d'Olivier hoped the education of women could be continued, not just within France but throughout Europe and further afield. The journal had to be published completely independently of the government and she suggested that perhaps the printing could be done in Turin, or later in Rome when the Society had extended there. Fundamental to her thinking was the conviction that women in her time were destined to renew society. She had told Sophie that she had discussed her ideas with Nicolas Loriquet. He encouraged her and told Sophie that Marie d'Olivier's ideas needed to be heard. Marie accompanied her paper with a rough outline of the proposed journal.[60]

Sophie knew Marie d'Olivier well and had watched her develop her ideas over several years, indeed she had encouraged her to speak and write. By 1826 Sophie had appointed Marie d'Olivier as superior of Beauvais, an appointment which needed both energy and skill in dealing with local authorities in the town. She succeeded quickly and established the school on a firmer footing, creating the conditions for future developments. In her letters during this period Sophie declared herself well satisfied with the school at Beauvais. She was less sure of the writings of Marie d'Olivier. In 1827 Sophie wrote to Adrienne Michel about d'Olivier's writings, basically moral tales for young women:

> I have not got the time to go into what you say in your letters about Mme d'Olivier. Write to her yourself whatever you wish. We correct her work here, for her tales are

rather like steel which has to be drawn from the earth and polished. She has not got a notion of the profound subtlety in expressing feelings, in use of speech, choice of epithets. She belongs to the age of Louis XIII. That has to be updated now. What a happy time it was, why has it disappeared?[61]

The following year Sophie received a letter from Nicolas Loriquet, commenting positively on the work of Marie d'Olivier. His opinion was important and Sophie admitted that she did not like either the work or the approach of Marie d'Olivier. She refused even to consider the publication of a periodical. In the context of the time, when the Jesuit schools were on the point of being suppressed and the Society of the Sacred Heart was linked with the Jesuits, any form of publication would have drawn unnecessary attention to the schools of the Society of the Sacred Heart. Instead Sophie asked Loriquet to encourage d'Olivier for the present and to defer any decision on making her work more accessible.[62]

During these years Sophie Barat's family in Joigny used her position of influence in Paris to advance their own careers. Sophie tried to get a position for Stanislas in Paris and asked Eugénie de Gramont to help her; but in the end both failed as Stanislas had not sufficient capacity for work nor was he suited to life in the capital.[63] Stanislas wanted to get married and he asked his aunt if she could recommend a young woman, but Sophie advised him to wait:

> You must wait until you have a suitable home, for since you cannot promise a fortune you must at least offer something to take its place. Without this precaution you will be refused by those families who belong to a higher class in society, and you must avoid a refusal. That is why I have held back. I cannot get any Sacred Heart pupil for you in your position, none would accept you. I have ideas, but I fear they will never come to fruition. We have so few to choose from the (court) nobility and from the provinces, either not a big enough dowry or other drawbacks.[64]

Sophie also tried to find jobs for her cousins, the Rambaud and Martineau families at Joigny.[65] Her own position as superior general as well as the success of the Society convinced her relations that she could win them favours. Not only her family held this view. Madame de Fars Fausselandry wryly remarked that in the 1820s in Paris:

> all I needed was to be associated with the Society of the Sacred Heart and then ministerial favours of every kind would be showered upon me.[66]

Yet over the years the close identification of the Society of the Sacred Heart with the aristocracy in Paris became restrictive. Slowly and painfully Sophie recognised that her work had been stifled and deflected from its original purpose. She had to accept that she had both initiated her imprisonment and enjoyed the captivity, at least for time. Had the Society not expanded so quickly, within France and beyond, this may not have caused undue tension in the long term. But even at this early stage in the Society's history its growth was rapid, within France and beyond. Indeed, the general council of 1820 had hardly ended when new foundations were being planned. In the course of a few years, between 1820 and 1825, houses were opened in France at Le Mans, Autun and Besançon; at Turin in the kingdom of Sardinia; at Grand Coteau in southern Louisiana. Two diocesan communities, at Metz and Bordeaux, asked to be fully integrated into the Society; and many of the former members of the community at Ghent, which had separated in 1814, wanted to rejoin. Sophie herself could hardly keep up with the pace of growth. Since they had abandoned the hope of having a foundation in St Louis, Philippine and Eugénie Audé decided to accept the offer of Mrs Smith, a wealthy widow, who honoured the wishes of her husband by founding a school in Lower Louisiana. Mrs Smith provided the property and after a long and laborious beginning Grand Coteau, the new school, began to grow. Sophie could only support this from afar, and help first with money and later in 1821 with more personnel. However, once Grand Coteau was established, Sophie urged consolidation rather than further expansion, even if it meant that for the time being Philippine could not go to the Indians at Providence (Rhode Island). Instead she advised Philippine to try and establish a centre in New Orleans or in St Louis. She also insisted that, as far as possible, borrowing of money for the communities and schools in Louisiana should be transacted in France as the rates of interest in Louisiana were exorbitant.[67]

In her letters Sophie told Philippine the extent of the developments in France:

> We are so urged to accept foundations, and we refuse a great number. However, we cannot let every opportunity pass us by. Le Mans has begun. Autun will begin in six months time. Since Autun is half way between Paris and Lyon, this house will be very useful to the Society. The house has been given to us with 600 francs annually and a small amount of money to help us begin. Formerly it was a Visitation convent.[68]
>
> The house at Turin has begun . . . The King and Queen are responsible for the finances of this school founded for the young noblewomen of their States. Mère de Charbonnel has just taken over the former government house at Besançon, and she will open the boarding school there sometime around November.[69]

The absorption of the community at Metz was effected in 1825. This diocesan community, the Dames de Sainte-Sophie de Metz, had been founded in 1807 by the local bishop. They had linked up with another community in Charleville, the Dames de la Providence. When the French dioceses were redrawn in 1821, the community at Charleville came under the jurisdiction of the archbishop of Rheims, rather than the bishop of Metz. In view of this the bishop of Metz broke the link between the two communities and he asked Sophie Barat to accept the community into the Society of the Sacred Heart. After a visit to Metz, Sophie accepted the proposal, since the community ran a good school. The experience also confirmed Sophie's own instinct about the need to remain independent from diocesan bishops whose policies could radically change the fortunes of any community.[70]

The situation in Bordeaux was somewhat different and went back to Sophie's early days. The community of Madame Vincent, known as the Sisters of Notre

Dame, originated in 1791, at the height of the Revolution. In 1807 Julie Billiart
integrated this community into her congregation and this lasted until she was
forced to leave Amiens in 1811. The community of the Dames Vincent then
asked Sophie Barat to accept them into the Society but some of the clergy
opposed this move. The community then, without consulting Sophie Barat, took
the name, the dress and way of life of the Society of the Sacred Heart as their
model. Sophie wrote to Emilie Giraud:

> My presence is needed in Bordeaux. Madame Vincent's community wants to join
> us and prudent friends tell us we should agree to this, if our conditions are accept-
> ed. This step will put an end to the scandal of having two communities in opposi-
> tion to one another. I must admit though that I would have left them free, without
> being in the least worried. God is the Father of us all, and I think the same as your
> Mère Geoffroy. I like to see God loved and glorified by all who wish to do so. Some
> think also that we should hold on to our rights. Alas! they are mistaken. How many
> abuses there are in the church on this pretext.[71]

In the midst of her concerns over Bordeaux, Sophie received a request for the
incorporation of several members of the former community at Doorseele in
Ghent. In the summer of 1822 the community had received an ultimatum from
the government of the Netherlands requiring that it submit within fifteen days
to new regulations regarding the school or leave the premises. Marie-Antoinette
de Peñaranda, a former member of the Association des Dames de l'Instruction
Chrétienne at Amiens, had become the superior general of the congregation and
had given each member the option of either leaving or staying in Ghent. The
headmistress of the school, Louise de Limminghe (1792–1874), left almost
immediately for Paris and asked Sophie to receive her back into the Society. De
Peñaranda also decided that she could not accept the constrictions placed on the
community by the Dutch government and decided to try and found a school in
Lille. This did not materialise and she too asked Sophie Barat to receive her into
the Society of the Sacred Heart. Others followed suit and during the year
between eighteen and twenty members of the community at Ghent asked to be
incorporated into the Society of the Sacred Heart.[72]

Sophie was quick to see the advantages the closure of the school in Doorsele
would have for the school at Amiens. Yet the fusion brought back difficult memories for Sophie:

> I did not believe then that I was a prophet. But when they broke off from us with
> so little tact and sensitivity, I wrote to them, and I have not forgotten my words:
> that it was not in my power to hold on to them, [that the] branch cut off from the
> trunk would wither and die . . . Of course, they could begin again someday; but you
> see now that they had to pay the price. What an example. The Society needs to
> understand this![73]

These three initiatives, from Metz, Bordeaux and Ghent, show that the
Society of the Sacred Heart was seen as young and promising, opening possibilities of survival to small groups trapped in a particular situation, either within a

diocese or in another country. Sophie did not seek such affiliations and was quite pragmatic, and indeed could be dismissive, of the quality of personnel which each group brought to the Society. She had specifically said in 1815 that she did not wish to have too many members of other congregations in the Society. It made the formation of the members too difficult and tended to dilute what Sophie saw as a new form of religious life. However this remained an ideal, for many other members of the Society, not from Metz, Bordeaux or Ghent, had spent some time in a religious congregation before asking to join the Society of the Sacred Heart. In a time of great change and upheaval this could not have been otherwise.

— 8 —

INNER JOURNEYS, CHURCH-STATE
RELATIONS, 1825-1826

As a general rule, Sophie accepted, planned and co-ordinated the new foundations in the Society, but once a decision had been taken, she discussed its implementation with several key members of the Society, especially Catherine de Charbonnel and Josephine Bigeu, and these carried out Sophie's wishes, even though it meant they were away from either Paris or their own communities for long periods of time. Once a new house was ready to open then Sophie sent the nucleus of the new community, with a named leader, to begin the new work. As the foundations increased Sophie retained direct contact with them through the letters she wrote to each superior. These letters were her means of forming those in leadership, many of whom had no experience at all of what it meant to run a house, run a school and a community, deal with local secular and church authorities, give spiritual guidance and support, and, most of all, model and maintain the spiritual vision of the Society. It was a daunting task for each leader, and one that Sophie herself understood. Her letters are a mixture of encouragement, correction, advice and trust, and they range over a variety of business and personal matters.

Adelaide de Rozeville was appointed the superior at Besançon in 1824. Sophie wrote to encourage her in her new task in a new house:

> What efforts you will have to make! how often you will have to put yourself aside, how often you will have to support others. And all this without a doubt brings us deeper into the ways of God and also ensures that we do not damage the work

which has been confided to us and for which we have, for the most part, the greatest responsibility . . . How many smaller issues we ought to overlook . . . and then we understand what *forgetfulness of self* means, and see only to the concerns of God . . . At that point . . . we need to expand our soul, fill our being with large vision, and stop being preoccupied with the self, except to sacrifice it. You will see that gradually you will lose your extreme sensitivity. You know its origin . . . I will ask the Heart of our good Master to fill your heart with his divine love. Following His example, become really kind to others, support them, excuse them, and do not be shocked by anything which comes your way. This is the true source of peace and of joy in the spirit.[1]

A month later Sophie wrote again:

You know how much I hold to order, cleanliness and economy, our way to live poverty. Hold to it without being parsimonious. The pupils especially should not want for anything. I will return to this important matter often, while you do not have the guidance and presence of Mère de Charbonnel with you. I have an abhorrence of debts and fortunately you have too. I shall be supported in this by you![2]

This mixture of spiritual and practical guidance was a hallmark of Sophie's leadership. With personal visits, these letters became the way Sophie retained contact with the communities and ensured, as far as she could, that the foundations succeeded. A great deal depended on the quality of the leaders in the houses and this proved a continual source of concern for Sophie. Many were natural leaders but needed time to develop their gifts. Time was not on their side as so many foundations were requested and most of the superiors had to learn by trial and error. Sophie's attention and honesty with them helped and she insisted they write regularly to her, giving detailed accounts of all the affairs and personnel of the house.

At the general council of 1820 Catherine de Charbonnel had been elected bursar general. She and Sophie carried the financial responsibility for the Society, and while de Charbonnel kept the accounts of what monies the Society had, Sophie worked closely with her in all major financial transactions. The income of the Society was composed of the legacies and/or revenues of the members of the Society; to this were added the fees of boarders and the gifts the Society occasionally received from wealthy lay people. Sometimes those who asked for a school in a particular area also offered a building and some income for the first few years. In that case Sophie could with a quiet mind agree to a new foundation. But as often as not little was offered and the Society had to find the money for the new work. The real financial burdens came when the school wanted to expand and new buildings were required. That was major capital expense and almost always the responsibility of the Society. Finance was key to all Sophie wished to do and she became adept at finding funds, often small amounts, and placing them where they were most needed. She dreaded debt and longed to pay off the money due for the purchase of the Hôtel Biron. Yet while debt deeply concerned her, she managed to retain, all her life, the capacity to risk a new foundation if she felt it would succeed. She counted on Providence to provide the money and, if that was not forthcoming, she was as ready to close a house as to open it.[3]

The houses in Louisiana were always a source of concern and Sophie told Philippine Duchesne in 1820:

> I have just sent you 3,000 francs. These are composed of 2,000 left over from Niort, and the rest are from divine Providence: 500 from Madame de Rollin, your cousin, so do not forget to thank her; 200fr from Madame de la Grandville, née de Beauffort, for whom I ask your prayers. Finally the last 300 are from my own resources, and I am happy to gather together some small sums of money so that I can send you my gift as well.[4]

When there was a possibility of buying more property adjoining La Ferrandière Sophie urged Catherine de Charbonnel not to delay in buying it:

> You must not hesitate. You need to make use of the chance and buy this part of the property beside us. There would be a host of problems if you had other neighbours . . . how happy you would be! What if you got a chapel already built! I really dread these projects but in your case I would have no regrets having another financial burden of 15,000 francs . . . for the land, alas! I dare say nothing. We need a rich person willing to help us. Where can we find such an amount of money! . . . Beauvais also worries me for we want to buy the maison Pain. The selling price is 80,000 frs. This is an impossible price for us, for we could end up losing all. We have to stop! Nevertheless I regret losing a good bargain! Let us pray and see what the good God wants, He is all powerful![5]

Even with the debt from the Hôtel Biron hanging over her head, as well as the project of building a chapel there, Sophie managed to pay back the loan that the businessman, John Mullanphy, had extended to Philippine Duchesne when she was in sore straits. But she warned Philippine that she should try to become solvent if at all possible since the Society in France was very stretched and Sophie had no way of guaranteeing money in the future.[6] Inevitably, over the years, Philippine's letters were filled with financial concerns, since the community in Louisiana had little income and they depended largely on the money Philippine and some of the others received from the Society and from their families in Europe. But by October 1822 Sophie had so many foundations to cater for that she complained to Marie Prevost:

> On every side I am asked for money and for personnel. People think that I am super-human, whereas I am just a poor zero.[7]

In December of the same year, Sophie confided to Marie Prevost again:

> Josephine Bigeu tells me that she is very short of money and needs some badly, and that I am not coming to her aid etc Alas! I am not the good God and I cannot create out of nothing . . .[8]

In the midst of so much intense work, in Paris, in planning new foundations with her assistants general, in training and supporting the leaders for the new communities and schools, in finding money or arranging loans, Sophie's energy and health were under pressure. She worried more than she showed especially over the financial situation of the Society. She suffered continual, severe headaches and sore eyes which forced her to stop working. She admitted that she suffered from overwork, from excessive weariness. Other signs of exhaustion appeared in the form of fevers, heavy colds, rheumatism and gastric upsets:

> I wrote to you with difficulty as I was suffering greatly from rheumatism in the gut and indeed almost everywhere in my body so that my system is badly shaken. I'm afoot fortunately but I suffer a lot when I try to work. My eyes simply will not function.[9]

Others too were working as hard as Sophie, and Sophie was aware of that too. She expected her colleagues to work hard and long and she could not understand laziness. When mistakes were made Sophie was generally understanding and fair. One of her most frequent phrases, over the years, was 'It's done' meaning: it has happened, it is over, let us move on, but learn from the experience. One of the people who could not seem to learn from her mistakes was Thérèse Maillucheau. She and Sophie were good friends and had shared a great deal over the years, especially on the spiritual level. In the course of 1822 Sophie began to suspect that all was not well in Grenoble. Despite her best efforts Thérèse Maillucheau simply was neither a leader nor a manager of community or school in Grenoble. Bad management over several years had brought the house close to bankruptcy. The presence of Marie de la Croix did not help, for she too had no sense of money or of economy. In October 1822 Sophie decided to remove Thérèse Maillucheau and send her to Quimper specifically as the superior, with no responsibility either for the finances of the house or for the running of the school. Personnel was scarce that year and Marie de la Croix was left in charge in Grenoble and could do nothing to pull the house back from disaster. Her health broke under the burden and Sophie realised that she had to go to Grenoble herself and retrieve the situation. The debts had accumulated over seven years, and the money borrowed by Thérèse Maillucheau had been set at a high interest rate of 7 per cent. The situation could only become worse and the house crashed into bankruptcy. Sophie spent some weeks in Grenoble early in 1823, reorganised the house and settled most outstanding debts. But it broke her health in the process and Sophie became very ill.

For forty-five days Sophie struggled with a tenacious fever and her life was in danger. News reached all the houses and her youngest niece, Dosithée, a student at Amiens, decided to offer her life for the life of her aunt. She was just fourteen at the time and affected by the cult of the day, that of dying a young, holy death. While she may have been ill prior to hearing of Sophie's condition in Grenoble, she contracted a fever in Amiens at this time and decided to offer her life to God for the cure of her aunt Sophie: 'If my aunt gets better, I could get worse.'[10] The day Dosithée died there was a remarkable improvement in Sophie's health and the doctor in Grenoble, Dr Bilon, wrote to Dr Terral at Amiens:

After forty-five days of illness, and several crises which did not peak, Madame Barat is now convalescing. . . . The illness was a sinus infection complicated by gastritis and a rheumatoid infection. This could be called, if you prefer, gastro-enteritis, with irritation of the liver and of the muscular system of the body, so severe that it produced a prolonged fever.[11]

Eugénie de Gramont and Catherine de Charbonnel travelled down from Paris to bring Sophie back to the rue de Varenne, when she was ready to leave Grenoble. Over the summer she regained her strength and was able to resume work. Later on that year Sophie confided to Philippine that while anxiety over the debts in the Society threatened at times to overwhelm her, those in Grenoble nearly killed her. She explained the changes she had made throughout France but recognised that some had been made too late.[12] Joseph Varin heard about her illness in Grenoble and wrote immediately to comfort her and assure her that all was going well in the Society, despite all the problems and difficulties and worries. And he urged her to speak more about her worries:

I saw from your last letter to Madame de Charbonnel that you did not dare even to mention that you were suffering. . . . maybe you keep your distress too much to yourself, and that is an old habit of yours . . .[13]

Sophie tended to make light of her worries with some people, particularly with Joseph Varin, and yet in letters to some friends she was quite frank about her burdens. But she missed the steady help of her old friend and spiritual director, Jean Montaigne. Since his illness and death she had found no one to talk to in depth about her inner life, her inner journey. Even Eugénie de Gramont and Thérèse Maillucheau were not admitted into that world. When Montaigne died in 1821, Sophie mourned his loss and told Thérèse Maillucheau:

We have just lost Father Montaigne. He was the only friend I had who really knew the depths of my soul and you understand what it has cost me to lose him . . . Fortunately he had been apart from us some time before his decease, so that his passing has affected me less, but I will feel the loss of his direction for a long time. So it is God alone. He wants our heart, without any human intermediary or support.[14]

The following year Sophie suffered another loss. Her mother, who had already begun to suffer from amnesia, became seriously ill and died on 21 June 1822. Sophie told Philippine 'I have lost my aged and revered mother'. In her reply Philippine comforted her, saying that she was sorry she had never met Madame Fouffé, 'I very much regret that I never met in Joigny she who gave birth to you, our very good mother'.[15] Life had been full of painful separations for Sophie's mother, and Sophie knew how lonely and bereft her mother had felt, especially when she and Louis had left Joigny.[16]

Sophie realised that now Marie-Louise Dusaussoy was quite alone in Joigny, though Stanislas visited her frequently. Sophie arranged to buy wine, fruit and nuts from her sister and in this way she was able to give Marie-Louise some financial support. By this time three of the girls had entered, Thérèse, Julie and Sophie Dusaussoy. Before she died Sophie had had great hopes for Dosithée;

Louis Barat too had cultivated her and sent her a copy of the *Practice of Christian Perfection* by Rodriguez, a text used in noviciate. This amused Sophie and probably brought back memories of Paris in 1795.[17] Louis Dusaussoy twice tried his vocation with the Jesuits, but in the end he was ordained a secular priest. He was restless and wanted to go on the missions to Louisiana. Sophie arranged for him to go there, asking both Philippine Duchesne and Eugénie Audé to help him. However, after a time this project failed and Louis had to return to France. In effect all his life Louis Dusaussoy was unstable and unable to take full responsibility for his life.[18] Sophie recognised this and provided him with light chaplaincy work in the houses of the Society, though these appointments often cost the community dearly.

By 1822 Louis Barat had left Bordeaux and had begun his final stage of formation at the Jesuit house in Montrouge, Paris. Between 1822 and 1825, when Joseph Varin was absent from Paris, Louis replaced him at the rue de Varenne, teaching religious instruction and acting as school confessor. Sophie was pleased about this and felt he was doing the children good. The school journal noted his presence in the house and the austerity of his way of life. Once, on 1 January 1824, just before the religious instruction class the girls wanted to wish him a happy new year in song. As they began singing he simply walked out of class and refused to return. Sophie heard about this and in the evening she met the class and asked them to sing for her instead.[19] The contrast between brother and sister was drawn and Sophie made the bridge needed into the affections of the pupils. If Louis was unable to communicate with the young women at the rue de Varenne he was better able to relate at a distance with Philippine Duchesne and some other members of the Society in Louisiana. He had given up all hope of going on the missions but kept close links with Philippine Duchesne and sent her what he thought could be of use. He composed hymns for the schools and communities and wrote often to encourage Philippine and her companions in all the trials they had to face. Sophie recorded one of the rare glimpses of Louis Barat laughing, when he read accounts of the children in Louisiana:

> Father Barat, to whom you are all very dear, laughed at the story of your pupils. He will look for more books for you, even though he cannot bring them out to you himself.[20]

Joy of another kind came into Sophie's life in the course of these years. In 1824, a year after her serious illness, Sophie made the acquaintance of Joseph-Marie Favre (1791–1838), a diocesan missionary in Chambéry and this meeting marked her life profoundly.[21] How they met is not known. It could have been when Sophie visited Chambéry briefly in August 1824, or Fr Favre may have given a retreat in one of the houses of the Society in France when she was there. In any event she found a spiritual friend and counsellor to whom she could write and occasionally see while on visitation. Favre's theological background was liberating for Sophie since he was trained in the spiritual school of St Francis de Sales and St Alphonsus of Liguori. Both these theologians advocated a gentle view of God which engendered trust especially in the matter of confession and communion. Throughout his life Favre gave parish missions and published books on the need of frequent communion. He also stressed that confessors should give absolution quickly in confession, rather than maintain the interminable examinations advocated by Jansenistic clerics with consequent prolonged withholding of absolution. This approach to God and the sacraments challenged the Jansenism which Sophie Barat had grown up with and replaced it with an image of God which was welcoming, warm and caring. Although the image of God which Sophie had imbibed at home and which had been actively inculcated by Louis Barat, had been somewhat modified and softened by the direction of Joseph Varin and Jean Montaigne, Sophie was ready for a deeper, and warmer vision of God.

Joseph-Marie Favre confirmed this in his guidance of Sophie and he helped her in the task of integrating them into her life. In 1824 Favre wrote to Sophie and asked her to reflect on her tendency to overwork:

> God is calling you to an intimate union with Him. You must overcome all that impedes this relationship. *YOUR CONTACTS WITH PEOPLE* are not the least of these obstacles. Keep them to a minimum and only when necessary. Let go of everything which does not absolutely require your involvement in the exercise of your responsibility. By being united to God you will do more in a quarter of an hour than in a whole day's *pouring out* of frenzied activity. Neither is *ENTHUSIASM* the least of obstacles: restrain yourself and moderate your actions in such a way that you are more attentive to God than to the chaotic nature of your occupations, which, however necessary, are less important than your great spiritual ideal. Furthermore your duty to God and to yourself comes before your duty to your neighbour. And you can only give out of what you have . . . Go to communion as often as you can; your poor soul needs it so much; every day would be best.[22]

This was clear, common-sense advice for Sophie, and all her life she struggled to maintain a balance between work and prayer. Favre's insistence that she give priority to her close union with God, as the essential focus of her life as well as her best contribution as leader, restored the balance which overwork and anxiety had damaged in 1823. It was an ideal to reach towards, a balance to attain. So, as in so many experiences and encounters in her life, Sophie's meeting with Joseph-Marie Favre was a catalyst, not just for her own personal growth but for her leadership of the Society of the Sacred Heart.

Indeed in meeting Favre in 1824 Sophie renewed contact with spiritual influences she had met first through Joseph Varin and the other members of the Fathers of the Faith, whose own spiritual roots reached back to Léonor de Tournély and the Fathers of the Sacred Heart. The line of continuity began in the late eighteenth century in Turin, in Piedmont in the kingdom of Sardinia where the former Jesuit, Nicholas de Diessbach, had initiated several secret groups of lay people and of priests. Through the provision of good spiritual reading, prayer and spiritual direction, de Diessbach had hoped to form a spiritual elite of both clergy and laity which would enable the Catholic church to survive the upheavals of the traumatic changes which were then happening all over Europe. De Diessbach was in contact with the Fathers of the Sacred Heart in Hagenbrunn near Vienna, and as confessor to the court in Vienna he had become director of Léopoldine Naudet. His death in 1798 occurred just before the Fathers of the Sacred Heart joined the Fathers of the Faith and accepted the leadership of Paccanari.[23]

The groups founded by de Diessbach in Turin were inspired by the theology of St Alphonsus of Liguori. This teaching gradually confronted the Jansenism, Gallicanism and rigorism of the clergy in Piedmont and Savoy, and slowly gained influence in France. There it met great resistance for the theology of Alphonsus of Ligouri ran counter to the spirit and practice of Jansenism and rigorism. Liguorian theology sought to breach the chasm between the individual and God, by urging the frequent practice of confession and communion. It presented an image of God and indeed a theology of Christ which was warmer and more attractive than that of Jansenism and rigorism which taught that no one could go to communion unless totally free from sin. Liguorians taught that (venial) sin:

> . . . far from being an obstacle to communion, it is a reason for approaching [the Holy Table] and whoever can receive communion once a year can also receive it daily . . . We must approach [Christ in communion] with trust, as the only support of our weakness and seek there the necessary strength to persevere. . . . It was Jansenism [which] . . . changed the former custom of frequent communion.[24]

To many of the clergy in France frequent communion was considered alien. It was literally from 'beyond the mountains', ultramontane, promoted by the church of Rome, and was rejected. But the new thinking could not be suppressed: some clerics in France were open and ready for it and appreciated its pastoral and spiritual importance. The canonisation process of Alphonsus of Liguori had begun in 1796 and the publication of his theological writings made his thinking more readily accessible. One of Diessbach's disciples, Pio Brunone Lanteri, was based in Turin and had wide influence through his writings and retreat work. These made an impact on Chambéry in the neighbouring kingdom of Savoy.[25] By 1815 some clergy there were ready and eager for the new theology. Indeed by this time Lanteri's writings and personal influence had begun to resonate with members of the clergy in France already in the stream of new thinking and theology. Among such clergy were first Eugène de Mazenod and Charles Leblanc, and later Fr Grousset, Villecourt and Delalle.[26] Indeed Favre himself was particularly influential not just in Savoy but in France. For a time he was superior of the Missionaries of Savoy and he received requests for preachers who used the theology of Alphonsus of Liguori as the basis of their teaching.

Thus when Sophie Barat met Favre she was reintroduced to the influences which had shaped both Léonor de Tournély and Joseph Varin when the spiritual associations founded in Turin had extended into Vienna. But now she entered a new phase of personal integration. Favre offered her an image of God which was warm and comforting, not harsh and severe. This connected with the image of the Sacred Heart which Louis sent his mother at the height of the Terror. But because Louis's direction did not emphasise the love of God revealed in the Heart of Christ, the inner meaning of the devotion did not affect her in a way that could influence her inner world, especially that of prayer. Neither did she explore the devotion with Joseph Varin, for at some deep level Sophie did not trust him. For several crucial years he had neither recognised, affirmed nor supported her authority. After 1815 Sophie only consulted him on matters regarding the governing of the Society of the Sacred Heart, rarely on personal matters. And while Joseph Varin acknowledged her inner turmoil and anxiety, and offered to help her spiritually, he could not win Sophie's confidence.

Favre's teaching and direction expanded her inner world into confidence and trust and since he had no direct bearing on the government of the Society, Sophie was freer to take his advice. They both shared similar experiences because Favre, like Sophie, had suffered from poor health since childhood and had struggled with scruples since adolescence, particularly from worries about sin and communion: 'anxieties which originated in the rigidity of certain principles . . . held by a few French theologians'.[27]

Favre's own conversion was slow for he was brought up within Jansenist influences at home and in the seminary. The theology of Liguori was a source of liberation and inner peace for Favre and he wanted to pass on that personal experience to others in the church. This liberation was symbolised and enacted by frequent confession and communion, by an approach to God that was trusting and intimate. Favre argued that since the church had not pronounced, either for or against frequent use of the sacraments, he was within orthodoxy in recommending frequency. In Chambéry he was consistently challenged by his own colleagues and had to defend his position vigorously:

> I am neither a heretic nor a Protestant; nor am I a Jansenist, not even a Gallican. I am Ultramontane with all my heart.[28]

This was the conviction within which Favre worked and within which Sophie Barat got to know and trust him. This new relationship came at a crucial period for Sophie when she needed something deeper and stronger to carry her forward in life's task. Through Favre, Sophie experienced something of the content of the devotion to the Sacred Heart, what it meant to love God and be loved by God, without any judgement, censure or threat. While comforting and strengthening, this teaching was an immense challenge to her own inner world, where all too easily she fell back into a Jansenistic, rigorist view of God and herself. Sophie was caught between these two ways of seeing God and the self. Not only was she deeply imbued with rigorist/Jansenistic views since childhood, but she also had to contend with a public world, especially Paris, where Favre's views were rejected. Thus Favre's position presented Sophie with an offer of great liberation which she could not easily take or sustain, especially when she dealt with many bishops and priests who were steeped in Gallicanism, Jansenism and rigorism.[29] Sophie did not speak to her friends about her new director, preferring to keep that part of her life private. Later on she would confide in Louise de Limminghe, when both were being guided by Favre. With her alone Sophie spoke about Favre's teaching and its influence on her life.

Favre's views had a further value for Sophie Barat at this time. They brought her into contact with a new energy, emanating from Rome. The papacy was steadily recovering its self-confidence and reasserting its authority. In this context, the distant image of Rome, of the Eternal City, of the city set upon a hill was immensely attractive after the profound disturbances in France since 1789. It was far away, over the mountains, beyond, ultramontane. It was, moreover, a Rome of three dimensions: classical and Renaissance Rome which had submitted to the yoke of Christianity; then Christian Rome, of the saints, of the martyrs, of the catacombs, which had the spiritual energy to renew the Catholic Church and win back the ground lost at the time of the reformation and enlightenment; and finally, it was a Rome of the Papal States, modelling the ideal city-state, with the pope, the Vicar of Christ on earth, as the focus for all truth and validity of doctrine.[30] This church, which had experienced humiliation at the hands of Napoleon, now began to move forward in confidence. Favre invoked the authority of Rome to support his views on frequent communion, and he called himself ultramontane in this context. But ultramontanism was more complex than merely representing Liguorian theology. In France it brought with it the threat of papal encroachment on long cherished Gallican rights and powers. Sophie would discover to her cost that Gallicanism was a force and tradition which would not easily cede power to Rome.

For good or ill, the Society of the Sacred Heart was firmly centred in Paris, closely linked with the nobility and episcopacy, caught into the worldliness of the Faubourg Saint-Germain, locked into a spirituality and view of God which would have nothing to do with Liguorian thought. Archbishop de Quelen had asked Favre to preach the retreat for the clergy in Paris in 1826 and did not ask him to return.[31] When Favre's book came out, *Le Ciel Ouvert*, it was criticised in Paris both for its content and for its style.[32] By instinct, though often with real difficulty, Sophie recognised the wholesomeness of Favre's teaching, but she had to work with those who saw it otherwise, both in the Society and in the episcopacy. This led Sophie to live a double life, caught between two images of God, one severe and the other gentle, one fashionable, the other rejected, and this made her journey into a gentler spirituality an enormous task and strain.

In the midst of this inner journey, Sophie continued to govern the Society of the Sacred Heart and once she had recovered from her illness of March 1823 she took up the process of seeking approval for the constitutions in Rome. Even before she met Favre her instinct was that the Society of the Sacred Heart needed formal approval from Rome sooner rather than later. Such approval would ratify her own authority, establish a certain independence and ensure easier access to dioceses outside France. At the same time she hoped it would finally neuter if not remove the capacity of Saint-Estève and those associated with him, to disturb and divide the Society. Thus while the work of the general council in 1820 was adequate for the governing needs of the Society, in Sophie's mind the general council of 1820 was only a stepping stone. Immediately after the council Sophie initiated the next phase of her plan. By the summer of 1823 she thought the time was ripe to open formal negotiations with Rome. Sophie wrote to Philippine Duchesne in August that year telling her confidentially that the Society had sent the constitutions to Rome for formal approval. She anticipated that the process could be long and possibly contentious and so she asked that it remain secret.[33] Sophie had good reason to do this, for Saint-Estève was still in Rome and could interfere with the process. Indeed the previous year Saint-Estève had been in France, travelling in the region of Grenoble. Sophie warned Thérèse Maillucheau not to allow him visit the community and 'maintain a cool attitude with him'.[34] Sophie contacted the Jesuit assistant general for France in Rome, Jean Rozaven, and asked him for advice on initiating the procedure for presenting the constitutions. Rozaven recognised the need for discretion, especially with regard to Saint-Estève, but he assured Sophie early in 1824:

> Up until now M. de S[ambucy]. knows nothing. Undoubtedly he will find out, but too late to interfere.[35]

However Rozaven had his own reservations about helping the Society of the Sacred Heart and he agreed to do so as long as his role remained private and that the Jesuits were not publicly involved in the process. He told Sophie that in Rome the Society of the Sacred Heart and Jesuits had become too identified and stories were being exchanged:

> The Jesuits certainly ought to be willing to help you in every way, according to our constitutions. But as you well know you are under particular scrutiny and so are we too. In certain quarters it was generally believed that your order had a special relationship with us. In Chambéry, for example, were you not called 'Jesuitesses'. It was difficult for us to scotch these rumours and the fathers had to withdraw completely [from the Society of the Sacred Heart]. The same thing could happen in other places too. In Amiens . . . there were far too many contacts between the Jesuits and the members of the Society of the Sacred Heart. [They had] visits, meals together. Did it not transpire that one of your religious took arithmetic or history lessons, I do not now which, from some Jesuit, who neither should nor could take on that kind of task.[36]

The petition accompanying the presentation of the constitutions and rules was drawn up in Paris and signed by Sophie Barat, two of her assistants general, Josephine Bigeu and Henriette Grosier, and one general councillor, Eugénie de Gramont. The application was supported by a letter from the ecclesiastical superior general of the Society, Mgr de Croy, who had succeeded Cardinal de Talleyrand-Périgord as grand aumônier of France, and by another from his delegate, Fr Perreau. These were supported by other letters of approval from several bishops in France. The dossier was sent to the congregation of bishops and religious in Rome and the process began almost immediately after the election of Pope Leo XII, who succeeded Pius VII in September 1823. Sophie had no part in the discussions at all. The church did not allow women the legal right to negotiate nor to become involved in affairs that concerned their own lives directly. That area of power and decision-making remained the preserve of the clergy. In that context Sophie was well served by her friends in Rome and France and as the process evolved she found clerics who were capable and ready to carry the matter to a conclusion.[37]

The actual goal and inspiration of the constitutions of the Society of the Sacred Heart caused no difficulties in Rome, for both the spirituality of the Society and the work of education it proposed to do in the church were highly valued at this time. The period after 1815 was a time of restoration and renewal for the church and any congregation of women which wished to restore Christian values in society was welcomed and supported. However, some modifications to the constitutions were required. This was symptomatic of the attitudes of church authorities which could not conceive of formal religious life for women as anything other than strictly cloistered. Again, this mindset was rooted in society in general and it reflected the assumption that women needed protection at all times and could not exercise freedom without the permission of a male figure. Thus when a congregation asked for formal recognition from the pope, it was assumed that papal enclosure with solemn vows would be observed. Papal enclosure, rather than approval by a diocesan bishop, required total separation of the women in the communities from all contact with society, often called 'the world'. This also implied grilles and other signs of total separation from the public, a form of life Philippine Duchesne had experienced when she had entered the Visitation convent in Ste Marie d'En Haut.

Sophie Barat wanted the members of the Society to take solemn vows which could only be dissolved by the pope, for papal approval would give the Society greater freedom to expand and some independence from diocesan bishops. But she did not want strict papal enclosure. Her petition to separate solemn vows which could only be dissolved by the pope from the obligation of strict papal enclosure was innovative at this period. Indeed, in the course of the general council of 1820, Mgr Frayssinous, the newly appointed ecclesiastical superior of the house in Paris, commented:

> Since you wish to be true religious while at the same time maintaining contact with the world, I can tell you that you have embarked upon a bold and even audacious undertaking. And it has made us realise how much we must be on our guard against the almost imperceptible influence which the world exerts [even] on the most devout people.[38]

What the Society of the Sacred Heart sought was not new in the church. From the seventeenth century many women in different countries in Europe had sought ways to redefine the form and structure of women's religious life within the Catholic church, especially in what concerned the issue of cloister. In that context, the Society of the Sacred Heart was by no means the most adventurous in the form of religious life it adapted.[39] Sophie Barat and her colleagues did not set out to redefine religious life, especially in the area of cloister, but they were pragmatic regarding the demands of the work of education itself and the need for a certain mobility for the religious as they moved around the houses of the Society, either in France or elsewhere. Sophie Barat was superior general for life and governed all the houses of the Society. She needed a structure of government which enabled her to move personnel from one diocese to another, from one part of the country to the other, or indeed to another part of the world. In addition Sophie also wanted the Society itself to be more accessible to parents and students and to present a less severe, less distant public image. For these two reasons alone, the Society had to be relieved of some of the constraints of cloister.

On the other hand, the Society of the Sacred Heart had opted for a monastic form of community life with relatively strict conditions of cloister. In the course of the general council in 1820 the question of cloister had been addressed within this perspective, and regulations had been drawn up regarding the journeys and visits which members could make. The occasions when visitors, clergy, doctors, family members could be permitted into private sections of the house were also determined. Sophie Barat had preferred this form of life as a way of ensuring the conditions community members needed to fulfil their commitment to inner spiritual growth. Her own attraction to Carmel stayed with her throughout her life and influenced her choices for the Society. She knew that to become women of prayer and reflection required time and space and Sophie understood this to be the function of cloister. Throughout her life Sophie saw no good reason to change that view and she tended to insist on cloister more rather than less at the end of her life. However, because of the actual work of education which the Society of the Sacred Heart wished to carry out, Sophie Barat resisted grilles from the beginning and rejected any form of cloister which could repel either parents or students. She never sought to have cloister removed, that was not part of her thinking. Rather she wished it to be modified in the view of the work of education, and the need to be free from local bishops who often interpreted the constitutions and work of the Society within a diocesan framework only. Indeed the documents presented to the authorities in Rome in 1823 described no role for local bishops in the question of cloister.

When presenting the petition for approbation to Rome, Fr Perreau explained why the Society of the Sacred Heart did not wish to have papal cloister. He argued that the parents of the students disliked grilles and strict cloister, to such a degree that they preferred secular schools to convents for these reasons:

> . . . after careful consideration of these serious obstacles, certain individuals, full of faith and of zeal for the greater glory of God, drew up a plan to establish a religious institute in honour of the Sacred Heart. This institute would be more adapted than the older orders to the morals, practices and needs of our time. It is envisaged that fervour and regularity of life will be maintained by all the means prescribed by faith, such as the obligation of prayer twice daily, examination of conscience, keeping great outward modesty and the practice of perfect obedience. God has blessed

the views of the founders. For almost twenty-four years of its existence this Society has maintained fidelity to its rules, and among the other orders in France it is held up as an example of fervour. Nor has there been any relaxation nor the abuses which usually result from the absence of strict cloister. Besides the safeguards contained in various articles of the rules, which I submit here for your inspection, appeared to have prevented this. The numbers of boarding school pupils in the houses of the Society have increased greatly. Many novices and professed sisters, as well as the pupils, belong to the most distinguished families of our time. Everything seems to point to the prosperity of this new Institute.[40]

Certainly the authorities in Rome did not wish to deter parents from sending their children to Catholic schools, especially in Paris – there were plenty of distinguished secular schools in the city at this time where girls could have been placed.[41] Over the following three years an agreement was worked out whereby the strict form of papal cloister was not imposed on the Society though further restrictions were imposed on the mobility of the members as well as on ease of access to the reserved areas of each community house of the Society. However the arrangement with Rome was a significant concession in the context of the day and it was given only in view of the work of education. Male control was retained over all the communities and over the superiors through underlining the role of the local bishop, something Sophie and her colleagues had hoped to get free of precisely by seeking formal approval from Rome.

The text which the Society presented for approval in 1823 was clear in its aims and assumptions:

> To glorify the Sacred Heart of Jesus the Ladies of the Society do not restrict themselves to working for their own personal perfection. They are also dedicated to working at their utmost for the salvation and perfection of their neighbour. For this reason they have adopted a normal life style, simple and ordinary in appearance, in such a way as to give no outward offence, frighten the imagination or drive away the very people they so much desire to win for God.
>
> . . . although they retain cloister with its most precious advantages, nevertheless this form of cloister cannot be the same as that in orders where one is exclusively dedicated to pursuing one's own personal perfection. It must be tempered, modified and adapted to the spirit and the aim of their Institute which sets out in a special way [to work for] the benefit and service of their neighbour.[42]

The first paragraph was accepted with minor changes but the second one was radically altered:

> . . . they retain cloister with its valuable benefits in order to preserve the integrity of their vows, a cloister however which must be tempered and modified in accordance with the spirit and aim of their Institute. Those dispensations which may be necessary to grant will be regulated by the local bishop [the Ordinary].[43]

The authorities in Rome could not conceive that religious women could decide on their own needs, act independently and travel freely. As in families, so in the church, women who had no male figure to supervise them were incomprehensible, inconceivable, and so indefinable. Besides Rome could not afford to ignore or alienate local bishops, especially French bishops, all of them jealous of their rights over religious communities. Sophie Barat had no option but to accept the modifications imposed. The approbation of the constitutions proceeded in two stages. In September 1825 the pope issued a decree granting the Society of the Sacred Heart approbation,[44] though the actual communication of the decree was so casual that neither Sophie nor Fr Perreau heard about it until some months later. In effect, the decree simply recognised the Society as a congregation doing important work in the church. Papal approbation was not granted since the Society could not observe papal enclosure. Fr Perreau was pleased at the outcome and urged Sophie to accept the approval as it stood. To him it solved the problem of cloister and the Society would be free to evolve in whatever way suited it best for its educational task. Within those terms this was very true. But Sophie herself was disappointed at the content of the decree. It left the Society under the jurisdiction of local bishops; the members of the Society made commitments which had the status of simple vows which could be dissolved by the authority of any local bishop. Clearly, over a period of time, her role of the superior general would be eroded, and the central structure of the Society would contract into diocesan forms. All that Sophie had struggled over for many years could be lost. She was also aware that while she needed scope and freedom to exercise her functions as superior general of a rapidly expanding congregation, individual communities also needed some protection from those bishops and clerics who wanted to change the constitutions of the Society to suit their local needs and personal views.

At this time Sophie had a particular case in hand, in Turin. In 1821 the king and queen of Sardinia had asked her to establish a house of the Society in Piedmont and offered a property in Turin to this purpose. The negotiations took place between the Court and the Society; the archbishop of Turin, Mgr Dom Colombano Chiavarotti had not been involved at all. Only after the community had actually arrived and taken up residence in the diocese did Sophie write a formal letter, apologising for the omission but by then it was too late. This was a tactical and diplomatic error on Sophie's part and the community was constantly made to feel the pique of the archbishop, as angry with the Court as with the Society for being overlooked. He belonged to a particularly austere branch of the Benedictines, the Camaldolites, and did not consider the Society a religious order properly speaking since it did not observe full papal cloister with papal vows. He was rigorist, rejected the theology of Liguori and harassed the communities founded by de Diessbach and Lanteri in Turin. Sophie had made an enemy and in time Rome heard about the strained relations between the Society and the archbishop.[45]

Rozaven warned Sophie that the views of the archbishop of Turin were not unique, and that she would have to reconsider her own views on cloister:

> If you insist on this point I can tell you honestly that that you will never obtain the
> kind of approval you seek nor will you get established in Italy. Everywhere you

will experience as much and indeed more difficulty than you had in Turin. That principle that you must adapt to the thinking of our time is valid. Yet the principle that we must resist the ideas of our age is in many instances no less valid. Wisdom consists in maintaining a balance between these two extremes, having neither too much rigidity nor too much concession. The laws of the Council of Trent on cloister seem to me to be really wise and important. I do not think they are less necessary for the times in which we live than they were in former times. . . . The founders of religious orders and congregations who have relied only on the fervour of first beginnings, without looking further to the future, have never established firm foundations . . . [46]

These views were confirmed when the authorities in Rome, clearly influenced by the views of the archbishop of Turin, refused to grant the Society full papal approbation. Josephine Bigeu was superior in Turin at the time and told Sophie that the situation was intolerable. She suggested to Sophie that she negotiate a form of approbation which would free the Society from some of the constrictions imposed by the archbishop.[47] Thus when Rozaven stated that the decree of September 1825 added nothing to the Society's former status within the church, Sophie decided to reopen negotiations with Rome and press for papal recognition of the Society. Realising that this time she needed a member of the Society present in Rome to act as her personal representative there, even if that person could not take an active part in any meetings, she asked Josephine Bigeu to go to Rome with Angélique Lavauden and Marie Fonsala and represent the Society's interests there.[48]

As in the previous application for papal approval, the question of cloister and solemn vows were key issues again. For a time it seemed it would be impossible to win concessions and yet with the help of persistent negotiators in Rome a compromise was reached. Rozaven summed it up in a letter to Léopoldine Naudet:

> The situation regarding the negotiation of the Ladies of the Sacred Heart is as follows: the Holy Father has received their petition with much consideration and interest and named a group of three cardinals to examine it. Everything leads one to hope for a favourable outcome within a few weeks. They will not take solemn vows because the circumstances prevailing in France do not permit the form of cloister required, but their vows and constitutions will be approved in a Brief. To the three ordinary vows of religion they will add a vow of stability from which they can be dispensed only by the pope. This approval will be very adequate for the moment. They reserve the right to request permission at a later date to take solemn vows, if happier circumstances permit a more complete form of cloister.[49]

The Society of the Sacred Heart was not granted the right to make the traditional solemn vows with full papal enclosure, since their way of life contradicted the traditional interpretation of solemn vows. Nevertheless it was recognised that the Society presented a particular and valid case. A compromise was reached whereby members of the Society would make a vow of stability (to remain in the Society of the Sacred Heart) at final profession and only the pope could dispense from that commitment. With the introduction of the vow of stability the Society gained papal recognition but Sophie still had to accept episcopal control over the travel arrangements of her members, as they moved from house to house, and from country to country. Rozaven saw it as a compromise, a way of achieving formal approval of the Society of the Sacred Heart by the pope, though clearly he did not at all approve of the type of cloister practised by the Society of the Sacred Heart in France, thinking it far too lax for women.

Papal authority was further strengthened in the Society of the Sacred Heart by another decision taken by the Roman commission examining the constitutions of the Society. A potential conflict of interests arose regarding who was to be the personal ecclesiastical superior of Sophie Barat. For just as in each diocese a male figure, the bishop or his delegate, had the right to supervise communities of religious women, church law also required the superior general to be accountable to a cleric. Since 1815 the ecclesiastical superior general of the Society of the Sacred Heart had been Cardinal de Talleyrand-Périgord and he had delegated this office to Fr Perreau. On his death, Mgr de Quelen succeeded de Talleyrand-Périgord as archbishop of Paris but the king, Louis XVIII, did not appoint de Quelen as grand aumônier of France. Rather he named the bishop of Strasbourg, Mgr de Croy, to this office.[50] This had created tensions for Sophie Barat. Mgr de Quelen in his capacity as archbishop of Paris claimed authority over the houses of the Society in Paris. Yet, in her role as superior general, Sophie was accountable to the grand aumônier. Archbishop de Quelen was aggrieved at what he perceived as a diminution of his rights and for a time withheld granting approval of the Society in his diocese, a necessary formality for the Society's request for approbation, though he did so finally in May 1825. The authorities in Rome were aware of this difficulty and of its potential for conflict, and to avoid such tensions in the future they decided to appoint a cardinal in Rome as Protector of the Society of the Sacred Heart. This suited Sophie Barat as it eased her relationship with the archbishop of Paris, further distanced her authority from that of bishops and clerics and gave her wider scope for action. While it removed the immediate tension between two roles, that of the archbishop of Paris and the grand aumônier of France, it did not resolve the basic grievance of French bishops who resented any interference from Rome in the internal affairs of the church, and religious women were considered internal affairs. Besides it was clear that, through its actions regarding the Society of the Sacred Heart, the pope and the court of Rome were reasserting authority after years of humiliation first during the Revolution and later at the hands of Napoleon. In any event, that agenda provided opportunities for Sophie Barat in her search for greater freedom of action within her own sphere and area. Ultramontanism of this sort suited her very well.

Sophie wrote a circular letter to the Society in August 1826[51] and announced that the pope had granted approbation to the constitutions, on the conditions that some modifications would be accepted by a general council of the Society. She convoked a general council to begin on 29 September, which would debate the modifications to the constitutions required by the examiners in Rome. It would also review the life of the Society since 1820. The members of the general council met in Paris in late September but they could not discuss the proposed modifications since the revised text of the constitutions had not arrived from Rome. Rozaven himself had taken on the task of drawing up the revised constitutions in Italian and this meant that there would be a further delay, for once the text had arrived in Paris it then had to be translated into French. In the interim the council dealt with ongoing business. It was clear in any event that the Society was going to accept all the modifications proposed by Rome and that approval by the general council was simply going through the legal motions.

Sophie used the interim to deal with another matter which needed the urgent attention of the general council. In 1824 the French government proposed to grant legal recognition to all religious congregations of women. Each congregation was invited to present its statutes for approval by the government before 1 January 1827. Any congregation which failed to present its statutes by that date would have no legal status in the country. It was a dilemma, for either option had advantages and disadvantages. Sophie's friend and adviser in government matters, Mgr Frayssinous, now minister of ecclesiastical affairs and public instruction, encouraged her to take this step and ensure the juridical position of the Society. Fr Perreau was against it, arguing that it would take away the liberty of the congregation. Félicité Lammenais saw it as a dangerous encroachment of the state in church matters and spoke against it in the Chambre des Pairs in January 1825. He argued that in the law of 1 January 1825 the government had all the powers it needed to dissolve religious life, if it so wished.[52] Any encroachment on religious rights was serious, and indeed the law of 1 January 1825 gave the government wide powers over the congregations and reinforced the power of civil authorities and of bishops, as agents of the state, over communities of women. These powers were unlikely to be abused, since the attitude of the government towards religious women at this period was benign.[53] Those bishops Sophie consulted over the matter advised her to make the presentation and she herself considered that the Society would be more stable if she did so.[54]

The general council debated the matter fully. The main concern of the council members was the knowledge that a formal process for approbation had just been concluded in Rome, another country as far as the French government was concerned. Had the French government known that the Society of the Sacred Heart was in the process of seeking formal approbation from Rome and that it had foundations outside France (in Louisiana, Savoy and Piedmont) then a conflict of powers and authorities would have emerged then. Yet having foundations in Savoy, Piedmont and especially in Louisiana actually helped the process of approbation in Rome. These two opposing views contained latent tensions which only became apparent later and provoked prolonged controversy. Sophie asked Rozaven what the opinion in Rome was regarding the law of 1 January 1825 and in particular the opinion of the pope on the matter. Rozaven replied that the pope did not interfere with the laws of other countries and on balance it was better to conform to the requirements of French law. He disagreed with

Lammenais and found his predictions gloomy and pessimistic.[55] Having weighed all points of view, Sophie proposed on 2 October 1826 that the Society apply for legal recognition and the motion was passed at the general council by a large majority. The statutes of the Society were presented in November 1826, and the royal ordinance of authorisation was granted on 22 April 1827.[56] Neither Sophie nor her colleagues could have ever imagined the conflicts which would arise from this procedure, how it would split the Society and create division.

Other business was dealt with during the council concerning the life and needs of the rapidly growing Society. As in 1820, so in 1826, Sophie asked the members of the council to forward any matters, queries or recommendations which they wanted to bring up at the general council, so that an agenda could be drawn up beforehand. In addition, each member of the council was asked to bring a list of the personnel needs of their houses and some indication of the personnel they could either give to or exchange with other houses. The financial state of the Society in general and of houses in particular was also examined as was the spiritual life of the membership and the work of education. One key decision was taken on the 10 October 1826. A member of the Society had written to Sophie and asked her to present a query to the council:

> Can we undertake work for the lower middle classes?
> The Council does not reject this project, but decides that, for the time being, this undertaking is impossible.[57]

For good or ill, this decision to concentrate on the nobility and upper middle classes and on the poor, confirmed the Society's reputation in the world of education. It was a decision only in principle, because the Society already had admitted pupils from the lower middle classes into a few of the schools as boarders both in France and in Louisiana.[58] The distinction between social classes in the schools of the Society was maintained. In 1829 Sophie told Madeleine du Chasteigner, at Niort, that while the orphans, like the boarders, could celebrate the superior's feast day in the school, the day pupils could celebrate the headmistress's feast day.[59] This indicated clearly that in Sophie's mind the wealthy and the poor were the major concern of the Society and that day pupils were another category, not having the same status.

The business of the general council was completed by the end of November and since the constitutions had still not arrived from Rozaven Sophie suspended their sessions until the new year. The general council resumed its work at the end of 1 March 1827, ratified the changes to the constitutions and concluded on 7 April with elections to offices. The members elected in 1827 reflected the further expansion of the Society in a few short years. In 1820 there were eleven houses of the Society: Amiens, Grenoble, Poitiers, Niort, Beauvais, Florissant, Paris, Quimper, Chambéry, Bordeaux and La Ferrandière. By 1827 these had increased to nineteen. Le Mans in France and Grand Coteau in Louisiana in 1821; Autun in France 1822; Besançon in France and Turin in Piedmont in 1823; St Michael's in Louisiana in 1825.

The figure who emerged from the shadows during the general council of 1826–27 was that of Jean Rozaven.[60] Through the process for the approval of the constitutions he had become more and more involved in the affairs of the Society of the Sacred Heart, even though Sophie herself had not met him. For his part Rozaven watched developments in the Society. He was the Jesuit assistant general for France, resident in Rome. Though geographically far way his knowledge of the affairs of the Society of the Sacred Heart was increasing all the time. He had been a Father of the Faith, based in London, and had publicly denounced Paccanari to the church authorities in Rome. The fall of Paccanari had forced the Fathers of the Faith to break all links with the centre in Rome and at that point, in 1804, Rozaven decided to join the Jesuits in Russia, the only country where the order had not been suppressed. Ironically, when the Jesuits were restored in Europe in 1814 they were suppressed in Russia in 1815 and Rozaven returned to France for a short time. In 1820 he was elected assistant general for France and he spent the rest of his life in Rome. There he renewed contact with the two Naudet sisters, since Louise had decided to live alone in Rome and Léopoldine founded a congregation, the Holy Family of Verona. Rozaven helped her draw up constitutions for her new community and when doing so he constantly referred to the Society of the Sacred Heart and to Sophie Barat.

In 1821 he wrote to Léopoldine Naudet:

> My thoughts on Madame Barat and her Society are quite close to yours, as you can judge from what I said to your sister. I think there is a bit too much glamour about its work, and while humility is not lacking in those who are in charge, the Society does not seem to have a sufficiently solid base. It is quite difficult for this beautiful virtue [of humility] to survive for long in an atmosphere of outward splendour and acclaim, undoubtedly not sought after, but which always pose a danger. What I particularly dislike are these public examinations, which take place in their boarding schools. I find these totally out of place and not without pitfalls for both pupils and teachers.[61]

In 1805 Joseph Varin criticised Saint-Estève when the school at Amiens celebrated feasts and school events in too elaborate a fashion. He referred in particular to the public examinations followed by distribution of prizes held in the school in September 1805.[62] Over fifteen years later and now in the context of the Faubourg Saint-Germain in Paris, the Society of the Sacred Heart continued this practice of holding examinations in public. Although small events in themselves, such practices presented young women in a public way and underlined the importance of their education. Rozaven rejected this change in the perception of women and echoed the thoughts of most of his contemporaries when he remarked to Léopoldine Naudet:

> I can see no necessity, nor useful purpose in a young girl, whose shyness and reserve ought to be her attraction, appearing in public and speaking with ease in the presence of one hundred or more people, only one of whom is her mother. All that she can gain from this are vain plaudits for which she will pay dearly, if as a

result her modesty should suffer and vanity find a place in her heart. I do not like
when a young woman draws attention to herself. I would rather that her merits
were ignored or remained unknown, except by those on whom she relies for her
own happiness . . . However I am assured that Madame Barat's establishments
achieve much good in France and I believe it. But I doubt that this good will last.
. . . I cannot blame you for following another route. On the contrary I urge you to
do so, with all my heart . . .[63]

Yet Rozaven gradually became the trusted friend of Sophie Barat. Contacts
were increased when Elizabeth Galitzine asked to enter the Society of the
Sacred Heart in 1825. She had been a member of the Russian Orthodox Church
and after instruction from Rozaven she asked to be admitted to the Roman
Catholic Church. She expressed an interest in joining a religious congregation
and Rozaven asked Sophie to consider receiving her into the Society. Elizabeth
Galitzine was not the first Russian to enter the Society. Natalie Rostapchine,
niece of the governor of Moscow who had set fire to the city rather than surrender to Napoleon, had been received into the noviciate in May 1821.[64]

Princess Elizabeth Galitzine was born in St Petersburg on the 22 February
1795, the daughter of Prince Alexis Galitzine and Countess Alexandra Pratasof.
Her father died when Elizabeth was four and then the little child entered a
bleak period:

Her mother's grief was so profound that people say she went mad. Madame
Elizabeth believed that the effect of this loss on her mother's spirit accounted for
the very great severity she used in bringing up her daughter. She was punished for
the least failures, with extreme harshness, she could not see her mother without
trembling. Her fear paralysed her and was taken for obstinacy, which only drew
unceasing, new punishments. She admitted herself later that this way of living was
unbearable, but that she really believed that she was a dreadful person since that
is what she was told. She never complained and did not judge those who made her
suffer. But seeing herself despised and detested by everyone, including the servants, she was only too vulnerable to the least sign of interest from anyone, from
wherever it came.[65]

Her mother became a Catholic secretly and was instructed in the faith by
Rozaven. For a time Elizabeth resisted but finally she was convinced of the
claims of the church of Rome and she asked Rozaven to instruct her too for baptism. This was the beginning of a remarkable relationship, which did not cease
when Rozaven, with his Jesuit colleagues, was expelled from Russia in 1815.
Guided by letters of spiritual direction from Rozaven, Elizabeth Galitzine lived
an intense spiritual life. He organised every least detail of her life, had access to
her every thought and desire, and expected her to keep a daily journal which
she sent him each week. To a child who had had such an austere upbringing
such attention and structure gave the security and safety she needed, and protected her from her mother and the demands that could be made upon her. Once
Rozaven had left Russia Elizabeth decided to become a religious. Her mother
resisted this decision for a time and then gave way, agreeing to bring her

daughter to wherever she had decided to enter. Elizabeth Galitzine asked Rozaven to choose a congregation for her, since she had no idea where to go, except that she wanted the most austere order he could find for her. Rozaven chose the Society of the Sacred Heart.

Rozaven contacted Sophie Barat in Paris and told her about Elizabeth Galitzine and the qualities she would bring to the Society of the Sacred Heart. Rozaven hoped that one day Sophie would thank him for his gift to the Society.[66] Rozaven then proceeded to tell Sophie how to deal with his protegée, and he overruled Sophie several times, especially in the spiritual and financial aspects of Elizabeth Galitzine's life. He insisted on knowing where she was to be received on arrival in France, and at first he dismissed the suggestion of Metz since it was a house where a fusion had taken place and so in his view was not suitable for Elizabeth Galitzine. Again he suggested to Sophie the manner in which Elizabeth Galitzine should administer her substantial fortune, especially the amount she should give to the Society of the Sacred Heart. Each time Sophie received this kind of letter from him she wrote to Elizabeth Galitzine and gave her a choice.[67] When Sophie asked Elizabeth Galitzine to continue her studies in view of the work she would do in the Society and in particular to study history, geography, literature and grammar, Rozaven advised against it. While Sophie came back on it and protested that studies were important in the Society of the Sacred Heart Rozaven won the day.[68] However, once Elizabeth Galitzine had entered the noviciate in the rue de Varenne a great silence descended and Rozaven was not kept informed of her progress. He complained bitterly about this, not only to Sophie Barat but also to Josephine Bigeu, whom he had met in Rome and on whom he had counted for news of 'ma fille'.[69] Although Rozaven found it difficult to relate to people and admitted to Joseph Varin that his personal manner was 'dry and cold . . . more likely to cause fear than inspire some trust'.[70] With Elizabeth Galitzine he was quite different. She was the daughter he never had and he was the father she had never known.

Thus through his help in the process for approbation of the constitutions and the detailed communications concerning Elizabeth Galitzine, Rozaven's influence over Sophie Barat was strengthened. In 1828 he welcomed the possibility of a house of the Society of the Sacred Heart in Rome and when it was established there at the Trinité des Monts he spent hours detailing the life and work of the community. Sophie welcomed this attention for she wished the Society of the Sacred Heart to have close links with the Jesuits. Throughout the 1830s Rozaven constantly offered his advice and Sophie gradually consulted him more and more. She certainly depended on that advice when dealing with the communities and with authorities in Rome. Those who either lived with Sophie or were involved in the government of the Society at this time watched with some apprehension the growing influence Rozaven had over Sophie Barat and some members of the Society.

— 9 —

ROME AND FURTHER EXPANSION, 1827–1829

In March 1827 Sophie knew the approbation from Rome would strengthen unity among the membership of the Society. She wrote to Philippine Duchesne just before the general council opened in 1826:

> I must tell you the happy news of our approbation in Rome. The Holy Father has made some changes in our constitutions, though I do not yet know what they are . . . The office of [ecclesiastical] superior general has been abolished. Now we have a Cardinal Protector in Rome, which brings us closer to the common father of the faithful. Our approbation is similar to that of the Jesuits; it is unique for an order of non-cloistered women.[1]

For Philippine and her companions the news of the approbation was a source of support and affirmation and, at such a distance from Sophie Barat and France, it strengthened the bonds of union between the Society present on two continents.[2] America was a very different reality from Europe and Philippine kept Sophie in touch through letters in which she graphically described the experiences of the little band which had left Bordeaux in March 1818. Throughout the course of these years Philippine and her companions had grappled with new cultures and a new language – English – and they had encountered a society which boasted of egalitarianism in ways Revolutionary thinking had hardly addressed in France. Yet racism was rife and just as divisive as the class structures were in Europe.

The missionaries' life was tough. It was a frontier, pioneer experience, shared with the people around them. It held constant hardships and offered challenges which though often exciting were daunting.[3] They worked doggedly to set up schools, first in St Charles and then, when that failed, in Florissant. Further expansion occurred in 1821 when Eugénie Audé went south to Grand Coteau and started a school there which soon flourished. In 1825 another school was established in St Michael's near New Orleans while in 1827, at last, a school was opened in St Louis, Missouri. By the time the general council met in 1826–27 the little nucleus which had left France in 1818 had grown considerably and in nine years could count four houses. There were already plans for two more in 1828, in La Fourche, Louisiana, and a return to St Charles, Missouri. The Society of the Sacred Heart was growing rapidly in the New World and the general council recognised this by deciding to appoint a fourth assistant general with special responsibility for America. Even though this decision was not implemented until 1833, nevertheless it was a formal consideration of the status and needs of the communities abroad.[4]

The approbation of the constitutions also gave the houses in Europe a sense of stability and confidence for the future. For Sophie too the approbation was a confirming experience personally. By the end of 1827 she was responsible for twenty-two houses of the Society and requests were coming in rapidly for new foundations. Sophie had safeguarded the founding impulse of the Society of the Sacred Heart. She had overcome the intrigues of Saint-Estève and had established her own authority. She had initiated the process of writing the 1815 constitutions and had seen that they were implemented in the houses, especially in Amiens where she carefully planned and executed a reform. She had moved the centre of the Society from Amiens to Paris and set out to establish there a model community and noviciate for the entire Society. She had held three general councils successfully in 1815, 1820 and 1826–1827; she had initiated and concluded negotiations which led to the formal approval of the constitutions by the pope. Thus when the general council closed on the 16 April 1827 the Society of the Sacred Heart had to a great degree come of age.

Along the way there had been many troubled times. Throughout, Sophie struggled with exhaustion and poor health, with rare periods when she felt really well.[5] From 1823 she had struggled with constant headaches, sore eyes, rheumatism and diarrhoea. She complained of fevers, insomnia and a general sense of weariness which dogged her and which she knew herself came from overwork.[6] With the papal approbation of the constitutions and the approval of the statutes of the Society of the Sacred Heart by the French government, Sophie experienced a sense of relief, the hurdle of recognition and legal existence for the Society achieved. That task completed, she expected to have less relentless work and that she could concentrate on governing the Society, overseeing the spiritual progress of communities and individuals, maintaining the already existing houses of the Society and planning future foundations. That was not to be. The negotiations took their toll, however, and from December 1827 until the summer of 1828 Sophie was ill with fever and had to keep business to a minimum.[7] The death of Josephine Bigeu in the winter of 1827 was an immense loss for Sophie and it left her bereft of an effective assistant general, capable of taking responsibility for business negotiations and overseeing new foundations.[8]

At the general council in 1826–27 a policy had been established whereby invitations for foundations would only be accepted if financial support was guaranteed, either from wealthy patrons or from local government authorities. Using these criteria established at the council, two new houses were founded in 1827, one in Lille and the other in Lyon.[9] In January 1828 Sophie was told by the papal nuncio in Paris, Luigi Lambruschini, that Pope Leo XII wanted to provide education for the girls of wealthy families in the papal states and wished her to establish a school of the Society in Rome. Sophie saw the value of this opening to the Society and, despite her illness, set about planning the new foundation immediately.

Lambruschini's proposal was not entirely new. The possibility of such a foundation had been mooted since 1824. Two years later, when Josephine Bigeu was in Rome, the subject was raised in the course of the process for approbation and Rozaven enthusiastically promoted the idea.[10] The possibility became a reality in the spring of 1828 and arose from two initiatives. One was taken in Rome by Rozaven and his fellow Jesuit, Giorgio Massa. They approached Pope Leo XII and proposed that Sophie Barat be asked to found a school in Rome. While both Rozaven and Massa had intended that this school would educate the wealthy families of the papal states, they also assumed that there would be a poor school for the children of the city of Rome, since that was integral to the constitutions of the Society of the Sacred Heart. They had two sources of income to offer the Society. One was the from the marchioness of Androsilla who had been left a substantial fortune by her husband, part of which was designated for some charitable purpose. She was prepared to consider endowing the poor school with that money. The other was a small legacy donated by a recently deceased priest, Fr Bellonte. Despite the approval in principle from the pope and the financial backing of two patrons, Rozaven and Massa found it difficult to find a suitable location for the school in Rome.[11]

While Sophie had been aware of Rozaven's plans for a school of the Society in Rome the initiative taken personally by the pope, through his nuncio in Paris, came to her as a surprise. Having received Sophie's agreement in principle Lambruschini wrote to Leo XII and suggested that Sophie Barat be formally asked to establish a school in Rome. He suggested that the former monastery of the Minimes, the Trinité des Monts in Rome, be considered as the most suitable location. It was French property, had been vacant since the French Revolution and Lambruschini hoped the French government would grant permission for a school to be established there. The pope took up these proposals with enthusiasm and asked Lambruschini to undertake negotiations both with Sophie Barat and with the French government. The French government was approached and it agreed to allow the Society of the Sacred Heart found a school in Rome at the Trinité des Monts, though it placed several strict conditions on the foundation, protecting its

1. *Birth-place of Madeleine Sophie Barat, 11 rue Davier, Joigny, France*

2. *Baptismal certificate of Madeleine Sophie Barat, born 12 December 1779 at Joigny*

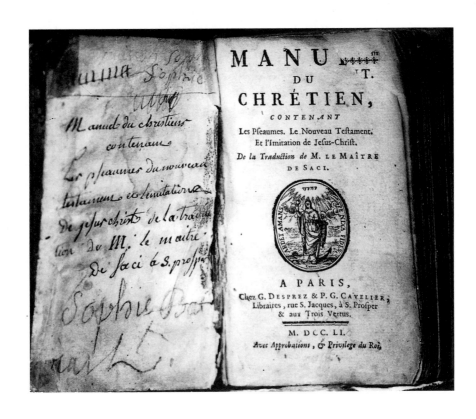

3.   *Sophie Barat's prayer book, given to her by her mother on her First Communion
      day. It contains the liturgy of the Mass, the New Testament and Psalms and the
      Imitation of Christ. Sophie used it all her life*

SUJETS DE
MEDITATIONS
SUR LE CAN·TIQUE
des Cantiques.

AVEC SON EXPLI-
cation selon le sentiment des
Peres de l'Eglise.

Pour l'usage des Religieuses Chartreuses.

A LA CORRERIE,
Par Claude Faure, Imprimeur & Libraire
à Grenoble.

M. DC. LXXXXI.
AVEC APPROBATION ET PRIVILEGE.

4.   *Meditations on the Song of Songs used by Sophie Barat. This was one of Sophie*
     Barat's favourite books of the Bible

5.   *Passport of Sophie Barat, 1843. Passports were needed for travelling within France during this period. This passport describes the height and facial characteristics of Sophie Barat.*

Si trova vendibile nella Tipografia G. Banzo via di S. Maria in Campomarzo N.34.
e via di Campomarzo N, 85

ROMA IL DI *24 maggio* 1845.

Colla presente privata scrittura stipolata in doppj Originali da valere , e tenere dalle infrascritte parti Contraenti nel più efficace modo di ragione, è stato fissato, e convenuto quanto appresso.

1. Il Proprietario di Vettura *Giorgio Mare* domiciliato a *Roma* in Via *della Nocetta* al N. *21* promette, e si obbliga di servire *Lad. Made Gle* *al suo Reggia con sei altre persone da Roma a Loreto e Benque da Loreto a Parma* nel Viaggio che vuole intraprendere da *Roma a Parma*

con mettere a sua disposizione durante il detto Viaggio *una buona carozza con i buoni cavalli che dovrà condurre egli stesso* ~~condotta da buoni Vetturino~~ pel prezzo convenuto di *Franchi Nocento Sessanta*

mediante il qual pagamento, che sarà eseguito *in tre rate cioè una terza parte a Roma, un altro in Loreto e l'ultimo terza parte cioè Parma* restano gli obblighi al detto proprietario di Vettura ~~o suo garzon~~ qui appresso dichiarati.

2. Ogni giorno , durante il detto Viaggio dovrà fornire a numero *7* Padroni *la mattina caffè con latte e pane a mezzo giorno un digunè alla Forchetta con minestra 3 piatte caldi e Frutta; la sera un buon Pranzo di nelle migliori locande. La notte un letto per ogni persona; con lumino da notte*

3. Tutte le spese d'ajuti nel passaggio di Fiumi, Ponti, e Montagne, come quelle di Barriere, saranno a carico del Vetturino Conduttore.

4. La Buonamano al Vetturino Conduttore sarà *a seconda della soddisfazione*

5. Che il prescritto Viaggio sarà eseguito nel corso di Giorni *quattro* compiti, o siano Notti *3 da Roma in Loreto e di giorno 4 e mezzo da Loreto fa carma* a contare dal giorno in cui è stata fissata la partenza.

6. La Partenza da *Roma* è fissata per la mattina del dì *10 Giugno 1845*

alle ore

7. Nel caso che la partenza venisse ritardata sarà pagato per ciaschedun giorno pel mantenimento delle Bestie.

8. Per tutti quei giorni di più che al predetto Signor gli piacesse di restar ferma in qualche Città , o che fosse costretto per casi fortuiti , è restato convenuto, che *si pagherà 2 scudi al giorno fra franchi*

9. Che il Vetturino Conduttore dovrà andar sempre in buoni Alberghi, partendo ogni mattina di buon ora per arrivare ogni giorno prima di notte all'Albergo ove dovrassi pernottare.

10. E per l'osservanza di ciò si sono volontariamente sottoscritte ambo le parti, come appresso

Roma li 24 maggio 1845

Croce di Giorgio Mare + che ha dichiarato essere illitterato

---

6.   Contract made by Sophie Barat with coachman Georgio Mare in Rome for her
     journey from Rome to Turin in May 1845

UN PAUVRE SIRE.

7.   *Un Pauvre Sire (Charles X, 1830). Charles X was exiled in 1830, during the July Revolution. The Society of the Sacred Heart, especially the rue de Varenne, was closely identified with the deposed king*

8. *Cachette des Royalistes les 27, 28 et 29 juillet (Paris). Cartoon showing royalists faithful to Charles X hiding in the Faubourg Saint-Germain*

S. G. M⁰ʳ Hyacinthe Louis DE QUÉLEN.

Archevêque de Paris.

Né à Paris, le 8 Octobre 1778.

9.   *Hyacinthe Louis de Quelen, archbishop of Paris (1817–1839). He lived at the rue de Varenne from 1832 until his death in 1839*

own interests in Rome.[12] However the advantages of the project outweighed the conditions placed on the Society by the French government. The fact that the pope had asked Sophie Barat to establish a school in Rome was prestigious for the Society and increased her own personal authority and reputation, within the Society and in general. It also strengthened her personal links with the papacy.

Both Lambruschini and Rozaven suggested to Sophie that Armande de Causans, then superior in Turin, be named to head the new foundation in Rome. When Lambruschini was archbishop of Genoa he had occasion to visit Turin and was impressed by the gifts and social skills of Armande de Causans.[13] From the time Armande de Causans had entered the Society of the Sacred Heart Sophie had recognised both her talents and her limitations. On appointing her to succeed Josephine Bigeu in Turin, Sophie explained why she had chosen her:

> Armande has great elegance, a sense of propriety and a charming manner when dealing with important people. In these respects she could suit Turin. Yet she has fewer gifts than Marie Prevost for looking after the internal matters of a house. . . . Mde de Causans is not efficient at expediting work. While she does whatever she has been asked to do very well, she cannot cope with several things going on at the same time.[14]

Marie-Louise-Armande de Causans was born in December 1785, at the château de Suzy near Soissons. Before the Revolution the marquis and marchioness de Causans were close to the French court and in particular to Madame Elizabeth, sister of Louis XVI. During the Revolution her parents had to go into exile and Armande was cared for by close family friends. She was a delicate child and poor health dogged her all her life. Her mother died in exile and for a time Armande lived with her father in the family home at Causans in the Vaucluse. One of her aunts, a canoness of the chapter of Saint-Louis de Metz, recognised the gifts and qualities of her niece and asked her to live with her in Paris. There she educated her niece in the social graces and in good works. In 1822, at the age of thirty-six, Armande de Causans entered the Society of the Sacred Heart at the rue de Varenne and soon after her profession Sophie appointed her as her private secretary.[15] Her appointment in 1826 to succeed Josephine Bigeu as superior of Turin was a difficult post to fill since the archbishop of Turin continued to be critical of the Society. Then, when Armande de Causans had been in Turin a short time, Sophie wrote to her former secretary:

> I am so excited about this matter [Rome] that if I were not held back by prudence I would tell the whole world. . . . The history of this foundation is wonderful. I will tell you the details when I am not so weak, [but today] I summarise. In Rome there is a beautiful house, with wonderful gardens, situated on a hill. It belongs to France. The pope has requested the King of France to give it and some of its revenues to the Dames du Sacré Cœur. [16]

Sophie asked for confidentiality until the agreement was formally concluded with the French government. In addition, the Christian Brothers congregation had been offered the Trinité des Monts previously and that conflict of interests had to be resolved. In fact, Sophie warned Armande de Causans that only the assistants general, Catherine de Charbonnel and Félicité Desmarquest, and Eugénie de Gramont knew of the foundation in Rome since they formed her advisory council in Paris. It was just fourteen years since Saint-Estève had invited Eugénie de Gramont to leave Amiens and establish a community in the Trinité. But by this time Eugénie de Gramont was a member of the general council, bound in friendship to Sophie Barat and fully committed to her own project in Paris at the rue de Varenne. Not even Joseph Varin knew of the foundation, nor was he told for some time. His indiscretion could have embarrassed Sophie and this she could not afford to risk.

The new foundation was planned in two phases. Initially, an advance party would go to Rome, take possession of the Trinité and put it into order, as the building had been deserted for some time. Then, after some months, a full community would be sent to Rome and the school could officially open. With Armande de Causans Sophie sent Euphrosine Faux (1790–1878), a member of the community at Bordeaux. She was a practical woman who became devoted to Armande de Causans and remained with her throughout most of her life. Sophie also sent a young woman, later to become her own secretary and biographer, Adèle Cahier (1804–1885).[17] The three left Turin for Rome in March 1828, and made their way slowly through Parma, Modena, Tuscany, until they reached the gates of Rome. There they were met by the Princess de Viano who guided them to the convent of St Sylvester where they were to stay until they could move into the Trinité.

It was a French foundation in the heart of Rome and the Society had undertaken obligations which soon proved both onerous and constricting. In return for the use of the property and its revenues, the Society had

> the power neither to alienate the property, nor to change in any way or cede it to anyone else, under any pretext. The property could only be occupied by French women. [18]

The little group remained with the community in St Sylvester for some time, a strictly enclosed Franciscan congregation. In this context, the daily exodus of the trio either to visit churches, attend ceremonies, visit the Jesuits, and on occasion meet with the pope and some of the cardinals, was in great contrast to the strict form of cloister which women religious observed in Rome and indeed in Italy. Armande de Causans received so many visitors in St Sylvester that the abbess, Madame Moroni, gave over a room outside the community enclosure area where all business could be transacted.[19] De Causans had experienced already the strict level of cloister expected by the archbishop of Turin and knew that since she had left Louise de Limminghe had had several further confrontations on the question with Mgr Chiavarotti, who threatened to excommunicate her. Within the world of the church in Piedmont as well as in Rome, the type of religious life lived by members of the Society of the Sacred Heart was different and Armande de Causans knew that confrontations on the issue led only to antagonism. She remarked to Sophie:

What a fuss they created in Turin over the question of cloister! I was happy to see that my view on the issue is in accord with yours . . . and that your opinion is to accede to the actual circumstances as they exist. Otherwise, what repercussions! We would place ourselves in a situation which would incur or bring about excommunications . . . these dreadful laws only concern orders which observe full [papal] cloister.[20]

When Armande de Causans finally got access to the Trinité she was daunted by the task of cleaning it and getting it ready for a school. Rozaven promised to help her and he became her constant support. Until she and her companions found their way in Rome and learnt more Italian they had to rely on Rozaven a great deal. He advised them with regard to audiences with the pope, with the cardinals and the bishops; he introduced them to the general of the Jesuits, Luigi Fortis, and arranged for visits to the Jesuit church in Rome, the Gesù. Rozaven was a constant presence in the Trinité. He examined the improvements in the house; he advised on the fees to charge, though this was overturned by the pope, who found them too high. On their arrival in Rome they had heard the Society of the Sacred Heart described as 'Jesuitesses'. When Armande de Causans met Cardinal Ostini he told her of: 'his enthusiasm for the Institute of the Sacred Heart, entirely modelled... on the Jesuits.[21] Armande de Causans knew this was due in great part to the enthusiasm with which Rozaven spoke of the Society in Rome. This pleased Sophie who wanted a closer link with the Jesuits. She told Philippine Duchesne: 'They want to put us on the same level as the Society of Jesus. Is this possible for women? Time will tell.'[22]

After the approbation of the Society of the Sacred Heart in 1827 Sophie had asked the general of the Jesuits, Fr Fortis, for a form of spiritual affiliation with the Jesuits, a devotional not a structural bond. This was granted in the form of a letter in September 1828 and Rozaven gave it to Armande de Causans. She told Sophie:

Father Rozaven undoubtedly drew up the document or at least negotiated it for us. . . . He told me that each house should have a copy of it and keep it carefully hidden away. Prudence is necessary in such matters and more than ever in the times we live in.[23]

Sophie asked Fr Fortis to ensure that the new community of the Trinité des Monts received spiritual help from the Jesuits in Rome. She drew his attention then to the influence of the Jesuit rule on the constitutions of the Society of the Sacred Heart but did not suggest that the constitutions of the Society of the Sacred Heart be more fully modelled on the Jesuit rule. Thus when Fortis wrote a positive reply, Sophie and her assistants general sent a letter of gratitude, it was simply that, a letter of thanks.[24] Nevertheless, and unknown to Sophie, already pressure was building up in Rome, from Rozaven and Armande de Causans for a more formal modelling of the Society of the Sacred Heart on that of the Jesuits.

Thus with the foundation of the Trinité in Rome, new elements entered into the Society of the Sacred Heart. The Jesuits in Rome, and indeed the second generation of Jesuits in France, had not experienced the bond between the first generation of Jesuits, many former Fathers of the Faith, and the Society of the Sacred Heart. These links had been forged during the years of Revolution and Empire, and emerged into the open at the restoration of the Bourbons and of the Jesuits in France. The 'new' Jesuits in Rome and in France tended to follow more strictly the line set down by Ignatius of Loyola and they distanced themselves from communities of religious women who wished to become more formally and structurally modelled on the Jesuit rule. Jean Rozaven, a former Father of the Faith, was the exception and he worked to model the constitutions of the Society of the Sacred Heart on that of the Jesuits. Sophie Barat did not object to his interest in the Society in Rome, but she had no idea of his plans for the Society of the Sacred Heart. Neither had she fully grasped the ascendancy Rozaven had over Elizabeth Galitzine, nor the extent of his infatuation with her. So while Sophie was satisfied with Fortis's reply to her request for spiritual affiliation with the Jesuits, for Rozaven it was only the beginning of a process. In that context, the arrival of the Society of the Sacred Heart was a personal triumph for Rozaven.

While Armande de Causans admitted that Rozaven was helpful in the early days in the Trinité, she found him both austere and forbidding in manner. He was used to being obeyed without question:

> He is so wise and full of knowledge regarding our true interests! Without a doubt . . . I have nothing to fear with him as a guide. . . . Fr Rozaven has many of the qualities of Fr Sellier. They both have hearts which no human affection, however little, can touch. Nevertheless the latter still lets slip some lively and vivacious characteristics which allow you to see human goodness combined with and transformed into burning love. But in the case of Fr Rozaven human nature is only born to die, whether we do it willingly or by force.[25]

Yet Armande de Causans also picked up Rozaven's infatuation with Elizabeth Galitzine, still a novice in Paris. In his eyes she could do no wrong. Whereas he was austere and distant in manner with most people, Rozaven was not so with Elizabeth Galitzine. As Armande de Causans drily remarked to Sophie

> For his [spiritual] daughter Elizabeth . . . I suspect he has a little weakness, but it is the only one. Apparently she is worthy of it.[26]

Rozaven was possessive of Elizabeth and she was totally devoted to him. She treated his every wish and opinion as her own, and appeared to have no thought or opinion of her own. Her letters were a source of joy to Rozaven and he showed them to Armande de Causans, ostensibly to encourage her in the way of perfection:

> Father Rozaven sent me his daughter Elizabeth's last letter, from which he tore off the first page. This was to edify and humble me no doubt by allowing me a glimpse of the exquisite inner life of a novice, already so advanced in the ways of perfection. [27]

Once the Trinité was ready for occupation, the new school opened officially but few pupils enrolled. Two obstacles prevented rapid growth. One was the condition laid down by the government to allow only French religious and students of French origin to reside in the Trinité. The other was that only families from the nobility could be received as pupils, whereas Armande de Causans was convinced that the school would expand quickly if they could accept pupils from the higher middle class.[28] These conditions made the running of the school difficult. Parents naturally wanted Italian to be taught in the school and permission had to be sought from the ambassador for an Italian teacher to live in the school. Other responsibilities had to be filled as the school grew and it was not always possible to find Frenchwomen to fill them. Yet each task had to be accounted for and each request queried.[29] Such constrictions blocked development and damaged the image of the Society of the Sacred Heart in Rome.

These problems only underlined the fact that if the Society of the Sacred Heart was to become established in the papal states and in the other kingdoms in Italy, then a noviciate needed to be established, independent from the Trinité. To this purpose a noviciate and poor school were planned, for another part of the city of Rome.[30] Armande de Causans confided to Sophie:

> This noviciate house (between you and me) is of greater consequence to the Society than the foundation of the Trinité . . . In brief, it will complete the task of making us more like the Jesuits, in the eyes of the public as well as in fact. [31]

The pope was hesitant at first when the proposal for a noviciate was mooted, fearing a confrontation with the French government. His reservations were removed by the information that the new house would be in a different location in Rome and funded by the money of the Marchioness de Androsilla and Fr Bellonte. Armande de Causans suggested to the pope that a poor school and noviciate would consolidate the work of the school at the Trinité, as well as serving the needs of the poor in the city. Then drawing on the recently approved constitutions, Rozaven and Armande de Causans wrote a justification of the Society's request to have a poor school. They explained that it was an integral part of the Society's practice to have a school for the wealthy and for the poor, if possible on the same property, but certainly in the vicinity:

> Indeed the education of the upper classes is one of the aims of their Institute but it is not the only one, nor is it that which they cherish most. The poor have always been too dear to the Heart of Jesus not to be the priority of the servants of this adorable Heart. They regard their establishments as incomplete when they do not benefit the poor. But, while the convent at the Trinité des Monts is not a suitable place to open classes for the poor, it is clear anyway that this good work of necessity has to be done by Italians. In consequence, a noviciate is indispensable to form candidates who can found and sustain in Rome and Italy this work so essential to the Society. From the moment the noviciate is established nothing will hinder the opening of schools for the poor, even in the noviciate itself.[32]

The pope's approval for a second house of the Society in Rome was crucial and strategic. While Sophie considered she had no choice about whether or not to accept the pope's invitation to establish a school in Rome, she recognised that the conditions imposed on the Trinité could prevent the Society's growth into Italy. The Trinité was perceived as an extension of France in Italy. Roman society tended to be anti-French and Armande de Causans was sensitive to this and made sure that some in the community began learning Italian. This was essential if the Society of the Sacred Heart was to take root in Rome and vocations flourish.[33] Another, quite different criticism of the Society which Armande de Causans and her companions had to deal with, when they arrived in Rome in March 1828, was that they were Paccanarists. It was a term of derision – the Society was associated with the Diletti di Gesù, founded by Paccanari. The case against Paccanari was still talked about in Rome. Indeed, the pope had considered asking the community of St Denys in Rome, founded by Saint-Estève, to take charge of a school for the daughters of the nobility in Rome. But he had decided against it on account of their former links with Paccanari. Now the Society of the Sacred Heart's former links with the Diletti caused Armande de Causans embarrassment and she felt the need to try and distance herself from that strand of the Society's history. When Louise Naudet arrived in the Trinité to see the community there was real panic, as Armande de Causans thought that Louise wanted to join the Society. But in fact she had come merely to greet them and to ask how they were settling into the house. Most of all she wanted news of Sophie:

> Madame Louise merely wanted to be friendly and spoke a great deal about Mother Barat, for whom she had the fondest memories and the highest regard.[34]

At this time, Louise Naudet was living alone in Rome and Rozaven was her confessor. For her part Sophie remembered Louise with affection and asked Armande de Causans to receive her kindly. Sophie did not tell Armande de Causans that it was Louise who had affirmed her leadership gifts in Amiens, many years ago. She simply said that the Society owed her a great deal.[35] She was more concerned about the community at St Denis for there were rumours abroad that they wished to be accepted into the Society, having been totally abandoned by Saint-Estève. Sophie was of the opinion that this should not happen, with the possible exception of Teresa Copina. Since she was Italian she could be useful in the new foundation but 'all the others are of poor quality'.[36]

Armande de Causans told Sophie that it would cause gossip in Rome if Teresa Copina were accepted into the Society. De Causans had little faith in fusions and perhaps had learnt from Euphrosine Faux how painful the situation in Bordeaux had been.[37] Sophie did not insist, since this case was more sensitive and delicate than any she had dealt with herself. As with Philippine Duchesne in Louisiana, so with Armande de Causans, Sophie handed over much of the decision-making, aware that it was difficult to judge a given situation from a distance. Besides she had unquestioning trust in Rozaven and advised Armande de Causans to follow his advice. Sophie herself deferred to most of his opinions, though not on the question of fees. She asked that they be kept at least as low as those requested by other religious schools in Rome. Rozaven ignored that advice but he was blocked by the pope who also asked that the fees be kept to a more modest scale.[38]

The amount of thought and planning, as well as the number of meetings and letters involved in establishing the new house in Rome, weighed heavily on Sophie. She wrote to Philippine Duchesne in April 1828:

> The long silence I have maintained between us . . . has been difficult for me. You know the reason for it; I was ill for more than three months. . . . You are aware of our new foundation in Rome . . . of the special marks of esteem shown us by the Holy Father. . . . I am frightened by the responsibility which weighs upon my weak shoulders, and which increases daily with foundations. We need at least fifteen religious to begin in Rome. . . . I have to stop now . . . for I am still unable to cope with work which taxes my nerves and give me terrible headaches.[39]

Her illness and the amount of work she had to do left Sophie feeling both desolate and alone, and also more sensitive to Philippine. She had hinted in her letters how isolated and lonely she felt in Louisiana. Sophie responded:

> . . . we have lived together on Thabor. How brief that vision was! Afterwards, the experience of Calvary . . . Will you believe me when I tell you that I look most often at Ste Marie [d'En Haut] when we lived together, and on Louisiana. If later on I were forced to flee from France my heart would fly to the land where you live. If God allows, I shall taste happiness again for a time. God's will be done. *Fiat.* You tell me a little of your solitude. I hope that Jesus compensates you for it and is your most faithful friend. Then one can take this solitude, for to tell you the truth when you have lived for many long years with people you get less attached to them. I myself, your mother, [though] surrounded with such love, live in that kind of solitude. I have admitted this to *you* alone. Few would understand. It is nevertheless the most precious gift: *God alone.*[40]

Sophie's illness in the winter of 1827–28 was the catalyst for these reflections. Yet for some time she had been feeling overwhelmed by the responsibility of her task. The area of finance was a source of deep concern for her and she spent many sleepless nights worrying about the Society's debts. She was torn between the real needs of communities and schools and the impossibility of finding enough money to help them all. She confided to Philippine Duchesne and Eugénie Audé in 1826 that if the general council did not take the financial situation of the Society in hand she would resign:

> How tortured I am . . . being unable to give each of you immediately the amount you need. If you knew our difficulties and my endless worries over heavy debts which we still have despite my care and continual recommendations . . . I tell you now (only you and Madame Duchesne) that I have decided that if the Assembly (general council) which is about to take place does not adopt the strictest measures to reduce these debts, which have increased by 200,000 frs in the past year, I will resign as superior general. I do not wish to see the Society perish through lack of order and because we did not wish to economise. What nights I have spent! What constant worries I carry in my soul![41]

When she was well and had energy Sophie was able to cope with the demands of her role. As soon as she was able to resume her work she became strong and decisive and could act with clarity and courage. But Sophie could be easily thrown by events. For example, in 1826 she was upset by the deaths of two young girls in Paris, and especially concerned about the effect such early deaths had on the families and students. Sophie admitted she had not the courage to face the families and left it to Eugénie de Gramont. She admitted to Josephine Bigeu that on such occasions:

> It is this cross which makes me regret not joining the Carmelites. An act of resig-
> nation steadies me, but it is hard.[42]

Sophie's total involvement in the task of governing the Society took priority over all else now and her involvement in family affairs lessened. She may have seen her role in the family completed when her nieces and nephews were edu-cated and grown up. While she never lost her interest and concern for each of them and indeed for her sister Marie-Louise, she of necessity had less time to devote to them now. All the Dusaussoy girls, except Dosithée (who had died in 1823) and Zoé, had joined the Society. Sophie expected them to blend into the general life of the Society and not to seek exceptions. She was annoyed with Stanislas Dusaussoy when he insisted on seeing his sisters in Paris whenever he wished.[43] However, it was with Stanislas most of all that Sophie continued cor-respondence, until the end of her life, realising that he most of all needed her support. When he complained that she had forgotten him, or had become indif-ferent towards him, Sophie wrote and explained that she simply was swallowed up by work:

> My work and responsibilities increase. All my time is devoted to my work. That is
> what you undoubtedly took for indifference. I still have as much affection for you
> now, especially when I pray, though it is not perhaps as demonstrative as before.[44]

Despite her illness, by June 1828 Sophie had named the new community for the Trinité, and, to fulfil the requirements of the French government, all were Frenchwomen. They were led by Catherine de Charbonnel and arrived in Rome in the autumn of 1828, in time for the opening of the new school.[45] Sophie still had to find a nucleus for the noviciate community which she wanted to have in place by the coming year. This would be much more difficult to compose for she had to find someone who was a gifted spiritual leader, who knew Italian and could both discern vocations and train Italian novices. While Armande de Causans and Rozaven sought a suitable property for the noviciate and poor school, Sophie kept searching for personnel. The plans were interrupted for a time by the death of Leo XII in 1829, the election of Pius VIII followed by his death two months later, and the election of Gregory XVI in 1831. By the time a property had been bought Sophie had decided to visit the new houses in Rome and she set off in mid-October 1832 to see for herself what had been happening there since 1828.

However, the new foundation in Rome was only one of the major concerns of Sophie since the general council of 1827. Other projects were in hand, such as a foundation in Perpignan, which she hoped would open the door to Spain, and another in Milan which she planned as an entry point to the Hapsburg Empire.[46] Yet Sophie was conscious that she simply did not have enough personnel trained and ready for responsibility. Three elements contributed to the crisis of personnel. One was the actual capacity of the individual women who asked to enter the Society. All came with certain ideals and gifts and some were capable after a short training of taking on the responsibility of founding new communities and schools. But these were very few and even those who were asked to take on this task had great difficulty all their lives in measuring up to the expectations of Sophie Barat. Most of those who entered needed time to develop a spiritual life and continue, or even begin their training as educators. Some of them were young; others were delicate and it took insight on the part of Sophie and those in charge of formation to discover what task each novice could do in the Society.

The superior was expected to be a spiritual leader and in this context would be expected to give spiritual direction to the members of the community; she would also give regular spiritual conferences, for feast days of the church. She was also responsible for the smooth running of the house and the school. She made the appointments to the several offices in the house, in particular the mistress of novices, the headmistress of the school, the bursar in the community as well as her own personal assistant who was also responsible for the coadjutrix sisters. The superior represented the community to the local government authorities and to the local bishop; with both she negotiated whatever business concerned the community and school and it was her task to safeguard the interests of the community and the wider commitments of the Society of the Sacred Heart. Finally, local superiors accepted new members into the Society and ensured that they received formation for their spiritual life and for the work they would do in the Society, whether it was teaching or domestic work. In a very real sense the quality of personnel in the Society depended on the judgement of the local superiors. It was an all-embracing role and it called for considerable managerial skills and personal gifts of communication. In the context of the role and place of women in nineteenth-century Europe, Sophie Barat's expectation and real need for such gifted women was a high ideal, and she found that if she wanted such women she had to train them herself. They rarely came ready-made. When the possibility of a foundation in Italy was mooted Sophie wrote to Marie de la Croix:

> Italy is beckoning us again. Already we have refused a really attractive institution owing to lack of leaders, for we have the numbers. Leadership requires so many qualities in one person, above all solid virtue, prudence etc and these are rarely found in one person! Pray that Heart of Jesus will give us a few.[47]

Sophie appreciated the gifts that each woman brought to the Society and indeed was skilled in the way she assessed them. Philippine Duchesne recognised that Sophie had this gift and wrote to her ruefully:

You are able to assign each one her place with that skill which creates harmony. I do not have that gift.[48]

When Sophie appointed Adelaide de Rozeville (1780–1855) superior of Besançon, Sophie trained her chiefly through her letters. Her method was a blend of encouragement, respect, esteem and affection. Sophie was frank when she reprimanded mistakes and errors of judgement, or any aspect of running the house which had failed because of mismanagement. She delegated as much as possible, and indeed advised others to do so too:

> After considering this in the presence of God I came to the conclusion that I must advise you to work towards relieving yourself of some of the details of your administration, by delegating to others . . . a portion of your responsibility. . . .
> You know . . . that the most perfect administrator is the one who can govern without getting lost in details. She sees all the mistakes made from a distance and can rectify them readily when they are committed by individuals in the community. She safeguards her time so as to have reasonable amount for her personal prayer and for the spiritual direction of the community. Hold to this form of government and you will see that your soul and your health will benefit.[49]

Normally Sophie did not formally consult individual members of the Society about moves from one house to another or from one occupation to another. She worked through the local superiors and changes were carried out that way. Nevertheless she displayed a high level of personal knowledge of the vast majority of the membership, something she was unable to retain as the Society grew. Her letters are full of endless proposals, ideas and plans, some of which materialised and others which proved inoperable. Sophie was flexible and inventive in her search to find solutions. Her practice was to try and match the need of a school or of community service with the capacity of the individual member.

Criticism of leadership in the communities and in the schools was inevitable and Sophie used it creatively. When community members or parents of the students complained about a superior, either to Sophie herself or to one of the assistants or councillors general, Sophie told the superior about them. When Catherine de Charbonnel visited Besançon in 1827 Sophie warned de Rozeville in advance that she had asked her to deal with the criticisms from the parents of the students:

> She will probably speak to you about complaints made by parents about some responsibilities regarding the pupils which were neglected. Pay attention to the quality of food, insist on good manners, that nothing is spared for what is necessary, and above all take no gifts from the children, even for the chapel. . . . People are fickle and always feel they will find better elsewhere. So if other schools are opened in your neighbourhood and there is something to complain about in yours, you will lose many pupils.[50]

Even if Sophie's procedure was honest and truthful, this did not make it any easier for the person concerned and certainly de Rozeville felt raw after de Charbonnel's visit. Sophie anticipated this and placed the criticism in another dimension:

Renew your courage and rely mostly on God, who will help you when your own resources fail, especially if you ask for this grace with faith and perseverance. Prayer and union with God will make this divine exchange easier. A superior cannot do without this, if she wants to carry out her responsibilities successfully. Pay particular attention also to the daily practice of gentleness and limitless patience . . . firmness is necessary yet it must be tempered by this quality [patience] which overcomes human nature by [God's] grace but does not destroy it.[51]

Yet the criticism undermined de Rozeville and Sophie some months later had to refer again to the visit made by de Charbonnel. While Sophie reminded her of the mistakes she had made, and indeed had tried to hide, she also urged her to keep all in proportion:

You are a little too sensitive and perhaps easily offended. How is it that you spend a day worrying over an unintentional mistake? Reproach yourself instead [for] showing your lack of patience, I do not mean in words, but when it shows in your manner, your face etc. . . . It is essential for a superior to maintain the most perfect evenhandedness and to govern with kindness. You must understand that this virtue is compatible with firmness, without which a religious house cannot maintain fervour and regularity for long. It is like a hand carved in cedar wood, inside a velvet glove. People are held but do not dare complain when all they feel is the softness of silk to the touch.[52]

When it was a question of criticism coming from the local civil authorities, Sophie was in no doubt as to what de Rozeville should do in Besançon:

I would really like to know what more these gentlemen expect of us. Must we be learned scholars, geniuses? Must their children achieve perfection in every way, as if we were fairies waving a magic wand?
These notions are ridiculous, but it is true that some abuses and carelessness have crept in among the teachers. Follow this up closely . . . wait until after the holidays and do not give any information other than the prospectus and the statutes approved by the government . . . having the Mayor and the Prefect on your side is the essential thing.[53]
Let there be no complaints over the content of the studies or the outward behaviour of the pupils.[54]

Sophie did not have a blueprint for leadership in her mind nor did she have a style which she attempted to implement throughout the Society. Rather she formed each superior according to the gifts of the individual. The values and role were the same throughout, but the manner in which they were implemented depended upon the capacity of each one. Inevitably the model she most advocated in her letters and conferences was the one she most tried to live out herself and in encouraging those she appointed she was acting on her own experiences and intuitions. For example, when she moved de Rozeville from Besançon to Amiens in 1828, she pointed out the adaptation needed, both for de Rozeville and for the members of the community, who had got used to the easy and informal manner of Marie Prevost:

Allow me to point out that I have noticed that in your style of government you are sometimes bad tempered and perhaps even severe. Mother Prevost is the type of character which feels the need to please everyone and make them happy. Undoubtedly this is a shortcoming when it is carried too far, especially in a religious. But at least she is trying to remedy this and the reprimands I give her will bring this about, I hope. At the same time I would like you to take a resolution, not to imitate her since we are trying to correct that, but I would like you to become more lenient, more good-natured actually. Your observance of the rule is too strict, especially just now at the beginning [of your mandate]. It contrasts with the excessive freedom which your predecessor established in that community [Amiens]. We must work towards this reform gently, and above all in gentle and unobtrusive ways. You are accused of doing exactly the opposite. Already in Besançon you gave good reason to be blamed in this way, for that harsh manner, impatient at times, for the tendency to see intent where there was only neglect or forgetfulness. Basically this negates the great good that can be done by a superior who blends both firmness and kindness. This latter virtue is absolutely essential in the running of the house confided to you and I often ask this of the Heart of Jesus for you and for all who have been called to govern.[55]

When Sophie appointed Laure des Portes, then at Poitiers, to be the new superior in Lyon in 1829 she asked Henriette Grosier to help initiate her into her new task:

Let her have no misunderstanding about this: kindness and gentleness are essential everywhere. *Firmness must be there without being obvious.* But alas, who understands this? What a wonderful skill good government is. The fact that it is rare and unknown distresses me![56]

The goodness Sophie asked for in leadership was real and comprehensive. It was based on Sophie's own experience of herself and of her own exercise of leadership. She told de Rozeville that she found her judgements of the women in her community far too severe and that she should not be surprised at anything:

Even the most saintly congregations of men and women can produce a host of troubles . . . Alas! Often crimes! Let us be patient and endure this calmly, [while] doing what we can. Let us pray and place our trust in God and he will do his work. We do not live with angels. So then we must put up with human nature and learn how to forgive. I have told you this often, and you are well aware of this. Yet these sisters, in whom you see serious and real faults, do not in the least heed your advice and actually conceal their faults. In this instance, and for the sake of harmony and accord, I would try to put myself where they are and only judge them through their own eyes. My own tendency towards laziness fits in with this attitude. In the end, what purpose would be served if I were to judge them in a harsher light, when I could [gradually] win them. I tend to wait.[57]

Women who wished to enter the Society of the Sacred Heart were examined by the local superior who decided whether or not to accept them. Over and over Sophie complained bitterly at the quality of candidates, both choir and coadjutrix, admitted by individual superiors:

It is certain that our Society would eventually deteriorate if we had continued to accept such a crowd of people so easily and with such little selection. We have to use them but they understand nothing about the education of the difficult children of our time. Such education requires not only virtue but good education, tact, good manners etc. and in this respect we are lacking![58]

The 1815 constitutions had legislated for a general noviciate in Paris, something Sophie had planned when moving to Paris from Amiens. In fact while there was a noviciate in Paris, in the rue de Varenne, it was not for the whole of France. The general council of 1820 accepted the reality that all novices could not be trained in Paris, and so permitted each house to accept novices and allow them to make final profession in the name of the Society. This decision was modified during the general council of 1826 when it was recommended that the choir novices at least spend some time in the general noviciate in Paris, or, if that was not possible, at its extension in Lyon. Sophie's hope of forming each novice in Paris was not possible due to the number of women who were entering. Nevertheless, Joseph Varin pointed out to Sophie as early as 1823 that:

The novices are still dispersed around the houses, and this does not help them imbibe the spirit of the Society.[59]

In her letters to superiors Sophie continually laid down the conditions for entry to the Society. She lamented over those superiors who allowed some women to enter too easily and who received an inadequate formation. Since she had to accept candidates for final vows in the Society, Sophie often only learnt about such women when they were presented to her for permanent admission into the Society. Normally they had been several years in a community. But as Sophie grew in experience she often asked that the person concerned be delayed for final vows or sent out of the Society. Too much damage was done to the person and to the Society by those unsuited for the life.[60] Sophie wished that superiors would actually abide by the conditions laid down in the constitutions of the Society and not be led by personal considerations or succumb to pressure, especially from priests. Above all they should accept candidates only after they had been well assessed.[61] Despite all her efforts and exhortations Sophie admitted:

We have a number who turn out to be useless through lack of talent and virtue, because each superior over a period of years has accepted all who asked to enter. In conscience we cannot send you [Philippine Duchesne] any of them. Thus we have a real need for new candidates whom we will train properly and who at the very least will have a sound vocation.[62]

But as she remarked to Philippine:

It takes ten years to train a choir sister and most of them die before their final vows.[63]

That was one of Sophie's biggest disappointments. So many of the young women died and she could only watch helplessly as this happened. In 1824 alone twelve were ill, 'they are the best educated, all our class teachers'. It took such a long time to prepare these women for teaching, at least ten to fifteen years Sophie thought, that early deaths dealt the Society a heavy blow.[64] She was concerned about the health-care of the religious in the community and when six young women were terminally ill in 1827, Sophie urged superiors to give health their priority.[65] She admitted to Adelaide de Rozeville:

> I do not dare to complain, but how many who cause me distress enjoy wonderful health and the best ones die . . . [66]

In her search for 'the best ones' Sophie concentrated on the formation of leadership in the communities. Yet this had its own drawbacks. Once she had trained a leader successfully for a particular house it was difficult to move her to another one. The community and the school often suffered from the lack of continuity, the parents and the clergy complained, and often the individual herself found it hard to move on once she had found her own style of government within a specific context. While Sophie held the overall picture of the Society she was often unable to act as she wished in practice. Philippine Duchesne had the same difficulties and Sophie empathised:

> Believe me, do not make the changes which have been contemplated. All the houses will be dissatisfied as well as the individuals and you will have a thousand setbacks. I have tried this and it cost me dear and yet it was necessary. You have no idea how much worry Amiens, Beauvais and Lyon gave me when I changed the superiors there. At the same time I had to transfer several sisters who did not like the new superiors. The public had got used to those who had been in charge for many years and were dissatisfied with the changes. Consequently, I would now remove only one superior at a time. Yet they do have to be changed sometimes precisely to avoid the situation that exists in [Poitiers]. A superior who fashions her own house and then runs it for more than three years becomes sovereign lady of her house and loses sight of the general good of the Society.[67]

While it was difficult for Sophie to move the superiors from one house to another, they constantly asked her to move those whom they found difficult to handle in the community. Sophie could not always do this, at least immediately and she suggested first that the person have a change of work in the house, to see if that helped. She also recommended a medical check-up to see if there was there a physical reason behind the difficulty. If neither of these led to a solution and the difficulties persisted, Sophie then tried to act but found her room for manoeuvre limited:

> Every community has some members like this and we cannot put them all together. So each one has to keep its quota of difficult sisters. I asked to be allowed to bring them all together in one house and I would be the superior. You will understand that then I would have more than enough to do, and so I said that someone else would have to govern the Society. My council just smiled and did not listen to me. Failing this solution, we all have to share the burden.[68]

The task of governing the Society, at all levels, was challenging and Sophie wryly remarked that 'it would take someone like Moses to lead the people entrusted to us, and I am far from that!'. [69] There were times when she was over-whelmed by the amount of work she had to do and this caused frequent collapses, due to exhaustion. This was not new. In 1823 Joseph Varin wrote to Sophie three times, telling her he could not imagine how she could survive the amount of work she had in hand. She had been seriously ill in March that year and was still recovering when he asked her to consider her position:

> Given your state of extreme weakness, as well as being separated from your assistants general, how can you carry the weight of present business as well as the backlog of work? However, you must realise now more than ever how necessary it is for you to have as much help as possible, so that you can concern yourself with the government of the Society as a whole and delegate many details of administration to others. And besides, the burden of that alone is enough to crush you if you do not share it with your assistants. Your Society has reached the stage when it needs a form of government which is active and vigilant, permanently in session. [70]

Some months later Joseph Varin voiced his concern again, pointing out that the very success of the Society of the Sacred Heart, especially its rapid expansion, was disconcerting. He was worried Sophie would collapse again and the whole enterprise founder:

> I am most anxious that you are supported by your assistants, so that you can carry the burden of office which daily becomes heavier. [71]

It was a valid concern and one that Sophie could appreciate and yet know that for the time being she could not change the system. Joseph Varin could point to the organisation implemented by the Jesuits since their restoration in France and wonder why Sophie Barat could not act likewise. The problem was that Sophie did not have enough leadership in the houses and for the new foundations to allow her the luxury of keeping her assistants general around her. She needed them as envoys, as visitors, as founders, as negotiators. Of necessity this meant they could not reside permanently with Sophie. Joseph Varin's advice was sound and expressed concern for Sophie, her health and the good governance of the Society of the Sacred Heart. It would be some years before Sophie could hope to implement it.

The years after the general council of 1826 were among the busiest in Sophie's life. After a brief spell of good health, her energy began to deteriorate and her former ailments reappeared. While these weakened her, they did not prevent her continuing to work and she negotiated the foundation of the Trinité in Rome in these circumstances. She also kept an eye on family affairs and was distressed when her niece Zoé became ill. She asked Stanislas to ensure that Zoé was cared for at home. Louis Barat was equally concerned for his niece and had told Sophie that he intended spending some days with her in Joigny. When Elisa Dusaussoy decided to enter the Society in 1829 Stanislas told his aunt that he was tired of his sisters entering religious life. He would not see them anymore and some of them in any case should get married. Sophie warned him:

Do not torment her, it would be useless. At least she will try her vocation. If you oppose her I shall send her to a faraway corner in France or maybe to Rome! I am telling you that she has taken her decision and I have too. Your mother is much more sensible than you. She knows the bitter pains of marriage and the dangers that a young woman risks in life, without money and later without support . . . [72]

Stanislas was well used to reprimands from his aunt and he told her he had accepted Elisa's decision but hoped he could see her regularly in Paris. He also asked her to approach the minister of education and religion, Mgr Frayssinous, and seek a post in Paris for his elder brother, Louis. Sophie refused both requests, and instead told him to watch his own financial affairs and leave her in peace.[73] It was a close relationship and one that Stanislas counted on progressively in his life.

But Sophie's life had become too busy and too demanding. In April 1829 she fell and hurt her right arm. In May she had another fall which was much worse since she damaged her foot seriously and she was badly bruised on one side of her body. In June she complained of being unable to use her left arm which had been damaged in the fall in May. In August she had another fall and in December yet another. Sophie claimed she had had seven falls in the one year. By the end of the year she was in pain and immobilised:

For several weeks now a seventh fall on the injured foot has forced me to stay in bed or in my basket-chair.[74]

Her foot was painful and no doctor in Paris seemed able to set it properly. Again and again she tried to walk with crutches but after a short time she had to return to bed or to the basket chair. It was a frustrating way to live and it forced her to pace herself somewhat, though there was no relief from pain and no genuine repose. The following year brought Revolution to Paris. In July 1830, Sophie was faced with decisions about the future of the Society and of the school in Paris and was, despite her handicap, once again on the road.

$-$ 10 $-$
PACE AND PROGRESS, 1830–1833

I n her letters after the general council of 1826 Sophie repeatedly referred to the growing restlessness in Paris and in France overall. The Bourbons under Louis XVIII (1815–24) had returned to power in 1815 as the harbingers of peace and stability, a welcome relief after the protracted period of the Revolution and Empire. A certain accommodation and balance between revolutionary and counter-revolutionary politics was achieved in the early days of Louis XVIII. However, the wave of good will had been gradually squandered and from the time Charles X (1824–30) acceded to the throne in 1824 the balance was tipped in favour of the counter-revolutionaries, the ultras. They yearned for the former glories of the ancien régime when, they fantasised, church and monarchy had worked together in close harmony. Such attempts to reinvent the past served to draw liberal and anti-clerical elements into unity, and to incite the more extreme revolutionary elements to action in Paris and in the major cities in France. This in turn evoked the worst memories of the Revolution. The dreadful days of the Terror were not so far away in time and the unrest created both dread and foreboding that these days could return. Certainly Sophie herself was acutely aware of the unrest in Paris and the potential this had to compromise or even destroy the work of the Society. The rue de Varenne, in the heart of the Faubourg Saint-Germain, was the home of the royalists, the ultras, and the Hôtel Biron was closely identified with the court and nobility.

One of the symptoms which directly threatened the Society of the Sacred Heart was the growing demand in both chambers of government that the Jesuits be banned from education in France. Sophie told Philippine Duchesne in 1827 that she was concerned about the political atmosphere and wondered if her communities in France would be suppressed.[1] By the following year Sophie told Philippine that the Jesuits were about to be expelled from their schools in France and she awaited the repercussion of this action. If the Society of the Sacred Heart was forced to close its schools Sophie promised that Louisiana would benefit from new personnel. Indeed she told Philippine:

> I continually dream of going to see you. But if I did make this long journey, then I would prefer never to return to France.[2]

In the context of the growing political emergency Sophie saw the advantage of foundations outside of France and she welcomed invitations to expand into new areas. She wrote to Louise de Limminghe lamenting lack of personnel for a possible foundation in Milan:

> ... we will definitely miss the opportunity of establishing the Society properly in this beautiful part of Italy, and consequently we will miss becoming known to the Emperor of Austria ... In fact this [a house in Milan] would be especially appropriate since we have been bearing the repercussions of the expulsion of the Jesuits and are losing much ground in France. Several orders have made unbelievable efforts to imitate us, and they even succeed in overtaking us quite easily. Perhaps God allows this to compel us to extend the Society beyond France, where other orders will not go. In a way these considerations persuade me to accept [a foundation in] Milan, if it is offered. So you may advise Madame, the wife of the Ambassador, to suggest the Society ...[3]

The imminent threat of expulsion from France made the new foundation at the Trinité des Monts in Rome even more important in Sophie's eyes, and she welcomed the possibility of a second house in the city, telling Philippine that she dared not think what the outcome of such an expansion in Rome could mean for her personally. Even then Sophie saw that some day she might move the centre of the Society of the Sacred Heart from Paris to Rome. She valued all contacts with Rome and complained when she had not heard from Armande de Causans. Letters from Rome were circulated among all the houses, with the suggestion that Jesuit communities in the vicinity be given a copy too. Indeed, Sophie and her colleagues continued to seek closer links with the Jesuits, although in Sophie's mind this still meant more a spiritual than a structural affiliation.

Certainly at this crucial time in Paris Sophie would not think of pressing for a closer link with the Jesuits. Further identification would only draw the Society of the Sacred Heart into disfavour. In the eighteenth century the Bourbon monarchy deeply resented the power of the Jesuits and had urged their suppression in 1763. When the order was restored by Pope Pius VII in 1814, the Jesuits, ironically, became identified with the restored Bourbon monarchy. The nobility sent their sons to be educated in Jesuit schools and the order became identified with conservatism and royalism. Indeed the hold of the Jesuits over boys' schools, as well as their clear ultramontanism, drew suspicion and criticism from government ministers and from the members of both chambers. Even if he had wanted to, Charles X was unable to protect the order in France and in June 1828 their eight schools were suppressed. Much was made of the secrecy and hidden power of the Jesuits which was viewed as sinister and dangerous to the state. Bizarre claims were spread abroad, suggesting that the Jesuits had turned their house of noviciate at Montrouge into an army camp, and that the house was connected to the Louvre by an underground tunnel. When the Comte de Montlosier, a royalist and Gallican, launched an attack on the Jesuits he found ready listeners.[4]

From 1828 general unrest in Paris had increased and a sense of foreboding hung over the city. Because the Society of the Sacred Heart was closely identified with the Jesuits[5] Sophie feared that the Society's schools in Paris and in other parts of France could be suppressed. She prepared contingency plans for Paris in particular since this would be the first to bear the impact of revolution. It was a difficult task: her series of falls had left her crippled and unable to move around freely. And while she spent most of 1829 and the spring of 1830 trying to recover from these falls, her incapacity made the task of government all the heavier. Despite various forms of treatment, no doctor in Paris seemed able to cure it. Weeks of rest had little effect for each time she tried to walk, with crutches, Sophie was soon forced to return to rest either in bed or in a basket chair which could be pulled around the house – hardly a position from which to plan and execute a quick exit from Paris.

Sophie found a possible solution through her contact with the marquis de Nicolay (1782–1871) and his family. After the suppression of the Jesuit schools in 1828, de Nicolay placed his sons at school in Fribourg, and, then anticipating the fall of the monarchy, he decided to move to Switzerland and rented a chateau at Givisiers. The de Nicolay family was closely linked with the destiny of the Bourbons. The memory of the Terror was still alive, when Théodore de Nicolay's father and elder brother had been guillotined. Madame de Nicolay, formerly Augustine de Lévis, had direct contacts with the families of the duc d'Angoulême and duc de Berry through her brother the duc de Lévis. In the turbulent atmosphere of the Revolution in July 1830 the family was too closely linked with the Bourbon dynasty to risk staying in Paris. Indeed when Charles X abdicated and left France, he asked Madame de Nicolay to join the court-in-exile in Austria and to tutor his granddaughter, the future duchess of Parma.[6] The two eldest daughters, Aymardine and Pauline de Nicolay, had been at school at the rue de Varenne since 1824 and through them Sophie had got to know the family well. Théodore de Nicolay told Sophie of his decision to leave Paris and settle in Switzerland. He offered Sophie, in the event of the Society having to leave Paris and continue the school and noviciate abroad, the possibility of staying with his family at Givisiers until she found accommodation for the religious and pupils. With this contingency plan Sophie remained in Paris, uneasy and waiting.

In late July 1830 the political situation became explosive. On 26 July Charles X invoked the powers given him in the Charter (the settlement hammered out

between revolutionary and counter-revolutionary interests after 1815), and
issued four Ordinances. These undermined the liberty of the press and restricted the parliamentary franchise to a tiny majority, composed almost exclusively
of the wealthiest landowners of France. Such measures virtually demolished the
constitutional monarchy and narrowed support for the king. By 27 July unrest
became so great in Paris that parents began to remove their daughters from the
rue de Varenne, so that in a few days the school which had numbered one hundred and sixty boarders was reduced to fifty. During this vital week the headmistress of the school, Eugénie de Gramont, had been unwell and was
convalescing at Conflans, in a house owned by Archbishop de Quelen, close to
the seminary of the diocese. Hearing of the unrest in the city she immediately
began her return journey with Catherine de Charbonnel and Henriette Ducis,
and had considerable difficulty in reaching the rue de Varenne on the evening
of 27 July. The following morning the city was in open revolution and there was
imminent danger that the Faubourg Saint-Germain would be a focus for the revolutionary crowd, being so closely linked with the king and the ultraroyalists.
Sophie was persuaded by Eugénie de Gramont and the councillors in the community to go to Conflans. She agreed reluctantly and left on crutches at midday
on 28 July and set out for the house of Archbishop de Quelen at Conflans,
accompanied by a member of the community and her nephew Stanislas
Dusaussoy.

The anger of the mob in Paris spread beyond the confines of the city of Paris
and on 29 July the seminary at Conflans was attacked. Sophie and her companions found alternative accommodation in the area and stayed there until 31 July
when the danger subsided and they were able to return to the rue de Varenne.
The long week of violence and unrest which ushered in the July monarchy
forced Sophie to plan moving the noviceship out of Paris. Charles X had fallen
in a few days, replaced by the Orleanist, Louis Philippe. The palace of the archbishop of Paris, beside Notre Dame, as well as the seminary at Conflans had
been sacked. Jesuit houses were attacked, ransacked and burnt, in Paris and
elsewhere. Their communities were dispersed and many Jesuits went into exile,
especially into Switzerland.[7] Sophie could only wonder if her turn was next.

By 8 August 1830 Sophie had decided to take up the offer of the marquis de
Nicolay and she asked him if Catherine de Charbonnel could stay with the family at Givisiers while seeking a suitable property for the noviciate and for the
school. Sophie and Eugénie de Gramont would follow on later, in the autumn.
In the meantime the noviciate in Paris would be divided and dispersed to
Besançon and La Ferrandière and later both groups would move to Switzerland
when a suitable property had been prepared. Sophie also offered places to the
pupils in the rue de Varenne if parents wished their daughters to continue their
education in Switzerland. She explored the possibility of a house in Tours, as
another alternative to the rue de Varenne, should the turmoil in the capital continue for some time. For the immediate future, when there was imminent danger in Paris, a house was rented in Versailles and the students taken there for

safety.[8] In fact no one had any idea how long the Orleanist monarchy would last and plans had to be made for all contingencies. Several possibilities were under consideration when Sophie, Eugénie de Gramont, Anna de Constantin (1779–1882) and Marie Patte (1795–1848)[9] set off from Paris on the morning of 10 August 1830, leaving Louise de Varax[10] in charge of the community and school, assisted by Madame de Marbeuf.

When Sophie and her companions arrived in Lyon they learnt that the house at La Ferrandière was under threat as were those in other parts of France, and this continued until the spring of 1831. For the most part the properties as well as the communities and pupils had been respected, due in great part to the courage of the members of the Society who faced the attackers and refused to show fear.[11] Sophie did not stay long in Lyon. Her foot was in poor condition after the prolonged travel and with Eugénie de Gramont she went to Aix les-Bains from 13 to 24 September, to take the waters.[12] By the time they had returned to Chambéry Catherine de Charbonnel had written to urge them to travel to Switzerland and view the properties she had found there. They set out on 8 October 1830 for Switzerland[13] and on their arrival Sophie, Eugénie de Gramont and Catherine de Charbonnel stayed with the de Nicolay family. By all accounts it was a pleasant, almost idyllic time. Aymardine de Nicolay (1810–86), the eldest daughter, remembered the experience very well. She recalled the shyness of Catherine de Charbonnel, the charm of Sophie and Eugénie, the bizarre dress they all arrived in, and how for some weeks life at home assumed the rhythm of a religious community. The chateau at Givisiers was somewhat like an émigré court and the family were visited by others who had also decided to leave Paris. These were nobility and clergy, among them Fr Perreau, former ecclesiastical superior general of the Society of the Sacred Heart, and Mgr Frayssinous, the former minister of public education and religion.[14]

By October 1830 two properties had been found, the château de Montet and the château de Middes. The decision was taken to rent Middes for a year and renovate Montet as the permanent residence. Catherine de Charbonnel, as she had so often done before for new foundations, made the necessary preparations for taking up residence. By November the novices began to arrive from La Ferrandière and from Besançon, led by Félicité Desmarquest and Henriette Coppens, and gradually they formed their life in new surroundings. By December 1830 Eugénie de Gramont was anxious to return to Paris and resume her work there. Sophie had intended to remain in Switzerland all winter but unrest in the area forced her to reconsider. Sophie decided to go to Chambéry and arrived there on 24 December 1830. She left the negotiations concerning Middes and Montet in the hands of Catherine de Charbonnel and these proved to be intricate. Unrest in the area focused on the presence of both the Society and the recently arrived French families, such as the de Nicolay family. Antagonism was expressed locally towards the new owners of Montet and cast doubts on its future as a school and noviciate. However this was modified by a formal letter of support from the commune of Montet, advising Catherine de

Charbonnel that she should proceed with seeking approval of her plans for the
new school. Nevertheless, the Prefect of Police at Fribourg had to be satisfied
with the proposals regarding the school and the teachers, and be assured that the
Jesuits were in no way involved. With the agreement of Sophie, Catherine de
Charbonnel stated in writing that the school she wished to establish was not run
by a religious congregation, that she had no intention of founding a monastery,
nor did the teachers in the school wear religious dress. She was also asked to
prove that the school was a new foundation, with a stable future, and not
dependent upon political events in France. All these she agreed to, despite the
fact that the Society was in fact setting up another house on a well-known model.
Catherine de Charbonnel declared:

> The Ladies of the Sacred Heart temporarily residing at Middes are not true relig-
> ious in the eyes of the church. The pope has refused to recognise them as such,
> owing to lack of cloister which is an essential condition [of religious life].
> The commitments they make here are only to one another. In Middes there are
> only two in the house who have made these pledges; that certainly does not con-
> stitute a community. We do not even intend to establish one here.
> We wear a semi-religious habit as a way of attracting more respect from the child-
> ren. Our houses are not at all like monasteries . . . Everyone in the house goes to
> recreation, goes for walks in the countryside and receive visitors at home, both men
> and women freely without having to seek prior permission. This would not be per-
> mitted if the group was a religious community.[15]

In the strict sense of the word what Catherine de Charbonnel claimed was
true: the Society of the Sacred Heart did not have full papal cloister in the way
understood by the authorities who questioned her. She knew that and used that
argument to win the approval for the school.

Meanwhile Eugénie de Gramont found it impossible to accommodate herself to the new realities in Paris, to the new government under Louis Philippe.
The de Gramont family was intimately linked to Charles X and Louis Philippe
could only be seen as a usurper. This was the view of Archbishop de Quelen
also. He refused to recognise the new government to the extent that he would
not attend any state functions or act in any way which gave credence to the new
régime. Despite diplomatic efforts by the pope, the archbishop refused to
change his point of view. He was linked to the Bourbons, to the old régime, and
tried to carry his diocese and church with him. When Archbishop de Quelen's
palace was sacked and destroyed by fire, several convents in Paris became temporary homes for the archbishop. One of them was the rue de Varenne, the Hôtel
Biron. While some judged Archbishop de Quelen's stance as stupidly perverse,
others saw it as heroic.

Sophie was aware of what could arise in Paris, especially in her absence, and
early in the new year, 1831, she wrote to Eugénie de Gramont and asked her to
tread carefully. She warned Eugénie de Gramont that she and the members of
the community in Paris should avoid all political comment either in the school
or in the course of visits received in the parlour at the rue de Varenne. While

opinions on the new government in France were discussed openly during their time at Givisiers, they could not be voiced so freely in Paris. Any comments made ought to

> support the present government, since God has given it to us and it is recognised by the Church and political powers. It would be folly to do otherwise. I told you about something I read on this subject from la Quotidienne. I would rather you did not subscribe to any newspaper.[16]

Pragmatic as ever, Sophie accepted the new order but Eugénie de Gramont could not act in an apolitical way, in the heart of the Faubourg Saint-Germain, surrounded by members of her family and by her friends, most of them convinced that the new order was illegal and should not be obeyed. Sophie and Eugénie did not agree on the outcome of the July revolution and 1830 marked the beginning of a change in their relationship. Gradually another, much more serious, polarisation than 1815 set in. As a presage of this impending storm, the pet names exchanged between Sophie and Eugénie increased. Sophie called Eugénie her 'Topina', her 'rat', 'chère petite rate' and Eugénie called Sophie 'merotte'. The terms of endearment were strong and affectionate yet the relationship seemed fragile. They were holding on to something they had had and which could not continue. Or perhaps Sophie was holding on to Eugénie for she knew by instinct the danger she and the Society ran if Eugénie de Gramont operated on her own.

Really serious disagreements still lay some months ahead and for the moment both felt the loss of each other's company, for now they were parted for the first time in over fourteen years. From 1816 they had lived together in the rue des Postes, then in the Hôtel Biron and together they ran the school at the rue de Varenne. In the two years prior to the July Revolution both Sophie and Eugénie had been very ill. Sophie's illness was centred on her seven falls. That of Eugénie de Gramont was chest and lung difficulties, compounded by her physical disability. Several times she was so near death that for a time Sophie feared that Eugénie could not survive her illness. Yet by the spring of 1831 Eugénie was restored to relative good health and was able to resume her work in the school, while Sophie had to continue treatment at Aix-les-Bains. So while Eugénie had reached Paris safely, Sophie had a disappointing experience on the journey to Chambéry. She told Eugénie wryly that she had had yet another fall, her eighth. She and her companions had stopped for a rest at St Genin. When it was time to get into the carriage again:

> as I was getting up from the sofa where I had been sitting, . . . I reached out for a chair to steady myself and pick up my crutches. [But] someone pulled the chair so quickly that I lost my balance because I was already leaning forward. I fell once again on my injured heel which took the weight of my body, which as you know is not as light as air [and] my heel snapped. I am in great pain.[17]

This was a huge disappointment. She spent three months in Chambéry resting her foot and in April visited the waters again at Aix. The process began all over again and promised to be long and painful. Sophie was feeling the frustration of being so immobile and she wrote to Eugénie:

> I tried to go to the right, then to the left, tra, tra, tra . . . and then I fell and I had to stay in bed for three months. This is how my life has been for two years and if our Lord does not want this to change I must resign myself to it all over again.[18]

Sophie spoke of her sense of loneliness and isolation to Eugénie de Gramont and asked that her letters be kept totally private. In this way she was able to express freely the sense of powerlessness she was feeling.[19] Sophie spent weekdays in Aix in the house of a doctor who looked after her foot and arranged the treatment she was to receive at the baths. The surroundings were pleasant, even beautiful; her solitude and isolation were, as she said, complete and absolute. She had a room on the ground floor of the house and at the end of a little corridor there was a door out to the garden, to a stream whose music soothed her and gave her peace. At the weekends she returned to Chambéry and caught up with her post and business.[20] In her loneliness and isolation Sophie poured her heart out to Eugénie, and passages from Ovid came to mind as she contemplated the stream in the garden. When they were both at Aix in September 1830, Eugénie had loved this stream:

> Yes it is indeed the stream you came to see. Every day I sit beside it and think about 'my rat'. I would like to see her here for a few moments. There is a little flow of water just now and a type of staircase [alongside]. I am sure that you would climb up there and *projectus in antro* [stretched full length in the cave] with what pleasure *dumosa pendere procul, de rupe videbo* [I shall [would] see you far off hanging from a thorny crag] . . . but alas! when shall we see each other again? You always bring me back to this sad thought by making me believe that you will not gather the fruits of the flowers which you are enjoying at this moment: *Barbarus has segetes (habebit)* [the barbarian will take possession of these cornfields]. I still hope, however, despite the threat of disaster: *cava praedixit ab ilice cornis* [a raven on the left warned me from the hollow holm-oak tree].[21]

Sophie's letter, while tender and full of longing to see Eugénie, was filled with foreboding. Sophie's choice of the raven's warning was an image that came to her in her solitude and which in sorrow she passed on, probably unaware of the meaning it held for her personally. Reaching into her own past she found ways of looking into the future and a way of talking which helped her recognise, even dimly, what she had intuited for some time: she was losing control of the Society of the Sacred Heart. Already circumstances in Paris had overtaken Sophie and letters advised her to return to Paris as soon as possible. A few days later the tension between Eugénie and Sophie erupted. Sophie had written to Eugénie saying that she had decided to return to Paris as soon as possible, that she had had enough of Aix and the sense of powerlessness and isolation. Eugénie read this as a mark of distrust of her leadership in Paris and wrote in this vein to Sophie at Aix. Sophie was astonished that this interpretation could be placed on her motives for returning to Paris and protested:

How could you have imagined that my complaints and my wish to return could have motives other than your health? . . . I who had been so happy that everyone appreciates and respects you. That was all I wanted in this world and I cannot imagine that you thought I had other ideas . . . if I had] would I speak to you with such tenderness and trust![22]

She assured her that the letters she had received from the rue de Varenne were positive about her leadership in the school and community, indeed Joseph Varin had urged her to name Eugénie an assistant general, something she could not do without calling a general council. All the letters showed concern for Eugénie de Gramont's health in such a tense situation. Nevertheless even though Sophie fed back positive comments from Paris, Eugénie sensed that criticism of her was being passed on to Sophie, and this created unease in their relationship. Paris at this time was tense and the threat of cholera was an added source of anxiety for both community and school there. In fact Sophie did not return to Paris until October 1831 and by then Eugénie's patience had run out. Sophie seemed unable to make up her mind when she was coming. Eugénie wrote to Sophie in early September that year, betraying her impatience. This exasperated Sophie and she replied sharply:

So it's my fault for being ill! It's my fault that I can't walk! It's my fault if I don't go [to Paris]! Soon it will be my fault if the cholera strikes! Really, it's a case of the vanquished paying the penalty. Nevertheless, I hope you do not doubt my eagerness to see you, though you have spoiled it for me somewhat![23]

While Sophie counted on returning to Paris, she did not intend staying there long. For some time she had been planning to travel to Rome to visit the Trinité des Monts and follow through the second foundation there. She wanted Eugénie to go with her and in her letters continually reminded her of this. As long as she had Eugénie by her side she could control her, to a degree at least. But Eugénie was not at all attracted to Rome, her whole interest was taken up with France, Paris, the Faubourg Saint-Germain. Nevertheless, Sophie continued to plan their journey together and she expected that they would set out together in 1832. Throughout these months Archbishop de Quelen continued to be present in rue de Varenne, for all kinds of reasons: to visit the school, to preside over school festivals, to hear confessions of the community, to speak with Eugénie de Gramont. Louis Barat was confessor to school and in this capacity met the archbishop several times in the grounds of the rue de Varenne. He mentioned this in his letters to Sophie, clearly letting her know that Archbishop de Quelen was a regular visitor to the rue de Varenne.

Sophie unwittingly encouraged this when she advised Eugénie to ask Archbishop de Quelen to be her spiritual director. The papal nuncio, Luigi Lambruschini, had acted in this capacity and Sophie had met Lambruschini at Aix, also taking the waters. He agreed that this was a positive move and encouraged it. Sophie conveyed this to Eugénie and hoped that maybe Archbishop de Quelen could succeed in making Eugénie obey someone, especially in the area of health:

I do not know how you understand obedience, but with regard to this matter [health] you have never understood it . . . you are only obedient when you are asleep. . . . You must realise that you are weak, that any illness will be your last. . . . But I'll say no more, because anything I say has no effect. [24]

Sophie too was in touch with her spiritual director, Joseph-Marie Favre. He wrote to her in late September, while she was at Middes. He asked her to watch her tendency to overwork, since this put a strain on her health, her prayer life and her capacity to fulfil her task as superior general. Sophie had asked him to allow her to make the vow of perfection and he had hesitated on account of her tendency to overwork which led to a certain decentring of her being. He urged her to go to communion daily as this would help her achieve balance in her day. These intimate times of prayer, he wrote,

will gradually subdue that liveliness of character which does you more harm than perhaps you imagine.

I would prefer that a dove-like simplicity should dominate the serpent's wisdom in you, so much so that you would have the manner, the ways and the characteristics of a child, rather than the manner, the ways and the characteristics of a quick-witted woman [femme d'esprit] or of a religious superior. But how difficult it is to be childlike in the midst of a scheming, cheating, proud world![25]

Sophie had told him that she wanted to have less activity and more time for prayer and asked him if he thought this was a call she should respond to personally. He thought not. Most busy people felt drawn to peace and quiet, especially when the work they were doing was difficult and demanding. Favre was more concerned with helping Sophie integrate her prayer and her work by way of learning to achieve a balance between the two elements in her life. So he encouraged Sophie to go on with her task and assured her of his prayer for that inner journey.

During this time Sophie was in regular contact with her family in Joigny. Stanislas kept her informed about Marie-Louise and Zoé, while Sophie told him about his brother, Louis. By now Louis was in Florence where he was tutor to a Russian family. Sophie doubted that he would settle there, remarking that he was only happy when on the move.[26] Stanislas still hoped to marry and told Sophie that he thought he had met the right person, Mlle d'Osler from Flanders.[27] Sophie was not so sure and told Stanislas that she had heard about a woman near Chambéry who wished to marry. She promised to meet her and see if there was a possibility of a marriage. Sophie found the woman charming but realised that she would not marry below her rank; she also wanted a pious, wealthy husband:

. . . then she would like more piety on your part, even though I described you as a quasi saint, and much more money than you have . . . We must accept that you are difficult to settle, for you have no rank or money. . . . You understand that I am disappointed that this did not work out! Maybe it is all for the best? You would need a lot of courage to get married just now. In a few months time you will congratulate yourself that you did not marry. You will have enough to do to save your own soul.[28]

Sophie often reminded Stanislas of the difficulties of family life, and asked him whether he was truly ready for them. She continued to listen to his hopes for marriage and helped him through his disappointments. She advised Stanislas to look after his mother and sister, to do some good work in Joigny and to lead a spiritual life. These were tasks he could fulfil in life and ones which Sophie assured him were worthwhile.

By October 1831 Sophie had begun to make her way back to Paris. After a visit to Montet she wrote to Marie-Louise and told her that she would visit Joigny on the journey from Montet to Paris, and would arrive on Saturday, 15 October. Sophie was still on crutches and told Stanislas:

> If you were not perched on the mountain I would be delighted to go to your house and stay there. But how could I climb up? I cannot with my crutches? Besides, how could I go to Mass on Sunday? We will go and stay in Sens or in Surville, with Mr de Beaurecueil, near Montereau. But my sister and Zoé will come with you to the post station for a little visit. Do not tell anyone we are coming. I dread the curious. . . . your mother would give me pleasure if she could bring us a gougère made that morning and a little pastry cake, as well as a little basket of grapes for my travelling companion, Mme de Varax.[29]

The visit was a pleasant oasis before facing into the situation in Paris. Letters between Eugénie and Sophie continued to be full of misunderstandings and Sophie hoped that her visit to Paris would help ease communication. But she could not hide her dismay when Eugénie proposed giving Archbishop de Quelen the permanent use of the house known as the Petit-Hôtel, situated in the grounds of the rue de Varenne, close to the Hôtel Biron. She wondered how the ever cautious and calculating Eugénie de Gramont could even think of such a proposition. Louise de Varax, Sophie's travelling companion and Eugénie de Gramont's assistant in the school at the headmistress of the rue de Varenne, certainly did not approve of such a move, and Sophie assured Eugénie that she would never agree to it either.[30] But Sophie was warned and a battle of wills had begun. Eugénie was a determined woman and knew what she wanted. As Sophie remarked some weeks later:

> I think I can see your wicked little finger laying down the law, and this forceful language does nothing to reassure me![31]

Sophie had suggested earlier on in the year that the rooms in the Petit-Hôtel could be rented out to two women who needed accommodation in Paris. After her visit to Paris in October 1831 she pursued this even more, in the hope of preventing Archbishop de Quelen taking up permanent residence there. She asked Eugénie not to give the Petit-Hôtel to any one without consulting her first.[32] But she knew that Eugénie de Gramont paid little attention her wishes and indeed that Eugénie ignored the other members of the community too.[33] Her hold in the house became even more complete when Louise de Varax became ill in February 1832 and died the following year. This was a serious blow to the school and the community. Now shadows of former days in Amiens gathered round

Sophie and she sensed that she was being displaced. She expressed it by talking about medical treatment. She remarked in January 1832, that she was getting used to different forms of medicine as she travelled in France and elsewhere. She took the reflection further, noting that it was an image of her life now that she had no definite residence: 'So I am now cosmopolitan in the full sense of the word.'[34]

Sophie was displaced too in her spirituality. Joseph-Marie Favre's theology and spiritual direction were far too liberal in the eyes of many priests and indeed of many religious as well. Sophie told Favre in January 1832 that his views on frequent, even daily, communion were considered quite wrong and damaging to the discipline of the church and of religious life. Some in Paris could not conceive of a God as accessible as that and they were scandalised. This led Sophie to doubt Favre's teaching and judgement but he held firmly to his views. He reminded Sophie of the insight she herself had gained during her retreat the previous year and how important it was to follow that path. Besides, he argued persuasively:

> I have great difficulty persuading myself that these spiritual directors have examined in depth and with care the particular needs of your soul, the attractions of grace which you have experienced for a long time [and] the fairly certain signs of God will for you.[35]

Favre asked Sophie to think back on her spiritual state when they first met in 1824 and on what had happened to her and her inner world since then. Her life had become very full, very busy. She had become absorbed in the world of high society, especially in Paris. She had stopped working on her inner world, had become cautious in the world of the spirit, had reverted to old patterns. She had been flattered by the success of the Society of the Sacred Heart, by its acceptance into powerful circles and she had become vain. The call to be and to live in this world fed into her own impetuosity and hyperactivity. She had travelled too much, written too many letters, taken too much care of her health. In sum she had been drawn away from her original call to follow Christ in prayer and in trust.

This was a strong letter which did not console or flatter Sophie. Favre reminded her of the purpose in her commitment to Christ. It was to have life of deep prayer, to have the marks of Christ in her life, experiencing humiliation and failure rather than enjoying marks of esteem and flattery. Then, with Christ, she would have peace and joy, courage and trust. He knew she was not happy, at peace with herself, that she had

> this inner disturbance, these reproaches of conscience, this dissatisfaction with yourself, this bitter remorse, this sadness, this despondency, this distrust and discouragement all of which have wreaked more damage on your temperament than all the mortifications and humiliations which you have dropped out of too much prudence and caution.[36]

He suggested that she return to the insights and resolutions of her retreat and change nothing until she had a further time of prayer, during which she could assess her inner state. He encouraged her to trust that she could regain her inner peace by prayer and he urged her to trust God especially in the area of confession and communion. Since 1827 Favre had advised Louise de Limminghe to try to get Sophie to practise less corporal penance. What she really needed was more trust in God, more courage to love God, less fear and anxiety, more liberty of spirit, of heart and conscience. He had no doubt that the task was difficult for de Limminghe.[37] She asked Favre for advice constantly and he explained:

> The pains, scruples and worries of your dear mother are partly due to her temperament and partly due to the false guidance she has been following for a long time. But they are due most of all to the devil who aims solely to make her waste precious time by useless self-occupation and by making her examine her conscience endlessly, like a squirrel going round in circles.[38]

Few would have guessed the inner struggles Sophie Barat had over these many years. She suffered from scruples and both Louise de Limminghe and Favre did their best to help her overcome them. It was a scourge and burden for Sophie, one that she hid very well, even from Eugénie de Gramont. In all of her letters to Eugénie there is no mention even of Favre's name, nor of her own inner turmoil. Sophie had rarely spoken to Eugénie of her inner, spiritual state, and confided even less so after January 1832, when Favre's theology had been so publicly criticised. In that sense Sophie had another life apart, with Joseph-Marie Favre and Louise de Limminghe. Just as she and Eugénie had names for each other, so had this trio. Favre was called John of the Cross, Sophie Madeleine of the Cross and Louise Addolorata, sometimes shortened by Sophie to Addo. It was a little community of support and care, mostly for Sophie's benefit.

Cholera hit Paris in March 1832 and Sophie was devastated by the news. In effect, the rue de Varenne escaped the plague but many in Paris died. During this time Archbishop de Quelen cut a heroic figure in the city, visiting the sick and dying, drawing attention to the plight of the poor and the orphaned. Eugénie told Sophie about this and indeed it was reported in the newspapers. From afar, Sophie wondered what she could do and the thought came to her that the Society could offer to take care of some orphans of the cholera, perhaps between ten and twenty children. She told Eugénie of her plan and asked her what she thought of the idea. She should discuss it with Archbishop de Quelen and see if it was feasible. The orphans could be housed in the area of the buildings reserved for the handicapped, and they could be dressed in the cast-off clothes of the boarders. She was sure donations would flow in for such a work, especially if Archbishop de Quelen patronised it and chose those who were to go to the orphanage.[39]

Eugénie's reaction to Sophie's proposal to have orphans at the rue de Varenne was immediate and positive:

> I cannot express in words, dear merotte, the pleasure your letter of the 27 gave me, in which you spoke about setting up an orphanage. . . . Besides we owe it to our unfortunate country and the [Society of the] Sacred Heart must set an

example. It is really up to us to get things going at present, all the other convents
will follow us . . . Your letter had such an effect on me that all I could do was weep
for the rest of the morning. I was in such a state that I could do nothing else than
write to Mgr [de Quelen] to inform him about this. . . . He came over that afternoon to discuss and settle the plan. . . . Once he had arranged all with me he went
to the boarding school, where the community also had gathered, and announced
the project.[40]

What Sophie could not have missed was the easy access Eugénie de Gramont
had to Archbishop de Quelen. In the course of a day she was able to contact him,
plan a strategy and jointly announce a new work of the Society in Paris.[41] Clearly,
despite Sophie's express wishes, the archbishop had taken up residence in the
Petit-Hôtel and moved freely in the boarding school and the community. While
Sophie tried to keep the initiative and the agenda in her hands, Eugénie had
already acted and created a situation which Sophie could not condone and which
inevitably would lead to serious confrontation.

If the situation in Paris, with the houses in France and Savoy and Italy, were
Sophie's only concern her energy and leadership would have been fully engaged
and stretched. Indeed the energies of a healthy, mobile woman would have been
absorbed by this work. But Sophie was ill and dogged by the inability to get
effective treatment for her foot. In spite of her handicap Sophie tried to keep in
touch with developments in Missouri and Louisiana, in Rome and Montet, as
well as plan, negotiate and execute new foundations. Since the general council
of 1826 she had agreed to a new house in Louisiana, at La Fourche, and to the
reopening of St Charles in Missouri. She was aware that the general council in
1833 would have to address the growing needs of the houses in America.

A new house had been opened in Perpignan in 1828 and Sophie was particularly happy with this foundation. She saw it as the Society's point of entry to
Spain, and she told both Philippine Duchesne and Eugénie Audé how important this would be in the future.[42] Over the following eighteen months a new
foundation was planned for Avignon. In Sophie's mind this house would replace
that of Ste Marie d'En Haut in Grenoble, for she knew that it could not continue much longer and warned Philippine of its imminent closure. Sophie
explained how the Society had lost out to two other educational institutions in
Grenoble, although the actual closure of Ste Marie d'En Haut in 1833 was due
to the town administration, which revoked rights once granted to Philippine
Duchesne on 26 January 1805. Thinking ahead, Sophie did not want to lose a
base in Provence which was a source of religious vocations. Indeed she had an
eye on that aspect of most foundations.[43]

Fusions of communities continued. A little community founded in 1800 at
Annonay in the Ardèche made contact with Sophie and asked if they could be
absorbed into the Society of the Sacred Heart. They had a flourishing boarding
and day school but had always wanted to join an established institute devoted
to the Sacred Heart. They heard of the events in Paris and how some houses of
the Society were closed for a time. Taking the opportunity to make contact they

approached Marie Prevost in La Ferrandière and asked if they could offer accommodation to the Society, in the hope of becoming part of the Society of the Sacred Heart. Sophie agreed to this request and delegated the negotiation to Marie Prevost.[44] Since the July Revolution Sophie had been interested in a foundation in Tours. In that year Sophie had been asked to consider accepting a group of women in Tours, called the Community the Holy Spirit, into the Society. This group had been established in Tours by Pulcherie Chobelet, the sister of Lydie Chobelet, one of the first members of the community at Poitiers in 1806. The request for a fusion came more from the local bishop than from the community itself and Sophie sensed in 1830 that the time was not right. Contact was retained with the little group over a period of years and the fusion with the Society took place in 1836.[45]

> While Eugénie and Archbishop de Quelen were planning the orphanage in Paris Sophie had arrived in Aix-en-Provence in March 1832, with Marie Prevost, in order to see if a foundation was possible there. A familiar pattern greeted Sophie there. Two women, former members of the dames de St Pierre, had started a school in Aix.[46] For a time the project had succeeded but it needed the stability and support of an institution. As in so many other situations Sophie had to examine the request carefully. She decided to agree to a fusion, partly because of the insistence of the pupils and the two founders of the school and partly because that area of France was rich in vocations. Sophie asked Catherine de Charbonnel to come to Aix and complete the negotiations for the fusion, thus allowing Sophie to proceed to Rome. When Eugénie asked her if it was wise to have two houses, Avignon and Aix, so close together, Sophie gave the reasons for her decision and remarked that it was a risk she had to take.[47]

Sophie arrived in Turin in May 1832. Her foot was still painful and she could not walk without crutches. The condition of her foot had deteriorated. Doctors in Paris had begun to fear that it would have to be amputated and this opinion was confirmed in Turin.[48] Sophie proposed that she return to Aix-les-Bains for treatment at the waters. But Louise de Limminghe asked Mr Rossi, a gifted surgeon and official doctor to the court to examine Sophie's foot:

> he discovered two bones still prised apart the width of a finger and a half, and by means of a bandage which he comes and applies every morning, he assures me I will be walking soon.[49]

Less than three weeks later Sophie wrote to Eugénie that the treatment had worked and that she would not have to go to Aix at all. All she would need was a bandage on the foot, to keep the ankle bone in place and prevent the bones from dislocating again. It took time for the foot to heal fully, and Sophie continued to have pain in her ankle for some time, especially after long journeys. Nevertheless, the treatment of Mr Rossi was a turning point and for the first time in nearly four years Sophie found she could walk. Eugénie had expressed doubts about the ability of the surgeon in Turin, but Sophie assured her that he was truly gifted. In August 1832 Sophie sent Eugénie the surgeon's report on her foot, to prove the success of his treatment.[50]

Sophie was not sure whether to go to Rome or defer her visit and visit Montet instead. But when Eugénie de Gramont urged her brusquely to proceed to Rome, Sophie was offended:

> You are of this opinion yourself, Madame. This has wounded my heart a little. But quite quickly I saw reason, which you personify, and I realised that you were right. As for going back to France, I would not have the time to catch up with all the work that awaits me there. It is better to leave everything the way it is and start again when I get back! But I will go to Rome without my little daughter, without 'my rat', and I will not see her perhaps for a year.[51]

Indeed with Archbishop de Quelen now residing in the rue de Varenne, in the Petit-Hôtel, the last person Eugénie needed to see was Sophie Barat. Sophie had not been told that the archbishop had moved to the rue de Varenne, the centre of the Society of the Sacred Heart. Indeed she still sought to fill the Petit-Hôtel herself for in Turin she found a child who needed treatment in Paris, and suggested to Eugénie that she be given two rooms for herself and a third for her maid in the Petit-Hôtel.[52] By this time Eugénie de Gramont and Archbishop de Quelen were playing a game of secrecy with Sophie Barat.

Sophie had planned to visit Joseph-Marie Favre in the autumn of 1832, on the way back from Turin, but when she decided to go directly to Rome from Turin, Sophie asked Louise de Limminghe to tell him that she would not be back in Chambéry until the following year. Aware of her inner struggles, Favre tried to help Sophie by letter. He suggested that her health was being damaged by her inability to trust God. He pointed out to her that trust and love are life-giving qualities, they expand the soul and give energy for life's tasks. How, he asked her, could she expect to be able to pray and be effective as a leader when she had such a deep fear and mistrust of God? This went to the heart of Sophie's Jansenistic upbringing and profoundly challenged her in her leadership of a Society devoted to the Heart of Christ:

> Trust and the love of God gladden the heart, uplift the soul and make it capable of the greatest undertakings, whereas fear and mistrust depress and sadden the soul, shrink the heart, dull the spirit, ruin the health of the body and disturb rhythm of the spiritual life. God did not come down upon the earth to be feared but to be loved. How . . . can you mistrust a God who infinitely loves you, who wishes only for your health and happiness. How can you mistrust your dear, kind brother Jesus, who has suffered so much to save you, who has made so many sacrifices, so that you could share in his glory and his treasures? . . . How can you mistrust this loving and gentle heart that only wishes to be loved and to give love? Such mistrust can only come from the devil. . . . Let it never be intentional.[53]

Favre understood the tyranny of Sophie's scruples and he asked her to take his advice on two matters. The first was to believe that the general confession she had made to him the previous year was 'completely good, adequately detailed, sufficiently inclusive and comforting for the moment of death'. Even were she to be in danger of death she was forbidden to make another general confession. Favre promised to take responsibility for her before God. He also ordered her to live consciously in the love of God, to trust in God's goodness and to put away all thoughts which saddened, upset or depressed her. He directly linked this with finding a proper rhythm for her prayer, work and recreation, and reminded her 'whoever does too much does nothing'.[54]

The same day Favre wrote to Louise de Limminghe and discussed Sophie and her needs at this time. Both had decided that Sophie be given an order of day, to help her find the balance she so evidently needed and which in turn could help alleviate her scruples. De Limminghe made out this order of day and sent it to Favre for comment. He insisted that Sophie got enough sleep so that she could pray and do her work. She was to eat whatever was set before her, even if she did not like it. As long as the food did not make her ill, she was to eat it. She was not to fast unless the doctor gave express permission to do so. Until her health improved she was to do no penance. If she did what she was told in the area of health and food she would be doing as much penance as the Trappists.

Thus in 1832 the patterns of Sophie's inner struggles show how difficult it was for her break out of the formation given her by Louis Barat in Joigny and later in Paris. Over the years she had received help from friends. Joseph Varin had indeed constantly encouraged her to trust God and look after her health. Jean Montaigne had helped her face Saint-Estève and the crisis at Amiens. Pierre de Clorivière supported her in the preparations for the general council of 1815. Yet none of them were able to help her deeper inner self. Moreover while the constitutions of the Society of the Sacred Heart contained beautiful sections on the love of God revealed in the Heart of Christ, these had yet to be experienced by Sophie herself, in her own life. The hold of Jansenism was deep, not just within her but within her colleagues in the Society and within the French church in general. No wonder then the teaching of Favre was controversial. It was not easy to accept a God as loving as that. It turned current theology on its head, put the practice of the sacraments of confession and communion into a new perspective, and called for a totally new image of God. Favre offered Sophie a new way of thinking about God, of praying and working. It was just what Sophie needed then though she struggled with the tension of being caught between this new, ultramontane spirituality and that of her childhood and early religious life.

In September 1832, Sophie wrote a letter to the Society, telling of the cure of her foot in Turin. She announced her visit to Rome, and she also proposed to convene the next general council in Paris in 1833. In view of this, Sophie asked all those in leadership to prepare their accounts regarding finance, personnel and the quality of religious life in the community, so that all would be ready in good time for the council. During her visit to Rome, Sophie delegated some of her authority. Catherine de Charbonnel would reside in Aix-en-Provence and look after Autun, Besançon, Lyon, Avignon, Aix, Perpignan and Grenoble. Henriette Grosier would take charge of Bordeaux and Niort, in addition to her own house at Poitiers. Marie Prevost would look after the new house at Annonay as well as La Ferrandière. Eugénie de Gramont was responsible for Paris, Amiens,

Beauvais, Le Mans, Quimper and Metz. Sophie herself retained personal responsibility for Montet, Italy, Piedmont and America.[55] When Eugénie protested at all the responsibility given her Sophie countered with the reality of the Society's rapid growth and pointed out the truth: 'I cannot do everything; you really need to help me'. In reality Eugénie de Gramont was not at all displeased to help Sophie out and she enjoyed her enhanced position as well as Sophie's absence from Paris.

Sophie set out from Turin accompanied by Louise de Limminghe and Marie Patte. On the way she stayed in the villa of the comtesse Cherubini whose daughter had been at school at Turin and who later joined the Society of the Sacred Heart. While there she burnt her foot badly on a warming pan. It proved quite a deep burn and when Sophie finally arrived at the Trinité des Monts on 25 October 1832 she had to go to bed immediately, exactly what she had hoped to avoid on her first visit to Rome. The cure of her foot in Turin had lifted her despondency over how to manage a visit to Rome, where a superior general arriving on crutches would cut a poor figure.[56] A few days after her arrival the pope called to see her at the Trinité and to her embarrassment she could not greet him at the front door. Instead he visited her in her rooms and arranged for a further meeting in the Vatican when she was better. However, a burn was quite different from a fall and by the spring of 1833 Sophie was fully mobile again.

The purpose of the Sophie's visit to Rome was to oversee the foundation of the second house in the city. The marquise of Androsilla and Jean Rozaven had planned the foundation and were anxious to pursue this to the end while Sophie was present in the city. The monastery in the Trastevere, called Sainte Rufine, had been chosen for the poor school and noviceship. Sophie viewed it and agreed that it would suit the purpose of the second foundation in Rome.[57] While the building was being prepared Sophie decided to visit Anne Baudemont. She told Eugénie de Gramont:

> We stopped at St Denis; there we were received graciously. Both Madames Baudemont and Copina are old; they suffer but do so valiantly. I do not think they want to change and I thank God for that as they would be more of a burden than of use to us. I invited them to come and see us, a permission they can arrange easily. St Denys is a real hole of a place and they still only have it on lease. I think it is such a shame that they separated from us and ended up here. They have well expiated for all they did and that is why I wanted to see them and to assure them that I have not harboured any resentment towards them. They asked me eagerly for news of you and of Madame Ducis. As for Mr de Saint-Estève, he has completely abandoned them. It had to end that way![58]

Sophie also made contact with Louise Naudet who was deeply moved to see Sophie Barat, so different from the shy young woman she had met in Amiens in 1804. So much had happened to them both since Louise's visit to Amiens in 1804. Sophie was touched to meet her old friend, the person who had recognised and encouraged her gift of leadership. Sophie wrote to Henriette Grosier that Louise:

is still the same for la Grosier and la Barat, she is unique! . . . What courage! But also how stubborn! she wants to live and die in Rome, alone in a room. I can just imagine it, she cannot live with others. You know how much she overdoes kindness and care for others.[59]

Sophie took daily lessons in Italian – she had already begun to study the language while she was at Aix-les-Bains in the previous year. She was able to speak to the pope in Italian and during the months in Rome she perfected her use of the language. By early May 1833 all was ready in Sainte Rufine and the noviciate gradually moved from the Trinité to the new premises in the Trastevere. Sophie decided that her work in Rome was completed for the moment and she made plans to leave for France and begin preparations for the next general council. Having paid the usual courtesy visit to the pope Sophie left the city on 3 June, setting out for Parma where she had been asked to make a foundation there by the archduchess, Marie-Louise.

Her time in Rome was an important learning experience for Sophie. She had three audiences with Pope Gregory XVI. She received him at the Trinité and he sent her several gifts in the course of her stay. While Gregory XVI made no secret that he wished all religious women to observe strict papal cloister, he valued the Society of the Sacred Heart's work of education. While she was in Rome Sophie met Jean Rozaven for the first time and was impressed. She called him the 'the best friend' of the Society.[60] His support in Rome was important for he had influence among the Jesuits and in the congregation of bishops and religious. Besides Sophie had valued his help in the approbation process for the constitutions in 1826. He had been an enthusiastic instigator of the foundation of the Trinité and had urged the second house at Sainte Rufina, seeing the noviciate as essential for the growth of the Society not just in Rome but throughout Italy.[61] Nevertheless, there were warning signs indicating that Rozaven had presumed he had the right to interfere in the internal workings of the Society. For example he and Elizabeth Galitzine, who by now had joined the Trinité community, urged Sophie to deal with Natalie Rostopchine, a member of the Society in Paris, a Russian, whose indiscretions had made the Tsar suspicious of some Russian families in St Petersburg. Eugénie de Gramont was furious at Rozaven's interference and Sophie responded:

I understood very well that it was Fr Rozaven who irritated you; in my case it was the Russians.[62]

While Rozaven was progressively insinuating himself into the affairs of the Society of the Sacred Heart in Rome, the Jesuits led by the general, Jean Roothan, wanted to distance themselves from communities of religious women, including the Society of the Sacred Heart. Rozaven appeared embarrassed at this development within the Jesuits, especially those in France, and he was unable to prevent new appointments which reflected the new views.[63] Sophie sensed this in the appointment of a new Jesuit Provincial for France, François Renault. He replaced Julien Druilhet, an old friend and loyal supporter of Sophie and the

Society. This appointment signalled the end of the relationships between the Fathers of the Faith, later the Jesuits, and the Dames de l'Instruction Chrétienne, later the Society of the Sacred Heart. Too close an identification of the Society of the Sacred Heart with the Jesuits had created problems for Sophie also. She was disappointed when she heard that a possible foundation in Florence had been refused by Louise de Limminghe simply because there were no Jesuits there. Sophie chided her for such imprudence and said it simply was not true that the Society of the Sacred Heart existed only in towns where there were Jesuit communities. Yet news of a decision like that

> spreads quickly and is doubly distressing. It is not at all necessary that there be Jesuit houses where we are established. How many towns are there in France where this is not so. We get on quite well [without them] and I would even say that in the cases where there are no Jesuits they are freer to help us.[64]

In Rome Sophie also obtained another view of Archbishop de Quelen. Over Easter Sophie met several Roman cardinals who criticised Archbishop de Quelen for his attitude to the government of Louis Philippe and for his unwillingness to listen to the views of Rome.[65] Before leaving Rome Sophie dealt with the situation in the Trinité. The school had not grown and its exclusive nature had alienated many families in Rome:

> This condition of holding to admitting only the nobility alienates a great number. We could have 60 or more boarders if we were allowed to receive both classes. It is true that the day we accept the first girl from the bourgeoisie that day the nobility will leave us. For here in the Holy City [of Rome] perfection does not exist any more than it does elsewhere. It is a prejudice which will always be there. Maybe they are right in the end.[66]

For some time Sophie had been uneasy about the leadership of Armande de Causans in Rome and wondered at her lack of communication. Sophie objected to the correspondence which Louise de Limminghe and Armande de Causans maintained and which excluded her from learning of events and developments in Italy.[67] Sophie's suspicions were confirmed when she arrived in the Trinité in October 1832. There, Armande de Causans held very much to her role as superior in the Trinité and Sophie noted her resentment when Félicité Desmarquest was present. An assistant general threatened the position of the superior and Armande de Causans showed it so publicly that she was forced to apologise. She appeared restless and Sophie was concerned about her:

> Fr Barelle is giving us an excellent retreat at the moment. Armande de Causans has had difficulty in getting into it; a dark spirit tried to turn her away from it. But she is holding out and I am sure she will benefit from this.[68]

When Sophie left Rome in early June 1833 she had been greatly enriched by her experience. Her health had improved; she could walk with ease and yet she felt burdened.

After almost four years of governing the Society of the Sacred Heart while unable to walk and to write letters in comfort, Sophie was depressed and low in spirits. In addition to years of physical stress, the Society had grown and developed very quickly and Sophie had to oversee this expansion within France, in Switzerland and Italy and in Missouri and Louisiana. The realities of each country were different and each foundation had its leaders and communities to be encouraged and formed and strengthened. It was an immense task. Sophie had learnt how to delegate to others but she always retained the formation of the leaders herself as far as possible. She held the threads of unity herself, she was the central figure and knew that very well. So she said to Louise de Limminghe that she was the mother who gave birth, she was the figure of maternal tenderness and that was her vocation. What she intuited now, just before the general council of 1833, was that some among the membership were not responding to her leadership.

– 11 –
CONSOLIDATION OR DISINTEGRATION, 1833–1836

Sophie journeyed from Rome to Parma and from there on to Turin, and she arrived in Chambéry on 17 July 1833. There, guided by Fr Favre, she made her retreat.[1] After the retreat Sophie wrote a letter to the Society giving an account of her visit to Rome. She spoke of the new foundation at Sainte Rufine and of her experience of the church in Rome. She noted how the Society of the Sacred Heart was associated with the Jesuits:

> the pope and the cardinals are convinced that . . . we are all saints, or at least on the road to becoming so and liken us to an Order [Jesuits] which produces as many apostles and saints as there are religious.[2]

Sophie was concerned about the disparity between how the Society was perceived and how it was in reality. But she also knew by instinct and through Favre's approach just how important encouragement was and so she ended her letter with a note of affirmation for all the good which individuals and communities were doing, often in difficult circumstances. She invited the members of the Society to commit themselves to living a deep inner life, taking time to pray and reflect and live out of a spiritual centre. She commented that a mediocre commitment only left the soul jaded and the spirit fettered.[3] While the spiritual state of the Society of the Sacred Heart was of paramount importance to her, Sophie was keenly aware that the work of education was in need of radical review and she intended that the council of 1833 would address this seriously. While in Rome Sophie learnt of a decision taken by Archbishop de Quelen:

some have written to me from Paris saying that Mr Combalot has many followers
. . .; they are astonished that Mgr [de Quelen] has authorised him. It is the
younger people most of all whom he [Combalot] attracts, and perhaps our students since they like his approach, having been formed this way in school. This
priest confided to one of his relations in la Ferrandière, whom he tried to entice,
that he wants to found an association like ours for women which he hopes will
replace it. [He claims] he will succeed in this by education, in encouraging studies for women more than we do, etc. . . . I am surprised that Mgr [de Quelen] has
tolerated him in Paris . . . this young man has real talent for drawing young people.
What losses we would suffer![4]

For several years there had been criticism that the level of studies in the
schools of the Society of the Sacred Heart were not serious enough and that the
teachers were not properly trained. In 1832 when Adelaide de Rozeville asked
Sophie's opinion about a new method of teaching which could help the weaker
child, Sophie replied:

Get acquainted with these teaching methods and see with our friends [Jesuits] if
they can be adopted at least for the backward children and those less able . . . In
this instance, even with more gifted children, we could use what could be adapted
to our plans, particularly with regard to spelling which we teach badly everywhere
. . . In this respect our pupils achieve less than the children in smaller day and
boarding schools . . . How many pupils we have lost for that reason. I have been
saying this ceaselessly. We do not pay enough attention to this at our council meetings, just to avoid innovation. I hope we will return to it, otherwise it would reveal
a lack of resolve. When it is a question of winning souls what does it matter to God
what is used: pen, pencil, wood or paper?[5]

Sophie left Chambéry on 1 August 1833 and travelled to Paris to prepare for
the general council, scheduled to meet at the end of September in the rue de
Varenne. The council opened on 29 September 1833, with the twelve governing members of the Society present.[6] As had happened in 1815, 1820 and 1826,
Joseph Varin spoke to the council on the first working day and recalled the origins of the Society of the Sacred Heart and its journey until then. The following day Sophie and the council visited Archbishop de Quelen nearby in the
grounds of the rue de Varenne. During Sophie's absence in Rome Eugénie de
Gramont had invited Archbishop de Quelen to take up residence in the Petit-
Hôtel, just a few yards from the Hôtel Biron. What Sophie and the council
members thought about this development is not recorded. The house journal
simply notes the arrival of the archbishop in the Petit-Hôtel, following on the
events in Paris of July 1830 and February 1831.[7]

The work of the council continued until 30 October and dealt with several
key issues in the Society. The council decided to draw up a directory, modelled
along that of the Jesuits. This directory would contain regulations for daily life
and work in the Society of the Sacred Heart. Once the constitutions and rules
had been approved in Rome there was no necessity to debate these in council.
The directory was a mark of the routine and stability which the Society had
reached in its development, rather like a book of instructions to keep a ship on

course.[8] It was also a way of effecting reform and change within the system whenever the council met to reflect on the life of the Society. However, two major concerns absorbed the meetings of the council, that of the quality of education given in the schools and the situation of the Society in America.

From 14 to 24 October the council debated the standard of education in the Society and the plan of studies was examined and revised. On 20 October Nicolas Loriquet visited the council and offered his advice on amendments to the plan of studies. The rule of life for the day-school and for the orphans in Beauvais was passed with some amendments.[9] However, Sophie pointed out that there was less problem with the actual plan of studies and more with the teaching personnel in the schools, mostly the members of the Society. In her letter to the Society after the general council Sophie spoke of her concerns regarding the quality of education in the schools:

> For years we have been complaining about this matter and we felt the sacred obligations which our calling demands were not totally fulfilled. The complaints we received from all quarters and the successes which secular boarding schools achieved over ours have caused us great pain. We have carefully investigated the causes of this failing. The first is the neglect of study. The second is the lack of enthusiasm for training pupils in good management, simplicity, love of order and useful work. Most of our pupils leave our schools having learnt many things but none of them in any depth. This is because none of the teachers has a sufficiently deep foundation in education and they can only dabble in the subjects, applying themselves only to those they like best and neglecting the others. Consequently a large number of our pupils lack a knowledge of spelling, of basic numeracy, and the way in which to write a correct and agreeable letter.[10]

Sophie urged the teachers to take their own training in hand and asked the superiors of communities to ensure that teachers got enough time to actually prepare their classes. She also asked those who worked in the schools not to pander to conceit and expensive tastes. Some of the parents had remarked that their daughters had learnt both at school and had become insufferable at home.[11] The snobbish reputation of the Society was well known and during the 1833 council Louise de Limminghe had proposed that members of the Society omit the 'de' in their names, denoting nobility. Though the proposal was debated, it was turned down on the grounds that such a change would make legal documents invalid when they were tested in the courts.[12]

Although the council of 1827 had decided that the houses in Louisiana and Missouri needed an assistant general, this decision had still not been implemented. Six years later the situation had become acute and action was needed. The little group of five which had gone out to Louisiana in 1818 had worked in frontier conditions and had achieved an enormous amount in a short time. Philippine Duchesne wrote to the community in Paris in 1827:

> We only realise our situation when we see our inadequate buildings, the poverty of our beginnings, how few we are in number, the difficulties which different religions, languages and customs bring. We encounter obstacles in establishing

discipline in the community and in the classes, discipline which is so necessary and which we can only work towards now with all our hearts.[13]

Philippine was an assiduous letter-writer and kept Sophie well informed of developments in the mission areas as well as the health and general well-being of the members. For her part Sophie followed all with interest, encouraged Philippine Duchesne and her companions, collected money for the mission and considered the presence of the Society in America of great importance for the future of the Society. When missionaries on leave in Europe called to see Sophie at the rue de Varenne they were welcomed with interest and their views on the Society were sought. In 1827 Sophie wrote her first formal letter to the professed members of the Society in America[14] and told them that she planned to visit them and only regretted that it could not be immediately.

The nature of the work and responsibility in the two mission areas, Louisiana and Missouri, called for courage, initiative and independence. The conditions of the time were frontier, basic and essential. Only the strong could survive and Philippine Duchesne admitted to Sophie that some had indeed faltered and weakened. Philippine Duchesne did not judge them harshly for this, but she pointed out to Sophie that leadership was confined to a few: to Eugénie Audé in Grand Coteau first and then later in St Michael's; to Xavier Murphy in Grand Coteau; to Hélène Dutour in La Fourche and Catherine Thiéfry in St Louis. Each one of them lived in areas miles away in distance from one another. Contact was erratic and each had to deal with the realities of different cultures, languages, backgrounds and education and at the same time initiate and establish schools in conditions which were daunting. And if the geographical distances were great within America, they were even greater between America and France. In addition, there was the distance created between a frontier church and the church in France, between the Society in France and that in America. Sophie tried to breach these and grasped some of the realities quickly, while others were difficult, almost impossible, to understand, at such a distance.

Sophie thought that four houses were enough in America for the moment and she wanted each to be consolidated before any further work was undertaken. However, this policy was tested in September 1827 when the Sisters of the Cross in La Fourche in Lower Louisiana asked to join the Society of the Sacred Heart. Most of the members of this community did not know French and found it impossible to teach the children in the school. Sophie agreed to this request and gave directions to Philippine as to how the fusion was to be carried out. The Sisters of the Cross were to be received individually, not as a group. Each would make a noviciate and be received into the Society of the Sacred Heart as a coadjutrix sister. La Fourche was to be modelled on the orphanages of the Society in France. Sophie asked Eugénie Audé to send the orphans at St Michael's to La Fourche, and the school there could admit boarders from the lower middle class. However, the level of studies was to remain below that of the boarding schools, in this case at St Michael's and Grand

Coteau. Fees at La Fourche could be paid either in money or in goods according to the preference of parents. The majority of the community were to be coadjutrix sisters with a few choir religious. Sophie insisted most of all that while Eugénie Audé was to oversee the fusion of the Sisters of the Cross: La Fourche was not to be added to St Michael's, as an extension of its work – they were to be kept quite separate, with separate purposes.[15]

This was quite a task for Philippine to oversee and Sophie reminded the communities that Philippine Duchesne had been delegated that authority in 1818. Philippine never found leadership easy but while the little group was centred in Upper Louisiana her role was unquestioned. When the Society expanded into Lower Louisiana, to Grand Coteau and then to St Michael's and now La Fourche, most issues had to be dealt with quickly and without reference to Philippine first. Besides, distances were vast, correspondence was difficult and erratic, and there simply was not time to consult and then decide. Besides, these were frontier women, unusual women, independent women, who were committed to their project. Sophie remained in contact with Eugénie Audé and Xavier Murphy and often dealt with them without telling Philippine, though in matters of long-term policy Sophie always insisted that Philippine had the final decision. Nevertheless, these double messages from Sophie undermined Philippine and made her feel increasingly inadequate for the task. When Hélène Dutour arrived in St Louis in 1827 she wrote back to Sophie complaining of Philippine Duchesne's administration in the house, and Sophie took this up with Philippine Duchesne:

> Madame Dutour complains of the excessive slovenliness of the house [St Louis] and of individuals in the community. It is a problem, I admit. See . . . that the washing is done more thoroughly and maintain discipline within the house.[16]

Philippine lived an abject form of poverty and austerity, shocking to newcomers, yet accepted by her own contemporaries. Sophie asked Philippine to pay attention to such criticisms, and indeed to take proper care of the house and grounds, but she knew Philippine well enough not to press too hard on the matter of austerity. Besides, she was aware that Dutour had only arrived in the country. She was in fact appointed superior of La Fourche the following year. Yet her first impressions of Philippine and her manner of administration were valuable and Sophie gave them some weight. Much more delicate was the manner in which Eugénie Audé treated Philippine Duchesne.

Philippine had complained of Eugénie Audé's independence and Sophie experienced what Philippine meant in an incident concerning St Michael's. Sophie only learnt of this indirectly, through Mr Rusand, the Society's agent in Lyon.[17] Sophie wrote to Audé:

> Monsieur Rusand who knows the rules of our Institute since he is printing them at the moment . . . has just sent me your letter which asked him for a whole list of classical books and 300 aulnes of woollen cloth for St Michael's. He wants to have my approval before sending these to you . . . I sent word to him that he was to send

you the classical books but not to get involved in the other order which is no concern of his. I told him it was my business and that I would speak to you about the matter.

... in such a hot country how can you choose woollen cloth which we have forbidden in the Midi and even in Paris in the summer? Then you have not considered that this very expensive material, which has often caused our parents to complain, will be even more expensive with transport costs and customs duties, and if an accident should occur to this delicate colour, this will be a loss of 4,000 francs. For that is how much your woollen cloth will cost. Then, by giving the commission to Mr Rusand, he would have to get the material from Rheims where it is made to Lyon, from Lyon to Bord[eaux] for shipping. Look at the amount it costs! I hope that these remarks will lead you to cancel this project.[18]

Clearly Eugénie Audé had forgotten her own dismay at the purchase of the Hôtel Biron in 1820 and now was establishing St Michael's as the Hôtel Biron of Lower Louisiana. She may have consulted Sophie on the matter of buying material for the school uniforms in previous letters and become impatient at the lack of response. Sophie admitted in April 1828 that she had lost all of Eugénie's letters, including her list of requests.[19]

Such independence on the part of Eugénie Audé, who not only ordered a vast amount of material from France, but used the Society's agent to carry it out without Sophie's prior consent, was an indication of the communication difficulties in the American mission. In September 1828 Philippine told Sophie that she felt the task of communicating with Eugénie Audé beyond her skills. Xavier Murphy also complained of Eugénie Audé's silence and apparent withdrawal into her own world at St Michael's at a time when she needed her advice and support. For some months there was question of moving Grand Coteau to Opelousas and such a major decision needed the corporate wisdom of all. Moreover, Hélène Dutour, only a year in La Fourche, wanted to upgrade the school, place it on a par with Grand Coteau and St Michael's and so undermine the policy set by Sophie in 1827. For this reason alone Eugénie Audé's co-operation was needed, to ensure that La Fourche retained the status set for it by Sophie. Philippine anticipated that in Upper Louisiana an experienced superior and headmistress was needed for the refoundation at St Charles, to ensure the success of the school. Philippine hoped Eugénie Audé could go there but she knew that a move as big as that could only be effected by Sophie herself:

Madame Xavier . . . complains, as I do, of Madame Eugénie's silence. I know nothing about it and am afraid that there is too much praise and flattery where she is, and this lessens and damages the union among us . . .

. . . if these changes are approved they will draw many complaints, and this could be prevented if you assign each one to her post, with your gift of softening it for each one. I do not have this ability.[20]

These letters reached Sophie at a time when she had been ill and then had a series of falls in the rue de Varenne. In October 1828 she told Eugénie Audé that she was worried in case she had misread the situation in Lower Louisiana and asked Eugénie to send her details, especially about La Fourche. Eugénie's own success in St Michael's astonished Sophie and she warned her not to expand too rapidly, as had happened to some houses in France, that it was good to have some financial reserves for emergencies. Immediate success had led some superiors to build too extensively and too rapidly and then:

> Expenditures and enterprises undertaken with hurried or unexpected approval have not been blessed by God; and these houses have almost declined, having no more than vast, very ornate buildings, without any pupils.[21]

By now Eugénie Audé had received Sophie's stern reprimand over her order to Rusand in Lyon, and she still smarted from it. She had written to apologise and Sophie took care to assure her warmly that the incident was forgotten. Nevertheless, Sophie urged Eugénie to treat the members of her community with gentleness, and to be both polite and generous with the other houses, especially those in greater need. Philippine warned Sophie that the wealthy reputation of St Michael's was affecting the mission in Upper Louisiana. Donations sent from France, for the Society of the Sacred Heart, were not being passed on by the bishop. Undoubtedly the reputation of the Hôtel Biron did not help Philippine's situation either.[22] Indeed, contrary to Sophie's understanding in November 1828, Eugénie did not easily give up her plan to buy cloth for the school uniforms and only by July 1829 was it clear to Sophie that the order sent to Mr Rusand had been cancelled.[23]

While chiding Eugénie for her high-handed actions, Sophie continued to take her into her confidence with regard to the situation in La Fourche. She explained that the question of that school was part of a wider concern of the Society, treated by the general councils of 1827 and 1833. She spelt it out for Eugénie Audé in November 1828, insisting that Dutour should not be allowed to raise the level of studies at La Fourche:

> Without a doubt it will be going against my wishes if La Fourche is raised to your level. It must remain a second level school and only teach little knowledge. It should teach *religion, crafts, reading, writing, a little spelling and counting*, as in our second boarding school in Bordeaux. That is why I wanted you to send your orphans there . . . what would have prevented you sending them your pupils' cast-off clothing and even the trousseaus to make? You must come to an understanding with Mother Duchesne, for the greater glory of God, to prevent this house harming yours. I will write to Mother Duchesne and convey these thoughts to her. I will invite her to go down river and visit your houses. You will meet the three superiors, in your houses if it is convenient: Mothers Xavier, Dutour and Mother Duchesne. And there gathered together for this little meeting, having invoked the Holy Spirit, you will consult one another and take decisions for the greatest good.[24]

Sophie did indeed write to Philippine and asked her to plan a visit to Lower Louisiana and establish some real form of communication between the superiors. Sophie had in mind a definite plan for Upper and Lower Louisiana. There were to be three boarding schools: Grand Coteau, St Michael's and St Louis or Florissant, and three secondary schools, 'for the poor, for orphans and for ordinary people, [and] in the north, for the Indians'. She asked Philippine to travel to St Michael's and hold a superiors' meeting there to determine the future of the Society in America. But Sophie meant the meeting to do more than that. She wanted Philippine to try and bring some uniformity in practice regarding the essentials of life in the Society of the Sacred Heart: the constitutions and rules, the ceremonial, the plan of studies.[25] She also wanted to ensure that St Charles would flourish and thought that in time 'perhaps this will be the house which will do the greatest good'.[26]

Sophie's greatest concern was over Eugénie Audé's attitude to La Fourche and especially to Philippine. In December 1828 Sophie chided Audé for sending a novice to La Fourche who was deaf and unable to take responsibility for work in the house. She pointed out that in a new foundation this was another strain for the community and Sophie also questioned Eugénie's sensitivity towards the handicapped person.[27] She also reproached her for treating Philippine badly:

> She [Philippine] tells me that you sent two from your community who were worse than useless; another is dying of consumption, which is a burden, and moreover, the cold climate there will shorten her life even further. It cost 500 francs to pay their travel expenses, notwithstanding their extreme poverty. It appears that you have not passed on the 2500 francs we paid into Mr Rustand's account for you. Yet I have asked you to be good enough to have that money passed on to that worthy mother immediately, for she is in extreme need. I find it difficult to understand how you can treat Mother Duchesne in this manner, who has suffered so much to establish the Society in this part of the world. . . . I hope that you will reflect on your somewhat harsh treatment of this good woman who has great need of being comforted.[28]

Sophie realised that communication had broken down between Philippine and Eugénie Audé and she asked Philippine to go to Lower Louisiana and try to resolve the difficulties in person. She knew that Philippine did not want either to travel south or meet with Eugénie Audé, Hélène Dutour and Xavier Murphy. Sophie comforted her and said she could not understand why Eugénie Audé was so difficult to deal with. Sophie recognised that Eugénie could well have a different point of view and valuable insights to offer, but nothing justified her attitude. While encouraging Philippine, Sophie wrote a sharp letter to Eugénie Audé, saying that she was extremely displeased at the way Eugénie had treated Philippine Duchesne, 'this woman who is the founder of the Society in Louisiana and who deserves consideration at the very least'.[29]

Sophie held out great hopes for this meeting in Lower Louisiana.[30] At the same time Sophie had begun to plan, not for the first time,[31] a new foundation on the east coast, in New York. She was caught between the conflicting views of both Philippine Duchesne and Eugénie Audé and had decided that a fresh focal point was needed in America, a centre where the true spirit of the Society could be nurtured. She told Eugénie Audé of her plan and asked for her co-operation:

You will do great work by contributing to the foundation in New York which has become essential for us. I will tell you my plan for it in another letter. I am sure you will like it for it will consolidate the Society in America and propagate its true spirit there in the ways that I envisage. But it is not yet time to communicate these to you. In the meantime, pray, become holy and gather money.[32]

The long planned visit of Philippine Duchesne to Lower Louisiana occurred in the winter of 1829 and Philippine sent Sophie an account of it. She spent some days in La Fourche in early November and from 16 November until 20 December in St Michael's. The first letter was written in Saint Michael's, on the 13 December, and Philippine reminisced that it was twenty-four years since Sophie arrived at the door of Ste Marie d'En Haut. Now she felt both the distance that separated her from Sophie, and the weight of her responsibilities in America. Philippine concentrated on the situation in La Fourche. Hélène Dutour wanted to have a noviciate in the house, and not have to send novices for their training to Grand Coteau. She wanted to have the level of studies equal to Grand Coteau and St Michael's, and she wanted to build more accommodation for the students and a chapel for both community and school. During the meeting in St Michael's the group decided that Dutour should not raise the level of studies in the school and that her building projects should be curtailed to what was necessary for the type of school envisaged. Sophie realised then that Philippine did not insist, in virtue of her role as Sophie's delegate, that Dutour abide by Sophie's plan for La Fourche.

Philippine told Sophie that Hélène Dutour's situation was not easy. It would be quite controversial in America to have two schools (La Fourche and St Michael's) close to each other, with one open to the lower class families and the other to the wealthy, middle class, each with a different scale of fees and different curriculum. Philippine knew that this had caused real difficulty in Missouri and she understood the problems which arose from the conditions that Sophie had placed on La Fourche. Earlier on that year Bishop Rosati visited La Fourche and wrote his impressions of the new foundation to Sophie in Paris:

I tell you without the least exaggeration that I was enchanted to see this house in a state of prosperity beyond my expectations. I found there thirty-three boarders and four religious, including Madame du Tour . . . Everything is run simply and economically, but yet with the greatest propriety and in the best possible order. People spoke a lot to me about Madame du Tour before I came here. All those who live here have the greatest veneration for her . . . This country offers many resources. Although the inhabitants are not wealthy, nonetheless they have the means to give a certain education to their children . . . They will never send them to a boarding school of the second class, because in a republican country where there is no distinction, their pride would be wounded.[33]

Bishop Rosati suggested to Sophie that, without calling it a second-class boarding school, a simpler curriculum could still be taught there. That would attract girls from modest backgrounds and at the same time avoid too direct a comparison with St Michael's.

The meeting of the four superiors ended in St Michael's on 20 December 1829 and while on the way to Grand Coteau with Xavier Murphy and Marie Lévêque, Philippine wrote her second report for Sophie. She discussed her impressions of St Michael's and of Eugénie Audé with Xavier Murphy and they both came to the conclusion that St Michael's was unlike most houses of the Society. All the key positions in the house were held by Eugénie Audé herself. She was superior, headmistress, mistress of novices and bursar. She also gave spiritual direction in the community and looked after visitors. Most of the community were young and inexperienced and Eugénie wanted it that way so that she could train the community herself. But Philippine considered that they were neither trained or supervised nor was there any order in the house. On the eve of 21 November none of the aspirants were aware that they would renew their commitment the following day. Philippine saw little evidence of spiritual reading or commitment to a serious prayer life. She felt diffident and inadequate when faced with situations like this:

> I have expressed my views on all that but I have been persuaded that I should not interfere anymore except out of sisterly friendship. What influence can I have here where everyone, both within and without, is in admiration of the spiritual and temporal aspect of the house, of the superior who leads and succeeds? I have a completely different attitude to this, which is explained away as me being the way I am.[34]

Philippine felt at ease with Xavier Murphy, closer to her than to Eugénie Audé or Hélène Dutour. She anticipated that the visit to Grand Coteau would be a pleasant affair and one that would cause her little difficulty. She was all the more shocked to discover that, in her view, 'the house is like a pretty family home'.[35] It was open to all, and people came in and out with facility. The community took walks in the woods and fields and talked to all whom they met. When Philippine asked how they lived out cloister she was told it was far too strict and off-putting for parents and children. Philippine did not remain silent and her criticism was resented and not welcome in the community. That did not daunt Philippine and she sent Sophie fifteen issues which she considered needed reform and asked for a response. Among the issues concerned were the observance of cloister, the use of the plan of studies of the Society (though Philippine herself did not know whether it was in force or not) and the teaching of religion which should not be neglected because there were so many Protestant pupils in the school. Philippine drew attention to the need for regular spiritual exercises, required by commitment to religious life. She was particularly critical of Xavier Murphy's treatment of the coadjutrix sisters in the community and requested specifically that their accommodation, in buildings apart from the house, be attended to and made safer. She suggested that more care be taken of visiting parents and Philippine could not understand why the chaplain was treated so badly in the house. She noted that Xavier Murphy was charming with the parents and somewhat curt with the community. Philippine left Grand Coteau with relief and her departure was as welcome as her arrival had been. Life in Lower

Louisiana was different and a source of puzzlement, even incomprehension, to Philippine.

When Sophie received Philippine's report on the superiors' meetings and on Philippine's visits to the communities she could not hide her disappointment. She also had letters from the other superiors, commenting on Philippine's visit and on the situation at La Fourche. Sophie realised that her initial plans for La Fourche could not work and proposed that, after all, La Fourche should teach in the senior classes to the same level of studies as at St Michael's. But she recommended that the arts d'agrément be taught in St Michael's only, and in La Fourche the accent be placed on practical formation and preparation for earning a living. Each school had a separate purpose and Sophie hoped that would reduce the possibility of conflict between the two. However, loyal to Philippine and aware of her position, she only authorised this policy if Philippine agreed to it. However, she warned Philippine that if her compromise was not accepted then neither Bishop Rosati nor the general public would be happy with La Fourche. It would also prevent confrontation and division between houses of the Society.

Sophie responded to Philippine's comments on Grand Coteau and suggested that a certain flexibility with regard to life in the houses in America was needed. She also replied to each of the twenty-four queries forwarded by Philippine, which concerned what she considered abuses in the school and communities. She asked Philippine to show latitude and to allow prayers in the schools to be said in English, not Latin; to permit English be taught in the afternoon classes; to ensure that Protestants not learn the Catholic catechism; to let the community walk in the woods and fields; to accept those of mixed blood, or born outside marriage, as members of the Society, as long as they fulfilled the other usual conditions for entry; to allow the coadjutrix sisters to wear the same kind of cloth as the choir sisters, on account of the climate; to allow the coadjutrix sisters be taught writing on Sundays.[36]

These issues were important and Sophie recognised that the needs in America were different in some aspects from those in Europe. They also showed her how much new leadership was needed in America. By 1831, Sophie had decided that it was time to ask Philippine to retire as superior at St Louis. She suggested that Philippine discuss the matter with Bishop Rosati and then go to either Florissant or St Charles, whichever house she preferred:

> I think . . . that at your age and having suffered so much, that the foundation of this American boarding school which demands so much attention in every way, is beyond your strength. For many years now all those who have seen St Louis have been complaining about the chaos, the untidiness and even the lack of cultivation of your land. . . . God knows I do not blame you. I know only too well all that you have accomplished and how much you have suffered. But times are changing and we too must adapt and change. I see also from my own experience that it is better for superiors not to spend long periods in the same houses. [37]

While Philippine was happy to be relieved from responsibility,[38] Bishop Rosati had a different reaction and wrote to Sophie, asking her to think again:

I believe that there is no one among your religious who can gain as much confidence as Mother Duchesne justly enjoys here. All who know her respect and venerate her because of her virtues, which joined to age and the experience she has acquired during her long sojourn in this country, make her truly esteemed by all. There are few people I esteem more than this holy religious. She has the true spirit of her vocation, and on many occasions, known only to me . . . has given the most striking proofs of this . . . I see from the complaints you heard about her and which have led you to the proposed change, that she has been misrepresented to you . . .[39]

Rosati explained the context of the complaints about Philippine, how she was coping with a situation quite different from France. The complaints about the few boarders in the school, about the land being left uncultivated and about Philippine's manner of dealing with a wealthy benefactor, Mr Mullanphy, were taken out of context. When Sophie received this letter defending Philippine so strongly, she had no choice but to revoke her decision and she told Philippine:

I accede fully and readily to his wish for it cost me to take that decision. I went along with the wishes you had expressed so forcefully for so long. Furthermore so many well informed people shared your thoughts on this point. I am delighted that they were mistaken, and that, for your part, it was merely a feeling of humility which influenced you to make this request.[40]

In the meantime the situation at La Fourche had become intractable. Hélène Dutour had insisted upon her building programme and in a few months had placed the house in serious debt. Sophie removed her from office in April 1831 and appointed Julie Bazire (1806–1883) as superior, though she asked Eugénie Audé to deal with the financial crisis. But this did not improve and caused tensions not only within the Society but with unpaid businessmen and workers. By March 1832 Sophie decided that it was best to close the house and disperse the community to St Michael's and Grand Coteau.[41] She asked Eugénie Audé to implement this decision and turned her attention once again to the overall needs of the American communities and to the situation in St Louis. Sophie confided her concerns to Eugénie de Gramont:

I am sending you . . . two letters for Opelousas. It will be helpful if you read them so that you are kept up to date. The letter of Madame de Coppens from St Louis could be exaggerated but the core of it is true regarding Madame Duchesne. She is no longer able to be in charge. Besides she never governed according to our spirit. You know that I tried to replace her with Madame Thiéfry and how the bishop complained. That is how our way forward is blocked. There is no doubt but that America needs to be visited by one of us.[42]

The following year Sophie wrote to Eugénie again:

Madame de Coppens is not completely wrong, for as long as Mother Duchesne is in this house it will never succeed. You know that I tried to change her and that the bishop opposed it. That is how I am always blocked! This good and holy woman will never change her Visitation spirit. What can we do? Have patience for I can send no one there. But a visit from one of us would be very useful in America.[43]

This urgent need was addressed at the general council in the autumn. Sophie had asked the American houses to send nominations for the office of assistant general of Louisiana and these were discussed on the last day of the council, when elections to offices were held. Nominations had been made for four candidates: Eugénie Audé (7); Philippine Duchesne (4); Xavier Murphy (5); Catherine Thiéfry (1).[44] Thus Eugénie Audé was appointed assistant general for America. Sophie wrote to Eugénie Audé once the council had formally closed:

> I hasten . . . to tell you that our general council concluded yesterday. Last evening, the 31 October, we proceeded to the nominations, a list of which is enclosed, and you were appointed to be assistant general in Louisiana. The council's decision was reached as a result of the majority of the votes cast by the professed sisters in America who know you well. We call upon . . . you to accept this burden . . . As soon as this letter arrives, and if your health permits, you should set about visiting the four houses of Opelousas, St Louis, St Charles, Florissant. Then take the boat and come to France, to give us an account of your mission. We will keep you here for as little a time as possible . . . [45]

But by this time Eugénie Audé's health had deteriorated. The cholera which had hit Upper and Lower Louisiana in the spring of 1833 had taken its greatest toll among the members of the community in St Michael's. Eugénie was shattered and crushed by the deaths of at least seven members of the community between May and August 1833, from the cholera and other related illnesses. She nursed each of the sick until death, and her heart was broken several times by the relentless pace of the plague. After all her years of hard, austere work, these weeks of stress and strain finally broke her health. She wrote to Sophie in September 1833 and asked if she could return to Europe, to see Sophie again and rest. She was a spent force.[46]

This letter arrived in Paris on the 9 November 1833, the morning Sophie had written to Eugénie to tell her of her election as assistant general. That evening she wrote again to Eugénie and asked her, despite her poor health, to accept the appointment, make the visits to the houses and then travel to Paris. A decision could be made regarding the future when they met and had time to talk together. If the task was beyond her strength then she would not be asked to continue in it. Sophie counted on Eugénie being able to visit the communities for she desperately needed a first-hand account of the actual situation in the American houses. Eugénie Audé made the visitation of the houses as requested and then embarked for Europe.[47] The information and experience which Eugénie brought would be of great importance to Sophie in her leadership of the houses in America. Yet the precarious state of Eugénie Audé's health presented Sophie with a more pressing problem, for who could she find to replace the new assistant general if Eugénie was too ill to return to America? Strong, administrative leadership was needed in America if unity between the houses and with the central leadership of the Society in France was to be achieved.

Eugénie Audé's appointment was a source of liberation for Philippine and in October 1833 she asked Sophie if now, finally, she could go to the Indians and fulfil the original impulse of her missionary vocation. Her request came at a time when Sophie had to convey sad news to Philippine, that Ste Marie d'En Haut had been closed. It was a huge break for Philippine, even if she would never return to France she always thought of Ste Marie d'En Haut as her spiritual home. Sensing what the loss of Ste Marie d'En Haut would be for Philippine, Sophie asked her to send her more details with regard to resources and the type of work a community would do with the Indians.[48] At Christmas time 1833 Sophie proposed once again that Philippine retire as superior of St Louis and remarked bluntly:

> I think . . . you must retain your position, at least until the return of Mother Eugénie. Then we will reorganise your houses. The order will be definite and I do not think anyone will want to oppose it. . . . [49]

Philippine was hurt at the sharpness of this remark and told Sophie so in her reply in April 1834:

> I was hurt by that remark in your letter: 'on Mother Eugénie's return the orders will be definite and I hope that no one will oppose them'. From whom was opposition expected? What gave rise to fears that there would be? [50]

Sophie realised that her manner had been abrupt and hurtful and she explained why to Philippine in July 1834:

> I wish to say a few words to you especially to explain, first of all, a remark in one of my letters which you mentioned in your last letter. It concerns the opposition I experienced to your transfer of house. You know that I was forced to give in. So it was not you that I had in mind then when I said that I hoped that Mother Eugénie could help me remove the obstacles. Indeed having one of the Society on the spot can judge better than I could. That is why, until now, I have been so hesitant about governing your houses.
>
> Now that I am more up to date I have not hesitated to take a decision regarding your change of house. Besides, it is one of our unwritten laws that we leave our superiors only six years in the same house unless it is impossible to do better. Moreover, my dear Philippine, you need rest and so an easier post of administration. You are to call Mother Thiéfry to your position in Saint Louis and you will take hers at Florissant. Mother Eugénie is writing by the same post to your good bishop, to advise him of this. If I can I will do the better thing and write myself.[51]

Eugénie Audé arrived in Paris on 26 May 1834 and gave Sophie a full account of the communities and schools, based on her recent visits to the houses and on sixteen years of experience. In the light of their conversations[52] Sophie wrote a letter to the religious of Louisiana, the first of a series she wrote to them between 1834 and 1836.

Sophie's letters to the members of the Society in general were the means she used to inform the communities of developments within the Society. She used letters to address issues that needed reform in the Society, either in community or in the schools. These letters were often blunt and direct in tone. But a good number of the membership in Europe knew Sophie personally, either through her personal letters or her visits to houses. Thus when her formal circular letters came, her voice could be heard and her meaning understood when she insisted on various aspects of life in the Society. She urged each to strive for a deep spiritual life, that superiors should facilitate this as their primary duty; that new members be properly trained for their work in the Society, either in the schools or in the household tasks; that (insistently) schools should be properly run and the teachers supervised; that economy and thrift should mark the administration of both communities and schools; that food should be wholesome and plentiful; that health of both religious and pupils should be properly cared for and preventive medicine practised. She drew attention to the need for each house to contribute a tenth of its income (*dixième*) to the centre, and to provide properly for those religious who were changed from one house to another; she regulated how dowries were to be administered, ensuring that they came within the requirements of the law and the wishes of families. In these years Sophie was establishing a certain rhythm within the Society, within the communities and within the schools, drawing on her intimate experience of leadership over many years.[53] It was this kind of communication she wanted to establish in America.

But the American houses had not got the advantage of personal contact with Sophie Barat, or even the knowledge that she was not very far away. Sophie herself was sensitive to this and repeated many times at this period that she wanted to visit the houses in Louisiana. By 1834 of the seventy-one members of the communities in America just seventeen had personally met Sophie Barat.[54] In her letters specifically for the American houses Sophie pointed out the deficiencies and weaknesses in the communities and in the schools. She signalled nineteen abuses, among them: criticism of authority and independence of superiors; informality at recreations; excessive stress on excellence in studies; distinctions made between races (especially between French and American) both in the schools and in the communities; interfering in one another's work, bickering and endless chattering; divisions and tensions within the communities which the boarders easily saw and talked about; several confessors for the one house, rather than the one appointed; dining with the priests; touching the children, or allowing the children to touch them, too affectionately; religious instruction omitted from the curriculum at any excuse; priority given to secular studies, rather than formation in piety; lack of proper supervision of the boarders and the orphans.[55]

A year later Sophie wrote another to the American houses, pointing out thirteen further abuses and issuing directive for the future. This time she concentrated on the schools. She insisted that the boarders be supervised, particularly when their parents visited them during the year; day and boarding school pupils should not mix, the orphans should not mix with either the boarders or the day pupils; the plan of studies should be followed in the composition of classes and the curriculum; religious rather than secular works of art should be displayed in the school; teachers should hold themselves with dignity and always show good manners; variations in dress gave bad example to the pupils and parents; there should be less ostentation regarding school achievements and prize-giving should be held in private, within the school; English must be taught to the level necessary in the schools. She suggested that every six months the superiors of the communities evaluate how these issues were being addressed and the results sent to her in Paris.[56]

Sophie wrote a further admonitory letter to the American houses in December 1836, in which she named six further abuses. Most of them were repetitions of former points: proper surveillance of the pupils and life in community. Two stood out, one dealing with the spirit of the American pupils in the schools and the other with the relationships between the members of the Society in America:

> That we should work tirelessly to teach the children docility of mind and heart all the more needed in their country where error [Protestantism] can only spread and hold sway with the help of independence and intellectual arrogance.
> Banish forever I beg you these odious distinctions between the Americans and the French.[57]

In these three letters, full of admonitions, Sophie presented herself as a superior general who was critical and negative with regard to the American houses. She spoke from her own context, from her French culture and mentality. The lists of abuses, sent out coldly, with no one to unpack them and explain the feeling and concern behind them, ensured they could not be heard easily. During this time Sophie wrote several letters of admonition to the Society in general yet none of them have the stern tone of these letters to the American houses. The distance certainly affected her as well as the anxiety to cover all the points brought up by Eugénie Audé. When she wrote to the houses in Europe she knew her people; when she wrote to America she wrote into the unknown. Language, too, was a barrier. Some of the members of the communities, especially the coadjutrix sisters, did not know French. A great deal depended on who translated the texts and how this was done. Sophie was aware of this and knew it put her at yet another remove from those she was trying to lead. This was a particular worry, for her concept of government was based on personal relationships and personal, ongoing contact. The impact of her letters on the communities was not apparent immediately but over the three years, Sophie gleaned some of the reactions to her letters and heard what the communities felt about her leadership.

If the years 1834–36 were the period when Sophie Barat wrote most of her circular letters to the Society, she was no less busy travelling and either founding new communities or accepting requests for fusion with the Society. From the time that general council had closed in November 1833, Sophie travelled in France almost continuously. In the space of a few months she had visited: Beauvais, Lille and Amiens (November–December 1833); Le Mans, Tours, Poitiers, Niort, Bordeaux, Lyon, Chambéry (February–May 1834); Charleville,

Besançon, Lyon, La Ferrandière, Chambéry, Montet, (August 1834–May 1835); Beauvais, Jette St Pierre (Belgium), Charleville (June–July 1835). During visits to already well-established houses Sophie reviewed the life of the community and the schools and made suggestions for changes or improvements. Foundations continued to be made and in August 1834, in response to some families in Lille, Sophie travelled to Brussels and initiated negotiations for a foundation there. Two months later Catherine de Charbonnel travelled to Belgium and found a suitable property in Jette St Pierre, outside Brussels. Renovations were necessary and the following year Sophie travelled again to Belgium, in June 1835, to see how these were progressing. By the spring of 1836 all was ready and the new house and school opened in March of that year.

More small communities continued to request integration with the Society. The Dames de la Providence at Charleville were founded in 1679, withstood the Revolution but found it progressively more difficult to survive alone. They had had some links with the Dames de Sainte Sophie de Metz and when that community joined the Society of the Sacred Heart in 1824, some of the Dames de la Providence at Charleville wondered if they could do the same. Finally, in 1834, they asked Sophie Barat if they could join the Society. After her visit to Charleville Sophie decided that the fusion could work and proceeded with the negotiations. She, then Marie Prevost and later Joseph Varin spent time introducing the community to the constitutions and spirit of the Society, a necessary process before finally confirming the fusion. These preparations were completed by September 1835.

Another community, the Dames de Saint Pierre at Marseilles also asked to join the Society of the Sacred Heart, in 1835. This community originated in Grenoble, when Pierrette de Bourcet de Lassaigne had set up a small school for the education of the girls of wealthy families in Grenoble. She began around the time that Philippine Duchesne tried to restore Ste Marie d'En Haut, and indeed Mlle de Bourcet's niece, Louise de Bourcet, went to school there. The work of Mlle de Bourcet grew after the Revolution, and she established the group as a religious community, with a rule, and persuaded her niece to join her work. When Mlle de Bourcet died Louise took over the leadership of the community in Grenoble in 1817 and one of the community, Geneviève Chaniac, left Grenoble to start a school in Aix-en-Provence. After some years Louise de Bourcet invited the community at Aix to affiliate with that of Grenoble, but this project failed. However, Louise opened a school of the Dames de Saint Pierre at Marseille, in 1828, where it was immediately successful. While the two communities could not agree to merge, they both agreed to ask to join the Society of the Sacred Heart. These negotiations began in 1832 and were completed by Eugénie Audé in 1834. When Sophie recognised that Eugénie Audé could not return immediately to America, she asked her to go to Marseille and effect the fusion of the Dames de Saint Pierre with the Society of the Sacred Heart.[58]

In the midst of her administrative work and constant travelling Sophie had not forgotten her family. In September 1833 she had heard with some dismay that Zoé was about to be married and she wondered how Marie-Louise could even encourage it. Zoé was delicate and while she had nothing against the young man himself, he had no money and depended on his father for work.[59] In the event the marriage did not take place though Zoé did not give up hope that she would marry someday. Sophie's next concern was Marie-Louise's health. Stanislas panicked and told Sophie that his mother was seriously ill. However it turned out not to be a grave illness though Marie-Louise was becoming frail. Since Stanislas lived and worked some of the year in Paris, Zoé was left alone for long periods in Joigny with responsibility for her mother and for the family vineyards. Sophie thought that the solution was to sell the family home and set up house in Paris but she recognised that this was an impossible move for her sister, who had neither the health nor the capacity to survive such an upheaval. Sophie urged Stanislas to relieve Zoé from time to time and to bring her to Paris for some weeks every year. Sophie herself promised to visit Joigny on her way back from Paris and to offer what help she could to the family. She consoled Stanislas by telling him that the new railway system would enable them to come to see her in Paris, once a month if necessary. She also ensured that the Society bought wine from Zoé annually.[60] Sensing that Zoé needed some work outside the home Sophie suggested that she find some work with the poor children in Joigny. Some years later, in 1837, the Sisters of Charity of Tours opened a school in the town and Sophie urged Zoé to help in the classes there.[61]

From the ending of the general council in November 1833 until January 1835 Sophie had had a gruelling schedule. By Christmas 1834 she was exhausted and from January to March 1835 she was seriously ill in Lyon. It was the effect of fatigue from travelling, from pressure of correspondence, from the burden of leadership of a fast growing enterprise and from her own inner struggles to come to terms with her life's task. It was an impossible task, trying to govern the Society and travel at the same time. A resolution was desperately needed, for as her letters to America showed, an edge had come into her voice and style. In 1823 she had collapsed in exhaustion in Grenoble. Then Joseph Varin had warned her that the structures of government were insufficient for the rapidly growing Society. That advice was even more pertinent in 1835. Her illness in Lyon was a gift to her and gave her time to work out the implementation of a strategy she had carefully thought out over a period of several months. She was convinced it could resolve the problem of governing the Society.

– 12 –

KEEPING HER NERVE, 1834–1835

fter the general council of 1833, Sophie began to seriously consider her position and role in the Society of the Sacred Heart, given its growth and increasing complexity. From a small beginning in 1800, through several crises which threatened to destroy her leadership, Sophie had steered the Society to a position of relative stability. It had a buoyant energy, was attracting young women and fulfilling some needs of education in society generally. The future seemed secure. The articulation and then approval of the constitutions gave further stability to the Society. All these factors caused Sophie to think about her role in the future development of the Society. She thought seriously about resigning as superior general. The task itself was daunting and Sophie continued to be burdened by inner struggles and poor health. She wrote to Joseph-Marie Favre and asked him how she could continue to lead the Society, considering her physical and moral state. Early in 1834 he replied, genuinely saddened to see Sophie so lost and uncertain:

> I am troubled and greatly saddened to see you still the unfortunate slave of anxiety, mistrust and fear. All these weaken your soul, undermine your courage, harden your heart and take up your time needlessly and painfully with your *poor* self. This ruins everything, distracts you from your essential duties, deprives you of the ability to communicate and of that gentleness of approach which wins people. It will undermine health both of mind and body, with no benefit to God, to yourself or to your good neighbour . . .
>
> In the name of our kind and loving Saviour, cast all your fears, all your anxieties into his Heart which burns with love for you.[1]

He repeated his advice to Sophie, not to go over her confessions, not to doubt God's forgiveness and love. Her scruples continued to cripple her profoundly and she lived in fear, convinced that she could not be forgiven by God. What Favre called her stubborn fear led her to turn on herself and go over all her actions endlessly, 'like a door on a hinge'. He told her this was no way to live, it was no compliment to God and no help to her in her life's task.

While Favre recognised he was in no position to give Sophie advice on how to actually govern the Society, he did offer three ways to help her cope with her task. He urged her to maintain a rhythm of prayer and reflection as a way of nourishing her inner world and keeping balance in all the activity she had as a matter of course. He asked her to try and delegate as much as she could: 'act as a *general*, not as a *foot soldier*'. Her role was to maintain the vision of the Society of the Sacred Heart and leave the details of administration to others. Finally he asked Sophie to place less importance on penance and listen more to the advice of those who cared for her. There was more than enough penance in the role she had and in the discipline of living a deep inner life of prayer and reflection, and he stressed once more the importance of eating properly.

Clearly Sophie's inner difficulties had not eased. She was dogged by self-doubt and by fear of God. Jansenism had entered deep into her being and she seemed unable to shift her consciousness into a new place of peace and self-acceptance, in the light of God's love, revealed in the Heart of Christ. The charism of the Society of the Sacred Heart was a profound challenge for Sophie Barat. She was forced to strain after inner freedom from a place of deep anxiety. Six months later Favre wrote again to Sophie, replying to one of her letters which indicated that not only was she no better in spirit but that she thought she should resign from the office of superior general. She asked him three questions: Were her confessions valid? Was she in the place in life planned for her by God? What kind of life should she lead as superior general?

Favre replied, as he so often done before, that her confessions were valid and that she must not be trapped by going over them. He asked her to trust him, promising Sophie that he would not deceive her. He had no doubt that she was in the place God wanted her to be in:

> Stay where you are and discharge your role to the best of your ability. Cast aside as genuine illusions all thoughts of abandoning this responsibility which God has entrusted to you, for this would be to follow a path of selfishness. Look back no longer lest you risk, like Lot's wife, being turned into a pillar of salt.[2]

He answered the third question by repeating the advice he had given in January, to maintain a rhythm of prayer, to look after her health and delegate as much as she could to avoid her continual overwork. He knew that Sophie thought that she ought to be a model in every way for the Society. In that context she wanted to live a life of extraordinary prayer, practise extraordinary penance and sustain an extraordinary schedule. Favre told her it was folly in the extreme, 'truly an illusion'. He told her it was impossible, she simply could not do this and deep down Sophie knew this. She had tried to be the model leader, as she saw it, from the early days in Poitiers and failed. She retained the ideal but could never realise it. The wish to be perfect led her to deny her frailty. Favre advised Sophie to live common life in the Society and keep to the ordinary ways and means for becoming holy. He challenged her to be humble enough to allow herself to let go of her illusions and live in the reality of her situation, to be led by God, as a little child, into this simple and ordinary path to holiness.

A few months later he invited Sophie again to reach into the freedom she could enjoy, if only she could learn to trust God and accept herself:

> I invite you, I beg you to set out on the path of love, obedience, trust and holy liberty . . . No more worries, no more deliberate turning back. Only joy, trust, love and courage in our good and loving Jesus who for so long has been asking for your heart. He only awaits the moment when you will quite gently, simply and lovingly, like a little child, abandon yourself to his sacred and loving care, with total, childlike trust, so that He can unlock and bestow upon you the indescribable treasures of his Heart which burns with love for you.[3]

This was the greatest challenge Sophie had faced in her life. She had to try to undo her image of God, of herself and of her imagined way of presenting herself to her colleagues and to the wider world in general. Could she be as vulnerable as that in life, and so mirror the spirituality of the Heart of Christ? Sophie and her colleagues had created the Society of the Sacred Heart. It had extended within France and beyond its frontiers, and there was every sign that it would reach the ends of the earth. The goals of the Society contained a great and large vision which had yet to be explored. Now Sophie was being asked to fill that vision and fill the spaces where the Society had rooted with a spiritual awareness of what the glory of the Heart of Christ might mean, for the religious and for those touched in any way by the work of the Society of the Sacred Heart.

Sophie's Jansenistic upbringing, as well as the influence of Louis Barat's formation, made such an inner journey an undoing of her being. It was frightening and she resisted it instinctively. Going towards the joy of liberation and inner peace was something she yearned to do, but even that was tainted by Jansenism and the fear of enjoyment. Here the split in Sophie's inner life was most painfully revealed. She had many friends whom she greatly loved and she wrote tenderly to them. In her letters and conferences, in her formation of the novices and of the professed, she had described the love of the Heart of Christ, graphically and attractively. But when it was a question of bringing that depth of love and affection into her own prayer life, Sophie was overwhelmed. Was God like that, for her? Could she let into her own being, into her own life, the love she talked about so eloquently?

Favre said yes and urged her to believe it and live in its light. In November 1834 he repeated his advice to Sophie and urged her to maintain a balance between her prayer life and her activity. In this way she would have the energy and depth required for her life's task. This was key and it was rooted in her daily life, possible to do, difficult to achieve but it was the ground of her own holiness and that of her members:

> In the normal course of Providence God only creates saints by saints. So you must become holy in order to make others holy. We can only give out of our abundance, so that we do not empty ourselves completely. . . . A mother who neglects her own nourishment kills herself and kills her children.[4]

In 1833 Louise de Limminghe had been elected Sophie's admonatrix, and in this capacity she had the duty to advise Sophie with regard to affairs in the Society. Since both of them were receiving spiritual direction from Favre, he had suggested that Louise de Limminghe become Sophie's spiritual director also. Both roles, of adviser in the affairs of the Society and spiritual director, were impossible to sustain, and soon the relationship between the two women became strained. Sophie refused to listen to Louise de Limminghe and Favre warned her that she was too intense with Sophie:

> . . . restrict yourself purely and simply to your role of adviser (admonatrix) as it is laid out, explained and regulated by your constitutions. Do not worry too much about minor indiscretions, too much penance, fears or anxieties. Sooner or later they will make her realise that an unguided life is like a ship without a pilot, exposed to all the winds and gales of passion, to all the hidden rocks of human fickleness, selfishness and indecision . . . Your guidance of her has been of no help either to her or to you . . . You have spent too much energy, enthusiasm, ardour and anxiety trying to get her to submit. She has not yet felt the need for dependence and obedience in such a way that she can profit from them and accept your advice and observations with good grace.[5]

By 1834 Louise de Limminghe had begun to consider leaving the Society of the Sacred Heart and entering a contemplative order. She thought then that the Society would founder unless it was radically reformed and she asked Favre for his advice. He insisted that her destiny was to stay and support Sophie Barat, that her relationship with Sophie was part of her way to God. However, he suggested that if the Society did fail (which he doubted very much) then she could choose where to go in the light of that reality.[6] By her love and care for Sophie:

> You will expand the shrivelled heart of your beloved superior, you will advance the glory of the Sacred Heart and the prosperity of your new-born Society . . .

> I wish, I desire with all my heart to see this soul act in complete trust and simplicity and in particular, with complete freedom in the way of obedience, despite her futile fears, her endless doubts and her confused views. Such open, courageous and obedient behaviour would rid her of this shroud of scruples which almost completely overcome her, divert her from her most important tasks and distance her from the love of the Sacred Heart and from religious perfection . . .[7]

Favre insisted that the best way to help Sophie was to encourage her to find a balance between her work and her prayer, because he knew that the task she faced as superior general was immense. No wonder she questioned whether she had the gifts and the qualities necessary to lead the Society at this time. If she felt fear and distrust of God in her inner world, she also faced the future of the Society apprehensively, especially after the council of 1833. By 1836, Sophie Barat was governing thirty-eight houses of the Society, not only in France but in America, Italy, Switzerland and Belgium. She was learning painfully that it was not possible to govern the houses personally, to visit them regularly, or remain in contact with every situation by ongoing correspondence. While she would have preferred to govern in this way, her constant bouts of ill health, her endless exhaustion, as well her repeated falls, indicated that she could not continue to use the model she had created.

New models of government were needed, but since the Society had secured a definitive approbation of the 1815 constitutions in 1826, Sophie had to abide by the structures of government contained in the text. She had no authority to change them unless a general council of the Society so wished and had the approval of the church authorities in Rome. Sophie came to the conclusion that she would have to find ways of radically changing the system of government in the Society which was proving inadequate to the reality of the Society's expansion. She thought she could do this by adopting further elements of the Jesuit form of government. Consequently, she and Louise de Limminghe wrote to Jean Rozaven asking his opinion on the governing structures of the Jesuits and the possibility of adapting them to the Society of the Sacred Heart. Rozaven was only too ready not just to advise but to actively direct Sophie's thoughts in the matter of effective governance.

However, Rozaven agreed to advise Sophie only on the condition that his role remained confidential and that his views were never cited in public. Sophie accepted this condition and Rozaven sent her suggestions on the future structures of government of the Society for the Sacred Heart. These were based on the model of the Jesuits. Rozaven was convinced that the authority of the superior general of the Society of the Sacred Heart was weak because the powers given the assistants general were too great. He warned Sophie that in Rome at least Félicité Desmarquest was deferred to as the authority in the Society of the Sacred Heart. She had trained a good number of the novices, from 1822–35, she was well known and loved, and Rozaven thought she had a much higher profile in the Society than Sophie herself. He asked her ironically if there were two sources of power in the Society of the Sacred Heart, the official source (Sophie) and the unofficial one (Desmarquest and the other assistants general).[8]

Sophie was aware of what Rozaven was pointing out. The expansion of the Society, the task of governing it, Sophie's constant travelling, the state of her health, particularly since 1828, inevitably meant that Sophie could not retain direct contact with every element and each person in the Society. She recognised that gradually she had lost touch with the second generation of women who had joined the Society and that she had to find ways of exercising influence over them. The enthusiasm and the bond which had held and formed the first generation around Sophie and her early companions had to be passed on to the next, if the work of the Society was to continue and prosper. Sophie's predicament gave the assistants general of the Society a higher profile and greater influence than Sophie realised. Rozaven underlined what Sophie already knew: the Society needed a new structure of government. Most of all, the ascendance of Eugénie de Gramont in the rue de Varenne, to somewhat the same status and reputation of Félicité Desmarquest in Rome, forced Sophie to think through her position. In several parts of the Society, clusters of power and leadership were growing. Her role was to centre them, lead them as a body, and in her role as superior general, she was the focus for unity. The alternative was the development of each centre in separate independent entities. From the beginning Sophie had intuited that the Society of the Sacred Heart was to be a centralised body of women, present all over the world and united in the common project of the glory of the Heart of Christ.

Sophie went back to her original intuition of 1815 of having a centre, a mother house, in Paris where she would live and govern the Society. There she would establish the formation centre of the Society, the general noviciate and the centre for preparation for final profession. There the spirit of the Society would be imbibed and then spread throughout the world. From the moment a woman entered a community, she would be caught into that atmosphere. Everything and everyone would gravitate towards Paris and all would emanate from Paris, with the superior general, whoever she was, present at centre of the Society. Sophie had not lost sight of that original design, but it had been greatly modified by events, by Eugénie de Gramont and Archbishop de Quelen in Paris and by the rapid expansion of the Society and the consequent dispersal of members, to parts of Europe and America.

In 1835 Sophie seized an opportunity to achieve what had eluded her for years. In the light of this and of her own long-term plans, Sophie decided to reopen the Paris noviciate, but not in the rue de Varenne. After the July Revolution, Sophie had moved the Paris noviciate to Montet in Switzerland. However, by 1834, relative stability had returned to France and to the capital in particular. Parents had begun to complain at the distances their daughters had to travel if they wished to enter the Society of the Sacred Heart. This time Sophie wanted a definite break and distance from the Hôtel Biron and indeed from Eugénie de Gramont and Archbishop de Quelen. A possible solution appeared when the number of orphans in the rue de Varenne became too numerous and more accommodation was needed. Archbishop de Quelen offered his property at Conflans and Eugénie de Gramont took this offer up with enthusiasm. She wanted to move the orphans immediately, but Sophie hesitated since the archbishop made the offer on the condition that only the orphans be housed at Conflans with the general noviciate of the Society. He opposed the establishment of a boarding school.

Sophie refused this offer, despite the pleas of Eugénie de Gramont, since neither the noviciate nor the orphanage could survive economically without a boarding school. In any event, both Félicité Desmarquest and Catherine de Charbonnel refused point blank to consider having the noviciate at Conflans, as did Joseph Varin when he heard about the proposal.[9] Sophie was under the impression that if Archbishop de Quelen conceded the boarding school to the Society their resistance to the noviciate at Conflans would fade. This was not so because when Eugénie de Gramont persuaded Archbishop de Quelen to change his mind and permit a boarding school, they still resisted placing the noviciate in Conflans. The real source of friction was the presence of Archbishop de Quelen in the Petit-Hôtel in the rue de Varenne and Eugénie de Gramont's cultivation of the archbishop and his entourage. Sophie was caught between the factions and she had to take a decision herself in the end.[10] She agreed to rent the property from the archbishop and hoped to win over those who opposed placing the noviciate at Conflans. Such was the devastation to the building and property during the July Revolution that it was impossible to move immediately. Ironically, the Society paid for the repairs at Conflans, as well as the annual rent, despite the fact that Archbishop de Quelen had been using the Petit-Hôtel for several years, a permanent guest of the Society.[11]

Eugénie de Gramont had further plans for the accommodation of the archbishop and when Sophie left Paris in February 1834 Eugénie arranged further living quarters for him in the rue de Varenne. Until then Archbishop de Quelen used the Petit-Hôtel during the day for business purposes only. Now, in addition to the Petit-Hôtel, Eugénie de Gramont furnished private rooms for Archbishop de Quelen within the Hôtel Biron itself. Both Félicité Desmarquest and Joseph Varin wrote and told Sophie that she would have to intervene. Sophie was deeply upset and told Eugénie that they had written to her, concerned about the reputation of the Society in Paris:

> The reason is the apartment which you have had so quickly furnished for your friend [Archbishop de Quelen]! Indeed, if you recall what I confided to you about the indiscreet rumours, they will undoubtedly increase . . . particularly in this latest situation and we will be unable to contain it for long. See to it then that your friend knows this and that for a year more or less he does not use the apartment, and certainly never spends the night there. . . . He will certainly guess the reason for my giving you this suggestion. No one respects him more than I do, and if I may be permitted to say, no one likes him better and wants to support him more . . . So, in preparing the apartment for him, let it be plain and let it not appear that it is his, at least not his bedroom, though there will be nothing to prevent him going there from time to time, to spend a day there.
> I will not dwell on the reasons for these reservations, you will guess them by recalling the remark I made to you before my departure. And I did not tell you all that I knew![12]

Sophie knew that Eugénie de Gramont paid little attention to her opinions when it concerned the archbishop of Paris. Eugénie considered that the Hôtel Biron, the goods and personnel of the Society were at the service of the archbishop. That priority transcended all other considerations, including the interests of the Society of the Sacred Heart and wishes of Sophie Barat. During the years of Sophie's absences or during her long illnesses, Eugénie's power and influence had increased and her position had become unassailable. The residence of Archbishop de Quelen in the rue de Varenne after the July Revolution identified the Society of the Sacred Heart with those in church and society who refused to recognise Louis Philippe as the legitimate king of France. Obstinate adherence to Charles X, to the Bourbons, to the duc de Bordeaux, and his refusal to compromise were the hallmarks of Archbishop de Quelen's stance in Paris. He still declined to appear at the court of the king, despite appeals from the pope and from those who argued for compromise. In the rue de Varenne, at the heart of the Faubourg Saint-Germain, surrounded by clerics who shared his views, Archbishop de Quelen was welcomed as a martyr and prophet, especially by Eugénie de Gramont. All sustained the fiction that nothing had changed since the July days of 1830.

By 1833 Sophie had recognised how the Society was being compromised by the archbishop's presence in the rue de Varenne. Her own leadership role was being eroded and Sophie was shrewd enough not to test the limits then. Indeed if Jean Rozaven had hinted that Félicité Desmarquest was exercising the power of a superior general in Rome, that may have seemed insignificant to Sophie when faced with the situation at the rue de Varenne. Despite Eugénie's protestations of affection, an incident occurred in 1834 which gave Sophie a clear indication as to where she stood, not only as superior general but also in relation to Eugénie de Gramont. In November that year Eugénie de Gramont had asked the Jesuits for a confessor, to help out the chaplain at the rue de Varenne, Fr Jammes.[13] The Provincial, François Renault, had named Louis Barat. But Eugénie de Gramont refused this appointment and Renault said he had no one else. Whatever the reason for Eugénie's refusal, Sophie was hurt at this action and told Eugénie that she could not understand why Louis was not acceptable, and indeed neither could the Jesuits in Paris. Other schools in Paris were satisfied with her brother:

> he was accepted at Les Oiseaux, at St Thomas etc., and there was astonishment at our refusal of him . . . In the position that you find yourself it would have been prudent to retain this old priest as spiritual director to about twenty of the best behaved and most easily led pupils.[14]

Already there were rumours about the school chaplain, Fr Jammes, which worried Sophie. He was far too familiar with the pupils and had easy access to the classes in the school as well as the dining room. He certainly would not have wanted an austere Jesuit, like Louis Barat, as a colleague. The contrast between the two would have been too marked. When Eugénie refused to have him, then Sophie insisted that when Jammes heard the confessions of the girls the door into the confessional remain open, that the chaplain should not be in the school late at night and that he should dine with the archbishop and not in the school dining room.[15] By refusing to have Louis Barat as confessor at the rue de Varenne

Eugénie had given tacit approval to the behaviour of her chaplain in the school. Indeed many clerics, who came to see Archbishop de Quelen, visited the school as well and often took part in school recreations.[16]

Sophie's advisers and friends still opposed moving the noviciate to Conflans. Not only were Félicité Desmarquest and Catherine de Charbonnel against it but Joseph Varin refused to consider the noviciate there, at any time.[17] Sophie knew that Varin was indiscreet about affairs of the Society and so knew the Jesuits in Paris were aware of the possible move of the noviciate to Conflans. They were highly critical of the plan, as were some members of the general public. Sophie received an anonymous letter, and sent Eugénie de Gramont a section of it:

> I have heard that you might be moving your noviceship to Conflans. I could not help regarding this step as unwise and I disapprove of it. I did not recognise your prudence in this move. How can you think of taking over this property in these difficult times? Everywhere there is a great deal of talk already about your wealth and vanity, real or supposed. The fact that in the view of the public Conflans is the archbishop's property, that it is situated in such an unfavourable district, adjacent to a much worse quarter, will make it a target for open malevolence. Your good friend [Archbishop de Quelen] has not given you proof of genuine friendship by unloading this burden on to your shoulders. It is a deadly gift . . .[18]

This was advice from a friend, but Sophie had accepted Archbishop de Quelen's clever offer already; the Society paid the costs of repairs and by March 1835 the boarding school and the orphanage opened in Conflans. The problem of where to place the noviciate had not yet been solved and the presence of the archbishop and his entourage, not only in the Petit-Hôtel but now in the actual Hôtel Biron, made it impossible for Sophie ever to consider reopening the noviciate in the rue de Varenne. In addition to tensions over Conflans, and over Archbishop de Quelen's residence in the Hôtel Biron, Eugénie de Gramont and Félicité Desmarquest themselves had regular disagreements over their respective rights as assistants general. Sophie settled them in favour of Desmarquest, who was the first assistant general, and she reproved Eugénie for over-stepping her limits. Yet such skirmishes signalled that Eugénie did not yield any of her power to another in the Society, not even to Sophie Barat. When Sophie heard that on the feast of the Good Shepherd, in April 1834, the entire community waited until 11 p.m. to convey good wishes to Archbishop de Quelen, she asked Eugénie to get sense. The Faubourg Saint-Germain was a hotbed of gossip and the activities at the rue de Varenne were a source of curiosity, to say the least.[19] A few months later Sophie had to reprimand Eugénie again, for it was clear that the life of the community and the school revolved around the timetable of Archbishop de Quelen:

> . . . let me warn you about something which creates a bad effect. It is the trouble and disturbance which Archbishop de Quelen's Mass causes in the boarding school. I can tell you without exaggeration that the pupils, the parents and many of the community do not like this. I have already mentioned this to you in the past! Undoubtedly you have had your reasons for acting otherwise. But since there are

so many pupils in the boarding school now and because the archbishop's timetable is unpredictable, it is really a waste of time for these children, for whom one Mass is quite sufficient.[20]

This situation had not developed overnight. From 1825 the house journal indicates increasing, frequent contacts with the archbishop and his entourage. In the beginning, the community, including Sophie Barat, had welcomed the gradual identification of the archbishop of Paris with the rue de Varenne. Over the years members of the community, including Sophie Barat, Eugénie de Gramont, Félicité Desmarquest and Catherine de Charbonnel, and some pupils in the school had spent time at Conflans, the country residence of the archbishop. When Sophie was ill Archbishop de Quelen offered her the use of Conflans to recuperate. The archbishop held many of his official functions in the rue de Varenne. Bishops and priests were ordained in the chapel of the rue de Varenne and meetings of bishops were convened in the Petit-Hôtel. Ferdinand Donnet recalled:

> In May 1833 I was consecrated in Paris as bishop of Rosa and coadjutor of Nancy by Mgr Forbin-Jeanson, in the chapel in the rue de Varenne. . . . I received the pallium as archbishop of Bordeaux, from the hands of Mgr de Quelen, delegated to do so by Gregory XVI. Mothers Barat and de Gramont occupied the first benches in the chapel.[21]

To all intents and purposes Archbishop de Quelen used the Petit-Hôtel regularly for business meetings in Paris. The archbishop administered first communions and confirmations in the school and distributed the annual prizes to the students. Occasionally, baptisms and often marriages were celebrated in the chapel of the rue de Varenne, officiated by Archbishop de Quelen himself.[22] He frequently officiated over the religious ceremonies of the Society, for entry, first and final profession. He sometimes heard the confessions of the community, gave spiritual conferences and presided over community recreations. When his palace in Paris and his private residence at Conflans were sacked, Archbishop de Quelen came to the rue de Varenne to give an account of what had happened to the assembled community and school. This increasingly familiar relationship between the archbishop and the Society of the Sacred Heart[23] was facilitated by Sophie's frequent absences from Paris. Sophie left Paris on the 10 August 1830, in the wake of the July Revolution, and only returned on 17 October 1831. In her absence Archbishop de Quelen had virtually taken up residence in the Petit-Hôtel, despite Sophie's misgivings expressed to Eugénie de Gramont. These were confirmed the evening of her return to the rue de Varenne, her base as superior general. Despite the fact that she had been away so long, the community did not greet her that evening. Archbishop de Quelen was presiding over community recreation.[24]

In any event, Sophie did not challenge the situation and indeed left Paris three weeks later, on 10 November 1831, not to return until 12 September 1833. Even then she did not stay long in Paris, but chose to visit houses in the north first, and then after a further short stay in Paris left for Bordeaux, Lyon and Chambéry, only returning to Paris on 7 May 1834. During these long absences the hold of the archbishop of Paris over the school and community was consolidated and Sophie was powerless to effect any change. She could only exhort Eugénie and plead with her, but in reality this had no consequence. She was both trapped and constrained by the presence of Archbishop de Quelen not just in the Petit-Hôtel but within the Hôtel Biron itself, in the midst of the school.[25]

By December 1834 Sophie realised that the noviciate could not be situated in Conflans nor in the rue de Varenne. She had to take an initiative and she knew this would polarise herself and Eugénie de Gramont more acutely. Shadows of the past loomed, when Saint-Estève, Anne Baudemont and Eugénie de Gramont had edged Sophie Barat out of Amiens. Archbishop de Quelen had taken Saint-Estève's place and Eugénie's first concern was his comfort, his concerns and his wishes. Sophie Barat was always second, in every regard. Sophie could not allow herself to acknowledge this situation consciously, so much was it bound up with her affection for Eugénie de Gramont, and with the development of the Society of the Sacred Heart in Paris. Despite all the time and energy Sophie had given Eugénie, over many years, their friendship could not reach a level of mutual trust. Yet Sophie realised that she had to manage the situation in Paris and not challenge it so starkly that a confrontation would ensue between the archbishop and herself. She had a dream in December 1834 which she hoped had no basis in reality. Perhaps it was a nightmare. It certainly disturbed her and she told Eugénie de Gramont that during the night she had:

> a type of revelation which increases my uncertainties although I rarely rely on such sources of knowledge, particularly if they emanate from my own imagination . . .[26]

No wonder then that throughout 1834 Sophie doubted her capacity to be superior general and that she had asked Favre if she was in the right place. He responded to her fears by encouraging her to trust in the love of God for her. He knew about her anxieties and uncertainties and tried to bring her to a place where she could live and act, at peace within herself:

> How can you still give in to these fears, to these anxieties, to such remorse and doubts, to these worries which so displease the Heart of Jesus! No, all these useless misgivings come from the devil who seeks to strangle our hearts and close them to love and trust; or else, they come from our arrogance which attempts to rely on our own good works . . . In the name of and for love of Jesus, open your heart, for so long crushed, shrivelled, vanquished and discouraged, to love and to trust. May neither past failures, nor present imperfections, nor the abuse of graces bring you the least distrust. [27]

Over the winter and spring of 1834–35 Sophie reached a solution with regard to the accommodation for the Paris noviciate. She spent the winter in Lyon, and in January became seriously ill with exhaustion and contracted a fever. She was unable to work for three months and during the period she had time to ponder and reach some conclusions for the future. As had happened before in Sophie's life, a prolonged period of poor health was followed by a key decision. By May she had recovered her energy and she went to Montet. There she met her old friend, the marquis de Nicolay, who agreed to rent his house on the rue Monsieur to the Society, on a short-term basis, until the Society could find a permanent home for the noviciate. The rue Monsieur was only a short distance from the rue de Varenne, but far enough away to make a break with the Hôtel Biron. Sophie decided to place not only the general noviciate of the Society there, but also the general administration of the Society and centre for final commitment. At one stroke, Sophie removed from the rue de Varenne not only the formation centre of the Society but also her own residence. The new house on the rue Monsieur would take precedence over the rue de Varenne, would be as she stressed twice that year in her formal letters, the centre of the Society, the mother house. In June 1835 she wrote to the Society:

> This little Society still in its infancy has already made considerable progress . . . but circumstances have created an obstacle to the fulfilment of the plans which as it were must complete our institute . . . To achieve this we have decided to have our own residence, which will be the *mother house* or headquarters of the Society. All business will converge there and all plans will emanate from there. The general noviciate, the juniorate and the tertianship year for all the French houses will be placed there, as far at this is possible. There also will be the general treasury, the secretariat and the archives of the Society. It will be our usual residence as well as that of the assistants general who will not travel around the houses anymore. In time we will try to ensure that as far as possible two of the assistants general are always there, with the admonatrix and a member of the general council . . . to help us in our work and form our regular council.[28]

None of the provisions in Sophie's letter were new since they were contained within the 1815 constitutions. Yet the implications of Sophie's decision were far-reaching. By setting up house outside the rue de Varenne, and taking the noviciate with her, Sophie signalled to Eugénie de Gramont that another path was being taken. By declaring her intention of implementing the regulations for assistants general, also laid down in 1815 (that they should reside in the mother house), Sophie signalled her intention to consolidate her authority over the Society. A month later she wrote a further letter, outlining her vision for the rue Monsieur:

> . . . this house [will be] the entire centre of the Society and consequently the source from which the true spirit should spring forth and spread, must inspire each and every member who makes up this great family.[29]

In January 1835 Sophie wrote a circular letter to the Society and encouraged the membership to live up to the high ideals they had embraced when they had entered religious life.[30] She noted three failings which pervaded communities, affected the quality of life the members were committed to and influenced the atmosphere in the houses. Some criticised where they were living and the work they were asked to do; others complained of those in leadership; many indulged in gossiping within the communities, forming small groups which became narrow and cynical, destroying the central thrust and purpose of living together. These were serious, basic issues and it was not the first time Sophie had pointed them out. She insisted they be faced and dealt with, by each individual looking at her own attitudes. No doubt she had Paris in her mind when she wrote such letters, for she knew about the complaints and the gossip and how both had spread abroad in other communities, damaging her own leadership. At the end of the letter she asked everyone to pray for a special intention that needed a great deal of wisdom and which concerned the well-being of the Society in general.

Sophie had come to the conclusion that even before the move to the rue Monsieur could take place, a new director of novices was needed. She had taken to heart Rozaven's comment that she had lost touch with the new generation in the Society. By appointing a new mistress of novices she was placing her stamp firmly on the formation of young women in the Society. She also hoped this might lessen the tensions between Desmarquest and Eugénie de Gramont. Both had dual roles, one as first assistant general and mistress of novices; the other as third assistant general and headmistress of the rue de Varenne. Again, Rozaven had pointed out to her that two powerful roles held by the same person were damaging to good government and indeed to Sophie's authority in the Society. Divesting Eugénie de Gramont was a step Sophie could not then contemplate. But that of finding a new mistress of novices could be implemented immediately and without too much offence. Sophie decided that Félicité Desmarquest would be superior of the new noviciate houses and that Eulalie de Bouchaud, then at Montet, would replace her as mistress of novices. Both would live in the rue de Varenne until alternative accommodation was found in Paris. Eulalie de Bouchaud (1802–44) certainly represented the second generation of women in the Society. She had entered at Lyon, with her sisters Emma (1779–1863) and Elisa (1804–81). Both Eulalie and Elisa travelled to Paris for their noviceship and finished their formation in Montet, where Eulalie made her final commitment in December 1833. Even then Sophie had remarked to Marie Prevost that Eulalie could succeed Félicité Desmarquest, that she was gifted in the area of spiritual guidance. After a year in Montet, working with Henriette Coppens, Sophie asked Eulalie de Bouchaud to come to Paris.

In December 1834 Eugénie de Gramont told the community at the rue de Varenne that Eulalie de Bouchaud had been appointed assistant superior of the community and would replace Desmarquest as mistress of novices.[31] This was a daunting task for such a recently professed member of the Society. At thirty-two she was considered quite young for the position in the Society, as well as the fact that her period of formation, after the noviciate, had been shortened from five years to three. Sophie expected Eulalie to keep her fully informed of all that was happening in the noviciate, especially when she was away from Paris. She knew that the task of replacing Félicité Desmarquest, who had been in that position since 1822 was indeed daunting and she wrote letters of encouragement:

You are pushing mistrust and timidity too far. I pray every day to our good Lord to grant you the courage to overcome this. In your position it is important that the novices are not aware that you are afraid of them and that you find relating to them difficult. Rest assured that you are working for the glory of the Sacred Heart and not out of pride . . . You will let me know in a few weeks time what progress you have made with regard to this holy resolution.[32]

Louise de Limminghe told Rozaven of Sophie's plans for the mother house and centre of formation in Paris. He saw them as only a first step in the process of establishing a sound, centralised administration in the Society of the Sacred Heart.[33] Sophie had implemented what was already in the 1815 constitutions but Rozaven thought that the permanent council of twelve members of the Society, established by the 1815 constitutions and approved of in 1827, was a moribund form of government. The Society, and Sophie Barat, needed further structures to consolidate its growth. Rozaven was convinced that the Jesuit model would suit best, especially in establishing the powers of the assistants general. He spoke of his own experience as an assistant general, with the power to advise and help, but not to make any decisions. Even when visiting houses of the order, a Jesuit assistant general had no power to change anything locally unless authorised specifically by the general of the Jesuits. He suggested that to strengthen the links between the local communities and herself, Sophie should plan towards having provincials, that is, leaders of areas in the Society who would be appointed by her and accountable to her directly. This, too, would curtail the power of the assistants general.

Rozaven invited Sophie to travel to Rome and discuss the structure of the Society with him:

> You should bring with you two or three of the people you trust most and who are best placed to help you with their advice. Choose them in view of the common good, with no concession to human respect, whether or not they are assistants generals or councillors. With the advice you will get here you will draft the relevant changes to be made [to the constitutions] and have them approved by the pope. Then on your return to France you will convene an extraordinary general council, without waiting until 1840. It will not be a council composed of only twelve members, but of delegates from all your houses, as far as this will be possible, and have the changes made in Rome adopted. This matter is important, believe me and requires the least possible delay. Only you can achieve this. . . . After your death a solution would be more difficult and perhaps impossible, because the Society will not have the same confidence in your successor; indeed it is to be feared that dissension will arise and certain parties would bring about the ruin of the good work you struggle to achieve.[34]

From 1835 onwards Sophie planned to centralise the Society and her own position by adopting the Jesuit model of government. Both Louise de Limminghe and Rozaven were eager to help her and indeed Rozaven awaited her return to Rome with some impatience. Louise de Limminghe was pleased and in her letters to Favre she spoke of her hopes that Sophie would grasp the nettle of reform and take decisive action. However, before Sophie could go any further in this process she needed to consolidate her position in the rue Monsieur and ensure that the noviciate had been well established in its new setting. The outward formalities of good relations between Sophie and Archbishop de Quelen were observed when the new noviciate opened on 22 July 1835. That day he paid a formal visit to the rue Monsieur and on the surface everything was pleasant and serene.[35] In fact Sophie's decision to install the noviciate and the mother house in the rue Monsieur facilitated his freedom of action in the rue de Varenne. In the future, Sophie had to announce her visits to the rue de Varenne some days in advance, and on the day she arrived the archbishop made sure he was not on the property.[36]

The most important task in the early weeks of the new foundation was to train the new members in the spirit of the Society. This was a time to retell the myths, the early stories of the foundation of the Society. When Sophie was asked about the early days she did not speak about Léonor de Tournély. She left that to Joseph Varin who visited the noviciate regularly and told them his stories and how the Society had evolved during and after the Revolution. Instead Sophie chose to tell the story of Suzanne Geoffroy, of the prophecies of Fr Nectoux about the Society of the Sacred Heart. This was a conscious choice, whereby Sophie placed the focus on herself and on the prophecies of the child, still playing with her dolls in 1787 and who was destined to bring the Society of the Sacred Heart to France. She recalled the early days in Amiens, Grenoble and Poitiers. Through this story-telling Sophie was consolidating her role and position, placing herself firmly at the centre of the Society's history, using herself as the point of reference. This is what she was best at, governing at the personal level, winning people by her charm and through that strengthening her hold on the future membership.[37]

But Sophie could only do this for the next generation of women in the Society by being present in Paris and she stayed as long as she could in the rue Monsieur. However, in April 1836 Sophie could no longer postpone visits to some of the houses in France, Savoy and Switzerland, and then travelling to Rome for her long-awaited discussion with Jean Rozaven concerning the government structures of the Society. This plan fitted in with the needs of the Society in Rome. Catherine de Charbonnel had been there since December 1834, and during her stay at the Trinité des Monts she managed to win the admiration of Armande de Causans, who was 'in no way inclined to exaggerate in her favour'.[38] By this time the situation in Sainte Rufine needed urgent attention for the Marquise Androsilla had spent all her resources and had become somewhat critical of the Society. Moreover, it was clear to Catherine de Charbonnel that Sainte Rufine was too small for both a noviciate and a poor school and she urged Sophie to come to Rome and see about founding a third house in the city.[39]

− 13 −

GATHERING CLOUDS, 1836–1838

Sophie spent from April 1836 to January 1837 in the south of France. Between April and July she visited the communities at La Ferrandière, Avignon, Perpignan, Marseilles, Aix-en-Provence and Annonay. From July until the end of December she travelled to Chambéry, Montet, Turin and Parma, finally arriving in Rome on 11 January 1837. While in Chambéry, in October 1836, Sophie asked Marie-Joseph Favre to direct her annual retreat. He was unable to do so and this was a disappointment to Sophie who wanted to consult her friend about a decision she had taken. She felt obliged to take an initiative and ask Archbishop de Quelen personally to consider what living in the rue de Varenne was doing to the reputation of the church and of the Society of the Sacred Heart.

Why Sophie did not confront Archbishop de Quelen personally before she left Paris is not known. It may have been too daunting a task or she may have feared Eugénie de Gramont's reaction. In any event she did not bring it up until she had been out of Paris for several months. On 14 October 1836, she addressed a formal letter to Archbishop de Quelen, from Chambéry:

> Having hesitated for a long time on whether or not to place before you the deep unease I experience, I decided finally to do so, convinced that it was an urgent duty of conscience.
>
> You are undoubtedly aware . . . of the shameful and derisive rumours concerning your residence, which are circulating everywhere and which confront and depress me wherever I go. The gutter press has carried these rumours as far as Rome. While the virtue of those concerned is not in question, people are surprised that such rumours can continue to be fuelled by failing to remove the cause of these vile

calumnies. I myself am spared neither reproaches nor threats. However, that is not what causes me most pain, Monsignor, but the sad certainty of the harm that this situation is doing to your own person . . . My conscience is alarmed also I must admit in seeing . . . the reputation, even the very existence of the Society so seriously compromised. I believe therefore that I have a duty before God to share my anxieties with you.[1]

Sophie received a prompt reply to her letter, on 23 October 1836.[2] Living in a world of fantasy, and a vain and arrogant man, Archbishop de Quelen could not grasp the reality of the situation which Sophie had outlined in her letter. He treated her letter with barely disguised contempt. He dusted off the gossip as quite beneath his consideration, as unworthy of him and, by implication, of Sophie Barat. He pretended that he had in fact already decided to leave the property of the rue de Varenne and return to his former lodgings at the convent of St Michel. Indeed Sophie's letter had arrived just as he was setting out for Conflans to give prizes to the orphans. Thanking her for her hospitality, praising her and the Society to the heights, Archbishop de Quelen pushed the irony further by quoting Sophie the gospel dictum: whoever receives a prophet will receive the reward of a prophet. He compared his life to that of the Old Testament patriarchs and to the apostles of Christ, and asked Sophie to pray for him. It was a disingenuous reply. Archbishop de Quelen had no intention of leaving the Petit-Hôtel or his quarters in the Hôtel Biron, provided by Eugénie de Gramont in 1834.

When she received this response, Sophie, who had hoped Archbishop de Quelen would show some consideration for the reputation of the Society, recognised that for the moment nothing could be changed. She told the archbishop that he was welcome to stay on the property as long as he wished, but repeated that her only concern was public opinion:

The purpose of my letter was solely to warn you of the public rumours about you. I was well aware that your wisdom and discretion would certainly suggest to you the means to banish them. Can we not then employ these means and maintain such contacts with the community at the rue de Varenne which prudence will allow in the difficult days we live in?[3]

She had little faith in the wisdom and prudence of the archbishop but she had to let matters in Paris rest as they were, unsatisfactory and increasingly drawing negative, public comment. The archbishop's defenders had poor arguments to offer:

Archbishop de Quelen knew that our public morals protect women more than men, and that a community of priests would be more seriously exposed to the insult, ill treatment and rage of protesters than a community of weak, retiring women.[4]

Archbishop de Quelen was well protected in the rue de Varenne. Indeed Sophie had to deal with Eugénie's fury when she heard of Sophie's first letter to the archbishop. She punished Sophie by not writing to her for some weeks and when she did finally write it was to remonstrate with her and defend the archbishop. She also complained to others, hinting that Sophie was devious and dishonest. Both Eugénie and Archbishop de Quelen thought that Sophie had been influenced by the views of Louis Barat and his friends and that they had urged her to write to the archbishop in November. Sophie strongly denied this and told Eugénie that she had felt for quite a long time that something had to be done; her letter was not written on sudden impulse or under pressure from others:

> I think that you know that it is neither in my style nor in my character to rush matters . . . I warned you of the necessity to take precautions but I was far from wishing to precipitate anything. So let us wait until I return and together we can weigh the pros and cons . . . [5]

Sophie spent Christmas in Turin and addressed a letter to the Society from there in December 1836.[6] In this letter Sophie spoke about the task of governing the Society and the increasing difficulty she had in maintaining personal contact with the membership, even with the superiors:

> Our travel and constant work . . . have deprived us of this pleasure. Indeed it would be a real joy to be able to correspond intimately with everyone and to show to each one, given us by the divine Heart [of Jesus] out of His goodness, the real interest and motherly care we have for them. But this is not possible since we cannot double our energy or increase the number of days. You will readily understand that this is truly impossible, seeing how the Society has extended.[7]

In this letter Sophie made it clear that her journey to Rome at the end of the month would be her last there and that she would return to Paris for good. She named Félicité Desmarquest to replace her in Paris in all matters pertaining to the government of the Society. This was a clear signal to Eugénie de Gramont and the communities in Paris that Sophie was only temporarily absent from her post and that in her absence Eugénie de Gramont held no official power. Sophie called the membership of the Society to greater kindness and goodness towards one another, and especially the way they spoke of and treated each other in public. The students were to receive the same care and affection. But this care, either within the communities or in the schools, were not to be soft or sentimental, but firm and truly loving in expression. Long after the students had left school they would remember how they were treated and they would talk about it, for good or ill. Sophie asked the superiors of the houses to ensure that the young religious received the help and guidance they needed for their work. To this end Sophie proposed to establish a training programme (*un Juvénat*) as soon as possible for the young teachers, where they could be formed properly and according to a common plan.[8]

Sophie arrived in Rome on 11 January 1837, accompanied by Louise de Limminghe, and their immediate task was to negotiate a purchase of property suitable for the noviciate. Sophie also learnt that the superior at Sainte Rufine had clashed with the Marquise Androsilla several times and communication had broken down. The benefactor of Sainte Rufine expected that she would be consulted at all times regarding all that concerned the house and the community.

The young superior, Adèle Cahier, could not consent to this and it was only a matter of time before the situation became critical. This happened when a novice, a protégée of the Marquise, became ill and was asked to leave the Society. Then another novice died and several became ill. Families in Rome began to talk and criticise the Society of the Sacred Heart. Adèle Cahier was blamed and considered too young and inexperienced for leadership. Sophie realised that Adèle Cahier would have to be replaced and in February 1835 she named Catherine de Charbonnel as superior in the hope that her experience would ease the situation for the community and mend public relations.[9]

While the Trinité was a foundation of the French government in Rome, made at the request of the pope, that of Sainte Rufine was a foundation within the city of Rome, with no connection at all with France. It was crucial that it make its way and be accepted by the Italian families in the city. Any antagonism or friction had to be resolved and so Adèle Cahier was sacrificed to that priority. De Charbonnel had the advantage of her experience as well as her office of assistant general and bursar general. Besides, she had been in Rome, from December 1828–July 1829, overseeing the foundation of the Trinité with Armande de Causans. On her return to Rome in 1834 Catherine de Charbonnel had found that the Society was being criticised in Rome. Many were puzzled by:

> religious women who describe themselves as cloistered though without grilles, who travel abroad without a chaplain, and who are superiors of houses before they are at least forty years of age etc, etc. . . . All this seems abnormal and almost suspect to them . . . Even the details of the way we live contrasts with some customs [here].[10]

Not only had Adèle Cahier come under scrutiny at Sainte Rufine, so also had the mistress of novices, Adèle Lehon (1806–94).[11] She too was considered far too young for her charge and complaints about her also had reached Sophie in Paris. However, Sophie could not remove both the superior and the mistress of novices at the same time. Instead she wrote to Adèle Lehon and warned her to act with prudence.[12] Catherine de Charbonnel's presence changed the situation in Sainte Rufine in any event and she told Sophie that Adèle Lehon had coped well in the circumstances. Within the year, 1835, Catherine de Charbonnel had stabilised the situation in Sainte Rufine and had begun to look around for a property for the noviceship. In the course of 1835 the Villa Lante and the Palais Lante, a vast property along the Tiber owned by the Borgèse family, appeared on the market. The family was ready to sell to the Society at an advantageous price if a quick agreement could be reached. Once Sophie had arrived in Rome in January 1837 the negotiations proceeded and by March that year the sale was concluded.[13] The Palais Lante had been empty for some time and had fallen into disuse so repairs were needed to the building. However the Villa Lante, a smaller building apart from the Palais, could be occupied immediately and Sophie moved there herself with the noviciate and Louise de Limminghe. Later Catherine de Charbonnel joined them there and Hypolite Lavauden (1792–1867) was appointed superior of Sainte Rufine.

Sophie was delighted with the new property along the Tiber. She wrote to Eugénie de Gramont:

> The view is enchanting. It overlooks all of Rome and is on the beautiful side of the city. We are very near St Peter's and we look down upon its fine cupola. The flower beds and pathways are lined with lemon and orange trees laden with fruit. . . . But since we found everything in a poor state of repair our initial expenses are considerable.[14]

From the moment of their arrival in Rome Sophie and Louise de Limminghe were absorbed in this new foundation at the Villa Lante, while keeping watch over Sainte Rufine too, a short distance away in the Trastevere. The Trinité where both stayed from January until May 1837 also presented urgent problems. In 1834 Sophie had thought of removing Armande de Causans from her role as superior of the house. While she had formed firm friendships with the church authorities and the nobility of Rome, she had also made some enemies, mainly because of her apparent laxity with regard to the observation of cloister. In addition, Sophie was aware that relations between the Trinité and Sainte Rufine were strained and that a change in leadership in both houses could ease the difficulties. However, in 1834 Rozaven advised Sophie to wait for a time before taking the step of replacing Armande de Causans.[15] There were enough problems to resolve in Sainte Rufine that year and too many sudden changes would give the Society an image of instability in Rome. When Sophie arrived in the Trinité in January 1837 she was still not in a position to consider the situation in the house and she let matters stand as they were for the time being, at least until the move to the Villa Lante was completed.

The polarisation between the houses in Rome was tragically demonstrated in the summer of 1837. Cholera had struck Italy that year and in early August Sophie wrote to Eugénie de Gramont with the news that it had appeared in Rome, in the height of summer. She described the processions in the city, the ceremonies in the churches, the presence of the pope in the streets of Rome, praying that the city would be spared devastation.[16] Some days later she wrote to Eugénie that while the cholera raged through Rome, the houses of the Society were safe. In fact she worried most about Sainte Rufine in the Trastevere as it was the first part of Rome to be infected by the plague.[17] In her solitude in the Villa Lante, overseeing the repairs at the Palais Lante, Sophie was sure that all was well and that the cholera had passed over all the houses of the Society. She was shocked to learn in early September that seven members of the community at the Trinité had died from cholera. She was not informed for a month and this caused her immense pain. She wrote to Eugénie:

> Now that I know the extent of our tragedy I need to talk to you about it. Can you believe that our mothers persisted in withholding from me, for a whole month, the news of how seven in the Trinité died cruel deaths by the destroying scourge of cholera? I was fully confident about the Trinité which seemed to be sheltered from the infection. While I feared for Sainte Rufine, which was surrounded by the dead

and dying, yet not one there as you know was affected while the other house was shaken to its foundations. I cannot describe to you how bitterly shocked I was. It nearly killed me . . . They believed that they were sparing me several shocks at so many deaths, but one like this was too much I think![18]

Who decided that Sophie Barat should not know about the deaths in the Trinité? And was it to protect Sophie who certainly would have insisted on visiting the dying? Sophie's health was always precarious, as she said to Eugénie de Gramont, at the height of the plague in Rome: 'you know that I catch every illness going'.[19] In any event, the isolation felt in the Trinité was deep, especially for Armande de Causans herself. Such a death toll in the community was profoundly depressing and the lack of moral support from Sophie at that time marked their relations then and in the future. Sophie admitted that her visit to the Trinité in early October was a difficult one. By then the death toll had reached nine:

> Yesterday I saw Mother de Causans and de Coriolis for the first time since our tragic events. What a painful meeting it was! Their house has been decimated. Nine at least have died.[20]

Some members of the Society in Rome, as well as Eugénie de Gramont and other members in France, did not hesitate to blame Louise de Limminghe for hiding the truth from Sophie. Sophie defended her and said she acted as she thought best. She knew that Sophie would not have remained in the Villa if she had known of the plight of the Trinité.[21] At this time strict quarantine was imposed in Rome, so that movements around the city were monitored. Yet given the already tense relations which existed between the Trinité and Sainte Rufine, the actions of Louise de Limminghe could only be viewed as a form of rejection and compounded the division between the houses.

Once it became permissible to move around Rome again, Sophie responded to the plight of the victims of the cholera and asked Sainte Rufine to open its doors to some of the abandoned children she met in the street. On the day she arrived at the Trinité, to visit the stricken community, Sophie met two children, begging at the front door:

> Why are you not at school? I asked.. 'Oh! Our teacher is dead . . . and the school is closed'. This was a grief, which in addition to the others, wounded me deeply at every moment. . . . I asked our mothers to reopen their classes and while awaiting more teachers, to use sisters in the meantime. Sister Adèle, whom you know, is capable of doing this. If these children were allowed to run in the streets for long our teachers would lose the fruits of their hard work of previous years. . . . The classes had already transformed these lazy and depraved children, and there is no country where the education of this class is more necessary. I only wish we could take on the responsibility for all the densely populated areas! It is impossible, but we must at least look after what we have![22]

When she went to Sainte Rufine Sophie found the same distressing situation of children left with neither father nor mother:

At Sainte Rufine, another equally distressing scene. My visit to the orphanage was heart rending. I was shown children who had lost both father and mother, left in the streets and picked up by other unfortunates who themselves were looking after families. All these children were huddled together, sharing the same straw mattresses. They were like a brood of chickens and in spite of myself I wept. I told our mothers to gather all those children who were abandoned; we will take them when we have our big house in order. But our mothers are in debt themselves for the poor people cannot pay any rent, the sole income of Sainte Rufine. No matter. They have been cared for; divine Providence will help us.[23]

While the Trinité and Sainte Rufine slowly recovered from the effects of the cholera, the problem of leadership had not been resolved at Sainte Rufine. Hypolite Lavauden found the task of superior beyond her capacity and she knew that Sophie was not satisfied with her leadership. Prior to her appointment as superior at Sainte Rufine she had been assistant in the house. Even then Sophie had written to reprimand her for the way she ran the house and cared for the community, especially the sisters:

As the Sisters here work so hard they should be given a meal in the morning with some soup or some milk on its own. It would be good to give milk three times a week. Make sure that it is not skimmed milk. It is better to add a *little* water if it is too thick in winter.[24]

Sophie was aware of the collusion between Lavauden and the mistress of novices, Adèle Lehon. Both had written discourteous letters to Sophie in September 1837 which she demanded an apology for immediately, though she recognised their fault was more out of ignorance and inexperience than malice.[25] Sophie recognised that the second generation in the Society needed further attention. The training of many women had been neglected, due to shortening their time of formation in view of pressing needs in the Society. She was reaping in Rome what she had lamented in France and heard echoes of from Philippine Duchesne.

The state of the Society in America continued to be a source of preoccupation for Sophie at this time. Her hopes that Eugénie Audé could return as assistant general were dashed for Eugénie had become seriously ill and pathologically dependent upon Sophie herself. She had been worn out on the missions and by the time she had returned to France her energy was spent. Her dependence on Sophie was an illness and a cry for help. It left Sophie with a great burden of worry. She searched in vain for someone to make a formal visit to Louisiana and Missouri and could not see anyone remotely ready for the task. She wrote to Eugénie Audé:

I am sending you . . . a little packet containing letters from America which I beg you to read carefully. . . . Send me back your comments and reflections on them. They greatly distress me. Every time I receive a letter from America it is as if a thorn pierces right through to my soul. This would mean nothing if I had a solution, but where am I to find a remedy? We need a strong leader for this country, one that could control all the houses under her charge. Write to them and encourage them. Unfortunately I have not done this![26]

Letters from Missouri and Louisiana bore grim news for Sophie. The situation of St Michael's was precarious and causing public scandal. Julie Bazire, who became the superior at St Michael's when La Fourche closed, had persuaded the Jesuits in the area to lend her money for her building projects. With the support of the chaplain, Fr Boué, she set about extending the property and when her plans were blocked by local interests in the area she entered into litigation. Newspapers in the region criticised the Society, 'the Jesuit Ladies of the Sacred Heart of Jesus' and described Bazire's 'Jesuitical gravity' as particularly offensive.[27] At the same time the Jesuits asked to be repaid the money they had lent Bazire and at this point Sophie heard of the problem. At such a distance Sophie did not know what to make of the situation and she wrote to Aloysia Hardey, (1809–86),[28] then assistant at St Michael's, to find out what was really going on. This opened a new correspondence with a new generation of women in America, with an American member of the Society.[29] On the strength of the views sent by Aloysia Hardey Sophie sent Bazire as superior to Grand Coteau and appointed Aloysia Hardey as superior in St Michael's. She told the Jesuits that they would have to wait for the Society's repayment of their loans, until she had time to amass the money in Europe.[30] Not only was Sophie alarmed by the situation at St Michael's but she had been distressed also by the tragic and sudden death of Xavier Murphy in Grand Coteau, after a short, fatal illness.[31] This was a serious blow for leadership of the communities in America had been weakened already by divisions in the houses. There was no one capable of defusing the tensions and taking the communities forward.

Acutely aware of the critical situation within the communities, and of the need to make a foundation in New York, Sophie proposed to Eugénie Audé that once the house in New York was established, Sophie herself would go to America for six months and consolidate the work of the Society there:

> It would be so convenient to have a house there [New York] for those arriving and departing. Later we could establish a foundation for Philadelphia. You do realise that I will only die content when we have a cradle in that part of America and I think that you must help me to set it up. . . . Then our work would be finished and others will do the rest. If we had a foundation in or near New York I would like to devote six months to going to visit it. It is hardly further away than going to Rome so what difficulties could there be? Fifty days travelling there and back and a stay of four months.[32]

She had good reason to want to go to America. She had heard several times from the community at St Louis how unhappy and divided the members were, how critical some were of Sophie Barat. Some resented her leadership, expressed in her several letters to the American houses, and most felt that she had abandoned them. Once they heard that Eugénie Audé would not return as assistant general then these feelings of being abandoned were only increased.[33] Eugénie Audé wanted to write a strong letter herself to St Louis and sent a draft of a letter to this effect for Sophie's approval. But Sophie found it too sharp and asked her not to deal with the situation that way. Severity from a distance would be disastrous and the written word was too bare and too strong on its own. If her own letters to America had caused some reactions, then Sophie knew letters of corrections would cause even further rancour.[34]

What Sophie was trying to understand was the particular difficulties of the houses in Missouri which had struggled for so long to survive.[35] She recognised that the houses in Lower Louisiana were more prosperous and secure. Yet Julie Bazire had placed the future of St Michael's in jeopardy. Such was Sophie's concern at this time that Elizabeth Galitzine offered to go as visitor to America, until a new assistant general was be named.[36] It was an offer which Sophie would accept. She wrote to Elizabeth Galitzine, then in Paris:

> Let us return to my cross: Louisiana. I no longer know what to do to reconcile the two superiors. I must confess that Mother Bazire is very imprudent. Then this behaviour of the Jesuits who allowed themselves to be led by her. . . . If I had not been protected by the Lord and had followed the advice of Fr de Vos, who is influenced by Mother Bazire, I would have quarrelled with Mr Jeanjean[37] and with the bishop as a consequence. And the letters from her community, written at her suggestion I am quite sure, are only to praise and vindicate her in my eyes. I know her excellent qualities and I hold no prejudice against her, but I cannot approve of her conduct regarding St Michael's, and the amount of money she owes the fathers [Jesuits] causes me great anxiety . . . what she owes them is out of proportion and totally beyond her means. . . . The demands of Mother Bazire and the Jesuits are unreasonable, and much less indeed would turn the Americans against the French, especially if they are told of this tactlessly.[38]

Sophie was referring not only to Bazire's handling of St Michael's but also to an offensive letter from the Jesuit, Fr de Vos, which she had received in the course of 1837. In it he warned Sophie that Aloysia Hardey and her assistant in the house, Aloysia l'Eveque, could separate from the Society, and then St Michael's would become an independent foundation. Sophie told Eugénie Audé that:

> a house composed totally of Americans could very well break away and that I must send a French superior there! But I have not got one, so I must leave all to Providence. Yet I cannot believe what they say. They both seem so attached to the Society. I refer to the two Aloysias. Tell me what you think as I need to be reassured as I do not believe what they tell me.[39]

For a time Sophie was suspicious and she gave some credence to de Vos. Yet even though Sophie knew about the American spirit of independence she could not believe that Aloysia Hardey would break from the Society. As the story about Bazire's extravagance emerged, and her financial loans to the Jesuits were exposed, Sophie realised that de Vos's letter about Aloysia Hardey was damaging and untrue.[40] Nevertheless, Aloysia Hardey had sensed Sophie's suspicions and only frequent letters of encouragement from her and from Eugénie Audé could clear those clouds of doubt.[41] Distrust between St Michael's and Grand Coteau continued and letters sent for Aloysia Hardey via Grand Coteau were sometimes opened there and their contents spread abroad. Aloysia Hardey complained about this, and she suspected that her letters were treated similarly in Paris. Sophie promised that at least within France she would try to prevent these indiscretions and told Eugénie Audé that all letters to Aloysia Hardey would have to bypass Paris.[42]

Clearly rumours had spread to Europe of the possibility of St Michael's withdrawing from the Society. Yet Sophie did not ask Aloysia Hardey directly if she had had any plan to separate from the Society. Instead she continued to write to her and show marks of trust and confidence in her government. Sophie made a point of saying how much she valued and appreciated American members of the Society, and she asked Aloysia to take the initiative of building bridges with all the houses in America, and especially with Julie Bazire and the community of Grand Coteau:

> Another word yet again on Grand Coteau. Do the impossible . . . to maintain unity between the two houses. Avail of opportunities to help them. And when you can, send some gifts. I would be saddened if the slightest coldness existed between you. The motto of the Society is: One Heart and One Mind, and each one must make the greatest sacrifices to put into practice these two precepts which is so pleasing to the Sacred Heart of Jesus![43]

Sophie told Aloysia Hardey not to believe or even listen to rumours about what she herself was reported to have said or written about her or about St Michael's. The only way to communicate directly and remain in harmony and maintain good government in the Society. In time she hoped that some American women who wished to enter the Society could be sent to France or Italy and be formed there, in either Paris or Rome:

> This is the best way to inculcate deeply the spirit of the Society in your country. Since you will only send us specially chosen candidates, suitable at a later date for key positions, I think this will be of inestimable value for our foundations in America. There would be closer union and uniformity at least in basic essentials, for I understand that customs can differ . . . Maybe you could escort these candidates! . . . I would like to get to know my first American daughter.[44]

While absorbed in the affairs of America Sophie also had to reckon with further criticisms of the rue de Varenne which had reached Rome and were conveyed to her from several quarters. The news of Archbishop de Quelen's residence not only in the Petit-Hôtel but now in the main building of the Hôtel Biron caused many a lifted eyebrow and Sophie could not ignore the remarks. She wrote to Eugénie de Gramont in January 1838 and offered the archbishop the sole use of the Petit-Hôtel. Up until now the archbishop had used some rooms of the Petit-Hôtel as his secretariat. Sophie now proposed that the archbishop set up his own household there and withdraw completely from the rooms he had in the Hôtel Biron. She requested that the main door of the Petit-Hôtel, which opened out on the street, be used by the archbishop and his visitors. The door of the Petit-Hôtel, giving on to the property of the Hôtel Biron and near the front door of the Hôtel Biron, was to be permanently closed and access to the key given to a few, specifically named persons. The Society would furnish the archbishop with household linen, silverware, fruit and vegetables from the garden in the rue de Varenne. Eugénie was charged to inform everyone that all communication between the Petit-Hôtel and the Hôtel Biron was to cease.[45] Sophie explained her reasons for this decision:

> I will say only this to you, my dear Eugénie, that you must not hesitate any longer now that our Father [Lambruschini] has agreed with the plan I suggest to you. Believe me, the reasons which compel me to urge this decision could not be more urgent. The present situation cannot possibly continue without causing the most serious problems. You can have no idea how much I hear or how much is written to me, I must tell you, from all quarters. Moreover, dear rat, even if these objections did not exist, I think my proposal is the most suitable in all respects. So why should there be any hesitation in accepting it?[46]

Eugénie replied on 26 January 1838, saying that the archbishop accepted Sophie's offer of the Petit-Hôtel for his sole use and would write to that effect soon. Sophie was pleased that he was so positive, though she dropped a pointed remark, regretting that the archbishop could not reach agreement with the government, which had already offered Archbishop de Quelen adequate, alternative accommodation in Paris.[47] Eugénie asked Sophie for the names of those who had criticised Archbishop de Quelen and the community at the rue de Varenne, especially herself. Sophie replied that there were too many and she refused to name them, but she told her they were cardinals, bishops and priests:

> A cardinal said to me one day: if the type of communications which have taken place [in Paris] happened in Italy, the person concerned [Eugénie de Gramont] and her house [rue de Varenne] would be placed under interdict. . . .
> Many priests who come here from Paris speak a great deal and make fun of the rue de Varenne etc., especially about the presence of the Dames du Sacré-Cœur at meals etc. . . . I abbreviate here . . . The pupils have spoken to their parents about visits you received when you were ill, towards nine o'clock in the evening and frequently.
> I say nothing about the reflections several French bishops communicated to me personally on this subject.[48]

This was plain talking indeed. Yet although Archbishop de Quelen wrote to Sophie he only thanked her for her continued hospitality and made no comment on her proposals. His attitude to her concerns was no different from his reaction in 1836, when Sophie asked him to consider the damage his presence in the rue de Varenne was doing to himself and to the Society of the Sacred Heart. Neither then nor now, in 1838, did he see there was a difficulty. It was the height of illusion and Sophie faced Eugénie with that:

> Believe me, dear rat, you and he are greatly mistaken. All who speak – or rather who speak to us – are for the most part devoted and attached to him [Archbishop de Quelen]. All respect him and complain about your delusion. In the end, what is required? That he should reside somewhere else. And since we are offering him the same services why not accede to the opinion of well-meaning people and eliminate

for us a wrong which can never be corrected. Several important people have said
this to me. I have offered him the Petit-Hôtel to prove that I do not share the prejudices against him. But it is hoped that he will accept this offer and leave [the Hôtel
Biron].[49]

When Sophie realised that Archbishop de Quelen had no intention of withdrawing from the Hôtel Biron, she made another offer to the archbishop. She
suggested that he move to the mother house, in rue Monsieur, and she guaranteed that the Society of the Sacred Heart would continue to pay the rent to the
comte de Nicolay. But even that offer did not convince the archbishop how seriously Sophie Barat considered the issue, how much in the public domain his residence in the rue de Varenne had become and that gossip was rife, not just in
Paris but in other parts of France and in Rome.[50] By July there was still no firm
indication that Archbishop de Quelen was going to move to the rue Monsieur
and Sophie warned Eugénie she intended to act to preserve the good name of
the Society.

The rue Monsieur had always been seen as a stopgap, rather than a permanent residence since it was not big enough for the noviceship and mother house
needs. Sophie told Eugénie that she had decided to build on the grounds of the
rue de Varenne. The question was whether to add a wing to the Petit-Hôtel or
build separately at the end of the gardens, on the side of the rue de Babylone.
She opted for the first possibility since it was cheaper, but also because it was
another way of giving notice to the archbishop that he would have to leave the
property. She continued to hint in any case that any accommodation offered the
archbishop must be temporary as he would surely wish to return to precincts of
Notre Dame, close to his cathedral.[51]

Sophie had to deal with another criticism regarding the rue de Varenne.
Eugénie de Gramont ran a marriage bureau for young and wealthy families. Over
several years Sophie had tried to stop having the marriages of past pupils in the
chapel at the rue de Varenne, to no avail. She admitted that she could do little
about it since the archbishop officiated at the weddings. In all, the rue de
Varenne was a most fashionable venue in Paris.[52] In Rome Sophie had heard,
more from friends rather then enemies of the Society, that Eugénie de
Gramont's activity in Paris was doing the Society's reputation real damage.
People spoke in Rome about

the religious in charge of the pupils of the Sacré-Cœur in Paris who ran an actual
marriage bureau. They said that she dealt with such business regularly and kept a
list of young ladies, with the extent of their fortune etc. This scandalised these for-
eigners as well as those they told about it. Added to other matters, this gives us an
unfortunate reputation in Rome. If it were not damaging our work we could put up
with it, but when it is doing us such fundamental harm, is it not necessary to apply
a remedy?[53]

Sophie's proposals regarding the residence of the archbishop and her criticisms of Eugénie's marriage bureau at the rue de Varenne, infuriated Eugénie

de Gramont. Sophie in turn was deeply angry and frustrated at being blocked in her role as superior general. She was rendered powerless by her oldest friend. She could not convince her how serious the situation had become in Paris. Sophie's own frustration was compounded by the awareness that their relationship had changed profoundly, boding ill for her imminent return to Paris:

> I am angry at the obstacles which have arisen concerning your worthy guest. Our situation regarding his proximity in the rue de Varenne remains most distressing. . . . I do not look forward to our next meeting . . . I can safely tell you in advance that I do not expect this meeting to be anything like the one we had before I left Paris.[54]

Her own inner world was desolate and the support she had found in her contacts with Fr Favre was coming to an end. He had become ill and was no longer able to write letters of encouragement and guidance. The last letter Sophie received from him was in February 1837. She was in the Trinité at the time and in poor health. Favre told her:

> I have learnt with great sorrow that you are in very poor health . . . Take some rest and relaxation as well as the remedies prescribed. Allow them [doctors] to treat you as they think best and not according to your own wishes. . . . Do you not need robust and vigorous health to fulfil the greatly increased and varied obligations, so complicated and *exhausting*, as those which you are responsible for? Heavens above, Mother, in running down your health by overwork, sleepless nights and mortification are you not also *weakening* the whole Society? . . . The devil only mocks your acts of penance which are becoming an obstacle to the exercise of your important responsibility.[55]

Almost twelve months later, Favre wrote to Louise de Limminghe, responding to her concern for Sophie. The advice which Favre had given Sophie so often apparently made no impact upon her. She continued to practise severe penance, and pushed herself to the point of illness. Favre told Louise de Limminghe that the only solution was to remain with Sophie, support her, encourage her and above all treat her very gently:

> You must realise . . . that only by a miracle of grace can your worthy Mother give up her long-standing tendency to guilt and penance which she has grown used to. It is a habit which must be treated like a chronic illness, with gentleness, care and patience . . . Sooner or later grace triumphs over all obstacles, no matter how great they seem.[56]

Sophie complained that her health deteriorated in Rome and that the climate did not suit her. She caught colds easily,[57] and from November 1837 to January 1838 she was quite ill with fever. Sophie felt she would not be fully cured until she had returned to France.[58] In September 1837 Sophie hurt a finger on her right hand badly enough to restrict her letter-writing for several weeks.[59] Although doctors told her to take walks for fresh air and exercise, Sophie found this difficult to do:

> My health needs . . . a little exercise and fresh air. Yet I take so little! work calls; and you know well that a walk without a definite purpose has no attraction for me.[60]

Concerns about the Society, its government and personnel, the specific crisis areas of Paris, America and Rome, all caused Sophie great anxiety and sleepless nights. She had no secretarial help as Elizabeth Galitzine was in the rue Monsieur in Paris, so that most letters had to be written by Sophie herself. No matter what Favre suggested as a remedy Sophie could not see a way to easing the workload. Her energy continued to be drained by her feelings of guilt and her sense of sin, which led to the exercise of penance which so concerned Louise de Limminghe. But Sophie bore the burden of responsibility for the Society of the Sacred Heart and that left her vulnerable to taking the blame inwardly when all did not go well. She had come to the painful awareness that it was no longer a question only of finding a government structure to facilitate her leadership of a rapidly extending Society. Some kind of deep, inner reform of the Society was needed, a recapturing of the original vision. Only in that way could the future of the Society be secure.

She spoke of this in February 1838 when Elizabeth Galitzine's niece was trying to choose between entering the Society of the Sacred Heart or the Visitation order. In Paris, Nicholas Loriquet, Sophie's old friend, was inclined to advise the Visitation and Sophie was distressed at this. Loriquet's attitude was, of course, as much a comment on the reputation of the rue de Varenne as on the qualities of the Visitation order:

> It is a mistake to think that only those called to an active life join the Society. If we lacked the contemplative life the active life would soon become a lifeless spectre, and deprived of that vitality what good could we possibly do then? Instead of driving away those who are attracted to contemplation and solitude the Jesuits should send them to us with even more enthusiasm because we need them more than others. . . . I do not hesitate to promise them that when they enter they will not be working in the school but that they will be occupied in the internal duties of the house and in helping to maintain adoration of the Blessed Sacrament day and night, when the general noviceship has sufficient numbers to sustain this . . . Your niece . . . will lead a solitary life as far from the world as at Port Royal . . . I am convinced that we lose our best candidates through the false notion that those who wish to enter our Society must be solely attracted to external work, yet almost all those attracted to the deal of the contemplative life have been successful with us . . .
> . . . an order composed of these two attractions is spiritually strong and this strength becomes a great support for the active of the Society . . . This is what I feel compelled to establish in our Society before I die. By this means everything will be renewed, we will maintain a strong contemplative life and this will not damage the works which the Society undertakes since unfortunately those entering with contemplative attractions are few. Moreover, the contemplative side of the Society will be a nursery for [future] superiors, mistresses of novices etc.[61]

During this period Sophie often reflected on her style of governing the Society. It was inevitable when her authority was being either challenged or ignored in some parts of the Society. By nature Sophie was cautious and slow to take up a definite position. She gathered as much information as she could about a person, a community, a school or any given situation which required a decision.

She tended to consult, seek advice and only quite slowly reached a decision. She was ready to change her mind, to reverse a decision, if new information surfaced. She told Elizabeth Galitzine:

> How many times, having thought out in advance such and such a change, have I been obliged to change my views once I have seen all and heard every point of view.[62]

She accepted the best that could be done in a given situation, rather than the most excellent or the most perfect. She continually adjusted her expectations to the actual circumstance and she remade her plans easily. Sophie knew what she was doing and though it looked weak at times, her form of government was truly and consciously hers. She had an ideal in mind, as she told Eugénie Audé:

> All those who govern should adhere to this maxim: govern the community with an iron hand in a velvet glove. We should govern firmly but in such a way that the members neither see nor feel the iron, which they could not tolerate if it were uncovered and seen.[63]

She trusted those in the Society who governed with her even when there were tensions and difficulties and assured Eugénie Audé:

> By nature I am neither suspicious nor demanding, provided that even while doing wrong people thought they were doing the right thing. I do not ask more of anyone.[64]

Sophie sought to model her government of the Society on the figure of Christ in the gospels:

> Gentleness is not weakness when it draws its source from the Heart of Jesus and flows like honey from the mouth of the lion. This is what we must bring into our way of governing, moderate structures and words of gentleness. But we must insist that people continue to grow.[65]

When she was in a house Sophie tried not to let her burdens show in the community. No matter what was happening in her own life, or what was going on in the Society, she did her best to hide even the slightest sign of worry from those she lived with. All was held within but her worries burst out in letters, in her scruples and in ill health. She told Adelaide de Rozeville:

> The important thing is that your worries and disappointment are not obvious to others and that your community [daughters] believe you to be invulnerable and above the *petty* weaknesses which obsess them. So you must practise great reserve and self-control. Keep your dignity . . .[66]

Her style of government suited a small group well but Sophie knew she had to find structures to help her govern the number of houses which were increasing all the time. It was becoming clearer daily that with the lack of direct, personal and consistent contact with the centre of the Society, some local superiors, whether they wanted to or not, were taking most decisions on their own. Sophie remarked wryly in 1838:

So what is the point of having a superior general if a local superior can appoint whomsoever she pleases, send back a member of her community to a certain houses without knowing whether the superior there can receive her. Consequently this exposes members of communities moving from house to house without purpose or reason. For no superior has the authority to receive them since they arrive without a formal letter of obedience from me, the first authority. . . . This is so . . . [67]

Such reflections, arising out of her experience over several years, only served to underline the urgency of a general council, convened specifically to address the issue of government structures. By Easter 1838, Sophie decided to return to Paris and begin the preparations for the council and decide where to hold it. She paid a visit to Pope Gregory XVI and left Rome on 16 May 1838. She had been there almost eighteen months. A month before Sophie's departure the treasurer general of the Cistercians, Fr Marie-Joseph de Géramb visited Rome. One day he was walking along the Tiber and asked an old man if he knew who lived in the Villa Lante:

'They are all princesses' he replied. 'and the mother abbess is related to the King of France'. 'Do you know her name?' I asked. 'I do not know her family name but since the cholera she has been renamed Benefactress . . .
The old man was correct in saying that she had been renamed Benefactress, a title that her charitable work in Rome had earned her, for she had showed herself to be a mother to a host of orphans. As for her being related to the King of France . . . this mother abbess is none other than the good and worthy Mother Barat.[68]

Armande de Causans and the Trinité had an equally high profile at this time in Rome. Fr Géramb noted that the school was

for the daughters of the Roman nobility. . . . The superior, Madame de Causans, governs this establishment with a wisdom and goodness which has earned her the affection of all who live there as well as the esteem of all who know her.[69]

Yet Sophie left Rome with a sense of foreboding. A crisis had been brewing in the Trinité since early January 1838 and it would affect the two other houses in Rome, as well as place the Society's future in Italy in question.

− 14 −

THUNDERSTORMS BREAKING, 1838−1839

In February 1838 Sophie noted in one of her letters to Eugénie de Gramont that the Society had become the focus of some negative comments in Rome, through a young woman: 'a novice from a distinguished Italian family, who left because of poor health, has spoken ill of us and done us great harm.'[1] These criticisms did not die down, but rather became a catalyst for gossip about the Trinité. This gossip concerned the internal life of the community, especially how Armande de Causans and Euphrosine Faux controlled everything in the house. Some parents criticised how Josephine de Coriolis ran the boarding school and Euphrosine Faux made no secret that she considered the headmistress inadequate to the post. Gossip spread throughout church circles in Rome, especially among the Jesuits and some of the Roman nobility. Armande de Causans had been superior since the foundation of the Trinité in 1828. Euphrosine Faux was her assistant within the house and she generally accompanied Armande de Causans to public functions in St Peter's or in the city of Rome. Both lived quite apart in the house and Faux in particular held all the key domestic positions in the community.

When she had appointed Armande de Causans to establish Trinité in Rome Sophie knew this was a task she could accomplish in terms of her capacity to negotiate with the papacy and the nobility. But Sophie was also aware of Armande de Causans's limitations, of her inability to look after the internal affairs of a house, especially the needs of a community. For this reason Sophie had chosen Euphrosine Faux as assistant to de Causans. Yet even in 1834 Sophie had sensed that it was time to change the leadership in the Trinité but lack of a suitable person to replace Armande de Causans prevented this move then. It

was not easy to find someone who had the qualities to fulfil the conditions set
down by the French government, as well as look after the spiritual needs of the
community and maintain good relations with parents and Italian society in general. Several years later, in 1853, Adèle Lehon was living in Sainte Rufine and
had regular contacts with the Trinité. Armande de Causans and Euphrosine
Faux were there, having had returned to Rome after an absence of some years.
Adèle Lehon told Sophie that little had changed:

> My contacts with the Trinité are getting somewhat more difficult as Mother Faux
> resumes more authority there, even though she is not the assistant [superior]. She
> runs everything. She is not the bursar, yet she runs the kitchen and even decides
> what is to be given to those who are ill. She has taken charge of the linen room
> again and everything is as it was before 1838. Since Mother de Causans is unable
> to attend community meetings or even the boarding school, she tends to see every-
> thing through Mother Faux's eyes. Whatever she says, I do not think the boarding
> school was badly run during Mother de Coriolis' time, nor that it was in need of
> reform . . . Mother Faux has many good qualities, but she is not renowned for her
> humility and capacity to live common life.[2]

In addition to the internal problems in the Trinité, Armande de Causans and
Euphrosine Faux continued to move freely around Rome, visiting cardinals,
bishops, religious communities and churches. Certainly Armande de Causans
was considered highly in church circles and she received invitations regularly to
ceremonies in St Peter's and other major churches in Rome. Some clerics in
Rome, and especially the Jesuits, viewed this as a breach of cloister. Long ago
in 1825 Rozaven had already voiced his disapproval of the Society of the Sacred
Heart's observance of cloister. He thought that all religious communities of
women should be fully cloistered, with grilles, a view generally held in Italy.
Whereas religious life, with solemn vows and strict papal cloister had been abolished at the beginning of the French Revolution, this had not happened in Italy.
There the strict conditions laid down by the Council of Trent continued to be
the norm and were expected to be observed by all religious women.

When the Society went to Turin in 1823 a clash was inevitable and the archbishop of Turin tried to impose papal cloister on the Society. In Rome Pope
Gregory XVI was a Camaldolite monk, and he held the same views as his colleague in Turin. The pope made no secret of his personal wishes regarding cloister for women, although when he met Sophie he did not ask her to change the
constitutions in this regard. Nevertheless, as the Society of the Sacred Heart
became more fully established in Rome the differences between the French
interpretation and the Italian interpretation of cloister became more apparent.
Sophie herself found the strict interpretation of cloister in Italy difficult to
understand: 'Grilles. Nothing will ever replace them in their eyes! This only
happens in Italy. What would they do anywhere else with grilles?'[3]

Yet Sophie had to take into account the criticism of the Society in Rome, on
the part of clerics and of some families there. This was not a passing phenom-
enon. Some years later, Adèle Lehon wrote to Sophie:

In Rome at the moment there are a great many sisters of every kind – grey, black, of St Joseph, of Providence, the daughters of the Sacred Heart of St Dorothy – who do not observe cloister at all and who are seen at all the ceremonies. People are very inclined to equate us with them, and I think because of that and to avoid the reproaches which Gregory XVI made against us previously, we have to observe cloister even more than before.[4]

Certainly in 1838 Sophie knew she had to be careful how she interpreted cloister in Italy and particularly in Rome. She knew that Armande de Causans and Euphrosine Faux received invitations to social events and occasions and had no intention of refusing to attend them.[5] Rozaven and two other Jesuits urged Sophie to send both women away from the Trinité but Sophie told him that she would deal with the situation herself, in her own time.[6] She had to find a way of removing them which avoided loss of face, especially for Armande de Causans. However, Sophie knew her departure should be organised quietly and she expressed misgivings at the effect an abrupt change would have on the Trinité community and school, on Armande de Causans herself and on the public perception of the Society in Rome. Instinctively she thought the move should be done at a later date, when the storm of criticism had lessened and the Trinité was no longer a subject of talk and rumour.[7] Soon Sophie would need help with the preparations for the general council and when Elizabeth Galitzine went to America she would need a secretary general. Armande de Causans had been her secretary before and a new appointment to her former post would cause no surprise.

While Rozaven and Louise de Limminghe continued to urge Sophie to remove Armande de Causans immediately, Sophie cautioned delay. She placed the implications of a sudden move before Louise de Limminghe:

What are you going to do and what decision will you make to remove these two from the Trinité? Consult the Fathers [Jesuits] again. It is impossible to send them away before they are replaced.[8]

But by now Sophie knew that the situation in the Trinité was more complicated than simply replacing Armande de Causans. Pressure and criticism had so affected Armande de Causans, Euphrosine Faux and Josephine de Coriolis that despite their personal tensions they had begun to consider separating from the Society and establishing the Trinité as an independent foundation. For this reason, Sophie had told the Trinité that novices could only be received at the Villa Lante.[9] She was even more apprehensive when she heard that the superior of Sainte Rufine, Hypolite Lavauden, supported Armande de Causans, and Sophie warned Louise de Limminghe:

What a cross this is and from where I least expected it! But what harm they are doing! How can they hope to succeed? If they do separate from the Society then one word from us to the Minister in Paris and they would soon be cast out themselves . . . The truth is that Mother de Causans has far too much sense to plan a separation. What would she do in isolation? I think this storm will calm down, provided that they are left alone until they receives obediences from me. That will be in two months' time.[10]

The Trinité was a French foundation in Rome and the presence of the Society there was a carefully negotiated agreement. Any deviation from that agreement would automatically break the contract. Armande de Causans was the founder of the Trinité and was aware of the Society's commitments. Yet since she was a well-known figure in Rome, much loved and respected, she could count on that reputation and support if she broke the relationship between the Trinité and the Society of the Sacred Heart. Apart from the fact that any separation was something Sophie instinctively avoided, she also knew the damage such a public act could do to the reputation of the Society generally. Not only that. She dreaded the financial implications of such a step, since Josephine de Coriolis in particular had brought in considerable capital when she entered the Society.[11]

Sophie also felt that Armande de Causans had been too severely criticised, especially by Jean Rozaven and Joseph Bellotti.[12] Armande de Causans had seen the Trinité through the founding days, built up its reputation and negotiated competently with the church and the nobility. She moved freely in these circles in Rome. She had worked hard to establish the Trinité and nothing could take away the pain of losing so many members of the community in the cholera in 1837. Worn out and weary, she resented Sophie's intention to have her replaced as superior, knowing that behind it was the pressure from Louise de Limminghe and Jean Rozaven.

By July 1838 Sophie sensed that Armande de Causans and Josephine de Coriolis were at the point of separating from the Society. By now the Jesuits in Rome had refused to serve the community at the Trinité, though the immediate reason for this decision is not known. In the hope of resolving the problem before it became finally intractable Sophie asked Louise de Limminghe to go to the Trinité and talk to Armande de Causans and Josephine de Coriolis and see if they could reach some accommodation with the Jesuits. The breakdown in communication was damaging the community in the Trinité as well as the reputation of the Society in Rome:

> We have to be fair, for there are only two who are out of step, being who they are and because of their health. But when I was there the community itself was running well. People exaggerate, you know.[13]

The most serious issue was the public nature of the tension between the Jesuits and the Trinité, and between the Trinité and Louise de Limminghe. Sophie's reactions to the nature of the problems in Rome showed her own style in dealing with controversial issues:

> . . . how sad it is that these petty disagreements have broken out between the two houses, and even between the most intimate friends! We should bear many painful things in silence, for with patience and the help of God they will be resolved. On the other hand when hearts are aggrieved, nothing can heal the wounds and if these

miseries come to light you know the consequences! So do all you can to reconcile both sides . . . [14]

Already both the Trinité and Sainte Rufine had lost confidence in Louise de Limminghe and felt she was colluding with the Jesuits in Rome, against them.[15] Whatever their differences, Sophie asked that they keep their problems within the family:

> I recall the noble discourse of Bonaparte, to the Senate at the moment of his fall from power. It is too true not to apply it to us: Sirs, do not reprimand me in public for my faults; that is imprudent . . . dirty linen should be washed in private . . . That is how we should have proceeded in this affair and we would have managed it without fuss.[16]

But she had difficulty in convincing Louise de Limminghe that she should take an initiative and go to the Trinité herself. Louise de Limminghe did not have the insight, the tact or the experience of Sophie Barat. In describing to Louise de Limminghe what she ought to do in Rome Sophie was representing her own style of government:

> What! Did you leave them in their pain and humiliation and not visit them, speak to them, encourage them to contact the Jesuits? Is that what charity is? Had they been even more at fault you would still have had to forget everything and take the first steps towards them. This is not the way that you should support my authority and make it loved. You are well aware of my style of government and you criticise any who follow it. No, I will never condemn anyone without hearing them out and I will not permit the extreme measures suggested to me. You yourself should have inclined gradually towards indulgence, but instead you follow the severe measures which the Jesuits proposed. I am deeply distressed by all this.[17]

Sophie disagreed with the severity of Rozaven's views concerning Armande de Causans and her leadership of Trinité. While she agreed that a change of superior was needed, Sophie was determined that that Armande de Causans should not leave the Trinité in disgrace. By August 1838 Sophie had lost her patience with the Jesuits and she wanted their part in the campaign against Armande de Causans to be known publicly.[18] They had taken an attitude towards the Trinité which Sophie could not endorse and she warned Louise de Limminghe that she had become too influenced by Rozaven and Bellotti. She did not doubt their good intentions but she found their actions unacceptable:

> Maintain your independence and imagine what I would do or what I would say in such and such a circumstance. Always seek advice but be sure that it is in tune with my way of thinking. I assure you that it is not because I think that my advice is the best, far from it, but God has promised me the help my responsibility demands. Because of this I advise you to follow my ideas and my way of acting.[19]

Sophie consistently maintained that the best strategy was to remove Armande de Causans by inviting her to Paris for the general council and then appointing her to her new office. Her instinct then, as always, was never to aggravate a situation so that it became confrontational and ultimately polarised. To the Jesuits and Louise de Limminghe this looked weak and ineffective, yet Sophie knew it was right and asked Louise to support her rather than follow the Jesuits. When, some weeks later, Louise de Limminghe asked Sophie if, in view of the situation in the Trinité, she would consider stricter rules of cloister for the Society in Italy, Sophie resolutely refused.[20] As far as she was concerned the real need was union and harmony between the houses in Rome and an end to gossip and rumour concerning the Society. However, by this time the situation had become more serious. Sophie was dismayed to learn that Gregory XVI had authorised Rozaven to choose a priest to investigate the quality of religious life and observance in the Trinité, and particularly the question of cloister:

> This is a blow for us in Rome. God's will be done! . . . What surprises me is Fr Rozaven's choice of inquisitor. Who exactly is this priest?[21]

While Gregory XVI may have authorised the visitation of the Trinité, there is no doubt that Rozaven had brought the matter to the attention of the pope. Yet Armande de Causans had powerful friends too in the church in Rome, especially among the cardinals. Cardinal Lambruschini, the Secretary of State, who had negotiated the founding of the Trinité with Sophie, took a personal interest in all the affairs of the house and was a friend of Armande de Causans. His visits increased notably that autumn. Sophie knew this and from Paris she had to tread this diplomatic tightrope carefully:

> I would need to really have trust in God not to fear for the Trinité! . . . Cardinal Lambruschini remains her strong supporter [Armande de Causans]. . . . The truth is that he esteems and likes Madame de Causans . . . I do not doubt that she has spoken to him. . . . [Lambruschini] did not have the habit of going so often to the Trinité. [22]

Armande de Causans prolonged the situation by telling Sophie that while she would readily travel to Paris her health would not allow her to do so immediately. Rozaven stepped in at this point and proposed that she stay on in the Trinité but no longer be the superior.[23] Sophie disagreed with this and asked that Armande de Causans be given time. Rozaven ignored Sophie's wishes and pressed ahead. He was critical of both the Trinité and of Sophie's leadership:

> If Fr Rozaven is not pleased with us, I have to say here and now that I am not very pleased with him in this affair. This good priest hardly considers my position nor does he even understand the situation of the Trinité. Besides I am following my conscience and I am at peace in this. I am convinced that if we hold to Madame de Causans leaving the Trinité as arranged, in the end that is what she will do. . . . Her refusal to leave Rome with her brother shows that she is trying to gain time. . . . I assure you that while our friends [Jesuits] render us services, which I certainly appreciate, they also cause us an amount of problems by their dictates. When there are only two or three months to wait, we need to be patient and so avoid endless difficulties and unpredictable consequences. [24]

Two days later, Sophie despaired of resolving the tensions in Rome. She told Louise de Limminghe to ask both Rozaven and Bellotti to withdraw from their involvement in three houses of the Society, the Trinité, Sainte Rufine and the Villa Lante. In any event she thought the Society of the Sacred Heart would not survive in Rome much longer:

> It is they [the Jesuits] who will destroy everything, and all through lacking a bit more patience and forbearance. I confess that I would not like to be responsible for this situation.[25]

Sophie had left Rome in May 1838, with Marie Patte and Catherine de Charbonnel, and she had still not fully recovered from her illness over the winter. She needed a change of air and had to return to Paris to prepare for the next general council. Yet by the time she reached Parma she was quite ill. The concerns over both Rome and Paris, as well as Louisiana burdened her; in addition she found the heat that summer unbearable. Marie Patte became ill on the journey and Sophie feared she would be unable to travel further with her to Paris. Sophie counted on Marie a great deal, and Marie cared for and understood Sophie's needs well and resented interference from others in this sphere. Another worry weighed on Sophie at this time. While travelling from Parma to Turin Sophie had caught a cold and soon developed an infection in her throat and chest which demanded careful treatment. She lost her voice and could not sleep. Her sense of isolation was extreme. She told Louise de Limminghe:

> Oh! How much I miss you for everything! . . . I feel so sad! The state I am in contributes to this. I see the work mounting up and my strength decreasing. No one to help me! This is a difficult moment to endure. Let us hope that the Lord will see me through it.[26]

To compound her feelings of isolation, Sophie heard that Fr Favre was seriously ill and in danger of death.[27] Still she continued to hope for a miracle. His direction was a support, he knew her well and would have understood that she dreaded her return to Paris:

> The Abbé is right, I am sad and worried about the present and future. This experience of isolation makes me ill. And yet I try very hard so that the grief which torments me is not perceived by others![28]

Sophie's recovery was slow. The doctor placed leeches on her throat and chest and this gave her some relief. She also had a vesicatory which brought down the inflammation, and though she was unable to continue her journey to Paris she began to resume some of her normal routine of letter-writing. She also completed the negotiations for a new house near in Pignerol, near Turin. This was intended as a house for the noviciate, with a school for the poor and later a boarding school for the middle class. Sophie was too ill to go and see the property, which was a former monastery, but she delegated the visit to Catherine de Charbonnel. There were silk mills in the area, indeed the former monastery had housed a spinning mill also, so it was easy to gather women workers for Sunday school. Such was the state of education in the area that the bishop asked Sophie to train bands of young women who could teach catechism in the parishes. It was a house in a beautiful setting which complemented the prestigious school for the nobility, established in Turin since 1823.[29]

Towards the end of June Sophie, although not fully cured, wanted to start out once again. The doctor had recommended baths and Sophie found them beneficial and strengthening. He also wanted her to take asses' milk but she found the weather too hot to be able to take that treatment. Before leaving she heard that Joseph-Marie Favre had died. She remarked laconically to Louise de Limminghe:

> No more hope of seeing our mutual friend now, he is in heaven . . . He is venerated as a saint.[30]

Sophie did not write about what the loss of Favre meant in her life. He had been a good friend and support and had understood her inner struggles. She referred briefly to her loss in November 1838, when she told Louise de Limminghe that she was struggling in her self and had neither a guide nor a friend to help her.

Since Catherine de Charbonnel had stayed on in Turin to see to the foundation of Pignerol, Sophie asked Eugénie Audé to travel from Marseilles to Turin and accompany Marie and herself to Lyon. Eugénie Audé's dependency on Sophie had not abated and she wanted to take charge of Sophie, something which Marie would not allow. She was so annoyed at Eugénie Audé's behaviour that she decided to write and complain to Louise de Limminghe. Sophie asked Louise de Limminghe not to take it all at face value, but admitted that the tension between the two was real enough.[31] They reached Lyon by mid-July and Sophie's voice was so weak that the doctor there forbade her to speak at all. He tried bringing up bile by vomiting but this only produced a worse fever. He decided to try purging Sophie and then treating her with quinine, in the hope that this could shift the fever. This treatment worked and Sophie felt much better:

> The two purgings have eliminated a good deal of bile and the fever seems to have been arrested, without having to use quinine.[32]

Her recovery permitted her to continue her journey to Paris. She deferred this for as long as possible, and the nearer she approached the rue de Varenne the more sick at heart she felt. Two issues awaited a decision there: the residence of Archbishop de Quelen and a choice of venue for the next general council. On the eve of her departure from Autun, for the last stage on her journey to Paris, Sophie told Louise de Limminghe that she was still unable to sleep, that she suffered tension in her head and stomach, signs of great anxiety:

> Sleep is always difficult, and rare. The nerves in my head are frayed and my stomach is very upset with anxiety. But both will settle with the relaxation of travelling. As you know, that is the only rest I will get. Once I arrive in any of our houses I cannot hope for any![33]

Sophie arrived in Paris on the 30 August 1838. Nothing had changed. Archbishop de Quelen was still in residence, though absent during the month of

September. Louis Barat told his sister what had happened during her absence and indeed he wrote to Louise de Limminghe himself with an account of it. Sophie resigned herself to resuming her campaign of persuading the archbishop to leave the property and began preparing for the next general council. Throughout these months she wondered constantly whether to hold it in Montet, Lyon or Paris.[34] For a time she thought Montet would be best; but then it was too cold in winter. Marie Prevost suggested Lyon as best, but Sophie did not pursue that possibility. For a time she felt that Paris would offer the best opportunities for the Society, especially if Joseph Varin could assist at the sessions. However, she hesitated for Sophie had sensed, even before her return to Paris, that Félicité Desmarquest had become powerful there and that she could mount opposition to the structural changes the Society needed for good government. These would directly affect her role as assistant general:

> Mother D. . . . having acquired such an ascendancy over the older members of the Society, during my absence in Rome, her way of seeing and judging will have the greatest significance . . . we can suppose that this excellent mother . . . will be totally opposed to the changes.[35]

In this context, Sophie thought that Eulalie de Bouchaud was too influenced by Félicité Desmarquest and that she should be removed as mistress of novices in Paris.[36] It was too sensitive an appointment to leave in the hands of someone whom Sophie did not trust, especially in view of the changes Sophie intended to introduce at the general council. Sophie still planned to have the general council in Paris but she soon changed her mind when Archbishop de Quelen returned to the rue de Varenne in October 1838. She saw that she could not hold the general council there, that her freedom and that of the Society would be compromised. Despite several requests for an appointment with him, between October and December, Archbishop de Quelen refused to meet Sophie even though he was her guest in the Petit-Hôtel. He simply ignored her and Eugénie de Gramont made no effort to mediate. It was a humiliating position for Sophie and it belittled her role as superior general. She told Louise de Limminghe that she felt alone and isolated in Paris, in the rue de Varenne.[37]

At this time too Sophie was concerned about her niece, Elisa Dusaussoy, whose health was deteriorating rapidly in Conflans. As a last resort Sophie wrote to the healer, the Prince de Hohenloe and asked him to pray from 21 to 28 January 1838 for her niece's recovery to health. She invited the family and the communities in Paris and Conflans, as well as those she wrote to at that time, to join in the novena. Elisa did not recover health and died on 17 February 1839.[38] Sophie's own health at this time was no better, easily explained by the tensions she was living with in the house. In September alone she continued to suffer from poor sleep, poor appetite and poor digestion. In general she felt weak and tired, with little energy to work. She was not surprised, since she had not a got 'a moment's peace'.[39] Her whole system was in crisis, reflecting the crisis within the Society. While Sophie had hoped to hold the general council before the end of the year, her advisers in Paris warned her that her health was not strong enough for such a project then. A further advantage for a delay was the possibility that Armande de Causans could be persuaded to leave for the council, and so avoid a confrontation in Rome. Thus in the autumn of 1838 everything pointed to holding the council in Montet, early in 1839.[40]

In the weeks before Christmas 1838 Sophie discussed with Elizabeth Galitzine, her secretary general, when to convene the general council later on in the year in Switzerland. They did not tell Eugénie de Gramont any of the details, though there were suspicions in the house that Sophie was about to leave Paris.[41] The agenda of the general council had been prepared while Sophie was in Rome, for both she and Louise de Limminghe had drawn it up with Rozaven. He had agreed to draw up the rules for provincials and for official visitors to provinces, following the Jesuit format. These had not been completed before Sophie left Rome in May so she asked that they be sent with Louise de Limminghe when she left Rome for the council. Only Louise de Limminghe, Elizabeth Galitzine and Jean Rozaven knew about these plans, and Sophie counted on their support when introducing the changes in government so badly needed for leading the increasingly expanding Society.[42] In her letter to the Society, in December 1838, Sophie announced the general council for the spring of 1839 but did not give any details of the agenda, other than expressing the hope that the plan of studies could be revised.[43] For different reasons, she could not trust either Eugénie de Gramont or Félicité Desmarquest to concur with her plans beforehand. Indeed in hoping to implement the new structures for the Society Sophie counted on the general goodwill and loyalty towards her which had characterised all previous councils, since 1815.

As Sophie waited in Paris and tried to regain some strength and energy for the spring, news from Rome confirmed her sense of foreboding. She learnt that both Armande de Causans and Euphrosine Faux had left the Trinité during the night of 7 December 1838, without a word to the community. They had managed to pack their cases quietly and no one in the houses suspected they were about to leave. The previous week Armande de Causans had applied to the ambassador for a travel permit. At first she gave no explanation as to why she was leaving the Trinité in early December. When the ambassador asked her why she was leaving Rome and who would remain in charge, Armande de Causans told the Comte Latour-Maubourg that she had been called to Paris by Madame Barat and that Josephine de Coriolis would replace her in everything regarding both school and community.[44] In fact while Josephine de Coriolis remained in the house and retained care of the boarding school, she had every intention of leaving the house too once she received permission from the pope. All three had been pushed too far and decided that they had had enough. By this time not only was Lambruschini fully aware of their decision, but so too was the pope. The decision to leave the Society was negotiated with Lambruschini and the pope, not with Sophie Barat. Nor was Sophie informed about it by Armande de Causans or Lambruschini. It was taken over her head, as if she had no part in the matter at all.

Sophie received a letter on Christmas Eve in Paris from Josephine de Coriolis telling her what had happened in Rome in early December. Sophie wrote immediately to Louise de Limminghe and asked to try and prevent the news from the Trinité becoming a source of gossip in Rome. She also wrote to Catherine de Charbonnel at Pignerol and asked her to travel to Rome immediately and take charge of the Trinité until the position of Armande de Causans and Euphrosine Faux became clearer.[45] At this stage Sophie hoped that the departure of both Armande de Causans and Euphrosine Faux could be passed off in public as simply their journey to Paris for the council. She had already written to Anna du Rousier in early December, warning her of the possibility that Armande de Causans would be travelling with her brother to the south of France, and asked her to look after Armande de Causans well. Now, without telling Anna du Rousier what had happened in the Trinité, Sophie wrote to her again and asked her to let her know when Armande de Causans arrived in Turin. At this stage Sophie still hoped that Armande de Causans and Euphrosine Faux had left with the intention of travelling to France and joining her in Paris.[46]

These swift moves held the Society's public position in Rome but she knew that it was temporary because Catherine de Charbonnel's health could not stand much pressure; she had become quite deaf and blind. On the 18 January 1839 Armande de Causans's brother wrote to Sophie and told her that he was taking his sister home, to Causans in Aix-en-Provence. He gave no details of his sister's health and the tone of his letter was cold and distant. Some days later Armande de Causans wrote to Sophie herself and gave her little information, except to say that she was staying at home for the time being. She acknowledged Sophie's letters but did not explain why she had left the Trinité so abruptly.[47] It was clear now that the flight had become public in Rome and would soon reach houses of the Society in France. Sophie felt now more than ever that Louise de Limminghe, Rozaven and Bellotti, had acted far too rashly and brusquely.[48] Another letter from Josephine de Coriolis confirmed this and Sophie told Louise de Limminghe:

> I am sending you this letter . . . which I think is both moderate and truthful. You realise that from the beginning I foresaw the indiscretions of the Jesuits. It is done now. They wanted to help, that is true, but the damage is great. Consider very carefully how we may repair the damage . . . it is clear that the Jesuits have done us harm.[49]

Sophie was sure that if her own wishes had been followed the situation would never have reached such an impasse. Certainly the news of Armande de Causans's flight from the Trinité would have been kept secret. Sophie hinted also that this was not the only area where interference from the Jesuits was unhelpful and she asked rhetorically who in fact was running the Society of the Sacred Heart.[50] Sophie's mode of government, and her way of treating individual members of the Society of the Sacred Heart, clashed with the Jesuit model. Paradoxically, however, she hoped to adopt the Jesuit structure of government at the next general council, for the sake of providing a government structure for the expanding Society of the Sacred Heart. Inevitably caught into a web of events not of her own making, Sophie decided that she would have to return to Rome quickly and deal with the Trinité directly herself. She asked Stanislas to get passports for herself, Marie Patte and Félicité Desmarquest and then made plans to leave Paris as soon as possible.[51]

Sophie left Paris accompanied by Félicité Desmarquest at the end of February 1839, bound for Montet. She stopped at Besançon on the way and there she wrote to Louise de Limminghe, telling her how shocked she was at the news that Armande de Causans, Euphrosine Faux and Josephine de Coriolis had decided to leave the Society and join a Visitation community in Rome. She learnt that they had asked the pope several months previously to be relieved of their vows. While Armande de Causans and Euphrosine Faux had received formal, written dispensation from the pope, Josephine de Coriolis had not, but clearly it was only a matter of time. Armande de Causans had written again to Sophie, who was upset at the cold, cursory and detached tone of the letter.[52] She thought all three were living in an illusory world and that their situation was untenable in the long run. But she accepted the reality of what had happened in Rome and she warned Louise de Limminghe:

> Do not be in the slightest way deceived with regard to the intentions of the of the three. They will stay in Rome, join the Visitation and from there try to supplant us. Then they will start another foundation in some other area. I have every reason to suspect this. It is important therefore to prevent them, either by ensuring that they do not enter the Visitation in Rome, or at least that Madame de Coriolis does not, and that they are not allowed to have a boarding school. If we do not get these terms then there is no point in our remaining in Rome. There would be endless problems stemming from rivalry, intrigue etc. and we would never have a moment of peace![53]

Both Louise de Limminghe and Catherine de Charbonnel urged Sophie to return to Rome immediately. She could see the wisdom of that and it was clear that the general council would have to be held there now, not in Switzerland. She set out immediately and proposed to travel in stages to Montet, Chambéry, Turin and so to Rome. At all points on that journey Sophie was be kept informed regarding events in Rome. At Montet she received news that while the Jesuit general, Roothan, and Rozaven considered that the council should be held in Rome, the pope thought it should be held in Montet. Sophie found the latter opinion impossible and hoped to explain her reasons when she got to Rome. Sophie could not count on the discretion of her secretary general, Elizabeth Galitzine, still in Paris, and so she told her to tell Eugénie de Gramont and the members of the community council in Paris, as well as Joseph Varin, that three members in Rome had decided to leave the Society. But she asked her not to tell Eugénie de Gramont that the general council would be held in Rome or that Sophie had decided to travel there immediately. In any event it was still not clear yet if she could persuade the pope that Rome would be a better venue than Montet for the council, on account of the crisis at the Trinité.[54]

Sophie wrote to Gregory XVI and explained the situation of the Society in Rome in the wake of Armande de Causans's sudden departure from the Trinité. She specifically asked that Armande de Causans, Josephine de Coriolis and Euphrosine Faux should not be allowed to enter the Visitation in Rome. The pope accepted this request and made their dispensation from vows in the Society conditional upon not entering the Visitation either in Rome or in Turin. They chose the city of Modena.[55] This had a profound effect on Armande de Causans in particular and Sophie realised that if she could be persuaded to reconsider her position, then both Josephine de Coriolis and Euphrosine Faux would return to the Society. In January 1839 Sophie had asked Marie Prevost to visit Armande de Causans at her home in Causans and ask her to join the community nearby, at Avignon. This plan failed. Then Sophie asked an old friend, the bishop of Nancy, Paul de Forbin-Janson, to approach Armande de Causans and urge her to consider returning to the Society.[56] He agreed to try and immediately set out to visit Armande de Causans at her family home.

When Sophie reached Rome she was made immediately aware of the impact of Armande de Causans's flight from the Trinité. Her many friends in Rome thought she had been forced out of the Trinité by Sophie Barat. Sophie was unable to tell the whole truth in public and she carried the blame for what had happened:

> I will tell little about the Armande affair. Her cousin will have brought you up to date, but you must take biased opinions into account. A scapegoat is required and it is she whom you mention. And yet I, on the spot and hearing both sides, have not been able to get to the depth of it. Both of them are as white as snow! What is clearer to me is the abuse of trust, and divulging of confidential matters, and that comes from outside the Society. What is most obvious is that there is a diabolical plot to destroy us and that is still going on. To survive in this country more discretion and caution are required and we have definitely lacked these. What is certain is that Armande's departure and all that either followed or preceded it, has done us real harm which we will be unable to efface completely. . . . Oh! if only a little prudence had been used everything would have been settled quite easily! God has permitted this to make me suffer. I can assure you that this journey and my stay in Rome have been difficult for me in every respect. However, I cannot regret it, since it has been in the design of God's Providence.[57]

What Sophie wanted most of all was the resolution of the problem, rather than a prolonged uncertainty regarding the leadership of the Trinité. Bishop Forbin-Janson persuaded Armande de Causans to reconsider her position and she decided to ask to return to the Society of the Sacred Heart.[58] Sophie agreed to accept her back, but not to the Trinité. It was impossible to reinstate her there, even if Sophie had wanted to at the time. In effect Sophie appointed Armande de Causans as superior of the community at Aix-en-Provence and sent Euphrosine Faux there with her. Josephine de Coriolis remained in the Trinité, in charge of the boarding school, and Sophie assumed the role of superior of the house until the general council opened in June 1839.

When she arrived in Rome, with a full schedule already in hand, family affairs intruded. Louis Barat wrote to Sophie announcing that Zoé wished to get married and that he had encouraged her to do so. Apparently Zoé's fiancé, Pierre Cousin, held to the family giving her a dowry of 20,000 francs, a sum which Sophie thought excessive. She felt that the request reflected badly on Cousin. However, Louis Barat suggested that Louis, Stanislas and Sophie Dusaussoy contribute to their sister's future. Louis Dusaussoy refused to give any money but Sophie thought she could arrange that Sophie Dusaussoy cede some of her income. Then another letter arrived saying that the marriage was called off, to Sophie's relief.[59] She was much more absorbed with handling the Society in Rome and she needed to give her attention to a plan of action.

As well as discussing new government structures for the Society, Sophie intended that the general council would reflect on the implications of the recent crisis at the Trinité. She had been taken aback at how easily three members of the Society could gain access to the pope and negotiate their separation without any reference to her as the superior general. In public she excused both sides, but she realised that she could not take for granted that her role was understood and accepted. It was not personal ill will against Sophie Barat which had led the pope to deal directly and solely with Armande de Causans, Josephine de Coriolis and Euphrosine Faux. They had gained access to him through the good offices of Lambruschini, who saw their case as exceptional and pertaining to Rome. Moreover the monastic model of separate, autonomous communities continued to be the mental framework within which church authorities operated. Indeed, until Sophie intervened personally in the case she was not even considered an element in the decision. In the light of this experience Sophie noted:

> I intend to have a clause on this matter inserted into either the decrees or the commentaries on the constitutions. For, as it stands at the moment, all those who have a notion or temptation to leave the Society under one pretext or another could just disappear without the superior general knowing anything about it! There is no contact or bond . . . The good God has allowed this unfortunate incident in the Trinité to happen, no doubt to enlighten us . . . It has happened. Let us hope that God will create some good out of it.[60]

While the crisis at the Trinité was a dramatic and public one, Sophie still had other serious problems to deal with. The residence of Archbishop de Quelen at the rue de Varenne remained a source of criticism and scandal which Sophie was never allowed to forget, especially in Rome.[61] Even before she had left Paris, one of the clergy, Denis Affre, had represented to Archbishop de Quelen how serious the position of the church and the Society of the Sacred Heart was in the eyes of the public:

> Monsignor, I prostrate myself at your feet to beg you, in the interests of your diocese, in your own interests and those of the religious communities, to take up residence somewhere else than in these houses. I assure you . . . that only the most sincere goodwill urges me to write this to you. Moreover, you cannot doubt that such advice is dictated by complete disinterested consideration. I would have

remained silent had I not been assured that my feelings were shared by those most devoted to your honour. These are very Christian people, well placed to judge the opinion of both the highest ranks in society and the bourgeoisie.[62]

This entreaty had no effect on Archbishop de Quelen and he remained in the rue de Varenne. It was a closed question and Sophie was powerless to do anything further. Sophie had great hopes that the general council could be held quickly and the changes she had planned for so long accepted and passed without difficulty. But she had a sense of foreboding, that she was facing into another storm:

I feel the Society, like the government, is on the brink of a crisis. May it endure it, overcome it and then emerge from it purer and stronger! [63]

In the previous year she had written to Aloysia Hardey, claiming that union existed in the Society in Europe:

Everything must be done in agreement and in a spirit of harmony and unity such as exists in Europe, where we [our mothers] work closely together in a spirit of harmony and union for the benefit of the Society and the glory of Jesus.[64]

By the end of that year Sophie was shocked by the events in the Trinité and now at the beginning of the general council Sophie was about to deal with issues far more difficult than any faced in the past. Indeed Sophie's own past, and that of Eugénie de Gramont, would come into view and force many in the Society to speak out in public. Evasion would no longer suffice. Situations would not disappear. They had to be faced, exorcised, dealt with, once and for all. Sophie would have to journey to the core of her own self and at the same time be exposed to the hearts and minds of her colleagues in a way she had never sought. What she saw was complex and difficult and what she learnt about herself was shattering and painful.

In May 1839 Sophie wrote to the council members of the Society and asked all to convene in Rome, at the Trinité, in the first week of June. She indicated in general terms why Rome had been chosen. Most of the members were aware that a crisis at the Trinité had precipitated Sophie's journey to Rome, though not all would have heard the details. Contrary to her practice in 1826 and 1833 Sophie did not outline the main issues she hoped to deal with at the council; even the renewal of the plan of studies, which the previous year she had taken as a priority for the council, was omitted. The letter of convocation was accompanied only by a list of instructions for travelling, including a warning to them and the communities to keep their journey and its destination confidential. The uncertain political situation France at the time caused Sophie to ask for this discretion. The Society continued to be linked to the legitimist party in France and was suspected of supporting the court of Charles X in exile. The Bourbon heir, the duc de Chambord, was travelling in the south of France, in Savoy and in Italy at this period, much the same route Sophie Barat travelled on her way to Rome.

Three members of the general council wrote to say they could not be present. Eugénie de Gramont said she could not leave the rue de Varenne for a prolonged period. Both Henriette Grosier and Geneviève Deshayes pleaded absence on the grounds of ill health. Sophie asked all three to sign a declaration that they would accept whatever was discussed and passed at the council in Rome:

> I have just asked you to send me in writing at least your written agreement to the decrees of the general council. This council will of necessity be decisive for the Society in establishing really solid foundations.[65]

This was an unusual step and Sophie explained that she acted in this way because of the cost of sending out the agenda ahead of time as well as the lack of time available before the council. In fact Sophie never intended sending out the agenda in advance since the matter for discussion was too sensitive. Moreover, by now Sophie not only hoped to establish new government structures in the Society. She had decided that for the sake of the Society's growth and her own freedom of action as superior general, the Society of the Sacred Heart should be centred in Rome. As Sophie requested, Eugénie de Gramont, Henriette Grosier and Geneviève Deshayes forwarded their agreement in advance to all the decisions of the council.[66] Eugénie de Gramont also stated that the council should not feel obliged to re-elect her assistant general. Clearly she had no idea of the agenda and Sophie certainly had not discussed it with her, knowing that her views would be resisted. She did not even tell Eugénie of her travelling plans when she left Paris in February 1839.

The general council opened in the Trinité on 10 June 1839. It consisted of: Sophie Barat, Félicité Desmarquest, Catherine de Charbonnel, Eugénie Audé, Henriette Coppens, Marie Prevost, Marie d'Olivier, Louise de Limminghe, Adelaide de Rozeville and Elizabeth Galitzine. Sophie had invited Thérèse Maillucheau to Rome, and at the opening session of the Council suggested that she and Elizabeth Galitzine be elected to replace two members unable to be present. This was accepted. In addition Elizabeth Galitzine was elected secretary to the council. Ten members of the council present ensured that the general council had sufficient numbers to proceed to business. From the beginning it was clear that Sophie Barat, Jean Rozaven, Louise de Limminghe and Elizabeth Galitzine had the agenda of the Council firmly in hand: planned, prepared and ready for the members to discuss.

At the first session Sophie asked Rozaven to present his views on the government of the Society of the Sacred Heart and to indicate what changes it would be necessary to make in the constitutions. Rozaven addressed the council and assured the members that he had the full approval of the general of the Jesuits, Roothan, for the work he was doing on the constitutions of the Society of the Sacred Heart. The documents, prepared well in advance by Rozaven, contained those issues which Sophie had discussed with him over several years: the creation of provinces to facilitate governing the Society; the appointment of the provincials, of the secretary general and the bursar general by the superior general; the election of the superior general, the assistants general and the admonatrix general for life by the general council; the convocation of the general council only on the death of the superior general or when the general good of the Society required it; the residence of the superior general and the assistants general permanently in Rome; the publication of a new edition of the constitutions of the Society of the Sacred Heart, modelled more closely on the government structures of the Jesuits. Three further points were included: solemn vows would be taken by choir religious after ten years of formation; coadjutrix sisters would make simple, not solemn vows; office in choir would be discontinued on account of the onerous work of teaching.

During the following days Rozaven presented his material, forty-seven articles in all, to the council. All were passed, with little debate. On the evening of Sunday 16 June Sophie had an audience with Pope Gregory XVI. She was accompanied by Félicité Desmarquest and Marie Prevost. Rozaven had also received an invitation from the pope to be present. Rozaven showed the pope the agenda he had prepared for the general council of the Society of the Sacred Heart. The document was written in Italian. The pope showed particular interest in the point regarding Sophie's residence in Rome. While not a formal approval of the business of the council, the visit added a certain weight to the proceedings, one that was used later to validate the work of the council.[67] By 5 July the work was complete and a document was drawn up, for communication to the whole Society and as an account to be sent to the pope for approval.[68] The preamble to the text explains why the changes were necessary in the rapidly growing Society. The needs of good government required some decisive action and the following decrees were passed unanimously. The key articles for the future government of the Society, recorded by Elizabeth Galitzine, were:

- the superior general of the Society resides in Rome.
- she is assisted in government by four assistants general, elected by the Society and as far as possible from different countries. They reside with the superior general in Rome.
- neither the superior general nor the assistants general visit the houses of the Society alone. This task is the work of Provincials whom the superior general appoints.
- the superior general decides on the number of provinces in the Society. The Provincials have a three year mandate, only rarely extended to six. The same applies to local superiors.

Changes regarding the members of the Society were basically:

- office in choir is abolished, though all are free to say it in private. It is considered not to be part of the Society's spirituality. Instead a half-hour of prayer, or the rosary is considered a more contemplative substitute for those who use their voice constantly during the day.

- no member of the Society is to be admitted to final vows before the age of thirty and they must have been in the Society for ten years[69]

No mention is made here of the decree passed regarding the difference in the vows taken by the choir religious and the coadjutrix sisters, nor the decision to allow both categories, choir and coadjutrix, to wear the cross and ring of profession from the time of first vows. However, in her letter to the Society, written on 13 July 1839, Sophie included both but significantly omitted to say that she would reside in Rome. She merely stated that the superior general would reside in one place and no longer visit the houses.[70] In her letter Sophie explained that all the decisions taken by the council had yet to be copied and sent to all the houses. In addition, guidelines were to be drawn up for the provincials. All the material would not be ready before the autumn. In the meantime, she enclosed the names of those newly elected to offices and a list of the new provinces of the Society. On 5 July Catherine de Charbonnel was elected unanimously; Louise de Limminghe by a good majority, and Elizabeth Galitzine and Eugénie de Gramont tied for the last place. Elizabeth Galitzine was elected on a second ballot, by a good majority. Sophie reappointed Elizabeth Galitzine as secretary general and Catherine de Charbonnel as bursar general, while Félicité Desmarquest became the admonatrix general, elected by the council. The Society was divided into provinces during the general council.[71]

The decrees of 1839 aimed at a radical restructuring of the Society. In less than three weeks, Sophie had achieved on paper what she had planned over many years and discussed with few members of the Society. There had been no general preparation either of the Society as a body, or of the members of the general council, for such radical changes. For Sophie the decrees of 1839 were the realisation of many years of thought. But for most members of the Society the decrees represented new ideas; they introduced a new structure of government into the Society, as well as several quite significant changes to the way of life they had known. But Sophie counted on her own capacity to communicate and convince her colleagues, by visits and by letters, and by the fact that she herself wanted the changes to the constitutions. However she had not counted on the dominant manner in which Rozaven took over the process of the council in Rome, nor was she aware of the antagonism felt towards him by many in the Society. She herself had found his treatment of Armande de Causans offensive and she did not hesitate to say so to Louise de Limminghe, though not to Rozaven himself. Nor did Sophie realise how Louise de Limminghe and Elizabeth Galitzine were viewed in the Society. Some felt that Louise de Limminghe had cut Sophie off from the membership; many did not trust Elizabeth Galitzine and saw her as the puppet of Rozaven. Thus while the content of the decrees were difficult enough for many to accept, the impact of Rozaven, Louise de Limminghe and Elizabeth Galitzine on the general council, and on Sophie herself, led some to doubt the wisdom of all that had transpired in Rome in the summer of 1839.

− 15 −

REPERCUSSIONS, JULY–DECEMBER 1839

The general council of 1839 closed on 5 July and the following day all the members had a visit with the pope, which some interpreted as formal approval of the deliberations. The Jesuit general, Jean Roothan, paid a courtesy call to Sophie at the Trinité and this too was taken as acceptance of the Society of the Sacred Heart's adoption of some Jesuit structures of government. Peace and harmony appeared to reign and Sophie prepared a circular letter for the Society, to accompany the text of the decrees. These were due for distribution in early September 1839.

While Sophie and Elizabeth Galitzine remained in Rome and prepared texts and letters for the Society, reaction to the work of the general council gathered momentum in Paris. Sophie had known that Eugénie de Gramont's acceptance was crucial and she had asked her several times to travel to Rome for the council. No doubt Eugénie's physical handicap made travelling painful and the long journey to Rome was a daunting prospect. In any event Eugénie was totally absorbed in the life of the Faubourg Saint-Germain and in her personal commitment to Archbishop de Quelen.[1] Sophie had written to Eugénie several times before and during the council, trying to keep her well informed. She also asked Marie d'Olivier to visit Eugénie on her way back to Beauvais after the council and tell her about the decisions taken in Rome. Sophie knew that if Eugénie de Gramont supported her then the decrees would be accepted in the Society. She learnt with dismay that Eugénie was determined to have nothing to do with them.

The general council only confirmed Eugénie de Gramont's misgivings. She was already suspicious of Sophie's plans and had complained that Elizabeth

Galitzine had taken all the archives of the Society, including those of the rue de Varenne, to Rome. In Elizabeth Galitzine's eyes Sophie's future residence in Rome was a foregone conclusion and so she had taken everything from the rue de Varenne. Sophie had warned Elizabeth Galitzine to leave the house archives in place but this was either forgotten or ignored. Sophie assured Eugénie that the archives of the rue de Varenne would be returned. But Eugénie had been alerted.[2]

On 4 July 1839 Sophie wrote a long letter to Eugénie, telling her the outcome of the council in detail. She admitted to feeling low and sad for the implications of her residence in Rome were weighing upon her. For several years Sophie had planned and spoken about modifications which had to be made to the constitutions, and in particular she spoke about her residence in Rome and the creation of provinces in the Society.[3] She told Eugénie about the creation of provincials, of provinces and confirmed her appointment as provincial of the houses in the north of France. She expressed great disappointment that Eugénie was not elected an assistant general again, though she reminded Eugénie that she had chosen to be absent.

Sophie had tried hard to have Eugénie elected assistant general and she told Aimée d'Avenas that she fought for this during the council. The community at the rue de Varenne were taken aback at the election of Elizabeth Galitzine and could not understand how Eugénie had been passed over:

> I have been expecting your observations on our nominations. It is clear that our Eugénie cannot be compared with the one who was preferred to her and although Eugénie only failed to be elected by a few votes my heart felt sad. I tried in vain to dispel the prejudices of some of the council members. One particular grievance, which you know about, could not be effaced. The consequences of those dinners, [held in the rue de Varenne], of the marriages which she [Eugénie] is held responsible for. . . . In the Provinces these things are exaggerated. . . . All this antagonised the members . . .How I have been mortified here over these matters. [4]

By way of comfort to Eugénie Sophie pointed out that, since the council, real executive power in the Society now lay with the superior general, the provincials and the local superiors. The assistants general were simply counsellors to the superior general and had no authority with regard to provinces or houses. In other words, Eugénie de Gramont would have more power in her new role than in the role of assistant general. It was a point which Eugénie took up with more enthusiasm than Sophie anticipated. Eugénie's nomination as provincial ensured that she could continue as superior of the rue de Varenne for the next three or even six years, despite the fact that she had been in the house virtually since 1818.[5]

By the middle of July detailed news of the council had been communicated first by Sophie herself and then by two of returning members, Adelaide de Rozeville and Marie d'Olivier. Both had complained quite openly that during the council they were put under great pressure to sign the decrees without proper discussion, that Rozaven was an overbearing presence throughout the entire proceedings, and that they were obliged to go to confession to him.[6] In her account of the general council Elizabeth Galitzine dismissed these complaints. She considered that de Rozeville and d'Olivier were disturbed by the Society of the Sacred Heart's adoption of the Jesuit model for the office of local superior. That model favoured brief, fixed mandates rather than prolonged periods of office.[7]

Sophie asked Eugénie not to judge the decrees too hastily and to wait until her return to Paris in the spring, when all would be much clearer and they could discuss the future together:

> You are my only support in France. The good God has left me so poor in person-nel! That is why he did not allow you to be assistant general for the time being. Everyone knows that you will be more useful to the Society in the post that you are about to assume. You were only a few votes short, but those present won the day. It had to be like that.[8]

Sophie asked Eugénie to look at the decrees in their totality and try and see the positive effect they could have in the Society. She went through them again, point by point.[9] While the question of residence was crucial, Sophie did not see it being implemented immediately but rather over a period of several years. Even then, if it did not prove effective she would return to France. This was already quite a significant shift in her thinking from July, when she actually out-lined to Eugénie how she saw her life in Rome evolving.[10] But she insisted that Eugénie look at the urgent need for provincials, as well as a permanent residence for the superior general and the assistants general. She simply could not carry on as before. It was not good either for her or for the Society. Sophie also argued that the self-perpetuating council of twelve, established by the 1815 constitutions, was totally inadequate to the needs of the Society. Most recognised this. As for changing local superiors, the need could not have been clearer throughout the Society as a whole and Sophie was spared having to say so to Eugénie directly, since her new office of provincial permitted her to stay on in the rue de Varenne:

> The change of superiors had become necessary. Several had become too firmly rooted in each house and were becoming like lady abbesses. A general move like this one will hurt no one.

Sophie concluded:

> I will finish with a short observation. If these changes, or rather improvements, are to be made, it would be better not to wait until I'm dead. Perhaps then they would become impossible to carry out. Anyway, now that we believe that we must adopt the government structures of the Jesuits, why adopt a truncated version? The Jesuits themselves have reproached us, saying that we were wrong to pride our-selves on resembling them when our constitutions and plan of government have little resemblance to theirs.
> That's enough of this petty justification. I can imagine your aversion.[11]

Indeed Eugénie had more than just repugnance for the decrees, she com-pletely rejected them and was unable to see any advantage in them at all. They had come as a surprise to her and she argued with Sophie that for twenty-three years the Society had lived according to the constitutions passed in 1826 and she had no idea that plans had been afoot for some time to change them. If Sophie had something better to offer the Society, surely three weeks in Rome was not enough time to effect such enormous changes. She could only conclude that Sophie had been dominated, indeed taken over by Rozaven, Elizabeth Galitzine and Louise de Limminghe and that she herself had had nothing to do with it.[12] Aimée d'Avenas, in charge of the studies in the school at the rue de Varenne, wrote graphically to Sophie:

> Your Council has imitated the Assembly of 1789: in a few days it has reduced the edifice to ruins. But when one destroys what was sacred in the eyes of all one exposes oneself to the destruction of one's own work in due time.[13]

Even more disturbing for Sophie was a letter from Joseph Varin. He had been informed of the changes by Eugénie de Gramont and on the basis of her account wrote in anger to Rome. He criticised Sophie and the members of the council in detail for the work they had done in Rome. In particular he accused them of destroying the foundations of the Society, treating the coadjutrix sisters shamefully, and changing the original aim and purpose of the Society of the Sacred Heart:

> This general council, established by the Society *solely* to guard the integrity and observation of its constitutions, constitutions approved by the sovereign pontiff . . . has itself overturned them from top to bottom and immediately afterwards proclaimed its own demise and destroyed itself forever.
> . . . I know what has been said, I hear the complaints made against the sisters. Yet if they have at times given cause for dissatisfaction, whose fault is that? Oh! if only they had been given a proper noviceship training, if care had been taken to teach them religion correctly and to form them in the spirit of the Society, as the constitutions required, we would have to praise them for their exemplary conduct.
> In the first constitutions it was stated – and it was the most fundamental article – that the Society was founded *solely* for the interests and glory of the Sacred Heart. That was its first and *only* purpose. Everything else which concerned the Society, whether it was the salvation and the perfection of the members, or the sanctification of the neighbour, ought to be considered as the means to achieve the end of the Society, that is, the glory of the Sacred Heart.[14]

Some days later, when Joseph Varin had had a long discussion with Marie d'Olivier, he wrote to Sophie again and repeated his concern that the general council had changed the aim of the Society of the Sacred Heart. He insisted that the aims of the Society of the Sacred Heart and the aims of the Jesuits were quite different and if the decrees were adopted by the Society of the Sacred Heart, all they had struggled for from the beginning would be lost. For the Society of the Sacred Heart

> is that which we saw being born thirty nine years ago, which received you as its first member in its lowly birthplace and which with the grace of God you have so wonderfully developed . . . Ask the Jesuits in Rome what the Society of Jesus would

think of a general congregation which would destroy the founding principles of the Society of Jesus . . . And when are you destroying the Society of the Sacred Heart? At the moment of its greatest prosperity. [15]

Indeed Joseph Varin had carried the spiritual vision of Léonor de Tournély faithfully and he had been with the Society of the Sacred Heart from its very beginnings in France. Both he and Sophie had journeyed together, perhaps not always easily but over the years they had reached a place of mutual respect. Joseph Varin had been present at all the general councils of the Society but had not been consulted for that of 1839. He was notorious for his indiscretion and Sophie could not have confided in him in the months leading up to her decision to hold the general council in Rome. However, his close involvement in the origins of the Society, as well as in its growth and flowering, gave him the moral authority to speak out. His source of information regarding the decrees was Eugénie de Gramont and then Marie d'Olivier. That Sophie had not written to him at all was a source of disappointment at least, though for several years Sophie had had less contact with Joseph Varin. In 1836 he had opposed even the discussion of her residence in Rome, though by 1839 he began to see it could have some advantages for the Society. He had asked Thérèse Maillucheau and Marie d'Olivier to tell Sophie of his change of view when they reached Rome for the council in June 1839. Generally, however, Sophie tended to filter information to Joseph Varin and cautioned others to do the same.

Joseph Varin's letters confirmed Sophie's worse fears, and when she wrote to Louise de Limminghe she admitted that mistakes had been made:

Pray hard to Our Lady of the Seven Sorrows. The Society is badly shaken. We have acted in every way with imprudence. We must proceed more slowly and disguise our plans. It has happened but what troubles I am going to reap! If only I suffer then it will not matter, but . . . [16]

Sophie was particularly sensitive to the accusation made by Joseph Varin that she had acted in a high-handed, arbitrary way. And she was even more annoyed when these views were conveyed not to her but to Félicité Desmarquest by Eulalie de Bouchaud. She reprimanded the mistress of novices and told her that information of that nature should come to her directly and not through someone else, even an assistant general. Sophie remained suspicious of Desmarquest and felt she wanted to replace her as superior general.[17] Yet the reprimand did not prevent Sophie speaking her mind about Joseph Varin to Eulalie de Bouchaud:

What weak arguments this good priest offers me. I hope that he will calm down. Time will tell that it is all for the best. So be steadfast as a rock and support us. But if you have to be as simple as a dove, you will also have to have the wisdom of a serpent.[18]

Sophie discussed with her assistants general in Rome how best to reply to both Joseph Varin's letters.[19] Some form of explanation was needed, not only because of Varin's unique position in the Society, but also because whatever was written would be spread around Paris and sent to other houses of the Society.

Moreover, Varin was due to give retreats in the houses in the west of France sometime in September. Sophie decided not to reply herself, but asked Elizabeth Galitzine to do so with the help of Rozaven. She also took the precaution of sending a copy of this letter to the superior of the houses where Varin was to stay.[20] By this time both Henriette Grosier and Geneviève Deshayes had heard about the content of the decrees and opposed them, with Eugénie de Gramont and Joseph Varin.

The letter drawn up by Elizabeth Galitzine was a systematic refutation of all of Joseph Varin's observations, in particular denying his charge that the council had changed the aim and the purpose of the Society of the Sacred Heart. The question of how the sisters were treated in the council was addressed and the reason given for such a decision:

> It is true that the coadjutrix sisters will no longer be admitted to final profession, yet how necessary this step was . . . and why should we not be allowed to adopt what was so wisely decreed by you, whereby the brothers are not admitted to final profession; nor are they less religious for that. But at least when we are in the sad position of having to send them out of the Society, if they do not have the vow of stability we do not have the distress of having to apply to the pope as has already occurred.[21]

Only some days previously Sophie herself had written a much clearer and softer explanation:

> People were wrong to have informed the sisters so quickly about matters concerning them. It was aimed directly at new entrants. The older sisters and those who are giving satisfaction could hope to have made their final profession. But if they are accepted do not go back on what has been decided. At the end of the day all the vows are the same and before God there is no difference. In the Jesuits the same arrangement [as proposed in 1839] applies to the brothers and all are happy and content. So I hope that this point will bring no difficulty, at least no more than the others. At least the sisters will be controlled, which will be a great help.[22]

Rozaven wrote a postscript to the letter drawn up by Elizabeth Galitzine and took Joseph Varin to task for basing his criticisms on false premises. He confirmed that he had helped the general council, with the full approval of Roothan. He rejected Varin's contention that the glory of the Heart of Christ was the unique aim of the Society of the Sacred Heart. One aim did not exclude another, one priority did not negate another. So the glory of the Heart of Christ did not exclude the perfection of the self or the service of the neighbour. It was a war of words and ideas. The style of the letter was not Sophie's, the words were not hers, the letter was cold and defensive, and Sophie's signature did not appear. The text expressed the attitudes of Elizabeth Galitzine and Rozaven, polemic, heady and determined. The role of Rozaven was only too evident. His postscript supported the letter written by Elizabeth Galitzine. Both had taken on Paris, Eugénie de Gramont, Joseph Varin and any who opposed the changes they viewed as so vital to the well-being of the Society of the Sacred Heart. This letter, originally intended for Joseph Varin alone, was sent to the provincials, vice-provincials, to those houses already disturbed by news of the decrees, and to the houses where Varin was due to give the community retreats in September: Tours, Niort and Poitiers.[23]

The question of both the choir and coadjutrix religious had long been a source of concern to Sophie Barat. She often lamented the quality of choir religious in the Society, the lack of leadership and teaching qualities in those who entered and the difficulty in forming so many who were lightweight and superficial. She complained about superiors who accepted such candidates easily and did not send them away soon enough. Most of all, Sophie Barat expected people to work when they entered, and she was critical of those, either choir or coadjutrix, who did not or would not work hard. Whatever the task assigned and regardless of their social background, Sophie expected the members to work earnestly. In 1827 she asked Favre if he thought that the coadjutrix sisters were receiving sufficient spiritual formation for their religious life. He thought it was adequate, though he could only go by the theory contained in the constitutions. Yet, since Sophie accepted the class divisions of the day, without question, she did not try to educate the sisters out of the class in which they had been born. Indeed the class structures, within which the Society of the Sacred Heart was born, were reflected in the life of the Society itself, not only in France but in every country and culture where the Society took root.

The skills of the coadjutrix sisters were vitally needed in the Society. No community or school could survive without the sustained gifts of those who could care for the sick, cook and clean, knit and sew, look after animals and see to the produce from the farm. It was an entire infrastructure which virtually sustained the lives of all. It was hard work and the sisters were often over-stretched. The ideal, contained in the constitutions, of the sisters' life mirroring the contemplative life of Jesus in Nazareth was attractive and many women entered for that reason. What intervened and affected the quality of life of both choir and coadjutrix religious was the rapid extension of the Society. There were too few members to sustain so much work. The temptation of superiors was to accept women into the Society, as much as for the work they could do as for their spiritual motivation. In the case of the coadjutrix sisters it became a mixture of a religious vocation to a congregation where their work was that of servants.[24] Sophie repeatedly told local superiors to maintain a balance in a community of two thirds choir and one third coadjutrix religious.

By 1843 there were almost as many coadjutrix as choir religious in the Society. In 1843, the first year that statistics were recorded, there were 148 professed coadjutrix religious and 405 professed choir religious. However, in the case of those still in formation the picture was quite different and it was this situation which the 1839 decrees sought to address. In 1843 there were 413 aspirant coadjutrix religious and 407 aspirant choir religious, with 175 novice coadjutrix religious and 156 novice choir religious. The picture showed the real imbalance creeping in that had to be addressed.[25] The solution was to enforce strict screening of all candidates at the moment of entry, and Sophie Barat constantly asked the superiors to carry this out. To her disappointment it was not done consistently. Moreover, since the coadjutrix sisters entered, made their noviciate and profession in the houses where they had entered, Sophie had little occasion to meet them personally, except while on visitation or if there was a crisis. Certainly the 1839 decree regarding the sisters caused much heart-searching and criticism throughout the Society.

This was merely one of the decrees which Eugénie de Gramont rejected. She continued to write irate letters to Sophie, rejecting the work of the general council. She asked Sophie how she could have accepted the proceedings and she reminded her of how in the past Sophie had criticised her assistants general, especially Elizabeth Galitzine and Félicité Desmarquest. This upset Sophie since she had spoken to Eugénie in trust:

> it is wrong for you to bring this up with me and to make use of it against me, particularly since these same people make up for their involuntary failings with genuinely great qualities.[26]

Their friendship had been at breaking point for some time. Now it was further stretched when Sophie received a detailed, scathing memoir. It was unsigned but clearly drawn up by Eugénie de Gramont and Aimée d'Avenas (in charge of the school studies) though sent in the name of the community at the rue de Varenne.[27] It showed, more than anything else, the model of religious life Eugénie de Gramont lived by and which she was determined to hold on to at all costs. Her memoir stressed the matters treated in the decrees. With regard to the residence of the superior general in Rome, Eugénie argued that the Society was French, most of its members were French and its reputation was French. Moreover the French bishops would not tolerate Sophie's residence in Italy and if Sophie insisted upon moving to Rome then a schism was possible. She rejected the suppression of office said in public, as giving the appearance of worldliness. Office was an integral part of her vision of religious life, and its omission was inexplicable, especially in the Faubourg Saint-Germain, where it was fashionable to attend vespers at the rue de Varenne. If the decree concerning the sisters was allowed to stand, the whole balance and indeed economy of religious life would be affected. Some would certainly leave the Society and then the communities and schools would have to get paid help. She did not accept that local superiors should be changed regularly and saw such an innovation as disruptive to the smooth running of a house.

These points, taken within the context of the Hôtel Biron, only exposed the contradiction in Eugénie de Gramont's position. She was entirely under the dominion of Archbishop de Quelen. Both were Gallican to the core and neither Eugénie de Gramont nor the archbishop wanted the Society of the Sacred Heart to be governed from Rome. As for the argument that the recitation of office safeguarded the religious life of the Society, Eugénie de Gramont could not see that the lifestyle of the community at the rue de Varenne caused scandal, though Sophie had told her time and time again. Although Eugénie complained that the sisters were badly treated, she herself was particularly demanding of them in the school and community.[28] But Eugénie de Gramont simply did not see that her way of life needed to be reformed, that it was a source of gossip and scandal and that she was at the centre of it. Her model of religious life was that of Saint-Estève. The Hôtel Biron was her Amiens and all Sophie's efforts over many years had not succeeded in modifying the views of her friend.

Eugénie rejected the 1839 decrees which had modelled the constitutions of the Society of the Sacred Heart much more closely on those of the Jesuits. She asked Sophie if the rumour was really true that each house of the Society was going to have a Jesuit named as superior. This was unthinkable and Eugénie saw the hand of Rozaven in this proposal, a man who had been out of France for fifty years. She repeated once more that Sophie should have consulted the entire Society about all the radical changes put through so rapidly in three short weeks. If the Society had taken ten years first to write and then to test the 1815 constitutions, should they not do the same now? This was a fair point. But the reality was that Sophie's ideas of modifying the constitutions had been well thought-out over a number of years. While Sophie saw the 1839 council as passing decrees which would allow her to govern better, Rozaven took the agenda out of her hands in Rome he had firm support in Elizabeth Galitzine and Louise de Limminghe. Eugénie de Gramont was at one extreme; Rozaven, Galitzine and de Limminghe were at the other. The next few months would see the aligning of forces on either side with Sophie forced to mediate between the two.

Sophie had no difficulty in receiving such a memoir but the stridency of its language troubled her. Sophie reminded Aimée d'Avenas:

> . . . I will never challenge your right to put forward your point of view. Your own character and that of the little mother [Eugénie de Gramont] are known to be genuine and true and you pursue your views in a straightforward manner. You might strike out to right and left, clashing with those who block your way; yet in expressing the truth we cannot tell all the truth and that is not at all lack of honesty.[29]

Sophie told Eugénie that the content of the memoir greatly saddened her. She knew Archbishop de Quelen's opposition to the decrees was influenced by that of Eugénie herself. Sophie sensed that the archbishop would not only block the decrees in Paris, but he would advise the other bishops in France to do likewise.[30] She knew that Eugénie would not await further explanation. She was tenacious and, as Sophie knew only too well, ready to fight her cause. Sophie wrote to Eulalie de Bouchaud, mistress of novices at the rue Monsieur, hoping to keep her loyal to the decrees of the council. This was difficult when Eugénie de Gramont was the newly appointed provincial and was responsible for the rue Monsieur. Sophie told Eulalie de Bouchaud to defer to Eugénie in all that pertained to the immediate running of the noviciate, but that in all else she was accountable to Sophie herself. She confided her worries to Eulalie:

> I have received your letter . . . and I thank you for it, for just now you cannot tell me too much of what you hear from your neighbours [in the rue de Varenne]. Their

opposition is definitely supported by Mgr de Quelen. This then is a disturbance from which we will be delivered by the Heart of Christ. Listen to all but say little and write and tell me everything you find out: that is your task. . . . If this fire spreads it may be necessary for me to go to Paris. Do not say a word about that. . . . Madame de Gramont is taking a path which she could well regret for she can do us harm. This is not her intention but once minds and hearts are divided who can prevent this? [31]

Sophie did not reply to Eugénie's memoir herself since it was not signed. Instead she asked Elizabeth Galitzine to draft a reply and to take particular care with the grammar and presentation in the document since every word would be scrutinised. Since Elizabeth Galitzine was resented in the rue de Varenne, Sophie told her to make sure that her handwriting did not appear in the final draft. She suggested that Eugénie Audé's would be acceptable to most in Paris. In her reply to the memoir from Paris Elizabeth Galitzine made no effort to disguise her delight that, with the passing of the decrees at the general council that year, the Society of the Sacred Heart had become more identified with the Jesuits, both in its spirit and in its form of government. Her reply was divided into three sections: the actual work of the general council; its authority to make decisions; the obligation of the members of the Society of the Sacred Heart with regard to the council. Basically the entire document claimed that the Society of the Sacred Heart was a universal congregation, not confined to France, and that the decrees of 1839 allowed it to become more truly what it was destined to be: a congregation, modelled on the Jesuits, and serving the universal church. As for the role of Jean Rozaven, the Society was privileged to have him present at the council, especially since the pope had appointed him to examine many recently founded religious congregations.[32] Indeed, while it was not a decree passed at the council, the Society of the Sacred Heart would be fortunate if each house had a Jesuit as its superior. The battle of words had begun and news of the growing divisions within the Society began to spread to the houses in France.

Geneviève Deshayes, one of the founding members of the Society, sent a letter of protest to Sophie and to Gregory XVI.[33] She had received copies of Elizabeth Galitzine's replies to Joseph Varin's letters and to Eugénie de Gramont's memoir. She voiced her fears that Sophie Barat and the Society were being taken over by the Jesuits, through the power of Jean Rozaven, Louise de Limminghe and Elizabeth Galitzine. The tone of Elizabeth Galitzine's replies only confirmed the rumours she had heard in France prior to Sophie's return to Rome in 1839: there was a plot afoot to push Sophie and the Society in another direction. The fact that three of the councillors, who could not attend the council in Rome, had been asked to sign their adhesion in advance was a gross abuse of trust and authority on Sophie Barat's part. They would never have agreed to sign their identity away. Deshayes asked Sophie who

ever ordered a Dominican to become a Carmelite? or a Jesuit to become a Capuchin? The pope would not force adherence or impose his authority by coercion, without the possibility of objecting to the Decrees which a small group of councillors drew up, approved and declared to be obligatory on all. . . . .They wish us to be perfect and suggest, or rather direct, that we imitate the Jesuits constitutions. We are not challenging those constitutions, but everything has its own perfect form, each religious order its own spirit. Women are not men and France is not Italy.[34]

Another letter arrived in Rome in late September which gave Sophie pause for serious thought. Césaire Mathieu, archbishop of Besançon and an old friend of Sophie Barat, wrote to tell her of his dismay at the 1839 decrees. When Adelaide de Rozeville had returned from Rome she had shown him the results of the council. He advised the community to accept and abide by them, but privately he was worried about the effect the decrees could have on the Society:

The reforms and innovations are still a very sensitive issue, especially for an order just beginning. These reforms and innovations create disquiet. They often raise storms which reach the foundation of religion which is meant to be like a safe port giving security. Just as reforms are introduced now after twenty years, so further changes can be brought in ten or in fifteen years, and those who entered the community in their youth may fear that they will see the fundamentals change during their lifetime.

He thought Sophie should not reside in Rome, because:

Most of your institutions are in France. Most of the members of the Society come from France, especially those who are the most suited for leadership. You are French and you know almost all the members personally. In this context to transfer the centre of the Society truly is unthinkable. The centre of Christianity is neither the physical centre of the work of the Society, *nor its spiritual centre.*

Césaire Mathieu did not think that provinces were really necessary and believed that she had enough scope in the 1826 constitutions to appoint more assistants general to help her govern. Nor did he see the need to change local superiors frequently and presumed that if she wanted to move one she would be obeyed. Césaire Mathieu was taken aback at how the coadjutrix sisters were treated in the decrees:

No more solemn vows for the coadjutrix sisters. What a retrograde step for these poor women, many of whom are saints and most of them so good! Why must there be such an enormous distinction between the choir and the lay religious in the humble Society of the Sacred Heart?
I am afraid . . . that [in Rome you] have been led in this matter by a badly thought out wish to resemble the Jesuits; [you did] not consider sufficiently the basic differences which have to exist between an order of men and a community of women . . . Was there no true friend there, able to give good advice and point out such simple observations and divert the members of the Council from collectively rushing into such a chasm?[35]

That letter was written on 14 September 1839, when the archbishop was travelling incognito by steamboat to Nîmes. Marie Prevost was on the same boat and by chance recognised him. They had a lengthy discussion on the subject of the decrees and Césaire Mathieu got a different picture from the one he had received from de Rozeville. Nevertheless, he did not write to Sophie again, to modify his views.

More letters arrived in Rome in the autumn of 1839, from four superiors, Gertrude de Brou at Tours, Aglae Fontaine at Autun, Antoinette de Gramont at Le Mans and Armande de Causans at Aix-en-Provence. The same points were raised in all four letters. They had been well informed by Eugénie de Gramont and had received copies of Elizabeth Galitzine's replies to Joseph Varin and Eugénie de Gramont. They told Sophie that the bishops of their dioceses were critical of the decrees, that they had agreed with Archbishop de Quelen's stance, and indeed some had complained to the pope.[36] One of the decrees particularly interested the diocesan bishops, that of the mandates of local superiors. The bishops saw that as interfering with their authority, placing the authority of the superior general beyond the control of the bishop. There was a particular case in point in Poitiers.

Sophie had been trying for some time without success to move Henriette Grosier from Poitiers, where she had been superior since 1815, with an exception of a short period in Amiens. In August 1839 Sophie decided, with the backing of the decrees, to try again. She explained to Henriette Grosier that she wanted to implement the decrees gradually in the Society, without unduly upsetting people, and that she had decided to ask Henriette to move from Poitiers to Bordeaux, though she promised that after three years she would try to arrange for her return to Poitiers. She counted on a favourable response since Henriette was one of the oldest in the Society and she ought to give a lead in obeying the new decree. She invoked the early days of the Society in Amiens, when they were asked to move quickly and anywhere, and she counted on Henriette to do the same now. Two weeks later Sophie realised that asking her to go to Bordeaux, out of the diocese of Poitiers, would be asking too much. She decided that Niort, which was in the diocese of Poitiers, needed a superior more urgently and asked Henriette to go there instead. [37]

In September the bishop of Poitiers, Jean Baptiste de Bouillé (1819–42) wrote to Sophie and asked her to justify the decrees of the general council. He particularly asked her to reconsider two things: her residence in Rome, and changing Henriette Grosier from Poitiers. The bishop argued that introducing regular changes of the local superior would have a bad effect on the parents of the pupils. Stability in leadership was important for the Society of the Sacred Heart, whose educational work was intended for the upper classes of society.[38] It was a clear message not to move Grosier. Sophie replied carefully. She expressed appreciation that the bishop had written directly to her and she answered his queries systematically. She explained that the constitutions of the Society of the Sacred Heart had not been changed as such, but that additional articles had been drawn up to reflect the reality of the growth of the Society throughout the world, not just in France. The additional articles were taken from the original source of the 1815 constitutions, that is to say, from the Jesuits. She considered that Rome was the right place for the mother house of the

Society. While in the political sense it was indeed another state, in the religious sense it was the centre of Christendom and the Society of the Sacred Heart was destined to be universal, not just confined to France. With regard to the question of changing superiors, Sophie told the bishop that she hoped the parents had confidence in the Society of the Sacred Heart as a body rather than in individuals. Indeed she regretted that she had to insist on Henriette Grosier moving to Niort but the superior there was needed elsewhere in the Society. However, she reminded the bishop that Niort was still in his diocese and that after her term of office was completed in Niort, it was possible that Grosier could return to Poitiers once more.[39]

Despite her letter, by November 1839 Sophie was obliged, under pressure from Henriette Grosier herself, some of the community in Poitiers, the local clergy as well as the bishop, to reverse her decision. Sophie permitted Henriette Grosier to remain as superior at Poitiers, but she was frustrated at how her authority had been thwarted:

> What will become of the Society if each one interferes in its government and believes that she has the right to object to all the operations of the superior general? The role of superior general would founder, for who would take it?[40]
> All these difficulties concerning changing superiors, have arisen even though I have the incontrovertible right to do so. I must admit that it is getting very difficult to govern a Society when I am blocked at every step.[41]

Sophie was concerned at the number of bishops who had written to the pope about the decrees of the general council. To counteract such complaints, she decided to present the Society's view and asked Elizabeth Galitzine to draw up a memoir and have Rozaven examine it before sending it to Gregory XVI.[42] Even Rozaven himself was taken aback at Elizabeth Galitzine's aggressive tone and he began to protect himself and the Jesuits. It was one thing to exercise power privately within the Society of the Sacred Heart, but quite different if this were to become known publicly. Already, Roothan in Rome and the Jesuits in Paris, were critical of Rozaven's role in the affairs of the Society of the Sacred Heart and wanted him to distance himself from further involvement with the Society of the Sacred Heart.

Elizabeth Galitzine presented two major points to the pope. One was Sophie Barat's understanding that the pope wished her to reside in Rome. The second was the wish of the Society of the Sacred Heart to adopt the Jesuit constitutions in full. When her document was complete she asked Rozaven to read it. He told Elizabeth Galitzine that he thought the pope had never formally said that Sophie Barat should reside in Rome. Though the pope had been pleased when Sophie was in Rome and had always urged her to return, he had not insisted that she move the centre of the Society there. Nevertheless, what Elizabeth Galitzine said was partially true. Ever since Sophie's first visit to Rome in 1832 the pope regularly expressed pleasure at her presence in Rome and hoped that her visits would be frequent. This had become a source of concern in France and more than once both Joseph Varin and Eugénie de Gramont had asked her not to consider living in Rome. As her problems in the rue de Varenne became more intractable the thought of living in Rome appealed to Sophie.

With regard to the Society's adoption of the Jesuits' constitutions, Rozaven had an even stronger reaction: 'You said that you wished to adopt our constitutions pure and entire, in so far as they could be adapted to your Society. I do not approve of this declaration.'[43]

Rozaven asked Elizabeth Galitzine and Sophie to consider the implication of such a statement to the pope. If the French government heard of this, the Society of the Sacred Heart would be even more identified with the Jesuits in France.[44] Rozaven was aware of the of the growing resistance in France to the 1839 decrees and he suggested that the three-year trial period, requested by Eugénie de Gramont in her memoir, be used as a way of easing the tension. Even Rozaven had recognised that the Society could be torn apart by dissent and division, and his further disengagement was signalled by his refusal to present the memoir to the pope in the name of the Society. Having taken part for some years in the project of modifying the constitutions of the Society of the Sacred Heart he found himself unable to own that role in public:

> Unfortunately I have too many good reasons . . . and I feel myself obliged to refuse. Surely you will not attribute this refusal to a lack of interest in your Society. God knows how much I have invested in it, but to be of benefit to you my involvement of necessity must be discreet.[45]

Rozaven did not recognise how fanatically loyal Elizabeth Galitzine was to him and that this blinded her to everything and everyone else, even (perhaps especially) Sophie Barat. As Armande de Causans had remarked long ago to Sophie, Rozaven's only apparent weakness was his infatuation with Elizabeth Galitzine. Elizabeth Galitzine had begun to imagine that she had the capacity to inspire others to follow her vision for the Society of the Sacred Heart. Sophie knew her better and she thought that while Elizabeth Galitzine's could function well as secretary general, she was not capable of being a leader. But Elizabeth Galitzine had been elected at the 1839 council and now held three powerful positions in the Society. She was secretary general, assistant general and provincial of the American houses.

By October 1839 the relationship between Sophie and Elizabeth Galitzine was deteriorating. Sophie found it difficult to moderate the intensity of Elizabeth Galitzine's commitment to the outcome of the council. She seemed consumed with her own mission of modelling the constitutions of the Society of the Sacred Heart as closely as possible on those of the Jesuits. For a long time she had been impatient with Sophie's cautious procedure. She wanted Sophie to assert her authority in the Society and to insist that all, especially Eugénie de Gramont, conform immediately to the decrees of 1839. She could not imagine why Sophie would hesitate, delay or modify anything which had been passed during the council and she expressed her frustration when signs of this began to appear in late August. Her total commitment to her vision for the

Society made her unaware of the effect she had on others. Sophie realised this herself:

> The reason I said nothing to you . . . about the pain you have caused me is precisely because you would not have been aware of what you had done. You might have thought then, as you undoubtedly still do, that you had the right to treat me like that. Maybe I could have been tricked by my own sensitivity, but our mothers here have let me know how saddened they were and one in particular left with her heart broken by your behaviour.
> Nevertheless, I am not demanding an apology. In your case it would be useless, since in your view you have done nothing wrong. You will do the same again at the first opportunity. I hope that I will not provide the occasion for you. What I need to do is take my own precautions.[46]

Louise de Limminghe tried to talk to Elizabeth Galitzine and asked her to apologise to Sophie. But as Sophie knew when she received the apology, it was a matter of going through the motions, a useless and empty exercise.[47] Elizabeth Galitzine had determined to follow what she was convinced was her duty and in this she was supported by her father-figure Jean Rozaven. Indeed Elizabeth Galitzine continued to deliberately block Sophie and when Sophie asked her to tell the provincials to implement the decrees slowly and by degrees, Elizabeth Galitzine conveniently forgot to include this wish in the letters sent out. Sophie had to face daily outright, personal antagonism of her secretary general, who treated her with impatience and rudeness.[48] By the autumn of 1839 Sophie realised with sadness that not only had the general council been taken over by Rozaven, Elizabeth Galitzine and Louise de Limminghe but that she herself had been pushed aside. News from France some few weeks later had confirmed her alarm and Sophie admitted there was a logic to the complaints, especially regarding the haste in which all had been presented and passed. She had tried to express her reservations at the council and these had been rejected then, as she reminded Louise de Limminghe:

> Our affairs are taking a bad turn. I am sorry that I did not follow my own feelings, or rather the insight that comes from my position, for that enables me to see what others fail to perceive. We need to pray more than ever.[49]

Sophie herself sent the memoir drawn up by Elizabeth Galitzine to Gregory XVI, in which the content of the decrees passed at the council were described in detail, but no mention was made of the Jesuits at all or of the verbal approvals which the pope had given to the possibility of Sophie's residence in Rome.[50] Thus both the pope and Rozaven were protected from been drawn into the debate, and Sophie was left alone to deal with the crisis. Yet while such a situation left Sophie isolated, in the long run it served her well. As she faced into the thickening clouds of division, dissent and rebellion in the Society she needed to be independent, alone and free. The next three years were to be the hardest of her life. She had reached her sixtieth year in December 1839. She would need all her wisdom, experience and inner vision to see herself and the Society across this threshold. The threshold was her of her own making and design. She had known for some time that change was needed in the Society. Most did not understand this, and several would try to wrest the plan from Sophie. She was comforted when Joseph Varin wrote to her in November 1839 and told her that he had realised that Sophie had not written the letter to him in September:

> Neither your spirit nor your style were recognisable in it, and one of our more learned Jesuits remarked that it is obvious that whoever wrote it does not know the Institute of the Jesuits . . . Oh! If only you had suppressed such an inconsiderate letter and if you had relied on the personal explanations which Mother Prevost gave me . . . In the explanations she gave me and in what your last letter dealt with, I could recognise you as the person I have known, and I have said several times: That is the true state of affairs, measures full of gentleness and wisdom.[51]

This letter was a great comfort to Sophie. Joseph Varin, as impulsive and indiscreet as ever, was also generous and honest enough to tell Sophie that he had jumped to conclusions. Generous too in not asking her why she had delegated such a vital letter to Elizabeth Galitzine. But few could understand why Sophie let the letter go as it was, signed not only by Elizabeth Galitzine but also containing a postscript written by Rozaven.

Once Marie Prevost had returned to Lyon after the council, she began hearing news of Eugénie de Gramont's reaction to the decrees and she told Sophie about it. Sophie replied and asked her and Catherine de Charbonnel to visit the rue de Varenne and explain the decrees to Eugénie de Gramont and the community. However, Marie Prevost saw immediately that this would not work. Eugénie de Gramont was the provincial of the houses in the north of France, appointed by Sophie herself. Eugénie had official authority but neither Marie Prevost nor Catherine de Charbonnel had any real power to effect change, other than as visitors appointed by Sophie. The only solution which Marie Prevost could suggest was for Sophie to replace Eugénie de Gramont as provincial. She could remain superior in the rue de Varenne and then Catherine de Charbonnel could make a formal visitation of the rue de Varenne as the assistant general, accompanied by Marie Prevost.

Sophie received further letters confirming Marie Prevost's view on the situation in Paris, and warning her as well that some of the French bishops were critical of the decrees. Basically the bishops objected to having any decisions from Rome foisted upon them in their dioceses, even when it concerned the inner life of the Society. The tussle between Rome and France, between Gallicanism and ultramontanism, was played out in their insistence on the right to be consulted. In that sense it was not a rejection of Sophie Barat and the Society of the Sacred Heart, but of its alignment with the authorities in Rome. Both Eugénie de Gramont and Aimée d'Avenas (despite their protestations to the contrary in letters to Sophie) continued to contact both bishops and communities in France, and they tried to form a solid group of opposition to the 1839 decrees. Whereas Joseph Varin initially had sided with Eugénie de Gramont, by the autumn of

1839 he stated firmly that he supported the decrees and urged all in the Society to do so.[52] Sophie did not trust this completely and indeed later discovered that he had veered once again and worked with Eugénie de Gramont to reverse the 1839 decrees:

> He [Joseph Varin] distresses and impedes us a lot . . . as you have seen, for you told me about his conversation with Mde de Gramont . . . What can we do? Place our trust in God and hope for help from Him alone! I have to tell you that we are being deserted on all sides.[53]

Rozaven was careful to disguise his role in the affairs of the Society of the Sacred Heart, at least in Rome, though in France those who opposed the decrees blamed Rozaven, Louise de Limminghe and Elizabeth Galitzine for the outcome of the 1839 council. Aimée d'Avenas defended Eugénie de Gramont and said she was being used as a scapegoat by Galitzine, and Rozaven:

> They want the little mother to take the blame for all the complaints and to maintain with you the artificial, gushy pretence of obedience. . . . We have really opened our hearts to you and have spoken to you according to our conscience. We urge them to do the same and not implicate us in their affairs. I have written on her [Eugénie de Gramont's] behalf. If the little mother was not so charitable and if prudence did not dictate otherwise, I could send you other copies [of documents] in which you will see strange things stemming from your flock. They take it upon themselves to denounce us as *dissenting from you*. The word *'dissenter'* means one who breaks away. Yet why would we wish to break away? We will remain attached to the original foundation. . . . All [here] are hurt by your silence towards them which is forcing them to write to the pope and to speak in public instead of approaching you. . . . The little mother is distressed about her position, but she has told you everything and you did not want to believe any of it. She asks me to say to you that while you have always loved her, yet you have preferred the advice of others to hers. And I must add *that you have given her hardly any support in all that she has suffered within the Society.*[54]

Aimée d'Avenas was Eugénie de Gramont's mouthpiece and her letter to Sophie contained veiled threats. She asked Sophie to return to Paris immediately in order to avoid a schism and warned of the danger should the government hear of Sophie's possible move to Rome. That would breach the statutes of 1827 and bring the Society into conflict with the government. D'Avenas was voice of the old Society, which Sophie wanted to renew and invigorate and bring forward into the future. There was a certain truth that the decrees of 1839 were a strategy on the part of Elizabeth Galitzine, Louise de Limminghe and Jean Rozaven to take Sophie away from the rue de Varenne, from France for good. The rue de Varenne had restricted Sophie for years. She had a continual battle with Eugénie de Gramont to retain her independence, rendered particularly difficult by the presence of Archbishop de Quelen. What the dissidents in Paris did not realise was that Sophie had planned the process herself over some years and wanted the changes in the government structures of the Society. However, what Sophie herself could not have anticipated was the number of those who, for several reasons, wished above all to implement the 1839 decrees. This group within the Society was much bigger and more widespread than merely Elizabeth Galitzine, Louise de Limminghe and Jean Rozaven. Many members of the Society had had enough of the rue de Varenne, of Eugénie de Gramont and of Sophie's inexplicable tolerance of her over so many years.

Marie Prevost voiced this when she wrote to Sophie in November 1839. She had arrived in Paris with Catherine de Charbonnel on 1 November and both stayed at the rue Monsieur, rather than the rue de Varenne. This visit was a difficult one for Catherine de Charbonnel. Even her travelling companion, Marie Prevost, as well as Eugénie de Gramont and Joseph Varin, expressed little confidence in her. As far as possible they ignored her. For a woman who was quite deaf and almost blind this was a painful, isolating experience.[55] Both Eugénie de Gramont and Joseph Varin, without reference to Sophie, advised Catherine de Charbonnel not to exercise her office as provincial in the west of France.[56] Yet, after several meetings with Marie Prevost Joseph Varin declared he understood the purpose of the decrees as well as the background to the decisions taken, and he would support them. Marie Prevost also learnt that other Jesuits, old friends of the Society and for the most part former Fathers of the Faith, also supported the 1839 decrees and thought they would be helpful for the growing needs of the Society of the Sacred Heart. All of them, particularly Joseph Varin, had decided that they would not enter into any of the debates opening up within the Society. Later they were ordered by their superiors in Paris and Rome to distance themselves from the Society of the Sacred Heart.

Significantly, in the course of her conversations with Archbishop de Quelen, Marie Prevost had discovered that if Eugénie de Gramont had accepted the 1839 decrees, he would not have interfered,

> which proves more than ever that she is [similar to] the [brother] Elias of St Francis of Assisi. But this saint, *while enfolding him [Elias] in the mantle of charity* never conceded to his wishes to abolish or even weaken what the *general assemblies* had decided. This poor Elias tried to get supporters to work against Francis to destroy what Francis had built up at great cost. But the Lord was there to hinder the arrogance of Elias, who wanted to supplant his father and his master.[57]

The comparison Marie Prevost made between St Francis of Assisi and Brother Elias showed Sophie how she and Eugénie de Gramont were seen by many in the Society. Marie Prevost reminded Sophie of what had happened in Amiens, in the early days of the Society. As some had planned to depose Sophie as superior general then, so there were plans afoot to do so now. She warned Sophie:

> They are trying to frighten you . . . just as Charles X was frightened and she who would willingly have taken your place twenty-five years ago is doing all in her power now to have people believe and to prove that you govern the Society only through her. She even takes it upon herself to censor your letters.[58]

Sophie was disturbed at what Marie Prevost had picked up during her visit to Paris and to the other houses of the north of France. It was clear that Eugénie de Gramont had expressed publicly her opposition to the decrees; that she had informed several bishops and priests of the council decrees and of her views on them; that she withheld some of Sophie's personal letters to members of the Society, as well as Elizabeth Galitzine's letters and Sophie's formal, circular letter to the Society, written in September 1839.[59] Sophie's forebodings were increased when Marie de la Croix wrote to her and told her that her own memories of 1815 in Amiens and Paris were disturbing her and she was reliving what had happened in 1815 in Amiens and Paris:

> When I recall the first attempts of the powers of hell to try and separate us from Sophie whom God gave us as our leader and mother, I want to cry tears of blood. Alas, these new problems are unfortunately true . . . It is like the remains of an old wine, still fermenting. It is an unfortunate affair which we must conceal from the members of the Society as far as possible. . . .
> Our Society . . . is no longer in its infancy. Now it contains mature and devoted members who are its ramparts . . . The defection of a few now can no longer threaten the ruin of the Society, and our mother general need no longer fear what caused her so much sorrow, apprehension and grieving in 1815.[60]

Marie Prevost, too, drew comparisons with the crisis of 1815. She remembered that when Eugénie de Gramont colluded with Saint-Estève, the affairs of the Society remained unknown to the general public. But now it was quite different. Eugénie de Gramont had brought the issue of the 1839 decrees to the notice of the French bishops and compromised both Sophie Barat and the Society of the Sacred Heart. The decrees had not even been printed and sent to Paris when complaints were made and Sophie's leadership denounced to the bishops.[61] Marie Prevost spoke at length with Louis Barat in Paris and like his colleagues he encouraged holding firm to the new decrees. More direct criticism of Sophie came from another Jesuit, Louis Sellier:

> He *is furious* at your indulgence. Mother de Gramont has spoken of what you said to her in private. For example, that you had done *all you could to sway [the council] so that she would be elected assistant general*. One of the councillors told him that you had said in Rome that looking around *the whole Society you saw only Mother de Gramont as capable of governing it*. You must realise . . . statements of this kind at such a moment give rise to unfortunate consequences. . . . Then he added: 'your mother general should recall what I told her so often, *that in supporting Eugénie de Gramont, who has betrayed the Society, means Sophie is contributing to its destruction herself.*' . . . I told him that you intended to hold firm to a trial period for the Decrees. . . . '*I will believe it when I see it*', he replied.[62]

In October 1839 Clement Boulanger wrote to the general of the Jesuits, to complain about the involvement of Rozaven in the affairs of the Society of the Sacred Heart. He referred in particular to the letter written by Elizabeth Galitzine to Joseph Varin which had included a postscript from Rozaven. Both had been indiscreet and had compromised the Jesuits in the eyes of the French bishops, most of whom were critical of the 1839 decrees. Neither the French bishops nor the French government would accept Elizabeth Galitzine's proposition that the

Society of the Sacred Heart be accountable to the Jesuits and that the superior general would, like the Jesuit general, live in Rome.[63] Roothan asked Rozaven to write to the Jesuit Provincial in Paris, Achille Guidée, and answer the charge that he had meddled in the affairs of the Society of the Sacred Heart and had compromised the Jesuits in Paris and indeed in France. In his letter to Guidée Rozaven presented his actions as both minimal and secondary and in his own defence was economical with the truth. He admitted that he had been approached by the Society of the Sacred Heart during the 1839 general council but made no mention of the years of negotiation with Sophie Barat prior to that, nor of his links with Elizabeth Galitzine and Louise de Limminghe. He confirmed that the decrees had been communicated to him but omitted to say that he had been present during the sessions of the council:

> I have a clear conscience and I am not worried about what they say. What does it matter to me that someone exaggerates and says *that I have overpowered the mother general and some others and that I have imposed what I wanted on them?* I would laugh at this nonsense . . . the enemy of all good is seeking to kindle the fire of discord in a congregation from which the church expects great results.[64]

Guidée accepted this explanation and wrote to the general at the end of November, agreeing with Roothan's assessment:

> So you have refuted the absurd fantasy of Mme XXX [Elizabeth Galitzine] who alleges that Fr Rozaven intends to appoint a Jesuit as superior and confessor of each house of the Society of the Sacred Heart. You know how fertile an imagination this good lady has in creating fanciful ideas, but this one is too much and exceeds the limits of ridicule and absurdity.[65]

Roothan was apprehensive when he saw the Jesuits were being dragged into the affairs of the Society of the Sacred Heart and thought the time had come for all Jesuits to cease all contact with any community or member of the Society of the Sacred Heart:

> . . . I have known for years that the seeds of division existed among these women, that with their present *form* of government this division seemed inevitably to perpetuate and bring about deplorable consequences. At least that is what is said. . . . And for that reason the mother general, on the advice of several of her councillors, thought a congregation [general council] should be held . . . [66]

When Jean Brumauld de Beauregard, former bishop of Orléans (1823–39) wrote to Roothan in November 1839, he outlined the problem as he saw it. While he admired the Society of the Sacred Heart, he thought that its structure of government was weak. He was critical of Sophie Barat, who hardly ever resided in Paris and continually travelled in France or in Italy. He hinted that she was authoritarian, that she rarely convened her members of council and most of them lived far away from one another, at great distances.[67] These remarks were quite valid, reflected Sophie's own way of governing the Society, and she herself had recognised that a more stable form of government was needed. Yet neither Roothan nor Beauregard were aware of the situation at the rue de Varenne, where Archbishop de Quelen, with the collusion of Eugénie de Gramont, had weakened Sophie's role and authority within the Society and in the perception of the public.

At this time the French government continued to be particularly antagonistic towards the Jesuits. If they were to survive another suppression they had to avoid all controversy, especially any regarding the authority of Rome. Nevertheless, the members of the Society of the Sacred Heart and of the Society of Jesus were old friends; they had come through a great deal together in revolutionary times and worked closely in the opening years of the nineteenth century. Those in Rome, especially Roothan and Rozaven, had not been through that particular experience. So many of the Jesuits in Paris and in Amiens continued to comment on the affairs of the Society of the Sacred Heart, sometimes in public and often in ways that disturbed Sophie herself.[68] The superior at Amiens, Laure de Portes, told Sophie how the Jesuits there reacted to Sophie's choice of Eugénie de Gramont as provincial:

> The choice of the little mother [Eugénie de Gramont] as Provincial has astonished all the Jesuits, including Fr Sellier. He says she will spread her own spirit to the other houses in her province and she does not have the spirit of the Society. All this is the result of her relationship with Archbishop de Quelen which for a long time has been the talk of the salons of Paris . . . [69]

All such correspondence showed Sophie how polarised the Society had become in France, and what awaited her when she returned to France. What astonished her was the amount of feeling aroused. Marie de la Croix had put her finger on it when she said it was an old wine still fermenting. This old wine, these old agendas, these contentious issues, surrounding the personal relationship between Sophie Barat and Eugénie de Gramont, the struggle with Saint-Estève and Eugénie de Gramont in Amiens, the situation at the rue de Varenne with Archbishop de Quelen living and working in the Hôtel Biron and the Petit-Hôtel, were finding their way into the public domain. The germ of destruction, the shadow side of the Society of the Sacred Heart, prophesied by Jean Montaigne in 1808, lived on after 1815. When the crisis broke in 1839, the old hurts and wounds resurfaced, demanding to be addressed.

At the end of this year Sophie could only be filled with dismay and foreboding. So much had happened between December 1838, when Armande de Causans fled the Trinité, and December 1839, when the body of the Society was in turmoil. Henriette Grosier wrote to her, expressing the hope that her health was standing up to all the pressure. Sophie, clearly irritated by the query from one who had certainly caused her stress, replied:

> No . . . my health is far from being good. You would not recognise me now. I have lost the capacity to sleep and to eat since the council, and I have been unable to regain either. I cannot digest the little I eat. I have to rest after every meal except lunch. The day before yesterday the doctor was alarmed at my weak state. The kind of life I lead could only have this effect. There is no point in saying this to those outside. Fortunately this condition does not prevent me from working as usual. When I have exhausted my strength, then that is the end.[70]

Despite the news that was coming in daily from France, Sophie refused to express any criticisms of others in public, especially of Eugénie de Gramont and Aimée d'Avenas. She knew that she could not blame other members of the Society for what had happened. She knew that during the council she had allowed herself to be overruled and for a time she had lost trust in her own intuitions. For years she had planned to modify the constitutions of the Society so that she had more effective executive power as superior general. The possibility of living in Rome had been mooted for some years and apart from consolidating her own position, it would give Sophie a way out of the impasse at the rue de Varenne. She knew that she would have to insist on stringent conditions for entry in to the Society, for choir and sister religious. In this context, she had insisted on a longer period of formation for both groups, and the simple vows of the sisters, rather than solemn profession. She never dreamt that such measures would take the Society into such division and dissent, and she was shattered by the effect of the decrees in some houses in France. Marie Prevost, Catherine de Charbonnel and Desmarquest supported such changes and made a powerful pressure group with Rozaven, Louise de Limminghe and Elizabeth Galitzine, especially since it seemed clear that Sophie wanted them. But the decrees were genuinely a shock in Paris, Tours, Poitiers, Autun and Beauvais. No agenda for the council had been circulated, no advance preparation had been asked for, no prior soundings taken. A great deal of the criticism stemming from France was true and based on common sense. No wonder then they thought that Sophie was virtually a prisoner in Rome and that she had been forced to act as she did. Indeed, Sophie admitted that she had acted out of character. Her style of government was usually to invite, suggest, rather than force or insist, and this was well known in the Society. In the wake of the general council of 1839 Sophie was taken aback at the harsh way she was being criticised:

> Undoubtedly . . . my procedure was forced, for this is not my usual way of acting at all. But should I . . . not show any bitterness at all the problems which several people have overwhelmed me with over these months past? It is not good enough to show me rudeness. Is it pleasant to have such insults sent to the rue de Varenne, instructing them there to pass them on to me anonymously, and yet I know that at the same time these very people are writing letters of obedience to me! Also, some call me obsequious, that is the word . . . I cannot suspect you of this. It is too far removed from your character and from your way of being with me. But you must realise that that this way of behaving [towards me] is not conducive to my acting in a gentle and cordial manner.[71]

Whatever about the way she handled the general council in Rome, Sophie would need all her skills of leadership in the future to steer her way through the currents flowing within the Society at this time. By Christmas 1839 it was clear to Sophie that the decrees had exposed attitudes and vested interests, as well as old agendas which reached back to 1815 and indeed even earlier. If these could be faced honestly it would cleanse the Society of its seed of destruction. Most of all Sophie Barat had to accept that she had allowed her better judgement to be overridden and her authority to be cast aside. She had to accept the outcome of her mistakes and try and remedy them. Despite her angry words to Henriette Grosier, Sophie recognised this and told Louise de Limminghe:

> so much is due to human weakness! I see this all the time! What draws me to towards this consideration is my own great need. People need a great deal of indulgence to put up with me.[72]

Sophie reflected wryly that in 1839 she thought she was introducing a new structure of government which would help the Society in its evolution. It turned out to be nothing as simple or straightforward as that. Instead she had evoked a whirlwind upon herself and upon many individuals within the Society and beyond it.

— 16 —

DIVISION AND DISSENT, 1839–1840

W hy did the general council of the Society of the Sacred Heart, convened in 1839, cause such disturbance? It affected the leadership of the Society; it drew the criticism of the French bishops, as well as the Jesuits in Rome and in Paris; it placed the relationship between the pope and Archbishop de Quelen (and later his successor, Archbishop Affre) under further strain than it had been for some time. The Society's internal agenda, the private world of women, became part of the public domain. It became caught in the Gallican/ultramontane controversy, reflected in the often tense relations between the pope and the French hierarchy, especially the archbishop of Paris. Sophie could not have anticipated such consequences. She had believed that reform was needed at many levels in the Society of the Sacred Heart, and the crisis that followed the general council of 1839 showed her only too clearly that it was more profoundly needed than she had realised. Marie Prevost gave her the clue in talking about the relationship between Francis of Assisi and Brother Elias, and Sophie was faced with the choices she had made since 1815, especially her strategy of almost boundless tolerance of Eugénie de Gramont. Faithful to a point of blindness, Sophie could no longer hold out any hope, even to herself, that finally Eugénie de Gramont would listen to her at the level of spiritual idealism, never mind at any other level. Thus the crisis of 1839 reached into several layers of the Society's story, into its history, into its shadow world. It exposed the Society for what it was, for what it had become; it questioned where it was going and by whom would it be led.

And Sophie Barat, so hesitant and unsure in 1833, as to whether or not she should be superior general, did not question her leadership of the Society at this time. In November 1839 she wrote another circular letter to the Society, her third that year, explaining the 1839 decrees further in the hope of putting an end to the unrest within France. She did not hide her disappointment that debates and arguments over the decrees had affected the Society and damaged

> the good spirit maintained until now . . . this close and intimate union which has constantly lightened the weight of my anxiety, has been my strength and support in the midst of innumerable oppositions pitched against the Society from its birth. The greatest assaults on the Society have been repulsed by this bronze wall, this impregnable bulwark of divine love. I cannot hide the fact that this wall has been weakened at the time of the [1839] Decrees.[1]

Most of all, Sophie deplored the fact that so many, rather than writing to her, had complained to the pope, to bishops and priests, and to those members of the Society who originally had taken a positive attitude towards the decrees. She announced that in view of the divisions created or exposed by the decrees, she had decided to take up a suggestion made by Eugénie de Gramont in her memoir: Sophie proposed that the 1839 decrees be tried for a three-year period. If they proved to be unhelpful, then a general council could annul them. But Sophie suggested that if they were accepted and tried with an open mind, the decrees would be experienced as both necessary and helpful to the life of the Society.

She signalled two issues which had caused misunderstanding. One was the recitation of office which some, particularly Eugénie de Gramont, held to as an integral part of religious life. Sophie repeated what she had said in the previous circular letters, that for those who taught and used their voices all day, she thought quiet, non-vocal prayer was more helpful than office. However, if some houses had the personnel and the ability to say office with dignity then she would not impede that in any way. The other issue was the decree concerning the coadjutrix sisters:

> I have something more to point out with regard to the article concerning the vows of our coadjutrix sisters. It is necessary to help them understand that, like Jesuits whose constitutions we have adopted for some time now, they will reach the grade of professed coadjutrix sisters at the end of ten years. They will then be as sure of remaining in the Society when they reach this stage as if they had made the vow of stability. The defects and failings which require release from simple vows, are the same defects and failings which require release from the vow of stability. This vow adds nothing to the [spiritual] value of simple vows. Since simple vows are perpetual, following the declarations of the popes, they are as perfectly religious as even solemn vows. So let our dear Sisters rest assured that the measure taken in their regard is not to their detriment. We appreciate their devotedness and their loyalty to the Society and they can count fully on our affection which has not changed in any way in their regard.[2]

It was the most Sophie could say in public, and as far as it went it was true. She could hardly have said that many sisters had been accepted too hastily into the Society and many were quite unsuited for religious life. On a more immediate level, the denial of final profession to the coadjutrix sisters had a practical objective. Sophie wanted to avoid as many cases as possible reaching authorities in Rome, causing endless correspondence as well as damaging both those concerned and the reputation of the Society. But she knew also that the same lack of discernment of candidates applied to the choir religious and their release from vows was troublesome too. However there was a key issue which could not be voiced at all. Over the years, Sophie had planned to create grades of membership within the Society, among the choir religious. At the centre of the Society, for the purpose of leadership and formation, there would be an elite group, carefully chosen and formed. Only they would make final profession, with the vow of stability. This was in function of the roles they would exercise in the Society, and in theory it did not imply a spiritual superiority. In practice, of course it would as the reaction to the decision regarding the sisters showed. As a way of preparing for this development in the Society, the period of formation was to be extended to ten years with the implication that this could be prolonged indefinitely. The taking of first vows was a true commitment, but not a binding one on the Society of the Sacred Heart. Thus, in the future in the Society there would be many coadjutrix sisters and choir aspirants who would only make profession of simple vows. The elite would go forward to final, solemn profession.[3]

Sophie knew that she could not reveal this plan at a time when there was so much criticism of the 1839 decrees. If there was a strong reaction to the proposal that the coadjutrix sisters would not make final profession then there would be uproar if choir aspirants were to be treated similarly. Such a radical regrouping of personnel was unthinkable and impossible to implement then. At the end of her letter Sophie added a personal note for the superiors of the houses, asking them to convey the contents of her letter to their local bishop verbally. She counted more on the good relationship she had cultivated over the years with the bishops than on written statements.[4]

From September 1839 Sophie's relationship with Eugénie de Gramont became progressively colder. Eugénie wrote to Sophie in October 1839:

> Again I have been obliged to delay writing to you for some time . . . absorbed by a multitude of business matters, the number of which I have no control to lessen. The days and the time are flying by and so too is life, fortunately. I must admit that that is the only comforting thought, and only the awareness that soon all problems will end is capable of giving me patience to wait for heaven . . . but I do not have the time to talk to you about that today. I have a number of details to tell you concerning some houses as well as several individuals to be placed or replaced, which will take all the time I can give to writing today.[5]

When Eugénie read Sophie's circular letter to the Society, announcing the trial period of three years for the decrees, she expressed satisfaction that her proposal had been taken up. She only regretted that Sophie had not suggested the trial period from the beginning. Eugénie told Sophie that in resisting the decrees, as they had been presented to her, she had acted according to her conscience. She promised to begin the trial period and to introduce the decrees in all the houses she was responsible for as provincial.[6]

Events in Paris gave Sophie some grounds to hope that she could return there in 1840. To the sorrow of Eugénie de Gramont and the relief of Sophie Barat, Archbishop de Quelen, who had been ill for most of 1839, died in the rue de Varenne on 31 December 1839. Sophie carefully disguised her feelings in her letter of sympathy to Eugénie:

> He is one more Saint in heaven and a Protector for us. Despite the assurance we can have, we will pray for him and have him prayed for in all our houses . . . What a loss for his flock . . . but how your heart must suffer . . . [7]

Eugénie gave Sophie no details of the Archbishop de Quelen's final days at the rue de Varenne. Nor did she send an account of the several days of official mourning there before his body was taken to Notre Dame and so to burial. It was Eulalie de Bouchaud and Aimée d'Avenas who kept Sophie informed of the events surrounding the death of the archbishop. One incident reported in the newspapers caused Sophie some concern. She asked Eulalie de Bouchaud:

> Have you heard of reports of an incident, said to have happened in Paris at the same time as the death of your worthy prelate? Nobody explained this to us, thinking that we knew like everyone else. The following came from Munich: Everyone here is talking about the report mentioned in three letters from Paris, referring to *'the woman dressed in black* and *the driver of the coach.'* [8]

The presence of this mysterious woman who visited the rue de Varenne when the archbishop was lying in state worried Sophie. She never found out who it was and Eugénie did not refer to the incident either. However, at this time all letters from Rome to Paris, including those from members of the Society, were being censored. The duc de Bordeaux had visited the Trinité and Sainte Rufine, and this aroused the suspicion of the French government.[9] Eugénie warned Sophie to avoid mentioning anything of a political or polemical nature in her correspondence as it was being censored by the government.

By the spring of 1840 Sophie thought that at least one obstacle had been removed from her path. She had not counted on Archbishop de Quelen being as powerful over Eugénie de Gramont in death as he had been in life. Eugénie de Gramont, Aimée d'Avenas and Elisa Croft collaborated in the writing of a life of Archbishop de Quelen. Indeed a cult of his memory was fostered by Eugénie, with cures and miracles attributed to him.[10] Since he had not wanted the decrees implemented in France, Eugénie now told Sophie that in conscience she had to wait until the new archbishop of Paris was appointed and had given his formal approval to the decrees. Since Sophie could not afford to confront her on these grounds, Eugénie's decision effectively prevented Sophie returning to Paris until at least the summer of 1840. Indeed Eugénie wrote an impertinent letter to Sophie in mid-January, condemning those members of the general council who had not stood up to the pressure from Sophie herself, and from Louise de Limminghe and Elizabeth Galitzine. She found all communication since the council quite inadequate but knew it had been in the hands of Elizabeth Galitzine and Marie Prevost and so she could not expect much from them. She interrupted her letter, on the grounds of other more urgent business, and instructed Sophie not to reply until she received the second part. Three weeks later Eugénie completed it and reprimanded Sophie for not communicating properly with the bishops in France. Finally she repeated that the decrees were not wanted either by the bishops or by the Society.[11]

Two weeks later Eugénie wrote again, in a warmer tone:

> I imagine . . . that my letters cause you pain. It is painful for me to write to you, yet I would find it impossible not to tell you all that I think . . . All that has been written to you about me are unkind conjectures and assumptions.[12]

All this time Sophie had no idea what was going on in the rue de Varenne and she had to rely on Eulalie de Bouchaud for information. A priest in Rome told Sophie he had heard rumours that the school chaplain, Fr Jammes was about to take up residence in the Petit-Hôtel. This drove Sophie to contact Eulalie de Bouchaud immediately and ask her to contact the vicar general, Fr Morel:

> Tell him on my behalf that if the chaplaincy at the Sacred Heart, rue de Varenne, is given to Mr Jammes this would be totally against my wishes, even if he did not live in the Petit-Hôtel . . . I suffered enough from Archbishop de Quelen's residence there and there would be even more problems having someone other than him. . . . Emphasise the distress I had from what happened at the rue de Varenne and say that I want to put an end to it.[13]

Sophie followed this up with a personal letter to Morel in which she asked him not to allow either Jammes or indeed anyone else to live in the Petit-Hôtel at least until either she returned to Paris or the new archbishop had been appointed. She explained the situation in the Society since the general council of 1839 and how the rue de Varenne had resisted the decrees. She asked him for his support in implementing the decrees. However, she asked that her letter remain confidential. He should say nothing to Eugénie de Gramont nor indicate at meetings of the cathedral chapter that she had made representations to him. In this instance Sophie had to chose between which was worse, either to oppose Eugénie in public or ask Morel for discretion. Either way she left herself open to criticism both from the clergy and from Eugénie de Gramont herself. She sent the letter to Eulalie de Bouchaud and asked her to show it first to Joseph Varin, before sending it on to Morel, just to ensure that what she had written from a distance was clear enough.[14]

Morel agreed to keep Sophie's letter confidential though he stated that he did not want to get involved in Sophie's difficulties with Eugénie de Gramont. He claimed he did not know the situation well enough and that his appointment in the diocese was temporary until the nomination of the new archbishop. Morel told Eulalie de Bouchaud that he wondered if Sophie was able to stand up to Eugénie de Gramont. He knew that Madame de Gramont is a very clever woman who never drops her reserve, especially with him . . . he only knew her because she was continually fluttering around Archbishop de Quelen in the Petit-Hôtel. . . . In the rue de Varenne they are only allowed to talk about the archbishop with ridiculous enthusiasm and admiration . . . One thing amazed him . . . that is, that you do not wish to speak openly to Mother de Gramont yourself about your problems with Mr Jammes, since you are perfectly within your rights to do so.[15]

The following day, 3 March 1840, Eulalie de Bouchaud wrote to Sophie and told her that Morel had visited Eugénie de Gramont in the rue de Varenne. He spoke to Eulalie de Bouchaud afterwards and told her that he could do very little to help the situation. Jammes had lived in the Petit-Hôtel with Archbishop de Quelen and it would be hard to put him out now. Besides, the parents of the pupils living in the Faubourg Saint-Germain would resent his removal as chaplain to the school. Morel himself wrote to Sophie a month later and told her that since she would not allow her letter to be read at the meeting of the cathedral chapter, then Jammes could not be removed from the Petit-Hôtel. While the clergy agreed with her that the situation was improper and needed to be addressed, they thought it best to wait until the appointment of a new archbishop. A few days later, when preaching at a ceremony of first vows in the rue de Varenne, Morel signalled that he had capitulated to Eugénie de Gramont. During his sermon he applauded the stance she had taken with regard to the 1839 decrees, and he told those making their vows to live according to the 1826 constitutions of the Society. When Eulalie de Bouchaud met him in the sacristy afterwards and asked him what he was going to do about Jammes, Morel told her he could nothing. He admitted that he could not face opposition from Eugénie de Gramont and from the lobby in the Faubourg Saint-Germain. Sophie would have to deal with Jammes herself. He and the members of the clergy simply could not do so.[16]

Bitterly disappointed but hardly expecting an easy resolution, Sophie wrote to Eulalie de Bouchaud:

If I was there on the spot I would fear nothing. I would install myself in the rue de Varenne and who then could prevent me from taking action? But without support and being so far away I have to proceed with caution. At least that is the advice of those whom I have been able to consult. So see with our two friends [Jean-Nicolas Loriquet and Louis Barat] if we can wait longer without taking action, or if the situation is so bad that we should take some steps, even though I can foresee that they will not succeed.[17]

Sophie relied on the advice of her brother, Louis, and of Nicholas Loriquet and told Eulalie de Bouchaud to consult them before taking any action.[18] Sophie did not consult Joseph Varin because although he had assured her of his support she knew that he still suspected that the 1839 decrees had displaced the primary aim of the Society, the glory of the Sacred Heart, enshrined in the 1826 constitutions.[19] Louis Barat told Sophie to hold firm and not concede to the pressure orchestrated by Eugénie de Gramont, not just in the rue de Varenne but in several houses of the Society in France. He warned her that Jean Roothan had written to the Jesuits in Paris and told them not to get involved in the affairs of the Society of the Sacred Heart nor to discuss them among themselves or with outsiders. In any event, by now Loriquet said he would not write to Sophie anymore since she paid no heed to his advice. He agreed with his colleague, Louis Sellier, that only Eugénie de Gramont's dismissal as superior would bring peace to the Society in France.[20]

In May 1840 Sophie asked for an audience with the pope, a customary courtesy when departing from Rome. By this time Gregory XVI was aware of the situation in the Society and agreed that Sophie should return to Paris and try to calm the unease. They spoke about Sophie's residence in Rome, a key decision of the general council of 1839 and the one most resisted in Paris. The pope told Sophie:

> I do not know the circumstances well enough to be able to judge the situation. I leave you completely free. If you think that you ought to delay [moving to Rome] on account of political circumstances, you may certainly do so. . . . Consult Cardinal Lambruschini. He knows France, and the situation there. He can advise you better about when to leave France. . . . Certainly the Holy See will protect you always, because of the good the Society does for the education of young women.[21]

Like other teaching congregations of women at this time, the Society of the Sacred Heart was fulfilling a need in the church, not just in France but in Europe and further afield. In this context the pope was interested in the survival of the Society of the Sacred Heart, especially in France, where the Society educated the young women of elite families. The education of young women in convent schools ensured that the church had a point of entry into such families. Gregory XVI had a good understanding of Archbishop de Quelen and knew that Sophie had been struggling for years to remove him from the rue de Varenne, to no avail. The pope had found Archbishop de Quelen just as stubborn with him and resistant to every form of persuasion. If the pope and the officials in Rome had been unable to persuade Archbishop de Quelen to concede any legitimacy to the government of Louis Philippe, they did not judge Sophie Barat harshly when she could not remove the archbishop from the rue de Varenne. Gregory XVI assured Sophie of his support and concern, and placed no conditions upon her as she left for Paris. On the other hand, Elizabeth Galitzine, Louise de Limminghe and Jean Rozaven insisted that once Sophie reached the rue de Varenne she should exercise her authority and deal once and for all with Eugénie de Gramont. This was an impossible demand. No one knew better than Sophie herself that any amount of official authority would not solve this problem. The rue de Varenne was Eugénie's empire and it could not be touched with impunity.

In February 1840 Sophie told Eugénie that she was planning to return to Paris. Despite her previous refusals to do so Sophie again asked Eugénie to put the decrees into practice in the rue de Varenne.[22] She expressed the hope that they could work together for the good of the Society. Commenting on the support given her by Catherine de Charbonnel, Sophie reminded Eugénie:

It used to be like that long ago with 'my rat'. Why has just one situation interrupted, I hope just temporarily, the precious harmony . . . which sustained us for so many years in the midst of the hardest crosses. When burdens are carried together you hardly notice the weight! I am asking you now to delay no longer in putting the Decrees into practice. I hope that you will reply at last and tell me you have acceded to my just desires![23]

By now there was rupture in their personal relationship and Sophie recognised this with sorrow. Eugénie continued to actively promote the resistance to the 1839 decrees in the rue de Varenne and in several houses in France. She refused to co-operate with Sophie's requests, not only over the decrees but also when Sophie asked her to release Henriette Ducis as a travelling companion and secretary to Catherine de Charbonnel. Even Catherine de Charbonnel's evident incapacity and yet urgent need to visit the houses in the west of France did not move her. Sophie did not realise yet how fully the houses in the west were being influenced by Eugénie de Gramont herself. The last thing Eugénie wanted was the visit of an assistant general who supported the 1839 decrees. Sophie tried every ploy to win Eugénie round, pointing out that the reputation of the rue de Varenne would suffer and Eugénie's good name would be damaged.[24]

Curiously, when Sophie and Eugénie were doing business which did not broach either the rue de Varenne or the 1839 decrees, they worked well together. They had functioned well this way for years, and Sophie continued to rely on Eugénie for some essential negotiations in France. At this level their relationship remained quite smooth and businesslike and Sophie could rely on Eugénie to find the information she needed and carry out transactions. A case in point occurred in April 1840 when Sophie heard about the dangerous state of the buildings in Beauvais. There the superior, Marie d'Olivier, warned both Sophie and Eugénie that the condition of the boarding school buildings were dangerous and needed immediate repair. Sophie asked Eugénie to visit the school and see what could be done to ensure the pupils' safety. The building was owned by the civil authorities and a series of complicated agreements had been drawn up between the authorities and the Society since 1817.[25] Sophie wondered if Marie d'Oliver had the capacity to deal with the situation, and she considered her removal as superior. She had been there a long time and a move would be in keeping with the spirit of the new decrees:

Mother d'Olivier gives no support to her colleagues, she does not maintain discipline and each one goes her own way. During your visit you will see how to remedy the situation.[26]

Eugénie went to visit Beauvais and her report to Sophie was clear, pointing out the difficulties and outlining the options Sophie had with regard to its future:

I am just back from Beauvais . . . and I returned tired, laden with a cold, and feeling unwell. . . . I was poorly the whole time I was there but this did not prevent me from working hard. First I dealt with the building which I found in such bad condition that a gust of wind, a storm, a torrent of rain could sweep it away and cause it to collapse and consequently crush all beneath it….that so frightened me the first night that I could not close an eye. Mother d'Olivier was not in the slightest bit concerned and laughed at my disquiet. . . . The architect says it is very serious and thinks that the entire building will have to be reconstructed. The mayor . . . [who] knows that the municipal coffers are empty tried to persuade me that simple repairs will be sufficient. But he is deluding himself; as soon as a hammer is used inside the building everything will collapse . . . If the financial outlay goes beyond 7–8 thousand, the town will not undertake the responsibility. They will leave the building to deteriorate and will asked us to rebuild at our expense. The town would be very keen . . . to sell us the land and so the building then would belong to us and we could build what we like on it. . . . If we decide to leave [Beauvais] the town will give us nothing but the price of the contents of the building. . . . Please let us know your decision and tell us how you would like this affair to be resolved.[27]

Two weeks later Sophie told Eugénie of her decision. The Society could not afford to rebuild the entire school, nor was it possible to close Beauvais suddenly. So the most practical solution was to close the second boarding school, intended for the middle class, and retain the boarding school for the nobility and wealthy bourgeoisie with school for the orphans of Beauvais. This arrangement would honour the agreements which the Society had with the local authorities and at the same time provide a sound economic basis for the future. The Society would accept the 8,000 francs from the mayor and pay the rest of the money needed for the repairs, as long as it was not too exorbitant. Fewer teachers would be needed and both schools would be better run and the pupils better cared for:

We shall see at the end of the year who we can get to replace Madame d'Olivier. Between ourselves, I do not think she capable any more of being a superior. She is so absorbed in her own writings, though they are so mediocre. It is impossible to get her away from them, yet as you pointed out she wants to run everything and allows no scope to others. It is impossible for a house to operate under such leadership. So please see to it that the roof is repaired. You could send Madame de Lemps to Beauvais with our instructions.[28]

Working together on administrative issues was harmonious and effective. Sophie's and Eugénie's difficulties were at the level of their vision of the church, of religious life and of the monarchy. The disagreement over Jammes and his residing in the Petit-Hôtel was yet another issue which revealed their further polarisation. Eugénie continued to defend Jammes, claiming that the rumours in Rome about him and the rue de Varenne were quite untrue. Besides, in Paris,

The French who return from Rome are not at all happy with the atmosphere in Rome itself, among the Romans, the cardinals, Cardinal Lambruschini. They have been bought over by [Louis] Philippe who is deceiving them as much as he likes.[29]

Sophie knew that from the moment she returned to the rue de Varenne she would meet Eugénie's resistance. That day was not far off as the new archbishop of Paris, Denis Affre, had been named in June 1840. However, prior to her return to France, Sophie prepared Elizabeth Galitzine for her formal visitation of the American houses. Sophie was convinced that the task of implementing the 1839 decrees there was particularly urgent, given the gap in leadership there since Eugénie Audé's departure in 1833. Sophie suggested that Elizabeth Galitzine leave for America in the summer of 1840, and that on the way to Le Havre she spend some time in Paris. There she could meet the new archbishop and give him a letter from Sophie, describing what the general council had set out to achieve the previous year in Rome.[30]

Elizabeth Galitzine met Archbishop Affre in July 1840 in the rue Monsieur and in the course of a conversation he appeared positive towards the decrees and agreed that Eugénie de Gramont should abandon her resistance.[31] Archbishop Affre was no friend to either Eugénie de Gramont or the rue de Varenne and Eugénie was dismayed when she heard his name mentioned as a possible future archbishop. Affre had been critical of Archbishop de Quelen's prolonged residence in the rue de Varenne.[32] The fact that Archbishop Affre had written to the archbishop was enough to win the disapproval of Eugénie de Gramont. Eugénie made no secret of her views, as Sophie learnt from Bathilde Sallion (1791–1875), a member of the community at the rue de Varenne:

> I have learnt . . . from my outside contacts that there is a good deal of talk in public about the hostility between Madame de Gramont and the new archbishop. They say that Madame de Gramont sets the tone throughout the faubourg Saint-Germain and that they consider it an honour to think as she does. On the feast of the Assumption there was fairly big dinner in the Petit-Hôtel. Mr Morel, [Mr] Jammes, [Mr] Molinier, [M] Surat and the young prince Galitzine were there. Madame de Kersabie, who follows the abbé Morel like a little puppy, was there all the time. They sent for Madame d'Avenas (who does not like to go there); she went there all the same.[33]

These dinners at the Petit-Hôtel were the occasion for criticism of the new archbishop and fervent reminiscing about Archbishop de Quelen. It was a closed world, turned in upon itself. When Denis Affre was recommended for the position of archbishop of Paris, one of the points in his favour was that he would not please the Faubourg Saint-Germain.[34] Archbishop Affre was equally critical of Eugénie de Gramont and the community at the rue de Varenne. He made no secret of this and in public spoke freely of the opposition to Sophie Barat's authority which was rife at the rue de Varenne. He was also critical of Eugénie de Gramont's autocratic style of government. She had no assistant and no councillors to advise her; she controlled communications so closely in the rue de Varenne that letters from those who were loyal to Sophie Barat were secretly given to friends to post, some of them Jesuits. Affre also accused Eugénie de Gramont of mismanaging the finances of the Society. He claimed that Antoinette de Gramont, had complained that Eugénie, her younger sister, retained the revenues that were her due. Consequently the house at Le Mans was deprived of some of its finances.[35] When the archbishop paid a visit to the rue de Varenne in mid-September 1840 he had a lively exchange with Eugénie de Gramont in the sacristy. During the stormy interview Archbishop Affre informed Eugénie that Jammes and Fr Surat, a former companion of Archbishop de Quelen in the Petit-

Hôtel, were being removed from their residence. There was no discussion, no possibility of redress. His actions demonstrated clearly that he intended to test Eugénie de Gramont's power and challenge her hegemony.

Sophie returned to Paris, to the rue Monsieur, some days after Archbishop Affre's visit to the rue de Varenne. Eugénie was still reeling from Affre's visit and she could not reconcile herself to the dismissal of Jammes.[36] She blamed Sophie and Elizabeth Galitzine for the removal of Jammes, since for Sophie had asked Elizabeth Galitzine to discuss the issue with Affre when she saw him in July. But Archbishop Affre had done exactly what Sophie hoped he would do and she was relieved to find the decision had been taken so quickly. However, it made her return to Paris even more difficult and her relations with Eugénie more strained and tense. She left Rome in early August and during the six-week journey through Italy, Savoy and France 1840 she had time to prepare for what she would face on her return to Paris. She was apprehensive and ill with anticipation, under no illusions about what lay ahead. She wrote to Louise de Limminghe:

> Mr Jammes has been dismissed already by Archbishop Affre. They await my return for the rest! . . . What will my situation be like in Paris, in *every respect* [?] But is not Jesus every where! Why fear! My health is holding up, that is a true protection for me since I can scarcely sleep. For sure my sleep pattern will not return in Paris. But once again, let us trust, we will not be tempted above our strength. Does God not look after his chosen ones![37]

Sophie did not hide from Eugénie what she was feeling. She knew that Eugénie did not want her in Paris, and she admitted: 'I'll do what schoolchildren do, I'll take the longest path'.[38] When she arrived in Paris Sophie decided to observe the situation before deciding on a plan of action. 'I watch, I listen and I pray and ask others to pray'. [39] Experienced as she was, Sophie Barat had not yet dealt with a set of issues as complex as those which awaited her in Paris. Within two weeks, however, she had decided to move from the rue Monsieur and take up residence in the rue de Varenne. At this point there was no question of demoting Eugénie de Gramont but by residing in the rue de Varenne Sophie hoped to be in a stronger position to implement the 1839 decrees and effect reform in the house.[40]

As she expected, the dismissal of Jammes was a source of discontent, though for a time it served to make relations with Archbishop Affre easier for Sophie. Louise de Limminghe had difficulty in understanding why the affair was so difficult, and why Sophie and the archbishop were being so criticised:

> No, you have only the faintest idea of the effect which the dismissal of Mr Jammes had here! The faubourg Saint-Germain will not forgive either me nor the archbishop. You know well that I take my share of the responsibility in this. Later on people will say that we did well to do it, because they are blown about by every wind. In any case they can do what like, for I have lost my reputation long ago! [41]

Indeed Sophie's reputation had been damaged in Paris, both within and without the Society. Gossip spread in the Faubourg Saint-Germain. Some said that

Sophie Barat had changed, that perhaps she was ill, that she had lost the capacity to govern the Society of the Sacred Heart. Others thought that she had been led astray by some members of the Society and said so to her when they visited her in the rue de Varenne. The opinion was spread around that Eugénie de Gramont would be a much more competent superior general. Sophie Barat could not continue in office. Sophie wrote laconically to Eugénie Audé that her return to Paris had been painful and that her situation could only get worse.[42]

By the winter of 1840–41 Sophie had some idea of how the 1839 decrees were being received in Rome and in Paris. She had yet to discover their impact in America. She counted a great deal on Elizabeth Galitzine's visit to the houses in upper and lower Louisiana and she eagerly awaited her letters. Sophie was aware that she had taken a risk in appointing Elizabeth Galitzine as provincial of the houses in America. She had often expressed doubts about her judgement, about her impetuosity, her fanatical devotion to Rozaven, as well as her independent way of working which led her to disregard the wishes of Sophie. Sophie gave Elizabeth Galitzine detailed instructions for her visit to America. She repeatedly counselled consultation and reflection before taking any decisions regarding personnel or houses. Most of all she urged discretion, moderation and gentleness. She warned Elizabeth Galitzine that these attitudes were essential in America:

> Take care not to let any moodiness or impatience to appear. These faults will ruin everything. Of all the peoples in the world the Americans and the Japanese are the best at maintaining their composure in difficult situations. So they will be very surprised to discover that people dedicated to God are less perfect than lay people or heretics . . . [43]

Sophie made no reference to the 1839 decrees in her letter of instruction to Elizabeth Galitzine, except to state that she was only to speak of those issues which Sophie Barat authorised. For the rest Elizabeth Galitzine was to use the constitutions and rules of the Society and other texts in circulation in the Society which commented on the work of education.[44]

Sophie also gave Elizabeth Galitzine instructions for her journey in Italy and France, on her way to the port at Le Havre. She advised her to be extremely discreet in Paris, both when staying at the rue de Varenne and when speaking to the Jesuits:

> Be ready for questions in the rue de Varenne . . . Be discreet also with the Jesuits especially regarding our contacts with their colleagues here [in Rome]. Everything is repeated, they write to their general and usually it is not very accurate. You can say a bit more to my brother, he is discreet. . . .
> I do not know what to say to you about the excellent Fr Varin. Let him see that you trust him, that you regret what hurt him in the past; tell him that I am on my way. He will be comforted and you will tell him that the reason for my delay is a chest fever, which I can use as an excuse since I have it at the moment.[45]

While counselling silence and discretion at the rue de Varenne, Sophie asked Elizabeth Galitzine to speak to Aimée d'Avenas privately and tell her how

Eugénie de Gramont's reputation was being damaged by her persistent refusal to implement the 1839 decrees. She hoped that Aimée d'Avenas could persuade Eugénie to implement the three-year trial period in the houses she governed as provincial.

In June 1840, Sophie wrote a formal letter to the communities in America, announcing the visit of Elizabeth Galitzine. Sophie admitted that she had hoped that such a visit would have taken place a long time ago and regretted that she could not travel herself to see them all. She urged them to accept whatever Elizabeth Galitzine advised and whatever she said in the name of the Society:

> The Society of the Sacred Heart, already so prosperous in Louisiana, is about to become more solid and perfect by the practice of these Decrees. That is what we had in mind when we added them to the constitutions.[46]

In November 1839, Eugénie Audé had written to Aloysia Hardey and told her about the general council decrees passed in Rome the previous July. She explained that while the decrees were what Sophie Barat wanted for the good government of the Society, she did not want them communicated widely until a proper, accurate edition had been printed. During the delay the superiors and their council could discuss the rather hastily drawn-up version which had been sent after the council had closed. They were free to make representations to Sophie over the decrees and these would be taken into account. However Eugénie Audé told Aloysia Hardey that if she or any other superior in America had already told the entire community about the decrees then it was best to let that situation stand until Sophie found someone to make a formal visit to the American houses.[47] By the time Sophie had decided that Elizabeth Galitzine could be released to go to America, the decision to allow a three-year trial period had been taken. Sophie then had to tell Aloysia Hardey to ignore the former, correct advice of Eugénie Audé, and instead put the decrees into practice, with enthusiasm.[48] However, in a letter some weeks later Sophie revealed some of her misgivings:

> I am happy at the consolation that you will have in seeing her and I am sure that soon you will give her the full trust and loyalty which she merits on so many accounts. All the care and attention that you take to help her, to share her burdens and lighten them for her, will be for me. If I had been able to visit you she would be simply my assistant and travel companion . . . It will not be contrary to the practice of perfect obedience to inform your visitor of the customs of the country, and of the problems that such and such a measure, regulation, practice could have etc. . . . She will benefit from your insights and observations. . . . [49]

At the general council in 1839 Sophie had asked that the decrees be communicated slowly over a period of time, and only fully when a formal edition had been printed, presented and approved by the authorities in Rome. However, she had been forced to change that strategy when Eugénie de Gramont demanded a trial period of three years. This forced Sophie to permit hurried, often uncorrected, versions of the 1839 decrees to be circulated to the provincials and local superiors. Even then Sophie did not want the communities to have personal copies of the decrees until they had been ratified by Rome. Elizabeth Galitzine ignored Sophie's wishes and gave out copies of the decrees in Rome, then in Lyon and in Paris, as she made her way to port.[50] She did the same in Missouri. Sophie was taken aback at this and told her that even Rozaven was surprised at her cavalier attitude:

> . . . you must certainly recall my conditions with regard to this matter? In conse-
> quence I could not understand your procedure in Louisiana . . . Discuss with your
> councillors how best to undo this misplaced communication you made in upper
> Louisiana.[51]

Such actions had created misunderstandings and unease in communities. In some parts of the Society the trial period for the decrees had begun; in others they had not even heard about them; and in other parts again they had heard about the decrees but the trial period had not been implemented. Sophie was dismayed to find that Elizabeth Galitzine was undermining her authority so blatantly in America and ruefully remarked that the chaplain at the Villa Lante, Fr Mitrail, knew her better than the Society. He had warned Sophie of the damage Elizabeth Galitzine could do the Society if she was placed in a position of authority.[52]

Elizabeth Galitzine had begun to undermine Sophie's authority immediately after the general council of 1839. It emerged later that at that time she had written a long, ill-judged letter to Eugénie de Gramont, criticising Sophie's leadership of the council. She asked Eugénie de Gramont not to reply, as she did not want that letter to fall by accident into Sophie's hands.[53] Elizabeth Galitzine criticised Sophie for refusing to allow anyone to raise the situation of Armande de Causans and the Trinité in Rome. To her dismay, Sophie appeared to trust Josephine de Coriolis, and was about to appoint Armande de Causans as superior in one of the houses in the south of France:

> The matter is settled. We can say nothing since we were not consulted. But if this
> misfortune takes place I rely on you to write to [Sophie] about it and tell her what
> you think. Whatever you say has more effect on her than what others say.[54]

Elizabeth Galitzine also told Eugénie de Gramont that it was Cardinal Lambruschini who warned Sophie that she could not say in writing that her residence in future would be in Rome as it would upset the bishops in France. This was mischievous and alerted Eugénie about what had happened in Rome. It points to a serious lack of judgement and an effort to damage Sophie's leadership at this time. A year later, when Elizabeth Galitzine was on her own in America, Sophie realised she was unable to control what her assistant general did there, despite the detailed instructions she had given her.

Throughout this time Sophie's volume of work increased as since Elizabeth Galitzine's departure for America, she had no secretarial help and she anticipated the toll this would have on her personally.[55] Catherine de Charbonnel had joined her in Paris, in the rue de Varenne, while Félicité Desmarquest returned to the rue Monsieur where she had resumed her former role as mistress of novices. Both of them helped Sophie with advice and Sophie delegated some letters to them. But there was a vast amount of correspondence which she normally did with the secretary general and this now had to be done alone. When particularly pressurised Sophie had to ask for help with her letters, either from the community at the rue de Varenne or at the rue Monsieur. None was offered spontaneously. Sophie told Louise de Limminghe how she managed to get through the day. She got up at 5 a.m. and prayed for two hours. After Mass and breakfast she began her letters at 8.30 and worked until midday or beyond if necessary. The afternoons were taken up with meetings and visits, and if time allowed further letter writing. She admitted that, contrary to the advice of all her doctors, she did not take time to relax, to walk, to rest.[56]

At the end of September 1840, Sophie wrote to Henriette Grosier:

> How much work awaits me! I will tell you about it later . . . Please pray that Jesus will help me. Without His help the work is really hard and for the present I have not been able to replace my industrious secretary, who I assure you, used to do the work of four people! [57]

In addition to her letter-writing and interviews with members of the Society and of the clergy, Sophie was planning to replace the superiors at Amiens, Beauvais, Conflans, Bordeaux and Niort, as she pointedly told Henriette Grosier.[58] The most difficult task by far was facing the community at the rue de Varenne, especially Eugénie de Gramont and Aimée d'Avenas. She told Eugénie Audé:

> Tomorrow I am going to the rue de Varenne. I will have a heavy, painful task. May God give me the strength and the ability to work. But . . . how easy it would have been to avoid all that has happened! Everyone says to me: Oh! If only you yourself brought back the Decrees! No one would have dreamed of protesting. Madame de Gramont said this to me the other day, and what sad consequences would have been avoided. . . . But it's done now, . . . can I heal the situation. I do not know.[59]

The work of healing the rift created by the manner in which the 1839 decrees were communicated was time consuming and exhausting. Her relationship with Eugénie de Gramont had changed and Sophie admitted that they had lost 'their former intimacy, at least on certain subjects'.[60] In addition Sophie was aware that her own reputation as a leader had been severely damaged, both in Paris and in Rome, and she remarked to Eugénie Audé that among the Roman cardinals, 'I am considered reckless'.[61] Yet despite all these pressures Sophie herself was surprised at how well she was in October 1840. But by December 1840 this had changed. Sophie had learnt of the extent of the opposition mounted against her and the 1839 decrees and her energy and stamina began to crumble. She caught a heavy cold which developed into a sinus infection and was confined to bed for several weeks.[62] During this time she could not work, or indeed govern the Society. Others however were hard at work pursuing their own agendas.

By the time Sophie began a slow convalescence in March 1841, the Society in France, in Italy and in America had become more polarised and divided. Eugénie de Gramont led the opposition in France; Elizabeth Galitzine continued to communicate the 1839 decrees to the communities of upper and lower Louisiana. Louise de Limminghe with Jean Rozaven held firmly to the 1839 decrees and kept both Cardinal Pedicini and Cardinal Lambruschini informed. In addition, Marie d'Olivier had rejected Sophie's decision to close the day school at Beauvais. With the help of the local bishop, she petitioned the pope for a separation of the house at Beauvais from the Society. In March 1841 Sophie wrote to Eugénie Audé, burdened by the seemingly unending spate of problems:

> My convalescence has begun but it is slow. Neither sleep nor my appetite have returned and I am still very weak. Then how could I recover with so many worries and so much distress? . . . try and find out as hard as you can which of the houses have linked up with the rue de Varenne in order to separate [from the Society]! . . . I suspect Le Mans, Autun, Beauvais, and only the superiors in the last two named . . .[63]

By the summer of 1841 Sophie realised that the situation in the Society was unravelling and that she needed to return to Rome and fix a date for the next general council. This was the only way to bring the members together and try to resolve the divisions and dissent which had grown within the Society.

— 17 —
MOVING TO DISINTEGRATION, 1841–1842

The winter of 1840 was a bleak time for Sophie. She was ill and miserable and felt her world falling about her. Letters from Louise de Limminghe were no help. She talked of future suffering, of dark days ahead and her own imminent death. This heaviness and depression burdened Sophie and she asked her friend to think more of her in Paris when she wrote so morosely. If Louise de Limminghe died then

> my soul will be *alone* in this world . . . You understand the full meaning of this word. If you only knew my position, how those on whom I should be able to count for support make it worse and torture me. You would be astonished if I told you . . . these details cannot be put on paper. . . . [1]

With so many problems on her mind Sophie found it difficult to regain energy. She had lost her sleep pattern and her appetite for food and she began to fear that she could not recover strength for her work. She wanted to visit the houses which were in league with Eugénie de Gramont, and through personal contact win back her leadership.[2] Yet even while ill Sophie was forced to deal with the question at Beauvais since the pope had received formal letters from the bishop of Beauvais, Mgr Pierre Cotteret (1838–1841) and from Marie d'Olivier. Initially they complained that Sophie Barat was about to close the second boarding school at Beauvais; then they requested permission for Beauvais to separate from the Society. Gregory XVI asked Cardinal Patrizzi, Prefect of the congregation of bishops and religious, to write to Sophie in Paris to get her views on the matter. Sophie drew up a memorandum, outlining her position and explaining why she had decided to suppress the second boarding school at Beauvais. She also outlined the financial state of the Society, informing the pope that the Society had suffered a loss of 500,000 francs in recent years, and simply could not afford to rebuild the school at Beauvais. She forwarded the documentation to Eugénie Audé in Rome and asked her to work closely with Louise de Limminghe and Jean Rozaven when presenting the Society's view on the matter.[3] At the same time Sophie asked Eugénie de Gramont, who had already dealt with Beauvais the previous year, to return there and speak frankly to the bishop about the situation. Eugénie's manner of resolving the impasse revealed the skill and charm which made her so successful in the rue de Varenne. She spent an hour and a half with the bishop, flattering him, listening to his endless jokes and she emerged from the interview having achieved all Sophie wanted:

> The conversation throughout was friendly, cheerful and lively; he told tales you would die laughing at. He has never been so charming. He consents to all and does not even insist on the second boarding school. Mother d'Olivier had persuaded him that the boarding school for the upper classes was supported by the school for the lower classes. I convinced him it was the contrary. He asked me to convey to you his most gracious good wishes. [4]

With regard to answering the queries from Cardinal Patrizzi in Rome regarding Beauvais, Sophie knew she had a strong case to present and had every confidence she would be vindicated there:

> It is important to get the pope to understand that if I am left to the caprices of either one or the other parties it will be impossible for me to govern the Society. . . . The bishop of Beauvais is not taken seriously by his own colleagues. One of them said to me recently, when we were discussing an entirely different matter: 'Ha! the bishop of Beauvais, his *head is full of nonsense*!' . . . This is just for yourself, of course.[5]

Sophie's careful presentation of the case in Rome was convincing and the pope concurred with Sophie's views, though it took until August 1841 to settle the matter finally.[6] Sophie had recognised the potential danger if the petitions from Marie d'Olivier and the bishop of Beauvais had been favourably received in Rome. If they had succeeded, other petitions from French bishops would have followed:

> Firstly because most of the bishops do not want the superior general to go to Rome at all, and, secondly, because they want a French bishop to be the [ecclesiastical] superior general [of the Society]. With the majority of the [French] bishops against us we will have only a few houses which will remain loyal . . . I am also aware that even in these houses there are some members who are only waiting for the opportunity to break away and join the others.[7]

Sophie was aware of this and appreciated Eugénie de Gramont's part in the resolution of the crisis at Beauvais. She told Eugénie Audé:

> Mother de Gramont acted admirably in this affair, she has been a great help to me. Everyone in Beauvais deferred to her and I am sure she acted honestly. She never says anything she does not mean. That would be the antithesis of her character and on this occasion she completely supported me.[8]

Indeed Eugénie de Gramont had no desire to destroy the Society or Sophie Barat. While she disagreed profoundly with Sophie over the 1839 decrees and led the opposition against them in France, she had no interest in supporting Marie d'Olivier. She had long disagreed with Marie d'Olivier's educational views and saw the growth of the second boarding school at Beauvais as a dangerous development, endangering its economic future. She knew that Marie d'Olivier's views had been dealt a severe blow at the 1826 general council, when the possibility of the Society educating the middles classes had been proposed. The response of the council then was negative, on the grounds of lack of personnel. Sophie recognised that Marie d'Olivier needed scope to develop her gifts and she was appointed to Beauvais for this reason. While Marie d'Olivier's educational ideas were far-seeing, she did not have the administrative capacity to run a community and three schools well. Had she retained the boarding school for the nobility and the wealthy middle class in good condition, and used it as the economic base for the second boarding school and the orphanage, Marie d'Olivier might have been able to show Sophie and indeed the Society, another model of education.[9] This was not to be and by 1841 Sophie realised that Marie d'Olivier would leave the Society that she had another path to follow which in the long term Sophie could not facilitate. It did not occur to Sophie either then or later to question why the Society of the Sacred Heart could not accommodate the views and aims of Marie d'Olivier, nor did she see what she had lost in her departure. Marie d'Olivier continued to write to Sophie, but due to the financial claims which the d'Olivier family made on the Society, their relationship became strained. Sophie replied rarely to d'Olivier's letters, and they never met again.[10]

Despite her general poor health at this time Sophie managed to work. She had little choice. Her convalescence was filled with problems urgently needing resolution. She still could not sleep or eat properly and yet she managed to deal deftly with the problem at Beauvais. But by May she was still weak and still could neither sleep properly nor digest food. She had a sore mouth and tried a vesicatory on her arm in the hope that this could help her.[11] Her nerves were on edge and the doctor in Paris suggested she try to rest elsewhere. She decided to visit Amiens, Lille and Jette, in the hope that the change of air would do her good, though she admitted that the actual travelling was stressful and tiring.[12] In Jette she caught yet another heavy cold and her body broke out in a rash which prevented both sleep and rest. The weather was wet and cold and she suffered from continual bouts of diarrhoea which left her without energy and quite depressed.[13] She wrote to Stanislas to ask him to be the executor of her will, in case of a sudden death.[14] By July 1841 Sophie complained that she had been unable to work for eight months. Consciously or not, she had begun to use her illness as a form of self-protection. In the course of her visits to Amiens and Lille in particular, Sophie was able to claim that she had not enough strength to speak to the communities there. Eugénie de Gramont had not implemented the 1839 decrees in any of the houses in northern France and Sophie's poor health allowed her to avoid confronting that issue in public. She wanted to avoid that at all costs, especially in Amiens, where the memories of Saint-Estève were easily evoked.[15]

Throughout this time Sophie knew that Jean Rozaven was impatient at what he viewed as her indecisiveness and weakness. He urged her to return to Rome as soon as possible. He had already complained to Louise de Limminghe that Sophie did not follow his advice and she in turn had passed this opinion round some of the houses. For her part Sophie realised that Rozaven was out of touch with France, with the reality of the Society of the Sacred Heart there. She recognised with regret that in the past she had been too influenced by him, and knew that if she acted on his advice now the Society would never recover its own way.[16] At the same time Sophie knew that she had to keep Rozaven on her side in Rome. He had influence as a member of the congregation of bishops and religious; he had a high profile among the clergy and was in good standing among the Jesuits. She could not afford to have him as an enemy and so she learnt of his disapproval with some apprehension. She knew how devoted both Elizabeth Galitzine and Louise de Limminghe were to Rozaven, and that she held little power and influence in that context. She had no choice then but to work with him, or find herself faced with many enemies. But he became progressively more impatient and could not understand how ill Sophie was or that she could not force the 1839 decrees upon the communities. Sophie remarked wryly to Elizabeth Galitzine: 'I cannot go any faster than the good God allows!'.[17]

Sophie's life had become bleak and lonely. Members of the Society in both France and Belgium seemed unaware of the chronic state of her health. But Sophie was forced to hide so much in public and she could not reveal the source of her anxieties. She told Elizabeth Galitzine:

> I am overwhelmed with work. I am still unwell and I feel that I will not recover. I have no secretarial help at all. On this latter point no one shows me any sympathy and rather than put themselves out I am left to carry on as best I can. All this does not matter to me. I will do as much as I can. I am looking forward to the General Council and once matters are settled I will have nothing else to do but to prepare for my imminent death I believe. Our Lord will allow me the time to complete my mission . . . [18]

Sophie had continually asked for secretarial help. Marie Prevost refused her request to have Adèle Cahier as secretary during the months of Elizabeth Galitzine's absence in America, on the grounds that there was no one to take her place in the school at La Ferrandière. Sophie did not insist and instead asked Eugénie de Gramont if she could find someone in Paris to help her. Despite some efforts on the part of Eugénie, a secretary could be not found and Sophie continued to do most of her correspondence herself.[19] This prevented her full recovery. Even while ill Sophie had remained in touch with key members and key movements within the Society, but she knew that this was not adequate leadership at such a critical time in the Society's evolution. She needed to be seen in the houses, explaining the 1839 decrees and generally asserting her own authority. She marked her official resumption of work by writing a circular letter

to the members of the Society in June 1841.[20] She explained that while she had
returned to France in the autumn of 1840, two illnesses had prevented her visiting the houses. However she drew attention to several issues in the Society
which needed urgent reform, noting that many members had ignored the recommendations of previous general councils, or those she had made in previous
letters.

Her letter did not deal directly with the 1839 decrees. Sophie concentrated
on practical issues in the Society, and on the conditions for good government and
discipline. She called the members of the Society to practise obedience to
authority, especially when they were asked to move from one house to another,
or to change the work they did in a particular school or community. Sophie
reminded all that the vow of poverty was expressed in the Society of the Sacred
Heart by the sharing of goods. None had the right to retain finances for their own
use. Yet she knew that some members retained money and other gifts received
from their families; others retained the payments they had received for special
tuition of the pupils. Others again insisted on designating how and where their
money was to be spent. All these attitudes ignored the general needs of the
Society, especially of new foundations and reinforced preoccupation with a local
area, a local situation, rather than seeing the wider needs of the expanding congregation. Sophie also questioned the over-dependence of many members of the
Society on their families. She also asked that those who had nieces in the schools
would not interfere with those teachers who looked after them.

These were practical recommendations from a woman in touch with her communities, with many practical things to say to them. By insisting on the sharing
of finances and on horizons wider than merely the local community, Sophie was
inviting the Society to think of itself as bigger and wider than France, than
Europe. She was also reinforcing the idea she had had from the beginning, that
the Society was composed of communities served by a central government; it
was not a federation, nor were the communities autonomous and independent.
All were to be interdependent and in communion with one another. Mobility of
personnel and sharing of financial resources as well as a certain freedom from
family ties, were essential to the realisation of this model of community. The circular letter was not a pious exhortation on Sophie's part. It was at the heart of
what she had always envisaged for the Society. It was also her understanding of
the spirit of the 1839 decrees: the Society of the Sacred Heart, led by a superi-
or general, who lived in Rome and governed communities all over the world. In
that spirit Sophie announced several new foundations, especially that in New
York and that of Philippine Duchesne to the Indians. Sophie was clearly moved
at this realisation of Philippine 's dreams and asked the members of the Society
to support the new venture which had few resources of its own.[21]

The same day, 16 June 1841, Sophie wrote a further letter just for the superiors and their councils and some members of the communities. In the letter she
went into greater detail concerning the financial state of the Society, the question of cloister in the Society, the supervision of younger members of the Society,

and especially the need to stop the practice of allowing wealthy women to spend their retirement years in houses of the Society. Finally, she reminded them that the general council of the Society would take place in 1842.[22]

Both sections of the letter were clear and strong and hit hard at abuses in the Society. Henriette Grosier was disturbed by the content of Sophie's circular letter, especially the section complaining of the difficulty of moving people. She wrote to Sophie in distress, saying that she felt it was aimed at her. Sophie replied diplomatically that it was not aimed at anyone in particular:

> I do not know why . . . the circular letter caused you so much pain. The abuses which were mentioned so circumspectly were not aimed at you, but at several members, scattered alas! throughout all the provinces and who are far from being true religious . . . Once and for all dear mother and friend, do not think any more about what once may have has caused us pain in the past. If we had been close at hand and able to see one another, how many of our mutual problems could have been eased by a face to face explanation![23]

By the summer of 1841 the Roman, ultramontane faction of the Society had gradually built up a power base in Rome, in Italy and in some of the houses in the south of France, particularly in Lyon, Aix, Marseilles and Bordeaux. The French, Gallican group was concentrated in Paris, Le Mans, Autun and Poitiers supported by the archbishop of Paris and most of the bishops in the dioceses of France where the Society had houses and schools. The personal relationship between Sophie and Eugénie became increasingly more difficult and fraught with tension. Sophie was irritated at Eugénie's cold, dry manner and her continual criticism of the 1839 decrees. Sophie told her that she was judging the decrees of 1839 in a superficial way and did not appreciate their inner value for the Society.[24] She asked her when would she ever learn to defer to another in her life, to Sophie as her leader

> but it is useless to say this to you, for *you want whatever you want*, is that not so, dear Eugénie? When I see you converted in this regard then I will believe that you are a saint. So hurry up![25]

But nothing changed and in the following month Sophie chided Eugénie again:

> Believe me, I am very happy when I am able to go along with you and I will always to do that if the reasons you give me are sound. . . . Later you will realise, I hope, what it has cost me to go against you, and all the pain and love I have expended in justifying and excusing you in front of several people. I will stop here, leaving to our Lord to choose the moment He pleases to reconcile you completely to one who has not altered in her affection for you. You must believe that![26]

Eugénie responded to this letter quickly and positively which comforted Sophie and gave her to hope that the roots of their friendship would help them both survive the divisions created after 1839.[27] In effect, opposition to the 1839 decrees had quietly hardened, during Sophie's illness and while she was visiting Amiens, Lille and Jette. When she returned to Paris in mid-August 1841 she had

decided that, if her health allowed, she would return to Rome to begin preparations for the general council the following year. During this time she had the
opportunity to talk at length with Joseph Varin. He had written to Roothan early
in August and asked if he could speak to Sophie Barat, despite the prohibition
on the Jesuits to have any contact with members of the Society of the Sacred
Heart. He explained that for forty-one years he had known and loved the Society
and that he was distressed to see it disintegrating before his eyes, at least in
France. The last two years had seen religious life in the Society fall apart:

> for a long time all hoped for the return of the superior general, convinced that her
> presence alone could bring healing to the pain which all were suffering. She has
> been back here about ten months and until now the enthusiasm which animates
> her has been paralysed by illness and relapses which have remarkably weakened
> her . . . Moreover she has little support from her assistants [general] some of whom
> are far away fulfilling various other functions; others are weakened by age or infir-
> mities. But the deepest source of all pain is the loss of the most gifted members of
> the Society at the height of their powers . . . by death; . . . and on the other hand .
> . . vocations have stopped . . . I will not go into the loss of considerable funds set
> aside in reserve, either for new foundations, or to help houses that may need aid,
> losses occasioned by bankruptcies or by injustice . . . Madame Barat said to me and
> repeated these words: On my return [from Belgium] I have to speak to you.[28]

Roothan replied quickly to Varin's request and told him that he had not
intended to place that kind of interdict on him. He was free to speak with Sophie
Barat, but he was not to take a leadership role in the Society of the Sacred Heart.
In particular he was to have no contact with the archbishop of Paris about either
Sophie or the Society.[29] No record exists of the meetings between Sophie and
Joseph Varin at this time. However some months later Sophie told Eulalie de
Bouchaud that Joseph Varin did not understand her position and that he was
working with Eugénie de Gramont to have the 1839 decrees suppressed.[30]
Undoubtedly, Varin spoke out of his position as a Jesuit in Paris and out of his
understanding of the needs of the Society of the Sacred Heart in France at this
time.

When Sophie announced in September that she would be absent from Paris
for some time, she gave no hint that she was going to Rome. Certainly Eugénie
de Gramont was unaware of this and wrote to Adèle Lehon in Sainte Rufine:

> Indeed you must miss not having our mother general with you now. But you have
> had her with you for long enough and it is our turn now. We were deprived of her
> for almost two years.[31]

Sophie left Paris on 16 September 1841, travelling with Marie Patte and
Félicité Desmarquest. On the way to Autun Sophie visited her sister, Marie-
Louise, at Joigny. Stanislas was not there and Sophie told him later in a letter
how overjoyed she was to see her sister again. It was a special visit, since earlier
in the summer of 1841 Zoé had announced her marriage to Pierre Cousin again
and this time it was definite. Sophie had accepted the fact and asked Stanislas

to help her write a letter of congratulation to the couple.[32] She met Pierre Cousin in Joigny and had time to make her own assessment. She enjoyed being at home in Joigny again, a rare moment of ease in her life. But she was still quite ill, with acute attacks of diarrhoea, and she cut her stay short:

> No doubt you will have heard about me from Joigny, which perhaps caused you worry? Indeed I arrived there very ill. Some hours of rest relieved me and since then I feel better . . . I found the family well. Your mother is happy at Zoé's joy. The young man is fine. I would like him to have more education and polish. He has the basics. Since Zoé is happy we must be too . . . As I have no time to write to Joigny it would give me pleasure if you would do this for me; give them my news and tell them how delighted I was to be with them.[33]

After spending ten days in Autun, Sophie continued south and visited the houses in Lyon, Chambéry and Turin. She set out for Rome in late October, spending some days in Parma and Lorette on the way. She arrived at the Trinité on 19 November where she found Eugénie Audé seriously ill. Sophie had this to deal with immediately while at the same time renewing contact in Rome with the pope, Lambruschini and Cardinal Pedicini. Although Cardinal Pedicini was the cardinal protector of the Society Sophie tended to seek Lambruschini's advice. He had a much greater knowledge of Paris than Pedicini. He was a friend of the Society, particularly of Eugénie de Gramont. He also had direct access to the pope. Moreover, he was not a member of the congregation bishops and religious, and so did not deal directly with Jean Rozaven. Unofficially he had frequent meetings with Josephine de Coriolis who kept him informed about developments within the Society.[34]

Meanwhile on her arrival in America Elizabeth Galitzine had introduced the decrees to every community she visited, and most members of the Society in America were aware of the content of the general council of 1839. Then in February 1841 Elizabeth Galitzine wrote to the communities informing them that Sophie had requested her to suspend reading the new edition of the constitutions until its inaccuracies could be corrected and the text formally approved by the next general council. However, Elizabeth Galitzine added her own observations, noting how the 1839 Decrees had been welcomed in America and she assured the communities that their value would not be lost: 'Later on I hope we will be able to put into practice the rule drawn up by St Ignatius, fully and without restriction.'[35] Elizabeth Galitzine had made an impact on the American members of the Society. Indeed her arrival had been welcomed, and she gave time and attention to communities and situations which had been neglected for several years. Her own personality was imposing and her Russian background a source of awe for some. Her triple role as assistant general, provincial and secretary general, were also a source of power and influence. She gave conferences to the communities, saw each one individually, visited the schools, met the local bishops and clergy. At the conclusion of her visit to each house she wrote a report for the superior in which she made detailed recommendations for the future.[36]

Her profile was high and she was respected. So when she invited the communities to write to Sophie Barat, and ask that the 1839 decrees be put into practice, there was no reason why the members would resist the request. They did not know then that this was part of a systematic form of lobbying, to ensure that Eugénie de Gramont and the rue de Varenne would not have the decrees reversed.

For example, in April 1841, when on a visit to St Charles, Elizabeth Galitzine told the community that Sophie Barat did not want her to comment further on the 1839 decrees. She advised them to give up the reading but not the spirit of the decrees, and she gave them a paper to sign, there and then, and promised to bring it back to Sophie personally. The same happened when Elizabeth Galitzine visited the new foundation among the Potawatami at Sugar Creek. Philippine Duchesne signed willingly, for she thought that Sophie had always wanted the Jesuit rule for the Society.[37] Thus while Elizabeth Galitzine obeyed Sophie Barat to the letter she continued to lobby for the decrees. By so doing, and by galvanising the petitions from the communities, Elizabeth Galitzine undermined Sophie's authority and led the communities to conclude that Sophie was not as effective a leader as Elizabeth Galitzine herself. It was a subtle form of character assassination, all the more damaging since Sophie had lost personal contact with the American houses.

During her visit, Elizabeth Galitzine explored possible new foundations in America and in Canada, and decisions had to be taken about them while she was in the country. Sophie had anticipated this and in November 1841 she gave Elizabeth Galitzine that authority, while requesting her to take into account the advice of her council there. This council consisted of Regis Hamilton and Catherine Thiéfry.[38] Sophie's only assurance in delegating her power to Elizabeth Galitzine was the knowledge that it was short-lived, since Galitzine would have to return to Europe in the late spring of 1842 for the general council.[39]

Sophie's delegation of authority gave Elizabeth Galitzine all the scope she needed. She continued to consolidate her position in America and to create expectations within the communities that the 1839 decrees were about to be formally adopted by the Society as a body. Sophie had her own suspicions about Galitzine's actions in the communities and in January 1842 Sophie reminded her that only the superiors were to have copies of the decrees, and these for reference only, not for implementation. Sophie told Galitzine that Rozaven agreed with her on this point and she hoped this would be the persuading factor. Bishop Rosati, an old friend of the Society and especially of Philippine Duchesne, was not impressed by either Elizabeth Galitzine's manner or her actions. Sophie told her that the Society could not afford to lose his support.[40]

Sophie was further alerted to Elizabeth Galitzine's extreme position with regard to the 1839 decrees when she got a lengthy epistle from her in which she urged Sophie to make a vow to obey the pope. This thought had come to Elizabeth Galitzine during her annual retreat in Grand Coteau, in December

1841, directed by Fr De Theux, an austere Jesuit, known and feared for his severity:[41]

> It came to me in prayer that in order to save the Society and to consolidate its form of government once and for all, the mother general, like St Ignatius, should make a special vow of allegiance to the Holy See. All the mothers general ought to make this vow personally to the pope and offer the Society [of the Sacred Heart] to his Holiness so that he can deploy the professed members of the Society for whatever mission he designates. The professed members of the Society will also make a vow to be ready to go wherever the pope sends them.[42]

Elizabeth Galitzine also proposed that the superior general of the Society of the Sacred Heart, and her council, submit all their decisions to the general of the Jesuits, since the pope could not personally direct the Society of the Sacred Heart in all the details of its life. In this way the Society of the Sacred Heart would be protected:

> by the court of Rome and by the Society of Jesus . . . the Society of the Sacred Heart in fact will be dependent upon the Society of Jesus but without the formal title as such . . . In this way all can be settled amicably, the Company of Jesus cannot take any offence at all.[43]

At the end of her retreat Elizabeth Galitzine made two vows. One was to work tirelessly for the Society of the Sacred Heart without concern for her own reputation. The other was a solemn vow, witnessed by Fr De Theux, to offer her life for the sake of having the 1839 decrees implemented in the Society, and to save it from the destructive forces at work within it and which she considered about to strike imminently.[44] Elizabeth Galitzine did not tell Sophie all the details she had considered regarding the future government structure of the Society. She confined herself in the letter to the question of Sophie vowing personal obedience to the pope. Sophie found this advice extraordinary. It was an attempt to make Sophie's role similar to that of the Jesuit general.

During this time Sophie began writing a journal, and in it she recorded some of the negotiations which were taking place in Rome in the spring of 1842.[45] In February 1842 she consulted Cardinal Lambruschini, the secretary of state, about her future residence and about the location for the general council in the summer of 1842. Lambruschini spoke to the pope about this and asked his advice on these two points. Both Gregory XVI and Lambruschini were of the opinion that she should fix her residence in France, not necessarily in Paris, and that the general council should take place in France, but in Lyon rather than Paris. Lambruschini arranged that Sophie should have access at all times to his private secretary, Mgr Gambaro, should she need to make urgent contact with him or with the pope. Lambruschini warned Sophie that there was a strong movement in Rome and elsewhere to separate the Society of the Sacred Heart from the houses in the north of France. He declined to say who exactly was behind the pressure but Sophie concluded that some of the French bishops thought she was orchestrating it herself.[46]

She noted in her journal that a memoir had been sent to Rome from the rue de Varenne and she did not know whether it was a copy of the protest written the previous year or a new one.[47] She wrote a candid letter to Aimée d'Avenas, suspecting that she had drawn up the text, with the approval of Eugénie de Gramont:

> . . . you have complained, written accounts, debated, done anything you wished. I have no difficulty with that. You were free to do so, I have never wanted to force a burden upon the will of anyone. You could say anything to me, send anything to me . . . but what you can never justify is the scandal you have created in France, in Rome etc., a scandal which has considerably damaged the Society and which we could have avoided by coming to understanding among ourselves! I have proof of what I am saying.[48]

Sophie had learnt that criticism of Eugénie de Gramont expressed by the community at Amiens, as well as by Marie Prevost, had been relayed to Eugénie by the bishop of Algeria, Mgr Dupuch. This only revived the enmities of the early days at Amiens and served to further polarise the communities in France. Sophie feared that if this continued all her work over the years would be destroyed and swallowed up in dissent, division and finally disintegration.[49] On 16 February 1842 Sophie held a meeting in Sainte Rufine with Félicité Desmarquest, Louise de Limminghe and Jean Rozaven. All present apparently agreed that the wishes of the pope in the matter of Sophie's residence had to be respected. They did not name Paris as the place of residence but they affirmed that Sophie was free to travel to Rome whenever she found it necessary. By now, de Limminghe, Desmarquest and Rozaven had recognised that Sophie herself would not take the initiative and announce that she was going to live in Rome. Instead they began to place all their hopes on the next general council. But Sophie herself was clear that her residence had to be the rue de Varenne. To do otherwise would jeopardise the unity of the Society. Sophie noted the options open to her:

> There are reasons for and against the rue de Varenne. For so many years it has been the centre of the Society, known by the government and the bishops as the mother house. Anyone who wanted to usurp authority by taking possession of the rue de Varenne would unfailingly succeed, or at least do a great deal of damage.[50]

In a letter written at the end of January 1842 Sophie conveyed her thinking to Eulalie de Bouchaud, indicating that she had taken a decision about her return to Paris, even before she saw Lambruschini in early February:

> It is very true that N. 41 [rue de Varenne] will always remain the focal point and centre of all. This is inevitable and any superior general far away from it will always have reason to be apprehensive.[51]

Some days later Sophie wrote a circular letter to the Society, convoking the general council in the summer of 1842, in France. She did not specify either the dates or the place where it would be held, promising to do so in May. In the meantime, she asked the provincials to forward any points they wished to raise so that the agenda could be prepared. The letter was a prolonged appeal for union and charity among the membership, as well as a call to come to the council with open minds and hearts. Sophie cited a text from the gospel of St John spoken by Christ on the eve of his Passion, ' I am the true Vine', and prayed that all would remain closely bonded, as branches of that vine. She also asked that the letter be given only to the older members of the Society as well as to those members who knew that a crisis existed. Under no circumstances was the letter to be given to outsiders, lay or cleric.[52]

On 1 April 1842 Sophie began to discuss the preparations for the general council with Rozaven, de Limminghe and Desmarquest. They decided that the best way to rebuild confidence within the Society was to invite a representative number of the membership of the Society to ensure that every point of view was heard. To this purpose not only those who had been at the 1839 council were asked but also those who had attended the 1833 general council. The provincials named in 1839 were invited and each could choose a member of their province to accompany them. In her capacity as superior general, Sophie had the right to call those members she thought should be present at the council. Some days later Sophie learnt that Elizabeth Galitzine had begun a war of words against Eugénie de Gramont and Aimée d'Avenas. Sophie noted in her journal:

> April the 5th. I have learnt the sad news of the faction which Madame Galitzine has formed against me in America, and of her efforts in France to draw in the members there. Our Lord inspired one of them, the angel of the Society, to send me the letter she received from Elizabeth Galitzine. Through this I know all.

> 8th. Council meeting on this subject, with Fr Rozaven and our mothers, as I need their light on this. All condemned and disapproved of Madame Galitzine's imprudent conduct. The way to repair the damage is to write wherever Madame Galitzine has written, and then to her herself, and then to refuse to accept any sealed packet of letters at the general council.[53]

In April 1842, Sophie wrote to Elizabeth Galitzine in a mixture of anger and despair at the

> reckless step which you took with the professed members in America, to force us, using the authority of the general council, to adopt your version of the constitutions! What a door to rebellion you have opened, and above all among the Americans! Fortunately I received warning in time to prevent the rest of your plan being carried out in Europe. I hastened to warn our provincials here to reject out of hand your proposals in this matter . . . [54]

Elizabeth Galitzine did not believe that Sophie would implement the 1839 decrees. This was confirmed when Sophie wrote in September 1841 telling her that Eugénie de Gramont was being co-operative and helpful, and that she herself would resign as superior general as soon as the general council was over. Elizabeth Galitzine was alarmed and she wrote to Louise de Limminghe telling her that Sophie had deserted the ultramontane party: Rome, the pope and the

Jesuits. Eugénie de Gramont had won the upper hand.[55] She was further alarmed to learn that the general council would not be held in Rome but in France,[56] and she read into this further evidence that Sophie had surrendered to the pressure from Eugénie de Gramont, Archbishop Affre and the majority of the French bishops. Elizabeth Galitzine's return to France became a crusade, to deliver the Society of the Sacred Heart from the tyranny of these pressures, keep faith with the American communities, and either rescue Sophie Barat or see to her demise. To her it was a clear case of the universal, ultramontane, Roman church against the independent, Gallican church.

When Sophie told Elizabeth Galitzine that 'Madame de Gramont is very good and is all I could wish her to be in our present position',[57] she was being loyal and discreet. In fact, she was having great difficulty in the rue de Varenne and many tussles with Eugénie. Her remarks about her friend were generous but not out of context. During these months when many wrote to Sophie complaining about others, she herself refused to join in the criticisms. It was an old trait in Sophie, that she was faithful to her friends and colleagues:

> Your well-meaning intention excuses you in the eyes of God and in mine, but many others will not be so indulgent![58]

Such discretion on the part of Sophie was necessary at this time, since everything she said or wrote was interpreted and critiqued, according to the position of those who read her letters.

While the news of Elizabeth Galitzine's activities shocked Sophie, de Limminghe and Rozaven merely pretended to be startled. Both were fully supportive of Elizabeth Galitzine and she maintained regular correspondence with them while she was in America. Sophie had recognised the potential danger of Elizabeth Galitzine's letters, containing proposals which had not been even discussed at the general council of 1839. The decrees of 1839 had not actually changed the constitutions of the Society approved in 1826. However, Galitzine's proposals were so radical that the Society of the Sacred Heart would have to seek a new approbation from Rome. Elizabeth Galitzine, frustrated by the resistance to the 1839 decrees on the part of some of the houses in France and by many of the French bishops, had taken the process further than the council of 1839. She had in effect lost confidence in Sophie's capacity to lead the Society. She claimed that Sophie was completely overpowered by Eugénie de Gramont. Sophie denied this and stated that Elizabeth Galitzine:

> . . . is completely wrong in suggesting that it is fear of Mother de Gramont which impels me to refuse to accept and to present Elizabeth Galitzine's work to the Society. My reasons are much higher than that and only have in mind, I dare to say, the greater good of the Society. [59]

Sophie could not believe that Eugénie would plot against her and excused her actions as mere imprudence; 'she has the Society's interests at heart'.[60] By this time Rozaven became aware that his involvement with the Society of the

Sacred Heart had become known in Rome and Paris, and was being severely criticised by his own colleagues and the French bishops. Elizabeth Galitzine's initiatives were public and Rozaven's name was linked with them. She made no secret of his support. In June 1842 Sophie wrote another circular letter to the Society, indicating that the general council would take place in Lyon towards the end of July that summer. She announced the composition and expressed once again the hope that union and peace would prevail during the council and that the divisions within the Society could be breached.[61] Both sides had written and said enough about each other. They now had to face one another, talk their differences through and reach some accommodation. As Sophie told them in her June letter; 'it depends on you to achieve this': the general council could either make or break the Society.

– 18 –

LEADERSHIP TESTED, 1842

arly in 1842 Sophie told Eugénie de Gramont that she hoped their relationship could be mended and that the happiness they had once enjoyed in their friendship would be restored in full. She liked to think that their recent tensions were as clouds in the sky which could be swept away and leave 'this tender union between us'.[1] But she soon learnt that could not happen easily when Eugénie reproached Sophie for leaving France without visiting Henriette Grosier, who was ill at Poitiers. Sophie was taken aback that Eugénie did not appreciate her position:

> I certainly do not wish to complain about your affection for her, but I should like you at least to be fair! When I was leaving [for Rome] I could not really bear any more emotion, and besides, how could I foresee her attacks? . . . At least you must believe . . . that I do not hold this against you and that your long affection for me will remain uppermost always.[2]

But there was little possibility that their relationship could heal – the source of their differences were so fundamental. Sophie asked Eugénie why she could not have remained silent and waited to express her opposition to the 1839 decrees at the next general council. This was disingenuous because the intention of the general council of 1839 had been to implement the decrees immediately and seek approbation of them in Rome. Initially there was no question of another general council to debate the decrees. This only arose when Eugénie de Gramont refused to accept them. Sophie decided to argue no more with Eugénie, for she realised that: 'All I gain from it are unpleasant remarks and I cannot satisfy you.'[3]

340

But she continued to grieve at the loss of their friendship. A few days later she admitted with deep sadness that her oldest and deepest friendship was broken. Their difficult parting in Paris in September 1841 remained with her, as a painful memory:

> It is better to remain silent with you . . . all goes back to these sad memories. Later perhaps it will be easier for us to understand one another. I long for this with all my heart. And our Lord knows that I will work towards this eagerly, as I have already done when I get the chance.[4]

This inner pain did not help Sophie's health and in the spring of 1842 she struggled to work and was continually exhausted. She caught colds and fevers and she could not get rid of a throat infection, even when leeches were applied.[5] Sophie slept poorly and had little time for exercise and for fresh air. In the Trinité Eugénie Audé was dying and Josephine de Coriolis was seriously ill. Louise de Limminghe was ill at the Villa Lante and neither house had anyone free and capable of helping Sophie with her work. Sophie remarked that the Trinité was like a small hospital,[6] and with no one, not even 'a cat to write a letter for me'. She asked Eugénie de Gramont again if she could find her someone to help with her letters.[7] There was no one free and this left Sophie burdened and depressed by the enormity of her task. She wondered wearily at the state of her life:

> Oh! If I had been able to foresee my destiny I would have stubbornly refused to learn nothing and I would have become a coadjutrix sister. It is a vain regret, I know. The best thing to do is to make use of the situation, to suffer and to love . . . [8]

When Sophie spoke about overwork in her letters she was referring not only to the amount of time and energy she had to give to the critical situation that had arisen in the Society since 1839. The administration of the Society's communities and schools continued in France, Italy, Savoy, America, Switzerland and Belgium. Sophie had to consult, take decisions and convey them, sometimes to the provincials, often to the local superiors and to individuals. The Society had not stood still since 1839 and several new foundations had been made, or were being planned for the immediate future. Between 1839 and 1841 new houses had been opened in Kientzheim (Alsace), in Loreto (Italy), in Nancy, Laval and Montpellier (France). The Society extended into new territories in America, to Sugar Creek, to New York, to McSherrystown (Pennsylvania); and into Canada, to Saint-Jacques de l'Achigan, near Montreal. Early in 1842 Sophie planned new foundations in Ireland, at Roscrea and in England at Berrymead, as well as in Italy, at Saluces, St Elpidio and Padua, in Lemberg in Galicia (Poland) and in Algeria. These were the houses which were actually founded, but Sophie had many other requests also from all over the world: Latin America (Peru), India (Calcutta), Australia (Sydney), Burma, North Africa (Tunis), as well as from several countries in Europe. The Society had never been so sought after since its foundation.

Sophie had to ask herself continually whether or not she had the personnel and finance to continue expanding. She never lost sight of the essential reality that the Society of the Sacred Heart had to be situated in marketable places and conditions. Sophie had a eye to that all her life and never lost the courage to branch out in a new area, a new country or a new continent. The Society was a business that had to keep moving in a market which had plenty of competitors. Once Sophie was asked why she continued to plan new foundations:

> In reality . . . we have to count on the good Master with a lively faith so that He will compensate for our poverty. On the other hand, we are accused of taking on too much, but if we do not make superhuman efforts others will take our place and we would gradually die. So that is why I have accepted Bourges and Rennes . . . [9]

However, as Varin had pointed out to Roothan, women were not entering the Society in sufficient numbers to sustain all the new foundations, and the financial state of the Society was precarious. There were individual members who needed care and attention. Sophie spoke in particular of those who were physically or mentally ill, and of those who had entered with no vocation or who had lost heart on the way. In 1841 Sophie told Anna du Rousier that she was worried that vocations were so few in the Society, especially in Belgium and Italy where the Society had relatively new foundations. She sensed that the clergy opposed young women entering the Society and remarked: 'we lack the gift of gaining the support of the clergy'.[10] When Elizabeth Galitzine was in the process of negotiating the new foundations in America Sophie warned her that she had no personnel to offer:

> All our best people are dying, I have counted ten in a few weeks . . . preceded by as many, at the beginning of the year. And just now eight are terminally ill and will leave us this winter, all young women. Add to this the few postulants entering the Society. Not one in the last four months in Paris and no hope of any. You see that we have to stop, that we are forced to do so here. I trust that you will have postulants in America, now that you are becoming known.[11]

While Sophie mourned the deaths of many young women in the Society, she deplored the quality of some who had been allowed to enter the Society too easily. She lamented that many had

> neither talent, refinement nor education and, worst of all, no religious vocation. If this goes on the Society will die out. We really need fewer foundations and more religious spirit and genuine integrity. Without these we will not achieve our goal and we will perish.[12]

Sophie wrote to Eulalie de Bouchaud, mistress of novices in the rue Monsieur, Paris, and warned her to be very careful when accepting women into the Society. Candidates had to have good health basically, show a capacity to grow in the understanding and practice of religious life, and have strong personalities:

> I believe . . . that we must not accept women who really do not have what is needed to understand religious life and live it. Later on these would frustrate rather

than help [the Society]. How much I prefer to have those who have difficult characters but who have soul and energy, to those wet hens who do us no good![13]

Sophie sent away many postulants, novices and aspirants and only wished other superiors would do the same. She grieved over what had happened:

Look at what our Society has become in twenty years. It has become unrecognisable! And what worries me most is that I cannot send away all who damage us … We have hardly any novices in rue Monsieur, very few postulants, and yet I prefer that to having numbers who are not truly religious. The source of vocations appears to be drying up, the best are in Heaven.[14]

Added to these concerns was the financial state of the Society, which by the autumn of 1841 had reached crisis point. As Sophie told Gregory XVI, mismanagement and misfortune had threatened the economic vitality of the Society and wiped out the resources which Sophie had gathered carefully. Sophie also complained that provincials and local superiors continued to build beyond their actual needs, had run into debt and consequently were unable to pay the annual tenth of their income to the central fund:

If this course continues the Society will not survive long. Each Provincial will only see her Province, the local superior her own houses and Society as a body tries to survive if it can![15]

Despite exhaustion and weariness, and with little administrative help, Sophie continued to govern the Society. As well as delegating the negotiations for the new foundations in America and Canada to Elizabeth Galitzine, Sophie also asked Eugénie de Gramont to assume responsibility for the foundations of Roscrea in Ireland and Berrymead in England, though she retained the correspondence with the bishops concerned. Both foundations were important in her eyes for they would provide English-speaking members of the Society, who in time would help foundations in America and Australia. England too as Protestant country was both a challenge and mission for Sophie and Ireland was seen as a way into England:

Of the two locations offered the [English] one would be more acceptable than that in Ireland as far as pupils are concerned. As for postulants, we would attract many more in Ireland! Also, it would be a true work of Providence to catch both. So may the little mother [Eugénie de Gramont] give good instructions to Mother Croft, whom she is sending there, so that these two fish fall into the nets of the Sacred Heart![16]

In the summer of 1842 Sophie made final preparations for the general council at Lyon, hopeful that at last the divisive issues within the Society could be resolved. She told Eugénie de Gramont that she expected her to travel to Lyon for the council and advised her not to choose Aimée d'Avenas as her companion for the council.[17] Eugénie refused to accept this directive, accusing Sophie of infringing her rights as a provincial to choose her own companion. However, Sophie knew that Eugénie's presence at the council would be difficult enough to absorb, but to have both there, after the opposition they had mounted to the 1839 decrees, would be intolerable.[18] This tension presaged ill for the council. With a sense of foreboding Sophie set out from Rome and travelled in stages, intending to arrive in Lyon by the end of July.

News concerning Archbishop Affre's attitude to the council awaited Sophie in Chambéry and it shocked her profoundly.[19] He had written to those bishops in France who had houses of the Society in their dioceses and explained that Sophie Barat had not informed him that she intended to hold a general council of the Society in Lyon; nor had she sought his permission to hold it outside of Paris. This was a side of Archbishop Affre which Sophie had not yet encountered. In 1840 they had worked together on removing Jammes as chaplain from the rue de Varenne, a matter of common agreement. It was quite a different matter when Sophie acted independently from him and ignored what he considered his rights as archbishop. One of Affre's priorities on his appointment as archbishop had been to set in motion a restructuring of the relations between the archbishop of Paris and the religious congregations of men and women in his diocese. The main purpose of this was to establish his authority over them in no uncertain terms.[20] Eugénie de Gramont and Aimée d'Avenas colluded with the archbishop since they preferred to have the 1839 decrees suppressed without having to hold the general council at all. They co-operated with the archbishop's request by forwarding a copy of their observations and comments on the 1839 decrees and he enclosed that document with his letter to the French bishops.[21] Eugénie wrote to Sophie in early July 1842, explaining her position:

> I must give you an account of something that is going on, which you will undoubtedly blame me for, if I do not explain it to you yet I am not to blame at all. The archbishop of Paris is very unhappy that the Council is being held in Lyon. He is very offended and expresses this very openly. At the same time, he declares his deep dissatisfaction with the new Decrees of the Council of Rome [1839] . . . Moreover, two years ago at his consecration when I asked his permission to start the trial period for the Decrees . . . he asked me to note the main points on paper . . . I did that two years ago and I did not speak to him about this anymore. Since he learnt that the Council was going to meet, he took the notes and wrote to all the bishops. Then he told me that he wanted to send my notes to all the bishops, to show them how flawed everything is . . . I begged him to do nothing of the sort, I did what I could to prevent him. . . . I can assure you that I am upset and it is not my fault. . . . The archbishop is not a man to displease or make angry. Be careful.[22]

Not only did Archbishop Affre criticise Sophie Barat for calling the council at Lyon, he also forbade Eugénie de Gramont to attend the council. Sophie found this intolerable and challenged Eugénie to demand the right to leave Paris.[23] But Eugénie either could not or would not face the ire of Archbishop Affre and she asked Sophie to move the council from Lyon to Paris, to the rue de Varenne or even Conflans, assuring her that this decision alone would appease Affre. While Eugénie de Gramont was pleased that she was spared facing her peers at the general council, she was enraged that she had been forced to support Affre. It was not so long ago since she was known to be a critic of Archbishop Affre, yet now she was forced to agree with him. Eugénie blamed Sophie and the members of the general council of 1839 for all these ills. When Henriette Grosier died in July 1842 Eugénie reminded Sophie that Henriette had always opposed the 1839 decrees, until her death:

> in the face of death and the judgement of God, she did not regret or retract her opposition to the Decrees, which she always regarded as quite wrong and disastrous for the Society . . . Let the [Dames] members of the Council know all this, let them meditate on it during their retreat, those who so thoughtlessly meddled with the constitutions, which they ought to respect and teach others to respect. That was their responsibility, not to change them.[24]

In the middle of July 1842 Sophie received a blunt letter from Archbishop Affre in which he forbade her to hold any council on the constitutions of the Society of the Sacred Heart and in future to obey him as her superior.[25] Sophie replied to Archbishop Affre on 24 July and defended her position. She told him that she had acted within her rights as superior general of the Society of the Sacred Heart, enshrined in its constitutions. She added that. in all that regarded her role as superior general, she was accountable to the cardinal protector in Rome. In that context, just as she had not informed the bishops in all the dioceses where the Society had houses, so she had not informed the archbishop of Paris of the meeting of the general council in Lyon. She reminded him that Archbishop de Quelen never challenged her right to convene general councils.[26] Archbishop Affre replied immediately informing her that her response was quite inadequate:

> I can see from the way in which you justify your oversight how convinced you are of your independence. It is clear that you believe it to be complete. For you the matter of notifying the archbishop of Paris is simply an issue of mere courtesy.[27]

Archbishop Affre rejected Sophie's argument that the cardinal protector in Rome was her superior and he insisted on his rights as archbishop of Paris over her and the Society of the Sacred Heart. He accused Sophie of using the role of the cardinal protector to remain independent of him and he threatened to destroy the Society unless she submitted to his authority. Sophie had grappled for years with the conflicting claims of bishops over houses of the Society within the dioceses, in France and elsewhere. By the terms of the Concordat and Organic Articles, which had been accepted by the Church in France, the powers of French bishops were controlled and circumscribed by the government. By writing a circular letter to the bishops Archbishop Affre had gone beyond his rights, since the government frowned upon internal correspondence between the bishops. In a sense, Sophie Barat had more scope for independent action than the bishops and this was a source of resentment, particularly when theoretically women's legal existence in France was so circumscribed. Furthermore, the French bishops were jealous of their corporate independence from the claims of Rome, and the fact that the Society of the Sacred Heart had a cardinal protector in Rome was a further source of tension. These issues were the subtexts of the struggle between Archbishop Affre and the Society of the Sacred Heart at this time. Affre took Cardinal de Bonald to task for allowing the Society of the Sacred Heart to meet in Lyon and wrote a menacing letter to his colleague

> the meaning of which was that he must not believe that his title of Primate of the Gauls gives him permission to trample the rights of the other bishops underfoot.[28]

The cardinal caved in and told Sophie that he could not allow the council to proceed in his diocese. He admitted that he could not face the aggression of Archbishop Affre and preferred to capitulate than enter into a battle of rights. Once Sophie received this news she realised that she had reached an impasse and that she had no choice but to write to Affre and put forward her own point of view again. Her letter was short and clear. She explained that until his intervention she had always understood she had the freedom to call councils of the Society, but evidently he thought differently. In the light of that she had decided to defer the council for the time being, until she had further clarification.[29] While she was laconic with Archbishop Affre, Sophie wrote a long letter to Eugénie de Gramont in which she made it clear that she thought Eugénie could have supported her more and explained the position to the archbishop:

> I notice that you often attribute to us intentions we do not have, I assure you. . . . I believed what you told me: that you had nothing to do with this affair, and our mothers agreed with me.[30]

A sense of impending doom hung over Sophie and she wondered just where the Society was going:

> Into what an abyss they are plunging a work which should be supported and protected wherever we are established.[31]

Sophie wrote to Cardinal Lambruschini and asked him to consult Gregory XVI on the matter of the claims of the archbishop of Paris over the Society of the Sacred Heart. She outlined the history of the Society, from the beginning in Amiens until 1839. At no time was the archbishop of Paris ever considered the superior general of the Society of the Sacred Heart. Sophie also outlined her powers as superior general and argued that she had not overstepped them. Finally, she described the role of the cardinal protector and asserted that this role was more suitable for a congregation which was destined to be worldwide and had official approbation from Rome. Sophie petitioned the pope for a statement which would make it clear that the superior general of the Society of the Sacred Heart was exempt from the authority of the archbishop of Paris.[32]

The relationship between the pope and the archbishop of Paris was a sensitive issue and Sophie presented Gregory XVI with a case which became a test of strength between a Gallican archbishop and ultramontane authority. Already, Archbishop Affre had contested his rights as archbishop of Paris with regard to foundations in Rome, and his manner and actions had evoked antagonism from the papal court. This only helped Sophie gain the sympathy of the pope.[33] He responded to her request for clarification by appointing eight cardinals to study Sophie's case. They found in favour of Sophie Barat's rights against the archbishop of Paris. On 16 August 1842 the pope conveyed the decision in a formal brief to Pedicini, the cardinal protector of the Society, who forwarded it to Sophie at Lyon.

In a separate letter, to accompany the pope's brief, Pedicini asked Sophie to convey the decision to the bishops in whose dioceses the Society had houses. Presuming that the council would now take place in Lyon, Pedicini also advised her to call Eugénie de Gramont once more to Lyon, to take part in the council. Unfortunately that accompanying letter was not sent and Sophie only received the brief of Gregory XVI in late August. Pedicini's letter finally arrived in September. By then, Cardinal de Bonald, under pressure from Archbishop Affre, had withdrawn his permission to hold the council in his diocese and Sophie had no choice but to cancel it. The members had a retreat together, followed by some meetings for general business. Then all dispersed and returned to their houses.[34]

Cardinal Lambruschini sent a copy of the papal brief to the internuncio in Paris, Antonio Garibaldi. He formally handed it over to Archbishop Affre who predictably was incensed. Mgr Garibaldi went to see Affre at his country house at St Germain-en-Laye and received a torrent of abuse from the archbishop.[35] Affre accused the pope of ignoring his point of view and his rights as archbishop of Paris. He felt that the Society of the Sacred Heart in the person of Sophie Barat had gained a victory over him and his authority as archbishop, and that in the eyes of his colleagues he had lost face. He continued to argue that Sophie Barat should be dependent upon him and threatened that he would

> inform the government that they must not consult him any more on matters generally pertaining to the Society of the Sacred Heart. That he will ask the superior general to come to Paris quite soon to explain herself . . . to state whether she intends to continue to reside in Paris and to regard herself as subject to the archbishop of Paris himself, and if otherwise . . . they [Society of the Sacred Heart] may go and reside in another diocese.[36]

Once the government became aware of Archbishop Affre's decision, news of the papal brief would become public. This was potentially serious, for no decrees from a foreign power, especially from the pope, could be received in France without the prior authorisation from the government. In view of this, Garibaldi urged moderation and prudence but Affre would have none of it. A few days later he paid a visit to the rue de Varenne and in the course of a long interview he expressed his views forcefully to Eugénie de Gramont. She took the archbishop's side completely and accused Sophie of placing the Society in great danger:

> What a false step . . . you have taken . . . How could you have compromised the dignity of the Holy See by making it act in such a cavalier way and make allegations

against the archbishop which are quite without foundation? What will you gain from this? . . . Why do you act like this with the bishops and always want to act without their consent? Now his [Archbishop Affre] displeasure with you has greatly increased . . .[37]

Eugénie accused Sophie of wanting to change the structures of the Society and change the residence of the superior general, without consulting the bishops and most of all without consulting Eugénie de Gramont. But Sophie had decided a long time ago to make a bid to free the Society from the constrictions which both Eugénie and Archbishop de Quelen had placed upon its growth and spiritual vitality. Sophie's bid for freedom was a gamble which she had taken for the sake of the Society, to take it beyond the confines of Paris, of France, into a wider world. She knew that unless the Society went forward into new places it would contract and die, and die it must in Paris unless some profound change was made. Eugénie de Gramont had resisted all change, sensing that the old world she had controlled would crumble. Yet now, just when Sophie was struggling to realise her vision, another archbishop of Paris threatened to limit her freedom to act and to direct the Society of the Sacred Heart.

Archbishop Affre sought to restore his wounded self-image among the bishops of France. He decided to write a second letter to them in mid-September, insisting that Sophie Barat had to be dependent upon his authority. The letter showed how seriously he meant it when he told Garibaldi that he would inform the French government.[38] As Affre understood it, once the statutes of the Society of the Sacred Heart, presented to the government in 1827, were granted approval, then the Society was dependent upon the government and the government exercised that authority through the archbishop of Paris. All requests for new foundations outside Paris, all matters concerning dowries and financial transactions regarding property, were negotiated through the archbishop of Paris. Archbishop Affre was quick to point out:

> The government consult him, not as a magistrate, [but] as the spiritual leader of the diocese. . . . [39]

Affre rejected the argument that a cardinal protector modified or transcended the authority of the archbishop of Paris over the Society of the Sacred Heart. Yet he assured the bishops he accepted the decision of the pope and cardinals, despite the fact that he had not even been consulted by Rome and had been misrepresented by Sophie Barat. He had decided to make no claim whatsoever over the Society of the Sacred Heart and would advise the government that he was not its superior, that this office was exercised from Rome. It was a vindictive and effective strike against the Society. The French government would not tolerate any community in France taking its orders from outside the jurisdiction, and especially from Rome, and Affre knew it. He included in the letter some of the views of the bishops all over France, and cited one especially critical of Sophie herself:

That which Madame Barat treats so lightly is of sufficient importance to warrant her serious reflection.[40]

Sophie did not learn of the contents of this letter for some weeks. During that time she had other concerns to deal with and fortunately by this time she had asked Césaire Mathieu, archbishop of Besançon, to help her find her way through the thicket of intrigue which was settling in all around her. In particular she needed to go to Besançon to talk through her next move with Affre:

I would like the help of your insights, to reassure myself that, in defending our rights, I am acting according to my conscience! [41]

Césaire Mathieu promptly replied that of course he would try to help Sophie, they were old friends and he knew how serious her position was with regard to the archbishop of Paris. He assured her that she was right to have postponed the general council in Lyon.[42] Sophie travelled to Besançon in the middle of September and found that Césaire Mathieu was absent temporarily on business. While awaiting his return, she received a letter from Pedicini which disturbed her profoundly and forced her to return immediately to Lyon. While the archbishop of Paris had denounced Sophie Barat for calling the general council in Lyon, Cardinal Pedicini took her to task for cancelling it.[43] He presumed that she had received his letter of instruction with the brief, sent to her from Rome in mid-August. But she had not received that letter and had presumed that she was to convey the contents of the brief to the Society and to the French bishops in whatever way she thought best.[44] The tone and content of Pedicini's letter astounded Sophie and when Césaire Mathieu returned to Besançon he wrote immediately to Rome to explain that Sophie had never received the letter of instruction from Pedicini.[45] Sophie was caught in a narrow place between the ultramontane position of Rozaven, de Limminghe and Galitzine, and the Gallican position of Affre and Eugénie de Gramont, new allies in a common cause, supported by the French bishops.

Sophie was aware that Elizabeth Galitzine, who had remained in Lyon when the general council was dispersed, kept Rozaven and de Limminghe informed with regard to events in France. In Rome both Louise de Limminghe and Rozaven kept up the pressure on Sophie by holding sway over Pedicini. They began to fear not only the impact of Archbishop Affre and Eugénie de Gramont on Sophie's leadership; they also feared that Sophie's health would buckle under the pressure. Elizabeth Galitzine had little hope for the future.[46] She thought that Sophie would be dead by Christmas and she urged Louise de Limminghe to find out how they were to proceed in France in the event of Sophie's death. The French government had already begun to enquire into the internal affairs of the Society. The French embassy in Rome confirmed an enquiry that Sophie Barat had been resident in Rome for regular periods since 1832.[47] Galitzine's worst nightmare was the possibility that Eugénie de Gramont would succeed Sophie as superior general. Rumour had it that the government would ask the mother general to resign in favour of Madame de Gramont. Indeed we have heard many times that the little lady had been selected to be superior general. Or, if this does not happen immediately, they will require that she be appointed assistant general, as Mother de Causans said to me . . . what role would we have in all that? . . . They treat us as if we are imbeciles.[48]

Elizabeth Galitzine had a vivid imagination and she conjured up a scene from a general council in Paris:

I presume that this august assembly will presided over by the archbishop of Paris, who will have on his right the Minister of religion or his delegate in soutane or otherwise. On his left, his theologian, the little lady [Eugénie de Gramont]. Further down [from her], the mother general. On the other side of the Minister, Madame d'Avenas . . . The archbishop will pronounce an excommunication, declaring the illegal Council of 1839 anathema. . . . The little lady will propose a toast to the great Churchman of France, and clink glasses with the Minister of Religion.[49]

Rozaven too had dismissed Sophie Barat. He told Elizabeth Galitzine that he agreed with her assessment of Sophie's leadership:

I very much agree with you that we must do everything to save the Society despite the mother general. But I fear that all our efforts will only be futile and founder due to the insurmountable apathy or weakness of the one who governs you. She only knows how to use petty means and petty stratagems, which in ordinary circumstances allow her to deal temporarily with a situation. But such means are totally inadequate and useless in serious matters where the salvation of the Society is concerned . . . I have asked the cardinal protector to write a letter and I enclose a copy or translation. The mother general herself will certainly not tell you about this letter, that is why I am passing it on to you.[50]

He also wrote to the archbishop of Bordeaux, Ferdinand Donnet (1837–82), who had been critical of Sophie's decision to postpone the general council at Lyon. At this time Donnet wanted to avoid any conflict with the French government, especially when he was finalising arrangements for Henri Lacordaire's visit to the city in November.[51] Rozaven admitted that he did not know why Cardinal de Bonald had withdrawn his agreement to having the council in his diocese and presumed that he had been intimidated by Archbishop Affre. Yet, while ignoring what had happened between de Bonald and Affre, Rozaven condemned Sophie Barat:

Here in Rome it is regretted that the superior general no longer has the strength and energy to maintain her authority. . . . Indecision and weakness have placed her in a difficult position from which she will have difficulty in extricating herself. Fear and faint-heartedness are poor counsellors. . . . She has allowed herself to be intimidated by the threatening and domineering tone which the archbishop uses towards her. She believed him to have more power than he actually had…But women are easily intimidated. They need support, encouragement, protection, and the bishops are those who can provide this for them.[52]

Rozaven dealt Sophie's leadership a further blow when he suggested to Pedicini that a strong letter to Sophie would solve the problem. Rozaven drew up the letter and Pedicini signed it. Its tone and content had taken Sophie by surprise, as she told Césaire Mathieu, but in time she recognised the source of the letter and could better understand the violence in it. When the internuncio in Paris, Garibaldi, saw a copy of the letter he remarked to his friend Césaire Mathieu:

> I am also of the opinion that the cardinal protector, Pedicini, could not bring himself to write in such a forthright manner. He is a quiet, easy-going person, indeed I would say he is almost indolent.[53]

In the letter Sophie was asked a series of questions and issued a series of barking orders, all of them to impress on her personal obedience to the pope. Rozaven insisted that Sophie hold the council in Lyon, and insist that Eugénie de Gramont attend it or remove her from office. Most of all, Sophie must refuse to return to Paris. All three orders missed the point, since the council had had to be postponed and all had dispersed. There was no point in asking Eugénie de Gramont to travel then and Sophie had to return to Paris to deal with Archbishop Affre and try to pacify the criticisms of the government. Even before she received this menacing letter Sophie had told Elizabeth Galitzine that she could no longer work with Rozaven. He was unable to understand her delicate position, he judged her harshly and he held rigidly to fixed ideas when flexibility would have helped generate a resolution. Sophie asked Elizabeth Galitzine to explain her position to Rozaven, especially the decision of Cardinal de Bonald, still not knowing the full extent of their collusion and their common view that Sophie Barat was no longer capable of being superior general.[54]

At the end of September 1842 Sophie wrote a long letter to Pedicini. She explained that she could not recall the members of the general council until the spring at the earliest. Neither could she simply remove Eugénie de Gramont from the rue de Varenne immediately. Such a move would have to be carefully planned if a public scandal was to be avoided. She defended Eugénie and said she had been willing to go to Lyon but Archbishop Affre had forbidden her to go. She assured Pedicini that she wanted to hold a general council as soon as possible herself. She had decided to resign as superior general:

> As a result of the position which they have placed me in and the constraints which they consider necessary to provoke me, I can no longer govern the Society. I intend therefore to give in my resignation. It will not be difficult to find a candidate among our mothers who assuredly will govern better than I can. I expect a reply before I leave for Paris.[55]

Sophie said nothing to Elizabeth Galitzine about the letter from Pedicini but Galitzine knew of its existence and questioned Sophie about the contents. Sophie refused to talk about it or to give any hint of what she was thinking. When Galitzine suggested that Sophie was flying in the face of the pope's express wishes and could be excommunicated for contempt, Sophie laughed wryly at that interpretation and refused to be drawn into further discussion, other than saying it was not the time to dismiss Eugénie de Gramont.[56] But Sophie told Césaire Mathieu that a pressure group originating in Rome wanted her to act in a way that was quite contrary to her style of leadership in the Society:

> It is true that in Rome there is a kind of conspiracy against me and my way of working, and since they are acting in the name of the Holy Father I find myself constricted and no longer able to move. So, they are insisting that I remove Madame de Gramont from Paris, that I relieve her of all responsibilities and consequently that I destroy her reputation. They also insist that I remove from several houses those who oppose [the Decrees], and these are exactly the people who need more prudent treatment. They insist that I remain out of Paris. Indeed they want to deprive me of every kind of liberty, and by this fact it is the assistants [general] who have been given the government of the Society now. This would be correct if they had wished me to resign. But worst of all, I must go against by own insights and my own conscience. This then is my position.[57]

Criticism of Sophie's leadership came not only from Rome but also from some of the bishops in France. In September 1842 the archbishop of Bordeaux, Ferdinand Donnet (1837–82), had not only written to Rozaven about the Society, he had also asked the superior in Bordeaux, Henriette Granon, about the crisis. Granon wrote to Sophie for advice and she told Granon that she had difficulties with some of the community at the rue de Varenne, and that her good working relationship with Archbishop Affre was over. But nothing merited the criticisms she received over her management of the rue de Varenne, and particularly of Eugénie de Gramont:

> Without doubt all would soon come to an end if No. 41 [rue de Varenne] came back. At the moment there is a slight rapprochement but the most effective way would be to reconcile the French bishops and the leader of the Society of the Sacred Heart. There are hardly any absurdities of which I have not been accused. Mockery of me became accepted. I am not accusing Mother de Gramont of this. She is not capable of doing it, but their friends are. This merry-go-round is nearly over. I thank the Lord for all these humiliations if they can draw upon us the mercy of his divine Heart.[58]

Sophie's public image and reputation were gradually being demolished, by both factions in the Society, for their own purposes. The criticisms emanating from the rue de Varenne were especially hurtful and Sophie was unable to face the fact that Eugénie de Gramont contributed to her character assassination just as much as Rozaven, Galitzine and de Limminghe. What further oppressed and saddened Sophie was the awareness that her every move and every word were being monitored. As the days went by Sophie realised Césaire Mathieu's letters aroused curiosity in Lyon and on 2 October 1842 Sophie proposed using the rue de Varenne as their postal address. On the same day she received a letter from Césaire Mathieu, telling her that Archbishop Affre had written a second letter to the French bishops, denouncing her, her convocation of the council at Lyon in the summer of 1842 as well as the general council of 1839.[59] It was too much and Sophie doubted that Césaire Mathieu would stand by her now. Césaire Mathieu sensed this and wrote to her immediately, assuring her that he would be steadfast and not walk away. Mathieu saw Sophie as a Christ-figure and his own role was to serve her as she needed at this critical point in the history of the Society of the Sacred Heart. He also suggested that the Society's own success and public profile in France and elsewhere may have drawn this crisis upon itself:

> Allow me in sharing your cross to experience also something of its weight. Simon of Cyrene was glad to have something himself to suffer when he helped our divine Master on the way to Calvary. . . . I can only be hopeful for your congregation. The present storm shows you what success means . . . and that of the Society is compromising its very existence. But in my opinion Providence is teaching you a lesson in humility. For that reason you must accept and carry this cross with great calm, great gentleness, in reverent silence and perfect trust.[60]

During the month of September Sophie's niece, Julie Dusaussoy, became seriously ill in Conflans. Both Eugénie de Gramont and Marie de la Croix looked after her but soon warned Sophie that Julie would die within a short time. She died on 21 September and when Sophie heard the news she wrote to both Stanislas and Sophie Dusaussoy, barely unable to hide her envy of Julie's death.[61] She spoke about it to Louise de Limminghe also and about her wish to resign as superior general. As if to hasten that day Sophie had decided to leave Lyon and return to Paris. With this plan in mind she left Lyon on 4 October 1842, accompanied by Félicité Desmarquest. They travelled to Autun, to await a reply from Pedicini. It was a risky journey. The authorities in Rome, led by Rozaven and de Limminghe, did not want her to go to Paris. Sophie knew that her travelling companion was sympathetic to the views of Elizabeth Galitzine and Louise de Limminghe and so she felt watched. She told Césaire Mathieu:

> [Félicité Desmarquest] has such fixed and false ideas that I do not think we can agree! . . . this array of obstacles, this resistance which I find all around me is hardening my spirit. Sometimes I am close to losing my patience!![62]

In Autun Sophie heard from Paris that the government was about to confront her over the issue of her residence. In the middle of October, the minister of justice and religion, Martin du Nord, wrote to Archbishop Affre outlining the situation regarding the Society of the Sacred Heart.[63] As far as he was concerned, the Society of the Sacred Heart had freely entered into an agreement with the government, enshrined in statutes signed by Charles X in 1827. The government had not been aware, either then or since, that the Society of the Sacred Heart had received approbation of its constitutions from the pope and that it had a cardinal protector in Rome. The minister reminded the archbishop that the French government had never recognised the role or the authority of a superior general, even if she lived in France. Authority over religious communities was held by the local bishop in each diocese. This applied to Sophie Barat and to the Society of the Sacred Heart. The recent general council [1839] ignored these realities and unless Sophie Barat could assure the government that the Society of the Sacred Heart observed the 1827 statutes, which they themselves had requested from the king, the Society of the Sacred Heart would be dissolved, by applying the law of 24 May 1825.

Sophie received a copy of this letter from Mgr Gros, vicar general of Paris, who conveyed Archbishop Affre's dismay that the government had acted so quickly. He asked Sophie to believe that he had not intended that she would be so directly confronted by the minister. Archbishop Affre certainly did not want the schools of the Society to be affected in Paris or elsewhere in France, but his hot words had reached their target. He urged her to travel to Paris as soon as possible.[64] Césaire Mathieu assured her that he would explain the reasons for her decision to Rome if any criticism arose. Indeed, Lambruschini had already told Césaire Mathieu that his role as Sophie's adviser in the affairs of the Society was seen positively in Rome.[65] By way of beginning a process of resolution, Sophie wrote to Archbishop Affre to tell him that she was planning to return to Paris soon and that she hoped to clarify her position with regard to the government. Archbishop Affre welcomed the decision and agreed to help her on condition that she accept his authority over her and the Society of the Sacred Heart, a role he still claimed as archbishop of Paris. This was an ominous threat which proved to be much more difficult to dispel than any from the government.[66] Sophie knew her presence was needed in Paris but she was not sure what step she would take when she got there. Her relationship with Eugénie de Gramont was strained and she admitted to Césaire Mathieu that 'there I have no true friend'.[67]

But Sophie did find support in Paris in the person of the internuncio, Antonio Garibaldi. He was a good friend of Césaire Mathieu and over the next three months both worked closely together with Sophie in the common task of saving the Society of the Sacred Heart. Garibaldi explained to Lambruschini on 15 October 1842 that Sophie Barat must return to Paris to deal with the minister of justice and religion, who sought a declaration from her in writing that she would conform to the statutes of 1827. Garibaldi told Lambruschini that by now it was not simply an infringement of the statutes of 1827 which the government objected to so strongly. Archbishop Affre's impulsiveness, which Garibaldi criticised as irresponsible, had placed the Society of the Sacred Heart in a position of real danger. Affre now regretted his actions, but the deed had been done and the government had acted. Indeed, Garibaldi felt that for some time the government had been waiting for an opportunity to attack the Society of the Sacred Heart:

> The government itself, as well as some friends and enemies, holds certain prejudices against this very distinguished congregation, of such benefit in France. In fact the government considers the Society of the Sacred Heart to be motivated by a spirit quite hostile to the current political order. [It is seen] as a type of congregation similar to the Society of Jesus, or an association over which the Jesuits exercise influence. You . . . well understand the impact which such prejudices are capable of exercising in France at the present time.[68]

− 19 −

INTO THE ABYSS, 1842−1843

Sophie returned to Paris on 4 November 1842 and the next three months proved to be among the most painful and stressful of her life. In her frequent, almost daily letters to Césaire Mathieu Sophie confessed that she doubted that her health could withstand such pressure. Most of all, she wondered if she had lost her way, or if she had taken a fundamentally wrong decision and so taken the Society down the path of destruction. What if she herself was the 'seed of destruction'? She told Césaire Mathieu that if she could be sure that she was following God's will and destiny for her and for the Society, then it would be possible to conserve her courage. This clarity was not given to Sophie and she had to make her way slowly and painfully, step by step, until she found a clearing and a place of peace for herself and for the Society.

Sophie's first appointment was with the internuncio, Antonio Garibaldi, and she admitted to him that she simply did not know how to control the ultramontane group within the Society, and she feared that they had fatally damaged her reputation in Rome. She also knew that some of the Jesuits in Paris were critical of her and had written about her negatively to their colleagues in Rome. In her isolation in Paris Sophie dreaded that those in Rome, especially the pope, would drop their interest in the affairs of the Society in Paris and leave her to resolve the crisis alone. This was hinted at first by threats of abandonment by Rozaven, and then by his silence, a form of punishment and pressure:

> I suspect that these threats come from Fr Rozaven, because nothing has been explained to me, and since he has great influence all will be lost if he withdraws.

What is certain is that what I see happening all around me is a deliberate plot . . . If this state of affairs continues, I feel I will capitulate . . . [1]

When Sophie heard that the French government was preparing to take issue with the Society over her proposed residence in Rome she informed Elizabeth Galitzine immediately. She indicated the gravity of the situation and spelt out the implications of the government's attitude. Sophie knew that unless the Society informed the government that it had formally abandoned the proposal that she live in Rome, all the schools of the Society in France would be secularised and placed under the authority of the University. She told Elizabeth Galitzine:

> My soul is under such pressure when I see the misfortunes which await us and I have not got the courage to speak about them any more . . . Every post bears news of upheavals which brings my nerves to breaking point. I can barely hold my pen. [2]

She asked Elizabeth Galitzine, in her capacity as secretary general of the Society, to inform the other assistants general, the provincials and Rozaven in Rome of the pressure she was under in Paris. Sophie was convinced that they would understand how critical the situation had become and that they would support her decision to return to Paris, to deal directly with the government and with Archbishop Affre. Elizabeth Galitzine took quite the contrary view. She told Sophie to hold firm to the 1839 decrees, to refuse to deal with the government and to remain outside Paris at all costs. To go there would signal to all in the Society, and certainly to the pope and cardinals, that she had ceded to the Gallican elements in the French church and in the Society. Since the summer of 1842, when Affre forced Sophie to cancel the general council, Galitzine considered that in the future the Society should look entirely to Rome for its support and refuse to allow Affre to control its affairs. Indeed, without informing Sophie beforehand, Galitzine had circulated a long, detailed refutation of Affre's September letter to the French bishops. Now, in an effort to frighten Sophie, she warned her dramatically that if she went to Paris she would be in danger of being excommunicated and the Society of the Sacred Heart could be suppressed by the pope. Sophie was taken aback at this reaction:

> You are very quick to come to a decision about our dissolution. I must admit that only for the love of our Lord would I tolerate this language, as well as the other dealings which stem from it. May God protect me from such pain for I could not bear it otherwise, I would die.
> The archbishop of Paris has been told that we sent a circular letter to all the houses which refuted his letter. He is trying by every means to get a copy of this letter. The only letter I have is the one which you drew up for the Decrees. Did you speak about Archbishop Affre's letter in that? To have done so is a great imprudence at the present time. If you have, you must write immediately to all the superiors you sent a copy to and tell them not to show it to anyone and even to burn it now so that no one can demand to see it! What a frightening crisis we find ourselves in . . . [3]

By now Sophie felt she could not accommodate the two factions pulling the Society apart. She came to the conclusion, with great regret and sorrow, that the only solution was a complete suppression of the 1839 decrees. Her only hope was that the structure of provinces and the office of provincials could be retained, for this was essential to good government.[4] A priest in Paris, possibly Fr Surat, offered to go to Rome immediately and ask the pope, in the name of Sophie Barat, to annul the 1839 decrees. Sophie discussed this with Césaire Mathieu and they decided that this would polarise the ultramontane group in the Society further and Sophie would certainly be scapegoated. Furthermore, such an independent action would also antagonise the French bishops. Yet Sophie knew that she had to act quickly. If she did not take a strong initiative, Elizabeth Galitzine and the assistants general most certainly would:

> Can you understand such assistants general? and what am I to do with such men-
> talities? It is so true that it only takes one with the capacity and even the power to
> upset all. Before Madame Galitzine was on the Council the greatest harmony exist-
> ed. Under pretext of her attachment to Rome she has egged the others on . . . and
> Fr Rozaven, who has such influence over the cardinal protector and leads him like
> a tame dog, is himself led by Madame Galitzine. Everyone knows that he has a
> weakness for her. This is nub of my changed situation. . . . So we do not know
> women . . . [until now] I have always controlled them. What is the solution? Only
> one and it is urgent: the abolition of the Decrees.[5]

In late November 1842 Sophie met the minister, Martin du Nord and Archbishop Affre. While she felt she could negotiate with the minister, the archbishop was in no mood for compromise. He presented Sophie with an ultimatum, in the form of two declarations which she was to sign. The first was to promise to reside in Paris and abide by the 1827 statutes. The second was to ask the pope to agree with Archbishop Affre that the constitutions of the Society of the Sacred Heart ought to be in accord with the 1827 statutes. Sophie had no difficulty in recognising that, while there was some possibility that she could sign an agreement to abide by the 1827 statutes, she could never agree to Archbishop Affre's terms regarding the constitutions of the Society. Even agreeing to abide by the 1827 statutes would effectively suppress the 1839 decrees and lead to a direct confrontation with the ultramontane group in the Society. It could also precipitate the separation of some of the houses from Sophie's leadership, cause the disintegration of the unity of the Society, and undo all that Sophie had struggled to establish over so many years.

Archbishop Affre knew that once Sophie signed documents pledging to abide by the 1827 Statutes, Sophie Barat and the Society of the Sacred Heart would come automatically under his jurisdiction. Sophie knew this too, and while over the next two months Affre continually put pressure on her to sign, she consistently refused to do so. She asked for time to reflect, to consult, seek advice.[6] This delaying tactic infuriated the archbishop and he threatened to expel the Society from his diocese unless she signed. Throughout this time Césaire Mathieu supported her by continual letters of encouragement and when she became weary of the battle of wits, he was there to assure her that she had taken the right stance. He told her that Archbishop Affre's tactics were those of the bully and that he would never take the final step of expelling the Society of the Sacred Heart from Paris.[7]

Sophie found Affre's aggressive manner disconcerting. She admitted to Césaire Mathieu that she felt 'flustered and frightened by the threats of the archbishop of Paris'.[8] He was rude, abrupt and abrasive in manner, jealous of his rights and ready to defend them. Garibaldi told Lambruschini that the key to understanding Affre was to recognise that he was Gallican to the core. He would protest any questioning by Rome of his rights as archbishop of Paris. Antonio Garibaldi thought that Affre's second letter to the French bishops, in September 1842 was a tactical error on his part. He was already in conflict with some of his colleagues and his letter would have won more sympathy for Sophie Barat than support for himself. Despite the appearances of weakness and powerlessness it was Sophie Barat who was defining the process, not just in Paris but in most of the dioceses of France. Antonio Garibaldi wondered how Affre could extricate himself from the mesh of bad relationships he had created 'despite the gestures of politeness etc. which Mother Barat shows him'.[9]

Sophie's resistance to Archbishop Affre was costly at every level of her being. During the months of November and December she struggled with this situation alone in Paris and with the help of letters to and from Césaire Mathieu. She was able to write freely to him and get a realistic assessment of what was happening. He reminded her of their conversations in Autun, when she had anticipated what lay ahead of her in Paris. He pointed out that she was too weary and too saddened by what had happened to her and to the Society to be able to trust those around her. And he convinced her that the rue de Varenne would not break with her, would not take that final step to separate from Sophie Barat herself. That bond was too strong and too deep, too well established over too many years. He affirmed her prudence and consistency in refusing to sign anything either the archbishop or the minister requested.[10] He repeated that both the pope and Lambruschini had assured him in writing that they had not abandoned Sophie to Archbishop Affre's schemes. Indeed, Rome could not afford to do so since the archbishop was in the process of contesting and asserting his rights both in Paris and in Rome. The Society was part of that testing process.

But Sophie was isolated in the rue de Varenne. Her every move was watched and reported to Archbishop Affre: the people she spoke to, the visitors she received, even her letters were intercepted:

> Here I am under constant surveillance. Archbishop Affre knows about everyone I see and from whom I get letters. He spoke to me about you, about the nuncio etc. Please write to me directly, getting someone else to write the address and use a plain seal. No one could imagine my situation. Everything is examined and reported. A letter I sent to the Minister which I wanted him to see has not been answered. I have strong reasons to believe that it was intercepted . . . I shall take other means to reach him![11]

Césaire Mathieu solved that difficulty by using his own secretary as courier. Fr Caverot travelled to and from Besançon during the months of November and December, to ensure that the letters between Sophie and Césaire Mathieu were completely private.[12] The internuncio, Garibaldi, realised that Sophie could not resist Archbishop Affre's pressure indefinitely. He asked Mgr Tharin, the former bishop of Strasbourg to mediate with the archbishop and he persuaded him to refrain from insisting, even for a time, on his rights over the Society of the Sacred Heart. Affre had become aware that the French bishops resented his actions and would not accept his claim over the Society of the Sacred Heart, basically because that would conflict with their rights over houses of the Society in their dioceses. Archbishop Affre had to mend bridges with the bishops. He also had to mend bridges with the pope but could not find the moral courage to do so, fearing to lose face. At his request Sophie Barat agreed to write to Gregory XVI:

> Not daring to do it himself, out of fear, as it is understood, of suffering some humiliation, he [Archbishop Affre] requested Mother Barat to ask his Holiness if the archbishop of Paris could continue to give his opinion to the government concerning matters relating to the Society of the Sacred Heart despite the . . . Brief [August 1842]. Mgr Affre should really have gone to the Holy Father himself about these matters, but it is well understood that he has not the courage. On the other hand, Mother Barat herself is in the embarrassing and humiliating situation of making such a request to his Holiness, but she actually needs the co-operation of the archbishop of Paris to run the financial affairs of the Society.[13]

As Sophie was to learn later on in 1843, Affre had no intention of abandoning his claims over the Society of the Sacred Heart. But at least in December 1842, when the issue of the government's claims demanded swift resolution Archbishop Affre withdrew his pressure on Sophie for a short time.[14] This gave her space to discuss at length with Garibaldi and Tharin the issue of signing a declaration for the government, in which she would undertake to observe the agreement enshrined in the statutes of 1827. Gradually a path forward emerged. The French ambassador to the Holy See, Comte Latour-Maubourg, conveyed a message to the French government that the pope would never insist that the superior general of the Society of the Sacred Heart should reside in Rome. He would welcome it only if the French government approved of it. The ambassador was critical of Archbishop Affre's reaction to the Papal brief in August 1842 which drew the attention of the government to the 1839 decrees of the Society of the Sacred Heart. He was critical of Sophie Barat, too. He accepted that she had to preserve her rights with regard to diocesan bishops, but considered she had acted in a strange way by proposing residing in Rome. He cited Affre's criticism of Sophie Barat's leadership as cavalier and impulsive. Yet the ambassador was aware of the background to the 1839 general council. In Rome the general opinion was that the Society of the Sacred Heart had become too influenced by the Jesuits, that Rozaven had taken over the general council of 1839 and that the pope in particular had expressed his disapproval of this.[15]

However, both the minister for justice and religion, Martin du Nord, and the minister for foreign affairs, François Guizot, still did not accept that the Society of the Sacred Heart had dropped the plan of moving the residence of the superior general to Rome. In the course of a meeting with Garibaldi, Guizot had expressed criticism of Sophie Barat and the Society. Bearing in mind the legitimist reputation of the rue de Varenne, especially of Eugénie de Gramont, as well as the residence of Archbishop de Quelen there for many years, and the long association of the Society of the Sacred Heart with the Jesuits, the suspicions of Guizot were well founded. Garibaldi managed to persuade the minister to let Martin du Nord work out an agreement with Sophie Barat and not bring the matter into the political limelight. Between mid-November and mid-December an understanding was reached and Guizot told the Comte Latour-Maubourg in Rome that Madame Barat intended to observe the statutes of 1827. She had accepted that the general council of the Society of the Sacred Heart had acted too quickly in 1839.[16]

It was not just the persuasion of Antonio Garibaldi which convinced Guizot that he should bide his time. Césaire Mathieu had pointed out to Sophie that the Society of the Sacred Heart was in a strong position to negotiate with the government, especially since she had taken the decision to seek to have the 1839 decrees annulled. Césaire Mathieu had no doubt that Martin du Nord would

> weigh the consequences of a dissolution which would close thirty houses of the Society, affect almost the same number dioceses, as well as more than 1200 heads of the most notable families in France. And all for the sake of a quarrel over words . . . [17]

While Sophie carried out these negotiations, diplomatic letters were exchanged between Luigi Lambruschini, Antonio Garibaldi and Césaire Mathieu, concerning the Society of the Sacred Heart, and by late November 1842 they had worked out the basic outline of a resolution. These ongoing contacts with Rome assured Sophie that Rozaven's warning that the pope and Lambruschini were about to abandon the Society were unfounded. Assured that the problem with the French government was well on the way to being resolved, Sophie knew that she still had to deal with Rozaven, Louise de Limminghe and Elizabeth Galitzine. She told Garibaldi and Tharin that while she had decided that the 1839 decrees would have to be abandoned, Sophie could not propose this herself as it undoubtedly would cause a split in the Society. She thought at first that a general council of the Society of the Sacred Heart should be convened to this purpose, but on reflection Sophie suggested that the pope be asked to abrogate the decrees. She thought that her name and wishes should be kept completely out of this process. She knew well that Rozaven, de Limminghe and Galitzine would never accept any decision, even of the pope, if they knew it had originated in a request from her.[18]

These views were readily understood and accepted by Mathieu, Tharin and Garibaldi. They decided that those bishops in France who had houses of the

Society in their dioceses would be asked to formally request the pope to suppress the decrees of 1839. Mathieu agreed to send Fr Caverot around the dioceses of France, to obtain their written agreement to this. In his capacity as archbishop of Besançon he was due to go to Rome for his *ad limina* visit in January 1843 and he would bring the petition to the pope personally. However, while the plan was good in theory it could not be executed. Personal tension had existed for some time between Denis Affre and Césaire Mathieu. Affre was piqued when he learnt that Mathieu was Sophie Barat's personal adviser, approved by the pope. Garibaldi and Tharin argued that this underlying tension had the potential to undermine their plan. Affre was quite capable of scapegoating Sophie Barat if letters emanating from Césaire Mathieu were sent to the French bishops.

Mathieu reluctantly accepted the reality of the situation and a threefold plan was drawn up. The archbishop of Rheims, the archbishop of Tours, the bishop of Nancy and Tharin would draw up a memoir for the pope, outlining the situation of Sophie Barat and the Society of the Sacred Heart in Paris. A letter, petitioning the pope to suppress the 1839 decrees, would be circulated to the bishops who had houses of the Society in their dioceses, asking for their agreement and signature.[19] The plan was quickly put in motion. Fr Caverot visited as many bishops as possible before Césaire Mathieu set off for Rome; Mathieu himself visited some bishops en route through France. Tharin dealt with the bishops in the north of France. Significantly, Fr Surat brought the petition to Le Mans, Poitiers, Toulouse and Bordeaux, indicating that the rue de Varenne and its friends knew about the plan. Affre received his copy and chose not to be party either to the memoir or to the letter.[20] When all had signed, it would be forwarded to Rome. Césaire Mathieu would represent the bishops in Rome when he went there for his *ad limina* visit in the New Year, 1843.[21] Lambruschini approved of this plan and he warned Garibaldi to maintain a low profile in this affair. This was in the interests of Sophie Barat and to ensure that the petition would appear to originate solely from the French bishops.[22]

Garibaldi wrote enthusiastically to Mathieu about the possibility of a speedy resolution to the impasse. He had spoken to the minister of religion, Teste, who was pleased with the initiative. The minister passed on the news to the French ambassador in Rome and informed him of Césaire Mathieu's role in the proceedings. Teste was a friend of the Jesuits and once had stayed with them in Rome for six months. He told Garibaldi that he knew the general, Jean Roothan, personally and that he had prepared a letter for Roothan, in case the Jesuits in Rome blocked the move to suppress the 1839 decrees. Garibaldi informed Mathieu about the existence of this letter, in case he needed to refer to it in Rome. It contained a warning:

> If the Society of the Sacred Heart falls, the whole wrath of the French bishops and others would fall on the Jesuits, and their houses too could be suppressed. The letter is quite lengthy and well composed and contains matters which are very true, capable of making an impression and striking fear.[23]

By this time Roothan had received letters not only from Clement Boulanger, provincial of the Jesuits in Paris, but also from Tharin, who wrote in the name of the archbishops of Rheims and of Tours and the bishop of Nancy. For the first time in all the correspondence the role of Rozaven and Bellotti at the general council of 1839 was spoken about in public:

> several of your Jesuits, without intending to, but in actual fact brought this respected and effective Society to within an ace of destruction.[24]

Tharin explained that one or two Jesuits (Jean Rozaven and Bellotti) had been asked by Sophie Barat originally to draft articles, based on the Jesuit constitutions, which could then be proposed to a general council of the Society of the Sacred Heart. These articles would provide government structures for the rapidly expanding Society. They had agreed enthusiastically and had presented their plans at the general council of the Society in Rome in 1839. After a short discussion the proposed changes were adopted as decrees by the general council and proposed to the body of the Society of the Sacred Heart. Some of the houses in France resisted the decrees and this had led to a serious crisis for the Society and for Sophie Barat in particular. Tharin told the general that the bishops in France held Rozaven particularly responsible for pushing through far more sweeping changes than Sophie Barat had ever envisaged. And he warned that if by any chance the petition of the French bishops did not succeed the Jesuits would be blamed. The influence of the Jesuits on the Roman Curia was well known at this time, especially Rozaven's power over Cardinal Pedicini. Boulanger also wrote from Paris and warned Roothan that the involvement of Rozaven in the affairs of the Society of the Sacred Heart had greatly compromised the Jesuits in France and especially in Paris. He also informed the general that Archbishop Affre was irked by the support that Loriquet gave the ultramontane faction in the Society of the Sacred Heart, and suggested that the Jesuits in Rome and in Paris distance themselves from the Society of the Sacred Heart.[25]

Roothan replied to Tharin and gave his version of the situation, arguing that for some years he had been trying to lessen contacts between the Jesuits and the Society of the Sacred Heart. He admitted that he had got involved himself with the preparations for the general council of 1839 but had no idea that some members of the Society of the Sacred Heart would take the proposed decrees to such an extreme. In addition, neither he nor Rozaven knew about the agreement between the French government and the Society of the Sacred Heart, enshrined in the statutes signed by the Society of the Sacred Heart in 1827. This was a strange claim on the part of Rozaven for he had been specifically consulted on this issue by Sophie Barat in 1826 and 1827. Roothan insisted that Rozaven only gave advice to the Society of the Sacred Heart, that he did not compose or sign the 1839 decrees. In frustration Roothan admitted:

> I want to have nothing more to do with the Society of the Sacred Heart . . . I have always thought that women religious are like the vine which needs complete support . . . Their role cannot be like that of men. The members of the Society of the

Sacred Heart would like to be supported by the Jesuit fathers. But this cannot be. There have never been women Jesuits ... Yet how can an order of women religious, dispersed in dioceses, with a superior general, remain at the same time in customary dependence on local bishops? There I admit we have a problem which I do not know how to resolve.[26]

Both the French ambassador to the Holy See, Latour-Maubourg, and Mathieu were convinced that Roothan never knew the extent of Rozaven's involvement in the affairs of the Society of the Sacred Heart. Writing to the minister of religion in Paris, in November 1842, the ambassador reported that the Society of the Sacred Heart had been badly advised by the Jesuits, and in particular by Rozaven. He was considered to have played the greatest part in the affairs of the Society of the Sacred Heart.[27] Sophie herself spoke frankly to Garibaldi in Paris. She told him that she continued to receive letters from Elizabeth Galitzine and Louise de Limminghe, accusing her of capitulating in Paris to Archbishop Affre and to Eugénie de Gramont. The longer the affair dragged out the harder her position became and she knew that her character and reputation were being destroyed in Rome, in Italy, in parts of France and in America. Antonio Garibaldi relayed this to Lambruschini in Rome:

Mother Barat said that the agitation of the religious in France stems in particular from the belief that they have support in Rome and that the superior general is disapproved of there and that the Holy Father and Your Eminence wish the enforcement of the decrees ... especially that which refers to the residence of the superior general in Rome. Mother Barat believes that these ideas were formed by Mother de Limminghe, by a religious from the illustrious society, the Father Rozaven ... .[28]

Lambruschini was no friend of Rozaven and Sophie's assessment of his role in the Society's affairs only confirmed the secretary of state's views.[29] While Sophie had convinced both Garibaldi and Lambruschini, she had no success with Elizabeth Galitzine. No matter how many times she explained the issues to her secretary general, nothing could move her to see the actual position of the Society of the Sacred Heart in France and the necessity for compromise.[30] Sophie explained how the brief sent in August 1842 was viewed as a breach in diplomatic relations between the pope and the French government, that a papal brief,

according to French law, should not enter France without being registered with the Council of State. The minister stated this in his letter to Archbishop Affre and this is only too true! During the reign of Louis XIV, I believe, France was on the verge of schism concerning a similar matter. And now that the government is leaning towards Protestantism they want nothing better than at least to create scandal.[31]

Even with this information Elizabeth Galitzine would not make any concession. All she would do was repeatedly urge Sophie to hold out against the pressure from the government and the archbishop. She told Sophie that any decisions she made in Paris would be considered null and void, since they would have been taken under pressure. Although she was the superior general, she had neither the authority nor the freedom to decide the Society's destiny alone.[32] Better that the Society was suppressed in France than that it should capitulate to the government and to the archbishop of Paris. Ultramontane to a point of fanaticism, Elizabeth Galitzine had found the test case of her life upon which to pour out her feverish activity, and prove her loyalty to the Roman Catholic Church which she had defected to in Russia at such a price. Adèle Lehon, who knew her well in Rome, commented years later that Elizabeth Galitzine was a gifted, intelligent woman but that she was autocratic and inflexible: 'Her *auto-cratic* upbringing seemed to convince her that people can be led like machines.'[33]

By now Sophie began to dread what Elizabeth Galitzine would do next. She knew that she was actively working against her:

> What predicament are you going to place us in? I do not know . . . It is painful to show Rome and the whole Society that you are working against me, while I sacrifice myself for the good of all![34]

A few days later Sophie learnt just what Elizabeth Galitzine had been orchestrating, in the south and west of France, in Rome and in the north of Italy. She had written to the assistants general, to the provincials and to some superiors, asking them to draw up petitions similar to those she had activated in America earlier on in the year. She informed Pedicini and Rozaven about it and invited the assistants general and the provincials to write letters of protest to Archbishop Affre, accusing him of keeping Sophie Barat in Paris as a prisoner and forcing her to act against her will and against that of the general council of the Society of the Sacred Heart.[35] Predictably, Affre was furious, first at Elizabeth Galitzine's letter, and then at the others which he received. Sophie bore the brunt of that and she told Galitzine:

> Archbishop Affre has just written to me to inform me of the incredible letter you wrote to him. . . . Can you imagine his astonishment, like that which I experience myself when I received the protests. . . .
> You are gravely mistaken with regard to the archbishop and myself. Up until now, 17 November, I have received nothing, I have signed nothing and I have refused everything. The only point on which I hesitated and for which I sought your advice, concerned the question of my residence to which the government holds to *tenaciously* . . . If I had known you then as I know you now I would have been wary of seeking your advice. Next time I will know better.[36]

Sophie was shocked when she learnt that all the assistants general were against her now and that they had written letters of protest to Archbishop Affre. The only exception was Félicité Desmarquest, who while critical of Sophie's actions especially since the summer of 1842, could not write to Affre since she knew Sophie had signed nothing. Elizabeth Galitzine reprimanded Sophie and reminded her again that even the founder of the Society of the Sacred Heart had to obey the decrees of a general council. It was not so long ago that Joseph Varin was invoked as founder of the Society, when Geneviève Deshayes argued against the 1839 decrees. Now Sophie's role as founder was used in a last bid to retain the 1839 decrees. Sophie was not moved by this and replied:

> In my grief and in trust I wrote to you as you do with friends, and I did not take time to re-read my letter. To be honest, I was far from suspecting such a swift and serious abuse of my trust on your part. . . .
> Yes . . . the Society will judge us. I am not afraid of giving it an account of my conduct. If it shares your sentiments I will readily console myself by the fact that having lost its trust I will more easily obtain what I long for so much: to be *nothing*.
> If, on the contrary, the Society recovers from this crisis, I will be happy to have suffered so much pain and humiliation. Besides, my death cannot be long in coming: one cannot suffer so much grief with impunity![37]

Elizabeth Galitzine left no stone unturned in her efforts to pressurise Sophie. She wrote several times to Louis Barat in Paris, asking him to talk Sophie into holding firm to the 1839 decrees, purely and simply, and to risk destruction of the Society in France. She blamed Eugénie de Gramont for the troubles of the Society and for the captivity of Sophie in Paris. Galitzine's contacts with Louis Barat were not new. In 1840, when Sophie had asked her not to circulate copies of the 1839 decrees in America, Elizabeth Galitzine had written to Louis in Paris and asked him for his advice. She explained that throughout the 1839 council in Rome Sophie had argued that Eugénie de Gramont would not accept her residence in Rome. She told Louis then that she had expressed her criticisms of Eugénie de Gramont and the rue de Varenne to some of the American superiors. She had also spoken to the Jesuit provincial there, Peter John Verhaegan, and he had questioned Sophie's capacity to govern the Society. Elizabeth Galitzine did not comment on that in her letter to Louis, but placed the blame for the Society's divisions on Eugénie de Gramont. She told Louis that Eugénie de Gramont had written a letter to Philippine Duchesne, critical of the decrees. Philippine never saw that letter for Elizabeth Galitzine had intercepted it. She told Louis:

> I have good grounds to fear the treacherous influence of Mother de Gramont. . . . This poor creature has become a viper which the Society has nourished and kept alive at its heart. . . . If she [Sophie Barat] had shown her teeth at the beginning she would not now be obliged to have recourse to extreme remedies. And if she does not adopt such measures then the gangrene will reach the vital part . . . Her far too kind nature is paralysing her firmness.[38]

Elizabeth Galitzine resumed her correspondence with Louis Barat in October 1842, when she presumed that he would support any movement within the Society of the Sacred Heart which placed priority on loyalty to the pope. She gave Louis Barat an account of events in the Society since the summer of 1842 and commented on his sister in some detail.[39] Elizabeth Galitzine portrayed Sophie as a woman unable to govern the Society, terrified by Archbishop Affre and Eugénie de Gramont, and unable or unwilling to heed the advice of her assistants general or of the Society's friends in Rome, especially that of Pedicini or of Rozaven, the latter 'such a devoted and zealous friend of our Society'. She invoked Louis Barat's favourite name for Paris – Babylon – and lamented that Sophie Barat was now a prisoner there.

Louis Barat replied to her letter and in general terms he assured her that he wished the Society of the Sacred Heart to be loyal to the pope. Delighted at this encouragement Elizabeth Galitzine further damaged Sophie's leadership by sending Louis a copy of Pedicini's letter of censure to Sophie, to show him how Sophie was viewed in Rome. She did not tell him the letter accompanying the papal brief had been lost, nor that Cardinal de Bonald had retracted his permission to hold the general council in Lyon. Names and accusations abound in Elizabeth Galitzine's letter and most of it focuses on Eugénie de Gramont, 'the lady of the manor at No. 41 [rue de Varenne]'. She asked that her letters remain totally confidential with the exception of Loriquet. Neither Joseph Varin nor Sophie were to know about her letters, but she urged Louis to talk to his sister. She feared that Sophie would remain in Paris, for good. Before she left Lyon in early October Elizabeth Galitzine told Louis that she was dismayed to hear Sophie declare her hand:

> The poor woman said with passion: If No. 41 separates from the Society I will go there myself and then we shall see where the Society will be.[40]

Galitzine wrote again to Louis Barat in December 1842. She had heard that Sophie had declared that soon the tensions within the Society would be resolved by the abrogation of the 1839 decrees. Due to the opposition of her assistants general, however, Elizabeth Galitzine knew that Sophie thought a schism was inevitable. Italy and France would separate. Italy would adopt the 1839 decrees and France would retain the 1815 constitutions.[41]

No record exists showing whether Sophie knew of Elizabeth Galitzine's correspondence with her brother, nor whether Sophie discussed the crisis in the Society with him. The only record of communication between them at this time was an account of one of the community at the rue de Varenne. She noted that Sophie went to confession to her brother several times during this period and that she had emerged from the confessional in tears. Another community member remembered that Sophie commented several times during this period that her brother had been severe with her as a child.[42] Certainly Louis would have supported the ultramontane view. Throughout his life he bitterly regretted that he had taken the constitutional oath, even though he had retracted it and paid the price by imprisonment. Moreover, he was critical of the lifestyle at the rue de Varenne and complained regularly to Sophie about it. His thinking and spirituality were centred on apocalyptic literature and theology, of the end time, of Antichrist and impending doom. Within these boundaries Louis could only counsel Sophie to side with the ultramontane party.[43]

The situation at the rue de Varenne remained acute and Sophie had to deal with the opposition mounted by Eugénie de Gramont and Aimée d'Avenas. Eugénie continued to complain that Sophie had treated her badly, something which Sophie rejected:

I am not unjust in your regard at all. One day perhaps you will grasp all that I have suffered. I permit myself this comment and it is the only one. I do not like putting such sensitive matters in writing. Prayer and silence. In the depths of my heart I have always held the hope that our Lord will come to help us after this time of trial, if we know how to learn from it.[44]

All these months Sophie journeyed alone. She described her return to the rue de Varenne as climbing the road to Calvary. When she told Eugénie that she would keep her counsel she meant it and this gave the impression that she was a prisoner. Many years later Virginie Roux (1810–78), a coadjutrix sister, who lived in the rue de Varenne during these years, spoke of those times.[45] She remembered that in the winter of 1842–43 Sophie arrived with Marie Patte at the rue de Varenne and that during that time Sophie lived totally apart from the community. She dined alone and did not take part in any community prayer or meetings. Not only that, Eugénie de Gramont told the community that on no account were they to speak to Sophie and for her part Sophie spoke to no one, greeted no one, and passed them on the corridors as if she had not seen them. When she walked in the gardens of the rue de Varenne, she chose its most secluded parts. Sophie was aware of the atmosphere all around her in the rue de Varenne, of mystery, silence and watching. She had no one she could trust and each day's post brought her news of further betrayals from all over the Society, by those she had thought were her friends.

Sophie chose this tactic of seclusion in order to protect herself and demonstrate her independence. She could not afford to be seen to favour either the views of Eugénie de Gramont or those Louise de Limminghe and Elizabeth Galitzine. She had to disengage entirely from everyone in the rue de Varenne. To those looking on it looked like prison and was reported as such and used in Rome by Louise de Limminghe as an argument for rejecting any decision Sophie would take in Paris. If Sophie signed any document in Paris it could not be considered valid and binding. Yet all this time Sophie signed nothing. She had regular meetings with ministers from the government, with the archbishop of Paris, with clerics and lay people. Withstanding pressure from both the archbishop and the government was exhausting. Virginie Roux remembered the cost of such endurance and that on leaving one of the meetings Sophie went to the sacristy and wept for two hours.

Sophie had requested her assistants general several times to join both her and Félicité Desmarquest in Paris. They refused. At first Elizabeth Galitzine pleaded ill health and that was true at the time. Later she said that even were she well enough she could not travel as her conscience would not allow her to go to Paris. Catherine de Charbonnel was inwardly torn when she wrote to Sophie, convinced by Elizabeth Galitzine that she had to choose between loyalty to the pope or to the Gallican church, and regretfully had to refuse Sophie's invitation. This refusal was a particularly heavy blow for Sophie, one that wounded her deeply. She wrote three times to Catherine de Charbonnel and each time she refused. It showed Sophie the extent of the disaffection within the Society. One of her oldest and most loyal companions would not support her, would not come to Paris. Only later did Sophie glimpse what it cost her old friend.[46] Louise de Limminghe told Sophie she could not collude with any proceedings that emanated from France:

> It is a matter of *life* or of *death*. It concerns the matter of being or of not being a religious. There is no middle ground. Oh! My dear and loving, and ever more beloved mother, I beg you to stop allowing yourself to be taken advantage of, listen to those who have never deceived you. See the good example just now of the Good Shepherd Sisters. Mother de Coriolis assured us yesterday that the cardinal vicar of Rome has the protest of their mother general and her four assistants concerning an issue almost similar to ours.[47]

Félicité Desmarquest had no option but to be in Paris with Sophie. She maintained a continuous correspondence with Louise de Limminghe and Elizabeth Galitzine and fed them news of Sophie's movements, decisions, letters and health. She was particularly critical of Eugénie de Gramont at this time, accusing her of trying to control Sophie in the rue de Varenne.[48] Elizabeth Galitzine assured Félicité Desmarquest and Catherine de Charbonnel that their stance was fully approved by the pope, personally; that Pedicini forbade them to travel to Paris and that the Society in Paris had been abandoned. Only those of the Roman party would be recognised as the true Society of the Sacred Heart and they could only lament the fact that Sophie Barat, despite every effort to help her, had been taken over by enemies of the Society.[49]

By December 1842 Sophie learnt that Rozaven, Galitzine and de Limminghe were planning a schism within the Society. Letters to the provincials and some local superiors had been prepared, and the assistants general had drawn up a formal letter to send to Sophie Barat explaining their position and the decision to secede.[50] This would effectively isolate Sophie Barat in Paris, with some of the French houses, and create a new centre in Rome for the rest of the houses in France, Italy, Savoy, Switzerland and America. This plan won the support of both Cardinals Pedicini and Patrizzi in Rome. Rumours were abroad that Antonio Garibaldi was about to be replaced in Paris and Sophie had heard it was in some measure due to his support of Sophie Barat and the Gallican elements in the French church.[51]

In October 1842 Félicité Desmarquest told Louise de Limminghe that Sophie was 'locked in deep depression'.[52] She felt abandoned at a time when she needed the support and the presence of her assistants general.[53] Sophie kept the letters she received from them, remarking to Césaire Mathieu that unless they were safeguarded for the archives no one would ever grasp what had happened.[54] He continued to be her steadfast friend and adviser and again assured her that she had acted with prudence and wisdom, whatever the appearances. He appealed to her best self, the self that had taken so many risks. He advised her to try and keep focused on the essential goal she had set herself:

The more complicated the situation becomes outside, the more you need to proceed with simplicity. Accept the information which is given you, but do not let it into the depths of your heart.[55]

But this was not easy and Sophie admitted that at times she exploded. Her own reactions to the flood of crises in the Society disconcerted her. She had discovered levels in her feelings which alarmed her and she admitted:

I lost the capacity to let go and remain calm, to forget their schemes, and I criticised their conduct with too much of my old self. I wrote like this to them, in no uncertain terms.[56]

Césaire Mathieu did not comment directly on this but recalled the story of the early days of the Society. He appealed to Sophie's memory and faith vision:

While you had a good number of crosses when founding the Society, its prosperity draws others. This is so that you will not be lulled into a false security.[57]

He did not underestimate the pain Sophie was suffering, calling it 'this unbelievable anguish.'[58] Sophie did not hide that anguish from him:

What a life I lead . . . my last days full of wrangling and quarrels! It would be unbearable if I did not remind myself that it is God's will! Then there is so much to make amends for! So I will resign myself and I will work as much as my strength allows me.[59]

Sophie was exhausted and weary all the time and could not pray. This disturbed her because she counted on her inner life of prayer to give her the courage to continue and persevere. She was deeply distressed within. Her old worries returned. She asked herself again and again if she had taken the wrong path in life, made the wrong choice:

For several years now I have been walking on a bed of thorns and my plans have had no success.[60]
I have hardly anytime for prayer during the day. I have to do it at night and I am worn out with fatigue and sleepiness. I believe the good God is punishing me for having abandoned my first call which was to Carmel. Can the cross of Jesus, the sufferings and humiliations I endure make amends for this? I have a lot of worries about so many of my failings and my natural reactions mixed up at this time of trial. Pray then . . . that I obtain from the Sacred Heart of Jesus a merciful pardon of which I have so great a need![61]
My heart swims in sorrow; what a responsibility if I am the author of so many evils! After Jesus, you are my only support.[62]

Mathieu told her not to push herself so hard to pray. Her task was to work to save the Society and if her health collapsed, all could be lost:

There is a very appropriate word in Scripture which will comfort you: It says that giving alms is prayer. And how could the cross you bear not be a source of prayer, since Our Lord prayed on the cross for us! So then it is not necessary that you pray during the day, for you have not got the time; nor is it necessary that you, worn out with fatigue, prolong your vigils into the night. That would put you in danger of not having the strength necessary during the day. But hold fast to the cross in surrender and love, and let this sacred cross, or rather let Our Lord, who remains on the cross out of love for us, pray for you. This thought, which is very gentle and very true, will set your heart at ease. [63]

One of Sophie's oldest friends, Adelaide de Rozeville, then superior at Amiens, wrote to Hypolite Lavauden, superior at Parma in December 1842. She defended Sophie's reputation and leadership and told her friend that the rumours emanating from Italy were false. As for Sophie herself:

> She works, she prays, she is calm, she is courageous. She suffers, there is no doubt about that . . . [she has] such breadth of spirit and such greatness of soul that she cannot let herself be trapped in a circle of narrow views. She leaves petty motives aside . . . From 1839 no one should have allowed herself to act apart from her . . . [64]

Alone in her inner world, Sophie was alone in her task. She prepared all the documentation for Rome personally, to avoid drawing attention to her involvement in the strategy. This was difficult: she found communicating with the Roman cardinals daunting at the best of times and had gladly used Elizabeth Galitzine's knowledge of Italian and of the diplomatic protocol used in Rome. This was no longer available to her, indeed Galitzine's knowledge was being used against her in Rome at this time by de Limminghe and Rozaven. Of all the cardinals Sophie felt best able to communicate with Cardinal Lambruschini and she asked Césaire Mathieu to help her draft a confidential letter to him, stating her reasons for asking that the 1839 decrees be abolished.[65]

Despite her weariness and disappointment with all the events happening around her Sophie did not cease to challenge Elizabeth Galitzine and asked her again and again to account for such defiance of her personal authority. Sophie wondered aloud if she had not trusted too much, if over the years she had given too much freedom to her colleagues.[66] Had her style of government been defective? She wrote a spirited letter to Galitzine taking her to task for her unimaginable indiscretion and lack of tact. When Galitzine protested she was only trying to help Sophie and the Society be faithful to its own path, Sophie replied tersely:

> While we are making the greatest efforts to avoid a schism which would destroy the Society, you still dare to demand, in a memoir sent to Rome, the separation of three houses; you speak in a most improper way of the bishops and even of [me] your superior . . . If that is how you help and support me you would do much better to pray and amend your ways.[67]

One of the greatest supports that Mathieu gave Sophie at this time was that he did not ever underestimate the gravity of the situation. In early January 1843 he wrote to Sophie, saying that he hoped to travel to Rome as soon as possible in the new year: 'the church in France has not had anything as serious as this in twenty years.'[68] In the meantime, Sophie persevered in her task of trying to hold the factions within the Society together until the pope had pronounced upon the petition from the French bishops. While she said nothing herself, such a major communications exercise was impossible to keep confidential and some bishops spoke about the petition they had sent to the pope and of the decision awaited imminently.[69] Conveniently for Sophie, her initiative and active part in the whole process was not recognised, though Elizabeth Galitzine and Louise de Limminghe had their own suspicions. The presumption that women did not take part in negotiations, within the church or in society in general, ensured Sophie's anonymity. Besides, her critics had created a blind. They had presented her as a leader who had become powerless and ineffective. In fact Sophie had moved to save the unity of the Society and had managed with the help of Mathieu, Tharin and Garibaldi, to persuade the French bishops, Lambruschini and the pope to agree on her strategy. In January 1843 the cardinal protector, Pedicini, and Cardinal Ostini, prefect of the congregation of bishops and religious, wrote to Sophie Barat, through the nuncio Garibaldi, and told her that the pope had agreed to have the decrees examined by a group of cardinals and that in due time the outcome would be communicated to her.[70] Césaire Mathieu set off for Rome, prepared to represent Sophie Barat's case there in case of need. It looked like the end of the tunnel.

Elizabeth Galitzine learnt of the memoir sent by the four French bishops,[71] which had accompanied the petition from twenty-five French bishops to have the 1839 decrees annulled. In a frenzy of activity she wrote offensive letters, criticising the rue de Varenne as a *'house of mad and angry women'* [72] She also drafted a long memoir to the pope, denouncing the French bishops as well as the leadership in the Society of the Sacred Heart.[73] Such activity undermined and discredited the cause to which she was so devoted and ensured that the process set in motion by Sophie, Mathieu and Garibaldi would succeed. Mathieu got a copy of her document from Cardinal de Bonald at Lyon. When he arrived in Rome he prepared a detailed reply, also in the form of a memoir to the pope. He refuted all Elizabeth Galitzine's points. He took the opportunity to vindicate Sophie Barat's character and good name. He explained that while Sophie Barat had wanted the 1839 decrees to be implemented originally, the difficulties which had arisen led her to the decision that she could no longer proceed to requesting official approbation from the pope. Quite the contrary, Sophie Barat had asked that the decrees be annulled:

> I helped her with my advice in this painful matter and she is not lacking in strength of spirit, wise vision, prudent conduct, attachment to the Holy See, dedication to her community and deep affection for her sisters, including those who, believing that are doing good, cause her such grave trouble and immense difficulties.[74]

After several meetings, on 17 February, 2 and 3 March, which Césaire Mathieu described to Sophie in some detail, the eight cardinals reached a decision. They recommended that the 1839 decrees be annulled and that the Society of the Sacred Heart revert purely and simply to the constitutions approved in 1826 by Leo XII. Mathieu was so excited by the news that on the evening of 3

March he ran round to the Trinité and rang the bell ten times. It was late in the evening and no one answered. He returned the following morning and announced the news, and then went to Sainte Rufine, to do the same and claimed that the ills of the Society were over. Adèle Lehon remarked dryly to him, 'but the convalescence will be long and dangerous'.[75]

$-$ 20 $-$

RECLAIMING HER PLACE, 1843–1844

To her great relief, by early March 1843 Sophie had the basis of a resolution to the Society's internal divisions and a decision which would satisfy the demands of the French government. In a long letter written on the way home from Rome, Césaire Mathieu told Sophie all that had happened and he gave her details of the final meeting of the cardinals on 4 March.[1] By virtue of the suppression of the 1839 decrees, the Society had automatically reverted to observance of the 1826 constitutions. However, the Society's rapid growth and expansion had also been recognised, as had Sophie's physical inability to make official visits to all the houses. So while the structure of provinces and the office of provincial had been abolished, Sophie was authorised to appoint delegates to visit houses or areas of the Society in her name. The other offices of government were to remain in place until the next general council, to be held in 1845. If any assistant general resigned before 1845, Sophie could appoint a successor, once her choice had been approved by the pope. Mathieu was aware that Sophie had intended to remove Elizabeth Galitzine from all responsibility, but he cautioned Sophie against such a move. He explained that the cardinals had wanted to dismiss Eugénie de Gramont, Antoinette de Gramont and Aglae Fontaine as superiors but that he had argued it was better to legislate in view of the actual needs of the Society and not to deal with individuals. He told Sophie the task was to create peace in the Society and not to favour one group over the other, and, most of all, to 'to reinvest you with the greatest possible authority in the eyes of your congregation'.[2] Like Sophie, he was concerned about how to communicate to the Society the decision taken in

Rome. To this purpose he had prepared models of letters which Sophie could adapt as she thought best.

Sophie read all the details, as well as Césaire Mathieu's drafts of letters, with relief and thankfulness. She owed him years of gratitude for his faithful support and his active intervention in Rome and she counted on that support in the future.[3] She knew that the task of leading the two factions in the Society was going to be difficult. She was aware that that her leadership of the Society had been severely criticised in Rome, and that she had been caricatured as weak and vacillating. In the weeks preceding the decision of the cardinals, Jean Rozaven, Louise de Limminghe and Elizabeth Galitzine (in Lyon), had spread the rumour that that Sophie and the houses led by Eugénie de Gramont were planning a schism. The context for this was the knowledge of the letter from the French bishops petitioning the pope to suppress the 1839 decrees. Both de Limminghe and Galitzine had written again to Louis Barat and asked him to intervene and advise his sister not to turn her back on Rome, as they saw it. They lobbied the cardinal protector, Pedicini, and the prefect of the congregation of bishops and religious, Cardinal Ostini. The success of their plans seemed assured when Jean Rozaven was formally appointed by Cardinal Ostini to act as canon lawyer for the examination of the decrees of 1839.[4]

By the spring of 1843, the number of superiors in the Society who belonged to the ultramontane lobby was substantial. Led by Louise de Limminghe and Elizabeth Galitzine, it was composed of Catherine de Charbonnel, Félicité Desmarquest, Marie Prevost, Armande de Causans, Eulalie de Bouchaud, Laure des Portes, Henriette Granon, Josephine de Coriolis, Adèle Lehon, Laure d'Aviernoz, Hypolite Lavauden, Anna du Rousier, Aloysia Hardey and Maria Cutts.[5] This was a powerful lobby within the Society and Sophie knew that she had a major task in hand to win their acceptance of her leadership. She knew them individually and knew also that their motivations for being part of the ultramontane lobby were complex. She understood the motivation of Marie Prevost, Louise de Limminghe and Elizabeth Galitzine. Marie Prevost saw the stance of the rue de Varenne as a rerun of the situation of Amiens in 1814 and 1815. Since 1830 Louise de Limminghe had hoped that Sophie would act firmly with Eugénie de Gramont, deal with the presence of Archbishop de Quelen in the rue de Varenne, and effect reform of the house. Elizabeth Galitzine agreed with Louise de Limminghe's assessment of the rue de Varenne, but in addition she had a fanatical adherence to the Roman church, and in particular to the person of the pope. Her own journey from Russian Orthodoxy to Roman Catholicism had meant that any stance independent from Rome, including gallicanism, was truly anathema to her. Coupled with this was her extreme devotion and loyalty to Jean Rozaven, her confessor and father figure.

Sophie also had to deal with the antagonism of many in the Society towards Eugénie de Gramont. The personal friendship of Sophie and Eugénie had always been a source of criticism. Sophie's manner of dealing with Eugénie de Gramont led her critics to consider her either weak or infatuated, or both. Few if any in the

10.   *Détails exacts sur la mort de Monseigneur de Quelen (31 décembre 1839).*
       Engraving of the death of archbishop de Quelen at the rue de Varenne in December
       1839

11.   *Césaire Mathieu, archbishop of Besançon (1834–1875) befriended Sophie Barat*
       during the crisis period of 1842–1843

Héritages sur le Territoire de Joigny

Barat Jacques gde fouffé tonnellier

Au lieu dit Champ-blanc 30 Perches. . . . . 30 Perches

Au lieu dit Pisse-vin 30 P. en 2 pièces . . . . 30 P.

Au lieu dit la Belle-Croix 55 P. sur les quelles

    il est dû une rente de 10 tt . . . . 55 Pas

Au lieu dit Pillier de St Jean 15 P. . . . . 15 P.

Au lieu dit la voie des Laiteux 37 P. . . . . 37 P.

Au lieu dit la Cote St Thibault 12 P. d'une pièce,

    9 d'une autre, 18 d'une troisième . . . . 39 P.

Au lieu dit Lassé 32 d'une pièce, et 40 d'une autre . . 72 P.

Au lieu dit Carrouge 22 P. . . . . 22 Pas

Au lieu dit Paradis 22 P. . . . . 22 P.

& au lieu dit Joigny la Ville . . . . 6 P.

     Héritages sur le Territoire de St Aubin   328 —

Au lieu dit Souvilliers d'en bas 12 Pas ½ . . . . . . 12 P. ½

au lieu Souvilliers la gran Borne 18 P. sur les quelles

    il est dû une rente de 15 tt de rente . . . . . . 18 P.

au lieu dit le Pillier 22 P. sur lesquelles il est

    dû une rente de 4 tt . . . . 22 P.

au lieu dit replat de Siaux 25 P. en 2 pièces . . . . 25 P.

au lieu dit les Tonnières 25 P. en 2 pièces . . . . . 25 P.

au lieu dit Siaux 40 P. . . . . 40 P.

                                     102 P ½

                                       470 P ½

— Bon à suivre —   = 4 arpens 70 Perches ½

                                       140 — ½

                                       328 — ½

                                     468 — ½

12. *Official description of Sophie Barat's home, drawn up in 1791. Heritages sur le territoire de Joigny. Barrat, Jacques gde Fouffée, tonnellier Archives Communales, Ville de Joigny*

13. *The First house of the Society of the Sacred Heart was founded in Amiens in 1801. Rue de l'Oratoire, Amiens*

14. *Visitation monastery where Sophie Barat met Philippine Duchesne in 1804 Ste Marie d'En Haut, Grenoble*

15. *Monastery of Les Feuillants, Poitiers. Poitiers was founded in 1806 and was the first noviciate house of the Society of the Sacred Heart*

16. *Gardens of the rue de Varenne (the Hôtel Biron) purchased by Sophie Barat in 1820 and now the Rodin Museum*

17. *Early 19th century print of the Trinité des Monts in Rome. Sophie Barat established a community and school there in 1828*

18.   *Noviciate at Conflans. The noviciate of the Society of the Sacred Heart was moved from Paris to Conflans in 1841*

19.   *Academy of the Sacred Heart, St Charles Missouri. Philippine Duchesne lived here from 1842–1852*

20.   *Kindergarten at Aix-en-Provence*

M̃

Monsieur DUSSAUSSOY, Monsieur et Madame COUSIN, Monsieur le Major RAMEAU RAMBAUD, Madame RAMBAUD, Monsieur Yveling RAMBAUD, Mademoiselle Elise RAMBAUD, Madame DAVIES, Messieurs Morris et Robert DAVIES,

Ont l'honneur de vous faire part de la perte douloureuse qu'ils viennent de faire dans la personne de la Très-Révérende Mère **Madeleine Louise-Sophie BARAT,** Fondatrice et Supérieure générale de l'Ordre du Sacré-Cœur, leur Tante et Grand'tante, décédée le 25 mai 1865, dans sa quatre-vingt-sixième année d'âge, et sa soixante-quatrième année de profession, munie des Sacrements de l'Église.

Requiescat in Pace.

PARIS, PAUL DUPONT.

21.   *Family death notice of Sophie Barat, placed in the newspapers by her nephew, Stanislas Dusaussoy*

Society knew the lengths to which Sophie had gone to try and reform the rue de Varenne. Sophie was loyal all her life to Eugénie and would brook no criticism of her in public. While she did pass on such criticism as she heard to Eugénie, Sophie would not discuss what she had heard about her with others. Undoubtedly, had this situation not been so intractable and the feelings around it so aroused, neither Elizabeth Galitzine nor Louise de Limminghe would have received such widespread support. One polarisation led to another. However, the polarisation represented a deeper tension within the Society. It had been founded in France and had extended beyond its borders, in Europe and beyond. The rue de Varenne symbolised all that was French and Gallican. It represented a cultural and spiritual imperialism which the growing Society both needed and resented. While it wanted to belong to the founding energy, held by Sophie Barat, beyond the confines of France the Society was different. Difference did not necessarily mean better but it demanded recognition and accommodation.

From February 1843 Sophie, confident that the 1839 decrees would be annulled by the pope, had been considering, with some apprehension, how to restore her own authority in the Society, but especially with her four assistants general. Sophie had to prepare herself for a new form of communication and co-operation with those who had opposed her leadership. Throughout the winter and spring of 1842–43 she continued to write to each of them but it was a strained and wary correspondence. Sophie was in a vulnerable position personally, on account of her relationship with Eugénie de Gramont and her apparent unwillingness or inability to remove her as superior in the rue de Varenne. She anticipated that some of the assistants general would resign and she was aware that there were few capable of taking their place immediately. Despite her reluctance to resume working with the assistants general, Sophie knew that the fewer resignations she received the better. If she had to replace an assistant general, then many members of the Society in France, as well as Archbishop Affre and most of the French bishops, would expect Eugénie de Gramont to be named. By the same token if she failed to name Eugénie and in fact removed her from office at the rue de Varenne then Sophie would equally be criticised by those same people.[6]

Césaire Mathieu suggested that Sophie take the initiative with Louise de Limminghe and Josephine de Coriolis in Rome by writing a warm letter to them, inviting their loyalty and support.[7] While Sophie agreed with him on the need to re-create unity in the Society she balked at the suggestion that she write to Louise de Limminghe:

> If I could give you the details of their procedures I think you would advise me to maintain a bit of dignity still. They doubted my faith, my allegiance to the Holy See and insinuated this to others, without asking me for a word of explanation . . . It seems to me that it would be somewhat difficult for me to write to them now, apologise and show them trust. I will certainly take advantage of all the overtures they make to me, to show them good will, understanding and even that the past is forgotten. But to write to them first, I do not think so![8]

For months Sophie had dreaded the moment when she would have to meet and work with her assistants general, all of whom had chosen to work against her. She had decided she could not bring herself to initiate contact with them but that she would be able to respond if they wrote to her. This is what she felt she could do with integrity, without distorting the reality of what had happened or doing violence to her own reading of their actions. Césaire Mathieu respected Sophie's feelings in the matter, yet while accepting her views, he invited her to reflect again:

> in a serious case such as yours, when human prudence is stretched to the limits, it is clear that you must act in the noblest manner possible and that what looks like folly in human eyes is wisdom in the sight of God.
> The most difficult task you have in your position now is to reconcile minds and hearts, which have been so deeply alienated from one another.
> To achieve this you must do two things, one concerns yourself while the other involves the government of the Society.
> In what regards yourself, now you must be more gentle, more humble, more loving, more patient, in the measure that others are less. You will achieve nothing by dominance, but a great deal by being affable. That is what I mean by the letters I advised you write. But it is not my intention that you should apologise. It is only that you speak kindly and gently as if you had nothing against them in your heart. Then do you not see that if you have to go farther towards them, you have to do it for the sake of Jesus Christ who is always the first to come to us despite our faults? As for the other matter which concerns the government of the Society; in as much as being gentle and kind towards all, so you must also act firmly and with authority in the fullest sense. To achieve this you must not compromise your freedom or your affection with anyone. You must open your arms to all in the love of Our Lord and nothing else.[9]

Césaire Mathieu had in mind the community at the rue de Varenne and specifically Eugénie de Gramont. Criticism of the house in Paris had not ceased and Lambruschini was particularly critical of Eugénie de Gramont and wanted Sophie to remove her from leadership of the house. Césaire Mathieu warned Sophie of this several times. He also told her that she would have to demonstrate her independence from Eugénie if she was to win back her authority in the Society. He advised her to hold herself

> entirely aloof from the friends around you. For despite all their good will they would have taken you to the abyss if you had given them a hold over you, since they see everything from their own perspective.[10]

He also warned Sophie that she would have to sign an agreement with the French government, agreeing to observe the 1827 statutes. If she did not act decisively as soon as the pope had ruled on the 1839 decrees, her reputation in Rome for indecisiveness would be justified:

> Do not forget that here in Rome you are regarded as an indecisive person who resorts to consultation in order to avoid taking action. This is an opinion I have had to fight. If you do not sign after consultation people will not fail to renew this accusation.[11]

While Sophie was considering how to move forward she received a letter of resignation from Louise de Limminghe.[12] She had informed the other assistants general of her decision and Sophie saw this as a deliberate tactic to lead the others to consider their position. Sophie's own pragmatism surfaced and she sent Césaire Mathieu a copy of de Limminghe's letter of resignation:

> It will be helpful if you can form an opinion yourself of her style and plan in letting the other assistants general know of her resignation. This is to provoke them into doing the same and if I accept this resignation I will have to agree to the others. That would put me and the Society in an awkward position particularly on account of Madame de Gramont. Archbishop Affre is not at all satisfied . . . and since I have to deal with all these people I have no idea how I will be able to reconcile them all! The more I see the problems and the opposition against me, the more I feel the need to go to Besançon and talk to you . . . If Madame Desmarquest decides not to resign I think I ought to bring her with me. Maybe you will do her good. Her presence will be a strain, since none of the assistants will rejoin me willingly. They will return under compulsion, because they will not understand that force of circumstances led us to this extremity and that we could only save the Society at this price.[13]

Sophie's major concern was the possible resignation of the four assistants general as a group. This would leave her with the enormous task of replacing them, without the option of appointing Eugénie de Gramont to that office. Indeed the pressure from Rome to remove Eugénie de Gramont from office seemed a contradiction to Sophie. While she measured the damage that both factions had caused in the Society she felt that the Roman party had done the most harm. The long weeks of waiting and searching had shown Sophie just where she stood in relation to her old friend:

> I think the demand of several in Rome who so ardently wish Madame de Gramont to be removed from all responsibility neither just nor consequent. Since the Congregation and the pope believed they had to annul the Decrees, on account of the problems they caused, why should they then hold it against the party [in the Society] who pointed out the flaws in the first place? If they were wrong in the way they treated their superior general, the Roman party have certainly made worse mistakes, done her more harm and reduced her to zero.
> I beg you to believe that in defending Madame de Gramont I am not weakened by any personal affection for her but do so in the genuine interest of the Society. Our Lord has effectively broken in me, indeed purified in me, all human attachment. I think I have learnt this lesson.[14]

However, Sophie recognised that many feared that the spirit of the rue de Varenne would become even more dominant in the Society. She also knew that one of the reasons the decrees of 1839 had been greeted with enthusiasm especially outside of France was precisely the weakening of the French influence, notably that of the rue de Varenne, in the Society.[15] In her own journal at this time Sophie noted the key issues she wished to discuss with Césaire Mathieu, once he had returned to Besançon:

Notes for M.xx

How can I replace all the Provincials?
Should I replace some assistants generals before the Council of 1845?
. . . How to reform a *specific* house? quote details and examples.
Would it not be better to postpone all organisation until the next Council and leave
matters as they are until then? I think nevertheless that it would be good to replace
Mme de Limminghe.
Talk about my situation in Paris, what stand to take. [Archbishop Affre][16]

On 25 March 1843 Sophie received a letter from Elizabeth Galitzine asking
permission to return to America and explain the situation personally to the communities there. She anticipated that the American communities would be bitterly disappointed at the decision taken by the pope to suppress the 1839 decrees.
The following day she wrote to Sophie again and asked to be relieved of the
offices of secretary general and assistant general. She asked Sophie to accept her
request because she knew that her appointment as assistant general had irked
the communities in the rue de Varenne, Autun and Le Mans and that they doubted her capacities for the task. She would find it impossible to live and work in the
rue de Varenne and her resignation was the only solution.[17] At this point Sophie
became alarmed. She wrote to Césaire Mathieu and asked him to visit Lyon on
the way home from Italy and try to persuade Elizabeth Galitzine not to resign, at
least until the next general council in 1845.[18] Mathieu warned Sophie from
Toulon that the situation remained critical and that he had several things to say
to her verbally which would show her that the crisis was by no means over. The
resignations of Galitzine and de Limminghe clearly hinted at this and he warned
Sophie that it was best to accept their decisions.[19] Indeed, he suggested that she
accept the resignations of all who offered and told Sophie it was time to act:

How will you be able to lead the Society with people who remain with you only
through pressure? How will you prepare for the Council of 1845 with such dissidents? How will you heal minds and hearts with those same people who almost
destroyed the Society?
Be strong in the face of all . . . do not lose the fruits of my efforts by proceeding cautiously, by indecision . . . You have what you need to act now . . . [20]

Sophie would have had an easier choice if there were available women whom
she could trust then as assistants general. The only person she could name confidently was Henriette Coppens and she was ill. Sophie did not trust Eulalie de
Bouchaud and she was not sure enough yet of Anna du Rousier. Sophie was conscious also that the American houses needed to be visited again and she could
not see anyone other than Elizabeth Galitzine for this task. Césaire Mathieu
advised against this appointment, suggesting instead that Galitzine be sent to a
house of the Society where she could cause no further harm:

I am sure that before the decision of the Congregation [in March 1843] the
American provinces, I mean the houses there, wrote very strong letters to Rome in
favour of the Decrees and I fear criticising the house in Paris [rue de Varenne].

There is genuine confusion there. It is not rash judgement to think that Madame Galitzine provoked all this . . . If she remains as assistant general and in charge of the American province, you could be creating problems for yourself.[21]

Césaire Mathieu met both Elizabeth Galitzine and Marie Prevost in Lyon and while they appeared to accept the decision from Rome he confessed to feeling uneasy indeed:

> they called me the *Saviour of the Society* and I do not think I am mistaken in think-ing that a month ago they would have wished me at the bottom of the sea. Madame de Galitzine's last letter, which I am keeping for you, is a total recantation, pro-voked I believe by Madame de Limminghe. It seems to me that there is a new plan afoot. There is not one word of regret from Madame de Galitzine about her behaviour towards you in the past. On the contrary Madame Prevost claims that she *only did her duty*. In my opinion all this seems to show little honesty and that a plan is being hatched. Take care, especially since Madame de Galitzine is anxious to set out for Paris next Wednesday.[22]

Some days later, finally back in Besançon, Césaire Mathieu warned Sophie again that definitely another plan was afoot and that sending Elizabeth Galitzine to America would be a fatal move.[23] Yet Sophie wanted Elizabeth Galitzine to go to America, perhaps to place as much distance between them as possible. Until Elizabeth Galitzine joined the council Sophie had never had any opposition from within the governing group of the Society.[24] She still had influence among the assistants general and overawed them with her energy and conviction. At the same time, since Eugénie Audé had returned to Europe in 1834, the only person who knew the members of the Society in America personally was Elizabeth Galitzine. Sophie hoped that Elizabeth Galitzine would do less damage to the Society in America than she could do in Europe.

While Archbishop Affre was satisfied with the suppression of the 1839 decrees, he had renewed his claims over the Society and conveyed this to her and to Antonio Garibaldi. Affre made it clear that he would not co-operate with Sophie when she sought government approval for the foundation or suppression of houses of the Society in France; nor would he support any legal or financial transactions of the Society in France until Sophie Barat acknowledged the rights of the archbishop of Paris over her and the Society. In addition, he forbade Sophie to convene a general council of the Society outside the diocese of Paris and required her to ask his permission if she wished to leave the diocese on any business whatsoever.[25] He was applying one of the laws enshrined in the Organic Articles to Sophie Barat. No bishop in France could travel outside his diocese without the permission of the government. Since women had no clerical status the law could not be applied to them, but bishops resented the mobility which women religious had and tried to control it. In this instance, Archbishop Affre tried at every stage to monitor the moves of Sophie Barat.[26]

Affre's stance prevented Sophie from carrying out her plans. She had hoped to gather a small group of key members of the Society in Besançon and there discuss the next steps with Césaire Mathieu. But Antonio Garibaldi advised Sophie not to do so and suggested that Sophie resume her usual practice of visiting communities and to take no more than one or at most two companions with her. She considered taking Félicité Desmarquest with her, but realised that that this would block her freedom of communication.[27] Just as Sophie was about to set out for Besançon Archbishop Affre intervened and forbade her to travel until she and her council had accepted his rights over her and the Society of the Sacred Heart.[28] At this stage Sophie felt that she could not sustain much more and she asked for an appointment with Affre and spoke to him about the impossible position he was placing her in. She soon realised that his basic objection lay in her travelling to Besançon to meet Césaire Mathieu. Sophie was caught again between the rivalries and tensions of the two prelates.[29] She resigned herself to the fact that she could not travel immediately, that she had to work alone in Paris and hope for a meeting with Césaire Mathieu later on in the year, when Affre might relax his threats. She judged this well enough, for in June his objections were temporarily lifted. However, almost like mood swings, Archbishop Affre had reverted once more to pressure and threats on Sophie, though by now she had begun to anticipate his behaviour towards her.[30]

But in April 1843 Sophie needed to remain in Paris and find someone to replace Louise de Limminghe. Eulalie de Bouchaud, the mistress of novices in Paris, was not suitable:

> . . . no one is less united to me in spirit, in her manner of seeing things, in the way of judging and in the way she forms the novices. On the contrary she is completely one with the assistants general, above all Madame Desmarquest. It is this narrow, constraining style of religious life, altogether like the Visitation Order though sometimes also from the point of view of religious spirit, which makes them such a contrast to the rue de Varenne and the other houses. I prefer a middle ground between the two expressions [of religious life] . . .[31]

At the same time, Sophie was painfully aware that the situation in the rue de Varenne continued to need reform. When Césaire Mathieu had visited Armande de Causans in Aix she had spoken to him about the rue de Varenne. Sophie assured him he had only heard a little of the story.[32] She acknowledged: 'I cannot move, even touch an iota here [rue de Varenne]'.[33] It was a humiliating admission of the manner in which Eugénie de Gramont had rendered Sophie's authority null and void in the rue de Varenne. She told Césaire Mathieu that she was sure the assistants general did not care who replaced Louise de Limminghe as long as it was not Eugénie de Gramont. Yet Mathieu thought that de Limminghe and Galitzine were far more dangerous to Sophie and the Society than Eugénie de Gramont and the rue de Varenne. Reform was needed there certainly but he warned Sophie that some of the criticism was mere gossip. On the other hand, Mathieu reproached Sophie for hesitating to deal with Louise de Limminghe and Elizabeth Galitzine. He could not understand why she delayed accepting both their resignations and told her she could lose the initiative if she did not act:

Do not allow yourself to be dejected . . . you must take heart. Now more than ever you must remain firm and keep control of affairs. I would go so far as to say that it is your duty to do so; otherwise all will be lost.[34]

Despite his insistence that she act, Césaire Mathieu, better than anyone else, knew what Sophie was enduring, in such a trapped position, with minimal information and no support from any of her colleagues. He knew she counted on him for advice which could only be given through the medium of letters until Affre relented and allowed Sophie to resume travelling in France. The constriction and the complexity of the situation affected her profoundly and she longed to speak in depth to someone she could trust, especially how to actually deal with Louise de Limminghe.[35] She knew that in Rome de Limminghe had great influence in the Villa Lante and over Sainte Rufine, especially with Adèle Lehon, the superior of Sainte Rufine. Sophie wondered if they continued to plan to separate from the Society. The Trinité was different now. There the superior, Josephine de Coriolis, had gradually recovered her position and remained loyal to Sophie. Sophie told Mathieu:

I will wait for your advice before I write to the superior of Sainte Rufine. She is guided by Mother de Limminghe, even repeating her very phrases. Her limited ability does not allow her to find other expressions and besides she is so used to doing everything under the guidance of her superior. That is one of the disadvantages of having Mother de Limminghe in Rome . . . [36]

Certainly the correspondence between Louise de Limminghe, Elizabeth Galitzine and Adèle Lehon at this time indicated how deeply disappointed they were at the decision taken in Rome. They had hoped that even if the 1839 decrees were not accepted in France that the houses in Rome, Piedmont and America might have been allowed to retain them. They decided to prepare for the general council in 1845 by continuing to lobby for the 1839 decrees in the hope that by 1845 a petition from the general council, supported by the houses outside of France, could overturn the decision of the cardinals. Adèle Lehon argued that this was the only way to restore the authority of a general council of the Society. Otherwise, decisions taken by general councils could be contested in the future.

As he had done in the past, so now Jean Rozaven moved to protect himself. He told Adèle Lehon that he had decided not to communicate directly with Elizabeth Galitzine as this could compromise him in the eyes of his general, Roothan, and in those of the congregation of regulars and bishops. Rather than write to her himself, he asked Adèle Lehon to explain this to Elizabeth Galitzine:

He will not be writing to you because he always wants to be able to say truthfully that since the sad state of affairs [the decision in March 1843] he has had no contact. His own position is more delicate than ever. He has been asked to state frankly that he is opposed to the decision of the Congregation, [but] if reports criticising the decision were heard they would certainly be attributed to him. This would compromise him seriously with the cardinals and with his father general. He asks you therefore to be more circumspect than ever on his account. [37]

In early April 1843 Césaire Mathieu agreed with Sophie that it was time to write a circular letter to the Society. Sophie had to explain the decision to suppress the 1839 decrees and call the Society to unity and peace.[38] She drafted the letter and sent Césaire Mathieu a copy for comment. Sophie outlined the major events in the Society since 1839, how she had tried to hold a general council in 1842; she explained the background of the statutes signed in 1827, and how the French government had seen the 1839 decrees as an infringement of these statutes; she told the members that the government had threatened to suppress all the French houses if the 1839 decrees were adopted. In view of this real possibility Sophie had appealed to the pope, who appointed a group of cardinals to study the issue. They advised the pope to suppress the 1839 decrees. Having outlined the context of the pope's decision, Sophie called the members of the Society to renew their loyalty to her. That month she noted laconically in her diary:

> It would take a volume to describe what I have suffered since my departure [from Rome, in June 1842] until now, April 1843.[39]

She took the opportunity of her letter to the Society to recount a little of what had happened to her since 1839:

> I will not tell you of all the pain and bitterness which these last months, these dangers, the state of affairs, have given me, as well as the grim anxieties which have torn my soul. Jesus knows it all and for me that is enough! If the Society is saved. If all members of the Society, putting aside their differences of opinion and overlooking what could hurt one another, recognising the will of God in the decision of his Vicar [the pope], forgiving one another and uniting themselves with me to work with greater zeal than ever, to consolidate charity in the Society, uniformity, fidelity to the constitutions and to religious perfection, then we will thank the Lord for the harsh sufferings which I and members of the Society had to undergo. We will recognise that the cross is always the tree of life, from which all that is good comes to us.[40]

Sophie's letter to the Society deeply disturbed Elizabeth Galitzine. It clearly stated a return to the 1826 constitutions and so confirmed that the superior general would live in Paris, in compliance with the government's interpretation of the statutes of 1827. Elizabeth Galitzine wrote to both Louise de Limminghe and Jean Rozaven, though she was careful to say in the letter that she was writing to Jean Rozaven as a member of the congregation of regulars and bishops. [41] She asked him to bring Sophie's letter to the attention of the cardinal protector, Pedicini, and of the congregation of regulars and bishops. She asked that Sophie's interpretation of the decision of the cardinals on 4 March be refuted. Her letters reveal what Césaire Mathieu had sensed on his visit to Lyon, that there was another agenda being drawn up in Rome and Lyon, based on a different interpretation of the decision of the cardinals in March. That interpretation arose from the understanding that the trial period of the 1839 decrees remained operative until the general council of 1845. In that context Elizabeth Galitzine read Sophie's letter to the Society as further evidence that she was being pressurised by Archbishop Affre and especially by Eugénie de Gramont.

Elizabeth Galitzine argued that even if the Society could do little in the immediate term to save the 1839 decrees, it would be possible to retrieve them after the death of Sophie Barat. For this reason she wanted Pedicini to lodge a confidential statement in the archives of the Society, addressed to the assistants general

> so that they could avail of it in happier times, to save the Society. If that is not possible during the lifetime of our superior general it could be possible after her death. It is part of our duty to provide for the safety of the Society by ensuring that decisions taken at a later date which will give it back its vitality and vigour which some at present seek to take from it.[42]

Galitzine also wrote to Mathieu, expressing her dismay at Sophie's circular letter to the Society, though asking that her letter to him remain confidential. Mathieu replied immediately and told her that she had completely misinterpreted the decision taken in Rome. The intention of the cardinals was that the Society of the Sacred Heart should revert to the 1826 constitutions approved by Leo XII, without exception. He told her that Jean Rozaven had agreed to this, during the meetings of the congregation, which he had officially attended. In particular, Césaire Mathieu told Elizabeth Galitzine that Jean Rozaven had accepted that Sophie Barat had no choice but to live in Paris for the time being:

> Fr Rozaven said to me that it was a just decision, since the government at that time [1827] had only given its authorisation on that condition.[43]

Mathieu reminded Galitzine that Sophie was within her rights in communicating to the whole Society the content of the decision taken in Rome. In fact she had sent him a draft of her letter, to ensure that she provided an accurate account of the proceedings in Rome:

> . . . so if there is anything which offends you place the blame on me, not on others . . . How sad I am. On account of you, the position of the Society, and I can add of the church in France, has been very serious. We can only recover from such an upheaval by charity, mutual trust, obedience and self-sacrifice. If each one continues to cut herself off, to probe and suspect the motives and actions of others, all is lost . . . The Society has scarcely emerged from the storm and the thunder is still rumbling over our heads. Time and the healing balm of charity will cure all the wounds. But the fact is that it is the Society itself which will decide on its own sentence of life or of death. If it goes on tearing itself apart and continues divided, it will perish. If it unites in mutual support it will be healed.[44]

It was this letter which made Mathieu so uneasy about Sophie's plan to send Galitzine to America. He was bound by the confidentiality she had requested, so all he could do was warn and advise Sophie who had no idea how opposed Elizabeth Galitzine was to the decision of the cardinals. When Sophie told him that Louise de Limminghe had expressed the view that the 1839 decrees had not been abolished Césaire Mathieu was able to express his views frankly. He advised Sophie to remove de Limminghe from Rome, as she would never be a focus for unity there.[45] Both she and Elizabeth Galitzine claimed that the decrees had not been abolished. They pinned their hopes on the general council of 1845. During these weeks Césaire Mathieu himself began to despair of peace and harmony ever being achieved in the Society of the Sacred Heart. Significantly, before Elizabeth Galitzine left for America, she arranged that her personal archive in Rome would be put aside and kept safe for her use when she returned to Europe, for the general council of 1845. This was important since there were documents and papers which Elizabeth Galitzine did not want Sophie to see. The archives of the Society were still in Rome, where they had been transported for the general council of 1839 and Elizabeth Galitzine knew that Sophie would arrange to have them brought back to Paris.[46]

While she was in Conflans, as she was preparing for her departure to America, Elizabeth Galitzine and Félicité Desmarquest made plans for the 1845 general council. Elizabeth Galitzine contacted Louis Barat again. He encouraged her plans, and he hoped that in 1845 the 1839 decrees would be fully implemented. Commenting on the decision of the cardinals in Rome, Louis Barat wrote:

> The best thing about this matter is the postponement of the assembly [Council] until 1845 . . . at that stage . . . there will be hardly anything to fear, either from legal or from the Gallican authorities . . . and there will be the opportunity to restore the true Institute which will then be definitive . . . [47]

He agreed to see Elizabeth Galitzine while she was in Paris, but only in Conflans. He detested the rue de Varenne.

As Césaire Mathieu had suspected, when Elizabeth Galitzine set sail for America in June 1843 she went with a definite plan to implement the 1839 decrees in the American communities. She would maintain contact with Félicité Desmarquest in Paris, Marie Prevost in Lyon and Louise de Limminghe and Adèle Lehon in Rome. The lobby which she had established in America in 1841 was intact and she hoped that by 1845 it would be strongly represented at the general council. Sophie knew that many of the American communities supported Elizabeth Galitzine but she did not know yet the extent of her influence. Sophie told Aloysia Hardey to warn Maria Cutts and Bishop Blanc about possible tensions in the communities. Both could be trusted, but she did not risk more:

> I did not dare write to Louisiana because I do not know any of the superiors there, and I did not know to what extent Madame Galitzine had indoctrinated them . . . [48]

Sophie had already written to Aloysia Hardey before Elizabeth Galitzine had left for America and explained that Galitzine's purpose in returning to America was to communicate the decision taken in Rome in March of that year. She hoped that there would be no opposition to the decision and asked Aloysia Hardey to tell her how the visit proceeded.[49] In June 1843 Sophie wrote a formal letter for the American communities in which she asked all to live according to the constitutions of the Society approved in 1826. It was a short letter but she assured the communities that Elizabeth Galitzine would explain everything in detail.[50] Which of course she did, but not in the way that Sophie had intended.

Once Elizabeth Galitzine had left in early June for America, Sophie decided to take advantage of Archbishop Affre's temporary goodwill towards her. She left Félicité Desmarquest in Conflans, in charge of the noviciate, since Eulalie de Bouchaud was quite ill and needed a change of air. Sophie set out with Eulalie de Bouchaud to visit the houses in Le Mans, Nantes, Tours and Autun and finally arrived in Besançon on the 24 July.[51] There she was able to discuss her plans alone with Césaire Mathieu and test her perceptions of the situation in the Society. He agreed with her decision to appoint Henriette Coppens as assistant general to succeed Louise de Limminghe, and with her idea of holding meetings for superiors in Montet and in Lyon. Her relief at being able to talk freely and confidently was profound and Sophie was able discuss her plans with him in detail.[52] She left Besançon on 9 August and travelled on to Montet, arriving there on 12 August. There she had good discussions with Thérèse Maillucheau, Henriette Coppens and Anna du Rousier. She was particularly happy to talk with Anna du Rousier and discover her position with regard to the Society. Since the summer of 1842 Louise de Limminghe and Elizabeth Galitzine had worked hard to include her in the plans to separate the houses of the Society in Rome and Piedmont from those in France. Sophie had noticed that Anna du Rousier had stopped writing to her and she knew that she and de Limminghe were in constant communication.[53] At Louise de Limminghe's suggestion, Anna du Rousier had written to the archbishop of Genoa, to the bishops of Saluces and Pignerol and to the archbishop of Chambéry, asking them to support the 1839 decrees.[54]

Once the decision of the cardinals was announced in March 1843, Sophie wrote to Anna du Rousier and asked her why she had stopped communicating with her. Du Rousier responded immediately and told Sophie that she had understood that Sophie was trapped in Paris by Archbishop Affre and Eugénie de Gramont and could not act freely. Sophie accepted this explanation and asked Anna du Rousier to convey to the archbishops and bishops she had written to previously the news of the suppression of the 1839 decrees. When they met in Montet in August 1843 Sophie was pleased to see that Anna du Rousier accepted her leadership. Sophie knew now that du Rousier could be entrusted with office and that the houses in Piedmont and the north of Italy would remain loyal.[55]

After three weeks in Montet, Sophie left for Lyon to meet Marie Prevost, Armande de Causans and the other superiors from the Midi. This meeting was strained and tense, but help came from an unexpected quarter. Eulalie de Bouchaud had changed her viewpoint. She now grasped something of the magnitude Sophie had been grappling with since 1839. Her sister, Emma de Bouchaud, who was superior at Besançon and loyal to Sophie from the beginning, was more than likely instrumental in her change. Henriette Coppens in Montet had also influenced her and so by the time she and Sophie had reached Lyon,

Eulalie de Bouchaud was ready to speak out in support of Sophie. Sophie herself noted that those in Lyon talked more freely with Eulalie de Bouchaud than with her.[56] This did not disturb her at all. Indeed she noted in her own journal that while her visits had been useful, they were only the beginning of the process of establishing peace and harmony.[57]

While she was in Lyon Félicité Desmarquest wrote and asked Sophie to return quickly to Paris. She found the strain of living there too much without Sophie. Sophie agreed with reluctance, and looked forward to the time when Henriette Coppens could come to Paris, for she at least 'will understand and support me'.[58] By the end of September Sophie was back in Paris and soon Archbishop Affre renewed his claims over her and the Society of the Sacred Heart. He sent Sophie a long statement, asserting his rights and her duties, and he asked her to send a written acknowledgement that she had received the document. She was too shrewd to do anything of the sort.[59] Instead she quietly set off for a short visit to Beauvais and Amiens and was back in Conflans by the end of October. By then her physical and emotional energies were spent and Sophie had no inner resources to fight infections. She first caught a cold and then a fever and on 2 November 1843 Sophie was forced to stop. She was gravely ill for two months and it took another three before she had fully recovered her strength. In October 1843 Charlotte Goold (1804–49), who had been helping Sophie with her letters, was needed urgently for the foundation at Cannington in England and once again Sophie had no secretarial assistance. In 1841 Sophie had asked Marie Prevost to release Adèle Cahier, then in Lyon, as her secretary during Elizabeth Galitzine's absence in America. That request was refused then, but Marie Prevost recognised now that Sophie could not continue without help. She suggested that Adèle Cahier become secretary general. The appointment of Adèle Cahier was a significant choice. Not only was she a gifted secretary but she kept meticulous records and detailed accounts of the history of the Society, especially of the period 1839–50.[60]

When Sophie resumed her correspondence with Césaire Mathieu in March 1844, several important changes had occurred within and without the Society.[61] One was the unexpected and sudden death of Elizabeth Galitzine in St Michael's in December 1843. She had sailed from Le Havre on 20 June 1843 and reached New York on 25 July. She had spent some weeks there and in McSherrystown and then had travelled north to eastern Canada to Saint Jacques. In September she had returned to New York and after two weeks there set out for Missouri. As winter approached she complained of fever and of the excessive cold in St Louis. She had suffered for some years from recurrent fevers and she was advised to travel south to St Michael's, where it was warmer. No one in St Louis knew then that yellow fever had struck in the south. It had hit St Michael's by the time Elizabeth Galitzine arrived on 14 November. For some days she seemed well and she helped to nurse the sick and dying. On 1 December she became ill and her condition deteriorated rapidly. By 7 December all hope of saving her was lost. Elizabeth Galitzine was forty-eight and much of her life was unfulfilled. She had so many plans, so much to do, and death by yellow fever would prevent her from striving to realise her dreams for the Society of the Sacred Heart. Those who helped her at her last moments admitted that Elizabeth Galitzine's anguish was intense and that it was difficult to remain at her bedside. She died on the afternoon of 8 December in pain and desolation.[62]

Sophie learnt of Elizabeth Galitzine's death in January 1844 and realised that whatever their differences, the circumstances of her death were tragic. Sophie admitted to Césaire Mathieu that he had been right, that Elizabeth Galitzine had never been reconciled to the decision of 4 March 1843. After her death Sophie learnt that Galitzine had continued to promote the 1839 decrees in America, convinced that in 1845 they would be formally adopted by the Society and approved by the church.[63] Although still weak and unable to work for any length of time Sophie decided to assume personal responsibility for the American houses and to establish a direct relationship between herself and three key women, Aloysia Hardey, Maria Cutts and Bathilde Sallion.[64] If she could be sure of their loyalty and leadership, the possibility of the American houses separating from the Society would be weakened. She wrote to Aloysia Hardey and asked her to send her all Elizabeth Galitzine's plans for the organisation of the houses in America, as well as accounts of any plans she had made with Aloysia Hardey. Sophie also asked that the private papers of Elizabeth Galitzine be sent directly to her in Paris, with the exception of private journals, which she suggested should be burnt.[65] Sophie's correspondence with Aloysia Hardey was blunt and direct. Sophie had been taken aback when she learnt of the extent of the correspondence of Aloysia Hardey with Elizabeth Galitzine, Louise de Limminghe and Laure d'Aviernoz. Sophie questioned Hardey's loyalty to her personally as well as her manner of dealing with her colleagues in America,[66] even though Sophie had originally urged Hardey to welcome Elizabeth Galitzine in 1840, affording her every help, and to see in her the representative of the superior general. Now Sophie continually tested Aloysia Hardey. This was so daunting that she asked Sophie why she retained her as superior. Sophie replied:

> My criticisms are more like warnings, and if I had not got confidence in you I would remove you from your office and say no more. It is said that the Spirit of God tests those whom it loves. And that is entirely the feeling which guides me, when I tell you what others say about you. Besides I do not believe a quarter of what they say . . . [67]

Sophie also wrote to Maria Cutts, the superior at Grand Coteau, asking her for her recollections of Elizabeth Galitzine's plans for the American communities, as well as her personal memories of Elizabeth Galitzine.[68] In May 1844 Sophie appointed both Aloysia Hardey and Maria Cutts to responsibility in America. Cutts was charged to look after the houses in Louisiana and Missouri, and Hardey those in New York, McSherrystown and St Jacques. Bathilde Sallion was appointed bursar for both areas. Sophie explained to them that Elizabeth Galitzine had misinterpreted the decision taken in Rome in March 1843 and she asked them to ensure that all the copies of the 1839 decrees were burnt. She admitted that this was a harsh measure, but she wanted to end all division within the Society. She explained that she herself had tried to retain some of the decrees but because of the factions within the Society no exception could be made even for her. Finally she asked all three to meet and discuss how best to settle the affairs of the communities and schools.[69]

While Sophie was placing her stamp of authority on America, she had received several letters from Josephine de Coriolis, telling her of the situation of the Society in Rome. The old strains and tensions between the Villa Lante and the Trinité continued and had become even more apparent than before, especially between Josephine de Coriolis and Louise de Limminghe. Josephine de Coriolis had decided to remain in the Society and admitted to Sophie that she had made a mistake in 1838 when she had considered leaving. She accepted the decision of the cardinals in March 1843, that the Society revert to the original constitutions of 1826. On the other hand, Louise de Limminghe continued to believe that the 1839 decrees had not been abolished. There was criticism of the Society in Rome and Josephine de Coriolis told Sophie about this in February 1844. The Princess Borgèse, a great friend of Louise de Limminghe openly denounced the Society of the Sacred Heart, and in particular Sophie Barat:

> It was mostly about you . . . you have been particularly blamed and it is claimed that you showed serious weakness of character in the whole affair, etc., etc. . . . that you have made the Society exclusively French...Then she inserted certain phrases in parenthesis, like these: I have complete confidence in Madame de Limminghe. She is my friend. The mother general is for France but Madame de Limminghe is the mother general for Italy. Etc., etc., etc. I am also aware that Fr Jean Rozaven may have said something to the princess about our affairs . . . I am afraid that the Italian houses, (except the Trinité and Loreto) will sooner or later be lost to the Society . . . [70]

The Princess Borgèse was ultramontane and closely allied with Lacordaire and Madame Swetchine in France. Though friendly with Sophie Barat and ready to carry letters from Paris to Rome on her frequent visits to France, she was critical of Sophie's presumed Gallicanism.[71] Some of the tensions within the Society in Rome were reported in the press and Cardinal Pacca asked Josephine de Coriolis to refute them.[72] The Princess Borgèse criticised the Society of the Sacred Heart in public in Rome, declaring her support for Louise de Limminghe. The strain between Louise de Limminghe and Josephine de Coriolis, between the Villa Lante and the Trinité, was played out in the tensions between the two noviceships. This was experienced directly by an American, Cornelia Connolly, who was living in the Trinité at this time and was in the process of considering entering the Society of the Sacred Heart.

Cornelia Connolly (1809–79) had lived on the property of Grand Coteau, with her husband Pierce and their family. Pierce Connolly felt called to the priesthood in the Catholic Church and he asked Cornelia if she was willing to end living together as a married couple and to cease looking after their children.

She agreed to this and they both went to Rome and discussed their plan with Gregory XVI who agreed to give them a dispensation. While Pierce asked to become a Jesuit, Cornelia at first, at Pierce's instigation, thought of the Society of the Sacred Heart. Both arrived in Rome, with their children, in the winter of 1843.[73] After some months, during which she was guided by Jean Rozaven, Cornelia entered as a postulant at the Trinité on 9 April 1844. The Princess Borgèse was a friend of the Connollys and she tried to persuade Cornelia to visit Louise de Limminghe in the Villa Lante and hopefully choose to do her noviceship there. The visit made no impression and Cornelia decided to remain at the Trinité.[74] However, she found the divisions between the Trinité and the Villa Lante too contentious, and the spirituality of the Society in Rome too severe and unattractive. A few months later she decided not to enter the Society of the Sacred Heart at all, but to travel another path.[75]

Sophie read Josephine de Coriolis's letters with concern and she told Césaire Mathieu that a journey to Rome was essential. She had also heard that the Princess Boutourline (who had a daughter in the Society) was openly hostile towards the Society in Rome and particularly towards Sophie herself. She was worried about the Society's affairs appearing in the press in Rome. Discussion of the need to modify the Society's internal structures was in effect a thinly veiled criticism of the pope and the decision of the cardinals of March 1843.[76] Since July 1842, the relationship between Sophie Barat and Louise de Limminghe had progressively become more strained and it is no accident that most of their letters, between October 1842 and January 1843, as well as between September 1843 and May 1844, have disappeared. By January 1843, the rift between them was deep. Sophie then expressed her disappointment with the stance her friend had taken, despite all Sophie's efforts to explain the gravity of the situation of the Society in Paris. She had warned Louise de Limminghe that if she persisted it would

> clearly lead to the ruin of the Society . . . a schism then would be inevitable and these two opposing factions will be like two birds who have only one wing each. Perhaps they can continue to function but only haltingly and rather disjointedly . . . I have made my decision and I will struggle on alone as long as I can, to prevent the disintegration which threatens us . . .[77]

A month later, when Césaire Mathieu was in Rome and had met Louise de Limminghe in the Villa Lante, Sophie wrote again to de Limminghe, hiding nothing of her pain and sense of betrayal:

> No one knows better than this true Friend what I have suffered, not just from the bitter troubles which have besieged me, but from the source they came from . . . How my heart suffers from being misunderstood, abandoned by friends whom I believed to be my other self, without explanation, or knowing all the facts, and trusting in everyone else but me to whom they owed at least a little trust. But let us leave all that in the heart of God, for it is He who has allowed this to happen and for purposes we will understand later.[78]

By June 1843, Sophie was ready to accept Louise de Limminghe's resignation.[79] Sophie knew that the resignation actually gave her more scope in Rome to work to maintain the 1839 decrees and to plan her strategy for the general council of 1845. When the artist Pauline Perdrau[80] travelled to Rome in May 1844, Sophie asked her to take a gift for Louise de Limminghe. In her letter to Louise de Limminghe Sophie asked her to explain her own conduct as well as how the Princess Borgèse was so familiar with the internal affairs of the Society. Louise de Limminghe denied that she had ever spoken to the Princess Borgèse about the internal affairs of the Society. The princess had heard a great deal about life in the Trinité from Cornelia Connolly. From her contacts in Paris, with Lacordaire and Madame Swetchine, she had become critical of some houses of the Society in France, especially the rue de Varenne. Louise de Limminghe assured Sophie that she had tried not to talk to the princess about the Society, but that the princess was not easily put off.[81]

This letter only convinced Sophie that she must travel to Rome herself and try to put an end to the divisions there, between the Trinité and the Villa Lante, and at the same time try and reconcile Louise de Limminghe to the abolition of the 1839 decrees. With the death of Elizabeth Galitzine in December 1843 Louise de Limminghe had lost her closest ally in her bid to retain the 1839 decrees. She was concerned about how the life of Elizabeth Galitzine would be presented to the Society and she worried if her role and that of Rozaven would appear in the recounting of the last years of Elizabeth Galitzine's life. Sophie assured her that Galitzine's opposition to Sophie personally and to the decision of the pope in 1843 would not appear in the obituary notice. The account of her painful death was modified somewhat, to make it less stressful to read, and Sophie assured de Limminghe that in America the memory of Elizabeth Galitzine would be held in the highest regard.[82]

Sophie's intention to visit Rome was not solely for the purpose of resolving the divisions there within the Society. According to the decision taken in March 1843, a general council was due to take place in 1845. While Sophie had said nothing about this in public, she knew that the council could not possibly meet then. The wounds of division were still open and sore, in all parts of the Society. Archbishop Affre persisted in his claims over the Society which had forced the previous council in Lyon in 1842 to be cancelled. If Sophie held the council in Rome, Affre would denounce her and the French government would dissolve the Society of the Sacred Heart immediately. If she held the general council in Paris, the houses outside France would separate, and perhaps some of the houses in France would join them. At the same time, on a wider canvas, the ultramontane/Gallican tension persisted and Sophie knew she had to tread carefully, both in Paris and in Rome. For all these reasons Sophie decided to discuss her predicament with Gregory XVI and Lambruschini, newly appointed cardinal protector of the Society since Pedicini's death in January 1844.[83] But before Sophie made plans for the journey to Rome, she decided to cross the channel and visit the new foundations in England.

– 21 –

IN HER OWN HOUSE, 1844–1849

In autumn 1843 Lord Clifford had asked Sophie to make a second foundation in England, at Cannington. Sophie hesitated, since personnel and finances were overstretched, and against her better judgement she was persuaded by Lord Clifford and the vicar apostolic in England to consent. A few months later she knew that the two foundations could not be sustained and she decided to travel to England herself in June 1844 and determine which of the houses to close during her visit. She spent a month in England and while there she decided to close Cannington. Contrary to the gloomy foreboding in Paris about her health and the hazardous sea journey, Sophie travelled well and the change did her a lot of good.[1] In July and early August Sophie visited the houses in Lille, Jette and Amiens. When she returned to Paris in mid-August she had a fall and hurt her right arm and for some time she was unable to work.[2] This delayed her departure for Rome and she was only able to travel in late October.

This time she was accompanied by Marie Patte and her secretary, Adèle Cahier. They set off for Bourges where Sophie discussed a possible foundation there with Bishop Jacques du Pont (1842–59). They then proceeded to Autun and arrived in La Ferrandière where she caught a heavy cold and spent the month of November recuperating. In early December they moved on again and visited the communities at Annonay, Avignon and Aix-en-Provence. On the 12 December, Sophie's birthday, while they were travelling between Avignon and Aix the weather deteriorated. Heavy snow fell and a mistral made the journey very uncomfortable. When they arrived in Aix the driver of the coach did not know where the community lived and he let Sophie down at some distance from

391

the house. The walk in the snow was too much for Sophie's frail condition and she caught another heavy cold.[3]

A month later, on 13 January 1845, Sophie was able to continue on her travels and she visited the two houses at Marseilles. From there Sophie wrote a short letter to the Society, giving an outline of her itinerary and requesting more accurate accounts for the annual letters and for the catalogues (lists of houses and community members in the Society). This in itself marked a return to normal business.[4] From Marseilles she also wrote to Stanislas for news of Louis Barat whose health had been deteriorating rapidly. On leaving Paris Sophie had sensed that Louis was near death and wondered if she would see him again. Stanislas kept her informed as she travelled and his news confirmed her premonition.[5] Then she embarked for Rome on 17 January 1845. On the way she visited the community at Genoa, a foundation recently begun by Anna du Rousier and Armande de Causans. The ship docked at Civita-Vecchia on the morning of the 23 January and that evening Sophie arrived at the Villa Lante, to be greeted by Louise de Limminghe. Their meeting was painful and difficult. They did not reach an understanding, either over the decrees of 1839 or the strained relations that existed between the houses of the Society in Rome.[6] While Sophie was in Rome Aloysia Hardey sent her the letters and papers of Elizabeth Galitzine. These confirmed what Sophie already knew about the ongoing communication between Elizabeth Galitzine, Aloysia Hardey, Louise de Limminghe and Laure d'Avernioz especially between 1841 and 1843. Sophie wrote to Hardey and suggested that she end her correspondence with Laure d'Aviernoz, the assistant superior at the Villa Lante since she could never be reconciled to the decision taken in March 1843. On the other hand, Sophie thought Hardey could write occasionally to Louise de Limminghe, even though she claimed she had done nothing wrong, that she was 'white as snow'.[7] Sophie told Hardey that she considered that Elizabeth Galitzine was responsible for Louise de Limminghe's blindness:

> She was wrong to allow herself to be influenced and led by Elizabeth Galitzine who was the instigator of our troubles. She is in heaven now. Let us say no more. She certainly had the best of intentions.[8]

Winter in Rome that year was severe and Sophie fell ill again and was confined to bed for several weeks. The stress and strain of the last five years had begun to take their toll and for the rest of her life, with rare exceptions, Sophie was ill generally from November to February/March of each year. Earlier in 1845 she admitted to Césaire Mathieu: 'I am getting old. The slightest fatigue brings me endless maladies.'[9]

Even though she was ill during the winter months in Rome, Sophie's presence alone gave peace and stability to the three communities there. She described to Césaire Mathieu how she had been received in Rome. Lambruschini was welcoming and visited her in the Villa Lante while she was convalescing. He continued to visit her when she moved to the Trinité later on in the spring. In general, most of the officials in Rome were friendly towards her though one member of the congregation of bishops and religious, a cardinal, was cold and distant. Sophie knew it was over her residence in Paris and the suspicion that she had Gallican tendencies.[10] When Sophie had recovered her energy she had several formal meetings with Lambruschini and she explained the situation within the Society as well as her ongoing difficulties with Archbishop Affre. Lambruschini had no difficulty in understanding that Sophie could not hold a general council that year. He advised her to wait until 1846 before making a decision. They agreed that Sophie would send him her views annually and on the basis of that a decision would be taken. In view of the attitude of Archbishop Affre and the political unrest in Europe which culminated in the 1848 revolutions, the general council of the Society was deferred annually until 1851. In the meantime, Sophie governed the Society according to the constitutions approved in 1826. However, using the powers given her in March 1843, formal visits to houses of the Society could be made in her name either by the assistants general or by individuals named by Sophie for that purpose.[11]

One issue could not wait until a general council. Lambruschini insisted that Sophie deal with the final source of division within the Society, the controversy around the rue de Varenne. Sophie was ready for this and proposed a strategy. She would begin by making a formal visitation of the house. Then she would take up residence there as superior general and as local superior. In this way Eugénie de Gramont would cease to be superior. Both Lambruschini and Sophie recognised that the situation in the rue de Varenne had in great part caused the polarisation within the Society over the 1839 decrees. In the measure that the rue de Varenne was reformed, criticisms within and from without would cease.[12] The decision of the cardinals in March 1843 had been welcomed, even expected, by Eugénie and the community at the rue de Varenne. To them, all had returned to normal but Sophie had tried to initiate reform of the community and the school. When she asked about how the school was being run she was blocked as much by Aimée d'Avenas, the headmistress of the school, as by Eugénie de Gramont. Virginie Roux, who lived in the rue de Varenne during these years, remembered painful community meetings when both Eugénie de Gramont and Aimée d'Avenas were discourteous to Sophie in public. She did not respond to such rudeness but remarked to the community in general that when St Paul spoke about practising charity it really was 'nothing more than what people in society call good manners or exquisite politeness.'[13] While Aimée d'Avenas expressed her irritation with Sophie by rudeness in public,[14] Eugénie tended to use irony. During a community meeting Sophie remarked that she wished the Society had women of greater spiritual depth rather than intellectual learning:

> Once she said to us that her great desire was to see us leading lives of inner depth, and that she based so many of her hopes on that . . . Mother de Gramont replied in the most ironic tone of voice: 'Well, what would you do with the Society if you did not have well-educated religious?'. Our. . . . Mother [Sophie] replied, very politely: 'I do not wish to say that we do not need scholarly sisters. But I do wish to say that only those united to God can do God's work in people's souls. This is

true especially in foundations, the work there is done by those who live a deep inner life, not by those who are learned'.[15]

Members of the community, like Virginie Roux, had been aware of the antagonism of some in the house towards Sophie. When she had arrived back from Rome in 1841 she was met by coldness and rejection. The same thing happened in November 1842, and it continued despite the abolition of the 1839 decrees in March 1843. Archbishop de Quelen's death had not ended the worldly lifestyle in the rue de Varenne. The marriage bureau established by Eugénie de Gramont was still in full operation. Aimée d'Avenas was a regular contributor to the newspapers in Paris though she wrote anonymously.[16] The school chaplains were constantly in the school, with the pupils, and this had caused many raised eyebrows and comments in Paris.[17] The school had a public profile, a reputation for grandeur and wealth, and moved among the elite of Paris with ease. Although Césaire Mathieu had told her that the most serious issue in the Society was addressing the faction led by Elizabeth Galitzine and Louise de Limminghe, Sophie knew that the situation in the rue de Varenne was also serious and that she would have to deal with it personally. Lambruschini's suggestion that the time had come to reform the rue de Varenne met with her assent, however painful the path ahead appeared.

From Rome Sophie began to prepare Eugénie de Gramont for change. She wrote to Eugénie and told her that the time had come to remove Aimée d'Avenas as headmistress in the rue de Varenne. While she had real gifts, directing a school was not one of them; neither the community nor the parents of the pupils had confidence in her. The reputation of the school and of the Society was being eroded. She suggested that Aimée d'Avenas be assigned the task of writing textbooks; she was a gifted writer and had already published several useful texts for the schools.[18] However, Sophie warned Eugénie that this was merely the beginning of the changes envisaged. She told her that she had received two visits from Lambruschini and they had talked long about the affairs of the Society. Sophie quoted what Lambruschini had said to her and put her own comments in brackets:

> Several people from France whose rank and probity make them respectable (. . . I understood that these were ecclesiastics, but there were also some lay people among them), when they learnt that I am the cardinal protector of your Society, came to see me to warn me of the totally unacceptable abuses which are happening at the rue de Varenne. Do you know about them?
> Firstly: The marriages in which these religious are involved; they receive these young people and their fiancés; these religious chaperone the young couples. It seems that these rumours have spread and scandalise people! (when people criticise us they always exaggerate).
> Secondly, within the rue de Varenne there is a religious [Aimée d'Avenas] who has neither the spirit nor the virtue of religious life, who has the complete confidence of the superior and does great damage. She is an author and writes in the newspaper. To sum her up in two words: she is a *Philosophe*. She was sent to England and there she attracted criticism etc. (This seems a bit hard to me).[19]

Sophie commented on Lambruschini's information and reminded Eugénie of the cases they had had in Paris, in the school, which were certainly talked about in the salons of Paris and indeed beyond. One in particular, which had involved a young suitor being rejected by a boarder in the rue de Varenne, caused a great deal of criticism. She received criticism wherever she went:

> I do not go to any town, I receive hardly any letters, in which I do not hear some complaints against this house [the rue de Varenne], I mean the boarding school. A creditable priest said to someone in the Society: several of the pupils at the rue de Varenne, who have a religious vocation, do not wish to enter there. They see great lack of unity among the community; some of them have so little spirituality and too much frivolity. Unfortunately this is only too true.[20]

This was not new. Over the years Sophie had spoken and written to Eugénie de Gramont, telling her of the complaints that she had heard everywhere about the rue de Varenne. Nothing had happened then and Eugénie had no reason to believe that anything would now. Indeed, when Sophie returned to Conflans in late September 1845 she heard that the marriages, arranged by Eugénie de Gramont in the rue de Varenne, had been celebrated in the school chapel.[21] However, Sophie had put up with enough rudeness and flouting of her authority and was now determined to finally show her hand. Besides her conversations with Lambruschini had shown her that fifteen years of criticism had to be addressed if only to show that she was the superior general of the Society.

Sophie left Rome in early June. During her stay she had met Gregory XVI twice and he called at the Villa Lante some days before she left the city, wishing her well and offering her gifts.[22] Sophie travelled with Adèle Cahier, Marie Patte, and a novice, Pauline Perdrau. Louise de Limminghe travelled with them for the first part of the journey, as far as St Elpidio and Lorette. After that Sophie and her companions continued north, visiting Parma and Turin. Sophie herself visibly relaxed when travelling and the four had a pleasant time together, with Giorgio, the driver, daily mapping out the stages of the journey.[23] On her arrival at Turin Anna du Rousier told her that Louis Barat had died on 21 June 1845. He had suffered from acute dropsy greatly during the last six months of his life. His legs were so swollen that he was confined to an armchair, day and night. In that context, Sophie could only be relieved that his pain was over.[24] Sophie asked to have a quiet day alone, to take in what had happened. No doubt she thought over their life together, first in Joigny and then in Paris. She remembered the early days of the Society when Louis supported the communities and wrote treatises and songs for them. She knew how he felt about the rue de Varenne. He had encouraged the ultramontane party in the Society. How much did Sophie know of Elizabeth Galitzine's and Louise de Limminghe's letters to Louis? Did she feel betrayed, undermined by him at the most difficult moment in her life? We shall never know. Six years after Louis' death Stanislas wanted to write a life of his uncle and he asked Sophie to get some information for him from the Jesuits. Sophie refused, saying that even though he wrote works of spiritual depth Louis's preaching style was poor and his thought was difficult to follow. Besides his life was a hidden one, spent mostly in the confessional.[25]

After spending a day alone Sophie continued her visits in Turin, proceeding to Genoa, Marseilles, Aix, Montpellier and Lyon. After a time in Lyon, Sophie set off on the final stage of her journey back to Paris, visiting Besançon, Montet, Kientzheim, Nancy and Metz, and she arrived in Conflans on 17 September 1845. Content with her stay in Rome and with her visits to the houses of the Society en route, Sophie set about dealing with the rue de Varenne almost immediately. This promised to be difficult. In two letters to Sophie Eugénie de Gramont had made it clear to Sophie that she would resist any encroachment on her territory. Sophie asked her why she resented even the least steps to reform the school and community. She reminded Eugénie that she had faithfully supported her in the rue de Varenne, over many years, perhaps too many years:

> You know that it is difficult to discuss certain matters with you, and that of the coadjutrix sisters is one of them . . . I have endured abuses at reception in the rue de Varenne, and in the running of the boarding school. I have certainly spoken enough about them to you! . . . I would be so happy to work in harmony with you and for us to work together to perfect the task which has been given you by the Heart of Jesus . . . Why can we not work together to restore the public opinion by removing the reasons [for criticism]. We will not succeed in this if I remove you from the rue de Varenne, but by strengthening the bond of union between us. . . . If I had to remove you nothing would give me more pain. Believe me that if this should happen it would be completely against my wishes and only through demand of duty! But believe me there are still certain abuses and accurate reports which you neither wish to accept nor to remedy. . . . If we do not apply remedies your house will founder completely and what grief for both of us who have worked there for so many years.
> It is such beautiful weather. Will you not come to see us?[26]

Eugénie did not go to Conflans to see Sophie, a tactic she had often used with Sophie. A month later Sophie wrote to Lambruschini in December 1845, giving him an account of the Society in general and of the rue de Varenne in particular. She admitted that so far she had been unable to make any impact on Eugénie de Gramont, and explained that she was trying to deal with the situation in such a way that worse consequences would not ensue.[27] Sophie gave Lambruschini no hint of the confrontation she had with Eugénie de Gramont or the subsequent letters of recrimination she had received. Nor did she go into detail about the problems in the school regarding chaplains. Archbishop Affre continued to forbid the Jesuits to act as chaplains, or in any spiritual capacity whatsoever, in the schools and communities.[28] In Sophie's view, the secular clergy whom Affre appointed to the rue de Varenne and to Conflans were not suitable. She told the archbishop that working in a school like the rue de Varenne, and ministering to a noviceship community, were both quite different from working in a parish. And while Affre admitted that his appointments were not satisfactory, this did not make relations any easier with him.[29] When she asked him, again, to remove a chaplain from the rue de Varenne, Affre was predictably furious and subjected Sophie to a stormy interview.[30]

During this period Eugénie de Gramont and Archbishop Affre also maintained an extensive, often combative, correspondence over the question of the appointment of chaplains. Until Affre's appointment in 1840 Eugénie de Gramont had usually presented the names of those priests she wanted as chaplains in the rue de Varenne, and Archbishop de Quelen had appointed them. Like Sophie, she too had asked Archbishop Affre to appoint Jesuits to the school, at least for retreats and special days in the year, but he refused. Another source of tension between Sophie and the archbishop was the proposal in March 1846 to hold a canonical visitation of the houses of the Society in Paris. Sophie resisted this and asked that Fr Gaume, who had been appointed the ecclesiastical superior of the houses in Paris and Conflans, not carry it out. Archbishop Affre was predictably furious and insisted that the abbé Gaume carry it out. All Sophie could do in the circumstances was hope that it would dispel the false reputation of the rue de Varenne.[31]

Earlier in the year Sophie had received a letter from Lambruschini, in response to hers, sent before Christmas 1845. He had been taken aback at Sophie's letter in December 1845, saying that she had not yet dealt with Eugénie de Gramont and her leadership at the rue de Varenne. His letter was brusque and he insisted that she execute the plan she had discussed with him in Rome. However, in view of Eugénie's outright resistance to any change, as well as the difficulties with the school chaplains, Sophie had not raised the subject with her since their last interview on the subject in October 1845.[32] In addition Sophie had become ill again after Christmas and was confined to bed for six weeks. Once she had recovered enough energy she explained the impossible situation to Lambruschini, remarking that she could no more in the circumstances. He replied quickly, assuring her that she had lost nothing of his esteem for her personally, nor did he underestimate the extent of the difficulties she was facing.[33] Indeed, Lambruschini had not forgotten that when he left Paris in 1830 it was he who had written to Archbishop de Quelen asking him personally to take special care of Eugénie de Gramont:

> she is a worthy person and I recommend her to you in full confidence, as a soul dear to God and requiring in her difficult position the sound advice and practical guidance of her holy pastor . . .[34]

In that context he had a certain responsibility for the situation. He also remembered the struggles which he and Gregory XVI had had with Archbishop de Quelen. Sophie was dealing with the final stages of an old problem. Lambruschini's letter arrived in Conflans in early July and Sophie sent it straightaway to Eugénie in the rue de Varenne, with an accompanying note:

> I wrote a letter to you this morning which will have distressed you. However, I hope you will understand my reasons for this and that you will not be too upset to live for some time with someone who you know is deeply and sincerely attached

to you. Please drop me a line to say that you got the very disturbing letter from the cardinal and even send it back to me. I want to burn it so that no one will ever know of its existence. . . . [35]

Eugénie responded immediately, upset at the letters from Lambruschini and Sophie. She was taken aback at the calumnies contained in the letter and she threatened to leave the rue de Varenne completely. Sophie reminded her that there were some grounds for the criticisms, though undoubtedly they were exaggerated. Sophie repeated that she was going to take up residence in the rue de Varenne and that she was appointing Emma de Bouchaud as headmistress of the school, to replace Aimée d'Avenas.[36] Over the next few weeks the relationship between Sophie and Eugénie was strained. Again and again Sophie asked Eugénie to trust her and to accept that she would not have asked for changes in the rue de Varenne unless they were really needed. Sophie reminded Eugénie that their relationship had always proved difficult for others to accept:

> For years I have been aware of a kind of jealousy which simmered against us. I did little about it. It was only general remarks, nothing was specified. But for the last two or three years facts, exaggerated of course, have been cited. They are believed and accepted, to our general discredit. It is a trial which we must bear with resignation, but I think we have to work at removing all the grounds for criticism . . . Oh! if you only knew how much I suffer from all that I hear and above all from your own grief . . . [37]

In July 1846 Sophie arrived in the rue de Varenne, to begin a formal visit of the house. She was accompanied by Emma de Bouchaud the new headmistress of the boarding school. Both Eugénie de Gramont and Aimée d'Avenas had been aware of the coming changes since the spring of 1845, when Sophie had written to them from Rome. For some time communication between Eugénie de Gramont and Aimée d'Avenas had been strained and this made Sophie's task of removing Aimée d'Avenas as headmistress somewhat easier. That summer she asked d'Avenas to visit the schools at Jette, Lille, Amiens and Beauvais and on her return to Paris, she would be put in charge of the studies only in the rue de Varenne.[38]

All Sophie's plans could not be implemented immediately. An epidemic broke out in the school and community the week she arrived and she spent the month of August waiting until all had sufficiently recovered. She noted that there was general goodwill in the house and she was relieved that her arrival had not been blocked by Eugénie de Gramont.[39] While Lambruschini had made it clear that he wanted Eugénie de Gramont removed from the rue de Varenne, Sophie was unwilling to take that step. It would bring public comment and condemnation on Sophie herself and on the Society and it would be a crushing blow for Eugénie de Gramont.[40] The arrival of Sophie, and her announcement of a prolonged visitation and her determination to act as the superior of the house, signalled change. When the school reopened in September, Sophie was living in the rue de Varenne, and while she did not say in public that she had taken over as superior from Eugénie de Gramont, her presence alone made that clear to the community.

In some way, Eugénie de Gramont realised her power had gone and she became ill in the autumn of 1846. She deteriorated rapidly and by Christmas 1846, despite every effort to cure her, Sophie realised that Eugénie was dying. This friendship which had cost her so much energy and concern, which had nurtured and enriched her powers of loving, was slipping away from her. Those who watched Sophie during the final stages of Eugénie de Gramont's illness admired the love and care she showed her old friend. She was constantly at her bedside, trying to alleviate her pain and moral suffering. Eugénie kept apologising to Sophie for all the pain she had caused her over the years. Sophie kept assuring her that it was all over and that she should let it go, that all was forgiven. Eugénie died during the night of 19 December 1846 at the age of fifty-seven.

The news of Eugénie de Gramont's death was an event in Paris and the daily papers printed long death notices, full of praise and admiration for this remarkable woman.[41] The funeral arrangements were taken over by the members of Eugénie's family. They made out the invitations to the funeral at the rue de Varenne and arranged that musicians from the Paris Conservatoire would play at the funeral Mass. Sophie was not consulted about the arrangements and when she found the orchestra in the chapel ready to play for the Mass she could do nothing about it. Sophie could not bring herself to greet the family after the service. She knew well their opinion of her and preferred to return to her room.[42] For many years now the family of Eugénie de Gramont and the residents of the Faubourg Saint-Germain had known that Sophie did not agree with Eugénie's manner of running the school. They had been aware of her difficulty with Archbishop de Quelen's residence in the rue de Varenne, with the residence of Fr Jammes in the Petit-Hôtel and with Eugénie de Gramont's marriage bureau for the young couples of Paris. One of the obituaries published in the newspapers contained scarcely veiled criticism of Sophie Barat.[43] Strange indeed if she had approved of the manner in which the obsequies of her friend were observed, when she was not consulted about them.[44]

Sophie herself commented on the significance of Eugénie de Gramont in the evolution of the Society of the Sacred Heart. In 1818 Sophie had chosen Eugénie to be headmistress of the school in Paris, because she knew that with her aristocratic background she would draw pupils from French noble families and from the higher middle class. Eugénie was necessary to Sophie's strategy; Eugénie de Gramont marketed the Society of the Sacred Heart, not just in Paris but in Europe and abroad. Through her friendship with Archbishop de Quelen Eugénie gained access to the French bishops and the power of those contacts was revealed in the crisis which followed the 1839 general council. Had the decrees not been abolished, the rue de Varenne, with the support of the French bishops, would have separated from the rest of the Society and possibly taken many houses with it.[45]

For good or ill, Eugénie de Gramont was one of the keystones in the foundation of the Society of the Sacred Heart and her life had been given to the house and the school in Paris. Sophie appreciated this and remained affectionately attached to a woman who had caused her immense personal grief and sorrow. She had always defended Eugénie from all criticism. When Anna du Rousier told her the nuncio in Turin thought that superiors in the Society were too worldly Sophie rejected this completely. But she recognised who was the focus of the criticism. She told Anna du Rousier that only one house in the Society gave the appearance of wealth, for it was in the heart of the Faubourg Saint-Germain:

> But Madame de Gramont is far from enjoying the trappings of grandeur which are due to the locality and to the type of pupil confided to the school by divine Providence . . . No one is more religious than Madame de Gramont. In all that concerns herself she lives a poor, even austere life-style. . . . She has such a scant regard for her noble birth that she never speaks about it . . .[46]

Years later, in 1858, when one of her cousins in Joigny told Sophie he had met a member of the de Gramont family, Sophie's memory came alive. She spoke warmly of the de Gramont family and confessed:

> I still cannot get used to the death of Madame Eugénie de Gramont, who was so dear to me and so indispensable in helping us provide education for our pupils in Paris where she was both superior and headmistress.[47]

Sophie was faithful to all her friends, most of all to Eugénie. In 1847 she remarked to Thérèse Maillucheau:

> among my few and feeble virtues, or maybe among my failings, constancy is perhaps the most notable.[48]

On 23 December 1846 Sophie wrote to Aimée d'Avenas, then staying briefly at Le Mans, and told her that she had returned to the rue de Varenne from a brief stay in Conflans the previous evening:

> . . . what a void I found. This morning I had the strength to gather the community. . . . I announced that the house would henceforth be the residence of the superior general . . . This arrangement will hold until the next General Council.[49]

While Sophie mourned Eugénie, she spoke frankly to the community and told them why she had moved from Conflans to the rue de Varenne. She had taken the reins into her own hand and intended to make changes in the school. Her presence in the house would not be forever as she thought a mother house should stand on its own and not be part of a school.[50] Sophie was free now to tell the community much more about the pain of the years 1839–43:

> I must tell you some facts . . . Gregory XVI was very much in favour of our mother house being in Rome. But obstacles arose when the French government was informed. . . . After much debate it was concluded that the mother house would be in Paris . . . Being the superior general I ought to be superior of the house here too. But Mother de Gramont loved this house where she had spent so many years and I did not wish to grieve her. So I left her in charge.[51]

Yet at the last moment, Sophie had walked into Eugénie's empire and taken it from her. She had done it before death took Eugénie away, and that was important for Sophie's peace of mind and integrity. Her colleagues watched her do it and the news travelled. What Sophie had done by letter in America and by visits to Rome had now been accomplished by taking up residence in the rue de Varenne: Sophie Barat had re-established her authority and her leadership was no longer under question. Many thought the rue de Varenne would fall apart when Eugénie de Gramont died.[52] Rather it took on another form of life and Sophie stayed there as long as was necessary to see it through. She would do the same for the Society as a whole, planning to resign at the next general council in 1851.

In the midst of so much turmoil within the Society, and at a time of great personal stress and loss, Sophie continued to monitor the plans for foundations, those recently begun and those in process of negotiation. She was particularly interested in the project of a foundation in Spain, at Sarria, near Barcelona, and with the expansion into Austria by the foundation at Gratz, and with the foundation of Blumenthal on the borders of Holland and Prussia. The foundations in Louisiana and Canada, as well as the transfer there of some works to more suitable premises, were a source of regular comment in her letters to Aloysia Hardey, Maria Cutts and Bathilde Sallion. In France she paid particular attention to the foundations at Bourges, Rennes, Montfleury, La Neuville at Amiens and the transfer from Tours to Marmoutier.[53] Certainly there was no question of the demand for the Society of the Sacred Heart in France, in Europe, in the Americas and north Africa. As Sophie had said many times, she received more invitations for foundations than she could ever respond to positively.

She continued to be preoccupied by three issues, vital to the life of the Society: the formation of the members, the quality of education in the schools, and good financial practice. While the works of the Society were expanding all the time, Sophie was concerned with the drop in vocations in the late 1830s and early 1840s. She knew that the number of those entering was not sufficient to maintain the works and initiate new ones. However by 1846 she noted that the noviciate in Conflans was growing again. There were now twenty-nine novices. However, to maintain all the works of the Society and start new ones, Sophie estimated that the Society needed to have fifty novices in Conflans, fifty novices in la Ferrandière, and one hundred more in the other noviciates of the Society, in Rome, Montet and St Michael's.[54]

After the death of Eulalie de Bouchaud in May 1844 Sophie reappointed Félicité Desmarquest as mistress of novices. While the number of novices had decreased in the Society, the number of deaths had increased and Sophie constantly mourned the death of those on whom she had counted for leadership and responsibility. Tragically, these deaths occurred during the troubled period of 1839–46, and were of immense loss at a time when Sophie needed colleagues and friends in government. She realised then that a whole new generation of leaders would have to be formed. The original circle of friends was almost empty as she lamented to Thérèse Maillucheau, then at Bourges.[55]

With regard to formation Sophie once again asked superiors to examine carefully all those who wished to enter the Society. She lamented the poor judgement shown by all in leadership in the Society, including herself, in accepting those who did not really have a vocation to the religious life. This applied to the choir religious and in Sophie's view even more to the coadjutrix religious. So many women had been accepted indiscriminately and then had to be sent away after several years in the Society. Sophie herself found it painful when she had to send many choir and sister religious away herself.[56] This turned priests and families against the Society. It was a bad public profile. She reminded the superiors of the houses that the number of coadjutrix sisters in any given community always be less than the choir religious.[57] A year later, December 1845, Sophie returned to the question and asked that the Society follow the model of the Jesuits. In the Jesuit community the brothers composed one-third of the members and the priests two-thirds. Sophie pointed out again that the Society had not achieved this balance and in some houses the number of sisters exceeded that of the choir religious.[58] Sophie cited the example of Teresa of Avila, who maintained strict criteria for entry to Carmel. If she had doubts over those who presented themselves she

> excluded them mercilessly from her order . . . She did not have the requirement of education that we have, which demands a special selection, even among the coadjutrix sisters who often work with the children. It would be good if this examination and weeding-out process was done during the time of noviceship, to avoid the serious problems which follow from release from vows . . . In some more religious countries, release from vows leaves a taint which is like a life long dishonour for these women.[59]

In 1839 Sophie had suggested that the coadjutrix sisters have a longer period of formation and that they make simple profession. This had caused a great deal of criticism at the time and since, from all quarters. From her own experience of government, Sophie held the view that too many women had been accepted as coadjutrix sisters in the Society and that many had not had sufficient preparation to allow them to make a real choice for religious life. She questioned their motivation and the judgement of the superiors who accepted them into the Society. In this Sophie was a woman of her time and accepted the class divisions and distinctions as given. Even within her own family, except for a short period in the 1820s, Sophie did not try to push them beyond their social position. In the Society it was a question of having the kind of women who could either take part in the teaching life of the Society and so be designated choir religious; or take part in the domestic life of the community and school and be designated coadjutrix sisters. No doubt Sophie was demanding with anyone who would not work hard. Her own work ethic was stringent, and well established since her childhood.

On a broader level, in the nineteenth century religious life was seen by some as a form of social promotion. For some women it offered scope and independence, for others it provided adventure and freedom from married life. For others, life was harsh and demanding and religious life could offer some security and comfort. Sophie Barat would have no difficulty with mixed motivations as

long there was positive, religious commitment. For these reasons she continually stressed the need to discern vocations carefully. The process of leaving the
Society after final profession meant applying to the pope for dispensation from
vows, a long procedure which often led to acrimony which Sophie wanted to
avoid. As she wrote to Thérèse Maillucheau:

> Yes . . . these women with little religious spirit, with only half-vocation do us harm!
> Please pay attention to this. Until my dying day this will be my *'delenda Cartago'*!
> I will close all my letters with this.[60]

While Sophie was concerned about the quality of commitment among the
professed of the Society and demanded high standards for entry, she also called
for high standards among the membership who persevered. In February 1844
she wrote a letter to the Society, repeating many points she had made over the
years. In the light of the stormy experience of 1839–43 they were made with new
vigour. She asked the members to reflect on their relationship with God; she
asked them to look at how they thought, acted and reacted in their relationships
with one another, with their leaders, and how they fulfilled the tasks for which
they were responsible. She listed questions for the communities to answer themselves, and made a strong call to all to trust leadership and most of all to trust her.
Sophie put her challenge in the context of why each one had originally entered
the Society and she invited the members to make a fresh start.[61]

The following year she wrote again to the Society and asked each one to
look at her life and to ask herself how she mediated her commitment to
Christ.[62] The Society of the Sacred Heart was often criticised for the arrogant
tone and independent manner of some of the members. Sophie acknowledged
that some of this criticism was exaggerated and knew well that many of the
clergy resented the independent spirit of the Society, yet she had enough
material to warrant that some of it was well merited. Since its foundation, the
Society of the Sacred Heart had chosen to educate two groups: the elite and
the poor. Sophie consistently asked that, in the education given in the elite
schools of the Society, responding to the needs of the poor was presented as a
social, Christian responsibility. That was the package which Sophie and her
colleagues had designed and developed. However, the fact that the Society
educated within an elite milieu and drew many vocations from wealthy families, meant that the ways and manners of society were often prevalent in the
communities. Sophie did not critique that as such. She did critique how the
members behaved in the Society when they had entered, for then they had
taken on the commitment to live the values of the gospel. She appealed to that
basic choice, which each one had made initially and she invited all to respond
to the love of God as revealed in the Heart of Christ. She assured them that
they would experience great personal happiness and they would find what
they needed to fulfil their vocation. She reminded each one that this was
something much more difficult than most realised and how easy it was to get
caught in darkness and negativity, a form of hell. Finally, she assured them that

by their lives and service, they would make an impact on their world and help to regenerate Christian values in society.[63]

In this connection, Sophie was concerned about the standard of education in the schools. She had heard complaints about poorly trained teachers and badly taught students. She warned that, if this continued, the other teaching congregations as well as the schools run by lay people would take pupils way from the Society. The task of education, of teaching, required endless hard work, and Sophie suggested that there lay true self-giving and sacrifice. The studies had to be of a high standard and she had long hoped to establish a type of teacher-training course for the young teachers. While this had not yet been realised she intended to ask one or two members of the Society to travel around the schools to help the teachers in their work and examine how the plan of studies was being implemented:

> This weakness is all the greater since we believe in conscience that we must refuse to be inspected by the University. If we weaken in the art of teaching we provide ammunition to be used against us. That is what happened in one of the towns of France where the parents were the first to arouse the interest of the inspectors, telling them that we needed their inspections.[64]

Coming to a theme which threads through her life and thought, Sophie asked the teachers to look at the quality of their reflection, of their capacity to live in silence and take the space and time to find a rhythm of work. If they could establish and retain that, they would work well and deeply and hard. She accepted that many were overworked and yet she challenged them to organise their time better. They would be surprised how they could find more time for both prayer and study. If they achieved that they would discover God in this experience:

> Nothing blocks the Spirit of God as much as a life of idleness. How do those who neither work nor study pass their time? With nothing regular or useful to do, chatting idly, running here and there . . . they spend their time watching all that happens, allowing free reign to their imagination.[65]

The question of finance was never far from Sophie's mind and rarely absent in her letters. In March 1844 she wrote a supplement to her letter of the previous month and in it she expressed her concern about the financial state of the Society. The debts were great and the interest the Society was paying on loans was too high. Yet she noticed that many houses had several works of charity which drew on the resources of the houses and prevented them paying the usual tenth part of their income to the central fund of the Society. One of the most serious sources of economic loss was the number of pupils who were educated free. Often the school was run at such a deficit that the maintenance of the house was affected and central funds were requested. Again in the houses where there were orphanages, often the numbers accepted were far beyond the resources of the house or of the patrons to sustain. This was unjust as much to the orphans as to the other works of the house. She warned that soon she would require from every house a list of those in the schools and orphanages who were being cared for gratis. The number of free pupils had to be restricted, for economic reasons, and Sophie suggested the criteria should be either the nieces of the members of the Society, or the children of the poor nobility. She had enough experience of her own nieces to be able to say:

> not that we make exception of persons. But because we have had the sad experience that our type of education does more harm than good to a young person destined by her position, or that of her parents, to marry within her own class, or to work in a shop and sometimes to earn her own living. One can easily see what is the effect of our education on them. It burdens them, or it makes them lazy; many cannot make use of the lessons received, lacking the capacity to do so.[66]

Sophie spoke frankly about the debts in the Society which had to be addressed. In 1844 the debt stood at 600,000 francs and the central fund was empty. The most the Society was able to do was pay the interest on the loans taken out to pay the debts. It was a precarious position to be in. Sophie warned that if there was a revolution, the properties of the Society would lose their value and bankruptcy would follow. The Society's debts had to be cleared as a matter of urgency. To this purpose Sophie asked that the houses refrain from building, from acquiring property or from buying any major items. She asked that the houses try to help each other out in order to lessen debt. The central fund had to be replenished and Sophie asked that each house aim at paying its tenth again or even a part of it until its own debt was cleared. Without central funds, new foundations could not take place and the Society's mission could dry up quickly. Sophie reminded the members that her recommendations were not new, she had made them many times over the years. She referred to past circulars on the question of financial responsibility.[67] Sophie then addressed the question of the disposable income of the members of the Society. Those who received money in the form of rents or gifts were invited to retain the first 1000 francs of the money (for use in the house where they lived) and to give the rest to the central fund of the Society. All who received legacies of money were reminded that these belonged without exception to the central fund and not to the individual house where the member of the Society lived. In letters to the houses Sophie had already suggested a sum of money which should be sent to the central fund that year. She admitted that she had decided this without consultation and that despite some criticism she would maintain it. The next general council could confirm or modify her decision.[68]

By concentrating on the key issues of the formation of the members, the quality of education and the centralisation of financial resources Sophie firmly gathered the reins of her leadership. She did not wait for a general council to legislate on the key elements which had to be addressed, for she knew that until relations with Archbishop Affre were resolved she could hold the council neither in Paris nor outside of Paris. When she was in Rome in 1845 she had recognised that for the time being she was forced to govern alone. Among her assistants general Sophie could only trust Henriette Coppens. Catherine de Charbonnel, Félicité Desmarquest, Louise de Limminghe and Elizabeth Galitzine opposed her in 1842–43. She also knew that from 1843 Desmarquest, de Limminghe and Galitzine had decided on a common plan to wait until the general council of 1845 and then press once again for the adoption of the 1839 decrees by the Society. Elizabeth Galitzine's death had dealt that plan a blow, and Sophie's visit to Rome in 1845 had lessened Louise de Limminghe's influence there.

Working together in Paris was not easy for any of them and Sophie consulted much less than she used to prior to 1839. Both the circumstances outside the Society's control and the experience of betrayal by her colleagues pushed Sophie towards a form of government which became increasingly more individual and apparently more autocratic. It was the opposite of what she had chosen, worked for and nurtured in the early part of her leadership. But now she was old and tired, without the structures she had hoped to introduce into the Society in 1839. Moreover, Catherine de Charbonnel, who was still officially the treasurer general, had become almost totally blind. She needed to be relieved of her responsibility but that had to wait until a general council. By necessity, therefore, Sophie had to make decisions over financial affairs and train others for that responsibility.[69]

By 1847, Sophie felt able to write to Lambruschini in a positive manner about the Society. She felt that the wounds of division were beginning to heal:

> Hearts have been reconciled and the painful effects which the unfortunate affairs of 1842 and 43 had left are gradually receding. There remains, however, a certain uneasiness which only a General Council can dispel. . . . [However] the negative attitude of authority [Archbishop Affre] has blocked the convening of this assembly . . . [70]

However, if the Society was ready for a general council, Sophie could see no hope of holding one in the immediate future. She was 'harassed and badgered once again by the one you know [Archbishop Affre]'.[71] As Sophie had foreseen, political events overtook the Society. Rumblings and unrest in Europe broke out into revolution in 1848 and 1849.[72] Several houses of the Society were forced to close and did not reopen: Turin, Pignerol, Saluces and Genoa. Garibaldi took over the Villa Lante for a time; Sainte Rufine was threatened. Both communities moved to the Trinité, which the French ambassador offered as an asylum for all the French families living in Rome. Sophie may have hoped that this would help bring the communities together. The tense relations which continued to exist between them weighed heavily on her.[73] Lemberg was closed for a year. Following three years of pressure from the canton authorities, Montet in Switzerland was closed in 1848. The revolution broke out in Paris in February 1848.[74] Sophie decided not to disperse the communities though she sent home the younger members of the Society whose families lived in the city. When Louis-Philippe abdicated she remarked in the rue de Varenne that it was a question of *déjà vu*.[75] Sophie had been through revolution so many times in her life but this did not make it any easier. She admitted in 1848 that the singing of the 'Marseillaise' had brought back the painful memories of the Terror in 1793.[76]

The rue de Varenne was not attacked but on at least two occasions severely wounded soldiers asked for help. They were nursed back to health, their families informed and welcomed for visits. An officer of the National Guard sent Sophie the formal thanks of the wounded and their families.[77] When a troop of soldiers arrived at the rue de Varenne, to plant a tree of liberty in front of the Hôtel Biron, Sophie negotiated with them. While she had a tree dug up in the garden, the soldiers were to dig a hole in the front of the Hôtel Biron where they could then plant it in the name of liberty. She gave them a good supply of wine, bread and cheese. By evening a mulberry tree had been planted in the rue de Varenne and the soldiers left the property well satisfied with their work.[78] Sophie also offered to educate six girls who had lost their parents during the Revolution in February and this was acknowledged in the press.[79]

The unrest in Paris intensified in June 1848. While trying to mediate at the barricades Archbishop Affre was fatally wounded by crossfire. It was not a deliberate attack on the church, rather a tragic accident. He did not die immediately and had time to send personal messages of farewell. He sent his apologies to Sophie Barat and expressed his regret for the manner in which he had treated her over the years.[80] His death ended a turbulent, difficult relationship for Sophie. It also saved her from making a serious decision. Archbishop Affre had made her life impossible since 1840 and she could see no end to this harassment. He was a relatively young man, in good health and could live for many years. Sophie had concluded that if she could not get the spiritual help which the communities and the schools needed in Paris, the Society would have to leave the diocese of Paris. She had prepared a statement for Archbishop Affre in which she outlined the ministerial services the Society of the Sacred Heart had received in Paris from the Jesuits since its origins. Since the archbishop had forbidden the Jesuits to minister in the communities and schools Sophie decided that she had the responsibility to seek such support in another diocese.[81]

Archbishop Affre's death released Sophie in another way. It meant that Sophie could begin thinking of holding a general council of the Society. However, even had she wished to hold a council immediately, revolutions in Europe prevented her convening one that year and again in 1849, when the papal states were undergoing profound upheaval and change.[82] Only in 1850 did Sophie consider the time had come at last to hold the general council postponed since 1845. Before convening it she decided to visit Lambruschini in Rome and discuss with him the modifications she still needed to make to the government structures of the Society. It was the year of jubilee and the year in which she dearly hoped to resign her responsibilities as superior general.

− 22 −

A STEADY PACE, 1850−1865

S ophie Barat was seventy-one in 1850 and she had been superior general for forty-six years. Her original stepping forth into the future dated from 21 November 1800 and the Society of the Sacred Heart had taken Sophie's commitment that day as the founding impulse which led to the birth of the Society. Certainly on 21 November 1800 neither Sophie nor her companions could foresee their personal and collective journeys, how life would unfold, what hurdles they would encounter. Sophie emerged gradually as the leader. Her authority was affirmed, tested over many years and finally accepted by the general body of the Society in 1851. It was a slow process, for Sophie's style of government was mediated in terms of friendship rather than invoked by virtue of role or authority. By 1850, however, Sophie had had a prolonged experience of the shadow side of her leadership. While her style of government tended to be inclusive and to engender trust, it allowed a great deal of scope to others in the Society, for personal growth and for decision making. The very expansion of the Society demanded that the women be strong, independent characters, capable of taking responsibility. This led to the building-up of personal bases of power which sometimes lost touch with the personal charisma of Sophie Barat. It was that gap which Sophie sought to address when she wished to establish a form of government which would ensure stability, interdependence and unity. The conflicts within the Society did not allow her to achieve her goal then but they certainly confirmed her conviction that she must persevere.

By the spring of 1850 Pope Pius IX had returned to Rome after several months of exile in Gaeta. This was a signal for Sophie that it was time to set out for Rome and resolve finally the structural imbalances in the Society's plan of government. She intended to present to the pope certain clauses for inclusion in the constitutions of the Society. Once this had been accepted she would be ready to convene a general council of the Society and propose that the clauses be formally adopted by the Society. However, before she left Paris Sophie had a visit to make to the cradle of the Society, Amiens. For some years the chaplain there, Fr de Brandt (1812–1903), had exercised progressively more influence in the community.[1] While Adelaide de Rozeville was superior this had not created difficulties, since she was a strong leader in the house and had long experience. Indeed when Archbishop Affre had forbidden the Society in Paris to have Jesuits as confessors or retreat givers Sophie herself had asked the abbé de Brandt to minister in Conflans.[2] However, Adelaide de Rozeville's health began to deteriorate after 1845 and in November 1847 Sophie had to find a new superior for the house. She chose Angélique de Boisbaudry.[3] She was the mistress of novices at Conflans with little experience of government. For some time she had been in poor health and Sophie hoped the change of air would help her. She appointed a new mistress of novices at Conflans, Josephine Gœtz, then thirty years of age and recently professed,[4] and Angélique de Boisbaudry went to Amiens. However, the combination of poor health and inexperience allowed the leadership in the house to be assumed by Fr Brandt. He achieved this with the collusion of several members of the community at Amiens who formed a coterie with him, not unlike that created formerly by St-Estève. Fr Brandt spent many hours of the day and night in Amiens with two or three members of the community, to such an extent that the rest of the community became suspicious of his presence there.[5] Sophie became aware of the situation through letters from within and without the community.

In November 1849 Louis Sellier, Sophie's old friend and critic, wrote to her expressing his concern at events at Amiens.[6] He sensed that the community was distressed and that the quality of religious life was being eroded. He had recommended a young woman to enter the Society as a coadjutrix sister and she had begun in Amiens in good heart. Although she had far too much work to do, this was not the source of her complaints. She was disappointed at the lack of commitment in the house at Amiens to a life of prayer and to serious work. She wanted to stay in the Society but needed a fervent community life to support her and to challenge her.[7] Alerted by this letter Sophie made some enquiries. She learnt that in recent years Fr Brandt and a little group in the community had planned the reform of the Society of the Sacred Heart. In 1850 de Brandt preached about this publicly in Amiens around the time of the feast of the Sacred Heart and he assured his hearers that the successor to Sophie Barat had already been chosen. He had also contacted houses of the Society in Paris, Bordeaux, Niort and Toulouse, telling the communities that he had the full confidence of Sophie Barat, who was behind all his ideas for a reform, and that she had entrusted him with a certain, most important task.[8]

In July 1850 Sophie asked Catherine de Charbonnel to travel to Amiens and find out exactly what was going on there. Sophie Dusaussoy accompanied Catherine de Charbonnel and she wrote an account of their visit.[9] She told her aunt that the house was full of mysterious silence and that no one would speak either to herself or to Catherine de Charbonnel. De Brandt had imposed the silence and he had told Catherine de Charbonnel that her visit was neither desired nor needed. However, by dint of perseverance Sophie Dusaussoy discovered that their plan was to force Sophie Barat to resign and have her replaced by either Emma de Bouchaud (1799–1863) or Olympe de Causans (1796–1867). De Brandt had already written new constitutions for the Society and he claimed his reform methods would be as dramatic as those of Luther in the sixteenth century.[10] Sophie decided that swift action was needed. Without warning either the bishop, the community or de Brandt, she arrived in Amiens with Marie Prevost and Adèle Cahier on 2 August 1850 and began a formal visit of the house immediately.[11] The report of her visit was comprehensive and severe. She decided to remove the superior and replace her with Esther d'Oussières (1799–1882). Until she could take up her position Sophie asked that Marie Prevost and Adèle Cahier remain in Amiens as a strong presence underlining Sophie's authority. While she was in Amiens Sophie met de Brandt and told him firmly of her plans for the house. He expected to see her again but Sophie returned to Paris on 15 August. She had left him in no doubt as to who was the superior general of the Society of the Sacred Heart. If anyone was to reform the Society of the Sacred Heart it would be Sophie Barat, not Fr Brandt.

Sophie's departure evoked an angry reaction from de Brandt and the storm broke when he met Marie Prevost. He accused Sophie Barat of disturbing the community, of visiting the house without his permission and making changes without his authority. She had no right to tell Marie Prevost to stay on in the house and he ordered her to leave. She refused to do so, saying that Sophie Barat had asked her to stay and that it was her incontestable right to make such a request of any member of the Society. He ordered her three times to leave the house and each time Marie Prevost replied negatively, raising her voice to make sure he could hear her. Realising that he could make no impression de Brandt stormed out of the room in rage, though, as Adèle Cahier remarked wryly, he had recovered himself sufficiently to take his breakfast.[12] De Brandt followed up this violent interview with a letter to Sophie, claiming that her visit had upset the house and in particular had distressed the ailing superior.[13] He also found Marie Prevost's manner both rude and insolent. Sophie replied in her usual calm rhetoric. She expressed surprise at his claim that her visit to Amiens had upset the community, and in particular the superior. After all, visiting communities was the normal business of a superior general. In all her life she could not remember seeing Marie Prevost ever behave badly or lose her temper. She was sure that de Brandt would admire her very real qualities. [14]

The following week Sophie wrote to the community at Amiens telling them that Angélique de Boisbaudry needed a complete rest in Paris and that, until the arrival of a superior, Marie Prevost would remain in the house.[15] The new superior, Esther d'Oussières (then at Besançon) was informed as to the nature of her task in Amiens and took up office there on 28 August 1850. The change in leadership in the community made no difference to Fr de Brandt, as he persisted in his claims over the house and over the Society of the Sacred Heart. In the summer Sophie had not asked the bishop to remove de Brandt; she now considered that this was necessary and by the end of the year de Brandt had been removed as chaplain by the bishop of Amiens.[16] This did not end his efforts to influence the Society of the Sacred Heart. He continued as chaplain to another religious community at Louvencourt until 1855 when, following similar difficulties, he was removed from there also.[17] While he was never forbidden to say Mass from 1856 until his death in 1872, he was forbidden to hear confessions. Some years later three members of the Society of the Sacred Heart, two from Amiens and one from Beauvais, with some members from the community at Louvencourt, left their respective congregations and formed a new community led by de Brandt. It was called the Reformed Society of the Sacred Heart.[18]

Sophie's visit to Amiens had delayed her departure for Rome but she was ready to set out in mid-October 1850, leaving Henriette Coppens in charge in the rue de Varenne and Félicité Desmarquest in Conflans. She wrote a short letter to the Society from La Ferrandière, explaining why she was going to Rome. Sophie made it clear it would be short visit and asked that all business correspondence be sent to Paris.[19] On 11 November Sophie and Marie Prevost embarked from Marseilles for Rome where they arrived on 16 November.[20] They went to the Villa Lante where preparations were afoot to celebrate the golden jubilee of the Society of the Sacred Heart on the 21 November. Sophie did not look forward to the jubilee of the Society with personal enthusiasm. She was tired and weary of struggling to establish unity and harmony within the communities. At the same time she was deeply concerned that she still had not managed to provide the Society with adequate structures of government. And with regard to her own, personal leadership, Sophie had just left France where she had experienced yet another effort to depose her. She had no doubt that de Brandt had a certain following in the Society though she knew that it had been diminished by her visit to Amiens in the summer. She had further reminders of her struggles in Rome and within the Society when Jean Rozaven visited Sophie on 17 November. He was now old and frail yet he called to see Sophie and offer his good wishes. No record tells of their actual meeting or of what was said. It was the first time they had met since 1841 and it was the last. He died on 2 April 1851.[21]

Any celebration of her leadership was a burden to Sophie and she was relieved to be away from Paris and from Amiens for 21 November, since both places were full of painful memories. The assistants general, with the approval of Sophie, had copies made of the picture of the Virgin Mary that was in the little chapel in Paris the day Sophie and her companions made their first commitment.[22] That was the focus Sophie wanted then, away from her personally and centred on the inner motivation which had led to that step and which had carried her and her colleagues into new spaces and new paths. Yet Sophie had to acknowledge the commemoration in Rome and on the eve of 21 November she spoke to the community for a time, expressing her feelings and recalling the early days of the Society. She spoke of Léonor de Tournély and Joseph Varin with affection. But she did not call either of them founders of the Society of the Sacred Heart. Instead, Sophie suggested that while other congregations had founders, who inspired the members to follow them, the Society of the Sacred Heart was different. A loving and compassionate God, revealed in the icon of the pierced Heart of Jesus Christ on the Cross at Golgotha, was the founding impulse of the Society of the Sacred Heart. There was the source and origin of the celebration of 21 November 1850. Sophie insisted on this throughout her conference and she cited the words of Christ: 'Learn from me for I am gentle and humble of heart.' The key to her thought lay in her conviction that in Christ all the energies of God were revealed and available to the members of the Society, who in turn would mirror this vitality in their own lives, in their communities and in their service to the world. That for Sophie was sanctity, that was the cause for celebration.[23]

The community in the Villa Lante were deeply moved by the conviction with which Sophie spoke and realised that she had really meant what she said, that she spoke in no sense out of a false humility. She had been at the centre of so much growth and success, so much failure and tragedy, so much humiliation and rejection, that when she came to the fifty years of the Society she could only make sense of it all by turning to the level of faith and conviction, to the primacy of the spiritual in all their lives. They went to sleep with this in their hearts. The following day was one of prolonged celebration and Sophie found it progressively more difficult. When the Jesuit general, Jean Roothan complimented her on the fifty years of leadership, remarking that it was rare to have a leader so long in office, Sophie replied wittily: 'That is no compliment to me . . . no one has been so well looked after!'[24]

However she appreciated the visit from Roothan and had occasion during her stay in Rome to ask his opinion on the negotiations with the congregation of bishops and regulars.[25] In the evening time a cleric came to the Villa Lante, for a ceremony of thanksgiving. He began to preach on the achievements of the Society and then to compliment Sophie Barat on her work. Sophie slipped out of the chapel and went to her room. Later on she asked Louise de Limminghe who the preacher was and when she learnt his name she asked that he would never be asked to return to the Villa Lante. She found that kind of adulation false and it disturbed Sophie to hear it.

After Christmas 1850 Sophie began her preparations for finally resolving the government problems of the Society. The cardinal protector, Lambruschini, was frail and ill and was not in Rome at this time. Sophie had no idea when Lambruschini could return to work and she decided to approach the pope directly and ask him to authorise modifications to the constitutions of the Society of the Sacred Heart. However, the pope refused to deal with the matter directly and requested Sophie to initiate the proceedings through the Society's cardinal protector, Lambruschini. By then Lambruschini had recovered health and was back at work in Rome. He was offended that Sophie had by passed him but after her explanations he agreed to present Sophie's wishes to the congregation of bishops and religious. Sophie could not take any short cuts around the required protocol. This did not disconcert her and she used her letter of apology to Lambruschini as an opportunity to outline once again what the Society needed for its long term good government:

> I know the general feeling in the Society and I tell you in all trust that I doubt the effects which half-measures would have at a time when all expect to see the Society established at last on solid and durable foundations. Indeed, I can only regard the exchange of [the name and office of] Visitors for Provincials as a half-measure.[26]

In her petition Sophie asked the pope to sanction three key changes to the structures of government of the Society of the Sacred Heart:

1. the division of the Society into geographical areas, to be called provinces and the appointment of provincials to govern them. Sophie specifically asked for provincials, not visitors, as the latter were a temporary appointment and the term was out of favour in France.
2. the abolition of the general council structure composed of twelve governing members of the Society, and its replacement by a general council composed of the superior general, the assistants general, the provincials and one or two professed members from each province of the Society.
3. the right of the superior general to nominate an interim successor, to govern the Society between the death of the superior general and the convocation of a general council which would elect her successor.[27]

Sophie was dismayed to hear in May that the members of the congregation had advised the pope to refuse her petition. They saw no good reason to change the government structure contained in the 1826 constitutions. Sophie said nothing publicly but Rome was a close-knit community and Pius IX heard that Sophie Barat was downcast at this refusal. He sent one of the members of the congregation, Mgr Lucciardi, to talk with her and find out from her personally what she viewed as the essential form of government for the Society.[28] In view of these conversations, the pope revoked the decision of the congregation, and appointed three cardinals to deliberate on Sophie Barat's petition and present their decision.

In the end, a compromise was reached. On 28 May a decree was issued, in reply to Sophie Barat's petition. The request to have provinces and provincials was refused. Instead the Society of the Sacred Heart was to be divided geographically into vicariates, with vicars named for life to govern them; the vicars would replace the council of twelve members. Sophie was authorised to name a vicar general who would replace her temporarily when she died, and govern the

Society until a general council met to elect a new superior general.[29] While it was not all that Sophie wanted it was sufficient and Sophie decided to convene a general council in the autumn. She left Rome on 14 June 1851. The visit to Rome had been much longer and more exhausting than she had anticipated and as soon as she reached Marseilles Sophie fell ill. It took her several months for her to recover enough energy to resume the task of implementing the decree granted in Rome.[30] She decided to call a general council in the autumn, to present the changes to the government structures and have them formally approved by the Society. She invited all those who had been appointed to visit areas of the Society in her name since 1839.[31]

From this group the general council would elect the assistants general. From it also, Sophie would appoint those who were to be the new vicars. Sophie decided that the best place to hold the general council was Lyon. She explained why to Alexis Gaume, the ecclesiastical superior of the Society in the diocese of Paris. Marie Dominique Auguste Sibour (1848–57), who succeeded Archbishop Affre in 1849, agreed that Lyon would be best, for the Society, away from the eyes of the government.[32] Although still frail from her illness, Sophie travelled to La Ferrandière and the general council opened there on 13 November, the first held in the Society since 1839. It was a businesslike affair with a large agenda, drawn up by Adèle Cahier and presented to the council at the opening session. From the outset Sophie indicated that there was no point in trying to get further concessions from Rome, though she did not hide her disappointment at the decree granted in Rome the previous May. The members accepted this and set to work. The council was divided into commissions for the constitutions, for studies and for formation. The findings of these commissions were deliberated in plenary sessions and decisions passed without acrimony.[33] Sophie was relieved and wrote two accounts of the proceedings to Lambruschini.[34]

She also wrote a long letter to the Society in which she expressed feelings long locked inside her. She expressed her sorrow at the loss of personal, individual contact with the membership in general, due in most part to the rapid expansion of the Society and the demands of administration.[35] Sophie explained why for some years she had stopped writing regular, circular letters to the Society. She passed over the difficulties with Archbishop Affre from 1843 to 1848 and merely remarked that she had continually hoped to convene a general council but was prevented by political events, in France first and then in the Papal States. Only when the general council had met to discuss and then adopt a form of government which she had negotiated with the pope and Lambruschini did Sophie feel ready to resume her formal letters to the members of the Society.[36]

Sophie's letter in December 1851 signalled that during the general council her own personal authority had been confirmed and that the body of the Society was united around her leadership. She gave the membership an account of the proceedings and invited each one to accept the outcome of the council. However, she saw the decisions taken were merely the outer form of the Society and so, before she gave the details, Sophie spoke to the inner, spiritual motivations of each member. Though probably few may have noticed, this part of her letter showed that Sophie had made an inner journey of immense significance for her and for the Society of the Sacred Heart. Her isolation, sense of betrayal, loss of friends, loss of reputation in a very public way had forced Sophie to stand alone. Her leadership had been in friendship and companionship and that had sustained her for many years and this had been severely tested for over ten years. The abyss which seemed so narrow and frightening had opened out into new, vast spaces which enlarged her heart and opened her to new dimensions. She had broken free of her old fetters and inner attachments which had both bound and trapped her. She had transformed her image of a Jansenist God to that of a warm, loving presence, the Heart of Christ. The years of encouragement from Fr Favre had prepared her for the years of isolation and rejection. All had borne their fruit. Now Sophie could live alone, with herself, with her God, and with the fruits of her life, both sweet and bitter to the taste.

One of the indications of the inner journey Sophie Barat had made between 1839 and 1851 was in the manner in which she renewed her relationship with Louise de Limminghe. While their meeting in Rome in 1845 had been tense and strained, by 1850 enough time had elapsed for both women to be able to meet again at some depth. It fell to Sophie to assure de Limminghe constantly that the past was over and that she trusted her. As a mark of this trust, in 1851 Sophie appointed Louise de Limminghe to be vicar of the Austrian houses. Now de Limminghe could leave Rome finally without a sense of being dismissed or demoted. However, it was at the inner level that Sophie revealed what had happened to her personally, what inner freedom she had reached. While Louise de Limminghe continued to be trapped by her anxieties and sense of inadequacy, Sophie urged her to move forward. She spoke to Louise de Limminghe in the terms Favre had used when Sophie struggled to inner freedom:

> . . . please, and I cannot repeat this too often, open out your soul, you hold your-
> self in a double stranglehold. Your faults, which are only sheer fragility upset you
> too much and constrain your heart! You must draw much more closely to the Heart
> of Jesus and not think about yourself. His glory, his work in people ought to be
> your dominant thought. A single disavowal of your failings is enough. Conserve all
> your powers of your soul for securing yourself in union and in love with Jesus!
> Believe that everything is useful for nurturing these virtues. It is like the way we
> throw dry wood, green wood, brambles and brushwood on the fire, . . . these mate-
> rials . . . feed the fire . . . and their nature is changed on account of the action of the
> fiery furnace! Jesus acts like that in our souls, if we surrender our being entirely to
> Him.[37]

Sophie reminded Louise de Limminghe of the times they had shared in Chambéry with Fr Favre, times that she looked back on now with nostalgia. She acknowledged that events since then had wounded their former friendship but that she wanted that relationship restored.[38] However, Sophie's life had changed and since she no longer could deal with all her correspondence she asked Louise de Limminghe not to use the intimate terms they had exchanged formerly.[39]

The amount of administrative work as well as her age, energy, and personal choice created a certain distance between Sophie and all members of the Society.

In her letter to the Society in December 1851 Sophie spoke of the Heart of Jesus as defender and protector from the wrath of God. While she could not remove the deeply embedded image of the father-God as an angry and dark presence, she had found in the human, wounded figure of Christ, suffering and risen from the dead, the bulwark against her own fears and frailties.[40] In the shade of that kind of love, pierced on the Cross, Sophie had found her peace. From there she spoke to the Society and asked the members to let themselves be touched by the oil of healing which came from the Heart of Christ. Convinced that more was done in the world by the quality of spiritual life than by words and good works, Sophie asked each one to look at her personal commitment to Christ and to the Society:

> You recognise that you will not achieve this renewal of love and devotion to the Sacred Heart of Jesus except by means of a deep inner life. A superficial, hollow person cannot understand the essence of this devotion, nor enter upon the path which leads to it.[41]

Turning to the work of the council Sophie did not hide that she was disappointed that the Society had not been allowed to adopt the structure of provinces with the office of provincials. But she asked all to accept the compromise of having vicariates with the office of vicars. She admitted that she did not know why Pius IX had refused her request to retain provinces/provincials. She knew that the Society had got used to those terms, for twelve years had elapsed since the general council had established them and now those terms were being changed. Sophie disingenuously remarked that it was merely a change in terms but that the realities remained. Characteristically she made the best of what she could not change and moved ahead with that into the future. She explained the other decisions of the council and wrote further letters to the vicars and to the local superiors.[42] She set about forming and shaping the unity of the Society after the long period of division and dissent. But she did it with good heart, sure finally that her leadership had been accepted by the general council without reservation. Forty-seven years since her election as superior general for life, Sophie Barat knew that her personal role had been ratified and that the Society was at peace with itself. This was her last major letter to the Society. In that sense it was her final statement about the community she had initiated and then nurtured over many years, in good and bad times. And when it was threatened with destruction, by forces from within and without the Society, Sophie had painfully found a path of reconciliation and peace.

She wrote to her old friend Césaire Mathieu, who understood well the importance of the council and would rejoice to hear that it had been a peaceful, positive experience:

I found a very good spirit among the members of the Council, there was complete union between them and with me. Then full acceptance of all that I thought necessary to consolidate the Society.[43]

This was the time when Sophie had planned to retire from office and pass on the responsibility to another. At the council she asked to be relieved of her role as superior general but the members refused even to consider it.[44] Sophie herself had become the focus for unity within the Society, she had become an icon, and she had yet to form the new leaders for the future. In her own mind she may have decided that for the sake of the unity of the Society she would continue in office. She may have looked around her and seen no one from the second generation of the Society capable of succeeding her. Perhaps she saw it as her destiny, as God's will for her. In 1853 Sophie wrote to Emma de Bouchaud:

What a life we have . . . and while we were young we thought that we would bury ourselves in a Carmelite monastery. The ways of God are unfathomable. I would always regret not going to Carmel if I did not have the assurance that God so designed it. But at least we must unite solitude to the work we do, and counter this whirlwind with a deep cavern where the soul can take refuge as often as possible. For us this cavern in the rock is the Heart of Jesus![45]

That task of formation would be carried out, as before, by letters and by visits. However, now the visits were from individual members of the Society to Paris to see Sophie. She travelled less and less and concentrated her energies on governing from her desk. Sophie's correspondence greatly increased in volume over these years and she relied on her letters to reach every country where the Society existed. Her health was permanently fragile. Most winters Sophie was confined to her room for two to three months, an annual hibernation, which gave her energy for the rest of the year. She had the help of Adèle Cahier whose method of work and efficiency established a continuity of correspondence and of information in the Society. Cahier had a secretariat which functioned well and by 1853 she had renewed the printing press, originally established in 1843, as well as the licence from the police to allow the Society to print its own material.[46]

All the while the Society continued to grow all over Europe and beyond. Foundations were made in France in Montfleury (1846);[47] La Neuville, near Amiens (1847); Marmoutiers (1849); Orleans (1851); Layrac (1851); in Moulins (1853); in St Brieuc (1854); in St Pierre les Calais (1854); in St Ferréol near Besançon (1856); in Angoulême (1856); in Lyon, Les Anglais (1859. In Prussia at Warendorf (1852). In England in Roehampton, London (1851). In Ireland in Armagh (1851) and in Dublin, Mount Anville (1853). In Holland at Blumenthal (1848) and Liège, Bois l'Évêque (1865). In Italy in Milan (1853). In the Tyrol at Riedenburg, near Bregenz (1854). In Poland at Posen (1857). In Spain in Chamartin (1859).

In America, the Society continued to expand. Houses were opened in Philadelphia, a move from McSherrystown (1846); in Manhattanville and in

Eden Hall (1847); in Natchitoches (1847); in St Mary's Kansas, among the Potowaomies (1848); in Buffalo (1849); in Baton Rouge (1851); in Detroit (1851); in Albany (1852); in Rochester, from Buffalo (1855); in Chicago (1858); in Kenwood, from Albany (1859). In Canada, further houses were opened at St Vincent de Montréal (1846); in Halifax (1849); in Sandwich (1852); in St John, New Brunswick (1854); in London, Ontario from Sandwich (1857); in Sault-au-Récollet, from St Vincent de Montréal (1858).

The most adventurous foundations were made in Cuba and in Latin America. Although Sophie had been asked for foundations in Latin America before, she was unable to find either personnel or the right opportunity for such initiatives. However the 1848 revolutions as well as those in 1859–60 in Europe, released personnel and Sophie took the decision to open houses of the Society in Chile in Santiago (1853), in Talca (1858) and in Concepcion (1865). Houses were opened in Cuba, in Havana (1858) and in Santo Espiritu (1863). In addition to new foundations, established houses often extended their works, to include another school or work considered possible and necessary. [48]

There was no doubting the Society's vitality and Sophie watched over its growth with care and vigilance. Those she governed with were a blend of three generations in the Society: the original founding group; the second generation in the Society; those from the third who were being prepared for leadership of communities. By this time, many of the first generation were dead. Philippine Duchesne died in the autumn of 1852. Contacts with Philippine had been less frequent once she had ceased to be a superior and between 1839 and 1847 letters between Sophie and Philippine were rare. It was unfortunate that Philippine wrote to Sophie in February 1842 and praised the leadership of Elizabeth Galitzine in America. Philippine rejoiced in the 'great assistance which she will bring to your immense undertakings'. [49] Sophie received that letter in Rome at exactly the time she had heard that Elizabeth Galitzine was orchestrating a movement against her not just in America but also in Europe. In addition, Elizabeth Galitzine had asked all the American communities to send letters, signed by each member, asking the general council of 1842 to ratify the 1839 decrees. Philippine had signed one such letter, and while Sophie may never have seen Philippine's signature, she was aware that the American members of the Society had supported Elizabeth Galitzine.

From 1842 to 1846 no letters were exchanged between the two friends. Philippine respected Sophie's general request to the Society at this time that only letters of strict necessity should be written to her. Philippine found that request difficult to accept and she broke her silence in 1846 when she realised that plans were in hand to close her beloved Florissant. She told Sophie that she had known a disaster would follow once Elizabeth Galitzine removed the picture and shrine in honour of St Francis Regis in the chapel at Florissant. She was not impressed when Galitzine replaced the picture of St Francis Regis with one of the Sacred Heart. She linked the sudden and painful death of Elizabeth Galitzine in St Michael's with this step. No blessing could have come from such an act of destruction.[50] Sophie had heard about it in Paris and, even in the midst of the crisis surrounding the 1839 decrees, she had chided Elizabeth Galitzine for the insensitive way in which she had crushed Philippine's feelings. Galitzine knew little of Philippine's experiences of the Revolution in Grenoble, nor that her call to the Society and to the missions was bound up with her devotion to St Francis Regis.[51]

Philippine's letter to Sophie in 1846 broke the silence and the following year her niece, Amélie Jouve, a member of the Society, set out for America. Although she was going to Montreal in Canada, Sophie asked her to make a long detour and visit Philippine in St Charles first. She wanted to assure her old friend of her continued affection, and she sent Philippine a letter and some personal gifts. These were a source of immense joy and Philippine responded immediately. Sophie had asked Philippine why she had not written to her for so long. This gave Philippine the opportunity to explain to Sophie what had been impeding their communication for some years. Philippine explained that she had being waiting for a general council of the Society, to calm the unease generated by that of 1839 in Rome. That council had not yet taken place and now, in 1847, Philippine tried to explain to Sophie how Elizabeth Galitzine had been perceived by the American members of the Society:

> All the houses in this country welcomed respectfully the changes wrought by Madame Galitzine because they were seen as your wishes. But I am sure you have only to say a word and the old order will be resumed . . . I regard the visit of Madame de Galitzine as a scourge. Invested with all authority she acted in a way that offended the bishops; inside and outside the Society too. And the poor sisters, like sheep, let themselves be led as if she was the superior general. No one spoke of the real superior general.[52]

Her letter showed Sophie that Philippine had not betrayed her and that she had agreed to sign the letters at Elizabeth Galitzine's request only because she thought it was what Sophie wished herself. With communications so slow at the time, and with the rapidly changing situation in the Society in France between the autumn and spring of 1842–43, no one in America could have been aware then of the polarisation which had set in between the ultramontane and Gallican groups in the Society. Nor did they fully understand the ultimate purpose of the lobby which Elizabeth Galitzine was creating within America and Europe. This Philippine and the other members only picked up afterwards from letters and from members of the Society who joined the communities in America and Canada. When Philippine had a long conversation with Bathilde Sallion in 1851 she learnt a great deal of the entire background. Later she told Sophie that she had had no idea of what had been going on in Europe in the Society and could only imagine what Sophie had endured.[53] Sophie did not refer to the past in her letters to Philippine. What mattered most of all was that the relationship between the two women had been restored and while neither wrote frequent letters their understanding and mutual respect were a source of comfort.[54] Sophie and Philippine did not always share the same vision of religious life, nor had Philippine been able to provide the type of administrative leadership which Sophie had hoped for in the early days of the Society in America. Yet Sophie never ceased to admire Philippine for her fidelity to her vocation, first in Grenoble in Ste Marie d'En Haut, and later in Missouri. And when Philippine finally reached the Indians at Sugar Creek, Sophie rejoiced and wondered at the miracle that had happened. In the essentials of following her call, at no matter what cost, Philippine's moral stature was unquestionable and this was her greatest gift to Sophie and to the Society of the Sacred Heart. In August 1852 Philippine realised that her health was failing and she wrote to Sophie, telling her of her condition. Some weeks later she became aware that she was losing her memory and that she must reach out to Sophie again. This act of turning to Sophie was a recognition that Philippine's final journey had begun. Death was imminent. It was also a last act of faithful friendship. By the time Sophie received her letters Philippine Duchesne had died, on 18 November 1852.[55]

Another friend died in 1850, Joseph Varin. For some years the relationship between Sophie and Joseph Varin had been strained. A year before he died Sophie wrote to him and this evoked an immediate, warm reply:

> Truly I am distressed when I think of the very long silence which has reigned between us. Not a word from either one of us for such a long time, and yet our union of heart has certainly not suffered. It was the good Master who drew them together, forty eight years ago.[56]

Their relationship had never been an easy one, although they had worked towards one of mutual respect. It was Joseph Varin who had introduced Sophie to the dream of Léonor de Tournély and it was Joseph Varin too who had helped her spiritually at a time when the austere formation of Louis Barat had left her unsure of herself spiritually. Yet it had taken Joseph Varin a long time to recognise what others had seen before him, that Sophie Barat was the leader of the little, emerging congregation. For a time Varin supported Saint-Estève and rejected Sophie's doubts and misgivings. But their estrangement ended when they were brought together in common opposition to Saint-Estève in 1814–15. During the crisis surrounding the 1839 decrees Sophie and Varin had become estranged again. He thought Sophie had modified the aims and purpose of the Society of the Sacred Heart and he supported Eugénie de Gramont in her bid to have the 1839 decrees suppressed. This had damaged Sophie's leadership of the Society and even Sophie's faithful biographer, Adèle Cahier, tried to suppress the letters of Eugénie de Gramont to Joseph Varin, written between 1839 and 1843.[57] A year before he died he reminisced with his friends and spoke once again of Léonor de Tournély's conviction that of a society of women devoted to the Sacred Heart would be founded:

> This thought which has never left my mind or my heart, is effectively found fulfilled in the Congregation of the Dames du Sacré-Cœur. They were known first as les Dames de la Foi, [an Association] begun . . . by four women with Madame Barat named as leader. She was the founder and the superior from the age of twenty-two.[58]

It was a final, unequivocal recognition of Sophie Barat though she never heard it from his own lips. He did express satisfaction that the crisis surrounding the 1839 decrees had been resolved[59] and in the summer of 1849 Sophie had renewed personal contact with him and saw him in Paris the following winter. When Joseph Varin died on 19 April 1850 Sophie was in the process of preparing a circular letter to the Society. She included the news of Joseph Varin's death in her letter. She told the Society that she had written to him before he died, expressing the hope that any hurt or wound would not remain between them. She made no secret of the fact that a certain strain and distance had entered into the relationship between Joseph Varin and the Society of the Sacred Heart. Sophie acknowledged that, after God, the Society of the Sacred Heart owed its existence to Joseph Varin.[60] It was a generous tribute.

By 1854 Sophie was assured that the reforms she had wished to implement in the rue de Varenne had been successfully carried out. The school was prosperous and expanding and urgently needed more space. In view of this Sophie began to consider moving to another property in Paris, where she could centre the administration of the Society and provide space for the final months of formation before members took their final vows. In 1854 Sophie and the assistants general, with the secretariat led by Adèle Cahier, left the rue de Varenne and moved to rue des Feuillants in the Faubourg St Jacques.[61] They had hardly settled there when Baron Haussmann announced his urban renewal programme for Paris. The Faubourg St Jacques was one of the areas included in the planning and the Society of the Sacred Heart was informed that its property would be expropriated, with compensation. After fruitless searches in the city for other suitable premises Sophie decided that the only solution was to build a mother house in the gardens in the rue de Varenne. She rented temporary accommodation in the rue Cassini, until the new buildings were ready. Built with the money received for the expropriation of rue des Feuillants, the new mother house was ready in June 1859.[62]

Quietly, in July 1852, Sophie formally requested the minister of education and religion in Paris to approve of the modifications to the 1827 statutes, passed at the general council in Lyon in 1851. Article III specifically stated that that the superior general resided in Paris. The statutes were approved with no difficulty and there was no reaction within the Society.[63] The fire had gone out of the controversy. Now Sophie could concentrate on consolidating her work and assuring firm foundations for the future. She governed the Society in concert with her assistants general with whom she met at least twice a week in council. She remained in close contact by letter with the vicars and with the local superiors. These wrote to her officially at regular intervals during the year and through this correspondence Sophie was able to maintain an overall view of the Society. Her working days were divided into council meetings, letter-writing and individual visits. Her official correspondence was organised by Adèle Cahier and the secretariat, though she retained a great deal of personal letter-writing. She only ceded that to Adèle Cahier when she was ill or too hard pressed. Her days were busy and full and gradually a sense of laughter and relief began to steal into her life. Sophie began to enjoy recreations, especially in the garden; she enjoyed having the children in the junior school around her when she had time to be with them.[64] She was a woman at peace with herself and with the task she had done; she lived now with the fruits of her labours.

In spite of her travels and the amount of business she had to deal with Sophie had never lost contact with her family in Joigny. Now in these later years of her life Sophie was more regularly with contact with them than she had been for some years. Her nephew, Stanislas Dusaussoy, was a regular correspondent and he had always kept her informed of family affairs, so that even when she was overwhelmed by events in the Society, Sophie knew what was going on at home. None of her nieces and nephews were strong characters and each continually needed care and attention, and indeed they looked to her for guidance and advice. The eldest, Louis Dusaussoy, although ordained a priest, was not attached to a particular diocese and he showed signs of progressive mental instability. Sophie had tried over the years to settle him as a chaplain in one of the houses of the Society, either in Europe or in America. It never worked for long and the communities managed him for a time and then asked him to leave. It was an embarrassment for Sophie yet she never blamed him for his illness. In 1848 she admitted to Stanislas that she wondered what would happen to his brother, especially in old age. Louis had been in La Ferrandière for six months and his behaviour and mood swings had been so bad that he was asked to leave the house:

> They tell me that he is on the way to our house near Colmar [Kientzheim]. You know that they will receive him out of love for me. But what kind of a life is it! It seems that his character, already demanding and difficult can only become worse. What will be the end of it all? I do not know. You understand that his mental state is responsible for a good deal of this. He allows himself to be so dominated by fear that he is no longer master of himself. He will go mad, and this will not surprise me. It is not his fault that he is afraid . . . [65]

Suffering from fear or not, Louis Dusaussoy went all over the world leaning on the reputation of his aunt. He travelled to Florence, Loreto and Rome; to America again, and later to Latin America when the Society opened houses in Chile. Each appointment would last some months, rarely longer, and then Louis would make his way back to France, relying on his aunt to find him a place in one of the houses of the Society. Occasionally he found work as a tutor and once he was offered a permanent appointment as the curé at St Aubin, near Joigny. Sophie saw this as the solution and made great efforts to persuade her nephew to settle down there.[66] She did not succeed and Louis was soon off on his travels again. By 1857, Sophie's patience had worn thin. At this time Louis was in Manhattanville in New York, where Aloysia Hardey had received him, for Sophie's sake. Sophie wrote to her nephew there and told him frankly that he was garrulous, self-centred and lazy. She outlined the kind of work she expected him to do while he was in New York and to keep to it.[67] But she doubted he would heed her advice and remarked wryly to Stanislas: 'I will never understand how anyone, who has reasonably good health, can be happy not to work.'[68]

Sophie was concerned about Zoé when after several years of marriage she and her husband still had no children. She suggested that they adopt a child in the hope that this might help their marriage which Sophie sensed was already in difficulty. However, a son, Oscar, was born in 1846 and this appeared to save the relationship for a time. Sophie took great interest in her grand nephew, at every stage of his life, and arranged for his schooling in Joigny and in Amiens. His sudden death on 20 March 1864 was a blow to everyone in the family, for he was the only member of the Dusaussoy/Barat family of that generation. His death could no longer hide the estrangement between Zoé and Cousin and the couple agreed to separate.[69] The fact that in 1876 Zoé asked the army for a formal separation from her husband which prevented him from ever returning to the home in Joigny indicates how seriously their relationship had deteriorated.[70]

Sophie's last surviving niece was Sophie Dusaussoy, a member of the Society. She taught in the schools and lived a great deal of her life in the rue de Varenne. There was a certain strain between aunt and niece. Perhaps Sophie Dusaussoy had seen too much of her aunt's humiliation in Paris during the crisis over the 1839 decrees. When Elisa Dusaussoy died in Conflans in 1842, Sophie told her niece that all her hopes rested in her.[71] But in fact she was disappointed in Sophie Dusaussoy's development. Although her niece was an adequate teacher Sophie did not feel able to entrust her with more responsibility. Like her brother, Louis, Sophie Dusaussoy tended to lean on the reputation of her aunt, especially after 1850, when Sophie deliberately ensured that her niece did not live in Paris. She tried to give her more responsibility in the Society but on the advice of those who lived and worked with her Sophie realised that this would not be possible.[72] Sophie wrote to her from time to time, sending her little gifts for her projects. In 1857 she sent her niece money for tobacco, though she hoped that she could break the habit, unless it was doing her health good. Sophie herself had taken snuff from 1830 and found it a help when she had head colds. She also tried smoking tobacco and decided to give it up as she liked it too well. Now she encouraged her niece to do likewise, telling her that Josephine de Coriolis, who had taken tobacco for years, had finally given it up and Sophie admitted that she had too.[73]

Sophie's sense of responsibility for her family increased as Marie-Louise's health deteriorated. She had kept her sister's needs in mind and every year she had sent her a gift of a pair of shoes and sometimes other gifts, such as a shawl or warm underclothes. By the time Louis Barat died in 1845 Marie-Louise had begun to lose her memory and in 1847 Sophie planed to visit her sister in Joigny that year, when she was en route to the Midi.[74] The following year she began to make plans for Sophie Dusaussoy to come from Bordeaux to Paris and then to Joigny, to see her mother. But by July 1849 it was clear to Sophie that Marie-Louise had lost her memory completely and that she would not recognise anyone who visited her.[75] Sophie was deeply upset at her sister's deterioration. In

July 1851 she passed through Joigny, on her way from Lyon to Paris, but she found it too painful to stop en route. She wrote to Stanislas:

> I greet all the family affectionately. Of course I would have been happy to see your mother again. But it would have caused me great distress to see her in the state she is in. Besides painful impressions affect me badly at the moment when my mental state is very exhausted by work and fatigue . . . [76]

A few months later Sophie left Paris to go to Lyon for the general council and she passed through Joigny. Again she did not stop to visit, but two of the assistants general got off the train at Joigny for a few minutes, missed their connection and had to wait for another train which only arrived at midnight. When they rejoined Sophie later at Chalon she reproached them for not contacting Stanislas who would have made sure they got a meal and a rest in his house before continuing their journey. [77] On her way back from the general council, in mid-January 1852, Sophie told Stanislas when their train would be passing through Joigny. He was at the station when the train stopped for a few minutes and gave her family news:

> The details about your mother upset me. It is a real death of the person and what care you will have to give her so that accidents can be avoided . . . and which could go on for years . . . a duty you are happy to fulfil in thinking of the care she gave you all during your early years. [78]

By August 1852 Marie-Louise's health had deteriorated rapidly and Stanislas kept Sophie informed of her condition. Sophie urged Stanislas to make sure that Marie-Louise received the last sacraments and to be aware of the fact that sometimes those who receive them in death may have moments of great lucidity. [79] Perhaps the clearest sign of Louis Dusaussoy's instability was shown at this time. While his mother was dying Louis decided to leave Joigny and go to Marmoutier where he expected to be received there by the community, again on account of his aunt Sophie. This attitude deeply upset Sophie and she asked Stanislas to see what he could do to persuade his brother to stay at home in Joigny until his mother died. He failed. When Sophie heard the news that Marie-Louise had died in September 1852, at the age of eighty-two, she was relieved to know that her sister's painful state was over, but she admitted that she found it hard to forgive Louis for leaving Joigny at such a critical time. [80]

When Marie-Louise had died Sophie continued an arrangement she had already established of having a family visit once a year in Paris. Sometimes she arranged to have Sophie Dusaussoy travel from Le Mans, and then later from Bordeaux for this event. She continued this custom until her death. She also continued to buy wine from Stanislas and Zoé for the community in Paris, a practice she had begun in 1820. [81] She supported both of them and wrote letters of encouragement regularly. At the same time Sophie retained contact with her cousins in Joigny, was interested in their lives and tried to arbitrate in family disputes. When they were needy she sent them money. [82] Some still expected her to do favours for them in Paris but she told them she had no influence in Paris, and that even in the time of the Bourbons she had not been successful in seeking favours.[83] As Sophie told Stanislas in 1852, she had lost that kind of contact with the Faubourg Saint-Germain, even though she continued to receive visits from a few old friends of former times.[84]

Sophie's fidelity to her family all through her life revealed that quality in her character which was both her greatest strength and her greatest vulnerability. She stood by her friends and her family to a point of folly. This mode of being had marked her friendship with Eugénie de Gramont. It also marked her relationship with her nieces and nephews. But it was not just close friends and family who experienced that kind of fidelity. In 1842 a young girl, Julia de Wicka, was found wandering near Marseilles, apparently without home or family and speaking a strange language.[85] The Countess Babinska placed this young girl in the rue de Varenne, at her own expense, and there Julia learned French. Sophie met her in the school, took an interest in her strange history and decided to take responsibility for Julia. The girl was an actress and played on Sophie's concern for her, refusing to speak to anyone but Sophie. She became impossible in the school in Paris, then in Beauvais and later in New York. Yet Sophie never wavered. She continued to support Julia in the thick of criticism. Sophie asked Josephine Goetz to look after Julia in Conflans, and there two novices were assigned to her. This did not succeed either and Julia went around the houses of the Society, Paris, Besançon, Conflans and Tours, rather like Louis Dusaussoy, leaning on the reputation of Sophie Barat. And all this time Sophie continued to support her and wrote to her regularly. Julia got to know Georges Augustin, who worked on Paris–Lyon railways, and she proposed to him that they marry. Sophie thought this was a good idea and encouraged the match.

The marriage took place in 1861 and lasted a few weeks. Julia became violent and abusive and was continually drunk. She spent days and nights on the streets and continually berated Sophie Barat. In the meantime government authorities discovered that Julia had already married someone else in August 1860. The state wanted to dissolve the marriage; Georges Augustin did not and went to Paris to discuss his misfortune with Sophie Barat. She encouraged him to try to keep the marriage going and wrote constantly to Julia to try to get her to change her way of being, to no avail.[86] The case had reached this point when Sophie died in 1865, and her successors had to retain contact with the couple, until Julia died in 1872. In all this time Sophie never wavered in her fidelity. It was a disastrous situation and a public scandal and yet Sophie continued to write to Julia and to Georges. She had begun the friendship and she would stand by her choice. Perhaps this bizarre set of relationships best portrays Sophie Barat's mode of being. There is something heroic in such fidelity, in such constancy; there is also something blind and stubborn in such persistence. Both tendencies were dominant in Sophie's character and temperament for good and ill in her life.

In the midst of trying to sort out this impossible situation Sophie continued to watch over the work of education in the Society. In the period after 1850 Sophie set about ensuring that each school had the required documentation in order, reflecting the agreements made with government authorities and with bishops.[87] The passing of the Loi Falloux in 1850 relieved Sophie from the immediate pressure of training teachers according to state regulations, since the law permitted members of religious congregations to teach without a certificate. Yet Sophie recognised that the teachers in the Society required proper training and in view of this, in 1862 she asked Josephine Gœtz, then mistress of novices at Conflans, to draw up a plan for training the young teachers in the Society. Even if the Society was never required to present its teachers for examination by the state, the teachers should be at least as well trained as their lay colleagues. Sophie continued to lament that this was not so in many cases. She continually urged that the quality of the education given in the schools be examined and in particular that the younger members be properly prepared for teaching. She wanted the pupils to receive a good, basic preparation for life.[88] In 1855 Sophie was concerned about the standard of studies in the school at Toulouse:

> This year we must make amends for the past. To do this successfully we must com-
> bine divine ways with practical ones, in caring for the education of the children, in
> all its dimensions. This includes knowledge in accordance with our plan of stud-
> ies, handicraft, inculcating the desire, even the love of learning; also the ornamen-
> tal arts of dancing, drawing and music (arts d'agrément), drawing especially. But
> before everything else they must learn spelling and art of letter-writing. The other
> attainments are rare in women but in our time a woman is obliged to write all her
> life. There are few exceptions to this. So make sure that your teachers instruct the
> pupils thoroughly in these two subjects. This should start in the 6th class. By teach-
> ing these youngsters to spell you will be helping them greatly. Insist on discipline
> and politeness; make sure the children are trained to have good taste, good man-
> ners, with true simplicity. We do not work enough on these essential qualities. Yet
> these will bind the pupils to us and win their trust, for without this simple and
> modest way of being, they will not make their way in the world. It is the finishing
> touch to a careful and sound education.[89]

By choosing Josephine Gœtz to prepare a system of intellectual training for the members of the Society, Sophie indicated her growing confidence in her mistress of novices. Since 1847 they had almost daily contact by letter or by visits and Sophie could see that the formation of new members was being carried out well. That in itself was a relief and became a source of Sophie's sense of freedom and joy at this time. In 1854 she appointed Josephine Gœtz superior of Conflans, in addition to her work with the novices. It was a popular choice and the house prospered under her leadership. Sophie decided to bring Josephine Gœtz into the inner circle of government of the Society and appointed her assistant general, to succeed Henriette Coppens when she died in 1863. Indeed by 1863 Sophie was acutely aware that her energies were ebbing away and that she must call a statutory general council that year. She wrote to the Society proposing to convene a council by the end of the year or early in 1864. That plan fell through when Sophie became ill and for some months was unable to deal with business affairs. In March 1864 she announced that the council would meet in June that year.[90]

The general council was composed of Sophie Barat, the assistants general and the vicars of the Society, nineteen members in all. The actual work of preparation was done by the assistants general and Adèle Cahier as by this time Sophie was too weak to sustain prolonged work. The council opened on 17 June and ended on 21 July 1864. During those weeks the council examined the life of the Society in all its dimensions, beginning with the spiritual life of the members and of the communities and then proceeding to the work of education in all its dimensions. Key issues emerged for debate:

- the need to train teachers in the Society properly, especially for the higher classes in the schools. To this purpose careful preparation of all teachers would begin immediately after the noviceship. Provision was made for a period of further training for a smaller group of teachers, those destined to guide the studies in the schools and develop the Society's educational philosophy.
- the founding of more city houses of the Society. Parents had complained that too many schools were in the countryside. These city schools were linked with the boarding school in the countryside; they were to be fee-paying boarding and day schools, open in particular to the children who wanted to go there before they made their first communion. The studies in these schools did not go beyond the third class, that is to say middle school studies.
- regular recruitment of members, or of lay helpers, was considered in three ways: the reintroduction of the idea of a third order, associated with the Society; the encouragement of retreat houses in the Society, to encourage spiritual growth and also to cultivate vocations to the Society; orphanages were to be maintained in areas of need or where it was difficult to recruit coadjutrix sisters.[91]

The Society was fast consolidating its position. It had become a large institution with growing needs. By 1864 recruitment of both choir and coadjutrix sisters through the schools, the retreat houses and the orphanages was crucial for both maintenance and expansion. By 1864 there were 3,500 members in the Society. There were eighty-six institutions of the Society: forty-four in France; fifteen in north America; five in Canada; four in Italy; three in the Austrian Empire; three in Ireland; two in Latin America; two in Cuba; two in Prussia; two in Belgium; two in Spain; one in England; one in Holland.

During the council Sophie once again offered her resignation and again this was refused. At this stage the members must have realised that Sophie's life was drawing to a close and that they could not easily convene again to elect a new superior general. They insisted that she continue in office. In 1851 Sophie was a focus for the unity of the Society – she had become a living legend. She was the story, the storyteller, the myth and the reality, all in one. She had been elected for life; she was the only surviving founding member and she had led the Society for sixty-two years. Sophie protested to the council that she could be superior general only in name, not in function. She told the members that she wished to use the power given her in 1851 and name a vicar general. She had carefully chosen Josephine Gœtz. Should Sophie become too ill to govern, or should she die, Josephine Gœtz would take her place until a general council could be convened and a new superior general be elected. Sophie had named her successor.

EPILOGUE: MAY 1865

In 1849, on the advice of her lawyer, Sophie revised her will and signed it in Paris on 27 June 1850. She left that aside for good and began to consider another type of legacy, her testament to the Society of the Sacred Heart. Between November 1852 and April 1863 Sophie drafted and redrafted this will and testament. It was a review of her life and a reflection of her prolonged administration of the Society since its foundation:

> I brought nothing into the Congregation other than 6 frs, left over, I think, from my journey from Paris to Amiens. I should have received 1000 frs from my parents' estate but I thought I ought not claim them, since my sister had ten young children to look after then. This was the advice I was given at the time.[1]

Sophie took stock and looked back over her administration and acknowledged the amount of responsibility she had held for so long. She did not comment on the extraordinary personal journey she had made in her life. Nor did she speak of her personal achievement of leading the Society for so long, seeing it through its foundation phases, its growth and expansion crises, and then its period of consolidation. She made no reference to the 3,359 women who belonged to the Society nor to the eighty-nine houses in Europe, North Africa, North and South America. Neither did she refer to the thousands of pupils being educated in the schools of the Society. Over the years, and especially after 1850, Sophie spoke frequently of the women who had created the Society, and did not focus on herself. Besides at eighty-five life looked very different and her focus was elsewhere.

She looked back over her life, not as superior general, but as Sophie Barat, the individual person. From that perspective, Sophie felt the weight of what she had carried and she recalled her mistakes and errors of judgement, at different stages of her life. What worried her even more was the way in which she had treated the members of the Society. She regretted that often she had been severe and demanding and had acted too quickly on the criticisms she had heard. She admitted that she herself had been moody and quick-tempered and made life difficult for others. Sophie always worried about formation of younger members and she had been severe in her reprimands of them. This was especially true after 1850, perhaps fearing that she had been too tolerant and casual in previous years. She was weary of unsuitable young women asking to enter the Society and at times lost her patience with them over their persistence. Sophie had an impulsive, energetic nature which even the strictures of Louis Barat had never curbed. It was that nature, that energy, which had seen the Society through so many critical phases and which in the end ensured that it would not disintegrate. She had kept faith and saw her work through to the end. She who appreciated hard work and commitment in others was the hardest, most committed worker herself. Sophie's faults were the shadow side of her own life and the shadow side of the Society of the Sacred Heart. Sophie reminded those who would succeed her that the central aim of the Society of the Sacred Heart was to make present in the world the knowledge and love of the Heart of Christ. That was the core of their lives and without that vision at the centre there was no point in its existence.

At different stages in the course of her life Sophie had taken many steps forward alone. She had found the courage to move out from the shadows of diffidence and to assume leadership. She used her unusual capacity for relationships and she inspired her companions. She learnt the joy and pain of deep friendship and the cost of possessiveness. She experienced rejection and ridicule from some of her closest companions and from some sections of society and of the church. In the course of it all she found her inner freedom and individual strength and demonstrated the impact of power exercised with reticence. Each stage of the journey brought its pain and its joy because her heart and courage were great enough to respond to life, even if at times she could barely imagine surviving another day. She found her source of strength in her faith in God and in the life of prayer which empowered her. That too was bought at a price, for she drew energy from a God mediated through the image of the Heart of Christ wounded on Calvary. This meant undoing the Jansenist image of God, not just for a time or during a phase in her life, but always.

Many years before Fr Favre had challenged Sophie to believe in the love of God, revealed in the pierced side of Christ on Golgotha. He had invited her to allow that kind of God into her life, replacing the God of the Jansenists, a God of fear and severity. Sophie accepted that challenge and began to open her inner spiritual world to this sunlight of resurrection. As she grew older hints of a lighter spirit within Sophie crept into her letters, in the period after 1830 and especially when she emerged from the prolonged crisis of 1839–51. This latter period coincided with the death of Eugénie de Gramont, the general council of 1851 and the restoration of her relationship with Louise de Limminghe. Yet her relationship with Louise de Limminghe had changed profoundly and perhaps this best signals the inner changes in Sophie herself. Sophie made it clear to Louise de Limminghe that she could not resonate with her old friend's spirituality, which had remained harsh and severe, thoroughly Jansenistic. Sophie had left that world behind her. This stance with her old friend represented the transition which Sophie had made, signalling that she had found a spirituality which was liberating and joyful. It had not been either easy to find or was it always simple to live out with congruence and consistency. She could readily fall back into her old images, especially in times of difficulty and depression, and then had to journey out into the light again.

But Sophie Barat's will and soul power were strong and she had the unique quality of living consciously from those places. From there she spoke to the members of the Society, either in her letters or in personal contacts. Of course, at times she erupted with anger or frustration and cried out in pain and fear, and she had difficulty restoring her inner peace and calm. And so in 1863, as Sophie looked back over her life, she inevitably saw the mistakes and errors she had made. Yet her avowal was not a type of self-flagellation or self-pity. These had disappeared from Sophie's life a long time ago. Pauline Perdrau, who lived in the rue de Varenne from 1845 until after Sophie's death, asked her why she went to confession every day of her life. Sophie was amused at her curiosity and explained to her that she found the community chaplain, Fr Jurines, helpful in confession. She had decided to evaluate her personal and working life daily and had arranged with the abbé Jurines to go to confession each morning before the community Mass. Sophie had found a way of gradually unburdening herself of her past, telling her story, of letting go of immediate anxieties and each day deepening her inner peace. It counterbalanced the daily confessions which Louis Barat had insisted on and which she had found so painful. Sophie had discovered a form of healing, indeed of therapy, which comforted her in old age and prepared her for death.[2]

Though absorbed in making preparations for her inner journey over the threshold of death Sophie did not lose touch with the wider world. In February 1865 Sophie wrote to Stanislas:

> What times we live in! We have two extremes before our very eyes: the view of unbridled luxury which swallows up wealth and yields merely instant pleasure. And alongside these crazy expenses, there are thousands, I ought to say millions, of people, of every class and every age and of every condition, who are dying of hunger. How can those generous Christians who still exist and are so few in number come to the aid of so much need and distress? Yet nearly all the calamities and needs of the world fall on this little group of people, to do what is needed and it is not enough: for America, for Poland, for the missions in the East. But even around us here, how many are destitute. Indeed some in the higher classes of society are in the most pressing want! . . . We are inundated with requests, I could not tell you of all the appeals we get from every side![3]

In April, Sophie wrote to Stanislas, commenting on the wonderful spring in Paris and hoping that no late frost would harm the blossoms. She also thanked him for paying her back a sum of money she had lent him. Now her money affairs were in order.[4] Early in May 1865, taking advantage of the warm spring weather, Sophie spent some of the mornings in the garden. Sometimes the children from the junior school would join her as she sat under her favourite tree. That month too Sophie decided to pay a visit to the Hôtel Biron. She went to her old room there, originally used by Eugénie de Gramont. For a time she was lost in thought and then in a remark, typical for its brevity, she said very quietly, almost to herself: 'Once again I see these places where I lived and suffered so much.'[5]

It was a final farewell to a place which had marked her life profoundly. Sophie was calmly putting her life in order, before she entered into the final fortnight of her life. On the morning of 22 May 1865 Sophie got up early and all was normal until she started breakfast. She complained of a pain in her head and decided to rest for a time, thinking it would pass. This was not to be. Sophie had a stroke, slipped slowly into unconsciousness and never spoke again. She remained in this condition for three days and for a time it was clear that while she could not speak she understood what was spoken around her. But her final journey had begun, and on the evening of Ascension Thursday, 25 May 1865, at 11 p.m., Sophie Barat died peacefully.[6] During her lifetime Sophie had refused to have her portrait done or her photograph taken. In the hours after her death Pauline Perdrau – a portrait artist – tried to do a sketch of Sophie but after three hours she had to admit that she could not do it. A photographer was brought in and he took the first and last photograph of Sophie Barat, in death, at eighty-five years of age.

Sophie had expressed the hope that she would die in silence. Her wish was granted. In 1839 she had written to Emilie Giraud, thinking then that death could not be far away for them both:

> Let us be like the swan. When it is dying it gathers all its inner forces and sings with more harmony than ever before in its life. That is how saints die. It is the purest act of their life, the one most burning with love, the most perfect.[7]

The image of the swan attracted Sophie then but she still had twenty-six more years to live. In 1865 another image came to play around Sophie. In 1779 she began her life dramatically in the midst of a fire. In 1865 Sophie ended it gently, rather like the embers of an evening fire which settle and glow, then gradually fade and finally die.

Postscript

Sophie Barat's death was noted in the press in Paris and the faithful Stanislas wrote an obituary for his aunt which was published in early June 1865 in Joigny. The funeral took place on Monday, 29 May 1865 in the rue de Varenne and Sophie Barat was laid to rest in Conflans.

Madeleine Sophie Barat was canonised a saint of the Roman Catholic Church on 25 May 1925.

ABBREVIATIONS

GA, Rome	Society of the Sacred Heart, General Archives, Rome
AF, Poitiers	Société du Sacré-Cœur, Archives Françaises, Poitiers
AD, Yonne	Archives Départementales de l'Yonne
ASV	Archivio Segreto Vaticano
A.A.Fr.	Archives de l'Ambassade de France près le Saint-Siège, Rome
ARSI	Archivium Romanum Societatis Iesu
AHSI	Archivium Historicum Societatis Iesu
AFSJ	Vanves Archives Françaises de la Compagnie de Jésus

Note: The punctuation and spelling in the quotations from letters and manuscripts have been modernised.

BIBLIOGRAPHY

General Archives, Society of the Sacred Heart, Rome[1]
Series A: Society as canonical religious institute
Series A-I: Origins
Series A-II: Early development
Series A-III: The Institute
Series A-IV: Approbations

Series B: Relations of the Society with the Church
Series B-I: With popes
Series B-II: With cardinal protectors
Series B-III: With Vatican congregations
Series B-IV: Relations with individual ecclesiastics
Series B-V: Relations with other congregations
Series B-VI: Relations with laity

Series C: Internal History of the Society
Series C-I: Central government
Series C-I., a- Generalates. Dossier I: St. Madeleine Sophie: canonisation; affairs of generalate; memoirs; letters (14, 000)
C-I., b- Continuing records of the Mother House
C-I., c- General Councils and Chapters
Series C-II: Inter-provincial affairs

---

[1] The archives of the Society of the Sacred Heart in Rome and Poitiers are extensive and for this reason only headings can be given in this bibliographical description. The archives in Rome are classified in English, those in Poitiers are classified in French.

434

Series C-III: History of provinces of the Society
Series C-IV: History of individual institutions
Series C-V: Formation of members
Series C-VI: Noviciates; Probation; Intellectual formation
Series C-VII: Individual RSCJ (Religieuses du Sacré-Cœur)
Series C-VIII: Deceased members; Ménologes

Series D: External history of the Society
Series D-I: Activities of the Institute: Work of Education; popular works;
    extended influence of the Society
Series D-II: Publications of the Society
Series D-III: Charts, Tables, Statistics

S E: Legal and financial affairs
Series E-I: Lawsuits
Series E-II: Legacies and gifts
Series E-III: Legal relations with governments
Series E-IV Central financial administration
Series E-V: Fortunes of members of the Society
Series E-VI: Property of the Society

H-I. 6: Papiers Jeanne de Charry

Biographical collection
Lettres Annuelles de la Société du Sacré-Cœur (Accounts of the houses and
    schools of the Society, and the obituary notices of members)
Archives

Société du Sacré-Cœur, Archives Françaises, Poitiers
A 2: Les fondateurs
A-4: Constitutions, Conseil de 1839
A- 8: Relations avec l'église, 1800–1865
Archives de la Maîtresse Générale des Etudes françaises 1820–1940. Exercices
    et distribution solennelle des prix dans la maison d'Institution d'Amiens,
    19, 20, 21 septembre 1805

B04/117: Niort [Louis Barat] Recueil de pratiques pieuses pour servir de suite
    au mois angélique (Bordeaux, 1818); Lettres du Père Barat, Communauté
    de Niort
B05/117: Beauvais
B06/115: rue de Varenne
B06/ 117: rue de Varenne
B06/119: Journal du Noviciat.
B06/151: rue de Varenne, Evêché
B06/ 215: rue de Varenne
B06/ 215: rue de Varenne

B/08/114/115: Chambéry
B10/117: Bordeaux
B 35/ 111, 115, 118: La Neuville
B 90/111, 114, 117: Montet

Archives de la Trinité des Monts, Rome
Histoire de la fondation de Rome en 1828.
Journal de la maison de la Trinité des Monts, 1836–38

Archivio della Provincia di Italia
Storia di Casa, Cartolario, 1837–1860
Society of the Sacred Heart National Archives, U.S.A.
Series I. A-b, Madeleine Sophie Barat. Events of her generalate, 1802–1843.
    Callan Collection, XIII, C, 2–11
Series III, Inter-provincial affairs, A, USA, 1) Pre IPB, History
Series III, Special Collections. Marie Louise Martinez Collection. RSCJ mis-
    sionaries sent to America during the lifetime of Sophie Barat
Series IV, St Louis Province, City House, St Louis; St Louis Province, E. Grand
    Coteau; St Louis Province, K. Potawatami Mission; St Louis Province, M:
    St. Charles.
Series II, Interprovincial affairs, Pre IPB, A., USA, Box 1, History France

Archives Nationales
Collège Mazarin (Collège de Quatre Nations) C 149, no 251; M 174, no 64; M
    715, nos 14, 19; MM 464; H3 2555; H3 2562
F/19/42992 Paris 24 janvier 1808, Déclaration du Père Varin, ex supérieure et
    liste des Pères de la Foi.
F/19/6287, Dossier 8, Demandes d'exception, Paris, 1812
F/17/12434/D Inspections des écoles, Paris, 26 Janvier 1854
Archives de la Maison de Gramont
101 Archives Privées, Série D, Cartons 3 et 4.

Archives Départementales de l'Yonne
2 E 206/21 Acte de baptême de Madeleine Sophie Barat, le 12 décembre 1779
    à Joigny
C 185, Département de Joigny. Procès Verbaux des séances du département de
    Joigny
C 187, Joigny, Départements des Années.
L. 195 Discours sur les avantages que peuvent procurer les établissements de
    sociétés patriotiques, le 14 avril 1791
L 196 Lettre de la Municipalité de Joigny au Directoire du Département, 6
    février 1792
L610, Collège de Joigny, Auxerre 20 août 1791; 16 janvier 1792.
L 826, 3e Registre, Séance du 11 mai 1792

L 828, 1793–1794 Sociétés populaires à Joigny

L 1124, Registre des délibérations et opérations du comité de surveillance de la section de St Thibault de la ville de Joigny, Année 1793

L 41, 16 juin 1792; L 47, 21 mars 1793.

L 831, Délibérations du Conseil du District de Joigny (18 Septembre 1793)

L 245, Lettre du Conseil Municipal de Joigny (31 mars 1794)

Série 2 E, II J 206/31 Registre des concessions des places et bancs de l'église Paroisse St Thibault 1761 à 1824; Archives de St Thibault à Joigny, Bancs 1774–1808; chaises 1810–1822; 1874.

Série 2 E, 11 J 206/16, Paroisse de St Thibault Catholicité, 1792–1800. Marriage notice of Marie-Louise Barat, 13 March 1793.

Archives Communales, Mairie de Joigny

Série G.

Sous-série 1 G, 1 G 15. Héritages sur le Territoire de … Héritages sur le Territoire de St Aubin. Barrat Jacques, gde Fouffé, tonnelier

Sous série G, 1 G 15, District de Joigny, De la division du territoire en sections

Sous série G, 1 G 17: Rôles des propriétaires 1791 Etats de sections. Déclarations des Propriétaires, Sections A-H, Nos 1450, 1466, 1478; cf nos 581 571

Sous série G, 1 G 18: Contribution foncières 1791 S.A. Joigny Numéros de Propriétés compris dans la section. S. A. 1564; S.B. 620; 938; Sous-série 2 G Impôts extraordinaires.

Sous série G, I G 16 Etat de section, Déclarations des Propriétaires. Also 1 G 21 and 1 G 22, Contribution mobilière, nos 581, 547; 2 G 1, Déclaration de la citoyenne Chollet veuve Piochard.

Sous-série 1 G Impôt Direct, 1 G 15 Etat de section, Procès verbaux 1791. Population de Joigny

Sous-série 2 G, 2 G 2 An IV et V de la République, Contribution personnelle et somptuaire, Art 21, Barrat Jacques gre Fouffé tonnelier

Sous série 1D Conseil Municipal 1789–1944: 1D*1 Délibérations du Conseil Municipales du 3 septembre 1789 au 22 août 1793, ff 76–77, 83–84

Archives Municipales de Joigny, Bibliothèque de Joigny

Paroisse de St Thibault, Registres des naissances no. 43, 2 mars 1792; no. 151, 4 septembre 1795

Archives du Ministre des Affaires Etrangères

Correspondance Politique, Rome, vo. 984, Rome, 1842–43

Archives Françaises de la Compagnie de Jésus

Carton Louis Barat

Notice sur l'enfance et la jeunesse du R.P. Barat avec lettre d'envoi autographe de Ste Sophie Barat, 1846

Correspondance Louis Barat à Marie-Louise Dusaussoy

Lettres à divers. A son neveu, de Bordeaux
Lettres de Elizabeth Galitzine
Ms 4204, Sur L'église, l'Europe, la France. Application de l'Apocalypse à l'histoire de France
Ms 4202, 4203, Idée de l'Apocalypse
Ms 4201, Sur N.S. Jesus Christ et son Eglise
Ms. 6861 Règles et avis pour un ordre religieux de femmes. Oeuvre de P. Louis Barat
Carton Joseph Varin
Journal de Mantes, 1846, 1848 et 1849, no. 11, Diverses anecdotes très intéressantes

Archives de l'Archevêché de Paris
Procès Madame Barat, 1873
Papiers de Quelen I D IV
Papiers Affre I D V

Archives et bibliothèques, Diocese d'Amiens
Dossier Alexandre, Charles Michel de Brandt, 1812–1903

Archives, Carmel de Clamart
Saint Barthélemy
Registres et circulaires.
Notice sur Béatrix de la Conception (Octavie Bailly)
Notice sur Anne de saint Barthélemy

Séminaire Saint-Sulpice
Séminaire Saint-Sulpice, MS 411, Manuscrits de Mr Montaigne, 10, Vie et Lettres
Fonds Frayssinous, Communautés Religieuses, Sacré-Cœur, Cuiginières/Beauvais 1815–1828 Italy

Archivio Segreto Vaticano
Fondo Segretario di Stato, Particolari Esteri, 1842–1844, 67, R. 284, B. 623
Fondo Segreteria di Stato Esteri, Busta 616, Rubrica 283, Fascicolo 1
Archivio della Congregazione per gli Istituto di Vita Consecrata e le Società di Vita Apostolica
R. I., [Césaire Mathieu] Memoria [1843]
Archives de l'Ambassade de France près le Saint-Siège, Rome
Dossier: Religieuses du Sacré-Cœur (1838–1904)
Dépêches du Département 1842–43

Archivium Romanum Societatis Iesu
Monial 1 – fasc., iv, De congregatione monialium, dicta Dames du Sacré-Cœur
  1828–1833
Monial 1- fasc., v. Monialium negotia. Dames du Sacré-Cœur. Graves difficul-
  tates....1839–1843
Francia 1005–1006
Responsa ad externos, V, 1840–1843
Registrarium Provinciae Franciae, Tom. II, 27 juillet 1836–26 novembre 1842

Contemporary works
Almanach historique de la ville, bailliage et diocèse de Sens 1782 (Sens, 1782)
Annuaire statistique et administratif du Département de la Somme, pour l'an 1806
  (Amiens, 1806)
Baunard, Louis, *Histoire de Madame Barat, fondatrice de la Société du Sacré Coeur*,
  2 vols. (Paris, 1876)
Bellmare, M., *M. de Quelen pendant 10 ans* (Paris, 1840)
Bertrand, L., *Bibliothèque Sulpicienne ou histoire littéraire de la Compagnie de Saint-
  Sulpice* (Paris, 1900)
*Vie de Julie Billiart, par ... Françoise Blin de Bourdon ou Les Mémoires de Mère Saint-
  Joseph* (Rome, 1978)
Bouchage, François, *Le serviteur de Dieu, Joseph-Marie Favre, maître et modèle des
  ouvriers apostoliques, 1791–1838* (Paris, 1901)
Cahier, Adèle, *Vie de la Vénérable Mère Madeleine-Sophie Barat, fondatrice et première
  supérieure générale de la Société du Sacré Coeur*, 2 vols. (Paris, 1884)
Cahier, *Notice de la Mère Adelaide*
Charbonnel, *Vie de la Mère [Catherine] de, assistante et econome générale de la Société
  du Sacre-Coeur* (Paris, c. 1870)
Condorcet, Marquis de, *Sur l'admission des femmes au droit de cité* (1790)
*Dictionnaire historique et statistique des paroisses catholiques du Canton de Fribourg,
  vol. 7*, (Fribourg, 1891)
*Mémoires de Madame la vicomtesse de Fars Fausselandry, ou souvenirs d'une octogé-
  naire*, 3 vols. (Paris, 1830)
Mémorial catholique, février 1868, Une vénérable religieuse [Marie d'Olivier]
Favre, Joseph-Marie, *Considérations sur l'amour divin* (Chambéry, 1827)
—— *Le Ciel Ouvert par la confession sincère et la communion fréquent* (Lyon, 1829)
—— *Théorique et pratique de la communion fréquente et quotidienne à l'usage des prêtres
  qui exercent le saint ministère*, 2 vols. (Lyon, 1840)
Galitzin, . . . *Notice sur Madame Elizabeth, Religieuse du Sacré Cœur, 1795–1843*
  (Tours, 1858)
Galitzin, Prince Augustin, 'Mélanges. Une religieuse Russe', *Le Correspondent*,
  août 1862
Geoffroy, Vie de Madame (Poitiers, 1854)
Géramb, Marie-Joseph, *Voyage de La Trappe à Rome* (Paris, 1838)

Gœtz, Josephine, *Première lettres et bulletins relatifs à la maladie et la mort de notre vénérée mère fondatrice* [mai, 1865]

Gondran, Chanoine, 'Eloge historique de M. l'abbé Favre' in Joseph-Marie Favre, *Théorie et pratique de la communion fréquente et quotidienne à l'usage des prêtres qui exercent le saint ministère*, 2 vols. (Lyon, 1840)

Gouges, Olympe de, *Les droits de la Femme* (1791)

Gramont, Notice sur la vie de Madame la Comtesse de, née de Boisgelin (Paris, 1836)

Gramont, Quelques traits de la vie et de la mort de Madame Eugénie de, par M. Le Calvimont, Comte Louis de, Extrait de la Quotidienne du 25 janvier 1847

Grandidier, P.F., *Vie du … Père Guidée de la Compagnie de Jésus* (Amiens/Paris, 1867)

Guidée, Achille, *Vie du R.P. Joseph Varin … suivie de Notices sur quelques-uns de ses confrères* (Paris, 1854)

Histoires des Catéchismes de Saint-Sulpice (Paris, 1831)

Lettres Circulaires de … Madeleine Sophie Barat, 1e partie (Roehampton, 1917); 2e partie (Roehampton, 1904)

Loquet, Marie-Françoise, *Cruzamante, ou la sainte amante de la Croix* (Paris, 1786)

—— *Voyage de Sophie et d'Eulalie au palais du vraie bonheur. Ouvrage pour servir de guide dans les voies du salut, par une jeune demoiselle* (Paris, 1789)

—— *Entretiens d'Angélique, pour exciter les jeunes personnes à l'amour et à la pratique de la vertu*, 2nd edn, (Paris, 1782)

—— *Le miroir des âmes*, 6th edn (Paris, 1822)

Loriquet, Vie du …Père (Paris, 1845)

Manuel du Chrétien, contenant les psaumes, le Nouveau Testament et l'Imitation de Jesus Christ. De la tradition de M le Maître de Saci (Paris, 1751)

Mémoires, souvenirs et journaux de la Comtesse d'Agoult, 2 vols. (Le Temps retrouvé, LVIII, Paris, 1990)

Mennais, Abbé de la, *Du projet de loi sur les congrégations religieuses des femmes* (Paris, 1825)

Molard, F., Charles Schmidt and Charles Porée, *Procès-verbaux de l'administration départementale de 1790 à 1800*, 7 vols. (Auxerre 1889–1913)

[Olivier, Marie d',] *Les Trois Paulines* (Lille, 1834)

—— *L'Imagination ou Charlotte de Drelincourt* (Lille, 1858)

—— *Dialogues des vivants au XIXe siècle* (Paris, 1859)

—— *Lettres aux jeunes femmes du monde élégant* (Avignon, 1866)

Perdrau, Pauline, *Les Loisirs de l'Abbaye, Souvenirs inédits de … Pauline Perdrau sur la vie de notre sainte mère* (Rome, 1934)

Pont, Abbé, *Vie de l'abbé Favre, Fondateurs des missions de Savoie* (Montiers, 1865)

Porée, Charles, *Sources manuscrites de l'histoire de la Révolution dans l'Yonne*, 2 vols. (Auxerre, 1918–1927)

Reynaud, François-Dominique de, Comte de Montlosier, *Les Jésuites, les congrégations et le parti prêtre, en 1827. Mémoire à M. le Comte de Villèle* (Paris, 1827)

Richardson, Samuel, *Clarissa, or the history of a young lady* (London, 1747–8)

Sand, Georges, *Histoire de ma vie* (Paris, 1993 edn)

Tournély, *Notice sur . . . Léonor François de, et sur son oeuvre La Congrégation des Pères du Sacré Coeur* (Vienne, 1886)

Wollstonecraft, Mary, *Vindication of the rights of women* (1792)

Other works consulted

Ainval, Christiane d', *Le couvent des Oiseaux. Ces jeunes filles de bonne famille* (Paris, 1991)

Arnaud-Duc, Nicole, 'The Law's Contradictions', in Geneviève Fraisse and Michelle Perrot (eds.), *A history of women in the West, IV, Emerging Feminism from Revolution to World War* (Harvard, 1993)

Arnold, Odile, *Le corps et l'âme. La vie religieuse au XIXe siècle* (Paris, 1984)

Baudier, Roger, *The Catholic Church in Louisiana* (New Orleans, 1972)

Baudouin, Marthe, *En avant quand même. La Société du Sacré-Cœur de Jésus au Canada* (Montréal, 1992)

Bedouelle, Guy, *Lacordaire, son pays, ses amis et la liberté des ordres religieux en France* (Paris, 1991)

Bonnard, Mgr Fourier, *Histoire du Couvent Royale de la Trinité du Mont Pincio à Rome* (Rome/Paris, 1933)

Boudon, Jacques-Olivier, *L'épiscopat français à l'époque concordaire, 1802–1905* (Cerf, 1996)

Byrne, Patricia, 'French roots of a women's movement: The Sisters of St Joseph, 1650–1836' (PhD Thesis, Boston College, 1985)

Callan, Louise, *Philippine Duchesne, Frontier missionary of the Sacred Heart, 1769–1852* (Maryland, 1957)

—— *The Society of the Sacred Heart in North America* (New York, 1937)

Careel, Marie France, *L'acte éducatif chez Madeleine-Sophie Barat, Fondatrice de la Société du Sacre-Coeur de Jésus* (Lyon, 1991)

Charry, Jeanne de, *Histoire des Constitutions de la Société du Sacré Coeur. La Formation de l'Institut*, 3 vols. (Rome, 1975)

—— *Histoire des Constitutions de la Société du Sacré Coeur, Second Partie, Les Constitutions définitives et leur approbation par le Saint-Siège.* 3 vols. (Rome, 1979)

—— (ed.), *Joseph Varin S.J., Lettres à Sainte Sophie Barat (1801–1849) Texte Intégral, d'après les manuscrits originaux, présenté avec une introduction, des notes et un index analytique* (Rome, 1982)

—— *Evolution canonique et légale de la Société du Sacré-Cœur de Jésus de 1827 à 1853* (Rome, 1991)

Chartier, Roger, *The Cultural origins of the French Revolution* (North Carolina, 1992)

Cholvy, Gérard, *Être chrétien en France au XIXe siècle, 1790–1914* (Paris, 1997)

Cholvy, Gérard and Chaline, Nadine-Josette, *L'enseignement catholique en France aux XIXe et XXe siècles* (Paris, 1995)

Cholvy, Gérard and Hilaire Yves-Marie, *Histoire religieuse de la France contemporaine, 1800–1880* (Privat, 1990)

Christophe, Paul, *Grandes figures sociales du XIXe siècle* (Paris, 1995)

Collingham, A.C., *The July Monarchy. A political history of France 1830–1848* (London, 1988)

Conrad, Glenn R.(ed.), Cross, *Crozier and Crucible: A volume celebrating the bicentennial of a Catholic diocese in Louisiana* (New Orleans, 1993)

Contassot, Félix, *La Congrégation de la Mission et les Séminaires aux xviie et xviiie siècles* (Paris, 1968)

—— *Les Lazaristes au Grand Séminaire de Sens avant la Révolution (1675–1791), Etude Documentaire* (Paris, 1962)

Conway, Jill Ker, *Written by Herself. Autobiographies of American women. An anthology* (Vintage, 1992)

Crampe-Casnabet, Michèle, 'A sampling of 18th century philosophy' in Natalie Zemon Davies and Arlette Farge (eds.), *A history of women in the West, iii, Renaissance and Enlightenment Paradoxes* (Harvard, 1994)

Davies, Natalie Zemon, *Women on the Margins, New Worlds: Marie de l'Incarnation* (Harvard, 1995)

Degert, Abbé A., *Histoires des séminaires jusqu'à la Révolution*, 2 vols. (Paris, 1912)

Delumeau, Jean, *L'aveu et le pardon. Les difficultés de la confession XIIIe–XVIIIe siècle* (Fayard, 1992)

Demoustier, Adrien and Julia, Dominique, *Ratio Studiorum. Plan raisonné et institution des études dans la Compagnie de Jésus* (Paris, 1997)

Dibie, Pascal, *Traditions de Bourgogne* (Verviers, 1978)

Driskel, Michael Paul, *Representing belief. Religion, art and society in nineteenth century France* (Pennsylvania, 1992)

Duffy, Eamonn, *Saints and Sinner. A history of the popes* (Yale, 1997)

Dufourcq, Elizabeth, *Les aventurières de Dieu. Trois siècles d'histoire missionnaire française*, 4 vols. (Paris, 1992)

Duhet, Paule-Marie and Ribérioux, Madeleine, *1789. Cahiers de doléances des femmes, et autres textes* (Paris, 1989)

Le Faubourg St Germain, La rue de Varenne, Musée Rodin (Paris, 1981)

Faucourpret, Benoit de, *Les Pensionnaires du Collège Mazarin ou des Quatre Nations, 1688–1794* (Paris, 1992)

Foley, William E., *The genesis of Missouri. From wilderness outpost to Statehood* (University of Missouri Press, 1989)

Franjou, Edmond, *La querelle janséniste à Joigny et dans le jovinien au xviiie siècle* (Auxerre, 1970)

Gadbois, Geneviève, ' "Vous êtes presque la seule consolation de l'Église". La foi des femmes face à la déchristianisation de 1789–1880', in Jean Delumeau (ed.), *La religion de ma mère. Le rôle des femmes dans la transmission de la foi* (Paris, 1992)

Garnier, Adrien, *Frayssinous. Son rôle dans l'Université sous la Restauration, 1822–1828* (Paris, 1925)

Gaustad, Edwin Scott, *A religious history of America* (Harper Collins, new rev. edn 1990)

Gibson, Ralph, *A social history of French Catholicism* (London, 1989)

Gilbert, Sandra M. and Gubar, Susan, *The mad woman in the attic. The woman writer and the Nineteenth-Century literary imagination* (Yale, 1984)

Gildea, Robert, *Barricades and borders. Europe* 1800–1914 (Oxford, 1987)

Goldberg, Rita, *Sex and Enlightenment: Women in Richardson and Diderot* (Cambridge, 1984)

Gough, Austin, *Paris and Rome, The Gallican Church and the Ultramontane Campaign* 1848–1853 (Oxford, 1986)

Gueber, Jean, *Le ralliement du clergé français à la morale liguorienne. L'abbé Gousset et ses précurseurs* (Rome, 1973)

Hamon, Léo, (ed.) *Du Jansénisme à la laïcité. Le Jansénisme et les origines de la déchristianisation* (Paris, 1987)

Heilbrun, Carolyn, *Writing a woman's life* (Woman's Press, 1989)

Hennessy, James, *American Catholics. A history of the Roman Catholic Community in the United States* (Oxford, 1981)

Heyden-Rynsch, Verena von der, *Salons Européens. Les beaux moments d'une culture féminine disparu* (Luçon, 1993)

Hildesheimer, Françoise, *Le Jansénisme* (Paris, 1992)

Hufton, Olwen, *Women and the limits of citzenship* (Toronto, 1992)

—— *The prospect before her. A history of women in western Europe, vol I, 1500–1800* (London, 1995)

Le Jansénisme dans l'Yonne. Les Cahiers des Archives no. 4 (Auxerre, 1986)

Jaurgain, Jean and Ritter, Raymond, *La Maison de Gramont, 1040–1967*, 2 vols. (Les Amis du Musée Pyrénéen, 1968)

Julia, Dominique, *Les trois couleurs du tableau noir. La Révolution* (Paris, 1981)

Käppeli, Anne-Marie, 'Feminist scenes' in Geneviève Fraisse and Michelle Perrot (ed.) *A history of women in the West, IV, Emerging Feminism from revolution to World War* (Harvard, 1993)

Kley, Dale K. Van, *The religious origins of the French Revolution. From Calvin to the Civil Constitution, 1560–1791* (Yale, 1996)

Langlois, Claude, *Le catholicisme au féminin. Les congrégations françaises à supérieure générale au XIXe siècle* (Paris, 1984)

Lerner, Gerda, *The creation of feminist consciousness. From the Middle Ages to Eighteen-seventy* (Oxford, 1993)

Limouzin-Lamothe, R., *Monsignor de Quelen, archevêque de Paris*, 2 vols., (Paris, 1955, 1957)

—— and Leflon, J., *Mgr Denys Affre, Archevêque de Paris, 1793–1848*, (Paris, 1971)

Loupès, Philippe, *La vie religieuse en France au XVIIIe siècle* (Paris, 1993)

Luirard, Monique, 'Madeleine Sophie Barat dans la tourmente Révolutionnaire' (Lille, 1996). Unpublished paper.

Maître, Jacques, *Mystique et féminité. Essai de psychanalyse sociohistorique* (Paris, 1997)

Mansel, Philip, *The Court of France 1789–1830* (Cambridge, 1991)

Manzini, Luigi M., *Il Cardinale Luigi Lambruschini* (Vatican, 1960)

Martin-Fugier, Anne, *La vie élégante ou la formation du Tout-Paris, 1815–1848* (Paris, 1990)

Martin, J.P., *La Nonciature de Paris et les affaires ecclésiastiques de France sous le règne de Louis-Philippe, 1830–1848* (Paris, 1949)

Mayeur, Françoise, *L'éducation des filles en France au XIXe siècle* (Paris, 1979)

Mégnien, C.P., 'La vigne, le vin et les vignerons de Joigny' in vol. 3 of *A travers notre folklore et son dialect*, 4 vols. (Dijon, 1974–1977)

Melville, A.M., *Louis William Dubourg: Bishop of Louisiana and the Floridas, bishop of Montauban and the archbishop of Besançon, 1766–1833*, 2 vols., (Chicago, 1986)

Mezler Sara E., and Rabine, Leslie W., *Rebel Daughters, Women and the French Revolution* (Oxford, 1992)

Mooney, Catherine M., *Philippine Duchesne, A woman with the poor* (Paulist Press, 1990)

Morrissey, Thomas, *As one sent. Peter Kenny SJ*, 1779–1841 (Dublin, 1996)

Moulinet, Daniel, *Les classiques païens dans les collèges catholiques? Le combat de Mgr Gaume* (Cerf, 1995)

Naudet, Leopoldine, Beatificationis et canonizationis servae Dei, Leopoldinae Naudet fundatricis sororum a Sacra Familia Veronae (1773–1834). Relatio et Vota, 5 novembre 1996 (Rome, 1996)

Newman, Barbara, *From Virile Woman to Woman Christ. Studies in Medieval Religion and Literature* (Pennsylvania, 1995)

Nicolay, Jean de, *Pauline de Nicolay, Tertiaire Franciscaine, 1811–1868* (Neuilly, 1991)

Nobécourt, Marie-Dominique, 'Un exemple de l'éducation des filles au 19e siècle par les congrégations religieuses: le Sacré-Cœur de Paris, 1816–1874' (Thesis, Ecole des Chatres, 1981)

Noirot, Alype Jean, *Le Département de l'Yonne comme diocèse*, 5 vols. (Auxerre, 1979)

Offen, Karen, Ruth Roach Pierson and Jane Rendall, *Writing Women's History. International perspectives* (Macmillan, 1991)

O'Malley, John W., *The first Jesuits* (Harvard, 1994)

Padberg, John W., *Colleges in Controversy. The Jesuit schools in France from revival to suppression 1815–1880* (Harvard, 1969)

Peletier, Denis, *Les catholiques en France depuis 1815* (Paris, 1997)

Pentini, Maria Aluffi, *Sante Magdalena Sophia Barat à travers sa correspondance* (Rome, 1968–69)

Le peintre de Mater Admirabilis. Mère Pauline Perdrau, 1815–1895 (Montauban, 1927)

Peri-Morosini, Mons., *La Sainte Mère Madeleine Sophie Barat, fondatrice de la Société du Sacré-Cœur et le chateau de Middes en Suisse* (Toulouse, 1925)

Perrot, Michelle 'Roles and characters' in Michelle Perrot (ed.), *A history of private life, vol IV, From the fires of Revolution to the Great War* (Harvard, 1990)

Pilbeam, Pamela, *Republicanism in Nineteenth-Century France* (London, 1995)

Poinsenet, Marie Dominique, *Rien n'est impossible à l'amour. Marie Euphrasie*

Porter, Roy, *The greatest benefit to mankind. A medical history of humanity from antiquity to the present* (London, 1997)

Positio: Documentary study for the canonisation of Cornelia Connolly (née Peacock), 1809–1879, 3 vols (Rome, 1983); *Informatio for the canonisation process of ... Cornelia Connolly (née Peacock), 1809–1879* (Rome, 1879)

Poupard, Paul, *Correspondance inédite entre Mgr Antonio Antonio Garibaldi, internonce à Paris et Mgr Césaire Mathieu archevêque de Besançon. Contribution à l'histoire de l'administration ecclésiastique sous la monarchie de juillet* (Rome, 1961)

Price, Roger, *A concise history of France* (Cambridge, 1993)

Rayez, André and Louis Fèvre, *Foi Chrétienne et vie consacrée. Clorivière aujourd'hui* (Paris, 1971)

Rémond, René, *L'anticléricalisme en France. De 1815 à nos jours* (Brussels, 1992)

Ribeton, Olivier, *Les Gramonts. Portraits de famille, XVIe –XVIIIe siècles* (J et D. Editions, 1992)

Ripa, Yannick, *Women and madness. The incarceration of women in nineteenth-century France* (Polity Press, 1990)

Robb, Graham, *Balzac* (London, 1994)

Roche, Maurice, *Saint Vincent de Paul and the formation of clerics* (Fribourg, Switzerland, 1964)

Roe, Mary, *The educational thought of Madeleine Sophie Barat* (Dublin, 1974)

Rogers, Rebecca, *Les demoiselles de la Légion d'honneur. Les maisons d'éducation de la Légion d'honneur au XIXe siècle* (Paris, 1992)

Sevrin, Ernest, *Les missions religieuses en France sous la Restauration 1815–1879* (Paris, 1959)

Showalter, Elaine *The female malady. Women, madness and English culture, 1830–1980* (London, 1985)

Smith, Bonnie G., *Ladies of the leisure class. The bourgeoisies of northern France in the nineteenth century* (Princeton, 1981)

Sonnet, Martine, *L'éducation des filles au temps des Lumières* (Paris, 1987)

Turin, Yvonne, *Femmes et religieuses au XIXe siècle* (Paris, 1989)

Vacquier, J, *Monographie du Faubourg Saint-Germain, Ancien Hôtel du Maine et de Biron, en dernier lieu Etablissement des Dames du Sacré Cœur* (Paris, 1909)

Venard, Marc, 'Du Roi Très Chrétien à la laïcité republicaine. XVIIIe –XIXe siècle' in Jacques Le Goff and René Remond (eds.), *Histoire de la France religieuse*, t. 3 (Paris, 1991)

Vincent-Buffault, Anne *The history of tears. Sense and sentimentality in France* (London, 1991)

Virnot, Marie-Thérèse, (ed.) *Sainte Madeleine-Sophie Barat, Journal, Poitiers 1806–1808. Texte Intégral* (Poitiers, 1977)

Weber, Alison, *Teresa of Avila and the rhetoric of femininity* (Princeton, 1990)

Webster, Kathryn (ed.), *The Correspondence between bishop Joseph Rosati and blessed Philippine Duchesne* (St Louis, 1950)

Weisner, Merry E., *Women and gender in early modern Europe* (Cambridge, 1995)

Woloch, Isser, *The new regime. Transformations of the French Civic Order, 1789–1820s* (Norton, 1995)

Woodrow, Alain, *The Jesuits. A study of power* (London, 1995)

Woolf, Virginia *A room of one's own* (London, 1929)

—— *Three Guineas* (London, 1938)

Periodicals/articles

Anderson, George K, 'Old nobles and noblesse d'Empire, 1814–1830: In search of a conservative interest in post-Revolutionary France', in *French History*, vol. 8, no. 2 (1994)

Byrne, Patricia, 'Sisters of St Joseph: The Americanisation of a French Tradition', in *US Catholic Historian*, 5 (1986)

Clements, Teresa, 'Les Pères de la Foi, in France, 1800–1814, spirituality, foundations, biographical notes' in AHSI, lvii, fasc. 114, Periodicum semestre (1988)

Davier, Edme, "Miscellanea eruditionis tam sacrae quam profanae", in S. Jossier, 'Notice sur Edme-Louis-Davier', in *Bulletin de la Société des Sciences de l'Yonne*, vol. 13 (1859)

Dougherty, M.P. 'L'Ami de la Religion et les évêques français sous le Concordat, 1815–1850', in *Revue d'Histoire Ecclésiastique*, lxxxix, nos. 3–4 (Louvain, 1994)

Gibson, Ralph, 'Le catholicisme et les femmes en France au XIXe siècle' in RHEF, vol. lxxix, no. 202 (janvier–juin, 1993)

Hasquenoph, Sophie, 'Faire retraite a couvent dans le Paris des Lumières', in *Revue historique*, no. 598 (avril–juin 1996)

Hayden Michael, J, 'States, estates and orders: The qualité of female clergy in early modern France', in *French History*, vol. 8, no. 1 (1994)

Joigny: 'La vie économique à Joigny', in *L'Echo de Joigny*, nos. 28–29, Numéro Spécial (1980)

'La Fête de la Fédération (14 juillet 1790)' in *L'Echo de Joigny*, no. 44 (1988)

'Le premier 14 juillet à Joigny', in *L'Echo de Joigny*, no. 1 (1970)

'La religion à Joigny', in *L'Echo de Joigny*, nos. 28–29 (1980)

'Réunion tumultueuse à Joigny pour obtenir la démission du principal du collège, Saulnier', in *L'Echo de Joigny*, no. 25 (1978)

'L'Insurrection de septembre 1792 à Joigny', in *L'Echo de Joigny*, no. 4 (1970)

Rassemblements tumultueux d'hommes dans les vignes. See 'Tentative d'émeute et rixe entre vignerons ' (6 février 1792) in L'Echo de Joigny, no 25 (1978)

Joigny sous la Terreur. Relation de voyage de Mallard [1793] in L'Echo de Joigny, no 16 (1975)

'Soldat Mallard, Relation de voyage de Mallard, 1794', (ed.) M.Vallery-Radot, in *L'Echo de Joigny*, no 16, Ier Trimestre (1975)

Mothe, Edme-Joachim de la, 'Eloge du climat de Joigny (1783)' in *L'Echo de Joigny*, no 7 (1971–2), pp. 13–18

'Notice sur Antoine-Joseph-André Sudan, premier maire de Joigny en 1798' in *L'Echo de Joigny*, no 1, 1st trimestre (1970)

'Un cas de possession diabolique à Joigny, en 1791 [1790]. Récit de l'abbé Fromentot' in *L'Echo de Joigny*, no 15 (1974)

Kilroy, Phil, 'The use of continental sources of women's religious congregations and the writing of religious biography: Madeleine Sophie Barat, 1779–1865', in Maryann Gialanella Valiulis and Mary O'Dowd (eds.), *Women and Irish History* (Dublin, 1997)

Korner, Barbara O., 'Philippine Duchesne: A model of Action', in *Missouri Historical Review*, vol. lxxxvi, no. 4 (July, 1992)

Langlois, Claude, 'La vie religieuse vers 1840: un nouveau modèle', in Guy Bedouelle, *Lacordaire, son pays, ses amis et la liberté des ordres religieux en France* (Paris, 1991)

—— 'Clorivière et la Révolution: Apocalypse ou apologétique?', in *Recherches autour de Pierre de Clorivière* (Paris, 1993)

Leroy, Michel, *Le mythe jésuite. De Beranger à Michelet* (Paris, 1992)

Morlot, François, Le Père Louis Barat, Supérieur du Grand Séminaire de Troyes. Extrait des Mémoires de la Société Académique de l'Aube, vol. cix, 1978 (Troyes, 1980)

O'Brien, Susan, 'French Nuns in Nineteenth Century England', in *Past and Present*, no. 154 (February 1997)

O'Brien, Susan, 'Terra Incognita: The Nun in Nineteenth-Century England', in *Past and Present*, no. 121 (November 1988)

Peltier, Henri, 'Le chanoine de Brandt', *Le Dimanche* [Amiens], 11–18 septembre 1949

Pudor, G, 'A propos de la guérison du P. Blanpin', in *Echos de Santa Chiara*, vol. xxxix (juillet–août 1939)

"Quelques personnages illustres. Edme-Louis Davier (1665–1746)", in Notre Saint-Thibault. Bulletin paroissial, 1e novembre 1937, no. 4.

Rapley, Elizabeth and Robert, 'The image of Religious Women in the *ancien régime*: the états des religieuses of 1790–1791', in *French History*, vol. 11, no. 4 (December 1997)

Rayez, André, 'Clorivière et les Pères de la Foi', in *AHSJ*, vol. xxi (1952)

Reynier, Chantal, 'Le Père de Clorivière et le rétablissement des jésuites en France (1814–1818)', in *Revue Mabillon*, n.s., t.6 (=t.67), 1995.

—— 'La correspondance de P.J. de Clorivière avec T.Brzozowski, 1814 à 1818. Le rétablissement de la Compagnie en France', in AHSI, vol. lxiv (1995)

Rogers, Rebecca, 'Competing visions of Female Education in Post-Revolutionary France', in *History of Education Quarterly* (summer 1994)

—— 'Boarding schools, Women teachers and Domesticity: Reforming Girl's Secondary Education in the First Half of the Nineteenth Century', in *French Historical Studies*, vol. 19, no. 1 (1995), pp. 153–81.

—— 'Retrograde or Modern? Unveiling the Nun in Nineteenth Century France', in *Social History* (GB), vol. 23, no. 2 (May, 1998)

Sainte Sophie Barat et le diocèse de Lausanne, Genève et Fribourg in La semaine catholique de la Suisse Romande, nos. 20, 21, 22 (1952)

Thompson, D.G., 'The Lavelette Affair and the Jesuit Superiors', in *French History*, vol. 10, no. 1 (June, 1996), pp. 206–39.

NOTES

Notes to Introduction

1 Gérard Cholvy, *Être chrétien en France au XIXe siècle, 1790–1914* (Paris, 1997), pp. 11–19, 143; Ralph Gibson, *A Social History of French Catholicism* (London, 1989), pp. 14–29.

2 Geneviève Gadbois, '"Vous êtes presque la seule consolation de l'Église". La foi des femmes face à la déchristianisation de 1789–1880', in Jean Delumeau (ed.), *La religion de ma mère. Le rôle des femmes dans la transmission de la foi* (Paris, 1992), pp. 301–25.

3 Claude Langlois, *Le catholicisme au féminin. Les congrégations françaises à supérieure générale au XIXe siècle* (Paris, 1984); Odile Arnold, *Le corps et l'âme. La vie religieuse au XIXe siècle* (Paris, 1984); Yvonne Turin, *Femmes et religieuses au XIXe siècle* (Paris, 1989); Denis Peletier, *Les catholiques en France depuis 1815* (Paris, 1997), pp. 28–30; Gérard Cholvy, op. cit., pp. 36–45; Ralph Gibson, 'Le catholicisme et les femmes en France au XIXe siècle', RHEF, vol. lxxix, no. 202 (janvier-juin, 1993), pp. 63–93; Elizabeth and Robert Rapley, 'The Image of Religious Women in the *ancien régime*: the états des religieuses of 1790–1791', *French History*, vol. 11, no. 4, (December 1997), pp. 387–410.

4 Alison Weber, *Teresa of Avila and the Rhetoric of Femininity* (Princeton, 1990).

5 Edme Davier, "Miscellanea eruditionis tam sacrae quam profanae", S. Jossier, 'Notice sur Edme-Louis-Davier' in *Bulletin de la Société des Sciences de l'Yonne*, vol. 13 (1859), p. 144; "Quelques personnages illustres. Edme-Louis Davier (1665–1746)", *Notre Saint-Thibault*. Bulletin paroissial, 1e novembre 1937, no. 4. Une femme ... est un[e] protégé[e] qui change de figure et de caractère comme il lui plaît. Dissimulée dans ses pensées, ingénieuse dans ses passions, politique dans ses vues, friponne dans ses discours, coquette dans ses manières, affectée dans ses airs, fausse dans ses vertus, intéressée dans ses libéralités, hypocrite dans ses épargnes; toujours rusée; toujours équivoque et toujours une contrevérité: du plus ou moins, voilà comme les femmes sont faites.

6 Michèle Crampe-Casnabet, 'A sampling of eighteenth century philosophy', Natalie Zemon Davies and Arlette Farge (eds.), *A History of Women in the West, iii, Renaissance and Enlightenment Paradoxes* (Harvard, 1994), pp. 315–47; Olwen Hufton, *The Prospect Before Her. A History of Women in Western Europe, vol. I, 1500–1800* (London, 1995), pp. 432–3.

7 Paule-Marie Duhet et Madeleine Ribérioux, *1789. Cahiers de doléances des femmes, et autres textes* (Paris, 1989); Marquis de Condorcet, *Sur l'admission des femmes au droit de cité* (1790); Olympe de Gouges, *Les droits de la Femme* (1791); Mary Wollstonecraft, *Vindication of the Rights of Women* (1792); Sara E. Mezler and Leslie W. Rabine, *Rebel Daughters, Women and the French Revolution* (Oxford, 1992).

8 Michelle Perrot, 'Roles and characters', in Michelle Perrot (ed.), *A History of Private Life, vol. IV, From the Fires of Revolution to the Great War* (Harvard, 1990), pp. 167–185; Pamela Pilbeam, *Republicanism in Nineteenth-Century France* (London, 1995), pp. 172–4. Anne-Marie Käppeli, 'Feminist scenes', in Geneviève Fraisse and Michelle

Perrot (eds.) *A History of Women in the West, IV, Emerging Feminism from Revolution to World War* (Harvard, 1993), 482–87; Hufton, op.cit., pp. 25–58.

9   Ultramontanism fostered papal supremacy, rather than the independence of national churches. In the first half of the nineteenth century ultramontanism in France was a reaction to Gallicanism, expressed in papalism, a romantic interest in early Christian Rome and an idealisation of the Middle ages.

10 Gerda Lerner, *The creation of feminist consciousness. From the Middle Ages to Eighteen-seventy* (Oxford, 1993), p. 17. Also, Barbara Newman, *From Virile Woman to Woman Christ. Studies in Medieval Religion and Literature* (Pennsylvania, 1995), pp. 2–3.

11 Gallicanism in France was an expression of the independent stance which the French government and/or the French bishops held with regard to the role, power and teaching of the papacy.

12 Phil Kilroy, 'The use of continental sources of women's religious congregations and the writing of religious biography: Madeleine Sophie Barat, 1779–1865', in Maryann Gialanella Valiulis and Mary O'Dowd (eds.) *Women and Irish History* (Dublin, 1997), pp. 59–70.

13 Adèle Cahier, *Vie de la Vénérable Mère Madeleine-Sophie Barat, fondatrice et première supérieure générale de la Société du Sacré Coeur*, 2 vols. (Paris, 1884).

14 Louis Baunard, *Histoire de Madame Barat, fondatrice de la Société du Sacré Coeur*, 2 vols. (Paris, 1876). This work had run to its sixth edition by 1892. An illustrated edition was published in 1900 for the centenary of the Society of the Sacred Heart and a second edition printed for the canonisation of Madeleine Sophie Barat in 1925.

Notes to Chapter 1

1   AD, Yonne, 2 E 206/21. While the birth certificate states that Sophie was baptised the day she was born, 12 December 1779, Sophie herself always referred to her birth on the evening of 12 December 1779. Corr. SB et Louise de Limminghe, Lettre 541, Paris, 19 décembre 1857; [Josephine de Coriolis] Histoire de la Société du Sacré Coeur de Jésus, fondée en 1800 par … Madeleine Louise Sophie Barat, f. 26v (G.A. Rome, A-II., 2-b).

2   Adrienne Michel, Journal du second voyage de … Mère Barat à Gand 1811. No pagination (G.A. Rome, C-I., A, 1-c, Box 1); de Coriolis, Histoire de la Société du Sacré Coeur, f. 26v. Pauline Perdrau, *Les Loisirs de l'Abbaye, Souvenirs inédits de … Pauline Perdrau sur la vie de notre sainte mère*, 2 vols. (Rome, 1934, 1936), i, 329.

3   Détails envoyés par Madame Cousin, 3 juin 1872 (G.A, Rome, C-I., A, 1-e, Box 1).

4   Archives Communales. Maire de Joigny, Sous série G, 1 G 15, District de Joigny, De la division du territoire en sections.

5   Edme-Joachim de la Mothe, 'Eloge du climat de Joigny' (1783) *L'Echo de Joigny*, no. 7 (1971–72), pp. 13–18. *Almanach historique de la ville, bailliage et diocèse de Sens 1782* (Sens, 1782), p. 49. Also, Soldat Mallard, *Relation de voyage de Mallard*, 1794, pp. 20, 22.

6   F. Molard, Charles Schmidt and Charles Porée, *Procès-verbaux de l'administration départementale de 1790 à 1800*, 7 vols. (Auxerre 1889–1913), i, 304; AD, Yonne, L 275; Soldat Mallard, *Relation de voyage de Mallard*, 1794, ed. M.Vallery-Radot, in *L'Echo de Joigny*, no. 16, Ier Trimestre (1975), p. 22; 'Notice sur Antoine-Joseph-André Sudan, premier maire de Joigny en 1798' *L'Echo de Joigny*, no. 1, Ier trimestre (1970), p. 14.

7   Perdrau, *Loisirs*, p. 390. 'D'un artisan, d'un tonnelier, on dit d'un vigneron … mon père faisait des tonnes et les vendait.'

8   Archives Communales. Maire de Joigny. Série G. Sous-série 1 G, 1 G 15. Héritages sur le Territoire de Joigny … Héritages sur le Territoire de St Aubin. Barrat Jacques, gde Fouffé, tonnelier; C.P. Mégnien, 'La vigne, le vin et les vignerons de Joigny', vol. 3 of *A travers notre folklore et son dialect*, 4 vols. (Dijon, 1974–1977); Pascal Dibie, *Traditions de Bourgogne* (Verviers, 1978).

9   Marie de Gloanic to Louise Douzon, Avigliana, 6 juillet 1927 (Archives de la Société du Sacré Coeur, Joigny).

10 Monique Luirard, 'Madeleine Sophie Barat dans la tourmente Révolutionnaire' (Lille, 1996). Unpublished paper, p. 2.

11 Marie de Gloanic to Louise Douzon, Avigliana, 22 juillet 1927 (Archives de la Société du Sacré Coeur, Joigny).

12 Désignation. Une propriété sise à Joigny, rue Davier (ancienne rue du Puits Chardon), 28 août 1886 (Archives de la Société du Sacré Coeur, Joigny). Also in Marie de Gloanic to Louise Douzon, Avigliana, 22 juillet 1927 (Archives of the Society of the Sacred Heart, Joigny).

13 Notice sur l'enfance et la jeunesse du R.P. Barat avec lettre d'envoi autographe de Ste Sophie Barat, 1846 (AFSJ, Vanves, Carton Louis Barat). 'Naquit de parents chrétiens mais peu riche, cependant ils jouissent d'une certaine aisance. Le père cultivait lui-même les vignes, exercissoit le double métier de vigneron et de tonnelier; il put assuré élever convenablement les enfants'.

14 Archives Communales. Maire de Joigny. Série G. Sous-série 1 G, 1 G 15. Héritages sur le Territoire de Joigny … Héritages sur le Territoire de St Aubin. Barrat Jacques, gde Fouffé, tonnelier. Also, 1 G 17: Rôles des propriétaires 1791 Etats de sections. Déclarations des Propriétaires, Sections A-H, Nos 1450, 1466, 1478; cf nos. 581 571; 1 G 18: Contribution foncières 1791 S.A. Joigny Numéros de Propriétés compris dans la section. S.

A. 1564; S.B. 620; 938; Sous-série 2 G Impôts extraordinaire. 2 G 1, Déclaration de la citoyenne Chollet veuve Piochard.

15 Archives Communales. Maire de Joigny. Séries G, Sous-série 1 G Impôt Direct, 1 G 15 Etat de section, Procès verbaux 1791. Population de Joigny; 1 G 16 Etat de section, Déclarations des Propriétaires. Also 1 G 21 and 1 G 22, Contribution mobilière, nos. 581, 547; Sous-série 2 G, 2 G 2 An IV et V de la République, Contribution personnelle et somptuaire, Art 21, Barrat Jacque gre Fouffé tonnelier. For a history of the taxes in the Département of the Yonne, and of Joigny in particular, at this time see: AD, Yonne, C 185, Département de Joigny. Procès Verbaux des séances du département de Joigny; C 187, Joigny, Départements des Années. Also, 'La vie économique à Joigny', *l'Echo de Joigny*, nos. 28–29, Numéro Spécial (1980), pp. 11–19.

16 Letters of Sophie Barat to Stanislas Dusaussoy, Lettre 63, Turin, 9 July 1832. 'Cependant je crois que c'est hier que j'ai commencé à penser, et que j'avais que dix-sept mois quand je me suis aperçue que j'existais; il y a donc 51 ans que je pense.'

17 La première initiation de Sophie Barat au culte du Sacré-Coeur. Récit de la Mère Barat ... 30 mai 1856. General Archives, Rome Journal de la probation 1855–1856, 36. Jeanne de Charry, *Histoire des constitutions de la Société du Sacré-Cœur. La formation de l'Institut*, 3 vols. (Rome, 1975, iii, *Textes*, nos. 10, 89, 89–90). 'Il est bon que vous sachiez ... que je suis née d'une famille Janséniste, et très attachée à cette Secte qui est toujours montrée l'ennemie jurée de la dévotion au Sacré-Coeur'.

18 Françoise Hildesheimer, *Le Jansénisme* (Paris, 1992); Philippe Loupès, *La vie religieuse en France au XVIIIe siècle* (Paris, 1993); Dale K. Van Kley, *The religious origins of the French Revolution. From Calvin to the Civil Constitution, 1560–1791* (Yale, 1996); Roger Chartier, *The Cultural origins of the French Revolution* (North Carolina, 1992). Sous la responsabilité de Léo Harmon, *Du Jansénisme á la laïcité. Le Jansénisme et les origines de la déchristianisation* (Paris, 1987); *Le Jansénisme dans l'Yonne. Les Cahiers des Archives No 4* (Auxerre, 1986).

19 Edmond Franjou, *La querelle janséniste à Joigny et dans le jovinien au xviiie siècle* (Auxerre, 1970) pp. 3–11.

20 He was the biographer of Margaret Mary Alacoque, who had received revelations of the love of God symbolised in the Heart of Christ, a counter to the severe image of God presented by the Jansensists.

21 Franjou, *La querelle jansèniste*, pp. 3–11; 30–45; 51–81.

22 Perdrau, *Loisirs*, p. 165. 'Comme on parlait devant l'enfant d'une communauté divisée par l'effet des idées jansénistes. Sophie se dit à elle-même "Je serai religieuse mais je n'entrerai que dans un ordre où l'on sera d'accord, pas en révolution" '.

23 Histoire de la Société du Sacré Coeur de Jésus, fondée en 1800 par ... Sophie Louise Barat (G.A. Rome, A-II, 2-b, ff. 27

24 AD, Yonne, 11 J 206/16, Paroisse de St Thibault Catholicité, 1797–1800. Marriage notice of Marie-Louise Barat, 13 March 1793.

25 Archives de la Congrégation de la Mission, Paris. Félix Contassot, *La Congrégation de la Mission et les Séminaires aux xviie et xviiie siècles* (Paris, 1968), pp. 95–211; Félix Contassot, *Les Lazaristes au Grand Séminaire de Sens avant la Révolution (1675–1791), Etude Documentaire* (Paris, 1962), pp. 51–52. Maurice Roche, *Saint Vincent de Paul and the Formation of Clerics* (Fribourg, Switzerland, 1964), pp. 76–77; also, Abbé A. Degert, *Histoires des séminaires jusqu'à la Révolution*, 2 vols. (Paris, 1912), ii, 251–3. A great number of archives of the Congregation of the Mission were destroyed during the French Revolution, including those pertaining to the seminary at Sens.

26 Roche, op. cit., pp. 188–95.

27 AD, Yonne, L 610, College de Joigny, Auxerre 20 août 1791; 16 janvier 1792.

28 De Coriolis, Histoire de la Société du Sacré Coeur, ff. 27–27v. The College of the Four Nations, which existed from 1688 to 1794, was founded by Cardinal Mazarin. It was destined for the sons of noble families, and though in principle open to the sons of the wealthy middle class who lived like the nobility, none in practice were admitted. Thus it is hard to see how Louis Barat gained admittance. However in the turbulent times after 1789, and before its closure in 1794, Louis Barat could have attended courses there by day as there was provision for extern students. Louis Barat is not listed in the list of resident or non-resident students at the College. (Archives Nationales, Paris, C 149, no. 251; M 174, no. 64; M 715, nos. 14, 19; MM 464; H3 2555; H3 2562). Benoit de Faucourpret, *Les Pensionnaires du Collège Mazarin ou des Quatre Nations, 1688–1794* (Paris, 1992).

29 The Society of Jesus, founded by St Ignatius of Loyola in the sixteenth century, had become a powerful order in the church by the seventeenth and eighteenth centuries, with many enemies. The order had already been banished from Spain, Portugal and Paraguay before its suppression in France.

30 Adrienne Michel, Journal du second voyage de ... Mère Barat à Gand 1811. 'Se chargea de suite de mon éducation et devint non seulement mon Maître mais celui de Papa et de Maman'.

31 Notes sur notre ... fondatrice et les commencements de la Société. Premiers jours de la Société du Sacré Coeur de Jésus (G.A. Rome, A-II, 1-a, Box 1), no pagination. 'Elle fut confiée aux soins d'un frère, plus zélé pour l'avancement de l'âme de sa soeur, qu'expérimenté dans les soins nécessaires à une constitution faible et délicate ... il songea à faire de sa soeur une Sainte et pour cela il ne dédaigna pas d'en faire une femme savante ... Il la faisait travailler sans donner la relâche nécessaire à son âge et à ses forces physiques. Là, cette

âme fut captive; peut-être moins retenue, elle eût été moins gagnée; mais toujours est-il que le corps en pâtit'. Also, Perdrau, *Loisirs*, pp. 93, 165–7, 239, 375.

32 De Coriolis, Histoire de la Société du Sacré Coeur, ff. 26–26v.

33 Cahier, *Vie*, i, 3.

34 Adrienne Michel, Journal du second voyage de ... Mère Barat à Gand 1811.

35 AD, Yonne, L 610, 16 janvier 1792.

36 There is no record of Sophie's Confirmation. Confirmations were rare at this period, especially between 1789 and 1820. See E. Sevrin, *Les missions religieuses en France sous la Restauration 1815–1879* (Paris, 1959), i, 300–1. Her baptismal certificate has the names Madeleine Sophie, but Sophie signed all formal papers Madeleine Sophie Louise Barat, which may indicate that she took the name Louise at confirmation.

37 Deshayes, Notes sur notre ... fondatrice et les commencements de la Société, f. 4. Other accounts say that Sophie made her First Communion at ten years of age. De Coriolis, Histoire de la Société du Sacré Coeur, f. 31. The prayer book was in French. *Manuel du Chrétien, contenant les psaumes, le Nouveau Testament et l'Imitation de Jesus Christ. De la tradition de M le Maître de Saci* (Paris, 1751). Madame Fouffé bought the prayer book in 1754 and noted that it was expensive. Sophie wrote her name inside the front cover in large, childish handwriting; Cahier, *Vie*, i, 8–9.

38 De Coriolis, Histoire de la Société du Sacré Coeur, ff. 30–30v. Jeanne de Charry (ed.), *Joseph Varin S.J., Lettres a Sainte Sophie Barat (1801–1849) Texte Intégral, d'après les manuscrits originaux, présenté avec une introduction, des notes et un index analytique* (Rome, 1982), pp. 3–4, 189–90.

39 Adrienne Michel, Journal du second voyage de ... Mère Barat à Gand 1811. Il fallait que je fusse prête pour aller à la messe des écoliers qui était à 7 heures. Un jour que j'avais envie de dormir, mon frère arrive et demande: "Où est Sophie ?" Je l'entends et de frayeur, je m'enfonçais dans mon lit. "Est-ce que tu crois qu'elle est si paresseuse ?", lui dit Maman. Lui, prenant cette affirmation pour une réponse ne dit plus rien; mais moi, je m'écriai: "Je suis ici". Alors il me dit: "Tâche de te lever tout de suite et d'être encore à la Messe aussi tôt que moi." Je ne fus pas cinq minutes à m'habiller tant j'avais peur.

40 'Un cas de possession diabolique à Joigny, en 1791 [1790]. Récit de l'abbé Fromentot' in *L'Echo de Joigny*, no. 15 (1974), pp. 13–18. Deshayes Premiers jours de la Société, [f 5]; Adrienne Michel, Journal du second voyage de ... Mère Barat à Gand 1811.

41 'Notice sur Antoine-Joseph-André Sudan, premier maire de Joigny en 1798', *L'Echo de Joigny*, no. 1, 1st trimestre (1970), pp. 13–15.

42 AD, Yonne, L. 195 Discours sur les avantages que peuvent procurer les établissements de sociétés patriotiques, le 14 avril 1791.

43 Soldat Mallard, Relation de voyage de Mallard, 1794, p. 21

44 AD, Yonne, L 610, Collège de Joigny 16 janvier 1792; L 826, 3e Registre, Séance du 11 mai 1792; L 1124, Registre des délibérations et opérations du comité de surveillance de la section de St Thibault de la ville de Joigny, Année 1793, f. 23; L 41, 16 juin 1792; L 47, 21 mars 1793. Archives Municipales de Joigny, Mairie de Joigny, Sous série 1D Conseil Municipal 1789–1944: 1D1 Délibérations du Conseil Municipales du 3 septembre 1789 au 22 août 1793, ff. 76–77, 83–84. Archives de la Société du Sacré Coeur, Joigny, Dossier Louis Barat. De Coriolis, Histoire de la Société du Sacré Coeur, ff. 27v-28v. De Coriolis omits the fact that Louis Barat first took the oath and then retracted. Louis Barat was released from prison on 19 January 1795.

45 AD, Yonne, L 1124, f 23. Madame Barat wrote to the town council, pleading the case on the basis that Louis Barat was not ordained. Fouffé femme Barat Aux citoyens membres de la municipalité de Joigny Fouffé, wife of Barat. To the citizen-members of the town council (n.d). The sequestration order placed on the Barat home and goods was lifted on 1 May 1793. Joigny le 2e prairial de l'an 2o, Département de l'Yonne, District de Joigny, Archives de la Société du Sacré Coeur, Joigny.

46 AD, Yonne, L 1124, f. 23 Département de l'Yonne. Administration du District de Joigny. Extrait du Procès Verbal de la séance du 1er de prairial de l'an 2e de la République Française (1 mai 1793). This was confirmed on 2 May 1793 in a letter to the town authorities of Joigny; Adrienne Michel, Journal du second voyage de ... Mère Barat à Gand 1811. 'On me montrait du doigt comme une aristocrate'.

47 'La fête de la Fédération (14 juillet 1790)', *L'Echo de Joigny*, no. 44 (1988); Le premier 14 juillet à Joigny in *L'Echo de Joigny* no. 1 (1970), pp. 13–15; La religion à Joigny in *L'Echo de Joigny*, nos. 28–29, 1980, pp. 47–48; Charles Porée, *Sources manuscrites de l'histoire de la Révolution dans l'Yonne*, 2 vols. (Auxerre, 1918–1927), i, 139.

48 AD, Yonne, L 831, Délibérations du Conseil du District de Joigny (18 Septembre 1793) 'pas un seul grain de bled sur le marché'; L 245, Lettre du Conseil Municipal de Joigny (31 mars 1794). The town council warned that if the people of Joigny did not receive food soon some would die from starvation.

49 AD, Yonne, L 195 Discours sur les avantages que peuvent procurer les établissements de sociétés patriotiques ... à Joigny ... le 14 avril 179. Also L 828, 1793–1794. The existence of four Sociétés Populaires in Joigny and the activity of the comités de surveillance were noted with approval. Even before his retraction, the rector of St Jacques Saulnier was being pushed out. AD, Yonne, L 25, 25 août 1790. 'Réunion tumultueuse à Joigny pour obtenir la démission du principal du collège, Saulnier', *L'Echo de Joigny*, no. 25 (1978), pp. 22–3. 'L'Insurrection de septembre 1792 à Joigny', *L'Echo de Joigny*, no. 4 (1970), pp. 7–9; AD, Yonne, L 196 Lettre

de la Municipalité de Joigny au Directoire du Département, 6 février 1792. 'Rassemblements tumultueux d'hommes dans les vignes.' See 'Tentative d'émeute et rixe entre vignerons' (6 février 1792)', *L'Echo de Joigny*, no. 25 (1978), pp. 23–4. Joigny sous la Terreur. Relation de voyage de Mallard [1793] in *L'Echo de Joigny*, no. 16 (1975), pp. 20–24.

50 Joigny le 6 fructidor 2me année Républicaine [6 August 1793], Les administrateurs du district de Joigny aux officiers de la commune de Joigny. The authorities were trying to find out the forenames of one Louis Barat, teacher at the Collège St Jacques, who had retracted his oath and whose name was on the list of emigré priests; they extended their search to Paris and Louis Barat was arrested there.

51 Corr. SB et Louise de Limminghe, Lettre 272, Paris 18 novembre 1840.

52 AD, Yonne Registre de St Thibault de Joigny, Série 2 E, 11 J 206/16, 1792–1800; Archives Municipales de Joigny, Bibliothèque de Joigny, Paroisse de St Thibault, Registres des naissances, no. 63, 2 mars 1792; no. 151, 4 septembre 1795. (ouvrière en linge; vigneronne). By custom, Sophie had her own seat in St Thibault's, which she paid for annually. AD, Yonne, Série 2 E, 11 J 206/31, Registre des concessions des places et bancs d'Eglise. Paroisse St Thibault, 1761–1824, No. 38, f. 38.

53 AD, Yonne, 11 J 206/16, Paroisse de St Thibault Catholicité, 1797–1800. Marriage notice of Marie-Louise Barat, 13 March 1793. In 1800 Etienne Dusaussoy was listed among the 100 most wealthy citizens of Joigny. (Archives de la Société du Sacré Coeur, Joigny.)

54 Adrienne Michel, Journal du second voyage de….Mère Barat à Gand 1811. 'Au sujet du plaisir qu'elle prenait à lire Virgile: Ce n'est pas une Chrétienne mais une Virgilienne'; Cahier, *Vie*, i, 7. Samuel Richardson, *Clarissa, or the history of a young lady* (London, 1747–8). This work was published in French in 1751.

55 De Coriolis, Histoire de la Société du Sacré Coeur, ff. 31–31v. Jean François Marmontel, *Contes Moraux* (Paris, 1765). The tales were about aspects of romantic love: fantasy, passion and desire. For a discussion of *Clarissa* and European culture, see Rita Goldberg, *Sex and Enlightenment: Women in Richardson and Diderot* (Cambridge,1984).

56 Adrienne Michel, Journal du second voyage de … Mère Barat à Gand 1811. 'a force de soins et de caresses elle revint à elle'; Cahier, *Vie*, i, 11–13.

57 Cahier, *Vie*, i, 9.

58 La première initiation de Sophie Barat au culte du Sacré-Coeur. Récit de la Mère Barat … 30 mai 1856. Il trouva dans un magasin d'images, deux fort belles gravures représentant l'une le Sacré-Cœur de Jésus et l'autre le Saint Cœur de Marie. Il les acheta et les envoya à Madame Barat qui, oubliant ses anciennes préventions, accueillit avec joie ce don de son fils bien-aimé, et, en dépit des observations de sa famille, d'une de ses sœurs surtout, très attachée à l'erreur, elle fit encadrer les deux images qui demeurèrent là tout le temps de la Terreur, sans être jamais insultées, ni même remarquées dans les fréquentes visites domiciliaires qui furent faites durant ce temps-là.

59 Van Kley, op. cit., pp. 114–18. It was widely believed that while awaiting execution Louis XVI promised to dedicate France to the Sacred Heart and certainly after the Revolution devotion to the Sacred Heart was linked with those who longed for a restoration of the Bourbons, of the ancien régime. Jacques Maître, *Mystique et féminité. Essai de psychanalyse sociohistorique* (Paris, 1997), pp. 330–1; Michael Paul Driskel, *Representing Belief. Religion, art and society in nineteenth century France* (Pennsylvania, 1992,) p. 47.

60 De Coriolis, Histoire de la Société, ff. 27v-28v.

61 Récits de … Thérèse Maillucheau, (c. 1846), ff. 9, 11. G.A. Rome, A-II, a-1, Box 1. According to this account, the only one which explicitly mentions the role of Jacques Barat in the development of Sophie, Jacques Barat was a man of good judgement and saw Sophie's potential and the possibility that this could be frittered away in Joigny. The account notes the fear Sophie had of Louis's authority.

62 Un cas de possession diabolique à Joigny, en 1791 [1790]. 'Récit de l'abbé Fromentot', *L'Echo de Joigny*, no. 15 (1974), p. 18.

63 De Coriolis, Histoire de la Société du Sacré Coeur, ff. 32–32v

64 Sophie certainly talked about religious life to her friend in Joigny, Adele Bardot. Adèle Bardot (1781–1828) later became a member of the Society of the Sacred Heart. When she died Sophie wrote her obituary. G.A. Rome, Lettres Annuelles, 1818–1836, 10, pp. 76–83.

65 Deshayes, Notes sur notre … fondatrice et les commencements de la Société, ff. 6–7; de Coriolis, Histoire de la Société du Sacré Coeur, ff. 32v.

66 Perdrau, *Loisirs*, pp. 170–71. Mes pauvres parents, conduits par un esprit supérieur au leur, subissaient blâmes, critiques, moqueries au sujet de ce que l'abbé mon frère au sortir de prison à la chute de Robespierre, me faisait apprendre le latin, l'histoire, les lettres. « Quelle folie, disait-on dans le voisinage, d'appliquer une jeune fille si frêle à des études qui ne sont point à sa condition » […] Lorsque mon frère vit la guerre qu'on faisait à mes parents, il proposa de m'emmener à Paris sous le Directoire, qui relativement après l'horrible Constituante semblait offrir quelques garanties […] Ma mère refusa net; mais à un second voyage à Joigny, mon frère trouvant que je perdais mon temps et voulant compléter mes études, décida mon père, et maman céda, car elle voyait avec complaisance naturelle quelque succès obtenu dans la société bien modeste de

Joigny, et Dieu se servit de cette vanité maternelle, des prétentions sans raisons apparentes de mon frère pour faire de sa petite sœur une espèce de savante.

67   De Coriolis, Histoire de la Société du Sacré Coeur, ff. 28–28v. Louis Barat was ordained secretly in Paris by Jean Baptiste Maillé de la Tour Landry, Bishop of Gap, S. Papoul et Rennes. Archives de l'archevêché de Paris, 4o r D 2 i, Ordinations 1795–1802. 19 septembre 1795. Ad presbyteratum: Ludovicus Barat, Senonensis. The discovery of Louis Barat's ordination in 1795 is due to the persistent research of Marie-Joseph Vie.

68   De Coriolis, Histoire de la Société du Sacré Coeur, f. 33 'à détruire dans sa soeur la vie de la nature et à y substituer celle de la grâce'. Récits de Thérèse Maillucheau, (c. 1846), ff. 15, 19. Deshayes, Notes sur notre … fondatrice et les commencements de la Société, ff. 6–7; Adrienne Michel, Journal du second voyage de … Mère Barat à Gand 1811 [f14]. Perdrau, *Loisirs*, p. 121.

69   Déposition Adèle Lehon, Paris, 23 février 1882, ff. 541–2 (G.A. Rome, Copia Publica, Transumpti processus apostolica auctoritate constructi in curia ecclesiastica Parisiensi … Magdalena Sophia Barat, vol. ii, 1897).

70   Deshayes, Notes sur notre … fondatrice et les commencements de la Société, f. 10. 'Je ne vois rien. Je ne pense rien. On me le dit, j'obéis'.

71   Philibert de Brouillard (1765–1860) studied for the priesthood in St Sulpice and was ordained in 1789. He ministered in Paris during the Revolution. He became bishop of Grenoble and died in one of the houses of the Society of the Sacred Heart at Monfleury near Grenoble. Cahier, *Vie*, i, 18–19.

72   Adrienne Michel, Journal du second voyage de … Mère Barat à Gand 1811, f. 15. 'je ne le recevrais pas toujours avec action de grâce. Je pleurais bien.' Also, de Coriolis, Histoire de la Société du Sacré Coeur, ff. 33–33v. Récits de … Thérèse Maillucheau, (c. 1846), f. 27.

73   De Coriolis, Histoire de la Société du Sacré Coeur, ff. 30–31v.

Notes to Chapter 2

1   Jacques-André Émery (1732–1811) was elected superior general of Saint-Sulpice in 1782. *Dictionnaire de Spiritualité*, no. 4. Fascicules xxvi–xxvii (1959), 609–610.

2   AFSJ, Vanves. Fonds Varin; Guidée, *Joseph Varin*; *Dictionnaire de Spiritualité*, fascicules CII–CIII, no. 16, 1992, 288–290; de Charry (ed.), *Varin Lettres*, Introduction, ii–v. Geneviève Varin d'Ainvelle, Marie Françoise Varin d'Ainvelle, 1735–1794 (AF, Poitiers, A2, Les fondateurs).

3   André Rayez et Louis Fèvre, *Foi Chrétienne et vie consacrée. Clorivière aujourd'hui* (Paris, 1971), pp. 118–22; André Rayez, 'Clorivière et les Pères de la Foi', AHSJ, vol. xxi (1952), pp. 300–28.

4   P. Fidèle de Grivel, Breve Ragguaglio de 'Principj e Progressi della Società del Sacro Cuore di Gesú, 18 à 20. Récit de la première inspiration du P. De Tournély concernant l'Institut féminin voué au Sacré-Coeur. Original text and translation in de Charry, *Histoire des constitutions*, ii, *Textes*, No. 1, pp. 1–7. Also, *Notice sur … Léonor François de Tournély et sur son oeuvre La Congrégation des Pères du Sacré Coeur* (Vienne, 1886), pp. 104–12.

5   His vision, however, was far removed from that of the Englishwoman Mary Ward in the seventeenth century, who had sought in vain to establish an active form of religious life for women, based on the Jesuit rule. Her radical vision was expressed through consciously seeking greater freedom of movement for women religious, reflecting a closer, simpler relationship to society in general. She intended that her religious would not be required to take solemn vows since this imposed strict papal cloister on nuns, and prevented mobility. However, her vision of religious life for women was unthinkable in the church in the seventeenth century and remained so in the eighteenth century. Certainly de Tournély did not envisage anything of that nature for the women in his association. *Notice sur … Léonor François de Tournély*, pp. 34–38. Merry E. Weisner, *Women and gender in early modern Europe* (Cambridge, 1995), pp. 197–99, 213; Hufton, *Prospect*, pp. 39, 379–80.

6   De Charry, *Histoire des constitutions*, i, 115–31.

7   *Beatificationis et canonizationis servae Dei, Leopoldinae Naudet fundatricis sororum a Sacra Familia Veronae (1773–1834). Relatio et Vota, 5 novembre 1996* (Rome, 1996), pp. 12–18; de Charry, *Histoire des constitutions*, i, 148–9.

8   Achille Guidée, *Joseph Varin … suivie de Notices sur quelques-uns de ses confrères* (Paris, 1854), pp. 48–60, 94–99. Notice xv, Le P. Nicolas Paccanari, pp. 323–35; de Charry, *Histoire des constitutions*, i, 149–51.

9   De Charry, *Histoire des constitutions*, ii, *Textes*, 70–76.

10   De Charry, *Histoire des Constitutions*, ii, 151–67.

11   De Charry, *Histoire des Constitutions*, ii, *Textes*, 8–16; 23–28.

12   *Beatificationis et canonizationis servae Dei, Leopoldinae Naudet*, pp. 18–23.

13   Teresa Clements, 'Les Pères de la Foi, France, 1800–1814, spirituality, foundations, biographical notes' in *AHSI*, lvii, fasc. 114, Periodicum semestre (1988), 233–62.

14   AFSJ, Vanves, Fonds Varin, Journal de Nantes, 1846, 1848 et 1849, No. 11, Diverses anecdotes très intéressantes (no pagination) [J'ai rencontré] une petite personne toute simple, toute modestement et presque toute rustiquement vêtue. Je la vois encore arrivant de son village dans la cour de la diligence où elle venait rejoindre son frère à Paris. Lequel voulant se consacrer à notre petite société des Pères de la Foi, n'éprouvait qu'un embarras, celui de savoir que faire de sa sœur laissée à ses soins.

15 De Coriolis, Histoire de la Société du Sacré Coeur, f. 25; Cahier, *Vie*, i, 28–29.

16 Octavie Bailly (1768–1825) was born at Forge les Eaux, near Rouen. In 1804 she entered the Carmelite community at rue St Jacques (later rue d'Enfer) in Paris where her sister (1765–1850) had entered in 1801. Notice sur Béatrix de la Conception (Octavie Bailly) et Notice sur Anne de saint Barthélemy. (Archives, Carmel de Clamart, Registres et Circulaires); Notice sur Octavie Bailly, Carmel rue d'Enfer (General Archives, Rome, A–II., 2–c, Biographical information); de Charry, *Histoire des constitutions*, i, 227, 245–6.

17 Geneviève Deshayes, Notes sur notre … fondatrice et les commencements de la Société No. 3, f. 10 (G.A. Rome, A–II, 1–a, Box 1); de Charry, *Histoire des constitutions*, iii, *Textes*, Extrait d'une lettre du P. Varin au P. Paccanari, 19 mars 1801, p. 100; de Charry, *Histoire des constitutions*, i, 245–6. Loquet published: *Cruzamante, ou la sainte amante de la Croix* (Paris, 1786); *Voyage de Sophie et d'Eulalie au palais du vraie bonheur. Ouvrage pour servir de guide dans les voies du salut, par une jeune demoiselle* (Paris, 1789); *Entretiens d'Angélique, pour exciter les jeunes personnes à l'amour et à la pratique de la vertu*, 2nd edn (Paris, 1782); *Le miroir des âmes*, 6th edn (Paris, 1822).

18 De Charry, *Histoire des constitutions*, iii, *Textes*, 96–103; Cahier, *Vie*, i, 30–31; Mario Colpo (d), Una lettera del P. Varin al P. Paccanari del [18 mars] 1801 in ARSI, vol. lvii (1988), 315–29. There was a fire in the house that day, which started in the chapel while they were eating their meal.

19 Adrienne Michel, Journal du second voyage de … Mère Barat à Gand 1811. 'Il me confessa avant son départ et ensuite il me dit de chanter à la Messe; il fallut le faire … il partit sans me dire adieu.'

20 SB à Marie-Louise Dusaussoy, lettre 1, Paris, 10 octobre 1800. J'espère que ta maladie n'aura pas de suite et tu souffriras beaucoup moins si tu prends un peu plus de force et que tu ne t'appesantisses pas tant à de tristes réflexions. Il faut considérer que l'état dans lequel la Providence t'a placé entraîne nécessairement ces pensées et ces afflictions après soi; ne les laisse pas inutiles, fais-toi un sujet de mérite en menant une vie vraiment Chrétienne et en supportant avec patience les souffrances que tu endures. Car, ma chère sœur, je ne te donnerai pas de consolations humaines, elles sont insuffisantes et vaines, je ne peux t'offrir que celles de la Religion … Tu sentiras bientôt qu'avec un peu d'effort on vient à bout de tout et même des choses les plus difficiles; crois-moi, j'en ai fait l'heureuse expérience et malgré que ma position ne ressemble pas à la tienne, il a fallu cependant qu'il m'en coûtât quelque chose et je t'avoue que j'ai toujours ressenti une grande consolation des petits efforts que j'ai faits … ma bonne sœur, épanche ton cœur dans le mien. Ah! Si tu savais combien je m'attendris sur ton sort et je voudrais s'il était possible, te décharger de la moitié de ton fardeau; il viendra ce moment; en attendant la Providence veut que tu le portes encore seule pour un peu de temps … Écris-moi donc lorsque tu auras un petit moment, tes peines, tes espérances, enfin tout ce qui t'occupe; malgré mon peu de temps je tacherai d'y répondre et surtout parle moi de tes enfants … embrasse tendrement pour moi toute ta petite famille et sois assurée que je suis toujours avec la même affection et ta sœur et ton amie … embrasse pour moi mon Papa et Maman.

21 Achille Guidée, *Les Pères de la Foi* (Paris, 1854), pp. 33–105; Teresa Clements, 'Les Pères de la Foi in France: 1800–1814', *AHSI*, anno LVII, fasc., 114, Periodicum semestre (Jul.-Dec., 1988), pp. 236, 255.

22 Hyacinthe Devaux was a former Benedictine nun from the abbey of St Paul at Beauvais who owned the house in Amiens where she and her niece Henriette Grosier were living. Henriette Grosier (1774–1842) was born in Beauvais and at this time helped her aunt run a school in Amiens. She hoped to become a Carmelite though there was no possibility of this at the time. Geneviève Deshayes (1767–1849) was born in Amiens and she wrote an account of the early years of the Society of the Sacred Heart in Amiens which is very valuable. G.A. Rome, A–II, 1–a, Box 1, Geneviève Deshayes, Notes sur notre … fondatrice et les commencements de la Société.

23 Deshayes, Notes … sur les commencements de la Société, ff. 33–34. See ff. 25–32 for Joseph Varin's long exposé on the new congregation and its new members in Paris, which he explained to both Grosier and Deshayes. Also, de Coriolis, Histoire de la Société du Sacré Coeur, ff. 35v–36.

24 Deshayes, Notes … sur les commencements de la Société, ff. 47–48. Quel bien produisit sur nos cœurs la seule vue de […] Sœur Sophie. La réputation de sa piété, de sa vertu, de ses talents avait devancé son arrivée et chacune l'aimait avant de la connaître. Mais sa douceur, son air de modestie angélique, quelque chose qui n'appartenait qu'à elle, lui gagna nos cœurs […] Octavie, très bonne, très vertueuse, n'eut cependant pas pour nous même charme, même liant.

25 De Coriolis, Histoire de la Société du Sacré Coeur, ff. 39v–40.

26 *Vie du … Père Loriquet* (Paris, 1845)

27 De Coriolis, Histoire de la Société du Sacré Coeur, ff. 35, 36v, 38–39v, 42; Deshayes, Notes … sur les commencements de la Société, ff. 57–62.

28 Deshayes, Notes … sur les commencements de la Société, ff. 33–34.

29 Ibid., ff. 50; 60–61.

30 Ibid., ff. 57–59; 72–73. Joseph Varin to SB, 28 décembre 1801, de Charry (ed.), *Varin Lettres*, pp. 1–4.

31 De Coriolis, Histoire de la Société du Sacré Coeur, ff. 39v–40v; Guidée, *Joseph Varin*, pp. 68–76. Adèle Jugon did not stay in Amiens and later married the comte de Larivière; she maintained warm relations with the community at Amiens. Another woman, Cécile de Cassini, stayed in Amiens until August 1804; she tried six

other communities after that but stayed in none. She retained good relations with the Society of the Sacred Heart and entered again in 1858 at the age of eighty-one. She died in Orleans in 1867.

32 De Coriolis, Histoire de la Société du Sacré Coeur, f. 41v. It was a choice made in favour of those who could pay. The thinking behind this choice was current throughout the lifetime of Sophie Barat, namely that if the higher classes were well educated this would benefit all classes of society. Besides the money paid by boarders financed the poor school too.

33 SB à Marie-Louise Dusaussoy, Lettre 2, Amiens, 5 octobre 1802. Donne-moi d'abord des nouvelles de ta santé et de celle de ta petite famille, je ne sais si elle est augmentée ou si elle est diminuée, enfin quand je serais dans un désert, je ne serais pas plus ignorante de ce que vous regarde, si j'en sais quelque chose c'est indirectement et par des étrangers. Croyez-vous que je ne m'intéresse plus à ce qui vous touche, m'êtes vous donc devenus tellement indifférents, que rien de chez vous ne puisse me fixer un moment. Oh! Non, ma chère sœur, il n'est pas ainsi, l'amitié que j'ai pour vous n'est point altérée et si je ne l'exprime plus par des sensibilités et par des larmes, elle n'existe pas moins dans mon coeur et elle n'en est que plus solide et plus épurée.

34 From 1801 to 1809 Louis Barat ministered in the area around Lyon, in the junior seminaries founded by the Fathers of the Faith.

35 SB à Marie-Louise Dusaussoy, lettre 2, Amiens, 5 octobre 1802. 'En lui faisant entendre que vous aimez mieux avoir quelque chose de moins et le posséder quelques années de plus; dites lui qu'il donne davantage aux pratiques de la religion et entretenez vous souvent sur cet intéressant objet.'

36 De Coriolis, Histoire de la Société du Sacré Coeur, ff. 42, 42v, 43, 43v, 43v, 44; de Charry, *Histoire des constitutions*, i, pp. 289–91.

37 De Coriolis, Histoire de la Société du Sacré Coeur, f. 49v. 'C'est moi qui l'ai fait nommer supérieure'.

38 Charles Bruson (1764–1838), joined the Fathers of the Faith in 1800 and was at this period rector of the college at Amiens. He joined the Jesuits in 1814. Louis de Sambucy-Saint-Estève (1771–1847) was at St Sulpice with Joseph Varin. He joined the Fathers of the Faith in France and at this period taught in the college at Amiens.

39 Joseph Varin to SB, Besançon, 27 June [1803]; Lyon 24 July [1803], de Charry (ed.), *Varin Lettres*, pp. 29, 43.

40 De Coriolis, Histoire de la Société du Sacré Coeur, f. 45; Joseph Varin to SB, Tours 22 March [1804], de Charry (ed.), *Varin Lettres*, pp. 101–2.

41 Louis Barat à Marie-Louise Dusaussoy, St Galmier [Loire], 9 septembre 1803. AFCJ, Fonds Barat.

42 De Coriolis, Histoire de la Société du Sacré Coeur, f. 45v (i), 'Menacée depuis quelque temps d'un cancer, cette âme généreuse était offerte à Dieu pour souffrir dans le secret … tout ce que cette maladie a de douloureux et de répugnant pour la nature … son excessive délicatesse de conscience sur l'article de la modestie, se joignait à ses autres répugnances.'

43 ibid., ff. 45v (i)–45v (ii); Joseph Varin to SB, Tours 6 March [1804]; Tours 10 March; Tours 13 March, de Charry (ed.), *Varin Lettres*, pp. 93–100. Despite searches in the archives of the Filles de la Charité de Saint Vincent de Paul in Paris it has proved impossible to discover which hospital Sophie Barat attended in Paris in 1804. Medical opinion would suggest that Sophie Barat suffered from a vaginal abscess at this time.

44 Corr. MSB et Philippine Duchesne, 1804–1818, lettre 14, SB à Philippine Duchesne, Poitiers, 1 août 1806, p. 52

45 *Vie de la Mère [Catherine] de Charbonnel, assistante et économe générale de la Société du Sacré-Cœur de Jésus* (Paris, c. 1870). Marie du Terrail was orphaned during the Revolution and was educated at St Cyr. She was professed at Amiens in 1804 and taught in Belley and then in Grenoble, where she died in on 30 November 1813. Corr. SB et Philippine Duchesne, 1804–15, p. 200, n.2.

46 De Coriolis, Histoire de la Société du Sacré Coeur, f. 44. See also ff. 44v, 45.

47 Jean Louis de Lessègues de Rozaven (1772–1851) had been a Father of the Sacred Heart, and when he joined the Fathers of the Faith Paccanari sent him to London to establish a community there. With twenty companions he left London in the spring of 1804 and went to Russia to join the Jesuits there. Guidée, *Joseph Varin*, pp. 225–35.

48 De Coriolis, Histoire de la Société du Sacré Coeur, ff. 46–49v; Joseph Varin to SB, Tours 22 March [1804], de Charry (ed.), *Varin Lettres*, pp. 103–6; de Charry, *Histoire des constitutions*, i, 310–14.

49 *Beatificationis et canonizationis servae Dei, Leopoldinae Naudet, Relatio et Voto*, pp. 23–25, 50–1; *Beatificationis et canonizationis servae Dei, Leopoldinae Naudet, Positio* (1994), pp. 584–6; André Rayez, 'Clorivière et les Pères de la Foi' AHSJ, vol. xxi (1952), pp. 323–4.

50 De Coriolis, Histoire de la Société du Sacré Coeur, f. 48; Joseph Varin to SB, Tours 22 March [1804], de Charry (ed.), *Varin Lettres*, pp. 105–6.

51 Maître, *Mystique et Feminité*, p. 331; Eamonn Duffy, *Saints and Sinner. A history of the popes* (Yale, 1997), pp. 199–203.

52 A monstrance is an ornamented receptacle in which the Blessed Sacrament is exposed in Catholic churches, for the adoration of believers.

53 Perdrau, *Loisirs* i, 422–4. La première idée que nous avons conçue de la forme à donner à la Société a été de réunir le plus possible de véritables adoratrices du Cœur de Jésus Eucharistie […] Au sortir de la terreur et des abominations de la Révolution vis-à-vis de la religion et du Saint-Sacrement […] tous les cœurs […] battaient à l'unisson …Venger Jésus-Christ au Saint-Sacrement de l'autel était un cri de ralliement […] Deux personnes pieuses ne causaient pas ensemble sans chercher quelques moyens à faire revivre Jésus-Christ dans les familles … Me voici à l'idée primordiale de notre petite Société du Sacré-Cœur, celle de me réunir à des jeunes filles pour établir *une petite communauté qui, nuit et jour, adorerait le Cœur de Jésus outragé dans son amour eucharistique;* mais, me disais-je, quand nous serons vingt-quatre religieuses en état de nous remplacer sur un prie-Dieu pour entretenir *l'adoration perpétuelle,* ce sera *beaucoup,* et bien peu pour un si noble but […] Si nous avions *de jeunes élèves* que nous formions à l'esprit d'adoration et de réparation, que ce serait différent! Je voyais des centaines, des milliers d'adoratrices devant un ostensoir[52] idéal, universel, élevé au-dessus de l'Église. « C'est cela », disais-je, devant un saint Tabernacle solitaire: « il faut nous vouer à l'éducation de la jeunesse; refaire dans les âmes les fondements solides d'une foi vive au Très Saint Sacrement, y combattre les traces du jansénisme qui a amené l'impiété et, avec les révélations de Jésus-Christ à la Bienheureuse Marguerite-Marie sur la dévotion réparatrice et expiatrice envers son Cœur Sacré au Très Saint Sacrement, nous élèverons une foule d'adoratrices de toutes les nations jusqu'aux extrémités de la terre.

54 De Coriolis, Histoire de la Société du Sacré Coeur, ff. 52–52v; Louise Callan, *Philippine Duchesne, Frontier Missionary of the Sacred Heart, 1769–1852* (Maryland, 1957), pp. 14–38.

55 Callan, op. cit., pp. 43–61; Catherine M. Mooney, *Philippine Duchesne, A woman with the poor* (Paulist Press, 1990), pp. 59–79.

56 De Coriolis, Histoire de la Société du Sacré Coeur, ff. 52–67; de Charry, *Histoire des constitutions,* ii, 349–51; Callan, op. cit., pp. 61–76; Mooney, op. cit., pp. 79–84.

57 Pierre-Aimé-Alexandre Roger (1763–1839) was born in Coutances and studied in Paris at the Collège de Navarre and then entered the seminary at Leon directed by J.A. Emery. He was ordained in 1788 and in 1795 joined the Fathers of the Sacred Heart at Haggenbrunn and in 1799 accepted to join the Fathers of the Faith under the leadership of Nicholas Paccanari. Roger and Joseph Varin were sent to Paris in 1800, where they ministered together in the Salpêtrière for eighteen months. In 1802 Roger and Louis Barat were sent to minister in Belley and it there that M. Rivet met Roger. *Dictionnaire de Spiritualité,* fascicules 89–90, no. 13, 1988, 871–75.

58 De Coriolis, Histoire de la Société du Sacré Coeur, ff. 68–70 'Je vous le promets notre infirme viendra' (f. 69v). At this time Sophie Barat was very ill in Paris.

59 De Charry, *Histoire des constitutions,* iii, *Textes,* No. 22, La Mère Barat raconte les debuts de la fondation de Grenoble, le 2 septembre 1860, p. 129. Also, Joseph Varin to SB, [Paris] 6 octobre [1804], de Charry (ed.), *Varin Lettres,* p. 115.

60 Journal de la maison de Grenoble. Depuis sa fondation, le 13 décembre 1804 jusqu'au 27 décembre 1813. Par la Mère Duchesne, 13 décembre 1804, f. 1 (G.A. Rome, A–II., 1–d). Catherine Maillard (1784–1854) was Geneviève Deshayes's chambermaid and entered with her in Amiens; she made her vows in November 1804 just before leaving for Grenoble. De Charry, *Histoire des constitutions,* ii, 400–401, n. 179. Marguerite Rosalie Debrosse (1786–1854) also made her vows in Amiens on 21 November 1804.

61 De Charry, *Histoire des constitutions,* iii, *Textes,* No. 22, p. 130.

62 Marie Rivet (1768–1841) was a native of Grenoble and sister of Pierre Rivet, the local priest. She had been a Carmelite before the Revolution and joined Philippine Duchesne in Ste Marie d'En Haut in October 1802; Emilie Giraud (1783–1856) was a boarder in the school from June 1802 and later asked to join the community as a novice; Marie Balastron (1783–1862) joined the community in November 1802; Adélaïde Second joined the community in July 1804.

63 De Coriolis, Histoire de la Société, f. 79; de Charry, *Histoire des constitutions,* iii, *Textes,* No. 22, pp. 128–33.

64 Journal de Grenoble, ff. 1–2; de Coriolis, Histoire de la Société, f. 81.

65 Anne Baudemont, a former Clarissan nun, had accepted that some monastic practices and forms had to be laid aside. De Charry, *Histoire des constitutions,* ii, 364–7.

66 De Charry, *Histoire des Constitutions,* ii, 370–82; iii, *Textes,* No. 22, pp. 132–33; Callan, op. cit., pp. 93–99.

67 De Charry, *Histoire des constitutions,* ii, 354–362; iii, *Textes,* No. 23, Le premier abrège de l'Institut rédigé à Grenoble en novembre 1805, pp. 134–139.

68 De Charry (ed.), *Varin Lettres,* pp. 177, 179, n. 4, n. 5, 187, 188, n. 3.

69 De Charry, *Histoire des constitutions,* iii, *Textes,* No. 20, 7 mars 1805, Directives du P. Varin aux mères de Baudemont et Grosier … à Amiens, pp. 118–122.

70 Joseph Varin to SB, Tours lettre 51 Paris 25 Dec. [1804], de Charry (ed.), *Varin Lettres,* p. 131.

71 Joseph Varin to SB, Tours lettre 69, 22 March [1804], de Charry (ed.), *Varin Lettres,* pp. 172–174.

72 De Coriolis, Histoire de la Société, ff. 39v–40; de Charry, *Histoire des constitutions,* ii, pp. 335–342.

73 R. Limouzin-Lamothe, *Monsignor de Quelen, archevêque de Paris,* 2 vols., (Paris, 1955, 1957), i, 28; de Charry, *Histoire des constitutions,* ii, pp. 342–44.

74 Joseph Varin to SB, lettre 74, 22 Sept. [1805] Belley, de Charry (ed.), *Varin Lettres,* pp. 184, 186 n. 6.

75   De Charry, *Histoire des constitutions*, ii, 390–91.

76   ibid., ii, 391–407.

77   Joseph Varin à SB, lettre 79 10 avril [1806] p. 197; 13 mai [1806]; 16 mai [1806]; 19 mai [1806] 29 mai [1806]; 31 mai [1806]; 9 juin [1806];14 juin [1806]; 19 juin [1806] (de Charry (ed.), *Varin Lettres*, pp. 197–228).

Notes to Chapter 3

1   Corr. MSB et Philippine Duchesne, 1804–1815, lettre 13, SB à Philippine Duchesne, Lyon, 15 mai 1806, p. 48.

2   Henriette Girard (1761–1828) was accepted into the Association in 1803 by Joseph Varin but was able to enter finally only in 1805 when she had become free of family responsibilities. Corr. MSB et Philippine Duchesne, 1804–1815, lettre 6, SB à Philippine Duchesne, Lyon, 19 avril 1805, pp. 18–19.

3   Marie-Thérèse Virnot (ed.), *Sainte Madeleine Sophie Barat, Journal, Poitiers 1806–1808. Texte Intégral* (Poitiers, 1977), pp. 15–26; de Coriolis, Histoire de la Société, 1806–1807, Ch. II, ff. 1–5; Souvenirs des recréations de notre … mère générale au Noviciat de la maison mère, juillet 1835. No pagination. (Society of the Sacred Heart National Archives, U.S.A., Series I., A-b, Madeleine Sophie Barat. Events of her generalate, 1802–1843).

4   Corr. MSB et Philippine Duchesne, 1804–1815, lettre 14, Poitiers, 1 août 1806, p. 52; see also lettre 15, Bordeaux, 30 août 1806, p. 62 where Sophie confirmed that she was completely cured. Vous savez, quand je vous quittai, en quel état j'étais; en arrivant à Lyon l'échauffement de la route avait encore augmenté mon mal, et j'étais pire que l'année dernière, éloignée de ma chère samaritaine, je croyais que personne autre ne pouvait me guérir, et je le croyais aussi nécessaire à mon corps qu'elle-même le croyait utile à son âme. Je m'en plaignis doucement à N[otre] S[eigneur] et je lui représentais combien cela serait désagréable dans une route et près de personnes qui pourraient s'en apercevoir; seule et sans vouloir me confier à personne, je demeurai tranquille après cette plainte […] Je n'étais point sortie de Lyon que tout avait disparu, et cependant je n'avais rien fait pour le guérir; au contraire, l'extrême chaleur qu'il faisait alors, le peu de repos que je pouvais prendre, la mauvaise nourriture et la malpropreté des auberges, l'époque à laquelle je touchais, tout contribuait à augmenter le mal, et cependant tout fut parti dans une nuit; je suis tout à fait guérie.

5   Virnot, *Journal, Poitiers*, pp. 20–21, 129. Gresset (1709–1777) wrote *La Chartreuse* in 1735 when he taught in the Collège Louis le Grand in Paris. Cette chambre ressemblait assez à celle que Gresset dépeint dans sa Chartreuse. L'université des rats y vint tenir ses assemblées au milieu de la nuit, et comme nous habitons une maison isolée, nous aurions eu bien peur si nous n'avions eu toute notre confiance en Dieu.

6   Virnot, *Journal, Poitiers*, p. 21. [Là] on chanta une grand-messe sur un ton si burlesque que, dans toute autre circonstance, il y aurait eu sujet de rire, […] le curé annonça la Fête de Sainte Madeleine pour le mardi suivant, et […] pour les exciter à venir entendre la messe ce jour-là, il leur promit une grand-messe de Mort!

7   ibid., p. 25. Also p. 24. Me voilà donc avec une introductrice, et dans ce bel équipage, qui n'était pas propre à donner de la vanité, j'arrive humblement à la maison des Feuillants, demeure de Mlle Choblet.

8   De Coriolis, Histoire de la Société, 1806–1807, Ch. II, ff. 5v–6v; Virnot, *Journal, Poitiers*, pp. 15–16, 25–28, 124.

9   The diocese of Poitiers had had no resident bishop for some years. Mgr de Pradt, a career bishop, lived for the most part in Paris. When he was named bishop of Malines by Napoleon in 1809 the diocese of Poitiers remained vacant until 1819. From the beginning all Sophie Barat's dealings in Poitiers were with the vicars general who governed the diocese in the absence of the bishop.

10   This rule was not the text which was presented to the bishop of Grenoble in 1805, based on the rule of the Diletti. The task of drawing up a new rule had begun early in 1806, during the election of Sophie Barat as superior general. The new rule took inspiration from two sources, the rule of the sisters of Notre Dame, founded in Bordeaux in 1607 by Jeanne de Lestonnac and that of the Institute of the Blessed Virgin Mary, founded by Mary Ward. de Charry, *Histoire des constitutions*, i, 30–31. For details of the rule presented in 1806 at Poitiers, see de Charry, *Histoire des constitutions*, ii, 410–21.

11   De Coriolis, Histoire de la Société, 1806–1807, Ch. II, f. 8v. Profitons donc de la circonstance de la mission et déterminons-nous généreusement à quitter nos familles sans les en prévenir. Toutes furent de cet avis. Une de ces jeunes personnes, nommée Angélique, qui n'avait plus de parents possédait dans les environs une vigne où il y avait une espèce de petite cabane. Ce fut là le lieu qu'elles choisirent pour leur retraite.

12   ibid., Ch. II, ff. 7–9v; Virnot, *Journal, Poitiers*, pp. 28–34, 125; Manuscrit de la Mère Thérèse Maillucheau. Premier noviciat de la Société, formé à Poitiers par ma Mère générale en année 1806, ff. 78–85; 03–5. (GA, Rome, A-II, a–1, Box 1). This is a blue notebook. A note inside the document, dated March 1876, indicates that this is a genuine manuscript but that the handwriting of Thérèse Maillucheau was scored out and replaced by that of a copyist; Souvenirs des recréations de notre … mère générale au Noviciat de la maison mère, juillet 1835, no pagination (Society of the Sacred Heart National Archives, U.S.A.).

13   De Coriolis, Histoire de la Société, 1806–1807, Ch. II, ff. 10v–11.

14 Virnot, *Journal, Poitiers*, p. 34. Il m'arriva cependant un petit accident: ayant mis pied à terre pendant la nuit, je marchai sur une pierre sur laquelle mon pied tourna avec force, et j'eus les nerfs foulés […] mon pied enfla et, arrivée à Poitiers, je ne pouvais marcher. Je n'aurais su comment me rendre à notre maison, qui est très éloignée du bureau de diligences où l'on débarque, si Mme de la Charpagne, notre excellente amie, qui est logée tout près, n'avait été à l'affût depuis plusieurs jours pour me recueillir en passant, comme elle l'avait fait envers celles de mes compagnes qui m'avaient précédée.

15 The ten novices were: Lydie Chobelet, Josephine Bigeu, Thérèse Maillucheau, La Croix Roger, Perpétue Mougette, Brigitte Berniard, Jeanne Gertrude Lamalière, Angèle [n.n.], Marinette Guiégnet and Louise Marqué Olivier. For detailed accounts of this period see: Virnot, *Journal, Poitiers*; Manuscrit de la Mère Thérèse Maillucheau; de Coriolis, Histoire de la Société, 1806–1807, Ch. II, ff. 11–21v; Souvenirs des recréations ... juillet 1835.

16 De Coriolis, Histoire de la Société, 1806–1807, Ch. II, ff. 18v.

17 Thérèse Maillucheau. Premier noviciat de la Société, 1806, ff. 102–3; 128.

18 ibid., f. 154. For further examples of Sophie's behaviour at this time see ff. 93, 97, 107, 109–13, 130, 140, 142; de Coriolis, Histoire de la Société, 1806–1807, Ch. II, ff. 12v–13,1v.

19 De Coriolis, Histoire de la Société, 1806–1807, Ch. II, ff. 11v,13v–17; Virnot, *Journal, Poitiers*, 28–29, 121, 123; Souvenirs des recréations ... juillet 1835.

20 Thérèse Maillucheau. Premier noviciat de la Société, 1806, ff. 83, 93, 95; Souvenirs des recréations ... juillet 1835.

21 De Coriolis, Histoire de la Société, 1806–1807, Ch. II, ff. 20v; Virnot, *Journal, Poitiers*, pp. 52, 53, 69, 71, 73, 75, 78, 108–109.

22 De Coriolis, Histoire de la Société, 1806–1807, Ch. II, ff. 21v; Virnot, *Journal, Poitiers*, pp. 73, 75, 96–97.

23 Virnot, *Journal, Poitiers*, pp. 47, 62, 69.

24 Ibid., pp. 98, 110

25 *Vie de Madame Geoffroy* (Poitiers, 1854).

26 Ibid., p. 17. 'celle qui est destinée à être en France la fondatrice de cette congrégation est encore occupée du soin de ses poupées.'

27 de Charry, *Histoire des constitutions*, i, 87–94; Virnot, *Journal, Poitiers*, pp. 99–101;108–110; *Vie de Madame Geoffroy*, pp. 7–30.

28 [Adrienne Michel], Journal du second voyage de ... Mère Barat à Gand 1811, f.15 (GA, Rome, C–I., A, 1–c, Box 1).

29 Exercices et distribution solennelle des prix dans la maison d'Institution d'Amiens, 19, 20, 21 septembre 1805 (Archives de la Maîtresse Générale des Etudes françaises, AF, Poitiers); Joseph Varin à SB, lettre 74, 22 septembre [1805] Belley, pp. 184, 186.

30 Jauffret à Portalis, Paris 27 décembre 1806. De Charry, *Histoire des constitutions, Textes*, No. 34, lettre de Mgr Jauffret à Portalis, Ministre des Cultes, pp. 161–164. See also no. 33, La Première Rédaction des Statuts destinés à l'autorisation légale, and no. 35, Les Statuts de l'Association et le Décret d'autorisation légale, 10 mars 1807, pp. 156–160, 165–169. André Jauffret (1759–1832), was vicar-general of Lyon and secretary to Cardinal Fesch. He was responsible for helping religious communities of women seek legal recognition from the government; Joseph Varin à SB, Letter 86, Vichy 14 juin [1806], pp. 219–220, n. 2, p. 223.

31 Virnot, *Journal, Poitiers*, pp. 60–61.

32 De Charry, *Histoire des Constitutions*, ii, 413–16.

33 *Annuaire statistique et administratif du Département de la Somme, pour l'an 1806* (Amiens, 1806), pp. 206–209.

34 Renseignements sur Ladies of Christian Instruction demandés par M. Le Préfet du Département de la Somme (General Archives, Rome Approbation Civile 1806–1807, A–IV, 1).

35 Joseph Varin à SB, lettre 54, [Amiens] 18 janvier [1805] p. 137. Vous me connaissez, et vous savez combien je suis ennemi de la dissimulation et du déguisement, je vous demande donc d'ajouter une pleine confiance à ce que je pourrai vous dire en diverses occasions sur l'état de votre famille, il importe trop à votre repos et à votre bonheur que vous sachiez absolument la vérité, et quel jugement vous devez porter. Du reste, je sais qu'auprès de vous, je n'ai pas besoin de préambule pour obtenir croyance.'

36 Joseph Varin à SB, lettre 78, Belley, 23 mars [1806] p. 192. Je ne vous ai pas écrit, mais je ne vous ai pas laissé dans l'ignorance de ce qui me concernait. M. le [Blanc] d'un côté et Mde Baudemont de l'autre vous ont donné des nouvelles de mon voyage qui a été très heureux. Quand, pressé par le temps, j'ai plusieurs personnes à qui je dois écrire, et que vous êtes du nombre, je consulte les bienséances, pour savoir par qui commencer, et je vous mets pour la dernière, preuve non équivoque d'une solide amitié.

37 Joseph Varin à SB, lettre 51, Paris, 23 décembre [1804], p. 131. J'ai oublié de vous parler d'une lettre pour vous, de Mde Louise, votre famille [communauté d'Amiens] me l'a envoyée, et je l'ai brûlée, elle était longuement au sujet de ses deux amies Marie-A[nne] et Julie, du reste très imprudente.

38 Joseph Varin à SB, lettre 52, Paris 3 janvier 1805, p. 134. N'ayez pas d'inquiétudes sur le changement de fonction de Mde Desh[ayes]. Je puis vous dire que c'est un changement qui m'a donné le plus de consolation. J'en ressens une joie véritable. On lui donne en place, des occupations plus analogues à sa santé, et qui lui

plaisent davantage. Elle m'avait envoyé pour vous une longue lettre, mais si difficile à lire que je l'ai brûlée pour épargner votre vue. Ne lui dites pas cela. J'ai jeté un coup d'œil, il n'y avait rien essentiel. Fathers, husbands and guardians had the right in law to intercept letters received or sent by women. Private correspondence for women was a source of legal controversy in nineteenth-century France. Nicole Arnaud-Duc, 'The Law's Contradictions', in Geneviève Fraisse, Michelle Perrot (eds.), *A History of Women in the West, IV, Emerging Feminism from Revolution to World War* (Harvard, 1993), pp. 99–100.

39 Joseph Varin à SB, lettre 56, Paris 31 janvier [1805], p. 142. Il faut que vous vous reposiez un peu plus sur la sagesse de celui qui connaît et dirige la conscience. Ce qui se passe dans l'intérieur et le secret entre l'âme et Dieu, par le conseil d'un directeur éclairé, n'a besoin d'aucun autre assentiment, lorsque cela ne blesse les droits de personne.

40 Joseph Varin à SB, lettre 84, Vichy, 31 mai [1806], pp. 208–9. Laissons en cette affaire agir l'aimable Providence, et ne nous défions pas de la sagesse du cher M. de S[ambuc]y qu'elle semble choisir pour instrument. Je lui ai déjà écrit en ce sens à ce sujet.

41 Joseph Varin à SB, lettre 87, Roanne, 19 juin [1806], pp. 224–5. Le cher M. de S[ambuc]y m'écrit à toutes les postes, et va toujours en avant pour la grande affaire qui vous regarde. Vous pensiez que j'allais l'arrêter dans sa marche; vraiment, non, j'y bien pensé devant le bon Dieu, et je me suis senti une grande confiance pour laisser agir la Providence, je l'ai donc encouragé.

42 Joseph Varin à SB, lettre 81, [Roanne] 16 [mai 1806], pp. 201–2. Ho! oui, dépouillez vous entièrement de votre volonté propre et n'en conservez aucune relique même sous prétexte de dévotion et d'une plus haute perfection. La plus grande perfection que je vous désire, est de supprimer tout à fait les violences intérieures que je remarque en vous quand votre volonté est contrariée, soit sur la place que vous occupez, soit sur l'article des mortifications, soit sur etc. […] et de tout recevoir enfin avec aisance et liberté d'esprit.

43 Paris 24 janvier 1808, Déclaration du Père Varin, ex supérieure et liste des Pères de la Foi (F/19/42992 Archives National de France). In this declaration Joseph Varin stated that in 1804 the Fathers of the Faith were dissolved and that the former members worked under the authority of the diocesan bishops. He declared that he was no longer a member of the Association, that he had no links with Jesuits and that he never thought of becoming one. It was clearly an effort to find acceptance by the government. In any event Joseph Varin stayed in Besançon from 1808 to 1814.

44 Cahier, *Vie*, i, 171–2.

45 Ibid., i, 170–1; de Charry, *Histoire des constitutions*, ii, 653–57.

46 Aristocratic women often rented quarters in religious communities. See Sophie Hasquenoph, 'Faire retraite à couvent dans le Paris des Lumières', *Revue historique*, no. 598, avril–juin 1996, 353–67.

47 Souvenirs de Mlle Herbert, f.13 (GA, Rome, C–I., A,1–e (bis), Box 1).

48 Antoine-Adrien-Charles de Gramont, comte de Gramont d'Aster (1758–1795) married Gabrielle-Charlotte-Eugénie de Boisgelin (1766–1836) in 1780. Both came from distinguished noble families of France. They had three children: Antoine-Louis-Raymond-Geneviève de Gramont, comte de Gramont d'Aster (1787–1825); Antoinette-Sainte-Eugénie-Cornélie de Gramont (1788–1846); Antoinette-Jeanne de Gramont (1792–1844). Although the family were loyal to the Bourbons, the comte de Gramont d'Aster fought for Napoleon during the Empire and was awarded the cross of the Legion of Honour for his bravery after the siege of Moscow in 1812. In 1814 he was ready to join the Bourbons and escorted Louis XVIII to Paris. In 1817 he received the cross of Chevalier de St Louis and in 1819 he was named a peer of the realm. Once her daughters had entered the community at Amiens, Madame de Gramont d'Aster first thought of entering the Visitation order in Paris. She changed her mind and joined the community at Amiens in 1814. By so doing she avoided being recalled to Court, a real possibility after the fall of Napoleon. *Notice sur la vie de Madame la Comtesse de Gramont, née de Boisgelin* (Paris, 1836); Jean Jaurgain et Raymond Ritter, *La Maison de Gramont, 1040–1967*, 2 vols. (Les Amis du Musée Pyrénéen, 1968), pp. 658–665; Olivier Ribeton, *Les Gramonts. Portraits de famille, XVIe–XVIIIe siècles* (J et D. Editions, 1992), pp. 41, 128; *Dictionnaire de Biographie Française*, 1985, pp. 916–26.

49 Manuscrit de la Mère Thérèse Maillucheau, ff. 158–174.

50 Séminaire Saint-Sulpice, MS 411, Manuscrits de Mr Montaigne, 10, Vie et Lettres; L. Bertrand, *Bibliothèque Sulpicienne ou histoire littéraire de la Compagnie de Saint-Sulpice* (Paris, 1900), p. 54.

51 *Histoires des Catéchismes de Saint-Sulpice* (Paris, 1831), pp. 150–1, 167, 182.

52 Manuscrit de la Mère Thérèse Maillucheau, f. 164. 'Il y a au milieu de vous un germe de destruction; mais une âme très puissante auprès de Dieu prie pour vous, pour votre ordre.'

53 Corr. SB et Marie Balastron, lettre 1, Amiens, 23 décembre 1808; lettre 2, Amiens, 11 mars 1809; Corr. SB et Emilie Giraud, lettre 22, Paris 19 juillet 1811.

54 Corr. MSB et Philippine Duchesne, 1804–1818, lettre 29, Amiens, 5 décembre 1808, p. 106; lettre 30, Amiens, 3 février 1809, p. 108.

Notes to Chapter 4

1 De Charry (ed.), *Varin Lettres*, lettre 1, [28 décembre 1801], p. 3. Je ne sais pas ce que votre et notre cher frère B[arat] aura pu vous mander capable de porter dans votre âme le trouble et l'inquiétude, mais je raye et efface entièrement les lignes et jusqu'au moindre mot qui n'aurait pas été une expression de joie, de félicitation et d'encouragement.

2 De Charry (ed.), *Varin Lettres*, lettre 76, Roanne, 20 octobre [1805], pp. 189–90. Ce qui m'étonne, c'est cet autre genre de peine que [vos] entretiens avec votre frère, loin de dissiper, n'ont fait qu'accroître. Quoi, vous n'en découvrez pas encore l'auteur, qui n'est autre que le malin esprit, et si vous l'avez découvert, vous en êtes encore la dupe! Ho! je vous en prie, que toutes ces vaines inquiétudes soient dissipées, lorsque j'arriverai. Vous faut-il donc un Ange du Ciel pour vous rassurer, et si vous refusez de croire à Jésus-Christ dans la personne de son ministre, croiriez-vous plus à un Ange ? Courage, confiance et une sainte hardiesse.

3 AFSJ, Vanves, Fonds Barat, Louis à Marie-Louise Dusaussoy, St. Galmier, 9 septembre 1803.

4 Archives Nationales, Paris, F/19/42992, Déclaration du Père Varin, ex supérieure, et liste des Pères de la Foi, Paris 24 janvier 1808.

5 Corr. SB et Emilie Giraud, lettre 15, Paris, 29 novembre 1809. Je ne suis nullement étonnée que mon frère ne préfère de plus longues oraisons à la broderie que vous faites et qu'il regrette le temps que vous y employerz lui qui autrefois déchirait tout ce que je faisais disant que c'était du temps perdu. Vous savez […] l'utilité de la broderie chez nous, je désire donc que vous appreniez bien à *nuancer*. Ce n'est pas la quantité d'ouvrages que je vous demande […] Je ne vous gêne pour sur le temps, employez-y ce que vous pourrez mais en faisant passer toujours avant vos exercices de piété, la grammaire et les autres sciences nécessaires.

6 François Morlot, Le Père Louis Barat, Supérieur du Grand Séminaire de Troyes. Extrait des Mémoires de la Société Académique de l'Aube, vol. cix, 1978 (Troyes, 1980), p. 3.

7 Corr. MSB et Philippine Duchesne, 1804–1815, lettre 30, Poitiers, juillet 1809, p. 120. See note 1, p. 121. Je vous remercie de la part que vous avez prise à la peine que nous avons faite. Elle a été sensible, il est vrai; mais la douleur a été tempérée par l'espérance, et par les prières que vous offrez pour cet excellent père.

8 Corr. SB et Emilie Giraud, lettre 15, Paris, 29 novembre 1809. Si vous saviez combien elle a aimé votre mère! S'en voir privée est le martyre que le Ciel lui a réservé. Priez pour elle et pour toute la famille. See also lettre 25, Paris 22 avril 1812.

9 Austin Gough, *Paris and Rome, The Gallican Church and the Ultramontane Campaign 1848–1853* (Oxford, 1986), pp. 25–6.

10 Morlot, op. cit., pp. 3–7. Oh! Comme ce Monsieur Barat est loin de savoir diriger et élever des jeunes gens destinés à devenir, dans ce siècle, les Ministres de la religion! Je connais mieux que personne la situation morale du Séminaire de Troyes et la grandeur du Mal que les travers d'esprit de cet illuminé y a produit […] La manie pour les singularités en dévotion, les révélations et les petits miracles. Hélas! que peut devenir un Séminaire ainsi conduit?

11 Archives Nationales, Paris F/19/6287, Dossier 8, Demandes d'exception, Paris, 26 juin 1812; 9 juillet 1812; 18 juillet 1812; 14 août 1812; 26 août 1812; 7 septembre 1812; 16 octobre 1812. Also, Morlot, op. cit., pp. 7–8.

12 AFSJ, Vanves, Fonds Barat, Louis à Marie-Louise Dusaussoy, St Galmier, 9 septembre 1803.

13 Corr. MSB et Philippine Duchesne, 1804–1815, lettre 40, Joigny, 30 novembre 1810, p. 136; lettre 47, Gand, 18 et 23 mars [1811], pp. 149–50.

14 Corr. SB et Marie Balastron, lettre 8, Paris, 5 juillet 1814. Ce que vous me dites d'Elisa me fait bien de la peine; ne pourrait-on essayer un moyen pour empêcher qu'elle ne soit aussi menteuse et dissimulée, celui de gagner sa confiance, de la traiter avec douceur, et de la convaincre qu'elle sera aimée et bien traitée quand elle dira sa vérité. J'ai remarqué dans cette enfant un amour-propre si excessif, et un désir de plaire si violent, que l'apparence d'être grondée ou désapprouvée pourrait bien produire ces détours. Sans doute ne faut-il pas l'applaudir pour le mal, mais peut-être qu'en la reprenant doucement, en lui donnant un peu de liberté quand elle est avec vous, elle chercherait moins à vous en imposer. Au reste, de loin, la suivant peu, personne ne m'en parlant plus qu'un mot, je ne puis donner aucun conseil […] c'est l'âge de corriger ces défauts qu'elle développe, plus tard ce sera aussi plus difficile […] Lui permet-on quelques petites sottises de temps en temps sur la montagne? See also, lettre 6, Paris, 14 décembre 1813; lettre 7, Amiens, 1 mars 1814; lettre 9, Paris, 18 août 1814; lettre 10, Amiens, 5 décembre 1814.

15 Corr. SB à Sophie Dusaussoy, lettre 1, Paris, 11 juillet 1811; lettre 2, Poitiers, 30 août 1811; lettre 3, Poitiers, 10 mars 1812; lettre 4, Grenoble, 5 février 1813; lettre 5, Grenoble 18 mars 1813; lettre 6, Grenoble, 24 juin 1813; lettre 7, [Grenoble, 1813]; lettre 8, Paris, 14 décembre 1813; lettre 9, Amiens, 4 mai 1814; lettre 10, Amiens 6 juin 1814; lettre 11, Grenoble, août 1814.

16 Corr. SB à Sophie Dusaussoy, lettre 3, Poitiers, 10 mars 1812.

17 Corr. SB à Marie-Louise Dusaussoy, lettre 7, Amiens, 27 mai 1814. En général tous vos enfants sont très difficiles à élever: l'humeur, l'entêtement et l'orgueil les dominent; Thérèse devenait insupportable, traitant ses compagnes et ses Maîtresses comme ses inférieures et avec le ton le plus malhonnête; juge la peine que j'en ai! On a été obligé de l'humilier publiquement, il a fallu que je reprise moi-même avec rigueur; elle est un peu mieux, mais, m'écrit mère Grosier, peu persuadée qu'elle aura besoin de son travail par la suite. C'est

vraiment un inconvénient d'élever des enfants au-dessus de leur état quand ils n'ont pas les sentiments déli-cats! j'avais presque envie de vous les rendre afin qu'elle vît de ses yeux ce qui l'attendait, le travail et la peine [...] Je pense quelquefois que vous avez de grandes grâces à rendre au Seigneur de vous avoir donné les moyens d'élever ces enfants loin de vous [...] surtout avec votre mauvaise manière, de tout accorder dans les moments, et de gronder ensuite à tort et à travers.

18 Renseignements sur Ladies of Christian Instruction demandés par M. Le Préfet du Département de la Somme (General Archives, Rome Approbation Civile 1806–180, A–IV, 1).

19 Cahier, *Vie*, i, 182–87.

20 De Charry, *Histoire des Constitutions*, ii, 495–502; 518–26.

21 Ibid., ii, 527–38.

22 Corr. SB et Philippine Duchesne, 1804–1815, pp. 128–9.

23 Corr. MSB et Philippine Duchesne, 1804–1815, lettre 64, Niort, décembre 1811, p. 185.

24 Souvenirs de Mlle Herbert, ff. 11–12 (General Archives, Rome Cahier, C–I, A, 1–e (bis) Box 1); Cahier, *Vie*, i, 199; de Charry, *Histoire des Constitutions*, ii, 550–551. Details of the reasons for Saintt-Estève's imprisonment have not been recorded.

25 Corr. SB et Philippine Duchesne, lettres 72, 73, 74, Paris, 6, 10, 29 décembre 1813, pp. 199–200; de Charry, *Histoire des Constitutions*, ii, 540, 544–48.

26 De Charry, *Histoire des Constitutions*, ii, 551–53.

27 Ibid., ii, 627–31.

28 Ibid., ii, 631–4.

29 Amiens Affaires, Lettre No.1, Lettre de l'abbé de St-Estève au P. Varin, Rome le 29 août 1814.

30 Amiens Affaires, Lettre No. 2, Lettre de la Mère Barat à l'abbé de St-Estève, Paris 11 septembre 1814. Permettez-moi à ce sujet de vous faire une observation; vous avez déjà donné nos règles à l'examen, peut-être à la suite, presserez-vous notre approbation? Avant d'aller plus loin, ne serait-il pas sage d'attendre que la dernière rédaction ait eu lieu et qu'elle ait été acceptée par le Conseil réuni de la Société; car pour répon-dre au vœu général de toutes les Maisons, à l'exception de celle d'Amiens qui est moins exigeante, toutes, depuis surtout que la liberté est rendue à la France, veulent l'Institut des jésuites adapté à des femmes aussi rapproché qu'il pourra l'être [...] aussitôt que cette dernière rédaction sera achevée et approuvée par la Société, nous vous l'enverrons, et c'est alors que vous pourrez la présenter à l'examen et à l'approbation [...] Il y a encore un article qu'il importe de vous faire observer, c'est au sujet du nom que nous devons prendre. Vous savez [...] que celui du Sacré-Cœur a été agréé de toutes, on pourrait dire dans une espèce d'enthousi-asme. Il sera bien difficile de leur en faire goûter un autre [...] Car vous le comprenez bien [...] de même que c'est à la Société de présenter au St Père ses Constitutions, de même aussi c'est à elle à se choisir son nom [...] Cet article du nom sera l'objet de la réunion comme tout ce qui regarde les Constitutions; le résultat vous sera envoyé comme nous en sommes convenus de vive voix avant votre départ [...] c'est le seul moyen [...] que nous puissions prendre de rétablir et de faire un tout de la Société.

31 Amiens Affaires, No. 3, Lettre de l'abbé St-Estève à Monsieur Varin, prêtre. Paris le 1 octobre 1814 'une route franche, dégagée de préjugés, pleine de confiance et indépendante des dictums de certaines de ses filles'; 'une bien mauvaise supérieure ou un mauvais conseil'.

32 Amiens Affaires, No. 7, Lettre de l'abbé St-Estève à Mr de Clorivière, Rome le 7 novembre 1814.

33 Amiens Affaires, No. 4, Lettre de l'abbé de St-Estève à la Mère Barat, Rome 23 octobre [1814] Mes prédécesseurs ont détruit les jésuitesses. Je n'en veux pas non plus, encore moins de Dames de la Foi; et je ne consentirai jamais à ce que les jésuites se mêlent de religieuses: c'est contraire aux règles de leur fondateur.

34 Chantal Reynier, 'Le Père de Clorivière et le rétablissement des jésuites en France (1814–1818)', in *Revue Mabillon*, n.s., t.6 (=t.67), 1995, 267–93; Chantal Reynier 'La correspondance de P.J. de Clorivière avec T. Brzozowski, 1814 à 1818. Le rétablissement de la Compagnie en France', *AHSI*, vol. LXIV, 1995, 83–167.

35 Amiens Affaires, No. 6, Lettre de l'abbé St-Estève au P. Varin, (Rome) le 2 novembre [1814].

36 Amiens Affaires, No. 8, lettre du P. Varin à Madame Barat. Paris, 23 novembre [1814]. 'Voici l'explosion de l'orage que je voyais se former depuis long-temps sur votre tête, je pourrais bien ajouter sur la mienne.'

37 Louis Panizzoni was provincial of the Jesuits in Rome and vicar of the superior general of the Jesuits in the regions outside of Russia, including France. At this time the general of the Jesuits still resided in Russia.

38 The abbé Perreau (1766–1837) was born in Savigny-sous-Beaune and ordained before the Revolution. During the Revolution he was tutor to several families, particularly that of the duc de Périgord. He had to go under-ground during the reign of Napoleon and was imprisoned in 1811. At the Restoration he was named chaplain to the king and secretary to Cardinal de Talleyrand-Périgord. He was well known in Rome.

39 Amiens Affaires, No. 10, Lettre de la Mère Barat au P. Panizzoni S.J., provincial d'Italie [Amiens] 27 novem-bre 1814.

40 Barat à Panizzoni, 27 novembre 1814. Qu'il me soit permis en mon nom et au nom de toutes mes compagnes qui habitent quatre de nos maisons, et d'une grande partie de celles de la cinquième, qui a été conduite par Mr de Sambucy, de vous conjurer d'engager Mr de Sambucy à suspendre ses poursuites et à attendre que tous les esprits soient réunis par des règlements communs, que la Société adoptera. Sans quoi j'ai tout lieu de

craindre par la disposition où je vois les esprits que l'autorité et les règlements de Mr de Sambucy ne soient reconnus que de quelques personnes. Il me semble que notre Société étant pour la France, et devant être composée de françaises, demande ce délai pour faire l'essai de ce qui lui parait le plus convenable d'après le but qu'elle se propose pour la gloire de Dieu avec le désir de porter le nom de Société du Sacré-Cœur et de lui être toute dévouée.

41   Amiens Affaires, No. 11, Copie de la réponse à trois lettres de M. de Sambucy. Paris 10 décembre 1814.

42   Copie de la réponse à trois lettres de M. de Sambucy. Votre ancien ami, Mr l'abbé de Tournély qu'on peut et qu'on doit regarder comme le premier instituteur de la Société de ces Dames, puisque c'est lui qui en a conçu le projet et le plan en Allemagne, et que l'exécution qui a été donnée en France, n'en est absolument que la suite. Mr de Tournély […] n'a jamais eu le projet de former des jésuitesses, mais seulement une Société des Dames, qui en se consacrant au Sacré-Cœur, s'emploieraient tout entière à l'Éducation, prenant dans l'Institut de St Ignace ce qui pourrait les aider à remplir leur but. Elles sont donc Dames du Sacré-Cœur, et non pas jésuitesses.

43   For an assessment of the character of Joseph Varin, and in particular his dramatic change of judgement at this time, see de Charry, *Histoire des Constitutions*, ii, 631–64.

44   Amiens Affaires, No. 12, A Madame Barat à l'oratoire. À Amiens. Paris 16 décembre 1814.

45   Amiens Affaires, Nos. 16, 17. Saint-Estève à Joseph Varin, Rome 16 février 1814, Rome 19 février 1814.

46   Cahier, *Vie*, i, 208–9.

47   De Charry, *Histoire des constitutions*, ii, 657–67; Cahier, *Vie*, i, 204–9.

48   De Charry, *Histoire des constitutions*, ii, 670; Cahier, *Vie*, i, 208. 'les symptômes avant-coureurs d'une fièvre muqueuse compliqué'. 'Si ma sœur succombe, envoyez-moi seulement une lettre blanche avec un cachet noir, je comprendrai'.

49   Amiens Affaires, No. 13, A Monsieur Sellier, prêtre au petit séminaire de Saint Acheul près de Amiens. Paris 12 janvier 1815. 'Madame Sophie si affaiblie par la souffrance et privée presque de tout secours n'est guères en état d'agir avec la fermeté que demanderait l'état des choses'.

50   Amiens Affaires, No. 14, [Joseph Varin] A Madame Barat, Maison de l'oratoire à Amiens. Paris 13 janvier 1815 Il me semble que vous ferez bien de réunir votre conseil et de représenter avec force et douceur, qu'il est temps de rétablir l'union dans les membres de la Société et pour conséquent l'unité d'autorité, l'esprit de subordination et l'observation des règles; dites clairement que M. de S[ambuc]y n'est pas et n'a jamais été le Supérieur, que la Société ne l'a jamais reconnu comme tel, qu'aucune autorité compétente ne lui a conféré cette place, que la Maison d'Amiens ne peut donc pas le reconnaître pour Supérieur à moins de vouloir faire schisme, qu'au surplus dans quelques mois, l'on convoquera une députation de la Société et qu'alors on prendra une marche uniforme […] la réponse faite à M. de S[ambuc]y et plus encore l'expérience de la funeste qu'il exerce […] semblent vous mettre dans l'obligation de vous montrer et d'agir en Supérieure.

51   Amiens Affaires, No. 15, [Varin to Sophie] ¿ Madame Barat à l'oratoire à Amiens. Paris 8 février 1815.

52   Notice sur la vie de Madame la Comtesse de Gramont, née de Boisgelin, décédée le 16 janvier 1836, religieuse du Sacré-Cœur et supérieure de la maison du Mans (Paris, c. 1836). Although she had entered only in 1813, Madame de Gramont asked that she be admitted to first vows the following year, fearing she could be recalled to court when the Bourbons were restored in April 1814.

53   Amiens Affaires, No. 18, de Madama d'Aster à Mgr de Pressigny [Amiens] avril 1815. L'on nous a dit, Monsieur, que quelques personnes avaient parlé au St Père de notre petite Société, et qu'il daignait nous destiner la Maison de la Sainte Trinité sur la Place d'Espagne, et que l'on avait indiqué Mme de Gramont ma fille aînée pour commencer cet établissement. Le zèle d'une grande entreprise peut exciter un moment l'illusion dans une jeune religieuse, mais ce choix n'étant pas fait par notre Supérieure Générale ne pourrait avoir lieu. J'ose prier Votre Excellence de vouloir bien faire agréer au Saint Pontife nos très humbles excuses de ne pouvoir nous charger de cet établissement, et de vouloir bien exposer à Sa Sainteté les besoins de notre société naissante, qui sent qu'elle doit s'occuper d'abord à se perfectionner et se consolider avant de s'étendre. Ne serait-il pas très imprudent, du moins pour quelques années, d'établir cette maison aussi loin de la Supérieure Générale et du centre d'une Société naissante, qui n'a été formée que pour la France, qui n'a que des règlements superficiels et qui doit s'appliquer à adopter les véritables constitutions qui lui serviront de base. Grâce importante qu'elle ne peut espérer que de Dieu, par la prière, le silence et l'obscurité.

54   Amiens Affaires, No. 12, [Joseph Varin] A Madame Barat, Amiens. Paris 16 décembre 1814. A year later when the crisis was abating somewhat Madame de Gramont d'Aster wrote a sharp letter to Gaston de Sambucy. Amiens Affaires, No. 49 [Louis Perreau] A Madame Barat [Paris] 13 février 1816.

55   Marie de la Croix, Récit historique de la scission de 1815 et des souffrances morales de notre bienheureuse Mère Fondatrice (GA, Rome, C–I., A, 1–d, Box 2 Notes envoyées par la Mère Marie de la Croix), ff. 2–5. There are several versions of the account written by Marie de la Croix. This one appears to be the original. The others are in A–II., 1–a; C-VII, C.

56   Notes envoyées par la Mère Marie de la Croix), f. 5. Toute communication avec les professes nous fut interdite. Sous prétexte que sa maladie exigeait le plus grand repos, notre Rde Mère fut séquestrée dans la petite

maison qu'elle habitait, et à l'exception des personnes qui ll soignaient, aucune des religieuses ne put plus parvenir jusqu'à elle.

57   Marie de la Croix, Notes sur Amiens 1812, ff. 4, 5–6 (GA, Rome, A–II., 1–a). Also, Notes envoyées par la Mère Marie de la Croix, ff. 5–6. Nous étudions en silence, lorsque notre sous-maîtresse sortant de sa chambre et fermant à clef sa porte [...] nous dit en passant très vite: Ah! Mes chères enfants! n'oubliez jamais qui n'est pas dans la barque de Pierre est dans l'eau! elle étoit disparue, nous laissant stupéfaites!
      Ma maîtresse des novices me prit à part et pendant une promenade assez longue [...] elle me dit [...] en gémissant d'une si cruelle nécessité qu'il étoit temps de me faire une triste et douloureuse confidence: qu'il existe en France une source d'erreurs et de dissidence avec le Saint-Siège, appelée les quatre articles de l'Église Gallicane; que beaucoup d'évêques s'en faisaient les zélés défenseurs et que, par un malheur qu'on ne pouvait assez déplorer, et qui devenait chaque jour plus inappréciable pour nous, l'adhérence de notre très révérende mère générale aux quatre articles et sa confiance illimitée dans les auteurs de cette hérésie nous mettaient à tous les instants à deux doigts de notre perte!

58   Récit historique, f. 6. Vous me forcez alors à vous dire ce que j'aurais voulu vous cacher: c'est que Notre Mère est excessivement politique; et que cette bienveillance qui vous enchante n'est qu'une apparence pour nous gagner et nous faire tomber dans le dernier des malheurs! Voilà ce que la charité ne me permettait pas de vous dire.

59   Marie de la Croix, Notes sur Amiens 1812, pp. 7–8 bis; Notes envoyées par la Mère Marie de la Croix, f. 7.

60   Récit historique, f.9. Ma mère, me dit-elle? mais son amitié naturelle pour notre Mère Barat l'a complètement aveuglée; j'ai fait l'impossible pour l'éclairer, je n'ai pas pu y réussir. Aussi, ne lui dis-je plus rien, mais je veux au moins sauver Antoinette.

61   Angélique Gillot (1793–1824) started her noviciate in Amiens and completed it in Paris. She died at Niort in 1824. Jeanne de Charry, Exposé historique, p. 214, n. 83; Ménologes 1800–1900.

62   Récit historique, ff. 9–10; Notes sur Amiens, p. 11.

63   Affaires Amiens, No. 19, lettre de Stephanelli à la Mère Barat. Rome, le 5 août 1815.

64   Affaires Amiens, No. 25, Lettre du P. Varin à la Mère Barat après l'arrivée de la lettre de Stephanelli, Paris 16 septembre [1815] Je ne crois pas qu'après Notre Seigneur, le premier de tous vos amis, vous en puissiez trouver deux plus dévoués et plus disposés à ressentir vos peines et à les adoucir autant qu'il est en eux.

Notes to Chapter 5

1   Affaires Amiens, no. 19, Lettre de la Mère Barat au P. de Clorivière [Été 1815] Les abus et les maux que je vous ai confiés n'ont pas diminué, je pourrais même dire qu'ils n'ont fait qu'augmenter. Ce qu'il y a de plus affligeant, c'est que plusieurs sujets d'Amiens, ayant été envoyés dans les autres maisons, y ont porté cet esprit, et ont gagné insensiblement ceux qui gouvernent, ce qui est une source de peines cuisantes pour les supérieures qui me restent attachées. Le remède [...] à ce germe de division qui s'étend dans presque toutes les maisons, est celui dont vous avez reconnu la nécessité, c'est de pouvoir présenter à toute la famille les Règles selon l'esprit de St Ignace auxquelles la plus grande partie aspire. Ce travail, que toutes me demandent avec instance, pourra seul les fixer, rattacher tous les cœurs à l'unité et réunir tous les esprits [...] J'avoue que si je ne conservais pas l'espoir de voir bientôt la fin de nos maux, je ne sais si je pourrais en conscience continuer à gouverner cette association.

2   Affaires Amiens, no. 20, À Madame Barat, Maison de l'Instruction Chrétienne à Cuignières. Paris 18 août 1815.

3   Affaires Amiens, nos. 21, 22, 23, Correspondance relative au départ pour Rome des mères de Sambucy et Copina.

4   Affaires Amiens, no. 24, Lettre de la Mère Eugénie de Gramont à la Mère Barat 9 septembre [1815]. J'espère que nous ne tarderons pas à en faire autant. Je crois [...] que ceci est essentiel. Ce serait pour le coup que la désunion se ferait, et malheur à celles qui ne se rendraient pas au désir du St Père, au reste [...] ne croyez pas que je pense à vous quitter [...] Je vous le répète [...] il n'y qu'un parti à prendre, c'est de nous réunir à ce que vous n'avez pu empêcher.

5   Affaires Amiens, no. 25, Lettre du P. Varin à la Mère Barat après l'arrivée de la lettre de Stephanelli, Paris 16 septembre [1815].

6   De Charry (ed.), *Varin Lettres*. No. 88, Paris, 23 novembre [1814], p. 231, and note 14, p. 236; no. 91, Paris 13 janvier [1815], p. 246 and note 10, pp. 248–9; de Charry, *Histoire des constitutions*, ii (1st edn), pp. 742–765; de Charry, *Histoire des constitutions*, iii, *Textes*, no. 61, p. 314, Lettre de la Mère Baudemont à la Mère Barat, Châlons, 19 mai 1816. ['son affreuse prison'].

7   Affaires Amiens, no. 28, [Robert Debrosse] à Madame Barat, Poitiers 8 octobre 1815. Robert Debrosse (1768–1848) had been a Father of the Faith and entered the Jesuits in Paris in 1814. He became rector of the junior seminary at Bordeaux.

8   Chantal Reynier (ed.), La Correspondence de P.J. de Clorivière avec T. Brzozowski 1814–1818. La rétablissement de la Compagnie en France. Textus Inediti, no. 28, Paris 28 juin 1817, de Clorivière à Brzozowski, pp.140–143 in A.H.S.J., vol. lxiv (Rome, 1995).

9   *Vie de Madame Geoffroy*, pp. 25–6.

10 De Charry, *Histoire des constitutions*, iii, *Textes*, pp. 309–313, 318–331; Affaires Amiens, Nos. 56 Soyer à Madame Bigeu, Poitiers 7 juillet 1816.

11 Affaires Amiens, no. 55, Première lettre de Stephanelli à Mère Duchesne, Automne 1815.

12 Affaires Amiens, no. 56, Seconde lettre de Stephanelli à la Mère Duchesne, Rome 28 octobre 1815. There is a detailed refutation of this letter in the GA, Rome, obviously written at a later date. Affaires Amiens, no. 35, Réponse à la seconde lettre de Stephanelli à la Mère Duchesne.

13 [Marie de la Croix] Récit Historique, f. 10.

14 Martine Sonnet, *L'éducation des filles au temps des Lumières* (Paris, 1987); Dominique Julia, *Les trois couleurs du tableau noir. La Révolution* (Paris, 1981), pp. 310–31. For an extensive treatment of the influences of other religious and educational traditions on the content of the 1815 Constitutions, see de Charry, *Constitutions définitives*, i, 80–115.

15 De Charry, *Histoire des constitutions, Textes*, pp. 307–308.

16 Affaires Amiens, no. 42 bis Les notes envoyées par l'abbé St-Estève et leur examen au Conseil Général de 1815.

17 Affaires Amiens no. 44, Mère Barat à ses soeurs, Paris, 17 décembre 1815. Il s'agissait d'étouffer un germe de division qui, introduit depuis plusieurs années parmi nous, pouvait avoir des suites les plus funestes, et de nous réunir toutes sous l'observance d'une même règle, conforme au dessein que le Seigneur s'est proposé dans la formation de notre petite Société [...] notre Société dans le principe, a été essentiellement fondée sur la dévotion au Sacré-Cœur de Jésus, et [...] doit être tellement dévouée et consacrée à la gloire et au culte de ce divin Cœur que tous les travaux et toutes les fonctions qu'elle embrasse s'y rapportent comme à leur fin principale [...] telle est la glorieuse et aimable fin de notre petite Société: nous sanctifier nous-mêmes en prenant pour modèle le divin Cœur de Jésus et en cherchant autant qu'il nous sera possible à nous unir à ses sentiments et à ses dispositions intérieures; et, en même temps, nous consacrer à étendre et à propager la connaissance et l'amour de ce divin Cœur en travaillant à la sanctification des âmes [...] je le répète, telle est la fin que Dieu s'est plu à manifester dans le principe de notre Société, et si les temps orageux où elle a commencé en France ne nous ont pas permis de faire une profession ouverte de cette consécration au Sacré-Cœur de Jésus, nous croirions maintenant manquer essentiellement au dessein de Dieu, si nous ne nous reportions à l'origine de notre Société pour en prendre le véritable esprit et en remplir le but [...] En voyant les Constitutions et les Règles [...] vous n'aurez pas de peine à reconnaître qu'on s'est rapproché de celles de Saint Ignace, autant qu'il était possible, et qu'on y a puisé tout ce qui pouvait nous convenir.

18 Amiens Affaires 1814–1816, no. 39, Paris 1 décembre 1815, Réponse à Mr Lambert, Chne de Poitiers, (General Archives, Rome A–II., 1–b). See Amiens Affaires, No 30 [Madame Barat] à Fontana, [Paris] 8 octobre 1815 for a similar account of the actions of Saint-Estève and the steps Sophie Barat took to re-establish her position as superior general.

19 Amiens Affaires 1814–1816, no. 39, Paris 1 décembre 1815, Réponse à Mr Lambert. Mon silence, sur ces nouveautés, ne peut être regardé comme une marque d'approbation, puisque mon autorité sur la maison d'Amiens se trouvait sans effet par celle qu'avait prise de lui-même M. de S. Pour le bien de la paix, je pris donc le parti de tolérer ce que je ne pouvais empêcher, espérant que le temps rapprocherait les esprits. Je crus, il y a deux ans, que le moment en était venu [...] C'est alors que dans le désir de la paix, j'engageai toutes les maisons à accepter le travail de M. de S. et voila ce que l'on objecte maintenant contre l'opposition que je montre, comme si j'étais en contradiction avec moi-même, tandis qu'on devrait regarder la conduite que je tins alors comme un sacrifice pénible que je faisais au bien de la paix.

20 Amiens Affaires, no. 30, [Sophie Barat] au R.P. Fontana, [Paris] octobre 1815.

21 Amiens Affaires 1814–1816, no. 39, Paris 1 décembre 1815, Réponse à Mr Lambert. Il n'y a malheureusement que trop de conformité entre sa conduite à l'égard de la Société de la bonne Julie et celle que depuis plusieurs années il tient envers la notre. En effet, il n'était que le confesseur de la maison d'Amiens, et bientôt il voulut s'en faire le supérieur et comme le nouveau fondateur de toute la Société, en changeant l'esprit et la Règle. Ce n'est pas moi qui lui prête cette intention, vous avez vu par la lettre qu'il m'adressa sous le nom de M. Stephanelli qu'il déclare en propres termes qu'il n'y a que lui qu'on doit regarder comme supérieur et fondateur de notre Société [...] par quels moyens s'est-il efforcé d'arriver à son but? vous demandez des faits, ceux ci sont connus: C'est en faisant un parti dans la maison d'Amiens au préjudice de l'autorité de la supérieure qui pendant longtemps n'a existé dans cette Maison d'Amiens que comme une étrangère. Also, AF, Poitiers, B01, 117, C, Amiens. Histoire de la maison.

22 Reynier, La Correspondance de P.J. de Clorivière avec T. Bzozowski, 1814–1818, no. 28, de Clorivière à Bzozowski, Paris, 29 juin 1817, pp. 140–43.

23 In 1825 Saint-Estève's 'busy, bustling, intriguing spirit interfered with negotiations between Propaganda Fidei in Rome and the bishop of Quebec. The pope has long had an aversion to him ... about three weeks

ago he received orders from the pope's government to leave Rome in twenty four hours.' Robert Gradwell to Jean-Octave Plessis, bishop of Quebec, Rome, 28 August 1825 (original in English). GA, Rome, A–II., 1–b, Amiens. In 1827 Saint-Estève was appointed chaplain to the Carmelite sisters, rue de Vaugirard, Paris, and created problems there so that he had to be removed quickly by Archbishop de Quelen. Limouzin-Lamothe, *Monseigneur de Quelen*, i, 327.

24 Corr. MSB et Philippine Duchesne, 1804–1815, Lettre 23, 7 septembre 1807, 91; Lettre 27, Poitiers, 4 mai 1808, p. 101; Lettre 46, Gand, 17 février 1811, p. 147; Lettre 49, Gand, 23 avril [1811], p. 154; Lettre 54, Poitiers, 19 août 1811, p. 164; Lettre 56, Poitiers 9 septembre 1811, p.171; Lettre 62, Poitiers, 7 octobre 1811, p. 181; Lettre 68, Niort, 14 février 1812, p. 191. Corr. SB et Emilie Giraud, Lettre 22, Paris, 19 juillet 1811; Lettre 40, Amiens, 14 janvier 1815.

25 Corr. SB et Madeleine Sophie to Madeleine du Chasteigner, Lettre 6, Grenoble, décembre 1812.

26 Corr. SB et Emilie Giraud, Lettre 31, Grenoble, 14 mars 1813.

27 Adrienne Michel, Journal du second voyage ... de Mère Barat à Gand, 1811, f. 12. Qu'est-ce que je vois là?. – Mais, mon père, […] j'étais bien embarrassée […] je lui avoue et lui dit […] Mais, mon père, je fais gras. – Comment, me dit-il, et vous avez de vos filles une si petite idée, vous craignez donc qu'elles aient de vous des soupçons. Allons, qu'on assemble la communauté. On alla chercher tout le monde, jusqu'à celles qui étaient aux enfants […] je puis dire que je fus bien mortifiée.

28 Pierre de Clorivière was steeped in apocalyptic literature and theology. This was a way of interpreting the dissolution of the Jesuits, the French Revolution, the rise and demise of Napoleon, the return of the Bourbons (who had instigated the suppression of the Jesuits) and the restoration of Jesuits in 1814. De Clorivière lent his commentaries on the Book of Revelation to Sophie Barat. Claude Langlois, 'Clorivière et la Révolution: Apocalypse ou apologétique?', in *Recherches autour de Pierre de Clorivière* (Paris, 1993). Louis Barat was also greatly influenced by this type of theological literature and wrote vast numbers of commentaries himself over the years.

29 Corr. SB et Emilie Giraud, Lettre 42, Paris, 26 septembre 1815.

30 Corr. SB et Madeleine du Chasteigner, Lettre 6, Grenoble, décembre 1812.

31 De Charry, *Histoire des constitutions, Textes*, 251. 'elle est profondément politique; elle ne dit jamais ce quelle pense, et feint toujours des sentiments qu'elle n'a pas!'

32 De Charry, *Constitutions définitives*, i, 8–18.

33 De Coriolis, Histoire de la Société, 1806–1807, ch II, f. 13. Les sœurs coadjutrices n'affluaient pas dans les commencements; il fallut remplir leurs propres emplois en les conciliant avec les charges dont chaque membre était revêtu.

34 Corr. SB et Emilie Giraud, lettre 38, Amiens, 5 octobre 1814. Vous demandez tout de suite trois Ma"tresses de classe, observant que vous n'avez que des sœurs qui augmentent votre surcharge. Trois Ma"tresses d'un coup, c'est un peu fort! Vous savez, ma chère fille, que les Ma"tresses de classes ne se forment pas à la douzaine! J'espérais que mère Grosier pourrait vous en envoyer une et plus tard on vous en aurait préparé une seconde […] Vous n'avez que des sœurs chez vous. Cela est vrai, et c'est un grand abus que vous sentirez davantage plus tard. Et dès maintenant vous concevez l'inconvénient d'en recevoir au-delà du besoin, ce que désormais il faudra bien éviter. Je vois bien sur le tableau de vos occupations que vous êtes toutes pressées par le travail.

35 Chantal Reynier (ed.), La Correspondance de P.J. de Clorivière avec T. Brzozowski, 1814–1818 *AHSI*, vol. LXIV (1995), no. 10 Paris, 4 juin 1816, p. 106; no. 20, Paris, 20 août 1816, p. 114–15; no. 14, [n.p.] 17/29 septembre 1816, p. 117. 'vu la démoralisation générale de cette classe d'hommes'.

36 Amiens Affaires, no. 39, Réponse à Mr Lambert, Paris 1 décembre 1815. On reçoit dans son institut toutes les anciennes Religieuses, tandis qu'il sait bien que dans notre Société on croit devoir, sinon les exclure absolument, du moins user d'une très grande réserve dans leur admission. Vous comprenez aisément […] qu'une maison d'Amiens ouverte aux religieuses de tous les ordres ne pourrait pas longtemps conserver un même esprit.

37 Pierre Ronsin (1771–1846), was born at Soissons and died in Toulouse. Through Saint-Estève he got to know the Fathers of the Faith and he joined the association in c. 1803. He taught in the colleges at Belley and Roanne. He was director of a congregation dedicated to the Blessed Virgin, whose membership was composed of the nobility and wealthy middle class in Paris. In 1814 he entered the Jesuit novitiate in Paris.

38 Notes sur Amiens 1812, f. 13; Récit historique, f. 13. Votre mère a fait le vœu de Sainte Thérèse; comment avec l'obligation du plus parfait, aurait-elle pu donner à son expression le sens dans lequel vous l'avez compris? For a discussion of the vow of perfection in the history of spirituality, *Dictionnaire de spiritualité*, fasc. lxxxvi–lxxxvii, no. 12 (1983), pp. 229–33.

39 Notes sur Amiens, f. 14.

40 Clorivière au Brzozowski, 29 juin 1817, AHSJ (lxiv), 1995, p. 142. Dans un moment de ferveur extraordinaire, elle a fait subitement à Dieu, des vœux inconsidérés tendant à ce qu'elle se figurait être le plus parfait. Elle en fut blâmée par le P. Ronsin, qui se chargea d'en conférer avec MM les Grands Vicaires et d'autres ecclési-

astiques de poids et d'autorité; et d'après ces consultations [...] la lettre qu'il a écrite à sa pénitente ne renfermait rien d'extravagant, comme le prétend M(onsieur) de Sambucy.

41 Limouzin-Lamothe, *Monseigneur de Quelen*, 33.

42 Récit Historique, f. 14. Ce fut un des plus cruels moments de ma vie. Le Père Ronsin lui-même, j'en suis sûre, aura regretté de nous avoir imposé à toutes deux un tel supplice [torture], et la mère E. de Gramont, qui était présente a dû elle-même en souffrir beaucoup, car elle savait trop bien la part qui lui en revenait et devait craindre à chaque ligne de se trouver compromise. Il n'en fut rien; mais la nature en ce moment fut plus forte que la grâce: elle n'eut pas le courage de dire un mot pour me soulager un peu et je bus le calice jusqu'à la lie.

43 GA, Rome, A–II., b–2, Amiens. Compte-rendu du Conseil général de 1815. La Mère Bigeu à la Mère d'Aster, Paris, 20 décembre 1815; Affaires Amiens, no. 41, De la Mère Barat à l'abbé Soyer, [n.d.]. Mme Eugénie n'a encore parlé à cœur ouverte à N. Mère'. that 'éclairée par vos dernières [lettres], paraît se rapprocher de nous'.

44 Récit historique, f. 15. 'J'étais étonnée d'y voir admise la mère E de Gramont qui je trouvais bien plus responsable que moi de toute cette affaire.'

45 The Abbé Manceau published four volumes concerning the life and writings of Marie de la Croix. The first volume contained her biography and the three following her writings. He also published his memorandum to Pope Leo XIII. GA, Rome, Affaires de Mr l'abbé Manceau, 1884–1885, Quadrille, Bordeaux. (GA, Rome, C–I., A–3, d. events; C–I., b–4, Box 1; C–IV., 4, Bordeaux, Box 6; C–VII, 2–c, de la Croix; B–II., Box 1, dossier 7. AF, Poitiers, B10, 115, Journal de la maison de Quadrille, 1877–1885). The four volumes were printed by the publisher Oudin in Poitiers in 1884 under the title *Vie et écrits spirituels de Rose Marie de la Croix*. Despite persistent searches in Poitiers, Rome and Paris all copies of these books seem to have been destroyed. In January 1998 books formerly placed on the Index were made available in the Vatican Library. To date the volumes written by the abbé Manceau have not been traced. However, at the beginning of the twentieth century the Vatican asked some of the libraries of the city of Rome to house quantities of books placed on the Index and it is possible that eventually the missing volumes may be found.

46 De Charry, *Constitutions définitives*, i, 62–83.

47 Récit historique, f. 15.

48 GA, Rome, A–II., 1–g, Box 2, Amiens, Journal de la Maison d'Amiens, ff. 2–3.

49 Journal de la Maison d'Amiens, f. 2.

50 ibid., ff. 4–15.

51 De Charry, *Constitutions définitives*, ii, no. 75, 102–4. Ordonnance des Vicaires Capitulaires de Poitiers au sujet des constitutions de la Société du Sacré Cœur.

52 De Charry, *Histoire des constitutions*, iii, 311, Réponse de Mgr Cortois de Pressigny, Ambassadeur du Roi de France près le saint Siège à l'abbé Soyer, Vicaire Général de Poitiers, Rome, 16 décembre 1815.

53 Affaires Amiens, no. 43, Extrait d'une lettre de la Mère Grosier à la Mère Barat, [Poitiers] 16 janvier 1816.

54 Affaires Amiens, no. 47, Directives de l'abbé Perreau, supérieur général délégué de la Société du Sacré Cœur à la Mère Grosier à Poitiers, 26 janvier 1816.

55 Réponse de M. Soyer au sujet des observations des vicaires généraux de Poitiers sur les constitutions de Sacré Cœur 1816. De Charry, *Constitutions définitives*, ii, no. 77, pp. 108–110.

56 Lettres de la Mère Barat à M. Soyer au sujet des Constitutions, mars et avril 1816. De Charry, *Constitutions Définitives*, ii, no. 79, pp. 118–22. Les explications franches et simples que Madame Grosier vient d'avoir avec vous, Monsieur, auront, je n'en doute pas, dissipé les nuages qui troublaient l'union et l'harmonie qui dévoient naturellement régner entre vous, ayant tous deux des vues si pures pour le bien.

57 De Charry, *Constitutions définitives*, i, 208–9.

58 Affaires Amiens, [n.n.] Réponse de Pie VII aux vicaires généraux de Poitiers, 15 juin 1816.

59 Corr. SB à Thérèse Maillucheau, Lettre 10, Paris, 7 juillet 1816. Partout le travail et les petites maladies m'atteignent; à Poitiers, Niort et Bord[eau]x j'ai été presque continuellement souffrante; en arrivant à Paris après avoir passé une nuit dans la voiture pénible par le frisson et la soif de la fièvre, j'ai pris le lit en arrivant et j'ai passé cette semaine entière sans pouvoir travailler. Voilà presque ma vie habituelle.

60 Affaires Amiens, no. 52, 52 bis, Joseph Varin à Madame Barat, Paris 19 février 1816; no. 54, L. Perreau à Madame Barat, 21 février 1816.

61 Affaires Amiens, no. 52, Joseph Varin à Madame Barat, Paris 19 février 1816. Vous savez ce que je vous suis parce que vous m'êtes Mère, Sœur, et fille, mes sentiments y répondent et se trouvent en abrégé dans ce seul mot: Votre tout dévoué en NSJC, Joseph

62 Cahier, *Vie*, ii, pp. 257–8; Journal de la maison d'Amiens, f. 16.

63 Letters of Madeleine Sophie Barat to Thérèse Maillucheau, letter 5, Amiens, 6 avril 1816.

64 Affaires Amiens, no. 48, L. Perreau à Madame Barat, Paris, 2 février 1816.

65 Affaires Amiens, no. 51, Abbé de Lamarche à Madame Barat, Cuignières, 17 février 1816. Je m'explique: je suis le plus ancien ami de votre Société. Avant sa naissance j'ai donné tout l'encouragement possible, j'en ai suivi toutes les opérations. J'ai gémi de toutes les variétés qu'elle a subi, les difficultés de tout genre [...] intimement persuadé depuis 30 ans que ce serait au Sacré-Cœur de Jésus qu'on serait redevable de la religion

en France (comme je l'ai prêché publiquement alors); j'ai toujours cru qu'il fallait une Société proprement dite du Sacré-Cœur, pour opérer ce miracle qui est le plus grand que jamais le Seigneur ait opéré en France.

66   L. Perreau à Madame Barat, Paris, 2 février 1816. Ce qui m'occupe toujours singulièrement, c'est la composition de la Maison de Paris, et l'inconvénient d'avoir dans la même maison avec vos novices une personne ou deux, qui pourront les entretenir dans l'espérance de vivre un jour sous d'autres Règles, celles de M. de Samb[ucy] [...] soyez persuadée, Madame, que si quelques-unes de vos sœurs entretiennent la pensée de se réunir à la maison de Rome, dès que les règles de M. de Sam[bucy] seront approuvées, vous n'obtiendrez jamais une union parfaite et un même esprit parmi vos dames [...] je redoute pour cette raison, la réunion dans votre noviciat de personnes ainsi disposées; et cependant la Maison de Paris est celle où il est le plus essentiel qu'il n'y ait aucun mélange.

Notes to Chapter 6

1   Jeanne de Charry, Exposé Historique, pp. 212-16. Saint-Estève criticised this move, suggesting that Joseph Varin had rented the house on the rue des Postes to Sophie Barat. De Clorivière told the Jesuit general that Sophie Barat considered the house as a stepping stone to a larger property. De Clorivière au Brzozowski, Paris 29 juin 1817, *AHSI* (lxiv) 1995, p. 142.

2   A.F. Poitiers, B06, 117, iii, rue de Varenne. Alexandrine de Riencourt. Note sur la Maison de Paris. Quand j'arrivai à la rue des Postes, le 16 octobre, le pensionnat, sans être nombreux était déjà florissant [...] Nous étions si à l'étroit que douze novices avaient son dortoir une toute petite chambre à laquelle on devait se rendre le soir, en traversant à tâtons, un grenier. La salle du noviciat servait elle-même de chambre à coucher à une grande élève. In the autumn of 1816 the duc de Gramont, uncle of Eugénie de Gramont suggested to Sophie that she take on the royal foundation school of St Denis, established by Napoleon. Sophie refused, probably fearing it too closely linked with the royal foundation of St Denys in Rome. Cahier, *Vie*, i, 262.

3   Corr. SB et Eugénie de Gramont, lettres 13 et 14, Paris, 3 et 4 octobre 1817. Caroline est bien mal; je ne vous cacherai pas, nous n'avons guère d'espoir de la conserver. C'est un ange. Elle a reçu tous les sacrements dimanche passé, ayant toute sa connaissance, on lui a donné la communion, aujourd'hui, le scapulaire [...] C'est notre unique consolation; mon déchirement est de voir la douleur du père.
     Elle n'est plus notre chère Caroline [...] ou plutôt elle commence à vivre la véritable vie dans le sein de son Dieu où elle s'envola hier soir à 10 heures, après une assez longue et paisible agonie [...] elle a paru devant Dieu riche d'innocence et de mérites, car on ne peut avoir été plus pieuse dans le cours de sa maladie; remercions donc le Seigneur, en même temps que nous sentons sa main, et ne nous affligeons pas comme des païens qui n'ont plus d'espoir de se revoir jamais. For the illnesses and deaths of young children in convent boarding schools, see Arnold, *Le corps et l'âme.*

4   Corr. SB et Thérèse Maillucheau, lettre 11, Paris 19 juillet 1816; lettre 17, Paris 18 septembre 1816; lettre 33, Paris 7 mai 1817; lettre 41, Paris 4 août 1817; Corr. SB et Marie Prevost, lettre 4, Paris 21 octobre 1817; lettre 11, Paris 25 mars 1819; Corr. SB et Stanislas Dusaussoy, lettre 24, Paris 2 novembre 1818; Corr. SB et Marie-Louise Dusaussoy, lettre 10, Paris 12 juillet 1819.

5   Corr. SB et Eugénie de Gramont, lettre 3, Beauvais, 16 septembre 1817. Combien ma Eugénie me manque! étendue dans mon lit trempée de sueurs et de douleur. Je n'osais point le désirer, je sentais que sa présence et ses doux soins auraient été un soulagement que je dois sacrifier en pensant que je ne mérite rien [...] j'ai reçu votre bonne petite lettre....je la lus avec attendrissement, néanmoins, j'aurais désiré que vous eussiez été plus forte et que les larmes n'eussent pas besoin de couler.

6   Corr. SB et Eugénie de Gramont, lettre 6, Paris, 21 septembre 1817. Vous vous affectez trop, ma chère Eugénie, et cette facilité que vous avez à vous inquiéter pour moi me cause du chagrin, pour moi qui ai un fond de santé qui résiste à tout ce qui me fait craindre de vivre jusqu'à 80 ans, de moi qui depuis le temps que je souffre y suis accoutumée et qui engraisse au milieu des peines [...] vous voyez que c'est vous affecter bien en vain que de pleurer sur mes souffrances, vous qui avez tant besoin de vous ménager, de refaire votre santé si délabrée [...] See also lettre 7, Paris 22 septembre 1817; lettre 8, Paris 24 septembre 1817; lettre 15, Beauvais, 3 avril 1818.

7   Corr. SB et Eugénie de Gramont, lettre 15, Beauvais, 3 avril 1818. Je pense à vous presque continuellement auprès du Cœur de Jésus, je fais pour vous de grands projets de perfection. Ah! ma bonne fille, le reste passe avec ce monde, avec nous, Dieu et toujours Dieu par dessus toute chose. Donnez-moi vite de vos nouvelles, la secousse de la voiture n'a émoussé ni mon cœur ni mon imagination; l'un remue l'autre [...]

8   Corr. SB et Eugénie de Gramont, lettre 5, Paris, [n.d.] septembre 1817. Mon oubli le voilà. Je ne vous ai pas recommandé de vous couvrir, et si le temps est pluvieux et froid, il faut vous vêtir davantage, surtout pendant la route; quittez vos bas de fil, prenez-en de filoselle, mettez deux jupons, des manches, enfin couvrez-vous raisonnablement de manière à éviter le rhume. See lettre 10, Paris, 27 septembre 1817.

9   Corr. SB et Thérèse Maillucheau, lettre 62, Paris 19 février 1818.

10   Corr. SB et Thérèse Maillucheau, lettre 55, Paris 26 novembre 1817. [...] mes peines particulières, combien je suis mal secondée, envoyant les meilleurs sujets dans les autres maisons, et les ennuis que me causent ceux

qui devraient m'aider, et qu'on croit qui me sont d'un grand secours […] les autres sentent de la tristesse que je porte dans le fond de l'âme, je ne suis plus assez douce, assez patiente, c'est un grand tort; chacune porte son petit paquet, mais elles ne doivent point payer pour toutes, et c'est cependant ce qui arrive souvent quand on ne sait pas assez se contenir. J'ai perdue toute ma gaieté, je suis comme un bonnet de nuit aux récréations […] je ne puis guère parler de mes misères avec personne. See also lettre 76, Amiens, 8 octobre 1818.

11   Corr. SB et Thérèse Mallucheau, lettre 69, Chambéry, 29 août 1818. J'étais en vous quittant si peinée et mon cœur se trouvait si serré que je ne pus presque rien dire pendant la route que je faisais tristement lorsque je pensais à vous, à vos ennuis, aux sollicitudes qui allaient vous accabler, j'avais peine à retenir mes larmes…tout mon être était demeuré près de vous […] Qu'il me serait doux de revenir habiter une demi année dans votre voisinage, d'aller vous voir plusieurs fois, et vous, peut-être, de revenir me donner votre aide […] Voilà une espérance […] qui diminue beaucoup l'amertume de notre séparation.

12   Corr. MSB et Philippine Duchesne, première partie (1804–1815), lettre 14, Poitiers, 1 août 1806, p. 57; lettre 26, Poitiers, 2 mai 1808, p. 99; lettre 36, Angoulême, 17 août 1809, p. 126. Corr. MSB et Philippine Duchesne, seconde partie, Période de l'Amérique, i (1818–1821) lettre 97, Grenoble, 6 juillet 1818, p. 98; lettre 99, Grenoble 21 juillet 1818, pp. 111–2. Corr. SB et Eugénie Audé, lettre 2, Grenoble, 22 août 1818; Corr. SB et Thérèse Mallucheau, lettre 69, Chambéry 29 août 1818; lettre 70, Chambéry, 3 septembre [1818]; lettre 76, Amiens, 8 octobre 1818; lettre 130, Lyon, 2 décembre 1819; lettre 134, Paris, 3 janvier [1820]; lettre 135, Paris, 9 janvier [1820]; lettre 100, Paris 5 avril 1819.

13   Anne Vincent-Buffault, *The History of Tears. Sense and Sentimentality in France* (London, 1991).

14   Corr. SB et Marie Balastron, lettre, 13, Paris, 9 November 1818. Au lieu de garder la discrétion et de ne parler de Paris qu'avec avantage, vous avez dit en pleine recréation que Madame de Gramont est toujours avec moi […] vous savez combien de rapports nécessaires je suis obligée d'avoir avec la Maistresse Générale et celle qui m'aide pour ma correspondance et dont la santé demande tant de soins […] un peu de justice commanderait le silence de votre part.

15   Corr. SB et Eugénie de Gramont, lettre 29 [Grenoble], 5 juillet 1818; lettre 39, Chambéry, 30 Juillet [1818].

16   ibid., lettre 35, Grenoble, 18 Juillet 1818.

17   ibid., lettre 67, Paris, 24 Octobre 1818. Toute à vous […] je crains que cette dernière phrase qui n'est souvent que politesse pour les autres ne soit trop vraie pour vous.

18   ibid., lettre 56, Chambéry, 31 août 1818; lettre 60, Paris, 13 octobre 1818; lettre 61, Paris, 14 octobre 1818. See also lettres ns., 21, 39, 62.

19   ibid., lettre 95, Lyon, 7 décembre 1819; Letter 100, [La Ferrandière] 17 décembre 1819.

20   Corr. SB et Thérèse Mallucheau, lettre 145, Paris, 3 avril 1820.

21   Corr. SB et Eugénie de Gramont, lettre 95, Lyon, 7 Décembre 1819; lettre 99, Lyon 16 décembre 1819.

22   Corr. SB et Marie Prevost, lettre 1, Paris 18 juillet 1817. Quand n'aurons-nous plus rien à démêler avec ce bon Monsieur? Il me tarde qu'il n'ait plus prétexte pour nous écrire […] [Anne Baudemont] ne parait point heureuse où elle est […] quelle triste vieillesse elle aura! Je la plains de tout mon cœur. See lettre 2, Paris, 2 octobre 1817. Also, GA, Rome, A-II, b-2, Amiens. Affaires d'intérêt; réclamations après la mort de Madame de Sambucy, 1817–29; de Charry, *Constitutions définitives*, i, 51, n. 173.

23   GA, Rome, A-II, 1-b, Amiens. Affaire de Chambéry. Also Corr. SB à Catherine de Charbonnel, lettres 1–3, Chambéry, 31 juillet, 2 août, 12 août 1818.

24   A-II, 1-b, Amiens. Affaire de Chambéry, 1818. M. de Sambucy à Madame Bien-aimée, Rome le 23 août 1818.

25   Affaires Amiens, no. 60 (bis), Saint-Estève à Eugénie de Gramont, Rome, le 7 novembre 1818.

26   Corr. SB et Eugénie de Gramont, lettre 42, 2 août 1818; lettre 54, Chambéry, 29 août 1818; lettre 55, Chambéry, 29 août 1818; lettre 65, Paris, octobre 1818. The ominous figure of Léonard made some people feel ill: *Vie de Julie Billiart, par … Françoise Blin de Bourdon ou Les Mémoires de Mère Saint-Joseph*, Manuscript published (Rome, 1978), p. 61. See also pp. 121, 159.

27   Affaires Amiens, no number, Réponses aux lettres de Mr de Sambucy. n.d. C'est au pied de la Croix que je mets le chagrin que me donnent ces malheureuses affaires et auxquelles par une trop grande crédulité et confiance, je n'ai que trop contribué. On a abusé de ma grande jeunesse, et j'ai le regret de l'avoir passée d'une manière bien peu utile à mon salut.

28   For continual references to the remorse of Eugénie de Gramont at this time see: Corr. SB et Eugénie de Gramont, lettres 41, 42, 43, 44, 45, 47, 49, 55 (July–August, 1818).

29   Corr. SB et Eugénie de Gramont, lettre 40, [Chambéry, 30 Juillet 1818] 'Qui aima plus tendrement ses amis que Jésus lorsqu'il était sur la terre?'

30   Corr. SB et Eugénie de Gramont, lettre 103, Lyon, 25 décembre 1819. Ah! Si vous saviez ce que j'ai souffert par les plaintes et les reproches que j'ai reçus à ce sujet, depuis, je suis loin de vous. Vous dire par qui et comment, je n'ai pas voulu moi-même l'approfondir, seulement j'ai senti la nécessité de prendre quelques mesures de prudence à l'extérieur et de vous conseiller de faire de même […] car il faut convenir que les femmes sont bien petites!

31   Corr. SB et Thérèse Mallucheau, lettre 42, Paris, 6 août 1817; Cahier, *Vie*, i, 264–65.

32   Cahier, *Vie*, i, 325–30.

33 ibid., pp. 330–36.
34 Corr. SB et Thérèse Maillucheau, lettre 42, Paris, 6 août 1817.
35 Corr. SB et Philippine Duchesne, lettre 31, Amiens, 12 mars 1809, p. 114.
36 Corr. MSB et Philippine Duchesne, 1804–15, lettre 9, Amiens, 3 février 1806; lettre 31, Amiens, 12 mars 1809; Natalie Zemon Davies, *Women on the Margins, New Worlds: Marie de l'Incarnation* (Harvard, 1995), pp. 63-179.
37 For a detailed account of Philippine Duchesne's inner journey and desire for the missions, see Jeanne de Charry, (ed.), *Correspondance Sainte Madeleine Sophie Barat et Sainte Philippine Duchesne, second partie, Période de l'Amérique, i, 1818–1821* (Rome, 1989), lettre 83, [Paris, janvier/février, 1818], pp. 11–24. Philippine Duchesne wrote this letter before leaving Paris and asked the abbé Perreau to give it to Sophie when she had left for Bordeaux, to sail for America.
38 Corr. SB et Thérèse Maillucheau, lettre 20, Paris 21 octobre 1816. Imaginez donc que Philippine pense toujours à sa maison d'outre-mer, que mon frère lui a presque aplani les voies et que malgré la frayeur que me cause cette entreprise nous allons peut-être la voir réussir. J'en tremble. Priez pour cela, n'en parlez pas, de peur que les têtes ne se montent, nous sommes dans un siècle où elles se déplacent pour un rien, et ce n'est une petite affaire de pouvoir contenir toutes les imaginations.
39 Elizabeth Dufourcq, *Les aventurières de Dieu. Trois siècles d'histoire missionnaire française*, 4 vols. (Paris, 1992).
40 A.M. Melville, *Louis William Dubourg: Bishop of Louisiana and the Floridas, bishop of Montauban and the archbishop of Besançon*, 1766–1833, 2 vols. (Chicago, 1986); Roger Baudier, *The Catholic Church in Louisiana* (New Orleans, 1972); Glenn R. Conrad (ed.) *Cross, Crozier and Crucible: A volume celebrating the bicentennial of a Catholic diocese in Louisiana* (New Orleans, 1993); James Hennessy, *American Catholics. A history of the Roman Catholic Community in the United States* (Oxford, 1981), pp. 31–35; William E. Foley, *The Genesis of Missouri. From wilderness outpost to Statehood* (University of Missouri Press, 1989), pp. 275–77; Edwin Scott Gaustad, *A Religious History of America* (Harper Collins, new rev. edn 1990), pp. 151–56.
41 Corr. MSB et Philippine Duchesne, 1818–21, lettre 82, Paris, 7 février 1818. Permissions pour l'Amérique, pp. 9–10. Considérant devant Notre Seigneur les distances énormes qui vont nous séparer de la communauté de St Louis, et la grande difficulté de donner les permissions nécessaires selon notre institut, je revêts Mère Duchesne, Supérieure de la maison que nous formons à la Louisiane (haute) des pouvoirs dont le détail suit.'
42 Callan, *Philippine Duchesne*, p. 193.
43 Corr. MSB et Philippine Duchesne, 1818–21, lettre 92, Cuba, 16 mais 1818 Philippine Duchesne et Sophie Barat, p. 58. Elle […] répétait souvent qu'elle avait bien dit au P. Sellier, à Madame Prevost et même à vous qu'elle ne se sentait pas le courage d'aller si loin. Je lui ai répondu que vous ne l'auriez pas choisie si elle n'eût bien voulu, et même demandé; sur cela elle s'est repliée sur ce *qu'elle avait bien demandé, la Martinique, parce qu'elle croyait que c'était près, mais toujours répugné à la Louisiane*. See lettre 94, Nouvelle-Orléans, 7 juin 1818, p. 94; lettre 98, Nouvelle-Orléans, commencée 9 juillet 1818, p. 104.
44 ibid., 1818–21, lettre 89, [Bordeaux, 28 février 1818], p. 46.
45 ibid., lettre 87, Bordeaux, 18 février 1818, pp. 39–40; lettre 88, Bordeaux, 20 février 1818; lettre 89, Bordeaux, 28 février 1818.
46 ibid., seconde partie i, 2–8; Barbara O. Korner, 'Philippine Duchesne: A model of Action', *Missouri Historical Review*, vol. lxxxvi, no. 4 (July, 1992), pp. 341–62. At this time both St Louis and St Charles were part of Missouri Territory and for some years St Charles was the state capital.
47 Corr. SB et Stanislas Dusaussoy, lettre 17, Paris, 13 février 1818; lettre 24, Paris, 2 novembre 1818; Corr. MSB et Philippine Duchesne, lettre 84, Paris, 16 février 1818, p. 31; Corr. SB et Thérèse Maillucheau, lettre 71, St Genis, 6 septembre [1818].
48 Corr. SB et Thérèse Maillucheau, lettre 83, Paris, 29 décembre 1818. Notre docteur prétend que ce sont les nerfs de l'estomac qui se retirent et que cela s'usera avec le temps; il paraît, d'après cette décision, qu'il n'y a pas de remède et qu'il faut souffrir ce mal souvent aigu aussi longtemps qu'il plaira à Notre-Seigneur. See also, lettre 92, Paris, 26 février 1819; lettre 119, Paris, 19 juillet 1819; lettre 132, Lyon, 8 décembre 1819.
49 Corr. SB et Stanislas Dusaussoy, lettre 1, Paris, 20 juillet 1816. Ils sont bien dans la peine, le mauvais temps enlève de la récolte du blé et du vin; la misère est si grande que le commerce ne va pas, et le peu qu'ils font pour vous les gène beaucoup. Corr. SB et Marie-Louise Dusaussoy, lettre 6, Amiens, 29 janvier 1814.
50 Corr. SB et Stanislas Dusaussoy, lettre 3, Paris, 14 octobre 1816. J'ai reçu ces jours derniers des nouvelles de votre famille, la misère est grande dans ce pays; le pain n'a jamais été si mauvais; point de vendanges à espérer et si le bois ne mûrit pas, encore deux années de perdues.
51 Corr. SB et Eugénie de Gramont, lettre 21, Lyon, 10 juin 1818. En passant à Joigny j'ai bien vue de la misère et dans ma propre famille; j'ai promis un peu de secours à des enfants nés pour être mieux. Sans dire qui, demandez à Père Perreau sa vielle redingote, vous l'adresserez à ma sœur qui l'enverra chercher; s'il peut ajouter culotte, etc., ce sera une bonne œuvre. Vous voyez […] que je compte bien sur votre dévouement pour tout ce qui me touche puisque je vous charge de toutes mes petites affaires […]
52 ibid., lettre 32, Grenoble, 9 juillet 1818. … Je vous remercie […] de votre attention à envoyer les habits à ma sœur, c'est pour en revêtir des parents autrefois les plus riches et tombés comme bien d'autres.

53 Corr. SB et Stanislas Dusaussoy, lettre 25, Paris, 11 juin 1820; Corr. MSB et Philippine Duchesne, 1818–21, lettre 136, Florissant, mai 1821, p. 361.

54 Corr. SB à Sophie Dusaussoy, lettre 53, Paris, 2 mars 1853.

55 Corr. SB et Stanislas Dusaussoy, lettre 2, Paris, 17 septembre 1816; lettre 3, Paris, 18 octobre 1816; lettre 7, Paris, 29 mars 1817.

56 Ibid., lettre 4, 22 novembre 1816. Quel bien promettez-vous à vos sœurs dans le monde? à quels dangers n'y seront-elles pas exposées? Sans doute, il ne faut point faire leur vocation, et en cela vous pouvez vous en rapporter à nous; mais si vous les aimez véritablement, ne devriez-vous pas les encourager dans la pratique de la vertu et dans les bons sentiments quelles expriment? Au moins elles ne suivent point votre exemple et elles profitent de la bonne éducation quelles ont reçue [...] *Mais* votre lettre [...] était encore mal écrite, sans orthographe et le style le plus plat et le plus négligé. Jamais on ne dirait que vous avez fait vos études! Hélas! quand la délicatesse des sentiments n'est pas dans une âme, sa culture est comme celle que l'on essaye sur la pierre, elle produit quelques plantes sauvages, sans racines, et qui sèchent ou s'abattent à la première tempête! [...] J'attends de vos nouvelles.

57 Ibid., lettre 5, Paris 22 décembre 1816. Vraiment [...] la description de votre courroux au sujet de ma lettre m'a amusée un moment, car j'ai pensé que cette mer en fureur était du genre de ces tempêtes dont parle le Prophète: *Iracimini et nolite peccare* [mets-toi en colère mais ne pêche pas]. Si elle avait été sérieuse, cela me prouverait que vous êtes d'un tempérament bien irascible.

58 Ibid., lettre 5 décembre 1816; lettre 7, Paris, 29 mars 1817; lettre 11, Paris 29 septembre 1817. Corr. SB et Thérèse Maillucheau, lettre 34, Paris, 20 mai 1817; lettre 45, Paris, 25 septembre 1817.

59 Corr. SB et Thérèse Maillucheau, lettres 4, 10, 16, 21, 24, 26, 38; Corr. SB et Stanislas Dusaussoy, lettres 1, 3, 4.

60 Corr. SB et Thérèse Maillucheau, lettre 29, Paris, 8 janvier 1817. Je suis si fatiguée de recommander aux novices la bonne tenue que je désespère d'y former celles qui apportent un mauvais maintien.

61 Ibid., lettre 34, Paris, 20 mai 1817; lettre 44, Beauvais, 16 septembre 1817.

62 Ibid., lettre 67, Paris, 2 avril 1818. Elle [Sophie] a moralement un besoin immense de quelques soins pour terminer son éducation qu'elle ne pourra jamais trouver à Amiens où le genre est si commun. C'est une vraie Picarde que cette petite pour le langage et les manières. La mettre à Paris, nous n'avons pas de place et d'ailleurs ce serait d'une extrémité à l'autre. Je veux éviter de la mettre avec cette noblesse presque sans mélange où elle serait ou trop élevée ou trop humiliée si elle a l'esprit de penser!

63 Corr. SB et Marie Balastron, lettre, 11; Corr. SB et Thérèse Maillucheau, lettres 44, 45, 51, 52, 54, 58, 63, 67, 75, 86, 89, 91, 98, 100, 127, 128, 129, 132 143, 160; Corr. SB et Marie Prevost, lettres 5, 9, 16, 17.

64 Corr. SB et Thérèse Maillucheau, lettre 65, Paris, 29 mars 1818. 'J'aurais moins de peine de perdre mes nièces. Hélas! J'aurais moins de peine de perdre mes nièces. Hélas! je les aurais volontiers données pour toutes celles qui nous ont été enlevées, au moins je serais tranquille sur leur sort et quel avenir se présente pour celles qui devront rester dans le monde! Julie, Thérèse and Elisa Dusaussoy entered the Society of the Sacred Heart. Dosithée died as a student in Amiens in 1823, and Zoé entered the Society for a short time and later married Pierre Cousin.

65 *Oeuvres spirituelles du Révérende Père Barat: La montagne de la Myrrhe* (Bordeaux, 1820); *Cantiques propres de la Société du Sacré-Cœur* (n.p., n.d.); *La colline de l'encens* (Bordeaux, 1819); *Cantiques propres aux Enfants de Marie* ... ([Paris], 1830). (GA, Rome, A-I., 2-c, Box 1); lettres sur la vie religieuse adressées aux dames religieuses du Sacré-Cœur par ... [Louis Barat] (GA, Rome, A-I., 2-c, Box 2). Règles et avis pour un ordre religieux de femmes. Oeuvre de P. Louis Barat (AFSJ, Vanves, Fonds Barat, Ms. 6861). [Louis Barat] Recueil de pratiques pieuses pour servir de suite au mois angélique (Bordeaux, 1818); lettres du Père Barat, Communauté de Niort (AF, Poitiers, Niort, B04/117).

66 Corr. MSB et Philippine Duchesne, 1818–21, lettres 87, 88, 89, 133, 138, 142.

67 Corr. SB et Thérèse Maillucheau, lettre 135, 9 janvier 1819; Alexandrine de Riencourt. Note sur la Maison de Paris.

Notes to Chapter 7

1 *Lettres circulaires ... Madeleine Sophie Barat, première partie, lettres adressés à toute la Société* (Roehampton, 1917), 9 juillet 1820, pp. 12–15; Corr. MSB et Philippine Duchesne, seconde partie, période de l'Amérique, i, lettre 129, Paris 10 juillet 1820; Corr. SB à Félicité de Lalanne, lettre 7, Paris 20 juillet 1820; de Charry, *Constitutions définitives*, i, 230–31.

2 *Lettres circulaires*, p. 13. La Société, par la grâce de notre Dieu, s'étant accrue de quelques nouvelles fondations, les règlements qui ont été faits dans les premiers temps ayant été augmentés ou diminués dans chaque maison, selon qu'on trouvait nécessaire pour le plus grand bien des élèves; sans s'en apercevoir, on a différé sur quelques articles; et comme un de nos soins les plus chers est de travailler à établir et à conserver l'uniformité dans nos établissements, il nous parait urgent, avant que la Société s'étende davantage, de consolider

les maisons déjà établies, en réglant tout ce qui pourra contribuer à leur bien, tant pour le spirituel que pour le temporel.

3 Corr. MSB et Philippine Duchesne, 1818–1821, lettre 129, Paris, 10 juillet 1820, p. 311.

4 *Le Faubourg Saint-Germain, La rue de Varenne, Musée Rodin* (Paris, 1981), pp. 80–2; J. Vacquier, *Monographie du Faubourg Saint-Germain, Ancien Hôtel du Maine et de Biron, en dernier lieu Etablissement des Dames du Sacré Cœur* (Paris, 1909), pp. 43–44.

5 Anne Martin-Fugier, *La vie élégante ou la formation du Tout-Paris, 1815–1848* (Paris, 1990), pp. 109–17; Philip Mansel, *The Court of France 1789–1830* (Cambridge, 1991), pp. 81–2; George K. Anderson, 'Old nobles and noblesse d'Empire, 1814–1830: In search of a conservative interest in post-Revolutionary France', *French History*, vol. 8, no. 2 (1994), 149–66.

6 Graham Robb, *Balzac* (London, 1994), pp. 168, 169, 214. Balzac was critical of the Faubourg Saint-Germain 'where thinking is kept to a minimum' and where dogs, monkeys and horses were treated better than servants. It was a miniature human comedy with a giant repertoire of unwritten rules and 'sheer undiscriminating snobbery'.

7 Archives de l'Archevêché de Paris, Procès Madame Barat, Sessio 1°, Paris, 9 mai 1873, ff. 1107–9; Cahier, *Vie*, i, 342.

8 Langlois, *Le catholicisme au féminin*; Claude Langlois, 'La vie religieuse vers 1840: un nouveau modèle', in Guy Bedouelle, *Lacordaire, son pays, ses amis et la liberté des ordres religieux en France* (Paris, 1991), pp. 39–49; Ralph Gibson, 'Le catholicisme et les femmes en France au XIXe siècle', RHEF, vol. lxxix, no. 2 (janvier–juin 1993), pp. 63–93; Marc Venard, 'Du Roi Très Chrétien à la laïcité republicaine. XVIIIe–XIXe siècle', Jacques Le Goff et René Remond (eds.), *Histoire de la France religieuse*, t. 3 (Paris, 1991); Cholvy, *Être chrétien*, pp. 40–2; Pelletier, *Catholiques en France*, pp. 28–30.

9 Cahier, *Vie*, i, 342–44; de Charry, *Constitutions définitives*, i, 236–7; Vacquier, op. cit., pp. 44–5.

10 Corr. SB et Marie Balastron, lettre 24, Paris, 28 octobre 1820. Je m'empresse […] de vous rassurer sur l'imprudente narration de notre conseil. Le plus grand accord a régné et les petites discussions nécessaires pour s'éclairer, ont été suivies des plus heureux résultats pour le bien de la Société. Dites cela a celles, qui comme vous, ont été affligées d'apprendre le contraire, car il est essentiel au bien de la Société que l'on ne prenne pas là-dessus des idées fausses.

11 AF, Poitiers, Archives de la maîtresse générale des Etudes françaises, 1820–1940, Maison d'Amiens, rue de l'Oratoire, no. 7, Programme des différents Exercices qui seront soutenus par les Elèves et suivie de la distribution solennelle des Prix, 19, 20, 21, 23 septembre 1805.

12 Françoise Mayeur, *L'éducation des filles en France au XIXe siècle* (Paris, 1979), especially pp. 34–46; Gérard Cholvy and Nadine-Josette Chaline, *L'enseignement catholique en France aux XIXe et XXe siècles* (Paris, 1995). For an in-depth study of one institution, Rebecca Rogers, *Les demoiselles de la Légion d'honneur. Les maisons d'éducation de la Légion d'honneur au XIXe siècle* (Paris, 1992).

13 GA, Rome Séries D. External History of the Society. D-1, Activities of the Institute: School Rule and Plan of Studies: Plan d'Etudes provisoire à l'usage de la maison d'Amiens. For a recent edition of the Jesuit plan of studies (1599), Adrien Demoustier et Dominique Julia, *Ratio Studiorum. Plan raisonné et institution des études dans la Compagnie de Jésus* (Paris, 1997).

14 Plan d'Etudes provisoire à l'usage de la maison d'Amiens.

15 John W. Padberg, *Colleges in Controversy. The Jesuit schools in France from revival to suppression 1815–1880* (Harvard, 1969), pp. 54–64.

16 Corr. SB et Thérèse Maillucheau, lettre 61, Paris, 17 février 1818. Nous sommes bien à court, peu de Maîtresses formées. Le pis est la difficulté de trouver un local plus vaste, nous sommes obligées de renvoyer les novices plus anciennes pour faire place aux nouvelles, et combien il s'en présente peu qui aient des moyens.

17 Corr. SB et Eugénie de Gramont, lettre 92, Grenoble, 25 novembre [1819]. Votre pensionnat va vous donner de l'ouvrage, à ce qu'il paraît. Le bon Dieu vous aidera et bientôt votre Mère [Sophie Barat]. Surtout de la modération et du courage; partout dans ce siècle les enfants donnent du travail; l'essentiel est que vous donniez du temps aux maîtresses pour vous parler et vous mettre au courant, de donner à chacune les avis nécessaires afin que la marche devienne uniforme et que l'on s'entende bien; elles ont toutes bonne volonté mais elles sont à former n'ayant encore guère d'expérience. See also lettre 97, La Ferrandière, 12 décembre 1819.

18 ibid., lettre 97, La Ferrandière, 12 décembre 1819. La Mère de Charbonnel me marque que vous avez montré une fermeté nécessaire et qui avait produit les plus heureux effets. Vous aurez besoin pour maintenir ce mieux de tenir fortement à l'ordre, de donner de l'autorité aux maîtresses et de les appuyer, de les entendre souvent afin d'agir de concert et de leur recommander sans cesse de veiller, de reprendre, mais sans heurter cette jeunesse et en leur parlant toujours le langage de la raison avec modération.

19 Corr. SB et Thérèse Maillucheau, lettre 93, Paris, 4 mars 1819.

20 Corr. SB et Marie Prevost, lettre 17, Lyon, 2 décembre 1819.

21 Corr. SB et Thérèse Maillucheau, lettre 61, Paris, 17 février 1818. 'une œuvre qui fait toujours ma desolation parce qu'elle tombe faute d'une bonne tête c'est la petite Providence de Niort, maison intéressante et qui

mériterait bien qu'on fît des sacrifices pour la soutenir … ne répondrons-nous pas devant Dieu d'avoir laissé souffrir et même périr un établissement plus utile que ceux que nous soutenons avec tant de sacrifices, car enfin nos enfants ne seraient pas sans resource, leur fortune leur donnera toujours la facilité d'avoir une bonne éducation; mais les orphelines, c'est un abandon absolu, et vraiment les pauvres ne nous touchent pas assez.'

22   Corr. SB et Eugénie de Gramont, lettre 97, La Ferrandière, 12 décembre 1819. 'il me parait bien important que vous ne permetriez pendant le cours de l'année aucune pièce de fêtes, qui les dérange, leur monte la tête et les éloigne de leurs devoirs; ces enfants qu'un rien enflamme doivent être conduites avec une grande simplicité, si elles jouent de charades, il me semble que ce ne doit être que quelques fois et sans cet attirail de costume qui met tout en l'air et qui les entretient dans le désordre le plus complet. Voilà … quelques réflexions que je vous soumets, il faut prendre tous les moyens pour essayer ce qui leur conviendra mieux; mais quelles enfants! quelles tiennent bien du siècle où nous sommes!'

23   Corr. MSB et Philippine Duchesne, lettre 91, Paris, 21 avril 1818. Rebecca Rogers, 'Boarding schools, Women teachers and Domesticity: Reforming Girl's Secondary Education in the First Half of the Nineteenth Century', *French Historical Studies*, vol. 19, no. 1 (Spring, 1995), pp. 153–81.

24   The Lancastrian method of teaching was initiated in the late eighteenth century by two Englishmen, one an Anglican, Andrew Bell, and the other a Quaker, Joseph Lancaster. According to this system, the teacher taught student monitors who in turn tutored groups of students. In this way vast numbers of pupils could be taught in small groups, rather than in huge halls. With this method one well trained teacher could effect a great change in a town. This method clashed with that of the Christian Brothers in France, who prior to the revolution had used a form of monitorial teaching which had long-proven results. However, the clash was more at the political level, as the Catholic church insisted on the right to control schools' appointments and the content of religious education. Isser Woloch, *The New Regime. Transformations of the French Civic Order, 1789–1820s* (Norton, 1995), pp. 224–29; Limouzin-Lamothe, *Monseigneur de Quelen*, i, 60–61.

25   Préfet du Département de l'Oise à Madame de Barat, supérieure des Dames de la Foi, Beauvais, 7 août 1817. Sophie Barat's reply is appended to this document. AF, Poitiers, B05/117, Beauvais. For details regarding the Catholic church's attitude to the Lancastrian method see: Archives de l'Archevêché de Paris, Papiers de Quelen, 1 D IV 7. Adrien Garnier, *Frayssinous. Son rôle dans l'Université sous la Restauration, 1822–1828* (Paris, 1925), pp. 458–9, 463.

26   Corr. SB et Thérèse Maillucheau, lettre 84, Paris, 6 janvier 1819. 'sur la nouvelle méthode dont vous m'avez parlé pour la musique, si on l'appelle à la Lancastre, malgré son avantage vous devez y renoncer, il y aurait de graves inconvénients à ce que l'on dise, comme c'est peut-être déjà arrivé, que les Dames du S.C. ont adopté ce mode d'enseignement … cette affaire tout votre attention, je l'ai refusée partout … Nous avons ici une méthode … où plusieurs apprennent à la fois. Ce n'est certainement point à l'école Lancastrienne qu'il a été puiser, et cependant elles avancent beaucoup.' See also lettre 91, Paris, 17 février 1819.

27   ibid., lettre 17, Paris, 18 septembre 1816; Corr. SB et Marie Prevost, lettre 3, Paris, 14 octobre 1817; lettre 4, Paris, 21 octobre 1817.

28   Corr. MSB et Philippine Duchesne, lettre 122, Paris, 29 février 1820, p. 295; Corr. Sophie et Eugénie Audé, lettre 4, Paris, 1 mars 1820.

29   Corr. SB et Thérèse Maillucheau, lettre 86, Paris, 13 janvier 1819. 'Nos élèves nous donnent surtout beaucoup de sollicitudes; elles sont pleines d'elles-mêmes et n'aiment que ce qui leur plaît; je les ai bien humiliées un jour, je leur dis que nous étions bien punies de n'avoir que de nobles, que dorénavant, je leur préférerais la bourgeoisie … une faisait les hauts cries à cette menace.'

30   De Charry, *Constitutions définitives*, ii, 148–50.

31   ibid., pp. 156–59.

32   Rebecca Rogers, 'Boarding schools', pp. 156–9.

33   Corr. Sophie et Eugénie Audé, lettre 5, Paris, 10 octobre 1821. 'Il faut bien que je vous dise ici en passant que vos réflexions au Père Barat, et je ne sais à qui, sur notre acquisition de l'hôtel de Biron étaient au moins déplacées; graces à Dieu nous n'y sommes pas mieux qu'ailleurs, et l'endroit des Ecuries que nous habitons, n'a rien de magnifique, j'espère que nous y pratiquerons la pauvreté et je ne crois pas qu'aucune de nous y soit plus attachée qu'à la plus pauvre maison. Il fallait se loger, impossible de trouver ailleurs. C'est cette difficulté qui a décidé le Conseil général à faire cette acquisition. Sans doute … si je pouvais choisir, je n'hésiterais pas entre votre modeste demeure et la nôtre.'

34   Corr. SB et Alida Dumazeaud, lettre 79, Paris, 29 novembre 1852. 'Hélas! nous n'effacerons peut-être jamais les funestes impressions qui se sont répandues d'un bout de la France à l'autre, et d'une partie de l'univers, de notre prétendu luxe dans le début du Pensionnat de Paris. L'hôtel doré y prêtait. Cela est vrai, quelques maîtresses n'arrêtèrent pas des dépenses inutiles aux élèves. Cette malheureuse réputation court encore le monde et nous enlève chaque année un grand nombre d'enfants dont les autres maisons d'éducation profitent … Chaque fois, donc, que ces personnes pieuses du monde nous voient, ou nous entendent attacher quelque prix aux usages du monde, à la noblesse, à la grandeur, si nos conversations ne sont pas graves, religieuses, remplies de zèle pour le salut de tous, on nous critique, on nous juge sévèrement, et souvent on cesse de nous estimer.'

35 D.G. Thompson, 'The Lavelette Affair and the Jesuit Superiors', *French History*, vol. 10, no. 1 (June, 1996), pp. 206–39; Alain Woodrow, *The Jesuits. A study of power* (London, 1995), pp. 84–5.

36 Ouverture du Conseil Général de 1820. Relations de la Mère de Gramont d'Aster, de Charry, *Constitutions définitives*, ii, 139. Also, p. 140. 'Je puis le dire ici, j'ai rencontré des personnes qui croyaient reconnaître encore dans votre Société trop d'esprit et d'habitudes du monde.
Il n'y a pas 6 semaines que l'on m'a encore dit, non pas seulement en me parlant d'une de vos maisons de province: <u>Je comptais entrer au Sacré-Cœur, mais je trouve qu'il y règne encore trop d'esprit du monde.</u> Cherchez donc ce <u>milieu</u> si difficile à trouver.'

37 GA, Rome A-II., 1-a, Box 2, Dossier 3. (pour la plupart nées dans les classes les plus élevées.

38 Cahier, *Vie*, p. 334. '... l'établissement de Mme Lalanne m'inspire quelque attrait, de préférence à d'autres fondations plus brilliants, précisément à cause de l'esprit de pauvreté, d'humilité et de simplicité qui y règne; il me semble que cette œuvre nous rapprochera davantage du Cœur de notre divin Maître, que des commencements humbles et obscurs sont plus conformes à son esprit et plus propres à attirer ses bénédictions sur notre Société. ... cette œuvre ne nous est point étrangère; il est conforme à nos Constitutions de nous livrer à l'éducation des pauvres; c'est dans cette vue que chacun de nos établissements possède une école gratuite, qu'à Grenoble et à Beauvais, nous tenons une classe de travail pour les jeunes filles pauvres à qui l'on apprend des métiers.'

39 De Coriolis, Histoire de la Société, f. 36. 'un article inséré dans une gazette d'Italie fut bientôt répété par les journaux français. On y lisait qu'une société de femmes savantes venait de s'établir, qu'animée du double esprit de St François de Salles et de Fénelon, elles se consacraient à l'éducation de la jeunesse sous le titre de Diletti di Gésu ... on parle diversement dans le monde à ce sujet: les uns en plaisantaient, surtout à cause du mot femmes savantes et de plusieurs prédictions que l'on citait, comme ayant annoncé le nouvel ordre et le bien qu'il était appelé à faire dans le monde. Les autres, mais c'était le plus petit nombre, bénissaient le Seigneur et exaltaient sa miséricorde à la vue d'un moyen qu'ils considéraient comme adapté aux besoins du siècle et destiné à préparer à la longue la régénération sociale qu'ils appelaient de tous leurs vœux.'

40 Louis Barat à Stanislas Dusaussoy [Bordeaux] Fête de l'Assomption [c. 1821] (AFSJ, Fonds Barat, lettres à divers. A son neveu, de Bordeaux). 'ce serait là pour vous la source et le canal des bénédictions qui vous donneraient la force de rester dans la fournaise de Babylone comme les trois enfants, sans brûler ... Vous aurez besoin d'une force héroïque pour vous soutenir contre les attaques de l'impiété et les amorces de la volupté; car Paris est la Babylone de l'Europe ...' See also letters of 29 April [1822]; 22 Octobre 1822; 23 Novembre 1822; 29 septembre 1826. Paul Christophe, *Grandes figures sociales du XIXe siècle* (Paris, 1995), pp. 25–34.

41 Corr. MSB et Philippine, (1818–1821), lettre 104, Saint-Charles du Missouri, 8 octobre 1818, p. 159. 'par l'influence des riches sur les pauvres'.

42 Corr. SB et Eugénie de Gramont, lettre 122, Grenoble, 28 février 1823. 'Vous savez que ces réflexions ne restent pas là, quelles sont portées à d'autres et que l'on vous juge sévèrement. Je vous le répète: gênez-vous! c'est nécessaire.' Also, lettre 123, [Grenoble, 4 mars 1823]; lettre 124, Grenoble, 5 mars 1823; lettre 126, Grenoble, 8 mars 1823.

43 *Mémoires, souvenirs et journaux de la Comtesse d'Agoult*, 2 vols. (Le Temps retrouvé, LVIII, Paris, 1990), i, 136. 'sous leur voile noir, avec leur croix d'argent sur la poitrine et leur long rosaire au côté, ne se piquent pas d'oublier leur origine. La plupart étaient d'ancienne maison, quelques-unes d'un sang illustre. Elles ne prennent leurs élèves, à des rares exceptions près, que dans les familles nobles de la cour ou de la province ... le ton général en était au plus haut point aristocratique.' For accounts of school life in two other convents in Paris during this period, Georges Sand, *Histoire de ma vie* (Paris, 1993 edn), pp. 131–239; Christiane d'Ainval, *Le couvent des Oiseaux. Ces jeunes filles de bonne famille* (Paris, 1991).

44 While families of the nobility did predominate during the time the comtesse d'Agoult was at the rue de Varenne, yet in time the ratio developed into one-third from aristocratic families and two-thirds from wealthy bourgeois families. Marie-Dominique Nobécourt, 'Un exemple de l'éducation des filles au 19e siècle par les congrégations religieuses: le Sacré-Cœur de Paris, 1816–1874' (Thèse, Ecole des Chatres, 1981), p. 372.

45 Corr. SB et Eugénie de Gramont, lettre 127, Grenoble, 14 mars 1823; lettre 139, Blaye [n.d.] mai 1825; lettre 140, Bordeaux, 31 mai [1825]; lettre 142, Bordeaux, 12 juin 1825.

46 ibid., lettre 148, Niort, 4 juillet 1825; lettre 149, Niort, 6 juillet 1825.

47 ibid., lettre 142, Bordeaux, 12 juin 1825.

48 *Mémoires de la Comtesse d'Agoult*, i, 143. 'Sa sœur Eugénie, altière dans sa petite taille bossue, avec ces yeux gris et secs, avec sa voix fêlée, ses longs doigts osseux et son dur accent de commandement.'

49 ibid., i, p. 145. 'La supérieure de la communauté, madame Barat, femme de grande autorité et qui se laissait peu voir, me fit mander auprès d'elle. Elle me donna, de sa voix sévère, de discrètes et chrétienne louanges. Elle vanta ma sagesse, ma foi sincère.'

50 ibid., i, pp. 150–51. 'Il fallut que madame Barat, la supérieure générale, dont l'autorité invisible et redoutée inspirait au pensionnat une sorte de terreur, vint elle-même à mon chevet, où depuis toute une semaine je ne trouvais plus le sommeil, et qu'elle rendît pleine justice à ma droiture. Elle me dit avec une simplicité très chrétienne que l'on s'était trompé à mon égard, que l'on m'avait fait tort, qu'on le regrettait, elle plus que

personne … Sans flatteries, sans caresses, ni promesses, par la simple vertu d'une parole vraie, madame Barat, me calma et me guérit. La main dans sa main, réconciliées, j'écoutai les réflexions qu'elle crut devoir faire, les avertissements qu'elle me donna sur les inconvénients, sur le danger des affections trop vives, sur la nécessité de modérer même les plus légitimes.'

51 Corr. SB et Eugénie de Gramont, lettre 144, Bordeaux, 18 juin 1825. 'Sur cet article important, ma chère Eugénie, vous n'êtes point sans quelque tort; il est certain que vous soignez à merveille les malades et tout le monde vous rend cette justice, ainsi qu'à Mer Recamier, mais vous secouez trop les indispositions et ne prévenez pas les maladies. Vos élèves le disent à leurs parents. Combien des ennuis et de peines j'ai à ce sujet, parce que je sais les plaintes et que vous ne les écoutez pas assez. Par exemple, j'ai été témoin de la manière dont vous avez soignez une des Moretus pour son rhumatisme au cou. Il fallait du chaud, le lit et la chambre … sans cesse vous l'envoyiez à la classe et enfin un jour la voyant plus couverte qu'à l'ordinaire, vous lui avez dit avec un ton d'ironie: bientôt vous mettrez un matelas. La petite blessée a été se dégarnir, ses compagnes ont murmuré, la jeune personne s'est plainte à une de nos Dames … de la manière dont vous la traitez … Sa mère est arrivée peu de jours après.

Je vous demande le résultat et comme tous ces traits réunis feront tort à la maison et d'ailleurs blessent la conscience puisque nous répondons de leur âme et de leur corps. Tous ces graves inconvénients disparaîtront si vous mettez de côté votre façon de voir, qui est bonne au fond … Je recommande partout que l'on excède plutôt dans le trop que dans le moins …

Pardonnez-moi ma bonne Eugénie cette ouverture de cœur. Il y a longtemps qu'elle me pèse …'

52 ibid, lettre 147, Niort, 30 juin 1825.

53 ibid, lettre 132, Metz, 3 septembre 1823. *Mémoires de la Comtesse d'Agoult*, i, 138–41.

54 Corr. SB et Eugénie de Gramont, lettre 126, Grenoble, 8 mars 1823.

55 She had her own salon in Paris, Verena von der Heyden-Rynsch, *Salons Européens. Les beaux moments d'une culture féminine disparu* (Luçon, 1993), pp. 202–6.

56 *Mémoires de la Comtesse d'Agoult*, i, 142; 146–7; 152–155.

57 A.F. Poitiers, Affaire d'Olivier, Mémoire présenté à ma Mère Barat, janvier 1823. (A.F. Poitiers, Beauvais, Affaire d'Olivier B05/117-2). Marie d'Olivier (1778–1866) entered the community at Amiens and made her first vows on 4 October 1806. After her vows she went first to Poitiers and then to Niort. In 1822 Marie d'Olivier was sent to Lyon, and there she made her final vows.

58 Mémoire présenté à ma Mère Barat, f. 17. 'le caractère du siècle est un esprit raisonner et hardi … la foi est à peu près bannie du monde. Pourront-elles conserver leur vertu, si elles n'ont des principes raisonnés et si elles n'ont pas des habitudes sérieuses, enfin si elles n'ont pas ce qui est en effet le but réel d'une sage éducation, si elles n'ont pas appris à réfléchir? Comment se défendront elles, je ne dis pas seulement des discours qu'on entend dans les assemblées du monde, mais des discours de leurs frères, de leurs maris, de leurs cousins, de leurs pères même. C'est à dire d'une société qu'elles ne peuvent ni ne doivent éviter.'

59 Marie d'Olivier, Motifs Secrets de l'ouvrage et canevas rapide soumis à ma Mère Barat. Septembre 1824 (A.F. Poitiers, Beauvais, Affaire d'Olivier B05/117-2). This document was sent to Josephine Bigeu, in view of the approbation process which she was due to represent in Rome.

60 Prospectus. Annales des dames chrétiennes ou journal d'éducation. Septembre 1824 (A.F. Poitiers, Beauvais, Affaire d'Olivier B05/117-2).

61 Corr. Sophie et Adrienne Michelle, lettre 71, Paris 9 novembre 1827. 'Je ne puis m'occuper de vos lettres de Mme d'Olivier; écrivez-lui vous même ce que vous voulez. On la corrige ici, car ces productions sont d'acier qu'il faut retirer de la terre et polir. Elle n'a point l'idée de l'extrême délicatesse de notre siècle pour les pensées, la diction, le choix des épithètes. Elle est du temps de Louis XIII. Il faut nécessairement la rajeunir; et quel heureux âge, pourquoi a-t-il passé pour nous?'

62 SB à Nicolas Loriquet, Paris, 5 juin 1828, (GA, Rome C-I., 1-F, Letters. Holographs. Carton XVII, lettres à divers ecclésiastiques (1814–1864), à des religieux et religieuses; Also, C-I., G. Box 28.B lettres aux ecclésiastiques).

63 Corr. SB et Stanislas Dusaussoy, lettres 27, 28, 29, 30 (1821); lettres 32, 33 (1822); lettre 37 (1824); lettre 51 (1829).

64 ibid., lettre 42, Paris, 9 mars 1826. 'il faudrait attendre que vous avez une place convenable, car n'ayant pas de fortune à offrir, il faut au moins présenter quelque chose qui remplace; sans cette précaution vous serrez refusé dans les familles élevées au-dessus du commun, et c'est ce qu'il faut éviter. C'est la raison qui retient mes démarches; je ne puis vous procurer aucune élève du Sacré Cœur dans votre position, aucune n'accepterait; j'ai des vues, mains je crains qu'elles ne s'effectuent jamais, nous en avons si peu à choisir parmi celles de la noblesse et en Province, pas assez de fortune ou d'autres inconvénients.' See also, lettre 48, Amiens, 23 décembre 1827. In 1819 Thérèse Maillucheau tried to persuade Sophie that Stanislas should marry her niece, Emeline. Corr. SB et Thérèse Maillucheau, lettre 132, Lyon, 8 décembre 1819.

65 Corr. SB et Stanislas Dusaussoy, lettre 39, Paris, 30 janvier 1826; lettre 41, [Paris, 2 février 1826]; lettre 47, Paris, 6 août 1827; lettre 48, Amiens, 23 décembre 1827. Corr. SB et Charles Martineau, lettre 1, Paris, 21 août 1828; lettre 2, Paris, 21 mai 1830.

66 *Mémoires de Madame la vicomtesse de Fars Fausselandry, ou souvenirs d'une octogénaire*, 3 vols. (Paris, 1830), iii, p. 83. 'il n'eût fallu que m'associer aux Dames du Sacré Cœur et j'aurais vu les grâces ministérielles pleuvoir de toute parte sur moi'.

67 Corr. Sophie et Eugénie Audé, lettre 6, Paris, 13 novembre 1821; lettre 7, Paris, 10 février 1822; Corr. MSB et Philippine Duchesne, 1818–1821, lettre 146, Paris, 23 novembre 1821, p. 409; Corr. MSB et Philippine Duchesne, 1821–1826, lettre 151, Paris, 10 février 1821, pp. 50–51; lettre 173, Paris, 30 août 1823, pp. 199–200; Corr. SB et Thérèse Maillucheau, lettre 182, Paris, 18 août 1821.

68 Corr. MSB et Philippine Duchesne, 1821–1826, lettre 146, Paris, 23 novembre 1821, pp. 408–9. 'Nous sommes si pressées d'accepter des établissements, et nous en refusons beaucoup. Cependant nous ne pouvons laisser passer toutes les occasions. Le Mans est commencé. Autun se fera dans six mois. Cette ville à moitié chemin entre Paris et Lyon, nous sera fort utile. On nous donne la maison, 600frs par an et un petit fonds pour commencer. C'est une ancienne maison de la Visitation.'

69 ibid., lettre 171, Paris, 7 août 1823, p. 192. 'Celle de Turin est commencé … ce sont le Roi et la Reine qui font les frais de cet établissement pour la jeune noblesse de leurs Etats. La Mère de Charbonnel vient de prendre, à Besançon, possession de l'ancienne maison du Gouvernement, et va aussi ouvrir le pensionnat vers novembre.'

70 Cahier, *Vie*, i, 405–8.

71 Corr. SB et Emilie Giraud, lettre 80, Paris, 8 avril 1825. 'Ma présence devient nécessaire à Bordeaux. Mmes Vincent demandent à se réunir à nous et toutes les personnes sages nous conseillent de le faire, si nos conditions sont acceptées pour mettre fin à l'espèce de scandale qui résulte de nos deux autels élevés l'un contre l'autre. J'avoue que je les aurais laissées libres sans m'en inquiéter. Dieu est le Père de toutes et je pense comme votre Mère Geoffroy, et j'aime à le voir aimé et glorifié par tous ceux qui le veulent. On croit aussi que nous devons défendre nos droits. Hélas! c'est ainsi que l'on se trompe. Que d'abus dans l'église sur ce prétexte.' For the details of Sophie Barat's conditions for integration, accepted by the Dames Vincent, see Corr. SB et Catherine de Charbonnel, lettre 4bis, Paris, 11 mai 1825; Document [lettre] 5, re Bordeaux 1825. Cahier, *Vie*, i, 408–11.

72 Corr. MSB et Philippine Duchesne, 1821–26, [Paris] 18 juin 1823. lettre 169, Marie Prevost à Philippine Duchesne, pp. 180–4. Twelve women in the community at Doorseele remained in Ghent and the congregation of the Dames de l'Instruction Chrétienne, under the leadership of Agnès Verhelle, was approved by Rome in 1827.

73 Corr. SB et Marie Prevost, lettre 26, Paris 1 août 1822. 'Je ne croyais pas être prophète; mais quand elles se séparèrent de nous avec si peu de ménagement et de délicatesse, je leur écrivis et je n'ai pas oublié ma phrase, qu'il ne fut pas en mon pouvoir de [les] retenir, [que la] branche détachée du tronc se dessécherait et périrait … Sans doute, elles pourront se relever un jour; mais vous voyez qu'il faut quelles expient. Quel exemple et que notre Société devra connaître.' Also, Corr. SB et Marie Prevost, lettre 35, Paris, 3 février 1823; lettre 36, Grenoble, 11 mars 1823.

Notes to Chapter 8

1 Corr. SB et Adelaide de Rozeville, lettre 2, Paris, 4 janvier 1824. Que d'efforts il faudra faire! que de renoncements habituels, quel support du prochain; et tout cela, sans doute, pour nous avancer dans les voies de Dieu, mais aussi pour ne point nuire à l'œuvre qui nous est confiée, et dont nous avons la responsabilité en grande partie […] sur combien de petites choses on devra passer, comme on comprend alors l'oubli de soi pour ne voir que les intérêts de Dieu […] C'est maintenant […] qu'il faut élargir notre âme, la remplir de grandes vues, ne plus nous occuper de ce moi, que pour l'immoler; vous verrez que vous perdrez peu à peu cette extrême sensibilité dont vous connaissez la source[…] . Je prie le Cœur de notre bon Maître de remplir le vôtre de sa divine charité. Devenez, à son exemple, tout à fait bonne pour toutes, les supportant, les excusant, ne vous choquant de rien qui ait rapport à vous. Voilà la vraie source de la paix et de la joie de l'esprit.

2 ibid., lettre 3, Paris, 22 février 1824. Vous savez combien je tiens à l'ordre, à la propreté et à l'économie, pour nous la pauvreté. Tenez-y sans parcimonie, que les élèves surtout ne manquent de rien. Je reviendrai souvent sur cet important article, lorsque vous serez privée de la conduite et de la présence de votre Mère [de Charbonnel]. J'ai les dettes en antipathie; heureusement vous les avez aussi; je serai secondée de votre côté!'

3 Extensive financial archives of the Society of the Sacred Heart are held in Rome and Poitiers. For a discussion of finance/religious congregations, Langlois, *Le Catholicisme au féminin*, pp. 342–95.

4 Corr. MSB et Philippine Duchesne, 1818–1821, lettre 128, Paris, 24 mai 1820, p. 309. Je viens de vous faire passer 3 000 francs; ce sont les 2 000 qui restaient de Niort; les autres sont de la Providence: 500 de Madame de Rollin, votre cousine; ne manquez pas de l'en remercier; 200 frs de Madame de la Grandville, née de Beaufort, que je recommande à vos prières. Enfin les 300 qui restent sont de la petite bourse de votre Mère [Sophie Barat], heureuse d'amasser quelques petites sommes pour vous offrir aussi son don.

5 Corr. SB et Catherine de Charbonnel, lettre 4, Paris, 11 mai 1821. Il n'y a pas à hésiter; vous devez profiter de l'occasion et acquérir cette partie qui nous touche et qui offrirait une foule inconvénients si vous devez avoir

d'autres voisins [...] Que vous seriez heureuse! si vous pouviez avoir une chapelle toute bâtie. Je crains tant maintenant ces entreprises [mais] [...] je ne regretterai pas pour vous cette nouvelle charge de 15.000 francs [...] Pour la terre, hélas! je n'ose en rien dire! il faudrait qu'une personne riche voulût aider; où trouver tant d'argent! [...] Beauvais me tourmente aussi de son côté pour acquérir la maison Pain; elle est à vendre 80 000 frs; c'est impossible, ou nous finirons par tout perdre; il faut enfin se borner! Cependant, comme je regretterais le beau champ! Prions si le bon Dieu le voulait, il est tout puissant! Sophie managed to get the price lowered, to 60,000 francs, and so bought the Maison Pain. Corr. SB et Thérèse Maillucheau, lettre 178, Paris, 31 juillet 1821.

6 Corr. MSB et Philippine Duchesne, 1818–1821, lettre 140, Paris, 4 septembre 1821, pp. 283–5; Mooney, *Philippine Duchesne*, pp. 141–2.

7 Corr. SB et Marie Prevost, lettre 28, Paris, 28 octobre 1822. On me demande de tout côté, argent, sujets, on me croit une puissance plus qu'humaine et je ne suis qu'un pauvre zéro.

8 ibid., lettre 31, Paris, 11 décembre 1822. [Joséphine] Bigeu me dit qu'elle est dans la peine pour de l'argent dont elle a besoin; que je ne viens pas à son secours, etc. hélas! je ne suis pas le bon Dieu et je ne puis pas créer [...]

9 Corr. SB à Thérèse Maillucheau, lettre 211, Paris, 15 avril 1822. Je vous écris avec peine étant très souffrante de mon rhumatisme dans les entrailles et, à peu près, dans toute la machine qu'il secoue terriblement. Je vais heureusement mieux, mais je souffre beaucoup lorsque je m'applique, mes yeux refusent leur service. See also, lettre 166, Paris, 20 [avril] 1821; lettre 193, Paris, 7 novembre 1821; lettre 194, [10 novembre 1821]; lettre 195, Paris, 16 novembre 1821; lettre 212, Paris, 20 avril 1822; Corr. SB et Marie Balastron, lettre 28, Paris, 17 avril 1821; lettre 31, Paris, 28 juin 1822; Corr. SB et Suzanne Geoffroy, lettre 6, Paris, 18 juillet 1822.

10 Cahier, *Vie*, pp. 392–3. 'Si ma tante va mieux, je pourrai aller plus mal'

11 ibid., pp. 393–4. Après quarante-cinq jours de maladie, après plusieurs crises incomplètes, Madame Barat est en convalescence[...] La maladie était une fièvre muqueuse compliquée d'un état gastrique et d'une affection de rhumatisme. Ce sera, si vous préférez une gastro-entérite, avec irritation du foie et du système musculaire, portée à un degré suffisant pour produire et entretenir la fièvre.

12 Corr. MSB et Philippine Duchesne, 1821–1826, lettre 169; 171; 179.

13 De Charry (ed.), *Varin Lettres*, lettre 97, Paris, 10 mars 1823, p. 272. 'j'ai vu par votre dernière lettre à Mde de Charbonnel que vous n'osiez même dire tout ce vous souffriez. ... peut-être concentrez-vous un peu trop vos peines dans votre cœur, c'est pour vous une vielle habitude ...'

14 Corr. SB et Thérèse Maillucheau, lettre 161, Paris 22 mars 1821. C'est le seul ami qui ait connu le fond de mon âme et vous comprenez ce qui m'en a coûté de le perdre [...] Heureusement, qu'il s'était séparé de nous avant de sa mort. Cette perte m'a été moins sensible, mais je sentirai longtemps le vide de sa direction. Dieu seul donc, il veut notre cœur et sans aucun mélange ni appui humain.

15 Corr. MSB et Philippine Duchesne, 1821–1826, lettre 159, Paris, 30 juillet, 1822, p. 87; lettre 166, [Florissant] 16 janvier 1823, p. 163. 'j'ai perdue ma veille et respectable mère'; 'Je regrette bien de n'avoir pu connaître à Joigny celle qui a donné le jour à notre si bonne mère'. Also, Corr. SB et Thérèse Maillucheau, lettre 215, Paris, 18 mai 1822; lettre 218, Paris 27 juin 1822.

16 Corr. SB et Emilie Giraud, lettre 15, Paris, 29 novembre 1809. 'Si vous savez combien elle [Madame Fouffé] a aimé votre mère [Sophie Barat]! S'en voir privée est le martyr que le Ciel lui a réservé. Priez pour elle et pour toute la famille.'

17 Corr. SB et Marie Prevost, lettre 25, Paris 7 juillet 1822. Alphonse Rodriguez (1538-1616), *Exercicio de perfección* (1609). Pratique de la Perfection Chrétienne. Zoé entered the Society and decided that religious life was not for her. Later Elisa Dusaussoy entered the Society in 1829.

18 Corr. MSB et Philippine Duchesne, 1821–26, note 1, pp. 289–90.

19 AF, Poitiers, B06, 215, I, Paris, Journal du Pensionnat, 1823–29, 1 janvier 1824; B06, 215, III, Journal de E de M [Enfants de Marie], rue de Varenne, 1820–32, f. 53.

20 Corr. MSB et Philippine Duchesne, 1821–26, lettre 210, Paris, 14 septembre 1825, p. 382.Le Père Barat, à qui vous êtes toutes si chères, a ri de l'histoire de vos enfants. Il vous cherchera encore des livres, puisqu'il ne peut vous les porter lui-même.

21 Joseph-Marie Favre was born at Samoëns in Savoy in 1791. He trained for the priesthood at the seminary in Chambéry and was ordained in 1817. He spent most of his life giving parish missions (or retreats). He advocated a less austere form of the Christian life, particularly with regard to the sacraments of penance and communion, which won him the rejection of many of the clergy. His publications include: *Considérations sur l'amour divin* (Chambéry, 1827); *Le Ciel Ouvert par la confession sincère et la communion fréquent* (Lyon, 1829); *Théorique et pratique de la communion fréquente et quotidienne à l'usage des prêtres qui exercent le saint ministère*, 2 vols. (Lyon, 1840). This work begins with a short biography of Favre by Chanoine Gondrin, 'Eloge historique de M. l'abbé Favre.' Biographies on Favre include: Abbé Pont, *Vie de l'abbé Favre, Fondateur des missions de Savoie* (Montiers, 1865); François Bouchage, *Le serviteur de Dieu, Joseph-Marie Favre, maître et modèle des ouvriers apostoliques, 1791–1838* (Paris, 1901); Cholvy, *Être chrétien*, p. 144. Also: *Dictionnaire de spiritualité*, fascicules CII-CIII (Paris, 1992), pp. 120–21.

22 Bouchage, op. cit., lettres à Madame Barat, Arith, 15 décembre 1824, pp. 513-14. No letters of Sophie Barat to Joseph-Marie Favre have survived. In his will Favre requested that his spiritual papers and letters concerning spiritual direction be destroyed at his death. Pont, op. cit., pp. 98–99. J.M. Favre's letters to Sophie Barat and Louise de Limminghe were printed in François Bouchage, *Le serviteur de Dieu, Joseph-Marie Favre, maître et modèle des ouvriers apostoliques, 1791–1838* (Paris, 1901). Despite extensive searches in Lyon, Paris, Chambéry, Toulouse and Rome, the original letters have not yet been found. Dieu vous appelle à une intime union avec lui. Il vous faut surmonter tout ce qui s'oppose à cette union. VOS RAPPORTS AVEC LES CRÉATURES ne sont pas un des moindres obstacles; rendez-les tant rares que possible, n'en ayez que par nécessité, et déchargez-vous de tout ce qui ne demande pas indispensablement votre intervention dans l'exercice de votre charge. Unie à Dieu, vous ferez plus en un quart d'heure, que dans un jour avec toute l'activité naturelle que vous pouvez mettre à contribution. L'EMPRESSEMENT n'est pas non plus le moindre des obstacles: modérez-vous et modérez-vous encore dans l'action et modérez-vous si bien que vous soyez plus attentive à Dieu qu'à ce fatras d'affaires qui, quoique nécessaires, passent après tout après votre grande affaire spirituelle; et vous vous devez à Dieu et à vous même avant de vous devoir au prochain; et vous ne pouvez donner que de votre abondance[...] . communiez aussi souvent que vous le pouvez; votre pauvre âme en a tant besoin; tous les jours sera le mieux.

23 Jean Gueber, *Le ralliement du clergé français à la morale liguorienne. L'abbé Gousset et ses précurseurs* (Rome, 1973), pp. 187–192; de Charry, *Histoire des constitutions*, i, 148.

24 Pont, op. cit., p. 190. [...] loin d'être un obstacle à la communion est une raison pour s'approcher et qui peut communier une fois l'an peut communier tous les jours [...] il faut aller à lui [Christ] avec confiance, comme l'unique soutien de notre faiblesse, chercher la force nécessaire pour persévérer [...] Le jansénisme [...] changeait l'ancien usage de la communion fréquente.

25 *Dictionnaire de spiritualité* (Paris, 1992), fasc. CII-CIII, pp. 238–42.

26 Gérard Cholvy and Yves-Marie Hilaire, *Histoire religieuse de la France contemporaine, 1800–1880* (Privat, 1990), p. 156; Jacques-Olivier Boudon, *L'épiscopat français à l'époque concordaire, 1802–1905* (Cerf, 1996), p. 270. For a similar development in Besançon, also inspired by a former Jesuit, see Daniel Moulinet, *Les classiques païens dans les collèges catholiques? Le combat de Mgr Gaume* (Cerf, 1995), pp. 31–33.

27 Chanoine Gondran, 'Eloge historique de M. l'abbé Favre' in Joseph-Marie Favre, *Théorie et pratique de la communion fréquente et quotidienne à l'usage des prêtres qui exercent le saint ministère*, 2 vols. (Lyon, 1840), i, L. Also, xviii. 'inquiétudes qui avaient leur source dans la rigidité de certain principes ... de quelque théologiens français.'

28 Bouchage, *Le serviteur de Dieu*, p. 234. 'Je ne suis ni hérétique ni protestant, ni janséniste, ni même gallicane. Je suis ultramontain de toute mon âme.'

29 Jacques-Olivier Bourdon, *L'épiscopat français à l'époque concordaire, 1802–1905* (Cerf, 1996), pp. 240–44; M.P. Dougherty, 'L'Ami de la Religion et les évêques français sous le Concordat, 1815-1850', *Revue d'Histoire Ecclésiastique*, lxxxix, nos. 3–4 (Louvain, 1994), p. 592.

30 Moulinet, op. cit., p. 35.

31 Archives de l'archevêché de Paris, Papiers de Quelen, ID IV 12, Retraites Pastorales, 1822-39, no. 9, 20 juin 1829.

32 Bouchage, *Le serviteur de Dieu*, pp. 452–3.

33 Corr. MSB et Philippine Duchesne, seconde partie, période de l'Amérique, 2 (1821-1826), lettre 172, M.S. Barat à Ph. Duchesne, Paris, 25 août 1823, pp. 197-8.

34 Corr. SB à Thérèse Maillucheau, lettre 218, Paris 27 juin 1822. 'faite lui froide mine'.

35 GA, Rome, H-I, 3, Corr. Jean-Louis Rozaven et Léopoldine Naudet, Rome. N.d. [janvier 1824]. 'Jusqu'à présent M.de S. n'en sait rien; il l'apprendra sans doute mais trop tard pour l'empêcher.' De Charry, *Constitutions définitives*, i, 304–5, 393–4.

36 Jean Louis Rozaven à SB, Rome, 19 août 1824 (GA, Rome, C-I., A, I-F, Box R.). Nos pères doivent certainement être disposés à vous rendre tous les services qui s'accordent avec nos constitutions, mais vous savez bien que vous êtes particulièrement en vue et nous aussi. Dans quelques endroits c'était l'opinion commune que votre ordre avait avec le nôtre des relations particulières. A Chambéry par exemple ne vous appelait-on des J[ésuites] [...] c'était pour nous un devoir de faire tomber ces bruits et nos pères ont du s'éloigner entièrement. La même chose peut avoir eu lieu en quelques autres endroits encore [...] A Amiens [...] il y avait des rapports beaucoup trop fréquents, des visites, des déjeuners, des dîners; n'était-il pas même arrivé que quelqu'une de vos religieuses a pris des leçons d'arithmétique ou d'histoire, je ne sais lequel, de quelqu'un qui ne devait ni ne pouvait se charger de cela [...]

37 Jeanne de Charry is the author of a major study of the constitutions of the Society of the Sacred Heart: *Histoire des Constitutions de la Société du Sacré Coeur, 1ère partie: La formation de l'Institut*, 2 vols. (Rome, 1975; 2de éd 1981; 2de partie: *Les Constitutions définitives et leur approbation par le Saint-Siège*, 3 vols. (Rome 1979). These have been translated into English as *History of the Constitutions of the Society of the Sacred Heart. Part 1: The Formation of the Institute*, 2 vols. (Rome, 1st edn 1975; 2nd edn 1981); *Part 2: The definitive Constitutions and their approbation by the Holy See*, 3 vols. (Rome 1979).

38 De Charry, *Constitutions définitives*, i, 240. Puisque vous voulez être de vraies religieuses en conservant autant de rapports avec le monde, je puis donc dire que vous avez fait une entreprise hardie et même audacieuse. Et il nous a fait sentir combien nous devons être en garde contre cette influence presque insensible que le monde exerce sur les âmes les plus pieuses. Frayissinous was vicar general of Cardinal de Périgord and later became bishop of Hermopolis and Ministère de l'Instruction Publique et des Cultes. ...'

39 ibid., p. 241, n. 179; Patricia Byrne, 'French roots of a women's movement: The Sisters of St Joseph, 1650-1836' (PhD Thesis, Boston College, 1985); Patricia Byrne, 'Sisters of St Joseph: The Americanisation of a French Tradition,' *US Catholic Historian*, no. 5 (1986), pp. 241-48; J. Michael Hayden, 'States, estates and orders: The qualité of female clergy in early modern France', *French History*, vol. 8, no.1 (1994), pp. 51, 76.

40 Jeanne de Charry, Documents et correspondances, no. 97, Réponses de l'abbé Perreau et de la Mère Barat aux Animadversiones de la S.Congrégation, octobre et décembre, 1824, p. 176. Tous ces graves inconvénients mûrement examinés inspirèrent à quelques personnes pleines de foi et de zèle pour la plus grande gloire de Dieu, le dessein de former à l'honneur du Sacré-Cœur de Jésus un Institut religieux plus adapté que les Ordres anciens aux mœurs, aux usages et aux besoins du siècle. On s'est proposé d'y maintenir la ferveur et la régularité par tous les moyens que la foi prescrit, tels que l'obligation de faire deux fois l'oraison par jour, de faire l'examen particulier, de garder une grande modestie extérieure, et de pratiquer une obéissance parfaite. Dieu a béni les vues des fondateurs. Depuis près de 24 ans que cet Institut existe, il s'est soutenu dans la fidélité à ses Règles, il est cité en France parmi les autres Ordres religieux pour sa ferveur, on n'y a vu ni relâchement, ni aucun des abus qu'entraîne ordinairement le défaut de clôture rigoureuse. Au reste les précautions prises par différents articles de la Règle, que je mets réunis sous les yeux de V.S. paraissent y avoir obvié. Les pensionnats des maisons de la Société sont devenus très nombreux, beaucoup de novices et de professes appartiennent, comme les enfants, aux familles les plus distinguées du siècle, tout semble concourir à la prospérité de ce nouvel Institut.

41 Rebecca Rogers, 'Boarding schools', pp. 153–181; Rebecca Rogers, 'Competing visions of Female Education in Post-Revolutionary France', *History of Education Quarterly* (summer 1994), pp. 147–70.

42 De Charry, *Les Constitutions définitives*, iii, *Constitutions, sommaire, cérémonial. Manuscrit de 1823* (Rome, 1979), pp. 90–91. This text has the modifications made to the manuscript by the authorities in Rome, which were accepted by the Society in 1827 and printed in 1828. See also *Constitutions et Règles de la Société du Sacré Cœur* (Lyon, 1852), pp. 113–14. Les Dames de la Société pour glorifier le Sacré-Cœur de Jésus ne se bornent pas à travailler à leur propre perfection, elles se sont consacrées à travailler, autant qu'il en est elle, au salut et à la perfection du prochain, c'est pour cela qu'elles ont embrassé un genre de vie ordinaire, simple et commun en apparence, de manière à ne rien présenter à l'extérieur qui puisse offusquer les yeux, effrayer l'imagination, et éloigner les âmes qu'elles désirent si ardemment gagner à Dieu.
[...] si elles gardent la clôture dont les avantages sont si précieux, cette clôture néanmoins ne peut être la même que dans les ordres où l'on est comme exclusivement attaché au soin de sa propre perfection; mais elle doit être tempérée, modifiée et adaptée à l'esprit et au but de leur institut qui se propose, d'une manière spéciale, l'utilité, et le service du prochain.

43 De Charry, *Constitutions définitives*, iii, 91, n.. 100. elles gardent la clôture, dont les avantages sont si précieux pour conserver l'intégrité de leurs vœux, clôture cependant qui doit être tempérée et modifiée selon l'esprit et la fin de leur Institut; les dispenses qui pourraient être nécessaires seront réglées par l'Ordinaire.

44 Decretum Laudis, 2 septembre 1825. Jeanne de Charry, Exposé historique, pp. 376–85.

45 Jeanne de Charry, Exposé historique, p. 299; *Dictionnaire de Spiritualité*, Fascicules CII-CIII, p. 240; Cahier, *Vie*, i, 404–5.

46 Jean-Louis Rozaven à SB, Rome, 23 janvier 1825 (GA, Rome, C-I., A, I-F, Box R). si vous vous obstinez sur ce point je crois pouvoir vous dire que vous n'obtiendrez jamais une approbation telle que vous la désirez et que vous ne vous établirez pas en Italie; vous y éprouverez partout autant et plus de difficultés que vous n'en avez à Turin. Le principe qu'il faut donner quelque chose aux idées du siècle est vrai; mais le principe qu'il faut résister en bien des choses aux idées du siècle n'est pas moins incontestable et la sagesse consiste à marcher entre les deux extrêmes, à n'avoir ni trop de raideur ni trop de condescendance. Les lois du concile de Trente sur la clôture me paraissent bien sages, bien importantes et je ne les crois pas moins nécessaires dans le temps où nous vivons que dans les siècles passés [...] les instituteurs d'ordres ou de congrégations religieuses qui ont compté sur la ferveur des premiers commencements sans porter leur vue plus loin, n'ont jamais travaillé solidement.49 - Voici où en est l'affaire des Dames du Sacré-Cœur: le Saint Père a accueilli leur supplique avec beaucoup de bonté et d'intérêt et a nommé une congrégation de trois Cardinaux pour l'examiner. Tout concourt à faire espérer une issue favorable, dans quelques semaines. Elles n'auront pas les vœux solennels, parce que les circonstances actuelles de la France ne permettent pas la clôture telle qu'elle est nécessaire, mais leurs vœux et leurs constitutions seront approuvés par un Bref et aux trois vœux ordinaires de religion, elles joindront un vœu de stabilité dont elles ne pourront être dispensées que par le Pape. Cette approbation leur sera très suffisante pour le moment et elles se réserveront la liberté de solliciter par la suite la permission d'émettre des vœux solennels si des circonstances plus heureuses leur permettent une clôture plus exacte.

47 Jeanne de Charry, Exposé historique, pp. 388–9.

48 Cahier, *Vie*, i, 419-29

49 Corr. Jean-Louis Rozaven et Léopoldine Naudet, Rome, 17 juin 1826 (GA, Rome, H-I, 3). 'Voici où on est l'affaire des Dames du Sacré Cœur: le Saint Père a accueilli leur supplique avec beaucoup de bonté et d'intérêt et a nommé une congrégation de trois Cardinaux pour l'examiner. Tout concourt à faire espérer une issue favorable, dans quelques semaines. Elle n'auront pas les voeux solennels, parce que les circonstances actuelles de la France ne permettent pas la clôture telle qu'elle nécessaire, mais leurs voeux et leurs constitutions seront approuvés par un Bref et aux trois voeux ordinaires de religion, elles joindront un voeux de stabilité dont elles ne pourront être dispensées que par le Pape. Cette approbation leur sera très suffisante pour le moment et elles se réserveront la liberté de solliciter par la suite la permission d'émettre des voeux solennels si des circonstances plus heureuses leur permettent une clôture plus exacte.'

50 Boudon, op. cit., p. 316.

51 *Lettres circulaires* … Madeleine Sophie Barat, Paris, 11 août 1826, pp. 15–20.

52 Abbé de la Mennais, *Du projet de loi sur les congrégations religieuses des femmes* (Paris, 1825).

53 Langlois, *Le catholicisme au féminin*, pp. 628–9, 644–5.

54 Corr. SB et Josephine Bigeu, lettre 31, Paris, 2 juillet 1826; lettre 34, Paris, 16 août 1826.

55 Jean-Louis Rozaven à SB, Rome, 1826. Réponse du Père Rozaven aux répugnances de la Société à demande l'approbation légale en France 1826. See also Rome, 18 juillet 1826; 12 août 1826. Guidée, *Joseph Varin*, Notice sur le Père Jean de Rozaven, p. 228.

56 Statutes de la Congrégation des Dames Religieuses du Sacré Cœur de Jésus (GA, Rome, Civil approbations, A-IV., I, Box 1). Jeanne de Charry, *The Canonical and Legal Evolution of the Society of the Sacred Heart of Jesus from 1827–1853* (Rome, 1991), pp. 2–3.

57 16ème séance, mardi 10 octobre [1826] (GA, Rome, C-I., c-3, Box 1. 1815; 1820; 1826; 1833). Peut-on embrasser l'œuvre de la classe moyenne? Le conseil n'a point rejeté ce projet, mais il décide que, pour le moment, cette entreprise nous est impossible.

58 Corr. SB et Philippine Duchesne, Philippine Duchesne à SB, [Florissant] 1 décembre 1822; Marie Prevost à Philippine Duchesne, [Paris] 18 juin 1823. Corr. SB et Philippine Duchesne, lettre 231, Paris, 29 novembre 1827.

59 Corr. SB et Madeleine du Chasteigner, lettre 25, Paris 16 août 1829.

60 This office was one of personal adviser to Sophie Barat on matters concerning her government of the Society. The election to offices in 1827 took place towards the end of the council and reflected the expansion. Catherine de Charbonnel was re-elected first assistant general and bursar general; Félicité Desmarquest, mistress of novices, was elected second assistant general and admonatrix to Sophie Barat; Josephine Bigeu was named third assistant general, though clearly quite ill. Except for Lydie Chobelet, the former general councillors were re-elected: Geneviève Deshayes, Eugénie de Gramont, Marie Prevost and Susanne Geoffroy. Henriette Grosier, former assistant general was elected councillor general, and four new members were elected for the first time: Marie-Antoinette de Peñaranda (1775–1830), who had returned to the Society in 1823 and was about to take responsibility for a foundation in Lille; Victoire Paranque (1782–1838), who had returned from Ghent in 1814 and was assistant to the superior in Grenoble and in charge of the school there; Aglae Fontaine (1791–1854), a founder member of the noviciate in Paris in 1816 and superior of Autun; and Armande de Causans (1785–1866), newly named superior at Turin. Henriette Ducis was re-elected secretary general.

61 GA, Rome, H-I., 3, Corr. Jean-Louis Rozaven et Léopoldine Naudet, Rome, 9 mai 1821. Ma façon de penser sur Madame Barat et sa Société est assez conforme à la vôtre, comme vous en pouvez juger par ce que j'ai dit à votre sœur. Il me paraît que dans cette œuvre il y a un peu trop d'éclat, et que si humilité ne manque pas aux personnes qui l'ont entreprise, elle semble n'avoir pas un fondement assez solide, car il est assez difficile que cette belle vertu puisse subsister longtemps au milieu d'un certain éclat extérieur et des honneurs qui sans doute ne sont pas recherchés mais sont toujours dangereux. Ce qui me déplaît surtout ce sont les exercices publics qui ont lieu dans leurs pensionnats. Je trouve cela tout à fait déplacé et je ne crois pas sans inconvénient, ni pour les élèves ni pour les maîtresses.

62 De Charry (ed.), *Varin Lettres*, lettre 74, Belly, 22 septembre [1805], 184, 186 n. 6.

63 Rozaven to Naudet, 9 mai 1821. Je ne vois aucune nécessité, aucune utilité à ce qu'une jeune fille dont la timidité et la retenue doivent faire l'ornement de la paroisse et parle avec assurance devant une assemblée de cent personnes et plus dont une seule est sa mère; tout ce qu'elle peut y gagner ce sont de vains applaudissements qu'elle payera trop cher, si sa modestie en souffre et qu'elle donne accès dans son cœur à la vanité. Je n'aime pas qu'une fille fasse parler d'elle, je veux que son mérite même soit ignoré ou ne soit connu que des personnes dont elle doit dépendre pour son propre bonheur […] Quoi qu'il en soit, on m'assure que les établissements de Madame Barat font beaucoup de bien en France et je le crois; mais je doute que ce bien soit durable […] je ne puis donc vous blâmer de suivre une autre voie; au contraire je vous y exhorte de tout mon cœur […].

64 Corr. SB et Philippine Duchesne, lettre 137, Paris, 14 juin 1821, 363; also, p. 365, n.3; Corr. SB à Thérèse Maillucheau, lettre 168, Paris, 13 mai 1821; Corr. SB et Catherine de Charbonnel, lettre 4, [Paris] 11 mai 1821. Natalie Rostopchine did not stay in the Society of the Sacred Heart then, but many years later, in 1858, she asked Sophie if she could enter again, at the age of seventy-one. She was professed in 1861 and died at the Trinité des Monts in Rome.

65 Notes sur la vie de Me. Elizabeth Galitzine (GA, Rome, C-VII., 2, Galitzine, Box 3). La douleur de sa mère fut si vive qu'elle faillit, dit-on, en perdre la raison et Mademoiselle Élizabeth attribuait à l'effet que cette perte produit sur le moral de la princesse, l'excessive sévérité dont elle usa dans l'éducation de sa fille. Punie pour les plus légers manquements avec une extrême rigueur, elle ne pouvait voir sa mère qu'en tremblant, et la sorte de stupeur que produisait cette crainte, étant prise pour entêtement, lui attirait sans cesse des nouveaux châtiments. Elle avouait elle-même plus tard que cette vie lui était insupportable, mais que se croyant sincèrement une créature exécrable, ainsi qu'on le lui disait, elle ne plaignait jamais et ne jugeait pas les personnes qui la faisaient souffrir, mais se voyant méprisée et détestée de tous, jusqu'aux domestiques, elle n'en était que plus sensible à la moindre marque d'intérêt de quelque part qu'elle lui vint. This is the only account of Elizabeth Galitzine's life which contains the details of her childhood. *Notice sur Madame Elizabeth Galitzin, Religieuse du Sacré Cœur, 1795-1843* (Tours, 1858); Prince Augustin Galitzin, 'Mélanges. Une religieuse Russe', *Le Correspondent*, août 1862 (GA, Rome,, C-VII, 2, Galitzine, Box 3).

66 Jean-Louis Rozaven à SB, Rome, 19 août 1824; also Rome, 7 octobre 1824.

67 Jean-Louis Rozaven à SB, Rome, 23 janvier 1825; 27 novembre 1825; 13 avril 1826; 21 juin 1826; 23 janvier 1827. Corr. SB et Elizabeth Galitzine, lettre 5, Paris, novembre 1825; lettre 6, Paris, 4 janvier 1826; lettre 13, Paris, 6 juillet 1826; lettre 14, 21 juillet 1826. The correspondence exchanged between Sophie Barat and Elizabeth Galitzine at this period is detailed and long. For Elizabeth Galitzine's letters to Sophie Barat, 1825-26, see GA, Rome, C-I., A, I-F, Box R.

68 Corr. SB et Elizabeth Galitzine, lettre 2, Paris 6 mai 1825; lettre 3, Paris, 26 août 1825; lettre 4, Paris, 2 octobre 1825.

69 Jean-Louis Rozaven à SB, 20 février 1827; Jean-Louis Rozaven à Josephine Bigeu, Rome, 13 mars 1827; 24 mars 1827; 7 mai 1827.

70 Jean-Louis Rozaven à Joseph Varin, Rome, 5 mars 1823 (GA, Rome, C-I., A, I-F, Box R). 'sec et froid … et plus propre à faire peur qu'a inspirer quelque confiance.'

Notes to Chapter 9

1 Corr. MSB et Philippine Duchesne, 1821-1826, lettre 212, pp. 426–7. See note 3 where Jeanne de Charry shows that this form of approval was not new in the church. J'ai à vous confier l'heureuse nouvelle de notre approbation à Rome. Le Saint Pontife a fait quelques changements dans nos Constitutions, que j'ignore encore […] on a supprimé le supérieur général. Nous avons un Cardinal protecteur à Rome, ce qui nous rapproche du Père Commun des fidèles. Notre approbation est dans le genre de celle des jésuites; elle est unique pour un ordre de femmes non cloîtrées.

2 ibid., lettre 215, Philippine Duchesne to SB, 25 novembre 1826, pp. 441–2.

3 Marie Louise Martinez, RSCJ missionaries sent to America during the lifetime of Sophie Barat (Society of the Sacred Heart National Archives, U.S.A. Series III, Special Collections. Marie Louise Martinez Collection). Society in Louisiana consisted of several, disparate ethnic groups: Creoles (those born in America, though originally of French or Spanish origin, or sometimes of both); mixed blood Creoles (who were either slaves or free persons of colour); Acadians or Cajuns (a large, French speaking group in Louisiana who originated in Nova Scotia and were expelled from there in 1765); Negroes (black people brought from Africa as slaves); Mulattos (of mixed bloods, of black and white ancestry); Native Americans (the Indian people of North America, called 'sauvages' then); Mestizos (of mixed bloods, of Indian and European peoples).

4 Jeanne de Charry, *Histoire des constitutions, Exposée historique*, p. 500.

5 Corr. SB et Philippine Duchesne, 1821–26, lettre 211, Paris, 6 août 1826, p. 422.

6 Corr. SB et Marie Prevost, lettre 46, Paris, 24 décembre 1823; Corr. SB et Philippine Duchesne, 1821–26, lettre 180, Paris, 27 décembre 1823, p. 228; Corr. Sophie et Eugénie Audé, lettre 15, Paris, 8 avril 1824; Corr. SB et Suzanne Geoffroy, lettre 12, Paris, 17 juin 1824; lettre 15, Paris 12 février 1825; Corr. SB et Stanislas Dusaussoy, lettre 38, Poitiers, 19 juillet 1825; Corr. SB et Adelaide de Rozeville, lettre 7, Paris 9 août 1824; lettre 30, Paris, 21 mai 1826.

7 Corr. Sophie et Eugénie Audé, lettre 41, Paris, 15 avril 1828; Corr. SB et Adelaide de Rozeville, lettre 57, Paris 31 mars 1828; lettre 59, Paris, 11 avril 1828; Corr. SB et Philippine Duchesne, 1821–26, lettre 235, Paris, Paris, 13 avril 1828.

8 Corr. SB et Henriette Grosier, lettre 8, Paris, [n.d.] novembre 1827.

9 Cahier, *Vie*, i, 436–43.

10 Corr. SB et Philippine Duchesne, 1821–26, lettre 190, Paris, 28 octobre 1824, p. 287; Corr. SB et Marie de la Croix, lettre 5, Paris, 6 décembre 1826.

11 Trinité des Monts, Rome, Histoire de la fondation de Rome en 1828, ff. 1-2; Mgr Fourier Bonnard, *Histoire du Covent Royale de la Trinité du Mont Pincio à Rome* (Rome/Paris, 1933), pp. 279–307.

12 The Society of the Sacred Heart was closely monitored by the French Embassy in Rome. Lists of the members of the community were submitted annually, as well as any planned changes in personnel. The presence of any non-French members in the community was viewed with suspicion and presumed to be transitory. Archives de l'Ambassade de France près le Saint-Siège. Dossier: Religieuses du Sacré-Cœur (1838-1904).

13 Archives de la Trinité des Monts, Rome, Histoire de la fondation de Rome en 1828, ff. 2-9. Cahier, *Vie*, i, 468–74; Luigi M. Manzini, *Il Cardinale Luigi Lambruschini* (Vatican, 1960), pp. 126–31; 438–42.

14 Corr. SB et Josephine Bigeu, lettre 27, Paris, 31 mai 1826; lettre 30, Paris, 28 juin 1826. Armande a le bon ton, le sentiment des convenances, une correspondance plein d'agrément pour traiter avec les grands; sous ce rapport elle pourrait convenir plus à Turin, elle offrira seulement moins de ressources pour l'intérieur que l'autre [Marie Prevost] [...] Madame de Causans n'est pas expéditive pour le travail; elle fait très bien ce dont elle est chargée, mais elle ne pourrait pourvoir à beaucoup de choses en même temps.

15 Cahier, *Vie*, i, 468–9

16 Corr. SB et Armande de Causans, lettre 1, Paris, 19 janvier 1828. J'en suis si remplie de confusion que si je n'étais tenue par la prudence, je le dirais à tout l'univers [...] L'histoire de cette fondation est admirable, je vous en réserve les détails quand je serai moins faible; j'abrège. Il existe à Rome une superbe maison, avec des jardins magnifiques, sur une montagne, elle appartient à la France. Le Souverain Pontife l'a demandée au Roi pour les Dames du Sacré-Cœur, avec une partie des revenus [...]

17 Euphrosine Faux. Lettres Annuelles, 1878–79, 2 partie, pp. 35-38; Adèle Cahier, *Notice de la ... Mère.*

18 Archives de la Trinité des Monts, Rome, Histoire de la fondation de Rome en 1828, f. 12. sans pouvoir ni les aliéner, ni les changer, ni les faire passer en d'autres mains sous quelque prétexte que ce fût; que cet établissement ne pourrait être occupé que par des françaises [...]

19 ibid., f. 44; Journal de la maison de Rome, 1828–45, ff. 13-14.

20 Corr. SB et Armande de Causans, Rome, 10 décembre 1829 (GA, Rome, C-IV, 4, Rome, Box 1). Quelles histoires ils ont faites à Turin pour la clôture! j'ai été heureuse de voir que mon opinion là-dessus était d'accord avec la vôtre [...] et que votre pensée soit de céder seulement aux circonstances actuelles. Autrement quelles conséquences! Nous mettre dans le cas d'encourir ou de faire encourir des excommunications [...] ces terribles lois ne regardent que les ordres qui ont véritablement la clôture.

21 Archives de la Trinité des Monts, Rome, Histoire de la fondation de Rome en 1828, f. 46. 'son enthousiasme pour l'Institut du Sacré Cœur, tout à fait modelé ... sur celui des jésuites.'

22 Corr. SB et Philippine Duchesne, lettre 236, Paris. 9 mai 1828. 'On veut nous mettre sur le même mode que la Société de Jésus. Est-il possible avec des femmes? La suite nous éclairera.'

23 Corr. SB et Armande de Causans, [Rome], 13 septembre 1828 (GA, Rome, C-IV, 4, Rome, Box 1. Le P[ère] R[ozaven] dont c'est sans doute l'ouvrage ou du moins la conquête [...] Il m'a dit que chaque maison devait en avoir une petite soigneusement cachée. La prudence étant nécessaire dans ces sortes de choses et plus que jamais dans le temps où nous sommes.

24 GA, Rome, Lettres aux religieux et religieuses: au Père Général, Compagnie de Jésus à Rome. Lettre 1, SB au Père Fortis, Paris, 15 juin 1828; lettre 2, SB et les assistantes générales au Père Fortis, Paris, 20 octobre 1828. (GA, Rome, C-I., 1-F, Letters. Holographs. Carton XVII, Lettres à divers ecclésiastiques (1814-1864), à des religieux et religieuses; Also, C-I., G. Box 28.B).

25 Corr. SB et Armande de Causans, Trinité des Monts, 11 juin 1828 (GA, Rome, C-IV, 4, Rome, Box 1). il est si sage et si plein des lumières pour nos véritables intérêts! Ah sans doute [...] je n'ai rien à craindre en l'ayant pour guide [...] le Père Rozaven a beaucoup de choses du Père Sellier. Ce sont deux cœurs qu'aucune affection tant soit peu humaine ne saurait plus aborder. Néanmoins il échappe encore de la part du dernier quelques traits vifs et pénétrants qui laissent entrevoir la bonté naturelle mêlée à une ardente charité et transformée en elle; mais chez le Père Rozaven la nature ne voit jour qu'à mourir, ou de gré ou de force.

26 Corr. SB et Armande de Causans, Trinité des Monts, 11 juin 1828 (GA, Rome, C-IV, 4, Rome, Box 1). pour sa fille Élizabeth [...] je lui soupçonne un petit faible, mais il sera l'unique. Il parait qu'elle en est digne.

27 Corr. SB et Armande de Causans, Rome, 20 septembre 1828 (GA, Rome, C-IV, 4, Rome, Box 1). Le Père Rozaven m'a envoyé hier la dernière lettre de sa fille Élizabeth dont il a seulement déchiré la première page pour m'édifier et m'humilier sans doute en me faisant pénétrer dans ce bel intérieur d'une novice déjà si avancée dans la perfection.

28 Corr. SB et Armande de Causans, Rome, 18 décembre 1828; Rome, 4 juillet 1829; 4 août 1829 (GA, Rome, C-IV, 4, Rome, Box 1).

29 For details of these request see Archives de l'Ambassade de France près le Saint-Siège. Dossier: Religieuses du Sacré-Cœur (1838–1904).

30 Corr. SB et Philippine Duchesne, lettre 236, Paris, 9 mai 1828.

31 Corr. SB et Armande de Causans, Trinité des Monts, 11 juin 1828 (GA, Rome, C-IV, 4, Rome, Box 1). Cette maison du Noviciat (soit dit entre vous et moi) est d'une plus grande conséquence pour notre Société que

l'établissement de la Trinité[…] Bref c'est lui qui achèvera de nous Jésuitiser dans les opinions comme dans la réalité.

32 Archives de la Trinité des Monts, Rome, Histoire de la fondation de Rome en 1828, f. 61. See also ff. 45, 46, 52, 58-60. L'éducation de la classe la plus élevée de la société est bien une des fins de leur institut mais ce n'est pas la seule, ni celle qui leur tien le plus au cœur. La classe indigente a été trop chère au Cœur de Jésus pour qu'elle ne soit pas l'objet des préférences des servants de ce Cœur adorable. Leurs établissements leur paraissent imparfaits lorsqu'ils sont inutiles aux pauvres. Or, outre que le couvent de la Trinité des Monts n'est pas convenablement situé pour que l'on puisse y ouvrir des classes publiques, il est clair que cette bonne œuvre demande nécessairement des italiennes, et que par conséquence une maison de noviciat est indispensable pour former des sujets qui puissent fonder et perpétuer à Rome et dans l'Italie cette partie essentielle de leur institut. Rien n'empêcherait dès que le noviciat serait formé que les écoles pour les pauvres ne fussent ouvertes dans la maison même du noviciat.

33 Journal de la maison de Rome, 1828–1845, 8 juillet 1828, f. 14.

34 Archives de la Trinité des Monts, Rome, Histoire de la fondation de Rome en 1828, ff. 52-3. Madame Louise se contenta d'être aimable, parla beaucoup de la Mère Barat, à laquelle elle conserva le plus tendre et le plus respectueux souvenir.

35 Corr. SB et Armande de Causans, [Paris], 21 avril 1828.

36 ibid., Paris, 28 mai 1828. 'tous les autres sujets étant des plus minces'. See also letters of Armande de Causans 18 novembre 1828 and 15 mai 1829 (GA, Rome, C-IV, 4, Rome, Box 1).

37 Corr. SB et Armande de Causans, Trinité des Monts, 11 juin 1828. (GA, Rome, C-IV, 4, Rome, Box 1).

38 Corr. SB et Armande de Causans, Paris, 28 mai 1828.

39 Corr. SB et Philippine Duchesne, lettre 235, Paris, 13 avril 1828. Le long silence que je viens de garder avec vous […] m'a été pénible. Vous en savez la raison; j'ai été plus de trois mois malade […] Vous connaissez notre nouvelle fondation à Rome […] les marques particulières d'attachement que le saint-père nous donne […] Je suis épouvantée de la responsabilité qui pèse sur mes faibles épaules et qui augmente tous les jours avec les fondations. Il faut au moins 15 sujets pour commencer Rome […] je suis obligée de vous quitter […] ne pouvant encore supporter le travail qui me porte sur les nerfs et me donne de grandes douleurs de tête.

40 Corr. SB et Philippine Duchesne, lettre 239, Paris, 6 juillet 1828. Nous avons habité ensemble le Thabor. Que cette vision a été courte! Depuis, le Calvaire a succédé […] Croiriez-vous que mes yeux se reposent le plus souvent sur Sainte-Marie, quand nous l'habitions ensemble, et sur la Louisiane. Si j'étais obligée, plus tard, de fuir ma patrie, mon cœur volerait vers le pays que vous habitez. Si Dieu le permettait, je goûterais encore un moment de bonheur. *Fiat*. Vous me dites un mot de votre solitude. J'espère que Jésus y supplée et qu'il est votre ami le plus fidèle. Alors on la supporte, cette solitude, car, à vous dire le vrai, quand on a vécu de longues années avec les hommes, on s'y attache moins. Votre Mère, entourée de tant d'affection, vit aussi dans cette solitude. Je n'ai encore fait cet aveu qu'à *vous*. Peu d'âmes le comprendraient. C'est cependant le bien le plus précieux: *Dieu seul*.

41 Corr. Sophie et Eugénie Audé, lettre 29, Paris, 28 février 1826. Combien je suis peinée […] de ne pouvoir vous donner de suite la somme dont vous avez besoin; si vous connaissez notre gêne et mes inquiétudes continuelles sur les dettes considérables que nous avons encore […] vous seriez effrayée de ces dettes, elles sont considérables, malgré mes sollicitudes et mes recommandations continuelles […] je vous dis (à vous seule et à Mme Duchesne) que je suis décidée, si l'Assemblée qui va avoir lieu ne prend pas les mesures les plus sévères pour diminuer les dettes encore augmentées de 200.000frs l'année passée, à me démettre de ma charge; ne voulant pas voir la Société périr par défaut d'ordre et parce qu'on ne veut pas se gêner. Quelles nuits je passe! Quelles inquiétudes continuelles je porte dans mon âme! This letter upset Eugénie Audé and in her reply in September 1826 Sophie did not deny her concern but admitted she may have carried it too far and left no room for Providence. Corr. Sophie et Eugénie Audé, lettre 33, Paris, 6 septembre 1826.

42 C'est cette croix qui me fait regretter parfois le Carmel. Un Fiat remet mon âme mais c'est cruel. For a study of attitudes to death among the young in nineteenth century France, see Arnold, *Le corps et l'âme*.

43 Corr. SB et Stanislas Dusaussoy, lettre 50, Paris, 17 mars 1829; lettre 51, Paris, 11 mai [1829].

44 Corr. SB et Stanislas Dusaussoy, lettre 52, Paris, 9 juillet 1829. Mon travail et ma responsabilité augmentent; je dois tous mes moments à mon devoir; voilà sans doute ce que vous avez pris pour l'indifférence; je vous porte autant d'amitié que lorsqu'elle était peut-être plus démonstrative, et c'est surtout devant Dieu.

45 Corr. SB et Armande de Causans, Paris, 16 juin 1828.

46 Corr. Sophie et Eugénie Audé, lettre 45, Paris, 14 septembre 1828; Corr. SB et Henriette Grosier, lettre 13, Paris, 25 mars 1829; Corr. SB et Louise de Limminghe, lettre 28, Paris, 29 octobre 1828; lettre 34, Paris 17 décembre 1828; lettre 54, Paris, 31 mai 1830; lettre 58, Fribourg, 26 octobre 1830.

47 Corr. SB et Marie de la Croix, lettre 5, Paris, 6 décembre 1826. L'Italie se remue davantage, déjà nous avons refusé un établissement bien intéressant, faute de têtes; car nous avons le nombre. Il faudrait tant de qualités réunies pour commander, surtout une vertu solide, prudente, etc. et ces qualités réunies sont si rares. Priez, au moins que le Cœur de Jésus nous en donne quelques-unes.

48   Corr. SB et Philippine Duchesne, lettre 243, St Louis, 11 septembre 1828. Notre Mère commune marquait à chacune sa place avec cet art qui fait tout adoucir. Je n'ai pas ce talent.

49   Corr. SB et Adelaide de Rozeville, lettre 34, Paris, [8 juillet] 1826. Après y avoir pensé devant Dieu j'ai cru que je devais vous donner le conseil de travailler à vous décharger des détails de votre administration en cédant à quelques unes […] une portion de votre charge […] Vous savez […] que le plus parfait est celui […] où le premier qui gouverne sans se consumer dans les détails, voit de loin tous les abus, peut les rectifier plus aisément quand ce sont les sujets qui les produisent, garde son temps pour en consacrer une partie raisonnable à la prière et à diriger les âmes. Tendez à ce mode de gouvernement et vous verrez que âme et votre santé s'en trouveront mieux. See also lettre 23, Paris, 5 mars 1826.

50   ibid., lettre 49, Paris, 18 mai 1827. Probablement cette mère [Catherine de Charbonnel] vous parlera de quelques plaintes qu'ont faites les parents sur certains soins qui ont été négligés par rapport aux élèves. Faites soigner la nourriture, exiger la bonne tenue, qu'il n'y ait pas d'épargne pour les choses nécessaires et surtout point de cadeau de la part des enfants, même pour la chapelle […] L'homme est changeant, il croit toujours trouver mieux ailleurs; si donc il se formait d'autres établissements dans les environs et qu'il n'y ait quelque chose à redire sur le vôtre vous perdrez beaucoup d'élèves […]

51   ibid., lettre 49, Paris, 18 mai 1827. Remontez votre courage et comptez beaucoup sur Dieu, qui mettra son assistance lorsque la vôtre manquera, surtout si vous Lui demandez cette grâce avec foi et persévérance. L'oraison, l'union avec Lui, vous faciliteront ce divin commerce dont une supérieure ne peut se passer si elle veut s'acquitter de sa charge avec fruit. Attachez-vous aussi à la pratique journalière de la douceur et d'une patience sans bornes […] la fermeté est nécessaire, encore faut-il qu'elle soit tempérée par cette admirable vertu qui sépare la nature de la grâce sans déchirer.

52   ibid., lettre 55, Paris 12 octobre 1827. Vous êtes encore trop sensible, et peut-être susceptible; comment vous troubler une journée pour une faute involontaire? Reprochez-vous davantage […] vos impatiences quand elles paraissent ne dis point dans les paroles, mais dans l'air, la figure, etc. […] Il est essentiel pour une supérieure de garder la plus parfaite égalité et de gouverner avec douceur, comprenez que cette vertu est tout à fait compatible avec la fermeté sans laquelle une maison religieuse ne peut subsister longtemps dans la ferveur et la régularité […] C'est une main de bois de cèdre couverte de velours, on est tenu mais on n'ose s'en plaindre quand on ne sent que la douceur de la soie au toucher.

53   ibid., lettre 53, Paris, 16 août 1827. Je voudrais bien savoir ce que ces Messieurs attendaient de plus de nous, que nous fussions des savantes, des merveilles, que leurs enfants devinssent des perfections en tout genre, comme les fées les tournoient avec une baguette?
       Ces prétentions sont ridicules, il est vrai pourtant que quelques abus et négligences se sont glissés parmi les Msses [maîtresses], voyez cela de près […] attendez après les vacances, ne communiquez aucune autre pièce que le prospectus et les statuts tels qu'ils ont été approuvés par le gouvernement […] le Maire et le Préfet étant pour vous, c'est l'essentiel.

54   ibid., lettre 54, Paris, 30 août 1827. Qu'on ne puisse faire aucune plainte fondée sur le fond des études, ni sur la tenue extérieure.

55   ibid., lettre 65, Paris, 29 mai 1828. Permettez que je vous dise que j'ai remarqué dans votre style un peu d'humeur ce me semble, et peut-être de la sévérité. Le caractère de la Mère Prevost est tout à fait ce besoin de rendre heureux et de faire plaisir à tout le monde; sans doute c'est un défaut quand on le porte trop loin, et surtout pour une religieuse, mais enfin elle travaille à s'en corriger; elle y tend et les avertissements que je vais lui donner achèveront je l'espère. Je voudrais bien en même temps que vous prissiez la même résolution, non pour imiter tout à fait son genre et ses manières, puisque nous voulons les rectifier, mais je voudrais que [vous] devinssiez plus indulgente, plus bonne enfin; votre régularité est trop serrée, surtout dans les commencements, qui contrastent avec l'extrême liberté que votre devancière avait établie dans cette famille [Amiens]. Il faut tendre à cette réforme mais doucement, et surtout avec des manières douces et insinuantes; on vous reproche le contraire. Déjà à Besançon vous aviez à vous le reprocher, ce ton sec, quelquefois impatient, cette susceptibilité qui voit une intention où il n'y avait que de l'oubli et de la distraction, nuit essentiellement au bien immense que pourrait faire une supérieure réunissant la fermeté avec la bonté. Cette dernière vertu est absolument nécessaire pour la conduite de la maison qui vous est confiée, aussi je le demande souvent au Cœur de Jésus pour vous et pour toutes celles qui sont appelées à gouverner.

56   Corr. SB et Henriette Grosier, lettre 15, 30 mai 1829. 'Qu'elle ne s'y trompe pas: il faut partout de la bonté, de la douceur. La fermeté doit se sentir sans paraître; hélas, qui le comprend? […] Quelle science que celle du gouvernement; qu'elle est rare et que son ignorance ne cause de tourments!

57   Corr. SB et Adelaide de Rozeville, lettre 82, Paris, 5 septembre 1828. Les sociétés les plus stes [saintes] d'hommes, de femmes, fournissent mille misères […] hélas! souvent les crimes. Ayons patience, supportons avec calme, faisons ce que nous pouvons, prions, mettons notre confiance en Dieu et il fera son œuvre.
       Nous ne vivons pas avec les anges; il faut donc supporter l'humanité et savoir lui pardonner. Je vous l'ai dit souvent, vous la connaissez trop à fond tandis que ces sujets, à qui vous apercevez de grands et réels travers, ne sont nullement de votre avis et ils se les dissimulent. Dans ce cas et pour avoir la paix, je tâche de me met-

tre à leur niveau et de ne les juger qu'avec leurs lunettes; ma paresse s'accommode de cette vue, à quoi, au fond, me servirait une lumière plus perçante puisque je ne pourrais les convaincre: j'attends.

58 ibid., lettre 124, Paris, 8 juin 1830. Il est certain que notre Société finissait par s'abâtardir si on eût continué de recevoir avec tant de facilité et si peu de choix, une foule de personnes qu'il faut employer cependant et qui n'entendent rien à élever des enfants si difficiles dans ce siècle et qui demandent non seulement de la vertu mais de l'instruction, du tact, de bonnes manières, etc. et sous ce rapport que nous sommes pauvres!

59 De Charry (ed.), *Varin* Lettres, lettre 99, Bordeaux, 29 mai 1823, p. 286. Also p. 291 n. 12. Les novices se trouvent encore dispersées dans toutes les maisons, et elles n'y prennent point l'esprit.

60 Corr. SB et Suzanne Geoffroy, lettre 18, Paris, 7 mars 1826.

61 ibid., lettre 14, Paris, 16 août 1824; Corr. SB et Adelaide de Rozeville, lettre 36, Paris, 18 juillet 1826; lettre 42, Paris, 14 septembre 1826; lettre 49, Paris, 18 mai 1827; Corr. SB et Philippine Duchesne, lettre 212, Paris, 2 septembre 1826, p. 428; Corr. Sophie et Eugénie Audé, lettre 52, Paris, 6 avril 1829. For a discussion on the recruitment of women for congregations, Rebecca Rogers, 'Retrograde or Modern? Unveiling the Nun in Nineteenth Century France', *Social History* (GB), vol. 23, no. 2 (May, 1998), pp. 146–64; Langlois, *Le Catholicisme au féminin*, pp. 519-62.

62 Corr. SB et Philippine Duchesne, lettre 254, Paris, 26 juin 1829. Nous en avons une quantité qui deviennent nulles par défaut de talents et de vertus, chaque supérieure ayant reçu tout ce qui se présentait pendant de longues années; et en conscience nous ne pouvons vous [Philippine Duchesne] en donner. Nous avons donc un besoin réel de nouveaux sujets que nous formons et qui auront, au moins, une bonne vocation. See also Corr. SB et Adelaide de Rozeville, lettre 119, Paris, 3 mai 1830; lettre 125, Paris, 21 juin 1830.

63 Corr. SB et Philippine Duchesne, 1821–26, lettre 201, Paris, 14 septembre 1825, p. 381.Il faut dix ans pour former une religieuse de chœur, et la plupart meurent avant d'atteindre leurs derniers vœux.

64 Corr. Sophie et Eugénie Audé, lettre 16, Paris, 16 juillet 1824; lettre 18, Paris, 20 août 1824. 'les plus savantes, toutes nos Mises [maîtresses] de classe.' Arnold, *Le corps et L'âme*, pp. 247–65.

65 Corr. SB et Adelaide de Rozeville, lettre 46, Paris, 13 avril 1827; lettre 52, Paris, 31 juillet 1827.

66 ibid., lettre 116, Paris, 11 février 1830. Je n'ose me plaindre mais que de sujets qui me désolent se portent à merveille et les parfaits nous sont ôtés.

67 Corr. SB et Philippine Duchesne, lettre 248, Paris, 12 février 1829. Despite her many efforts, Sophie Barat never succeeded in changing Henriette Grosier as superior in Poitiers. This became a serious issue in 1839–40. Croyez-moi, ne faites pas les changements qui ont été médités; toutes les maisons seront mécontentes, ainsi que les sujets, et vous aurez mille déboires. J'ai fait cet essai et combien il m'en a coûté, et cependant c'était nécessaire. Vous ne pouvez vousfaire l'idée combien Amiens, Beauvais et Lyon, dont j'ai changé les supérieures, m'ont donné des soucis. Il a fallu, en même temps, déplacer plusieurs sujets, qui ne goûtaient pas les remplaçantes. Le public, accoutumé à celles qui conduisaient depuis des années, était mécontent[…] par la suite, je n'ôterai qu'une seule supérieure à la fois; car faut-il les changer quelquefois, précisément pour empêcher l'abus qui existe à [Poitiers]. Une supérieure qui crée sa maison et qui gouverne plus de trois ans devient souveraine maîtresse et perd l'intérêt général.

68 Corr. SB et Emilie Giraud, lettre 90, Paris, 3 septembre 1827. Chaque maison en a de ce genre et on ne peut les mettre tous ensemble, il faut donc que chacun garde les siens. J'ai demandé que l'on me laisse les réunir et j'en serais supérieure; vous comprenez que j'aurais assez à faire et qu'il en faudrait une autre pour le gouvernement de la Société. Nos Mères ont souri et ne m'ont point écoutée. Dans ce cas il faut partager le fardeau.

69 Corr. SB et Adelaide de Rozeville, lettre 60, Paris, 16 avril 1828. 'il faudrait un Moïse pour conduire le peuple qui nous est confié, et j'en suis éloignée!'

70 De Charry (ed.), *Varin Lettres*, lettre 99, Bordeaux, 29 mai 1823, p. 284. Comment dans cet état de faiblesse extraordinaire et éloignée de toutes vos assistantes, pourrez-vous porter le poids et de toutes les affaires courantes et de tout l'arrière? et cependant jamais vous ne dûtes mieux le sentir qu'à présent, combien il est nécessaire que vous soyez puissamment assistée, et vous reposant sur d'autres d'une multitude de détails, vous donniez tous vos soins au Gouvernement Général de votre Société; et encore ce poids seul suffirait-il pour vous accabler, si vous ne le partagez pas avec vos assistantes. Votre Société est venue à ce point où elle a besoin d'un gouvernement actif et vigilant et toujours en permanence. See also lettre 100, Bordeaux, 9 juin 1823, pp. 292–4.

71 ibid., lettre 101, Dole, 25 novembre 1823, pp. 297–8. 'Combien je désire que vous soyez secondée par vos assistantes, pour supporter un fardeau qui tous les jours devient plus pesant.

72 Corr. SB et Stanislas Dusaussoy, lettre 50, Paris, 17 mars 1829. Ne la tourmentez pas, ce serait inutile. Elle fera au moins un essai. Si vous la contrariez je l'envoie au bout de France et peut-être à Rome. C'est vous dire que son parti est pris ainsi que le mien. Votre mère plus raisonnable que vous en est bien aise. Elle connaît les amers chagrins du mariage et les dangers que courrait une jeune personne dans le monde sans fortune et plus tard sans appui […]

73 ibid., lettre 51, Paris, 11 mai [1829]; lettre 53, Paris, 27 septembre 1829.

74   Corr. SB et Emilie Giraud, lettre 98, Paris, 8 décembre 1829. Une septième chute sur la partie malade m'a
     forcée de garder encore le lit ou une corbeille, depuis plusieurs semaines. See also, Corr. SB et Adelaide de
     Rozeville, lettre 105, Paris, 22 avril 1829; lettre 108, Paris, 18 mai 1829; lettre 111, Paris, 17 juin 1829; lettre
     117, Paris, 19 mars 1830; lettre 122, Paris, 26 mai 1830; lettre 123, Paris, 7 juin 1830; lettre 124, Paris, 8 juin
     1830; Corr. SB et Henriette Grosier, lettre 14, Paris, [n.d.] mai 1829; lettre 17, Paris, [n.d.] décembre 1829;
     lettre 18, Paris, 28 décembre 1829; lettre 20, Paris, 11 février 1830; lettre 22 [Paris], 18 avril 1830; lettre 25,
     Paris, 26 juillet 1830; Corr. Sophie et Eugénie Audé, lettre 53, Paris, 12 juin 1829; Corr. SB et Louise de
     Limminghe, lettre 43, Paris, 22 juin 1829; lettre 45, Paris, 31 août 1829; lettre 48, Paris, 12 octobre 1829; let-
     tre 55, Paris, 7 juillet 1830; Corr. SB et Madeleine du Chasteigner, lettre 25, Paris, 16 août 1829.

Notes to Chapter 10

1   Corr. SB et Philippine Duchesne, lettre 218, Paris, 8 mars 1827.
2   ibid., lettre 244, Paris, 14 septembre 1828. Je rêve toujours d'aller vous voir; mais si je faisais ce long voyage,
     je ne voudrais plus revenir en France. Also lettre 247, Paris, 9 décembre 1828; lettre 237, Paris, 6 juin 1828.
     Corr. SB et Eugénie Audé, lettre 44, Paris 10 juin 1828.
3   Corr. SB et Louise de Limminghe, lettre 28, Paris, 29 octobre 1828. […] pas de doute que nous manquerions
     l'occasion la plus favorable pour établir la Société d'une manière convenable dans cette belle partie de l'Italie;
     puis, de nous faire connaître chez l'Emp[ereur] d'Autriche […] Enfin, ce serait d'autant plus convenable que,
     depuis le renvoi des jésuites, nous en portons le contrecoup et nous perdons beaucoup en France, plusieurs
     ordres religieux ayant fait des efforts incroyables pour nous imiter et même nous surpasser; ce à quoi on finit
     par réussir très aisément. Dieu le permet peut-être pour nous forcer de nous étendre hors de France où
     d'autres sociétés n'iraient pas; ces considérations me forcent pour ainsi dire à accepter Milan, si on nous l'of-
     fre; vous pouvez donc conseiller à Mme l'Ambassadrice de nous proposer […]
4   François-Dominique de Reynaud, Comte de Montlosier, *Les Jésuites, les congrégations et le parti prêtre, en 1827.*
     Mémoire à M. le Comte de Villèle (Paris, 1827); René Rémond, *L'anticléricalisme en France. De 1815 à nos jours*
     (Brussels, 1992), pp. 81–104; Padberg, *Colleges in Controversy*, pp. 2–11; Woodrow, *Jesuits*, pp. 86–88.
5   Michel Leroy, *Le mythe jésuite. De Béranger à Michelet* (Paris, 1992), pp. 192–3.
6   Jean de Nicolay, *Pauline de Nicolay, Tertiaire Franciscaine, 1811–1868* (Neuilly, 1991), pp. 5–7, 11, 15–16. Journal
     de Genève, 17 juin 1871. Union du 23 juin 1871.
7   Padberg, *Colleges in controversy*, pp. 11–13.
8   Cahier, *Vie*, i, 518–20.
9   Marie Patte was Sophie's travelling companion at this period. GA, Rome, C–VII, 2–P.
10   Cahier, *Vie*, 328, 518.
11   ibid., i, 520–22.
12   Chambéry, Journal de la maison, 1818 jusqu'à 1836 (copie), ff. 112–3 (AF, Poitiers, Chambéry, B08, 114/115).
     On the 8 September Sophie went on a pilgrimage with Eugénie de Gramont and Hypolite Lavauden to the
     shrine St Pierre d'Albigny to pray for a cure for her foot. Chambéry, Journal de la maison, f. 112.
13   Chambéry, Journal de la maison, ff. 114–5. (AF, Poitiers, Chambéry, B08, 114/115).
14   Cahier, *Vie*, i, 527–31. Sainte Sophie Barat et le diocèse de Lausanne, Genève et Fribourg in La semaine
     catholique de la Suisse Romande, nos. 20, 21, 22 (1952), pp. 306–8; 323–5, 338–9. *Dictionnaire historique et sta-
     tistique des paroisses catholiques du Canton de Fribourg*, vol. 7, (Fribourg, 1891), pp. 498–500. Chambéry, Journal
     de la maison, f. 111.
15   A.F. Poitiers, B 90 /111,114,117 Montet; Archives de l'État, Fribourg. Dames du Sacré Cœur, [Middes,
     juin–septembre 1831]. Les dames du Sacré-Cœur établies provisoirement à Middes ne sont point de vraies
     religieuses aux yeux de l'Église. Le pape a refusé de les reconnaître pour telles, à défaut de cloître, condition
     de rigueur.
     Les Professions qui s'y font ne sont que des engagements entre elles. Il n'y a à Middes que deux personnes
     qui aient pris ces engagements; ce qui ne constitue point une communauté. Nous n'avons pas même l'in-
     tention d'en établir une.
     Nous avons un costume semi-religieux comme moyen de nous attirer plus de vénération de la part des
     enfants. Nos maisons ne ressemblent point aux monastères […] Toutes les personnes de la maison vont aux
     récréations, se promènent dans la campagne et reçoivent chez elles hommes et femmes indistinctement sans
     avoir demandé pour cela aucune permission; ce qui ne serait pas tolérable si leur réunion formait une com-
     munauté.
16   Corr. SB et Eugénie de Gramont, lettre 166, [Chambéry], 1 janvier 1831. appuyer le gouvernement actuel;
     puisque Dieu nous l'a donné et qu'il est reconnu par l'église et par les puissances, ce serait une folie d'en-
     tretenir d'autres espérances. Je vous ai dit à ce sujet un mot de la Quotidienne, je préférerais que vous ne
     fussiez abonnée à aucun journal.
17   ibid., lettre 166, [Chambéry], 1 janvier 1831. en me levant du canapé où j'étais assise à Saint-Genin, […] au
     moment où j'atteins la chaise pour me poser et prendre mes béquilles on me la tire si vite que déjà penchée,

je perdis l'équilibre et je tombai encore sur mon malheureux talon qui eut à soutenir le poids du corps qui comme vous le savez, n'est pas à souffler dessus, un craquement eut lieu encore dans cette partie. J'en souffris beaucoup.

18 ibid., lettre 202, Chamb[éry], 22 mars 1831. Je voulais aller à droite, à gauche, tra, tra, tra, et voilà que je tombe et qu'il me faut demeurer 3 mois au lit. Depuis 2 ans je ne connais que cette route et si notre Seigneur ne veut pas que j'en sorte il faudra bien encore m'y résigner.

19 ibid., lettre 207, Cham[éry], 3 avril 1831; lettre 210, Aix, 8 avril (1831).

20 ibid., lettre 209, Aix, 6 avril 1831. In 1830 Sophie went to Aix three times: 5–22 April; 22 May–1 June; 22 July–13 August. Chambéry, 1831–1852: Notes des passages de notre … Mère Générale au Sacré-Cœur de Chambéry, 1818–1842 (AF, Poitiers, B08, 114/115).

21 Corr. SB et Eugénie de Gramont, lettre 213 (Aix), (14 avril 1831). Oui, c'est bien le torrent que vous êtes venue voir. Je vais m'asseoir tous les jours sur son bord et là je pense à ma rate; je voudrais l'y voir quelques instants; il y a peu d'eau dans ce moment et une espèce d'escalier; je suis sûre que vous y monteriez et *"projectus in antro"* avec quel plaisir, *" dumosa pendere procul, de rupe videbo"* […] mais hélas! quand nous reverrons-nous? toujours vous me ramenez à cette triste pensée en me faisant entendre que vous ne recueillerez pas les fruits des fleurs qui vous réjouissent dans ce moment: *Barbarus has segetes (habebit).* J'espère encore cependant malgré le sinistre *" cava praedixit ab ilice cornis".* The Latin quotations are from *The Eclogues* of Ovid, I, lines 70–71,75–76; IX, line 15 (Virgil, *The Eclogues* (Penguin Classics, 1987), pp. 34, 96). My gratitude to Joan Stephenson for pointing out the source of the quotations in this letter and providing the texts cited in the letters. See also lettre 271, Aix, 6 août 1831. For the classical allusions in Sophie Barat's letters, Maria Aluffi Pentini, *Sante Magdalena Sophia Barat à travers sa correspondance* (Rome, 1968–69), *Sa Culture*, ii, 104–113.

22 Corr. SB et Eugénie de Gramont, lettre 216, Chambéry, 26 avril 1831. Comment avez-vous pu penser que mes plaintes et mon désir de retour pouvaient avoir d'autre but que celui de votre santé? […] Moi qui eus été si heureuse de savoir que tout le monde vous apprécie, vous goûte. C'était tout ce que je désirais en ce monde, et je ne conçois pas que vous ayez cru que j'avais une autre pensée […] Est-ce que je vous parlerais avec cette tendresse et cette confiance!

23 ibid., lettre 282, 6 septembre 1831. C'est ma faute d'être malade! C'est ma faute si je ne marche pas! C'est ma faute si je n'arrive pas! Bientôt ce sera ma faute si le choléra arrive. Vraiment, c'est le cas de dire que les battus paient l'amende, car, enfin, j'espère que vous ne doutez pas de mon empressement à vous voir. Vous l'avez assez rabattu!

24 ibid., lettre 234, [Aix] 29 mai 1831; lettre 334, Lyon, 6 février 1832.

25 Joseph-Marie Favre à SB, Chambéry, 25 septembre [1831]. Bouchage, *Le serviteur de Dieu*, pp. 284–7. amortiront peu à peu cette vivacité de caractère qui vous fait plus de mal que vous ne le pensez peut-être.
Je voudrais que la simplicité de la colombe dominât si bien en vous sur la prudence du serpent que vous eussiez plutôt l'air, les façons et le caractère d'un enfant, que l'air, les façons et le caractère d'une femme d'esprit ou d'une supérieure. Mais qu'il est difficile d'être simple au milieu d'un monde rusé, fourbe, orgueilleux!

26 In 1833 Sophie commented on the instability of Louis, especially his wanderings all over Italy between 1831 and 1833. Corr. SB et Stanislas Dusaussoy, lettre 70, Rome, 23 avril 1833.

27 Corr. SB et Stanislas Dusaussoy, Chambéry, lettre 55, 23 avril 1831.

28 Enfin elle veut plus de piété et cependant je vous avais peint un quasi saint, et plus de fortune. Cependant il faut convenir que vous serez difficile à établir sans rang et sans fortune […] Vous comprenez que je suis fâchée de la non réussite, peut-être est-ce un bien. Se marier dans ce moment, il faut avoir du courage. Dans quelques mois vous vous féliciterez de ne l'être pas! Vous aurez assez de vous à sauver.

29 Corr. SB et Stanislas Dusaussoy, lettre 59, Besançon, 11 octobre 1831. Si vous n'eussiez pas été perché sur la montagne, j'aurais eu bien du plaisir à aller chez vous nous reposer, mais comment monter? Je ne puis avec mes béquilles. Puis, comment aller à la messe le dimanche? Nous irons nous coucher à Sens ou au château de Surville, chez M. de Beaurecueil, près Montereau. Mais ma sœur et Zoé viendront vous voir à la poste nous souhaiter un petit bonjour. Ne dites à personne notre arrivée. Je crains les curieux […] si votre mère peut nous apporter une gougère, elle me fera plaisir, mais cuite du matin; et un petit gâteau feuilleté pour ma compagne qui sera Mme de Varax, un petit panier de raisins.

30 Corr. SB et Eugénie de Gramont, lettre 297, Montet, 5 octobre 1831.

31 ibid., lettre 304, La Ferrandière, 29 novembre (1831). Il me semble que je vois votre méchant petit doigt passer sur l'autre, et ce langage énergique est loin de me rassurer!

32 ibid., lettre 186, Chambéry, 10 février 1831; lettre 320, Lyon, 3 janvier 1832.

33 ibid., lettre 326, Lyon, 17 janvier 1832; lettre 334, Lyon 6 février 1832.

34 ibid., lettre 322, Lyon, 9 janvier 1832. 'je suis donc cosmopolite dans toute la force du mot'

35 Joseph-Marie Favre à SB, Chambéry, 25 janvier, 1832. Bouchage, *Le serviteur de Dieu*, p. 514. J'ai bien de la peine à me persuader que ces guides aient examiné, de près à loisir, les besoins particuliers de votre âme, les attraits de la grâce qu'elle éprouve depuis longtemps, les indices assez certains du bon plaisir de Dieu à votre égard.

36 Joseph-Marie Favre à SB, Chambéry, 25 janvier, 1832. Bouchage, *Le serviteur de Dieu*, p. 515. L'agitation intérieure, ces reproches de la conscience, ce mécontentement de vous-même, ces remords cuisants, cette tristesse, cet abattement, cette défiance et ce découragement […] ont plus fait de mal à votre tempérament que toutes les mortifications et humiliations que vous avez laissées, par trop peut-être de prudence et de ménagement.

37 Joseph-Marie Favre à Louise de Limminghe, Chambéry, 1 mars 1827. Bouchage, *Le serviteur de Dieu*, p. 534.

38 Joseph-Marie Favre à Louise de Limminghe, Chambéry, 5 mai [1830/31/32]. Bouchage, *Le serviteur de Dieu*, p. 282. Les peines, scrupules et inquiétudes de votre bonne mère tiennent un peu à son tempérament, un peu à la fausse direction qu'elle a suivie depuis longtemps, mais surtout au démon qui ne vise qu'à lui faire perdre un temps précieux en l'occupant inutilement d'elle-même et en la faisant sans cesse tourner comme un écureuil autour de sa conscience.

39 Eugénie de Gramont à SB, Paris 29 avril [1832]; Corr. SB et Eugénie de Gramont, lettres 368, 369, 370, Avignon, 27, 28, 29 avril 1832. Also, lettre 374, Aix, 7 mai 1832.

40 ibid., Paris, 3 mai (1832). Je ne puis vous exprimer, chère merotte, le plaisir que m'a fait votre lettre du 27 où vous me parlez de commencer un établissement d'orphelines […] Puis nous le devons à notre malheureuse patrie et le Sacré-Cœur doit donner l'exemple. C'est vraiment à nous à donner le branle dans ce moment, tous les autres couvents nous suivront […] votre lettre m'a fait éprouver une telle sensation que je n'ai fait que pleurer tout le reste de la matinée. Je n'ai pas été en état de faire autre chose que d'écrire à Monseigneur [de Quelen] pour lui rendre compte de tout cela […] il est venu dans l'après-midi causer de ce projet et le fixer […] Mgr, après avoir fixé avec moi sur tout ce qui regardait cette œuvre, alla jusqu'au pensionnat, la communauté y était aussi réunie et annonça l'œuvre […]

41 For details on the orphanage founded in 1832, see A.F. Poitiers, Conflans, B21,117, Documents sur les orphelines, le pensionnat et le noviciat de Conflans. Also, Archbishop de Quelen à une religieuse de Conflans [Eugénie de Gramont], Paris, 29 mai 1832 (Archives de l'Archevêché de Paris, Papiers de Quelen, I D IV 8, no. 8).

42 Corr. SB et Philippine Duchesne, lettre 244, 14 décembre, 1828; Corr. SB et Eugénie Audé, lettre 45, Paris, 14 septembre 1828. Cahier, *Vie*, i, 496–99.

43 Corr. SB et Philippine Duchesne, lettre 248, Paris, 12 février 1829; Corr. SB et Adelaide de Rozeville, lettre 124, Paris, 8 juin 1830. Cahier, *Vie*, i, 499–501

44 Cahier, *Vie*, i, 549–552.

45 Between 1830 and 1836 Sophie entrusted the negotiations regarding Tours to Henriette Grosier, Geneviève Deshayes, Joseph Varin, Louis Barat and Eugénie de Gramont. Corr. SB et Henriette Grosier, lettres 28–42, octobre 1830–avril 1831; Corr. SB et Eugénie de Gramont, lettres 419, 420, 421, septembre 1832; lettre 514, février 1834; Cahier, *Vie*, i, 553, 606, 632.

46 Cahier, *Vie*, i, 561–65.

47 Corr. SB et Eugénie de Gramont, lettre 367, Perpignan, 20 avril [1832]. Cahier, *Vie*, i, 561–65.

48 Notes dictées par … [Louise] de Limminghe, sur les voyages de notre … mère fondatrice, f.7 (GA, Rome, C–I., A, 1–c, Box 1).

49 Corr. SB et Eugénie de Gramont, lettre 383, Turin, 1 juin 1832. Il a trouvé les deux os encore écartés de la largeur d'un doigt et demi en travers, et par le moyen d'un bandage qu'il vient me poser tous les matins, il assure que je marcherai bientôt. Sophie also told Emilie Giraud of her relief in finding a surgeon who could help her. Corr. SB et Emilie Giraud, lettre 106, Turin, 17 juin 1832. Cahier, *Vie*, i, 566–9.

50 Corr. SB et Eugénie de Gramont, lettre 389, Turin, 18 juin 1832.

51 ibid., lettre 400, Turin, 28 juillet 1832. Vous-même, Madame, vous êtes de cet avis; il m'a un peu blessé le cœur. Mais bien vite j'ai recouru à la raison qui vous personnifie et j'ai vu que vous aviez raison: rentrer en France, je n'aurai pas le temps d'y faire tout le travail qui m'attend. Il vaut mieux laisser tout comme cela est et remettre le tout à mon retour! Mais j'irai donc à Rome sans ma fillette, sans ma rate, et je ne la reverrai donc plus que dans un an, peut-être.

52 ibid., lettre 392, [Turin] 3 juillet 1832.

53 Joseph-Marie Favre à SB, Chambéry, 25 août, 1832. Bouchage, *Le serviteur de Dieu*, p. 517. La confiance et l'amour de Dieu dilatent le cœur, agrandissent l'âme et la rendent capable des plus grandes entreprises, tandis que la crainte et la défiance abattent et attristent l'âme, rétrécissent le cœur, hébètent l'esprit, ruinent la santé du corps et troublent toute l'économie de la vie spirituelle. Dieu n'est pas venu en ce monde pour se faire craindre mais pour se faire aimer. Comment […] pouvez-vous vous méfier d'un Dieu qui vous aime infiniment, qui veut votre salut et votre bonheur. Comment pouvez-vous vous méfier de votre cher et bon frère Jésus qui s'est donné tant de peine pour vous sauver, qui a fait tant de sacrifices pour faire part de sa gloire et de ses richesses? […] Comment pouvez-vous vous méfier de ce cœur aimant et aimable qui ne demande qu'à être aimé, pour aimer? Une telle méfiance ne peut venir que du démon […] Qu'elle ne soit jamais volontaire.'

54 Joseph-Marie Favre à SB, Chambéry, 25 août,, 1832. Bouchage, =, pp. 517–8. 'suffisamment bonne, suffisamment expliquée, suffisamment comprise et rassurante pour le moment de la mort'. 'qui fait trop ne fait rien'.

55 *Lettres circulaires*, premier partie, Turin, septembre 1832, pp. 32–4. See also, *Lettres circulaires*, premier partie, Paris, novembre 1831, pp. 20–31.

56 Corr. SB et Eugénie de Gramont, lettre 406, Turin, 6 août 1832. 'mal figuré en tout sens'.

57 Cahier, *Vie*, i, 580–1, 587–8, 590–2.

58 Letters of Madeleine Sophie Barat and Eugénie de Gramont, lettre 431, Rome, 24 novembre 1832. Nous nous sommes arrêtées à St Denys; nous y avons été reçues cordialement. Mme Baudemont et Copina sont vieillies; elles souffrent mais avec courage. Je ne crois pas qu'elles pensent à changer de position et j'en remercie le Seigneur, car elles seraient plus à charge qu'à profit. Je les ai invitées à venir nous voir, ce qu'elles obtiendront facilement. Quel trou que cette maison de St Denys! et encore ne l'ont-elles qu'à bail. Lorsque je songe que c'était pour ce trou que la séparation s'est faite, cela fait pitié. Au reste, elle l'ont bien expié, c'est pour cela que j'ai voulu les voir et les assurer que je n'en conservais aucun ressentiment. Elles m'ont demandé de vos nouvelles avec empressement, ainsi que de Madame Ducis. Pour M. de St-Estève, il les a tout à fait abandonnées, cela devait finir ainsi! Also, Notes dictées par … [Louise] de Limminghe, sur les voyages de notre … mère fondatrice, ff. 21–2 (GA, Rome, C–I., A, 1–c, Box 1).

59 Corr. SB et Henriette Grosier, lettre 66, Rome, 8 janvier 1833; lettre 69, Rome, 26 février 1833. [Elle] est toujours la même pour la Grosier, la Barat, elle est unique! […] Quel cœur! Mais quelle tête! elle veut vivre et mourir à Rome, seule dans une chambre; je le conçois, elle ne pourrait vivre avec d'autres, vous savez que ce serait toujours par excès de soins et de charité. Also, Notes dictées par …' [Louise] de Limminghe, sur les voyages de notre … mère fondatrice, ff. 22–3 (GA, Rome, C–I., A, 1–c, Box 1).

60 Corr. SB et Louise de Limminghe, lettre 146, Rome, 2 avril 1833. 'l'ami des amis'.

61 Jean Rozaven à SB, Rome, 8 janvier 1833; Rome, 3 février 1833 (GA, Rome, B–IV, 3, Box 9).

62 Corr. SB et Eugénie de Gramont, lettre 397, Turin, 14 juillet 1832. J'ai très bien compris que c'était le P[ère] R[ozaven] qui avait échauffé votre bile, pour moi, ce sont les Russes. See also lettres 394, 395, 396.'

63 Corr. SB et Louise de Limminghe, lettre 123, Rome, 22 janvier 1833; lettre 133, Rome, 23 février 1833.

64 ibid., lettre 138, 12 mars 1833. 'court le monde, et c'est doublement fâcheux […] il n'est pas du tout nécessaire qu'il y ait des J[esuites] où nous sommes. Combien de villes en France où ils ne sont pas! nous nous en tirons, je vous dirai même qu'ils sont alors plus libres pour nous donner des secours.

65 Corr. SB et Eugénie de Gramont, lettre 482, Rome, 30 avril 1833; lettre 485, 9 mai 1833.

66 ibid., lettre 463, Rome, 9 mars 1833; lettre 447, Rome, 15 janvier 1833. Cette condition de tenir à la seule noblesse en éloigne un grand nombre. Elles seraient 60 et plus si on admettait le mélange parmi les élèves. Il est vrai que le jour où il entrerait une bourgeoisie, la noblesse partirait. Car dans la ville S[ain]te la perfection n'existe pas plus qu'ailleurs. C'est un préjugé qui subsistera toujours; peut-être a-t-on raison au fond.'

67 Corr. SB et Louise de Limminghe, lettre 48, Paris, 12 octobre 1829; lettre 82, Aix-les-Bains, 13 avril 1831; lettre 83, Chambéry, 29 avril 1831.

68 ibid., lettre 149, Rome, 13 avril 1833. Dans le moment le P. Barelle nous donne une excellente retraite. M[adame] Ar[mande] a eu de la peine à se mettre en train, le démon a fait effort pour l'en détourner; elle tient bon, j'ai la confiance quelle tirera des fruits. Also, lettre 148, Rome, 9 avril 1833.

Notes to Chapter 11

1 Chambéry, Journal de la maison, 17 juillet 1833, f. 158 (AF, Poitiers, Chambéry, BO8, 114/115).

2 *Lettres circulaires*, i, Turin, 10 juillet 1833, p. 42. Le pape et les Cardinaux sont persuadés que […] nous sommes toutes des saintes, ou du moins dans la voie pour le devenir, et nous assimilant à un Ordre [les jésuites] qui produit autant d'apôtres et de saints que de religieux.

3 ibid., pp. 43–44.

4 While Combalot initiated the idea for this congregation its actual foundation was carried out in 1839 by Eugénie Millaret de Brou in Paris, under the name of Dames de l'Assomption. At that point Combalot lost his influence and Denis Affre, future archbishop of Paris, was named by de Quelen to be their superior. See Langlois, *Le Catholicisme au féminin*, pp. 166, 702. Corr. SB et Eugénie de Gramont, lettre 483, Rome, 4 mai 1833. On m'a écrit de Paris que M. Combalot faisait des prosélytes […]; on s'étonne que Mgr [de Quelen] lui ait donné des pouvoirs. Ce sera surtout les jeunes personnes qu'il entraînera et peut-être nos élèves qui, ayant instruction, aiment ce genre. Ce prêtre a confié à sa cousine qui est à la Ferrandière et qu'il s'efforçait de gagner, qu'il voulait faire une société de femmes comme la nôtre et pour l'effacer; qu'il s'y réussirait par la science, en poussant les études plus que chez nous, etc. Je suis étonnée que Mgr [de Quelen] l'ait souffert dans votre ville […] ce jeune homme a ce talent par excellence de gagner les jeunes personnes; quelle perte nous ferions!

5 Corr. SB et Adelaide de Rozeville, lettre 156, Avignon, 12 mars 1832. Prenez connaissance de ces modes d'enseignement et voyez avec les amis [les jésuites] si l'on peut les adopter au moins pour les élèves retardées et qui n'ont pas de moyens[…]. Dans ce cas et même avec plus de moyens on pourrait prendre ce qui s'adapterait à nos plans, surtout pour l'orthographe que nous montrons mal partout […] Nos élèves acquièrent moins sous ce rapport que les enfants des petits externats et pensionnats […] combien d'élèves nous avons

perdues pour cette raison. Je n'ai cessé de le dire; dans nos conseils, on n'y a pas assez fait attention, et cela pour n'y point innover! On y reviendra j'espère, car se serait une faiblesse d'esprit: quand il s'agit de gagner des âmes, que fait à Dieu une plume ou un crayon, du bois ou du papier? [...]

6   Cinquième Congrégation, 1833. Journal des Séances, 30 septembre, 1833. Notes pour le journal du Conseil (GA, Rome, C–I, C–3, Box 3, 1815, 1820, 1826, 1833).

7   Notes pour le journal du Conseil, 1 octobre 1833. 'par suite des événements, habite le Petit–Hôtel.'

8   Arrêts, Décrets, 1833 (GA, Rome, C–I., C–3, Box 3, 1815, 1820, 1826, 1833). Also C–I., C–3, Box 2, 1834, 1851, 1874, 1894).

9   Journal des Séances, 14–24 octobre, 1833.

10   *Lettres circulaires*, ii, Paris, 11 novembre 1833, pp. 21–2. Depuis longtemps nous gémissions à ce sujet, nous sentions que les obligations sacrées que nous impose à cet égard notre vocation, n'étaient pas entièrement satisfaites. Les réclamations que nous recevions de toutes parts, les succès que les pensionnats séculiers obtenaient sur les nôtres excitaient notre douleur. Nous avons recherché avec soin les causes du mal. La première est la négligence des études. La seconde, le peu de zèle à former les élèves à l'économie, à la simplicité, au goût de l'ordre et des ouvrages utiles. La plupart de nos élèves sortent de nos maisons ayant appris beaucoup de choses, n'en sachant aucune, parce les maîtresses n'ayant pas elles-mêmes un assez grand fonds d'instruction, ne font qu'effleurer les matières, et ne s'attachant qu'aux plus agréables, négligent les autres; de là dans une grande partie de nos élèves, l'ignorance de l'orthographe, de l'arithmétique pratique, de la manière d'écrire correctement et agréablement une lettre.

11   ibid., pp. 22–23.

12   Notes pour le journal du Conseil, 5 octobre 1833.

13   Corr. SB et Philippine Duchesne, lettre 228, Philippine Duchesne à la communauté de Paris, St Louis, 7 octobre 1827. Nous ne nous apercevons de notre situation que lorsque par la petitesse des bâtiments, la pauvreté des commencements, le petit nombre des sujets, la difficulté qu'apportent les différentes religions, les différentes langues, les usages du pays, nous rencontrons des obstacles pour établir l'ordre dans la communauté et les classes, ordre si nécessaire et auquel nous ne pouvons que tendre maintenant de tout notre cœur.

14   ibid., SB aux religieuses d'Amérique, lettre 221, [Paris], 12 juin 1827

15   ibid., lettre 231, Paris, 29 novembre 1827.

16   ibid., lettre 232, Paris, 13 décembre 1827. Madame Dutour se plaint de l'excessive malpropreté de la maison [St Louis] et des individus. C'est un inconvénient, je l'avoue. Tâchez [...] que l'on fasse mieux les lessives et tenez à l'ordre dans l'intérieur de la maison. Callan, *Philippine Duchesne*, p. 471; Mooney, *Philippine Duchesne*, p. 184.

17   Mr Rusand was a publisher and bookseller in Lyon, and old friend of Sophie Barat and Joseph Varin. He had helped the foundation of La Ferrandière. In 1828, in collaboration with a Parisian publisher, Poussielgue, he printed the constitutions of the Society of the Sacred Heart.

18   Corr. SB et Eugénie Audé, lettre 42, Paris, 25 avril 1828. Monsieur Rusand qui connaît les Règles de notre Institut, car il les imprime dans ce moment [...] vient de m'envoyer votre lettre, qui lui demande une liste de livres classiques et 300 aulnes de mérinos pour votre maison de Saint-Michel. Il veut voir mon agrément avant de vous expédier ces objets [...] Je lui fais répondre d'exécuter votre commande pour les livres classiques, mais qu'il ne se mêle pas de l'autre, qui n'est nullement son affaire. Je lui dit que c'est la mienne, et que je m'entendrai avec vous sur ce dernier article.

       [...] comment choisissez-vous dans un pays brûlant une étoffe de laine que nous avons proscrite dans tous nos établissements du Midi et même à Paris l'été? Vous n'avez pas donc pas réfléchi que cette étoffe si chère et qui a si souvent fait murmurer les parents, deviendra chez vous plus chère encore par le port, la douane, et si quelque accident a lieu pour cette couleur si fragile, ce sera une perte de 4000 francs; car vos 300 aulnes coûteront cette somme énorme. Ensuite en donnant la commission à Monsieur Rusand, il faudrait qu'il fît venir l'étoffe de Reims où elle se fabrique, à Lyon; de Lyon à Bord[eaux] pour l'embarquement. Voyez quels frais! J'espère que ces réflexions vous feront renoncer à ce projet. See also Corr. SB et Eugénie Audé, lettre 43, Paris. 30 avril 1828; lettre 44, Paris, 10 juin 1828.

19   ibid., lettre 41, Paris, 15 avril 1828.

20   Corr. SB et Philippine Duchesne, lettre 243, Saint Louis, 11 septembre 1828. Madame Xavier [...] se plaint, ainsi que moi, du silence de Madame Eugénie. Je n'y comprends rien, et crains que trop d'encens, là où elle est, ne relâche les liens de notre union et ne lui nuise [...]

       [...] si ces changements sont approuvés, cela va exciter bien des réclamations, qui seraient prévenues si notre Mère commune marquait à chacune sa place avec cet art qui fait adoucir. Je n'ai pas ce talent. See also, Corr. SB et Philippine Duchesne, lettre 242, Saint Louis, 25 août 1828.

21   Corr. SB et Eugénie Audé, lettre 47, Paris, 8 novembre 1828.[elles] s'emparèrent de notre nom et même de nos règles et ont fini par nous surpasser! Les dépenses et entreprises faites un peu par les permissions forcées ou surprises, n'ont pas été bénies de Dieu, et ces maisons sont presque tombées, n'ayant plus que de vastes bâtiments, bien ornés, sans élèves. Also, lettre 46, Paris, 23 octobre 1828.

22   Corr. SB et Philippine Duchesne, lettre 246, Saint Louis, 28 novembre 1828.

23 Corr. SB et Eugénie Audé, lettre 49, Paris, 20 décembre 1828; lettre 55, Paris, 17 juillet 1829.

24 ibid., lettre 47, Paris, 8 novembre 1828. Pas de doute qu'on ira contre mon intention, si on met La Fourche à votre niveau. Il faut ne faire là qu'une maison secondaire et n'enseigner que très peu de science. Apprendre la religion, le travail, lire, écrire, un peu d'orthographe, compter, comme dans notre second pensionnat de Bord[eau]x; c'est pour cela que je désirais que vous y missiez vos orphelines [...] qui aurait empêché que vous eussiez pu leur envoyer les dépouilles de vos élèves, et même leurs trousseaux à faire? Il faudrait vous entendre avec Mère Duchesne et voir s'il ne faudrait pas, pour la plus grande gloire de Dieu empêcher que cette maison ne fasse tort à la vôtre [...] Je vais écrire ces réflexions à Mère Duchesne. Je l'inviterai à descendre le fleuve et à aller visiter vos maisons. Vous réunirez si vous le pouvez commodément, les trois supérieures: Mère Xavier, Dutour et Mère Duchesne, chez vous; et là, dans cette petite réunion, ayant invoqué le Saint Esprit, vous vous consulterez et vous prendrez des mesures pour le plus grand bien

25 Corr. SB et Philippine Duchesne, lettre 247, Paris, 9 décembre 1828. 'pour les pauvres, les orphelines et les petits particuliers [et] au nord les Indiennes.'

26 ibid., lettre 251, Paris, 5 avril 1829. 'ce sera peut-être la maison qui fera le plus de bien'.

27 Corr. SB et Eugénie Audé, lettre 49, Paris, 20 décembre 1828.

28 ibid., lettre 50, Paris, 1 février 1829. Elle m'apprend que vous avez envoyé deux sujets plus que nuls, un autre se mourant de consomption, ce qui est une charge, et d'ailleurs le froid de ce climat abrégera encore ses jours. Il a fallu qu'elles payassentt 500 frs pour les frais de voyage, malgré leur pauvreté qui est extrême. Il paraît que vous ne lui avez pas fait passer les 2500 francs que nous avons soldés à Monsieur Rusand pour votre compte. Je vous ai cependant bien prié de faire tenir cette somme de suite à cette bonne mère, qui est dans un embarras extrême. J'ai peine à concevoir comment vous traitez ainsi cette bonne Mère Duchesne qui a tant souffert pour établir la Société dans cette partie du monde [...] J'espère que vous réfléchissez à votre conduite un peu sévère envers cette bonne Mère qui a bien besoin de consolation.

29 ibid., lettre 51, Paris, 5 mars 1829. 'Cette fondatrice de la Louisiane et qui mériterait au moins des égards'; Corr. SB et Eugénie Audé, lettre 52, Paris, 6 avril 1829.

30 Corr. SB et Philippine Duchesne, lettre 251, Paris, 5 avril 1829; lettre 253, Paris, 10 juin 1829; lettre 254, Paris, 26 juin 1829; lettre 256, Paris, juillet 1829. Corr. SB et Eugénie Audé, lettre 54, Paris, 26 juin 1829; lettre 55, Paris, 17 juillet 1829.

31 Society of the Sacred Heart National Archives, USA, *The correspondence between bishop Joseph Rosati and blessed Philippine Duchesne*, trans. and annotated by Kathryn Webster (St Louis, 1950), Letter 59, Philippine Duchesne to Joseph Rosati, St Louis, 24 January 1828, p. 65.

32 Corr. SB et Eugénie Audé, lettre 56, Paris, 22 octobre 1829. Vous ferez une très bonne œuvre de contribuer à cet établissement de New York qui nous devient absolument nécessaire. Je vous dirai dans une autre lettre mon plan à ce sujet. Je suis sûre qu'il vous plaira car il affermira la Société en Amérique et son véritable esprit s'y propagera avec les moyens que j'entrevois. Mais il n'est pas encore temps de vous les communiquer. En attendant, priez, sanctifiez-vous, amassez les fonds. Also, Corr. SB et Philippine Duchesne, lettre 259, Saint Michel, 11 décembre 1829. Philippine was enthusiastic about the possibility of a foundation in New York and recommended Xavier Murphy to lead it.

33 Joseph Rosati à SB, New Orleans, 14 April, 1829 (Society of the Sacred Heart National Archives, U.S.A., Callan Collection, XIII, C, 2–11). Je vous dirai sans la moindre exagération que j'ai été enchanté de voir cette maison dans un état de prospérité, au-delà de mes espérances. J'y ai trouvé 33 pensionnaires et quatre religieuses, y compris Madame du Tour. Le tout dans la plus grande simplicité et économie, mais aussi avec la plus exquise propreté et le plus bel ordre possible. Avant d'y arriver, on m'avait parlé beaucoup de Madame du Tour. Tous les habitants des environs ont pour elle la plus grande vénération [...] Ce pays offre beaucoup de ressources, les habitants qui ne sont pas riches, ont cependant ici les moyens de donner une certaine éducation à leurs enfants [...] Ils ne les enverraient jamais dans un pensionnat du second ordre, parce que dans un pays républicain où il n'y a pas de distinction, leur orgueil en serait blessé.

34 Corr. SB et Philippine Duchesne, lettre 260, steamboat, 22 décembre 1829. Saint-Michel ne prenait point la forme de nos maisons [...]. J'ai dit sur tout cela mon avis, mais j'ai été persuadée que je devais du reste me tenir entièrement de côté sans m'ingérer en rien que par amitié de sœur. Quel crédit pouvais-je attendre dans une maison où tout est admiration, au dehors et au-dedans, du côté spirituel et temporel, pour celle qui conduit, qui réussit, moi qui suis dans une position toute contraire, ce qu'on ne manque d'attribuer à ma manière.

35 ibid., lettre 261, Saint Michel, 20 janvier 1830. 'La maison est comme une jolie maison séculière'.

36 ibid., lettre 263, Paris, 14 février 1830. Annexe [Pour les maisons d'Amérique] Articles approuvés dans la précédente lettre (ou seulement permis). See Ch. 9 for a discussion of people of mixed blood at this period.

37 ibid., lettre 277, Paris, 30 novembre 1831. Je conçois [...] qu'à votre âge, et ayant tant souffert, cette fondation d'un pensionnat américain, qui exige tant de soins et de perfection, en tout genre, surpasse vos forces. On se plaint depuis de longues années, toutes celles qui ont vu Saint-Louis, du désordre, de la malpropreté, et même du défaut de culture de votre terrain [...] à Dieu ne plaise que je vous blâme. Je sais trop ce que vous avez fait et souffert; mais les temps changent, et il faut aussi modifier et changer. Je vois aussi, par expéri-

ence, qu'il devient nécessaire de ne pas laisser passer de longues années les mêmes supérieures dans les mêmes maisons.

38 ibid., lettre 278, St Louis, 1 février 1832.

39 Letter 137, Joseph Rosati to SB, St Louis, 1 February 1832 (1829 (Society of the Sacred Heart National Archives, U.S.A. Callan Collection, XIII, C, 2–11). Je ne crois pas qu'une autre quelconque de vos Dames puisse jouir de la confiance dont la Mère Duchesne jouit ici. Tous ceux qui la connaissent la respectent et la vénèrent à cause de ses vertus et de ses qualités qui jointes à son âge, à l'expérience qu'elle a acquise par un très long séjour fait dans le pays, la rendent véritablement respectable à tout le monde. Il y a peu de personnes que je vénère autant que cette sainte religieuse, qui a l'esprit de son état et qui, dans bien des occasions qui me sont connues particulièrement, m'en a donné les preuves les plus évidentes [...] Je vois par les plaintes qui ont pu vous engager au changement projeté, qu'on suppose bien des choses qui ne sont pas telles qu'on vous les a représentées [...]. Callan, *Philippine Duchesne*, pp. 526–36; Mooney, *Philippine Duchesne*, pp. 200–9.

40 Corr. SB et Philippine Duchesne, lettre 283, Aix, 8 mai 1832. Je cède avec d'autant plus de facilité, à son désir, qu'il m'en avait coûté beaucoup de prendre cette décision. Je consentais à vos désirs, si longtemps et si énergiquement exprimés. Et puis, tant d'autres personnes éclairées pensaient comme vous sur cet article. Je suis ravie qu'elles se soient trompées, et que, de votre part, il n'y ait qu'un sentiment d'humilité qui vous ait portée à me faire cette demande.

41 Callan, *The Society of the Sacred Heart in North America*, (New York, 1937) pp. 176–79; Mooney, *Philippine Duchesne*, pp. 183–88.

42 Corr. SB et Eugénie de Gramont, Rome, lettre 438, 20 décembre 1832. Je vous envoie [...] deux lettres pour les Opelousas, il ne sera pas inutile que vous les lisiez afin que vous soyez au courant [...] Celle de Madame de Coppens de Saint-Louis peut exagérer, mais le fond est vrai pour Madame Duchesne; elle n'est vraiment plus en état de gouverner, jamais d'ailleurs elle ne l'a fait selon notre esprit. Vous savez que j'ai essayé de mettre Madame Thiéfry à sa place et comment l'évêque a réclamé. C'est ainsi que l'on est arrêté dans sa marche. Pas de doute qu'il faudrait dans ce pays une visite d'une des nôtres.

43 ibid., lettre 464, [Rome], 9 mars [1833]. Madame de Coppens n'a pas tort en tout, tant que Mère Duchesne sera dans cette maison, elle n'ira pas. Vous savez que j'ai essayé de la changer et que l'évêque s'y est opposé. C'est ainsi que l'on est toujours contrarié! Jamais cette bonne et sainte mère ne changera son esprit de Visitandine. Que faire? avoir patience puisque je ne puis y envoyer personne; mais une visite de nous serait bien utile dans ce pays.

44 Cinquième Congrégation, 1833. 31 octobre 1833, Dépouillement des scrutins d'Amérique pour un assistante générale où visitatrice dans ces contrés; Journal des Séances, Notes pour le journal du Conseil, 14 octobre 1833. (GA, Rome, C–I, C–3, Box 3, 1815, 1820, 1826, 1833).

45 Corr. SB et Eugénie Audé, lettre 75 a, Paris, 2 novembre 1833. Je me hâte [...] de vous annoncer que notre conseil général fut clos hier. La veille, 31 octobre, on avait procédé aux nominations dont je joins ici la liste, et vous avez été désignée pour être assistante g[énéra]le de la Louisiane. Le conseil fut décidé d'après la pluralité des voix des professes d'Amérique qui vous connaissent particulièrement. Nous vous enjoignons [...] d'accepter ce fardeau [...] Aussitôt cette lettre reçue, si votre santé le permet, procédez à la visite de quatre maisons: des Opelousas, Saint-Louis, Saint-Charles, Florissant; puis embarquez-vous et venez en France nous rendre compte de votre mission; nous vous retiendrons le moins possible [...]

46 Corr. SB et Philippine Duchesne, lettre 289, St Louis, 23 juin 1833; Cahier, *Vie*, i, 397–603.

47 Corr. SB et Eugénie Audé, lettre 75 b, Paris, 2 novembre 1833; lettre 76, Paris, 6 novembre 1833. Callan, *Philippine Duchesne*, pp. 562–3.

48 Corr. SB et Philippine Duchesne, lettre 289, St Louis, 23 juin 1833; lettre 320, Paris, 16 octobre 1833.

49 ibid., lettre 296, Paris, 29 décembre 1833. Je crois [...] que vous devez encore conserver votre position, au moins jusqu'au retour de Mère Eugénie. Alors nous organiserons de nouveau vos maisons. L'ordre sera précis et je ne crois pas que l'on veuille s'y opposer [...]

50 ibid., lettre 300, St Louis, avril 1834. J'ai été affectée de cette phrase de votre lettre: " Au retour de M[èr]e Eugénie les ordres seront précis et j'espère qu'on n'y mettra pas d'opposition ". De qui pouvait-on attendre des oppositions? Comment a-t-on donné lieu de les craindre?

51 ibid., lettre 301, Paris, 29 juillet 1834. Je [veux] vous dire quelques mots en particulier, pour vous expliquer, d'abord une phrase d'une de mes lettres, que vous me relatez dans votre dernière. C'est au sujet des oppositions que j'ai trouvées à votre changement de maison. Vous savez comment je fus obligée de céder. Ce n'est donc pas vous [...] que j'avais en vue en vous disant que j'espérais que Mère Eugénie m'aiderait à lever les obstacles. En effet, une personne de nous, sur les lieux, juge mieux, que je ne pourrais le faire. Voila pourquoi, jusqu'au présent, j'ai été si timide pour la conduite de vos maisons.
Maintenant que je suis plus au courant, je n'ai pas hésité à décider votre changement de maison. D'ailleurs, c'est un de nos arrêtés secrets, de ne laisser nos supérieures que six ans dans la même maison, à moins l'impossibilité de faire mieux. D'ailleurs, chère Philippine, vous avez besoin de repos; et par conséquent, d'une administration plus facile. Vous appellerez M[èr]e Thiéfry à votre place à Saint-Louis et vous irez prendre la

sienne à Florissant. M[èr]e Eugénie écrit par le même courrier à Monseigneur votre digne évêque, afin de le prévenir. Ou, si je puis, je le ferai moi-même, ce qui sera mieux.

52 Corr. SB et Eugénie Audé, lettre 83, Lyon, 28 novembre 1834.

53 *Lettres circulaires*, i, Lyon, janvier 1835, pp. 47–52; Paris, 4 juin 1835, pp. 53–60; Paris, 28 juillet 1835, pp. 61–4; Paris, 28 décembre 1835, pp. 65–7; Turin, 6 décembre 1836, pp. 68–79. *Lettres circulaires*, ii, Lyon, janvier, 1835 (second partie), pp. 37–41; Paris, 28 décembre 1835, (seconde partie), pp. 49–51; Paris, 26 janvier 1836, pp. 52–61.

54 Society of the Sacred Heart National Archives, U.S.A. Catalogue 1833–1834; Marie-Louise Martinez, Missionaries sent to North America … by Madeleine Sophie Barat, 1818–1865.

55 *Lettres circulaires*, ii, Paris, 31 juillet 1834, pp. 28–36. Sophie wrote a short letter to the American houses, prior to Eugénie Audé's arrival in Paris. *Lettres circulaires*, ii, Paris, 4 avril 1834, pp. 25–27.

56 *Lettres circulaires*, ii, Paris, 11 septembre 1835, pp. 41–49.

57 *Lettres circulaires*, ii, Turin, décembre 1836, pp. 61–4. Qu'on travaille sans cesse à former les enfants à cette docilité d'esprit et de cœur d'autant plus nécessaires dans leur pays que l'erreur ne s'y propage et n'y règne qu'à l'aide de l'indépendance et de l'orgueil des raisonnements.
Bannissez à jamais, je vous en conjure, ces odieuses distinctions d'Américaines et de Françaises.

58 Cahier, *Vie*, i, ch. xxxvi (1833–34), xxxvii (1834–36).

59 Corr. SB et Stanislas Dusaussoy, lettre 71, Metz, 2 septembre 1833.

60 ibid., lettre 76, Lyon, 10 novembre 1834; lettre 82, Turin, 16 novembre 1836; lettre 86, Rome, 8 avril 1837; lettre 87, Rome, 7 septembre 1837.

61 ibid., lettre 83, Turin, 17 novembre 1836. Alype Jean Noirot, *Le Département de l'Yonne comme diocèse*, 5 vols. (Auxerre, 1979), i, *Un feu pour illuminé la nuit (1790–1843)*, 326–7, 329. The Sisters of Charity, Dominicans of the Presentation of Our Lady of Tours opened a day school in Joigny in 1837; a boarding school was added in 1846. (Sœurs de Charité, Dominicanes de la Présentation de la Sainte Vierge de Tours).

Notes to Chapter 12

1 Joseph-Marie Favre à SB, Tamié, par Conflans, 12 Jeanvier 1834. Je suis affligé et véritablement peiné de vous voir toujours la pauvre esclave de l'inquiétude, de la méfiance et de la crainte qui vous rétrécissent l'âme, vous abattent le courage, vous refroidissent le cœur, vous occupent péniblement et inutilement de votre pauvre rien, qu'il faut abîmer dans le tout, vous détournent de vos devoirs essentiels, vous ôtent cette grâce de parole, cette douceur de procédure qui gagnent les âmes, vous minent de la santé de l'âme et de corps sans aucun profit pour Dieu, pour vous, ni pour le cher prochain […] Au nom de notre cher et bon Sauveur, jetez toutes vos craintes, toutes vos inquiétudes dans son cœur brûlant d'amour pour vous.

2 Joseph-Marie Favre à SB, Tamié, par Conflans, 27 juin 1834. Reste donc à vous en acquitter du mieux qu'il vous est possible et à repousser comme de véritables illusions les pensées d'abandonner ce poste que Dieu vous a confié pour suivre les vocations de l'amour-propre. Ne regardez donc plus en arrière pour ne pas vous exposer à être changée en statue de sel comme la femme de Loth.

3 Joseph-Marie Favre à SB, n.d. [Tamié, par Conflans, juillet–septembre 1834]. Je vous invite, je vous engage à entrer dans cette voie d'amour, d'obéissance, de confiance et de sainte liberté […] Plus d'inquiétudes, plus de retours volontaires. Mais joie, confiance, amour, courage en notre bon, aimable et aimant Jésus qui vous demande depuis si longtemps votre cœur et qui n'attend que le moment où vous vous abandonnerez tout doucement, tout bonnement, tout simplement, comme une petite enfant, à sa divine et aimable conduite, à une confiance toute filiale, pour vous ouvrir et vous communiquer les trésors ineffables de son Cœur enflammé d'amour pour vous.

4 Joseph-Marie Favre à SB, Chambéry, jour de St. Jean de la +, 24 novembre 1834. Dans le cours ordinaire de la Providence, Dieu ne fait des saints que par des saints. Il faut donc nous sanctifier pour sanctifier les autres et ne donner que de notre abondance, pour ne pas nous épuiser […] Une mère qui ne se nourrit pas se tue elle-même et tue ses enfants.'

5 Joseph-Marie Favre à Louise de Limminghe, Tamié, 27 juin 1834. […] bornez-vous purement et simplement à votre emploi d'admonitrice tel qu'il est tracé, expliqué et réglé par vos constitutions, sans trop vous inquiéter de ses petites indiscrétions, excès de pénitences, craintes et inquiétudes qui lui feront comprendre tôt ou tard qu'une âme sans guide est comme un vaisseau sans pilote, exposé à tous les vents et tempêtes des passions, à tous les écueils de l'inconstance humaine, de l'amour propre, de l'indécision […] Sa direction n'a été utile ni à vous ni à son âme […] Vous avez mis trop de zèle, d'empressement, d'ardeur et d'inquiétude à l'y soumettre. Cette âme ne sentait pas assez le besoin de la dépendance, de l'obéissance […] pour en profiter et recevoir de bonne grâce et avec une sainte avidité vos avis et vos corrections. Also, Joseph-Marie Favre à Louise de Limminghe, Chambéry, 14 septembre [1834]. Chambéry, 30 septembre [1834].

6 Joseph-Marie Favre à Louise de Limminghe, Chambéry, 30 septembre [1834].

7   Joseph-Marie Favre à Louise de Limminghe, Chambéry, 24 novembre 1834. vous élargirez le cœur rétréci de votre bien aimée supérieure, vous avancerez la gloire du Sacré-Cœur et la prospérité de votre Société naissante. [...]
Je voudrais, je désirerais de tout mon cœur voir cette âme agir en toute confiance, en toute simplicité et, surtout, en toute liberté, dans les saintes voies de l'obéissance, en dépit de ses craintes vaines, de ses doutes éternels et de ses vues embarrassées. Cette conduite franche, courageuse et soumise l'aurait débarrassée de ce maillot de scrupules qui l'absorbent presque tout entière et la détournent de ses devoirs les plus importants, l'éloignent de l'amour du Sacré-Cœur et de la perfection religieuse [...] See also Joseph-Marie Favre à Louise de Limminghe, Tamié, 27 juin 1834; Chambéry, 24 septembre 1834; Chambéry, 30 septembre 1834.

8   Jean Rozaven à SB, [octobre 1834–Jeanvier 1835]. (GA, Rome, C–I., c–3, Box 7).

9   Corr. SB et Eugénie de Gramont, lettre 512, 17 janvier 1834; lettre 513, Tours, 14 février 1834; lettre 522, Bord[eau]x, 28 mars 1834; lettre 527, [Lyon], 15 avril 1834.

10   Corr. SB et Eugénie de Gramont, lettre 512, Paris, 17 janvier 1834; lettre 532, Chambéry, 4 mai 1834.

11   Cahier, *Vie*, i, 608.

12   Corr. SB et Eugénie de Gramont, lettre 528, Lyon, 15 avril 1834. Le motif est l'appartement que vous faites meubler si vite pour votre ami! [Monseigneur de Quelen] En effet, si vous vous rappelez ce que je vous ai confié sur les bruits indiscrets, ils redoubleront certainement dans cette seconde position, et nous ne pourrons y tenir longtemps. Tâchez donc que votre ami le sache, et que pendant un an, plus ou moins, il ne vienne que très rarement dans cet asile, et que surtout il n'y couche point [...] il devinera bien le motif qui me fait vous donner cet avis. Personne ne le vénère et s'il m'était permis de m'exprimer ainsi, ne lui est plus affectionnée, plus *attachée* [...] Donc, tout en lui préparant son appartement, qu'il soit simple et qu'il ne paroisse pas être pour lui, au moins pour la nuit, car rien n'empêchera qu'il n'y aille passer une journée de temps à autre.
Je n'insiste pas sur les motifs de cette réserve, vous les devinerez en vous rappelant le mot que je vous ai dit avant mon départ, et je ne vous ai dit tout ce que je savais.

13   The abbé Jammes was chaplain at the rue de Varenne and was a frequent presence at the Petit-Hôtel. In 1834 Archbishop de Quelen appointed him superior of the junior seminary of Saint-Nicolas in Paris and one of the vicars general of the diocese. The government refused to ratify the appointment on the grounds that Jammes was identified with the légitimiste party, faithful to Charles X. After prolonged correspondence the government finally accepted the appointment. Limouzin-Lamothe, *Monseigneur de Quelen*, ii, 150–52.

14   Corr. SB et Eugénie de Gramont, lettre 538, La Ferrandière, 1 novembre [1834]. On le prise aux Oiseaux, à St Thomas, etc., et on est étonné de notre refus [...] il eût été prudent, dans la position où vous vous trouvez, de garder encore ce vieux père pour une vingtaine de vos élèves les plus sages et les plus dociles à conduire.

15   ibid., lettre 538, La Ferrandière, 1 novembre [1834].

16   Souvenirs de la Sœur Virginie Roux. Notes confidentielles, f. 139 (GA, Rome, A–II., 1–a, Box 1).

17   Corr. SB et Eugénie de Gramont, lettre 530, Lyon, 17 avril 1834. Also, lettre 529, Lyon, 16 avril 1834.

18   ibid., lettre 531, Lyon, 25 avril 1834. J'ai appris que vous alliez transporter un noviciat à C[onflans]. Je n'ai pu m'empêcher de trouver cette mesure imprudente et de la blâmer. Je n'ai pas reconnu votre prudence à ce trait. Comment penser dans ces temps si difficiles, à occuper cette propriété? On parle tant déjà dans le monde de vos richesses et de votre vanité, vraies ou supposées. Avoir celle de l'Archevêque qui est plus en vue que toute autre, et qui servira de point de mire à la méchanceté publique; qui est située dans un pays si mauvais, et près d'un faubourg plus mauvais encore, il me semble que c'est s'exposer volontairement à désagréments de tout genre, et votre digne ami ne vous a pas donné une preuve de véritable amitié en se déchargeant de ce fardeau sur vos épaules. C'est un don funeste [...]

19   ibid., lettre 530, Lyon, 17 avril 1834.

20   ibid., lettre 547, La Ferrandière, 4 décembre 1834. Il ne sera pas inutile que je vous avertisse d'une chose qui fait mauvais effet. C'est le dérangement que la messe de Monseigneur occasionne au pensionnat. Je puis vous dire sans exagération que cela déplaît aux élèves, aux parents et à beaucoup des sœurs de la maison. Je vous en avais déjà dit un mot par le passé! Vous avez eu sans doute des raisons d'agir autrement. Mais maintenant que votre pensionnat est si nombreux, et Monseigneur à cause de ses affaires étant si peu exact, c'est vraiment une perte pour ces enfants à qui une messe suffit bien.

21   Ferdinand Donnet à Louis Baunard, Lorette, 2 mai 1876 (GA, Rome, C–I., A, 1–e). J'ai été sacré à Paris dans la chapelle de la rue de Varenne en mai 1833 en qualité d'évêque de Rosa et coadjuteur de Nancy, par Mgr Forbins-Jeanson [...] J'ai reçu dans la même chapelle le pallium d'archevêque de Bordeaux, des mains de Mgr de Quelen, délégué par Grégoire XVI. Les Mères Barat et de Gramont occupaient les premiers rangs dans la chapelle.

22   Sophie herself had suggested originally that the marriages of past pupils be celebrated in the chapel at the rue de Varenne. She bitterly regretted this later. Corr. SB et Eugénie de Gramont, lettre 151, Poitiers, 19 juillet 1825; lettre 154, Lille, 24 janvier 1827.

23 Paris, rue de Varenne, Journal de la maison, 1829–1835, ff. 1, 39, 79–80, 86–91, 97, 100, 103–4, 106–10, 115, 118 (AF, Poitiers, B06, 115, II).

24 Paris, rue de Varenne, Journal de la maison, 1829–1835, f. 90.

25 Corr. SB et Eugénie de Gramont, lettre 543, La Ferrandière, 19 novembre 1834; lettre 551, Lyon, 14 décembre 1834.

26 ibid., lettre 546, La Ferrandière, 1 décembre 1834. une *espèce de révélation* qui augmente mes incertitudes, quoique je ne m'appuie guère sur ces sortes de connaissances, surtout si elles sont de mon cru […]

27 Joseph-Marie Favre à SB, Conflans, 27 février 1835. Pourriez-vous encore vous laisser aller à ces craintes, à ces inquiétudes, à ces remords, à ces doutes, à ces anxiétés qui déplaisent tant à son Cœur! Non, toutes ces vaines appréhensions viennent du démon qui cherche à rétrécir nos cœurs et à les fermer à l'amour et à la confiance; ou de l'amour-propre qui cherche à mettre sa confiance en ses bonnes œuvres […] Ouvrez […] au nom et pour l'amour de Jésus, votre cœur si longtemps froissé, rétréci, abattu, découragé à l'amour et à la confiance. Que ni les fautes passées, ni les imperfections présentes, ni l'abus des grâces ne vous portent à la moindre méfiance […]

28 *Lettres circulaires*, i, Paris, 4 juin 1835, pp. 54–5. Cette petite Société, encore dans son enfance, a déjà reçu des développements essentiels […] mais les circonstances ont mis obstacle à l'exécution des projets qui doivent, pour ainsi dire, compléter nos institutions […] Pour y parvenir, nous avons résolu d'avoir notre maison, qui sera la maison mère ou chef-lieu de la Société. Ce sera là où toutes les relations doivent aboutir, et d'où elles sortiront toutes. C'est dans cette maison que seront placés le noviciat général, le juvénat et le troisième an pour toutes nos maisons de France, autant que cela sera possible; on y mettra aussi l'économat général, le secrétariat et les archives de la Société; ce sera notre résidence habituelle et celle de nos assistantes générales qui ne seront point en mission. On tâchera avec le temps, qu'il y en ait toujours deux autant que possible, avec l'admonitrice et une conseillère générale si la première ne l'était pas, pour nous aider dans nos travaux et former notre conseil habituel.

29 *Lettres circulaires*, i, Paris, 28 juillet 1835, p. 61. […] cette maison [rue Monsieur] tout entière, devenue le chef-lieu de la Société, et, par conséquent, la source d'où devra jaillir et se répandre le véritable esprit qui doit animer chacun des membres qui compose cette grande famille.

30 *Lettres circulaires*, i, Lyon, janvier 1835, pp. 47–52.

31 Paris, rue de Varenne, Journal de la maison, 1829–1835, f. 22; Cahier, *Vie*, i, 615.

32 Corr. SB et Eulalie de Bouchaud, lettre 1, La F[errandière], 1 décembre 1834. Vous poussez trop loin la méfiance et la timidité. Je prie tous les jours notre Seigneur de vous donner le courage de la surmonter. Dans la position où vous vous trouvez, il est important que cette jeunesse ne puisse deviner que vous la craignez ou que vous souffrez de vos rapports avec elle. Prenez donc un peu d'assurance; c'est pour la gloire du S[acré]-Cœur et non par orgueil […] vous m'apprendrez dans quelques semaines, les progrès que vous aurez faits dans cette s[ain]te hardiesse. See also lettre 2, Lyon, 12 janvier 1835.

33 Jean Rozaven [à Louise de Limminghe], [Rome] 24 juin 1835.

34 Jean Rozaven à SB, Rome, 15 octobre 1835. Vous amèneriez avec vous deux ou trois des personnes en qui vous avez le plus de confiance et qui soient les plus en état de vous aider de leurs conseils, qu'elles soient assistantes, conseillères ou non, sans aucun respect humain et dans l'unique vue du bien. Avec les conseils que vous trouveriez ici, vous rédigeriez les changements qu'il serait à propos de faire, vous les feriez approuver par le saint-père, puis retournant en France vous assembleriez un conseil extraordinaire, sans attendre l'an [18]40. Mais un conseil composé non seulement de deux, mais de députés de toutes vos maisons, autant que la chose serait possible, pour les faire adopter. Croyez-moi la chose est importante et demande le moins de délai que possible. Il n'y a que vous qui puissiez faire la chose […] Après votre mort le remède deviendra plus difficile et peut-être impossible, parce qu'on n'aura pas la même confiance dans celle qui vous succédera et qu'il est à craindre qu'il ne naisse des dissensions et des parties qui causeraient la ruine de la bonne œuvre vous à laquelle vous travaillez.

35 Journal du Noviciat du 9 juillet 1835 au décembre 1835 (AF, Poitiers, B06, Paris, 119, II); Cahier, *Vie*, i, 614–21.

36 Souvenirs de la Sœur Virginie Roux. Notes confidentielles, f.133.

37 Noviciat souvenirs des récréations avec notre Sainte Mère. Noviciat de la maison mère, 1835 (GA, Rome, A 34).

38 *Vie de la Mère [Catherine] de Charbonnel, assistante et économe générale de la Société du Sacré-Coeur* (Paris, c. 1870), p. 193. 'nullement disposé à exagérer en sa faveur'.

39 ibid., pp. 191–204.

Notes to Chapter 13

1 SB à Archevêque de Quelen, lettre 1, Chambéry, 18 octobre 1836. (Archives de l'Archevêché de Paris, Papiers de Quelen, I D IV 10, No. 19 a). Après avoir hésité longtemps si je déposerais dans votre cœur le profond chagrin qui pénètre le mien, je me décide enfin, croyant reconnaître en cela un impérieux devoir de conscience.

Vous n'ignorez plus sans doute [...] les horreurs et les infâmes plaisanteries qui circulent partout, et dont on m'accable dans tous les lieux où je m'arrête, au sujet de votre habitation; de malheureux journaux ont porté ces scandaleuses calomnies jusqu'à Rome, et quoiqu'on ne doute pas de la vertu des personnes qui en sont l'objet, on s'étonne que l'on puisse y prêter en ne faisant pas cesser la cause ou l'occasion de ces épouvantables bruits; on ne m'épargne ni les reproches ni les menaces; ce n'est pas là cependant, Monseigneur, ce qui me fait souffrir davantage, mais bien la triste certitude du tort immense que cette position fait à votre grandeur elle-même [...] Ma conscience s'alarme aussi en voyant, il faut bien vous l'avouer, [...] la réputation et l'existence même de la Société aussi fortement compromises; j'ai donc cru devant Dieu devoir vous confier mes angoisses [...]

2   Archbishop de Quelen to SB, 23 octobre 1836. (Archives de l'Archevêché de Paris, Papiers de Quelen, I D IV 10, 19 b); Limouzin-Lamothe, *Monseigneur de Quelen*, 229–30.

3   SB à Archevêque de Quelen, lettre 2, Turin, 2 novembre 1836. (Archives de l'Archevêché de Paris, Papiers de Quelen, I D IV 10, 19 c); Le but de ma lettre a été seulement de vous avertir des bruits publics, sachant bien que votre sagesse et votre prudence vous suggéreraient certainement les moyens de les éloigner. Mais ne peut-on pas les employer, ces moyens, et conserver avec la famille si dévouée [...] les rapports que la prudence permettra en ces malheureux temps où nous vivons?

4   M. Bellmare, *M. de Quelen pendant 10 ans* (Paris, 1840). Il [Archevêque de Quelen] savait que nos mœurs protègent plus les femmes que les hommes et qu'une communauté de prêtres serait plus gravement exposée à l'insulte, aux sévices et aux emportements de l'anarchie qu'une faible et timide congrégation de l'autre sexe. L'Ami de la Religion, v.104, 31 mars 1840, 613.

5   Corr. SB et Eugénie de Gramont, lettre 594, Turin, 24 novembre 1836. Vous saviez, ce me semble, qu'il n'est ni dans ma manière d'agir, ni dans mon caractère de brusquer les affaires [...] Je vous ai avertie parce qu'il est urgent de prendre des précautions, mais j'étais loin de vouloir rien précipiter. Nous attendrons donc mon retour; nous pèserons ensemble le pour et le contre [...] See also lettre 596, Turin, 15 décembre 1836; lettre 597, Parme, 23 décembre 1836.

6   *Lettres circulaires*, i, Turin, 6 décembre 1836, pp. 68–79.

7   *Lettres circulaires*, i, Turin, 6 décembre 1836, p. 68. Nos courses et le travail soutenu [...] nous ont privée de cette jouissance; car c'en serait une vraie pour nous de pouvoir correspondre cœur à cœur avec chacune et de témoigner à toutes celles que le divin Cœur nous a données, dans sa bonté, le vif intérêt et l'attachement maternel que nous leur portons. Mais la chose n'est pas possible, nous ne pouvons doubler ni nos forces ni les jours; on comprendra sans peine qu'il devient moralement impossible, vu l'extension que prend la Société.

8   *Lettres circulaires*, ii, Turin, 6 décembre 1836, Pour les supérieures et leur conseil, pp. 63–71.

9   Notice sur ... Marie Adélaïde Cahier (n.p; n.d), pp. 26–34; *Vie de la Mère [Catherine] de Charbonnel, assistante et économe générale de la Société du Sacré-Cœur de Jésus* (Paris, c. 1870), pp. 196–204.

10 ibid., p. 191. des religieuses qui se disaient cloîtrées sans grilles, qui voyageaient sans leur aumônier, qui gouvernaient une maison sans avoir au moins quarante ans etc. etc. Tout cela paraît anormal et presque suspect. Les détails même de notre manière de vivre contrastaient avec certains usages.

11 Vie de la ... Mère Adèle Lehon (Roehampton, 1895). Adèle Lehon became the third superior general of the Society of the Sacred Heart (1874–1894).

12 Corr. SB et Adèle Lehon, lettre 1, Paris 19 octobre 1835.

13 *Vie de la Mère [Catherine] de Charbonnel, assistante et économe générale de la Société du Sacré-Cœur de Jésus* (Paris, c. 1870), pp. 208–9.

14 Corr. SB et Eugénie de Gramont, lettre 615, Rome, 20 mai 1837. La vue est délicieuse; on domine tout Rome et par le beau côté. Nous sommes tout près de St Pierre et nous planons sur sa belle coupole. Le parterre et autres allées sont bordés de citronniers et d'orangers en plein rapport [...] mais comme nous avons trouvé tout cela en mauvais état, les 1ers frais sont considérables. Also, lettre 618, Rome, 7 juin 1837.

15 ibid., lettre 519, Bord[eau]x, 20 mars 1834.

16 ibid., lettre 625, Rome, 12 août 1837.

17 ibid., lettre 626, Rome, 31 août 1837.

18 ibid., lettre 628, Rome, 28 septembre 1837. Maintenant que je sais tout notre désastre, j'ai besoin de vous en parler. Concevez-vous que nos mères ont eu la constance de me cacher, un mois entier, la mort cruelle des sept enlevées à la Trinité par ce fléau destructeur? J'étais dans une pleine sécurité pour cette maison qui me paraissait à l'abri de toute contagion, et tandis que je tremblais pour Sainte-Rufine qui était entourée de morts et de mourants, aucune, comme vous le savez, n'a été attaquée, et l'autre maison ébranlée jusque dans ces fondements. Je ne puis vous peindre ma cruelle surprise; elle faillit m'être funeste [...] On crut devoir m'épargner plusieurs secousses et une seule était trop, ce me semble!

19 ibid., lettre 625, Rome, 12 août 1837. 'vous savez que je prends toutes les maladies régnantes.'

20 ibid., lettre 630, Rome, 7 octobre 1837. 'Hier, je vis pour la 1ere fois depuis nos tristes événements les mères de Causans et de Coriolis. Quelle entrevue pénible! leur maison est dépeuplée; 9 personnes de moins.'

21 Corr. SB et Adelaide de Rozeville, lettre 208, Rome, 24 octobre 1837; Corr. SB et Eugénie de Gramont, lettre 631, Rome, 26 octobre 1837.

22 Corr. SB et Eugénie de Gramont, lettre 631, Rome, 8 octobre 1837. Pourquoi n'êtes-vous pas à l'école, leur dis-je? Ah! notre maîtresse est au ciel [...] et l'école est fermée. Ce fut une épine qui, ajoutées aux premières, me perçoit l'âme à tout moment [...] j'ai engagé nos mères à rouvrir leurs classes et à y employer des sœurs en attendant. La Sœur Adèle que vous connaissez, est en état. Si on les laissait, ces enfants, courir les rues longtemps, nos maîtresses perdraient leurs années précédentes de travail et fruits [...] Ces classes avaient déjà changé cette jeunesse paresseuse et viciée, car pas de pays où l'instruction de cette classe soit plus nécessaire. Je voudrais que nous puissions nous charger de tous les quartiers populeux! C'est impossible [...] mais au moins devons-nous garder ce que nous avons! See also, Corr. SB et Adélaide de Rozeville, lettre 208, Rome, 24 octobre 1837.

23 Corr. SB et Adélaide de Rozeville, lettre 208, Rome, 24 octobre 1837. A Sainte-Rufine, autre spectacle aussi déchirant: ma visite à la salle d'asile fut des plus touchantes. On me présente des enfants privées de père et de mère, laissées dans la rue et recueillies par d'autres pauvres chargés eux-mêmes de famille; alors tous ces enfants sont pêle-mêle sur les mêmes paillasses. C'est comme des couvées, mes larmes coulaient malgré moi. J'ai dit à nos mères de recueillir les abandonnées, nous le prendrons lorsque nous aurons notre grande maison. Mais elles-mêmes sont les unes sur les autres, endettées parce que les pauvres gens ne payent pas leurs loyers, seuls revenus de Sainte-Rufine. N'importe, elles sont prises, la divine providence viendra à l'aide. Also Corr. SB et Eugénie de Gramont, lettre 631, Rome, 26 octobre 1837.

24 Corr. SB et Hypolite Lavauden, lettre 1, Chambéry, c. 1835. Comme les Sœurs ici travaillent beaucoup, qu'on leur donne un plat avec la soupe le matin, ou du lait seul. On ferait bien d'en mettre trois fois la semaine; tenir à ce qu'il ne soit pas d'écrémé; il vaut mieux mettre un peu d'eau lorsqu'il est trop épais l'hiver.

25 Corr. SB et Hypolite Lavauden, lettre 10, Rome, [septembre] 3 [1837]. See lettres 2–29, Rome, juin 1837–28 juillet 1838.

26 Corr. SB et Eugénie Audé, lettre 113, La Ferrandière, 18 juillet 1836. Je vous envoie [...] un petit paquet qui contiendra ces lettres d'Amérique que je vous prie de lire attentivement [...] Renvoyez-moi vos notes sur ces lettres et vos réflexions: elles me tuent; chaque fois que je reçois un courrier de ce pays c'est une épine qui perce l'âme [...] Si j'avais le remède, ce ne serait rien, mais où le trouver? Il faudrait dans ce pays une âme forte de corps et d'âme et qui tînt toutes ces maisons sous sa tutelle; écrivez-leur pour les encourager, je ne l'ai hélas pas fait!

27 SB à Anthony Blanc, bishop of New Orleans, Montet, 27 septembre 1836; Turin, 9 novembre 1836. Passage from an American newspaper sent by Mother Bazire. St James Parish, 17 September 1836. Jesuitical Spoliation (Society of the Sacred Heart National Archives, U.S.A., St Louis. Series 1, A–C, Generalates. St Madeleine Sophie Barat, 1779–1865).

28 Vie de ... Mary Ann Aloysia Hardey, assistante générale de la Société du Sacré-Cœur (Paris).

29 Corr. SB et Eugénie Audé, lettre 117, Montet, 20 août 1836; Corr. SB à Aloysia Hardey, lettre 1, 22 octobre 1836.

30 Corr. SB et Elizabeth Galitzine, lettre 63, Rome, 14 octobre 1837.

31 Corr. SB à Aloysia Hardey, lettre 2, Turin, 4 décembre 1836.

32 Corr. SB et Eugénie Audé, lettre 131, Turin, 26 novembre 1836. Il serait si commode d'avoir là [New York] une maison pour les arrivantes et les partantes. Plus tard on pourrait s'établir à Philadelphie. Voyez, je ne mourrai contente que lorsque nous aurons un berceau dans cette partie de l'Amérique, et il me semble que vous devez m'aider à le fonder. Puis notre mission sera achevée, d'autres feront le reste. Si nous avions une fondation à New York ou dans les environs, je voudrais consacrer six mois pour aller la visiter. Ce n'est guère plus loin que Rome par terre, quelle difficulté y aurait-il? 50 jours pour l'allée et la venue, et quatre mois de séjour.

33 ibid., lettre 135, Turin, 9 décembre 1836.

34 ibid., lettre 148, Rome, 18 mars 1837.

35 The Jesuit mission was also carved out of pain, hard work and exhaustion. The Jesuit general, Jean Roothan, sent out a visitor, Peter Kenny, in 1832, to gain information about the Jesuit houses on the east coast of America. Once he had received the report, Roothan decided to organise the Jesuits into one province, Maryland, but that the Jesuits communities in Missouri, being a special case, would be a vice-Province directly under the general.

36 Corr. SB et Elizabeth Galitzine, lettre 80, Rome. 17 février 1838.

37 The abbé Auguste Jeanjean knew the Society well and had been chaplain in Grand Coteau and St Michael's.

38 Corr. SB et Elizabeth Galitzine, lettre 81, Rome, 20 février 1838. Revenons à ma croix: la Louisiane. Je ne sais plus comment faire pour rapprocher les deux supérieures. Il faut avouer que Mère Bazire est bien imprudente. Puis cette conduite des jésuites qui se laissent mener par Mère Bazire [...] Si le Seigneur ne m'eût gardé et que j'eusse suivi les conseils du Père de Vos, toujours dirigé par elle, je me brouillais avec Monsieur Jeanjean, avec l'évêque par suite [...] Les lettres de ses filles, qu'elles n'écrivent que pour son insinuation, j'en suis sure, ne sont que pour me faire son éloge et la justifier [...] Je connais ses excellentes qualités, et je n'ai contre elle aucune prévention, mais il m'est impossible d'approuver sa conduite envers Saint-Michel, et tout ce quelle débite aux Pères [jésuites] etc. me fait un grand chagrin [...] elle donne aux Pères au-delà de ses

facultés et sans mesure [...] les exigences de Mère Bazire et des jésuites ne sont pas raisonnables et qu'il en faudrait moins pour dégoûter les Américaines des Françaises, surtout lorsqu'on le leur dit sans ménagement. See also, lettre 91, Rome, 4 avril 1838; lettre 150, Rome, 29 juillet 1840.

39   Corr. SB et Eugénie Audé, lettre 158, Rome, 25 mai 1837. Une maison composée de toutes américaines pourrait bien se séparer, et que j'eusse à y envoyer une supérieure française! or je n'en ai pas, ainsi il faut que j'abandonne le tout à la Providence, mais je ne puis croire ce que l'on dit, elles me paraissent toutes deux si attachées à la Société, je veux parler des Aloysias! Vous me direz ce que vous en pensez [...] car j'ai besoin d'être rassurée, quoique je ne crois pas ce que l'on m'a dit.

40   Corr. SB et Elizabeth Galitzine, lettre 59, Rome, 28 septembre 1837. Philippine Duchesne felt that Julia Bazire, then with her at Florissant, had been misjudged and wrote a defence of her to Sophie Barat in May 1841. She outlined the work that Julia Bazire had done in La Fourche, St Michael's and Grand Coteau in difficult circumstances. Philippine admitted that Bazire had lent a large sum of money (300,000 briques/old francs) to the Jesuits, as well as all the lime and wood they needed for their building projects. Corr. SB et Philippine Duchesne, lettre 322, [St Louis], 10 mai 1841.

41   Corr. SB et Eugénie Audé, lettre 167, Rome, 20 juillet 1837; lettre 184, Rome, 16 janvier 1838; lettre 188, Rome, 29 février 1838.

42   Corr. SB à Aloysia Hardey, lettre 8, Rome, 26 février 1838; Corr. SB et Eugénie Audé, lettre 188, Rome, 20 février 1838.

43   Corr. SB à Aloysia Hardey, lettre 5, Rome, 30 décembre 1837. Encore un mot de G[rand] Coteau. Faites l'impossible [...] pour conserver l'union entre vos deux maisons. Profitez des occasions pour lui rendre service. Quand vous le pouvez, envoyez quelques dons. Je serais désolée s'il existait le plus petit froid entre vous. La devise de la Société, vous le savez, est: *cor unum et anima una* et chacune doit faire les plus grands sacrifices pour tenir à la pratique de ces deux préceptes qui plaît tant au Cœur S[acré] de Jésus. See also, lettre 3, Rome, 12 juillet 1837; lettre 4, [Rome] 14 octobre, 1837; lettre 6, Rome, 9 janvier 1838.

44   Corr. SB à Aloysia Hardey, lettre 10, Rome, 16 mai 1839. Ce moyen sera meilleur pour inculquer profondément l'esprit de la Société dans vos parages; comme vous ne nous enverriez que des sujets d'élite, propres plus tard aux 1ers emplois, il en résulterait, ce me semble, un avantage inappréciable pour nos établissements chez vous. L'union serait plus étroite et l'uniformité, au moins dans l'essentiel, car je conçois que les usages peuvent différer [...] peut-être vous pourriez être leur conductrice! [...] je voudrais connaître ma première fille américaine.

45   Corr. SB et Eugénie de Gramont, lettre 633, Rome 4 janvier, 1838.

46   ibid., lettre 634, Rome, 18 janvier 1838. Je vous dirai seulement ce mot, chère Eugénie, que vous ne devez pas hésiter non plus que votre Père à prendre le parti que je vous conseille, croyez que les motifs qui me forcent à vous pousser à ce parti ne peuvent être plus absolus. Il est impossible que cette manière d'être se prolonge davantage sans les plus graves inconvénients. Vous ne pouvez vous faire l'idée de tout ce que j'entends et de tout ce que l'on m'écrit, je puis dire, de tous côtés. D'ailleurs, chère rate, lors même que ces réclamations n'auraient pas lieu, il me semble que la proposition que je fais est plus convenable sous tous les rapports. Pourquoi donc hésiterait-on à l'accepter.

47   ibid., lettre 635, Rome, 6 février 1838.

48   ibid., lettre 637, Rome, 1 mars 1838. Un cardinal me disait un jour: si les communications qui ont lieu chez vous existaient en Italie, la personne et la maison seraient interdites [...]
beaucoup de prêtres qui viennent de Paris parlent beaucoup et tournent en plaisanteries etc. et surtout la présence des dames pendant les repas etc. [...] j'abrège. Les élèves ont parlé à leurs parents des visites faites pendant que vous étiez malade, vers 9 heures du soir, et fréquemment. Je ne vous dis rien des réflexions de plusieurs évêques de France à moi-même à ce sujet.

49   ibid., lettre 643, Rome, 10 avril 1838. Croyez, chère rate, que vous et lui vous abusez grandement. Toutes les personnes qui parlent ou plutôt qui nous parlent lui sont dévouées et attachées plus ou moins, mais toutes l'estiment et vous plaignent tous de votre illusion. Car enfin, que demande-t-on? Qu'il se loge ailleurs, et puisque nous lui offrons les mêmes secours, pourquoi ne pas céder à l'opinion des bons, et éloigner pour nous un tort qui ne se réparera jamais. Plusieurs personnes de poids me l'ont dit. Je lui ai offert le Petit-Hôtel pour lui prouver que je ne partage pas les préventions, mais il serait à désirer qu'il acceptât tout et qu'il s'éloignât.'

50   ibid., lettre 644, [Rome, avril 1838].

51   ibid., 648, Lyon, 19 juillet 1838.

52   Corr. SB et Stanislas Dusaussoy, lettre 92, Paris, 23 novembre [1838]. Even Sophie's relations in Joigny heard about it and one of them wrote to Sophie asking if he could hold a funeral service there.

53   Corr. SB et Eugénie de Gramont, lettre 641, Rome, 4 avril 1838. la dame chargée des élèves du S[acré] C[œur] à Paris tenait un vrai bureau pour les mariages, qu'elle s'en occupait habituellement, qu'elle avait la liste des jeunes personnes et l'état de leur fortune etc. ce qui a scandalisé ces étrangers ainsi que ceux à qui ils les rapportaient. Ceci joint au reste, nous donne une triste réputation [...] S'il ne faisait pas de tort à l'œuvre, il faudrait s'y résigner, mais quand elle nuit essentiellement, ne faut-il pas apporter remède?

54 ibid., lettre 649, La Ferrandière, 1 août 1838. Je suis fâchée des obstacles qui s'élèvent au sujet du changement de votre digne hôte. Restera notre position tout à fait pénible à l'égard du voisinage? […] Je ne tiens
pas pour le moment à notre réunion […] Je suis pourtant bien aise de vous dire d'avance que je n'entends
nullement cette réunion comme elle était avant notre départ.

55 Joseph-Marie Favre à SB, Albertville, 14 février 1837. J'ai appris avec une peine extrême que votre santé est
en fort mauvais état […] Prenez le repos, les délassements, les remèdes qu'ils prescrivent, laissez-vous traiter
comme ils entendent et non pas comme vous l'entendez […] ne vous faut-il pas une santé forte, vigoureuse,
pour remplir des obligations aussi étendues, variées, aussi compliquées, aussi tuantes que celles dont vous
êtes chargées? Mon Dieu, ma mère, en vous faisant languir par des excès de travail, de veille, de mortifica-
tion, ne faites-vous pas languir toute la Société? […] Le démon ne peut que rire de vos mortifications qui
deviennent un obstacle à l'exercice de votre importante charge.

56 Joseph-Marie Favre à Louise de Limminghe, Conflans, 24 décembre 1837. Ne croyez pas […] qu'à moins
d'un miracle de la grâce, votre digne Mère quitte tout à coup cette longue habitude de crainte et de péni-
tence qu'elle s'est faite. C'est une habitude qu'il faut traiter comme une maladie chronique, avec douceur,
avec soin, avec patience […] La grâce triomphe tôt ou tard de tous les obstacles, quelques grands qu'ils vous
paraissent.

57 Corr. SB et Eugénie de Gramont, lettre 625, Rome, 12 août 1837; lettre 636, Rome, 15 février 1838.

58 Corr. SB et Philippine Duchesne, lettre 317, Rome, 25 janvier 1838. Corr. SB et Eugénie Audé, lettre 182,
Rome, 23 décembre 1837. Also, lettre 183, Rome, 30 décembre 1837.

59 Corr. SB et Adélaïde de Rozeville, lettre 206, Rome, 12 septembre 1837. Corr. SB et Eugénie Audé, lettre
173, Rome, 14 septembre 1837.

60 Corr. SB et Louise de Limminghe, lettre 150 bis, Rome, 24 janvier 1838. ma santé aurait[…]un peu besoin
d'exercice et d'un air libre. J'en prends si peu! Le travail commande; puis vous le savez que pour moi une
promenade sans but n'a pas d'attrait. Also, lettre 155, Parme, 25 mai 1838.

61 Corr. SB et Elizabeth Galitzine, lettre 78, Rome, 6 février 1838. On se trompe si on croit qu'il ne faut à la
Société que des âmes appelées à la vie active. Si la contemplative nous manque, l'autre sera bientôt un spec-
tre, et privées de la vie, quel bien pourrions-nous opérer? Au lieu donc de nous éloigner les sujets qui ont de
l'attrait pour la vie contemplative et la solitude, on devrait nous les donner avec encore plus d'empressement
parce qu'ils nous sont plus nécessaires qu'ailleurs […] je n'hésite pas à leur promettre qu'on ne les emploiera
pas aux élèves, mais qu'elles seront pour les emplois intérieurs, et pour nous aider à l'adoration du Saint
Sacrement du jour et de la nuit, quand le noviciat sera assez nombreux pour le soutenir […] votre nièce […]
sera, dans la Société du Sacré-Cœur aussi solitaire, aussi séparée du monde qu'à Port-Royal […] Je suis persuadée que nous perdons nos meilleurs sujets par l'idée fausse qu'il faut, pour entrer chez nous, le seul attrait
des œuvres extérieures, tandis que toutes celles qui avaient pour principe la vocation des contemplatives ont
presque toutes réussi chez nous […]
[…] un ordre composé de ces deux attraits, à une vie de grâce forte et qui soutient admirablement la partie
active, […] c'est ce que je me sens poussée fortement d'établir dans notre Société avant que Dieu m'appelle
à Lui. Par ce moyen tout sera réparé, la vraie vie intérieure se maintiendra et je dois ajouter que ceci ne fera
pas de tort pour les travaux qu'embrasse la Société, parce que malheureusement le nombre de ces âmes est
petit, et que, d'ailleurs elle serait la pépinière des supérieures, maîtresses des novices etc.

62 Corr. SB et Elizabeth Galitzine, lettre 60, 30 septembre 1837. Combien de fois, ayant médité d'avance tel ou
tel changement, je fus obligée d'y renoncer après avoir tout vu et tout entendu.

63 Corr. SB et Eugénie Audé, lettre 69, Rome, 7 mars 1833. Tous ceux qui gouvernent devraient s'attacher à
cette maxime: tenir ses sujets avec une main de fer couverte d'un gant de velours. On doit tenir fortement,
mais de manière que les sujets ne voient ni se sentent le fer qu'ils ne pourraient supporter s'il était nu et
découvert.

64 ibid., lettre 138, Rome, 16 janvier 1837. Je ne suis pas par caractère, ni soupçonneuse, ni exigeante, pourvu
que même en faisant mal, on ait voulu bien faire. Je n'en demande pas plus. Also, Corr. SB et Eugénie Audé,
lettre 98, Paris, 11 novembre 1835.

65 Corr. SB et Adélaïde de Rozeville, lettre 154, Avignon, 23 février, 1832. la douceur n'est pas la mollesse quand
elle se puise dans le Cœur de Jésus et qu'elle sort comme le miel de la gueule de lion. C'est celle-ci qu'il faut
introduire dans le gouvernement, des formes et des paroles douces, mais tenir à ce que l'on avance […]

66 ibid., lettre 235, Rome, 23 novembre 1839. L'essentiel est que vos ennuis, vos peines de cœur, ne paraissent
point au dehors, et que vos filles vous croient invulnérable et au-dessus des petites passions qui les obsèdent.
Donc une grande réserve, tenue; conservez votre dignité.

67 ibid., lettre 213, Chambéry, 5 juillet 1838. A quoi sert alors une Sup[érieu]re générale si une locale peut mettre en charge celle qui lui plaît, renvoyer tel sujet et dans telle maison sans savoir si la sup[érieu]re peut la
recevoir, et alors exposer ces personnes à aller de maison en maison sans but et sans raison, aucune des
sup[érieu]res n'ayant droit de les recevoir puisqu'elles arrivent sans obédience de la première autorité? […]
C'est fait […]

68 Marie-Joseph Géramb, *Voyage de La Trappe à Rome* (Paris, 1838), pp. 394–5; Guy Bedouelle, *Lacordaire, son pays, ses amis et la liberté des ordres religieux en France* (Paris, 1991), pp. 103–4. Ce sont autant de princesses, me répondit-il, et la mère abbesse est cousine du roi des Français. Savez-vous son nom, repris-je? Son nom de famille je l'ignore, mais depuis le choléra on l'a surnommée l'aumônière […]
Mon interlocuteur avait eu raison de dire qu'elle était surnommée l'aumônière, car c'est un titre que sa charité lui a mérité à Rome, où elle s'est montrée la mère d'une foule d'orphelines. Quant à sa parenté avec le roi des Français […] cette mère abbesse est simplement la bonne et respectable mère Barat.
69 Géramb, op. cit., p. 396. des nobles filles romaines […] La supérieure, madame de Causans, dirige cet établissement avec une sagesse et une bonté qui lui ont concilié l'affection de toutes les personnes qui y vivent, et l'estime de toutes celles qui la connaissent.

Notes to Chapter 14

1   Corr. SB et Eugénie de Gramont, lettre 635, Rome, 6 février 1838. Sophie did not name the family in her letter. 'une novice d'une famille distinguée de ce pays, sortie à cause de sa santé, a parlé assez mal de nous et nous fait grand tort.'
2   Adèle Lehon à SB, Rome, 24 août 1853 (GA, Rome, C–1., A, 1–F, Box R–6). Mes rapports avec la Trinité deviennent un peu plus difficiles à mesure que la Mère Faux y reprend plus autorité. Et elle en a. Sans être assistante, elle règle tout. Sans être dépensière, elle commande la cuisine et décide même ce qu'il faut donner aux malades; elle a repris le vestiaire, et c'est enfin comme avant 1838. La Mère de Causans ne pouvant présider les exercices communs, voire le pensionnat, juge souvent par les yeux de la Mère Faux. Quoiqu'en dise cette bonne Mère, je ne crois pas que le pensionnat allait mal du temps de la Mère de Coriolis, ni qu'il eut besoin de réforme […] La Mère Faux a sans doute beaucoup de qualités, mais ce n'est pas pour la dépendance et la régularité qu'elle brille.
3   Corr. SB et Eugénie de Gramont, lettre 775, Rome, 13 mai 1842. 'Les grilles, rien ne peut remplacer à leurs yeux! Ce n'est qu'en Italie, car partout ailleurs que ferait-on des grilles?'
4   Adèle Lehon à SB, Rome, 24 août 1853. Il y a maintenant à Rome une quantité de sœurs de toutes les couleurs: grises, noires, de St Joseph, de la providence, filles du Sacré-Cœur, de S. Dorothée et qui n'ont pas de clôture du tout et que l'on rencontre à toutes les cérémonies. On est très disposé à nous assimiler à elles et je crois à cause de cela, et pour éviter les reproches que nous a faites autrefois Grégoire XVI, qu'il faut ici plus encore qu'ailleurs observer la clôture.
5   Corr. SB et Louise de Limminghe, lettre 172, La Ferrandière, 17 juillet 1838.
6   ibid., lettre 157, Parme 2 juin, 1838.
7   ibid., lettre 165, Turin, 27, juin 1838.
8   ibid., lettre 173, Lyon, 21 juillet 1838. Qu'allez vous faire et quel parti prendre pour ôter ces deux [Armande de Causans et Euphrosine Faux] de la Trinité? Consultez encore les Pères. Impossible de leur donner une obédience avant qu'elles soient remplacées.
9   ibid., lettre 159, Turin, 9 juin 1838.
10 ibid., lettre 173, Lyon, 21 juillet 1838. Quelle croix et d'où je l'attendais le moins. Mais quel tort elles se font. Comment [ont-elles] l'espoir de l'emporter. Si elles se séparaient, nous n'avons qu'un mot à dire au ministère à Paris et elles seraient bientôt dehors […] A vrai dire Mère de Causans a trop d'esprit pour avoir le projet d'une séparation, que ferait-elle isolée? Je pense que cet orage se calmera moyennant qu'on les laisse tranquilles jusqu'aux obédiences, c'est encore deux mois.
11 ibid., lettre 177, La Ferrandière, 1 août 1838. Details of Josephine de Coriolis's finances are discussed by Sophie Barat in her correspondence with Thérèse Maillucheau, in Grenoble.
12 Joseph Bellotti SJ (1785–1876) had been rector of the Collegium Romanum in Rome (1832–35) and then vicar general to Jean Roothan's (1835–1842). He ministered regularly in the Trinité, from 1836–38; and in the Villa Lante, from 1842–51. Archives de la Trinité des Monts, Journal de la maison de la Trinité des Monts, 1836–38; Archivio della Provincia d'Italia. Storia di Casa, Cartolario, 1837–1860, ff. 24–83. In July 1842 Bellotti gave a copy of the 1839 Decrees of the Society of the Sacred Heart to the Italian Congregazione Figlie Maria Immacolata, suggesting it as a model for their constitutions.
13 Corr. SB et Louise de Limminghe, lettre 174, La Ferrandière, 26 juillet 1838. Il faut être juste, ces deux seules sont irrégulières par leur genre et leur santé, mais la communauté marchait lorsque j'y fus; on exagère, croyez-le.
14 ibid., lettre 175, La Ferrandière, 27 juillet 1838 […] qu'il est triste que ces petites discordances entre les deux maisons aient percé, même parmi les amis les plus intimes! Il vaudrait mieux souffrir beaucoup de choses pénibles dans le silence, elles se remettent toujours avec l'aide de Dieu et la patience. Au contraire, lorsque les cœurs sont aigris, rien ne peut guérir ces plaies, et si ces misères se découvrent, vous en savez le résultat. Faites donc tout ce qui sera en votre pouvoir pour ramener les opposants […]
15 ibid., lettre 176, La Ferrandière, 30 juillet 1838; Corr. SB à Hypolite Lavauden, lettre 34, Paris, 31 octobre 1838.

16 Corr. SB et Louise de Limminghe, lettre 177, La Ferrandière, 1 août 1838. Je me suis rappelée non le noble discours de Bonaparte, au Sénat au moment de sa décadence, mais [il est] trop juste cependant pour ne pas l'appliquer ici: Messieurs, vous me reprochez mes fautes en public, c'est imprudent [...] il faut laver son linge sale en famille etc. [...] Croyez que c'est ainsi qu'il eût fallu procéder dans cette affaire et nous l'eussions emportée sans bruit.

17 ibid., lettre 178, La Ferrandière, 4 août 1838. Quoi! Les avoir laissées dans leur peine et humiliations sans avoir été visiter, leur parler, les encourager à rappeler les Pères? Est-ce de la charité? Elles eussent été plus coupables encore, que vous deviez tout oublier et faire les premières démarches. Ah! Ce n'est pas de cette manière que vous soutiendriez mon autorité et que vous la ferez aimer. Vous connaissez cependant assez mon mode et vous devriez tendre à l'imiter. Non, jamais je ne condamnerai sans entendre et je n'admettrai les mesures violentes que l'on me propose. Vous eussiez dû vous-même ramener peu à peu à l'indulgence, et au contraire vous suivez les avis de sévérité que l'on vous donne [les jésuites]. J'en ai un vrai chagrin. Sophie said the same to Hypolite Lavauden, chiding her for deserting the Trinité 'dans le moment de leurs disgrâces'.' Also, Corr. SB à Hypolite Lavauden, lettre 30, Autun, 20 août, 1838.

18 Corr. SB et Louise de Limminghe, lettre 182, Autun, 19 août, 1838. Also, lettre 179, La Ferrandière, 9 août 1838; lettre 180, Autun, 14 août, 1838; lettre 207, Paris, 12 novembre 1838.

19 ibid., lettre 184, Autun, 27 août 1838. Conservez-vous libre et pensez à ce que je ferais ou dirais dans telle ou telle circonstance, en prenant toujours conseil, mais en vous rapprochant des miens. Ce n'est assurément pas que je les crois meilleurs, loin de là. Mais Dieu m'a promis le secours dû à ma charge, et c'est sous ce rapport que je vous dis de vous rapprocher de mes pensées et de ma manière d'agir. See also, lettre 207, Paris, 12 novembre 1838.

20 ibid., lettre 188, Paris, 8 septembre 1838.

21 ibid., lettre 189, Paris, 10 septembre 1838. C'est un coup pour nous à Rome. Fiat! [...] Ce qui m'étonne c'est le choix de l'examinateur par le P[ère] R[ozaven] [...] Quel est donc ce prêtre?

22 ibid., lettre 201, Paris, 19 octobre 1838. Vraiment il me faut de la confiance en Dieu pour ne pas craindre pour cette pauvre maison! [Trinité] [...] le cardinal Lambruschini est tout pour elle [Armande de Causans] [...] au fond il estime et aime Madame de Causans [...] je ne doute pas qu'elle ne lui ait parlé [...] [Lambruschini] n'avait pas coutume d'y aller si souvent [...]

23 ibid., lettre 209, Paris, 19 novembre 1838.

24 ibid., lettre 212, Paris, 26 novembre 1838. Si le R[évérend] P[ère] R[ozaven] n'est pas content de nous, je ne puis vous avouer ici que je le suis médiocrement de lui dans cette circonstance. Ce digne père ne se met guère à ma place, ni même comprend la position de la Trinité; au reste, je suis ma conscience et je me tranquillise. Je suis persuadée qu'en tenant au départ de Madame Armande, elle finira par partir [...] Ayant refusé de venir avec son frère, il est évident qu'elle cherche à gagner du temps [...] Je vous assure que si nos amis [jésuites] nous rendent des services, que j'apprécie certainement, ils nous causent aussi bien des ennuis par leurs exigences. Quand on n'a que deux ou trois mois à attendre pour éviter des inconvénients sans fin, et dont on ne peut prévoir les suites, on devrait bien prendre patience [...] See also Corr. SB et Louise de Limminghe, lettre 213 (2), Paris, 3 décembre 1838.

25 ibid., lettre (non-numérotée), Paris, 28 novembre 1838. Il sera donc eux [Rozaven et Bellotti] qui nous auront détruits, et cela pour n'avoir pas eu un peu plus de support et de patience. J'avoue que je ne voudrais pas avoir cette responsabilité.

26 ibid., lettre 158, Turin 8 juin 1838. Oh! Comme vous me manquez pour tout! [...] je suis si triste! L'état où je suis y contribue. Je vois le travail croissant et mes forces s'épuisent. Personne pour m'aider. C'est un moment pénible à passer. Espérons que le Seigneur me soutiendra. See also, lettre 159, Turin 9 juin 1838.

27 ibid., lettre 157, Parma, 2 juin 1838.

28 ibid., lettre 162, Turin 16 juin 1838. L'abbé a raison, je suis triste, inquiète pour le présent et pour l'avenir; cet isolement me fait mal, et cependant je prends beaucoup sur moi afin que le chagrin qui me domine ne paroisse pas au dehors!

29 Cahier, *Vie*, i, 654–6; *Vie de la Mère [Catherine] de Charbonnel, assistante et économe générale de la Société du Sacré-Cœur de Jésus* (Paris, c. 1870), pp. 219–26. Corr. SB et Louise de Limminghe, lettre 163, Turin, 20 juin 1838; lettre 164, Turin, 21 juin 1838.

30 Corr. SB et Louise de Limminghe, lettre 165, Turin, 27 juin 1838. Plus d'espoir de rencontrer notre ami commun, il est au Ciel [...] Il est vénéré comme un saint; ibid., lettre 209, Paris, 19 novembre 1838.

31 ibid., lettre 166, Turin, 28 juin 1838; lettre 167, Turin, 30 juin 1838.

32 ibid., lettre 182, Autun, 19 août 1838. Les deux purgations ont évacué beaucoup de bile et la fièvre paraît coupée sans être obligée d'employer la quinine. See also, lettre 175, La Ferrandière, 27 juillet 1830.

33 ibid., lettre 184, Autun, 27 août 1838. le sommeil est toujours pénible, rare; j'ai les nerfs de la tête et de l'estomac si souffrants. Mais ils se calmeront avec le repos de la route. C'est comme vous le savez le seul que je puisse trouver. Une fois dans nos maisons il ne faut plus l'espérer!

34 ibid., lettres 164; 169; 171; 183–6; 199; 211; 213; 220; 224, juin 1838–février 1839.

35   ibid., lettre 175, La Ferrandière, 27 juillet 1838. Mère D [...] ayant acquis pendant mon absence une telle prépondérance parmi nos anciennes que, certainement sa manière de voir et de juger aura le plus grand poids; [...] nous pouvons supposer que cette excellente mère [...] sera tout opposée aux changements.

36   ibid., lettre 207, Paris, 12 novembre 1838.

37   ibid., lettre 198, Paris, 10 octobre 1838; 199, Paris 12 octobre 1838; lettre 202, Paris, 27 octobre 1838; lettre 215, Paris, 12 décembre 1838; lettre 216, Paris, 14 décembre 1838.

38   Corr. SB et Stanislas Dusaussoy, lettre 93, Paris, 21 janvier 1838; lettre 93 (bis), Paris, 23 janvier 1839. Corr. SB et Louise de Limminghe, lettres 211, 213, 219, 221, 226 (2), novembre 1838–février 1839. Sophie had asked Prince Hohenloe many times for prayers. Alexandre–Léopold, prince de Hohenloe-Schillingsfürst (1794–1849) lived in Huttenheim in the Upper Rhine. He had a reputation for holiness and healing. He prayed for the requests which people sent him at certain, fixed times each day.

39   Corr. SB et Louise de Limminghe, lettre 200, Paris, 14 octobre 1838. Also, lettre 187, Paris, 7 septembre 1838; lettre 189, Paris, 10 septembre 1838; lettre 192, Paris, 17 septembre 1838; lettre 194, Paris, 24 septembre 1838.

40   ibid., lettre 192, Paris, 17 septembre 1838.

41   ibid., lettre 216, Paris, 14 décembre 1838.

42   ibid., lettre 163, Turin, 20 juin 1838; lettre 185, Paris, 31 août 1838.

43   *Lettres circulaires*, i, Paris, 10 décembre 1838, pp. 80–84.

44   Journal de la maison du Sacré Cœur de Jesus à Rome. Trinité du Mont (1828–45), 7 décembre 1838 (Archives de la Trinité des Monts); Trinité du Mont, Armande de Causans à Comte Latour-Maubourg, 4 décembre 1838 et 6 décembre 1838 (Archives de l'Ambassade de France près le Saint-Siège, Dossier: Religieuses du Sacré-Cœur (1838–1904).

45   Trinité du Mont, Catherine de Charbonnel à Comte Latour-Maubourg, 20 janvier 1839 (Archives de l'Ambassade de France près le Saint-Siège, Dossier: Religieuses du Sacré-Cœur (1838–1904).

46   Corr. SB et Anna du Rousier, lettre 12, Paris, 5 décembre 1838. Also, lettre 14, 24 décembre 1838; lettre 16, Paris, 7 janvier 1839. All the details of this case cannot be reconstructed as a vital set of letters from this period, concerning the Trinité, Armande de Causans, Josephine de Coriolis and Sophie Barat, were destroyed by Victorine Bois (1808–94) in 1864. lettres Annuelles, 1894–95, 2o partie, pp. 5–13. She lived in the Trinité for sixty two years. GA, Rome, Copia Publica Transumpti Processus apostolica auctoritate Romae constructi super virtutibus et miraculis in specie ... Magdalena Sophia Barat, Vol 11, 1897, Sessio 105, 28 Jan. 1899, f. 845–7; 14 February 1899, ff. 849–50. Sophie Barat retained good relations with the de Causans family and some members testified during the process of canonisation.

47   Corr. SB et Louise de Limminghe, lettre 224, Paris, 6 février 1839; lettre 225, Paris, 13 février 1839; lettre 226, Paris, 15 février 1839.

48   ibid., lettre 220 (bis), Paris, 18 janvier 1839.

49   ibid., lettre 221, Paris, 21 janvier 1839. Je vous envoie cette lettre [...] qui me parait modérée et vraie. Vous savez que, dès le principe, j'ai entrevu des imprudences des Pères. C'est fait, ils veulent se soutenir, c'est juste, mais le mal est grand. Voyez avec prudence comment on pourrait le réparer [...] il est évident que les P[ères] nous ont nui.

50   ibid., lettre 219, Paris, 31 décembre 1838. 'Qui donc est à la tête de la Congrégation?' Also lettre 222, Paris, 23 janvier 1839.

51   Corr. SB et Stanislas Dusaussoy, lettre 93, Paris, 21 janvier 1839; lettre 4, Paris, 24 janvier 1839.

52   Corr. SB et Eugénie de Gramont, lettre 652, Montet, 10 mars 1839.

53   Corr. SB et Louise de Limminghe, lettre 227, Besançon, 3 mars 1839. Ne vous faites point illusion sur le dessein des trois, c'est à Rome qu'elles resteront et c'est la Visitation où elles essayeront de nous supplanter. Puis elles iront faire une fondation dans un autre quartier. Ceci je le suppose avec raison. Donc il importe de les prévenir, soit en obtenant qu'elles n'entrent pas à Rome à la Visitation, au moins Mme de Coriolis, et que l'on ne permette pas un pensionnat. Si ces conditions ne sont point obtenues, croyez qu'il est inutile que nous restions à Rome. Ce seront des ennuis éternels, à cause de l'émulation, des intrigues, etc. nous n'aurons pas alors jamais un moment de paix. Also, Corr. SB et Elizabeth Galitzine, lettre 104, Besançon, 3 mars 1839.

54   Corr. SB et Elizabeth Galitzine, lettre 105, Besançon, 5 mars 1839; lettre 107, Montet, 10 mars 1839; lettre 109, Montet, 13 mars 1839.

55   Corr. SB et Eugénie de Gramont, lettre 654, Turin, 7 avril 1839.

56   Corr. SB et Louise de Limminghe, lettre 221, Paris, 21 janvier 1839; Corr. SB et Eugénie de Gramont, lettre 654, Turin, 7 avril 1839; lettre 655, Rome, 23 avril 1839.

57   Corr. SB et Eugénie de Gramont, lettre 657, Rome, 30 avril 1839. Je vous dirai peu de choses sur l'affaire d'Ar[mande]; son cousin vous aura mise au courant, mais tenez-vous en garde contre les préventions, il faut un bouc émissaire, et c'est celle que vous nommez. Et moi, qui suis sur les lieux et qui entends les deux parties, je ne puis encore voir le fond. Tous deux sont blancs comme neige. Ce qui me paraît le plus clair, sont les abus de confiance, des secrets redits, et ceci vient du dehors. Le plus évident est une opération du démon pour nous nuire et qui dure encore. Dans ce pays il faut plus de prudence et de réserve qu'ailleurs pour se maintenir, et certainement on en a manqué. Ce qui est certain c'est la sortie d'Ar[mande] et tout ce qui a

suivi ou précédé, nous fait un tort réel et qui ne pourra se réparer entièrement [...] Ah! Si l'on eût eu un peu de prudence, tout se serait calmé aisément! Dieu l'a permis pour me faire souffrir. Je vous assure que ce voyage et mon séjour à Rome me sont pénibles sous tous les rapports. Néanmoins je ne le regrette pas, puisqu'il était dans l'ordre de la Providence. See also, lettre 656, Rome, 27 avril 1839.

58   Corr. SB et Eugénie de Gramont, lettre 659, Rome, 11 mai 1839; lettre 660, Rome, 21 mai 1839; lettre 664, Rome, 13 juin 1839; lettre 665, Rome, 15 juin 1839.

59   Corr. SB et Stanislas Dusaussoy, lettre 95, Rome, 21 juin 1839; lettre 96, Rome, 29 juin 1839; lettre 97, Rome, 2 juillet 1839; lettre 98, Rome, 2 juillet (bis) 1839.

60   Corr. SB et Eugénie de Gramont, 660, Rome, 21 mai 1839. Je compte bien dans les déclarations ou explications des constitutions, faire insérer une clause à ce sujet, car de cette manière, toutes celles qui auraient une imagination ou une tentation de sortir, sous un prétexte ou sous [un] autre, pourraient ainsi disparaître sans que la sup[érieu]re g[énéra]le n'en sut rien! Il n'y a donc plus de contrat, ni de lien. Le bon Dieu a permis cet incident fâcheux, sans doute pour nous éclairer [...] C'est fait, espérons que notre Seigneur en fera tirer un bien [...]

61   Archbishop de Quelen's stance towards the government of Louis Philippe was considered inexcusable and the Ambassador in Rome was asked to register a complaint with the pope. Dépêches du Département, 1839–41. Ministère des Affaires Etrangères, no. 10, 1 février 1839 (Archives de l'Ambassade de France près le Saint-Siège, Dossier: Religieuses du Sacré-Cœur (1838–1904).

62   Denis Affre à Archbishop de Quelen, Paris, 9 janvier 1839 (Archives de l'Archevêché de Paris, Papiers de Quelen, I D IV 10, 19 d). Limouzin-Lamothe, *Monseigneur de Quelen*, ii, 231. Monseigneur, Je me jette à vos pieds pour vous conjurer, dans l'intérêt de votre diocèse, dans votre propre intérêt et dans celui des communautés religieuses, de prendre un logement ailleurs que dans ces maisons. Croyez, [...] que le dévouement le plus sincère a pu seul m'engager à vous écrire ceci. Vous ne pouvez, d'ailleurs douter qu'un tel avis ne soit dicté par un sentiment parfaitement désintéressé. Si je n'étais assuré qu'il est partagé par les personnes les plus dévouées à votre gloire, les plus chrétiennes, les plus à même juger de l'opinion de la première classe de la société et de la bourgeoisie, j'aurais gardé le silence.

63   Corr. SB et Louise de Limminghe, lettre 224, Paris, 6 février 1839. La Société comme les gouvernements est à la veille d'une crise, je le sens, puisse-t-elle la supporter, la surmonter et en sortir plus pure et plus solide!

64   Corr. SB à Aloysia Hardey, lettre 6, Rome, 9 janvier 1838. tout doit se faire en s'entendant et dans un esprit de concorde et d'union, comme il existe en France où nos mères ne font qu'un pour l'avantage de la Société et la gloire de Jésus.

65   SB à Eugénie de Gramont, Rome, 26 mai, 1839 (A.F. Poitiers, A–4, Constitutions, Conseil de 1839). *Lettres circulaires*, ii, Aux Mères Conseillères, Rome, 2 mai 1839, pp. 71–75; Aux Mères Conseillères empêcher de se rendre au Conseil, Rome, 16 mai 1839, pp. 76–78. Je viens vous prier de m'envoyer du moins par écrit votre adhésion aux décrets de ce conseil, qui devra nécessairement être décisif pour la Société, en l'établissant sur des bases vraiment solides.

66   [Elizabeth Galitzine], Histoire secrète de la Société du Sacré Cœur depuis 1839 jusqu'à juillet 1840 (GA, Rome, C–I, c–3, Box 2, 1839, ff. 2–4).

67   Articles relatifs au gouvernement de la Société du Sacré Cœur de Jésus, pour lesquels nous demandons humblement le consentement et la bénédiction de sa Sainteté. Histoire secrète de la Société ff. 4–6. This point was argued by Elizabeth Galitzine when the decrees of the 1839 council were questioned.

68   Histoire secrète de la Société (new pagination in manuscript), ff. 2–4. Décrets du Conseil Général du religieuses du Sacré Cœur de Jésus. Tenu à Rome en juin 1839.

69   Histoire secrète de la Société, ff. 2–3.

70   *Lettres circulaires*, ii, Rome, 13 juillet 1839, pp. 78–87.

71   For 1839 Decrees and results of the voting, GA, Rome, C–I, C–3, Box 3 1839; Box 4 1839; Box 6 1839. Rome (Trinité, Sainte Rufine, Villa Lante); Piedmont, vice-Province (Turin, Pignerol, Chambéry, Parme); Switzerland, vice-province (Montet, Besançon, Metz, Colmar, Munich [projected]); Belgium, vice-province (Jette, Lille, Charleville); France, northern province (rue de Varenne, rue Monsieur, Conflans, Beauvais, Amiens, Autun, Le Mans); province of Midi (Lyon, La Ferrandière, Annonay, Avignon, Aix, Marseille, Toulouse, Perpignan); province of the west (Poitiers, Niort, Tours, Nantes, Quimper, Bordeaux); America (St Michael's, Grand Coteau, St Louis, St Ferdinand, St Charles). All but two of the provincials were named immediately, Eugénie de Gramont (France, northern province), Marie Prevost (France, province of Midi), Catherine de Charbonnel (France, western province), Henriette Coppens, (Switzerland, vice-provincial), Eulalie Gonthyn (Belgium, vice-provincial). Provincials had yet to be appointed for Rome and for America.

Notes to Chapter 15

1   Corr. SB et Eugénie de Gramont, lettre 653, Chambéry, 3 avril 1839; lettre 660, Rome, 21 mai 1839.

2   ibid., lettre 669, Rome, 22 juin 1839.

3   Corr. SB et Emilie Giraud, lettre 120, Rome, 16 mai 1839.

4   Corr. SB et Aimée d'Avenas, lettre 5, Rome, 30 juillet 1839. Je me suis attendue à votre réflexion sur nos nom-
    inations. Il est certain que notre Eugénie ne pouvait se mesurer avec celle qui lui a été préférée et quoiqu'il
    ne lui ait manqué que peu de voix, mon cœur a été blessé. J'ai essayé en vain de détruire les préventions dans
    quelques-unes de nos mères; un seul grief que vous connaissez n'a pu s'effacer, les suites, les dîners, en
    Province on augmente, ces mariages que l'on a mis sur son compte, tout cela a indisposé [...] Combien j'ai
    eu d'humiliations ici a ce sujet [...] See also, Corr. SB et Henriette Grosier, lettre 134, Rome, 8 juillet 1839.
5   Corr. SB et Eugénie de Gramont, lettre 671, Rome 4 juillet 1839.
6   Histoire secrète de la Société, ff. 7–8.
7   ibid., ff. 8–10.
8   Corr. SB et Eugénie de Gramont, lettre 677, Rome, 25 juillet 1839. Vous êtes toute ma ressource pour la
    France, le bon Dieu me laisse si pauvre en sujets! C'est pour cela qu'il n'a point permis que vous fussiez
    assistante générale pour le moment; toutes savaient que vous seriez plus utile à la Société au poste que vous
    allez occuper. Néanmoins, il vous a manqué peu de voix, mais les présentes l'ont emporté, cela devait être.
9   ibid., lettre 681, Rome, 17 août 1839.
10 ibid., lettre 671, Rome, 4 juillet 1839; lettre 683, 6 septembre 1839.
11 ibid., lettre 681, Rome, 17 août 1839. Le changement des supérieures fixées devenait nécessaire. Plusieurs
    commençaient à bien s'ancrer dans chaque maison et a en devenir les abbesses. Une mesure générale ne
    blessera personne.
    Je finirai par une courte réflexion. Si ces changements, ou plutôt améliorations étaient à faire, il importait de
    ne pas attendre ma mort. Ils eussent été impossibles à cette époque, peut-être. Puis, dès que nous avons cru
    devoir nous approprier le gouvernement des J[ésuites] pourquoi le tronquer? Eux-mêmes nous l'ont reproché,
    que nous avions tort de nous vanter de leur ressembler, quand nous avions si peu de ressemblance avec eux
    pour nos constitutions et notre plan de gouvernement.
    C'est assez de cette petite justification, je conçois votre répugnance [...] See also, Corr. SB et Aimée d'Avenas,
    lettre 6, Rome, 28 août 1839. Sophie pointed out that Armande de Causans's twelve-year mandate at the
    Trinité had created serious problems.
12 Eugénie de Gramont à SB, Paris, 28 août 1839, Histoire secrète de la Société, ff. 15–16.
13 Aimée d'Avenas à SB, Paris, [n.d. c. août] 1839. Histoire secrète de la Société, ff. 16–17. Votre conseil a imité
    l'assemblée de 1789: en quelques jours il a jeté l'édifice à bas; mais quand on détruit ce qui était sacré aux
    yeux de tous on s'expose à voir à son tour détruire son propre ouvrage.
14 De Charry (ed.), *Varin Lettres*, lettre 108, Paris, 19 août 1839, pp. 327–28, n. 4–5, pp. 332–3. Ce conseil général,
    établi par la Société uniquement pour veiller à l'intégrité et à l'application de ses Constitutions, Constitutions
    approuvées par le Souverain Pontife [...] les ait lui-même renversées de fond en comble, et immédiatement
    après ait prononcé sa propre dissolution et se soit anéanti à jamais.
    [...] Je sais ce qu'on a pu dire à ce sujet, j'entends les plaintes formées contre elles [les sœurs coadjutrices].
    Mais si elles ont donné parfois des sujets de mécontentent, à qui la faute? Ah! Si on leur eût fait faire à toutes
    un bon noviciat, si on se fût fait un devoir de bien les instruire de leur religion et de les former à l'esprit de
    la Société, comme le demandaient les Constitutions, on n'eût eu qu'à se louer de leur bonne conduite.
    Dans les premières constitutions il était dit - et c'était l'article le plus fondamental - que la Société n'était for-
    mée uniquement que pour les intérêts et la gloire du Sacré-Cœur, que c'était là sa première et unique fin, et
    que tout le reste qui regardait, soit le salut et la perfection des membres, soit la sanctification du prochain, ne
    devait être considéré que comme les moyens pour procurer la fin, c'est à dire, la gloire du Sacré-Cœur.
15 De Charry (ed.), *Varin Lettres*, lettre 109, Paris, 24 août 1839, pp. 335–6. C'est celle que nous avons vu naître,
    il y a 39 ans et qui vous reçut pour la première dans son humble berceau, et dont avec la grâce du Seigneur,
    vous avez procuré le développement d'une manière si admirable [...] Demandez aux Pères [Jésuites] de
    Rome ce que la Société de Jésus penserait d'une Congrégation générale qui aurait changé et anéanti les points
    fondamentaux de la Société.... et dans quel moment détruit-on la première Société? C'est dans le moment
    de sa plus grande prospérité [...]
16 Corr. SB et Louise de Limminghe, lettre 233 (bis), Rome, 7 septembre 1839. At this time Sophie was in the
    Trinité and Louise de Limminghe in the Villa Lante. Priez beaucoup Notre Dame des Sept Douleurs, la
    Société est bien secouée. Nous avons agi en tout imprudemment, il fallait aller plus doucement et cacher nos
    projets. C'est fait, mais que d'ennuis je vais recueillir! Si je souffre seule, ce ne sera rien, mais [...]
17 Corr. SB et Eulalie de Bouchaud, lettre 39, Rome, 17 août 1839.
18 Corr. SB et Eulalie de Bouchaud, lettre 43, Rome, 6 septembre 1839. Quels pauvres raisonnements ce bon
    Père m'adresse. J'espère qu'il se calmera. Le temps fera voir que tout sera pour le mieux. Soyez donc [...]
    ferme comme un roc et soutenez-nous. Mais si vous devez être simple comme la colombe, il vous faut aussi
    la prudence du serpent.
19 From July 1839 Sophie held council meetings consisting of the assistants general and the secretary general.
    Rozaven was often present. For an account of these meetings, [Elizabeth Galitzine] Conseils particuliers,
    avec les assistants [générales], 7 juillet–8 juin 1840 (GA, Rome, C–I., C–3, Box 3, 1839).

20 Elizabeth Galitzine à Joseph Varin, Rome, 16 septembre 1839, Histoire secrète de la Société, ff. 20–24. Also, Copie d'une réponse au P[ère] V[arin]. Pour les seules supérieures, Rome, 14 septembre 1839 (GA, Rome, C–I., c–3, Box 3).

21 Elizabeth Galitzine à Joseph Varin, Rome, 16 septembre 1839. Les sœurs coadjutrices ne seront plus admises à la Profession, c'est vrai, mais combien cette mesure n'était-elle pas nécessaire, […] et pourquoi ne nous serait-il pas permis d'adopter ce qui a été si sagement arrêté chez vous, où les frères ne sont point admis à la Profession; ni sont-ils moins Religieux pour cela. Mais au moins quand on se trouve dans la triste nécessité de les renvoyer, on n'a pas, quand elles ne sont pas liées par le vœu de Stabilité, la douleur de devoir recourir au Chef de l'église, comme c'est déjà arrivé

22 Corr. SB et Eulalie de Bouchaud, lettre 42, Rome, 5 septembre 1839. On a eu tort de dire aux sœurs si promptement ce qui les concernait. C'était particulièrement pour les nouvelles. Les anciennes et celles dont on est content, pouvaient espérer leur profession. Mais si elles sont acceptées ne revenez pas sur ce qui est décidé. Enfin ce sont les mêmes vœux et devant Dieu il n'y a pas de différence. Chez les Jésuites c'est la même chose pour leurs frères et tous sont heureux et contents. J'espère donc que cet article ne fera aucune difficulté, pas plus que les autres; au moins elles seront tenues, ce qui sera un grand moyen.

23 Corr. SB et Louise de Limminghe, lettre 234, Rome, 16 septembre 1839. Also, lettres 235; 236; 237, Rome septembre 1839.

24 This happened in the Jesuits also. Reynier, La Correspondance de P.J. de Clorivière avec T. Brzozowski, pp. 114–19.

25 De Charry (ed.), *Varin Lettres*, note 4, pp. 331–2.

26 Corr. SB et Eugénie de Gramont, lettre 684, 20 10 septembre 1839. C'est mal à vous de me le rappeler et de vous en servir contre moi, surtout si ces mêmes rachètent ces défauts involontaires par de grandes et solides vertus.

27 Paris, 12 septembre 1839. Histoire secrète de la Société, ff. 25–9.

28 Souvenirs de Sœur Virginie Roux, ff. 81, 104–14, 118–21 (General Archives, Rome. A–II., 1–a, Box 1).

29 Corr. SB et Aimée d'Avenas, lettre 11, Rome 16 novembre 1839. […]jamais je ne contesterai ce que vous avancez, votre caractère, celui de petite mère, est connu pour être vrais, droits et pour aller votre chemin en ligne directe. Dussiez-vous heurter à droite et à gauche ceux qui gêneraient votre marche; mais en disant la vérité on ne peut pas dire toute la vérité et ce n'est point manquer de droiture.

30 Corr. SB et Eugénie de Gramont, lettre 686, Rome, 19 septembre 1839; lettre 687, Rome, 29 septembre 1839; lettre 688, Rome, 5 octobre 1839.

31 Corr. SB et Eulalie de Bouchaud, lettre 45, Rome, 5 octobre 1839. Je reçois votre lettre […] et je vous en remercie, car je ne puis dans ce moment être trop au courant de ce que vous apprendrez de vos voisines dont décidément l'opposition se manifeste appuyée par Mgr [de Quelen] […] C'est donc une secousse qui va s'élever, mais dont le divin Cœur nous délivrera. Écoutez tout, parlez peu et écrivez-moi tout ce que vous apprendrez: voilà votre tâche […] Si cet incendie s'étend, il sera peut-être nécessaire que je vous arrive; n'en dites pas mot […] Madame de Gramont va se mettre dans une voie dont elle pourra bien se repentir puisqu'elle peut nous faire du mal. Ce n'est point son intention, mais une fois les esprits divisés, qui pourrait les arrêter? See also, lettre 44, Rome, 23 septembre 1839; lettre 48, Rome, 22 octobre 1839.

32 Elizabeth Galitzine à Eugénie de Gramont, lettre, Rome, 18 septembre 1839. Histoire Secrète de la Société, ff. 30–34. Also, Réponse au mémoire contre le Conseil général de 1839, adressé à la Mère Générale, par quelques membres d'une seule maison, dont voici les propositions (GA, Rome, C–I., c–3, Box 3 1839).

33 Réflexions sur l'état de la Société du Sacré Cœur. Réclamations à adresser à la mère générale et au S[aint]e Père, par la maison de Tours. Histoire Secrète de la Société, ff. 34–8.

34 Histoire Secrète de la Société, ff. 35–6. [Qui aurait] jamais ordonné à un Dominicain de se faire Carme? à un Jésuite de se faire Capucin? Le pape […] n'imposerait pas d'autorité, de force, sans possibilité de réclamation, une adhésion à des Décrets qu'un petit nombre de conseillères, forge, approuve et déclare d'obligation pour toutes[…]. On veut notre perfection, et l'on nous propose, ou plutôt on nous enjoint d'imiter celles des Jésuites. Nous ne contestons par celle-ci, mais chaque chose a sa perfection propre, chaque Ordre son esprit. Les femmes et la France ne sont pas des hommes et l'Italie.
La plupart de vos établissements sont en France. C'est de France que vous viennent les sujets les plus nombreux, et surtout les plus propres à alimenter vos maisons. Vous êtes française, vous connaissez presque toutes vos filles. En cette position transférer le siège de l'établissement, c'est vraiment une mesure inouïe. Le centre de la Chrétienté n'est pas le centre physique de votre œuvre, ni même son centre moral.

35 Césaire Mathieu à SB, 14 septembre 1839, Histoire Secrète de la Société, ff. 38–41. Plus de vœux solennels pour les Sœurs coadjutrices. Ah! Quel retranchement pour ces pauvres filles, parmi lesquelles se trouvent tant de saintes et qui sont en général si bonnes! Quoi faut-il que dans la Société du Sacré-Cœur de Jésus si humble, il y ait de si énorme différence entre les Mères et les Sœurs […]
Je crains bien […] qu'on n'ait été dirigé en cela par un désir peu mûr de ressembler tout aux Jésuites, sans considérer assez les différences essentielles qui doivent exister entre un ordre d'hommes et une communauté

de femmes […] N'y a-t-il donc pas eu un véritable ami, un bon conseil pour vous faire ces observations si simples et pour détourner le conseil d'aller unanimement s'enfourner dans de pareille fondrière?

Plus des vœux solennels pour les Sœurs coadjutrices. Ah! Quel retranchement pour ses pauvres filles, parmi lesquelles se trouvent tant de saintes et qui sont en général si bonnes! Quoi faut-il que dans la Société du Sacré Cœur de Jésus si humble, il y ait de si énorme différence entre les Mères et les Sœurs …

Je crains bien … qu'on n'ait été dirigé en cela par un désir peu mûr de ressembler tout aux Jésuites, sans considérer assez les différences essentielles qui doivent exister entre un ordre d'hommes et une communauté de femmes … N'y a-t-il donc pas eu un véritablement ami, un bon conseil pour vous faire ces observations si simple et pour détourner le Conseil d'aller unanimement s'enfourner dans de pareille fondrière?'

36   Histoire Secrète de la Société, ff. 42–9.
37   Corr. SB et Henriette Grosier, lettre 137, Rome, 30 août 1839; lettre 138, Rome, 14 septembre 1839. Also, lettre 139, Rome, 28 septembre 1839; lettre 140, Rome, 8 0ctobre 1839.
38   Jean Baptiste de Bouillé à SB, Poitiers, 24 septembre 1839.
39   Histoire Secrète de la Société, ff. 47–48.
40   Corr. SB et Henriette Grosier, lettre 142, Rome, 18 octobre 1839. 'Que va donc devenir la Société si chacune s'insère dans le gouvernement, et si chaque particulière se croit en droit de réclamer contre toutes les opérations de la sup[érieu]re gén[éra]le? C'est à renoncer au poste, qui pourrait y tenir?' Also, lettre 143, Rome, 9 novembre 1839; lettre 144, Rome, 14 novembre 1839.
41   ibid., lettre 146, Rome, 18 décembre 1839. Que va donc devenir la Société si chacune s'insère dans le gouvernement, et si chaque particulière se croit en droit de réclamer contre toutes les opérations de la sup[érieu]re gén[éra]le? C'est à renoncer au poste, qui pourrait y tenir?

Toutes ces difficultés élevées pour le changement des supérieures, lorsque j'en ai le droit incontestable? J'avoue qu'il devient très difficile de gouverner une Société où l'on se trouve des entraves à chaque pas. See lettres 163, Paris, 29 août 1839; lettre 164, Paris, 12 septembre 1839, in which Sophie recognises and accepts that Henriette Grosier felt embarrassed by the way her change of house had been reversed in 1839.
42   Histoire Secrète de la Société, ff. 51–55.
43   Jean Rozaven à SB, Rome, [octobre] 1839. Histoire Secrète de la Société, f. 49. 'Vous dictes que vous avez voulu adopter purement et simplement nos constitutions en tout ce qui pouvait s'adapter à votre Société. Je n'en approuve pas cette déclaration.'
44   Leroy, *Le mythe jésuite*, pp. 192–4.
45   Jean Rozaven à SB, Rome, 7 octobre 1839. Histoire Secrète de la Société, ff. 50–51. J'ai malheureusement de trop bonnes raisons […] et je me vois contraint de refuser. Vous n'imputerez sûrement pas ce refus à un défaut d'intérêt pour votre Société, Dieu sait à quel point je m'y intéresse, mais pour vous être utile, cet intérêt même exige que je ne le manifeste pas [que] indirectement.
46   Corr. SB et Elizabeth Galitzine, lettre 129, Rome, 30 septembre 1839. La raison pour laquelle je ne vous ai rien dit […] de la peine que vous m'avez faite, c'est précisément parce que vous ne vous en êtes pas aperçue. Vous eussiez pensé, comme vous le croyez sans doute encore, que vous aviez droit de me traiter comme vous l'avez fait. Peut-être ma susceptibilité aurait pu me tromper, mais nos Mères m'en ont témoigné leur vif chagrin, surtout une qui est partie avec le cœur bien malade de vos procédés.

Néanmoins, je n'exige aucune excuse, elles seraient inutiles dans votre cas, puisque n'ayant fait aucune faute, et c'est vrai pour vous! A la première occasion, vous en ferez de même. J'espère donc ne plus vous la fournir. C'est à moi maintenant à prendre mes précautions.
47   Corr. SB et Louise de Limminghe, lettre 238 (bis), Rome, 30 septembre 1839.
48   Corr. SB et Henriette Grosier, lettre 147, Rome, 31 décembre 1839.
49   Corr. SB et Louise de Limminghe, lettre 239, Rome, 2 octobre 1839. Nos affaires tournent mal, j'en suis au regret de n'avoir pas suivi mon sentiment, ou plutôt les lumières dues à mon Poste, et qui me font connaître ce que les autres ne peuvent apercevoir. Prions plus que jamais, nous en avons besoin. Also, lettre 242, Rome, 12 novembre 1839.
50   Histoire Secrète de la Société, ff. 51–54.
51   De Charry (ed.), *Varin Lettres*, lettre 110, Paris, 9 novembre 1839, pp. 342–3. On n'y reconnaît ni votre esprit, ni votre style, et un de nos plus graves Pères ajoutait: on voit bien que celle qui écrit ne connaît pas l'Institut des J[ésuites][…]. Oh! Si vous eussiez supprimé cette lettre si inconsidérée, et que vous vous fussiez reposée sur les explications de vive voix que devait, si peu de temps après, me donner la Mère Prevost […] dans les explications qu'elle m'a données et dans la communication de ce qui à trait à votre dernière lettre, je vous ai retrouvée telle que je vous connaissais, et j'ai répété plusieurs fois: Voila, dans l'état actuel des choses, des mesures pleines de douceur et de sagesse.
52   Histoire Secrète de la Société, ff. 57–65.
53   Corr. SB et Eulalie de Bouchaud, lettre 162, Rome, 25 janvier 1842. Il [Joseph Varin] nous gêne et nous entrave bien […] comme vous l'avez vu par ce que vous m'avez rapporté de sa conversation avec M[adame] de G[ramont] […] que faire? Mettre notre confiance en Dieu et espérer le secours de Lui seul! […] je vous assure notre abandon de toute part est grand […]

54 Aimée d'Avenas à SB, Paris, 30 octobre 1839, Histoire Secrète de la Société, ff. 58–60. On veut que la petite mère se charge de tout l'odieux des réclamations, et garde avec vous l'air confit et sucré en obéissance[…]. Nous avons épanché devant vous notre cœur selon notre conscience et nous les exhortions à faire de même sans nous mêler de leurs affaires. Si la charité de la petite mère et aussi la prudence ne s'y opposaient pas, je vous enverrais d'autres copies où vous verriez de drôles de choses de la part de vos brebis, qui s'affectent de nous appeler devant vous dissidentes. Le mot dissidentes veut dire qui se sépare: or de quoi nous séparons-nous? Nous restons attachées à la vieille roche […] Toutes sont blessées de votre silence à leur égard et c'est ce qui fait que la plupart au lieu de s'adresser à vous […] écrivent au Saint Père ou parlent en public […]. La petite mère s'afflige de peine à son sujet, mais elle vous a tout annoncé et vous n'avez voulu la croire en rien. Vous l'avez toujours aimée, me charge-t-elle de vous dire, mais vous avez toujours préféré l'avis des autres au sien, et moi j'ajoute que vous ne l'avez guère soutenue dans tout ce qu'elle a souffert au milieu de la Société.

55 Corr. SB et Eulalie de Bouchaud, lettre 55, Rome, 21 novembre 1839.

56 Corr. SB et Eugénie de Gramont, lettre 692, Rome, 24 décembre 1839; Histoire Secrète de la Société, ff. 66–7; Eugénie de Gramont à SB, [Paris] 17 février 1840 (GA, Rome, C–IV., 4, Box 3, Paris (Closed Houses).

57 Marie Prevost à SB, Paris, 4 novembre 1839. Histoire Secrète de la Société, ff. 68–9. Ce qui plus que jamais prouve qu'elle est Héli de S. François d'Assise; mais ce saint *tout en le couvrant du manteau de sa charité*, n'a jamais déféré à son sentiment pour abolir ou même affaiblir ce que *les Assemblées G[énéra]les* avaient réglé. Ce pauvre Héli cherchait à se faire des partisans contre son Père St François d'Assise pour détruire ce qu'il édifiait à grand frais. Mais le Seigneur était là pour réprimer l'arrogance de celui qui voulait supplanter son Père et son maître. Francis of Assisi (1181–1226) founded the Franciscan order. During Francis's lifetime he appointed his close friend, Brother Elias, to succeed him as leader of the order. This appointment proved an unfortunate choice; Brother Elias moved away from the spirit of Francis and was eventually excommunicated.

58 Marie Prevost à SB, Histoire Secrète de la Société, f. 69. On cherche à vous effrayer […] comme l'on effrayait Charles X, et c'est celle qui se serait volontiers mise à votre place il y a 25 ans qui travaille de tout son pouvoir à faire croire et à prouver que vous ne nous gouvernez que par elle. Elle se permet même de supprimer vos lettres.

59 Histoire Secrète de la Société, ff. 69, 74.

60 Marie de la Croix à SB, Lille, 20 novembre 1839, Histoire Secrète de la Société, ff. 74–5. Quand je me rappelle les premiers efforts de l'Enfer pour nous séparer de celle que Dieu nous a donnée pour Chef et pour Mère, je voudrais les pleurer avec des larmes de sang. Hélas! ces nouveaux troubles en sont un fait malheureux. C'est un reste du vieux vin qui fermente. Exemple funeste qu'il faut dérober autant que possible à la connaissance de nos membres […]
Notre Société […] n'est plus à son berceau. Elle renferme maintenant dans son sein des âmes mûries et dévouées qui en sont les remparts […] le temps n'est plus où la défection de quelques sujets […] pouvait occasionner la ruine, et notre Mère générale n'a point à craindre ce qui l'a fait si cruellement souffrir, appréhender et gémir en 1815.

61 Marie Prevost à SB, Paris, 25 novembre 1839. Histoire Secrète de la Société, ff. 76–7.

62 Marie Prevost à SB, Paris, 25 novembre 1839. Histoire Secrète de la Société, f. 77.Il est furieux de votre trop grande bonté. La Mère de Gramont a donné connaissance de ce que vous lui dites de particulier, ainsi par exemple, que vous aviez fait tout ce que vous aviez pu pour l'influencer afin qu'elle soit assistante générale; une conseillère a dit aussi à ce père que vous lui aviez dit à Rome, que vous ne voyez dans toute la Société que la Mère de Gramont capable de gouverner la Société. Vous comprenez […] que des communications de ce genre dans un moment comme celui-ci font tirer de tristes conséquences […] Puis il ajoute: " Que votre Mère générale se rappelle de ce je lui ai dit si souvent, que soutenir celle qui trahissait la Société, c'est travailler soi-même à la détruire " […]. je lui ai dit que votre intention était de tenir ferme à l'essai de décrets […] " Je le croirai lorsque je le verrai ", m'a dit-il.

63 Clement Boulanger à Jean Roothan, 27 octobre 1839 (ARSI, Rome, Monialium negotia. Dames du Sacré-Cœur. Graves difficultates … 1839–1843, Monial 1–f.v. Ka). Clement Boulanger became Jesuit provincial in Paris in 1842.

64 Jean Rozaven à Achille Guidée, Rome, 9 novembre 1839. J'ai la conscience tranquille et ne m'inquiète guère de ce que l'on peut dire. Que m'importe qu'une extravagante dise que j'ai gagné la M[ère] générale et quelques autres, et que j'ai imposé ce que j'ai voulu? Je rirais de cette folie […] l'ennemi de tout bien tâche d'allumer le feu de la discorde dans une Société religieuse dont l'église peut attendre de grands fruits. See also, E. Solente à Jean Roothan, 12 janvier 1840, Dames du Sacré-Cœur. Graves difficultates … 1839–1843, M. (Francia, 6–xi, 23).

65 Achille Guidée à Jean Roothan, 30 octobre 1839. Dames du Sacré-Cœur. Graves difficultates … 1839–1843, Monial 1–f.v.I. (ARSI, Francia 1005–I, 34) Vous aurez fait donc justice de la sotte imagination de Mme XXX [Elizabeth Galitzine] qui prête à P[ère] Rozaven[aven] l'intention de placer un Jésuite dans chacune des maisons du Sacré-Cœur comme supérieur et confesseur. Vous savez jusqu'à quel point cette bonne Dame est féconde à créer des chimères, mais celle-ci est vraiment trop forte et dépasse les limites du ridicule et de l'absurde.

66 Jean Roothan à Achille Guidée, Rome, 5 novembre 1839. Dames du Sacré-Cœur. Graves difficultates ... 1839–1843, Monial 1–f.v. H (ARSI, Registrarium Provinciae Franciae, Tom. II, 27 juillet 1836–26 novembre 1842, f. 149). [...] J'ai su depuis des années que les germes de division existant parmi ces D[ames], qu'avec le mode de gouvernement établie cette division semblait devoir nécessairement se perpétuer et porter enfin des suites déplorables, au moins, c'est là ce qui se disait [...] que c'est pour cela que la Mère générale, d'après le conseil de plusieurs de ses conseillères, pensa devoir tenir une congrégation [conseil général] [...]

67 Jean Brumauld de Beauregard to Jean Roothan, Poitiers, 30 novembre 1839 (ARSI, Dames du Sacré-Cœur. Graves difficultates ... 1839–1843, Monial 1–v, 17. L).

68 Corr. SB et Eulalie de Bouchaud, [Rome, 9 novembre 1839].

69 Laure de Portes à SB, Amiens, 17 décembre 1839. Histoire Secrète de la Société, ff. 79–80. Le choix de petite mère pour provinciale les a tous étonnés, entre autres le P. Sellier, qui dit qu'elle donnera son esprit aux maisons de sa Province, et qu'elle n'a pas celui de la Société. Tout cela est à cause de ses rapports avec l'Archevêque, dont depuis longtemps on s'entretient dans les salons de Paris [...]

70 Corr. SB et Henriette Grosier, lettre 144, Rome, 14 novembre 1839. Non [...] ma santé est loin d'être bonne; vous ne me connaîtriez pas à ce trait. J'ai perdu le sommeil et l'appétit depuis le conseil, sans pouvoir recouvrer ni l'un ni l'autre, et je ne puis digérer le peu que je prends. Il faut me coucher après tous mes repas, à l'exception du déjeuner. Le médecin avant hier fut effrayé de ma faiblesse. La vie que je mène ne peut produire d'autre effet. Il est inutile d'en parler à l'extérieur. Heureusement cet état ne m'empêche pas d'ailleurs de travailler comme de coutume. Quand j'aurai tout épuisé ce sera la fin. Corr. SB et Elizabeth Galitzine, lettre 137, Rome, 9 décembre 1839. Sophie suffered from toothache at this time.

71 Corr. SB et Henriette Grosier, lettre 147, Rome, 31 décembre 1839. Sans doute [...] j'ai forcé mon style, ce genre ne m'est point ordinaire. Mais pouvais-je [...] ne point témoigner d'amertume de tous les ennuis dont plusieurs m'abreuvent depuis des mois? Ce n'est pas assez de m'adresser des impertinences; est-ce joli de les faire passer par la rue de Varenne en les chargeant de me les adresser sans les nommer, et, dans ce même temps, les mêmes m'écrivent des lettres de soumission. Aussi, on me les désigne sous le nom de "chien-couchant", c'est le mot [...] je n'ai pu vous en soupçonner; c'est trop éloigné de votre caractère et de votre manière d'être avec moi. Mais convenez que ces procédés ne sont point faits pour me donner un style doux et indulgent.

72 Corr. SB et Louise de Limminghe, lettre 246, Rome, 10 décembre 1839. Il faut tant en passer à la faiblesse humaine! Je le reconnais à tout moment! Ce qui m'incline à cette indulgence est ma propre misère; il en faut tant pour me supporter.

Notes to Chapter 16

1 *Lettres circulaires*, ii, Rome, 19 novembre 1839, pp. 109–10. [le] bon esprit maintenu jusqu'ici [...] cette union si étroite, si intime, qui a constamment allégé le poids de ma sollicitude, fait ma force et mon soutien au milieu des innombrables contradictions élevées contre la Société dès son berceau; les plus grands obstacles venaient se briser contre ce mur d'airain, ce rempart inexpugnable de la divine charité. Je ne puis me le dissimuler, elle a été malheureusement entamée à l'occasion des Décrets.

2 *Lettres circulaires*, ii, Rome, 19 novembre 1839, pp. 115–16. J'ai à observer de plus pour l'article des vœux de nos sœurs coadjutrices, qu'il est nécessaire de leur faire comprendre que comme dans l'Institut [jésuite], dont nous avons adopté depuis longtemps les Constitutions, elles passeront au grade de coadjutrices formées au bout de 10 ans; elles seront donc aussi sûres de demeurer dans la Société quand elles parviendront à ce grade, que si elles faisaient le vœu de stabilité, puisque les vices ou les défauts qui engageraient à les délier des vœux simples, détermineraient également à les faire relever du vœu de stabilité, lequel, par le fait, n'ajoute rien à leur mérite. Les vœux simples étant perpétuels, elles sont, suivant les bulles des Souverains Pontifes, aussi parfaitement religieuses que les professes même des vœux solennels. Que nos bonnes sœurs se rassurent donc, la mesure prise à leur égard n'est pas à leur détriment; nous savons apprécier leur dévouement et leur attachement à la Société, et elles peuvent compter pleinement sur l'affection de leurs premières Mères qui ne souffrira point d'altération.

3 This had resonances with vows and grades of membership within the Jesuits. John W. O'Malley, *The First Jesuits* (Harvard, 1994), pp. 6, 60–2, 345–56. These were considered important when the Jesuits were restored in France after the Revolution. Reynier, La Correspondance de P.J. de Clorivière à T. Brzozowski, p. 90.

4 *Lettres circulaires*, ii, Rome, 19 novembre 1839, Pour les supérieures seules, pp. 117–18.

5 Eugénie de Gramont à SB, [Paris] 30 octobre 1839 (GA, Rome, C–IV, 4, Box 3, Paris (Closed Houses). J'ai encore été obligée d'être longtemps sans vous écrire [...] emportée par une multitude d'affaires dont je ne suis pas la maîtresse de diminuer le nombre. Mes journées s'envolent, le temps aussi, et heureusement la fin de la vie aussi. J'avoue qu'il n'y a plus que cela de doux, et la pensée que bientôt tout ennui cessera est la seule capable de faire prendre patience en attendant le ciel [...] mais aujourd'hui je n'ai pas le temps de vous parler de cela. J'ai mille détails à vous dire sur quelques maisons et plusieurs sujets à placer et replacer, qui me prendront tout le temps dont je puis disposer aujourd'hui pour écrire.

6 Eugénie de Gramont à SB, Paris, 12 décembre 1839 (GA, Rome, C–IV., 4, Box 3, Paris) (Closed Houses).

7 Corr. SB et Eugénie de Gramont, lettre 695, Rome, 9 janvier 1840. C'est un Saint de plus dans le ciel et un Protecteur pour nous. Malgré cette assurance autant qu'on peut l'avoir, nous prions et faisons prier dans toutes nos maisons […] Quelle perte pour le troupeau […] mais que votre cœur doit souffrir […]

8 Corr. SB et Eulalie de Bouchaud, lettre 64, Rome, 23 janvier 1840. Avez-vous entendu parler d'un événement que l'on dit être arrivé à Paris en même temps que la mort de votre digne prélat? On n'a pas su nous l'expliquer, croyant que nous le savions comme tout le monde. On écrit de Munich ces mots: "Tout le monde parle ici de l'anecdote rapportée dans trois lettres de Paris de *la dame habillée en noir, et du conducteur de la diligence* […]" See also, lettre 65, Rome, 28 janvier 1839.

9 Corr. SB et Elizabeth Galitzine, lettre 139, Rome, 2 janvier 1840; Journal de Ste Rufine, 31 January 1840 (GA, Rome, C–IV, Santa Rufina, Box 2).

10 Eugénie de Gramont à SB, Paris, 17 février 1840 (GA, Rome, C–IV, 4, Box 3, Paris (Closed Houses); Histoire Secrète, f. 82; Archives de l'Archevêché de Paris, Papiers de Quelen, I D IV 9, no. 46, a, b. Elisa Croft (1792–1879) was a member of the community at the rue de Varenne.

11 Eugénie de Gramont à SB, Paris, 12 janvier 1840 et Paris 3 février 1840, Histoire Secrète, ff. 80–2.

12 Eugénie de Gramont à SB, Paris, 24 février 1840, Histoire Secrète, f. 86. Je conçois […] que mes lettres vous fassent de la peine, elles m'en font à vous écrire, cependant il me serait impossible de ne pas vous dire tout ce que je pense […] tout ce qu'on vous écrit sont des conjectures [peu] charitables et des suppositions qu'on fait sur moi […]

13 Corr. SB et Eulalie de Bouchaud, lettre 68, Rome, 18 février 1840. Dites-lui de ma part que l'aumônerie du Sacré-Cœur de la rue de Varenne, donnée à Monsieur Jammes, serait entièrement contre mes intentions, même quand il ne logerait point au Petit-Hôtel […] J'ai assez souffert du séjour de Mgr [de Quelen] et il y aurait encore plus d'inconvénient pour un autre que pour Monseigneur […] Insistez sur mes douleurs de ce qui s'est passé au Sacré-Cœur et je veux y mettre fin. For the significance of Jammes and his presence in the Petit-Hôtel, especially towards the end of Archbishop de Quelen's life, L'Ami de la religion, v.104, mardi 7 janvier 1840, pp. 32–6.

14 SB à Mr Morel, Rome, février 1840, Histoire Secrète, ff. 87–89. For details of this case. AF, Poitiers, Paris, B06, 151, ii, Evêché.

15 Eulalie de Bouchaud à SB, Paris, 2 mars 1840. Histoire Secrète, ff. 89–90. que Madame de Gramont est une femme très habile, qui n'a aucune espèce d'abandon surtout avec lui […] qu'il ne la connaissait que parce qu'il la voyait habituellement papillonner chez Monseigneur [de Quelen] […] dans cette maison il ne fallait parler des vertus de l'archevêque qu'avec un enthousiasme, une admiration ridicule […] Une seule l'étonnait […] c'est que vous ne vouliussiez pas dire ouvertement à la Mère de Gramont vos griefs contre Monsieur Jammes puisque vous êtes parfaitement en droit de le faire […]

16 Eulalie de Bouchaud à SB, Paris, 3 mars 1840; Mr Morel à SB, Paris, 4 avril 1840; Eulalie de Bouchaud à SB, Paris, 28 mars 1840. Histoire Secrète, ff. 90–91; 94–97.

17 Corr. SB et Eulalie de Bouchaud, lettre 83, Rome, 12 mai 1840. Si j'étais sur les lieux je ne craindrais rien; je m'installerais rue de Varenne et qui pourrait alors m'empêcher d'agir? Mais sans soutien, si loin, il faut procéder avec prudence; au moins c'est l'avis de ceux que j'ai pu consulter. Donc voyez avec nos deux amis [Jean-Nicolas Loriquet et Louis Barat] si nous pouvons attendre encore sans agir, ou si le mal exige que l'on procède à quelques démarches, dont pourtant je prévois le non succès.

18 ibid., lettres 87, 90, 97, 99, 102, Rome, juin–septembre 1840.

19 ibid., lettre 83, Rome, 12 mai 1840.

20 Histoire Secrète, ff. 92–6.

21 ibid., ff. 98–9. Je ne connais pas assez les circonstances pour en juger. Je vous laisse parfaitement libre. Si vous croyez devoir attendre à cause des circonstances politiques de la France, vous le pouvez certainement […] Consultez le cardinal Lambruschini. Il connaît la France, la situation des affaires. Il pourra vous mieux conseiller par rapport à votre départ […] Assurément le Saint Siège vous protégera toujours, à cause du bien que fait votre ordre pour l'éducation de la jeunesse.

22 Corr. SB et Eugénie de Gramont, lettre 699, Paris, 22 février 1840. See also in Corr. SB et Eulalie de Bouchaud, lettres 60, 64, 70, 71, 72, 75, 81, Rome, décembre 1839–avril 1840.

23 Corr. SB et Eugénie de Gramont, lettre 700, Rome, 27 février 1840. Il était ainsi autrefois avec ma rate, pourquoi une seule circonstance est-elle venue interrompre, un moment j'espère, cette douce harmonie […] qui nous a soutenues tant d'années, au milieu des croix les plus pesantes. Lorsqu'on les porte de concert, on en sent à peine le poids! Je vous demande dans ce moment de ne plus tarder la pratique des décrets. J'espère que vous me répondrez enfin que vous vous êtes rendue à mes justes désirs!

24 Corr. SB et Eugénie de Gramont, lettres 700–705, février–avril 1840.

25 Bibliothèque de la Compagnie de Saint-Sulpice, Paris. Fonds Frayssinous, Communautés Religieuses, Sacré-Cœur, Cuiginières/Beauvais 1815–1828.

26 Corr. SB et Eugénie de Gramont, lettre 706, Rome, 2 mai 1840. Cette bonne Mère d'Olivier n'appuie pas ses officières, elle n'a aucune tenue, tout va comme chacune l'entend. Vous verrez dans votre visite les remèdes

à apporter. Also, lettre 707, Rome, 14 mai 1840; Eugénie de Gramont à SB, [Paris, 18 avril 1840] (GA, Rome, C–IV., Box 3, Paris (Closed Houses)).

27   Eugénie de Gramont à SB, [Paris] 4 mai [1840]. GA, Rome, C–IV., Box 3, Paris (Closed Houses). J'arrive de Beauvais […] et je reviens fatiguée, enrhumée, mal à mon aise […] J'y ai été souffrante tout le temps que j'y ai été, ce qui ne m'a pas empêchée d'y travailler beaucoup. D'abord je me suis occupée de la maison que j'ai trouvée en si mauvais état qu'un coup de vent, un orage, une grande ondée peut l'entraîner et la renverser et par conséquent écraser tout ce qui est dessous […] cela m'effraya à un tel point que je ne pus fermer l'œil la première nuit. La Mère d'Olivier n'avait aucune inquiétude et elle riait de la mienne […] L'architecte […] dit que c'est très grave et croit qu'il faudra reconstruire tout ce bâtiment. Le maire[…] sait que la bourse de la ville est vide, veut me persuader qu'un simple raccommodage suffira. Mais il se fait illusion, quand on mettra le marteau là-dedans tout tombera […] si la dépense passe 7 à 8 mille francs, la ville ne voudra pas la faire. Elle laissera ce bâtiment en dégradation, nous demandera de le faire à nos frais […] La ville aimerait beaucoup […]nous vendre cette partie du terrain qui deviendrait alors notre propriété et sur laquelle nous bâtirons à notre volonté […] Si nous quittons cette maison, la ville ne nous en donnera rien que le prix brut des matériaux […] Veuillez donner une décision et nous dire de quelle manière vous voulez que cette affaire se fasse.

28   Corr. SB et Eugénie de Gramont, lettre 708, Rome, 19 mai 1840. Nous verrons à la fin de l'année par qui nous pourrions remplacer Madame d'Olivier. Entre nous, je ne la crois plus en état d'être supérieure; elle est tellement absorbée dans ses compositions, pourtant si médiocres. Impossible de l'en tirer, puis, comme vous le remarquez fort bien, elle veut tout gouverner et ne laisse aucune latitude; impossible qu'une maison marche ainsi dirigée. Voyez donc à traiter cette réparation de cette toiture; vous pourriez envoyer Madame de Lemps avec nos instructions.

29   Eugénie de Gramont à SB, [Paris] 13 mai 1840] GA, Rome, C–I., c–3, Box 7. Les Français qui reviennent [de Rome] ne sont guère contents de l'esprit de Rome, des romains, des cardinaux, du cardinal Lambruschini. Ils sont vendus à [Louis] Philippe qui les trompe tant qu'il peut.

30   SB à Archbishop Affre, Rome, juin 1840; Mémoire présentée à Mgr Affre, Archevêque de Paris. Histoire Secrète, ff. 100–104; Mémoire de la supérieure générale de la Société [du Sacré Cœur] à Mgr l'archevêque nommé de Paris, GA, Rome, C–I., c–3, Box 7.

31   Histoire Secrète, f. 105; Elizabeth Galitzine à Archbishop Affre, [Paris, juillet 1840]; GA, Rome, C–I., C–3, Box 7.

32   Limouzin-Lamothe, *Monseigneur de Quelen*, ii, 231.

33   Bathilde Sallion à SB, Paris, 19 août 1840. (GA, Rome. C–VII, 2, Box S). J'ai appris […] par mes rapports avec les personnes du monde qu'on parle beaucoup dans le public de l'opposition qui règne entre Madame de Gramont et le nouvel archevêque. On dit que Madame de Gramont donne le ton à tout le faubourg Saint-Germain et qu'on fait un honneur de penser comme elle. Le jour de l'Assomption il y a encore eu un dîner assez nombreux au Petit-Hôtel. Il y avait Monsieur Morel, Jammes, Molinier, Surat et le jeune prince Galitzine. Madame de Kersabie qui suit l'abbé Morel comme un petit chien, assista à tout le dîner. On envoya chercher Madame d'Avenas (qui n'aime pas y aller) elle y alla néanmoins. See also, Bathilde Sallion à SB, Paris, 5 septembre 1840.

34   Boudon, *L'épiscopat français*, p. 335.

35   Bathilde Sallion à SB, Paris, 27 août 1840. General Archives, Rome. C–VII, 2, Box S.

36   Bathilde Sallion à SB, Paris, [octobre] 1840. General Archives, Rome. C–VII, 2, Box S.

37   Corr. SB et Louise de Limminghe, lettre 264, Besançon, 24 septembre 1840. Monsieur Jammes est remercié déjà par Mgr de Paris, on m'attend pour le reste! […] dans quelle position je vais me trouver dans ce pays, sous tous les rapports. Mais Jésus, n'est-il pas partout! et pourquoi craindre? Ma santé se soutient, c'est une vraie protection, car je ne dors presque pas, et certes! ce ne sera pas à Paris que le sommeil reviendra. Mais encore une fois, ayons confiance, nous ne serons pas tentés au-dessus de nos forces. Dieu ne veille-t-il pas sur ses élus.

38   Corr. SB et Eugénie de Gramont, lettre 718, Chambéry, 14 septembre 1840. Non, vous ne pouvez vous faire qu'une faible idée de l'effet qu'a produit le renvoi de Monsieur Jammes! Le faubourg Saint-Germain ne peut le pardonner ni à Monseigneur [Affre] ni à moi. Vous comprenez que j'en prends facilement mon parti; plus tard, on dira que nous avons bien fait, car les hommes tournent à tout vent. Dans tous les cas, c'est comme ils voudront, il y a longtemps que j'ai fait le sacrifice de ma réputation! See also, lettre 717, Turin, 9 septembre 1840.

39   Corr. SB et Elizabeth Galitzine, lettre 151, Paris, 1 octobre 1840. 'Je vois, j'écoute, je prie et fais prier'. See also, Corr. SB et Louise de Limminghe, lettre 269, Paris, 25 octobre 1840.

40   Corr. SB et Louise de Limminghe, lettre 267, Paris, 13 octobre 1840. Also lettre 268, Paris, 22 0ctobre 1840.

41   ibid., lettre 272, Paris, 18 novembre 1840. 'Non, vous ne pouvez vous faire qu'une faible idée de l'effet qu'a produit le renvoi de Mr Jammes! Le faubourg Saint-Germain ne peut le pardonner ni à Monseigneur [Affre] ni à moi. Vous comprenez que j'en prends facilement mon parti; plus tard on dira que nous avons bien fait, car les hommes tournent à tout vent. Dans tous les cas, c'est comme ils voudront, il y a longtemps que j'ai fait le sacrifice de ma réputation!'

42 Adèle Lehon, *Récit historique des événements de 1839–1843*, ff. 10–11 (GA, Rome, C–I., C–3, Box 2 1839); Corr. SB et Eugénie Audé, lettre 193, Paris, 30 septembre 1840).

43 Avis de la petite servante de toute la Société à sa chère mère et fille Madame Elizabeth Galitzine, nommé visitatrice de la Louisiane en juin 1840, Rome, 16 juin 1840. (GA, Rome, C–I., A, 1–F, Box XVII). Gardez-vous de laisser paraître de l'inégalité ou de l'impatience; ces défauts gâteraient tout: les Américains sont de tous les peuples de l'univers avec les Japonais ceux qui gardent le plus de sang froid dans les événements contraires. Ils seront donc très étonnés de trouver des personnes consacrées à Dieu moins parfaites que des séculiers et même des hérétiques […]

44 Avis de la petite servante de toute la Société à sa chère mère et fille Madame Elizabeth Galitzine, nos. 8 and 15.

45 Avis de la petite servante de toute la Société à sa chère mère et fille Madame Elizabeth Galitzine. Souvenirs pour la route, nos. 2 and 3. A la rue de Varenne soyez sur vos gardes pour les questions […] Soyez aussi très discrète avec les pères jésuites surtout pour ce qui concerne nos rapports ici avec leurs frères. Tout est répété, on écrit à leur général et ordinairement avec peu d'exactitude. Vous pourrez dire un peu plus à mon frère, il est discret […]

Je ne sais que vous dire au sujet de l'ex[cellent] Père Varin. Témoignez-lui de la confiance, du regret du passé pour ce qui l'a froissé; dites-lui que j'arrive. Il sera consolé et vous motiverez le retard sur un échauffement de poitrine dont il faut profiter puisque je l'ai dans ce moment.

46 Lettres des notre mère générale à la communauté [27 juin 1840], (Society of the Sacred Heart National Archives, U.S.A., Series I., A–c, Generalates, Madeleine Sophie Barat, 1779–1865). La Société du Sacré-Cœur de Jésus, déjà si prospère en Louisiane, va acquérir plus de solidité et de perfection par la pratique des décrets, c'est ce que nous avons en vue en les ajoutant aux Constitutions.

47 Eugénie Audé à Aloysia Hardey, Rome, 39 novembre 1839. (Society of the Sacred Heart National Archives, U.S.A., Series II., A–Pre–IPB. History, Box 1).

48 Corr. SB et Aloysia Hardey, lettre 12, Rome, 14 mai 1840.

49 ibid., lettre 13, Rome 20 juin 1840. Je me réjouis de la consolation que vous aurez à la voir et je suis assurée que vous lui accorderez bientôt votre entière confiance et votre attachement qu'elle mérite à tant de titres. Tout ce que vous prodiguerez de soins, d'industries pour l'aider, partager ses travaux, les adoucir, sera fait à moi-même, car s'il m'eût été permis de vous visiter, elle n'eût été que mon aide et ma compagne […] ce ne sera pas contre la perfection de l'obéissance d'instruire votre mère visitatrice des usages du pays, des inconvénients que pourrait avoir telle ou telle mesure, règle, usage, etc. […] [elle] profitera de vos lumières et de vos remarques […]

50 Corr. SB et Elizabeth Galitzine, lettre 152, 20 octobre 1840.

51 ibid., lettre 156, Paris, 7 décembre 1840. Et vous vous rappelez certainement mes défenses à ce sujet? Je n'ai donc pas pu comprendre votre manière d'opérer en Louisiane […] Voyez avec vos conseillères ce qu'il y a faire pour réparer cette communication intempestive dans la haute Louisiane […]

52 ibid., lettre 155, Paris, 3 décembre, 1840.

53 Elizabeth Galitzine à Eugénie de Gramont, Rome, 18 juillet 1839 (Society of the Sacred Heart National Archives, U.S.A., Collection Marie Louise Martinez).

54 Elizabeth Galitzine à Eugénie de Gramont, Rome, 18 juillet 1839. La chose est arrêtée; nous ne pouvons rien dire car nous ne sommes pas consultées, mais si cette mésaventure a lieu, je compte sur vous pour en écrire à [Sophie] comme vous en pensez. Ce que vous lui dites lui fait plus d'impression que ce que disent les autres.

55 Corr. SB et Henriette Grosier, lettre 152, Rome, 11 juin 1840.

56 Corr. SB et Louise de Limminghe, lettre 268, Paris 22 octobre 1840; lettre 273, Paris, 23 novembre 1840.

57 Corr. SB et Henriette Grosier, lettre 154, Paris 1 octobre 1840. Quel travail m'attend! je vous en parlerai plus tard […] priez que Jésus m'aide; sans aide le travail est bien fort, car jusqu'à présent je n'ai pu remplacer mon active secrétaire, qui faisait, je puis l'assurer, du travail pour quatre.

58 ibid., lettre 156, Paris, 10 novembre 1840.

59 Corr. SB et Eugénie Audé, lettre 195, Paris, 21 octobre 1840. Je vais demain rue de Varenne. J'aurai un travail considérable et pénible. Le bon Dieu me rend des forces et la facilité du travail. Mais […] comme il eût été facile d'éviter tout ce qui s'est passé! Toutes me disent: Ah! Si vous étiez venue vous-même apporter ces décrets. Personne n'eut songé à réclamer. Madame de Gramont me le dit l'autre jour et quelles suites funestes on eût empêché […] C'est fait […] pourrai-je guérir? Je ne sais […] Also, lettre 196, Paris, 22 octobre 1840; lettre 198, Paris, 31 octobre 1840.

60 Corr. SB et Eugénie Audé, lettre 200, Paris, 12 novembre 1840. lost 'la même intimité qu'autrefois au moins pour certains sujets'.

61 ibid., lettre 198, Paris, 31 octobre 1840. 'je passe … pour une imprudente'.

62 Cahier, *Vie*, ii, 17.

63 Corr. SB et Eugénie Audé, lettre 209, Paris, 13 mars 1841. Ma convalescence marche mais lentement. Le sommeil et l'appétit ne reviennent guère et la faiblesse est grande encore. Puis comment se refaire avec tant d'ennuis, d'amertumes? […] vous devriez faire l'impossible pour tâcher de découvrir les maisons qui se sont

unies à la rue de Varenne pour se séparer! [...] Je soupçonne le Mans, Autun, Beauvais et les seules supérieures pour ces deux dernières.

Notes to Chapter 17

1 Corr. SB et Louise de Limminghe, lettre 274, Paris, 30 novembre 1840. mon âme se trouvera seule dans ce monde [...] Vous comprendrez certainement toute l'étendue de ce mot. Si vous saviez ma position, comme celles, sur qui j'aurais dû compter et m'appuyer, l'aggravent et me crucifient! Vous en seriez étonnée, si je vous le disais [...] ces détails ne peuvent se confier au papier [...]

2 Corr. SB et Eugénie Audé, lettre 210, Paris, 16 mars 1841; lettre 211, Paris, 25 mars 1841.

3 ibid., lettre 212, Paris, 30 mars 1841; lettre 213, Paris, 2 avril 1841. [Adèle Cahier] Notes sur Madame Olivier (AF, Poitiers, B05/117 Beauvais); Jeanne de Charry, Dossier: Affaires des maisons, Beauvais, nos. 6–7 (GA, Rome H–I, 6, Box 1) Bishop Cotteret was succeeded in Beauvais in December 1842 by Joseph Gignoux (1842–78).

4 Eugénie de Gramont à SB, [mars/avril 1841] (AF, Poitiers, B05/117, Beauvais). La conversation a été tout le temps aimable, gaie, originale; il a raconté des histoires à mourir de rire. Jamais il n'avait été si charmant. Il consent à tout; ne tient même pas beaucoup au pensionnat second. La M[ère] d'Ol[ivier] l'avait persuadé que le 1er [pensionnat] ne pouvait se soutenir que par le second. Je lui ai prouvé le contraire. Il m'a chargé pour vous des choses les plus gracieuses.

5 Corr. SB et Eugénie Audé, lettre 213, Paris, 2 avril 1841. Il importe de faire comprendre à sa Sainteté [Grégoire XVI] que si nous sommes livrées au caprice des uns et des autres, il me sera impossible de gouverner [...] Mgr de Beauvais n'a qu'une médiocre considération parmi ses confrères. Un d'eux me disait un jour pour des affaires étrangères à celles-ci: 'Ah! Mgr de Beauvais, sa tête chante!' [...] Ceci n'est que pour vous comme de raison.

6 Corr. SB et Eugénie Audé, lettre 219, Paris, 5 juin 1841; lettre 220, Paris, 11 juin 1841; lettre 223, Lille 28 juin 1841; lettre 225, Jette, 8 juillet 1841; lettre 229, Paris, 23 août 1841.

7 ibid., lettre 214, Paris, 5 avril 1841. 1° parce que les évêques, la plupart, ne veulent point une supérieure générale à Rome; et 2° qu'ils désirent que l'un d'eux soit le supérieur général. Donc ayant la plus grande partie de l'épiscopat pour adversaire, il ne nous restera que peu de maisons fidèles [...] Je sais encore que même les maisons fidèles recèlent quelques sujets qui n'attendent que l'occasion pour se séparer et se joindre aux autres. See also, lettre 215, Paris, 6 avril 1841.'

8 ibid., lettre 219, Paris, 5 juin 1841. La Mère de Gramont s'est parfaitement conduite dans cette affaire, elle m'a été un grand secours. Tout a plié devant elle à Beauvais, et je suis sûre qu'elle a agi franchement. Jamais cette mère n'a parlé contre sa pensée. C'est l'antipode de son caractère et elle m'a tout à fait soutenue dans cette occasion.

9 *Mémorial catholique, février 1868, Une vénérable religieuse* [Marie d'Olivier], pp. 71–74; Papiers Hypolite Martin sj (AF, Poitiers, Beauvais, B05/117, Box 2). Marie d'Olivier published several works in the course of her life: *Les Trois Paulines* (Lille, 1834); *L'Imagination ou Charlotte de Drelincourt* (Lille, 1858); *Dialogues des vivants au XIXe siècle* (Paris, 1859); *Lettres aux jeunes femmes du monde élégant* (Avignon, 1866). Marie d'Olivier tried to found another community at Saignes (Cantal), which she called religieuses du Sacré-Cœur de Marie. This project did not succeed.

10 AF, Poitiers, Beauvais, B05/117, Box 2; Corr. SB et Eugénie de Gramont, lettre 726, Paris, 2 juin 1841; lettre 727, Paris, 9 juin 1841.

11 Roy Porter, *The Greatest Benefit to Mankind. A medical history of humanity from antiquity to the present* (London, 1997), pp. 313–14.

12 Corr. SB et Eugénie Audé, lettre 216, Paris, 23 mai 1841; lettre 217, Paris, 26 mai 1841; lettre 221, Paris, 15 juin 1841. Corr. SB et Eulalie de Bouchaud, lettre 109, Amiens, 20 juin 1841; Corr. SB et Louise de Limminghe, lettre 282, Paris 22 mai 1841; Corr. SB et Anna du Rousier, lettre 41, Lille, 2 juillet 1841.

13 Corr. SB et Eugénie de Gramont, lettre 737, Jette, 21 juillet 1841; Corr. SB et Adèle Lehon, lettre 49, Jette, 17 juillet 1841; Corr. SB et Eulalie de Bouchaud, lettres 112, 114, 120, 121, 123, 127, juin–juillet 1841.

14 Corr. SB et Stanislas Dusaussoy, lettre 104, Jette, 15 juillet 1841.

15 Corr. SB et Eugénie de Gramont, lettre 731, Amiens, 25 juin 1841.

16 Corr. SB et Eugénie Audé, lettre 218, Paris, 29 mai, 1841.

17 Corr. SB et Elizabeth Galitzine, lettre 161, Jette, 16 juillet 1841. 'Je ne puis aller plus vite que le bon Dieu ne le veut!'

18 ibid., lettre 160, Lille, 1 juillet 1841. Je suis accablée de travail, encore souffrante, je ne me remets pas. Je n'ai point de secrétaire; sous ce rapport, on ne me témoigne guère de regret et on me laisse m'en tirer comme je peux plutôt que de se gêner. Tout cela ne me fait rien. J'irai tant que je pourrai. Je ne désire qu'atteindre le conseil général et une fois les affaires arrangées, je n'aurai plus qu'à me préparer à la mort qui approche, je crois. Notre Seigneur ne me laissera que pour terminer ma mission [...]

19 Corr. SB et Louise de Limminghe, lettre 263, La Ferrandière, 18 septembre 1840; lettre 266, Paris, 7 octobre 1840; lettre 273, Paris, 23 novembre 1840; lettre 286, Lille, 28 juin 1841. Corr. SB et Henriette Grosier, lettre 156, Paris, 10 octobre 1840.

20 *Lettres circulaires*, i, Paris, 16 juin 1841, 84–95.

21 *Lettres circulaires*, i, Paris, 16 juin 1841, 95; Corr. SB et Phillipine Duchesne, lettre 325, Paris, 23 août 1841.

22 *Lettres circulaires*, ii, Second partie de la lettre de Paris, 16 juin 1841. Pour les supérieures, leur conseil et celles des professes à qui les supérieures trouveront à propos de les communiquer, 120–25

23 Corr. SB et Henriette Grosier, lettre 163, Paris, 20 août 1841. Je ne sais pourquoi [...] la circulaire vous a fait de la peine. Les abus indiqués avec tant de ménagements ne vous avaient pas pour objet. Mais plusieurs de nos religieuses hélas! éparses dans toutes les provinces et qui sont loin d'être de vraies religieuses [...] Une fois pour toutes, chère mère et amie, ne pensez plus à ce qui a pu nous peiner un moment; si nous eussions été à portée de nous voir alors, combien d'ennuis mutuels eussent été adoucis par une explication de vive voix!

24 Corr. SB et Eugénie de Gramont, lettre 729 (Paris, rue Monsieur, 13 juin 1841).

25 ibid., lettre 730, Amiens 20 juin [1841]. Mais il est inutile de vous le dire, ce que vous voulez, vous le voulez. N'est-ce pas, chère Eugénie, lorsque je vous verrai convertie sous ce rapport, vraiment je vous croirai une sainte. Hâtez-vous donc!

26 ibid., lettre 734, Jette, 5 juillet 1841. Croyez que je suis trop heureuse lorsque je puis m'accorder avec vous, et je le ferai toujours lorsque les motifs que vous m'exposerez seront raisonnables [...] Vous saurez plus tard, je l'espère, tout ce qu'il m'en a coûté de vous contrarier et tout le zèle et l'affection que j'ai employés à vous justifier et vous excuser devant plusieurs. Je me borne à ce seul motif, laissant à notre Seigneur le moment où il lui plaira de vous rapprocher tout à fait de celle qui n'a pas changé pour vous, croyez-le!28 - Depuis longtemps on soupirait après le retour de la supérieure générale, dans la conviction que sa présence seule pourrait apporter le remède au mal dont tout gémissait. Voilà à peu près dix mois qu'elle est de retour, et jusqu'ici tout le zèle dont elle est animée a été paralysé par la maladie et des rechutes qui l'ont singulièrement affaibli [...] du reste, très peu secondée par ses assistantes dont quelques-unes sont éloignées pour remplir diverses fonctions; d'autres sont affaiblies par l'âge et les infirmités. Mais ce qui le navrait de douleur était la perte d'un certain nombre de sujets les plus distingués et dans la force de l'âge [...] par la mort [...] et d'un autre côté [...] les vocations sont arrêtées [...] Je ne parle pas de la perte des fonds considérables mis en réserve, soit pour les nouvelles fondations, soit pour aider les maisons qui peuvent être dans le besoin, pertes occasionnés soit par les banqueroutes, soit par l'injustice [...] Mme Barat m'a dit et me répéta ces paroles: A mon retour [de Belgique] j'aurai besoin de vous parler [...]

27 ibid., lettre 737, Jette, 21 juillet 1841.

28 Joseph Varin à Jean Roothan, Paris, 2 août 1841. (ARSI, Monialium negotia. Dames du Sacré-Cœur. Graves difficultates ... 1839–1843, Monial 1–f.v, 18). 'depuis longtemps on soupirait après le retour de la supérieure générale, dans la conviction que sa présence seule pourrait apporter le remède au mal dont tout gémissait. Voilà à peu-près dix mois qu'elle est de retour, et jusqu'ici tout le zèle dont elle est animée a été paralysé par la maladie et des rechutes qui l'ont singulièrement affaiblie ... du reste très peu secondée par ses assistantes dont quelques unes sont éloignées pour remplir diverses fonctions; d'autres sont affaiblies par l'âge et les infirmités. Mais ce qui le navrait de douleur était la perte d'une certain nombre de sujets les plus distingués et dans la force de l'âge ... par la morte ... et d'un autre côté ... les vocations sont arrêts ... Je ne parle pas de la perte des fonds considérables mis en réserve, soit pour les nouvelles fondations, soit pour aider les maisons qui peuvent être dans le besoin, pertes occasionnés soit par les banqueroutes, soit par l'injustice ... Mde Barat m'a dit et me répéta ces paroles: A mon retour [de Belgique] j'aurai besoin de vous parler ...'

29 Jean Roothan à Joseph Varin, Rome, 17 août 1841. (ARSI, Reg. Franc. Tom II, f. 255).

30 Corr. SB et Eulalie de Bouchaud, lettre 162, Rome, 25 janvier 1842.

31 Eugénie de Gramont à Adèle Lehon, Paris, 1 juillet [1841] (GA, Rome A 6, Box R. lettres reçues par Madeleine Sophie Barat). Vous voilà sans notre Mère générale, vous la regrettez sûrement beaucoup, mais vous l'avez assez longtemps, c'est notre tour de la posséder. Depuis près de deux ans nous en sommes privées.

32 Corr. SB et Stanislas Dusaussoy, [Paris] 26 août, 1841. Sophie told Stanislas again that she could not understand why Zoé wanted to marry. Lettre 104, Jette, 15 juillet 1841.

33 ibid., lettre 107, Autun, 20 septembre 1841. Vous aurez eu sans doute [...] de mes nouvelles de Joigny, qui peut-être vous auront inquiété. J'y suis arrivée en effet très souffrante. Quelques heures de repos m'ont soulagée et depuis je suis mieux [...] J'ai trouvé la famille bien; votre mère heureuse du bonheur de Zoé. Le jeune homme est bien; je lui eusse désiré plus d'éducation et de bon ton; il a l'essentiel. Il faut s'en contenter puisque Zoé est contente [...] Comme je n'ai pas un moment pour écrire à Joigny, faites-moi le plaisir de me suppléer et de leur donner de mes nouvelles en leur exprimant le plaisir que j'ai eu à les embrasser. For another account of this visit to Joigny, Corr. SB et Eulalie de Bouchaud, lettre 131 Autun, 19 septembre 1841.

34 Josephine de Coriolis à Luigi Lambruschini, Trinité des Monts, 27 décembre 1842. Also 13 octobre 1842 (Archivio Segreto Vaticano, Fonds Segretario di Stato, Particolari Esteri, 1842–1844, 67, R. 284, B. 623).

35   Elizabeth Galitzine [aux communautés d'Amérique] Grand Coteau, 17 février 1841. (Society of the Sacred Heart National Archives, U.S.A. Series 1, Society as a whole. Generalates. 1. Madeleine Sophie Barat. Ms Books, No. 1, ff. 115–6). 'Plus tard je l'espère ... il nous sera donné de pratiquer à la lettre et sans restriction cette règle tracée par l'Ignace.'

36   Visite en octobre 1840 par M.E. Galitzine, Assistante Générale et Provinciale, M. Thiéfry étant supérieure. (Society of the Sacred Heart National Archives, U.S.A. Series IV, St Louis Province, City House St Louis–1, Box 1, Community. Visitation Book, 1840–1859); Mémorial de la visite de M[ère] Elizabeth Galitzine, Assistante Générale et provinciale des maisons d'Amérique. Avis particulières à Mère Cutts, nommée supérieure de la maison de Grand Coteau, le 8 février 1841 (Society of the Sacred Heart National Archives, U.S.A, Series IV, St Louis Province, E. Grand Coteau, Box 4). Maria Cutts told Sophie Barat how vital Elizabeth Galitzine's visit had been in Grand Coteau and how she personally regretted that she could not live by the 1839 decrees immediately and hoped the general council would pass them; Notes de la Mère de Galitzine sur l'Amérique. (GA, Rome C–III., Provinces. US Early History). Visits of Mother Galitzine to the houses of North America, 1840–1843. (Society of the Sacred Heart National Archives, U.S.A, Series IV., St Louis province, K. Potawatami Mission, Journal, Sacred Heart Convent, St Mary's Kansas, Notes sur nos fondations des sauvages de Sugar Creek et St Mary's, mars 1842, no pagination). Catherine Thiéfry à SB, New York, 22 mai 1841 (GA, Rome C–IV., 4, USA East. Letters).

37   Journal of the Society of the Sacred Heart, 1818–1840, St Charles, April 12 1841 (Society of the Sacred Heart National Archives, U.S.A. Series IV, St Louis Province, M: St. Charles, Box 1), p. 76. See also, Grand Coteau, English Translation of the House Journal, 1821–1884, January 14 1841, p. 73. For the letter from the American houses, petitioning the general council to retain the 1839 decrees: GA, Rome C–I., c–3, Box 5 1839.

38   Elizabeth Galitzine à SB [n.d] (Society of the Sacred Heart National Archives, U.S.A., Series II, Interprovincial affairs, Pre IPB, A., USA, Box 1, History).

39   Corr. SB et Elizabeth Galitzine, lettre 166, Rome, 27 novembre 1841. Also, lettre 165, Rome, 23 novembre 1841; lettre 169, Rome, février 1842.

40   ibid., lettre 168, Rome, 19 janvier 1842; lettre 170, Rome, 22 février 1842.

41   Thomas Morrissey, *As one sent. Peter Kenny SJ, 1779–1841* (Dublin, 1996), pp. 283–88.

42   Journal de la retraite commencée au Grand Coteau le 13 décembre 1841, achevée le 22 décembre, f. 28 (GA, Rome C–VII., 2, Galitzine, Box 3). il m'est venu dans l'esprit que pour sauver la Société et affermir à tout jamais son gouvernement il fallait que la mère générale fît comme St Ignace un vœu particulier de dévouement au Saint-Siège, que pour cela toutes les Mères générales doivent faire vœux d'obéissance entre les mains du pape et offrir la Société à Sa Sainteté afin qu'il puisse disposer des Professes de l'Ordre pour les missions qu'il désignerait. Les Professes feraient vœu également d'être prêtes à aller partout où le Sainte Père les appellerait.

43   ibid., f.28. par la Cour de Rome [et] par cette Société de Jésus [...] elle se trouverait sous la dépendance de son gouvernement sans y être en titre [...] De cette manière tout peut s'arranger à l'aimable, la Compagnie de Jésus ne peut prendre aucun ombrage [...]

44   Grand Coteau, 29 décembre 1841; 12 janvier 1842 (GA, Rome C–VII., 2, Box 3). For a discussion on victim spirituality in the nineteenth century, see *Dictionnaire de Spiritualité*, fasc. CII–CIII, no. 16 (1992), 537–45.

45   Notes en forme de journal écrites par la ... Mère Barat de 1842–1846. Copie collationnée sur l'autographe (GA, Rome, C–VII., 2, Box 3; C–I., A, 1–F, Box XVII).

46   Notes en forme de journal, ff. 2–3. The bishops of Turin, of Pinerolo and the vicar general of Chambéry had written to support the 1839 Decrees. Antonio Garibaldi told Lambruschini that the majority of French bishops were against the Decrees (Archivio Segreto Vaticano, Rome. Fondo Segreteria di Stato Esteri, Busta 616, Rubrica 283, Fascicolo 1. Nos 17862, 16393/6, 1369).

47   Notes en forme de journal, f. 4.

48   Corr. SB et Aimée d'Avenas, lettre 38, Rome, 11 février 1842. [...] que vous avez réclamé, fait des mémoires, disputé, tout ce que vous voudrez. Ce n'est pas là ce que je blâme. Vous étiez libre de le faire, je n'ai jamais voulu imposer un joug malgré la volonté d'aucune. Vous pouviez-me tout dire, tout adresser [...] mais ce dont vous ne vous justifieriez jamais, c'est l'éclat que vous avez donné en France, à Rome etc., éclat qui a produit un mal considérable à la Société et que nous eussions pu éviter en nous entendant entre nous! J'ai les preuves de ce que j'avance [...]

49   Corr. SB et Eulalie de Bouchaud, lettre 162, Rome, 25 janvier 1842.

50   Notes en forme de journal, f. 4. Il y a du pour et du contre car la rue de V.[arennes] étant le centre depuis des années, et connue par le gouvernement et les évêques comme le chef-lieu, une intrigante qui voudrait usurper l'autorité en s'emparant de ce poste, réussirait immanquablement, ou du moins, ferait bien du mal.

51   Corr. SB et Eulalie de Bouchaud, lettre 164, Rome, 29 janvier 1842. Il n'est que trop vrai que la position du 41 [rue de Varenne] restera toujours le Poste, le centre de tout. C'est inévitable et une la supérieure générale loin de ce Poste aura toujours à appréhender [...]

52   *Lettres circulaires*, i, Rome, 21 février 1842, 96–105; *Lettres circulaires*, ii, Rome, 5 mars 1842, 125–6.

53 Notes en forme de journal, ff. 6–7. Avril [1842]; lettre de Elizabeth Galitzine aux Provinciales, St Michel, 24 janvier 1842 (GA, Rome C–I., C–3, Box 6. 1839). Le cinq, J'ai reçu la pénible nouvelle du parti que M[adame] G[alitzine] avait formé en Amérique contre moi, et ses essais en France pour entraîner nos Mères. Notre-Seigneur a inspiré à l'une d'elles, l'ange de la Société, de m'envoyer sa lettre. J'ai tout su par ce moyen. 8 Conseil à ce sujet, avec le R[everend] P[ère] Roz[aven] et nos mères, ayant besoin de lumières. Tous ont blâmé et désapprouvé la conduite imprudente de M[adame] Galitzine. Les moyens de la réparer seront d'écrire partout où elle l'aura fait; puis à elle-même, et enfin de refuser au conseil général toute espèce de paquet cacheté.

54 Corr. SB et Elizabeth Galitzine, lettre 173, Rome, 25 avril 1842. l'imprudente démarche que vous avez faite auprès des professes de votre Province, pour nous forcer, par l'autorité du conseil général à adopter votre rédaction des Constitutions! Quelle porte vous ouvrez à la révolte, et surtout chez les Américaines! Heureusement j'ai été avertie à temps pour empêcher que le reste de votre plan s'exécutât en Europe, en me hâtant d'avertir nos Provinciales de rejeter bien loin vos propositions à cet égard [...]

55 ibid., Paris, 7 septembre 1841.

56 ibid., lettre 169, Rome, 18 février 1842.

57 ibid., lettre 163, Paris, 7 septembre 1841. 'Madame de Gramont est très bien et tout ce que je puis désirer dans la position où nous sommes.'

58 ibid., lettre 173, Rome, 25 avril 1842. Votre excellente intention vous excuse devant Dieu et à mes yeux, mais tant d'autres ne seront pas si indulgents!

59 Corr. SB et Marie Prevost, [Rome, avril/mai 1842]. [Elizabeth Galitzine] est tout à fait dans l'erreur, en avançant que c'est la crainte de Mère de Gramont qui me pousse à refuser d'accepter et de présenter son travail à la congrégation. Mes motifs sont bien supérieurs et n'ont en vue, j'ose le dire, que le plus grand avantage de la Société.

60 Corr. SB et Adelaide de Rozeville, lettre 267, 5 mai 1842. 'son cœur est attaché à la Société.'

61 *Lettres circulaires*, ii, Rome, I juin 1842, 127–32.

Notes to Chapter 18

1 Corr. SB et Eugénie de Gramont, lettre 753, Rome, 6 janvier 1842. 'cette union si douce entre nous'.

2 ibid., lettre 756, Rome, 19 janvier 1842. Je ne veux certainement pas me plaindre de votre prédilection pour elle, mais je voudrais au moins que vous fussiez juste! lorsque je partis je ne pouvais réellement pas encore supporter d'émotion, et d'ailleurs pouvais-je prévoir ses attaques? [...] croyez au moins [...] que je n'en garde aucun souvenir et que celui de votre ancien attachement dominera toujours. See also, lettre 768, Rome, 7 février 1842; lettre 761, Rome, 25 février 1842.

3 ibid., lettre 758, Rome, 7 février 1842. 'j'y gagne rien que des phrases désagréables et je ne vous convaincs pas'.

4 ibid., lettre 761, Rome, 25 février 1842. il vaut mieux passer sous silence avec vous [...] tout ce qui tient à ces tristes souvenirs; peut-être plus tard il sera plus facile de nous entendre. Je le désire de toute mon âme et notre Seigneur sait que j'y travaillerai avec zèle, comme je le fais déjà à l'occasion.

5 Corr. SB et Louise de Limminghe, lettres 331–33, Rome, 15–17 avril 1842; Corr. SB et Eulalie de Bouchaud, lettre 172, Rome, 1 mars 1842; lettre 173, Rome, 9 mars 1842.

6 Corr. SB et Eulalie de Bouchaud, lettre 172, Rome, 1 mars 1842.

7 Corr. SB et Eugénie de Gramont, 758, Rome, 7 février 1842. 'un chat pour m'écrire une lettre'.

8 Corr. SB et Louise de Limminghe, lettre 324, Rome, 12 février 1842.Ah! Si j'avais pu étant enfant prévoir ma destinée, je me serais entêtée à ne rien apprendre et j'aurais été Sœur. C'est un regret inutile, je le sens. Le mieux serait de profiter de cette position pour souffrir et aimer.

9 ibid., lettre 360, Conflans, 3 janvier 1846. Vraiment [...] il faut compter sur le bon Maître avec une foi bien vive afin qu'il supplée à notre pauvreté; d'un autre côté, on nous blâme de tant entreprendre, mais si nous ne faisons pas des efforts surhumains, d'autres prennent la place, enlevant les sujets et alors nous périrons insensiblement. Voilà pourquoi j'ai accepté Bourges et Rennes [...]

10 Corr. SB et Anna du Rousier, lettre 42, Lille 29 juillet 1841. 'nous n'avons pas le talent de nous attacher le clergé'. Also, lettre 64, Rome, 3 mars 1842.

11 Corr. SB et Elizabeth Galitzine, lettre 162, Paris, 22 août 1841. Tous nos meilleurs sujets meurent, j'en ai compté dix en quelques semaines [...] précédées par autant, dans le commencement de l'année, et, à l'heure qu'il est, plus de huit sont désespérées et vont nous échapper cet hiver, toutes jeunes. Joignez à cela la rareté des postulantes. Plus une seule depuis quatre mois à Paris et aucun espoir. Vous voyez [...] qu'il faut nous arrêter, nous y sommes forcées. Je crois que vous en aurez en Amérique, maintenant que vous allez être connues. Also, Corr. SB et Louise de Limminghe, lettre 277, Paris, 8 décembre 1840.

12 Corr. SB et Elizabeth Galitzine, lettre 168, Rome, 19 janvier 1842. Ni talent, ni délicatesse, ni éducation, et le pis de tout cela, sans vocation. Si on continue, la Société se perdra: croyez qu'il vaut mieux moins de fon-

dations et plus d'esprit religieux, de solidité, de vertu. Sans cela nous manquerons notre but et nous nous perdrons [...]

13 Corr. SB et Eulalie de Bouchaud, lettre 67, Rome, 15 février 1840. Je crois [...] qu'il ne faudrait point admettre les sujets qui n'ont réellement pas ce qu'il faut pour comprendre la vie religieuse et la pratiquer. Plus tard ces âmes nuisent plutôt quelles n'aident Ah! Combien je préfère des caractères un peu difficiles mais qui ont de l'âme, de l'énergie, à ces poules mouillées dont on ne tire rien de bon! Also, lettre 137, Turin, 15 octobre 1841; lettre 149, Rome, 16 décembre 1841; lettre 169, Rome, 18 février 1842.

14 Corr. SB et Louise de Limminghe, lettre 271, Paris, 12 novembre 1840. Quelle Société eut été la nôtre dans vingt ans. Elle eut été méconnaissable. Et ce qui me tourmente c'est que je ne puis [renvoyer] tout ce qui nuit [...] Nous n'avons presque plus de novices rue Monsieur, très peu de postulantes, et cependant je le préfère au nombre qui n'est pas religieux. La source paraît tarir [...] Nos meilleures sont au Ciel. Also, lettre 272, Paris, 18 novembre 1840; lettre 273, Paris, 23 novembre 1840.

15 Corr. SB et Elizabeth Galitzine, lettre 164, Lyon, 5 octobre 1841.Si cette marche continue la Société ne se soutiendra pas longtemps. Chaque provinciale ne voit que sa Province, la supérieure locale sa maison, et la Société va si elle peut!

16 Corr. SB et Aimée d'Avenas, lettre 39, Rome, 19 février 1842. Car des deux positions offertes, celle-ci [d'Angleterre] serait plus propice que celle d'Irlande quant aux élèves. Pour les postulantes nous en aurions beaucoup plus en Irlande! aussi serait-ce un vrai coup de Providence de les enfiler toutes deux. Que petite-mère [Eugénie de Gramont] donne bien ses instructions à celle qu'elle envoie, Mère Croft, afin que ces deux poissons tombent dans les filets du Sacré-Cœur. See also lettre 36, Rome, 13 janvier 1842; lettre 37, Rome, 21 janvier 1842; lettre 38, Rome, 11 février 1842.

17 Corr. SB et Eugénie de Gramont, lettre 780, 31 mai 1842.

18 ibid., lettre 784, Lorette, 28 juin 1842.

19 Notes en forme de journal, Lyon, 22 juin 1842, f. 8.

20 Ordonnance de Monseigneur l'archevêque de Paris qui établie un conseil pour la direction des communautés religieuses 1841 (Archives de l'Archevêché de Paris, Fonds Affre, I D V 2, 1840–1848). R. Limouzin-Lamothe and J. Leflon, *Mgr Denys Affre, Archevêque de Paris*, 1793-1848 (Paris, 1971), pp. 241–80.

21 Affaires concernant la Société de 1839 43. No. 1 (GA, Rome, C–I., c–3, Box 2 1839, ff. 1–8). There are copies of these and subsequent documents in other collections in the General Archives, Rome: Affaires de 1839. Recueil No. 1. Pièces datées de 1842 (C–I., c–3, Box 2, 1839; Also Box 7). While there is an extensive record of correspondence between Sophie Barat and Archbishop Affre in the archives of the Society of the Sacred Heart, there is none at all in the archives of the archdiocese of Paris.

22 Eugénie de Gramont à SB, [Paris], 4 juillet 1842. (GA, Rome, C–IV., 4, Box 3, Paris, Closed Houses). Je dois vous rendre compte d'une chose qui se passe, dont vous m'accuserez très probablement si je ne vous l'explique pas, mais je ne suis coupable du tout. L'archevêque de Paris est très mécontent de ce que le conseil se tienne à Lyon. Il est très blessé et s'exprime très hautement; en même temps il exprime son très grand mécontentement des nouveaux décrets du conseil de Rome [1839] [...] De plus, il y a deux ans quand après son sacre je lui demandai la permission de mettre en exécution ces nouveaux décrets à l'essai [...] il me pria de lui faire une note des choses principales [...] J'ai fait cela il y a deux ans et depuis je ne lui en avais reparlé. Depuis qu'il sait que le conseil va s'assembler il a repris ses notes et a écrit aux évêques; puis il m'a dit qu'il voulait envoyer ces notes à tous les évêques pour leur montrer combien tout cela était mauvais. Je l'ai supplié de n'en rien faire, j'ai fait ce que j'ai pu pour l'en empêcher [...] Je vous assure que j'en suis fâchée et que ce n'est pas ma faute [...] l'archevêque n'est pas un homme à mécontenter ni à fâcher. Prenez y garde.

23 Corr. SB et Eugénie de Gramont, lettre 785, La Ferrandière, 25 juillet 1842; lettre 786, 27 juillet 1842; lettre 787, Lyon, 31 juillet 1842.

24 Eugénie de Gramont à SB, [Paris] 1 août 1842 (GA, Rome, C–IV., 4, Box 3, Paris, Closed Houses). Devant la mort et le jugement de Dieu elle n'a point regretté ni rétracté cette opposition à des décrets qu'elle a toujours regardés comme très mauvais et chose fatale à la Société [...] que les Dames du conseil sachent tout cela, qu'elles fassent une méditation de leur retraite, celles qui si légèrement ont porté la main sur des constitutions qu'elles devaient respecter et apprendre aux autres à respecter. C'était là leur charge et non de les changer. Also Eugénie de Gramont à SB, [Paris] 12 août [1842] (GA, Rome, C–IV., 4, Box 3, Paris, Closed Houses).

25 Denys Affre à SB, Paris, 12 juillet 1842. Affaires concernant la Société de 1839 43. No. 1, ff. 9–11.

26 SB à Denys Affre, Lyon, 24 juillet 1842. (Affaires concernant la Société de 1839 43. No. 1, ff. 11–15).

27 Denys Affre à SB Paris, 28 juillet 1842. (Affaires concernant la Société de 1839 43. No. 1, ff. 27–30). Je voie dans la manière dont vous justifiez votre oublie à quel point vous êtes persuadée de votre indépendance. Il est clair que vous la croyez entière. Vous ne regardez un avis donné à l'archevêque de Paris que comme une simple politesse.

28 Récit historique des événements de 1839–1843, [Adèle Lehon] f. 16; also ff. 14–15 (GA, Rome, C–I., c–3, Box 2 1839). Dont le sens était qu'il ne devait pas croire que son titre de Primat de Gaules lui permit de fouler aux pieds les droits des autres évêques [...], ff. 8,14 (GA, Rome, C–I., c–3, Box 2 1839).

29   SB à Denys Affre, [Lyon], 2 août 1842.(Affaires concernant la Société de 1839 43. No. 1, f. 31.)
30   Corr. SB et Eugénie de Gramont, lettre 788, Lyon, 3 août 1842. Je remarque que vous nous prêtez souvent des intentions que nous n'avons pas, je vous assure […] J'ai cru ce que vous m'avez dit, que vous n'étiez pour rien dans cette affaire, et nos Mères ont partagé mon opinion.
31   Corr. SB et Eulalie de Bouchaud, lettre 196, Les Anglais, 4 août 1842. Dans quel abîme on précipite une œuvre qui devait trouver appui et protection partout où nous sommes établies.
32   Copie du mémoire envoyé au cardinal Lambruschini et qui a été présenté à la congrégation des Réguliers: Réclamations faites à notre … Mère Général par 'Archevêque de Paris. (Affaires concernant la Société de 1839 43. No. 1, ff. 32–43); Notes en forme de journal, Lyon, 18 août, 1842, f. 9.
33   Archives du Ministre des Affaires Etrangères, vol. 984, 1841–43, ff. 98–99, 102–102v, 112–13. Also, Boudon, *L'épiscopat français*, pp. 446–50.
34   Cahier, *Vie*, ii, 26–9.
35   Antonio Garibaldi à Lambruschini, 27 agosto 1842 (ASV, Fonds Segretario di Stato Esteri, Busta 616, Rubrica 283, Fascicolo 1, No. 1718).
36   Antonio Garibaldi à Lambruschini, 27 agosto 1842.
37   Eugénie de Gramont à SB, Paris, 30 août 1842. Affaires concernant la Société de 1839 43. No. 1, ff. 32–43). Quelle démarche fausse […] vous avez faites […] comment pouvez vous compromettre ainsi la dignité du Saint-Siège et le faire agir avec autant de légèreté et faire peser sur un archevêque une imputation qui n'a aucun fondement? Que gagnerez-vous […] Pourquoi agir ainsi avec des évêques et vouloir toujours agir sans eux. Enfin son mécontentement contre vous en est très augmenté.
38   Lettre de Mgr l'Archevêque de Paris à tous les Evêques, Paris, 16 septembre 1842. (Affaires concernant la Société de 1839 à 43. No. 1, ff. 61–74). Corr. SB et Eulalie de Bouchaud, lettres 207, 208, Autun, 6, 10 octobre 1842. Archbishop Affre did not send a copy of his letter to Sophie. However, she received one from the internuncio, Antonio Garibaldi.
39   Lettre de Mgr l'Archevêque de Paris à tous les Evêques, Paris, 16 septembre 1842, ff. 62–3. 'Il le consulte, non comme magistrat, … comme chef spirituel du diocèse …'
40   Lettre de Mgr l'Archevêque de Paris à tous les Evêques, Paris, 16 septembre 1842, f. 73. Ce que Madame Barat traite si légèrement a une importance sur laquelle elle doit faire de sérieuses réflexions.
41   Corr. SB à Césaire Mathieu, (Lyon, 12 août 1842). Ce serait pour m'assurer que j'agis selon ma conscience, en défendant nos droits, que je voudrais […] m'aider de vos lumières!
42   Corr. Césaire Mathieu à SB, lettre 1, Besançon, 12 septembre 1842.
43   Cardinal Pedicini à SB, Rome, septembre 1842 (GA, Rome, C–I., c–3, Box 2).
44   Corr. SB et Elizabeth Galitzine, lettre 179, Autun, 22 octobre 1842.
45   Corr. SB à Césaire Mathieu, lettre 4, (Lyon, 20 septembre 1842). Sophie finally received Pedicini's letter on 21 October 1842.
46   Elizabeth Galitzine à Louise de Limminghe, Lyon, 4 septembre 1842.
47   Affaires concernant la Société de 1839 à 43. No. 1, ff. 77–78.
48   Elizabeth Galitzine à Louise de Limminghe, Lyon, 4 septembre 1842. [prié] la Mère générale de donner sa démission en faveur de Madame de Gramont. Car plus d'une fois nous avons entendu que la petite dame était désignée pour être supérieure générale; ou bien si on ne vient pas de suite on exigera qu'elle soit nommée assistante générale comme me l'a dit Mère de Causans […] Quel rôle devons nous jouer dans tout cela […] on nous traite d'imbéciles.
49   Elizabeth Galitzine à Louise de Limminghe, Lyon, 4 septembre 1842. Je présume que cette auguste assemblée sera présidée par Mgr l'Archevêque [de Paris] qui aura à sa droite le ministre des Cultes ou son délégué en soutane ou autrement; à sa gauche, son théologien, la petite dame. Plus bas la mère générale; de l'autre côté du ministre, Madame d'Avenas […] Mgr prononcera une excommunication anathème contre le conseil irrégulier de 1839 […] la petite dame boira à la santé du grand Prélat de France et trinquera avec lui et le ministre des Cultes.
50   Elizabeth Galitzine à Louise de Limminghe, Lyon, 16 septembre 1842. Je suis bien de votre avis de tout faire pour sauver la Société malgré la Mère générale. Mais je crains bien que tous nos efforts ne soient [qu']inutiles et ne viennent échouer contre l'insurmontable apathie ou faiblesse de celle qui vous gouverne et qui ne sait employer que de petits moyens, de petites ruses, capables dans les occasions ordinaires de la tirer momentanément d'affaire, mais absolument insuffisants et nuls dans les circonstances importantes où il s'agit du salut de la Société […] J'ai engagé le cardinal Protecteur à écrire une lettre dont vous trouverez ci-joint la copie ou traduction […] La Mère générale ne vous la communiquera certainement pas, c'est pour cela que je vous la transmets […]
51   Bernard Peyrous, 'La prédication de Lacordaire à Bordeaux en 1841 et 1842', in Guy Bedouelle, *Lacordaire, son pays, ses amis et la liberté des ordres religieux en France* (Paris, 1991), pp. 119–38. Lacordaire wished to restore the Dominican order in France. However, while Archbishop Donnet had invited him to preach in Bordeaux that year he did not accept Lacordaire's request to make a Dominican foundation there.

52   Jean Rozaven à Ferdinand Donnet, Rome, 13 octobre 1842 (GA, Rome, Fonds Jeanne de Charry, H–I., 6. Box 1). On regrette ici que la supérieure générale n'ait pas non plus de vigueur et d'énergie à soutenir son autorité […] l'indécision et la faiblesse l'ont mise dans une situation difficile dont elle aura de la peine à sortir. La peur et la pusillanimité sont de mauvais conseillers […] [elle] s'est laissée intimider par le ton menaçant et impérieux que l'archevêque a pris avec elle. Elle lui a cru plus de pouvoir qu'il n'en avait réellement […] Mais les femmes sont faciles à intimider, elles ont besoin d'appui, d'encouragement, de protection, et à qui appartient-il de leur en donner sinon aux évêques […]

53   Paul Poupard, *Correspondance inédite entre Mgr Antonio Antonio Garibaldi, internonce à Paris et Mgr Césaire Mathieu archevêque de Besançon. Contribution à l'histoire de l'administration ecclésiastique sous la monarchie de juillet* (Rome, 1961), lettre 99, Paris, 26 septembre 1842, p. 377. Je suis moi aussi d'autant plus d'avis que le cardinal Pedicini, protecteur, n'est pas porté de lui-même à écrire d'une manière si forte, que c'est un homme très tranquille, très pacifique et je dirais presque indolent.

54   Corr. SB et Elizabeth Galitzine, lettre 174, Besançon, 14 septembre 1842.

55   SB à Cardinal Pedicini, Lyon, 22 septembre 1842. (GA, Rome, C–I., c–3, Box 2, 1839). A la manière dont on vient de faire ma position et par les entraves que l'on juge à propos de me susciter il ne m'est plus possible de gouverner la Société. Je compte donc donner ma démission. Il ne sera pas difficile de trouver un sujet parmi nos mères, qui gouvernera assurément mieux que moi. J'attendrai la réponse avant de me rendre à Paris.

56   Elizabeth Galitzine, à Louise de Limminghe, Lyon, 22 septembre 1842.

57   Corr. SB à Césaire Mathieu, lettre 5, Lyon, 25 septembre 1842. Il est vrai que l'on fait une espèce de trame à Rome contre moi et mes opérations et comme on agit au nom du Saint Père je me trouve étranglée et je ne puis plus bouger. Ainsi, on exige que j'ôte Madame de Gramont de Paris, que je lui enlève ses charges; par conséquent que je lui ôte sa réputation et que je soulève plusieurs maisons, précisément les opposants qui ont besoin de plus de ménagements, que je reste loin de Paris […] enfin, on veut m'ôter toute espèce de liberté et par le fait ce sont les assistantes [générales] à qui l'on confie le gouvernement, ce qui serait dans l'ordre si on voulait que je me retire. Mais ce qui est pis, je dois obéir contre mes lumières, ma conscience. Voilà ma position […]

58   Corr. SB à Henriette Granon, lettre 28, Besançon 15 septembre 1842. Sans doute tout serait bientôt terminé si le N° 41 revenait; dans ce moment il y a quelque rapprochement, mais le moyen le plus efficace serait de rattacher nos seigneurs évêques au chef de la Société. Il n'y a point d'absurdités que l'on n'ait débitées contre moi. Il faillit me ridiculiser. Je ne dis pas Mère de Gramont. Elle n'en est pas capable, mais leurs amis. Ce manège touche à sa fin. Je bénis le Seigneur de toutes ces humiliations si elles doivent nous attirer la miséricorde du divin Cœur.

59   Corr. SB à Césaire Mathieu, Lyon, 2 octobre 1842.

60   Corr. Césaire Mathieu à SB, lettre 2, Paris, 8 octobre 1842. Permettez-moi en prenant part à votre croix, d'en éprouver aussi un peu la pesanteur. Ce fut le bonheur de Cyrène d'avoir lui-même quelque chose à souffrir en aidant notre divin Maître dans le trajet du calvaire […] Je ne puis ne pas espérer en faveur de votre congrégation. L'orage présent vous montre ce qu'est la prospérité Celle de la Société compromet son existence, mais il me semble que c'est une leçon d'humilité que vous donne la Providence. C'est pour cela qu'il faut prendre et porter la croix présente avec un grand calme, une grande douceur, un religieux silence et une parfaite confiance.

61   Corr. SB et Stanislas Dusaussoy, lettre 109, Lyon, 2 octobre 1842; Corr. SB à Sophie Dusaussoy, lettre 22, Lyon, 2 octobre 1842; Corr. SB et Louise de Limminghe, lettre 339, Lyon, 3 octobre 1842; Corr. SB et Eugénie de Gramont, lettre 800, La Ferrandière, lettre 800, 24 septembre 1842.

62   Corr. SB à Césaire Mathieu, lettre 9, (Autun, 28 octobre 1842) [Félicité Desmarquest] a les idées si arrêtées et si fausses, ce me semble que nous ne pouvons nous accorder! […] cette réunion d'obstacles, cette résistance que je trouve de tout côté me dessèche. Ma patience est quelquefois près de m'échapper!

63   Ministère de la Justice et des Cultes à Mgr Affre, Paris, 17 octobre 1842 (Affaires concernant la Société de 1839 à 43. No. 1, ff. 79–82).

64   Mgr Gros à SB, Paris, 21 octobre 1842. (Affaires concernant la Société de 1839 à 43. No. 1, ff. 83–4).

65   Corr. SB à Césaire Mathieu, lettre 3, Vesoul, 6 novembre 1842.

66   Antonio Garibaldi à Lambruschini, Paris, 4 novembre 1842. (ASV, Fonds Segretario di Stato Esteri, Busta 616, Rubrica 283, Fascicolo 1, No. 1750).

67   Corr. SB à Césaire Mathieu, lettre 9, (Autun, 28 octobre 1842). 'personne de véritable ami'.

68   Antonio Garibaldi à Lambruschini, Paris, 15 octobre 1842. (ASV, Fonds Segretario di Stato Esteri, Busta 616, Rubrica 283, Fascicolo 1, No. 1738); also Antonio Garibaldi à la, Paris, 28 octobre 1842 (ASV, Fonds Segretario di Stato Esteri, Busta 616, Rubrica 283, Fascicolo 1, No. 1746).

Notes to Chapter 19

1 Corr. SB à Césaire Mathieu, lettre 10, Paris, 7 novembre 1842. Comme ces premières notions sont venues par le P[ère] R[ozaven], du moins je l'ai deviné, car on ne m'a rien expliqué, et comme il a une très grande influence, en se retirant, tout sera brisé [...] Il est certain que je crois m'apercevoir que tout ce qui se passe autour de moi a l'air d'un complot fait à dessein [...] Si cet état de choses se prolonge, je sens que je succomberai.

2 Corr. SB et Elizabeth Galitzine, lettre 182, Autun, 29 octobre 1842; lettre 183, Autun, 1 novembre 1842; lettre 183 (bis), Autun, 1 novembre 1842. Mon âme est sur le pressoir à la vue des maux qui nous attendent, et je n'ai pas le courage d'en dire plus [...] J'ai à chaque courrier des révolutions qui me donnent sur les nerfs, à peine si je ne puis tenir ma plume.

3 Corr. SB et Elizabeth Galitzine, lettre 185, Paris, 7 novembre 1842. Vous prenez votre parti bien facilement sur notre destruction. J'avoue que je ne supporterais jamais ce langage que pour amour de notre Seigneur, ainsi que tous les autres procédés qui y ont trait. Fasse le ciel que je n'ai pas cette douleur, je ne pourrais la supporter sans mourir, je le sens. On a dit à Monseigneur de Paris que nous avons envoyé une Circulaire à toutes nos maisons, qui était une réfutation de la sienne. Il cherche par tous les moyens à se procurer cette Circulaire. Je n'ai que celle que vous avez faites pour les décrets. Serait-ce dans celle-là que vous en auriez parlé? Ce serait une grande imprudence dans ce moment. Si vous l'avez fait, écrivez de suite à toutes les supérieures où vous l'avez envoyée de ne la montrer à personne, de la brûler même pour le moment afin qu'on ne puisse commander! Dans quelle crise affreuse nous nous trouvons [...] Sophie wrote to superiors asking them to destroy Elizabeth Galitzine's refutation of Archbishop Affre's letter. Corr. SB et Henriette Granon, Letter 30, Paris, 14 novembre 1842.

4 Antonio Garibaldi à Lambruschini, Paris, 12 novembre 1842. (ASV, Fonds Segretario di Stato Esteri, Busta 616, Rubrica 283, Fascicolo 1, No. 1752).

5 Corr. SB à Césaire Mathieu, lettre 16 [Paris, 17 novembre 1842]. Comprenez-vous [...] de telles assistantes? et que faire maintenant avec ces têtes? Tant il est vrai qu'il ne faut qu'une qui ait des moyens, de la vertu même, pour tout brouiller, car avant que Madame Galitzine fût dans le conseil, le plus intime accord y régna. Sous prétexte de son attachement à Rome, elle a entraîné les autres [...] et le Père Rozaven qui a tant d'influence sur le cardinal protecteur, qu'il mène comme un instrument docile, et lui-même mené par Madame Galitzine, dont tout le monde connaît le faible pour elle. Voici le nœud de ma position changée [...] Nous ne connaissons pas les femmes alors: je les avais toujours dominées [...] Quel remède? Un seul et il presse: l'abolition des décrets [...] Also lettre 15, Paris, 15 novembre 1842; Corr. Césaire Mathieu à SB, lettre 10, Besançon, 16 novembre 1842.

6 Corr. SB à Césaire Mathieu, lettre 13, Paris, 12 novembre 1842.

7 Corr. Césaire Mathieu à SB, lettre 4, Besançon, 9 novembre 1842.

8 Corr. SB à Césaire Mathieu, lettre 14, Paris, 13 novembre 1842. 'frappé et comme terrifiée des menaces de Mgr de Paris'.

9 Antonio Garibaldi à Césaire Mathieu, lettre 99, Paris, 26 septembre 1842, Poupard, *Correspondance*, p. 379. 'même à la suite de politesse etc que ferait envers lui mère Barat'.

10 Corr. Césaire Mathieu à SB, lettre 6, Besançon, 11 novembre 1842.

11 Corr. SB à Césaire Mathieu, lettre 13, Paris, 12 novembre 1842. Je suis ici sous une surveillance active. Mgr sait tous les personnages que je vois et même de qui je reçois des lettres. Il [Monseigneur Affre] m'a parlé de votre grandeur, du Nonce etc. Veuillez [...] m'écrire directement, en faisant mettre l'adresse par une autre main et le cachet simple. On ne peut se faire une idée de ma position; tout est examiné, rapporté. Une lettre au ministre que je voulais voir est demeurée sans réponse. J'ai de fortes raisons de croire quelle a été interceptée [...] Je vais prendre d'autres moyens pour parvenir jusqu'à lui!

12 Louis Marie Joseph Caverot (1806–87) was born in Joinville (Haute-Marne) and studied in Troyes, Dôle and St Sulpice. He ministered in Besançon while Césaire Mathieu was archbishop. He later became bishop of Saint Dié and later archbishop of Lyon.

13 Antonio Garibaldi à Lambruschini, Paris, 17 novembre 1842. (ASV, Fonds Segretario di Stato Esteri, Busta 616, Rubrica 283, Fascicolo 1, No. 1753.)

14 Antonio Garibaldi à Césaire Mathieu, Paris, 30 mars 1843, Poupard, *Correspondance*, pp. 394–96; 399.

15 Ambassadeur de France à Rome à Monsieur le Ministre, Rome, 8 novembre 1842 (Archives du Ministre des Affaires Etrangères, vol. 984, 154–56).

16 Monsieur le Ministre à Monsieur le Comte (Latour-Maubourg), Ambassadeur de France à Rome, Paris, 14 décembre 1842 (Dépêches du Département 1842–43, 15, No. 133 (A.A.F.). Antonio Garibaldi à Lambruschini, Paris, 17 novembre 1842. (ASV, Fonds Segretario di Stato Esteri, Busta 616, Rubrica 283, Fascicolo 1, No. 1753).

17 Corr. Césaire Mathieu à SB, lettre 5, 10 novembre 1842. [peser] les conséquences d'une révocation qui anéantira trente maisons, intéressera presque autant de diocèses et plus de douze cents chefs de familles les plus honorables de France. Le tout pour une dispute de mots.

18 Antonio Garibaldi à Lambruschini, Paris, 17 novembre 1842. (ASV, Fonds Segretario di Stato Esteri, Busta 616, Rubrica 283, Fascicolo 1, No. 1753). Also Antonio Garibaldi à Lambruschini, Paris, 18 novembre 1842.

No. 1754; 19 novembre 1842. No. 1756; 7 décembre 1842. No. 1761 (ASV, Fonds Segretario di Stato Esteri, Busta 616, Rubrica 283, Fascicolo 1, Nos 1754, 1756, 1761.)

19 Corr. Césaire Mathieu à SB, lettre 58, Lyon, 3 avril 1843.

20 Elizabeth Galitzine à Louis Barat, Lyon, 19 décembre 1842 (AFSJ, Fonds Barat. Correspondance de Madame Galitzine avec le Père Barat, lors de la crise de 1840–43.

21 Affaires concernant la Société de 1839–43, No. 2, ff. 5–11 (General Archives, Rome, C–I., c–3, Box 2, 1839). See also Affaires de 1839. Recueil No. 1. Pièces datées de 1842 (General Archives, Rome, C–I., c–3, Box 2, 1839).

22 Antonio Garibaldi à Lambruschini, Paris, 13 décembre 1842, No. 1766; Antonio Garibaldi à Lambruschini, Paris, 17 décembre 1842. No. 1767; Antonio Garibaldi à Lambruschini, Paris, 20 décembre 1842. No. 1768 (ASV, Fonds Segretario di Stato Esteri, Busta 616, Rubrica 283, Fascicolo 1) no. 1766.

23 Antonio Garibaldi à Césaire Mathieu, lettre 102, Paris, 30 décembre 1842. Poupard, *Correspondance*, pp. 382–5. There were successive Ministers of Religion at this time. For details, see Poupard, *Correspondance*, p. 63, Si la Société des Dames du Sacré-Cœur tombait, on ferait en France, de la part des évêques et des autres, tomber tout l'odieux sur les jésuites, et leurs maisons pourraient bien y passer aussi. La lettre est assez longe et bien faite et contient des choses très vraies et capables de faire impression et peur.

24 Paul Tharin à Jean Roothan, Paris, 10 janvier 1843. 1843 (ARSI, Monialium negotia. Dames du Sacré-Cœur. Graves difficultates, Monial 5–I, 19). Plusieurs de vos Pères, sans le vouloir, mais très réellement, ont placé cette respectable et utile congrégation à deux doigts de sa perte.

25 Clement Boulanger à Jean Roothan, [Paris], 1 janvier 1843; 19 janvier 1843; 25 juin 1843 (ARSI, Monialium negotia. Dames du Sacré-Cœur. Graves difficultates … 1839–1843. Franc. 5–II, 16, 18, 27). For the difficulties the Jesuits were having with Archbishop Affre at this time and their appeal to Gregory XVI, see, P.F. Grandidier, *Vie du … Père Guidée de la Compagnie de Jésus* (Amiens/Paris, 1867), pp. 192–204; 404–10.

26 Jean Roothan à Paul Tharin, Rome, 6 février 1843. (ARSI, Responsa ad externos, 1840–43, vol. v, 292–4). Je désire bien […] de n'avoir plus à écrire sur les Dames du Sacré-Cœur […] Je pense toujours que les religieuses sont comme la vigne qui a un besoin absolu d'un soutien. Cette fonction pour les religieuses ne peut être de genre masculin. Les Dames du Sacré-Cœur le voudraient avoir dans les Pères de la Compagnie. Or cela ne peut être. Il n'y a jamais eu, il ne peut y avoir de Jésuitesses […] Mais comment combiner un ordre religieux de femmes répandu en tant de diocèses, avec une générale, et en même temps cette dépendance ordinaire des évêques. C'est là, j'avoue, un problème auquel je ne saurais répondre.

27 Ambassadeur de France à Rome à Mons. Le Ministre, Rome, 8 novembre 1842 (Archives des Affaires Etrangères, Paris. Correspondance Politique, Rome. Vol. 984, Rome, 1842–43, f. 156). See, A.A.F. Dossier: Religieuses du Sacré-Cœur (1838–1904), Dépêches du Département 1842–43, No. 133, Paris, 14 décembre 1842. Also, Jean Roothan to Césaire Mathieu, Rome, 28 mars 1843 (ARSI, Responsa ad externos, 1840–43, vol. v, 312).

28 Garibaldi à Lambruschini, Paris, 20 décembre 1842. (ASV, Fonds Segretario di Stato Esteri, Busta 616, Rubrica 283, Fascicolo 1, No. 1768).

29 For an instance of the personal conflict between Lambruschini and Rozaven, over the affairs of the Society of the Sacred Heart, see Conseils particuliers, 17 novembre 1839.

30 Corr. SB et Elizabeth Galitzine, lettre 186, Paris, 8 novembre 1842; lettre 187, Paris, 9 novembre 1842; lettre 188, Paris, 9 novembre 1842.

31 Corr. SB et Elizabeth Galitzine, lettre 187, Paris, 9 novembre 1842. selon les lois françaises [le dossier du pape] ne doit pas pénétrer en France sans être registré au conseil d'État. Le ministre l'a écrit ainsi dans sa lettre à Monseigneur, et ce n'est pas que trop vrai! Sous Louis XIV, je crois, la France fut sur le point de devenir schismatique pour une affaire de ce genre; et maintenant que l'on penche vers le Protestantisme, on ne demanderait pas mieux que de faire au moins du scandale.

32 Elizabeth Galitzine à SB, Lyon, 12 novembre 1842 (Affaires concernant la Société de 1839 à 43. No. 1, ff. 86–88).

33 Adèle Lehon, Récit historique des événements de 1839–1843 (General Archives, Rome, C–I., c–3, Box 2, 1839, f. 8). 'Son éducation à *l'autocrate* semblait lui persuader qu'on peut conduire les hommes comme des machines.'

34 Corr. SB et Elizabeth Galitzine, lettre 190, Paris, 15 novembre 1842. Dans quelle passe vous allez nous mettre, je l'ignore? […] il est pénible de montrer à Rome et à toute la Société que vous travaillez contre moi, lorsque je me sacrifie pour le bien de toutes!

35 Affaires concernant la Société de 1839 à 43. No. 1, ff. 88–135. This material is extensive and indicates that Elizabeth Galitzine had galvanised the support of the assistants general, the provincials and many superiors, as well as Pedicini and Rozaven. For the protests of Adèle Lehon (Sainte Rufine), Josephine de Coriolis (Trinité), Anna du Rousier (Turin), Hypolite Lavauden (Parma), see General Archives, Rome, C–I., C–3, Box 5, 1839.

36 Corr. SB et Elizabeth Galitzine, lettre 191, Paris, 17 novembre 1842. Monseigneur l'archevêque de Paris [...] m'écrit à l'instant pour me faire part de l'inconcevable pièce que vous lui avez adressée [...] Vous concevez son étonnement comme celui que j'ai éprouvé moi-même, lorsque j'ai reçu les mêmes protestations [...] Vous vous êtes grossièrement trompée et par rapport à moi et à Monseigneur. A l'heure qu'il est, 17 novembre, je n'ai rien reçu, rien signé, et j'ai tout refusé. Le seul article pour lequel j'ai hésité et pour lequel je vous demandais votre avis était celui de la résidence, auquel le gouvernement tient mordicus [...] Si j'avais pu, hélas, vous connaître au point où je le fais maintenant, je me serais bien gardée de vous demander le conseil. Bonne leçon pour une autre fois.

37 Corr. SB et Elizabeth Galitzine, lettre 192, Paris, 6 décembre 1842. Dans ma peine et ma confiance, je vous écrivis comme à des amis, et ne pris pas le temps de relire. A vous dire vrai, j'étais loin de penser à un abus de confiance de votre part aussi majeur et aussi prompt. Oui [...] la Société nous jugera, je ne crains pas de lui rendre compte de ma conduite: si elle partage vos sentiments, je m'en consolerai aisément parce qu'alors ayant perdue sa confiance, j'obtiendrai plus facilement plus tôt ce que je désire si ardemment, de n'être plus rien. Si au contraire la Société se relève de cette crise, je serai encore heureuse de mes souffrances et de mes humiliations. D'ailleurs ma fin ne peut être longue à venir: on ne souffre pas impunément tant de chagrins!'

38 Elizabeth Galitzine à Louis Barat, St Charles, 17 octobre 1840 (AFSJ, Fonds Louis Barat, Corr. de Madame Galitzine avec le Père Barat, lors de la crise de 1840–43). J'ai tout lieu de craindre la perfide influence de la Mère de Gramont [...] Cette pauvre mère est devenue un serpent que la Société a nourri et réchauffé dans son sein [...] Si elle [Sophie Barat] avait montré les dents au commencement elle ne serait pas obligée maintenant d'en venir aux remèdes violents, et si elle ne les adopte pas la gangrenée gagnera la partie vitale [...] Sa trop grande bonté paralyse sa fermeté.

39 Elisabeth Galitzine à Louis Barat, Lyon, 25 octobre 1842 (AFSJ, Fonds Louis Barat).

40 Elizabeth Galitzine à Louis Barat, Lyon, 25 octobre 1842. 'La chatillaine de No 41' [...] La pauvre dame dit avec chaleur: si le n° 41 se sépare j'irai la rejoindre et on verra alors où sera la Société.

41 Elizabeth Galitzine à Louis Barat, Lyon, 19 décembre 1842 (AFSJ, Fonds Louis Barat). See also, Note, janvier 1843. (General Archives, Rome, C–I., C–3, Box 5, 1839).

42 Testimony of Matilde Garabis, Paris, 4 juin 1884 (General Archives, Rome, Processus apostolicus in causa beatificationis et canonisationis ... Magdalena Sophiae Barrat, vol. iii, sessio 74, f. 1405).

43 AFSJ Vanves, Fonds Louis Barat, Sur L'eglise, l'Europe, la France. Application de l'Apocalypse à l'histoire de France, Ms 4204; Idée de l'Apocalypse, Ms 4202, 4203; Sur N.S. Jesus Christ et son Eglise, Ms 4201.

44 Corr. SB et Eugénie de Gramont, lettre 811, Autun, 21 octobre 1842. Je ne suis point injuste à votre égard. Un jour peut-être vous saurez tout ce que j'ai souffert. Ce mot m'échappe et il sera le seul. Je n'aime pas à confier ces choses si délicates au papier. Prier, me taire, j'ai toujours l'espérance au fond de l'âme que notre Seigneur viendra à notre secours après l'épreuve, si nous savons en profiter.

45 Souvenirs de Sœur Virginie Roux (General Archives, Rome, A–II., 1–a, Box 1), ff. 134–6. Lettres Annuelles, 1877–78, pp. 31–5. All the house journals of the rue de Varenne exist with the notable exception of the crucial years 1842–52. A note in the archives at Poitiers indicates that after extensive searches the journal for that period was considered to have been lost. (AF, Poitiers, Paris, rue de Varenne, BO6, 115, II.) In 1877 Stéphanie Cardon (1806–79), who lived in the rue de Varenne at the same time as Virginie Roux, refuted some of the 'Souvenirs' (Stéphanie Cardon à Adèle Cahier, Lille, 26 janvier 1877.) However, by this time Sophie Barat's canonisation process had commenced and hagiography had begun to take over from historical fact.

46 Corr. SB à Césaire Mathieu, lettre 21, Paris, 27 novembre 1842; lettre 23, 2 décembre 1842; lettre 27, Paris, 10 décembre 1842; lettre 28, Paris, 11 décembre 1842; lettre 30, Paris, 14 décembre 1842; lettre 31, Paris, 16 décembre 1842. Corr. SB et Elizabeth Galitzine, lettre 195, Paris, 21 décembre 1842. Catherine de Charbonnel à SB, Laval, 26 mars 1843 (General Archives, Rome, C–I., C–3, Box 3, 1839).

47 Louise de Limminghe à SB, Rome, 25 novembre 1842 (General Archives, Rome, C–I., c–3, Box 3). C'est...une question de *vie* ou de *mort*. Il s'agit d'être religieuse ou de n'être plus. Il ne peut exister de milieu. Ah! Je vous en conjure ma digne mère, ma toujours, toujours plus aimée mère, cessez de vous laisser abuser; écoutez celles qui ne vous ont jamais trompées. Voyez le bel exemple que donne en ce moment les religieuses de Bon Pasteur. Madame de Coriolis nous a assurées hier que le cardinal vicaire tient dans ses mains la protestation de leur mère générale et ses quatre assistantes par une circonstance presque semblable à la nôtre. For the case of the congregation of the Good Shepherd of Angers (Notre-Dame de Charité du Bon Pasteur, Angers) see: Marie Dominique Poinsenet, *Rien n'est impossible à l'amour. Marie Euphrasie Pelletier, Fondratrice du Bon Pasteur* (St Paul, 1992) pp. 151–86. Claude Langlois, 'La vie religieuse vers 1840: un nouveau modèle', in Guy Bedouelle (ed.), *Lacordaire, son pays, ses amis et la liberté des ordres religieux en France* (Paris, 1991), pp. 45–6. Also Langlois, *Le catholicisme au féminin*. For the contacts between Sophie Barat and Marie Euphrasie Pelletier, AF, Poitiers, A 8, Relations avec l'église, 1800–1865.

48 General Archives, Rome. C–I., C–3, Box 6. lettres: Félicité Desmarquest à Louise de Limminghe, 1842–1843.

49 Elizabeth Galitzine à Félicité Desmarquest, Lyon, 24 décembre 1842. (Affaires concernant la Société de 1839 à 43. No. 2, ff. 1–5. Also ff. 50–65).

50 General Archives, Rome, C–I., C–3, Box 5, 1839.

51   Corr. SB à Césaire Mathieu, lettre 33, Paris, 20 décembre 1842; Corr. Césaire Mathieu à SB, lettre 27, Besançon, 23 décembre 1842. Also, Notes sur les lettre de ... [Elizabeth] Galitzine et Louise] de Limminghe, 1841–42 (General Archives, Rome, C–I., C–3, Box 6, 1839).
52   Félicité Desmarquest à Louise de Limminghe, Conflans, 8 octobre 1842 (General Archives, Rome, C–I., c–3, Box 6). 'enfermée dans une profonde tristesse'.
53   Corr. SB à Césaire Mathieu, lettre 31, Paris, 16 décembre 1842.
54   ibid., lettre 23, Paris, 2 décembre 1842; lettre 28, Paris, 11 décembre 1842; Corr. Césaire Mathieu à SB, lettre 20, Besançon, 13 décembre 1842.
55   Corr. Césaire Mathieu à SB, lettre 25, Besançon, 21 décembre 1842. Plus les affaires s'embrouillent au dehors, plus il faut y aller avec simplicité. Recevez les renseignements qui vous sont adressés, sans les laisser descendre jusqu'à votre cœur.
56   Corr. SB à Césaire Mathieu, lettre 35, Paris, 24 décembre 1842. Je suis sortie de mon calme d'abandon, d'oubli de leurs procédés et j'ai blâmé leur conduite avec trop de nature. Je leur ai écrit aussi assez vertement.
57   Corr. Césaire Mathieu à SB, lettre 6, Besançon, 11 novembre 1842. Quoique vous ayez eu beaucoup de croix pour la fondation de votre ordre, sa prospérité en appelait d'autres, pour ne pas vous laisser endormir dans une sécurité funeste.
58   Corr. Césaire Mathieu à SB, lettre 14, [n.p.] 30 novembre 1842. 'cette inconcevable tourmente'.
59   Corr. SB à Césaire Mathieu, lettre 17, Paris, 19 novembre 1842. Quelle vie je mène [...] sur mes vieux jours tant de tracasseries! ce serait pénible si je ne me disais sans cesse Dieu le veut! puis il fait expier! Je me résigne donc et je travaillerai tant que j'aurai des forces.
60   ibid., lettre 25, [Paris, 5 décembre 1842]. Depuis plusieurs années je ne marche que sur les épines et je réussis mal dans mes plans.
61   ibid., lettre 23, Paris, 2 décembre 1842 [check]. Je n'ai presque pas le temps de prier dans le jour. Il faudrait le faire la nuit, et je suis accablée alors de fatigue et de sommeil. Je crois que le bon Dieu me punit d'avoir abandonné ma première vocation qui était le Carmel. Sa croix, les humiliations, les souffrances peuvent-elles supplier? J'ai encore bien des inquiétudes sur tant d'imperfections et de mélanges de nature dans cette épreuve. Priez donc [...] afin que j'obtienne du Cœur Sacré de Jésus un pardon de miséricorde dont j'ai un si immense besoin!
62   ibid., lettre 36, Paris, 27 décembre 1842. Mon cœur nage dans l'affliction; quelle responsabilité si je suis l'auteur de tant de maux! Vous êtes [...] mon unique appui après Jésus.
63   Corr. Césaire Mathieu à SB, lettre 16, Besançon, 6 décembre 1842.Il y a un mot de l'Écriture bien propre à vous consoler: Il est dit que l'aumône prie; et comment la croix ne prierait-elle pas, puisque c'est sur elle que Notre Seigneur a prié pour nous! il n'est donc nécessaire que vous fassiez dans la journée des oraisons, pour lesquelles vous n'avez pas le temps, ou que vous prolongiez malgré votre accablement les veilles de la nuit, ce qui vous mettrait en danger de n'avoir plus les forces nécessaires pendant le jour. Mais attachez-vous à la croix par la résignation et par l'amour, et laissez cette divine croix, ou plutôt Notre Seigneur, qui y demeure attaché pour notre amour, laissez-le prier pour vous. Cette considération très douce et très vraie calmera votre cœur.
64   Adelaide de Rozeville a Hipolyte Lavauden, Amiens, 16 décembre 1842 (General Archives, Rome, C–VIII, 2, K.L.) 'Elle travaille, elle prie, elle est calme, elle est courageuse. Elle travaille, elle prie, elle est calme, elle est courageuse. Elle souffre, il ne faut pas en douter [...] [elle] a une étendue d'esprit et une grandeur d'âme qui ne se laissent pas resserrer dans un cercle de vues étroites. Elle laisse les petits mobiles [...] Dès 1839 personne n'aurait dû se permettre d'agir en dehors d'elle [...]
65   Corr. SB à Césaire Mathieu, lettre 25, Paris, 5 décembre 1842.
66   Corr. SB et Elizabeth Galitzine, lettre 201, Paris, 27 janvier [1843].
67   ibid., lettre 204, Paris, 9 février 1843. Lorsque nous faisons les plus grands efforts pour éviter un schisme qui perdrait la Société [...] vous osez encore, dans un mémoire, envoyé à Rome, demander la séparation de trois maisons, parler des évêques très peu convenablement, de votre supérieure même [...] Si c'est ainsi que vous m'aider et me soutenez, vous feriez bien mieux [...] de prier et de vous guérir.
68   Corr. Césaire Mathieu à SB, lettre 29, Besançon, 3 janvier 1843. 'aucune affaire plus grave pour l'église de France n'ayant été engagé depuis 20 ans'
69   Corr. SB à Césaire Mathieu, lettre 36, Paris, 27 décembre 1842.
70   Garibaldi à Lambruschini, Paris, 24 janvier 1843 (ASV, Rome, Dispacci di Mons. Internunzio di Parigi alla Segretaria di Stato, Busta 67, no.1790; Garibaldi à Lambruschini, Paris, 17 février 1843. No. 1797).
71   Mémoire sur la situation actuelle de la Société des Dames du Sacré-Cœur (Affaires concernant la Société de 1839 à 43. No. 2, ff. 5–11).
72   Corr. SB à Césaire Mathieu, lettre 43, Paris, 13 janvier 1843; lettre 47, Paris, 26 janvier 1843; lettre 49, Conflans, 5 février 1843. 'maison de fous et enragés'.
73   Représentation faites sur le Mémoire adressée sa Sainteté sur la situation actuelle de la Société des Dames du Sacré-Cœur (Affaires concernant la Société de 1839 à 43. No. 2, ff. 12–25).
74   [Césaire Mathieu] Memoria (CRIS R–I).

75   Adèle Lehon à Elizabeth Galitzine, Sainte Rufine, 14 mars 1843 (Affaires concernant la Société, No.2, 1839
      à 43, ff. 65–66 General Archives, Rome, C–I., c–3, Box 2, 1839) 'mais la convalescence sera longue et dan-
      gereuse'.

Notes to Chapter 20

1   Corr. Césaire Mathieu à SB, lettre 49, Florence, 9 mars 1843; lettre 50, Florence, 10 mars 1843.
2   Corr. Césaire Mathieu à SB, lettre 50, Florence, 10 mars 1843. 'vous revêtir aux yeux de votre Congrégation
      de la plus grande autorité possible'.
3   Corr. SB à Césaire Mathieu, lettre 56, Paris, 17 mars 1843.
4   [Rome, Villa Lante. Diary of events. December 1842–September 1843] (GA, Rome, C–I., c–3, Box 5 1839);
      Corr. SB à Césaire Mathieu, lettre 59, Paris, 24 mars 1843; Corr. SB et Marie Prevost, [Paris], 15 mars 1843.
      (Affaires concernant la Société de 1839 à 43, No. 2 f. 63. Also, Storia di casa, 'Cartolario', 1837–1860, ff. 25–29
      (Archives de la Villa Lante, Rome).
5   For a record of the correspondence between these women during this period: GA, Rome, C–I., C–3, Box 6, 1839.
6   Corr. SB à Césaire Mathieu, lettre 56, Paris, 17 mars 1843.
7   ibid., lettre 50, Paris, 18 février 1843; lettre 51, [Paris, 15 février 1843]. Corr. Césaire Mathieu à SB, lettre 38,
      Rome, 2 février 1843; lettre 40, Rome, 8 février 1843.
8   Corr. SB à Césaire Mathieu, lettre 51, [Paris, 15 février 1843]. Si je pouvais vous donner les détails de leurs
      procédés, je crois que vous me conseilleriez de garder cependant un peu de dignité. Avoir soupçonné ma foi,
      mon attachement au St Siège, l'avoir insinué à d'autres, et cela sans m'avoir demandé un mot d'explication
      […]! Il me semble […] que les prévenir, m'excuser auprès d'elles en faisant des actes de foi aurait quelque
      inconvénient. Je profiterai certainement de toutes les ouvertures qui me seront faites pour leur témoigner de
      la bonté, de l'indulgence, l'oubli même du passé. Mais les prévenir, je ne le crois pas.
9   Corr. Césaire Mathieu à SB, lettre 42, Rome, 17 février 1843 […] dans une affaire majeure comme la vôtre et
      où la prudence humaine est à bout de voies, il est évident qu'il faut prendre son point de conduite plus haut,
      et ce qui serait folie souvent devant les hommes devient sagesse devant Dieu. Le plus difficile de votre posi-
      tion est maintenant de concilier des esprits et des cœurs aussi profondément aliénés au regard les uns des
      autres. Pour cela vous avez deux choses à faire, l'une qui regarde vous-même, et l'autre qui regarde le gou-
      vernement de la communauté. Celle qui vous regarde vous-même, c'est d'être plus douce, plus humble, plus
      charitable, plus patiente, à mesure que les autres le sont moins. Vous ne ramènerez rien par empire, mais bien
      par débonnaireté. C'est à cela que tendent les lettres que je vous ai conseillées. Mais mon intention n'est
      point que vous fassiez des excuses. Seulement vous parlerez bonnement et doucement comme si vous n'aviez
      rien sur le cœur. Puis, ne voyez-vous pas que si vous avez un peu à excéder, il faut le faire du côté de Notre
      Seigneur qui vient toujours à nous le premier malgré nos fautes? Quant à l'autre chose qui concerne le gou-
      vernement de la Société: autant que vous serez douce et bonne pour toutes, autant il faudra être ferme et
      supérieure dans toute la force du terme. Pour cela, il ne faut engager votre liberté et votre affection avec per-
      sonne; il faut les embrasser toutes dans l'amour de Notre Seigneur et pas autre chose.
10   ibid., lettre 43, [Rome] 20 février 1843. Grandement au large avec les amis qui vous entourent, et qui malgré
      toute leur bonne volonté ne laisseraient pas de vous entraîner dans le précipice, si vous leur donniez prise sur
      vous, parce qu'ils voient les affaires à travers de leur prisme.
11   ibid., lettre 45, [Rome, 23 février 1843]. N'oubliez pas qu'on vous a donné ici la couleur d'une personne incer-
      taine et qui consulte pour de ne pas faire. Opinion que j'ai dû combattre. Si, après la consultation, vous ne
      signez pas on ne manquera pas de renouveler cette accusation.
12   Louise de Limminghe à SB, Rome, 11 mars 1843 (Affaires concernant la Société, No. 2, 1839 à 43, ff. 69–70.
      GA, Rome, C–I., c–3, Box 2, 1839.)
13   Corr. SB à Césaire Mathieu, lettre 58, Paris, 22 mars 1843. Il ne sera pas inutile que votre grandeur juge de
      son style et de son dessein en avertissant de sa démarche les autres assistantes générales. C'est les provoquer
      à en faire autant et si je reçois cette démission, il me faudra l'accorder aux autres, ce qui me mettra dans l'em-
      barras et la Société dans une fâcheuse position, surtout à cause de Madame de Gramont. Mgr l'archevêque
      n'est point apaisé […] et lorsque j'aurai tout ce monde sur les bras je ne sais trop comment je pourrai tout
      concilier. Plus je vois les ennuis et les oppositions qu'on va me susciter, plus je sens la nécessitée d'aller vous
      trouver […] Si Madame Desmarquest me reste, je pense que je devrai la conduire avec moi; peut-être [vous]
      lui ferez du bien, elle me gênera beaucoup, car aucune d'elles ne reviendront de bonne foi. Ce sera par force,
      parce qu'elles ne veulent comprendre aucunement, que la force des choses nous a conduit à cette extrémité
      et que nous ne pouvions sauver la Société qu'à ce prix.
14   ibid., lettre 59 [61], Paris, 24 mars 1843. Je trouve que l'exigence de plusieurs à Rome qui désirent si ardem-
      ment l'éloignement de Madame de Gramont de toute charge n'est point juste ni conséquente. Car si la
      Congrégation et le très saint Père ont cru devoir supprimer des décrets à cause de leurs inconvénients,
      pourquoi en veut-on au parti qui précisément en a saisi plus vite que l'autre la défectuosité? et faut-il le punir

d'avoir éclairé? S'il a eu tort dans les procédés vis-à-vis de leur supérieure générale, le parti romain en a eu certainement de plus graves et bien davantage l'a molestée et réduite à zéro.

Je prie votre grandeur de croire qu'en défendant Madame de Gramont il n'y a aucune faiblesse d'attachement sensible, mais le pur intérêt de la Société. Notre Seigneur a pris des moyens vigoureux pour rompre et même pour châtier chez moi tout attachement humain. Je crois que j'en ai profité.

15 ibid., lettre 65, Paris, 2 avril 1843.

16 Notes en forme de journal, ff. 11–12. 'Notes pour M.xx.
Que faire pour suppléer aux provinciales?
Faut-il remplacer quelques assistantes générales avant le conseil de 1845?
[…] Que faire pour la réforme de telle maison? détails et exemples à citer.
Ne faudrait-il pas remettre toute cette organisation au prochain conseil et jusque là laisser les choses comme elle sont? Je crois néanmoins qu'il sera utile de remplacer Mme de Limminghe.
Parler de ma position à Paris - quelle marche y tenir.

17 Elizabeth Galitzine à SB, Lyon, 25 mars 1843; Lyon 26 mars 1843 (Affaires concernant la Société, No. 2, 1839 à 43, ff. 73–78. GA, Rome, C–I., c–3, Box 2, 1839).

18 Corr. SB à Césaire Mathieu, lettre 61, Paris, 29 mars 1843. Also, lettre 60, Paris, 27 mars 1843.

19 Corr. Césaire Mathieu à SB, lettre 52, Toulon, 26 mars 1843.

20 Corr. SB à Césaire Mathieu, lettre 57, 2 avril 1843. Comment conduirez-vous la Société avec des personnes qui ne resteront avec vous que par force? Comment préparerez-vous le conseil de 1845 avec ces opposantes? Comment guérirez-vous les esprits et les cœurs par les mêmes personnes qui ont failli perdre la Société? Soyez forte contre tous […] ne perdez pas le fruit de mes efforts en tâtonnant, en hésitant […] vous avez à la main le pain et le couteau.

21 ibid., lettre 57, Lyon, 2 avril 1843. Je crois être sûr qu'avant la décision de la Congrégation, les provinces d'Amérique, c'est à dire les maisons, ont écrit à Rome des choses très fortes en faveur des Décrets, et, je le crains, contre la Maison de Paris. C'est là un véritable désordre. Ce n'est pas un jugement téméraire de penser que Madame Galitzine a provoqué tout cela. Si elle demeure assistante et chargée de la province, vous pour-rez vous donner pour la suite beaucoup de tablature. Also, Corr. SB à Césaire Mathieu, lettre 62, Paris, 30 mars 1843; lettre 64, Paris, 1 avril 1843.

22 Corr. Césaire Mathieu à SB, lettre 58, Lyon, 3 avril 1843. On m'a appelé *Sauveur de la Société* et je ne crois pas me tromper en pensant qu'on aurait voulu, il y a un mois, me voir au fond de l'eau. La dernière lettre de Madame de Galitzine, que je garde pour vous la rendre, est une palinodie complète, provoquée, je crois, par Madame de Limminghe. Il me parait qu'il y a un nouveau plan sous roche. Aucune parole de regret de Madame de Galitzine sur sa conduite passée envers vous; au contraire Madame Prevost dit qu'elle n'a fait que son devoir. Tout cela me semble montrer peu de franchise et cacher un plan subséquent. Prenez y garde, et d'autant plus que Madame de Galitzine s'empresse de partir pour Paris mercredi prochain.

23 ibid., lettre 58, Lyon, 3 avril 1843; lettre 59, Besançon, 8 avril 1843.

24 Corr. SB à Césaire Mathieu, lettre 72, Conflans, 5 mai 1843.

25 Denys Affre à SB, Paris, 19 avril 1843; 20 avril 1843; 30 juillet 1843. Denys Affre à Antonio Garibaldi, Paris, 23 mars 1843. GA, Rome, C–I., c–3, Box 7; AF, Poitiers, Paris, BO6, 151, II, Evêché. Limouzin-Lamothe and Leflon, *Affre*, pp. 255–7.

26 M.P. Dougherty, 'L'Ami de la religion et les évêques français sous le Concordat, 1815–1850', *Revue d'Histoire Ecclésiastique*: vol. lxxxix, nos. 3–4, Louvain, 1994, pp. 578–621; Cholvy, *Être chrétien*, pp. 22–4.

27 Corr. SB à Césaire Mathieu, lettre 68, Conflans, 12 avril 1843.

28 Denys Affre à SB, Paris, 19 avril 1843; also 20 avril 1843 (GA, Rome, C–I., c–3, Box 3).

29 Corr. SB à Césaire Mathieu, lettre 69, Paris, 20 avril 1843; lettre 70, Paris, 25 avril 1843; lettre 71, Paris, 30 avril 1843.

30 ibid., lettre 76, Conflans, 2 juin 1843; lettre 78, Nantes, 6 juillet 1843; lettre 83, Paris, 22 septembre 1843.

31 Corr. SB à Césaire Mathieu, lettre 71 bis, Paris, 30 avril 1843. Si c'est par Madame [Eulalie] de Bouchaud la place ne sera plus tenable; dans ce pays je mets contre moi tous les entourages etc.[…] Personne n'est moins unie à moi d'esprit, de manière de voir, de juger, de former son monde. Elle ne fait qu'un au contraire avec les assistantes [générales], surtout Madame Desmarquest, et c'est ce genre étroit, rétréci, tout à fait de la Visitation mais aussi parfois sous le rapport de l'esprit religieux qui les fait un contraste avec la rue de Varenne et les autres. Je voudrais le milieu […]

32 ibid., lettre 72, Conflans, 5 mai 1843. See also, lettre 73, Conflans, 11 mai 1843.

33 ibid., lettre 72, Conflans, 5 mai 1843. 'Je ne puis bouger, ni toucher à un iota'.

34 Corr. Césaire Mathieu à SB, lettre 61, Autoreille (en tournée) 11 mai 1843. Ne vous laissez pas abattre […] reprenez courage. Il faut que maintenant plus que jamais vous teniez d'une main ferme le timon des affaires. J'ajoute même que c'est votre devoir de conscience; autrement tout sera perdu. See also, lettre 62, Dampierre sur Salon, 15 mai 1843; lettre 63, Vesoul, (en tournée), 27 mai 1843; lettre 64, Besançon, 10 juin 1843; lettre 65, Besançon, 20 juin 1843. Corr. SB à Césaire Mathieu, lettre 74, Conflans, 20 mai 1843; lettre 75 [bis], Conflans, 20 mai 1843.

35　Corr. SB à Césaire Mathieu, lettre 76, Conflans, 3 juin 1843.
36　ibid., lettre 72, Conflans, 5 mai 1843. J'attendrai [votre] avis pour écrire à cette supérieure de Sainte-Rufine, dirigée par la Mère de Limminghe, qui me reproduit ses mêmes phrases. Que son génie étroit ne lui aurait pas suggéré, d'ailleurs accoutumée comme elle l'était à n'agir que sous l'influence de sa première Supérieure. C'est un des inconvénients de Mère de Limminghe à Rome […] See also, lettre 73, Conflans, 11 mai 1843; lettre 75, Conflans, 20 mai 1843. Corr. Césaire Mathieu à SB, lettre 64, Besançon, 10 juin 1843; lettre 65, Besançon, 20 juin 1843.
37　Adèle Lehon à Elizabeth Galitzine, St Rufine, 14 mars 1843 (Affaires concernant la Société, No. 2, 1839 à 43, ff. 67–8 GA, Rome, C–I., c–3, Box 2, 1839). Il ne vous écrit pas parce qu'il veut toujours pouvoir dire avec vérité que depuis ces tristes affaires il ne l'a point fait. Sa position dans ce moment est plus délicate que jamais. Comme il a été appelé à dire franchement son avis contraire aux décisions de la congrégation, si l'on rapportait des paroles de blâme etc. on ne manquerait pas de les lui attribuer, ce qui le compromettrait étrangement auprès des cardinaux et du père général. Il vous prie donc d'être plus circonspecte que jamais sur son compte.
38　Corr. Césaire Mathieu à SB, lettre 54, Aix, 29 mars 1843.
39　Notes en forme de journal, f. 11. Il faudrait un volume pour décrire ce que j'ai souffert depuis mon départ jusqu'à cette époque, avril 1843.
40　*Lettres circulaires*, ii, Paris, 6 avril 1843, pp. 155–6. Je ne vous dirai pas […] tout ce que ces mois derniers, ces dangers, cet état de choses, ont eu pour moi de pénible et d'amer, et les cruelles angoisses qui ont déchiré mon âme. Jésus le sait, cela suffit! Si la Société est sauvée, si tous les membres de la Société, mettant de côté les divergences d'opinion, et oubliant ce qui a pu réciproquement les blesser, reconnaissant la volonté de Dieu dans la décision de son Vicaire, se pardonnent mutuellement et s'unissent à leur chef pour travailler avec plus de zèle que jamais à affermir dans la Société la charité, l'uniformité, la fidélité aux Constitutions et la perfection religieuse, nous remercions le Seigneur des cruelles tribulations par lesquelles il nous a fait passer, ainsi que la Société, et nous reconnaîtrons que la croix est toujours l'arbre de la vie et que tous les biens nous viennent avec elle.
41　Affaires concernant la Société, No. 2, 1839 à 43, ff. 67–8 GA, Rome, C–I., c–3, Box 2, 1839, ff. 94–99.
42　Elizabeth Galitzine à Jean Rozaven, Lyon, 14 avril 1843. Affaires concernant la Société, f. 98.afin qu'elles puissent s'en prévaloir dans des temps plus heureux, pour sauver la Société. Si cela ne se peut durant la vie de notre supérieure générale actuelle, cela se pourra après sa mort, et il est de notre devoir de pourvoir à la sûreté de l'Institut, en obtenant des décisions qui plus tard lui rendront cette vie et cette vigueur qu'on cherche à lui ôter.
43　Césaire Mathieu à Elizabeth Galitzine, Besançon, 21 avril 1843. Le Père Jean Rozaven m'a dit que cela était de justice, puisque le gouvernement n'avait donné dans le temps son autorisation que sous cette condition […]
44　Césaire Mathieu à Elizabeth Galitzine, Besançon, 21 avril 1843. Affaires concernant la Société, ff. 105–6. […] ainsi si quelque chose vous déplaît, jetez-m'en la faute, mais pas à d'autres[…]. Hélas, que je suis peiné. La position de la Société, et je puis même dire de l'église de France, à votre occasion, a été des plus graves. C'est une commotion dont on ne peut se remettre que par la charité, la confiance mutuelle, l'obéissance et l'abnégation de soi. Si chacune continue à se retrancher à part, à sonder, soupçonner les intentions, les démarches des autres, tout est perdu […] la Société est à peine sortie [de l'orage] et le tonnerre gronde encore sur nos têtes. Le temps et le baume de la charité guériront bien des blessures. Mais on peut dire que c'est la Société elle-même qui va prononcer maintenant son arrêt de vie ou de mort. Si on se déchire, si on se divise, tout se perdra; si on s'unit, si on se supporte, tout se guérira.
45　Corr. Césaire Mathieu à SB, lettre 64, Besançon, 10 juin 1843. A letter from Louise de Limminghe to SB is enclosed with this letter, Rome, 1 juin 1843; lettre 65, Besançon, 20 juin 1843.
46　Elizabeth Galitzine à Laure d'Avernioz, Conflans, 13 juin 1843 (GA, Rome, C–I., c–3, 1839, Box 6.) Félicité Desmarquest wrote the last page of this letter. Laure d'Avernioz was assistant superior at the Villa Lante. Elizabeth Galitzine addressed the letter to her, but it was intended for Louise de Limminghe. Elizabeth Galitzine had a similar arrangement with the chaplain at the Villa Lante, the abbé Mitrail.
47　Louis Barat à Elizabeth Galitzine, [Paris, juin 1843], Affaires concernant la Société, ff. 85–6. Le plus avantageux dans cette affaire c'est le renvoi de l'assemblée à 1845 […] on n'aura guère à craindre ni l'ordre légal, ni l'ordre Gallican […] et la facilité sera laissée en entier de reprendre le vrai Institut qui alors sera définitif […] Elizabeth Galitzine cited part of this letter when she wrote to d'Avernioz in June 1843: Elizabeth Galitzine à d'Avernioz, Conflans, 13 juin 1843 (GA, Rome, C–I., c–3, 1839, Box 6). Also, Rome, Villa Lante. Diary of events. December 1842–September 1843. Elizabeth Galitzine also received letters from Louis Barat in December 1842 and February 1843.
48　Corr. SB et Aloysia Hardey, lettre 18, Paris, 30 janvier 1843. Je n'ai point osé écrire à la Louisiane, ne connaissant aucune des supérieures et ne sachant pas jusqu'à quel degré Madame Galitzine les a endoctrinées […]
49　ibid., lettre 20, Paris, 24 mai 1843. See also, lettre 21, Conflans, 25 septembre 1843.
50　*Lettres circulaires*, ii, Conflans, 14 juin 1843, pp. 159–65.
51　Corr. SB à Césaire Mathieu, lettre 78, Nantes, 6 juillet 1843; lettre 70, Tours, 18 juillet 1843.

52   ibid., lettre 80, Besançon, 7 août 1843.
53   Corr. SB et Anna du Rousier, lettre 81, Autun, 24 octobre 1842.
54   ibid., lettre 94, Paris, 9 mars 1843; lettre 95, Paris, 18 mars 1843.
55   Corr. SB à Césaire Mathieu, lettre 81, Montet, 16 août 1843.
56   ibid., lettre 82, La Ferrandière, 2 septembre 1843
57   Notes en forme de journal, f. 12.
58   Corr. SB à Césaire Mathieu, lettre 81, Montet, 16 août 1843. 'me comprehenda et me soutiendra.'
59   ibid., lettre 83, Paris, 22 septembre 1843.
60   Vie de la Mère Adélaide Cahier (1804–1885). Adèle Cahier wrote a biography of Sophie Barat which appeared
       in 1884. [Adèle Cahier], *Vie de la vénérable Mère Barat, Fondatrice et première supérieure générale de la Société du
       Sacré-Cœur de Jésus*, 2 vols. (Paris, 1884). For a discussion of the contribution of Adèle Cahier to the history of
       the Society of the Sacred Heart, see Phil Kilroy, 'The use of continental sources of women's religious con-
       gregations and the writing of religious biography: Madeleine Sophie Barat, 1779–1865', in Maryann Gialanelle
       Valiulis and Mary O'Dowd (eds.), *Women and Irish History* (Dublin, 1997), pp. 59–70.
61   Corr. SB à Césaire Mathieu, lettre 86, Paris, 18 mars 1844.
62   Relation de la dernière traverse de ... Mère Galitzine; Notes sur la vie de Madame Elizabeth Galitzine; Extrait
       d'une lettre de St Michel, du 12 décembre 1843; 'Mélanges. Une religieuse russe.' *Le Correspondant*, août 1862
       (GA, Rome, C–VII., 2, Galitzine, Box 3); Notes sur la Mère de Galitzine (GA, Rome, C–I., c–3, Box 5).
63   Corr. SB à Césaire Mathieu, lettre 86, Paris, 10 mars 1844; Aloysia Hardey to Adèle Cahier, New York, 17 juin
       1844 (GA, Rome, C–IV, USA. East (Letters).
64   *Lettres circulaires*, ii, Paris, 24 janvier 1844, pp. 165–7.
65   Corr. SB et Aloysia Hardey, lettre 23, Paris, 24 janvier 1844; lettre 24, Paris, 25 janvier 1844.
66   ibid., lettre 26, Paris, 8 mars 1844; lettre 28, Conflans, 21 mai 1844; lettre 29, BerryMead, 5 juin 1844; lettre
       30, BerryMead, Acton, près Londres, 17 juin 1844.
67   ibid., lettre 37, Conflans, 13 novembre 1845. Mes reproches sont plutôt des avertissements, et si je n'avais pas
       de confiance en vous je vous retirerais de votre place et me tairais. L'Esprit dit qu'il châtie celui qu'il aime.
       C'est absolument ce sentiment qui me guide, en vous tenant au courant de ce que l'on dit de vous. D'ailleurs,
       je ne crois pas le quart [...]
68   Corr. Sophie et Maria Cutts, lettre 2, Paris, 24 janvier 1844.
69   ibid., lettre 3, Paris, 2 mai 1844; lettre 4, Lille, 14 Juillet 1844. At this time Sophie sometimes wrote the same
       letters to Aloysia Hardey, Maria Cutts and Bathilde Sallion, but added her own personal notes to each. See
       also, *Lettres circulaires*, ii, Paris, 1 mars 1844, pp. 180–3; Paris, 13 juillet 1844, pp. 189–97; Corr. SB, Aloysia
       Hardey et Bathilde Sallion, 1840–1846 (GA, Rome, C–IV., USA. East (Letters)). Also, Society of the Sacred
       Heart National Archives, U.S.A. Series III, Inter-provincial affairs, A, USA, 1) Pre IPB, History, Box 1; Series
       III, Special Collections, Marie Louise Martinez Collection.
70   Josephine de Coriolis à SB, Rome, [février] 1844. Il a été grandement question de vous [...] on vous a grande-
       ment blâmée, on a dit que vous aviez montré dans tout cela une grande faiblesse de caractère etc., etc.[...]
       que vous aviez rendu la Société exclusivement française [...] puis elle a entremêlé ses phrases de certaines
       parenthèses telle que celles-ci: J'ai toute la confiance de Madame de Limminghe. C'est mon amie. La Mère
       Générale reste pour la France, mais Madame de Limminghe est la Mère Générale de la Société d'Italie etc.,
       etc., etc.[...] Je sais bien que le Père Jean Rozaven peut avoir aussi dit quelque chose au sujet de nos affaires
       à la princesse [...] Je crains que les maisons d'Italie (excepté la Trinité et Lorette) ne soient un jour ou l'autre
       perdues pour la Société.
71   Guy Bedouelle, *Lacordaire, son pays, ses amis et la liberté des ordres religieux en France* (Paris, 1991); Corr. SB et
       Stanislas Dusaussoy, lettre 103, Paris, 26 octobre 1840.
72   Josephine de Coriolis à SB, Rome, 4 mars 1844. Also, Laure de Ste Colombe (1806–1886) à SB, Rome, [n.d.
       c. 1846], contains details of the unrest within the community at the Trinité at this time (GA, Rome, C–IV., 4,
       Rome, Box 1).
73   Two years later, in 1846, Sophie Barat came across a similar case herself in Lyon. She advised the couple to go
       to Rome. Corr. SB et Louise de Limminghe, lettre 362, Paris, 13 février 1846; lettre 364, Conflans, 24 février
       1846; lettre 365, Paris, 3 mars 1846; lettre 366, Paris, 9 mars 1846; lettre 367, Conflans, 14 avril 1846; lettre 368,
       Conflans, 26 avril; lettre 371, Conflans, 23 mai 1846. For a study of the theology which led the church to accept-
       ing the abandonment of marriage and children in favour of religious life, see: Newman, *Virile Woman*, pp. 78–105;
       Natalie Zemon Davies, *Women on the Margins. Three Seventeenth Century Lives* (Harvard, 1995) pp. 71,–3;83.
74   Josephine de Coriolis à SB, Rome, 26 mars, 28 mars, 29 avril 1844.
75   In effect Cornelia Connelly founded the Society of the Holy Child Jesus. *Positio: Documentary study for the
       canonisation of ... Cornelia Connolly (née Peacock), 1809–1879* (Rome, 1983), I, pp. 212–13. Also, pp. 120–166
       (Grand Coteau 1838–1843), 167–211 (Matrimonial Separation and Religious Life (Rome, 1843–46). Positio:
       III, Notes, Appendices, Archival Sources, Biography, Index (Rome, 1983), pp. 1257–1274. I acknowledge with
       gratitude the gracious gift from the Society of the Holy Child Jesus of the documentation process for the
       canonisation of Cornelia Connolly.

76 Corr. SB à Césaire Mathieu, lettre 86, Paris, 10 mars 1844; lettre 87, Paris, 16 mars 1844; lettre 88, Paris, 9 avril 1844.
77 Corr. SB et Louise de Limminghe, lettre 340 (bis), Paris, 13 janvier 1843. Tend évidemment à la ruine de la Société [...] un schisme est alors inévitable, or ces deux portions divisées seront comme deux oiseaux, qui n'auront chacun qu'une aile. Elles marchent peut-être encore, mais en boitant, ou se déboîtant plutôt [...] J'ai pris mon parti et je lutterai seule, tant que je pourrai, pour empêcher la destruction qui nous menace [...]
78 ibid., lettre 341, Paris, 15 février 1843. Personne ne sait plus que ce véritable ami ce que j'ai souffert, non des peines cruelles qui m'ont assiégée, mais de la source d'où elles sont venues [...] combien le cœur souffre d'être méconnue, abandonnée d'amitiés que l'on pensait être d'autres soi-même, et cela sans connaissance des choses, sans explication, s'en rapportant à tout autre qu'à la personne à qui l'on devait au moins quelque confiance. Mais laissons tout cela dans le sein de Dieu, c'est Lui qui a tout permis et pour des fins que nous connaîtrons plus tard.
79 ibid., lettre 343, Paris, 22 mars 1843; lettre 345, Paris, 15 juin 1843.
80 *Le peintre de Mater Admirabilis. Mère Pauline Perdrau, 1815–1895* (Montauban, 1927); Pauline Perdrau was a portrait artist in Paris before she entered the Society of the Sacred Heart. Her portrait of Archbishop de Quelen hangs in the Treasury of Notre Dame, Paris. (Archives de l'Archevêché de Paris, Papiers de Quelen, I D IV 3, No. 19; I D IV 5). A fresco by Pauline Perdrau which depicted Mary as a young girl was called Mater Admirabilis and became a popular shrine at the Trinité. Bonnard, *Histoire*, pp. 301–4; G. Pudor, 'A propos de la guérison du P. Blanpin', *Echos de Santa Chiara*, vol. xxxix (juillet–août 1939) pp. 280–93.
81 Louise de Limminghe à SB, Rome, 17 mai 1844. This is a fragment of the letter from Louise de Limminghe. Sophie Barat's letter to Louise de Limminghe has not been found.
82 Corr. SB et Louise de Limminghe, lettre 349, Lille, 3 juillet 1844 lettre 350, Lille, 9 juillet 1844.
83 *Lettres circulaires*, I, Paris, 15 janvier 1844, pp. 106–11.

Notes to Chapter 21

1 Corr. SB et Charlotte Gould, lettre 11, Conflans, 19 mai 1844; Cahier, *Vie*, ii, 125–30; Susan O'Brien, 'French Nuns in Nineteenth Century England', *Past and Present*, no. 154 (February 1997), pp. 142–80; Susan O'Brien, 'Terra Incognita: The Nun in Nineteenth-Century England', *Past and Present*, no. 121 (November 1988), pp. 110–40.
2 *Lettres circulaires*, ii, Marseille, 16 janvier 1845, p. 198.
3 Notes en forme de journal, ff. 14–15. Cahier, *Vie*, ii, 131–33; Corr. SB et Eugénie de Gramont, lettre 909, La Ferrandière, 21 novembre 1844; lettre 913, Aix, 3 janvier 1845; lettre 914, Aix, 7 janvier 1845; lettre 915, St Joseph [Marseille] 15 janvier 1845.
4 *Lettres circulaires*, ii, Marseille, 16 janvier 1845, pp. 198–9.
5 Corr. SB et Stanislas Dusaussoy, lettre 116, Marseilles, St Joseph, 15 janvier, 1845. Also lettre 117, Rome, 10 mai 1845; lettre 118, Rome, 8 juin 1845.
6 Corr. SB et Louise de Limminghe, lettre 351, [Trinité] 9 avril 1845.
7 Corr. SB à Césaire Mathieu, lettre 94, Rome, 27 février 1845. 'blanche comme neige'
8 Corr. SB et Aloysia Hardey, lettre 34, Rome, 18 avril 1845. Elle a eu tort de se laisser influencer et mener par celle qui a été le moteur de nos ennuis. Elle est au Ciel. N'en parlons plus. Elle avait certainement les meilleures intentions. See also, Corr. SB et Aloysia Hardey, lettre 35, Paris, 25 septembre 1845; lettre 37, Conflans, 13 novembre 1845 and *passim*.
9 Corr. SB à Césaire Mathieu, lettre 93, Aix, 8 janvier 1845. 'Je deviens vieille, la moindre fatigue me donne des maladies interminables.' Also, Corr. SB et Eugénie de Gramont, lettre 922, Rome, 28 mars 1845.
10 Corr. SB à Césaire Mathieu, lettre 94, 27 février 1845.
11 Notes en forme de journal, f. 17.
12 Corr. SB à Césaire Mathieu, lettre 95, Rome, 1 mai 1845.
13 Souvenirs de Sœur Virginie Roux, f. 61 (GA, Rome, A–II., I–a, Box 1) 'rien autre chose que ce que l'on appelle dans le monde le bon ton ou l'esquisse politesse.'
14 Souvenir de Sœur Virginie Roux, Notes confidentielles, f. 139
15 Souvenir de Sœur Virginie Roux, Notes confidentielles, ff. 138–9. Une fois elle nous disait que tout son désir était de nous voir religieuses vraiment intérieures, qu'elle fondait sur cela tant d'espérances [...] La Mère de Gramont reprit avec un ton des plus ironiques: " Eh! bien, que feriez-vous de votre Société si vous n'aviez pas de religieuses savantes? " [...] Notre [...] Mère [Sophie] répondit avec beaucoup de douceur: " Je ne veux pas dire que nous n'avons pas besoin de religieuses savantes; mais je veux dire que l'œuvre de Dieu dans les âmes ne se fait que par celles qui lui sont unies, surtout pour les fondations, elles ne sont pas faites par des savantes, mais les âmes intérieures."
16 Quelques traits de la vie et de la mort de Madame Eugénie de Gramont, Louis de Calvimont (La Quotidienne, 25 janvier 1847) p. 12. (Comment on Aimée d'Avenas in the obituary for Eugénie de Gramont, 1847).
17 Souvenir de Sœur Virginie Roux, Notes confidentielles, ff. 139–40.

18   Corr. SB et Eugénie de Gramont, lettre 917, Rome, 10 février 1845; lettre 920, Rome, 26 février 1845.

19   ibid., lettre 922, Rome, 28 mars 1845. Plusieurs personnes venues de France, que le rang et les vertus rendent respectables ([…] j'ai compris que c'étaient des ecclésiastiques, mais il y a aussi des personnes séculières) ayant appris que j'étais le cardinal protecteur de votre Société, sont venues me trouver pour m'avertir des abus tout à fait répréhensibles qui se passent rue de Varenne. Les connaissez-vous?
Premièrement: des mariages dont ces dames s'occupent, recevant les jeunes gens avec les Promises. Les religieuses accompagnent; il parait que ces bruits sont répandus et scandalisent! (lorsque l'on parle contre nous, on exagère toujours)
Deuxièmement: Il y a dans cette maison une religieuse qui n'en a ni l'esprit, ni les vertus, qui a toute la confiance de la supérieure et qui fait bien du mal. C'est un auteur. Elle écrit dans les journaux. Pour la peindre en deux mots: c'est une *Philosophe*. On l'a envoyée en Angleterre. Elle s'y est attiré la critique etc. (Ceci m'a paru fort.) See also, lettre 923, Rome, 7 avril 1845; lettre 925, Rome, 18 avril 1845. Barbara Hogg, *Society of the Sacred Heart in England, 1842–1870*, (Provincial Archives, Society of the Sacred Heart, London), p. 27.

20   Corr. SB et Eugénie de Gramont, lettre 922, Rome, 28 mars 1845.[…] je ne vais pas dans une ville, je ne reçois presque pas de lettres, où je n'entends quelques plaintes faites contre cette maison [rue de Varenne]: je veux dire le pensionnat. Ainsi un prêtre de mérite disait à une des nôtres: plusieurs élèves de ces Dames, qui ont la vocation, ne veulent pas y entrer, voyant si peu d'union parmi elles, et même pour plusieurs, si peu de piété et tant de légèreté. Malheureusement, ceci n'est que trop vrai.

21   Corr. SB et Eugénie de Gramont, lettre 945, Conflans, 28 septembre 1845.

22   Notes en forme de journal, f. 17.

23   ibid., f. 18; Pauline Perdrau wrote an account of this eventful and happy journey. Perdrau, *Loisirs*, pp. 56–107.

24   Corr. SB et Eugénie de Gramont, lettre 938, Turin, 7 juillet 1845.

25   Corr. SB et Stanislas Dusaussoy, lettre 194, [Paris], 29 juillet [1851]. Joseph Varin wrote a long account of Louis Barat's life for Jean Roothan, yet in it he made no reference at all to Sophie. Joseph Varin à Jean Roothan, Paris, 30 décembre 1845 (ARSI, Rome, Franc., 6–IX, 43).

26   Corr. SB et Eugénie de Gramont, lettre 956, Conflans, 3 novembre 1845. Vous savez qu'il est difficile de vous aborder sur certains points, et celui des Sœurs est de ce nombre […] combien d'années j'ai souffert les abus de la porterie, de la direction du pensionnat. Assurément, je vous en ai parlé souvent! […] Je serais si heureuse […] de m'entendre avec vous, de ne faire qu'un pour tâcher de perfectionner la mission que le Cœur de Jésus vous a confiée […] Pourquoi ne travaillerions-nous de concert à ramener l'opinion, en ôtant les prétextes. Ce n'est pas en vous retirant que nous réussirons; mais c'est en resserrant l'union entre nous […] rien ne peut égaler la peine que j'ai à vous en faire, et si cela arrive, croyez que c'est contre mon gré et par la force du devoir! Car croyez encore qu'il est certains abus, des rapports vrais que vous ne voulez ni voir ni remédier […] si nous n'appliquons les remèdes, votre maison tombera tout à fait, et quels regrets pour vous, pour moi, qui y travaillons depuis tant d'années […]
Il fait si beau, ne viendrez-vous pas nous voir?

27   Corr. SB et Luigi Lambruschini (GA, Rome, B–II., Box 1, Dossier 3).

28   AF, Poitiers, Paris, B06, 151, II, Evêché. The role of chaplains was under discussion in the diocese of Paris at this time. Note demandée Monseigneur l'Archevêque sur les communautés Religieuses et sur les prêtres attachés aux dites communautés. 1843 (Archives de l'Archevêché de Paris, Fonds Affre, 1840–1848, 1 D V 2).

29   Corr. SB à Césaire Mathieu, lettre 98, Conflans, 23 février 1846. See also, lettre 96, Paris, 20 septembre 1845. Archbishop Affre to SB, Paris, 20 octobre 1846 (AF, Poitiers, Paris, B06, 151, II, Evêché); Notes en forme de journal, ff. 19–22; Souvenirs de Sœur Virginie Roux, Notes confidentielles, ff. 139–40.

30   Corr. SB à Césaire Mathieu, lettre 99, Paris, 15 mars 1846. For the conflict between the Society of the Sacred Heart and Archbishop Affre over the appointment of chaplains from 1845–46, Copie d'un journal fait par [Sophie Barat] depuis octobre jusqu'au novembre 1846 (GA, Rome, C–I., A, 1–c, Box 1); Corr. SB à Césaire Mathieu, lettre 105, Paris, 24 décembre 1847.

31   Corr. SB à Césaire Mathieu, lettre 100, Conflans, 6 mai 1846. Also, SB à Luigi Lambruschini, [Conflans], mai 1846 (GA, Rome, B–II., Box 1. Dossier 3). Notes en forme de journal, ff. 24–5; Lettres de Alexis Gaume (AF, Poitiers, Paris, B06, 151, I, Evêché); Limouzin-Lamothe and Leflon, *Affre*, pp. 257–8.

32   SB à Luigi Lambruschini, [Conflans], décembre 1845; [Conflans] 28 janvier 1846 (GA, Rome, B–II., Box 1. Dossier 3); Notes en forme de journal, 3 septembre 1846, f. 30.

33   Luigi Lambruschini à SB, Rome, 20 mai 1846 (GA, Rome, B–II., Box 1, Dossier 3); Notes en forme de journal, f. 21.

34   Luigi Lambruschini à Archbishop de Quelen, Rome, 12 avril 1833 (Archives de l'Archevêché de Paris, Fonds de Quelen, 1 D IV, 8, 1833, N°8). elle est bien digne et je vous la recommande de tout mon mieux, étant une âme bien chère à Dieu et ayant dans sa position dure le besoin des sages conseils et des utiles injonctions de son saint pasteur […]

35   Corr. SB et Eugénie de Gramont, lettre 1003, Conflans 7 juillet 1846 (mardi soir). Je vous ai écrit ce matin […] une lettre qui vous aura affligée. Pourtant j'ose espérer que vous apprécierez mes motifs et que vous ne serez pas trop peinée de vivre de temps à autre avec une mère dont vous connaissez le profond et sincère

attachement. Je vous prie de m'adresser une ou deux lignes pour m'accuser réception de cette lettre si pénible du cardinal et même de me la renvoyer. Je compte la brûler afin que personne n'en ait jamais connaissance
36 ibid., lettre 1003 bis, Conflans, 8 juillet 1846.
37 ibid., lettre 1019, Conflans, 29 août 1846. Il y a des années que je connais l'espèce de jalousie qui se couvait contre nous. Je m'en occupais peu. On ne spécifiait que des généralités. Mais depuis deux à trois ans, on cite des faits, exagérés sans doute. On les croit, et comme on y donne lieu, la défaveur est générale. C'est une épreuve que nous devons porter avec résignation, mais aussi, nous devons, ce me semble, travailler à en ôter les prétextes [...] Ah! si vous saviez ce que je souffre de tout ce que j'entends et surtout de votre douleur [...]
38 Corr. SB et Aimée d'Avenas, lettre 86, Rome, 10 mars 1845; lettre 88, Rome, 20 avril; lettre 93, [Conflans], 21 mai 1846; lettre 96, [Conflans], 14 juin 1846; lettre 97, Conflans, 23 juin 1846.
39 ibid., lettre 98, Conflans, 6 juillet 1846; lettre 99, Paris, 31 juillet 1846.
40 Notes en forme de journal, 22 juillet 1846; août 1846, ff. 28–9; Corr. SB à Césaire Mathieu, lettre 103, Paris, 17 août 1846.
41 L'Ami de la religion, t. 131, 22 décembre 1846, 735; L'Ami de la religion, t. 131, 26 décembre 1846, 767–9; Quelques traits de la vie et de la mort de Madame Eugénie de Gramont, par M. Le Comte Louis de Calvimont. Extrait de la Quotidienne du 25 janvier 1847. The Society of the Sacred Heart wrote a longer than usual death notice for Eugénie de Gramont. Lettre Annuelles, Maisons du Nord, Paris. Décembre 1846. Eugénie de Gramont (1788–1846), pp. 1–12. Perdrau, *Loisirs* (Rome, 1934), pp. 138–9.
42 Perdrau, *Loisirs*, pp. 140–1.
43 Louis de Calvimont, Quelques traits de la vie et de la mort de Madame Eugénie de Gramont, pp. 8, 11.
44 Testimony of Marie du Chélas, Paris, 8 février 1886 (GA, Rome, Processus apostolicus in causa beatification-is et canonisationis ... Magdalena Sophiae Barrat, vol. iii, sessio 107a, f. 1896).
45 Deposition of Adèle Lehon, Paris, 23 février 1882 (GA, Rome, Processus apostolica auctoritate constructi in curia ecclesiastica Parisiensi ... ii, 1897, Sessio 3a–34a, f. 395). For an assessment of the character of Eugénie de Gramont, attributed to Sophie Barat, Peri-Morosini, *La Sainte Mère Madeleine Sophie Barat, fondatrice de la Société du Sacré-Cœur et le château de Middes en Suisse* (Toulouse, 1925), p. 5.
46 Corr. SB et Anna du Rousier, lettre 121, Paris, 15 mars 1844. Mais Madame de Gramont est loin de goûter ces apparences de grandeur qui tiennent au local et au genre de personnes que la divine providence a confié à cet établissement. Personne de plus religieuse que madame de Gramont. Elle est pauvre pour tout ce qui la concerne, même sévère pour elle[...] Elle a si peu plaie de sa naissance que jamais elle n'en ouvre la bouche[...] However, Sophie told du Rousier that the school of 180 students was not being properly run and she admitted that on that count the rue de Varenne was poor indeed. Corr. SB et Anna du Rousier, lettre 156, Paris, 24 décembre 1846. Also lettre 121, Paris, 15 mars 1844.
47 Corr. SB et Mr Rameau Rambaud, Paris, 26 mai 1858. Je ne puis encore m'accoutumer à la privation, au vide, que me laisse la perte de Madame Eugénie de Gramont, qui m'était si chère et si nécessaire pour nous aider dans l'éducation de nos élèves de Paris dont elle était supérieure et maîtresse générale.
48 Corr. SB à Thérèse Maillucheau, lettre 271, Paris, 24 août 1847. parmi mes rares et minces vertus, ou peut-être mes défauts, la constance est peut-être la plus marquée.
49 Corr. SB et Aimée d'Avenas, lettre 101, Paris, 23 décembre 1846. [...] quel vide j'ai trouvé. Ce matin j'ai eu la force de réunir la communauté [...] J'ai annoncé que la maison serait dorénavant la résidence de la Supérieure générale [...] Cet arrangement tiendra jusqu'au Conseil Général.
50 Perdrau, *Loisirs*, pp. 141–44.
51 Souvenir de Sœur Virginie Roux, Notes confidentielles, ff. 136–7. Il faut que je vous dise les choses [...] Grégoire XVI voulait absolument que la maison mère de notre Société fût à Rome. Mais le gouvernement de France en ayant été informé y a mis obstacle [...] Après de longs débats il a été conclu qu'elle serait à Paris [...] Etant Supérieure générale je devais être supérieure de cette maison. Mais la Mère de Gramont aimait cette maison où elle était depuis si longtemps, je n'ai pas voulu la contrister. Je l'ai donc laissée dans sa charge.
52 Perdrau, *Loisirs*, pp. 140.
53 Notes en forme de journal, ff. 22–26. Details of all these foundations are found in Adèle Cahier, *Vie*, ii, Chs. XLV–XLVII.
54 Notes en forme de journal, f. 30. Also, f. 22.
55 Corr. SB à Thérèse Maillucheau, lettres 234–69, septembre 1845–décembre 1846.
56 Corr. SB et Anne Marie Granon, lettre 36, Paris, 11 mars 1843; lettre 44, Paris, 1 avril 1844; lettre 47, Rome, 25 avril 1845. Corr. SB et Emma de Bouchaud, lettre 4, Rome, 6 septembre 1839; lettre 6, 8 octobre 1839; lettre 139, Paris, 3 juin 1849; lettre 154, Paris, 9 mars 1850.
57 *Lettres circulaires*, ii, Paris, 10 février 1844, p. 172.
58 *Lettres circulaires*, ii, Conflans, 29 décembre 1845.
59 *Lettres circulaires*, ii, Paris, 10 février 1844, pp. 170–71. Les excluait de son ordre sans miséricorde et elle n'avait pas comme nous l'éducation qui exige un choix bien spécial, même parmi les Sœurs coadjutrices, souvent employées près des enfants. Il serait bon que cet examen et cette épuration se fissent pendant le noviciat, pour éviter les graves inconvénients qui suivent le relevé des vœux [...] et qui [...] impriment, dans certains

pays plus religieux, une tache et comme un déshonneur sur toute la vie de ces personnes [...] See also, *Lettres circulaires*, ii, Conflans, 29 décembre 1845, pp. 200–2; Paris, 5 avril 1848, p. 224.

60   Corr. SB à Thérèse Mailucheau, lettre 228, Lille, 5 juillet 1844. Oui [...] que les sujets peu religieux, avec des demi-vocations, nous font du mal! De grâce faites-y attention; jusqu'à ma mort ce sera ma *delenda Cartago*! Je finirai toutes mes lettres par là. See also lettres 229, Conflans, 19 septembre 1844; lettre 230, La Ferrandière, 30 novembre 1844. Corr. SB et Olympie Rombau, lettre 60, Paris, 3 juillet 1857; lettre 61, Paris, 23 septembre [1857]; lettre 72, Paris, 10 juillet 1858. Delenda est Cartago. Carthage must be destroyed. (Cato the Elder, 234–149 BC).

61   *Lettres circulaires*, i, [Conflans] février 1844.

62   *Lettres circulaires*, i, Conflans, 29 décembre 1845, pp. 120–1.

63   ibid., pp. 130–1. Also, pp. 122–5.

64   ibid., p. 126. ce mal est d'autant plus grand que, croyant, par principe de conscience, devoir refuser les inspections de l'université, si nous faiblissons dans la science de l'enseignement nous fournissons des armes contre nous. C'est ce qui est arrivé dans une des principales villes de France, où les parents [...] étaient les premiers à exciter les inspecteurs, disant que nous avions besoin de leurs examens. See Marie Prevost à Louise de Limminghe, Aix, 24 décembre 1844 (GA, Rome, C–I., C–3, Box 3, 1839).

65   *Lettres circulaires*, i, Conflans, 29 décembre 1845, p. 128. Rien ne s'oppose à ce divin Esprit comme une vie de désœuvrement. Ces personnes qui n'aiment ni le travail, ni l'étude, à quoi passent-ils leur temps? A rien de fixe et d'utile, parlant sans motifs, allant à gauche et à droite [...] voyant tout ce qui se passe, donnant un libre cours à leur imagination [...]

66   *Lettres circulaires*, ii, Paris, 26 mars 1844, pp. 186–7. Also pp. 184–5. non que nous fassions acception de personnes, mais parce que nous avons eu la triste expérience que notre mode d'éducation nuit plus qu'il n'est utile à une jeune personne destinée par sa condition, ou celle de ses parents, à contracter des alliances dans son rang, ou à être dans un magasin, quelquefois même à travailler pour vivre. On devine aisément ce qui résulte de cette éducation qui les humilie ou les rend paresseuses, beaucoup n'ayant pu profiter des leçons reçues, faute de moyens [...]

67   *Lettres circulaires*, ii, Paris, 10 février 1844, pp. 173–6. Corr. SB et Louise de Limminghe, lettre 364, Conflans, 24 février 1846; lettre 383, Paris, 31 mai 1847. Corr. SB et Anne Marie Granon, lettre 52, Conflans, 20 février, 1846. Corr. SB et Anna du Rousier, lettre 151, Conflans, 3 juin 1846.

68   *Lettres circulaires*, ii, Paris, 10 février 1844, pp. 176–8.

69   Corr. SB et Matilde Garabis, lettres 1–9, mai 1844–mai 1845. Sophie had appointed Matilde Garabis (1810–92) to be the bursar in Conflans in 1845.

70   SB à Luigi Lambruschini, Paris, 24 juin 1847 (GA, Rome, B–II, Box 1, Dossier 3). Les esprits se sont rapprochés et les impressions pénibles qu'avaient laissés nos tristes affaires de 1842 et 43 s'effacent peu à peu. Il reste cependant un certain malaise qu'un conseil général pourra seul cesser [...] Les dispositions peu favorables de l'autorité [Monseigneur Affre] ont mis obstacle à la convocation de cette assemblée [...]

71   Corr. SB à Césaire Mathieu, lettre 99, Paris, 15 mars 1846. 'tracassée et harcelée de nouveau par ce genre [Archbishop Affre] qui vous connaissez'.

72   Robert Gildea, *Barricades and Borders. Europe 1800–1914* (Oxford, 1987), pp. 83–92; 255–62; H.A.C. Collingham, *The July Monarchy. A political history of France 1830–1848* (London, 1988), pp. 403–15; Roger Price, *A Concise History of France* (Cambridge, 1993), pp. 168–82.

73   Corr. SB et Louise de Limminghe, lettre 383, Paris, 31 mai 1847.

74   Corr. SB et Stanislas Dusaussoy, lettre 150, Paris 19 février 1848.

75   Perdrau, *Loisirs*, p. 161: 'Nous savons le métier d'assister aux déchéances.'

76   Perdrau, *Loisirs*, p. 172.

77   Gardes Nationales de Département de la Seine, Paris, 26 février 1848 (GA, Rome, C–I., A, 1–c, Box 2).

78   Perdrau, *Loisirs*, p. 162–4; Cahier, *Vie*, ii, 181–4; 191–202. GA, Rome, A–II., 2–d, Fondations.

79   L'Ami de la Religion, t. 136, 2 mars 1848, 516; Notes demandées par Mgr l'archevêque de Paris au moment de la proclamation de la république, février 1848 (AF, Poitiers, Paris, rue de Varenne, BO6, 151, I, L'évêché).

80   Limouzin-Lamothe and Leflon, *Affre*, p. 258; Cahier, *Vie*, ii, 145.

81   Notes sur la position des maisons du Sacré-Cœur de Paris et Conflans. Elles n'ont pas été envoyée. (AF, Poitiers, Paris, B06, 151, I, Lettres de l'Archevêché).

82   Gildea, op. cit., pp. 91, 101, 255.

Notes to Chapter 22

1   Cahier, *Vie*, ii, 205. Affaire ecclésiastique. Secret. Monsieur l'abbé de Brandt (GA, Rome, France, Amiens, C–IV., 2). Alexandre, Charles, Michel de Brandt was born in Amiens in 1812 and studied for the priesthood in St Sulpice. Ordained in 1838 he became private secretary to Bishop Mioland (1838–1849) and then Bishop de Salinis (1849–1861). Henri Peltier, 'Le chanoine de Brandt', *Le Dimanche* [Amiens], 11–18 septembre 1949.

The abbé de Brandt wrote several books of meditations and devotions (Archives et bibliothèques, Diocese d'Amiens).

2   Archives de l'Archevêché de Paris, Procès de Madame Barat, Sessio 1o, 28 mai, f. 348; 18 mai 1873, ff. 1135–6.

3   Corr. SB et Adelaide de Rozeville, lettre 390, Paris, 24 novembre 1847.

4   Josephine Gœtz (1817–1874) was born in Alsace. Her mother died when she was three years old and Josephine was brought up by her aunt Odile Gœtz, even though her father married again and he died in 1830. She went to school with the Society in Besançon where she was an independent and wilful pupil. In 1835 she entered the Society of the Sacred Heart and taught for nine years in Besançon. Sophie Barat had already recognised her leadership qualities and when she was finally professed in 1847 Sophie named her mistress of novices that year, to succeed Angélique de Boisbaudry. She succeeded Sophie Barat as superior general in 1865.

5   [Adèle Cahier] Extrait de notes sur la maison d'Amiens (GA, Rome, C–IV, 2, Amiens, Letters, Box 1, ff. 1–4).

6   Louis Sellier à SB, St Acheul [Amiens], 18 novembre 1849 (GA, Rome, C–IV, 2, Amiens. Letters, Box 3).

7   Notes données par la Sœur Adélaide Edouard, en 1896 (AF, Poitiers, La Neuville, B35, 111, 115, 118).

8   Adèle Cahier à SB, Amiens, c. septembre 1850 (GA, Rome, C–IV, 2, Amiens, Letters, Box 1, ff. 5–6).

9   Sophie Dusaussoy à SB, Amiens, 27 juin 1850; 3 juillet 1850 (GA, Rome, C–I., C–3, Box 6, 1839).

10 Sophie Dusaussoy à SB, Amiens, 27 juin 1850; 3 juillet 1850; 7 juillet 1850 (GA, Rome, C–I., c–3, Box 6).

11 Résultat de la visite faite dans la maison d'Amiens par la révérende mère générale en août 1850 (GA, Rome, C–IV., 2, Amiens. Letters, Box 3). See also, General Archives, Rome. C–I., A, I–c, Box 3; AF, Poitiers, Amiens, B01, 114, Visites des Supérieures Majeurs.

12 Adèle Cahier à SB, Amiens, [16 août 1850]. Secrète (GA, Rome, C–IV, 2, Amiens, Letters, Box 1).

13 Angélique de Boisbaudry died in Paris on 15 November 1850. Her sisters, Elisa (1813–87) and Camille (1817–58) remained in the Society. Corr. SB à Elisa de Boisbaudry, lettre 3, Rome 27 novembre 1850. Lettres Annuelles, 1850–51, I, Amiens, pp. 13–15.

14 Abbé de Brandt à SB, Amiens, 16 août 1850; 28 août 1850. (GA, Rome, C–IV, 2, Amiens, Letters, Box 3). SB à l'abbé de Brandt, [Paris], 18 août 1850, Série 'ecclésiastiques', Box 28.

15 SB à la communauté d'Amiens, Paris, 27 août 1850 (GA, Rome, Séries des lettres aux diverses communautés, Amiens).

16 Corr. SB et Esther d'Oussières, Rome, 9 février 1851.

17 Marie-Joachim-Elizabeth de Louvencourt (1747–1778) was born in Amiens and she founded a community there, Les Sœurs des Sacrés Cœurs de Jésus et de Marie in 1776. La dévote Marie de Louvencourt d'Amiens (+ 1778) et ses écrits conservés à Courtrai (Archives et bibliothèques, Diocese d'Amiens).

18 Affaire ecclésiastique. Secret. Monsieur l'abbé de Brandt (GA, Rome, France, Amiens, C–IV, 2); Copie d'une lettre de la Secrétaire Générale au sujet de Madame de Stassart, 23 octobre 1861 (AF, Poitiers, Economat General. Lettres d'affaires. Adèle Cahier 1844–1865); Lettres [de SB] aux personnes sorties de la Société, vol. 67. Also letters exchanged between the bishops of Beauvais, Tournai and Amiens in 1861, concerning the activities of de Brandt and the women who followed him, in GA, Rome, C–1, A, 1–c, Box 3.

19 *Lettres circulaires*, ii, La Ferrandière, 1 [novembre] 1850, 232–4.

20 Marie Prevost aux communautés de Midi, Rome, 20–21 novembre 1850 (GA, Rome, C–III, 3, Europe: France (before 1971). All Provinces. Circular Letters of Provincials, 1833–1855).

21 Archivi della provincia di Italia. Storia di Casa: Villa Lante. Cartolario 1837–1860. Diario 1850–52, 17 novembre 1850, f. 58; Marie Prevost aux communautés de Midi, Rome, 20–21 novembre 1850.

22 Catherine de Charbonnel, Félicité Desmarquest et Henriette Coppens, Paris, 4 novembre 1850 (GA, Rome, C–I., e–I., Box 8).

23 Cahier, *Vie*, ii, 206. 'Apprenez de moi que je suis doux et humble de Cœur.'

24 ibid., p. 207. 'Cela ne fait pas mon éloge … c'est qu'aucun ne s'est ménagé autant que moi.'

25 SB à Jean Roothan, Trinité du Monts, 11 février 1851 (ARSI, Monial, I–VI, 2).

26 SB à Luigi Lambruschini, Trinité du Mont, 8 mars 1851. Je connais la disposition générale des esprits et je confie à votre Eminence que je redouterais les suites de demi-mesures prises dans un moment où toutes s'attendent à voir enfin cette Société s'asseoir sur des fondements solides et durables. Or, je ne puis m'empêcher de regarder comme demi-mesures la substitution des Visitatrices aux provinciales […]

27 Objet de la supplique présentée à … Pius IX … en 1851 (GA, Rome, C–I, c–3, Box 8, 1851; 1864; B–II., Box 1, Dossier 3). Also, Notes ou mémoire pour son eminence le Cardinal Protector [Lambruschini], vol. 67.

28 Exposé remis par la … mère générale à monseigneur Lucciardi, Document 24, vol. 67.

29 Cahier, *Vie*, ii, 208–211.

30 SB à Luigi Lambruschini, Paris, 14 août 1851. lettre 10, vol. 67

31 *Lettres circulaires*, ii, Paris, 1 août 1851; Paris, 20 octobre 1851 (aux conseillères); Paris, 20 octobre 1851 (pour les seules supérieures), 234–41. Twenty in all were invited to the general council: Catherine de Charbonnel; Félicité Desmarquest; Marie Prevost; Henriette Coppens; Emilie Giraud; Olympe Rombau; Louise de Limminghe; Josephine de Coriolis; Adèle Cahier; Aimée d'Avenas; Henriette Granon; Anna du Rousier;

Aloysia Hardey; Maria Cutts; Adèle Lehon; Elisa de Bouchaud; Gertrude de Brou; Esther d'Oussières; Pauline de Valencise; Emma de Bouchaud.

32 Adèle Cahier à Alexis Gaume, Paris, 12 octobre 1851; Alexis Gaume à SB, Paris, 13 octobre 1851 (GA, Rome, C–I., c–3, Box 8, 1851; 1864).

33 For a full account of the general council of 1851 GA, Rome, C–I., c–3, Box 8, 1851; 1864.

34 SB à Luigi Lambruschini, La Ferrandière, 10 décembre 1851; 16 décembre 1851 (GA, Rome, C–I., c–3, Box 8, 1851; 1864).

35 *Lettres circulaires*, i, La Ferrandière, 13 décembre 1851, 142.

36 ibid., 143. [...] de grâce, et je ne puis trop vous le répéter, élargissez votre âme, vous la tenez entre deux étaux. Vos fautes qui ne sont que de pure fragilité, vous alarment trop et resserrent votre cœur! Vous devriez vous tenir plus près de celui de Jésus et ne plus penser à vous. Sa gloire, son œuvre dans les âmes devraient être votre pensée dominante. Un seul désaveu suffit pour vos misères. Réservez toutes les puissances de votre âme pour vous établir dans l'union et l'amour de Jésus! Croyez que tout est bon pour alimenter ces deux vertus. Comme on jette dans un foyer où le feu subsiste, bois sec, vert, épines, broussailles [...] ces matières [...] l'entretiennent [...] et changent de nature pour l'action du brûlant élément! C'est ainsi que Jésus opérera dans nos âmes, si nous lui livrons notre Être tout entier.

37 Corr. SB et Louise de Limminghe, lettre 424, Paris, 25 février 1852 [...] de grâce, et je ne puis trop vous le répéter, élargissez votre âme, vous la tenez entre deux étaux. Vos fautes qui ne sont que de pure fragilité, vous alarment trop et resserrent votre cœur! Vous devriez vous tenir plus près de celui de Jésus et ne plus penser à vous. Sa gloire, son œuvre dans les âmes devraient être votre pensée dominante. Un seul désaveu suffit pour vos misères. Réservez toutes les puissances de votre âme pour vous établir dans l'union et l'amour de Jésus! Croyez que tout est bon pour alimenter ces deux vertus. Comme on jette dans un foyer où le feu subsiste, bois sec, vert, épines, broussailles [...] ces matières [...] l'entretiennent [...] et changent de nature pour l'action du brûlant élément! C'est ainsi que Jésus opérera dans nos âmes, si nous lui livrons notre Être tout entier.

38 Corr. SB et Louise de Limminghe, lettre 430, Paris, 2 juillet 1852.

39 ibid., lettre 454, Paris, 27 août 1853.

40 ibid., lettre 445, Paris, 4 avril 1853.

41 *Lettres circulaires*, i, La Ferrandière, 13 décembre 1851, 150. Also, 148–9. Vous le savez vous n'arriverez à ce renouvellement dans l'amour et la dévotion au Sacré-Cœur de Jésus, que par le moyen de la vie intérieure. Jamais une âme légère et superficielle ne pourra comprendre l'essence de cette dévotion, ni entrer dans la voie qui y conduit.

42 *Lettres circulaires*, ii, La Ferrandière, 13 décembre 1851, Pour les supérieures et leur conseil, 242–48; pour les seules supérieures vicaires, 248–58.

43 Corr. SB à Césaire Mathieu, lettre 108, La Ferrandière, 27 décembre 1851. 'J'ai trouvé dans les membres du Conseil le meilleur esprit, l'union la plus entière entre elles et avec l'autorité première. Enfin une pleine adhésion à tout ce que j'avais cru nécessaire à la consolidation de l'œuvre.'

44 Corr. SB et Philippine Duchesne, lettre 334, Paris, 16 février 1852. J'ai trouvé dans les membres du conseil le meilleur esprit, l'union la plus entière entre elles et avec l'autorité première. Enfin une pleine adhésion à tout ce que j'avais cru nécessaire à la consolidation de l'œuvre.

45 Corr. SB et Emma de Bouchaud, Paris, lettre 213, 18 juin 1853. Quelle vie que la nôtre [...] lorsque dans notre jeunesse nous croyions nous ensevelir au Carmel. Les voies de Dieu sur les âmes sont impénétrables. Je le regretterais toujours si je n'avais l'assurance que Dieu l'a ainsi voulu. Mais il faudrait au moins unir la solitude au travail et opposer à ce tourbillon un trou profond où l'âme puisse se réfugier le plus souvent possible. Ce devrait être pour nous [...] ce trou de la pierre, le Cœur de Jésus! [...]

46 Adèle Cahier au Ministre de la Police Générale, Paris, février 1853; Ministre de la Police Générale, à Adèle Cahier, Paris, 11 février 1853 (GA, Rome, C–I, A–1, c, Box 2).

47 This foundation was a fusion of the Dames de St Pierre with the Society of the Sacred Heart.

48 Cahier, *Vie*, ii, 184–91; 215–224; 233–49; 256–62; 281–95.

49 Corr. SB et Philippine Duchesne, lettre 327, Sugar Creek, 28 février 1842. 'grand soulagement qu'elle apportera á vos immenses travaux'.

50 Corr. SB et Philippine Duchesne, lettre 328, St Charles, 5 juin 1846.

51 Corr. SB et Elizabeth Galitzine, lettre 193, Paris, 13 décembre 1842.

52 Corr. SB et Philippine Duchesne, lettre 329, St Charles, 10 septembre 1847. Toutes les maisons de ce pays ont accueilli respectueusement les changements opérés par Madame Galitzine, parce qu'on voyait vos intentions. Mais à votre seule parole, je suis sûre, qu'on reprendrait l'ancien ordre [...] Je regarde la visite de Madame de Galitzine comme un fléau. Revêtue de tout pouvoir, elle agissait de manière à blesser les évêques; le dedans et le dehors. Et les pauvres Sœurs, comme des brebis, se laissaient conduire, comme si elle eut été supérieure générale. On ne parlait plus de celle qui l'était.

53 ibid., lettre 333, St Charles, 18 août 1851.

54 ibid., lettre 330, Paris, 16 septembre 1849.

55 ibid., lettre 337 [St Charles], 17 août, [1852]; lettre 338 [St Charles], 1852.

56 De Charry (ed.), *Varin Lettres*, lettre 112, [Mantes, Seine-et-Oise], 20 [juillet] 1849, p. 349–50. O vraiment […] que je suis tout chagrin quand je pense à ce si long silence qui règne entre nous. Depuis si longtemps, pas un mot de part et d'autre, et, cependant il est bien certain que l'union de cœurs n'en souffre pas. C'est le bon Maître qui les a unis, il y a 48 ans […]

57 The existence of these letters was noted in 1886 but they have not been found in the archives of the Society of the Sacred Heart or in those of the Jesuits (France and Rome). Testimony of Marie du Chélas, Paris, 15 février 1886 (GA, Rome, Processus apostolicus in causa beatificationis et canonisationis … Magdalena Sophiae Barrat, vol. iii, sessio 108a, f. 1906).

58 Joseph Varin, 1846, 1848 et 1849. Journal de Mantes. Diverses anecdotes très intéressantes, no. 11 (AFSJ, Vanves, Fonds Varin). Cette pensée qui n'est jamais sortie de mon esprit ni de mon cœur, s'est effectivement trouvée remplie par la Congrégation des Dames du Sacré-Cœur, dite d'abord des Dames de la Foi, qui commença […] par quatre dames à la tête desquelles fut mise Madame Barat qui fut la fondatrice et supérieure dès l'âge de 22 ans.

59 Joseph Varin à Mathilde Garabis, Paris, 24 mars 1843 (AF, Poitiers, Bordeaux, B10, 117, ii. Lettres à la Mère Garabis).

60 *Lettres circulaires*, ii, Paris, 30 avril 1850, pp. 139–40.

61 Cahier, *Vie*, ii, 251–6.

62 ibid., pp. 295–300.

63 Statuts de la Congrégation des Dames du Sacré-Cœur de Jésus, approuvés par Décret du 5 août 1853 (GA, Rome, A–IV., 1, Box 2); for Sophie Barat's dealings with the archbishop of Paris, Marie Dominique Auguste Sibour (1848–57) at this time, AF, Poitiers, Paris, rue de Varenne, BO6, 151, I, L'Evêché.

64 Perdrau, *Loisirs*, pp. 251–95, 481–4.

65 Corr. SB et Stanislas Dusaussoy, lettre 161, Paris 29 septembre 1848. On m'apprend qu'il s'est dirigé vers notre maison près de Colmar [Kientzheim]. Vous comprenez qu'on le recevra par affection pour moi. Mais quelle vie que celle-là! Il paraît que son caractère déjà exigeant et difficile n'a fait que s'accroître. Qu'en sera-t-il à la fin? Je l'ignore. Vous comprenez […] que le physique est pour beaucoup dans cet état. Il s'est tellement laissé dominer par la peur qu'il n'est plus maître de lui. Il perdrait la tête que je n'en serais pas étonnée […] ce n'est pas sa faute […] Also, lettre 108, Rome 12 avril 1842; lettre 162, Bordeaux, 19 novembre 1848. See also, Corr. SB à Sophie Dusaussoy, lettre 16, Turin 3 novembre 1836; lettre 18, Rome, 1 mars 1838; lettre 39, Paris, 22 avril 1849.

66 Corr. SB à Zoé Dusaussoy, lettre 3, 1853; Corr. SB et Stanislas Dusaussoy, lettres 213, 214, 217, février–juillet 1853.

67 Corr. SB et Louis Dusaussoy, Paris, 31 janvier 1856.

68 Corr. SB et Stanislas Dusaussoy, lettre 270, Paris, 5 août 1857. 'Jamais je ne comprendrai que l'on puisse être heureux sans le travail quand on se porte passablement.'

69 The correspondence regarding Zoé's marriage, the birth of Oscar, the child's upbringing and the failure of the marriage is extensive. See Corr. SB et Stanislas Dusaussoy, Lettres, *passim*.

70 Archives de l'Armée de terre à Vincennes (Archives de la Société du Sacré-Cœur, Joigny). The army paid Zoé a widow's pension until her death in 1894.

71 Corr. SB à Sophie Dusaussoy, lettre 22, Lyon, 2 octobre 1842.

72 Corr. SB et Olympe Rombaud, lettre 96, Paris, 11 août 1860; lettre 97, Paris, 16 août 1860. For the replies AF, Poitiers, Bordeaux, BI0, 117, II, Lettres importantes ou d'affaires courantes de la maison 1853 à 1864 inclusivement.

73 Corr. SB à Sophie Dusaussoy, lettre 63, Paris, 16 février 1857; Corr. SB et Adèle Lehon, lettre 207, Paris, 6 février 1857; Corr. SB et Louise de Limminghe, lettre 55, Paris, 7 juillet 1830.

74 Corr. SB et Stanislas Dusaussoy, lettre 147, Paris, 19 novembre 1847; lettre 148, Paris, 28 décembre 1847.

75 ibid., lettre 179, Conflans, 25 septembre 1849. Also, lettre 170, Paris, 12 juillet 1849; lettre 178, Paris, 7 septembre 1849.

76 ibid., lettre 193, Paris, 15 juillet 1851. J'embrasse affectueusement toute la famille. J'aurais sans doute été bien contente de revoir votre mère. Mais dans l'état où elle est, c'eut été un grand chagrin pour moi. Or les impressions pénibles me font beaucoup de mal dans ce moment où mon physique est très ébranlé par le travail et la fatigue […] Also, lettre 200, Paris, 30 janvier 1852.

77 ibid., lettre 196, La Ferrandière, 20 novembre 1851.

78 ibid., lettre 200, Paris, 30 janvier 1852. Les détails sur votre mère m'ont fait de la peine. C'est une vraie mort morale, et quelle surveillance il vous faut employer pour lui éviter les accidents […] et qui peut se prolonger des années […] un devoir que l'on aime à remplir en pensant aux soins qu'elle a pris de vous tous dans vos premières années.

79 ibid., lettre 204, Paris, 16 août 1852; lettre 205, Paris, 23 août 1852.

80 ibid., lettre 208, Paris, 25 septembre 1852.

81 ibid., lettres 132, 141, 154, 157, 1846–1847.

82 Corr. SB à Elisa Rambaud, lettre 1, Paris, 3 février 1857; lettre 2, Paris, 5 novembre 1857.

83 Corr. SB à Rameau Rambaud, lettre 4, Paris, 11 octobre 1854; lettre 5, Paris, 1 février 185.
84 Corr. SB et Stanislas Dusaussoy, lettre 203, Paris, 3 juillet 1852; lettre 279, Paris, 29 janvier 1859.
85 Histoire de Julia de Wicka (GA, Rome, C–I., A, 1–d, Box 2). This history was written by Josephine Augustin (1823–84).
86 Corr. SB et Julia de Wicka, lettre 1, Rome, 12 mai 1845–lettre 144, Paris, 28 avril 1865. Corr. SB et George Augustin, lettre 1, Paris, 14 juin 1860– lettre 7, Paris, 12 janvier 1864; Corr. SB et Josephine Augustin, lettre 2, Paris, 25 novembre 1859 – lettre 56, Paris, 12 mai 1865. Corr. SB et Aloysia Hardey, lettres 53, 58, 75, mai 1852–mars 1857; GA, Rome, C–I., A, 1–d, Box 2.
87 GA, Rome, A–IV., 1, Box 1 and 2; D–I., 1–f.
88 Archives Nationales, Paris, F/17/12434/D Inspections des écoles, Paris, 26 janvier 1854; Perdrau, *Loisirs*, ii, 254–63. *Lettres circulaires*, i, La Ferrandière, 13 décembre 1851, pp. 155–6; *Lettres circulaires*, ii, Paris, 1 août 1856, pp. 292–303; Paris, 21 septembre 1859, pp. 303–5; Paris, 5 août 1863, pp. 309–18.
89 Corr. SB et Pauline Pellisson de Valencise, lettre 5, Paris 26 octobre 1855.Il faut, cette année, réparer le passé, et, pour y réussir, joindre aux moyens divins ceux raisonnables de soigner l'éducation de ces enfants, en tout genre, science selon nos plans, travaux des mains, leur en inculquer le goût et même l'amour, arts d'agrément, surtout le dessin, mais avant tout l'orthographe et l'art épistolaire, car les autres connaissances paraissent peu dans une femme, tandis que, dans notre siècle, elle est obligée d'écrire toute sa vie; il y a peu d'exceptions. Appliquez donc vos maîtresses à bien enseigner ces choses à leurs élèves et que l'on commence dès la 6^c classe; en apprenant à lire à ces petites, les faire épeler les aiderait beaucoup. Tenez à l'ordre et à la politesse, que l'on forme ces enfants au bon ton, aux bonnes manières, avec une noble simplicité. On ne les travaille pas assez sous ces rapports essentiels. Ce sera toujours ce qui nous attachera les élèves et nous attirera la confiance, car sans cette tenue simple et modeste, elles ne plairont pas; c'est le vernis d'une éducation soignée et solide.
90 *Lettres circulaires*, i, Paris, 17 mars 1863, 184–94; Paris, 10 mars 1864, 194–201. *Lettres circulaires*, ii, Paris, 5 août 1863, 309–318.
91 Decisions prises dans la 8eme Congrégation générale et modifications apportées par elle à plusieurs de celles des Congrégations précédentes [1864]; Procès Verbaux des Séances, juin–juillet 1864; Notes concernant la Société [Sophie Barat] (GA, Rome, C–I., c–3, Box 8, 1851; 1864); *Lettres circulaires*, i, Paris, 24 juillet 1864, 201–5; Paris, 4 novembre 1864, 205–212; *Lettres circulaires*, ii, Paris, 25 août 1864, 327–32; Paris, 4 novembre 1864, 332–5; Cahier, *Vie*, ii, 630–38.

Notes to Epilogue

1 [Sophie Barat] Quelques pensées que je n'ai pu expliquer dans mon testament (GA, Rome, C–I., A, 1–d, Box 1). N'ayant rien apporté à la Congrégation que six francs, je crois, restes de mon voyage de Paris à Amiens. J'aurais eu à recueillir quelque 1000 francs de la succession de mes père et mère, j'ai cru ne devoir pas les réclamer, ma sœur ayant eu à cette époque dix enfants à soigner dans leur bas âge. On me le conseilla ainsi dans le temps.
2 Perdrau, *Loisirs*, pp. 151–2. This was a habit Sophie had for most of her life. Corr. SB et Eugénie de Gramont, Lettre 990, Conflans, 15 mai 1846; Lettre 1001, Conflans, 4 juillet 1846.
3 Corr. SB et Stanislas Dusaussoy, Lettre 322, Paris, 27 février 1865. […] Dans quels temps nous vivons! Nous avons sous nos yeux ces deux extrêmes: la vue d'un luxe effréné qui engloutit des richesses sans seul résultat qu'un plaisir d'un instant, et à côté de ces folles dépenses, des milliers, je devrais dire millions, d'individus de toutes les classes, de tous les âges, de toutes conditions qui meurent de faim, et comment ce qui reste de chrétiens charitables en si petit nombre peuvent-ils suffire à soulager tant de besoins et de misères? Car presque toutes les infortunes et les besoins du globe tombent sur ce petit nombre pour leur procurer le nécessaire et on ne peut suffire: c'est l'Amérique, la Pologne, les missions de tout l'Orient. Mais autour de nous, combien des infortunés même de la classes élevée dans le plus pressant besoin! […] on nous dévore, je ne puis vous dire ce qui tombe sur nous de tout côté!
4 ibid., Lettre 323, Paris, 25 avril 1865.
5 Perdrau, *Loisirs*, p. 481. 'Encore une fois … je revois ces lieux où j'ai tant vécu et souffert.'
6 Josephine Gœtz, *Première lettres et bulletins relatifs à la maladie et la mort de notre vénérée mère fondatrice*, I–VII, pp. 1–17.
7 Corr. SB et Emilie Giraud, Lettre 120, Rome, 16 mai 1839. Faisons comme le cygne qui, près de mourir, recueille ses forces et chante avec plus d'harmonie que jamais. C'est ainsi que les saints finissent. C'est l'acte de leur vie le plus pur, le plus brûlant d'amour, le plus parfait.
L'abbé Auguste Jeanjean connaissait bien la Société et avait été aumônier à Grand Coteau et à Saint-Michel. *Correspondance Sophie Barat et Henriette Grosier*, lettre 142, Rome, 18 octobre 1839. Aussi, lettre 143, Rome, 9 novembre 1839; lettre 144, Rome, 14 novembre 1839.
Correspondance Sophie Barat à Césaire Mathieu, lettre 108, La Ferrandière, 27 décembre 1851.

INDEX

Affre, Denis: urges de Quelen to leave rue de Varenne 282; and Gregory XVI 310; appointed archbishop of Paris 318; and de Gramont 319–20, 375, 377; dismisses Frs Jammes and Surat 319–20; and general council 338, 344, 345, 346, 390, 393, 405, 406; dispute with SB and Society 348–52, 356–65; renews claims to rights over Society 379–81, 383, 386; improvement in relations with SB 385; fatally wounded in 1848 disturbances 407; SB passes over difficulties in letter to Society 414

Alacoque, Margaret Mary 20

Albany 417, 418

Amiens: Diletti di Gesù established in 31–2; Varin and 31–2, 34; Fathers of the Faith 31–3, 139; school 32, 33, 34, 37, 62, 63, 69, 139; Loquet as superior 33; Diletti's early difficulties in 33–4; SB and Louise Naudet 35–6, 216; Diletti and Paccanari scandal 37–8; Baudemont comes to 39–40; possible merger with Grenoble 42; Grenoble order of the day based on 44; Deshayes leaves for Grenoble 45; Varin's authoritarianism 46; extravagance of school criticized 47, 177; SB in poor health 49; and Bordeaux foundation 53; SB draws on experience of 59, 60; SB leader in 61; Saint-Estève and 63; expands 63–4; SB sidelined from 64, 68–9; SB visits 64, 67, 68–9, 131, 236, 328, 332, 386, 391; Deshayes removed from school 65; and Ghent and Cuignières 67; Marie-Louise Dusaussoy's children educated at 72, 73, 74, 161; clash between Billiart and Saint-Estève 75, 98–9, 156; and proposed constitution 77, 93–4; St Acheul's 86, 90; 'inner circle' 88, 106, 107, 147; SB removed from on grounds of ill health 89; de la Croix in 90; SB criticizes Saint-Estève's role in 91; SB sees constitution as remedy to discontent 92–3; unrest in 1815 95, 374; general council of 1815 96, 117; separation from Diletti 96;

tensions in 101; story of origins of Association silenced in 104; de Gramont and 108, 110, 114–16, 118, 119, 121, 125; bishop of 109; SB resolves divisions 109; novices brought to Paris 117; SB's missionary hopes 127; Stanislas Dussaussoy at 132; Prevost 136; school's high reputation 146; move to Paris 181; de Rozeville 193; change of superior 196; Montaigne helps SB deal with crisis 215; SB's later recollections of 252; SB plans to change superior 324; de Rozeville superior at 370; SB asks d'Avenas to visit school 398; new foundation 401; de Boisbaudry appointed superior 409; difficulties in 1849-50 409–11

Androsilla, marchioness of 182, 187, 216, 252, 255–6

Annonay 212, 215, 253, 391

Armagh 417

Association des Dames de l'Instruction Chrétienne: emerges from Diletti di Gesù 38; elects superior general 44, 47; SB asks Varin for rule of life 44; structures 44; lack of episcopal control 52; lack of mother house 52; Poitiers foundation 52; noviciate 55, 56; Fr Nectoux's prophecy 60, 139; Jesuit influences 62; Napoleon approves 62–3; difficulties trouble SB 71; Saint-Estève assumes role of founder 74–5; proposed constitution 75–85; name of Association 80; attempts to found house in Rome 82; and Fathers of the Faith 83, 218; founding myth 97, 139; Fr Soyer and 110–13; location of mother house 111

Audé, Eugénie: embarks on Louisiana mission 129; critical of purchase of Hôtel Biron 145; Grand Coteau 155, 181, 223, 224–5; SB asks to help Louis Dussaussoy 163; SB and 189, 212, 267, 321, 324; SB criticizes for extravagance 224–5, 226; breakdown of relations with Duchesne 227; unusual powers in St Michael's 229; illness 232, 333; elected